Ocean and Coastal Resources Law

ASPEN CASEBOOK SERIES

Ocean and Coastal Resources Law

Josh Eagle
Solomon Blatt Professor of Law
University of South Carolina School of Law

Shi-Ling Hsu
D'Alemberte Professor
Florida State University College of Law

Wolters Kluwer

Printed in the United States of America.

1 2 3 4 5 6 7 8 9 0

ISBN 978-1-5438-0111-8

Library of Congress Cataloging-in-Publication Data

Names: Eagle, Josh, author. | Hsu, Shi-Ling, author.
Title: Ocean and coastal resources law / Josh Eagle, Solomon Blatt
  Professor of Law, University of South Carolina School of Law; Shi-Ling
  Hsu, D'Alemberte Professor and Associate Dean for Environmental
  Programs, Florida State University, College of Law.
Other titles: Coastal law
Description: Third edition. | New York : Wolters Kluwer, [2019] | Series:
  Aspen casebook series | Includes bibliographical references and index. |
  Summary: "Casebook for teaching a course on Ocean and Coastal Law, or
  courses on either Ocean Law or Coastal Law" — Provided by publisher.
Identifiers: LCCN 2019028649 (print) | LCCN 2019028650 (ebook) | ISBN
  9781543801118 (hardcover) | ISBN 9781543815177 (ebook)
Subjects: LCSH: Coastal zone management — Law and legislation — United
  States. | Law of the sea. | LCGFT: Casebooks (Law)
Classification: LCC KF5627 .E15 2019 (print) | LCC KF5627 (ebook) | DDC
  346.7304/6917 — dc23
LC record available at https://lccn.loc.gov/2019028649
LC ebook record available at https://lccn.loc.gov/2019028650

SUSTAINABLE FORESTRY INITIATIVE Certified Sourcing www.sfiprogram.org SFI-01051

About Wolters Kluwer Legal & Regulatory U.S.

Wolters Kluwer Legal & Regulatory U.S. delivers expert content and solutions in the areas of law, corporate compliance, health compliance, reimbursement, and legal education. Its practical solutions help customers successfully navigate the demands of a changing environment to drive their daily activities, enhance decision quality, and inspire confident outcomes.

Serving customers worldwide, its legal and regulatory portfolio includes products under the Aspen Publishers, CCH Incorporated, Kluwer Law International, ftwilliam.com, and MediRegs names. They are regarded as exceptional and trusted resources for general legal and practice-specific knowledge, compliance and risk management, dynamic workflow solutions, and expert commentary.

Josh Eagle

In memory of Jimmy Chandler, Esq. of Georgetown, South Carolina

Shi-Ling Hsu

For Debby, Katharine, and Allen

Summary of Contents

Contents

chapter 2

U.S. Law for Living Resources of the Oceans 65

chapter **3**

Marine Protected Species   149

chapter 4

Offshore Industrial Development   219

chapter **5**

The Coastal Law Context: Uplands, Shoreline, Water   345

chapter **9**

The Coastal Zone Management Act and State Coastal Programs   689

chapter **10**

Coastal Disasters, Climate Change, and the Future of Coastal Law   891

Preface to the Third Edition

This third edition, an extension of earlier editions of *Coastal Law*, adds four new chapters and a new co-author, Shi-Ling Hsu, and is now titled *Ocean and Coastal Resources Law*. With the addition of new subject matter covering the domestic and international law of oceans, we aim to create a more complete treatment of the law. Very clearly, activities on the seas affect coastal land activities, and vice versa. We wish that our casebook could provide shining examples of how the law holistically integrates the legal treatment of land and water, but then we would have to classify our book as fiction. Instead, what we hope to impress upon the reader is how the law of oceans and the law of coastal lands attempt to grapple with forces and effects much larger than what litigants bring before a tribunal or court. Tribunals, courts, and other lawmakers do indeed struggle, sometimes with seemingly little success, but often gamely, to account for the interaction between the oceans and the land adjoining them, and quite often land far removed from them. The ambition of this casebook is to aid in that struggle, and to help a new generation of lawmakers develop the law of ocean and coastal resources as it should be, not as it has been.

Josh Eagle is grateful to Vanessa McQuinn for her help in preparing the manuscript and to the University of South Carolina for its support over the past fifteen years.

Shi-Ling Hsu is always grateful for the singularly excellent law library faculty and staff of the Florida State University Law Library, for institutional support of the Florida State University College of Law, and for the support of the Rocky Mountain Mineral Law Foundation, which helped fund the first-ever meeting of the two co-authors.

August 2019

Acknowledgments

Books and Articles

AMERICAN ASSOCIATION FOR PORT AUTHORITIES, THE LOCAL AND REGIONAL ECONOMIC IMPACTS OF THE U.S. DEEPWATER PORT SYSTEM, 2006 (2007), reprinted with permission from Martin Associates.

ARCHER, JACK H. ET AL., THE PUBLIC TRUST DOCTRINE AND THE MANAGEMENT OF AMERICA'S COASTS (1994), reprinted from *The Public Trust Doctrine and the Management of America's Coasts*, Copyright © 1994 by the University of Massachusetts Press.

Arnold, Chester, L. & James Gibbons, *Impervious Surface Coverage: The Emergence of a Key Environmental Indicator*, 26 J. AM. PLAN. ASS'N 243 (1996), reprinted by permission of Taylor & Francis Ltd., http://www.tand.co.uk/journals.

Bagstad, Kenneth J., Kevin Stapleton & John R. D'Agostino, *Taxes, Subsidies and Insurance as Drivers of United States Coastal Development*, 63 ECOL. ECON. 285 (2007), Copyright © 2007, reprinted with permission by Elsevier Limited, Oxford via Copyright Clearance Center.

Barry, Dan, *A Quiet Escape on the Rivers, and an Endangered Species*, NEW YORK TIMES A-12, July 8, 2007, reprinted with permission from the New York Times / PARS International. All rights reserved.

Barton H. Thompson, Jr., *Tragically Difficult: The Obstacles to Governing the Commons*, 30 ENVTL. L. 241 (2000), reprinted with permission from the author and Environmental Law, Copyright © 2000.

Boyd, James W., *Lost Ecosystem Goods and Services as a Measure of Marine Oil Pollution Damages*, in MARITIME POLLUTION LIABILITY & POLICY (Michael G. Faure et al. eds., 2010), reprinted with permission by Kluwer Law International © 2010.

EASTERLING, WILLIAM E., III, BRIAN H. HURD & JOEL B. SMITH, COPING WITH CLIMATE CHANGE: THE ROLE OF ADAPTATION IN THE UNITED STATES (2004), reprinted with permission from the Pew Center of Global Climate Change.

Faulkenberry, Lisa V. et al., *A Culture of Servitude: The Impact of Tourism and Development on South Carolina's Coast*, 59 HUM. ORG. 86 (2000), reprinted with permission by the Society for Applied Anthropology.

FLORIDA ATLANTIC UNIVERSITY CENTER FOR URBAN AND ENVIRONMENTAL STUDIES, FLORIDA'S RESILIENT COASTS: A STATE POLICY FRAMEWORK FOR ADAPTATION TO CLIMATE CHANGE (2010), reprinted with permission by the Bipartisan Policy Center, Copyright © 2010.

Griggs, Gary, Kiki Patsch, Lauret Savoy, *Understanding the Shoreline, in* LIVING WITH THE CHANGING CALIFORNIA COAST (Gary Griggs, Kiki Patsch & Lauret Savoy eds., 2005), Copyright © 2005, reprinted with permission by University of California Press via Copyright Clearance Center.

Hardin, Garrett, *The Tragedy of the Commons*, 162 Science 1243 (1968), reprinted with permission by AAAS via Copyright Clearance Center.

Healy, Robert G. & Jeffrey A. Zinn, *Environment and Development Conflicts in Coastal Zone Management*, 51, J. AM. PLANNING ASSOC. 299 (1985), reprinted by permission of Taylor & Francis Ltd., http:www.tandf.co.uk/journals.

Jenkins, Robert E. & Jill Watry Kastner, *Running Aground in a Sea of Complex Litigation: A Case Comment on the* Exxon Valdez *Litigation*, 18 UCLA J. ENVTL. L. & POL'Y 151 (1999), reprinted with permission by the UCLA Environmental Law Society and UCLA Journal of Environmental Law & Policy.

Liebesman, Lawrence R., Rafe Petersen & Michael Galano, Rapanos v. United States: *Searching for a Significant Nexus Using Proximate Causation and Foreseeability Principles*, 40 ENVTL. L. REP. NEWS & ANALYSIS 11242 (Dec. 2010), reprinted with permission by the Environmental Law Institute.

Lowry Kem, Casey Jarman & Susan Machida, *Federal-State Coordination in Coastal Management: An Assessment of the Federal Consistency Provision of the Coastal Zone Management Act*, 19 OCEAN & COASTAL MANAGEMENT 97 (1993), Copyright © 1993, reprinted with permission by Elsevier Limited, Oxford via Copyright Clearance Center.

Meltz, Robert, *Takings Law Today: A Primer for the Perplexed*, 34 ECOLOGY L. Q. 307 (2007), Copyright © 2007 by the Regents of the University of California.

NATURAL RESOURCES DEFENSE COUNCIL, HARBORING POLLUTION (2004), reprinted with permission from the Natural Resources Defense Council.

Nie, Martin, *State Wildlife Policy and Management: The Scope and Bias of Political Conflict*, 64 PUB. ADMIN. REV. 221 (2004), reprinted with permission by John Wiley & Sons, Inc. via Copyright Clearance Center.

Note: *The Public Trust in Tidal Areas: A Sometime Submerged Traditional Doctrine*, 79 YALE L. J. 762 (1970), reprinted with permission by The Yale Law Journal via Copyright Clearance Center.

Perruso, Richard, *The Development of the Doctrine of Res Communes in Medieval and Early Modern Europe*, 70 L. HIST. REV. 69 (2002), reprinted with permission by the author and The Legal History Review.

Poirier, Marc R., *A Very Clear Blue Line: Behavioral Economics, Public Choice, Public Art and Sea Level Rise*, 16 SOUTHEASTERN ENVTL. L. J. 83 (2007), reprinted with permission by the Southeastern Environmental Law journal, University of South Carolina School of Law, Copyright © 2007.

Photographs

Photograph of the sign at Higbee Beach, reprinted with permission by Mr. Bert Filemyr, photographer.

Photograph of Gidget, TV Guide Magazine, May 28-June 3, 1966, cover courtesy of TV Guide Magazine, LLC.

Photograph of Hurricane Katrina, Copyright © McClatchy-Tribune Information Services, all rights reserved. Reprinted with permission.

Photograph of Pee Dee River Shack, reprinted with permission, Angel Franco / New York Times / Redux Pictures.

Photograph of Eve Mosher applying a lightblueline in Brooklyn, reprinted with permission by Hose Cedeno, Eve Mosher, HighWaterLine.

List of Figures and Tables

Ocean and Coastal Resources Law

chapter 1

International Law for the Oceans

International law is a unique subject in law school because it is only considered law to the extent that nations are willing to recognize it as such. There is no sovereign overseeing all nations to ensure compliance with international law. There is no international police force or sheriff. So where does international law originate? Generally speaking, there are four sources of international law, listed here in descending order of authoritativeness:

1. International conventions
2. International custom, as evidence of a general practice accepted as law
3. General principles of law recognized by nations
4. Judicial decisions and the teachings of the most highly qualified international law scholars as subsidiary means for the determination of rules of law

This chapter focuses on the first two sources of international law. International conventions, or treaties, are agreements among sovereigns. To the extent that they reflect the *consent* of the parties, they are natural extensions of a sovereign power to bind its own people to its rules; it so happens that those rules are agreed to by international negotiations. Treaties need to be internally *ratified* by a participating country before that country becomes obligated to align its behavior with a treaty's rules and procedures. In the United States, treaties are ratified by the U.S. Senate, upon which they bind us to treaty commitments and, within the United States, become equal in authority to federal statutes. But sometimes international law need not be codified to be considered binding. If certain norms widely reflect the general practice of nations, then it may be considered customary international law even without a treaty.

Figure 1-1.
A 1665 map of the world's oceans, as drawn by Athanasius Kircher, a German scholar. The map is believed to be the first to depict ocean currents.

Treaty negotiations are often intractably contentious. Take, for example, treaties meant to address global climate change. The global mean temperature of the Earth is warming, with potentially catastrophic ecological and human consequences. Treaties by which nations agree to reduce their emissions of the greenhouse gases that cause global warming are necessary to avoid some very plausibly dystopic futures. Despite the desperate need for international agreement, climate treaties have been extremely difficult to negotiate and consummate.

A. INTERNATIONAL OCEANS AND COASTAL LAW

With respect to international law pertaining to the oceans and coasts, countries have been at times willing and able to recognize mutual interests in international agreement. The set of treaties that form the foundation of international ocean law, the International Law of the Sea, is a comprehensive set of rules that are widely accepted as law binding on all signatories, and even non-signatories.

How can countries be bound by a treaty to which they are not a party? The answer lies in the second-most authoritative source of international law, *international custom*. The following case is one of the U.S. Supreme Court's earliest pronouncements on the role of international custom, also known as customary international law.

The Paquete Habana

175 U.S. 677 (1900)

Mr. Justice GRAY delivered the opinion of the Court.

These are two appeals from decrees of the District Court of the United States for the Southern District of Florida condemning two fishing vessels and their cargoes as prize of war.

Each vessel was a fishing smack, running in and out of Havana, and regularly engaged in fishing on the coast of Cuba; sailed under the Spanish flag; was owned by a Spanish subject of Cuban birth, living in the City of Havana; was commanded by a subject of Spain, also residing in Havana, and her master and crew had no interest in the vessel, but were entitled to shares, amounting in all to two-thirds, of her catch, the other third belonging to her owner. Her cargo consisted of fresh fish, caught by her crew from the sea, put on board as they were caught, and kept and sold alive. Until stopped by the blockading squadron, she had no knowledge of the existence of the war or of any blockade. She had no arms or ammunition on board, and made no attempt to run the blockade after she knew of its existence, nor any resistance at the time of the capture. . . .

Both the fishing vessels were brought by their captors into Key West. A libel for the condemnation of each vessel and her cargo as prize of war was there filed on April 27, 1898; a claim was interposed by her master on behalf of himself and the other members of the crew, and of her owner; evidence was taken, showing the facts above stated, and on May 30, 1898, a final decree of condemnation and sale was entered,

> "the court not being satisfied that as a matter of law, without any ordinance, treaty, or proclamation, fishing vessels of this class are exempt from seizure."

Each vessel was thereupon sold by auction. . . .

We are then brought to the consideration of the question whether, upon the facts appearing in these records, the fishing smacks were subject to capture by the armed vessels of the United States during the recent war with Spain.

By an ancient usage among civilized nations, beginning centuries ago and gradually ripening into a rule of international law, coast fishing vessels pursuing their vocation of catching and bringing in fresh fish have been recognized as exempt, with their cargoes and crews, from capture as prize of war.

[The Court undertakes a lengthy review of past international incidents in which fishing boats had been captured in times of war.]

International law is part of our law, and must be ascertained and administered by the courts of justice of appropriate jurisdiction as often as questions of right depending upon it are duly presented for their determination. For this purpose, where there is no treaty and no controlling executive or legislative act or judicial decision, resort must be had to the customs and usages of civilized nations, and, as evidence of these, to the works of jurists and commentators who by years of labor, research, and experience have made themselves peculiarly well acquainted with the subjects of which they treat. Such works are resorted to by judicial tribunals not for the speculations of their authors concerning what the law ought to be, but for trustworthy evidence of what the law really is. . . .

This review of the precedents and authorities on the subject appears to us abundantly to demonstrate that, at the present day, by the general consent of the civilized nations of the world, and independently of any express treaty or other public act, it is an established rule of international law, founded on considerations of humanity to a poor and industrious order of men, and of the mutual convenience of belligerent states, that coast fishing vessels, with their implements and supplies, cargoes and crews, unarmed and honestly pursuing their peaceful calling of catching and bringing in fresh fish, are exempt from capture as prize of war. . . .

This rule of international law is one which prize courts administering the law of nations are bound to take judicial notice of, and to give effect to, in the absence of any treaty or other public act of their own government in relation to the matter. . . .

Figure 1-2.
The sinking of the *USS Maine* in Havana harbor in 1898 led to the eruption of the Spanish-American War.

points for discussion

1. *Customary international law. Paquete Habana* is frequently cited for the proposition that widespread international custom can be considered international law that is binding even in the absence of formal agreement. Sufficient evidence must support customary international law as a widely agreed-upon norm of international behavior. The Court's lengthy review of incidents involving the treatment of fishing boats in wartime, dating back to the 1600s, convinced the Court that capturing fishing boats, even in wartime, was contrary to customary international law.

2. *Jurists.* In addition to his deep dive into the history of the laws of war and civilian boats, Justice Gray also spent considerable effort reviewing the writings of international legal scholars. French, Italian, Spanish, German, Dutch, Austrian, and Argentinian jurists are cited by Gray. Does this provide some insight as to the relationship between customary international law and "teachings of the most highly qualified publicists" (the fourth source of international law)?

3. *Duration.* Justice Gray left no stone unturned, and found, on the basis of hundreds of years of experience and hundreds of years of writings by eminent scholars, that customary international law forbade the capture of civilian fishing boats as prizes of war. Must custom be so long-standing to qualify as customary international law?

4. *In a peaceable manner.* As you will learn, the modern law of the sea guarantees each country a right to "innocent passage" through ocean areas adjacent to other countries. Under the innocent passage provisions of the Law of the Sea treaty, vessels must transit continuously and expeditiously. Coastal nations retain the authority to determine whether foreign vessels are innocent or pose a threat. Are there any circumstances under which the United States could have asserted that the *Paquete Habana* was a threat?

B. A BRIEF HISTORY LEADING UP TO THE LAW OF THE SEA CONVENTIONS

The evolution of international law governing oceans has a little bit of something for everyone. For legal philosophers, there is an ancient debate among eminent scholars over the nature of the sea; for example, do you think that the ocean should be owned by private parties, governments, or no one? For economic historians, there is the importance of commerce and the economics of shipping and mineral extraction as drivers of law. For military buffs, differentials in naval strength and strategic considerations have animated many developments in law.

Following the voyages of Christopher Columbus, Pope Alexander VI proclaimed the entire hemisphere east of a longitudinal line drawn through Brazil to be the property of Spain, while the hemisphere to the west would belong to Portugal.

That's quite a lot of chutzpah, even for a Pope. In response, a Dutch jurist named Hugo Grotius, who is commonly considered to be the father of international law, argued in his 1609 treatise *Mare Liberum* (Latin for "open sea") that the seas were no more susceptible of territorial appropriation than the air — too vast to reduce to possession:

> The air belongs to this class of things for two reasons. First, it is not susceptible of occupation; and second its common use is destined for all men. For the same reasons the sea is common to all, because it is so limitless that it cannot become a possession of any one, and because it is adapted for the use of all, whether we consider it from the point of view of navigation or of fisheries.

The more important principle arising out of *Mare Liberum* is the notion that the seas were meant to be open to all for purposes of navigation and trading, an acute sensibility of the mercantilist Dutch. This debate was joined by numerous Scottish, Italian, and English scholars, most of whom indignantly objected to such a radically egalitarian concept. These included Lord Chief Justice Coke, and his colleague, John Selden, who published *Mare Clausum* ("closed sea") in 1635, arguing that long-standing practice of asserting dominion over the oceans was a basis for territorial claims.

Grotius won out. Over time, nations recognized their mutual interests in trading, and observed the dampening of unilateral claims to sovereignty over important seafaring routes. What Grotius understood clearly — that his opponents failed to grasp — is that commerce through open shipping lanes was even *better* than "owning" the seas. So great is the benefit from commerce it outweighed the benefits of sovereign ownership, for example, the ability to charge foreign ships a fee for the right to enter national waters. "Freedom of the Seas" is a principle that survives largely intact to this day, continuing to influence the development of the international law of the sea.

That said, coastal nations did still worry about self-defense, and sought to exercise some control over ships passing too close to their shores. A prevailing norm seemed to emerge that coastal nations could claim the ocean up to three nautical

Hugo Grotius, whose real name was Hugo de Groot, was not only a legal scholar, but a statesman and dissident. As a member of the *Remonstrants*, a mostly affluent class urging religious tolerance, Grotius was arrested following a *coup* by the opposing *Gomarists*, a populist faction urging Calivinist orthoxy. Grotius's fellow *Remonstrant* Johan van Oldenbarnevelt was arrested and beheaded, but Grotius was spared and instead jailed in Loevenstein castle, now a universal field trip destination for Dutch schoolchildren. His captors allowed him many books, which were brought in and out of his confinement using large bookcases. Grotius escaped by hiding in one of the empty bookcases. To avoid detection, he practiced lying motionless in a bookcase for hours at a time. Once safely away, he fled to France, where he eventually won freedom for his wife, on the condition that he never return to his native Netherlands. He never did.

Figure 1-3. Hugo Grotius

miles from its coastline. That happened to be the distance that a cannon could reach when fired from land, giving rise to the popular labeling of that norm, the "cannon-shot rule." Controlling the ocean waters close to shore was deemed to be a proper prerogative of a coastal nation to defend itself against attack. All fisheries in what has become known as the "territorial sea" were also deemed to be the property of the coastal state.

Cannon shots have of course given way to more sophisticated military technologies and claims to territorial seas have changed. Different countries laid claim to oceanic waters up to 12 nautical miles to better protect themselves from naval attack, and to expand their economic prospects as well. Fishing has been an important economic activity throughout history, and countries sought to maintain some control over fishing in their near-shore waters, both to prevent overfishing and to favor their own fishermen. Over time, countries began to navigate around this new 12-mile-wide area, and it became a customary, *de facto* territorial sea.

But the significance of the ocean is not limited to navigation, shipping, and fish. In the earlier part of the twentieth century, the technology for mining resources from the seabed developed, and now the oceans had another role to play: as a site for the extraction of oil, gas, and other resources. Extraction activities would take place much farther out than the territorial sea; they would take place on the shallow, relatively flat parts of the seabed that extended out from the coastlines, sometimes for hundreds of miles, before it dipped into the deep canyons of the oceans. This area extending out beyond the territorial waters became known as the continental shelf and is the subject of the following Presidential Proclamation. As mining technologies matured, countries such as the United States sought to establish some legal foundation for their resource extraction activities.

Proclamation No. 2667, 28th September, 1945 Policy of the United States with Respect to the Natural Resources of the Subsoil and Sea Bed of the Continental Shelf

Executive Order 9633, September 28, 1945

Whereas the Government of the United States of America, aware of the long range world-wide need for new sources of petroleum and other minerals, holds the view that efforts to discover and make available new supplies of these resources should be encouraged; and

Whereas its competent experts are of the opinion that such resources underlie many parts of the continental shelf off the coasts of the United States of America, and that with modern technological progress their utilization is already practicable or will become so at any early date; and

Whereas recognized jurisdiction over these resources is required in the interest of their conservation and prudent utilization when and as development is undertaken; and

Whereas it is the view of the Government of the United States that the exercise of jurisdiction over the natural resources of the subsoil and sea bed of the continental shelf by the contiguous nation is reasonable and just, since the effectiveness of measures to utilize or conserve these resources would be contingent upon cooperation and protection from shore, since the continental shelf may be regarded as an extension of the land mass of the coastal nation and thus naturally appurtenant to it, since these resources frequently form a seaward extension of a pool or deposit lying within the territory, and since self-protection compels the coastal nation to keep close watch over activities off its shores which are of their nature necessary for utilization of these resources;

NOW THEREFORE I, HARRY S. TRUMAN, President of the United States of America, do hereby proclaim the following policy of the United States of America with respect to the natural resources of the subsoil and sea bed of the continental shelf.

Having concern for the urgency of conserving and prudently utilizing its natural resources, the Government of the United States regards the natural resources of the subsoil and sea bed of the continental shelf beneath the high seas but contiguous to the coasts of the United States as appertaining to the United states, subject to its jurisdiction and control. In cases where the continental shelf extends to the shores of another States, or is shared with an adjacent State, the boundary shall be determined by the United States and the State concerned in accordance with equitable principles. The character as high seas of the waters above the continental shelf and the right to their free and unimpeded navigation are in no way thus affected.

points for discussion

1. *Why a continental shelf?* President Truman's proclamation was surely inconsistent with international law at the time it was made. No legal concept in international law in existence in 1945 supported such a claim. But rather than meet with resistance, Truman's proclamation that minerals embedded in the naturally appurtenant continental shelf were the property of the coastal state became widely accepted among nations. Why do you think that was the case? For a discussion, see Ann L. Hollick, *U.S. Oceans Policy: The Truman Proclamations*, 17 Va. J. Int'l L. 23 (1976). What is the economic benefit of the effective enclosure of such vast tracts of submerged lands?

2. *Customary international law, again.* Within a decade, any disputes about the concept of a continental shelf had disappeared. The 1958 Law of the Sea Convention (the first one) included a Convention on the Continental Shelf, which proclaimed that the continental shelf was the "natural prolongation" of the coastal state (something like "naturally appurtenant"), and that rights to the seabed existed *ab initio*, without need for a formal claim. It did not settle the boundaries of the continental shelf but affirmed the concept. Does the rapidity (for international law) of adoption of the continental shelf concept affect your notions about customary international law?

> An international "convention" is *both* a meeting of countries and the resulting agreement among them. For the most part, the word convention is identical in meaning to the word "treaty," except that oftentimes, as in the case of the law of the sea, many, many lengthy meetings among delegates are required to hammer out the details of the agreements. "Convention" is thus understood to encompass both the meetings that took place and the ensuing treaty.

C. THE LAW OF THE SEA CONVENTIONS

As commerce, resources, and military considerations increased in relevance for coastal nations, the stakes also increased, giving impetus for international agreement. Twenty years of negotiations would eventually result in the 1982 Law of the Sea Conventions, a comprehensive set of treaty provisions governing activities at sea or taking place in the seabed and setting forth the jurisdictional boundaries of coastal nations.

Often, international conventions reflect a practice that has become commonplace, and thus are just codifications of what has already become customary international law. To some extent, that is the story of how the Law of the Sea Conventions emerged. Created in 1947 by the United Nations, the International Law Commission is a body of legal experts charged with codifying existing international law pertaining to oceans, in addition to proposing some new, additional rules. Ultimately, the Law of the Sea Conventions would consist of three separate efforts, the last of which is the most ambitious and comprehensive, going well beyond customary international law.

The first Law of the Sea Convention, held in 1958 in Geneva (UNCLOS I), yielded four separate agreements:

- the Convention on the Territorial Sea and Contiguous Zone,
- the Convention on the Continental Shelf,
- the Convention on the High Seas, and
- the Convention on Fishing and Conservation of the Living Resources of the High Seas.

The Convention on the Continental Shelf was an affirmation of the Truman Proclamation, even if it failed to settle the question of where the continental shelf ends. Similarly, the Convention on the Territorial Sea and the Contiguous Zone affirmed the conceptual validity of these two maritime zones. While the territorial sea is the band of water immediately adjacent to coastal land, the contiguous zone is the next band of water out, in which a coastal state would still have some enforcement powers, but in fewer areas of regulation. These two zones had already attained status under customary international law anyway, but the convention failed to establish their boundaries. And finally, the Convention on the High Seas was most clearly a codification exercise, setting forth the accepted practice at the time, and the key "freedoms" of the high seas: navigation, overflight, fishing, laying cables and pipelines, and scientific research.

The one agreement from UNCLOS I that broke somewhat new ground, away from customary rules, was the Convention on Fishing and Conservation of the Living Resources of the High Seas, which obligated signatories to "cooperate with other States in adopting, such measures for their respective nationals as may be necessary for the conservation of the living resources of the high seas." This was one of the earliest instances in which international law hinted at the need for countries to coordinate their fishing to avoid depleting fish stocks. The convention did no more than state that vague aspirational notion, but it laid an important foundation for future measures and future agreements to protect fish stocks. The second Convention on the Law of the Sea (UNCLOS II) was held in 1960 and focused only on establishing the boundaries of the territorial sea and establishing fishing limits. In neither case were the parties successful.

The last of the Conventions on the Law of the Sea (UNCLOS III) was not at all like the first two conventions. It was historic in scope and breadth—over 160 nations convened at the outset, in 1973. Its 320 articles and its several annexes took nearly a decade to negotiate, and now forms the corpus of international law as it pertains to the oceans. Considering that virtually every aspect of ocean governance was up for negotiations and considering that process was intentionally made to focus on consensus, the process was remarkably productive. At the outset, the parties agreed that UNCLOS III would have to be an up-or-down proposition on the *entire* convention, without cleaving off individual parts.

A number of emerging global issues could have doomed the effort. The Cold War between the United States and the Soviet Union became more ominous. The development of submarines capable of launching nuclear strikes loomed large over negotiations. An embargo imposed by oil-producing nations against the United States raised the importance of oil and gas exploration, even as the marine environment shared center stage after a disastrous blowout of an offshore oil rig off the coast of California. And while fishing might seem to pale in comparison to nuclear annihilation and energy, its influence over policy has always been outsized. Nevertheless, when UNCLOS III was concluded in 1982, it truly represented a historic compact. Rarely have the nations of the world made as much international law by compact as they did with UNCLOS III.

The United States, with the largest navy, the most important shipping fleet, the greatest energy needs, and a powerful fishing industry, was a central player in almost all of the parts of UNCLOS III. Under a consensus-based process, every provision of UNCLOS III had to have the assent of the United States. The United States agreed to every provision except one: the provision pertaining to the mining of the deep seabed, the areas beyond the continental shelf. UNCLOS III created an International Seabed Authority to authorize seabed exploration and mining. Along with other developed nations that had the need for deep sea minerals and the technology to mine them, the United States led a push to reduce United Nations' control or adjudication over seabed mining. By 1980, the parties appeared near agreement.

However, the election of Ronald Reagan in 1980 changed everything. Having ridden an electoral wave that was suspicious of international cooperation, President Reagan promptly reversed course on UNCLOS III. His administration would not sign UNCLOS III, in large part because Reagan rejected the idea of international governance over deep seabed mining.

UNCLOS III was completed in 1982 and entered into force in 1994. The United States signed the treaty then, but still has not ratified it. Three U.S. Presidents — Bill Clinton, George W. Bush, and Barack Obama — pushed for ratification, but none succeeded. Nevertheless, because UNCLOS III has been so widely and consistently observed — including by the United States — most of its provisions have attained the status of customary international law.

points for discussion

1. *U.S. dissent.* The provisions of the deep seabed are not customary international law in part because of the United States' objection. As recently as 2012,

then-Secretary of State Hillary Rodham Clinton testified before Congress, urging it to belatedly ratify UNCLOS III, and enter into the regime of deep seabed mining. As parties to the convention, Russia and China were securing leases from the International Seabed Authority for oil, gas, and other valuable minerals such as rare earth elements needed for technology products. *See* Testimony of Hillary Rodham Clinton, Secretary of State, Before the Senate Committee of Foreign Relations (May 23, 2012). Did the United States make a mistake in refusing to sign UNCLOS III? What would it gain from binding itself to the deep seabed mining provisions?

2. *Up-or-down on the entire UNCLOS III.* Do you think that the "package deal" structure of treaty negotiations helped the many countries reach negotiation? Why might such a restriction, reducing flexibility, induce more agreement?

1. Jurisdictional Zones

Perhaps the most fundamental thing that UNCLOS III accomplished was to divide the ocean into maritime zones, and to specify rights and obligations in each type of zone. Recall that customary international law held that a coastal nation could claim an area of sea up to three nautical miles from its coastline as its territorial sea. This would be a marine area over which countries would have jurisdiction and control, and ownership of resources such as seabed minerals and fish. That number varied. Some South American countries made claims of up to 200 miles as their territorial seas. UNCLOS III settled the maritime boundaries of not only the territorial sea, but the band of sea beyond that, the "contiguous zone" (that was the subject of the UNCLOS I treaty), over which the coastal nation had some limited jurisdiction and control. UNCLOS III also created a new band of sea, extending up to 200 nautical miles from the coast, that would be known as the Exclusive Economic Zone ("EEZ"). Within the EEZ, coastal nations would not have ownership of resources, but the exclusive right to harvest or extract those resources. UNCLOS III requires, however, that coastal states make EEZ resources available to "landlocked and geographically disadvantaged" countries.

Figure 1-4 shows the different maritime zones that were the product of UNCLOS III. This useful graphic also shows the boundaries established by the domestic law of the United States, setting forth the delineation between state and federal waters, and the locus of private land ownership. The graphic is not intended to show the actual extent of the continental shelf.

All of the international maritime zone boundaries are determined by distance from shore. But what is the shore? Tides rise and fall, so which point serves as the marker? The answer is contained in Article 5, which provides that the normal *baseline* is the "low-water line . . . as marked on large-scale charts officially recognized by the coastal State." Conceptually, this is the low tide line. But tides occur twice daily and differ throughout the season. Which one? The answer is, under

Figure 1-4.
Maritime jurisdiction under the United Nations' Law of the Sea Conventions.

the rules adopted by the National Oceanic and Atmospheric Administration ("NOAA"), that it is the lower of the two tides each day but averaged over every day in an 18.6-year period known as the Metonic cycle. The U.S. government calls its official averages "National Tidal Datum Epochs"; the current data in use is from the epoch running from 1983 through 2001. Soon after the current epoch (2001-2019) ends, the government will calculate new mean lower-low-tide elevations. The line formed by the projected elevation of the average lower-low tide into the shore is known as the Mean Lower Low Water line, often denoted MLLW. The "baseline," the line that one would draw on a map demarcating the legal coastline, would consist of all of the MLLW marks, strung together into a line. While the United States uses the MLLW for defining the extent of international zones such as the EEZ, states use different "datums," or sea-level measurements, for determining their own ocean boundaries.

Measuring the low-tide line under Article 5 has not been particularly contentious. However, the drawing of the baseline, the line from which all the maritime zones extend, has generated a number of disputes. It is not hard to see why. Coastlines are never straight, and often contain geographic features that make it impossible to draw a parallel line 12, 24, or 200 miles out. For example, when should a baseline be drawn across, rather than along the shoreline of a bay? How would one define a bay? Article 10 of UNCLOS III provides that

> a bay is a well-marked indentation whose penetration is in such proportion to the width of its mouth as to contain land-locked waters and constitute more than a mere curvature of the coast. An indentation shall not, however, be regarded as a bay unless its area is as large as, or larger than, that of the semi-circle whose diameter is a line drawn across the mouth of that indentation.

Figure 1-5.
Illustration of Article 10. Note, however, that if the mouth of the bay is less than 24 miles across, even if it is smaller than an imaginary dotted semicircle drawn from the "corners" of the mouth, it would be impossible to draw a territorial sea boundary that would be indented to reflect the bay. In such cases, the baseline is drawn straight across the mouth of the bay after all.

In addition to "juridical bays" that meet the definition within Article 10, "historic bays" are recognized on the basis of long-standing recognition and practice. These include the Delaware Bay between New Jersey and Delaware, the Chesapeake Bay, the Long Island Sound, Spencer Gulf in Australia, and Hudson's Bay in Canada.

However, other issues arise. How about archipelagic countries such as Indonesia? How about the Hawai'ian Islands? Articles 46-54 contain a complex set of rules on drawing baselines connecting islands and setting out all kinds of other rules regarding passage, fishing, and other matters. Those provisions attempt to strike a balance between providing security and economic benefit to an archipelagic state, and keeping the seas open for transit.

point for discussion

1. *Climate change and baselines.* Global climate change is the suite of large-scale climatic effects caused by an increase in the Earth's atmospheric temperature, caused by emissions of so-called "greenhouse gases" that, suspended in the air, act like a pane of glass and trap heat within the Earth's atmosphere. There are several different greenhouse gases, but carbon dioxide and methane are the most important ones. The nations of the world have made some small steps toward reducing emissions of greenhouse gases but are not close to making sufficient progress to avoid significant, and possibly catastrophic, global climate changes. One of the more certain changes is a rise in global mean sea levels. Sea levels will rise globally, at different rates in different places, and the exact amount is still very much uncertain. What would be the effect on the baseline regime?

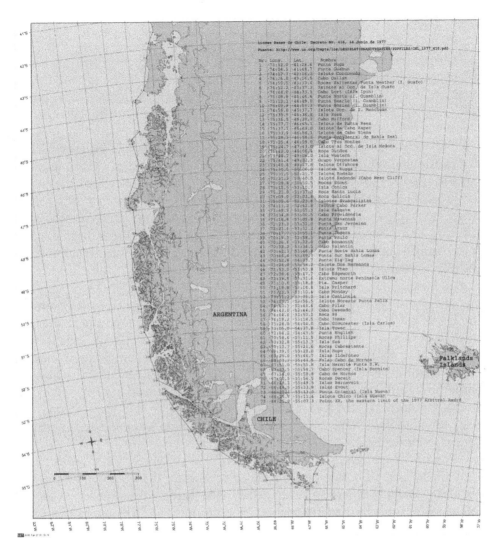

Figure 1-6.
Baselines of Chile. Read the UNCLOS rules and see whether you can find examples
of how bays, islands, and the like affect the baseline location.

What *should* change with respect to the baseline regime and the system of
maritime zones?

a. Internal Waters

There are certain waters that are recognized by UNCLOS III as being under the
complete control and sovereignty of the coastal nation, as if it were terrestrial territory. "Internal waters" includes the waters inside of baselines, such as rivers, juridical
and historic bays, and areas otherwise enclosed by baselines drawn in accordance
with Article 10, such as deltas and seas marked by fringing reefs. Any person in or
on internal waters is subject to the jurisdiction and the laws of the coastal nation.

b. Territorial Sea

Coastal nations have complete control and sovereignty over their territorial waters, just as they do over internal waters, with two important exceptions: (1) the right of innocent passage, and (2) the right of transit passage. As with other provisions in UNCLOS III, these mechanisms attempt to strike a balance between the security of the coastal nation and traditional passage rights.

"Innocent passage" is a concept that dates back centuries, and so at some levels had clearly attained the status of customary international law. As warship technology became more sophisticated, and the nature of conflict more global, the notion of innocent passage became more complex. In the 1949 *Corfu Channel* case, the newly formed International Court of Justice heard a dispute between the United Kingdom and Albania over the mining of Albanian territorial seas that led to the severe damage of two British warships and the death of 44 British sailors. What were British warships doing in Albanian territorial waters? Good question. See the map in Figure 1-7.

The Corfu Channel is *not* the 70-mile-wide opening between Italy, on the top left of the figure, and Albania, on the right; it is the tiny little channel to the *inside* of the small Greek island of Corfu off the coast of both Albania and Greece, therefore placing it within one mile of the Albanian coast. The Royal Navy, whatever its intentions (it had conspicuously trained its guns in non-battle positions), could have easily sailed around the outside of the Island of Corfu. Nevertheless, the International Court of Justice held that Albania was not entitled to mine the strait (it denied doing so) and was liable to the United Kingdom for damages.

The *Corfu Channel* case actually produced several principles that became codified in UNCLOS III. Coastal nations can enact laws for the territorial sea (as they obviously can for their territory), but they cannot "hamper the innocent passage of foreign ships through the territorial sea." Passage must be "continuous and expeditious." "Innocent" means "not prejudicial to the peace, good order or security of the coastal State." Prejudicial actions include threats of force, weapons exercises, any information collection or propaganda affecting the security of the coastal state, "willful and serious pollution" contrary to UNCLOS, and fishing. Submarines — an important consideration in

Figure 1-7. Map of Adriatic Sea, Ionian Sea, and Corfu

the height of the Cold War between the United States and the Soviet Union — must navigate on the surface and show their flag when passing innocently through another country's territorial sea.

This definition of "innocent" was the product of extensive negotiations and was heavily influenced by American negotiators who wanted to make sure that its superior naval fleet had the maximum amount of freedom. By this fairly expansive definition of "innocent," British passage through the Corfu Channel was innocent. Importantly — because this is a difference between innocent passage and "transit passage" that is discussed below — innocent passage can be temporarily suspended if "such suspension is essential for the protection of its security, including weapons exercises," and only after publication.

"Transit passage" is a separate but related concept, focusing more on the preservation of certain straits "used for international navigation" and connecting up

Corfu Channel was in fact the case first heard by the International Court of Justice and concerned a more involved series of events than is described in the case. A civil war in Greece between an American-backed government and a socialist one had drawn the concern of the United States and the United Kingdom. Two British cruisers first passed through the Corfu Channel in May 1946, and were fired upon by forces in Albania, which was wary of being drawn into the Greek conflict. No damages were inflicted. After lodging a formal protest, the United Kingdom announced it would send more ships, and return fire if attacked. Two cruisers and two destroyers did in fact return in October, with guns "fore and aft," in non-combat positions. One of the destroyers struck a mine, sustaining heavy damages and 36 casualties. The other destroyer also struck a mine, leading to another eight sailors' deaths. More protests were lodged. Weeks later, the Royal Navy again entered the Corfu Channel in a mine-sweeping operation. The International Court of Justice held partly for the United Kingdom and partly for Albania, but importantly ruled that the United Kingdom was entitled to pass through the Corfu Channel, given that it was a passageway between two parts of the High Seas, even if it was the much less obvious one than steering clear of the island of Corfu. Albania was ordered to pay damages to the United Kingdom. However, the Court also held that subsequent minesweeping operations by the United Kingdom violated international law.

different parts of the high seas or exclusive economic zones. The *Corfu Channel* case found that the Corfu Channel was a strait, because although it was not commonly used for transit, it was "useful." This case seemed to trouble the drafters, as Article 38 provides that "transit passage shall not apply if there exists seaward of the island a route through the high seas or through an exclusive economic zone of similar convenience." This would seem to preclude the provocative testing of waters undertaken by the Royal Navy as "transit passage," although its passage may still be "innocent."

The important difference between transit passage and innocent passage is that transit passage cannot be suspended. Straits must always be open for transit. But transit passage is somewhat narrower, as it only provides for freedom of navigation and overflight "*solely* for the purpose of continuous and expeditious transit" through the strait (emphasis added). Additionally, ships and aircraft exercising transit passage must "proceed without delay" and "refrain from any threat or use of force against the sovereignty, territorial integrity or political independence of States bordering the strait," and refrain from any activities other than those incident to their normal modes of continuous and expeditious transit.

Together, innocent passage and transit passage are important qualifications to a coastal nation's right to otherwise secure its territorial sea. To a large extent, they reflect the negotiating power that comes with being a naval power. Countries such as the United States, Russia, and the United Kingdom had a great deal of influence on the UNCLOS language, given their interest in maintaining the right to sail in as much of the sea as possible.

c. Contiguous Zone

Just beyond the territorial sea, the contiguous zone is the band of sea that is between two lines drawn 12 and 24 nautical miles from the baseline. In this zone, a bit farther out from land, international law gives coastal nations less authority to regulate. Article 33 provides that a coastal nation may "prevent infringement of its customs, fiscal, immigration or sanitary laws and regulations" within the 12-to-24-nautical-mile band. As noted above, the notion that coastal nations have this intermediate level of regulatory control over this area was a part of customary international law before UNCLOS I.

Additionally, coastal nation jurisdiction in the contiguous zone is limited. Pursuant to Article 33, coastal nations may only interdict ships that they reasonably believe are using the seas to violate these four types of laws (which are liberally construed to include drug smuggling and unauthorized fishing). For example, Australia's 2013 "Operation Sovereign Borders," an effort to stop ships suspected of depositing migrants and refugees on Australian shores, intercepted those ships in its contiguous zone, and towed them into the EEZ. The following case illustrates another example, pertaining to fishing.

Figure 1-8.
A Japanese fishing vessel of the 1970s, similar to the *Taiyo Maru 28*; the boat in the picture is adrift at sea after being ripped from the dock by the Fukoshima tsunami of 2011.

United States v. F/V Taiyo Maru, Number 28

395 F. Supp. 413 (D. Me. 1975)

Judge GIGNOUX delivered the opinion of the United States District Court, District of Maine.

There is no dispute as to the events, recited above, which led to the seizure of the TAIYO MARU 28. For the purposes of the instant motions, the following undisputed facts are significant: (1) On September 5, 1974, the United States Coast Guard sighted the TAIYO MARU 28, a commercial Japanese fishing vessel, within waters which the United States claims as part of its contiguous fisheries zone, and had reasonable cause to believe that the vessel was fishing in the zone in violation of United States fisheries law; and (2) at that point, the Coast Guard signaled the TAIYO MARU 28 and, after giving immediate and continuous hot pursuit, effected seizure of the vessel on the high seas.

The United States contends that, by fishing in the contiguous fisheries zone, the TAIYO MARU 28 and her captain violated the Bartlett Act, 16 U.S.C. § 1081 et seq., and the Contiguous Fisheries Zone Act, 16 U.S.C. § 1091 et seq., and that international law permits, and United States law authorizes, the hot pursuit of a foreign vessel from the contiguous fisheries zone and the seizure of the vessel on the high seas for violation of domestic fisheries law. Defendant's position is that this Court lacks jurisdiction over the TAIYO MARU 28 and her master, because the vessel was seized on the high seas in violation of the 1958 Geneva Convention on the High Seas, . . . a multilateral treaty agreement to which both Japan and the United States are parties signatory.

By the Bartlett Act, enacted in 1964, Congress made it unlawful for any foreign vessel, or for the master of such a vessel, to engage in fishing within the territorial waters of the United States, or "within any waters in which the United States has the same rights in respect to fisheries as it has in its territorial waters . . . except . . . as expressly provided by an international agreement to which the United States is a party." 16 U.S.C. § 1081. In enacting the Bartlett Act, the intent of Congress was to fill a gap in existing law by making it clear that foreign vessels are denied the privilege of fishing within the territorial waters of the United States and by providing effective sanctions for unlawful fishing by foreign vessels within territorial waters. H.R.Rep. (Merchant Marine and Fisheries Committee) No. 1356 (1964), U.S.Cong. & Admin. News, 1964, pp. 2183, 2183-84. The Bartlett Act did not define the width of the territorial sea, "thereby leaving the opportunity for the United States to follow the lead of Canada and other nations in establishing a limit beyond the present 3 miles for fishery purposes." *Id.* at p. 2187. The words "within any waters in which the United States has the same rights in respect to fisheries as it has in its territorial waters" were added in anticipation of the United States extending its fishery jurisdiction out to 12 miles. . . .

By the Contiguous Fisheries Zone Act, enacted in 1966, Congress established a fisheries zone contiguous to the territorial waters of the United States and provided with respect to such zone:

> The United States will exercise the same exclusive rights in respect to fisheries in
> the zone as it has in its territorial sea, subject to the continuation of traditional

fishing by foreign states within this zone as may be recognized by the United States. 16 U.S.C. § 1091.

The contiguous fisheries zone was defined by Congress in the Contiguous Fisheries Zone Act as having "as its inner boundary the outer limits of the territorial sea and as its seaward boundary a line drawn so that each point on the line is nine nautical miles from the nearest point in the inner boundary." In so defining the contiguous zone, Congress recognized that the territorial sea of the United States extends three miles from the United States, which is where Thomas Jefferson set the outer limit in 1793 and where "it has remained unaltered to this day." It was the expressed intent of Congress in the 1966 legislation to "unilaterally establish a fishery zone contiguous to the present 3-mile territorial sea of the United States by extending our exclusive fisheries rights to a distance of 12 miles from our shores." H.R.Rep.No.2086, *supra* at p. 3285.

Defendant makes no contention that the contiguous fisheries zone created by the United States in the Contiguous Fisheries Zone Act violates customary international law. Defendant also recognizes that, within the three-mile territorial sea, the United States has the right to prohibit foreign fishing and that Article 23 of the Convention on the High Seas provides express authority for the United States to conduct hot pursuit from the territorial sea onto the high seas for the purpose of apprehending foreign ships which have violated domestic fisheries law within the territorial sea. And defendant does not contest that the Contiguous Fisheries Zone Act extended to a zone nine miles from the seaward limit of the territorial sea all the rights with respect to fisheries which the United States previously had in its territorial sea, and that, unless restricted by treaty, the United States has the right to conduct hot pursuit from a contiguous zone onto the high seas for violations of its domestic law. Defendant's sole contention is that the United States had no right to conduct hot pursuit from the contiguous zone and to effect seizure of the TAIYO MARU 28, because the vessel was seized on the high seas in violation of Article 23 of the 1958 Convention on the High Seas.

Defendant asserts that Article 23 of the Convention on the High Seas must be read in conjunction with Article 24 of the Convention on the Territorial Sea and the Contiguous Zone. The argument is that since Article 24 only authorizes the establishment of a contiguous zone for the purposes of enforcing the coastal State's customs, fiscal, immigration or sanitary regulations, and since Article 23 permits hot pursuit of a foreign ship from such a contiguous zone only for the four purposes listed in Article 24, the United States was without authority to commence hot pursuit of the TAIYO MARU 28 from within the contiguous fisheries zone for the purpose of enforcing its fisheries regulations.

***

Analysis of the text of Article 23 of the Convention on the High Seas shows that the Article provides general authority to undertake hot pursuit from a contiguous zone when the authorities of the coastal State have good reason to believe that a foreign vessel has violated the coastal State's laws and regulations. It is true that

Article 23 permits hot pursuit from a contiguous zone, created for one of the four purposes enumerated in Article 24 of the Convention on the Territorial Sea and the Contiguous Zone, only if there has been a violation of the rights for the protection of which the zone was established. But Article 23 does not in terms deny a coastal State the right to commence hot pursuit from a contiguous zone established for a purpose other than one of the purposes listed in Article 24. Nor does Article 24 in terms prohibit the establishment of a contiguous zone for a purpose other than one of those specified in the Article. The language of Article 24, relating to the purposes for which a contiguous zone may be established, is permissive, rather than restrictive. It provides that a coastal State "may" establish a contiguous zone for the purposes of enforcing its customs, fiscal, immigration or sanitary regulations. Although Article 24 only affirmatively recognizes the right of a coastal State to create a contiguous zone for one of the four enumerated purposes, nothing in the Article precludes the establishment of such a zone for other purposes, including the enforcement of domestic fisheries law. . . .

***

It is apparent that Congress was well aware of its obligations under the 1958 Conventions when the 1966 Contiguous Fisheries Zone Act was enacted, and that Congress perceived no conflict between the Act and the treaty provisions. This is evident from the House Report, which discusses the Conventions and their relationship to the proposed legislation:

> In 1958, and again in 1960, the Law of the Sea Conferences held in Geneva, Switzerland, left unresolved the twin questions of the width of the territorial sea and to the extent to which a coastal state could claim exclusive fishing rights in the high seas off its coast. At the second conference in 1960, the United States and Canada put forward a compromise proposal for a 6-mile territorial sea, plus a 6-mile exclusive fisheries zone (12 miles of exclusive jurisdiction in all) subject to the continuation for 10 years of traditional fishing by other states in the outer 6 miles. This compromise proposal failed by one vote to obtain the two-thirds vote necessary for adoption.
>
> Since the 1958 Law of the Sea Conference, there has been a trend toward the establishment of a 12-mile fisheries rule in international practice. Thirty-nine countries acting individually or in concert with other countries have extended their fisheries limits to 12 miles since 1958.

The Report also notes that, as of July 1, 1966, of the 99 United Nations coastal nations, slightly more than 60 countries asserted a 12-mile exclusive fishery zone, either as territorial sea or as territorial sea plus a contiguous zone.

Since the seizure of the TAIYO MARU 28 on the high seas following hot pursuit from the contiguous zone was not in violation of Article 23 of the 1958 Convention on the High Seas, and, moreover, was sanctioned by domestic law and in conformity with the prevailing consensus of international law and practice, this Court has jurisdiction to decide the present proceedings on their merits. Defendant's motions to dismiss for lack of jurisdiction are therefore denied.

points for discussion

1. *Extent of contiguous zone.* This case took place in 1975, before UNCLOS III established the contiguous zone as a belt 12 to 24 nautical miles from the baseline. In 1975, the territorial sea was only 3 nautical miles wide, and the contiguous zone 9 nautical miles wide, immediately seaward of the territorial sea. Was the court influenced by the fact that other countries were claiming a fishing zone of up to 12 nautical miles from their coasts?

2. *Contiguous zone purposes.* Notice the court upholds the expansion, by domestic U.S. law, of the allowable laws that can be enforced in the contiguous zone. And yet, defendant did not challenge this, but limited his defense to seizure on the high seas. Was this expansion permissible under international law?

3. *Hot pursuit.* Article 111 of UNCLOS now provides that

   > [H]ot pursuit of a foreign ship may be undertaken when the competent authorities of the coastal State have good reason to believe that the ship has violated the laws and regulations of that State. Such pursuit must be commenced when the foreign ship or one of its boats is within the internal waters, the archipelagic waters, the territorial sea or the contiguous zone of the pursuing State, and may only be continued outside the territorial sea or the contiguous zone if the pursuit has not been interrupted. . . . If the foreign ship is within a contiguous zone, as defined in article 33, the pursuit may only be undertaken if there has been a violation of the rights for the protection of which the zone was established.

   Does this suggest that coastal nations can define their contiguous zone purposes as they wish? Are there any limits? Article 111 also provides that "[t]he right of hot pursuit ceases as soon as the ship pursued enters the territorial sea of its own State or of a third State." *Taiyo Maru* was intercepted off the coast of Maine. If you were a sailor on board, and if this rule were in effect at the time, what would you have advised the captain?

4. *Drug smuggling.* Can a coastal nation intercept ships in its contiguous zone that it suspects of illegally smuggling drugs? What about beyond the contiguous zone? Why or why not? Consider Article 108 of UNCLOS III, which provides:

Illicit traffic in narcotic drugs or psychotropic substances

   1. All States shall cooperate in the suppression of illicit traffic in narcotic drugs and psychotropic substances engaged in by ships on the high seas contrary to international conventions.

   2. Any State which has reasonable grounds for believing that a ship flying its flag is engaged in illicit traffic in narcotic drugs or psychotropic substances may request the cooperation of other States to suppress such traffic.

What would a coastal nation do if it suspected a vessel of smuggling drugs outside of its contiguous zone? What if it had passed through its contiguous zone?

d. Exclusive Economic Zone

The Exclusive Economic Zone (EEZ) was a concept developed in UNCLOS III. As noted above, some nations had claimed up to 200 nautical miles as their territorial sea, so that distance had some basis in state practice. But the codification of that number, and the detailed enumeration of the rights and responsibilities of coastal nations, was an ambitious undertaking in international lawmaking.

The EEZ runs from the line separating the outer limit of the 12-nautical-mile territorial sea to a distance 200 nautical miles from the baseline. It thus contains within it the contiguous zone. Where coastal nations are close enough to have overlapping EEZs, the boundary is drawn halfway in between the competing EEZ lines. The State of Florida is close enough to Cuba and the archipelagic state of the Bahamas so that the U.S. EEZ line is much closer than the normal allotment of 200 nautical miles. See Figure 1-9.

Figure 1-9.
The lines show the extent of Exclusive Economic Zones in the Caribbean region. Note the many cases in which a country's EEZ does not appear to extend to the full 200 nautical miles.

The provisions in UNCLOS III pertaining to the EEZ are unprecedented in terms of scope, and the extent to which they codified the rights and obligations on all the world's countries, even the land-locked ones. New provisions were added to provide for environmental protection and marine scientific research. A quick summary of the major UNCLOS III provisions follows.

i. Living Resources

UNCLOS Article 56 provides that the coastal state has in its EEZ the "sovereign rights" over the "natural resources, whether living or non-living, of the waters superjacent to the seabed and of the seabed and its subsoil. . . ." It should come as no surprise that the "living resources" with which the parties were most concerned were fish. Fishing industries throughout the world wield enormous political power, in part because of the jobs and revenue they provide, but also because many countries view their fishermen as an important part of their culture and history. A key driver for the establishment of the EEZ was continuing irritation on the part of American fishermen that foreign flag fishing vessels were very active in waters close to the United States. This led to a widespread perception that foreign fishermen were taking fish that "rightfully" belonged to Americans. In fact, even before UNCLOS III established the 200-mile limit in 1982, Congress had passed the Magnuson-Stevens Act, also known as the Fisheries Conservation and Management Act. (We will cover this Act in detail later in this book.) The Act established a management system and authorized the setting of catch limits and the development of fisheries management plans. It also claimed that the United States had the right to exclude foreign flag vessels from the area within 200 nautical miles from the coast. Here, as with the continental shelf, a unilateral act by the United States wound up serving as customary international law, which then wound up being codified in a multilateral convention. Indeed, UNCLOS III authorized coastal nations to enact exactly the kinds of fishing regulations set out in the Magnuson-Stevens Act. With the exception of some highly migratory fish and marine mammals, the coastal nation has the sole authority to regulate the taking of living resources in its EEZ.

ii. Non-living Resources

Until relatively recently, the term "non-living resources" in UNCLOS referred to oil and gas and mineral resources in the seabed. Article 56 confers to coastal nations the exclusive right to extract these resources from their EEZs. But in a very forward-looking moment of drafting, Article 56 also vests coastal nations with the exclusive right to "produc[e] energy from the water, currents and winds." Article 56 thus explicitly vests in the coastal state all harnessed renewable energy sources, such as wind turbines (floating and fixed) and marine hydrokinetic generators, which use currents and tides to generate electricity. This ownership in the coastal state was almost certainly implicit from the other language and provisions of UNCLOS, but with the free travel and overflight provisions in other parts, it might have been prudent to state it explicitly.

iii. Vessel Navigation

Article 58, "Rights and duties of other States in the exclusive economic zone," provides that all states, coastal or land-locked, enjoy the freedoms of the high seas with respect to navigating through an EEZ and for laying submarine cables and pipelines. Submarines may pass without surfacing, as they must in a territorial sea, and overflight is permitted through the airspace.

iv. Marine Scientific Research

UNCLOS III recognizes the importance of research, and provides that all nations, coastal or not, have the "right to conduct marine scientific research," provided that it is for peaceful purposes, is done with appropriate scientific methods, does not unjustifiably interfere with other legitimate uses, and otherwise complies with UNCLOS III. Researchers must request *express consent* to conduct marine scientific research in another country's EEZ six months in advance. This consent should be granted "in normal circumstances." What exactly that means is unclear, but they are certainly broader than the list in Article 246(5) of circumstances under which coastal nations may withhold consent. Express consent is implied if the coastal nation fails to respond to a request within four months.

v. Artificial Islands and Structures

Article 60 grants coastal nations the right to construct artificial islands and other structures in their EEZ for all of the purposes discussed above, and "other economic purposes." So clearly, offshore rigs and wind turbines are permissible, as they are under the Convention on the Continental Shelf. But coastal nations may go further than that and construct much larger structures. Dubai has constructed artificial islands for housing and for tourism that are so large they are fringing at the edges of their territorial sea, but no worry: They are permitted to build out to their EEZ. Moreover, coastal nations can enact customs, fiscal, health, safety, and immigration laws and regulations with respect to such islands.

As with other rights in the EEZ, coastal nations are to have "due regard" for "fishing, the protection of the marine environment and the rights and duties of other States." For example, while coastal nations may construct artificial islands, they are also obligated to keep in mind the freedoms of the high seas, including travel and overflight. In *Artic Sunrise* (*Kingdom of the Netherlands v. Russian Federation*) (2014), 53 I.L.M. 607, a case before the International Tribunal for the Law of the Sea, the Netherlands sought the release of a Greenpeace ship that had approached a Russian oil drilling platform in Russia's EEZ. Knowing full well what it intended to do, Russian forces boarded the Dutch-flagged ship, and detained the crew and ship. The Netherlands sought their release. The Tribunal ordered the release of the ship and crew, but some dissenting opinions were filed. Notably, the arbitrators of the Tribunal reached different conclusions about how to balance the freedoms of the high seas with the rights of coastal nations to protect their artificial islands and structures.

Coastal nations are not permitted to construct artificial islands and structures for military purposes. China has, however, done so in the South China Sea, much to the consternation of its neighbors and strategic adversaries (such as the United States). This violation of UNCLOS III is additionally irritating because while China lays claim to an enlarged part of the South China Sea, some of the Chinese artificial islands are really within the EEZ of Vietnam, not China.

e. Continental Shelf

The UNCLOS provisions on the new EEZ might not have been necessary, and some are actually redundant, because of the 1958 Convention on the Continental Shelf, which provided that a coastal nation had the exclusive right to "mineral and other non-living resources of the seabed and subsoil," as well as "living organisms belonging to the sedentary species." UNCLOS III repeats much of the language in the 1958 Convention, while adding considerably more detail about several other matters, including the outer boundary of the continental shelf.

While the continental shelf had attained the status of customary international law by 1958, the question of exactly where it ended remained unsettled all the way up to UNCLOS III. To some extent it is still unsettled. The original 1958 limit was the isobath at which the depth reached "200 metres or, beyond that limit, to where the depth of the superjacent waters admits of the exploitation of the natural resources." But as marine drilling technology standards improved, more and more seabed could be said to "admit of exploitation." UNCLOS III was the product of extensive jockeying among developed and developing nations, and nations with differing geographic features in their adjoining seas.

Article 76 provides that every coastal nation gets a minimum of 200 nautical miles as its continental shelf, unless (as in the case of the EEZ or the territorial seas) coastal nations have overlapping continental shelf zones. A coastal nation can claim a larger continental shelf as a "submerged prolongation of the land mass" (reminiscent of President Truman's "naturally appurtenant" language), which can be determined by reference to the "foot" of the continental slope, the point at which the *gradient* changes most quickly — the ocean floor changes most abruptly from a steep drop-off to a flat plain. See Figure 1-4 and the "kink" in the ocean floor. Using that point as a reference, a coastal nation can use either one of two formulas to delimit its continental shelf. First, it can find the line at which the thickness of sedimentary rock is at least 1 percent of the distance from the foot of the slope. For example, if a coastal nation wanted to define its outer continental shelf limit to be 100 miles from the foot of the slope, it would have to find that the sedimentary rock was 1 mile thick at that point. The second formula is simply to claim an outer continental shelf limit of 60 nautical miles from the foot of the slope. In neither case can the outer limit of a continental shelf be more than the greater of 350 nautical miles or the 100 nautical miles past the 2,500-meter isobaths.

As you can imagine, these formulas are not only complicated, but the evidence needed to support these claims is significant, and the potential for dispute great.

UNCLOS III thus establishes a body called the Commission on the Limits of the Continental Shelf, which makes recommendations to coastal nations on their outer limits. If the coastal state adopts them, they become the established outer limit of their continental shelf. Whew!

All of this calculation is to determine the extent to which a coastal nation has "sovereign rights" that are not conferred by the UNCLOS III provisions on the EEZ. The continental shelf may confer upon a coastal nation the exclusive right to extract oil or gas or mineral resources farther out than 200 nautical miles. The continental shelf may also confer upon a coastal nation the right to take sedentary living organisms from the seabed. Unlike other maritime zones, exclusive rights in the continental shelf need not be affirmatively claimed; they are vested in the coastal nation *ipso jure.*

f. The High Seas

The high seas — those areas outside of the territorial seas and EEZs of coastal nations — remain the last bastions of Grotius's view that the oceans are *res nullius,* the property of no one. The reality is, however, that multinational conventions, some discussed below, have been eroding the traditional freedoms of the high seas for decades. Treaties dealing with whaling, migratory fish stocks, and pollution have curtailed, but not completely eliminated, those freedoms.

Article 87 provides that "[t]he high seas are open to all States, whether coastal or land-locked, [and] comprises, *inter alia,* . . . freedom of navigation . . . overflight . . . to lay submarine cables and pipelines . . . to construct artificial islands and installations permitted under international law . . . fishing . . . [and] scientific research." These freedoms are to be exercised, as are other rights under UNCLOS III, "with due regard" for other countries.

On the high seas, ships must bear a flag, and jurisdiction over ships lies only with the country of that flag. Duties attach to the flagged country, including a duty to cooperate in the suppression of illicit traffic in narcotic drugs and psychotropic substances," and to "take effective measures to prevent and punish the transport of slaves. . . . " States other than that of the ship flag can assert jurisdiction on the high seas in the cases of piracy, hot pursuit, and unauthorized broadcasting.

g. The Deep Seabed

Until the 1960s, the deep seabed was considered a wasteland. At that time, mining technologies could not reach the depths of the ocean floor beyond the continental shelf. The most sensible conception of the deep seabed was to simply consider it part of the high seas, *res nullius* as Hugo Grotius would have argued. However, as mining technologies advanced, and as the deep seabed no longer seemed out of reach, the prospect of an uncontrolled free-for-all began to emerge. The need for an international legal regime became obvious, at least to some nations, and they looked to UNCLOS III to create rules for deep seabed mining.

Because the boundaries of the continental shelf are not coterminous with that of the EEZ, the deep seabed does not cover the same surface area as the high seas.

The deep seabed is thus referred to in UNCLOS III as "the Area." A very large and complicated regime, consisting of 59 articles, is contained in Part XI of UNCLOS III, which governs the deep seabed, or "Area."

The Area contains oil and gas deposits, but even more importantly, it contains valuable mineral deposits, useful for many technological applications. Nickel, copper, manganese, cobalt, aluminum, and other minerals are wrapped up in *polymetallic nodules*, small clumps, mostly about 2 to 4 inches in diameter, half-buried and littered about the seabed at depths of 12,000 to 20,000 feet. At such great depths and in such small clumps, only highly industrial and potentially damaging mining techniques are economically viable. "Hydraulic mining" employs automated devices that dredge up the sea floor where large concentrations of polymetallic nodules exist, crushes it into a slurry and pumps them in a flexible hose to the surface. It is reminiscent of gold-mining in the nineteenth century, in which huge quantities of earth were removed to extract a small amount of a valuable substance, a wasteful and destructive process. The prospect of economically viable mining of the seabed raises two concerns: (1) that a wasteful free-for-all might ensue in a race to collect these precious nodules, and (2) the environmental consequences of mining. A convention was badly needed.

Figure 1-10.
Polymetallic nodules lie on the seabed, as seen from a French research submarine.

UNCLOS III negotiations over the deep seabed were extremely contentious. The United States persistently held out when it objected to proposals, and many provisions of Part XI, pertaining to the deep seabed, were changed to accommodate the United States. In the end, however, the United States refused to sign on. The Reagan Administration took the position that the acceptable parts of the Deep Seabed regime were really customary international law, and the ones it objected to were not. However, other nations overwhelmingly approved the deep seabed provisions, along with the rest of UNCLOS III, over the objection of the United States.

To understand why the United States seemed so determined to play the role of spoiler, it is important to understand, if only through a very brief description, what the deep seabed provisions do. First, UNCLOS III establishes the International Seabed Authority, which in the treaty is shortened to the somewhat Orwellian-sounding "the Authority." The Authority has extensive powers to regulate mining in the Area and is charged with developing rules and procedures for licensing mining in the Area. Article 136 states simply, opaquely, that "[t]he Area and its resources are the common heritage of mankind." The Authority is supposed to carry out its regulatory activity in observance of this principle, though exactly what it means is a bit unclear. One sticking point for the United States was that the Authority "shall take measures . . . to promote and encourage the transfer to developing States of . . . technology and scientific knowledge so that all States benefit therefrom," and that "the . . . Parties shall cooperate in promoting the transfer of technology and scientific knowledge relating to activities in the Area." Although that final language was softened from a firmer mandate (at the behest of the United States), that language still rankled.

Perhaps even more of a problem for the United States, Part XI of UNCLOS also creates another Orwellian-sounding body, the "Enterprise." The Enterprise is a production arm of the Authority, mining, transporting, processing, and marketing minerals from the Area, which places it in direct competition with private mining companies. The Enterprise is theoretically on equal footing with private mining companies, but several provisions suggest otherwise, such as an initial production reservation of 38,000 tons, and provisions that "ensure that the Enterprise is able to carry out activities in the Area . . . to keep pace with States and other entities."

Over time, the concerns of the United States have waxed and waned in importance. As mineral prices plummeted, deep seabed mining became irrelevant; as production of electronics becomes more prevalent, mineral prices increase again, raising the stakes again. The United States takes the position that it is not bound by Part XI of UNCLOS III. As recently as 2012, then-Secretary of State Hillary Clinton testified before the Senate Foreign Relations Committee on accession to UNCLOS III, urging ratification.

Written Testimony of Hillary Rodham Clinton, Secretary, U.S. Department of State, Before the Senate Foreign Relations Committee on May 23, 2012

Accession to the 1982 Law of the Sea Convention and Ratification of the 1994 Agreement Amending Part XI of the Law of the Sea Convention

U.S. interests are deeply tied to the oceans. No country is in a position to gain more from the Law of the Sea Convention than the United States. . . . It is no wonder then that there is such a strong and wide-ranging coalition supporting U.S. accession. The U.S. military has consistently and unequivocally supported the Convention for its national security benefits. Affected U.S. industries, including shipping, fisheries, telecommunications, and energy, have consistently supported U.S. accession for its economic benefits. Non-governmental organizations concerned with the protection of natural resources have consistently supported U.S. accession. And both Republican and Democratic Presidents have supported U.S. accession. I have never seen another treaty with such intensive and broad support. . . .

. . . I would like to highlight [provisions relating] to mining in the deep seabed areas beyond any country's jurisdiction. Only as a Party to the Convention could the United States sponsor U.S. companies like Lockheed Martin to mine the deep seabed for valuable metals and rare earth elements.

These rare earth elements — essential for cell phones, flat-screen televisions, electric car batteries, and other high-tech products — are currently in tight supply and produced almost exclusively by China. While we challenge China's export restrictions, we must also make it possible for U.S. companies to develop other sources of these critical materials. They can only do this if they can obtain secure rights to deep seabed mine sites and indisputable title to minerals recovered. While we sit on the sidelines, companies in China, India, Russia, and elsewhere are securing their rights, moving ahead with deep seabed resource exploration, and taking the lead in this emerging market.

I want to make two additional points about deep seabed mining. First, we cannot rely on customary international law here. For companies to obtain security of tenure to deep seabed mining sites, they must be sponsored by a Party to the Convention. And without such security of tenure, industry has told us that it will not risk the significant investment needed to extract these valuable resources. I want to be clear that there is no means for the United States to support its domestic deep seabed mining industry as a non-Party.

Second, once the United States becomes a Party, we would have an unprecedented ability to influence deep seabed mining activities worldwide. In revising the Convention's deep seabed provisions in the 1994 Agreement, our negotiators obtained a permanent U.S. seat on the seabed Council. This is the key decision-making body established by the Convention on deep seabed matters. I know of no other international body that accords one country, and one country only — the United States — a permanent seat on its decision-making body. In this way, the Convention's institutions provide the United States with a level of influence commensurate with our interests and global standing.

Until we join, however, our reserved seat remains empty. As a result, we have limited ability to shape the rules and no ability to help U.S. companies pursue their job-creating initiatives to exploit deep seabed resources.

points for discussion

1. *In or out?* Do you agree with Secretary Clinton's assessment (shared by former President George W. Bush) that the United States is better off in UNCLOS III than outside of it? Do you think with so many signatories to UNCLOS that the United States is correct in asserting that it is protected by customary international law?

2. *The Authority and the Enterprise.* Concerns that the Authority and the Enterprise would serve an allocative function advantaging developing countries have not generally materialized. China has raced ahead without benefiting materially from UNCLOS III's redistributive provisions. In part, the 1994 Implementing Agreement for Part XI (pertaining to the Deep Seabed) provided that the Enterprise will only conduct deep seabed mining projects as part of joint ventures submitted for approval to the Authority, so that the Enterprise only operates as part of some other private venture. Aline Jaeckel, *Current Legal Developments, International Seabed Authority*, 31 Int'l J. Marine & Coastal L. 706 (2016). Though nascent, some efforts are afoot to establish some environmental regulations for deep

seabed mining. *See, e.g.*, Verena Tunnicliffe et al., *Strategic Environmental Goals and Objectives: Setting the Basis for Environmental Regulation of Deep Seabed Mining*, __ MARINE POL'Y __ (2018).

Problem Exercise

The notorious drug kingpin "El Guano" has escaped his Central American jailors again. The U.S. Drug Enforcement Agency (DEA) believes that he is being shuttled out of Centroamericano by boat to Canada, where he can consolidate his power and his lieutenants. DEA boats spot a suspicious yacht, flying the Centroamerican flag, cruising north parallel to the Pacific Coast, about 210 miles off of the west coast of the State of Washington. DEA agents believe that El Guano is headed for a "safe house" — a place of refuge safe from detection — in the Canadian city of Vancouver. To get to Vancouver, however, the boat carrying El Guano must enter the narrow Strait of Juan de Fuca, a narrow passageway between the U.S. State of Washington and the Canadian Province of British Columbia, that is about 17 miles wide, and which is split right down the middle by the U.S.-Canada border (see map in Figure 1-11). DEA agents believe that eventually, the yacht carrying El Guano must eventually pass very close to American shores.

Figure 1-11. Map of Juan de Fuca Strait

You are a lawyer with the U.S. Department of State and are summoned to advise the DEA as to their possible legal courses of action. When and where can they capture El Guano — if they can — if he sails toward Washington State and into Strait of Juan de Fuca? Provide legal analysis for all possibilities. Does El Guano have alternatives, if he wishes to avoid possible interdiction by the United States?

2. Protection of the Marine Ecosystem

UNCLOS III confers rights and imposes duties upon coastal nations with respect to protection of the marine environment in their respective EEZs. Coastal nations may adopt laws and regulations to prevent marine pollution in their EEZ but must work through rules and procedures "established through competent international organizations." That "competent international organization" for most international marine pollution issues is the International Maritime Organization (IMO), which is a standard-setting body with respect to marine pollution.

The "rules and procedures" that are promulgated by the IMO include the 1973 International Convention for the Prevention of Pollution from Ships, which was modified by the Protocol of 1978. As shorthand, the modified convention is known simply as MARPOL 73/78, which has been updated several times. They also include the London Convention of 1972, which regulates the dumping of wastes at sea. While these conventions exist independent of UNCLOS III, and are not specific to the EEZ, UNCLOS III sets forth numerous provisions that incorporate these treaties by reference, and either reinforce or strengthen existing provisions in these treaties. For example, Article 210 provides that "[d]umping within the territorial sea and the exclusive economic zone or onto the continental shelf shall not be carried out with the express prior approval of the coastal State, which has the right to permit, regulate, and control such dumping. . . . " The contribution of UNCLOS III is to operationalize some pollution control standards, as well as that of other marine pollution standards adopted by IMO.

Although UNCLOS III strengthens some environmental provisions, enforcement is still difficult to ensure. Generally, UNCLOS III provides that enforcement is to be undertaken by the vessel's flag country (its home country). Only in a narrow set of conditions, involving a "substantial discharge," "clear grounds" for believing a violation has occurred, and "clear objective evidence" of the discharge, are coastal nations permitted to detain foreign flag vessels.

In addition to creating new rights, UNCLOS III also imposes new duties on coastal nations to protect the marine environment. UNCLOS III requires coastal nations to "adopt laws and regulations to prevent, reduce, and control pollution of the marine environment" from land-based sources, vessels, and seabed activities. The list of duties is long; the prospect for sanctioning noncompliance is somewhat remote.

Also part of the aspirations to protect the marine ecosystem is the conservation of fisheries in each country's territorial sea and EEZ. Article 61 provides that "the coastal State shall determine the allowable catch of living resources within its [EEZ]," and shall, "taking into account the best scientific evidence available," ensure that its living resources are "not endangered through over-exploitation." Article 62 provides that laws and regulations to protect fisheries *may* relate to a long list of factors and provisions, such as licensure, allowable equipment, fixing the age and size of fish, or the allowable seasons for fishing. However, UNCLOS III makes clear that the details of regulation and the stringency of regulation in its EEZ are up to the coastal state.

D. OTHER MULTINATIONAL CONVENTIONS

While the Law of the Sea Conventions form a governance structure for the world's oceans, other international conventions govern certain practices, and certain species of special concern. The Law of the Sea Conventions being a prominent exception, international lawmaking tends to be, like domestic lawmaking, reactive in nature. When the nations of the world can actually find some agreement, however, the international law made in treaties is an important form of governance that trickles down to the individual nations. Several of the most prominent examples of multilateral agreements relating to the ocean are reviewed in this section.

1. Whaling

Humans have hunted whales for thousands of years for their oil, meat, and bones. The earliest organized whale hunts were believed to have been undertaken by the Basques as early as 700 A.D. Whale oil, for example, has been used as a smoke-less lamp fuel, for cosmetics, and as a lubricant. As ships became more seaworthy and expanded their ranges, and as the uses of whale products expanded, whaling expanded. By the mid-1800s, whaling employed more than 70,000 people world-wide, and over 700 ships. As you can imagine, traditional whaling required a large, cooperative effort but yielded a large bounty. Modern technologies have rendered traditional whaling practices anachronistic, but the act of whaling itself, even with exploding-tip harpoons launched from a gun, retains cultural significance. Three countries in particular — Japan, Norway, and Iceland — have fiercely defended their whaling communities and resisted international efforts to control whaling.

Concerns with "overharvesting" have emerged in the last century, as some whale species have been pushed to the brink of extinction. Some are actively hunted by Japan, Norway, and Iceland, and some are the victims of commercial fishing and other marine activities that cause indirect but serious, sometimes lethal harm. More recently, since the 1970s, when scientists first began to appreciate the intelligence and complexity of whales, ethical concerns have broadly emerged over the harm, direct and indirect, that humans have imposed on them.

Developments in international law with respect to whales reflect these changing conditions and more. The League of Nations tried, unsuccessfully, to introduce standards in the 1920s, but two agreements emerged in the 1930s: the Geneva Convention for Regulation of Whaling in 1931, and the Agreement for the Regulation of Whaling in 1937. Recognizing the rapidly depleting populations of many species of whales, the agreements were predicated on the "principle of international regulation of a common property resource in the high seas." While ineffective, these agreements formed a precedent for future limits on whaling. It is worth noting that even those weak agreements were driven by a sharp drop in demand for whale products. Far too many whales were being killed. But the impetus for agreement stemmed from the supply glut and low prices caused by excessive whaling, not the depletion of whale stocks.

By the end of the second World War, the need for a more effective international agreement was clear. The result was the 1946 International Convention for the Regulation of Whaling. The most important outcome of the 1946 Convention was the creation of the International Whaling Commission (IWC), a body authorized to enact regulations and limits on whaling binding on signatories. The IWC was charged with a number of regulatory and fact-finding duties and, in theory, had the authority to impose binding restrictions on signatories to the 1946 Convention.

At the outset, however, the 1946 Convention was focused on managing whale harvesting, not conservation of whales. Two paragraphs in the preamble are illuminating:

> *Recognizing* that the whale stocks are susceptible of natural increases if whaling is properly regulated, and that increases in the size of whale stocks will permit increases in the number of whales which may be captured without endangering these natural resources;
>
> *Recognizing* that it is in the common interest to achieve the optimum level of whale stocks as rapidly as possible without causing widespread economic and nutritional distress;

The 1946 Convention gives signatory nations the ability to "opt out" of any IWC regulations. Signatories can simply file a timely objection and be exempt *themselves* from whaling regulations. Whaling countries do not even have to necessarily avail themselves of this provision; another provision in the 1946 Convention provides that "any Contracting Government may grant to any of its nationals a special permit authorizing that national to kill, take and treat whales for purposes of scientific research. . . . " In other words, the government of a whaling nation may assert that its whaling is for scientific purposes, and issue permits to its nationals to hunt whales. There are no limits to "scientific" whaling.

The ineffectiveness of the 1946 Convention became clear in the 1970s, as several whale stocks

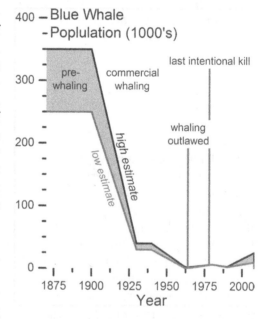

Figure 1-12.

Blue whale populations have rebounded only slightly despite 50 years of a moratorium on hunting.

became gravely endangered. But not only was the 1946 Convention and the IWC facing its failure to manage whaling for whaling's sake, it was facing a new source of opposition: a powerful environmental movement in the 1970s, which did not seek to just manage whaling, but to end it altogether. By the 1980s, the prohibition forces managed to prod the IWC to enact a five-year moratorium on commercial whaling altogether. Japan objected, thereby removing itself from the obligation to cease commercial whaling.

Perhaps nowhere has the movement to ban whaling altogether been as strong as it has been in the United States. Congress enacted domestic laws designed to try to punish whaling nations. The amendments, called the Pelly and Packwood Amendments, created certain mandatory duties on the part of the Secretary of Commerce with respect to whaling nations. The following case sets out the context of the amendments, and their operation with respect to international law.

Japan Whaling Association v. American Cetacean Society

478 U.S. 221 (1986)

Justice WHITE delivered the opinion of the Court.

In these cases, we address the question whether, under what are referred to in these cases as the Pelly and Packwood Amendments . . . the Secretary of Commerce is required to certify that Japan's whaling practices "diminish the effectiveness" of the International Convention for the Regulation of Whaling because that country's annual harvest exceeds quotas established under the Convention. . . .

Based on concern over the effects of excessive whaling, 15 nations formed the International Convention for the Regulation of Whaling (ICRW). The ICRW was designed to "provide for the proper conservation of whale stocks and thus make possible the orderly development of the whaling industry," and today serves as the principal international mechanism for promoting the conservation and development of whale populations. . . .

To achieve its purposes, the ICRW included a Schedule which, *inter alia*, regulates harvesting practices and sets harvest limits for various whale species. In addition, the ICRW established the International Whaling Commission (IWC), which implements portions of the Convention and is authorized to amend the Schedule and set new harvest quotas. The quotas are binding on IWC members if accepted by a three-fourths' majority vote. Under the terms of the Convention, however, the IWC has no power to impose sanctions for quota violations. Moreover, any member country may file a timely objection to an IWC amendment of the Schedule and thereby exempt itself from any obligation to comply with the limit unless and until the objection is withdrawn. All nonobjecting countries remain bound by the amendment.

Because of the IWC's inability to enforce its own quota, and in an effort to promote enforcement of quotas set by other international fishery conservation programs, Congress passed the Pelly Amendment to the Fishermen's Protective Act of 1967. 22 U.S.C. § 1978. Principally intended to preserve and protect North American Atlantic salmon from depletion by Danish fishermen in violation of the ban imposed by the International Convention for the Northwest Atlantic Fisheries, the Amendment protected whales as well. The Amendment directs the Secretary of Commerce to certify to the President if "nationals of a foreign country, directly or indirectly, are conducting fishing operations in a manner or under circumstances which diminish the effectiveness of an international fishery conservation program. . . . " 22 U.S.C. § 1978(a)(1). Upon certification, the President, in his discretion, may then direct the Secretary of the Treasury to prohibit the importation of fish products from the certified nation. § 1978(a)(4). The President may also decline to impose any sanctions or import prohibitions.

After enactment of the Pelly Amendment, the Secretary of Commerce five times certified different nations to the President as engaging in fishing operations which "diminish[ed] the effectiveness" of IWC quotas. None of the certifications resulted in the imposition of sanctions by the President. After each certification, however, the President was able to use the threat of discretionary sanctions to obtain commitments of future compliance from the offending nations.

Although "the Pelly Amendment . . . served the useful function of quietly persuading nations to adhere to the decisions of international fishery conservation bodies," Congress grew impatient with the Executive's delay in making certification decisions and refusal to impose sanctions. As a result, Congress passed the Packwood Amendment to the Magnuson Fishery Conservation and Management Act, 16 U.S.C. § 1801 *et seq.* This Amendment requires the Secretary of Commerce to "periodically monitor the activities of foreign nationals that may affect [international fishery conservation programs]," . . . "promptly investigate any activity by foreign nationals that, in the opinion of the Secretary, may be cause for certification . . . ," and "promptly conclude; and reach a decision with respect to; [that] investigation." § 1978(a)(3)(C).

To rectify the past failure of the President to impose the sanctions authorized — but not required — under the Pelly Amendment, the Packwood Amendment removes this element of discretion and mandates the imposition of economic sanctions against offending nations. Under the Amendment, if the Secretary of Commerce certifies that "nationals of a foreign country, directly or indirectly, are conducting fishing operations or engaging in trade or taking which diminishes the effectiveness of the International Convention for the Regulation of Whaling," the Secretary of State must reduce, by at least 50%, the offending nation's fishery allocation within the United States' fishery conservation zone. Although the Amendment requires the imposition of sanctions when the Secretary of Commerce certifies a nation, it did not alter the initial certification process, except for requiring expedition. It was also provided that a certificate under the Packwood Amendment also serves as a certification for the purposes of the Pelly Amendment.

In 1981, the IWC established a zero quota for the Western Division stock of Northern Pacific sperm whales. The next year, the IWC ordered a 5-year moratorium on commercial whaling to begin with the 1985-1986 whaling season and last until 1990. In 1982, the IWC acted to grant Japan's request for a 2-year respite — for the 1982-1983 and 1983-1984 seasons — from the IWC's earlier decision banning sperm whaling.

Because Japan filed timely objections to both the IWC's 1981 zero quota for Northern Pacific sperm whales and 1982 commercial whaling moratorium, under the terms of the ICRW, it was not bound to comply with either limitation. Nonetheless, as the 1984-1985 whaling season grew near, it was apparently recognized that under either the Pelly or Packwood Amendment, the United States could impose economic sanctions if Japan continued to exceed these whaling quotas.

Following extensive negotiations, on November 13, 1984, Japan and the United States concluded an executive agreement through an exchange of letters between the Chargé d'Affaires of Japan and the Secretary of Commerce. Subject to implementation requirements, Japan pledged to adhere to certain harvest limits and to cease commercial whaling by 1988. In return and after consulting with the United States Commissioner to the IWC, the Secretary determined that the short-term continuance of a specified level of limited whaling by Japan, coupled with its promise to discontinue all commercial whaling by 1988, "would not diminish the effectiveness of the International Convention for the Regulation of Whaling, 1946, or its conservation program." Accordingly, the Secretary informed Japan that, so long as Japan complied with its pledges, the United States would not certify Japan under either Amendment.

Several days before consummation of the executive agreement, several wildlife conservation groups filed suit in District Court seeking a writ of mandamus compelling the Secretary of Commerce to certify Japan. Because in its view any taking of whales in excess of the IWC quotas diminishes the effectiveness of the ICRW, the District Court granted summary judgment for respondents and ordered the Secretary of Commerce immediately to certify to the President that Japan was in violation of the IWC sperm whale quota. Thereafter, Japan's Minister for Foreign Affairs informed the Secretary of Commerce that Japan would perform the second condition of the agreement — withdrawal of its objection to the IWC moratorium — provided that the United States obtained reversal of the District Court's order.

A divided Court of Appeals affirmed. Recognizing that the Pelly and Packwood-Magnuson Amendments did not define the specific activities which would "diminish the effectiveness" of the ICRW, the court looked to the Amendments' legislative history and concluded, as had the District Court, that the taking by Japanese nationals of whales in excess of quota automatically called for certification by the Secretary. We granted certiorari, and now reverse.

***

III

The issue before us is whether, in the circumstances of these cases, either the Pelly or Packwood Amendment required the Secretary to certify Japan for refusing to abide by the IWC whaling quotas. We have concluded that certification was not necessary and hence reject the Court of Appeals' holding and respondents' submission that certification is mandatory whenever a country exceeds its allowable take under the ICRW Schedule.

Under the Packwood Amendment, certification is neither permitted nor required until the Secretary makes a determination that nationals of a foreign country "are conducting fishing operations or engaging in trade or taking which diminishes the effectiveness" of the ICRW. It is clear that the Secretary must promptly make the certification decision, but the statute does not define the words "diminish the effectiveness of" or specify the factors that the Secretary should consider in making the decision entrusted to him alone. Specifically, it does not state that certification must be forthcoming whenever a country does not abide by IWC Schedules, and the Secretary did not understand or interpret the language of the Amendment to require him to do so. Had Congress intended otherwise, it would have been a simple matter to say that the Secretary must certify deliberate taking of whales in excess of IWC limits.

Here, as the Convention permitted it to do, Japan had filed its objection to the IWC harvest limits and to the moratorium to begin with the 1985-1986 season. It was accordingly not in breach of its obligations under the Convention in continuing to take whales, for it was part of the scheme of the Convention to permit nations to opt out of Schedules that were adopted over its objections. In these circumstances, the Secretary, after consultation with the United States Commissioner to the IWC and review of the IWC Scientific Committee opinions, determined that it would better serve the conservation ends of the Convention to accept Japan's pledge to limit its harvest of sperm whales for four years and to cease all commercial whaling in 1988, rather than to impose sanctions and risk continued whaling by the Japanese. In any event, the Secretary made the determination assigned to him by the Packwood Amendment and concluded that the limited taking of whales in the 1984 and 1985 coastal seasons would not diminish the effectiveness of the ICRW or its conservation program, and that he would not make the certification that he would otherwise be empowered to make.

The Secretary, of course, may not act contrary to the will of Congress when exercised within the bounds of the Constitution. If Congress has directly spoken to the precise issue in question, if the intent of Congress is clear, that is the end of the matter. *Chevron U.S.A. Inc. v. Natural Resources Defense Council, Inc.,* 467 U.S. 837, 843 (1984). But as the courts below and respondents concede, the statutory language itself contains no direction to the Secretary automatically and regardless of the circumstances to certify a nation that fails to conform to the IWC whaling Schedule. The language of the Pelly and Packwood Amendments might reasonably be construed in this manner, but the Secretary's construction that there are circumstances in which certification may be withheld, despite departures from the Schedules and without violating his duty, is also a reasonable construction of the language used in both Amendments. . . .

IV

Contrary to the Court of Appeals and respondents' views, we find nothing in the legislative history of either Amendment that addresses the nature of the Secretary's duty and requires him to certify every departure from the IWC's scheduled limits on whaling. . . .

In the House Report for the 1978 amendment, the Merchant Marine and Fisheries Committee specifically addressed the "diminish the effectiveness" standard and recognized the Secretary's discretion in making the initial certification decision:

> "The nature of any trade or taking which qualifies as diminishing the effectiveness of any international program for endangered or threatened species will depend on the circumstances of each case. In general, however, the trade or taking must be serious enough to warrant the finding that the effectiveness of the international program in question has been diminished. An isolated, individual violation of a convention provision will not ordinarily warrant certification under this section."
> *Id.,* at 15, U.S.Code Cong. & Admin.News 1978, p. 1779.

This statement makes clear that, under the Pelly Amendment as construed by Congress, the Secretary is to exercise his judgment in determining whether a particular fishing operation "diminishes the effectiveness" of an international fishery conservation program like the IWC.

***

We conclude, therefore, that the Secretary's decision to secure the certainty of Japan's future compliance with the IWC's program through the 1984 executive agreement, rather than rely on the possibility that certification and imposition of economic sanctions would produce the same or better result, is a reasonable construction of the Pelly and Packwood Amendments. Congress granted the Secretary the authority to determine whether a foreign nation's whaling in excess of quotas diminishes the effectiveness of the IWC, and we find no reason to impose a mandatory obligation upon the Secretary to certify that every quota violation necessarily fails that standard. Accordingly, the judgment of the Court of Appeals is
Reversed.

Justice MARSHALL, with whom Justice BRENNAN, Justice BLACKMUN, and Justice REHNQUIST join, dissenting.

Since 1971, Congress has sought to lead the world, through the repeated exercise of its power over foreign commerce, in preventing the extermination of whales and other threatened species of marine animals. I deeply regret that it will now have to act again before the Executive Branch will finally be compelled to obey the law. I believe that the Court has misunderstood the question posed by the case before us, and has reached an erroneous conclusion on a matter of intense worldwide concern. I therefore dissent.

Congress began its efforts with the Pelly Amendment, which directs that "[w]hen the Secretary of Commerce determines that nationals of a foreign country, directly or indirectly, are conducting fishing operations in a manner or under circumstances which diminish the effectiveness of an international fishery conservation program, the Secretary of Commerce shall certify such fact to the President." 22 U.S.C. § 1978(a)(1). That Amendment, although apparently mandatory in its certification scheme, did not provide for a mandatory response from the President once the certification was made. Rather, the President was empowered, in his discretion, to impose sanctions on the certified nations or not to act at all. § 1978(a)(4).

This executive latitude in enforcement proved unsatisfactory. Between 1971 and 1978, every time that a nation exceeded international whaling quotas — on five occasions — the Secretary of Commerce duly certified to the President that the trespassing nation had exceeded whaling quotas set by the International Whaling Commission and had thus diminished the effectiveness of the conservation program. Although the offending nations had promised immediate compliance, the Secretary apparently believed that he was obliged to certify the past violations. Yet on the basis of those assurances, the President each time exercised his option under the Pelly Amendment to impose no sanctions on the violators.

Unhappy with the President's failure to sanction clear violations of international whaling agreements, Congress responded in 1979 with the Packwood Amendment. That Amendment provides that if the Secretary of Commerce certifies that a country is diminishing the effectiveness of the International Convention for the Regulation of Whaling, the Secretary of State must reduce the fishing allocation of the offending nation by at least 50 percent. It also provides certain time limits within which the Executive Branch must act in imposing the mandatory sanctions. The automatic imposition of sanctions, it seemed, would improve the effectiveness of the Pelly Amendment by providing a definite consequence for any nation disregarding whaling limits.

In 1984, the Secretary of Commerce for the first time declined to certify a case of intentional whaling in excess of established quotas. Rather than calling into play the Packwood Amendment's mandatory sanctions by certifying to the President Japan's persistence in conducting whaling operations, Secretary Baldrige set about to negotiate with Japan, using his power of certification under domestic law to obtain certain promises of reduced violations in future years. In the resulting compromise, the Secretary agreed not to certify Japan, provided that Japan would promise to reduce its whaling until 1988 and then withdraw its objection to the international whaling quotas. Arguing that the Secretary had no discretion to withhold certification, respondents sought review of the Secretary's action in federal court. Both the District Court and the Court of Appeals found that Congress had not empowered the Secretary to decline to certify a clear violation of International Whaling Commission (IWC) quotas, and ordered the Secretary to make the statutory certification. This Court now renders illusory the mandatory language of the statutory scheme, and finds permissible exactly the result that Congress sought to prevent in the Packwood Amendment: executive compromise of a national policy of whale conservation.

The Court devotes its opinion to the question whether the language of the Pelly or the Packwood Amendment leaves room for discretion in the Secretary to determine that a violation of the whaling quota need not be certified. Although framed in the same way by the Court of Appeals and by the parties before this Court, that issue is not the most direct approach to resolving the dispute before us. Indeed, by focusing entirely on this question, the Court fails to take into account the most significant aspect of these cases: that even the Secretary himself has not taken the position that Japan's past conduct is not the type of activity that diminishes the effectiveness of the whale conservation program, requiring his certification under the Pelly Amendment. In the face of an IWC determination that only a zero quota will protect the species, never has the Secretary concluded, nor could he conclude, that the intentional taking of large numbers of sperm whales does *not* diminish the effectiveness of the IWC program. . . .

I would affirm the judgment below on the ground that the Secretary has exceeded his authority by using his power of certification, not as a means for identifying serious whaling violations, but as a means for evading the constraints of the Packwood Amendment. Even focusing, as the Court does, upon the distinct question whether the statute prevents the Secretary from determining that the effectiveness of a conservation program is not diminished by a substantial transgression of whaling quotas, I find the Court's conclusion utterly unsupported. I am troubled that this Court is empowering an officer of the Executive Branch, sworn to uphold and defend the laws of the United States, to ignore Congress' pointed response to a question long pondered: "whether Leviathan can long endure so wide a chase, and so remorseless a havoc; whether he must not at last be exterminated from the waters, and the last whale, like the last man, smoke his last pipe, and then himself evaporate in the final puff." H. Melville, Moby Dick 436 (Signet ed. 1961).

points for discussion

1. *"Diminishing the effectiveness."* What is the argument that forging the compromise was lawful under the Pelly and Packwood Amendments? Do you agree? As a normative matter, would you tighten the requirements to make the certification by the Secretary of State mandatory? Would it truly matter that much, if the President still retains the discretion to impose sanctions? Or does certification carry with it some other political significance?

2. *Postcript.* Japan did indeed end commercial whaling as promised. However, it continued extensive whaling under a provision that allows whaling for "scientific research." Excluding aboriginal subsistence whaling (which is exempt from the commercial whaling moratorium), over 20,000 whales have been killed under the scientific research exemption since the 1946 Convention. Japan takes on average 500 whales per year under the scientific research exemption. Most recently, Japan took 333 minke whales for scientific research, including 120 pregnant females and 114 juveniles.

   However, as it turns out, just the international outcry was too much for Japan to bear. In 2018, Japan announced its withdrawal from the International Whaling Convention, and its intent to resume commercial whaling in 2019, presumably without limits or international scrutiny. Whaling is an old tradition in Japan, and old traditions die hard. The one force that may ultimately destroy that tradition is the market: Whereas Japanese consumed over 200,000 tons of whale meat per year in the 1960s, they consume less than 7,000 tons per year today. Withdrawal from the IWC may thus only represent a last gasp for a dying industry in Japan.

3. *The Convention.* The original 1946 Convention was quite weak, as the case explains, and Japan's recent withdrawal suggests why. For a history of the debate surrounding the 1946 Convention, see Cinnamon Pinon Carlarne, *Saving the Whales in the New Millennium: International Institutions, Recent Developments, and the Future of International Whaling Policies,* 24 Va. Envtl. L.J. 1 (2005).

4. *Scientific research.* Even with Japan's withdrawal, whaling remains an ongoing enterprise, and other countries such as Norway or Iceland may take advantage of the scientific research exemption so ruthlessly exploited by Japan. If you were to narrow the scientific research exemption, how would you do it? Who would decide whether whale kills would further the cause of science? For a critique of the scientific research exemption, see Rachel N. Wichert & Martha C. Nussbaum, *Scientific Whaling? The Scientific Research Exception and the Future of the International Whaling Commission,* 18 J. Hum. Dev. & Capabilities 356 (2017).

5. *Duty to cooperate.* Article 62(2) of UNCLOS III requires signatories to cooperate in the conservation of living resources. Is Japan's intransigence a failure to cooperate? For one view, see Howard S. Schiffman, *The International Whaling Commission: Challenges from Within and Without,* 10 ILSA J. Int'l & Comp. L. 367 (2004).

Source: Australian Customs and Border Service

Figure 1-13.
A Japanese whaler caught this whale in 2008, in the name of scientific research.

2. Highly Migratory Fish Species

UNCLOS III sets out new obligations with respect to the conservation of living resources. Signatories are expected to undertake measures to "prevent, reduce, and control pollution of the marine environment" (Article 194), including measures "necessary to protect and preserve rare or fragile ecosystems as well as the habitat of depleted, threatened or endangered species and other forms of marine life" (*id.*), and generally to "protect and preserve the marine environment" (Article 192). These obligations have probably attained the status of customary environmental law. But as revolutionary as UNCLOS III was with respect to protection of the marine environment, the specifics were and still remain difficult to flesh out. Moreover, while UNCLOS III set forth new obligations with respect to the territorial seas and the EEZ — albeit incompletely — it left unaddressed the problem of fishing in the high seas, and fishing for highly migratory fish, such as tuna and swordfish, which wander in and out of EEZs and the high seas. Almost 70 percent of global fish harvests are of species that "straddle" EEZs and the high seas.

These unresolved problems, along with the urgency of increasing overexploitation, led to the 1995 Conference on Straddling Fish Stocks and Highly Migratory Fish Stocks. The agreement is often referred to as the "1995 UN Fish Stocks Agreement," or just the "Fish Stocks Agreement." Formally, it was an implementing agreement for UNCLOS III, but it clearly expanded the ambit of state obligations with respect to protecting highly migratory fish. Parties to the Fish Stocks Agreement are required to assess the impacts of fishing and other human activities, adopt conservation and management measures, minimize waste and pollution, and "take measures to prevent or eliminate overfishing and . . . ensure that levels of fishing effort . . . commensurate with the sustainable use of fishery resources." (Article 5.)

Perhaps the most important effect of the Fish Stocks Agreement was to help give impetus to the formation of regional fisheries management organizations, or "RFMOs." Article 8, paragraph 1 of the Fish Stocks Agreement provides:

> Coastal States and States fishing on the high seas shall, in accordance with the Convention, pursue cooperation in relation to straddling fish stocks and highly migratory fish stocks either directly or through appropriate subregional or regional fisheries management organizations or arrangements, taking into account the specific characteristics of the subregion or region, to ensure effective conservation and management of such stocks.

Not only does the Fish Stocks Agreement call for "cooperation" among fishing countries, but it explicitly calls for regional fisheries management organizations. Twenty RFMOs have assumed responsibility for studying and managing migratory stocks on the high seas, tuna being the most prominent but not the only one.

In general, the RFMOs are failing at their mandate of controlling overfishing. Two-thirds of tuna stocks and other highly migratory species are overfished or depleted. In 2012, the stock of Pacific bluefin tuna reached the shockingly low level of just 2.6 percent of its historical biomass. One independent auditor for the International Commission for the Conservation of Atlantic Tunas (an RFMO) actually wrote that management of the bluefin tuna in the Atlantic was "widely regarded as an international disgrace." This is uncommon bluntness for auditors of international organizations, which tend to give such organizations the benefit of the doubt.

Why has the record of RFMOs been so poor? The answers would be both familiar and complicated for those familiar with fisheries regulation. Enforcement is challenging, as illegal, unreported, and unregulated (IUU) fishing has increased. RFMOs have limited powers of enforcement. RFMOs rely upon member states for data, which are sometimes doctored. Russia and Japan have been caught red-handed, but these are likely not isolated incidents. The "freedom to fish" is still a dominant paradigm and rooted in a strong and insular fishing culture worldwide. Finally, within fishing countries, fishing industries invariably wield outsized political influence. And for fishermen, the explanation for smaller and smaller catches is never overfishing; it is always that the fish have gone elsewhere, a delusion much easier to hold for highly migratory stocks.

The experiences with one RFMO, the Southern Bluefin Tuna Commission, created under the Convention for the Conservation of Southern Bluefin Tuna, seems to encapsulate many of the problems encountered by RFMOs, and with protecting highly migratory stocks. Southern bluefin tuna had been harvested commercially since the 1950s, and by the 1980s a sharp decline in the population became obvious. The following case involves a compulsory dispute mechanism whereby parties are required to settle disputes over the interpretation of UNCLOS III using one of several approved methods under Article 287. However, the UNCLOS tribunal, the International Tribunal on the Law of the Sea, only hears disputes "arising under" UNCLOS. What if it arises under UNCLOS as well as one of the RFMOs? The International Tribunal on the Law of the Sea awarded Australia and New Zealand provisional relief, but the Arbitral Tribunal found otherwise.

Southern bluefin tuna are only one of many overfished tuna species. Pacific bluefin tuna, a related species that migrates across the North Atlantic Ocean from Japan to North America, reached a low of 2.6 percent of its unfished level. By comparison, the Atlantic bluefin tuna, at half its 1974 levels, is comparatively healthy but still falling in the category of "overfished." Part of the reason that bluefin are so depleted worldwide is because of their high value (particularly for sushi) and because of their biological characteristics: They are long-lived and slow-growing, so that fishing can easily outpace reproduction.

Figure 1-14.
Frozen bluefin tuna at the Tsukiji fish auction in Tokyo. In 2019, a Japanese restaurateur paid a record $3,000,000, about $5,000 a pound, for a single bluefin tuna.

Southern Bluefin Tuna Case: Australia and New Zealand v. Japan Award on Jurisdiction and Admissibility

August 4, 2000

Rendered by the Arbitral Tribunal constituted under Annex VII of the United Nations Convention on the Law of the Sea.

Southern Bluefin Tuna (Thunnus maccoyi, hereafter sometimes designated "SBT") is a migratory species of pelagic fish that is included in the list of highly migratory species set out in Annex I of the United Nations Convention on the Law of the Sea. Southern Bluefin Tuna range widely through the oceans of the Southern Hemisphere, principally the high seas, but they also traverse the exclusive economic zones and territorial waters of some States, notably Australia, New Zealand and South Africa. They spawn in the waters south of Indonesia. The main market for the sale of Southern Bluefin Tuna is in Japan, where the fish is prized as a delicacy for sashimi.

It is common ground between the Parties that commercial harvest of Southern Bluefin Tuna began in the early 1950s and that, in 1961, the global catch peaked at 81,000 metric tons ("mt"). By the early 1980s, the SBT stock had been severely over-fished. . . . In 1982, Australia, New Zealand and Japan began informally to manage the catching of SBT. Japan joined with Australia and New Zealand in 1985 to intro-duce a global total allowable catch (hereafter, "TAC") for SBT. . . . But the SBT stock continued to decline. In 1997, it was estimated to be in the order of 7-15% of its 1960 level. . . . Whether, in response to TAC restrictions, the stock has in fact begun to recover is at the core of the dispute between Australia and New Zealand, on the one hand, and Japan, on the other. They differ over the current state and recovery prospects of SBT stock and the means by which scientific uncertainty in respect of those matters can best be reduced. . . .

In 1993, Australia, Japan and New Zealand concluded the Convention for the Conservation of Southern Bluefin Tuna (hereafter, "1993 Convention" or "CCSBT"). The provisions most pertinent to these proceedings are the following:

Article 16

1. If any dispute arises between two or more of the Parties concerning the inter-pretation or implementation of this Convention, those Parties shall consult among themselves with a view to having the dispute resolved by negotiation, inquiry, mediation, conciliation, arbitration, judicial settlement or other peaceful means of their own choice.

    2. Any dispute of this character not so resolved shall, with the consent in each case of all parties to the dispute, be referred for settlement to the International Court of Justice or to arbitration; but failure to reach agreement on reference to the International Court of Justice or to arbitration shall not absolve parties to the dispute from the responsibility of continuing to seek to resolve it by any of the various peaceful means referred to in paragraph 1 above.

    3. In cases where the dispute is referred to arbitration, the arbitral tribunal shall be constituted as provided in the Annex to this Convention. The Annex forms an integral part of this Convention.
    [Other cited provisions of CCSBT omitted.]

 . . . Japan from 1994 sought an increase in the TAC and in its allotment but any increase has been opposed by New Zealand and Australia. While the Commission initially maintained the TAC at existing levels due to this impasse, since 1998 it has been unable to agree upon any TAC. In the absence of a Commission deci-sion, the Parties in practice have maintained their TAC as set in 1994. At the same time, Japan pressed in the Commission not only for a TAC increase, initially of 6000 tons and then of 3000 tons in its allotment, but also for agreement upon a joint Experimental Fishing Program ("EFP"), whose particular object would be to gather data in those areas where fishing for SBT no longer took place, with a view to reducing scientific uncertainty about recovery of the stock. . . .

At a Commission meeting in 1998 Japan stated that, while it would voluntarily adhere to its previous quota for commercial SBT fishing, it would commence a unilateral, three-year EFP as of the summer of 1998. Despite vigorous protests by

Australia and New Zealand over pursuance of any unilateral EFP, Japan conducted a pilot program with an estimated catch of 1,464 mt. in the summer of 1998.

In response, Australia and New Zealand formally requested urgent consultations and negotiations under Article 16(1) of the 1993 Convention. Despite intensive efforts within this framework to reach agreement on an experimental fishing program for 1999, an accord was not achieved. . . . [Australia and New Zealand] informed Japan that, if it recommended unilateral experimental fishing on June 1, 1999 or thereafter, they would regard such action as a termination by Japan of negotiations under Article 16(1) of the 1993 Convention. Japan, which resumed its EFP on June 1, 1999, replied that it had no intention of terminating those negotiations. . . .

On June 23, 1999, Australia restated its position that the dispute did not relate solely to Japan's obligations under the 1993 Convention, but also involved its obligations under UNCLOS and customary international law. It considered that there had been a full exchange of views on the dispute for the purposes of Article 283(1) of UNCLOS, which provides that, "When a dispute arises between States Parties concerning the interpretation or application of this Convention, the parties to the dispute shall proceed expeditiously to an exchange of views regarding its settlement by negotiation or other peaceful means."

. . . Japan declared that it was ready to have the dispute resolved by arbitration pursuant to Article 16(2) of the 1993 Convention, indicating however that it was not prepared to halt its unilateral EFP during its pendency though it was prepared to resume consultations about it. Thereafter Australia notified Japan that it . . . had decided to commence compulsory dispute resolution under Part XV of UNCLOS. . . . Australia emphasized the centrality of Japan's obligations under UNCLOS and under customary international law to the dispute and the need for those obligations to be addressed if the dispute were to be resolved. . . .

The provisions of UNCLOS centrally invoked by Australia and New Zealand were the following:

Article 64
Highly migratory species

1. The coastal State and other States whose nationals fish in the region for the highly migratory species listed in Annex I shall cooperate directly or through appropriate international organizations with a view to ensuring conservation and promoting the objective of optimum utilization of such species throughout the region, both within and beyond the exclusive economic zone. In regions for which no appropriate international organization exists, the coastal State and other States whose nationals harvest these species in the region shall cooperate to establish such an organization and participate in its work.

[A number of other UNCLOS III articles are cited that call for States to cooperate with each other with respect to conserving the living resources on the high seas.]

In seeking provisional measures, Australia and New Zealand among other contentions argued that Article 64, read in conjunction with other provisions of

UNCLOS, imposes an obligation on Japan, as a distant water State whose nationals fish for SBT, to cooperate with Australia and New Zealand, as coastal States, in the conservation of SBT. The Commission established under the 1993 Convention is "the appropriate international organization" for the purposes of Article 64. Japan's unilateral actions defeat the object and purpose of the 1993 Convention. In such a case, the underlying obligations of UNCLOS remain. While the 1993 Convention was intended as a means of implementing the obligations imposed by UNCLOS in respect of highly migratory fish species, it is not a means of escaping those obligations. . . .

Japan . . . maintained that the gravamen of the claims asserted concern the 1993 Convention, not UNCLOS, and that those claims turned not on issues of law but matters of scientific appreciation. [Japan pointed out that Australia and New Zealand] in August 1998 specifically invoked dispute resolution under the 1993 Convention, not UNCLOS; they had treated the dispute as one arising under the CCSBT, and sought consultations not under UNCLOS but under Article 16 of the 1993 Convention. The . . . Parties were required to continue to seek resolution of their dispute pursuant to those procedures. . . . For all these reasons, Japan argued that the proposed Annex VII arbitral tribunal lacked jurisdiction prima facie. . . . The only remedy that made sense, if there were to be any, would be to call on Australia and New Zealand to resume negotiations under the 1993 Convention with a view to reaching agreement on the TAC, annual quotas, and the continuation of the EFP on a joint basis. . . .

. . . [I]f UNCLOS is regarded as the earlier treaty and as the framework or umbrella convention that sets out broad principles that in practice are to be realized by the conclusion and application of specific implementing agreements, then the CCSBT is the exemplar of such an implementing agreement. It then is not only the lex posterior but the lex specialis. In accordance with generally accepted principles, the provisions of a lex specialis not only specify and implement the principles of an anterior framework agreement; they exhaust and supplant those principles as long as the implementing agreement remains in force. The provisions of UNCLOS on which the Applicants rely, Article 64 and 116-119, are fully covered by the more specific provisions of the CCSBT. The function of the CCSBT is to fulfill and implement UNCLOS and discharge its obligations in respect of SBT by providing the necessary institutional structure which UNCLOS contemplates and the substantive detail that amplifies the outlines laid down in UNCLOS. . . .

From the record placed before the Tribunal by both Parties, it is clear that the most acute elements of the dispute between the Parties turn on their inability to agree on a revised total allowable catch and the related conduct by Japan of unilateral experimental fishing in 1998 and 1999, as well as Japan's announced plans for such fishing thereafter. Those elements of the dispute were clearly within the mandate of the Commission for the Conservation of Southern Bluefin Tuna. It was there that the Parties failed to agree on a TAC. It was there that Japan announced in 1998 that it would launch a unilateral experimental fishing program; it was there that that announcement was protested by Australia and New Zealand; and the higher level protests and the diplomatic exchanges that followed refer to the

Convention for the Conservation of Southern Bluefin Tuna and to the proceedings in the Commission. The Applicants requested urgent consultations with Japan pursuant to Article 16(1) of the Convention. . . .

There is in fact no disagreement between the Parties over whether the dispute falls within the provisions of the 1993 Convention. The issue rather is, does it also fall within the provisions of UNCLOS? The Applicants maintain that Japan has failed to conserve and to cooperate in the conservation of the SBT stock, particularly by its unilateral experimental fishing for SBT in 1998 and 1999. . . . They contend that Japan's unilateral EFP has placed it in breach of its obligations under Articles 64, 116, 117, 118 and 119 of UNCLOS, for the specific reasons indicated earlier in this Award (in paragraphs 33 and 41). Those provisions, they maintain, lay down applicable norms by which the lawfulness of Japan's conduct can be evaluated. They point out that, once the dispute had ripened, their diplomatic notes and other demarches to Japan made repeated reference to Japan's obligations not only under the 1993 Convention but also under UNCLOS and customary international law.

[UNCLOS] Article 286 provides that, "Subject to section 3, any dispute concerning the interpretation or application of this Convention shall, where no settlement has been reached by recourse to section 1, be submitted at the request of any party to the dispute to the court or tribunal having jurisdiction under this section". Article 286 must be read in context, and that qualifying context includes Article 281(1) as well as Articles 279 and 280. Under Article 281(1), if the States which are parties to a dispute concerning the interpretation or application of UNCLOS (and the Tribunal has just held that this is such a dispute) have agreed to seek settlement of the dispute "by a peaceful means of their own choice", the procedures provided for in Part XV of UNCLOS apply only (a) where no settlement has been reached by recourse to such means and (b) the agreement between the parties "does not exclude any further procedure".

The Tribunal accepts Article 16 of the 1993 Convention as an agreement by the Parties to seek settlement of the instant dispute by peaceful means of their own choice. It so concludes even though it has held that this dispute, while centered in the 1993 Convention, also implicates obligations under UNCLOS. It does so because the Parties to this dispute—the real terms of which have been defined above—are the same Parties grappling not with two separate disputes but with what in fact is a single dispute arising under both Conventions. To find that, in this case, there is a dispute actually arising under UNCLOS which is distinct from the dispute that arose under the CCSBT would be artificial.

. . . [T]he Tribunal is of the view that Article 16 falls within the terms and intent of Article 281(1), as well as Article 280. That being so, the Tribunal is satisfied about fulfillment of condition (a) of Article 281(1). The Parties have had recourse to means set out in Article 16 of the CCSBT. Negotiations have been prolonged, intense and serious. . . . Manifestly, no settlement has been reached by recourse to such negotiations, at any rate, as yet. It is true that every means listed in Article 16 has not been tried; indeed, the Applicants have not accepted proposals of Japan for mediation and for arbitration under the CCSBT, essentially, it seems, because Japan was unwilling to suspend pursuance of its unilateral EFP during the pendency of such recourse. It is also true that Article 16(2) provides that failure to reach agreement on reference of a dispute to the International Court of Justice or to arbitration "shall not absolve parties to the dispute from the responsibility of continuing to seek to resolve it by any of the various peaceful means referred to in paragraph 1 above". But in the view of the Tribunal, this provision does not require the Parties to negotiate indefinitely while denying a Party the option of concluding, for purposes of both Articles 281(1) and 283, that no settlement has been reached. To read Article 16 otherwise would not be reasonable. . . .

SEPARATE OPINION OF JUSTICE SIR KENNETH KEITH

While I agree with much of the Award, I have the misfortune to disagree with my colleagues on one critical issue. I have accordingly prepared this opinion.

Each of the treaties in issue in this case sets up substantive obligations and obligations relating to peaceful settlement. The parallel and overlapping existence of the obligations arising under each treaty is fundamental in this case. I conclude that the one has not excluded or in any relevant way prejudiced the other. . . .

. . . [D]oes article 16 "exclude" the UNCLOS set of obligations? It does not say that it does. It could have, given the timing of the drafting of the two treaties as the preamble reflects. Next, it does not say that disputes concerning the CCSBT must be resolved *only* by procedures under it and *must not* be referred to any tribunal or other third party for settlement. Again it could have said that, as treaty parties have. But does it impliedly exclude the UNCLOS procedures? To do that, article 16 would have to be capable of dealing with *all* the disputes relating to Southern Bluefin tuna arising between CCSBT parties and concerning the interpretation and application of the relevant provisions of UNCLOS. And, as well, it would have to *exclude* (impliedly) the UNCLOS procedures. I consider those two points in turn.

The structure of Part XV and three elements of section 3 of that Part also contribute to an understanding of article 281(1) and the compulsory binding procedures of section 2 of Part XV. They too are part of the relevant context, Section 1, "General Provisions", begins with the obligation of the State Parties to settle UNCLOS disputes by peaceful means (article 279). Within that overall obligation, which is supported by obligations to exchange views about means of settlement (article 283) and the availability of a conciliation procedure (article 284 and Annex V), the emphasis of the section is on the Parties' freedom of choice of means (articles 280-282). If the Parties' chosen means does not lead to a settlement then one Party can submit the dispute to "Compulsory Procedures Entailing Binding Decisions" . . . . That structure itself supports the need for States to include clear wording in their agreements if they are to remove themselves from their otherwise applicable compulsory obligations arising under section 2 to submit to procedures entailing binding decisions. . . .

Finally, in terms of the object and purpose of UNCLOS as a whole, I refer to the widely stated and shared understanding, expressed throughout all the stages of the Conference which prepared the Convention, about the critical central place of the provisions for the peaceful settlement of disputes. The States at that Conference moved decisively away from the freedom which they generally have in their international relations not to be subject in advance to dispute settlement processes, especially processes leading to binding outcomes. The processes in significant part were not to be optional. . . .

The objects and purposes of UNCLOS in general and its comprehensive, compulsory and where necessary, binding dispute settlement provisions in particular, along with the plain wording of its article 281(1) and of article 16 of the CCSBT lead me to the conclusion that the latter does not "exclude" the jurisdiction of this tribunal in respect of disputes arising under UNCLOS.

points for discussion

1. *UNCLOS vs. CCSBT.* This case is largely about a technical point, whether the compulsory jurisdiction provisions under UNCLOS III were superseded by a provision in another convention with a more specific subject matter, and in the context of an RFMO. Conservationists may decry the divestment of jurisdiction in the International Tribunal on the Law of the Sea (ITLOS), because this compulsory dispute resolution was an important victory in UNCLOS III. But might there be a good reason to remove disputes that are more subject matter–specific, such as over Southern Bluefin Tuna, to another track? Might you have drafted Article 16 of the CCSBT differently? Or might you take Justice Keith's view, that for parties of UNCLOS III to "opt out" of the compulsory dispute resolution mechanism, clear and unambiguous language in the alternative treaty is required?

2. *Endless negotiations.* The Tribunal acknowledged that Article 16 "does not require the Parties to negotiate indefinitely while denying a Party the option of concluding, for purposes of both Articles 281(1) and 283, that no settlement has been reached. To read Article 16 otherwise would not be reasonable." Isn't that what was already happening? Could the Tribunal have expected more negotiations to bear fruit? Had the parties already reached their firewalls?

3. *Japan vs. Australia and New Zealand.* This trio of countries, while nominally allies in many global affairs, find themselves in disagreement quite a lot when it comes to marine issues. Whaling is another area in which Japan often finds itself on the other side of the two Oceanic countries. Japan is a very densely populated country, without the capacity to engage in livestock farming like Australia and New Zealand, and is thus more dependent upon fishing and whaling. From a conservationist point of view, it is easy to sympathize with Australia and New Zealand. But can Japan make its own case that Australia and New Zealand are acting unilaterally themselves? Can you try to justify Japan's experimental fishing program?

E. THE IMPACT OF INTERNATIONAL TRADE ON OCEAN RESOURCES

Why do nations trade? Most economists agree, *in principle*, that international trading can make all trading partners better off. Putting aside for the moment the many concerns and problems with globalization, free trade can create wealth. Consider a simple illustrative example. Let's say that two countries, the United States and Canada, produce only two goods: fish and computers. In the United States, it requires three units of labor to catch and produce a fish, and two units of labor to produce a computer. In Canada, it requires four units of labor to produce a fish, and six units of labor to produce a computer.

	Units of Labor to Catch a Fish	Units of Labor to Produce a Computer
United States	3	2
Canada	4	6

The United States is said to have an *absolute advantage* with respect to both fish and computers, meaning it is more efficient at producing both. Does that mean that there is no point in trading with Canada? No! The United States enjoys a *comparative advantage* in producing computers, and Canada enjoys a *comparative advantage* in producing fish. While the United States is more efficient at producing fish than Canada, it has an even better opportunity if it concentrates on producing computers, in which its efficiency advantage is larger. Canada might be less efficient at producing fish but can still contribute to trade by relieving the United States of the need to produce fish, so it can put more of its workers in the computer industry. By focusing on what each country does best, the two countries can still realize gains from trade.

Suppose each country has 1,200 units of labor. If each country uses half of its labor (600 units) to produce fish and half to produce computers, they will produce the following:

No Trading

	Fish	Computers
United States	200	300
Canada	150	100

But the countries can do better by trading with each other. What if Canada just did what it does best — catch fish — and the United States spent most of its labor making computers? Say the United States spent 300 units of labor catching fish and 900 making computers. Then the countries would produce the following:

Specializing

	Fish	Computers
United States	100	450
Canada	300	0

Now, suppose the United States traded with Canada 125 computers for 125 fish. Then they wind up with:

Trading

	Fish	Computers
United States	225	325
Canada	175	125

Compare these levels of consumption with the second table ("No Trading"), the one representing the situation in which there was no trade, and each country tried to spend half its labor force making each of the two commodities. Both United States and Canada are consuming 25 more fish and 25 more computers than without trade.

Depending on your perspective, the results of freer international trade range from being disastrous to miraculous. One downside that has been made obvious by the political turmoil surrounding globalization is that the gains from trading have been very uneven, and exacerbated economic inequality within countries, the United States and China being prominent examples. You noticed, no doubt, that in moving from the no-trading world to the trading world, 300 fish jobs were lost in the United States. Dislocation is part of efficiency, unfortunately. But international trade has lifted many parts of the world out of poverty, and has made economic juggernauts out of South Korea, Taiwan, Israel, Hong Kong, Singapore, and Ireland. China was considered a developing country not so long ago and is now an economic powerhouse with the world's second-largest economy.

Free trade agreements themselves are an outgrowth of the Great Depression, widely believed to have been linked, among other things, to the U.S. imposition of tariffs to protect domestic industries from competition. The infamous Smoot-Hawley Act led to a disastrous trade war that closed markets and contributed to the downfall of thousands of companies, resulting in a cascade of bad economic news that ultimately led to decades of hard times around the world. After World War II, the world vowed never to allow that to happen again. A series of multilateral agreements culminated in the General Agreement on Tariffs and Trade, or the GATT, and is still the basic international legal instrument that prevents signatory nations from unreasonably insulating its markets from international trade. The GATT is one of the most enduring treaties in the history of international law and has served to keep markets open and discourage the imposition of duties. Until 1995, the GATT referred to both a treaty and an organization — the GATT organization was the world body headquartered in Geneva that administered the GATT treaty, including the adjudication of disputes that arise under the treaty. The GATT organization was replaced in 1995 by the World Trade Organization (the WTO).

There are two major problems with this free trade paradigm. First, as noted above, economic growth has been very uneven, and it does cause job losses, even as it creates jobs in other sectors. Second, when producing goods for trade has caused harm to the environment, freer trade means more environmental harm. Implicit in this free trade paradigm is the assumption that baseline environmental regulations are, if not roughly equal, at least the rational political choice made by a country. Suffice it to say, that is not remotely true. Biofuels, for example, were touted as an environmentally superior alternative to refining crude oil into gasoline, but global trading in biofuels has led to the destruction of vast tracts of Indonesian and Brazilian rainforest that were cleared to grow biofuel feedstocks. Trade often has the effect of exacerbating environmental harms imposed by some industries, particularly those exploiting ocean resources.

This tension between trade and the environment has played out very prominently with respect to ocean resources. Seafood is a vigorously traded good. But countries have widely differing views on the environmental and ecological impacts that should be tolerated in catching it, and that can run up against international trade laws such as the GATT, which try to keep open channels of trade. In order to prevent countries from blocking trade like the Smoot-Hawley Act did, international trade law has overturned the domestic laws of some countries if they have the effect of limiting trade. This has been the case even when the laws were meant to protect the environment or animals, not limit trade. It is hard to distinguish the two, but the effect can be to overrule domestic environmental laws.

A notable example pertains to a GATT Panel decision in 1993 in favor of Mexico and against the United States, which found that an American rule under the Marine Mammal Protection Act to protect dolphins from brutal methods of tuna fishing violated the GATT. The rule — prohibiting the fishing for tuna by encircling dolphins — was ruled to be contrary to the GATT and could not be used to exclude Mexican-caught tuna from U.S. markets. Environmentalists were outraged — what right did the GATT panel have to overturn a considered political judgment made in the United States about what kind of tuna they could eat and not eat?

The General Agreement on Tariffs and Trade

(1947)

Article XI

1. No prohibitions or restrictions other than duties, taxes or other charges, whether made effective through quotas, import or export licences or other

measures, shall be instituted or maintained by any contracting party on the importation of any product of the territory of any other contracting party or on the exportation or sale for export of any product destined for the territory of any other contracting party.

Article XX

Subject to the requirement that such measures are not applied in a manner which would constitute a means of arbitrary or unjustifiable discrimination between countries where the same conditions prevail, or a disguised restriction on international trade, nothing in this Agreement shall be construed to prevent the adoption or enforcement by any contracting party of measures:

(a) necessary to protect public morals;

(b) necessary to protect human, animal or plant life or health;

* * *

(g) relating to the conservation of exhaustible natural resources if such measures are made effective in conjunction with restrictions on domestic production or consumption;

General Agreement on Tariffs and Trade (G.A.T.T.) Secretariat Report of the Panel United States — Restrictions on the Importation of Tuna

September 3, 1991

... On 5 November 1990, Mexico requested consultations with the United States concerning restrictions on imports of tuna. . . . [T]he sixty-day period for consultations had expired without a mutually satisfactory adjustment having been reached [prompting this request by Mexico for a GATT Panel to review the U.S. restrictions.]

Purse-Seine Fishing of Tuna

The last three decades have seen the deployment of tuna fishing technology based on the "purse-seine" net in many areas of the world. A fishing vessel using this technique locates a school of fish and sends out a motorboat (a "seine skiff") to hold one end of the purse-seine net. The vessel motors around the perimeter of the school of fish, unfurling the net and encircling the fish, and the seine skiff then attaches its end of the net to the fishing vessel. The fishing vessel then purses the net by winching in a cable at the bottom edge of the net, and draws in the top cables of the net to gather its entire contents.

Studies monitoring direct and indirect catch levels have shown that fish and dolphins are found together in a number of areas around the world and that this may lead to incidental taking of dolphins during fishing operations. In the Eastern Tropical Pacific Ocean (ETP), a particular association between dolphins and tuna has long been observed, such that fishermen locate schools of underwater tuna by finding and chasing dolphins on the ocean surface and intentionally encircling them with nets to catch the tuna underneath. This type of association has not been observed in other areas of the world; consequently, intentional encirclement of dolphins with purse-seine nets is used as a tuna fishing technique only in the Eastern Tropical Pacific Ocean. When dolphins and tuna together have been surrounded by purse-seine nets, it is possible to reduce or eliminate the catch of dolphins through using certain procedures.

Marine Mammal Protection Act of the United States
(Measures on Imports from Mexico)

The Marine Mammal Protection Act of 1972, as revised (MMPA), requires a general prohibition of "taking" (harassment, hunting, capture, killing or attempt thereof) and importation into the United States of marine mammals, except where an exception is explicitly authorized. Its stated goal is that the incidental kill or serious injury of marine mammals in the course of commercial fishing be reduced to insignificant levels approaching zero. . . . These provisions govern the taking of marine mammals incidental to harvesting of yellowfin tuna . . . as well as importation of yellowfin tuna and tuna products harvested. . . .

Section 101(a)(2) of the MMPA also states that "The Secretary of Treasury shall ban the importation of commercial fish or products from fish which have been caught with commercial fishing technology which results in the incidental kill or incidental serious injury of ocean mammals in excess of United States standards". This prohibition is mandatory. Special ETP provisions in section 101(a)(2)(B) provide that importation of yellowfin tuna harvested with purse-seine nets and products therefrom is prohibited unless the Secretary of Commerce finds that (i) the government of the harvesting country has a program regulating taking of marine mammals that is comparable to that of the United States, and (ii) the average rate of incidental taking of marine mammals by vessels of the harvesting nation is comparable to the average rate of such taking by United States vessels. . . .

The Dolphin Protection Consumer Information Act (DPCIA) specifies a labelling standard for any tuna product exported from or offered for sale in the United States. "Tuna products" covered include any tuna-containing food product processed for retail sale, except perishable items with a shelf life of less than three days. Under this statute, it is a violation of section 5 of the Federal Trade Commission Act (FTCA) for any producer, importer, exporter, distributor or seller of such tuna products to include on the label of that product the term "Dolphin Safe" or any other term falsely suggesting that the tuna contained therein was fished in a manner not harmful to dolphins, if it contains tuna harvested in either of two situations. The two situations are (1) harvesting in the Eastern Tropical Pacific Ocean by a vessel using purse-seine nets which does not meet certain specified conditions for being considered dolphin safe, and (2) harvesting on the high seas by a vessel engaged in driftnet fishing. . . .

Mexico requested the Panel to find, with respect to the MMPA import prohibition imposed on yellowfin tuna and tuna products from Mexico, that inter alia:

> (a) the embargo provisions in MMPA section 101(a)(2) as well as relevant provisions of the corresponding regulations were inconsistent with the general prohibition of quantitative restrictions under Article XI; the provisions of MMPA section 101(a)(2)(B) and relevant implementing regulations established discriminatory specific conditions for a specific geographical area, in violation of Article XIII. . . .

With respect to the Dolphin Protection Consumer Information Act, Mexico requested that the Panel find this legislation was inconsistent with Articles IX and I by virtue of its establishment of discriminatory and unfavourable specific conditions for a specific geographical area. . . .

The United States requested the Panel to find that:

> (a) The measures imposed under the MMPA with respect to certain domestic yellowfin tuna from Mexico were internal regulations affecting the sale, offering for sale, purchase, transportation, distribution or use of tuna and tuna products consistent with Article III:4; and
> (b) even if these measures are not consistent with Article III, they were covered by the exceptions in Article XX(b) and XX(g). . . .

The United States further requested that the Panel find, with respect to the Dolphin Protection Consumer Information Act, that . . . because the Act discriminated on the basis of the waters in which the tuna is caught, not the origin of the tuna, it was consistent with the requirements of [the GATT].

The United States [argued] . . . that the MMPA specified the requirements for tuna imported into the United States. It did not subordinate the jurisdiction of one contracting party to the legislation of another contracting party. The United States also noted that dolphin roamed the seas and were therefore common resources within the jurisdiction of no one contracting party. . . . The United States stated that the MMPA embargo was necessary to protect the life and health of dolphins.

Mexico . . . stated that the text and prior interpretation of Article XX(b) indicated that it referred to protection of the life and health of humans and animals within the territory of the contracting party protecting them. Otherwise, one contracting party could arrogate to itself the right to protect the life or health of humans and animals in international areas or within the territory of other contracting parties. Such a case had never arisen in GATT, was not provided for in the General Agreement, and above all would be contrary to international law.

The United States responded that a government could prohibit imports of a product in order to protect the life or health of humans, plants or animals outside its jurisdiction. The United States assumed that Mexico shared this view, since Mexico too prohibited the importation of dolphins and dolphin products in order to protect dolphin outside its jurisdiction. . . .

The United States stated that the MMPA embargo was necessary to protect the life and health of dolphins. No alternative measure was available or had been proposed that could reasonably be expected to achieve the objective of protecting the lives or health of dolphins. Purse-seining for tuna in the ETP meant deliberate encirclement of schools of dolphin with nets. Without efforts to protect them, they would be killed when the tuna was harvested. In order to avoid these needless deaths, the United States had established requirements for tuna production: yellowfin tuna harvested in the ETP using purse-seine nets and imported into the United States must have been produced under a program providing for harvesting methods to reduce dolphin mortality. . . .

Mexico responded that the MMPA embargo was not "necessary" in the sense of Article XX, as the lives and health of dolphins could be protected consistently with the General Agreement. Mexico's own dolphin-protection measures had been taken in conformity with the General Agreement, demonstrating that the General Agreement did not oblige its contracting parties to adopt measures contrary to the environment. . . .

Mexico also stated that the text and prior interpretation of Article XX(b) indicated that it referred to protection of the life and health of humans and animals within the territory of the contracting party protecting them. Otherwise, one contracting party could arrogate to itself the right to protect the life or health of humans and animals in international areas or within the territory of other contracting parties. Such a case had never arisen in GATT, was not provided for in the General Agreement, and above all would be contrary to international law. . . .

The Panel proceeded to examine whether Article XX(b) or Article XX(g) could justify the MMPA provisions on imports of certain yellowfin tuna and yellowfin tuna products, and the import ban imposed under these provisions. . . .

Article XX(b)

The Panel noted that the basic question raised by these arguments, namely whether Article XX(b) covers measures necessary to protect human, animal or plant life or health outside the jurisdiction of the contracting party taking the measure, is not clearly answered by the text of that provision. It refers to life and health protection generally without expressly limiting that protection to the jurisdiction of the contracting party concerned. The Panel therefore decided to analyze this issue in the light of the drafting history of Article XX(b), the purpose of this provision, and the consequences that the interpretations proposed by the parties would have for the operation of the General Agreement as a whole.

The Panel noted that the proposal for Article XX(b) dated from the Draft Charter of the International Trade Organization (ITO) proposed by the United States, which stated in Article 32, "Nothing in Chapter IV [on commercial policy] of this Charter shall be construed to prevent the adoption or enforcement by any Member of measures: . . . (b) necessary to protect human, animal or plant life or health". [But] the record indicates that the concerns of the drafters of Article XX(b) focused on the use of sanitary measures to safeguard life or health of humans, animals or plants within the jurisdiction of the importing country.

The Panel further noted that Article XX(b) allows each contracting party to set its human, animal or plant life or health standards. The conditions set out in Article XX(b) which limit resort to this exception, namely that the measure taken must be "necessary" and not "constitute a means of arbitrary or unjustifiable discrimination or a disguised restriction on international trade", refer to the trade measure requiring justification under Article XX(b), not however to the life or health standard chosen by the contracting party. The Panel recalled the finding of a previous panel that this paragraph of Article XX was intended to allow contracting parties to impose trade restrictive measures inconsistent with the General Agreement to pursue overriding public policy goals to the extent that such inconsistencies were unavoidable. The Panel considered that if the broad interpretation of Article XX(b) suggested by the United States were accepted, each contracting party could unilaterally determine the life or health protection policies from which other contracting parties could not deviate without jeopardizing their rights under the General Agreement. The General Agreement would then no longer constitute a multilateral framework for trade among all contracting parties but would provide legal security only in respect of trade between a limited number of contracting parties with identical internal regulations. . . .

On the basis of the above considerations, the Panel found that the United States' direct import prohibition imposed on certain yellowfin tuna and certain yellowfin tuna products of Mexico and the provisions of the MMPA under which it is imposed could not be justified under the exception in Article XX(b).

Article XX(g)

The Panel proceeded to examine whether the prohibition on imports of certain yellowfin tuna and certain yellowfin tuna products from Mexico and the MMPA provisions under which it was imposed could be justified under the exception in Article XX(g). The Panel noted that the United States, in invoking Article XX(g) with respect to its direct import prohibition under the MMPA, had argued that the measures taken under the MMPA are measures primarily aimed at the conservation of dolphin, and that the import restrictions on certain tuna and tuna products under the MMPA are "primarily aimed at rendering effective restrictions on domestic production or consumption" of dolphin. The Panel also noted that Mexico had argued that the United States measures were not justified under the exception in Article XX(g) because, inter alia, this provision could not be applied extrajurisdictionally.

The Panel noted that Article XX(g) required that the measures relating to the conservation of exhaustible natural resources be taken "in conjunction with restrictions on domestic production or consumption". . . . A country can effectively control the production or consumption of an exhaustible natural resource only to the extent that the production or consumption is under its jurisdiction. This suggests that Article XX(g) was intended to permit contracting parties to take trade measures primarily aimed at rendering effective restrictions on production or consumption within their jurisdiction.

The Panel further noted that Article XX(g) allows each contracting party to adopt its own conservation policies. The conditions set out in Article XX(g) which limit resort to this exception, namely that the measures taken must be related to the conservation of exhaustible natural resources, and that they not "constitute a means of arbitrary or unjustifiable discrimination . . . or a disguised restriction on international trade" refer to the trade measure requiring justification under Article XX(g), not however to the conservation policies adopted by the contracting party. . . .

On the basis of the above considerations, the Panel found that the United States direct import prohibition on certain yellowfin tuna and certain yellowfin tuna products of Mexico directly imported from Mexico, and the provisions of the MMPA under which it is imposed, could not be justified under Article XX(g).

Dolphin Protection Consumer Information Act (DPCIA)

The Panel noted that Mexico considered the labelling provisions of the DPCIA to be marking requirements falling under Article IX:1, which reads:

> "Each contracting party shall accord to the products of the territories of other contracting parties treatment with regard to marking requirements no less favourable than the treatment accorded to like products of any third country."

The Panel noted that the DPCIA is based inter alia on a finding that dolphins are frequently killed in the course of tuna-fishing operations in the ETP through the use of purse-seine nets intentionally deployed to encircle dolphins. The DPCIA therefore accords the right to use the label "Dolphin Safe" for tuna harvested in the ETP only if such tuna is accompanied by documentary evidence showing that it was not harvested with purse-seine nets intentionally deployed to encircle dolphins. . . . According to the information presented to the Panel, the harvesting of tuna by intentionally encircling dolphins with purse-seine nets was practised only in the ETP because of the particular nature of the association between dolphins and tuna observed only in that area. By imposing the requirement to provide evidence that this fishing technique had not been used in respect of tuna caught in the ETP the United States therefore did not discriminate against countries fishing in this area. . . .

The Panel found for these reasons that the tuna products labelling provisions of the DPCIA relating to tuna caught in the ETP were not inconsistent with the obligations of the United States under Article I:1 of the General Agreement.

points for discussion

1. *Mexican tuna fishermen.* The Mexican tuna fishing industry, which had become the dominant supplier for U.S. tuna markets, was incredulous that the United States was truly concerned about dolphin welfare, as opposed to protecting its own tuna fishermen. Do they have a point? Should tuna

fishing methods be the subject of an international treaty rather than United States legislation? Or is it truly up to Americans as to how their tuna is caught?

2. *Epilog—tuna labeling.* The GATT panel decision excerpted above was not nearly the last word. The United States lifted its ban and replaced it with a policy requiring tuna caught in the ETP to have "comparable" rates of dolphin mortality than the U.S. boats that were adopting dolphin-friendlier tuna fishing methods. Another GATT panel struck that measure down. The United States did enjoy some success pursuing labeling measures. The requirements of the Dolphin Protection and Consumer Information Act now require that tuna caught within the ETP be accompanied by a certification that "[n]o dolphins were killed or seriously injured during the sets in which the tuna were caught; and [n]one of the tuna were caught on a trip using a purse seine net intentionally deployed on or to encircle dolphins." 50 C.F.R. § 216.91(a)(1)(ii)-(iii). Mexico challenged this regulation on the grounds that it was discriminatory toward Mexico and managed to get a WTO panel to strike it down, but only because it *insufficiently* regulated tuna caught outside of the ETP. Eventually, the restriction took effect, along with some lesser requirements for tuna caught outside of the ETP.

3. *Epilog—sea turtles and shrimp.* In a strikingly similar parallel trade dispute, the United States sought to protect sea turtles from shrimpers, who often catch sea turtles in their shrimp trawl nets. The United States required U.S. shrimp trawlers to deploy turtle excluder devices, commonly referred to as "TEDs," that shunt sea turtles up and out of a shrimp trawl net. TEDs reduce the efficiency of shrimp trawling, however, so American shrimpers, believing they were at a competitive disadvantage vis-à-vis foreign shrimpers, lobbied Congress to pass a law banning the import of shrimp from any country lacking a TED requirement. This restriction was deemed to be a violation of GATT, much the same way that the U.S. tuna-fishing ban failed. However, in an interesting twist, the WTO Panel found that the TED requirement was discriminatory, but that there was nothing in principle wrong with the TED requirement as a reasonable "measure relating to the conservation of an exhaustible natural resource," and hence something that could be fixed. That remains to be tested. For an analysis of the Tuna-Dolphin and Shrimp-Turtle disputes, see Robert Howse, *The World Trade Organization 20 Years On: Global Governance by Judiciary*, 27 EUR. J. INT'L L. 9 (2016).

4. *Epilog—international trade and ocean resources.* How might international trade law be changed to better accommodate the environmental laws of countries? Should a country be able to regulate the behavior of fishermen of another country, and imports of fish from that country? What might the pitfalls be? It might be possible that a country might use its leverage in international trade to coerce other countries to adopt more sustainable fishing practices. For this view, see Katrina Wyman, *Unilateral Steps to End High Seas Fishing*, 6 TEX. A&M L. REV. 259 (2018).

F. CHAPTER SUMMARY

1. **International law.** The backdrop for any issue pertaining to governance of the oceans is the long and sometimes meandering history of international law. International law for the oceans has adapted itself to changing realities, including commerce, militarization, regional conflicts, and the ever-evolving technology of fishing, whaling, and armed conflict.

2. **The United Nations Law of the Sea Convention.** While it is always easy to find fault with this series of conventions — there are many — it remains an unusually successful model for international lawmaking, having obtained agreement from such a large number of countries for such a large and wide-ranging set of issues. Perhaps most importantly, the definition of different maritime zones has facilitated trade and commerce, and provided a framework for international disputes. The conventions also serve as a good illustration of the relationship between treaty law and customary international law, and the delicate balance that sometimes needs to be struck between international relations and domestic politics.

3. **Other multinational agreements.** The United Nations Law of the Sea Convention also provided a framework for which further agreements could be negotiated. This second generation of multinational agreements show an increasing concern for the marine environment and the welfare of cetaceans.

4. **International trade.** Mirroring the development of international law itself, the United Nations Law of the Sea and all subsequent agreements are negotiated in the context of an impulse for nations to trade, for which maritime transport is indispensable. The General Agreement on Tariffs and Trade, while not specific to the oceans, is uniquely impacted by the international law of oceans, and also impacts activities governed by the international law of oceans.

G. SUGGESTED READING

David J. Bederman, *The Old Isolationism and the New Law of the Sea: Reflections on Advice and Consent for UNCLOS*, 49 HARV. INT'L L.J. 21 (2009).

DAVID J. BEDERMAN, GLOBALIZATION AND INTERNATIONAL LAW (2008).

Daniel Bodansky, *Protecting the Marine Environment from Vessel-source Pollution: UNCLOS III and Beyond*, 18 ECOL. L.Q. 719 (1991).

David D. Caron, *The International Whaling Commission and the North Atlantic Marine Mammal Commission: The Institutional Risks of Coercion in Consensual Structures*, 89 AM. J. INT'L L. 154 (1995).

Robert Howse, *The Fair Trade-Free Trade Debate: Trade, Labor, and the Environment*, 16 INT'L REV. L. & ECON. 61 (1996).

MARK JANIS & JOHN NOYES, INTERNATIONAL LAW (5th ed. 2016).

Millicent McCreath, *Report of the Conference on Climate Change and the Law of the Sea: Adapting the Law of the Sea to Address the Challenges of Climate Change,* 33 INT'L J. MARINE & COASTAL L. 836 (2018).

chapter 2

U.S. Law for Living Resources of the Oceans

The living resources of the ocean, especially fish and marine mammals, have always featured prominently in the development of ocean law. This is not surprising, given that people have for millennia depended on the ocean for food. This is still true today: Living resources (mostly fish and shellfish) make up about 17 percent of human protein consumption worldwide and up to 70 percent in some countries.

It should also not be surprising that conflicts have arisen over the exploitation of these living resources. Fish and other living resources have been abundant at times in history; but humans have proven to be relentless and ingenious hunters and have decimated populations of living resources in relatively short periods of time. This raises the question of the role of law, and how it might mediate conflicts. Fishermen, governments, conservation organizations, and other stakeholders — such as industries that pollute and may face regulation to protect fish — each have different priorities when it comes to governance of the oceans. As this chapter will illustrate, the law of living ocean resources has evolved over time and continues to do so.

A. INTRODUCTION

Humans' attempts to use national and international law to control exploitation of the living resources of the oceans have always bumped up against four stark realities. First, jurisdiction over oceans has always been contested. Up until the twentieth century, the dominant rule was "freedom of the seas," which meant that countries could permit their own fishing and whaling fleets to fish anywhere, for anything, and without any numerical limit on take.[1] The 1982 Law of the Sea Convention modified this rule to some degree, giving countries bordering the ocean ("coastal states") up to 200 nautical miles of exclusive jurisdiction over living resources. Exclusive jurisdiction meant that coastal states could prohibit fishing in this area, known under the Law of the Sea as the "exclusive economic zone" (EEZ). About 60 percent of the world's oceans, however, still do not fall under the exclusive jurisdiction of any single country.

A second challenge to effective regulation of take is the sheer size of the ocean — about 40 times the size of all land in the United States. This vast area, together with unforgiving weather, have made it difficult for authorities to monitor the activities of fishing vessels and to catch violators. Satellites and other new technologies have made monitoring and enforcement easier, but it remains a challenge.

Third, even if jurisdiction were clear and rules were enforceable, scientific uncertainty makes it difficult to craft sensible and politically acceptable rules. The living biota of the oceans are complex creatures that inhabit a complex and poorly understood environment. Predicting how their populations will respond to fishing is a challenging exercise. It is hard enough to predict how humans will behave, let alone bottom-dwelling fish! Uncertainty is the only constant.

A final, but still important, challenge is that harm to the living organisms of the ocean is difficult to observe. The same tough weather conditions that hamper law enforcement also make ocean research challenging and expensive. It has always seemed less broadly repugnant to pollute the oceans and destroy its life, than it has to foul our own terrestrial nests. "Out of sight, out of mind" is the unfortunate maxim that comes to mind. As a consequence of the disconnect, there is less political will to make needed sacrifices, such as reduced levels of fishing.

Despite these daunting challenges, the history of controlling overexploitation in the ocean has seen some victories. Even in the notoriously intractable international realm, coastal states have made treaties to limit fishing, whaling, and pollution. Federal U.S. law has brought an end to the most egregious instances of overfishing and has curtailed some of the injuries fishing causes to habitats like hard corals. To be sure, there remain many, many tragic outcomes, both economically and ecologically. But in what is surely one of the most vexing challenges facing any regulator, fisheries and marine mammal conservation efforts have at least managed to forge some paths forward.

The following excerpt from a foundational article lays out a natural resources dilemma that is particularly applicable to the conservation of living ocean resources.

---

1. For purposes of convenience, we will use the term "fishing" in the rest of this chapter to mean hunting for any kind of marine life, including marine mammals. We will use more specific terms, like "whaling," where necessary for clarity.

Garrett Hardin, The Tragedy of the Commons

162 Science 1243 (1968)

Tragedy of Freedom in a Commons

. . . The tragedy of the commons develops in this way. Picture a pasture open to all. It is to be expected that each herdsman will try to keep as many cattle as possible on the commons. Such an arrangement may work reasonably satisfactorily for centuries because tribal wars, poaching, and disease keep the numbers of both man and beast well below the carrying capacity of the land. Finally, however, comes the day of reckoning, that is, the day when the long-desired goal of social stability becomes a reality. At this point, the inherent logic of the commons remorselessly generates tragedy.

As a rational being, each herdsman seeks to maximize his gain. Explicitly or implicitly, more or less consciously, he asks, "What is the utility *to one* of adding one more animal to my herd?" This utility has one negative and one positive component.

> The positive component is a function of the increment of one animal. Since the herdsman receives all the proceeds from the sale of the additional animal, the positive utility is nearly +1.
>
> The negative component is a function of the additional overgrazing created by one more animal. Since, however, the effects of overgrazing are shared by all the herdsmen, the negative utility for any particular decision-making herdsman is only a fraction of −1.

Adding together the component partial utilities, the rational herdsman concludes that the only sensible course for him to pursue is to add another animal to his herd. And another; and another. . . . But this is the conclusion reached by each and every rational herdsman sharing a commons. Therein is the tragedy. Each man is locked into a system that compels him to increase his herd without limit — in a world that is limited. Ruin is the destination toward which all men rush, each pursuing his own best interest in a society that believes in the freedom of the commons. Freedom in a commons brings ruin to all. . . .

In an approximate way, the logic of the commons has been understood for a long time, perhaps since the discovery of agriculture or the invention of private property in real estate. But it is understood mostly only in special cases which are not sufficiently generalized. Even at this late date, cattlemen leasing national land on the western ranges demonstrate no more than an ambivalent understanding, in constantly pressuring federal authorities to increase the head count to the point where over-grazing produces erosion and weed-dominance. Likewise, the oceans of the world continue to suffer from the survival of the philosophy of the commons. Maritime nations still respond automatically to the shibboleth of the "freedom of the seas." Professing to believe in the "inexhaustible resources of the oceans," they bring species after species of fish and whales closer to extinction. . . .

Pollution

In a reverse way, the tragedy of the commons reappears in problems of pollution. Here it is not a question of taking something out of the commons. But of putting something in — sewage, or chemical, radioactive, and heat wastes into water; noxious and dangerous fumes into the air and distracting and unpleasant advertising signs into the line of sight. The calculations of utility are much the same as before. The rational man finds that his share of the cost of the wastes he discharges into the commons is less than the cost of purifying his wastes before releasing them. Since this is true of everyone, we are locked into a system of "fouling our own nest," so long as we behave only as independent, rational, free-enterprisers.

The tragedy of the commons as a food basket is averted by private property, or something formally like it. But the air and waters surrounding us cannot readily be fenced, and so the tragedy of the commons as a cesspool must be prevented by different means, by coercive laws or taxing devices that make it cheaper for the polluter to treat his pollutants than to discharge them untreated. . . . Indeed, our particular concept of private property, which deters us from exhausting the positive resources of the earth, favors pollution. The owner of a factory on the bank of a stream . . . often has difficulty seeing why it is not his natural right to muddy the waters flowing past his door. The law, always behind the times, requires elaborate stitching and fitting to adapt it to his newly perceived aspect of the commons.

How to Legislate Temperance?

Analysis of the pollution problem as function of population density uncovers a not generally recognized principle of morality, namely: the morality of an act is a function of the state of the system at the time it is performed. Using the commons as a cesspool does not harm the general public under frontier conditions, because there is no public; the same behavior in a metropolis is unbearable. A hundred and fifty years ago a plainsman could kill an American bison, cut out only the tongue for his dinner, and discard the rest of the animal. He was not in any important sense being wasteful. Today, with only a few thousand bison left, we would be appalled at such behavior. . . .

Mutual Coercion Mutually Agreed Upon

The social arrangements that produce responsibility are arrangements that create coercion, of some sort. Consider bank-robbing. The man who takes money from a bank acts as if the bank were commons. How do we prevent such action? Certainly not by trying to control his behavior solely by a verbal appeal to his sense of responsibility. Rather than rely on propaganda we . . . insist that a bank is not a commons; we seek the definite social arrangement that will keep it from becoming a commons. That morality of bank-robbing is particularly easy to understand because we accept complete prohibition of this activity. We are willing to say "Thou shalt not rob banks," without providing for exception. But temperance also can be created by coercion. Taxing is good coercion device. To keep downtown shoppers temperate in their use of parking meters for short periods, and traffic fines for longer ones.

We need not actually forbid a citizen to park as long as he wants to; we need merely make it increasingly expensive for him to do so. . . . The only kind of coercion I recommend is mutual coercion, mutually agreed upon by the majority of the people affected.

To say that we mutually agree is not to say we are required to enjoy it, or even to pretend we enjoy it. Who enjoys taxes? We all grumble about them. But we accept compulsory taxes because we recognize the voluntary taxes would favor the conscienceless. We institute and (grumblingly) support taxes and other coercive devices to escape the horror of the commons. . . .

Recognition of Necessity

Perhaps the simplest summary of this analysis of man's population problems is this: the commons, if justifiable at all, is justifiable only under conditions of low-population density. As the human population has increased, the commons has had to be abandoned in one aspect after another. . . .

[We see] that the commons as a place for waste disposal would also have to be abandoned. Restrictions on the disposal of domestic sewage are widely accepted in the Western world; we are still struggling to close the commons to pollution by automobiles, factories, insecticide sprayers, fertilizing operations, and atomic energy installations. . . .

Every new enclosure of the commons involves the infringement of somebody's personal liberty. Infringements made in the distant past are accepted because no contemporary complains of a loss. It is newly proposed infringements that we vigorously oppose; cries of "rights" and "freedom" fill the air. But what does "freedom" mean? When men mutually agreed to pass laws against robbing, mankind became more free, not less so. Individuals locked into the logic of the commons are free only to bring on universal ruin; once they see the necessity of mutual coercion, they become free to pursue other goals. I believe it was Hegel who said, "Freedom is the recognition of necessity."

points for discussion

1. *Two kinds of commons.* Why do you think Garrett Hardin chose to use a common pasture "open to all" to illustrate the tragedy of the commons? What is "tragic" about it?

   Hardin's pasture was unregulated; there was no law in place, no agency responsible for rationally managing resources. Where there is no law (or private agreement) possible, herders can do as they please. This situation is often called "open access."

   Hardin also presents "cattlemen leasing national land on the western ranges" as an example of the tragedy of the commons. But grazing on federal public lands is not technically a commons: It is ostensibly regulated by the provisions of the Taylor Grazing Act of 1934, which mandates rational management. In using federal land grazing as an example, Hardin was illustrating a different kind of commons, what some have called the "tragedy of the regulated commons." How does a regulated commons become tragic? Under the Act, federal regulators may, for a fee, issue grazing permits that allow private parties to graze on federal public lands. The fees, however, are often lower than market rates, and the government sometimes has a difficult time collecting them. Studies have shown that federal lands where grazing is permitted are in poor condition, that is, overgrazed, like Hardin's pasture. During congressional debate over passage of the 1978 Public Rangelands Improvement Act members of Congress lamented that federal rangelands were in terrible condition. About 10 percent of those rangelands are in a state of virtual desertification. Why? Charging ranchers under-market grazing fees is a form of subsidy; subsidies result in greater demand for grazing than would occur in a free market. As demand increases, so too does the pressure on managers to allow more grazing. As a result of this pressure, federal land managers have often permitted too much grazing, ignoring evidence of overuse. Moreover, even when managers set sustainable grazing levels, the government does not fully enforce those limits. Ironically, some federal land is today so overgrazed and unproductive that grazing fees that were once too low have become justified. The result is poor productivity for everyone, most of all ranchers dependent upon federal lands. *See, e.g.,* WELFARE RANCHING (G. Wuerthner & M. Mollie Mattison eds., 2002).

As you will learn later in this chapter, U.S. fisheries are also a regulated commons. Is there a difference between the resource depletion tragedies — overgrazing, overfishing — and pollution tragedies?

2. *Solutions.* List the different types of solutions for the tragedy of commons. What does Hardin mean by "mutual coercion, mutually agreed upon"? What might mutual coercion mean?

Hardin also mentions private property as one potential way of solving the commons problem. In a part of the essay not excerpted above, he suggests that maybe national parks ought to be privatized. Do you agree? Is private property the only form of "enclosure" that could solve a tragedy of the commons? For a treatment of different property regimes surrounding Hardin's imagined regimes, see Shi-Ling Hsu, *A Two-Dimensional Framework of Property Rights Regimes,* 36 U.C. DAVIS L. REV. 813 (2003), and Abraham Bell & Gideon Parchomovsky, *Reconfiguring Property in Three Dimensions,* 75 U. CHI. L. REV. 1015 (2008).

Perhaps the best known nongovernmental alternative to private ownership is community-based management, in which people with a shared interest in the resource come together to manage it, without the help of government. The concept of community ownership is closely associated with the scholar who spent her career studying the idea, Elinor Ostrom. Like Hardin, Ostrom was an economic giant who was not an economist. (Hardin was a biologist, while Ostrom was a political scientist.) In 2009, she became the first woman to receive the Nobel Prize in Economics. Her defining work, *Governing the Commons* (1990), described several instances in which a common-pool resource was exploited sustainably for long periods of time, sometimes hundreds of years. The result was so surprising because these potential tragedies had been avoided without government intervention or the use of privatization. What Ostrom discovered is that groups of people can form very sophisticated and robust cooperative arrangements, even in the absence of any legal mandate to do so. Indeed, a wide variety of resources, such as groundwater, fish, trees, and irrigation systems, were cooperatively managed in Turkey, Switzerland, Philippines, and California, demonstrating the universality of informal, extra-legal cooperative institutions.

3. *Problem not solved.* Yet another giant of a noneconomist, law professor Carol Rose, coined the term "comedy of the commons" to describe the notion that some common-pool or open access resources must *necessarily* be open to all (or at least many), because their very usefulness lies in their public accessibility. Consider the beach, for example. Is the value of going to the beach not bound up in its social nature? Or consider shipping lanes. If a shipping lane were under the private ownership of a single mogul, what would be the implications for commerce? Professor Rose argued that there is "inherently public property" that is best left relatively free and unfettered, because the highest and best use of such property was to have it used quite intensively. Inherently public property *increases* in value if more people use it (to a point). Carol Rose, *The Comedy of the Commons: Custom, Commerce, and Inherently Public Property*, 53 U. Chi. L. Rev. 711 (1986). Consider also the case of early telephones. What good is having a telephone unless there are many other people to talk to at the other end? *See, e.g.*, Jon Gertner, The Idea Factory: Bell Labs and the Great Age of American Innovation (2012).

4. *Expansion of the commons.* The Hardin essay is one of the most cited works of all time, with over 35,000 citations in books and academic journals. For a time, it was the most cited work in the economics literature, which is stunning considering that Hardin was not an economist. The notion of the tragedy of the commons has been applied to countless varieties of other policy situations, including traffic congestion, overuse of antibiotics (Aidan Hollis & Peter Maybarduk, *Antibiotic Resistance Is a Tragedy of the Commons That Necessitates Global Cooperation*, 43 J.L. Med. & Ethics 33 (2015)), digital privacy (Dennis Hirsch, *Privacy, Public Goods, and the Tragedy of the Trust Commons*, 65 Duke L.J. Online (2016), https://dlj.law.duke.edu/2016/02/privacy-public-goods-and-the-tragedy-of-the-trust-commons/), social media, campaign finance, the use of performance-enhancing substances (Shi-Ling Hsu, *What IS a Tragedy of the Commons? Overfishing and the Campaign Spending Problem*, 69 Alb. L. Rev. 75 (2005)), and global climate change (Nicholas Stern, The Stern Review: The Economics of Climate Change (2007)), to name just a few.

5. *Fishing commons.* Overfishing is perhaps one of the most apt illustrations of the tragedy of the commons. Throughout the thousands of years of fishing

history, continuing up to the modern era, fishermen have overfished fish stocks ranging from the easy-to-overfish oyster to the much-more-difficult-to-catch swordfish. As you will see later in this chapter, regulatory interventions have saved or recovered some fisheries from this fate. But left to their own devices, humans have been uncannily consistent in catching an unsustainable number of fish.

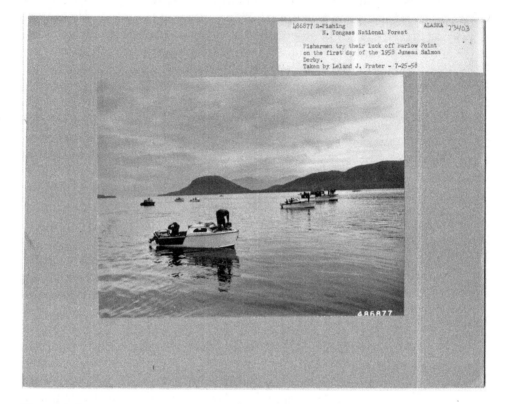

Figure 2-1.
These salmon fishermen are waiting for the gun to sound, signaling the beginning of the fishing season. Once the gun sounds, they will race to catch as many fish as they can until the season ends. Can you see the parallels between the "salmon derby" and Hardin's pasture?

Overfishing is also uniquely apt because fishermen, by fishing too much (or lobbying too much for high catch limits), are acting against their own long-term self-interest. Consider Table 1, pertaining to the Northern Pacific Halibut. Fish are extremely hard to count, for obvious reasons. Fish abundance is therefore estimated by a variety of proxies. One of the most widely used proxies is "catch-per-unit effort" (CPUE). The idea is to be able to compare stock status in different time periods by comparing how easy it is to catch fish in each period. If fishermen caught 15 fish in an hour 10 years ago but can only catch one an hour today, then

Table 1. CPUE for the Northern Pacific Halibut fishery between the years 1890 and 1930

Year	CPUE
1890	1000
1910	271
1915	118
1920	84
1925	51
1930	35

Source: JAMES A. CRUTCHFIELD, REGULATION OF THE PACIFIC COAST HALIBUT FISHERY 45 fig. 2 (1961), https://hdl.handle.net/2027/uc1.31822024036162?urlappend=%3Bseq=7.

it might be reasonable to conclude that stocks have declined. Table 1 shows the CPUE for the Northern Pacific Halibut fishery between the years 1890, when it was unfished, and 1930, by which time it had experienced a boom in the entry of new boats.

Hardin's theory explains why fishermen end up in the tragedy of the commons (too much fishing) and the regulated tragedy of the commons (too much lobbying).

1. Biological Principles of Fishery Management

Informed regulation of fish requires at least a very basic understanding of how fish spawn, feed, grow, migrate, and die. Obviously, it is impossible to generalize about the many fish species in the oceans of the world, but fisheries managers have usually used some very simple ecological principles that govern, to some extent, every fish species as a starting point.

Fish need space, food, and reproductive partners. If you were to go back millennia and measure the development of an entirely new fish species, you could graph its population over

> What is a fishery? A "fishery" is defined in the Magnuson-Stevens Act as "one or more stocks of fish which can be treated as a unit for purposes of conservation and management and which are identified on the basis of geographical, scientific, technical, recreational, and economic characteristics." 16 U.S.C. § 1802(13). A fishery typically has a location, although that location can be very large (e.g., North Pacific) and typically has some group of fishermen. We will use the term to refer to the taking of some *species*, or group of species, e.g., the "Alaskan salmon fishery," or the "Pacific Coast Groundfish Fishery."

time. What would such a timeline of population growth look like, absent any fishing? Conceptually, scientists think of fish populations as having a "logistic growth curve," shaped like an "S," as shown in Figure 2-2.

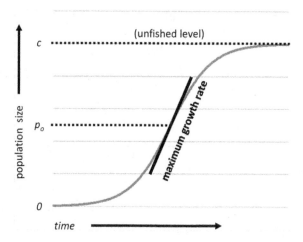

Moving from left to right, then, the S-shaped curve traces out the adult, reproductive population of the fish species over time. At first, the species' population would grow very slowly. This is because, when there are only a few members of a new species, it is difficult to

Figure 2-2. Reproductive Population of Fish Species over Time

find reproductive mates. Those first few members of the new species do have some advantages: They have access to as much food and space as they need, as there are very few others to compete with. And being small in number, they may also be safer from the attention of predators. With plenty of food and space available, the fish stock grows, and the increasing population makes it easier to find mates. Spawning rates increase, and the population increases more rapidly, which is why the S-curve in its middle region begins to rise more quickly. But as population increases, so does competition for food and space. Also, at higher population levels, predators take notice and with more competition among this newly enlarged population, hiding from predators becomes more difficult. At some point, the advantage of having many more fish around—the ease of reproducing—begins to be outweighed by the disadvantage of less available food and space. As a result, the rate of population growth slows on the right side of the graph. The population is still increasing, but at a slower rate. Finally, the adult population becomes high enough that competition among species members for food and space makes it harder for juvenile fish to reach maturity. At very high population levels, fish mortality (the number of fish deaths) will just cancel out recruitment (fish reaching maturity). At that point, the population will remain stable indefinitely, with the growth rate at zero. This is the maximum possible population, or "carrying capacity," denoted c.

At any given point on the S-curve, there exists a distinct population (total number of adults) and a population growth rate (change in the number of adults over a specific period of time). Adjusting the amount of fishing simultaneously adjusts both the population and the rate of population growth. Managing a fishery is trying to maintain a desirable population and population growth rate and choosing the amount of fishing that achieves that.

What is the rate of population growth? It is the *rate* at which population is growing, or the slope, or *steepness* of the S-shaped curve—slowly at first on the left side, speeding up in the middle, and slowing down again on the right side, as it tapers off to the carrying capacity. At which point is the population growing the fastest? At the midpoint p_o, the abundance of reproductive partners is high, and yet mortality due to food or space constraints has not yet peaked. At that point, the fish stock is adding p_o fish every year, the most it can.

This midpoint p_o in fact has legal ramifications. If the fish population is growing the fastest at p_o, then p_o is the point at which you can harvest the greatest amount of fish and still keep stocks at the same overall levels from year to year. For a given fish stock, the maximum growth rate translates to a number of fish that fishermen can catch in each time period without the stock levels being different at the end of the time period. In other words, fishing at the optimal rate theoretically lays the foundation for a fishing industry — businesses ideally need access to a consistent number of fish from year to year so they can make good decisions about how much to invest in boats, nets, and other fishing gear. Fishing at the optimal rate also is the most efficient use of the fish stock (from a fishing perspective): The greatest number of fish are being harvested without compromising the long-term health of the fishery. Fisheries laws and treaties refer to both the harvesting rate p_o and the number of fish produced annually by fishing at rate p_o as the *maximum sustainable yield* of the fishery.

Obviously, this is only a conceptual model. Especially in the era of climate change, many complexities interfere with a neat, simple account of fish growth and harvesting. Changes to the ecological environment in which a species lives, for example, a sudden decline in the abundance of prey or a change in water temperatures, can impact population growth. Many other irregular events, including disease, also cause fish deaths. Ecologists call such events disturbances. Fisheries scientists, who specialize in building computer models that estimate the response of fish stocks to disturbances, treat "fishing mortality" (fish killed by fishermen) as a disturbance. So, fishing policy is something that can be adjusted (in theory) to achieve a certain population and rate of population growth. Fishing policy should account for the fact some fish are caught as *bycatch*, which means that they are not the intended target for fishermen but are caught incidentally while fishing for something else. It is never as easy as simply finding out the carrying capacity and the maximum growth rate and setting the catch limit at that level. Uncertainty pervades many, many aspects of managing fish stocks. But the value of this model is in providing a framework within which a fisheries regulator can at least aim for a "sustainable" level of harvest of a fish species.

How do scientists and regulators know how many fish there are in the sea? They don't. Terrestrial animals that can be seen (if you know where to look) are hard enough to count. The ocean poses even more daunting challenges, and fish are mobile and evasive. As noted above, estimating fish populations is done by proxies such as catch-per-unit effort. Another common proxy is age-structure: Scientists examine batches of caught fish and study the age distribution of the batch. If too many batches consist of relatively young fish, it suggests the stock is in poor condition, as few fish are able to grow to full maturity.

Figure 2-3. A Modern Factory Trawler

2. Fishing Technologies and Techniques

Technological innovation in the fishing industry may not seem quite so obvious and breathtaking as in consumer electronics or high-tech industries, but it has been taking place for a long time, and has profoundly changed the way people fish, and therefore, the ecology of oceans. At every turn, some technological advance has enabled fishermen to catch fish more efficiently.

Before the mid-1850s, fishing either took place from shore, or on boats that were powered by oar or sail. The advent of **steam-powered trawlers** opened up an entirely new world to fishermen: Fishing the high seas, covering over half of the Earth's surface, became possible. The practice of trawling — dragging a net through the water — is much more efficient than passively waiting for a fish to attack bait. Later, after World War I, the advent of the **diesel** engine, adopted for other uses, made fishing fleets more powerful and efficient. **Radar**, developed for military purposes during World War II, became standard equipment on fishing boats to help with navigation and collision avoidance. All of these technologies allowed fishermen to travel farther and longer to catch fish. In allowing fishermen to range farther, these technologies produced international conflicts over fishing, and indirectly led to the first efforts to control overfishing.

Sonar technology, long used for detecting submarines, was declassified in the 1970s, and rapidly became an important tool in fishing for pelagic fish, mid-depth fish that can be detected much the same way that submarines can be detected. GPS technology became widely available in the 1990s, again facilitating long-range travel in the quest for fish. It should be noted that GPS can be a double-edged sword for illegal fishermen — environmental organizations have employed GPS technology developed by Google to detect when fishermen illegally entered closed waters for the purpose of poaching.

One of the most disruptive innovations has been evolution of **factory ship processing**. Starting in the 1960s, flash-freezing technology was used to replace ice and salt to immediately preserve caught fish. Once that became possible, fishing boats began to incorporate aspects of fish processing on board to add value to landed catch. With diesel power, machines could be installed on boats to scale and fillet fish. A modern freeze trawler will employ dozens of on-board workers on an assembly line that removes fish heads, and will scale, fillet, weigh, and package fish into boxes marked "Frozen at Sea," ready for distribution as soon as the boat docks. Discards and leftover parts are ground into fishmeal.

Fish and other edible ocean life reside just about everywhere there is a sufficiently clean body of water. They are near shores, in the high seas, swimming through straits, in shallow waters and deep; they are sedentary, bottom-dwelling, highly migratory, predator and prey. Given the diversity of edible ocean life, it is not surprising that fishermen employ a variety of technologies. What follows is a review of the different kinds of fishing techniques.

Figure 2-4. Longlining

Longlining is the fishing method most like traditional pole fishing, except that instead of setting one hook, longliners set lines as much as 40 miles long, with thousands of hooks. Longline boats are of all sizes and need not be very large — as small as 12 meters — but large enough to haul in, store, and transport the catch back to the dock. Longline fishing is quite different depending on whether the fisherman is searching for swordfish, cod, hake, tuna, halibut, or the many other species that can be caught by hook and bait. Setting hooks can take hours, as does hauling it all up, so lines are only set once or twice every 24 hours. Generally, longlining is less damaging to ocean ecology than other techniques, but baiting a hook does predictably catch unintended species: sea turtles, sharks, and sometimes, when baiting hooks, seabirds. Catching one species of fish when fishing for another can be a problem because the vessel may not be equipped to handle the bycatch, or have a permit for it.

Trawling, like longlining, is a very broad category with all kinds of trawlers catching all kinds of fish at all depths. Trawling can be by one boat or two traveling in parallel and each dragging one end of a large net ("pair trawling"). Midwater trawling is simply towing a very large net along, catching whatever happens to be in its path. Typically, sonar technologies are used to more precisely target fish, moving down current from the school, and then turning around and towing against the current to minimize fish escape. At midwater and shallow depths, pair trawling has the advantage of minimizing disturbance to the fish, as the two boats can move around a school of fish; a single trawler must move over it. Bycatch of midwater trawling tends to be low, since boats usually identify a discrete school of fish before setting their net.

Bottom trawling is much more destructive, both in terms of habitat and bycatch. Bottom trawling is exactly what it sounds like: towing a large net across the bottom of the ocean floor. Nets are cone-shaped and the mouth is kept open by some structure, sometimes a beam known as an "otter board." Bottom trawling targets bottom-dwelling species, such as roughy, halibut, whiting, lobster, and rockfish. Bycatch is very common; a single net can contain many different species of fish. As well, bottom trawling disrupts the ocean floor, displacing sediment, damaging or destroying other bottom-dwelling species, sometimes including coral reefs. Estimates of bycatch in shrimping range from 4 to 10 pounds of bycatch (of all sorts) for every *one* pound of shrimp caught.

Figure 2-5. Bottom Trawling

Figure 2-6. Dredging

Something like bottom trawling is the technique of **dredging**, which is as harmful as it sounds. Bottom-dwelling species can be efficiently caught with dredging. Scallops are commonly caught by dredgers. The difference between bottom trawling and dredging is that an inherent part of dredging is the disruption of the ocean bottom, to more actively scoop up bottom-dwelling marine life.

Figure 2-7. Purse seining

If trawling nets are not large enough for a fisher, he or she can resort to **seining**. Some seine nets are structurally similar to trawl nets, but the net openings are uncoiled to surround an area. So a "purse" seine from a single boat will drop one end of a net opening and then travel around a school of fish while dragging the other end of the net opening. Once a school of fish is encircled, the opening is closed. A purse seine net involves a drawstring that encloses the net. Seining can be used to catch near-surface, midwater, or bottom-dwelling fish. Bycatch is highly dependent on the operation, as many variations of seining exist. One of the

THE GILL-NET COD FISHERY.

Way in which cod gill-nets are set for underrunning in Ipswich Bay, Mass   (Sect. v, vol. i, p. 232.)

1, End of the gang of nets. 2, Anchor-line, also called the "underrunning line." 3, Anchor. 4, Buoy-line. 5, Buoy.

Drawing by Capt. J. W. Collins.

Figure 2-8. Gillnetting

most notorious chapters in the history of fishing involved the fishing for tuna while enclosing nets around dolphins, who then drown in the nets or worse yet, are killed as the net is hauled up.

For both trawling and seine nets, mesh size matters. In order to avoid ensnaring juveniles, which are needed to return to the ocean to grow and spawn, mesh sizes should be large enough to allow them to escape. Regulation of mesh size is common.

Gillnetting employs nets that are vertically hung from buoys on the surface, to catch passing fish. Gillnets can drift or be fixed. Sizes vary, as do the species caught. Traditional gillnetting involved ensnaring fish in the mesh, so that encirclement was unnecessary. Mesh size is thus a central regulatory issue with gillnets. Done properly, most gillnetting can be a fairly selective fishing method, but bycatch is a significant concern. Sea turtles, sharks, and marine mammals are frequently ensnared. New England gillnets have been known to ensnare Northern right whales, of which there exist only a few hundred; only litigation forced the Massachusetts Division of Marine Fisheries to more tightly regulate the use of gillnets to avoid fatal encounters with right whales. *See Strahan v. Coxe* on p. ◆◆◆. In 1991, the United Nations banned the use of high seas drifting gillnets of more than 2.5 kilometers long.

Trapping is the strictly passive baiting and setting of traps, in which fish enter and are prevented from coming out. Traps are set for lobster, crabs, shrimp, octopus, and eels. Bycatch and juveniles can be released relatively unharmed. Lost or abandoned traps, however, continue to "ghost fish" after their useful life, but regulations now mandate that some escape panels be installed on new traps.

Figure 2-9. Senators Ted Stevens and Warren
Magnuson, Representing Alaska and
Washington, Respectively

Warren Magnuson was a Democratic politician from Washington, serving as
U.S. Representative from 1936 to 1944, and as Senator from 1944 to 1981. He
helped found the National Cancer Institute, sponsoring legislation for its formation in 1937, and his work on the Magnuson-Moss Warranty Act helped
bring about an era of consumer protection regulations. He was a powerful senator serving on Appropriations committees, and securing federal dollars for
his home state, including for the Bonneville Dam. In addition to his work on
public health and the conservation of fisheries, Magnuson spoke out on behalf
of Asians. He authored the Chinese Exclusion Repeal Act of 1943, also known
as the Magnuson Act, which overturned a 61-year ban on immigration from
China, and allowed many Chinese residents of the United States to become natural citizens.

Ted Stevens was a Republican politician from Alaska, who also excelled at
securing federal dollars for Alaska for roads, airports, and other important infrastructure for the state. Stevens defended his 1,452 earmarks for Alaskan projects,
citing Alaska's special needs as a remote state with very high federal ownership
of land. While his work on fisheries conservation was notable, he also worked to
facilitate oil extraction in Alaska and settle claims by Native Alaskans. Stevens
was convicted of violations of government ethics rules regarding some home
renovation gifts just days before his last reelection bid, but that conviction was
later overturned after discovery of severe prosecutorial misconduct, prompting
Judge Emmet Sullivan to berate Justice Department lawyers, and order an investigation into the prosecution itself. A Justice Department lawyer investigated for
his conduct on Stevens's case later committed suicide. Stevens died in a plane
crash in 2010, one year after leaving the U.S. Senate.

B. THE MAGNUSON-STEVENS FISHERY CONSERVATION AND MANAGEMENT ACT

1. An Overview

Before 1976, fisheries management in the United States was done almost exclusively by the states. The Submerged Lands Act of 1953 gave the states jurisdiction over fishing out to three nautical miles from shore. Until the mid-1970s, international law did not recognize exclusive national jurisdiction over ocean areas more than three miles from shore.

Although there was no national fisheries management until 1976, there were some federal treaty obligations that required states to impose (or not to impose) certain kinds of regulations. The Supremacy Clause of the U.S. Constitution requires states to comply with international treaties to which the United States is a party. For example, the United States had treaty fishing agreements with other countries, such as Canada, that required states such as Washington to honor reciprocal fishing and port privileges between American and Canadian nationals. The United States also had entered into treaties in the 1800s with Indian tribes in the Pacific Northwest that guaranteed the tribes fishing rights. In a landmark 1974 case, a federal court interpreted one of these treaties as requiring the State of Washington to divide fishing opportunities equally between tribal and non-tribal fishermen. *See United States v. Washington*, 384 F. Supp. 312 (W.D. Wash. 1974), *aff'd*, 520 F.2d 676 (9th Cir. 1975). (In 2018, the Supreme Court affirmed a Ninth Circuit decision holding the state responsible not only for dividing fish, but for protecting and restoring fish habitat. *Washington v. United States*, 584 U.S. ___ (2018).)

Notwithstanding these exceptions, the vast majority of regulations faced by fishermen were of state origin. In *Corsa v. Tawes*, 149 F. Supp. 771 (D. Md. 1957), Delaware and corporate plaintiff fishermen challenged the constitutionality of a Maryland statute prohibiting the use of very large purse seine nets, hundreds of yards deep and hundreds of yards across, that encircle large schools of fish (see Figure 2-7). The court held that the measure did not offend due process, and that Maryland could legitimately regulate fishing in its territorial waters to prevent overfishing and depletion of its fish stocks. Absent something like a treaty obligation, state law was generally the locus of fishing regulation.

That changed dramatically when Congress passed the Fishery Conservation and Management Act of 1976. The Act created a plethora of new regulatory authorities and responsibilities, which were vested in the National Marine Fisheries Service (NMFS), a branch of the National Oceanic and Atmospheric Administration (NOAA). We will refer to the Act as the Magnuson-Stevens Act, its title since 1996.

The Magnuson-Stevens Act was a sweeping piece of federal legislation that dramatically re-made fisheries management in the United States, and even influenced management in other countries. Although the idea of national control out to 200 nautical miles would not be adopted by the international community until the 1982 conclusion of the U.N. Law of the Sea Convention, Congress made a unilateral U.S. claim in the Magnuson-Stevens Act to a 200-mile "Fishery Conservation Zone." Fisheries economists cheered: As we learned from Hardin's article, exclusive control (private or governmental) is a prerequisite to solving commons problems. Most American fishermen were also pleased because they no longer had to share the 200-mile belt around the United States with foreign vessels. A few U.S. fishermen were opposed to the expansion of jurisdiction: For example, Southern California tuna fleets that fished within 200 miles of the west coast of South America were concerned that South American countries would kick them out.

The legislative history of the original Act is replete with allegations that foreign fishermen were decimating stocks off our coasts. As it turned out, excluding foreign boats did not save the stocks. American boats proved to be more than capable of wreaking their own havoc on fisheries. By 1995, over 30 percent of the fish stocks managed under the Magnuson-Stevens Act were classified as "overfished."

In addition to creating the Fishery Conservation Zone, the second major feature of the Magnuson-Stevens Act is its creation of new regulatory institutions to manage fisheries. Congress vested primary management responsibility in eight regional fishery management councils composed mainly of citizens "who . . . are knowledgeable regarding the conservation and management, or the commercial or recreational harvest, of . . . fishery resources." Congress limited NMFS' role to assisting the councils with information gathering and deferential review of council decisions. Figure 2-10 shows the states that are represented in each of the eight

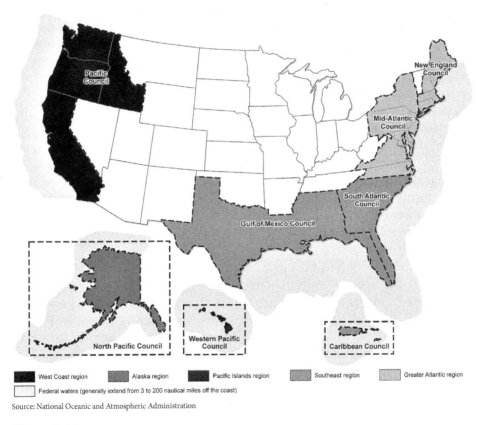

Source: National Oceanic and Atmospheric Administration

Figure 2-10.
This map shows the eight councils' jurisdictional areas.

regional councils. States retain jurisdiction over their "marginal seas," the ocean up to three nautical miles from shore. The councils have primary management authority over fishing from 3 to 200 nautical miles from shore. While the councils manage fish stocks within their respective areas, the Act gives NMFS the responsibility to manage fish that travel great distances and cross jurisdictional boundaries frequently — "highly migratory" species, such as tuna, swordfish, and sharks.

As part of their regulatory authority and responsibility, a regional council must develop a fishery management plan (FMP) for "each fishery under its authority that requires conservation and management." 16 U.S.C. § 1852(h). Regional councils have a great deal of autonomy in fashioning FMPs; we will learn about them in more detail later.

Congress amended and reauthorized the Magnuson-Stevens Act in 1996, with passage of the Sustainable Fisheries Act, which mostly strengthened fisheries regulation, that is, made the law more protective of fish stocks. But the Sustainable Fisheries Act also inserted new language requiring the NMFS and regional councils to take into account the economic interests of fishing communities. In the abstract, conserving fish is synonymous with protecting the *long-term* economic interests of fishing communities, but fishermen often have a hard time seeing it that way.

The 1996 Sustainable Fisheries Act also waded into a debate that was heated at the time, over the use of *individual fishing quotas* as a tool for limiting annual catches. Historically, the councils had attempted to limit catches almost exclusively by setting a total allowable catch (TAC), sometimes referred to as total allowable landings (TAL), a cap on fishing by all of the boats in a fishery in a given year. Unlike TACs, individual quotas give each fishermen, boat, or company, the right to catch a specific amount of fish each year, indefinitely. Quotas are usually not issued in units of fish, but instead as percentage shares of the overall fishery limit. Using shares increases quota-holders' stake in the future of the fishery in a way that fixed amounts could not. Do you see why? Individual fishing quotas can be transferable (sold or given away) or nontransferable. Transferable quotas (individual transferable quotas (ITQs)) are more controversial than nontransferable quotas, because of community concerns about who will end up "owning" the fishery, although the Magnuson-Stevens Act specifically states that ITQs are not property. Communities are often worried that transfers will result in local job losses. This chapter discusses ITQs in more detail later.

The Magnuson-Stevens Act was reauthorized again in 2007. Like the 1996 reauthorization, this latest Act mostly strengthened conservation mandates. Fishery management plans now *must* include annual catch limits for every fishery, and those annual catch limits may not exceed the level recommended by the "scientific and statistical committee," 16 U.S.C. § 1852(h)(6), typically a subcommittee convened to focus on fish populations. The upshot is that some discretion to loosen fishing restrictions has been removed. Fishery management plans must also set those annual catch limits in such a way that "overfishing does not occur in the fishery, including measures to ensure accountability." 16 U.S.C. § 1853(a)(15). These "accountability measures" have served as an effective tool for conservation organizations to force fishery management plans to account for potential gaps in monitoring, enforcement, and accounting for disturbances such as bycatch. Also like in the 1996 reauthorization, measures to acknowledge impacts on fishing industries were added. The 2007 reauthorization imposed a new requirement that each fishery management plan include a "fishery impact statement" that assesses the impacts of conservation and management measures, and "possible mitigation measures," on "participants in the fisheries and fishing communities affected by the plan or amendment." 16 U.S.C. § 1853(a)(9).

2. National Standards

The Magnuson-Stevens Act now contains ten national standards that the councils and NMFS must follow, respectively, in writing or reviewing FMPs. The original version Act contained only seven national standards; Congress added standards 8, 9, and 10 in 1996.

National Standards for Fishery Conservation and Management

16 U.S.C. § 1851

(a) In general — Any fishery management plan prepared, and any regulation promulgated to implement any such plan, pursuant to this subchapter shall be consistent with the following national standards for fishery conservation and management:

(1) Conservation and management measures shall prevent overfishing while achieving, on a continuing basis, the optimum yield from each fishery for the United States fishing industry.

(2) Conservation and management measures shall be based upon the best scientific information available.

(3) To the extent practicable, an individual stock of fish shall be managed as a unit throughout its range, and interrelated stocks of fish shall be managed as a unit or in close coordination.

(4) Conservation and management measures shall not discriminate between residents of different States. If it becomes necessary to allocate or assign fishing privileges among various United States fishermen, such allocation shall be (A) fair and equitable to all such fishermen; (B) reasonably calculated to promote conservation; and (C) carried out in such manner that no particular individual, corporation, or other entity acquires an excessive share of such privileges.

(5) Conservation and management measures shall, where practicable, consider efficiency in the utilization of fishery resources; except that no such measure shall have economic allocation as its sole purpose.

(6) Conservation and management measures shall take into account and allow for variations among, and contingencies in, fisheries, fishery resources, and catches.

(7) Conservation and management measures shall, where practicable, minimize costs and avoid unnecessary duplication.

(8) Conservation and management measures shall, consistent with the conservation requirements of this chapter (including the prevention of overfishing and rebuilding of overfished stocks), take into account the importance of fishery resources to fishing communities by utilizing economic and social data that meet the requirements of paragraph (2), in order to (A) provide for the sustained participation of such communities, and (B) to the extent practicable, minimize adverse economic impacts on such communities.

(9) Conservation and management measures shall, to the extent practicable, (A) minimize bycatch and (B) to the extent bycatch cannot be avoided, minimize the mortality of such bycatch.

(10) Conservation and management measures shall, to the extent practicable, promote the safety of human life at sea.

Compliance with the national standards is mandatory, and plaintiffs can challenge non-compliance in court. At the same time, plaintiffs will sometimes run into issues because of vague language ("to the extent practicable") and conflicts between standards. For example, taking into account the impact on fishing communities and minimizing adverse economic impacts (standard 8) may well conflict with efficiency in the utilization of fishery resources (standard 5).

C. FISHERY MANAGEMENT PLANS AND MANAGEMENT MEASURES

In the Act, Congress gave the councils the obligation to draft FMPs for all fish species under council management. Some FMPs cover one species, while others govern multiple species that make up a single fishery. The Northeast Groundfish FMP, for example, covers species like haddock, cod, and hake that are generally caught in the same nets.

FMPs are documents that, generally speaking, are meant to provide a comprehensive history of the fishery, a summary of relevant science, and—most important—the numerical framework for future management decisions. So, for example, the FMP will include a council's best estimate of the population target, that is, the level that can produce the optimum yield of the fishery. Although the councils establish specific management measures in separate "annual specification" regulations, all management measures in annual specifications must conform to both the FMP for that fishery and, of course, to the Act and general fisheries regulations.

Congress mandated that councils include in FMPs a number of informational elements, including "a description of the fishery, including, but not limited to, the number of vessels involved, the type and quantity of fishing gear used, the species of fish involved and their location, . . . actual and potential revenues from the fishery, [and] any recreational interests in the fishery. . . . "

In addition to required background information, FMPs must by law also "contain the conservation and management measures . . . necessary and appropriate for the conservation and management of the fishery, to prevent overfishing and rebuild overfished stocks, and to protect, restore, and promote the long-term health and stability of the fishery." 16 U.S.C. § 1853. What is a management measure? As an example, a simple conservation and management measure would be a catch limit on the number of fish that can be caught in a given year. Management measures can also be quite complex, as you shall see later in this chapter.

The Act also sets forth a variety of discretionary components for FMPs, including permitting requirements, limits on the number of vessels that can participate in the fishery, reporting requirements for vessels and fish processors, on-board observer requirements, and ocean "zoning" that may prohibit or limit the fishing methods and the times during which fishing is allowed. FMPs may also set out "limited access privilege programs" (LAPPs), "individual fishing quota" (IFQ), or individual transferable quota (ITQ) programs, all of which are meant to reduce the number of boats or fishermen participating in a fishery.

All of the standards are important, in that any FMP can be challenged on the grounds that it is inconsistent with one or more of the standards. The first standard in particular, however, serves as a fundamental starting point for NMFS and the regional councils because it specifies that FMPs "shall prevent overfishing while achieving, on a continuing basis, the optimum yield. . . ." Preventing overfishing is straightforward enough. Optimum yield, as it turns out, has been the source of litigation and general heartburn.

Section 2 of the Magnuson-Stevens Act provides that "optimum yield" is the amount of fish that

> (A) will provide the greatest overall benefit to the Nation, particularly with respect to food production and recreational opportunities, and taking into account the protection of marine ecosystems;
> (B) is prescribed on the basis of the maximum sustainable yield from the fishery, as reduced by any relevant social, economic, or ecological factor; and
> (C) in the case of an over fished fishery, provides for rebuilding to a level consistent with producing the maximum sustainable yield in such fishery.

So, the term "optimum" ties back into the concept introduced earlier in this chapter: *maximum sustainable yield* (MSY) — the maximum amount of fish that can be taken, year after year, with new recruits annually replacing the fish lost to harvest. Before 1996, the Act had defined optimum yield as MSY "as modified" to take into account social and economic considerations. During that period, the councils frequently set optimum yield higher than MSY. This placated the fishing industry, which consistently lobbied in favor of less stringent fisheries regulation,

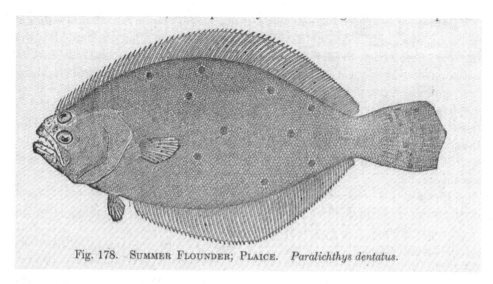

Fig. 178. SUMMER FLOUNDER; PLAICE. *Paralichthys dentatus.*

Figure 2-11. Summer Flounder

but created a high risk that management measures could lead to an overfished stock. In 1996, Congress changed "as modified" to "as reduced," making it possible for the councils to be more conservative, but not less conservative, than the scientific advice on MSY.

First and foremost, FMPs are supposed to prevent overfishing or, if necessary, rebuild depleted stocks. But beneath the words in National Standard One are great uncertainties lurking at the intersection of science and law. For example, how certain must the management measures be to reduce overfishing? And by how much? The following cases highlight the difficulties the councils, NMFS, and the courts confront in trying to manage fish (really, fishermen) in the face of ambiguity and uncertainty.

Natural Resources Defense Council v. Daley

209 F.3d 747 (D.D.C. 2000)

Chief Judge EDWARDS delivered the opinion of the D.C. Circuit Court of Appeals.

Paralichthysdentatus, or summer flounder, a commercially valuable species of flounder, dwell off the Atlantic coast and are harvested primarily between May and October from North Carolina to Maine. The summer flounder fishery is an "overfished" fishery, in the process of recovering from severe depletion prevalent during the late 1980s and early 1990s. The Secretary of Commerce, advised by the National Marine Fisheries Service ("the Service"), the principal appellee in this case, annually sets a fishing quota limiting each year's summer flounder catch, pursuant to the Magnuson-Stevens Fishery Conservation and Management Act ("the Fishery Act"). This case involves appellants' challenge to the Service's quota for the 1999 summer flounder harvest.

Before the District Court, appellants alleged that the 1999 quota did not provide sufficient assurance that it would meet the conservation goals of the Fishery Act and attendant regulations. . . . On cross-motions for summary judgment, the District Court granted judgment in favor of appellees.

***

The Fishery Act was enacted to establish a federal-regional partnership to manage fishery resources. Under the statute, there are eight Regional Fishery Management Councils "to exercise sound judgment in the stewardship of fishery resources." Management Councils propose and monitor fishery management plans "which will achieve and maintain, on a continuing basis, the optimum yield from each fishery." Management Councils submit management plans to the Secretary of Commerce (functionally the Service), who may then adopt them through notice and comment rulemaking. An "optimum yield" under the statute is defined as the "maximum sustainable yield from the fishery." If a fishery is "overfished," the management plan must "provide [] for rebuilding to a level consistent with" the maximum sustainable yield. A fishery is "overfished" if the rate of fishing mortality "jeopardizes the capacity of a fishery to produce the maximum sustainable yield on a continuing basis."

The Service defines overfishing and optimum yield according to the fishing mortality rate ("F"). F represents that part of a fish species' total mortality rate that is attributable to harvesting by humans, whether through capture or discard. Fish are "discarded" for many reasons, including, for example, when they are the wrong species, undersized, or not valuable enough. . . . There is a specific F, termed "Fmax," that is defined as that fishing mortality rate that will maximize the harvest of a single class of fish over its entire life span. Overfishing is fishing in excess of Fmax. Therefore, the basic goal of a management plan is to achieve Fmax, thereby preventing overfishing and assuring optimum yield.

. . . All parties agree that the summer flounder fishery is "overfished" and has been for some time. The Mid-Atlantic Fishery Management Council (Mid-Atlantic FMC), covering New York, New Jersey, Delaware, Pennsylvania, Maryland, Virginia, and North Carolina, developed the original summer flounder management plan with the assistance of two other regional Management Councils and the Atlantic States Marine Fisheries Commission ("the Commission"), a consortium of 15 coastal states and the District of Columbia. The Service approved the original management plan in 1988; however, the Service has amended the plan several times. At the time relevant to the instant case, the plan was designed to achieve a fishing mortality rate equal to Fmax by 1998.

Pursuant to the management plan, the Service must set a quota each year fixing the total weight of summer flounder that may be harvested by commercial and recreational fishermen. This quota is referred to as the "total allowable landings" for the year, or "TAL." The Service allocates 60% of the TAL to commercial fisheries and 40% of the quota to recreational fisheries, and states receive allocations based upon their share of the summer flounder fishery. States may subdivide their allocated commercial quota between "incidental" and "directed" catch. Directed fisheries intentionally harvest summer flounder. Fishermen who catch juvenile flounder, or who are part of the directed fishery for another species and catch summer flounder unintentionally, have harvested incidental catch.

The TAL must meet several requirements. It must be consistent with the 10 national standards of fishery conservation and management set out in the Fishery Act. Most relevant to the instant case, the quota must embody conservation measures that "shall prevent overfishing while achieving, on a continuing basis, the optimum yield from each fishery for the United States fishing industry." The quota must also be "consistent with" the fishery management plan. Finally, under the applicable regulations, the Regional Administrator of the Service must annually adopt a final rule "implement[ing] the measures necessary to assure that the applicable specified F will not be exceeded." The "applicable specified F" is also referred to as the "target F."

There is a relatively direct relationship between the TAL and the likelihood of achieving the target F. In general, the higher the TAL, the less likely a plan is to achieve the target F. In other words, the lower the target F, the lower the TAL must be to attain the target F. The basic dispute between the parties concerns whether the 1999 TAL provides a sufficient guarantee that the target F for summer flounder will be achieved.

For 1999, the summer flounder fishery management plan mandated a target F equivalent to Fmax, which was 0.24. The Summer Flounder Monitoring Committee, a Mid-Atlantic FMC committee, had recommended a TAL of 14.645 million pounds, while Mid-Atlantic FMC had recommended a TAL of 20.20 million pounds. The Service rejected Mid-Atlantic FMC's recommendation as "unacceptably risk-prone" for several reasons: (1) it had an "unacceptably low probability" of 3% of achieving the target F; (2) it had a 50% probability of achieving an F of 0.36, which was "significantly higher" than the target F; (3) the proposal relied on unpredictable data; and (4) Mid-Atlantic FMC had "yet to specify a harvest level that has achieved the annual target F." The Service also rejected the Summer Flounder Monitoring Committee's recommendation of a 14.645 million pound TAL. Although the Committee's recommendation had a 50% chance of achieving the target F, the Service rejected the proposal without any meaningful explanation.

On October 21, 1998, the Service proposed a TAL of 18.52 million pounds. All parties agree that, at most, the Service's proposal afforded only an 18% likelihood of achieving the target F. The Service also proposed an incidental catch restriction "to address discards in this fishery that should further reduce the overall mortality." . . . The Service also considered recent changes in minimum mesh size. On this point, the Service noted that, while Mid-Atlantic FMC felt that the "recently adopted mesh provision requiring 5.5 inch" mesh throughout the net would "substantially reduce discard and discard mortality," the alleged benefits of mesh had yet to be verified by anyone.

Between the time of proposal of the 1999 TAL and its adoption, the Service concluded that it did not have the authority to impose any incidental catch restrictions on the states. Therefore, the Service merely recommended that the states adopt the incidental catch proposal, making the proposal entirely voluntary. . . . According to an advisor to the Service's Assistant Administrator for Fisheries, this development "result[ed] in an unknown but probably substantial reduction in the likelihood that [Mid-Atlantic FMC's] rebuilding schedule will be achieved," and he therefore recommended that the Service adopt the Summer Flounder Monitoring Committee's recommended 14.645 million pound TAL.

The Service rejected this recommendation and, on December 31, 1998, issued the final TAL, adopting its initial proposal. The Service acknowledged that the Summer Flounder Monitoring Committee's recommended quota had a 50% chance of achieving the target F, while the Service's TAL had only an 18% chance of achieving the target F.

. . . The Service suggested that the 5.5 inch minimum mesh provision might ameliorate other mortality concerns, but acknowledged that the requirement had not been in effect long enough to determine its efficacy.

Appellants filed suit in District Court on January 29, 1999, seeking, inter alia, (1) a declaratory judgment that defendants violated the Fishery Act, the Administrative Procedure Act ("APA") . . . and (2) remand to the agency to impose a new summer flounder TAL. . . . The District Court upheld the Service's adoption of the 18.52 million pound TAL, deferring to the agency under *Chevron U.S.A. Inc. v. Natural Resources Defense Council, Inc.* The District Court first determined that §§ 1851(a)(1) and (a)(8) in the Fishery Act evinced competing interests between advancing conservation and minimizing adverse economic effects and that Congress offered no insight as to how to balance these concerns.

***

[W]e will defer to [an agency's] interpretation [] if [it is] reasonable and consistent with the statutory purpose and legislative history. However, a court will not uphold [an agency's] interpretation "that diverges from any realistic meaning of the statute."

This case presents a situation in which the Service's quota for the 1999 summer flounder harvest so completely diverges from any realistic meaning of the Fishery Act that it cannot survive scrutiny under *Chevron* Step Two.

As an initial matter, we reject the District Court's suggestion that there is a conflict between the Fishery Act's expressed commitments to conservation and to mitigating adverse economic impacts. Compare 16 U.S.C. § 1851(a)(1) (directing agency to "prevent overfishing" and ensure "the optimum yield from each fishery"); with id. § 1851(a)(8) (directing agency to "minimize adverse economic impacts" on fishing communities). The Government concedes, and we agree, that, under the Fishery Act, the Service must give priority to conservation measures. It is only when two different plans achieve similar conservation measures that the Service takes into consideration adverse economic consequences.

The real issue in this case is whether the 1999 TAL satisfied the conservation goals of the Fishery Act, the management plan, and the Service's regulations. In considering this question, it is important to recall that the Service operates under constraints from three different sources. First, the statute requires the Service to act both to "prevent overfishing" and to attain "optimum yield." Overfishing is commonly understood as fishing that results in an F in excess of Fmax. Since Fmax for 1999 was equivalent to 0.24, this constraint required the Service to issue regulations to prevent F from exceeding 0.24. Second, any quota must be "consistent with" the fishery management plan adopted by the Service. In this case the fishery management plan called for an F of 0.24. Therefore, the quota had to be "consistent with" achieving that F. Third, the Service is required to adopt a quota "necessary to assure that the applicable specified F will not be exceeded." The "applicable specified F" for 1999 was Fmax, or 0.24.

All of these constraints, then, collapse into an inquiry as to whether the Service's quota was "consistent with" and at the level "necessary to assure" the achievement of an F of 0.24, and whether it reasonably could be expected to "prevent" an F greater than 0.24. . . .

***

The 1999 quota is unreasonable, plain and simple. Government counsel conceded at oral argument that, to meet its statutory and regulatory mandate, the Service must have a "fairly high level of confidence that the quota it recommends will not result in an F greater than [the target F]." We agree. We also hold that, at the very least, this means that "to assure" the achievement of the target F, to "prevent overfishing," and to "be consistent with" the fishery management plan, the TAL must have had at least a 50% chance of attaining an F of 0.24. This is not a surprising result, because in related contexts, the Service has articulated precisely this standard.

The disputed 1999 TAL had at most an 18% likelihood of achieving the target F. Viewed differently, it had at least an 82% chance of resulting in an F greater than the target F. Only in Superman Comics' Bizarro world, where reality is turned upside down, could the Service reasonably conclude that a measure that is at least four times as likely to fail as to succeed offers a "fairly high level of confidence."

Rather than argue that the quota alone provided enough assurance, the Service contends instead that two additional measures were adopted to increase the likelihood of achieving the target F. These measures were: (1) the provision relating to minimum mesh size; and (2) the recommendation that states voluntarily allocate a certain portion of the directed commercial fishery toward incidental catch. There is nothing in this record, however, to indicate that the proposals on mesh size and voluntary state action would improve the level of confidence so as to assure a reasonable likelihood of achieving the target F.

The Service's reliance on its provision regarding minimum mesh size for fishing nets is rather perplexing. We do not question the Service's rational conclusion that it is important to reduce the number of undersized flounder being captured, given recent observations, in a species with a potential 20-year life span, that very few adult fish survive past three years of age. At the time the 1999 TAL was proposed, however, the Service acknowledged that the mesh size provision's "benefits have not yet been analyzed." . . . In the final rule, the Service stated only that the minimum mesh size provision was "intended to address" discarding due to undersized catch; the Service acknowledged, however, that the mesh provision had "not been in operation long enough to determine if an adjustment to the mesh size is warranted." In short, there are no meaningful data (or even well-founded predictions) to support the assertion that a larger mesh size would reduce the number of undersized fish caught. . . .

The Service's second recommendation, that states set aside a certain percentage of the commercial fishing quota for incidental catch instead of directed commercial catch, also fails to ameliorate the deficient 18% figure. . . . The second, and more serious, flaw in the Service's reliance on its incidental catch proposal is that the proposal is merely a recommendation to the states, not a mandatory requirement. . . . This is manifestly insufficient.

As we noted at the outset of this opinion, the Service's quota for the 1999 summer flounder harvest so completely "diverges from any realistic meaning" of the Fishery Act that it cannot survive scrutiny under *Chevron* Step Two. The Service resists this result by suggesting that we owe deference to the agency's "scientific" judgments. While this may be so, we do not hear cases merely to rubber stamp agency actions. . . . Indeed, we can divine no scientific judgment upon which the Service concluded that its measures would satisfy its statutory mandate.

For the reasons articulated herein, we reverse the District Court's judgment and remand the case to the Service for further proceedings consistent with this opinion.

points for discussion

1. *Total mortality and fishing mortality.* A plan "designed to achieve a fishing mortality rate equal to Fmax by 1998" means that the original goal was to lower fishing and allow the stock to recover, so that by 1998 the stock could once again produce its maximum sustainable yield. Using "target F" and "Fmax" is a way of focusing on total fish mortality, not just from fishing. Mortality can occur naturally, from targeted fishing, and due to bycatch. The amount of targeted fishing that can be allowed is reduced by higher levels of natural mortality or bycatch.

2. *Management complexity.* The *Daley* case was complicated by the number of groups involved in the total allowable landing (TAL)-setting process. There were NMFS, the Mid-Atlantic Fishery Management Council, the Summer Flounder Monitoring Committee (a subcommittee of the Mid-Atlantic FMC), and the Atlantic States Marine Fisheries Commission (a multistate management commission for regulating fishing out to three miles offshore). What roles do you think each of these groups played? Why did the Summer Flounder Monitoring Committee produce the most cautious TALs?

3. *Working with probabilities.* Eighteen percent was clearly not a sufficiently high probability to satisfy the court that the plan would serve the goals

of "preventing overfishing." What about 50 percent? Where did the court come up with that number? Would a 50-50 chance of timely recovery be consistent with the national standards or with Congress's overarching goals in the Act? Imagine that scientists opine that a 5,000-pound annual quota for Hummingfish would lead to a 60 percent chance of being overfished, while a 1,000-pound annual quota would lead to a 40 percent chance of the stock being overfished. Are these choices consistent with the "*shall* prevent overfishing" language in National Standard One? (Emphasis added.) If the scientists say that the only way to be 100 percent sure that the quota won't lead to overfishing is to close the fishery, how should the council proceed? What is the acceptable level of risk of overfishing? Or the risk of giving up fishing revenue when it might turn out in the future that a 5,000-pound quota would not have endangered stock health?

4. *What's the backstory?* What was NFMS's rationale for such a low probability — 18 percent? Do you think the companion measures — the larger mesh size (allowing juveniles to escape) and the recommendation that states allocate some of their TALs share to bycatch — justified the low probability of timely recovery? Is it arbitrary and capricious if NMFS knows of a helpful measure, but simply does not know how well it works?

5. *Courts and science.* How are these probabilities calculated? Fisheries scientists have developed many models that take into account stock health, the probability of disturbances, predator-prey interactions, and many other factors (but by no means all of them!) that come into play in estimating fish populations. The regional councils and the NMFS can choose from several models, giving them the ability to pick the model that suits their political interests best, and not necessarily the most accurate or appropriate one. In *Oceana v. Evans,* 2005 WL 555416 (D.D.C. Mar. 9, 2005), the court upheld the use of a model that the plaintiffs believed was too optimistic, holding that a model need not be perfect to constitute the "best scientific information available." It continued: "It is simply not the Court's role to interject itself into this extremely technical scientific debate; indeed, this is precisely the type of issue in which the Court should properly defer to Defendants' expertise" (citing *CLF v. Mineta,* 131 F. Supp. 2d 19, 28 (D.D.C. 2001)).

6. *Illegal fishing.* As can be seen from the graph in Figure 2-12, the stock of summer flounder rebounded from its lows in the early 1990s, but the spawning stock biomass remains well below the target level that would yield MSY. More troubling, after a period of leveling off following the *Daley* case, the stock appeared headed for trouble again by 2014. TALs have only been exceeded by small amounts, so the Atlantic States Marine Fisheries Commission suspects that illegal, unreported fishing is occurring. Do you think that an FMP should take account of illegal fishing, or be responsible for finding ways to curb it?

Figure 2-12. Summer Flounder Population Trends

1. Rebuilding Depleted Fish Stocks

Definitions

16 U.S.C. § 1802

(34) The terms "overfishing" and "overfished" mean a rate or level of fishing mortality that jeopardizes the capacity of a fishery to produce the maximum sustainable yield on a continuing basis.

National Standard One has always provided that the councils "shall prevent overfishing." Until 1996, however, the Act did not specify what a council should do if the councils began management of a stock when overfishing was already occurring or when stocks had previously become overfished. The 1996 amendments introduced new requirements relating to the latter situation, that is, requirements

Source: National Oceanic and Atmospheric Administration. For more on the incredible diversity of rockfish on the West Coast, go to http://lovelab.msi.ucsb.edu/

Figure 2-13. A Darkblotched Rockfish

for rebuilding an overfished stock. The rebuilding provisions, simply put, required that the councils rebuild stocks in as short a time as possible, but no longer than ten years. As the following case illustrates, the ten-year requirement was subject to several important exceptions.

Natural Resources Defense Council v. National Marine Fisheries Service

421 F.3d 472 (7th Cir. 2005)

Judge FISHER delivered the opinion of the Ninth Circuit Court of Appeals.

Congress enacted the Magnuson-Stevens Act to "conserve and manage the fishery resources found off the coasts of the United States." The Agency is charged with developing and implementing rebuilding plans for overfished fish species. In 1996, Congress amended the Act by passing the Sustainable Fisheries Act (SFA). The SFA added new requirements to the Act to accelerate the rebuilding of overfished species.

The Act, as amended by the SFA, contains a provision the proper interpretation of which is the main subject of this appeal. Section 1854 of the Act provides in part that when any species is found to be overfished, the Agency must approve a rebuilding plan that:

> (A) specif[ies] a time period for ending overfishing and rebuilding the fishery that shall
>> (i) be as short as possible, taking into account the status and biology of any overfished stock of fish, the needs of fishing communities, . . . and the interaction of the overfished stock of fish within the marine ecosystem; and
>> (ii) not exceed 10 years, except in cases where the biology of the stock of fish, [or] other environmental conditions . . . dictate otherwise.

§ 1854(e)(4).

The Act also sets forth a series of "national standards" with which any rebuilding plans must be "consistent," and provides for the establishment of National Standards Guidelines ("NSGs") that must be "based on the national standards" for use in "assist[ing] in the development of fishery management plans." The Act provides that NSGs "shall not have the force and effect of law."

There is some ambiguity to § 1854(e)(4). Section 1854(e)(4)(i) specifies that the rebuilding time period be as "short as possible," but also directs that the Agency "tak[e] into account the status and biology of [the] . . . overfished stock" and "the needs of fishing communities." Section 1854(e)(4)(ii) in turn plainly mandates that the rebuilding plan be no longer than 10 years, so long as biologically or environmentally possible. However, if it is not possible to rebuild within 10 years, the Act is not clear as to the exact limits on the length of the rebuilding period.

Seeking to clarify the proper interpretation of § 1854(e)(4), the Agency in 1997 sought "comment on whether or not it is correct in its interpretation that the duration of rebuilding programs should not be unspecified and, if so, what factors should be considered in determining that duration." The Agency propounded two alternate interpretations for public comment: that whenever it would take longer than 10 years to rebuild an overfished species, either (1) all fishing of that species would be banned until the rebuilding was complete or (2) the Agency would set a ceiling on the rebuilding duration that would be reached by adding the shortest possible time to rebuild plus "one mean generation time . . . based on the species' life-history characteristics." A "mean generation time" is a scientific term, not mentioned in the Act itself, measuring how long it will take for an average mature fish to be replaced by its offspring. After notice and comment, the Agency adopted the second interpretation in a NSG. The Agency reasoned that:

> "[f]or stocks that will take more than 10 years to rebuild, the guidelines [adopted] impose an outside limit that is objective, measurable, and linked to the biology of the particular species. . . . The guidelines strike a balance between the Congressional directive to rebuild stocks as quickly as possible, and the desire . . . to minimize adverse economic effects on fishing communities. For stocks that cannot be rebuilt within 10 years, the guideline allows flexibility in setting the rebuilding schedule beyond the no-fishing mortality period, but places a reasonable, species-specific cap on that flexibility by limiting the extension to one mean generation time."

The Pacific Coast Groundfish Fishery is one of the fisheries the Agency oversees, covering the bottom-feeding fish species dwelling in the waters off the coasts of California, Oregon and Washington. In 2000, the Agency assessed the status of one species of Pacific groundfish within the fishery — darkblotched rockfish. It found that the species was at 22% of its unfished population level (its predicted level absent any fishing), and therefore concluded that the species was "overfished" within the meaning of the Act. The Agency further concluded that the species could be rebuilt in 10 years or less, triggering § 1854(e)(4)(ii)'s mandatory requirement that the rebuilding take place within 10 years. The Agency then set a 130 metric ton "fishing harvest level," or quota, i.e., a set limit of darkblotched rockfish that could be fished in 2001.

In 2001, the Agency updated its assessment of darkblotched rockfish and concluded that it had significantly overestimated the health of the species. The Agency now estimated that the species was almost twice as depleted as previously thought — it was at only 12% of its unfished population level. In the Agency's calculations, rebuilding therefore could not be accomplished within 10 years; the minimum period for rebuilding was now 14 years.

This increased rebuilding time meant, by necessity, that the rebuilding plan was no longer limited by § 1854(e)(4)(ii)'s mandatory 10-year cap; instead, the only applicable statutory time limit was § 1854(e)(4)(i)'s command that the rebuilding period be "as short as possible." Further, according to the interpretation of the Act set forth in the 1998 NSG, the revised minimum rebuilding period triggered a new ceiling that was the 14-year period *plus* "one mean generation time," which in the case of the long-lived darkblotched rockfish was 33 years. The Agency, in short, switched from operating under the statutory constraint of *10 years* rebuilding time to a new constraint, dictated by the 1998 NSG, of *47 years*. The Agency then set a "target" rebuilding time of 34 years, and in accordance with this target, *raised* the fishing level harvest for 2002 from the previous year's 130 metric tons to 168 metric tons.

NRDC brought suit alleging that the new quota violated the Act, the Administrative Procedure Act and the National Environmental Policy Act. The district court concluded that the quota violated none of these statutes and granted summary judgment for the Agency.

* * *

We should not defer to an agency's interpretation of a statute if Congress' intent can be clearly ascertained through analysis of the language, purpose and structure of the statute. If, however, Congress' intent is not clear, and if "Congress delegated authority to the agency generally to make rules carrying the force of law, and [] the agency interpretation claiming deference was promulgated in the exercise of that authority," then we must defer to the agency's construction of the statute so long as "the agency's answer is based on a permissible construction of the statute."

The Agency arrived at its increased 2002 darkblotched rockfish quota by applying its interpretation of § 1854(e)(4) of the Magnuson-Stevens Act as set forth in the 1998 NSG. NRDC argues that this interpretation of the Act is not entitled to *Chevron* deference for two separate reasons.

First, NRDC argues that Congress' intent in this section of the Act is clear, thereby precluding the need for any deference to the Agency's interpretation of the statute. We disagree. As we noted above, § 1854(e)(4)(ii) is explicit that *if* a species can be rebuilt within 10 years, it must be. But § 1854(e)(4)(i), which states that the rebuilding period must be as "short as possible, taking into account the status and biology of any overfished stock of fish [and] the needs of fishing communities," introduces an ambiguity into the calculus. When it is not biologically possible to rebuild within 10 years, may the Agency extend the rebuilding period beyond the shortest possible rebuilding time to account for the needs of fishing communities? It would be possible to resolve the ambiguity by concluding that the Act as a whole makes it clear that the needs of fishing communities are perfectly aligned with the environmental goal of rebuilding fish stocks in as short a time as possible. But if this were the case, the language "the needs of fishing communities" would be redundant (as these needs would be no different than the need to rebuild stocks in as short a time as possible). There is therefore an ambiguity in this part of the statute, requiring interpretation.

* * *

The interpretation of § 1854(e)(4) stated in the 1998 NSG, as applied in the 2002 quota, is not a permissible (or reasonable) construction of the statute; it is directly at odds with the text and purpose of the Act. Section 1801 of the Act contains its "Findings, purposes and policy." The "Findings" section states that the nation's fishery resources "constitute valuable and renewable natural resources," that many of these species' "survival is threatened" and that others' survival will soon be threatened by "increased fishing pressure . . . the inadequacy of fishery resource conservation and management practices and controls." The next subsection recognizes "commercial and recreational fishing" as a "major source of employment" that "contributes significantly to the economy of the Nation." § 1801(a)(3). But even here, the Act urges that the economies of many coastal areas "have been badly damaged by the overfishing of fishery resources at an ever-increasing rate over the past decade." The Act goes on to explain that "[i]f placed under sound management before overfishing has caused irreversible effects, the fisheries can be conserved and maintained so as to provide optimum yields on a continuing basis." § 1801(a)(5). These observations lead to the conclusion that "[a] national program for the conservation and management of the fishery resources of the United States is necessary to prevent overfishing, to rebuild overfished stocks, to insure conservation, to facilitate long-term protection of essential fish habitats, and to realize the full potential of the Nation's fishery resources." § 1801(a)(6). The "purposes" section adds that "[i]t is therefore declared to be the purposes of the Congress in this chapter . . . to take immediate action to conserve and manage the fishery resources. . . ." § 1801(b)(1).

The purpose of the Act is clearly to give conservation of fisheries priority over short-term economic interests. The Act sets this priority in part because the longer-term economic interests of fishing communities are aligned with the conservation goals set forth in the Act. Without immediate efforts at rebuilding depleted fisheries, the very long-term survival of those fishing communities is in doubt. This background provides helpful context for interpreting § 1854. However, even if we turn to the plain language of § 1854(e)(4) and, without such context, ask how its two subsections interact, we still must reject the interpretation of the Act contained in the 1998 NSG as it was applied to this species.

Section 1854 contains two significant mandates that constrain the Agency's options in adopting a rebuilding plan for an overfished species. First, the time period must be *as short as possible*, although the Agency may take into account the status and biology of the overfished species and the needs of fishing communities. Subsection (i)'s commands apply to *all* rebuilding periods, whatever their length. Second, Congress specified a presumptive *cap of 10 years* on any rebuilding period, subject to exceptional circumstances beyond the Agency's control — such as an international treaty or, relevant here, "the biology of the stock of fish."

We have noted some ambiguity in subsection (i)'s mandate to rebuild a species in "as short [a time period] as possible" while giving consideration to "the needs of fishing communities." The natural reading of this language, however, is that Congress intended to ensure that overfished species were rebuilt as quickly as possible, but wanted to leave some leeway to avoid disastrous short-term consequences for fishing communities. To use an example relevant here, even if a fishing community is actively seeking not to fish for a certain species, it will inevitably catch some of the overfished species in the process of fishing for other, more plentiful fish — what is known as "bycatch." Because almost no groundfish that are caught as bycatch survive even if they are thrown back into the ocean, an absolute ban on catching any of a species of groundfish could mean a total moratorium on all fishing in the parts of the fishery containing groundfish, with obvious adverse consequences for fishing communities. Section 1854(e)(4)(i), then, allows the Agency to set limited quotas that would account for the short-term needs of fishing communities (for example, to allow for some fishing of plentiful species despite the inevitability of bycatch), even though this would mean that the rebuilding period would take longer than it would under a total fishing ban.

Reading subsection (i) in this light, it is apparent that Congress intended subsection (ii) as a limit on the Agency's discretion. The Agency may consider the short-term economic needs of fishing communities in establishing rebuilding periods, but may not use those needs to go beyond the 10-year cap set by subsection (ii). To breach this cap, the Agency may only consider circumstances that "dictate" doing so. One such circumstance, albeit not relevant here, would be an international agreement. Another that *is* relevant is "the biology of the stock of fish" — that is, when the current number of fish in the fishery and the amount of time required for the species to regenerate make it impossible to rebuild the stock within 10 years, even with a total moratorium on fishing. In such cases, subsection (ii) recognizes that the presumptive 10-year cap cannot apply. That said, it is manifestly unreasonable to conclude, as the Agency apparently has, that Congress intended in such circumstances to relieve the Agency of its continuing obligation to rebuild the species in a time frame that is "as short as possible."

The 2002 quota was not based on a permissible construction of the Act, because the Agency altered dramatically the balance between the needs of a species and of fishing communities with no statutorily grounded justification. NRDC argues that if the rebuilding period must exceed 10 years, the Act mandates a total moratorium on all fishing — the alternative interpretation of § 1854 that the Agency rejected when it adopted the 1998 NSG. Although NRDC's interpretation of the statute is reasonable, it is not the only reasonable one. It is also reasonable to conclude that the needs of fishing communities may still be taken into account even when the biology of the fish dictates exceeding the 10-year cap — so long as the weight given is proportionate to the weight the Agency might give to such needs in rebuilding periods under 10 years. This interpretation would allow the Agency's rebuilding periods to account for short-term concerns such as bycatch in the same manner whether the rebuilding period exceeds 10 years or not.

The 2002 darkblotched rockfish quota is patently unreasonable, however, and reflects no such measured proportionality. Freed from the 10-year cap because of the biology of the rockfish (its long regeneration time and its dire condition), the Agency simply applied the 1998 NSG's formulaic approach and *increased* the annual take. In 2001, the Agency set a quota of 130 million tons of darkblotched rockfish because it believed the species had been reduced to only 22% of its unfished population. When its revised estimate revealed that the species was doing much worse, the Agency expanded the fishing of the species from 130 million tons to 168 million tons, a 29% increase. Whatever the outer limits of the range of permissible constructions of the Act, we are certain that what lies beyond them is an interpretation allowing the Agency, upon discovering that a species is in significantly worse shape than previously thought, to increase dramatically the fishing pressure on that species. Increasing the annual take in these circumstances is simply incompatible with making the rebuilding period as short as possible.

We are not prepared to accept NRDC's argument that once the 10-year cap is lifted because the biology of the fish dictates it, the Act in turn dictates that the Agency can no longer consider the short-term economic needs of fishing communities at all. Such an argument, although plausible, does not appear to give due consideration to the continuing operation of subsection (i)'s command to take the needs of fishing communities into account. But neither are we prepared to accept the Agency's interpretation, which would ignore the primary mandate of subsection (i) — that the rebuilding period be "as short as possible." At least as applied here, the Agency's interpretation not only increased the fishing take by almost 30% but extended the maximum rebuilding period from less than 10 years to 47 years. Plainly, the Act does not contemplate that the Agency grant the least protection to the fish species in the worst shape.

The arguments of the Agency and Intervenors regarding potentially dire consequences for fishing communities seem persuasive at all only because they assume that the sole alternative is NRDC's strict moratorium. The district court made this same flawed assumption:

> Faced with a choice between an interpretation of the [Act] that requires a moratorium on harvesting of fish species that take more than ten years to regenerate naturally, and an interpretation that permits limited harvesting over the course of a longer rebuilding period, [the Agency] selected . . . the latter interpretation. In light of [the Act's] dual conservationist and commercial objectives, an interpretation that accommodates both objectives, rather than selecting one to the exclusion of the other, is permissible.

The Agency was "faced with [this] choice" only because it proposed these two extreme interpretations, and no others.

Our rejection of the Agency's interpretation is compelled by the language of § 1854, which requires that rebuilding take place in "as short [a time] as possible" and, if biologically possible, in less than 10 years. That simple command cannot be reconciled with a rebuilding period that is from 20 to 33 years longer than the biologically shortest possible rebuilding period (and that increases the annual take in the meanwhile). We hold that even granting the Agency some leeway in extending rebuilding periods when the 10-year cap is not applicable, the 2002 darkblotched rockfish quota was based on an impermissible construction of the Act.

We reverse the district court's holding that the Agency did not violate the Magnuson-Stevens Act in setting its 2002 fishing quota for darkblotched rockfish. We remand to the district court for any further proceedings consistent with this opinion.

points for discussion

1. *The power to define terms.* When is a species considered "overfished" under the Act? When the population is below P_{MSY}? Below 50 percent of P_{MSY}? Does the statutory definition help? Can you see how those in favor of more (or less) conservative management might put a great deal of lobbying effort into getting an "overfished definition" that suits their goals?
2. *Your choice.* What were the two "extreme positions" rejected by the court? After this case, if you were charged with setting a new TAL, what would it be? How would you arrive at your number?

3. *Reasonable alternatives.* The court opined, in dicta, that NRDC's interpretation that § 1854(e)(4) required a moratorium on all fishing was reasonable,
   but was "not the only reasonable one." Do you agree that because of the
   bycatch problem, a total moratorium would have been a reasonable interpretation? Might you have suggested other measures instead of a total moratorium on all fishing?
4. *The West Coast rockfish fisheries.* The darkblotched rockfish is now one of
   19 species that are managed collectively under an Individual Fishing Quota
   program (see below) that regulates the quantity that can be caught for all of
   the species. The darkblotched rockfish was declared "rebuilt" in 2017. Notably,
   reducing catch of darkblotched rockfish was very difficult for fishermen because
   they tend to commingle with other abundant species, that fishermen had to
   avoid for fear of darkblotched rockfish as bycatch. *See Two More Rockfish Species
   Declared "Rebuilt,"* ENVTL. DEFENSE FUND BLOG (July 13, 2017), http://blogs
   .edf.org/edfish/2017/07/13/two-more-rockfish-species-declared-rebuilt/.

Problem Exercise

The Batfish is a long-lived, bottom-dwelling species once abundant but now overfished. In addition to being overfished, it is often caught as bycatch by fishers fishing for Mauve Snapper. The National Marine Fisheries Service estimated in 2013
that the population of Batfish had declined to 20 percent of its pre-harvest levels.
A 75 percent reduction on TAC of Batfish would produce a recovery — such that it
would no longer be considered overfished — in 18 years; a complete ban on fishing
for Batfish would produce a recovery in 12 years; a complete ban on not only tar-
geting Batfish but also Grouper would produce a recovery of the Batfish in 10 years.
What should the Service do to produce a recovery of the Batfish?

Suppose that in answer to the above question, the Service reduced the total
allowable catch by 75 percent, with a view toward rebuilding the stock to a recovery
level in 18 years. *Now,* consider that after further study, the Service discovers that
the Batfish are much less healthy; that the population is only at 10 percent of its
pre-harvest levels, instead of 20 percent; and that at this rate, recovery can only be
achieved in 28 years, not 18. A complete ban on fishing for Batfish would produce a
recovery in 15 years, not 12, and a complete ban on fishing for Batfish and Grouper
would produce a recovery in 13 years, not 10. *Now* what should the Service do to
produce a recovery of the Batfish?

2. Bycatch

The Magnuson-Stevens Act defines "bycatch" as "fish which are harvested in a
fishery, but which are not sold or kept for personal use, and includes economic
discards and regulatory discards." 16 U.S.C. § 1802(2). A broader definition is possible: "discarded catch of any living marine resource plus unobserved mortality

due to a direct encounter with fishing gear." *See* Nat'l Marine Fisheries Serv., U.S. National Bycatch Report First Edition Update 1 (2013). This broader definition includes not just fish, but also marine mammals, seabirds, and sea turtles. Economic discards are fish thrown back because the fishermen can't sell them for more than the cost of storing them and taking them back to port. Regulatory discards are fish thrown back because the law does not permit them to be caught.

Bycatch is wasteful, economically and ecologically. An estimated 27 million tons of fish are discarded by commercial fisheries worldwide. The environmental organization Oceana estimates the market value of discarded fish in the United States at $1 billion annually. *See* Oceana, Wasted Cash: The Price of Waste in the U.S. Fishing Industry (2014). This estimate might even be too low, because some commercial fish are also sportfish, which is a much more lucrative and valuable industry than commercial fishing. The recreational fishing industry dwarfs the commercial fishing industry in value, so the estimate of swordfish bycatch loss at $1.3 million is likely too low. Fish that are caught and thrown back have varying mortality rates, but are typically very high. Some, including halibut, sablefish, pollock, and lingcod, have mortality rates that are at or near 100 percent.

Bycatch can occur in a number of ways and for a number of reasons. Fish or wildlife can be inadvertently caught while fishing for some other target fish species. They can be caught on longline hooks, ensnared in driftnets, or gathered up in seine nets with a school of other fish. In fisheries where the fisher has an incentive to catch large fish (such as in quota programs, discussed below), fishermen may discard small fish and keep fishing for larger ones. This practice is known as "highgrading," and is particularly wasteful because the small, young discarded fish die instead of growing to maturity and reproducing. Driftnets set by New England fishermen, with the blessing of Massachusetts regulators, have ensnared and killed dozens of Northern right whales, of which there are fewer than 500 left. Sometimes regulations prohibit retention of certain species, sexes, or sizes, and therefore mandate the discard of some fish.

Some overfished stocks also suffer from bycatch, and so managing such a stock requires not only managing the targeted species, but also the fishery in

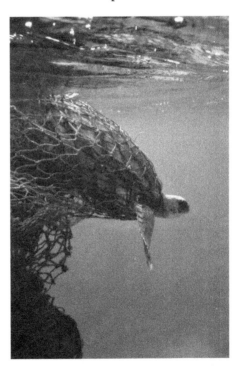

Figure 2-14.
Bycatch, or unintentional catch, can include endangered species, such as this sea turtle. The turtle here was a victim of a "ghost net," that is, a fishing net that breaks free from a boat and floats around in the ocean.

which bycatch is occurring. Several of the cases in the chapter involve disputes over how much the allowed annual catch must be set aside to account for fish lost to bycatch. But how much?

Bycatch is notoriously hard to monitor and to measure. Unless there are observers on board to check up on the fishermen, or electronic monitors to constantly film fishing activity, regulators have a very limited ability to make sure that fishermen aren't skirting regulations. Regulators can prohibit certain kinds of fishing gear that is particularly destructive, or insufficiently selective for the target fish species and size. Regulators can examine fishing logbooks. Regulations can require the retention of all catch, with an accounting to be done on the docks. All of these suffer from imperfect enforcement.

The Act requires FMPs to have certain provisions, including a "standardized bycatch reporting methodology," and "accountability measures," which must ensure that catch limits are observed, and not breached by excessive and uncounted bycatch.

Contents of Fishery Management Plans

16 U.S.C. § 1853

> (a) **Required provisions.** Any fishery management plan which is prepared by any Council, or by the Secretary, with respect to any fishery, shall—
> (11) establish a standardized reporting methodology to assess the amount and type of bycatch occurring in the fishery, and include conservation and management measures that, to the extent practicable and in the following priority—
> (A) minimize bycatch; and
> (B) minimize the mortality of bycatch which cannot be avoided;
> (15) establish a mechanism for specifying annual catch limits in the plan (including a multiyear plan), implementing regulations, or annual specifications, at a level such that overfishing does not occur in the fishery, including measures to ensure accountability.

Recall also that national standard 9 provided that "[c]onservation and management measures shall, to the extent practicable, (A) minimize bycatch and (B) to the extent bycatch cannot be avoided, minimize the mortality of such bycatch."

National Standard 9 — Bycatch

50 C.F.R. § 600.350

> (3)(i) A determination of whether a conservation and management measure minimizes bycatch or bycatch mortality to the extent practicable, consistent with other national standards and maximization of net benefits to the Nation, should consider the following factors:

(A) Population effects for the bycatch species.

(B) Ecological effects due to changes in the bycatch of that species.

(C) Changes in the bycatch of other species of fish and the resulting population and ecosystem effects.

(D) Effects on marine mammals and birds.

(E) Changes in fishing, processing, disposal, and marketing costs.

(F) Changes in fishing practices and behavior of fishermen.

(G) Changes in research, administration, and enforcement costs and management effectiveness.

(H) Changes in the economic, social, or cultural value of fishing activities and non-consumptive uses of fishery resources.

(I) Changes in the distribution of benefits and costs.

(J) Social effects.

These statutory and regulatory provisions are at issue in the following case. This case involves an *amendment* to an FMP, which must be approved by NMFS just like an FMP. Like FMPs, amendments must be published and noticed for public review and comment.

Pacific Marine Conservation Council v. Evans

200 F. Supp. 2d 1194 (N.D. Cal. 2002)

United States Magistrate Judge LARSON delivered the opinion of the United States District Court, Northern District of California.

Plaintiffs Pacific Marine Conservation Council, Natural Resources Defense Council, and Ocean Conservancy move for summary judgment on the grounds that the National Marine Fisheries Service ("NMFS") violated the Magnuson-Stevens Fishery Conservation and Management Act ("MSA") by approving Amendment 13 to the Pacific Coast Groundfish Fishery Management Plan ("FMP"). Plaintiffs allege that Amendment 13 does not comply with MSA's requirement to regulate bycatch. . . .

***

. . . In enacting the SFA, Congress sought to address the issue of bycatch in America's fisheries by adding important new bycatch requirements.

First, Congress added to the [Magnuson-Stevens Act, or] MSA a requirement that fishery managers assess the amount and type of bycatch occurring in each fishery. Congress required each fishery management plan to "establish a standardized reporting methodology to assess the amount and type of bycatch occurring in" each fishery managed. Second, Congress required fishery managers to take affirmative steps to minimize bycatch and bycatch mortality. Specifically, [the Act] mandates that any fishery management plan which is prepared by any Council, or by the Secretary, with respect to any fishery, shall: "[I]nclude conservation and management measures that, to the extent practicable and in the following prior-ity: (A) minimize bycatch; and (B) minimize the mortality of bycatch which cannot be avoided." 16 U.S.C. § 1853(a)(11).

Congress further mandated quick action by fishery managers to implement these and other SFA requirements by requiring fishery management councils to submit to NMFS proposed FMP amendments to NMFS. These amendments were intended to bring each existing FMP into compliance with new statutory require-ments no later than two years after enactment of the SFA. . . .

[T]he Pacific Council [] prepared Amendment 13 to the Pacific Groundfish FMP and submitted the proposed amendment to the NMFS in 2000. The purpose of Amendment 13 is to bring the FMP into compliance with the bycatch-related requirements of the MSA. Unfortunately, as discussed below, Amendment 13 falls short of what is required by the MSA.

To comply with MSA's requirement that each plan establish a standardized reporting methodology to assess the amount and type of bycatch, Amendment 13 *permits* but does not *require* an observer program.[2] Amendment 13 pro-vides: "The Regional Administrator *may* implement an observer program through a Council-approved federal regulatory framework." Amendment 13 does not make the observer program mandatory despite the NMFS' own conclusion that an at-sea observer program is essential for adequately assessing bycatch in the Pacific groundfish fishery.

Similarly, to attempt to comply with MSA's requirement to minimize both bycatch and bycatch mortality, Amendment 13 *lists* but does not *require* certain types of bycatch reduction techniques for the non-whiting groundfish fishery. The sentence in Amendment 13 that introduces this list of potential bycatch reduction techniques reads:

> These [bycatch reduction measures] may include but are not limited to: Full reten-tion or increased utilization programs; setting shorter-than-year-round fishing season in combination with higher cumulative landing limits; allowing permit stacking in the limited entry fleet; gear modification requirements; catch alloca-tion to, or gear flexibility for, gear types with lower bycatch rates; re-examining/improving species-to-species landings limit ratios; and time/area closures.

Amendment 13 did not make these techniques mandatory ("may include"), despite MSA's unambiguous intent to minimize bycatch and bycatch mortality to the extent practicable.

The MSA confines the scope of judicial review of agency regulations and actions to that provided in the [Administrative Procedure Act]. Section 706 of the APA requires reviewing courts to "hold unlawful and set aside agency action, find-ings, and conclusions found to be arbitrary, capricious, an abuse of discretion, or otherwise not in accordance with law." An agency decision may be invalidated if

---

2. An observer program documents bycatch by placing trained individuals in fishing boats for the duration of a fishing trip. While at sea, the observer records the numbers and species of fish that are discarded overboard, giving fishery managers hard and reliable data on the amount and type of bycatch that is occurring in the fishery.

it fails to consider important aspects of a problem, uses criteria Congress did not intend, or is not explained well enough for a reviewing court to identify the agency's response to major policy issues raised in preliminary proceedings. . . .

***

Adequate Bycatch Assessment Methodology

First, Plaintiffs challenge Amendment 13 for failing to adopt an adequate bycatch assessment methodology in violation of MSA's requirement that each FMP "establish a standardized reporting methodology to assess the amount and type of bycatch occurring in the fishery." 16 U.S.C. § 1853(a)(11). Plaintiff directs this court's attention to NMFS's admission that it lacks adequate data on the amount and type of bycatch in the Pacific ground fishery; that this absence of bycatch data seriously harms its ability to manage the Pacific groundfish fishery and to protect overfished groundfish species; and that an at-sea observer program is essential for adequately assessing bycatch in the Pacific groundfish fishery. While the administrative record makes it clear that an adequate groundfish observer program is essential to account for bycatch in the Pacific, NMFS has yet to implement such an observer program.

Amendment 13 discusses the possible use of observers to assess bycatch at some point in the future. However, it contains no requirement to adopt either an observer program or any other bycatch assessment methodology. As NMFS admits in its Federal Register notice announcing its approval of Amendment 13, the rule "itself does not require implementation of an observer program."

Defendants argue that Amendment 13 provides for an at-sea observer program and that implementation of this program is underway. NMFS contends that its observer program provides adequate bycatch assessment as required by MSA. This court finds the program legally insufficient to meet NMFS's bycatch assessment duties under 16 U.S.C. section 1853(a)(11), because it is not mandated by Amendment 13. That section of MSA requires that bycatch assessment methods be established in the fishery management plan itself. Because the observer program is optional under Amendment 13, NMFS in theory could decide not to implement an observer program for the ground fishery, and nothing in Amendment 13 would prohibit the agency from making that decision.

Furthermore, NMFS admits that its observer program cannot provide the data necessary to assess the amount and type of bycatch occurring in the fishery. NMFS calls the current observer program "a limited observer program," and the agency admits that at the current level of funding, the observer program will not be able to provide sufficiently accurate new discard estimates for each area/time/gear strata.

MSA requires that a fishery management plan establish a bycatch assessment methodology sufficient to assess the amount and type of bycatch occurring in the fishery. 16 U.S.C. § 1853(a)(11). Because Amendment 13 fails to establish a mandatory and adequate observer program — a program that the NMFS itself concedes is critical — this court finds that Amendment 13 is "not in accordance with" the MSA.

Accordingly, this court grants Plaintiffs motion for summary judgment on this claim and remands Amendment 13 to NMFS for further consideration and action.

***

Plaintiffs also challenge NMFS's dismissal of two additional bycatch reduction methods as "impracticable without an observer program." The first of these potential measures is the use of incentives for vessels with lower bycatch rates, such as allowing higher landing limits (and thus greater fishing profits) for fishing vessels that fish selectively and thus have relatively low discard rates. The second potential measure is the use of discard caps to manage the fishery.

In response, NMFS argues that these bycatch reduction measures were "reasonably found impracticable without 100 percent observer coverage." As Plaintiffs correctly point out, this argument begs the question of whether full observer coverage is itself practicable in the groundfish fishery in light of the criteria for practicability set forth at 50 C.F.R. 600.350(d)(3)(i). . . .

Defendants argue that "both alternatives are deemed impracticable without a full observer program, since both would require individual vessel monitoring." NMFS states [in the rule] that: "While a limited observer program is practicable at current funding levels, the type of observer program that would be needed to implement a vessel incentive program is not practicable." With respect to the discard caps, NMFS opines that:

> [A] discard cap program with only limited observer coverage tends to exaggerate the observer effect in information about vessels sampled, meaning that the vessels carrying observers have a significant incentive to change their fishing behavior to lower their bycatch rates and keep the entire fishery open. Unobserved vessels do not have this same incentive to reduce discards; thus, there is a strong chance that the whole fleet would reach the discard cap before the observed fleet's expanded data indicated that the cap has been reached. Stronger observer effect under incentives like discard cap management leads to less scientific accuracy from the observer program.

NMFS did not fully consider the practicability of the more comprehensive observer program necessary to administer vessel incentives or discard caps in light of the factors set forth in 50 C.F.R. 600.350(d)(3)(i). Consequently, NMFS has engaged in unreasoned decision-making in dismissing these two potential bycatch reduction measures. Defendants' failure to minimize bycatch and bycatch mortality is arbitrary, capricious, and contrary to law, and in violation of the MSA, SFA and APA. . . . This court also remands Amendment 13 to NMFS for further consideration in light of these requirements.

points for discussion

1. *Very observant.* Observers have been a part of fisheries monitoring since the 1970s. Their job is to make sure that fishermen comply with regulations. Observers go out on fishing vessels, spending days, weeks, and even months at sea, monitoring fishing practices. They make sure that fishing

gear complies with regulations, such as mesh size, line length, and net size, and they make sure that practices conform to regulation — that nets are placed in the right places and depths, and that bycatch is handled and logged appropriately. As you learned from the above cases, it is difficult to learn what happens on board with fish unless they are brought back to port for sale (although the advent of electronic monitoring, discussed below, is an alternative). So, if fishermen haul aboard fish they intend to discard, observers must be able to identify the species to ensure that it would be legal. Observers also collect data for fisheries scientists and for the regulating council. Observers are required to have a bachelor's degree in a natural science field, have training in math and statistics, and must attend a three-week course covering species identification, data collection, regulations, safety, and survival skills. There were about 900 observers working in 2016, who logged over 70,000 days at sea.

2. *Monitoring.* What is, and how do you know if you have, an adequate bycatch reporting methodology? Do you see alternatives to observers for monitoring fishermen behavior? In the age of ubiquitous portable recording devices and automation, it should not be surprising that one method of monitoring that obviates the need for human observers is the electronic video camera. Cameras can record boat activity round the clock, and if positioned correctly, can record the actions of fishermen bringing fish on board, or throwing them overboard. This can be useful if, for example, estimating bycatch is accomplished by requiring fishermen to retain their full catch, and counting the bycatch on shore. Fishermen are forbidden to switch off or tamper with cameras, and may be punished if unexplained gaps in recording appear. Advocates of electronic monitoring point out that human observers are vulnerable to bias, intimidation, and bribery. However, human observers are sometimes also charged with identifying bycatch as it is hauled on board, requiring training and human judgment. NMFS has, at the time this edition went to press, only made limited use of electronic monitoring, limiting its use to only a few fisheries, including some pelagic longline fisheries and groundfish fisheries. In *Oceana v. Ross*, 275 F. Supp. 3d 270 (D.D.C. 2017), Oceana challenged NMFS's reluctance to more widely employ electronic monitoring for the incorrigible New England fishermen, but the court deferred to NMFS's judgment that electronic monitoring cameras were more costly and less effective in the fisheries in question. At this point, the official NMFS position is the standardized bycatch reporting methodology varies greatly from fishery to fishery, and electronic monitoring is only appropriate for some fisheries.

3. *Complying with national standard 9.* How many fishing trips must have an observer on board to monitor bycatch? In *Oceana v. Pritzker*, 26 F. Supp. 3d 33 (D.D.C. 2014), a court upheld a plan instituted by the New England Fishery Management Council (following litigation) to ensure that 22 percent of all trips of covered fisheries were staffed by observers. This was an increase over the 8 percent previous coverage level. The point of observers is not only to monitor fishermen behavior, but to estimate, as a statistical matter,

how much bycatch is landed with a typical fishing trip. From that perspective, something far less than 100 percent is required, because one can infer how much bycatch is caught for all of the other trips. Conservation organizations have argued that trips without observers on board would fish longer and possibly use illegal gear, which might

Being a fisheries observer can be dangerous business. In 2015, a 41-year-old fisheries observer named Keith Davis, working for the Inter-American Tropical Tuna Commission, failed to return with the Panamanian boat he was working 500 miles west of Peru. Panamanian authorities took charge of the investigation, frustrating the FBI and Coast Guard, and no charges have been filed in what is suspected to be a murder. Davis's disappearance coincides with two other observer deaths in the same year, of unusual illnesses.

produce more bycatch. The council estimated that the level of bias was between 1 and 4 percent, but it is unclear how it arrived at that estimate.

4. *The big picture.* An extensive, sweeping fishery management plan is in place that covers over 90 species of fish, including 19 species of groundfish and that includes, by the way, the darkblotched rockfish at issue in *Natural Resources Defense Council v. National Marine Fisheries Service*, presented above. In addition to observer requirements, the plan includes a variety of other measures to reduce overfishing and bycatch.

Figure 2-15. An NOAA Observer Examines Catch

3. Essential Fish Habitat

Contents of Fishery Management Plans

16 U.S.C. § 1853

> (a) **Required provisions.** Any fishery management plan which is prepared by any Council, or by the Secretary, with respect to any fishery, shall —
>
> (7) describe and identify essential fish habitat for the fishery based on the guidelines established by the Secretary under section 1855(b)(1)(A) of this title, minimize to the extent practicable adverse effects on such habitat caused by fishing, and identify other actions to encourage the conservation and enhancement of such habitat.

The following case illustrates how one court attempted to interpret the phrase "minimize to the extent practicable the adverse effects on such habitat caused by fishing." Note that words like "adverse" and "caused" require scientific input that will likely be data-poor. Moreover, "practicable" means "able to be done." But what does that word mean when it comes to evaluating specific bycatch measures?

Natural Resources Defense Council v. Evans

254 F. Supp. 2d 434 (S.D.N.Y. 2003)

Judge BERMAN delivered the opinion of the United States District Court, Southern District of New York.

In 1998, the National Marine Fisheries Service ("NMFS") declared tilefish (Lopholatilus chamaeleonticeps) to be overfished, thus triggering the need for an FMP. The Mid-Atlantic Fisheries Management Council ("Mid-Atlantic FMC") issued a draft tilefish FMP and [Environmental Impact Statement] in May 1999 for comment. The draft considered, among other things, the impact of bottom-tending mobile gear on tilefish habitat and, despite the paucity of evidence in respect of adverse effects on tilefish habitat, stated:

> Based on the best available scientific information, it can be inferred that trawling is causing long-term physical adverse impacts to tilefish EFH [i.e., "essential fish habitat"]. It is further implied that in some cases those adverse impacts may be severe, at least locally. The draft FMP cited studies of the impact of bottom-tending mobile gear on other (i.e., non-tilefish) habitats.

The draft recommended changes to the use of bottom-tending mobile gear.

The draft FMP gave rise to a great deal of comment. . . . Fisherman Dan Farnham argued that "gear impacts are not specifically identified for tile fish" and that "[t]he best tilefish landings occur where bottom gear is fished heavily." Maggie Raymond, a representative of Garden State Seafood and other organizations, commented that the Council should research the gear impacts on tilefish habitats before implementing the draft FMP or "[t]here will be lost revenues with this alternative." Fisherman Joe Nolan believed the conclusions in the draft "would destroy historic fishermen."

Commenters who opposed the "inference" that bottom-tending mobile gear negatively impacts tilefish habitat generally based their arguments on the lack of available evidence. Commenters who supported the inference generally sought a precautionary approach, that is, limiting or banning the use of bottom-tending mobile gear despite the lack of evidence of its effects on tilefish habitat.

Interested parties, including Dr. Ken Able, a recognized expert on tilefish, representatives from the NMFS and Mid-Atlantic FMC, and others met in September 1999 as a working group to discuss, among other things, bottom-tending mobile gear's impact on tilefish habitat. Dr. Able was "unaware of any work on the east coast that would address gear impact questions for tilefish. . . . Theoretically, trawls could pass over the burrows without destroying them or could potentially cause sediments to fill the burrows. Able ha[d] not seen evidence of burrows filled in by trawls in his submersible work." In short, no scientific data existed which proved a negative impact on tilefish habitat, according to Dr. Able. The Mid-Atlantic FMC acknowledged that they lacked evidence for their opinion that bottom-tending mobile gear had an adverse impact on tilefish habitat.

At an October 14, 1999 meeting of the Mid-Atlantic FMC, the chairman of the Council stated that "what [Dr. Able] said and what the rest of the researchers concluded was that there really is nothing definitively known on tilefish gear or on bottom tending gear impacting tilefish habitat. . . . We can make all the associations we want, but we don't have any direct evidence. There's nothing in the literature. He knows of nothing."

At a November 1999 meeting of the Mid-Atlantic FMC, one staff member noted that "the conclusion of the working group was that nothing definitively was known directly about tilefish being directly impacted by bottom tending mobile gear. There is nothing direct in the literature. Unquestionably, trawl gear-patterns are found in tilefish burrows. . . . What the working group and the tilefish technical team now is recommending is that there not be gear impact measures in this FMP at this time, that there be a research approach." A Council member noted: "The fact is there is no evidence as to what mobile gear does. It's not that there isn't much. There isn't any. . . . We simply have no information to justify . . . the proposals we went out to public hearing with. We just had nothing." Consequently, the Council voted to "eliminate the recommendation [from the draft FMP] to close ocean areas to protect tilefish habitat from supposed impact from mobile gear at this time." Rather, the Council approved a plan to implement a research program to study the impact of bottom-tending mobile gear on tilefish habitat within two years.

The Council submitted the revised tilefish FMP and [Environmental Impact Statement], to the NMFS in March 2000. The final FMP states:

> It was concluded that there is nothing definitively known about tilefish-mobile fishing gear interactions. There is nothing specifically described about the sensitivity of tilefish burrows in the scientific literature. Unquestionably, from submersible vessel research, there are trawl door patterns observed in areas with

tilefish burrows, but how much of an impact the doors have and how quickly tile-fish can reopen their burrows, if sediment closed, is completely unknown at this time.... [I]mpacts of bottom tending mobile gear specifically to tilefish habitat are unquantifiable at this time.

The Secretary approved the FMP on May 10, 2001. Based on the adverse economic effects that a prohibition on the use of bottom-tending mobile gear in tilefish HAPC ["Habitat Area of Particular Concern"] would have upon several other fisheries and on the lack of scientific evidence showing identifiable adverse effects caused by such gear on tilefish [essential fish habitat], the Council did not propose gear prohibitions in the HAPC on other than limited access tilefish vessels. NMFS and the Council support a cooperative research program to further investigate this issue.

Plaintiffs claim that (i) Defendants wrongly concluded that bottom-tending mobile gear does not cause an identifiable adverse effect on tilefish habitat; and (ii) the [Environmental Impact Statement] included in the tile fish FMP was inadequate. The Court addresses these claims in turn.

(i) Effects of Bottom-Tending Mobile Gear

Plaintiffs advance a number of arguments to support their claim that Defendants acted arbitrarily in concluding that bottom-tending mobile gear does not have an identifiable adverse effect on tilefish habitat. Plaintiffs argue that Defendants ignored evidence of physical disruption to tilefish habitat, which is an adverse effect; that Defendants failed to explain their change in position from the draft FMP to the final one; and that Defendants wrongly declined to act without definitive proof, among other things. Defendants respond that Plaintiffs have not established physical disruption to tilefish habitat, and even if they had, physical disruption does not necessarily reduce "quality or quantity of essential fish habitat," as required by the regulations under the Magnuson-Stevens Act and that Defendants changed their position based on the best scientific information available, i.e., the "absence of *any* evidence that trawl gear is actually causing any adverse effects to the [essential fish habitat], as defined by the regulations."

The implementing regulations for the Magnuson-Stevens Act provide that "Councils must act to prevent, mitigate, or minimize any adverse effects from fishing, to the extent practicable, if there is evidence that a fishing practice is having an identifiable adverse effect on [essential fish habitat]." 50 C.F.R. § 600.815(a)(3)(iii). Section 600.810(a) defines "adverse effect" as "any impact which reduces quality and/or quantity of [essential fish habitat]. Adverse effects may include direct (e.g., contamination or physical disruption), indirect (e.g., loss of prey, or reduction in species' fecundity), site-specific or habitat-wide impacts." "Identifiable" means "both more than minimal and not temporary in nature." To make the adverse effect determination, "[c]ouncils should use the best scientific information available."

Ample record evidence including, among other things, the comments and reports of academics and fishing industry representatives establishes clearly that the Defendants arrived at the conclusion that no identifiable adverse effects on tilefish essential fish habitat from bottom-tending mobile gear exists upon a rational analysis of the best scientific information available. The preparers of the FMP concluded that studies of mobile gear's effects on other habitats were not sufficiently analogous and there was a complete lack of evidence to prove an identifiable adverse effect on tilefish habitat.

Plaintiffs note that the final FMP states: "Unquestionably, from submersible vessel research, there are trawl door patterns observed in areas with tilefish burrows." Plaintiffs claim that this observation constitutes per se evidence of physical disruption, and that adverse effect may include a "physical disruption." 50 C.F.R. § 600.810(a). Thus, Plaintiffs contend, the Defendants missed an identifiable adverse effect. Defendants argue that door patterns do not prove physical disruption and, even if they did, Defendants' conclusion was correct because there is no evidence of an impact that reduces "quality or quantity of essential fish habitat."

Record evidence indicates unequivocally that in hundreds of submersible dives, Dr. Able, a renowned expert on tilefish, observed bottom-tending mobile gear patterns in active twenty- to thirty-year old tilefish burrows. ("These fish survived multiple annual trawling during the most intense time of fishing. . . . We can safely postulate that trawling does not impact the local environment or food chain to the detriment of the Tilefish lifecycle. This is a more reasonable hypothesis than the assumption that trawling does significantly impact the habitat or food chain to the detriment of Tile fish. Our hypothesis of low impact is based upon what we know from trawl surveys and from what has been observed during submersible dives, while the draft plan's assumptions of significant impact on the [essential fish habitat] has no direct evidence or basis other than pure conjecture." Based on these observations, Defendants reasonably found no evidence of a reduction in quality or quantity of essential fish habitat and did not deem "doormarks" an identifiable adverse effect. The Court defers to the Defendants' expertise, which is supported by the record. *See American Oceans*, 183 F. Supp. 2d at 11-12 (stating that a court must "look at the decision not as the chemist, biologist, or statistician that we are qualified neither by training nor experience to be, but as a reviewing court exercising our narrowly defined duty of holding agencies to certain minimal standards of rationality").

Plaintiffs' argument that Defendants' changed position from the draft FMP to the final FMP reflects Defendants' arbitrary decision-making process is unpersuasive. The record demonstrates that Defendants based the original inferred hypothesis on studies of other habitats, and that this hypothesis was, subsequently, called into question by Dr. Able, the fishing industry and the Council. . . . Defendants based their final conclusion upon the lack of any evidence of effects on tilefish habitat ("[N]one of the existing literature discusses or documents specific impacts to subterranean burrow communities such as those used by tilefish."). Moreover, "an agency does not have a burden to explain a change in position from a proposed rule to the final rule, and . . . a lack of an explanation for the change is not in itself evidence of arbitrariness."

Plaintiffs' arguments that Defendants declined to act without definitive proof, that Defendants yielded to fishing industry pressure, and that Defendants used the impracticability of implementing precautionary measures as an excuse to reverse their original hypothesis, are equally unpersuasive. The record clearly supports Defendants' conclusion that no evidence existed that bottom-tending mobile gear caused an identifiable adverse impact upon tilefish. At oral argument, in response to the Court's question whether there is evidence of an impact on tilefish habitat, Plaintiffs'

Figure 2-16. Tilefish

counsel acknowledged that "there is no information[], besides inferences, based on the kind of evidence that the Council considered and that is in the record." The Court finds that it was reasonable for Defendants not to impose new restrictions on bottom-tending mobile gear given the lack of evidence that the gear had an identifiable adverse effect.

For the reasons stated herein, the Court denies Plaintiffs' motion for summary judgment and grants Defendants' cross motion for summary judgment. . . .

points for discussion

1. *More on tilefish.* Tilefish are a long-lived bottom-dwelling fish that can be found from Nova Scotia to Florida, and in the Gulf of Mexico. They live to be about 50 years old, and are slow to sexual maturity—about six years. Spawning season in the Gulf of Mexico is January to June, and March to November in the Atlantic. Tilefish can be caught by longlining and by pole lines, but have been more efficiently caught by bottom-tending mobile gear. Tilefish live at depths of 250 to 1,500 feet, where they burrow in small groups, sometimes sharing their burrows with groupers and snappers. Essential fish habitat for tilefish was established in 2001, and in 2009, NOAA prohibited the use of bottom trawling in certain areas designated as essential fish habitat for tilefish. 74 Fed. Reg. 42,580, 42,585 (2009). Most commercial tilefish harvesting is now done by longline and pole line. Most tilefish stocks are managed under Individual Fishing Quota programs (see below). According to NOAA, neither the blue tilefish nor the golden tilefish are overfished. Seafood Watch, an organization that publishes fish consumption recommendations for consumers who want to avoid eating fish that are not sustainably fished, lists blue (a.k.a. golden) tilefish as "best choices," but generally cautions against blueline tilefish.

2. *Getting to the bottom of it.* What do you make of the testimony of the people at the hearing, and the testimony of Dr. Ken Able? Were you convinced that the decision not to prohibit the use of bottom trawling was based on

the best scientific information available? If you were either the NMFS or an environmental advocacy group, what would be your next steps in determining whether bottom trawling was harmful to tilefish habitat?

3. *Other approaches.* In *Oceana v. Evans*, 2005 WL 555416 (D.D.C. 2005), a court emphasized that area closure was only one of several ways of protecting essential fish habitat. In particular, Judge Huvell cited with approval the report's conclusion that "effort reduction, *not* area closures, is the 'cornerstone' for mitigating the adverse effects of trawls and dredges on seafloor habitat." Magnuson-Stevens Fishery Conservation and Management Act Provisions; Fisheries of the Northeastern United States; Northeast (NE) Multispecies Fishery; Amendment 13, 69 Fed. Reg. 22,906-01, 22,922 (citing Nat'l Research Council, Effects of Trawling and Dredging on Seafloor Habitat (2002) ("Effort reduction" is also known as "input control," or a regulatory method aimed at reducing the amount of effort — be it in crew, hours, or vessel numbers, size, or power — in fishing.)).

NOTE ON NEPA

As seen from the previous case as well as others, claims made under the National Environmental Policy Act (NEPA) are a frequent companion to claims made under the Magnuson-Stevens Act. For every "major federal agency action," NEPA requires some environmental analysis be done on its environmental effects, unless it falls under some categorical exemption. FMPs and significant amendments are "major federal agency actions" triggering NEPA requirements. An analysis can be a full-blown "Environmental Impact Statement" (EIS) or an abbreviated "Environmental Assessment" (EA), which either could find that the environmental impact could be significant, triggering a full-blown EIS, or could make a "finding of no significant impact" (FONSI), which would terminate the NEPA process.

The requirement that has proven to be the most complementary to Magnuson-Stevens Act claims is the NEPA requirement that the acting agency analyze a reasonable number and range of alternatives. In *Oceana v. Evans*, excerpted above, the court wrote:

> The heart of an EIS is its analysis of a reasonable range of alternatives to the agency's proposed action. These alternatives should be presented so as to "sharply defin[e] the issues and provid[e] a clear basis for choice." The range of options considered by the agency is "bounded by some notion of feasibility," and a "detailed statement of alternatives cannot be found wanting simply because the agency failed to include every alternative device and thought conceivable by the mind of man." Thus, courts apply a "rule of reason" in assessing whether an agency considered a sufficient range of alternatives. . . . Courts accord "considerable deference to the agency's expertise and policy-making role" that defined the scope of the action in the first place. In addition to setting forth alternatives, an EIS must also analyze an action's direct, indirect and cumulative impacts, detail the action's purpose and need, and describe the affected environment. A court's role in evaluating a NEPA challenge is "not [to] substitute its own policy judgment for those of the agency,"

but to "ensure that the agency took account of [the relevant] factors and that its decision was not arbitrary and capricious."

The alternatives requirement has been so useful for challenging FMPs because it forces the regional FMCs to consider alternative conservation measures. The Magnuson-Stevens Act mandates often contain limiting language to enable the FMCs to consider tradeoffs in setting catch limits and seasons, regulating gear, monitoring bycatch, or designating essential fish habitat. For example, the designation of "essential fish habitats" must "minimize *to the extent practicable* adverse effects on such habitat caused by fishing." 16 U.S.C. § 1853(a)(7) (emphasis added). Also, FMCs must establish a "standardized reporting methodology to assess the amount and type of bycatch occurring in the fishery, and include conservation and management measures that, *to the extent practicable*" minimize bycatch. 16 U.S.C. § 1853(a)(11) (emphasis added). This common language "to the extent practicable" releases some of the pressure on FMCs and NMFS to focus too much on conservation, but the vagueness is a fertile source of litigation. Litigants invoke NEPA to make sure that of all of the different ways that FMCs might carry out all of their mandates under the Magnuson-Stevens Act, they have considered a sufficient variety of alternatives. Environmental organizations might argue for more expansive designations of essential fish habitat, or call for a closure of a fishery, or the prohibition of destructive gear.

Because judicial review under NEPA tends to be deferential, challenges are more often unsuccessful than successful. However, the NEPA mandate that agencies thoroughly consider different alternatives continues to have a disciplining effect on FMCs. FMCs tend to be biased in favor of the fishing industries, so a procedural counterweight such as NEPA has likely moderated many of the decisions made by FMCs and NMFS.

4. Quantity Limits

The history of fishing regulation is replete with examples of fishermen outsmarting regulators by finding loopholes. Certainly, fishing technologies have evolved to help fishermen catch fish more efficiently, which has been the source of almost perpetual crisis in so many fisheries. (Being efficient allows fishermen to increase their CPUE and, thus, catch more fish.) But what is interesting, almost comical, is how fishing technologies have evolved in many cases simply to avoid regulation.

The oldest type of fishing regulation sought to prohibit certain types of gear that were thought to be particularly destructive or just too efficient at catching fish. Gear that is so brutally efficient at catching fish poses the threat of catching so much fish so quickly that stocks have no time to recover. Gear restrictions can include rules requiring trawling nets to have a minimum mesh size in order to allow juveniles to escape. Regulators can also ban certain gear altogether. In order to protect sensitive ocean floor habitats, for example, some jurisdictions have outlawed bottom trawling. Gear restrictions such as these can reduce certain types of mortality, but by themselves do nothing to curb overfishing, because fishermen can usually substitute other gear for prohibited gear, and find other ways to continue fishing in the most profitable manner. Fishermen can also increase their vessel size, increase their engine power, and increase their crew to compensate for gear restrictions, unless there are separate rules limiting "fishing power." Fishermen 1, Regulators 0.

Regulating fishing power is another way to try to control overfishing. However, fishermen have figured out ways around those rules as well. Limits on the number of boats that could fish led to the replacement of the fleet with larger, faster boats with greater fishing capacity. Restrictions on boat length led to the entry of *rounder* boats. Fishermen 2, Regulators 0.

Limiting access to a fishery, by putting a cap on the number of licenses to fish, by boat or by person, is another incomplete method of controlling overfishing. It does have some benefits. It can reduce the number of boats in the race for fish. And, it has the potential to improve conservation. When there are too many fishermen in a fishery, so that not all permit holders can operate profitably within the constraints of MSY, there are obviously added pressures not to practice good conservation, for example, by allowing too much fishing. Economists call the condition of too many boats (or too much investment) in the fishery "overcapitalization," and they see it as the root of many fisheries problems. While limited access can restrict the number of parties that can enter a race to fish, it does not prevent overfishing because it does not control the total amount of fish caught. And even when there are fewer fishermen, a race for fish, with negative consequences such as excessive investment in fishing power, could still occur.

Temporary closures, that is, rules that prohibit fishing for a period of days, weeks, or months, are another way to control overfishing. Closures take pressure off fish stocks, allowing them time to recover, and are simpler to enforce than many other kinds of fisheries regulations. One common use of closures is to protect fish during the time they are reproducing. (This is also common in terrestrial hunting regulations.) Many species of fish will benefit significantly from spawning closures because they aggregate (meet in one location) to reproduce, making the population highly vulnerable to fishing effort. Closures, too, are an incomplete regulatory method. As with other kinds of effort limits — rules on fishing power, limits on the number of boats, days-at-sea rules — fishermen can offset the conservation benefits of a closed season by fishing more in the open season. In the Pacific halibut fishery in Alaska, the fleet proved that it could catch the entire annual quota in 48 hours! (That fishery now lasts all year because, in 1995, it became an individual quota fishery.)

Effort limits, also known as "input controls," seek to control the amount of time and money that goes into catching fish. Some combination of input controls could be effective in curbing overfishing by making it impossible for the fleet to catch more than MSY. But there is never any guarantee that this will actually occur, because there are no hard limits on the number of fish caught intentionally or as bycatch.

The only sure-fire way to ensure against overfishing is to directly control the amount of fish caught, an "output control." This is the genesis of modern catch limits. These go by a variety of names, such as "total allowable landings," "total annual catch," "annual quota," or "annual catch limit," but they all seek to cap fishing mortality for a 12-month fishing year. (Regulators often begin a fishing year not on January 1, but on the day of the year that the fishery ordinarily begins.)

Output rules set limits on the amount of fish the fishery can catch in a given year. But, who — which fishermen, type of vessel, or community — should have the right to catch them? In a derby or race, the answer is simple: first in time, first in right. Is there a better way? In other words, could regulators use rules that give each fisherman or boat the annual right to catch a part of the total annual catch? How should those privileges (access to valuable public resources) be divided up? What is fair? What is efficient? Those questions are at the crux of the problem of how to institute individual quota systems such as the "LAPP" system described below.

Contents of Fishery Management Plans

16 U.S.C. § 1853

(b) Discretionary provisions

Any fishery management plan which is prepared by any Council, or by the Secretary, with respect to any fishery, may —

(6) establish a limited access system for the fishery in order to achieve optimum yield if, in developing such system, the Council and the Secretary take into account —

(A) present participation in the fishery;

(B) historical fishing practices in, and dependence on, the fishery;

(C) the economics of the fishery;

(D) the capability of fishing vessels used in the fishery to engage in other fisheries;

(E) the cultural and social framework relevant to the fishery and any affected fishing communities;

(F) the fair and equitable distribution of access privileges in the fishery; and

(G) any other relevant considerations.

Limited Access Privilege Programs

16 U.S.C. § 1853a

(c) Requirements for limited access privileges
(1) In general

Any limited access privilege program to harvest fish submitted by a Council or approved by the Secretary under this section shall —

(A) if established in a fishery that is overfished or subject to a rebuilding plan, assist in its rebuilding;

(**B**) if established in a fishery that is determined by the Secretary or the Council to have over-capacity, contribute to reducing capacity;

(**C**) promote —

(**i**) fishing safety;

(**ii**) fishery conservation and management; and

(**iii**) social and economic benefits;

(**D**) prohibit any person other than a United States citizen, a corporation, partnership, or other entity established under the laws of the United States or any State, or a permanent resident alien, that meets the eligibility and participation requirements established in the program from acquiring a privilege to harvest fish, including any person that acquires a limited access privilege solely for the purpose of perfecting or realizing on a security interest in such privilege;

(**E**) require that all fish harvested under a limited access privilege program be processed on vessels of the United States or on United States soil (including any territory of the United States);

(**F**) specify the goals of the program;

(**G**) include provisions for the regular monitoring and review by the Council and the Secretary of the operations of the program, including determining progress in meeting the goals of the program and this chapter, and any necessary modification of the program to meet those goals, with a formal and detailed review 5 years after the implementation of the program and thereafter to coincide with scheduled Council review of the relevant fishery management plan (but no less frequently than once every 7 years);

(**H**) include an effective system for enforcement, monitoring, and management of the program, including the use of observers or electronic monitoring systems;

(**I**) include an appeals process for administrative review of the Secretary's decisions regarding initial allocation of limited access privileges;

When Congress introduced this second provision in 2006, the term "Limited Access Privilege Program" (LAPP) was a new entry into the established lexicon of quota-dividing systems. At the most basic level, a right to catch an amount of fish is known as a "catch share." Catch shares can be held by vessel owners, captains, crew, whole communities, or fishery sectors (a "sector" is a group of fishermen who use the same type of fishing gear or who fish for the same purpose, e.g., subsistence or commercial). Community-owned quotas are used in the world's largest fishery, the Alaska pollock fishery, and are known there as "community development quotas." These rights to catch a quantity of fish are usually referred to as Individual Fishing Quotas (IFQs) or Individual Transferable Quotas (ITQs). Technically, these are two different types of rights — the latter being transferable, the former not — but in the literature, the terms are often conflated and generally refer to fishing rights that are transferable. The Magnuson-Stevens Act defines an IFQ as "a Federal permit under a limited access system to harvest a quantity of fish, expressed by a unit or units representing a percentage of the total allowable catch of a fishery that may be received or held for exclusive use by a person." 16 U.S.C. § 1802(23). Can you figure out why shares are almost always in the form of a percentage of the TAC rather than a fixed amount of fish?

Despite their many advantages over a pure TAC, IFQ programs are always controversial, primarily because individual fishermen have very different ideas about which fishermen should receive how many shares in the initial allocation. It is possible to allocate shares based on average catches over a time period, length of time in the fishery, and so forth. Without any certainty about whether they will emerge from the allocation process as winners or losers, individual fishermen will often fight to keep IFQs from even being discussed. The following excerpt highlights some of the advantages and challenges for IFQ programs.

Shi-Ling Hsu & James E. Wilen, Ecosystem Management and the 1996 Sustainable Fisheries Act

24 Ecology Law Quarterly 799 (1997)

A few fisheries have adopted a measure that attacks the fundamental property rights problem: individual fishermen quotas (IFQs). IFQs grant rights to harvest a given percentage of the biologically determined total annual allowable catch. They are, in effect, a property right to the potential harvest. As a result, they change the incentives fishermen face in a radical way. Under IFQs, a fisherman does not need to build a bigger boat to outfish her competitors before regulators close the season; he may fish whenever it is efficient to do so during the season. While IFQs have only been adopted in three fisheries in the U.S., they have been adopted in over fifty fisheries worldwide.

The impacts of IFQs on fisheries are a remarkable counterpoint to the status quo in traditional fisheries managed by closed seasons and gear restrictions. IFQs have reversed the race to overcapitalize, because they encourage fishermen to downsize and adopt fishing practices more suitable to producing higher valued products year-round. Reduced overcapitalization offers many benefits. First, the product itself improves, as fish formerly frozen because of short seasons are available fresh throughout the year. Second, fishermen begin to act as stakeholders of the resource, since detrimental actions more clearly impact their own potential revenues. This is an important byproduct since fishermen and regulators tend to view most modern regulated fisheries as an adversarial struggle. Finally, in fisheries where there were formerly significant amounts of bycatch and discards, fishermen reduce waste, particularly if bycatch is included in their quota.

Support for IFQs is by no means universal, however, and there are many detractors who point to potential problems. While IFQ programs can theoretically deliver substantial ecological and economic benefits, they will almost certainly have distributional consequences. In systems where quota shares are transferable, the most efficient fishermen will bid up prices and purchase the quota shares. These more efficient fishermen will also probably hire fewer crewmen, resulting in a decrease in numbers employed. In regions that are heavily dependent upon the fishing industries, like remote areas of Alaska, IFQ programs could potentially impact not only working crewmen, but also persons supported by secondary industries associated with fishing. Moreover, the prospect of larger, more efficient operations — some of which are corporate entities like Tyson Foods or Con-Agra Corporation — capturing a large percentage of quota shares is an outcome that most local residents of fishing communities and some managers wish to prevent in order to save smaller family fishing operations. Opponents of IFQs also fear that smaller fishing operations may receive too small of an initial allocation of quota shares to be able to fish economically, and yet will be outbid by larger entities in their attempts to buy more quota shares. In addition, smaller operations tend to have less access to credit for buying quota shares than larger operations.

Provincialism also creates opposition to IFQs. Programs that risk transferring fishing rights on a permanent basis to "outsiders" predictably evoke strong reactions from local fishermen. Intra-cultural and intra-community conflicts over the use of IFQs have also become pointed. However, because IFQ programs create a valuable property right that can be sold by those choosing to sell out, substantial numbers of fishermen are inclined to support IFQs. Some fishermen have also supported IFQs because they see them as the only way to manage fisheries effectively and avoid the inevitable growth in fishing capacity that occurs under open access.

––––––––––––––

As the article noted, fishermen sometimes furiously oppose new IFQ programs. Anxious fishermen led Congress, in the 1996 Sustainable Fisheries Act, to impose a moratorium on any new IFQ programs pending the results of a National Academy of Sciences study on their ecological and economic effects. That study, a 437-page report entitled *Sharing the Fish: Toward a National Policy on Individual Fishing Quotas*, comprehensively summarizes the many potential ecological, social, and economic effects, direct and indirect, of IFQ programs. Although the report takes great pains to acknowledge and document the objections raised against IFQ programs, it concludes that the "value [of IFQ programs] in matching harvesting and processing capacities to the resource, slowing the race for fish, providing consumers with a better product, and reducing wasteful and dangerous fishing has been demonstrated repeatedly." *Id.* at 12.

While the introduction of IFQs has been controversial, they are now common. In most cases, NMFS and the regional councils have overcome stakeholder opposition to IFQ programs. New England fisheries are an exception. By and large, the New England Regional Fishery Management Council has governed by working with the sector system, described above.

The following case concerns the first IFQ program instituted in the United States, which was unsurprisingly met with litigation.

Sea Watch International v. Mosbacher

762 F. Supp. 370 (D.D.C. 1991)

Judge BOUDIN delivered the opinion of the United States District Court, District of Columbia.

In 1977, the Mid-Atlantic Regional Fishery Management Council ("the Council") began to regulate the surf clam and ocean quahog fisheries [including the separate New England surf clam industry]. . . . The Council regulated the three fisheries under different plans. . . . In 1988, the Council proposed Amendment 8 to the Fishery Management Plan for Surf Clams and Ocean Quahogs ("Amendment 8"). This Amendment was the culmination of several years of work by the Council, and reflected numerous concerns about the viability of existing regulations, the migration of vessels from the surf clam fishery to the less-regulated quahog fishery, and the resultant increase in the quahog harvest. Amendment 8 was approved by the Secretary and implemented by regulations published in the Federal Register on June 14, 1990. The regulations became effective on September 30, 1990. Amendment 8 brought the three fisheries under a single limited access scheme built around individual transferable quotas ("ITQs"), which are transferable permits to fish for a fixed percentage of the annual aggregate catch quota for the species and area. Thus, although the annual quota for all fishermen may vary from year to year depending on the Council's determination of an optimum yield, the holder of, e.g., a 5% ITQ would be entitled to catch up to 5% of that quota.

For each of the fisheries, ITQs were allocated on the basis of vessel fishing history, although the data used to calculate that history and the weight assigned to it varied between the fisheries. For example, in the Mid-Atlantic surf clam fishery, eighty percent of the ITQ was derived by averaging vessel catch history from 1979 to 1988, with the last four years counted twice, and the lowest two years deleted. The other twenty percent was based upon the vessel's dimensions, as a proxy for the owner's capital investment. The results were divided by the total for all vessels in the fleet, producing an ITQ expressed as a percentage of the annual quota.

After Amendment 8 went into effect, two groups of fishermen and seafood processing companies brought these actions, alleging serious economic harm from the ITQ assignments. Their most salient arguments are, first, that the ITQ system exceeded the defendants' statutory authority and, second, that the decision to limit access to the quahog fishery was unsupported by the administrative record. In each case, there are additional arguments that the challenged action also violated the National Standards for the other applicable provisions of the Magnuson-Stevens Act.

***

"Property Rights" Claim. Plaintiffs argue that implementation of the ITQ system for the three fisheries exceeds the Council's and the Secretary's statutory authority, and should therefore be set aside under Section 706(2)(C) of the Administrative Procedure Act. . . . The gist of plaintiffs' claim on this point is that an ITQ system "amount[s] to privatization of the surf clam and quahog resource," and that such a "transfer of private ownership interests in a fishery" is both unauthorized by the Magnuson-Stevens Act and in conflict with an express prohibition on the assessment of fees in excess of costs.

The difficulty with plaintiffs' argument is that Congress did authorize the creation of quotas. The Act expressly authorizes the Council and the Secretary to impose permit requirements and to establish limited access systems.

16 U.S.C. § 1853(b)(1), (6). The legislative history of this section refers specifically to the possibility of dividing "the total allowable catch into shares or quotas which are then distributed among the fishermen." Even without this legislative history, the language of the section broadly embraces the possibility of quotas. Nothing in its terms, and nothing else in the Magnuson-Stevens Act cited to this Court, precludes making quotas transferable. Indeed, transferable permits were precisely the method utilized in the Mid-Atlantic surf clam fishery prior to adoption of Amendment 8, although transfer was linked to sale of the vessel. The present ITQ system differs only in degree from the system of aggregate quotas and transferable permits previously in use and unchallenged by plaintiffs, and the interests created by it fall short of actual full-scale ownership.

* * *

National Standard 4. Plaintiffs contend that the ITQ system is contrary to National Standard 4, which reads in its entirety:

> (4) Conservation and management measures shall not discriminate between residents of different States. If it becomes necessary to allocate or assign fishing privileges among various United States fishermen, such allocation shall be (A) fair and equitable to all such fishermen; (B) reasonably calculated to promote conservation; and (C) carried out in such manner that no particular individual, corporation, or other entity acquires an excessive share of such privileges. 16 U.S.C. § 1851(4).

Plaintiffs claim the system contravenes subsection (A) of this Standard by treating similarly situated fishermen unequally; by rewarding violators of prior regulations; and by discriminating against owners of smaller fishing fleets. . . .

The argument that the ITQ system treats similarly situated fishermen unequally begins with the fact that ITQ assignments were calculated from vessel catch histories rather than individual catch histories. Thus, plaintiffs assert, the assignments ignored the high rate of vessel turnover in the industry, excluding individuals with a substantial catch history who recently sold a vessel, and awarding a "windfall" to individuals with little or no history who recently purchased a vessel. They claim this result is inherently unfair and inequitable under subsection (A) of Standard 4.

However, National Standard 4 does not require that allocations of quotas to fishermen be made by calculating the exact historical catch of each fisherman on an individual basis. In fact, previous regulation of the Mid-Atlantic surf clam fishery also was based on vessel data, insofar as moratorium permits were awarded to vessels with a history of participation in the surf clam fishery, and were transferable only along with those vessels. The record supports defendants' claim that vessel catch data, used as a surrogate for individual catch history, was the only accurate data available. The high rate of vessel turnover only serves to underscore the difficulty of obtaining data organized by individual owner. The decision not to do so reflects not mere administrative convenience, but a consistent and reasonable regulatory scheme.

***

Plaintiffs next contend that the ITQ system violates National Standard 4 because it is intended to drive a particular group of individuals, the single vessel and small fleet owners, out of the fisheries. Since Amendment 8 permits owners to catch their entire ITQ with a few vessels, the argument runs, it will result in lower average costs to the owners of large fleets, and provide them with an unfair competitive advantage. Moreover, it is alleged, small fishermen lack the capital to purchase sufficient ITQs to operate their vessels at full capacity, and ultimately will be driven out of business. It is quite possible that scale economies and transferability of ITQs will produce some consolidation. It is also possible that small fishermen enjoy advantages of their own, and nothing prevents coalitions of small owners from pooling their allocations to obtain efficiencies. Moreover, single vessel or small fleet owners may happen to have substantial allocations depending upon their history. Even where a fisherman with a small allocation decides to exit, transferability of the ITQ provides at least some compensation. There is nothing intentionally invidious or inherently unfair in the plan adopted by the Council and the Secretary. "Inherent in an allocation is the advantaging of one group to the detriment of another."

Limitation of Access to the Quahog Fishery

Aside from the general challenges to the ITQ system described above, plaintiffs make several specific challenges to the decision to limit access to the ocean quahog fishery by bringing it under the same regulatory scheme as the two surf clam fisheries. . . . Plaintiffs contend that the decision to include ocean quahogs in the ITQ system lacks support in the administrative record and was arbitrary and capricious. . . . [T]he Court concludes that the Secretary's decision, though based on conflicting, even speculative, evidence about trends affecting the ocean quahog resource in the future, nonetheless had a rational basis, and was not arbitrary or capricious.

In brief, plaintiffs' argument is that any regulation of the resource is responding to a "problem that does not exist." They dispute the Council's claim of an upward trend in the ocean quahog harvest data, and its prediction that the same "overcapitalization" that required restriction of access to the surf clam fisheries eventually will occur in this fishery. They cite the lower market demand for quahogs, and the undisputed fact that the annual quahog catch quota has never been reached. . . .

However, the administrative record shows that the Council's Scientific and Statistical Committee recommended the inclusion of quahogs in a comprehensive fishery management plan for several years prior to adoption of Amendment 8, and that the Council considered other alternatives. The ultimate decision to adopt this recommendation was based on several related grounds, including the fact that surf clams and quahogs had become substitute goods for certain uses, that existing surf clam restrictions had already resulted in movement of vessels from that fishery into the quahog fishery, and that the potential for further migration to and increased catches in the quahog fishery would be heightened by placing the surf clam fishery under the ITQ system while leaving the quahog fishery unregulated. The Council coupled these long-term concerns with evidence of a recent increase in the quahog harvest.

In sum, the threat to the ocean quahog resource is reflected in the need for the existing annual quotas. An increase in this threat is posed by the diversion of ships from the surf clam to the quahog fishery as surf clam restrictions tighten. Both regulators and fishermen have an interest in having ground rules established before any problem matures. Contrary to plaintiffs' arguments, the Act does not mandate any finding of necessity before fishery access can be limited. The accompanying regulations state that "[i]n an unutilized or underutilized fishery, [limited access] may be used to reduce the chance that [overfishing or overcapitalization] will adversely affect the fishery in the future." The issue thus turns on predictions about the future in an area of technical and scientific expertise, where special deference is due to regulatory agencies. Although plaintiffs' attack on this determination is by no means a frivolous one, the Court holds that the Council and the Secretary did have a rational basis for their action.

***

For all the reasons detailed above, the Court finds that the Secretary's decision to limit access to the ocean quahog fishery was not arbitrary and capricious or an abuse of discretion within the meaning of the Magnuson-Stevens Act.

In accordance with this Memorandum Opinion, an Order will be entered granting the defendants' motion for summary judgment and dismissing this case.

points for discussion

1. *A history of litigation.* While this was the first IFQ program and the first case, subsequent litigation has revisited some of the themes in this case. In *Alliance Against IFQs v. Brown*, 84 F.3d 343 (9th Cir. 1996), the court upheld a plan to institute an IFQ program for the taking of sablefish and halibut. Quota were allocated only to fishermen who landed halibut or sablefish in 1988, 1989, or 1990, but their quota share was based on their highest total landings from 1984 to 1990. In rejecting the plaintiffs' claim that the program violated national standard 4 because it was not "fair and equitable to all fishermen," the court found that the IFQ program and the process by which it was developed was not "arbitrary or capricious," and was "rationally connected with the achievement of optimum yield." *Id.* at 349. Similarly, litigation over the "control dates" in which fishermen's catches are used to determine their quota shares has continued to be a point of contention. In *Pacific Dawn v. Pritzker*, 831 F.3d 1166 (9th Cir. 2016), the court upheld an IFQ plan for all of the Pacific groundfish, more than 90 species in all, some of which were the subject of *Pacific Marine Conservation Council v. Evans*, discussed above. A control date of November 6, 2003 was the subject of litigation; the process of developing the plan was so long and drawn-out that by the time the plan was to take effect in 2010, many changes had already taken place in the fisheries. In upholding the plan, the court stated that the plan took adequate notice of "present participation," even though it assigned it less

weight than other factors. *Id.* at 1175. It was not arbitrary or capricious that "while 'the Council did examine present participation levels, the Council gave greater weight to historic participation in determining the initial allocation.'" Can you see why historic participation might be a better measuring stick than "present participation"? What would happen if IFQ programs assigned too much weight to "present participation"? Litigation over catch shares and IFQs continues apace. For a review of the history and the ongoing litigation on catch shares and IFQs, see Suzanne Iudicello & Sherry Bosse Lueders, *A Survey of Litigation over Catch Shares and Groundfish Management in the Pacific Coast and Northeast Multispecies Fisheries*, 46 ENVTL. L. 157 (2016).

2. *Scope of the program.* The court acknowledged that ocean quahogs were not in nearly as much jeopardy as surf clams. Why then, were they included in the IFQ program? Do you agree that it was worth being proactive in covering quahogs under the IFQ program? What factors would lead you to conclude that, or the opposite?

D. THE REGIONAL FISHERY MANAGEMENT COUNCILS

In most of the U.S. fisheries in federal waters, the chief regulatory body is one of the eight regional fishery management councils (councils). For fisheries within their jurisdictions, the regional councils study fisheries, set catch limits, and draw up the Fishery Management Plans. Enforcement is carried out by the NMFS and the U.S. Coast Guard.

The structure of the NMFS, with its eight regional councils, reflects a political compromise made during the drafting of the Magnuson-Stevens Act. A widespread perception that foreign fishermen were overfishing stocks vital to U.S. fishermen provided impetus for the declaration by Congress, through passage of the Act, to declare exclusive fisheries jurisdiction in Fishery Conservation Zones that went out 200 nautical miles. In 1976, this was in contravention of international law, but as far as federal-state relations were concerned, the Act declared federal control over fisheries in that belt extending from the outer edge of state waters at 3 nautical miles out to 200. Fishermen were willing to accept federal regulatory authority if it was necessary to force foreign fishermen out of this 197-mile belt. Senator Stevens, the primary author of the Act, had sour memories of federal management of salmon fisheries in Alaska when it was still a federal territory, before 1959. As a result, he believed that management of the Fishery Conservation Zones should not be left to a federal agency, and that the power to regulate fisheries in federal waters should be vested in bodies composed of industry representatives and the states. Those federally recognized bodies that had regulatory authority, but were a step removed from a Washington-based federal agency, would be the eight regional councils.

For each council, the Act spells out the total number of councilmembers and the make-up of voting and nonvoting membership. The councils range in size from 7 to 21 voting members, with a varying number of nonvoting members. As noted above, NOAA gets one voting seat on each council. The rest of the voting membership is broken down to mandatory and appointed members. Mandatory members are state officials from states in the region, specifically "[t]he principal State official with marine fishery management responsibility and expertise." 16 U.S.C. § 1852(b)(1)(A). Appointed members are chosen by the Secretary from lists submitted by the governors of each represented state, and are required to be "individuals who, by reason of their occupational or other experience, scientific expertise, or training, or knowledgeable regarding the conservation and management, or the commercial or recreational harvest, of the fishery resources of the geographical area concerned." 16 U.S.C. § 1852(b)(2)(A).

In practice, more than 80 percent of appointed members since 1976 have been representatives of various sectors of the fishing industry: captains, lobbyists for commercial fisheries trade associations, recreational fishermen, even owners of food processing compa-nies. This number reflects the fact that only the indus-try has the resources and degree of incentive to lobby state governors for inclusion on the critical nomination lists. Studies have shown that more than half of all appointed members have direct financial interest in

> Each council consists of voting members and nonvoting members. The nonvoting mem-bers include: (i) a NOAA designee, usually the regional administrator; (ii) a state fisher-ies administrator from each of the states with membership in the council; and (iii) at-large members representing some mix of representa-tives nominated by the governors.

the fisheries they are charged with regulating. This would be a big problem under federal conflict of interest rules, but Congress specifically exempted the councils from these rules under the Act.

The Act gives NOAA the authority to review council FMPs and annual specifica-tions, but not the authority to substitute its judgment for that of the councils. In other words, NOAA reviews the plans for consistency with the Act, but must send noncom-pliant plans back to the council for the council to change. Meanwhile, the previous plan remains in effect. In practice, FMPs are very rarely disapproved at the federal level.

The following case was highly complex and involved many parties, many of whom made motions and counter-motions. The excerpt here involved a motion for summary judgment by the Trawlers' Survival Fund (TSF), a fishermen's organization, challenging proposed Amendment 13 to the New England groundfish plan because they believed it to be too stringent. The following excerpt involves the fund's claim that NMFS was acting outside of its authority and attempting to usurp the regulatory prerogative given by the Act to the New England Fishery Management Council.

Oceana v. Evans

2005 WL 555416 (D.D.C. Mar. 9, 2005)

Judge HUVELLE issued the memorandum opinion of the United States District Court, District of Columbia.

Plaintiff relies on the legal principle that the Secretary has only limited pow-ers in reviewing a Council's recommendations: he may only approve, disapprove, or partially approve an Amendment, and any disapproval or partial approval must be based on an identified inconsistency with governing law, including the ten National Standards....

***

The TSF alleges that the Secretary acted illegally in promulgating 50 C.F.R. § 648.85(a)(2)(i)(D), which authorizes the NMFS Regional Administrator to implement the [Trans-Boundary Management Guidance Committee]'s recommended hard TACs in the event that they differ from those recommended by the Council. TSF argues that this measure was not a part of Amendment 13, and its promulgation was therefore not authorized by the [Magnuson-Stevens Act] and thus *ultra vires* because the power it purports to confer "eschew[s] legally-mandated processes for approving or disapproving Council regulations."

TSF's objection is well taken.... In effect, the challenged regulation allows the Secretary to do an end run around the Council. It provides that "[i]f the recommendation of the Council is not consistent with the recommendation of the [Trans-Boundary Management Guidance Committee], the Regional Administrator may select either the recommendation of the [Trans-Boundary Management Guidance Committee], or the Council." The plain language of the regulation is clearly inconsistent with Amendment 13.

In response, defendants argue that the Secretary has broad authority to promulgate regulations in order to effectuate a FMP.... Although it is indisputable that the Secretary has "general responsibility to carry out" Amendment 13 and that he may "promulgate such regulations, in accordance with [the Administrative Procedure Act], as may be necessary to discharge such responsibility," 16 U.S.C. § 1855(d), his powers are limited. "The [Magnuson-Stevens Act] is clear that when the Secretary is presented with proposed amendments and regulations, he does not have the independent authority to, *sua sponte*, add a regulation that is inconsistent with the proposal from the Council." In particular, although the Secretary has broad authority to implement a FMP, he may not deviate from a council's recommendation except as provided by statute. He may only "approve, disapprove, or partially approve a plan or amendment," 16 U.S.C. § 1854(a)(3), and where he takes any action other than to fully approve a plan or amendment, he must give the council written notice of his action, as well as state the legal flaw in the council's proposal and recommend corrective action to the council. *Id.* In short, the more specific terms of § 1854 serve as a limit on the Secretary's broad regulatory powers described in § 1855.

In this case, the Secretary never gave notice that he was deviating from Amendment 13's recommendation that the Council must assent to [Trans-Boundary Management Guidance Committee]'s annual TAC proposals before they could be implemented by the Secretary.... In light of the Secretary's improper substitution of his own recommendation in place of the Council's, the Court is constrained to hold that the third sentence of 50 C.F.R. § 648.85(a)(2)(i)(D) was adopted in violation of the [Magnuson-Stevens Act] and therefore cannot be enforced.

Therefore, the Court grants summary judgment in favor of TSF....

points for discussion

1. *Default positions.* What is the effect of only giving NMFS a mostly up-or-down approval authority? Does this up-or-down authority improve or detract from effective fishery management?

2. *Political economy.* "Regulatory capture" theory posits that sometimes (maybe quite often) regulatory agencies become "captured" by the industries they regulate, in that the industries get to have too much influence over the regulations that affect them. Some back-and-forth and give-and-take is not only inevitable — regulatory officials may spend most of their time dealing with people in the regulated industries, giving rise to some natural kinship — but also desirable. Agencies often *need* information possessed only by the industry. Moreover, regulated industries are more likely to comply with rules in which they have had some say.

   Regulatory capture in fisheries regulation, however, is more problematic. A bias toward catching more fish than is sustainable is a recipe for long-term disaster, which has never seemed to be much of a deterrent for fishermen. A study published in 2010 showed that the state representatives on regional FMCs have indeed tended to vote in a manner that suggests they are unduly influenced by commercial or recreational fishing interests. This was not true of the federal representatives. *See* Craig W. Thomas et al., *Special Interest Capture of Regulatory Agencies: A Ten-Year Analysis of Voting Behavior on Regional Fishery Management Councils*, 38 Pol'y Stud. J. 447 (2010).

   It has been suggested that one source of this pro-overfishing bias stems from the dual mandate of regional FMCs of conservation and allocation of fishing rights. The painful task of allocating fishing rights creates an incentive to make the task less painful by increasing the catch, so that a larger overall pie can be allocated. *See* Josh Eagle et al., Taking Stock of the Regional Fishery Management Councils (2003).

E. RECREATIONAL FISHING

Fishery conservation efforts have traditionally been focused on commercial fishermen and not as much on recreational fishermen. There are some historical reasons for this orientation: In 1970, the old Bureau of Sportsfisheries and Wildlife were merged into the newly created and commercially focused NMFS, in which it lost much standing and independence. There are also good ecological reasons for this orientation: Commercial fishermen catch much more fish, and their fishing methods — driftnetting, bottom trawling, and purse seining — are much more damaging than recreational methods, which are typically still hook-and-line. In fact, recreational fishermen can often be heard to complain about lax regulation of commercial fishing that they believe harms stocks in a way that recreational fishing cannot. There are also some economic reasons for regulating recreational fishermen less stringently: While recreational fishermen may catch fewer fish than their commercial counterparts, each fish is much more valuable in the context of recreational fishing. Examine Table 2. "Value" can be an elusive concept, but this table adopts two reliable measures. For commercial fishermen, the value of their catch is their revenue, the amount of money they receive for their catch. Recreational fishermen don't sell their catch, of course, but the amount of money they *spend* on their experience is one measure of their value. Actually, considering how much enthusiasm recreational fishermen often have for their avocation, they may place a much *higher* value on the recreational fishing experience than the figures in Table 2 indicate. But that consumer surplus — the excess value consumers have over and above the price of recreational fishing — cannot be easily measured.

Table 2. Regional Fisheries Management Councils

Regional Fisheries Management Council	States & Territories	Commercial Landings Revenue (in $million)	Recreational Fishing Expenditures (in $million)
New England	ME, NH, MA, RI, CT	953	1,874
Gulf	TX, LA, MS, AL, FL	674	16,177
Pacific	OR, WA, CA, ID	472	4,637
North Pacific	OR, WA, AK	1,400	499
Mid-Atlantic	NY, NJ, DE, PA, MD, VA, NC	362	4,616
South Atlantic	NC, SC, GA, FL	141	10,481
Caribbean	Virgin Islands, Puerto Rico	No data	No data
Western Pacific	HI, Samoa, Guam, Marianas	66	750

Adapted from Craig W. Thomas et al., *Special Interest Capture of Regulatory Agencies: A Ten-Year Analysis of Voting Behavior on Regional Fishery Management Councils*, 38 Pol'y Stud. J. 447 (2010).

Excluding Caribbean fisheries, the value of recreational fisheries is generally an order of magnitude greater than the value of commercial catch. If the third and fourth columns were totaled up, the national total value of commercial catch would be about $4 billion, and the total amount spent nationally on recreational fishing would be about $39 billion. In the Gulf of Mexico, the value of recreational fishing is *23 times* that of the commercial catch. But that means that recreational fishing is big business, and it turns out that the scale of recreational fishing means that it has the potential to overfish stocks and cause other forms of ecological harm.

Recreational fishermen sometimes complain that they compete for fish with a commercial fishing fleet that faces lax regulation, but recreational fishermen create their own ecological problems. A major problem with recreational fishing is the lack of counting and monitoring. While observer and electronic monitoring programs and fish distributors help ensure that commercial fish are counted, few such mechanisms exist to ensure that recreationally caught fish are counted, or that recreational practices are monitored. Recreational fishing is too dispersed for reliable counting and monitoring. NMFS relies mostly on telephone interviews and dockside inspections for its information.

One fishery in which commercial and recreational fishermen have clashed is the Gulf of Mexico red snapper fishery.

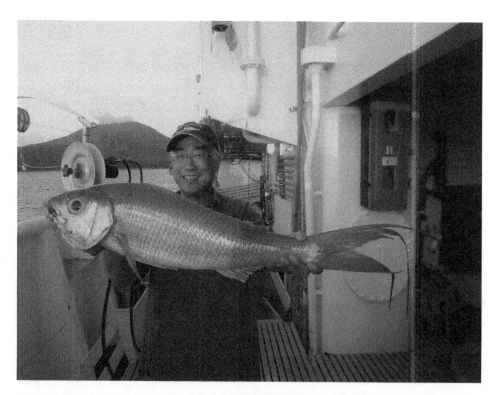

Figure 2-17. NOAA Fisherman with a Red Snapper

Guindon v. Pritzker

31 F. Supp. 3d 169 (D.D.C. 2014)

Judge ROTHSTEIN delivered the opinion of the United States District Court, District of Columbia.

This case concerns management of the red snapper fishery in the Gulf of Mexico. . . . Plaintiffs are commercial fishermen challenging three NMFS regulations that set quotas and fishing season lengths for the recreational sector of the fishery. Plaintiffs bring claims under the Magnuson-Stevens Fishery Conservation and Management Act ("MSA"), the Administrative Procedures Act ("APA"), and the National Environmental Policy Act ("NEPA"). [T]he Court grants Plaintiffs' Motion for Summary Judgment and denies Defendants' and Defendant-Intervenor's cross-motions.

***

Section 407(d), [a Magnuson-Stevens Act] provision specific to the Gulf of Mexico red snapper fishery, requires that any [Fisheries Management Plan], FMP amendment, or implementing regulation must contain conservation and management measures that "establish separate quotas for recreational fishing . . . and commercial fishing that, when reached, result in a prohibition on the retention of fish caught during recreational fishing and commercial fishing, respectively, for the remainder of the fishing year."

***

B. Management of the Gulf of Mexico Red Snapper Fishery

1. How NMFS Establishes Quotas and Sets Season Length

Each year, before the red snapper season begins, the Council receives a recommendation as to that year's Acceptable Biological Catch from the Council's Scientific and Statistical Committee (SSC). The Council then proposes to NMFS a red snapper "quota" for the year. The recommended quota is intended to serve as the total [annual catch limit (ACL)] for red snapper in the Gulf of Mexico fishery. Because the quotas include fish harvested in adjoining state waters, NMFS must take those state harvests into account in managing the Gulf of Mexico red snapper fishery. Pursuant to Section 407(d) of the [Magnuson-Stevens Act], the fishery is subdivided into recreational and commercial sectors, with separate quotas for each. Thus, the Council will also specify the allocation of the total quota between the commercial and recreational sectors. Currently, the FMP specifies that the commercial sector receives 51 percent of the quota and the recreational sector receives 49 percent.

NMFS manages the commercial and recreational sectors differently. In the commercial sector, each participant receives an Individual Fishing Quota ("IFQ"), which entitles that participant to a fixed, specific portion of the annual commercial catch. Commercial vessels must install geographical monitoring systems and may only sell their catch to authorized dealers. Since 2007, these management measures have assured that the commercial sector does not exceed its quota. In fact, as the 2010 Amendment to the Reef Fish FMP observed, "there is no possibility of a quota overrun for the commercial sector."

By contrast, NMFS manages the recreational sector using only size limits, bag limits, and length of season. The only [Accountability Measures] currently in place for the recreational sector is in-season closure of the fishery. NMFS estimates in advance how long it will take for the recreational sector to harvest its quota, based on historical data, then sets the season length according to that projection.

The primary data source for estimating recreational "landings" (total weight of red snapper caught) is the Marine Recreational Information Program (MRIP). NMFS implemented MRIP several years ago in an effort to improve the quality of the agency's landings estimates. MRIP data are collected in two-month "waves," with data available 45 days after the wave ends. MRIP produces an estimate of red snapper landings through a combination of "dockside intercepts" (referred to as "landings data") and phone surveys (referred to as "effort data").

The dockside intercept program, known as the Access Point Angler Intercept Survey (APAIS), involves communicating with recreational fishermen when they return from fishing trips. Of particular relevance to this case is an alteration to the APAIS sampling design that NMFS made in March 2013. The change allowed NMFS to capture data from fishing trips at time intervals during the day that the agency had not previously sampled.

2. Recent History of Recreational Sector Management

Red snapper stock is managed under the Reef Fish Fishery Management Plan ("Reef Fish FMP"), first implemented by the Secretary in 1984. At that time the agency had already observed declines in the adult population of red snapper. The Council first amended the Reef Fish FMP in 1990 ("Amendment 1"), with the goal of stabilizing long-term population levels by 2000. Red snapper is currently designated as "overfished," and is subject to a rebuilding plan. Over time NMFS has extended the target date to complete rebuilding of the stock. Currently the target is 2032.

Amendment 1 to the Reef Fish FMP required that the annual catch be allocated between recreational and commercial sectors based on historical percentages. The regulations implementing Amendment 1 set the allocation at 51 percent commercial and 49 recreational, an allocation that survives to the present.

Prior to 1997, the Secretary permitted recreational red snapper fishing year-round, with catch levels constrained only by bag and size limits. From 1997 to 1999, NMFS used in-season monitoring, along with data from prior seasons, to project when the quota would be reached and when to close the season. "In-season monitoring" meant that, during the fishing season, an NMFS "quota monitoring team" tracked available landings data and combined that data with past patterns to project when recreational sector would reach its quota. The agency would announce the closure date several weeks in advance.

For the 2000 season NMFS abandoned its in-season quota monitoring operation and began setting fixed season lengths in advance, based only on projections of when the quota would be reached. . . . [R]ecreational landings exceeded the quota in some years and fell below in others.

In 2008, the Council amended the Reef Fish FMP with the goals of ending red snapper overfishing by 2009 or 2010 and rebuilding the stock by 2032. To that end, the Council prohibited fishing from January 1 to May 31 and from October 1 to December 31. This meant that NMFS could not open the season until June 1, and could not keep it open past September 30. The recreational quota for the 2008 season was reduced to 2.45 million pounds. NMFS set a 66-day season for 2008, closing August 5 rather than September 30. . . . Even so, recreational landings exceeded the 2008 quota by 1.26 million pounds, or about 51 percent.

For 2009, with the same recreational quota of 2.45 million pounds, NMFS set the season at 75 days. The recreational landings exceeded the quota by 2.175 million pounds, or about 88 percent. For 2010 NMFS raised the recreational quota to 3.403 million pounds, and set the season at 53 days. The Deep Water Horizon spill cut the season short.

NMFS set the 2011 recreational quota at 3.521 million pounds, and projected a 48-day season on the basis of that quota. After the season ended, but before NMFS had received preliminary landings estimates, the Council authorized raising the recreational quota by 0.345 million pounds and suggested reopening the season in the fall. NMFS adopted the Council's recommended quota increase. However, preliminary June and July landings estimates indicated that recreational landings had exceeded not only the original quota but also the newly increased quota. For that reason, NMFS did not reopen the 2011 season. The final estimates revealed that recreational landings exceeded the 2011 quota by 734,000 pounds. . . . The 2012 recreational quota was set at 3.959 million pounds. . . . The 2012 recreational landings exceeded the quota by 1.187 million pounds, or about 30 percent.

C. The Challenged Agency Actions

A 2012 regulatory amendment to the Reef Fish FMP set total quotas for both 2012 and 2013. The total quota for 2013, including commercial and recreational, was set at 8.69 million pounds, an increase over 2012. The 2012 FMP amendment specifically stated that the 2013 quota increase was contingent on the acceptable biological catch not being exceeded in 2012, and provided that "[i]f NMFS determines the 2012 Acceptable Biological Catch is exceeded, NMFS will maintain the 2012 commercial and recreational quotas in the 2013 fishing year."

As discussed above, the recreational sector did exceed its quota in 2012, by 1.187 million pounds. The Council's [Scientific and Statistical Committee (SSC)] nevertheless set the 2013 Acceptable Biological Catch at 8.46 million pounds, rather than at the 2012 quota level (8.08 million)....

The Council met in February 2013 to consider the SSC's recommendations.... The Council cited preliminary data indicating that the recreational sector had exceeded the 2012 quota of 3.959 million pounds by over a million. Three quota alternatives for 2013 were considered: (1) no action (*i.e.*, leaving the 2013 quota at 2012 levels), (2) setting the quota at the level of the 2013 Acceptable Biological Catch (8.46 million pounds), and (3) implementing a 20 percent buffer for the recreational sector. The Council chose the second alternative, recommending a quota of 8.46 million pounds, equal to the Acceptable Biological Catch, with no buffer. Though, as the Council recognized, this was "not as biologically conservative" as the buffer alternative, the Council observed that it "ha[d] managed the recreational red snapper sector based on the Acceptable Biological Catch for several years."

***

A new stock assessment arrived in May of 2013, as anticipated. The SSC reviewed the stock assessment and determined that the Acceptable Biological Catch for 2013 could be increased to 13.5 million pounds total, as long as it fell to 11.9 and 10.6 million pounds in 2014 and 2015, respectively. Because the Acceptable Biological Catch was set very close to the overfishing limit (OFL), with only a small affordance for scientific uncertainty, the SSC also recommended a 20 percent buffer to account for management uncertainty.

The full Council did not meet until July 2013, after the 28-day June fishing season had closed. The Council published another framework action (the "July Framework Action") recommending that NMFS set the 2013 quota below the Acceptable Biological Catch, at 11 million pounds rather than 13.5 million pounds, in order to achieve a "constant catch" in 2014 and 2015. The Council determined that setting the 2013 quota at 11 million pounds would reduce the likelihood that NMFS would have to decrease quotas in 2014 and 2015.

The Council also suggested reopening the season in the fall to allow for harvesting of the additional quota amount, but only contingent upon there being unused quota available.... Though the Council considered the SSC's suggestion of a 20 percent buffer, it did not adopt the proposed buffer. The Council explained that the distance between the Acceptable Biological Catch (13.5 million) and the 2013 quota (11 million), which the Council recommended in order to achieve a constant catch through 2013, 2014, and 2015, would also function as a "de facto buffer" against overages in the recreational sector....

***

On August 14, 2013, NMFS published a Notice of Proposed Rulemaking, describing the proposal to increase the 2013 quota to 11 million pounds total.... In late August, NMFS received the June 2013 landings estimates. As it turned out, MRIP landings estimates indicated that recreational fishermen actually caught 6.13 million pounds of red snapper during the June 2013 season. This exceeded NMFS's estimate of what would be caught during the 28-day June season by 1.985 million pounds. . . .

A question emerged as to the cause of the large overage. Ned Cyr, the Director of the NMFS Office of Science and Technology (OST), analyzed the MRIP landings estimates to determine why they were "higher than anticipated." Cyr noted as a possible cause that NMFS had recently implemented several improvements to the MRIP sampling methodology, specifically the change to APAIS sampling design. OST analyzed whether any of the 2 million pound overage "could be attributable to any changes in the sampling design." The analysis indicated that "sampling under the new design was capturing charter and private boat angler fishing trips in time intervals that had no sampled trips in the previous years." In other words, the staff conducting dockside interviews had reached fishermen at new times of day. This "raised concern that the improved temporal coverage may have been partly responsible for the big increase in red snapper catch, especially if trips returning in these previously uncovered time intervals tended to be more directed to offshore fishing and red snapper."

***

On September 18, 2013, NMFS published a final rule (the "September Final Rule") increasing the 2013 quota to 11 million pounds and setting a 14-day fall fishing season. The final rule describes the June 2013 landings estimates as "unexpectedly high relative to previous years." NMFS stated that "[i]t is misleading to make a direct comparison between these numbers, however, because if the new MRIP methodology had been available to use in the 2013 stock assessment on which the current Acceptable Biological Catches and quotas are based, then the original quotas may have been set much higher." The September Final Rule includes NMFS's conclusion that "the best scientific information available to determine landings during the June season is the projection used to set the season length."

***

1. NMFS Failed to Prohibit the Retention of Fish After the Recreational Quota Had Been Reached, in violation of Section 407(d)

Section 407(d) requires NMFS to "establish . . . quotas for recreational fishing . . . that, when reached, result in a prohibition on the retention of fish . . . for the remainder of the fishing year."[] The provision's first clause imposes on NMFS an obligation to "establish a quota," and the second clause essentially explains how the quota must function — *i.e.,* to "result in a prohibition on the retention of fish." Thus, the Court concludes that under Section 407(d), NMFS must close the season, and may not reopen it, whenever the agency determines that the quota has been reached. The Court will also presume that NMFS has complied with the statute if it implements some effective mechanism to prohibit the retention of fish above the quota. This might include setting a season length in advance based on a projection of when the quota will be met, but such a projection must be accurate and conservative enough to effectively accomplish the statutory mandate.

Plaintiffs claim that NMFS violated Section 407(d) by approving a 28-day season based on a "flawed projection model," without adequate accountability measures, and by reopening the season in the fall when the recreational quota had already been reached and exceeded. NMFS contends that its method of complying with Section 407(d) was, and has been, to project when the quota will be met and set the length of the fishing season accordingly. . . .

The Court agrees with Plaintiffs that NMFS violated Section 407(d) in setting the June 2013 season, and in reopening the recreational fishing season in the fall. If NMFS's estimates in previous years had come at all close to accurately predicting recreational landings, or if NMFS had some credible reason to believe that 2013 would be different, the Court might have been limited to sympathizing with Plaintiffs' frustrations at watching an agency fail to accomplish a statutory mandate. But by 2013 at least, if not sooner, the agency had experienced many years of recreational overage, and possessed several remedial tools to effectuate its statutory responsibility. At a certain point NMFS was obligated to acknowledge that its strategy of incrementally shortening the season was not working. Administrative discretion is not a license to engage in Einstein's definition of folly—doing the same thing over and over again and expecting a different result. Section 407(d) required NMFS to implement management measures with a fighting chance of "result[ing] in a prohibition on the retention of fish"—be that a buffer, a dramatically shortened season, or some other strategy. Failing to do so was arbitrary and capricious.

The agency's conduct in reopening the fishing season in fall 2013 was yet more egregious. To summarize the sequence of events: (1) in July 2013, the Council proposed increasing the 2013 quota and suggested reopening the season in the fall, contingent on there being unused quota available; (2) in early August, NMFS published a proposal discussing the possibility of reopening the season, contingent on available quota; (3) in late August, NMFS received MRIP landings estimates indicating an overage that exceeded both the current and proposed quota; (4) NMFS reopened the fall season anyway.

In July 2013, when the Council authorized reopening the season in the fall, it did so "contingent upon there being unused quota available," and observed that "[b]ecause of the potential for a quota overage during the June season, the full amount of a quota increase may not be available." The Council intended the length of the reopened season to be "based on the landings from the June season subtracted from the total recreational quota (original quota plus increase)." In fact, the Council expected the break in time caused by the split season to "result in more accurate projections for 2013," because NMFS could "better determine how much quota is available before setting the closing date for the supplemental season." The Council also specifically noted in the July Framework Action that "the system for collecting recreational data has improved." All this suggests that the Council expected NMFS to use the June 2013 MRIP landings estimate, or at least some estimate based on recreational data from the 2013 season, when deciding whether to reopen.

In August 2013, NMFS proposed increasing the recreational quota from 4.145 to 5.39 million pounds, with a possible supplemental season contingent on the availability of additional quota "after the June landings are known." Then NMFS received the June landings estimate of 6.13 million pounds, which exceeded the quota then in effect by 2 million pounds, or about 48 percent. It also exceeded the proposed 5.39 million quota by over 700,000 pounds.

At that point the agency changed course. NMFS characterized the 48 percent overage as "unexpectedly high relative to previous years," though in the previous five years the average overage was 42 percent. OST was asked to explore the effect of sampling design on the MRIP landings estimates, but found no indication that the massive overage occurred as a result of those design changes. Despite OST's "inconclusive" finding, NMFS declared the 2013 MRIP landings estimates "non-comparable" to the 2013 quota. The agency then determined that, according to the "best scientific information available," the recreational sector caught exactly what the agency expected it would catch during the 28-day June season, *i.e.* 4.145 million pounds. This allowed NMFS to reopen the fishing season in the fall.

The agency's decision makes very little sense. NMFS decided to reopen the season without accounting in any way for the possibility that *some,* if not most or all, of the estimated overage was due to fishing effort. Assuming that the recreational sector caught exactly what the agency predicted it would, despite "more accurate" evidence of a massive overage — was a glaring dismissal of the "relevant factors," and a "clear error of judgment." [R]eopening the season was arbitrary and capricious.

NMFS attempted to justify its action by explaining that "if the new MRIP methodology had been available to use in the 2013 stock assessment on which the current Acceptable Biological Catchs and quotas are based, then the original quotas may have been set much higher." In other words, NMFS disregarded the 2013 MRIP landings estimates not because they were inaccurate but because they raised the possibility that NMFS had set the prior quotas unnecessarily and unfairly low. It is not clear to the Court why the possibility of unfairness in prior quotas, or even in a current quota, would justify disregarding accurate and reliable information. NMFS never revised or disavowed those earlier quotas. Instead it chose to adopt a landings estimate that it knew to be inaccurate, apparently to avoid punishing fishermen who might have been permitted to catch more under a hypothetical prior quota.

2. NMFS Failed to Use the Best Scientific Information Available, in Violation of National Standard 2

NMFS's dismissal of the 2013 MRIP landings estimates also violated National Standard 2, which requires NMFS to base all conservation and management measures on the "best scientific information available." National Standard 2 obligates NMFS to make "a thorough review of all the relevant information available at the time." NMFS may not "disregard superior data in reaching its conclusion." Challenges brought under National Standard 2 will normally fail, unless there is "some indication that superior or contrary data was available and that the agency ignored such information."

"Superior or contrary data" is precisely what NMFS ignored in promulgating the September Final Rule. NMFS conceded in the Rule itself that the June 2013 landings estimates were "more accurate and less biased than those produced in past years." Though NMFS insists that it never ignored that data, merely tabled it for further evaluation, the record demonstrates that the agency disregarded the estimate entirely in formulating the September Final Rule. Faced with reliable data as to how many fish were landed in the recreational sector, NMFS did not even factor the possibility of a massive overage into its decision to reopen the fall season.

NMFS scientists made clear that they could not attribute the "unexpectedly high" landings to differences in sampling methodology. Even the Director of NMFS's Southeast Fisheries Science Center, who originally deemed the 2013 MRIP estimates "non-comparable," still recognized the uncertainty concerning what was actually caught in June 2013 and recommended that such uncertainty "should be factored into decisions about season length for the fall season." NMFS nevertheless reopened the season, as if there remained any possibility that the recreational sector had actually landed only 4.145 million pounds of red snapper. This is a quintessential example of ignoring "superior or contrary data."

***

Conclusion

For the reasons given above, the Court finds that the May Final Rule, June Temporary Rule, and September Final Rule were arbitrary and capricious and not in accordance with the [Magnuson-Stevens Act]. Under the [Magnuson-Stevens Act], NMFS has a statutory duty to: prohibit the retention of fish after quotas are reached in the Gulf of Mexico red snapper fishery; use the best scientific information available when making management decisions; require whatever accountability measures are necessary to constrain catch to the quota; avoid decisions that directly conflict with the FMP's allocation of catch; and, where sectors are managed separately, avoid penalizing one sector for overages that occur only in another.

points for discussion

1. *Casting blame.* This case is somewhat unusual in that it is the commercial fishermen who are complaining that recreational fishermen are overfishing and depleting the stock. As noted above, it is usually the other way around. In a part of the case not excerpted above, the court ruled that the behavior of the council, enabling the constant overfishing in the recreational sector to the detriment of the commercial sector, violated both § 304(b) of the Act as well as national standard 4 (§ 301(a)(4)):

   > Plaintiffs argue that NMFS violated Section 304(b) by creating a "de facto reallocation" of quota from the commercial to the recreational sector, such that the actual allocation of quota did not reflect the 51/49 split established in the FMP. NMFS contests Plaintiffs' statement that the agency has accomplished a "*de facto* reallocation," emphasizing the agency's shortening of the fishing season in recent years. NMFS seems to argue that as long as the 51/49 split remained on paper, and the agency did *something* to carry it out, there could not be a "de facto reallocation." The Court views this contention with some skepticism. ... . NMFS essentially guaranteed that the actual catch allocation would skew widely from the 51/49 allocation, as indeed it did. This violated Section 304(b). . . . Plaintiffs also claim that the "de facto reallocation" runs afoul of National Standard 4, which provides that allocation of fishing privileges must be fair and equitable to all fishermen, and reasonably calculated to promote conservation. . . . When an agency blinds itself to the high likelihood that its actions will cause overharvesting, the Court cannot characterize those actions as "reasonably calculated to promote conservation." For that reason, the September Rule, at least, violates National Standard 4.

   The opinion in this case was an unusually sharp rebuke to the council for its management of the red snapper fishery. Why do you think the council enabled recreational overfishing so persistently? Was it favoritism toward recreational fishermen? Why would that be?

2. *The facts.* Even better than Judge Rothstein's compelling narrative account of the history of the red snapper fishery, Table 3, excerpted from a 2015 report by the Gulf of Mexico Fishery Management Council and NOAA, makes clear just how habitual and severe was recreational overfishing for red snapper. Two things to note as background: First, the Deepwater Horizon spill occurred in 2010, which resulted in closure of the fishery. Second, remember that the commercial sector went under an IFQ system in 2007.

   Why do you think it was so difficult to both measure recreational landings and to enforce limits? How might you design a scheme to avoid these recurring recreational overages? How might you try to accommodate the interests of the recreational fishing industry? What do you think recreational fishing interests would value?

Table 3. Red snapper landings and overage/underage by sector, 1986-2014. Landings are in mpww. Commercial quotas began in 1990. Recreational allocations began in 1991 and recreational quotas began in 1997.

Year	Recreational			Commercial		
	Alloc. Quota	Actual Landings	Difference	Quota	Actual Landings	Difference
1986	na	2.770	na	na	3.700	na
1987	na	1.814	na	na	3.069	na
1988	na	2.568	na	na	3.960	na
1989	na	2.656	na	na	3.098	na
1990	na	1.614	na	3.1	2.650	−0.450
1991	1.96	2.917	+0.957	2.04	2.213	+0.173
1992	1.96	4.618	+2.658	2.04	3.106	+1.066
1993	2.94	7.161	+4.221	3.06	3.374	+0.314
1994	2.94	6.076	+3.136	3.06	3.222	+0.162
1995	2.94	5.464	+2.524	3.06	2.934	−0.126
1996	4.47	5.339	+0.869	4.65	4.313	−0.337
1997	4.47	6.804	+2.334	4.65	4.810	+0.160
1998	4.47	4.854	+0.384	4.65	4.680	+0.030
1999	4.47	4.972	+0.502	4.65	4.876	+0.226
2000	4.47	4.750	+0.280	4.65	4.837	+0.187
2001	4.47	5.252	+0.782	4.65	4.625	−0.025
2002	4.47	6.535	+2.065	4.65	4.779	+0.129
2003	4.47	6.105	+1.635	4.65	4.409	−0.241
2004	4.47	6.460	+1.990	4.65	4.651	+0.001
2005	4.47	4.676	+0.206	4.65	4.096	−0.554
2006	4.47	4.131	−0.339	4.65	4.649	−0.001
2007	3.185	5.809	+2.624	3.315	3.153	−0.162
2008	2.45	4.056	+1.606	2.55	2.461	−0.089
2009	2.45	5.597	+3.147	2.55	2.461	−0.089
2010	3.403	2.651	−0.752	3.542	3.362	−0.180
2011	3.866	6.734	+2.868	3.664	3.562	−0.102
2012	3.959	7.524	+3.565	4.121	4.000	−0.121
2013	5.390	9.639	+4.249	5.610	5.399	−0.211
2014	5.390 4.312 ACT	3.896	−1.494	5.610	5.568	−0.042

Excerpted from NOAA, 2015 RED SNAPPER FRAMEWORK FOR ACTION (2014).

3. *The function of national standard 2.* Is the "best available science" mandate only as good as the councils or the NMFS are willing to abide by it? Are "outside" parties, such as environmental groups, to participate meaningfully?

4. *Reasonable horizons.* Is recovery by 2032 ambitious enough? Is it the prevention of "overfishing" to set a recovery plan 17 years into the future?

Monitoring commercial catch of red snapper is manageable: Selling it to fish markets requires documentation, including possession of the required quota, precluding much of the illegal fishing that plagues some other fisheries. However, monitoring recreational fishing of red snapper is much more difficult. Recreational fishermen do not sell their catch, and cannot be logistically required to hold quota, given their large numbers and disparate sailings. Impromptu dockside inspections by wildlife officials is the main deterrent, but also a key data collection tool. Dockside inspections are a statistical sampling, which can be used to infer recreational catches in other places and other times. Dockside inspections dropped precipitously as funding was severely cut, undermining not only the data quality but also the deterrent effect. One method employed to compensate for fewer inspections was supplementing of inspection data with phone survey data. The statistical methods to extrapolate from relatively little data can be quite complex, and part of what caught the regional fishery management council off-guard was the result of the sampling. Clearly, however, funding for enforcement and monitoring is a key ingredient in monitoring fishing and estimating stock populations.

F. AREA-BASED REGULATION OF OCEAN USE

With some exceptions, federal ocean law currently works by regulating particular activities, such as summer flounder fishing or oil extraction, without regard for where they occur. This is an understandable approach from the legal standpoint, as legal rules and institutions seem familiar when they focus on a single kind of behavior. But as you have learned from this chapter, these laws do not generally provide effective protections. Fish, sea turtles, marine mammals, and other living organisms of the oceans are all parts of much larger and complex ecosystems, so protecting an individual species from harmful or excessive practices may not save it from severe harm and population crashes. Moreover, regulating certain behavior may neglect regulation of other behaviors that may indirectly harm individual fish species, as in the example of bycatch.

An alternative approach is to set aside *areas* in which an entire suite of harmful behaviors is prohibited, for the purpose of conservation. This was an approach championed by some conservationists and marine scientists in the 1990s to better protect wildlife and ocean habitat. They advocated for the creation of "marine reserves," areas in which activities harmful to fish and other living organisms would be prohibited. This was the beginning of a new approach to marine conservation.

Marine reserves are areas of the sea where all extractive uses—including fishing and mineral development—are prohibited by law. From a conservation viewpoint, marine reserves could provide several benefits that would help ensure the success of fisheries management. First, reserves would increase fish populations by protecting areas of important, rare, or sensitive fish habitat from human impacts. Improved habitat means better feeding and breeding environments that, obviously, will improve the condition of populations, especially those populations that require rare or very specific feeding and breeding conditions. Second, reserves would increase populations by giving fish a safe haven, a break from fishing pressure. Havens work particularly well where the species of concern are not migratory. Third, reserves would provide an insurance policy against mistakes made by fisheries management agencies in the other parts of the sea. Even if a fisheries management plan incorporated a dreadful mistake in overestimating a fish population, a marine reserve could provide a refuge to allow a stock to recover. Importantly, scientists emphasize the benefits of marine reserves for fishermen, pointing out that reserves would have spillover effects by producing fish that could be caught outside the reserves.

"Marine reserve" is not a term with legal significance, but a category. It is an area in which extractive uses are prohibited for the purpose of conservation. An example of a marine reserve is Biscayne National Park, an area of ocean off the coast of Florida that, like other national parks, is reserved for conservation and recreation. Other National Park Service units, such as Cumberland Island National Seashore in Georgia, include within their boundaries oceanic waters. Marine reserves make up about 3 percent of all U.S. waters.

A related, less ambitious concept is that of "marine protected areas," which might not ban all extractive uses. A marine protected area is just an area with different rules than its surrounding area. For example, fishing in a marine protected area could just be an area in which certain fishing gear is banned. By Executive Order 13,158, President Clinton directed the Departments of Interior and Commerce to develop a process for identifying and monitoring marine protected areas. The executive order describes marine protected areas as ". . . any area of the marine environment that has been reserved by federal, state, territorial, tribal, or local laws or regulations to provide lasting protection for part or all of the natural and cultural resources therein."

The fishing industries as well as the regional fishery management councils constituted under the Magnuson-Stevens Act have strongly opposed the creation of marine reserves and even areas that might be recognized as marine protected areas. For fishing industries, the argument that such areas might protect fish populations for more sustained fishing was evidently unpersuasive. For regional fishery management councils, it represented potential encroachment on their regulatory domain. California passed its own state law for establishing marine reserves, the 1999 California Marine Life Protection Act, which authorized the creation of reserves as well as areas where some fishing would be allowed. But fishing groups mounted substantial opposition, delaying implementation of the law by ten years. Scientists and marine conservation groups had underestimated the combined political strength of the fishing industries.

In addition to state law, like California's, marine reserves and marine protected areas are created under a variety of federal statutes. The Magnuson-Stevens Act authorizes the imposition of a variety of restrictions that offer varying levels of protection to fish and other living organisms. The National Park Service Organic Act allows for the establishment of marine national parks. Two federal statutes are noteworthy for their role in the creation of marine reserves and marine protected areas.

1. National Marine Sanctuaries

The 1972 National Marine Sanctuary Act creates a legal framework for establishing a wide range of marine protected areas. The Act authorizes the Secretary of Commerce to designate an area a national marine sanctuary if the area is

> of special national significance due to its conservation, recreational, ecological, historical, scientific, cultural, archaeological, educational, or esthetic qualities, the communities of living marine resources it harbors; or its resource or human-use values.

16 U.S.C. § 1433(a).

Each of the 13 national marine sanctuaries is unique, and each has its own management plan and sanctuary-specific regulations. National marine sanctuaries may permit extractive activities such as commercial fishing and mineral leasing, but require that they be permitted for a maximum of five years and "compatible with the purposes for which the sanctuary is designated and with protection of sanctuary resources." 16 U.S.C. § 1441(c)(1). Some sanctuaries allow fishing and mineral extraction, others not at all.

The broad discretion granted to the Secretary of Commerce through the NOAA has led to a fairly passive administration of the national marine sanctuaries. Wary of encroaching upon the domain of regional fishery management councils, the NOAA has left most of the fisheries management contained within the sanctuaries under council management. Even with the considerable permissiveness with which NOAA manages national marine sanctuaries, the political opposition is vigorous, and few sanctuaries have been created since the 1980s.

2. The Antiquities Act

The Antiquities Act is better known for its controversial applications on federal public lands, where national monuments have been designated by presidents without the need for congressional consultation. Presidents Bill Clinton, George W. Bush, and Barack Obama have all made designations of marine areas as national monuments. President Obama took two of President George W. Bush's Antiquities Act designations and greatly expanded them: the Northwestern Hawai'ian Islands was redesignated as the Papahānaumokuākea Marine National Monument, and enlarged to over 442,000 square miles, while the Pacific Remote Islands National Monument was enlarged to over 409,000 square miles. Together, these two monuments constitute about 75 percent of all marine protected areas within the U.S. Exclusive Economic Zone waters.

The Antiquities Act offers flexibility, in that prohibitions and permitted uses are largely determined by the presidential designation. The Papahānaumokuākea Marine National Monument, home to unusually important and beautiful coral reefs, prohibits commercial or recreational fishing, and requires permits for snorkeling or diving. Over 7,000 species live within the monument, including the endangered monk seal, and green, leatherback, and hawksbill sea turtles, to name just a few. In the Pacific Remote Islands Marine National Monument—aptly named for the distance from these islands to any mainland—commercial fishing is prohibited, but recreational fishing is generally allowed.

While some consultation is often undertaken, it is often not to the satisfaction of some stakeholders, and still has the potential to stoke political controversy. President Bush's first invocation of the Antiquities Act was said to have been inspired by a state dinner including ocean explorer Jean-Michel Cousteau, who convinced the President and the First Lady that the hundreds of islands forming the northwestern strand of the Hawai'ian archipelago were in desperate need of conservation. Of course, fishing industries disagreed, and have challenged establishment of the monuments in court, arguing for example that the Antiquities Act applies only to lands owned by the United States, and that international law does not grant the United States ownership of the lands beneath its EEZ. To date, both National Monuments still exist.

3. Marine Spatial Planning and Ocean Zoning

Beyond the need to provide for conservation, a broader mandate is possible, one that may avert some of the political controversy surrounding conservation-oriented designations of ocean areas: the concept of "ocean zoning," or "marine spatial planning," borrowing from the land use context. Zoning could be used to create zones focused on the protection of natural areas, as they are when marine reserves, some national marine sanctuaries, or some national monuments are created. But zoning represents a more comprehensive approach because it aims to create benefits for all ocean user groups, not just conservationists. Areas rich in mineral deposits might be "zoned" for mineral development, while the site of fragile coral reefs might be zoned as a marine reserve. While reserves or marine protected areas are spatial exceptions to broader management, zoning could replace the current system of ocean regulation. Expanding the range of uses for oceans holds the promise of offering some certainty for the commercial fishing and the energy industries. For example, areas might be designed for renewable energy, allowing offshore wind developers to plan on permitting for an offshore wind farm with far fewer regulatory hurdles. Land use zoning is meant to head off litigation over land uses; so too, might marine spatial planning. The idea of marine spatial planning is similar to the concept of zoning in the land use context: physically separating uses to avoid conflict and establish some certainty over a longer term, and avoiding the costly and time-consuming default option of litigation.

A federal effort convened by President Obama, by Executive Order 13,547, called on the Departments of Commerce and Interior and other federal agencies to engage in Coastal and Marine Spatial Planning. The idea was to mimic the multiple-use planning adopted by federal land management agencies and involve regulated industries such as commercial fishermen and oil and gas firms in zoning areas of the ocean. This effort foundered due to a lack of participation by regulated industries and was subsequently revoked by executive order.

Although ocean zoning has yet to be widely adopted at the federal level, states have moved ahead. As noted above, California enacted the Marine Life Protection Act, which not only created the authorization for marine reserves, but a statewide network of four different kinds of conservation zones, which range from limited conservation ("state marine conservation areas") to strict preservation ("state reserve"). Other states have focused on other industries, most notably renewable energy. Oregon adopted a "Territorial Sea Plan" in 1991, and implemented it finally in 2013, with an emphasis on developing tidal wave energy, or "hydrokinetic energy," from the ocean's waves to generate electricity. Massachusetts adopted a framework with three types of management areas: Prohibited, Renewable Energy, and Multi-use. "Prohibited" means that most industrial uses are prohibited, and that the area is to be dedicated to conservation. "Renewable Energy" is aimed at permitting use for the generation of offshore renewable energy. Massachusetts has some of the highest retail electricity rates in the country, and it would desperately like to avoid a replay of the Cape Wind debacle of decades past (discussed in Chapter 4). Other states have adopted a variety of different types of spatial marine planning, all suited to their own unique state needs and priorities.

G. CHAPTER SUMMARY

1. **Economics, technology, and biology.** The exploitation of living resources of the oceans has always been driven by the economics of human behavior and cooperation (or lack thereof), the technologies of ocean harvest, and the biological responses of the living resources. The interaction of these three almost immutable forces has often left legal rules and institutions behind in terms of trying to preserve order in a chaotic seafaring world.

2. **The Magnuson-Stevens Fishery Conservation and Management Act.** While the states have jurisdiction over the first three nautical miles of ocean from shore, the federal government has jurisdiction of the remaining 197

nautical miles out to the edge of the country's exclusive economic zone. The main federal statute governing harvest in this zone is the 1976 Magnuson-Stevens Fishery Conservation and Management Act. The Act divides up authority over the U.S. ocean territory into eight regional fishery management councils, which have responsibility for managing fishing activities in their respective assigned regions. Each regional fishery management council is required to implement a fishery management plan for each fishery that carries out certain national standards and includes mandatory measures to prevent overfishing, while and protecting living resources from non-targeted mortality, or "bycatch."

3. **Area-based ocean management.** An alternative to behavior-based ocean regulation is to designate areas of the ocean for specific uses. Marine reserves might be created in which fishing and mineral development are prohibited to allow for the recovery of fish and other living organisms of the ocean. Under a more comprehensive marine spatial planning regime, other areas could be designated for mineral development or commercial fishing.

H. SUGGESTED READING

Christopher J. Carr & Harry N. Scheiber, *Dealing with a Resource Crisis: Regulatory Regimes for Managing the World's Marine Fisheries*, 21 Stan. Envtl. L.J. 45 (2002).

Josh Eagle et al., Taking Stock of the Regional Fishery Management Councils (2003).

Suzanne Iudicello et al., Fish, Markets, and Fishermen: The Economics of Overfishing (1999).

Alison Rieser, *Property Rights and Ecosystem Management in U.S. Fisheries: Contracting for the Commons?*, 24 Ecol. L.Q. 813 (1997).

Jon G. Sutinen et al., *Measuring and Explaining Noncompliance in Federally Managed Fisheries*, 21 Ocean Dev. & Int'l L. 335 (1990).

James E. Wilen, *Common Property Resources and the Dynamics of Overexploitation: The Case of the North Pacific Fur Seal*, 33 Marine Res. Econ. 218 (2018).

chapter **3**

Marine Protected Species

In addition to laws protecting the living organisms of the ocean from overharvest, two federal statutes provide especially powerful protections from harm. The Marine Mammal Protection Act (MMPA), enacted in 1972, and the Endangered Species Act (ESA), enacted in 1973, were in some ways motivated by very different problems, and yet turned out to be very similar in structure and orientation. The MMPA was enacted out of a concern over the treatment of higher-order marine species with a greater sentience than fish. The ESA was enacted out of a concern over the extinction of species. And yet, the two statutes, enacted less than a year apart, look similar, especially given overlap in regulatory targets: Many marine mammals are endangered and thus enjoy protection under both statutes. But the similarities go beyond superficialities. It is true that Congress may have made a moral judgment unaware of some very significant unintended consequences. *See* Michael J. Bean, *Endangered Species, Endangered Act?*, 41 ENVT. 12 (1999). That said, these statutes have survived well into their fifth decade. The ESA has been much more controversial than the MMPA, as it has impacted many more people and businesses, and has seen more legislative assaults over the years. But it remains.

A. ENDANGERED SPECIES ACT

The precursor to the ESA was the 1966 Endangered Species Preservation Act, which did little more than provide for the compilation of a list of species at risk of extinction. President Richard Nixon, courting environmental voters, argued that the 1966 Act "simply does not provide the kind of management tools needed to act early enough to save a vanishing species" and called for "a stronger law to protect endangered species of wildlife." Less than a year later, Congress delivered to Nixon the Endangered Species Act, which passed the House by a vote of 390 to 12, and the Senate by a vote of 92 to 0.

If there was any doubt that the ESA was serious business, it was swept away by the U.S. Supreme Court's decision in *TVA v. Hill*, 437 U.S. 153 (1978), in which the Court held that the Tennessee Valley Authority, a federal governmental entity, could not complete construction of the Tellico dam because it would inundate the only known habitat of the endangered snail darter. The juxtaposition was striking: Over $100 million had already been spent on a nearly completed dam, and the snail darter was an unsightly fish that had seemingly no commercial use or economic value. Justice Burger, in a 7-to-2 decision, wrote:

> It may seem curious to some that the survival of a relatively small number of three-inch fish among all the countless millions of species extant would require the permanent halting of a virtually completed dam for which Congress has expended more than $100 million. . . . We conclude, however, that the explicit provisions of the Endangered Species Act require precisely that result.

The case involved Section 7 of the ESA, which barred federal entities from taking actions that jeopardized the continued existence of a listed species. Following the Court's decision in *TVA v. Hill*, Congress passed an amendment providing for an "Endangered Species Review Committee," a committee of cabinet-level officials that could grant exemptions to Section 7 prohibitions for certain projects. 16 U.S.C. § 1536(e).

The ESA protects species listed as "endangered," which is defined as "any species which is in danger of extinction throughout all or a significant portion of its range," 16 U.S.C. § 1533(6), or "threatened," which is defined as "any species which is likely to become an endangered species within the foreseeable future throughout all or a significant portion of its range." 16 U.S.C. § 1533(20). Among other things, the remainder of the Act explains what the federal government and other parties, including state governments, firms, and individuals, must do (or not do) to avoid the Act's civil and criminal penalties.

The ESA has many parts, but four aspects are worth emphasizing: (1) listing a species, (2) designating its critical habitat, (3) Section 7 consultations, and (4) the Section 9 "take" prohibition.

1. Listing

The ESA provides that the "Secretary" — of Interior in the case of terrestrial species, or Commerce for marine species — can list a species as threatened or endangered if its population has been reduced due to:

(A) the present or threatened destruction, modification, or curtailment of its habitat or range;

(B) overutilization for commercial, recreational, scientific, or educational purposes;

(C) disease or predation;

(D) the inadequacy of existing regulatory mechanisms; or

(E) other natural or manmade factors affecting its continued existence.

16 U.S.C. § 1533(a)(1).

Listing triggers the ESA's substantial protections. The process can begin in one of two ways. It can begin within either the Department of the Interior (for terrestrial species) or the Department of Commerce (for marine species), which can investigate the need for protection. It can also begin with a citizen petition. Any "person" — which is broadly defined to include not only individuals but corporations and other business associations and any employees or agents of any federal, state, or local governmental entity — may petition the Secretary for a listing. A petition is a request that the agency investigate whether the species should be listed. The petitioner must set forth the "scientific or commercial information" necessary for the agency to determine if listing is warranted. The ESA provides that "[t]o the maximum extent practicable, within 90 days after receiving the petition . . . the Secretary shall make a finding as to whether the petition presents substantial scientific or commercial information indicating that the petitioned action may be warranted." Utilizing the same five factors listed above, the Secretary determines whether the listing is (i) warranted, (ii) not warranted, or (iii) warranted but "precluded," meaning that there is some other sufficient reason to avoid listing. The terms of the statute only specify that preclusion can be due to "pending proposals to determine whether [a] species [is listed], and expeditious progress is being made to add qualified species to . . . such lists. . . ." 16 U.S.C. § 1533(b)(3).

Listing determinations are to be made "solely on the basis of the best scientific and commercial data available." 16 U.S.C. § 1533(b). As in the Magnuson-Stevens Act, the frequent appearance of this phrase underscores Congress's intent that decisions should not be political, but rather should be based solely on available evidence.

The following case illustrates how these factors might be utilized in a decision to list a species.

State of Alaska v. Lubchenco

825 F. Supp. 2d 209 (D.D.C. 2011)

Judge LAMBERTH delivered the opinion of the United States District Court, District of Columbia.

Thirty years ago, the number of beluga whales in Cook Inlet — a glacial fjord reaching 180 miles from Anchorage to the Gulf of Alaska — likely exceeded 1,300, but now hovers around 350. Although the population dwindled steadily through the 1980s and early 1990s, its decline was accelerated between 1994 and 1998 by Alaska Natives, who depend to some extent on beluga whales for subsistence. Aided by modern technology, Alaska Natives decimated the beluga population in Cook Inlet, harvesting nearly half of the remaining 650 whales in only four years. This unregulated harvest led to what could fairly be described in conservation terms as an emergency.

The Service initially responded by designating the stock of Cook Inlet beluga whales as "depleted" under the Marine Mammal Protection Act ("MMPA"), allowing the agency to regulate subsistence hunting. The Service also considered a petition to list the Cook Inlet beluga under the ESA, which defines an "endangered species" as one that is in "danger of extinction throughout all or a significant portion of its range." Relying on the assumption that the legislative and regulatory action already taken to control subsistence hunting would allow the population to recover, the Service determined that ESA listing was not warranted at that time. That decision was previously upheld by this Court. However, the Service determined that the stock of beluga whales in Cook Inlet is a distinct population segment ("DPS"), making it eligible for future listing under the ESA despite the existence of healthy populations in other parts of the world.

The fundamental assumption on which the Service based its 2000 decision proved too optimistic. Aerial surveys performed annually over Cook Inlet — the state-of-the-art method for estimating abundance of marine mammals — indicated that the population had not shown any appreciable signs of recovery since 1999, when hunting restrictions began. Instead of the 2 to 6 percent annual population growth the Service expected, the abundance estimates for the next several years indicated that the population was still declining at a rate of 4.1 percent. Concerned that the cause of the species' decline was more complicated than the residual effects of subsistence whaling, the Service initiated a status review of the Cook Inlet beluga whale in March 2006.

To determine the probability of extinction, the Service developed a time-series model that extrapolated the negative population trend observed in Cook Inlet over 50, 100, and 300 years. The parameters for this model — which include a "constant mortality effect" for killer whale predation and an "unusual mortality effect" for irregular (but devastating) events such as mass strandings and oil spills — were subject to extensive peer review by independent researchers, including representatives from Alaska's own Department of Fish and Game. The Service also tested the model's sensitivity to these parameters by varying assumptions about growth rates, mortality effects, and the optimum sustainable population size for Cook Inlet (known as the "carrying capacity"). After performing over ten thousand trial runs, the Service selected a model that best fit the observed trend in the abundance estimates. The most realistic model resulted in a 1 percent risk of extinction in 50 years, a 26 percent risk of extinction in 100 years, and a 70 percent risk of extinction in 300 years. The Service concluded that "[t]aken as a whole, these modeling results indicate clearly that it is likely that the Cook Inlet beluga population will continue to decline or go extinct over the next 300 years unless factors determining its growth and survival are altered in its favor."

Following another petition to designate the stock as endangered, the Service published a Proposed Rule to list Cook Inlet belugas under the ESA. The effect of this publication was to initiate the public notice and comment process required by the Administrative Procedure Act ("APA"). The majority of comments supported listing the Cook Inlet beluga whale as endangered. However, and of particular importance to this case, the State of Alaska opposed the listing determination, arguing that nothing had changed with respect to potential threats to the population since the Service's 2000 determination that listing was not warranted. Alaska also disputed whether the population was actually trending downward, arguing that the ban on subsistence hunting had effectively stopped the population slide, and that growth could not reasonably be expected until the breeding age component of the population had stabilized.

In April 2008, the Service extended the one-year deadline for a final listing determination to October 2008, noting "substantial disagreement" regarding the population trend. This six-month extension allowed the Service to incorporate into its population viability analysis the results of the June 2008 aerial survey of Cook Inlet. When the 2008 abundance estimate was included in the model, however, the rate of population decline was still 1.45 percent annually — not significantly less than zero, but significantly less than the expected growth rate of 2 to 6 percent for a healthy population.

Satisfied that listing the species as endangered was now appropriate, the Service published its Final Rule on October 22, 2008. Alaska then sued for declaratory and injunctive relief under the APA and the ESA's citizen-suit provision, seeking to have the Service's listing determination vacated by this Court. The State's six-count complaint alleges that the Service failed to consider the relevant statutory factors and did not conform to the required procedures for making a listing determination. . . . The parties then moved for judgment on the administrative record, and the case is now ripe for summary judgment. For the reasons that follow, the Court will deny plaintiffs' motions for summary judgment and grant defendants' cross-motions for summary judgment.

***

Defendants are entitled to summary judgment because the administrative record demonstrates that the Service acted rationally in listing the Cook Inlet beluga whale as endangered. Plaintiffs attack this determination on three fronts, challenging the rationale behind the Service's decision, its basis in science, and the procedures through which it was promulgated. The record amply reflects, however, that the Service considered the statutory factors and articulated a rational basis for its listing determination, grounded that decision in the best available scientific data, and provided a full opportunity for public comment before publishing its Final Rule. These activities suffice to allow the agency's decision to survive judicial review under the "highly deferential" standard that applies to this case.

A. The Service Rationally Considered the ESA's Listing Factors

The Service's decision to list the Cook Inlet beluga whale as endangered is rational because the small, isolated population has not shown any appreciable signs of recovery since 1999, when hunting restrictions began. Everyone agrees that the already-declining population suffered unsustainable losses from the mid- to late-1990s. Although the Service reasonably expected that the regulation of subsistence whaling would result in immediate population growth, the most recent estimates show unmistakably that the population is not recovering and that there is a meaningful risk that the number of beluga whales in Cook Inlet is actually continuing to decline. As the Service explained, this unexpected development "strongly suggests other factors may now be involved in the lack of recovery," and that "cessation of excessive harvests is not enough to bring about recovery." Because the regulation of subsistence whaling failed to reverse the downward trend in population numbers, the Service acted rationally in looking beyond this factor as the sole cause of the species' decline.

Recall that in identifying species that qualify for protection under the ESA, the Service must consider five statutorily prescribed factors, any one of which is sufficient to support a listing determination. These factors include:

(A) the present or threatened destruction, modification, or curtailment of its habitat or range; (B) overutilization for commercial, recreational, scientific, or educational purposes; (C) disease or predation; (D) the inadequacy of existing regulatory mechanisms; or (E) other natural or manmade factors affecting its continued existence.

The Service must list a species as endangered or threatened if "any of § 1533(a)(1)'s five factors are sufficiently implicated." Here, the administrative record demonstrates that the Service thoughtfully considered each of the § 1533(a)(1) factors and found that all five factors support a listing determination.

First, the Service found that the "habitat for this species has been modified by municipal, industrial, and recreational activities in upper Cook Inlet, where belugas concentrate." 72 Fed. Reg. 19857. The Service cited examples of significant projects — including port expansions and coal mining — that threaten to destroy or modify beluga habitat. at 19858. The Service also identified a number of ongoing activities that may impact this habitat, including:

(1) continued oil and gas exploration, development, and production; and (2) industrial activities that discharge or accidentally spill pollutants (e.g., petroleum, seafood processing waste, ship ballast discharge, effluent from municipal wastewater treatment systems, and runoff from urban, mining, and agricultural areas).

In addition, the Service noted that with the contraction of the species' range into the upper Cook Inlet, the population was more vulnerable to losses due to stranding, predation, or disease. Thus, the Service reasonably concluded that the cumulative effects of this development along Cook Inlet weigh in favor of listing the beluga as endangered because these activities could result in the "present or threatened destruction, modification, or curtailment of its habitat or range."

Second, the Service found that "[s]ubsistence removals reported during the 1990s are sufficient to account for the declines observed in this population and must be considered as a factor in the proposed classification of the Cook Inlet beluga whale DPS as endangered." Indeed, the agency found that residual effects from past subsistence hunting were "significant" and were sufficient — by themselves — to account for much of the decline observed in the Cook Inlet beluga population. As the Service explained:

While subsistence harvest occurred at unknown levels for decades, the observed decline from 1994 through 1998 and the reported harvest (including estimates of whales that were struck but lost, and assumed to have perished) indicated these harvest levels were unsustainable. Annual subsistence take by Alaska Natives during 1995-1998 averaged 77 whales. The harvest was as high as 20 percent of the population in 1996.

The Service also noted that there may be other residual effects on the stock from commercial and sport whaling operations that existed prior to the enactment of the MMPA in 1972. Thus, the Service reasonably concluded that the "overutilization for commercial, recreational, scientific, or educational purposes" also contributed to the Cook Inlet beluga's status as endangered.

Third, the Service considered whether "disease or predation" might be contributing to the population decline. The Service noted that "killer whales are thought to take at least one Cook Inlet beluga per year." Compared to the enormous impact on the species from subsistence whaling, the mortality effects of killer whale predation are obviously slight. But the Service was particularly concerned that mortality due to killer whales may be underestimated, and that the loss of more than one beluga whale annually could impede recovery. And in any event, the precariously low level of beluga whales predisposed the population to significant consequences from any increase in killer whale predation. Thus, the Service reasonably concluded that this factor too weighed in favor of an endangered designation.

Fourth, the Service found that the "absence of legal authority to control subsistence harvest prior to 1999 is considered a contributing factor" to the Cook Inlet beluga whale's decline. The Service noted that subsequent regulations promulgated pursuant to the MMPA "constitute an effective conservation plan regarding Alaska Native subsistence harvest, but they are not comprehensive in addressing the many other issues now confronting Cook Inlet beluga whales." Thus, the Service acted rationally in finding that the "inadequacy of existing regulatory mechanisms" contributed to the Cook Inlet beluga's status as endangered.

Fifth, the Service found that the small population of beluga whales in Cook Inlet was vulnerable to "other natural or manmade factors" — including strandings, oil spills, noise from oil and gas exploration, ship strikes, and the effects of pollutants and urban runoff — that could affect its continued existence. Specifically, the Service found:

> Cook Inlet beluga whales are known to strand along mudflats in upper Cook Inlet, both individually and in number. The cause for this is uncertain, but may have to do with the extreme tidal fluctuations, predator avoidance, or pursuit of prey, among other possible causes. We have recorded stranding events of more than 200 Cook Inlet beluga whales. Mortality during stranding is not uncommon. We consider stranding to be a major factor establishing this DPS as endangered.

Of particular concern was a fundamental ecological shift: "[t]he contraction of the range of this population northward into the upper inlet," which "makes it far more vulnerable to catastrophic events with the potential to kill a significant fraction of the population." In sum, the Service concluded that each of the five statutory factors supports — to some extent — a determination that the Cook Inlet beluga whale is currently "in danger of extinction throughout all or a significant portion of its range;" considered together, these factors present a strong case for listing under the ESA.

Plaintiffs' principal argument in opposition is that nothing has changed with respect to potential threats to the population since the Service's 2000 determination that listing was not warranted. Plaintiffs characterize the Service's 2008 decision as an "about face" that was not justified by any change in circumstances. There is some appeal to this argument. After all, if it was rational to conclude that listing was "not warranted" in 2000, why is the opposite conclusion — that listing is now required — not "arbitrary and capricious" when nothing has changed in the intervening eight years? But it is precisely the lack of changed circumstances that led the Service to conclude in 2008 that listing was now appropriate. The key assumption underlying the agency's 2000 decision — that subsistence whaling was the only factor responsible for the decline in beluga abundance — has proven false. Instead of the expected 2 to 6 percent annual increase in abundance, the population has shown no appreciable signs of recovery, and the best available scientific data indicate a very high probability that the population is continuing to decline (albeit at a statistically insignificant rate). Under these circumstances, and after nearly a decade during which the expected recovery failed to materialize, the Service could rationally conclude that the species warranted protection under the ESA.

***

To be sure, the record reflects that excessive whaling by Alaska Natives remains the most significant factor in the declining whale population over the past thirty years. But that does not undermine the Service's choice to look beyond this factor after the regulation of subsistence harvest failed to reverse the negative population trend. Although subsistence hunting occurred at unknown levels prior to 1994, there is very little reliable information for the period between 1979 and 1994 to identify a mechanism for the apparent decline of this population from approximately 1,300 to 650 whales. And although listing is not required "simply because the agency is unable to rule out factors that could contribute to a population decline," there is a world of difference between an inability to eliminate certain factors, on one hand, and a determination that a *single* factor no longer explains the observed population trend, on the other. Indeed, the agency affirmatively found that all five statutory factors were implicated to some extent. Under the circumstances, what the agency did here makes sense and therefore passes muster under the "highly deferential" standard of review that applies to this case.

***

For these reasons, plaintiffs' motions for summary judgment are denied and defendants' cross-motions for summary judgment are granted. A separate order memorializing these conclusions will issue this day.

Figure 3-1. A Beluga Whale Surfaces

points for discussion

1. *Subjective science?* Aboriginal subsistence hunting halted in 2005. Are you sympathetic with the argument that listing is unwarranted because the population is not declining? The court noted that the Service was entitled to a "highly deferential" standard of review. If this was not a challenge by the State of Alaska to a listing decision, but instead a challenge by an environmental organization of the Service's decision to *not* list the Cook Inlet beluga whale, how do you think it would come out?

2. *Distinct population segments.* The case makes reference to the Cook Inlet beluga whales as a "distinct population segment" (DPS). A DPS is a vertebrate population that is "discrete from other populations" and "significant," in that it is separate and distinct from other populations, but important to the overall survival of the entire species. 61 Fed. Reg. 4,722 (Feb. 7, 1996). In other words, a subpopulation can be listed under the ESA as endangered or threatened. The Cook Inlet is one of five stocks of beluga whales in the United States, all in Alaskan waters. The health of this stock has not improved: In 2016, a NOAA stock assessment estimated the population at 328. Is the Cook Inlet population an example of why DPSs should be listed under the ESA, or the opposite?

3. *You list.* This opinion makes reference to a number of conditions that can be related to the five factors to be considered in a listing (or delisting) decision. As an exercise, list the five factors and write alongside them the conditions considered by NOAA that contributed to the decision to list the beluga whale.

4. *Climate change pressures.* Global climate change is expected to raise average ambient air temperatures, but most dramatically in the Arctic. The extent of Arctic Ocean sea ice, a key indicator of changing climate conditions in the Arctic region, has been declining quite regularly and dramatically for decades. Given that the beluga whale, like the polar bear, is uniquely adapted to an Arctic environment that is changing rapidly — and will continue to change — how would that figure into a listing decision? Which of the five statutory factors would capture climate change? Can you make an argument that such polar species are doomed anyway, and that listing is futile?

2. Designation of Critical Habitat

More than half of species on the endangered and threatened lists are there because of the first of the five factors: specifically, "the present destruction, modification, or curtailment of [their] habitat or range." If loss of habitat caused the species' population to decline, it is logical to conclude that, if the species' population is to recover, lost habitat must be restored or new habitat must be created. Toward this end, the Act requires that the Secretary designate "critical habitat" for each listed species. The ESA's protections for critical habitat apply only in the context of Section 7: to federal construction, spending, and permitting decisions. Section 9, as we will see, also limits habitat modification or destruction, applies to public and private entities, but is not necessarily connected to critical habitat designation.

The ESA requires the Secretary to designate "critical habitat" for listed species "to the maximum extent prudent and determinable." 16 U.S.C. § 1533(a)(3). Critical habitat is defined as the "specific areas . . . on which are found those physical or biological features essential to the conservation of the species." 16 U.S.C. § 1532(5)(A). Critical habitat does not need to be space presently occupied by the species; it could be habitat formerly occupied or necessary to support a larger population. The U.S. Fish and Wildlife Service states that "physical or biological features" include

- space for individual and population growth and for normal behavior;
- cover or shelter;
- food, water, air, light, minerals, or other nutritional or physiological requirements;
- sites for breeding and rearing offspring; and,
- habitats that are protected from disturbances or are representative of the historical geographical and ecological distributions of a species.

Listing and Critical Habitat, Critical Habitat, Frequently Asked Questions, U.S. Fish & Wildlife Serv., https://www.fws.gov/endangered/what-we-do/critical-habitats-faq.html (last updated Dec. 6, 2018).

As we saw in *TVA v. Hill*, some parts of the Act — at least in their words — seem to eschew consideration of politics or the negative economic consequences of protecting species from extinction. The critical habitat provisions are somewhat different:

> The Secretary shall designate critical habitat, and make revisions thereto . . . on the basis of the best scientific data available and after taking into consideration the economic impact, the impact on national security, and any other relevant impact, of specifying any particular area as critical habitat. The Secretary may exclude any area from critical habitat if he determines that the benefits of such exclusion outweigh the benefits of specifying such area as part of the critical habitat, unless he determines, based on the best scientific and commercial data available, that the failure to designate such area as critical habitat will result in the extinction of the species concerned.

16 U.S.C. § 1533(b)(2).

Even by the standards of the perpetually beleaguered ESA, the listing and critical habitat designation of the Steller sea lion seemed to be unusually controversial. So bitter were the feelings over listing that Steller sea lions were shot as pure acts of vandalism. It was not even as if the impacts upon competing interests were greatly affected; but it did infringe upon the commercial pollock fishing industry. As you read through this critical habitat designation, consider what might have created such hard feelings.

Figure 3-2. Steller Sea Lions at a "Haulout"

58 Fed. Reg. 45269-01
RULES and REGULATIONS

DEPARTMENT OF COMMERCE
National Oceanic and Atmospheric Administration

50 CFR Part 226

Designated Critical Habitat; Steller Sea Lion
Friday, August 27, 1993

AGENCY: National Marine Fisheries Service (NMFS), NOAA, Commerce.
ACTION: Final rule.
SUMMARY: Pursuant to the Endangered Species Act (ESA), NMFS is designating critical habitat for the Steller (northern) sea lion (Eumetopias jubatus) in certain areas and waters of Alaska, Oregon and California. The direct economic and other impacts resulting from this critical habitat designation, over and above those arising from the listing of the species under the ESA, are expected to be minimal.

EFFECTIVE DATE: September 27, 1993.

Background

Counts of Steller sea lions on rookeries and major haulouts during the breeding season have indicated that extensive declines have occurred within the Alaskan and the Russian portions of their range over the last 30 years. A 1989 range-wide survey of Steller sea lions indicated that about 70 percent of the Steller sea lion population during the summer resides in Alaska. A series of counts in the Gulf of Alaska (GOA) and the Bering Sea/Aleutian Islands (BSAI) between the mid-1970s and 1991 indicated a 70 percent decline in the Alaskan portion of the population over this time period. Counts in Southeast Alaska, British Columbia, and Oregon have remained stable over the same period; Steller sea lion numbers in California have declined. The causes of the Steller sea lion population decline are unknown. Potential causative factors include disease, incidental takes in fishing gear, direct mortality (shooting), and natural or human induced changes (through fishing) in the abundance and species composition of the sea lion prey.

***

Terrestrial Habitat

Because of their traditional use and the relative ease of observation, terrestrial habitats are better known than aquatic habitats. Steller sea lion rookeries and haulouts are widespread throughout their geographic range and the locations used change little from year to year. Factors that influence the suitability of a particular area include substrate, exposure to wind and waves, the extent and type of human activities and disturbance in the region, and proximity to prey resources.

The best known Steller sea lion habitats are the rookeries (Table 1), where adult animals congregate during the reproductive season for breeding and pupping. Rookeries are defined as those sites where males defend a territory and where pupping and mating occurs on a consistent annual basis. Rookeries typically occur on relatively remote islands, rocks, reefs, and beaches, where access by terrestrial predators is limited. A rookery may extend across low-lying reefs and islands, or may be restricted to a relatively narrow strip of beach by steep cliffs. Rookeries are occupied by breeding animals and some subadults throughout the breeding season, which extends from late May to early July throughout the range. Female sea lions frequently return to pup and breed at the same rookery in successive years, and this site may be the same rookery, or approximate rookery (same island) as the female's natal site.

Steller sea lion rookeries are found from the central Kuril Islands around the Pacific Rim of the Aleutian Islands to Prince William Sound (Seal Rocks, at the entrance to Prince William Sound, Alaska, is the northernmost rookery) and south along the coast of North America to Ano Nuevo Island, California, the southernmost rookery (figure 1). . . .

***

Food Resources

Adequate food resources are an essential component of the Steller sea lion's aquatic habitat. Steller sea lions are opportunistic carnivores that prey predominantly upon demersal and off-bottom schooling fishes. Invertebrates, e.g., squid and octopus, also appear to be regular components of their diet (Pitcher 1981). Prey consumption is expected to vary geographically, seasonally, and over years in response to fluctuations in prey abundance and availability.

Data on Steller sea lion prey consumption are fairly limited. Results of limited diet studies conducted in Alaska since 1975 indicate that walleye pollock has been the principal prey in most areas over this time period, with Atka mackerel, Pacific cod, octopus, squid, Pacific herring, Pacific salmon, capelin, and flatfishes also consumed. In recent years Atka mackerel appears to be the principal prey consumed in the Aleutian Islands. Few data are available on Steller sea lion prey preferences in Alaska prior to 1975; however, those data available indicate that pollock may have been a less important component of the diet in previous years. Limited food habitat data from California and Oregon show a predominance of rockfish and hake in the diet, with flatfish, squid, octopus, and lamprey also eaten.

Foraging Habitats

Specific foraging areas, and their constancy over time, have not been well defined. NMFS' ongoing studies in the central [Gulf of Alaska] and Aleutian Islands using satellite telemetry are providing more detailed information on feeding areas and diving patterns in Alaskan waters. The following summarizes the findings to date: NMFS has deployed 52 satellite-linked time depth recorders on Steller sea lions since 1989. The results of this tagging indicate that waters in the vicinity of rookeries and haulouts are important foraging habitats, particularly for post-parturient females and young animals. These investigations strongly suggest that sea lion foraging strategies and ranges change seasonally, and according to the age and reproductive status of the animal.

Need for Special Management Considerations or Protection

. . . NMFS has prohibited vessel entry within 3 nm of all Steller sea lion rookeries west of 150 degrees W. longitude, the area where the greatest population decline has occurred, primarily to protect sea lions using these habitats from intentional and unintentional harassment. The Recovery Team recommended that waters extending 3,000 feet (0.9 km) from rookeries and major haulouts throughout the range of Steller sea lions be considered essential habitat that merits special management consideration.

***

Reduction in food availability, quantity, and/or quality is considered to be a possible factor in the Steller sea lion population decline. Most of the data on proximate causes of the Alaska sea lion decline point to reduced juvenile survival as a significant causative agent. There are also indications that decreased juvenile survival is due to a lack of food post-weaning and during the winter/spring of the first year. Calkins and Goodwin (1988) found that Steller sea lions collected in the [Gulf of Alaska] in 1985-1986 were significantly smaller (girth, weight, and standard length) than same-aged animals collected in the [Gulf of Alaska] in the 1970s. Reduced body size at age was interpreted as an indicator of nutritional stress.

Conservation and management of prey resources and foraging areas appears essential to the recovery of the Steller sea lion population. The quality and quantity of these resources may be degraded by human activities, e.g., pollutant discharges, habitat losses associated with human development, and commercial fisheries. . . . Presently, there is insufficient information to identify any specific geographic areas where additional management measures to protect sea lion food resources from contaminant inputs and habitat loss, beyond the existing state and Federal regulations, are necessary.

The relationship between commercial fisheries and the ability of Steller sea lions to obtain adequate food is unclear. The BSAI/[Gulf of Alaska] geographic region where Steller sea lions have experienced the greatest population decline is also an area where large commercial fisheries have developed. Many of the Steller sea lion's preferred prey species are harvested by commercial fisheries in this region, and food availability to Steller sea lions may be affected by fishing. At present, NMFS believes that the exploitation rates in federally managed fisheries are unlikely to diminish the overall abundance of fish stocks important to Steller sea lions. However, spatial and temporal regulation of fishery removals in some areas has been determined to be necessary to ensure that local depletion of prey stocks does not occur.

***

Activities That May Affect Essential Habitat

A wide range of activities by several private, state, and Federal agencies may affect the essential habitats of Steller sea lions. Specific human activities that occur within or in the vicinity of the essential sea lion habitat defined above, and that may disrupt the essential life functions that occur there, include, but are not limited to: (1) Wildlife viewing (primarily south-central and southeastern Alaska and California); (2) boat and airplane traffic (throughout the range of the Steller sea lion); (3) research activities (on permitted sites and during specified times throughout the year); (4) commercial, recreational, and subsistence fisheries for groundfish, herring, salmon, and invertebrates, e.g., crab, shrimp, sea urchins/cucumbers (throughout the range of the Steller sea lion); (5) timber harvest (primarily southeastern and south-central Alaska); (6) hard mineral extraction (primarily southeastern Alaska); (7) oil and gas exploration (primarily Bering Sea and [Gulf of Alaska]); (8) coastal development, including pollutant discharges (specific sites throughout range); and (9) subsistence harvest (Alaska).

points for discussion

1. *Foraging and critical habitat.* As the rulemaking notes, Steller sea lions have a varied diet, but seem to rely quite a lot, especially for nursing females, upon pollock and Atka mackerel, two important commercial fisheries. This critical habitat designation identified areas in which commercial fishermen fish for pollock and Atka mackerel. Is NMFS obligated to limit catch of these fish in order to preserve them as a food source for Steller sea lions? Can fishing be considered the adverse modification of habitat?

2. *Does commercial fishing for pollock and Atka mackerel pose a threat to the Steller sea lion?* As so often seems to be the case, there does not seem to be sufficient data for NMFS to confidently make a decision. As the rulemaking notes, it is easier to identify "rookeries" and "haulouts" — places where sea lions have been observed to use as breeding grounds and non-breeding resting places — than it is to identify where they forage for food and what they eat. In this case, the uncertainty of fish stocks is compounded by the uncertainty about the Steller sea lion's feeding habits, which are difficult to observe. As we have seen in earlier parts of this chapter, the default action seems to be for agencies to refrain from regulation in the absence of data that the regulator deems to be sufficient. Does that effectively reverse the presumption created by the Fisheries Conservation Management Act, the ESA, and the MMPA? How much information is enough? How little is too little? How does the certainty of information relate to the consequences of action or inaction?

3. *Cost-benefit analysis.* As *TVA v. Hill* made abundantly clear, Section 7 of the ESA "admits of no exception," and thus does not permit any balancing of costs and benefits. But designation of critical habitat *may* be determined

in part by cost-benefit analysis. 16 U.S.C. § 1533(b)(2). Does it make sense to exclude cost considerations for listing decisions but not critical habitat designation?

4. *Cost-benefit analysis, continued.* Executive Order 12,291 requires of all "major" federal rulemakings a "regulatory impact analysis" of the costs of a new rule. "Major" is defined as: (1) an annual effect on the economy of $100 million or more; (2) a major increase in costs or prices for consumers, individual industries, federal, state, or local government agencies, or geographic regions; or (3) a significant adverse effect on competition, employment, investment, productivity, innovation, or on the ability of U.S.-based enterprises to compete with foreign-based enterprises in domestic or export markets. NMFS concluded that this designation of critical habitat was not "major." Given the "Activities That May Affect Essential Habitat" section, do you think that evaluation was realistic?

5. *Shoot, shovel, and shut up.* The ESA can be very difficult to enforce when listed species are found in remote places. Paradigmatically, restrictions on logging imposed to save the Northern spotted owl have, on occasion, caused private landowners to engage in illegal self-help, shooting Northern spotted owls before they can be sighted and reported to wildlife officials. Once the evidence is safely buried, logging can continue without fear of federal or state restrictions. Steller sea lions are also vulnerable to illegal shooting. Steller sea lions are notorious for grabbing fish right off hooks set by commercial fishermen. Fishermen respond by shooting Steller sea lions they suspect of stealing their fish. Designation of critical habitat is especially important in these cases because the illegal act of killing is so difficult to monitor and prevent. If it is so difficult to catch someone in the act of killing, then the next best solution is to prohibit the underlying activity, fishing, in a designated area. However, depending on the breadth of the designated area, that could place a large area off-limits to fishing, which would be a hardship on those who might not kill sea lions.

> Sea lions are clever, smart enough to bite off bait without snagging on the fish hook. Some fishermen have tried non-lethal methods of discouraging sea lions from stealing their catch, like slingshots, rubber bullets, fireworks, electric cattle prods, and even broadcasting sound recordings of the feared killer whale. But sea lions are not easily deterred. Between 1998 and 2017, more than 700 sea lions were found in California with gunshot or stab wounds. Few of the perpetrators were ever charged, all of them fishermen. One Newport Beach man was convicted for repeatedly stabbing a sea lion to death with a steak knife. *See* Annie Roth & Jeremy Rehm, *California Sea Lions Keep Getting Shot by Fishermen*, NAT'L GEOGRAPHIC (Aug. 17, 2018). California sea lions are not considered endangered under the Endangered Species Act but are still protected under the MMPA.

3. Section 7

Perhaps the hallmark of the ESA is its Section 7 duties imposed on all federal agencies undertaking any "agency action" — actions that are "authorized, funded, or carried out by such agency." Agencies must "insure" [sic] that the action does not jeopardize endangered species nor destroy or adversely modify their critical habitat. 16 U.S.C. § 1536(2). Section 7 also requires that a federal agency undertaking such an action *consult* with an "expert agency" — the U.S. Fish and Wildlife Service or the National Marine Fisheries Service, or some office therein (such as the National Marine Fisheries Service Office of Protected Resources), to determine whether the agency action is likely to jeopardize the "continued existence of any endangered species or threatened species or result in the destruction or adverse modification of [critical] habitat."

The product of the consultation process is a Biological Opinion, the expert agency's findings and conclusions as to whether the federal agency action will jeopardize the species or destroy or adversely modify critical habitat. Given the complexity and uncertainty surrounding many listed species, the Biological Opinion can be quite long. The Biological Opinion ultimately produced by NMFS pursuant to the case below was 206 pages, but it references hundreds of pages of other, supporting documents. Some Biological Opinions address multiple species in a region, potentially impacted by a program of activity, such as commercial fishing for multiple species, or a program of offshore oil drilling (Chapter 4).

If the Biological Opinion concludes that jeopardy or destruction or adverse modification of habitat will result from the federal agency action, then the expert agency may suggest "reasonable and prudent alternatives," which can be undertaken without violating Section 7 of the ESA. 16 U.S.C. § 1536(b)(3)(A).

The Steller sea lion presents a case in which the science changed several times in the course of multiple consultations. The Steller sea lion was first listed as threatened in 1991, generating the need for a Biological Opinion. It was re-listed as endangered in 1997, triggering another round of consultation, and the need for a new Biological Opinion. For the most part, all of the Biological Opinions offered up quite gloomy assessments of the state of the species. The following case explores one phase of this fraught series of actions.

Greenpeace v. National Marine Fisheries Service

80 F. Supp. 2d 1137 (W.D. Wash. 2000)

Judge ZILLY delivered the opinion of the United States District Court, Western District of Washington.

The Gulf of Alaska (GOA) and the Bering Sea/Aleutian Islands region (BSAI), collectively referred to as the North Pacific ecosystem, is home to the largest commercial fishery in the United States. The ecosystem is also home to the western population of Steller sea lions which in 1990 were listed under the ESA as a threatened species, and in 1997 were reclassified as endangered.

* * *

The groundfish fisheries at issue in this case are regulated under two Fishery Management Plans — one for the Bering Sea and Aleutian Islands and the other for the Gulf of Alaska. According to NMFS, these FMPs "utilize a myriad of interrelated regulations to manage the fisheries." The FMPs address all the factors affecting when, where, and how the fisheries are conducted and include such measures as optimum yield for each fishery, overfishing, total allowable catch limits for targeted species (TAC), time and area closures, gear restrictions, bycatch limits of prohibited species, and allocations of TACs among vessels delivering to different types of processor groups, gear types, and qualifying communities.

Since the time of their original implementation, there have been dozens of formal amendments to the North Pacific groundfish FMPs. In addition, discrete annual decisions such as setting the yearly TAC for each fishery, establishing the prohibited species catch limit, and apportioning the TAC into fishing seasons and among various sectors of the industry are implemented by regulation each year.

Prior ESA Compliance

Under the ESA, all federal agencies must insure that action taken by the agency does not jeopardize the existence or recovery of endangered species or adversely modify their critical habitat. Section 7 of the ESA requires the "action" agency to consult with an "expert" agency to determine whether jeopardy or adverse modification is likely to result from the proposed agency action. The final product of a formal consultation is a biological opinion (BiOp), which sets forth the expert agency's conclusions regarding jeopardy and adverse modification, as well as the reasoning supporting the opinion.

Since 1990, when the Steller sea lion was first listed as threatened, NMFS's Office of Sustainable Fisheries (the "action" agency for ESA purposes) has engaged in both informal and formal consultation with NMFS's Office of Protected Resources (the "expert" agency) regarding the effect of the North Pacific groundfish fisheries on the Steller sea lion and other marine mammals. These consultations have varied in scope from addressing the overall effects of the groundfish FMPs in their entirety, to addressing the effects of discrete amendments to the FMPs or annual catch limits.

NMFS has twice before consulted on the environmental effects of the BSAI and GOA groundfish FMPs. In April 1991, NMFS issued two biological opinions addressing the overall impacts of the fisheries on the Steller sea lion and other marine mammals listed under the Endangered Species Act. Each opinion expressly stated that the "Activity Considered" was the "Fishery Management Plan (FMP) for the Gulf of Alaska (GOA) Groundfish" and the "Fishery Management Plan for the Bering Sea/Aleutian Islands Groundfish." According to NMFS, each opinion considered "all aspects of the fishery." Each opinion concluded that "as currently managed and conducted" the respective groundfish fisheries were not likely to jeopardize or adversely modify the Steller sea lion or its critical habitat.

In 1995, NMFS reinitiated consultation and, in January 1996, again issued biological opinions that addressed the overall impacts of the North Pacific groundfish Fishery Management Plans on listed species. Like their 1991 predecessors, the 1996 biological opinions expressly considered the "Fishery Management Plan for the Gulf of Alaska Groundfish Fishery" and the "Fishery Management Plan for the Bering Sea and Aleutian Islands Groundfish Fishery." Because it had been more than four years since the "overall" effects of the BSAI and GOA groundfish fisheries had been examined, the express purpose of the 1996 biological opinions was to "reconsider" the overall effects of these fisheries on Steller sea lions, "including the adequacy of fishery management regulations to protect them." As in 1991, the 1996 opinions concluded the groundfish management plans for the GOA and BSAI were not likely to jeopardize Steller sea lions or adversely modify sea lion critical habitat.

In 1997, NMFS reclassified the western population of Steller sea lion from threatened to endangered. Nevertheless, in January 1997 NMFS issued a Decision Memorandum that concluded the 1997 fisheries "were not likely to affect Steller sea lions in a way or to an extent not already considered in previous section 7 consultations." In 1998, NMFS concluded "that the 1996 biological opinion remained valid for the 1998 BSAI groundfish fishery." However, due to a 60% increase in the GOA pollock total allowable catch for 1998, NMFS reinitiated consultation on the GOA groundfish fisheries and, in a March 1998 biological opinion, once again concluded the GOA fishery was not likely to result in jeopardy or adverse modification.

Procedural History

In April 1998, plaintiffs filed suit in this Court. Plaintiffs . . . challenged the January 1996 biological opinion for the BSAI and the March 1998 biological opinion for the GOA, [claiming that] these biological opinions did not meet the requirements of the ESA because the "cumulative impacts of the total groundfish catch of multiple species" were not adequately analyzed in the 1996 BSAI opinion, and because the 1998 GOA opinion was "limited to considering a single year, rather than the impacts of the past, present, and reasonably foreseeable fishing under the current management regime."

In August of 1998, plaintiffs moved for summary judgment on these claims. In response NMFS moved for a stay of litigation. NMFS argued a stay was proper because it was preparing a new Supplemental Environmental Impact Statement (SEIS) addressing "the Fishery Management Plan for the Bering Sea and Aleutian Islands Groundfish Fishery (FMP BSAI) and the Fishery Management Plan for the Groundfish Fishery of the Gulf of Alaska (FMP GOA)." In conjunction with the SEIS, NMFS represented to the Court that it was consulting on a biological opinion pursuant to section 7 of the ESA that would "examine all Federally-managed fisheries in the BSAI and GOA," including all "the issues that will be addressed in the SEIS."

. . . NMFS's legal counsel [declared that] the scope of the consultation "will be broad and will examine all Federally-managed fisheries in the Gulf of Alaska and Bering Sea and Aleutian Islands and the manner in which the total allowable catch levels are set as well as the issues referenced in [the SEIS]." In other words, the promised biological opinion was to be coextensive with the groundfish FMPs, including "a detailed discussion" of the effects of the fisheries on listed species and critical habitat. . . .

In December of 1998, NMFS issued the promised documents: a Supplemental Environmental Impact Statement, a biological opinion dealing specifically with the Atka mackerel and pollock fisheries (hereinafter "BiOp1"), and a biological opinion dealing with the entire groundfish fisheries (hereinafter "BiOp2"). Plaintiffs amended their complaint to challenge the sufficiency of these documents under NEPA and the ESA. .

***

. . . [P]laintiffs claimed that BiOp2 was insufficient under the ESA because it analyzed only the 1999 total allowable catch (TAC) specifications "without adequate discussion or consideration of the likely cumulative impacts of all these fisheries on Steller sea lions." Plaintiffs now claim they are entitled to summary judgment "because the Endangered Species Act requires a programmatic biological opinion on the entire groundfish fishery management program," and NMFS has not prepared such an opinion.

NMFS's motion to dismiss is based on the fact that, subsequent to this Court's order of remand for preparation of revised RPAs and a comprehensive SEIS, NMFS has once again reinitiated consultation on the effects of the entire groundfish management scheme. Because consultation has been reinitiated, NMFS argues dismissal is proper on the theory that BiOp2 has been "taken back" and, thus, there is no longer any "final agency action" and nothing for this Court to review. In the alternative, NMFS asks for yet another stay of this litigation pending the completion of its renewed groundfish consultation. . . .

Plaintiffs' Motion for Summary Judgment

***

Plaintiffs correctly assert that NMFS must prepare a biological opinion equal in scope to the FMPs. The Ninth Circuit has unequivocally held that biological opinions under the ESA must be "coextensive" with the agency action. In *Conner v. Burford,* 848 F.2d 1441, 1458 (9th Cir. 1988), the Ninth Circuit rejected the argument that a federal agency could meet its ESA obligations by addressing portions of the agency action incrementally as each portion went into effect. According to the *Conner* Court, the ESA provides a "clear mandate" that a "comprehensive" biological opinion addressing "all phases of the agency action" must be completed before initiation of the agency action. Although *Conner* was decided in the context of oil and gas leases in national forests, its holding is based on a legal interpretation of the ESA and is applicable here.

The ESA requires a biological opinion to detail how the "agency action" affects the species or its critical habitat. Consequently, the scope of the "agency action" is crucial "because the ESA requires the biological opinion to analyze the effect of the entire agency action." The meaning of "agency action" under the ESA is a matter of statutory interpretation that is ultimately to be decided by the court. The Ninth Circuit has consistently held that "agency action" is to be construed broadly. Under the ESA, "agency action" means "all activities or programs of any kind" authorized, funded or carried out by federal agencies, including "the promulgation of regulations." Thus, section 7 of the ESA "on its face" requires the agency to analyze all aspects of the agency action in a biological opinion.

***

. . . [T]here is no doubt the FMPs in their entirety, constitute agency action subject to consultation under ESA section 7. By law, fishery management plans contain "all of the rules, regulations, conditions, methods, and other measures" required to maintain the fisheries and prevent long-term adverse effects on fishery resources and the marine environment. All regulations implementing the plans must be consistent with them. By definition, the rules, regulations and other measures that comprise the Fishery Management Plans constitute "agency action." The plans as a whole authorize and regulate all the activities involved in fishing. Thus, these plans not only set forth criteria for harvesting resources within sea lion habitat, but guide and constrain all aspects of the groundfish fisheries in the BSAI and GOA. As such, they have a significant on-going effect on the ocean environment in general, as well as sea lion habitat in particular.

Based on the foregoing, the Court concludes the BSAI and GOA FMPs in their entirety constitute on-going agency action under the ESA. Consequently, the ESA requires a comprehensive biological opinion coextensive in scope with the FMPs.

***

[T]he January 1996 and the March 1998 biological opinions are no longer legally sufficient. The ESA requires an agency to reinitiate consultation and to issue a new biological opinion when a new species is listed, when the agency action is modified, or when new information reveals the action may affect a listed species in a manner or to an extent not previously considered. In this case, both of the 1996 opinions were issued prior to the listing of the Steller sea lion as endangered. Since the 1996 opinions were issued, significant changes have been made to the fishery management plans and NMFS has concluded the pollock fishery may jeopardize the Steller sea lion. These changes alone render continued reliance on the 1996 biological opinions legally impossible. Similarly, the March 1998 biological opinion is out-dated. Although it ostensibly reviewed the fishery plan for the GOA in its entirety, the opinion is only 10 pages in length and was necessary only because of a 60% increase in the TAC for 1998.

Based on the law and the prior history of this case, the Court concludes the proper subject of consultation in BiOp2 should have been the overall groundfish Fishery Management Plans for the BSAI and GOA in their entirety. Given the foregoing, the only remaining question is whether BiOp2 is legally adequate in scope.

***

Given the broad and complex nature of the FMPs and the numerous significant issues NMFS itself recognizes these management plans raise, a comprehensive biological opinion addressing the full scope of the FMPs should, at the very least, identify all the relevant management measures and explain how these measures individually, and in combination, affect the listed species and its marine environment. While BiOp2 does mention many of the relevant management measures, it does so only in the context of a general, background discussion. Although useful, general background information does not substitute for focused and meaningful analysis of how the numerous individual management measures, or the management scheme as a whole, affect listed species. Of the issues identified by NMFS itself, BiOp2 fails to meaningfully analyze such things as the processes by which annual catch limits are determined, the methods by which changes to these processes are implemented, the distribution of the fishery over time and space, exploitation rates, overfishing levels, groupings of exploited species, habitat alterations, relative impacts on the environment, individual and cumulative effects of all activities related to the fisheries, direct impacts on target species, incidental impacts on other species, and mechanisms for assessing environmental impacts. . . .

BiOp2 fails to critically analyze how core management measures such as the processes for deriving acceptable biological catch, overfishing, and total allowable catch, impact endangered species. While BiOp2 does include a description of these processes, the discussion is general in nature and does not explain how these measures, or the processes for deriving them, relate to the conservation of the Steller sea lion. A proper analysis in this area seems important and necessary. Acceptable biological catch and overfishing levels are based on stock assessment techniques. These levels, in turn, constrain the TAC. At least theoretically, therefore, the process ensures that no fish stock will be overfished. Nevertheless, in its 1996 BSAI FMP biological opinion, NMFS concluded that "these processes cannot ensure that the amount of food available to sea lions will not be diminished by fishing." . . .

***

The requirement that an agency evaluate the effects of its actions on critical habitat is mandatory under the ESA. With respect to this crucial issue, BiOp2 contains no meaningful analysis. BiOp2 states its analysis of this issue was "limited by the lack of available information on the distribution of fishing effort relative to Steller sea lions rookeries and haulouts and designated critical habitat." As a consequence, BiOp2 does not even include such basic information as the estimated level of fishing in critical habitat, information that is key to analyzing the effects of fishing in those areas NMFS itself has designated as critical to sea lion recovery and survival. Moreover, NMFS admits that at least some of the information it needed "could be developed after several months of analysis" but the needed analysis "could not be completed in the time allowed for this consultation." Thus, it appears that necessary data was available but simply not analyzed.

***

A biological opinion which is not coextensive in scope with the identified agency action necessarily fails to consider important aspects of the problem and is, therefore, arbitrary and capricious. Here, BiOp2 not only fails to consider important aspects of the problem, the analysis it does contain is simply not adequate. Although an agency need not rely on conclusive scientific proof in a biological opinion, its conclusions must be based on "the best scientific and commercial data available." Thus, an agency "cannot ignore available biological information or fail to develop projections" which may indicate potential conflicts between the proposed action and the preservation of endangered species.

In this case, NMFS admits that at least some of the information it needed was available but could not be analyzed in the time allowed. A federal agency, however, is not "excused from [fulfilling the dictates of the ESA] if, in its judgment, there is insufficient information available to complete a comprehensive opinion and it takes upon itself [a more limited analysis]." This is not a situation where NMFS fully addressed the problem based on uncertain scientific data. Rather, NMFS entirely ignored relevant factors and admittedly failed to analyze and develop projections based on information that was available.

In sum, the ESA requires a comprehensive biological opinion that addresses the full scope of the agency action — in this case the groundfish fishery management plans in their entirety. BiOp2 was to be that opinion. It is not. Because these management plans constitute on-going agency action, the Court concludes NMFS is in continuing violation of the ESA until such time as a comprehensive opinion adequately addressing the full impact of the FMPs is completed.

***

Defendant's motion to dismiss . . . is DENIED. Plaintiffs' motion for summary judgment . . . is GRANTED.

points for discussion

1. *Prolog.* As is clear from the opinion, this case was not the National Marine Fisheries Service's first run-in with Judge Zilly, who became quite an expert on the Steller sea lion. He wrote just a year previous in *Greenpeace v. National Marine Fisheries Service*, 55 F. Supp. 2d 1248 (W.D. Wash. 1999):

   > Steller sea lions are closely related to other types of sea lions and to fur seals. The genus to which Steller sea lions belong is thought to be at least 3 million years old. Female Steller sea lions average 2.3 meters in length and 263 kilograms . . . , while males are somewhat larger, at 2.8 meters and 566 kilograms. Males live to about 20 years old, and females can reach 30 years old. In 1965, the population of the western stock of Steller sea lions was estimated at 230,000 animals. They inhabit coastal areas around the North Pacific Rim, from Southern California to Japan. Before the recent population decline, approximately 75% of the world's population of Steller sea lions were found in Alaska. The majority of Steller sea lions are still found in Alaska, primarily in the Gulf of Alaska and Bering Sea/Aleutian Islands area. . . . Over the last three decades, however, the population of Steller sea lions in the North Pacific has declined approximately 85%. In 1990, NMFS

listed the Steller sea lion as a threatened species under the ESA, and established emergency protective regulations in an attempt to stop the population decline and to begin the process of recovery. In 1993, NMFS designated "critical habitat" for the Steller sea lion, based in significant part on protecting food resources for the sea lions. This critical habitat consists of the area around 40 rookeries and 82 haulouts, which provide areas for reproduction, feeding, rest, and protection from predators and weather. In 1997, based on genetic distinctions, the Steller sea lion species was separated into the western and eastern populations; the western population's status was then changed to endangered. During the 1990s, the rate of decline has slowed to single-digits, but nevertheless continues. NMFS has determined that the next twenty years will likely be crucial for Steller sea lion survival and recovery.

Id. at 1254. And although *TVA v. Hill* emphatically held that Section 7 of the ESA does not permit any balancing of interests, it is still highly advisable for a federal judge to familiarize him- or herself with the impacted industry. Apart from the practicality of understanding the mitigation measures, critical habitat designation permits, unlike Section 7, consideration of the cost impacts of designation (hence that relevant, if somewhat optimistic assessment in the federal rulemaking designating critical habitat). Judge Zilly also wrote in the previous case:

The North Pacific is home to the largest commercial fishing industry in the United States. The most abundant fish in the region, and the major component of the North Pacific fishing industry, is the walleye pollock (pollock). Pollock is a bottom-dwelling fish and a member of the cod family. S1-55 at 21. Mature female pollock are approximately 40 cm in length, and males are longer. Pollock have a fairly short life-span and a high mortality rate, in part because they are sometimes highly cannibalistic. . . . The estimated biomass of pollock in the North Pacific ecosystem has fluctuated significantly since the 1960s. In the east Bering Sea, for example, the estimated biomass was less than 2 million metric tons (mmt) in the mid-1960s, rose to nearly 8 mmt in 1971, declined to 4 mmt in 1978, peaked at 14 mmt in 1984, declined to 8 mmt in 1990, increased again to over 12 mmt in 1993, and dropped to 7 mmt in 1997. The fishing effort directed toward pollock has also fluctuated. From 1964 to 1970, the pollock catch in the BSAI rose from approximately 200,000 to 1 million mt. In the late 1980s, the total catch peaked at approximately 2.7 mmt. A significant portion of this catch came from what later was designated as Steller sea lion critical habitat. By the mid-1990s, the total pollock catch in the Bering Sea /Aleutian Islands had declined to approximately 1.25 mmt, but much of the catch came from within Steller sea lion critical habitat. Scientists believe that the pollock population changes stem in large part from climate changes which have [a]ffected the rest of the North Pacific ecosystem as well. In part because of these changes, Steller sea lions have become increasingly dependent on pollock as their major source of prey.

In the Aleutian Islands, atka mackerel (mackerel) also form a very significant part of the sea lions' diet. Mackerel are a pelagic, dense schooling fish. They reach a maximum size of 50-55 cm, at age 4 to 6 years. Biomass trends for the atka mackerel are similar to those for pollock: in 1977, the biomass in the Bering Sea/Aleutian Islands I was approximately 300,000 mt. It rose in the early 1980s, fell again, then peaked at approximately 1.3 mmt in 1991. In the 1990s, the biomass has declined steadily, to approximately 600,000 mt in 1998. The amount of mackerel caught has been generally rising since the late 1970s, with a brief peak in the mid-1980s at 30,000 mt, a decline in the late 1980s to approximately 18,000 mt, then sharp and steady growth throughout the early 1990s. By 1996, the total atka mackerel catch reached nearly 80,000 mt. Since 1980, the percentage of the catch occurring in Steller sea lion critical habitat has been almost always above 75%, and in many years was well over 90%.

In the previous case, Judge Zilly upheld the NMFS finding that the pollock fishery was likely to jeopardize the Steller sea lions but that the mackerel fishery was not. The case was remanded to the NMFS to prepare a new Biological Opinion, which became the focus of the instant case. Because the Steller sea lion had been upgraded from just "threatened" to "endangered," the old Biological Opinions, most recently the 1998 opinion, were out-of-date, and a "re-initiation" of consultation was required. What NMFS sought was a stay, to allow it time to complete the re-initiation. They lost. Do you think that a stay, pending examination of the completed re-initiation and updated Biological Opinion, was justifiable?

2. *Epilog.* Nor was this Judge Zilly's last word on the Steller sea lion. Just five months later, all of the parties were back in court. The plaintiffs were back in court seeking a ban on groundfish trawl fishing in the critical habitat of the Steller sea lion. Plaintiffs' motion for injunction was granted, again pending completion of a Biological Opinion of satisfaction to the court. *Greenpeace v. Nat'l Marine Fisheries Serv.,* 106 F. Supp. 2d 1066 (W.D. Wash. 2000). The standard for injunctive relief under the ESA resembles that of a permanent injunction, except that there is no balancing under the ESA, because "the balance of the hardships has already been struck in favor of endangered species." *Id.* at 1072. In an illustration of the importance of expert testimony, the court was more persuaded by plaintiffs' expert, who opined that "the combined and cumulative effects of groundfish trawling are almost certainly greater than the individual effects of any one fishery, and are likely quite substantial. . . . [F]ished areas may take days, weeks, or months to recover." *Id.* at 1079.

A 2002 rule imposed stronger restrictions on groundfish fisheries for pollock, Pacific cod, and Atka mackerel, to mitigate the Steller sea lion's competition for food. Steller sea lion critical habitat near rookeries and haulouts (resting places) were completely closed, and trawl fishing was prohibited in critical habitat.

A revised recovery plan was implemented in 2008, but Steller sea lion populations continued their decline. The western population of Steller sea lions slid another 45 percent. More regulations were implemented in 2010-2011 limiting the harvest of Atka mackerel and Pacific cod primarily in the Aleutian Islands. In the meantime, the eastern population of Steller sea lions — those not in Alaska — were removed from the threatened list in 2013.

3. *The trigger.* Do you find convincing the court's rationale that the "agency action" is the FMP, but not the annually set catch limits? What if a catch limit is set that is inconsistent with the FMP? What would be the dividing line between significantly important "agency actions" triggering Section 7 consultation, and more routine actions that do not?

4. Section 9 "Take"

Section 9 of the Act provides that it is "unlawful for any person subject to the jurisdiction of the United States to —

(A) import any such species into, or export any such species from the United States;

(B) take any such species within the United States or the territorial sea . . . ;

(C) take any such species upon the high seas;

(D) possess, sell, deliver, carry, transport, or ship, by any means whatsoever, any such species taken in violation of subparagraphs (B) and (C);

(E) deliver, receive, carry, transport, or ship interstate or foreign commerce, by any means whatsoever and in the course of a commercial activity, any such species;

(F) sell or offer for sale in interstate or foreign commerce any such species; or

(G) violate any regulation pertaining to such species or to any threatened species of fish or wildlife listed [under] this chapter."

The term "take" is ambiguous. The ESA defines it as "harass, harm, pursue, hunt, shoot, wound, kill, trap, capture, or collect, or to attempt to engage in any such conduct." 16 U.S.C. § 1532(19). The terms "harass" and "harm" are ambiguous, and are not defined in the statute. The Department of Interior issued regulations that establish how the agency will interpret those words in implementing the ESA.

Definitions

50 C.F.R. § 17.3

Harass in the definition of "take" in the Act means an intentional or negligent act or omission which creates the likelihood of injury to wildlife by annoying it to such an extent as to significantly disrupt normal behavioral patterns which include, but are not limited to, breeding, feeding, or sheltering.

Harm in the definition of "take" in the Act means an act which actually kills or injures wildlife. Such act may include significant habitat modification or degradation where it actually kills or injures wildlife by significantly impairing essential behavioral patterns, including breeding, feeding or sheltering.

This regulation was challenged in the case *Babbitt v. Sweet Home Chapter of Communities for a Great Oregon*, 515 U.S. 687 (1995), brought by an association of small landowners and logging companies. The plaintiffs argued that these regulations, and that a set of logging regulations that were based on these broad definitions, were impermissibly broad. The plaintiffs were concerned that the regulations, written to protect that habitat of the Northern spotted owl, a species listed as threatened under the ESA, would interfere with their ability to harvest trees, which would arguably be "significant habitat modification or degradation [that] actually kills or injures wildlife. . . ." The suit against the Interior Secretary sought a declaratory judgment that the definition of "harm" in 50 C.F.R. § 17.3 was an impermissibly broad interpretation of the statutory definition of "take."

Writing for a 6-3 majority, Justice Stevens cited three reasons for finding the regulation lawful. First, as a textual matter, the broad definitions of "harm" and "harass" are justified because of the expansive list of actions included under the definition of "take," strongly suggesting that "take" is not limited to actions that result in physical capture or killing. Second, the ESA calls for a broad interpretation of the prohibitions on "take," because it would defeat the broad conservation purposes of the ESA if species could be indirectly harmed. It would make little sense to outlaw the shooting of species, if one could indirectly harm them by destroying their habitat or depriving them of food sources. And finally, Section 10 of the ESA, concerning "incidental take permits" (this is discussed below), would not be necessary unless the term "take" was broadly defined to include actions that cause indirect harm to listed species.

In so doing, the Court upheld the Ninth Circuit decision in *Palila v. Hawaii Dep't of Land & Natural Resources*, 852 F.2d 1106 (9th Cir. 1988), in which the court found the State of Hawai'i liable for failing to control the grazing of sheep of vegetation that was vital to the survival of the endangered Palila bird. Even the omission, by a state, of failing to control feral animals that caused indirect harm — the depletion of a food source of a listed species — was a prohibited "take" under the ESA. In short, broad regulations have prevailed and have supported broad interpretations by U.S. Fish and Wildlife Service and the National Marine Fisheries Service to protect species listed under the ESA and, as we shall see later, the Marine Mammal Protection Act.

Broad definitions of "harm" and "harass," are inevitably ambiguous, given the widely varying needs of different species, and their habitat requirements. How is a regulatory agency to protect species as diverse as northern spotted owls, desert tortoises, polar bears, Florida scrub jays, and marine species?

The following case touches upon many of the themes in litigation and advocacy surrounding terrestrial species listed under the ESA. The job of protecting marine species is often more complicated than protecting land-based species, because of the difficulty of observing them, the unfamiliarity of their habitat and behavioral patterns, and the political power of the fishing industries that oppose species protections.

Strahan v. Coxe

127 F.3d 155 (1st Cir. 1997)

Chief Judge TORRUELLA delivered the opinion of the First Circuit Court of Appeals.

Strahan is an officer of GreenWorld, Inc., an organization dedicated to the preservation and recovery of endangered species. Strahan brought suit on behalf of the Northern Right whale, listed as an endangered species by the federal government. Northern Right whales are the most endangered of the large whales, presently numbering around 300. Entanglement with commercial fishing gear has been recognized as a major source of human-caused injury or death to the Northern Right whale. Collision with ships is also a significant cause of Northern Right whale death.

The majority of Northern Right whales are present in Massachusetts waters only during spring feeding. The district court found, based on statements made by defendants as well as on affidavits from three scientists, that Northern Right whales have been entangled in fixed fishing gear in Massachusetts coastal waters at least nine times. . . .

The NMFS issued a final interim rule proposing to close off entirely the critical habitat of the Northern Right whale and to modify fishing practices to enhance the viability of the Northern Right whale. The report accompanying the proposed rule recognized that entanglement with fishing gear is one of the leading causes of the depletion of the Northern Right whale population and indicated that more than half of the Northern Right whale population bear scars indicating unobserved and unrecorded earlier entanglement. The report calls for a ban on gillnet fishing and lobster pot fishing, the two manners of fishing at issue in this case, during the Northern Right whales' high season in the Cape Cod Bay Critical Habitat from January 1 to May 15 of each year, and in the Great South Channel from April 1 to June 30, until modified fishing equipment is developed that will diminish the risk of injury and death to the Northern Right whale.

II. Massachusetts' Regulatory Authority Scheme

The Massachusetts Division of Marine Fisheries ("DMF") is vested with broad authority to regulate fishing in Massachusetts's coastal waters, which extend three nautical miles from the shoreline. Nearly all commercial fishing vessels must receive a permit from DMF in order to take fish, including shellfish, from Massachusetts coastal waters. DMF is a division of the Department of Fisheries, Wildlife and Environmental Law Enforcement, which is part of the Executive Office of Environmental Affairs. The Division of Fisheries and Wildlife, a subcomponent of the Department of Fisheries, Wildlife and Environmental Law Enforcement, "has authority over all endangered species of Massachusetts including marine mammals."

The DMF has limited the use of gillnets and lobster pot fishing gear in certain areas. See [] 322 C.M.R. § 4.09 (restricting use of gillnets south and west of Cape Cod), § 4.11 (restricting use of gillnets in Massachusetts Bay), § 4.13 (regulating fixed gear marking and maximum length requirements), § 6.13 (setting lobster trap limit), § 8.10 (fixed gear restrictions). In 1994, in response to the alarming depletion of the Harbor porpoise, DMF ordered that all sink gillnets be removed from coastal waters north of Cape Ann every November and from Massachusetts Bay and Cape Cod Bay every March.

***

The district court's reasoning, in finding that Massachusetts' commercial fishing regulatory scheme likely exacted a taking in violation of the ESA, was founded on two provisions of the ESA read in conjunction. The first relates to the definition of the prohibited activity of a "taking," and the second relates to the solicitation or causation by a third party of a prohibited activity, such as a taking. The district court viewed these provisions, when read together, to apply to acts by third parties that allow or authorize acts that exact a taking and that, but for the permitting process, could not take place. Indeed, the district court cited several opinions that have also so held. See, e.g., *Sierra Club v. Yeutter*, 926 F.2d 429, 438-39 (5th Cir. 1991) (finding Forest Service's management of timber stands was a taking of the red-cockaded woodpecker in violation of the ESA); *Defenders of Wildlife v. EPA*, 882 F.2d 1294, 1301 (8th Cir. 1989) (holding that the EPA's registration of pesticides containing strychnine violated the ESA, both because endangered species had died from ingesting strychnine bait and because that strychnine could only be distributed pursuant to the EPA's registration scheme); *Palila v. Hawaii Dep't of Land and Nat. Resources*, 639 F.2d 495, 497-98 (9th Cir. 1981) (holding state's practice of maintaining feral goats and sheep in palila's habitat constituted a taking and ordering state to remove goats and sheep); *Loggerhead Turtle v. County Council of Volusia County*, 896 F. Supp. 1170, 1180-81 (M.D. Fla. 1995) (holding that county's authorization of vehicular beach access during turtle mating season exacted a taking of the turtles in violation of the ESA). The statute not only prohibits the acts of those parties that directly exact the taking, but also bans those acts of a third party that bring about the acts exacting a taking. We believe that, contrary to the defendants' argument on appeal, the district court properly found that a governmental third party pursuant to whose authority an actor directly exacts a taking of an endangered species may be deemed to have violated the provisions of the ESA.

The defendants argue that the statute was not intended to prohibit state licensure activity because such activity cannot be a "proximate cause" of the taking. The defendants direct our attention to long-standing principles of common law tort in arguing that the district court improperly found that its regulatory scheme "indirectly causes" these takings. Specifically, the defendants contend that to construe the proper meaning of "cause" under the ESA, this court should look to common law principles of causation and further contend that proximate cause is lacking here. The defendants are correct that when interpreting a term in a statute which is, like "cause" here, well-known to the common law, the court is to presume that

Congress intended the meaning to be interpreted as in the common law. We do not believe, however, that an interpretation of "cause" that includes the "indirect causation" of a taking by the Commonwealth through its licensing scheme falls without the normal boundaries.

The defendants protest this interpretation. Their first argument is that the Commonwealth's licensure of a generally permitted activity does not cause the taking any more than its licensure of automobiles and drivers solicits or causes federal crimes, even though automobiles it licenses are surely used to violate federal drug laws, rob federally insured banks, or cross state lines for the purpose of violating state and federal laws. The answer to this argument is that, whereas it is possible for a person licensed by Massachusetts to use a car in a manner that does not risk the violations of federal law suggested by the defendants, it is not possible for a licensed commercial fishing operation to use its gillnets or lobster pots in the manner permitted by the Commonwealth without risk of violating the ESA by exacting a taking. Thus, the state's licensure of gillnet and lobster pot fishing does not involve the intervening independent actor that is a necessary component of the other licensure schemes which it argues are comparable. Where the state has licensed an automobile driver to use that automobile and her license in a manner consistent with both state and federal law, the violation of federal law is caused only by the actor's conscious and independent decision to disregard or go beyond the licensed purposes of her automobile use and instead to violate federal, and possibly state, law. The situation is simply not the same here. In this instance, the state has licensed commercial fishing operations to use gillnets and lobster pots in specifically the manner that is likely to result in a violation of federal law. The causation here, while indirect, is not so removed that it extends outside the realm of causation as it is understood in the common law.

The defendants' next argument need only detain us momentarily. They contend that the statutory structure of the ESA does not envision utilizing the regulatory structures of the states in order to implement its provisions, but that it instead leaves that implementing authority to NMFS. The point that the defendants miss is that the district court's ruling does not impose positive obligations on the Commonwealth by converting its regulation of commercial fishing operations into a tool of the federal ESA regulatory scheme. The Commonwealth is not being compelled to enforce the provisions of the ESA. Instead, the district court's ruling seeks to end the Commonwealth's continuing violation of the Act.

We review the district court's findings of fact for clear error. The district court found that entanglement with fishing gear in Massachusetts waters caused injury or death to Northern Right whales. Indeed, the district court cited several of the Commonwealth's documents in support of this finding, including its statement that " '[f]ive right whales have been found entangled in fixed fishing gear in Massachusetts waters; three in gillnets and two in lobster lines.' " The court further cited to affidavits of three scientists that suggested that entanglement of Northern Right whales had harmed, injured, or killed those whales. The court cited eleven occasions on which Northern Right whales had been found entangled in fishing gear in Massachusetts waters between 1978 and 1995. The court also indicated that at least fifty-seven percent of all Northern right whales have scars indicating prior entanglement with fishing gear and noted that, even where the whale survives, the entanglement still wounds the whale. Although these findings indicate only that entanglements have occurred in Massachusetts waters, the district court determined that three whales had been found entangled in gear deployed in Massachusetts waters.

***

The defendants next contend that the district court ignored evidence of the significant efforts made by the Commonwealth to "minimize Northern right whale entanglements in fishing gear," and evidence of other causes of takings of Northern Right whales. With respect to the determination of whether a taking has occurred, the district court quite rightly disregarded such evidence. Given that there was evidence that any entanglement with fishing gear injures a Northern Right whale and given that a single injury to one whale is a taking under the ESA, efforts to minimize such entanglements are irrelevant. For the same reasons, the existence of other means by which takings of Northern Right whales occur is irrelevant to the determination of whether the Commonwealth has engaged in a taking.

Finding neither any error of law nor any clear error with respect to the factual findings, we believe that the district court properly applied the ESA to the facts presented and was correct in enjoining the Commonwealth so as to prevent the taking of Northern Right whales in violation of the ESA. . . .

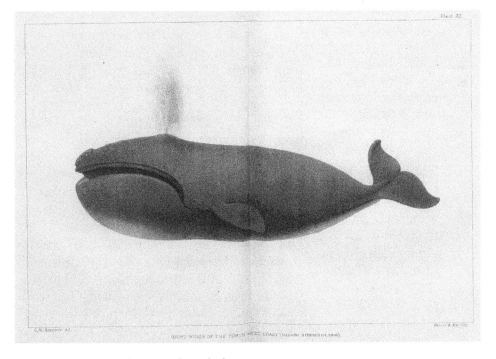

Figure 3-3. A Northern Right Whale

points for discussion

1. *Epilog.* There is some uncertainty whether any Northern right whales still exist outside of the North American population. Population estimates by NOAA tend to place the population at over 400, while conservation organizations think the population is in the low 300s. Vessel collisions and fishing gear entanglements remain the largest cause of mortality among right whales, although ocean noise and climate change, which disturbs their food chain, also pose threats that are difficult to assess.

   The Northern right whale is also protected under the MMPA, which requires "take reduction plans" to protect marine mammals from harm from commercial fishing practices. NOAA has developed an Atlantic Large Whale Take Reduction Plan, covering the Northern right whale, the humpback whale, the fin whale, and the minke whale. A 1997 regulation required all ships to try to maintain a 500-yard distance from any right whales, avoid them, and if within 500 yards, move away from them at a "slow, safe speed." Unfortunately, regulations to reduce

   Right whales are the rarest of all large whales. They were actually so named because early whalers, who valued their rich oil deposits, considered them to be the "right" whales for hunting. The species at issue in the above case is actually the North Atlantic right whale, a subspecies related to other baleen whales more abundant in the Southern hemisphere and the Pacific Ocean. North Pacific right whales are even more endangered, with about 100 surviving in the wild. North Atlantic right whales are slow swimmers, and tend to swim close to land, making them easier targets than other, more elusive whale species. They are filter feeders, straining huge volumes of ocean waters through their enormous mouth, and using their baleen teeth to catch krill, shrimp, and other small ocean life. North Atlantic right whales feed and mate off the coasts of New England and the maritime provinces of Canada, then migrate south for calving grounds, off the coasts of South Carolina, Georgia, and northern Florida. NOAA has designated two critical habitat areas, the New England coastal waters, and the coastal waters running from Cape Fear, North Carolina, down to Cape Canaveral, Florida. North Atlantic right whales have been protected from hunting since the 1950s but have not increased in population. The first North Atlantic right whale calf sighting in over two years occurred in December 2018, a troublingly long hiatus. In 2017, twelve North Atlantic right whales were killed in Canada and five in the United States, from ship strikes and net entanglements. Canada subsequently proposed additional measures to protect right whales, like speed limits in the St. Lawrence River, where many of the fatal ship strikes take place.

entanglements, which kill Northern right whales much more often than ship strikes, have been ineffective. Regulations mandate more traps per vertical fishing line (reducing the number of vertical lines in the ocean), sinking groundlines for fixed-gear fisheries, and gear visibility requirements. About 3,000 square miles of right whale habitat off the coast of Massachusetts are seasonally closed to fishing. An Atlantic Large Whale "Take Reduction Team" (see below, under discussion of the Marine Mammal Protection Act) meets yearly via webinar to discuss possibilities such as requiring the use of weaker ropes, so that right whales might break away if entangled. NOAA somewhat generously describes progress as "incremental." In 2014, seven Northern right whales were known to be entangled in fishing gear, two of them dying.

2. *Conscription or regulation?* The court makes short work of the argument by the State of Massachusetts that it was being asked to carry out the ESA. It is worth taking note that the State of Massachusetts is a defendant. Its regulations are being challenged as being insufficiently protective of endangered species. Does it surprise you that a state can be guilty of a "take" under Section 9 of the ESA for failing to protect listed species? Do you see any logical limits to what a state might be required to regulate to protect listed species?

Figure 3-4. Monk Seals in Hawai'i

Not only can states be guilty of a Section 9 "take," but so too can the federal government, as the following case illustrates.

Greenpeace Foundation v. Mineta

122 F. Supp. 2d 1123 (D. Haw. 2000)

Judge KING delivered the opinion of the United States District Court, District of Hawaii.

The Hawaiian monk seal (*Monachus schauinslandi*) ("monk seal") is an endangered species. Statistics on the status of the monk seal paint a grim picture. Recent population estimates indicate that the current monk seal population numbers at approximately 1,300 to 1,400. A 1997 National Marine Fisheries Service ("NMFS") report noted that the seal population at French Frigate Shoals ("FFS") atoll, which is home to one of the largest monk seal colonies, has declined nearly 55% since 1989. The survival rate of monk seal pups is another portent of the bleak outlook for the monk seal. In the mid-1980's, approximately 90% of seal pups at FFS survived to age two. The survival rate declined to about 10% in the mid-1990's. Indeed, NMFS scientists agree that "[t]he overall status of the Hawaiian monk seal is extremely grave."

The monk seal is endemic to Hawaii. It inhabits eight areas in the Northwestern Hawaiian Islands ("NWHI"). . . . Defendant NMFS has designated the NWHI as the monk seal's "critical habitat."

An active lobster fishery and bottomfish fishery operate in the NWHI. NMFS and the Western Pacific Regional Fishery Management Council ("Council") manage each fishery via separate Fishery Management Plans ("FMP") prepared pursuant to the Magnuson-Stevens Fishery Conservation and Management Act, NMFS adopted the FMP for the Crustacean Fisheries of the Western Pacific Region ("Crustacean FMP") in 1983, and the FMP for the Bottomfish and Seamount Groundfish Fisheries of the Western Pacific Region ("Bottomfish FMP") in 1986. The lobster fishery harvests spiny lobster (*Panulirus marginatus*) and slipper lobster (*Scyllarides squammosus*). The bottomfish fishery targets snappers, groupers, and jacks. Monk seals are known to prey on the species harvested by the fisheries.

Plaintiffs Greenpeace Foundation, Center for Biological Diversity, and Turtle Island Restoration Network ("Plaintiffs") brought this suit against Defendants Norman Mineta, Secretary of Commerce; and Penelope D. Dalton, Assistant Administrator of the NMFS (collectively, "Defendants"). The target of the suit is the embattled NMFS, whom Plaintiffs allege is violating the Administrative Procedure Act ("APA"), by managing the fisheries in a manner that does not comply with Sections 7 and 9 of the Endangered Species Act ("ESA"), and the National Environmental Policy Act ("NEPA").

The crux of the ESA claims is that the fisheries are depleting the monk seal's food supply and interacting with monk seals in an injurious manner. Cast in the language of the ESA, the claims allege that (1) NMFS has been remiss in performing its Section 7 duty to consult with the Secretary of Commerce regarding the impact of the FMPs on protected species, and (2) the operation of the fisheries has resulted in "takes" of monk seals in violation of Section 9.

***

II. Endangered Species Act

A. Section 7

Section 7 of the ESA requires every federal agency to "insure that any action authorized, funded, or carried out by such agency . . . is not likely to jeopardize the continued existence" or "result in the destruction or adverse modification of habitat" of listed species. To fulfill its obligation under Section 7, an agency must consult with the Secretary of Commerce. An agency must use "the best scientific and commercial data available" in conducting the consultation.

***

After consultation is complete, the Secretary must prepare a biological opinion. The biological opinion must include a "detailed discussion of the effects of the action on listed species or critical habitat" and the Secretary's "opinion on whether the action is likely to jeopardize the continued existence of a listed species or result in the destruction or adverse modification of critical habitat," (a "jeopardy opinion"), or whether the proposed action poses no threat of jeopardy or adverse modification (a "no jeopardy opinion"). If new information reveals effects of the action that may affect listed species or critical habitat in a manner or to an extent not previously considered, the agency must reinitiate consultation. Consultation must also be reinitiated if the action is modified in a manner that causes an effect to a listed species or its habitat that was not previously considered.

Plaintiffs contend that NMFS ignored the best scientific and commercial data available in preparing the biological opinions on the Crustacean FMP. In reviewing whether NMFS's past consultation efforts satisfied Section 7 requirements, the Court applies the standard set forth in the APA, which requires that an agency action be set aside if it is "arbitrary, capricious, an abuse of discretion or otherwise not in accordance with law."

NMFS issued the first biological opinion on the Crustacean FMP in 1981. The theme pervading the opinion is that insufficient information prevented detailed assessment of the impact of the FMP on the monk seal. The opinion identified spiny lobster as a prey species for monk seals, but it could not ascertain its relationship to the monk seal diet. The opinion stated that monk seals are "opportunistic feeders supported by a diverse prey base." NMFS believed that monk seals could adapt to other prey species if lobster were to become unavailable. However, the available information did not permit NMFS to assess the amount of shift in the monk seal's diet from lobster to other prey caused by lobster fishing or the impact of that stress. NMFS opined that the lobster fishery did have the "potential of reducing the lobster populations to levels at which lobsters are no longer available to monk seals." NMFS further admitted that the maximum sustainable yield ("MSY") and optimum yield ("OY") estimates of the lobster population calculated by the Council were too high and rested on the erroneous assumption that the lobster stocks in the NWHI were unexploited. The opinion warned: "[I]f OY is overestimated the fishery could result in depletion of the lobster resources. Therefore the FMP does not insure the availability of lobster to monk seals." The opinion concluded that "[t]here is insufficient information available for the Council to be able to insure that the proposed activity will not jeopardize the continued existence of the monk seal. . . ." NMFS stressed that the opinion was not to be construed as a "no jeopardy opinion" and that it "in no way alleviate[d] the Council of its obligation under Section 7(a) (2) of the ESA to insure that the activities conducted under the spiny lobster FMP are not likely to jeopardize the continued existence of the threatened and endangered species which occur in the NWHI. . . ." Despite this conclusion, the opinion paradoxically recommended implementation of the FMP.

The conclusions of the 1981 biological opinion are difficult to reconcile with the recommendation of NMFS that the FMP be implemented. NMFS has an affirmative obligation under Section 7(a) (2) to insure that agency action will not jeopardize the continued existence of listed species or adversely modify their habitat. Certainly, an agency's assessment of proposed action is limited by the best scientific and commercial information available. Data on the role of lobster in the monk seal's diet was admittedly sparse at the time the 1981 biological opinion was prepared. Nonetheless, when an agency concludes after consultation that it cannot insure that the proposed action will not result in jeopardy, and yet proceeds to implement such action, the agency has flouted the plain requirements of Section 7.

The next biological opinion prepared in connection with the lobster fishery, issued in 1996, assessed the impact of Amendment 9 to the Crustacean FMP. Amendment 9 established a new harvest guideline system that allowed fishermen to retain berried and undersized lobsters in a catch. The rationale was that the retention limits then in effect resulted in waste from mortality of lobsters that are captured and released without contributing to the protection of the reproductive potential of lobster stocks. The new proposed harvest management program was based on the existing model for calculating the exploitable lobster population. The models indicated that stocks of spiny lobster would remain healthy over the long term. At the same time, the opinion noted a "continuing decline in pup production, and total seal counts over the past six years, [which] is cause for significant concern." Id at 6. NMFS attributed the decline to several factors, one of which was the reduction of the availability of prey such as lobster due to lobster fishing. The availability of lobster had been particularly low at FFS for a number of years. NMFS maintained, as it did before and does today, that "monk seals appear to be very opportunistic and catholic feeders." However, NMFS still had not elucidated the importance of lobsters to the monk seal's diet. . . .

The 1996 opinion in many ways perpetuated the errors of the 1981 opinion. As a memorandum from one NMFS scientist to another regarding the 1996 opinion reveals, NMFS takes the position in the opinion that its knowledge of monk seal behavior had not advanced much in the past fifteen years. And so management of the lobster fishery remained relatively unchanged. The harvest management system under Amendment 9 was predicated on the existing model of calculating the exploitable population of lobster, with the addition of a guideline permitting retention of berried and undersized lobsters. NMFS ignored the flaws of that model, as evidenced by its observation in the 1996 opinion that the status of the lobster stocks was relatively healthy. In fact, the lobster stocks showed signs of stress. From 1983 to 1991, the catch per unit effort ("CPUE") declined from 2.71 to 0.56 legal spiny and slipper lobsters per trap haul. NMFS closed the lobster fishery in 1991 and 1993. It reopened the fishery briefly in 1994, but aborted the season shortly after it began when it realized that its harvest quota was too high. In the year before the 1996 biological opinion issued, the CPUE was an anemic 0.60. Such data should have alerted NMFS that the existing model of calculating the exploitable lobster population was in need of revision. NMFS ignored the data.

***

A review of the 1996 opinion convinces the Court that NMFS did not adequately discharge its duties under Section 7(a)(2). If, in the 1981 opinion NMFS was uncertain of the impact of the FMP because it knew too little about the monk seal diet, by 1996 it was emboldened by its ignorance to draw definitive conclusions about the impact. NMFS reiterated in the 1996 opinion that the available information still had not clarified the importance of lobster in the monk seal diet; yet, in a departure from its conclusion in 1981, NMFS this time concluded that no jeopardy to the monk seal would result. . . .

***

NMFS has failed to fulfill its "rigorous" affirmative duty under Section 7 to "insure" that implementation of the Crustacean FMP does not result in jeopardy or adverse modification. NMFS cannot speculate that no jeopardy to monk seals or adverse modification of their critical habitat will occur because it lacks enough information regarding the impact of the fishery on seals.

B. Section 9

Section 9(a)(1)(B) of the ESA makes it unlawful for any person to take any endangered species of wildlife within the United States or the territorial seas of the United States. "Take" is defined as "harass, harm, pursue, hunt, shoot, wound, kill, trap, capture, or collect, or to attempt to engage in any such conduct." The term "harm" includes "significant habitat modification or degradation which actually kills or injures fish or wildlife by significantly impairing essential behavioral patterns, including breeding, spawning, rearing, migrating, feeding or sheltering."

1. The Lobster Fishery

Plaintiffs claim that the lobster fishery adversely modifies the habitat of the monk seal by depleting the lobster population in the NWHI. It is undisputed that the fishery removes prey from the critical habitat of the monk seal. The question is whether the removal of prey results in adverse habitat modification. Plaintiffs offer circumstantial evidence that it does. One study revealed that monk seals at FFS dive deeper and travel farther to forage than seals at Pearl and Hermes Reef because there is less food available at FFS. Another study found that monk seals at FFS consume more cephalopods than seals elsewhere because other prey is less available to them. Decreased prey availability has been hypothesized to be a cause of the decline in the reproduction, survival, and condition of surviving immature seals. Plaintiffs also rely on studies of the monk seal's diet. One study found that lobster contains amino acids and macrominerals important to bodily functions of the monk seal. Fatty acid signature analysis of monk seal blubber suggests that lobster comprises a significant part of the monk seal's diet.

The information in the record is insufficient to establish as a matter of law that lobster is absolutely critical to the diet of the monk seal. Plaintiffs may of course rely on circumstantial evidence to show a causal link between lobster fishing and the monk seal population. Circumstantial evidence was the basis for the findings of adverse habitat modification in *Palila v. Hawaii Department of Land & Natural Resources*, and *Sierra Club v. Lyng*. The difference is that the agency action in those cases destroyed or modified a feature of the species' habitat that was decidedly critical to the continued existence of the species. In *Palila*, this Court found that mamane trees were clearly essential to the endangered Palila's survival. In *Lyng*, the court found that the very shelter upon which the red-cockaded woodpecker depended for survival was threatened by the Forest Service's management of the Texas national forests.

Here, it is not certain that lobster plays such an essential role in the monk seal diet that a reduction of lobster prey dooms the monk seal to extinction. The studies Plaintiffs rely upon do not prove otherwise. Studies of monk seal foraging behavior may indicate a decrease in prey availability in general, but they do not show that it is a reduction in the availability of *lobster* that causes monk seals to consume other prey. Indeed, one study hypothesized that monk seals were consuming more octopi because fewer teleosts (ray-finned fish) were available. Nor do the data based on fatty acid signature analysis prove that the monk seal relies heavily on lobster as part of its diet. Dr. Sara Iverson, the researcher conducting the studies, submits a declaration to the Court in which she states that her findings "cannot be conclusive and should not be used as a basis for decisions concerning possible interactions between fisheries and monk seals." Dr. Iverson emphasizes that her research is "preliminary" and that it has not been peer reviewed. She anticipates an additional three years of research before she can make "firm and defensible conclusions" about the importance of various prey in the monk seal diet.

The Court agrees that preliminary findings are not a basis for a conclusive determination that lobster comprises a significant and essential portion of the monk seal diet. On the basis of the currently available scientific information, this Court cannot find as a matter of law that the removal of lobster from the monk seal's critical habitat results in "harm" to the monk seal within the meaning of Section

9. The role of lobster in the monk seal diet is a question of fact that precludes summary judgment on the Section 9 claim.

The ruling does not assure victory for NMFS. NMFS's position is essentially that it is innocent of Section 9 violations because it is not aware of any data that confirms that it is in violation of Section 9; such is a head-in-the-sand attitude we do not condone. It is also a position in conflict with the underlying philosophy of the ESA. But to this problem we assign the requirements of NEPA and Section 7 of the ESA, not section 9.

Because a material question of fact exists, the Court DENIES summary judgment to Plaintiffs and DENIES summary judgment to Defendants on the Section 9 claim with respect to the lobster fishery.

2. The Bottomfish Fishery

Plaintiffs claim that the bottomfish fishery "takes" monk seals within the meaning of Section 9 of the ESA. Harm to the monk seal allegedly occurs in several ways. First, fishermen sometimes respond violently to monk seals that attempt to take fish from their lines. According to NMFS, there have been incidents of fishermen clubbing or shooting monk seals in response to catch theft. In 1990, an anonymous informant alleged that one monk seal per day was being killed and discarded by fishermen. NMFS investigated into the allegations and could not confirm any mortality or injury to monk seals as a result of interaction with bottomfish vessels. Second, bottomfishing gear can harm monk seals. There are reports of monk seals being injured by bottomfish hooks. . . . Third, bottomfish fishermen are known to discard unmarketable fish near monk seals for them to consume in order to distract them away from fishing lines. Such fish often contain ciguatera toxin, which is poisonous to seals.

NMFS is aware of the potential for harmful interaction between bottomfish fishermen and monk seals. In a 1986 biological opinion on the implementation of the Bottomfish FMP, NMFS acknowledged the possibility that bottomfish fishermen might harm monk seals, but dismissed it as an insignificant concern given the low rate of interaction anticipated and the fact that NMFS planned to conduct an education program for fishermen. NMFS issued another biological opinion on the fishery in 1991, this time addressing an amendment to the Bottomfish FMP which would place observers on selected fishing vessels in the NWHI and expand the number of islands and atolls that required a 50 nautical-mile study zone. NMFS adopted the amendment. Enforcement of the observer policy has been lax, however. From 1991 to 1993, NMFS placed observers on approximately 12% of bottomfishing trips in the NWHI. No observers were placed on any bottomfish vessels in the NWHI in 1996 and 1997. Without the aid of significant observer coverage, accurate measurement of the incidence of harmful interaction is elusive.

The evidence in the administrative record confirms that monk seals have been killed, hooked, and poisoned in connection with bottomfishing. Such documented interactions are "takes" within the meaning of Section 9 of the ESA. It is immaterial that certain of these incidents might be accidental. NMFS has not authorized any incidental takes of monk seals, nor could it, since the monk seal is designated as a "depleted" species under the Marine Mammal Protection Act of 1972. Takes of depleted species are permitted for scientific purposes only. Any takes of monk seals as a result of bottomfishing are a violation of Section 9.

Accordingly, the Court GRANTS summary judgment to Plaintiffs and DENIES summary judgment to Defendants on the Section 9 claim in connection with the bottomfish fishery.

points for discussion

1. *Litigation strategy.* The court is quite critical of NMFS for its actions pertaining to lobsters under Section 7 but finds plaintiffs' evidence of a "take" under Section 9 wanting. Why would standards under Sections 7 and 9 differ? Can you evaluate the tradeoffs of seeking relief under those two particular sections?

2. *Where's the harm?* What do you think is the nature of the "take" regarding the bottomfish fisheries? If NMFS is found to be violating Section 9 by failing to sufficiently regulate bottomfish fisheries, what measures would absolve it from liability? Like Steller sea lions, Hawai'ian monk seals are victims of human violence: Four monk seals were killed by gunshot in 2017, including a pregnant female. NOAA also reported that three were killed by gunshots in 2009 and 2010.

3. *Seal conservation.* Hawai'ian monk seals are one of the few seal species that thrive in warm, tropical waters rather than frigid waters. The related Caribbean monk seals are now extinct. The Hawai'ian monk seal population continued to decline after this case, dropping to about 900 in 2010. NOAA estimated in 2017 a population of approximately 1,400 Hawai'ian monk seals, approximately the same population as when the above case was litigated. In addition to spiny lobster depletion, Hawai'ian monk seals are also killed by entanglement in nets. In general, a population by the Northwest Hawai'ian Islands seems to be increasing, while populations closer to the main, populated Hawai'ian Islands seem to be suffering. In fact, NOAA has a "translocation" program that seems to be funneling seals from treacherous habitat near the main Hawai'ian Islands to the Northwest Hawai'ian Islands area. NOAA efforts seem to be focused on these sorts of strategies that try to mitigate the problem after the fact, such as rescuing seals that are entangled, malnourished, or injured by fishing hooks. Is this approach justified by local resistance to fishing restrictions? Would some of the funding for saving endangered seals be better spent on observers?

NOTE ON ESA INCIDENTAL TAKE PERMITS

The necessarily vague standards of "take," "harm," and "harass" have given both regulators and regulated persons fits over what should and should not be allowed. An amendment to the ESA in 1982 provided a key, although it would be over a decade before the U.S. Fish and Wildlife Service realized its usefulness. While former Arizona governor Bruce Babbitt served as Interior Secretary, in the Clinton Administration, the agency began to use Section 10 of the ESA to issue "incidental take permits," which permit "any taking otherwise prohibited [by Section 9] if such taking is incidental to, and not the purpose of, the carrying out of an otherwise lawful activity." 16 U.S.C. § 1539(a)(1)(B). What that means is that the Fish and Wildlife Service or the National Marine Fisheries Service may issue a permit to engage in some legal activity — such as land development, fishing, oil and gas exploration, or any number of things — that *might* cause indirect harm to listed species and thus expose the actor to Section 9 liability under the ESA.

Interior (or Commerce) can only issue a Section 10 permit if the applicant first submits "a conservation plan" that specifies —

(i) the impact which will likely result from such taking;

(ii) what steps the applicant will take to minimize and mitigate such impacts, and the funding that will be available to implement such steps;

(iii) what alternative actions to such taking the applicant considered and the reasons why such alternatives are not being utilized; and

(iv) such other measures that the Secretary may require as being necessary or appropriate for purposes of the plan.

16 U.S.C. § 1539(a)(2)(A).

These plans have become known as "habitat conservation plans." As opposed to land-based endangered or threatened species, which may have specific needs for specific plots of land, the word "habitat" is somewhat less intuitive for marine species, but the idea is the same: In order to allow the incidental take of endangered or threatened species, the applicant must agree to do certain things to enhance the survival of the species, as compensation for this limited license to violate Section 9. In addition, in order for a permit to issue, the Secretary must find that:

(i) the taking will be incidental;

(ii) the applicant will, to the maximum extent practicable, minimize and mitigate the impacts of such taking,

(iii) the applicant will ensure that adequate funding for the plan will be provided;

(iv) the taking will not appreciably reduce the likelihood of the survival and recovery of the species in the wild; and

(v) all of the measures in the habitat conservation plan will be met.

16 U.S.C. § 1539(a)(2)(B)(i)-(v).

Through the habitat conservation planning process, the details of mitigation measures can be fleshed out, and expectations for land management and public and private behavior made concrete. For example, land developers in southern

Alabama, in the habitat of the endangered Alabama beach mouse, have been required to encumber subdivided lots with a variety of restrictions, such as a prohibition on cat ownership, the adoption of approved lighting plans, and a prohibition on planting non-indigenous plants. These restrictions are recorded, making them binding on all future owners.

Since state and local governments can be liable under Section 9, state and local governments may be the applicants for incidental take permits. Following *Babbitt v. Sweet Home*, discussed briefly above, the State of Washington entered into a habitat conservation plan that allowed some logging to proceed as long as the state and private logging companies regulated by the state agreed to abide by a list of complex measures to protect Northern spotted owls. For example, the plan sometimes specified different amounts of logging that could be permitted within certain distances of known owl nesting sites. As long as the State of Washington enforced those limits, and logging companies abided by them, no prosecution for a Section 9 take would occur.

By the same token, following the decision of *Loggerhead Turtle v. Volusia County*, 148 F.3d 1231 (11th Cir. 1998), the defendant county was required to undertake regulatory measures to protect sea turtles that might nest on beaches within the county, including private beachfront property. When sea turtles hatch at night and emerge from their nest, they instinctively swim toward light, which on undeveloped beaches is the moonlight reflecting off the ocean. Light from residential and commercial properties confuses the sea turtle hatchlings, causing them to crawl in the wrong direction. Volusia County thus entered into a habitat conservation plan in which the county was required to develop beachfront lighting regulations. The lighting ordinance identifies sea turtle nesting areas and specifies that light should not be visible by a person standing on the beach. Volusia County is also home to an odd tradition of driving motor vehicles on public beaches. Under its habitat conservation plan, the county agreed to restrict the times, places, and seasons in which beach driving would be permitted.

In all of these habitat conservation plans, the Fish and Wildlife Service agrees to refrain from prosecution as long as the permittees abide by the conditions. No one expects habitat conservation plans to work perfectly; deaths, injury, and other "incidental takes" will still occur. But the issuance of an incidental take permit reflects the judgment of the Service that some harm to listed species will inevitably occur, and that the habitat conservation plan will mitigate the harm, and "will not appreciably reduce the likelihood of survival and recovery of the species in the wild."

B. MARINE MAMMAL PROTECTION ACT

Like the ESA, the run-up to passage of the Marine Mammal Protection Act (MMPA) had strong moral undercurrents. For years, tuna fishermen had been exploiting the fact that certain species of dolphins tend to swim over or near schools of tuna. As dolphins are marine mammals that must surface to breathe, this made tuna easy to locate, and to catch. Tuna fishermen used large purse seine nets to encircle the tuna and, incidentally, the dolphins, with the result that dolphins were often casualties of tuna fishing. A report from the House Merchant Marine and Fisheries Committee estimated that more than 400,000 dolphins were being killed each year in this way, often dying gruesome deaths that shocked members of Congress. Dolphins weren't the only victims of casual cruelty. A House Committee report concluded:

> Recent history indicates that man's impact upon marine mammals has ranged from what might be termed malign neglect to virtual genocide. These animals, including whales, porpoises, seals, sea otters, polar bears, manatees and others, have only rarely benefited from our interest; they have been shot, blown up, clubbed to death, run down by boats, poisoned, and exposed to a multitude of other indignities, all in the interest of profit or recreation, with little or no consideration of the potential impact of these activities on the animal populations involved.

H.R. REP. No. 92-707, at 15 (1971).

Like the ESA, the goal of the MMPA is to protect (not utilize) sea life. The Act does not, by its terms, contemplate any trading-off between marine mammals and industrial interests. "The primary purpose of the MMPA is to protect marine mammals; the [MMPA] was not intended as a 'balancing act' between the interests of the fishing industry and the animals." *Comm. for Humane Legislation v. Richardson*, 414 F. Supp. 297, 306 (D.D.C. 1976). So, the MMPA provides that "[t]here shall be a moratorium on the taking and importation of marine mammals and marine mammal products . . . " and that "any person or vessel subject to the jurisdiction of the United States may not take, possess, transport, purchase, sell, export, offer to purchase, sell or export any marine mammal or marine mammal product."

The term "take" in the MMPA is similar to that in the ESA, and is defined as "harass, hunt, capture, or kill, or attempt to harass, hunt, capture, or kill." The term "harassment" is defined as "any act of pursuit, torment, or annoyance which (i) has the potential to injure a marine mammal or a marine mammal stock in the wild; or (ii) has the potential to disturb a marine mammal or a marine mammal stock in the wild by causing disruption of behavioral patterns, including, but not limited to, migration, breathing, nursing, breeding, feeding, or sheltering." 16 U.S.C. § 1362(18)(A).

It is worth noting that the MMPA applies to all marine mammals, endangered or not. Marine mammals that are listed under the ESA as either endangered or threatened enjoy the protections of both statutes, although the ESA is generally more protective. But abundant marine mammals, which include several species of dolphin, are only protected under the MMPA.

The take moratorium admits of a number of exceptions. Under a variety of conditions of varying complexity, the MMPA allows takes to occur:

- incidentally in the course of commercial fishing. 16 U.S.C. § 1372(a)(2), and 16 U.S.C. § 1387.
- for scientific research, public display, photography for educational and commercial purposes, or enhancing the survival or recovery of a species or stock. 16 U.S.C. § 1372(a)(1).
- as expressly provided for by an international treaty, convention, or agreement to which the United States is a party. 16 U.S.C. § 1372(a)(2).
- by nonlethal means, to deter a marine mammal from damaging gear, catch, or private property, or from endangering personal safety, and for a government

employee to deter a marine mammal from damaging public property. 16 U.S.C. § 1372(a)(4)(A).

- incidentally, by U.S. citizens only, of a small number of marine mammals in a specified geographic region, for a five-year period, if the Secretary, after notice and opportunity for comment, finds that the taking will have a negligible impact, or an unmitigable adverse impact. 16 U.S.C. § 1372(a)(5)(A)(i).
- during military readiness activities, provided that they are conducted with the "least practicable adverse impact on such species or stock." 16 U.S.C. § 1372(a)(5)(A)(ii).
- by any Indian, Aleut, or Eskimo who resides in Alaska and who dwells on the coast of the North Pacific Ocean or the Arctic Ocean if such taking is for subsistence purposes, or is done for purposes of creating and selling authentic native articles of handicrafts and clothing, and is not accomplished in a wasteful manner. 16 U.S.C. § 1372(b).

1. Incidental Take Permits for Commercial Fishing

The most significant exemption, in terms of impacts on marine mammals, pertains to the exemption for incidental takes in the course of commercial fishing. This is the direct analog to Section 10 incidental take permits under the Endangered

Figure 3-5.
Fishermen have long engaged in "fishing over dolphins," because dolphins often congregate to feed on fish such as tunas.

Species Act. As noted above, the incidental take of dolphins was a strong motivation for passage of the MMPA. The controversy over dolphin mortality and tuna fishing did not abate after passage.

Committee for Humane Legislation v. Richardson

540 F.2d 1141 (D.C. Cir. 1976)

PER CURIAM, United States Court of Appeals, District of Columbia Circuit.

Prior to 1960 the most common method of fishing for yellowfin tuna was use of pole, line, and live bait. In the Eastern Tropical Pacific yellowfin tuna fishery, fishermen observed in the late 1950's that yellowfin habitually associate with certain species of dolphin (commonly called porpoise), and began setting their nets "on porpoise." When porpoise are spotted at the ocean surface, speedboats are deployed to herd them to where the net will be set. The tuna follow below the porpoise. The porpoise then are encircled with a cup-like purse-seine net, the open bottom of which is then drawn closed in the manner of a drawstring purse, trapping both the porpoise and the tuna beneath.

Although efforts are made to free the trapped porpoise, purse-seine fishing has resulted in substantial incidental deaths of porpoise. Porpoise are air-breathing mammals, and may be suffocated if they become entangled in the net, or drowned as a result of shock or physical injury. The number of incidental porpoise deaths in recent years has been as follows:

1971	312,400
1972	304,600
1973	175,000
1974	97,800
1975	130,000 (est.)

The average number of porpoise killed each time purse-seine nets are "set" was 70 in 1971, 43 in 1972, 19 in 1973, 12 in 1974, and 17 in 1975.

The effectiveness of purse-seine fishing has led to dramatic increases in its use by the United States tuna fishing fleet. The catch of yellowfin tuna caught by United States purse-seiners on porpoise was 99,000 tons in 1974, or 60 percent of the total United States yellowfin catch (of 165,000 tons) and about 43 percent of the total United States tuna catch. For the period 1971-1974 purse-seiners fishing on porpoise accounted for 72 percent of the total catch of yellowfin.

The Marine Mammal Protection Act of 1972 was addressed in part to the growing problem of porpoise deaths incidental to commercial fishing. The Act was founded on a concern that certain species of marine mammals were in danger of extinction or depletion as a result of man's activities, and a concomitant belief that those species "should not be permitted to diminish below their optimum sustainable population." A moratorium was imposed on taking and importation of all marine mammals, with a two-year exemption from the moratorium for taking of marine mammals incidental to the course of commercial fishing operations.

Although the Secretary of Commerce was permitted to license incidental taking of marine mammals subsequent to the two-year exemption, the statute directs that "[i]n any event it shall be the immediate goal that the incidental kill or incidental serious injury of marine mammals permitted in the course of commercial fishing operations be reduced to insignificant levels approaching a zero mortality and serious injury rate."

The permits to be issued after the exemption period expired on October 21, 1974 were authorized under 16 U.S.C. § 1374, which in turn required compliance with regulations issued under Section 1373. Section 1374 requires that the permit specify, inter alia, "the number and kind of animals which are authorized to be taken or imported," and the location, period, and method of the authorized taking. The applicant for a permit "must demonstrate to the Secretary that the taking or importation of any marine mammal under such permit will be consistent with the purposes of this chapter and the applicable regulations established under section 1373 of this title."

Section 1373, in turn, authorizes the Secretary to promulgate regulations "on the basis of the best scientific evidence available" for permits for taking marine mammals, "as he deems necessary and appropriate to insure that such taking will not be to the disadvantage of those species and population stocks and will be consistent with the purposes and policies set forth in section 1361 of this title." The Act requires that prior to promulgating any such regulations the Secretary shall publish and make available to the public either before or concurrent with the publication of notice in the Federal Register of his intention to prescribe regulations under this section (1) a statement of the estimated existing levels of the species and population stocks of the marine mammal concerned; (2) a statement of the expected impact of the proposed regulations on the optimum sustainable population of such species or population stock; (3) a statement describing the evidence before the Secretary upon which he proposes to base such regulations; and (4) any studies made by or for the Secretary or any recommendations made by or for the Secretary or the Marine Mammal Commission which relate to the establishment of such regulations.

On March 13, 1974 NMFS published notice of its intent to prescribe regulations for taking porpoise incidental to commercial fishing. It took this action despite its professed lack of knowledge as to the actual populations of porpoise, the optimum sustainable populations, or the effect of the takings on the optimum sustainable populations of porpoise. Final regulations were promulgated on September 5, 1974, and the American Tunaboat Association was granted a general permit for the period October 21, 1974 to December 31, 1975 under which fishermen holding certificates of inclusion in the general permit were permitted to take an unlimited number of porpoise.

Despite subsequent warnings by the Marine Mammal Commission that the levels of incidental porpoise deaths would remain unacceptably high, NMFS did not impose a quota, although it later amended its regulations to require improved gear and techniques. The number of porpoise killed by commercial fishermen increased from 97,800 in 1974 to about 130,000 in 1975.

The American Tunaboat Association's application for renewal of its permit was granted on December 19, 1975. Although NMFS published population estimates for two species of porpoise, it again stated that it could not make any statement as to the optimum sustainable populations or the effect of the proposed taking, and determined to set no quota as to incidental deaths unless it appeared that the total number of deaths would exceed 70 percent of the final 1975 estimate. Although the Marine Mammal Commission again warned that there was no basis for assurance that porpoise stocks would not be harmed by the taking, NMFS expressed its belief in proposing regulations that existing porpoise populations would neither increase nor decrease as a result of the taking.

Appellees, various environmental protection organizations, filed suit in 1974 and 1975 to challenge the legality of the permits issued the American Tunaboat Association. The suits were consolidated, and on May 11, 1976 the District Court entered summary judgment for plaintiffs. The court found that the overriding purpose of the Marine Mammal Protection Act was protection of the animals' interests, and held that the Act required (1) that NMFS find that the effect of any proposed taking on the optimum sustainable populations of the species involved not be to the disadvantage of the animals, (2) that the permit specify the number and kind of animals which may be taken, and (3) that the applicant for a permit demonstrate that the taking will serve the purposes of the Act. The court declared the American Tunaboat Association's general permit void and ordered that no further permit be issued until the Act has been complied with. The effect of the decision has been stayed pending further order of this court.

The first major issue presented by this appeal is whether NMFS has discretion under the Marine Mammal Protection Act of 1972 to issue permits for incidental taking of marine mammals in the course of commercial fishing when estimates of the optimum sustainable populations of the species involved and of the effect of that taking upon the optimum sustainable populations are not available.

As a preliminary matter, we may state our agreement with the District Court's conclusion that the Act was to be administered for the benefit of the protected species rather than for the benefit of commercial exploitation. That general legislative intent, however, is not dispositive of the instant question. Congress was confronted directly with the conflict between protection of the porpoise and protection of the American tuna fishing industry; one result of that conflict was the express two-year exemption granted commercial fishermen from the moratorium on taking marine mammals. More significantly for this case, the committee reports contain strong language indicating that the Act was not intended to force tuna fishermen to cease operations:

> (Section 1373(b)) lists the general criteria which may be considered by the Secretary in the process of prescribing regulations under the Act. These include a wide range of factors such as the effect of limitations on present and future animal populations, U.S. treaty requirements, ecological and environmental considerations, the conservation and development of fishery resources and economic and technical feasibility. The Secretary, for example, in regulating the operations of the tuna industry with respect to the incidental catching of porpoises must consider

the technical capability of these fishermen to avoid injury to porpoises. It is not the intention of the Committee to shut down or significantly to curtail the activities of the tuna fleet so long as the Secretary is satisfied that the tuna fishermen are using economically and technologically practicable measures to assure minimal hazards to marine mammal populations.

***

The specific requirements of the Act are indeed so clear as to require little discussion. 16 U.S.C. § 1373(d) requires that the Secretary publish, inter alia, a statement of "the estimated existing levels of the species and population stocks" of the marine mammals to be taken, and a statement of the expected impact of the takings on the optimum sustainable populations of the species. As the House committee report explained, the Act was deliberately designed to permit takings of marine mammals only when it was known that that taking would not be to the disadvantage of the species:

> In the teeth of this lack of knowledge of specific causes, and of the certain knowledge that these animals are almost all threatened in some way, it seems elementary common sense to the Committee that legislation should be adopted to require that we act conservatively that no steps should be taken regarding these animals that might prove to be adverse or even irreversible in their effects until more is known. As far as could be done, we have endeavored to build such a conservative bias into the legislation here presented.

In promulgating the instant regulations in both 1974 and 1975, NMFS did not fulfill the requirement that it determine the impact of the takings on the optimum sustainable populations of the species of porpoise involved. The statement that "[t]here is no evidence that the porpoise populations would substantially increase or decrease as a result of the regulations and reissuance of the general permit" is not at all responsive; the fact that actual stocks may be stable may supply little or nothing to the determination of effect on optimum sustainable populations. We therefore affirm the judgment of the District Court on this issue.

***

The remaining statutory requirement relevant to this appeal is contained in 16 U.S.C. § 1374(d)(3): an applicant for a permit for taking marine mammals must demonstrate that the taking "will be consistent with the purposes of this chapter and the applicable regulations established under section 1373 of this title." Again, the purpose of the requirement was stated clearly in the legislative history: "[i]f that burden is not carried and it is by no means a light burden the permit may not be issued. The effect of this set of requirements is to insist that the management of the animal populations be carried out with the interests of the animals as the prime consideration."

The court has carefully examined the American Tunaboat Association's 1974 permit application and its 1975 renewal application. Neither contains any discussion of the predicted impact of the proposed takings on the optimum sustainable population of the porpoise species involved, or otherwise displays consistency with the purposes of the Marine Mammal Protection Act. We concur in the judgment of the District Court that the applications were deficient under the terms of the Act and should not have been granted. We therefore affirm the judgment of the District Court.

points for discussion

1. *Approaching?* The case makes reference to a "zero mortality rate goal." The MMPA provides that "it shall be the immediate goal that the incidental kill or incidental serious injury of marine mammals permitted in the course of commercial fishing operations be reduced to insignificant levels approaching a zero mortality and serious injury rate." 16 U.S.C. § 1371(a)(2). This "zero mortality rate goal" was significant in forcing the regulating agencies to set very low tolerance levels for incidental take. Considering that the MMPA is strictly a conservation statute with a "zero mortality rate goal," is the required backdown procedure adequate? Does it not still simply reflect a balancing of fishing versus marine mammal protection interests, rather than a mandate to avoid killing marine mammals?

2. *MMPA goals.* The case also makes reference to the phrase "optimal sustainable population," which is defined as with respect to any population stock, the number of animals which will result in the maximum productivity of the population of the species keeping in mind the carrying capacity of the habitat and the health of the ecosystem of which they form a constituent element." 16 U.S.C. § 1362(9). Optimum sustainable population is thus analogous to the optimal population p_0 at which a fishery can be maintained indefinitely (in theory). But does such a concept go against the idea of a zero mortality rate goal?

3. *Epilog.* The tuna industry succeeded in pushing through Congress a relaxation of the stringent requirements of 16 U.S.C. § 1371(a)(2) for incidental take permits. The procedure for issuing permits to commercial fishermen that incidentally "take" marine mammals is generally quite strict, as discussed below. So, a special provision was added to 16 U.S.C. § 1371(a)(2) for yellowfin tuna harvested with purse seine nets

> The MMPA provided legal protection for all marine mammals, including dolphins, but urging Congress to take action on foreign boats was a different matter. The difference maker was Sam LaBudde, once a biologist employed with the National Marine Fisheries Service. LaBudde got himself a job on a Panamanian tuna fishing boat as a cook, posing as a curious American wanderer. He carried a video camera, and to disarm the fishing crew, he filmed himself and the sailors socializing, joking, and performing routine fishing tasks. He also filmed, however,

in the Eastern Tropical Pacific Ocean: Provided that the tuna fishing vessels are registered under a country complying with the International Dolphin Conservation Program, and that dolphin mortality limits are observed, a general permit may issue. 16 U.S.C. § 1371(a)(2)(B).

the gruesome process by which the Panamanian boat enveloped tuna and dolphins together. Dolphins were not only drowned, but crushed and mangled alive. The footage was aired on the major TV networks, and eventually shown in Congress. With the support of tuna companies, Congress eventually passed the Dolphin Protection Consumer Act of 1990, which set out standards for a tuna company affixing the now-ubiquitous *dolphin-safe* logo on all cans of tuna sold in the United States. For his work, LaBudde won the Goldman Environmental Prize in 1991.

However, additional regulations were required to protect dolphins. Regulations governing tuna fishermen in the Eastern Tropical Pacific Ocean were to include a variety of provisions, including those requiring observers on *each* vessel; requiring use of the backdown procedure (in which purse seine nets are allowed to sink below the surface of the water to give dolphins a choice to swim out) or other procedures equally or more effective; requiring the use of special equipment, including dolphin safety panels in nets and monitoring devices; ensuring that the backdown procedure during sets of purse seine netting on marine mammals is completed and rolling of the net to sack up has begun no later than 30 minutes before sundown; and the establishment of per-vessel mortality limits and per-year mortality limits. None of this special treatment applies if fishing threatens dolphins listed under the ESA. By most accounts, this regime has succeeded in keeping dolphin mortality far below those levels seen in the 1970s.

NOTE ON THE 1994 AMENDMENTS FOR INCIDENTAL TAKE PERMITS

Apart from tuna taken from the Eastern Tropical Pacific Ocean by purse seine nets, the procedure for commercial fishermen to obtain a permit for the incidental take of marine mammals is set forth in 16 U.S.C. § 1387. Known as a "general permit," the process under the original MMPA was quite stringent. A permit could only be issued if, based on the best scientific information available, it was demonstrated that the incidental take level would not disadvantage the species or be inconsistent with MMPA's conservation purposes or policies. 16 U.S.C. § 1373(a). Note that this language is analogous to the standard for the issuance of incidental take permits under Section 10 of the ESA: that the incidental taking "will not appreciably reduce the likelihood of the survival and recovery of the species in the wild."

The burden of proof was on NMFS, if it was issuing a permit, to show that the incidental take permit would not "disadvantage the species." A bias in favor of conservation was to be applied. 16 U.S.C. § 1371(a)(2). Incidental take permits could only be issued after a formal noticed hearing before an administrative law judge, provided for under 16 U.S.C. § 1373(d), and a general permit must set forth detailed information, such as an estimate of the existing levels of the species, and a statement of the expected impact on the optimum sustainable population of the species or stock, and relevant evidence. Following the decision in *Kokechik Fisherman's Ass'n v. Secretary of Commerce*, 839 F.2d 795, 802 (D.C. Cir. 1988), it became clear that permits would be difficult to obtain:

> The MMPA does not allow for a Solomonic balancing of the animals' and fisheries' interests such as the Secretary attempted. The interest in maintaining healthy populations of marine mammals comes first and the Secretary cannot ignore the fur seals. He can include the northern fur seals in the permit only if he makes the requisite findings. Lacking such findings, the permit cannot issue.

839 F.2d at 803. This strong bias in favor of protecting marine mammals did exactly what it was supposed to do: dramatically reduce the number of marine mammals incidentally taken in the course of commercial fishing. But commercial fishermen chafed. As it did at the behest of the tuna industry, Congress intervened. Gone are the stringent requirements of the old general permit process, with its burden of proof and conservation bias working against issuance of permits. The zero mortality rate goal still applies, and is even included in the new provisions, but rather than revoke permits, NMFS is required to undertake extra regulatory measures.

An amendment in 1994 shunted the commercial fishing permit process to a complicated new system of assessing the health of marine mammal stocks, and the threat posed by commercial fisheries. NMFS must periodically (typically every three years) undertake stock assessments of marine mammals. Similar to the concept of "maximum sustained yield" under the Magnuson-Stevens Act, the MMPA requires NMFS to determine each stock's "potential biological removal level" (PBR), that maximum level incidental take that would allow the stock to stay at its optimum sustainable population. The PBR must take into account natural mortality, so that it is only a measure of human-caused marine mammal mortality and is lower than total mortality. 16 U.S.C. § 1362(20). NMFS must also identify especially vulnerable "strategic stocks," stocks for which:

(i)   incidental takes exceed the PBR,
(ii) the population is below optimum sustainable population, or
(iii) the species is listed under the Endangered Species Act.

Fisheries are classified by their frequency of injuring marine mammals. Fisheries are either category I (frequently), category II (occasionally), or category III (rarely). Boats in category I or category II fisheries must register and comply with a number of regulatory and tracking provisions, like reporting takes, accommodating observers, and other take reduction measures. 16 U.S.C. § 1387(c)(3). For all category I fisheries, NMFS must develop "take reduction plans," packages of regulations that are supposed to reduce the level of takes to below PBR within six months. Take reduction plans must also be developed for category II fisheries that impact strategic stocks. Take reduction plans are in place for several marine mammals, such as bottlenose dolphins, and groups of marine mammals, such as Atlantic large whales. The plans incorporate a variety of gear, timing, and area restrictions, to go along with the usual reporting and licensing requirements. Larger plans incorporate restrictions for groups of fisheries.

Problem Exercise

Aquaculture is the raising of fish in an enclosed pen, rather than having to go out and find them and catch them. Since fish are artificially spawned and raised, eliminating predation, competition, and starvation, a large amount of fish can be grown in a relatively small space. Since many fisheries have been overfished, aquaculture is sometimes held out as an alternative to traditional capture fishing. There are downsides, of course. Fish defecate, so aquaculture pens, concentrating a large amount of fish, also concentrate a large amount of fish excrement. Fish grown in aquaculture pens have not been swimming around competing for food, and are thus less healthy, and less healthful as a food source.

Fish-doo is a company that proposes to build a salmon fish farm in the state waters of Washington, about half a mile off the shore of the Olympic Peninsula, in the 17-mile-wide Juan de Fuca Strait, the passageway leading into Puget Sound and Seattle, the fourth-busiest port in the United States. A salmon "farm" is typically about four football fields, but the proposed Fish-doo farm will be three times that size.

Several species of Pacific salmon are listed as endangered or threatened under the ESA. Farmed salmon can be very different from wild native salmon. They are usually genetically different, and when Atlantic salmon are grown in Pacific Ocean waters, they are usually more aggressive than wild native Pacific salmon. If farmed salmon escape from their pens, which happens with some regularity, they can get out into the wild and compete with native wild salmon for food. They can also interbreed in a way that threatens the viability of the native wild salmon. Farmed and interbred salmon have been caught by commercial and recreational fishermen in significant numbers.

Second, the Juan de Fuca Strait is home to a population of orcas, killer whales, which are distinct from other populations of orcas in that they do not migrate; instead they stay resident in Puget Sound and the Juan de Fuca Strait. The salmon pens are an attractive nuisance to these orcas, who try to steal some of those farmed salmon but become entangled in the mesh netting, and drown. There are only 3 pods totaling 40 whales in this population, and a Washington environmental organization has petitioned the National Marine Fisheries Service to list the Juan de Fuca population.

Advise Fish-doo as to the legal issues faced by its proposed mega-salmon-farm.

2. Aboriginal Exemptions

The MMPA contains an explicit exemption from the take moratorium for Alaskan natives. Section 1371(b) provides that the take moratorium "shall not apply with respect to the taking of any marine mammal by any Indian, Aleut, or Eskimo . . . and who dwells on the coast of the North Pacific Ocean or the Arctic Ocean if such taking is done for substance purposes, or for purposes of creating and selling authentic native articles of handicrafts and clothing. . . ." This is provided that the taking is not accomplished in a wasteful manner. 16 U.S.C. § 1372(b).

There is another way that aboriginal groups can be exempted from the take moratorium, or at least be relieved of normal permitting requirements: by treaty. But at least by the terms of the MMPA, the treaty must pre-date passage of the MMPA. 16 U.S.C. § 1372(a)(2). Many U.S. treaties with aboriginal groups pre-date 1972, but even then, it can be a complicated matter to determine the applicability of the MMPA, as the following case demonstrates.

Before first European contact, the Makah population ranged between 2,000 and 4,000, divided into about five villages throughout Washington State's Olympic Peninsula. Makah culture centered upon its proximity to the Juan de Fuca Strait between Washington and British Columbia, the present gateway to Seattle. The Makah signed a treaty in 1855 with Governor Isaac Stevens, on behalf of the United States, in which the Makah ceded over 300,000 acres of tribal land, in exchange for the right to continue whaling. Whaling is a central aspect of Makah culture, as it is a dangerous (see below) and highly cooperative activity, requiring many tribal members to successfully bring in one whale. The Makah effectively abandoned the practice by the 1920s, only to experience a resurgence in interest in the 1990s, leading to the legal dilemma that is the backdrop to the *Anderson v. Evans* case.

Figure 3-6. A 1910 Photo of Makah Examining a Beached Whale

Anderson v. Evans

371 F.3d 475 (9th Cir. 2002)

Judge BERZON delivered the opinion of the Ninth Circuit Court of Appeals.

The [Makah] Tribe, a traditional Northwest Indian whale hunting tribe, had given up the hunt in the 1920s. In recent years, the Tribe's leaders came to regret the cultural impact on the Tribe of the lapse of its whale hunting tradition. As part of a general effort at cultural revival, the Tribe developed plans to resume pursuing gray whales off the coast of Washington State and in the Strait of Juan de Fuca. The worldwide hunt for whales in the years the real-life Captain Ahabs roamed the high seas, however, seriously depleted the worldwide stock of the cetaceans. As a result of the near extinction of some species of whales, what had been a free realm for ancient and not-so-ancient mariners became an activity closely regulated under both federal and international law. This case is the second in which we have considered whether the federal government's approval of the Tribe's plans to pursue once again the Leviathan of the deep runs afoul of that regulation.

The plaintiffs, citizens and animal conservation groups, challenge, as did the plaintiffs in Metcalf, the government's failure to prepare an environmental impact statement ("EIS") pursuant to the National Environmental Policy Act of 1969 ("NEPA"), 42 U.S.C. § 4321 et seq. They also contend that the Tribe's whaling plan cannot be implemented because the Tribe has not complied with the Marine Mammal Protection Act of 1972 ("MMPA"), 16 U.S.C. § 1361 et seq. Having reviewed the environmental assessment ("EA") prepared by the government agencies and the administrative record, we conclude that there are substantial questions remaining as to whether the Tribe's whaling plans will have a significant effect on the environment. The government therefore violated NEPA by failing to prepare an EIS before approving a whaling quota for the Tribe. We also conclude that the MMPA applies to the Tribe's proposed whale hunt.

***

The Tribe is composed of Native Americans whose traditional territory is in Washington State, on the northwestern Olympic Peninsula. In 1855, the United States entered into a treaty with the Tribe, the Treaty of Neah Bay, providing that the Tribe would give up most of its land on the Olympic Peninsula. In exchange, the Tribe was given, inter alia, the "right of taking fish and of whaling or sealing at usual and accustomed grounds and stations. . . ." That the Treaty of Neah Bay is the only treaty between the United States and a Native American tribe that specifically protects the right to hunt whales suggests the historic importance of whaling to the Makah Tribe.

Despite the central place of whaling in their lives, the Tribe ended their whaling expeditions in the late 1920s. Explanations regarding the reasons for the abandonment of this custom include: the federal government's discouragement and lack of assistance; a decline in demand for whale oil; social and economic dislocation within the Tribe; and the drastic decline of the gray whale population.

Then came, in the early 1990s, both a renewed interest within the Tribe in reviving its traditional whaling customs and the removal of the California gray whale from the Endangered Species Act list. The Tribe therefore determined to resume its traditional whale hunting. In the seventy years since the last hunt, however, whaling had become an activity tightly regulated internationally, through the International Whaling Commission, and domestically, through the Whaling Convention Act, and the MMPA, as well as through more general federal environmental legislation. Pursuant to the ICRW, aboriginal subsistence whaling is permitted, but such whaling must conform to quotas issued by the IWC for various whale stocks.

In 1996 the NOAA entered into a written agreement with the Tribe committing the NOAA to seek an aboriginal subsistence quota from the IWC. The United States presented a proposal for such a quota at the annual IWC meeting in June 1996. The proposal proved controversial, however, and some members of the IWC blocked its passage. . . . In the face of this opposition the United States withdrew its request.

* * *

A few months later, the NOAA and the Tribe entered into a new agreement similar to the prior one except that the new version required that the Tribe's management plan provide time and area restrictions "including . . . confining hunting activities to the open waters of the Pacific Ocean outside the Tatoosh-Bonilla Line." This provision sought to reduce the likelihood that the Tribe would take nonmigrating whales. Four days after this agreement was reached, the NMFS issued a final EA and a finding of no significant impact ("FONSI") concerning the proposed hunt. . . . In March 1998, the NMFS announced a quota permitting the Tribe to take five gray whales in a one-year period and allowing no more than thirty-three strikes over a five-year period.

Meanwhile, on the day the 1997 FONSI was released and before the IWC and NMFS quotas were issued, a group of concerned citizens and animal conservation organizations filed a complaint in federal court against the federal defendants for violations of NEPA, the WCA, and the Administrative Procedure Act. The primary allegation was that the EA was a deficient effort, put together simply to justify the prior agreement allowing the Tribe to hunt whales. After the district court granted summary judgment for the defendants, the Tribe began whaling and in 1999 killed one whale.

The whale's demise did not bring this prolonged dispute to an end, for this court reversed the district court. . . . We held that the EA was invalid because it was not produced until after the agreement with the Tribe had been consummated. A new EA must be drafted, we ordered, "under circumstances that ensure an objective evaluation free of the previous taint." Because we viewed the government defendants' actions as having been undertaken improperly, we stated that when the new EA was completed and returned to the courts for evaluation, it should be subject to "additional scrutiny [and] the burden shall be on the Federal Defendants to demonstrate . . . that they have complied with [the] requirement" to evaluate the environmental impact of the proposal objectively and in good faith.

***

The plaintiffs filed this action in January 2002, alleging violations of both NEPA and the MMPA [and requesting a preliminary injunction]. Concluding that the federal agencies had taken the requisite "hard look" at the risks associated with the whale hunt and that the court was required to defer to their decision, the district court determined that the plaintiffs did not have a probability of success on the merits. The district court also held that the Treaty of Neah Bay's preservation of the Tribe's whaling rights takes precedence over the MMPA's requirements; the plaintiffs therefore were unlikely to prevail on their MMPA claim as well. The plaintiffs appealed these rulings.

Under the CEQ regulations, we must consider whether the effects of the Tribe's whaling on the human environment are "likely to be highly controversial," and also whether the "possible effects . . . are highly uncertain or involve unique or unknown risks." A proposal is highly controversial when there is "a substantial dispute [about] the size, nature, or effect of the major Federal action rather than the existence of opposition to a use." Put another way, a proposal can be considered controversial if "substantial questions are raised as to whether a project . . . may cause significant degradation of some human environmental factor."

***

In sum, given the substantial uncertainty and controversy over the local impact of the Makah Tribe's whaling and its possible precedential effect, an EIS should have been prepared. Of course scientific inquiry rarely yields certainty. But here the agencies' inquiry itself was deficient. Thus, an EIS is required.

***

Because the agencies have not complied with NEPA, we set aside the FONSI, suspend implementation of the Agreement with the Makah Tribe, and vacate the approved whaling quota for the Tribe.

GOULD, Circuit Judge, with whom HILL and BERZON, Circuit Judges, concur:

In addition to arguing their NEPA claim, plaintiffs maintain that the federal defendants issued a gray whale quota to the Tribe in violation of the Marine Mammal Protection Act (MMPA) which prohibits the taking of marine mammals absent a permit or waiver. The Tribe has not applied for a permit or waiver under the MMPA. Defendants maintain that the MMPA does not apply because the Tribe's whaling quota has been expressly provided for by an international treaty, or, in the alternative, because the Tribe has an Indian treaty whaling right that is not affected by the MMPA.

A. Exemption

The federal defendants, including NOAA, and the Makah Tribe as defendant-intervenor first assert that § 1372(a)(2) of the MMPA exempts the Tribe's whaling from the MMPA moratorium. Section 1372(a)(2) provides an exception to the MMPA's blanket moratorium on the taking of marine mammals when takes have been "expressly provided for by an international treaty, convention, or agreement to which the United States is a party and which was entered into before [1972] or by any statute implementing any such treaty, convention, or agreement." 16 U.S.C. § 1372(a)(2). Defendants argue that § 1372(a)(2) applies here because the International Whaling Commission (IWC) approved a gray whale quota for the Tribe in 1997. We reject this argument for several reasons.

First, there is the problem of timing. Defendants recognize that a 1997 approval does not pre-date the MMPA as required by § 1372(a)(2), but argue that the 1997 approval relates back to the International Convention for the Regulation of Whaling (ICRW), which the United States signed in 1946. The ICRW enacted a schedule of whaling regulations (Schedule) and granted the IWC the power to amend the Schedule by adopting subsequent regulations, including quotas. International Convention for the Regulation of Whaling, 62 Stat. 1716, 1717-19 (1946). Defendants argue that, because the IWC was given the power to adopt quotas in 1946, the Tribe's quota approved in 1997 should be considered a right under the 1946 Convention that pre-dates the MMPA.

We disagree. The 1997 Schedule was adopted more than twenty-four years after the MMPA became effective. Section 1372(a)(2) exempts only international treaties that pre-date the MMPA, without also exempting amendments to those treaties. If Congress wanted to exempt subsequent amendments, then Congress could have done so explicitly. But Congress did not do so. That Congress did not intend to exempt subsequent amendments is clear when § 1372(a)(2) is considered alongside the mandates of § 1378(a)(4). Section 1378(a)(4) requires "the amendment of any existing international treaty for the protection and conservation of any species of marine mammal to which the United States is a party in order to make such treaty consistent with the purposes and policies of this [Act]." Far from intending amendments of international treaties to escape the restrictions of the MMPA moratorium by relating back to the treaties' pre-MMPA inception, Congress mandated that existing treaties be amended to incorporate the conservation principles of MMPA. It would be incongruous to interpret § 1372(a)(2) to exempt the amendments that were mandated by § 1378(a)(4). And, if we accepted the defendants' view, then we would read the MMPA to disregard its conservation principles whenever in the future the IWC made unknown decisions for unknown reasons about the killing of unknown numbers of whales. We do not believe that Congress subordinated its goal of conservation in United States waters to the decisions of unknown future foreign delegates to an international commission.

Second, there is a problem of specificity. Even if we were to read the 1997 Schedule to relate back to the 1946 Convention and thus to pre-date the MMPA, § 1372(a)(2) still would not apply here because the Schedule fails expressly to provide any whaling quota for the Tribe. Defendants do not dispute that the Schedule fails to mention the Tribe on its face. But defendants argue that IWC Schedules in practice never mention particular aboriginal tribes, but rather provide general quotas based on specific needs of particular tribes. Whatever may be the IWC's practice, the MMPA unambiguously requires express approval for § 1372(a)(2) to apply and to excuse the takings of marine mammals without a permit.

Third, there is a problem of uncertainty. We cannot tell whether the IWC intended a quota specifically to benefit the Tribe. Even if timing and specificity were no problem, the surrounding circumstances of the adoption of the Schedule cast doubt on the intent of the IWC to approve a quota for the Tribe. The Schedule extends the quota only to those aborigines whose "subsistence and cultural needs have been recognised." This language was inserted into the Schedule after some IWC delegates questioned whether the Tribe qualified for the aboriginal subsistence quota. Whether recognition must formally come from the IWC or from the United States is not clear.

In light of the circumstances giving rise to this language, the IWC presumably intended that such recognition, whether it came from the IWC or the United States, would depend on the Tribe's ability to satisfy the definition of aboriginal subsistence whaling. When the United States presented its request for a quota for the Makah Tribe to the IWC, the United States, in response to issues raised by the IWC during subcommittee, represented that the IWC had adopted the following definition of aboriginal subsistence whaling:

> whaling, for purposes of local aboriginal consumption carried out by or on behalf of aboriginal, indigenous, or native peoples who share strong community, familial, social, and cultural ties related to a continuing traditional dependence on whaling and on the use of whales.

While NOAA issued a Federal Register Notice in April 1998 recognizing the Tribe's subsistence and cultural needs, it is not clear that the IWC anticipated such recognition, given that the United States relied on a definition of subsistence whaling that requires a "continuing traditional dependence" on whaling and given that the Tribe had not engaged in whaling since 1927.

Because the IWC adopted the "has been recognised" language in response to opposition to the Tribe's whaling, and because it was not a foregone conclusion that the Tribe would satisfy the definition of aboriginal subsistence whaling, the IWC's intent to approve a whaling quota for the Tribe has not been demonstrated. The "expressly provided for" requirement of § 1372(a)(2) is not satisfied.

Fourth, § 1372(a)(2) does not apply in this case by way of a statute implementing an international treaty because there is no domestic statute implementing the ICRW that expressly permits the Tribe's whaling. The Whaling Convention Act (WCA), 16 U.S.C. § 916, implements the ICRW domestically, making it unlawful to take whales without first obtaining a quota from the IWC. 16 U.S.C. § 916c. The WCA does not mention quotas or aboriginal subsistence whaling, much less the Tribe's whaling, and therefore is of no assistance to defendants.

In sum, the defendants' reliance on § 1372(a)(2) to exempt the Tribe's whaling from the MMPA's general moratorium is misplaced. The federal defendants' view so clearly offends the express, unambiguous language of the statute that the statutory interpretation offered by NOAA and the federal defendants cannot properly be afforded deference under *Chevron*. . . .

B. Conservation Necessity

We consider whether the MMPA must apply to the Tribe to effectuate the conservation purpose of the statute. In *Fryberg*, we set out a three-part test for determining when reasonable conservation statutes affect Indian treaty rights: (1) the sovereign has jurisdiction in the area where the activity occurs; (2) the statute is non-discriminatory; and (3) the application of the statute to treaty rights is necessary to achieve its conservation purpose. Applying this rule, the MMPA may regulate any pre-existing Makah Tribe whaling rights under treaty if (1) the United States has jurisdiction where the whaling occurs; (2) the MMPA applies in a non-discriminatory manner to treaty and non-treaty persons alike; and (3) the application of the statute to regulate treaty rights is necessary to achieve its conservation purpose.

As to the first prong of the test, the MMPA extends to "any person subject to the jurisdiction of the United States," and reaches 200 nautical miles outward from the seaward boundary of each coastal state. Thus, the MMPA would clearly apply to the Tribe's whaling off the coast of Washington State in the Strait of Juan de Fuca. As to the second prong, the MMPA places a general moratorium on all persons except certain Native Alaskans with subsistence needs. The MMPA cannot be said to discriminate between treaty and non-treaty persons because members of the Tribe are not being singled out any more than non-treaty people in the lower forty-eight states.

The third prong of the *Fryberg* test requires that the application of the MMPA to the Tribe be necessary to achieve its conservation purpose. This prong frames for us the critical issue under this test: whether restraint on the Tribe's whaling pursuant to treaty rights is necessary to effectuate the conservation purpose of the MMPA. In assessing this issue, we are mindful that the major objective of the MMPA is to ensure that marine mammals continue to be "significant functioning elements in the ecosystem." In fact, "[marine mammals] should not be permitted to diminish below their optimum sustainable population." To carry out these conservation objectives, the MMPA implements a sweeping moratorium in combination with a permitting process to ensure that the taking of marine mammals is specifically authorized and systematically reviewed. For example, the MMPA requires that the administering agency consider "distribution, abundance, breeding habits, and times and lines of migratory movements of such marine mammals" when deciding the appropriateness of waiving requirements under the MMPA. And, when certain permits are issued, the permit may be suspended if the taking results in "more than a negligible impact on the species or stock concerned." One need only review Congress's carefully selected language to realize that Congress's concern was not merely with survival of marine mammals, though that is of inestimable importance, but more broadly with ensuring that these mammals maintain an "optimum sustainable population" and remain "significant functioning elements in the ecosystem." The MMPA's requirements for taking are specifically designed to promote such objectives. Without subjecting the Tribe's whaling to review under the MMPA, there is no assurance that the takes by the Tribe of gray whales, including both those killed and those harassed without success, will not threaten the role of the gray whales as functioning elements of the marine ecosystem, and thus no assurance that the purpose of the MMPA will be effectuated.

. . . The tribal council of the Makah Tribe has shown admirable restraint in limiting its aim to a small number of whales, and seeking the umbrella approval of the United States for a share of a quota approved by the IWC. But it is not clear the extent to which the Tribe's treaty right is limited to the approvals of the IWC or the Tribe's Gray Whale Management Plan. The intent of Congress cannot be hostage to the goodwill or good judgment or good sense of the particular leaders empowered by the Tribe at present; it must be assumed that Congress intended to effectuate policies for the United States and its residents, including the Makah Tribe, that transcend the decisions of any subordinate group.

If the MMPA's conservation purpose were forced to yield to the Makah Tribe's treaty rights, other tribes could also claim the right to hunt marine mammals without complying with the MMPA. While defendants argue that the Makah Tribe is the only tribe in the United States with a treaty right expressly guaranteeing the right to whale, that argument ignores the fact that whale hunting could be protected under less specific treaty language. The EA prepared by the federal defendants notes that other Pacific Coast tribes that once hunted whales have reserved traditional "hunting and fishing" rights in their treaties. These less specific "hunting and fishing" rights might be urged to cover a hunt for marine mammals. Although such mammals might not be the subject of "fishing," there is little doubt they are "hunted."

***

The application of the MMPA to the Tribe to uphold the conservation purpose of the MMPA goes hand in hand with the principles embedded in the Treaty of Neah Bay itself. The treaty language, when considered on its face, supports our conclusion that the conservation purpose of the MMPA requires it be applied to the Tribe. The Treaty of Neah Bay provides the Tribe with a right to fish and hunt whales "in common with all citizens of the United States." 12 Stat. 939, 940 (1855). We have recognized that the "in common with" language creates a relationship between Indians and non-Indians similar to a cotenancy, in which neither party may "permit the subject matter of [the treaty] to be destroyed." While this "in common with" clause does not strip Indians of the substance of their treaty rights, it does prevent Indians from relying on treaty rights to deprive other citizens of a fair apportionment of a resource. In *Washington Commercial Passenger Fishing Vessel Ass'n*, the Supreme Court concluded that: "Nontreaty fishermen may not rely on property law concepts, devices such as the fish wheel, license fees, or general regulations to deprive the Indians of a fair share of the relevant runs of anadromous fish in the case area. Nor may the treaty fishermen rely on their exclusive right of access to the reservations to destroy the rights of other 'citizens of the Territory.' Both sides have a right, secured by the treaty, to take a fair share of the available fish. That, we think, is what the parties to the treaty intended when they secured to the Indians a right of taking fish in common with other citizens." This holding might be read to suggest that the Tribe's treaty right gives the Tribe a right to a "fair share" of whales that are to be taken. The "fair share" formula, however, does not provide a ready answer in this case, which involves now-protected marine mammals rather than salmon and other fish available, within limits, for fishing. The question presented to us is not how whaling rights can be fairly apportioned between Indians and non-Indians. Rather, the Tribe asserts a treaty right that would give the Tribe the exclusive ability to hunt whales free from the regulatory scheme of the MMPA. Just as treaty fisherman are not permitted to "totally frustrate . . . the rights of the non-Indian citizens of Washington" to fish, the Makah cannot, consistent with the plain terms of the treaty, hunt whales without regard to processes in place and designed to advance conservation values by preserving marine mammals or to engage in whalewatching, scientific study, and other non-consumptive uses. The Supreme Court has recognized that regulation for the purpose of conservation is permissible despite the existence of treaty rights. Mindful of that recognition, we conclude that to the extent there is a "fair share" of marine mammal takes by the Tribe, the proper scope of such a share must be considered in light of the MMPA through its permit or waiver process. The MMPA will properly allow the taking of marine mammals only when it will not diminish the sustainability and optimum level of the resource for all citizens. The procedural safeguards and conservation principles of the MMPA ensure that marine mammals like the gray whale can be sustained as a resource for the benefit of the Tribe and others.

Having concluded that the MMPA is applicable to regulate any whaling proposed by the Tribe because the MMPA's application is necessary to effectuate the conservation purpose of the statute, and because such application is consistent with the language of the Neah Bay Treaty, we conclude that the issuance by NOAA of a gray whale quota to the Tribe, absent compliance with the MMPA, violates federal law. Whether or not the Tribe may have sufficient justification to gain a permit or waiver allowing whaling under the MMPA, we must now set aside NOAA's approval of the Tribe's whaling quota absent MMPA compliance as "arbitrary, capricious, an abuse of discretion, or otherwise not in accordance with law."

Of course, in holding that the MMPA applies to the Tribe, we need not and do not decide whether the Tribe's whaling rights have been abrogated by the MMPA. We simply hold that the Tribe, to pursue any

Like their related baleen whale, the right whale, gray whales are slow swimmers, but unlike their cousins, they ferociously defend their calves when threatened, sometimes attacking boats. Whereas the right whale was named by New Englanders because they were the "right" whale to hunt, gray whales were named "devil-fish" (they are not, of course, fish) by New England whalers because of their propensity to resist. Their reputation for cantankerousness did not stop them from being extirpated in the North Atlantic Ocean, where Yankee whalers found shallow lagoons where gray whales calved their young, cornering and slaughtering them. The Eastern Pacific population of gray whales is relatively healthy; a Western Pacific Ocean population near Asia is considered critically endangered.

treaty rights for whaling, must comply with the process prescribed in the MMPA for authorizing a "take" because it is the procedure that ensures the Tribe's whaling will not frustrate the conservation goals of the MMPA.

point for discussion

1. *Treaty rights.* The MMPA provides an exception for matters "expressly provided for by an international treaty, convention or agreement to which the United States is a party, and which was entered into before the effective date of [the MMPA]." The Treaty of Neah Bay was entered into in 1855. Article 5 of the treaty provides that "[t]he right of taking fish and of whaling or sealing at usual and accustomed grounds and stations is further secured to said Indians in common with all citizens of the United States." 16 U.S.C. § 1372(a)(2). Are you satisfied with the court's reconciliation of the MMPA with the treaty?

3. Import and Public Display

"Take" includes possession of marine mammals but possessing them for public display is permitted under the MMPA, subject to, of course, a variety of restrictions. But how does one go about obtaining a whale? Captive breeding programs for marine mammals are on the decline, but popular demand for viewing them is not. Aquariums and other zoological facilities thus turn to import. But that is a difficult way to obtain marine mammals, as these statutory and regulatory excerpts and the following case demonstrates.

Importation of Pregnant or Nursing Mammals; Depleted Species or Stock; Inhumane Taking

16 U.S.C. § 1372(b)

Except pursuant to a permit for scientific research, or for enhancing the survival or recovery of a species or stock . . . , it is unlawful to import into the United States any marine mammal if such mammal was —

(1) pregnant at the time of taking;

(2) nursing at the time of taking, or less than eight months old, whichever occurs later;

(3) taken from a species or population stock which the Secretary has, by regulation published in the Federal Register, designated as a depleted species or stock; or

(4) taken in a manner deemed inhumane by the Secretary.

Notwithstanding the provisions of paragraphs (1) and (2), the Secretary may issue a permit for the importation of a marine mammal, if the Secretary determines that such importation is necessary for the protection or welfare of the animal.

Prohibited Importation

50 C.F.R. § 216.12

(a) Except as otherwise provided in subparts C and D of this part 216, it is unlawful for any person to import any marine mammal or marine mammal product into the United States.

(b) Regardless of whether an importation is otherwise authorized pursuant to subparts C and D of this part 216, it is unlawful for any person to import into the United States any:

(1) Marine mammal:

(i) Taken in violation of the MMPA, or

(ii) Taken in another country in violation to the laws of that country;

(c) Except in accordance with an exception referred to in subpart C and §§ 216.31 (regarding scientific research permits only) and 216.32 of this part 216, it is unlawful to import into the United States any:

(1) Marine mammal which was pregnant at the time of taking.

(2) Marine mammal which was nursing at the time of taking, or less than 8 months old, whichever occurs later.

(3) Specimen of an endangered or threatened species of marine mammal.

(4) Specimen taken from a depleted species or stock of marine mammals, or

(5) Marine mammal taken in an inhumane manner.

Issuance Criteria

50 C.F.R. § 216.34

(a) For the Office Director to issue any permit under this subpart, the applicant must demonstrate that:

(1) The proposed activity is humane and does not present any unnecessary risks to the health and welfare of marine mammals;

(2) The proposed activity is consistent with all restrictions set forth at § 216.35 and any purpose-specific restrictions as appropriate set forth at § 216.41, § 216.42, and § 216.43;

(3) The proposed activity, if it involves endangered or threatened marine mammals, will be conducted consistent with the purposes and policies set forth in section 2 of the ESA;

(4) The proposed activity by itself or in combination with other activities, will not likely have a significant adverse impact on the species or stock;

(5) Whether the applicant's expertise, facilities, and resources are adequate to accomplish successfully the objectives and activities stated in the application;

(6) If a live animal will be held captive or transported, the applicant's qualifications, facilities, and resources are adequate for the proper care and maintenance of the marine mammal; and

(7) Any requested import or export will not likely result in the taking of marine mammals or marine mammal parts beyond those authorized by the permit.

Georgia Aquarium, Inc. v. Pritzker

134 F. Supp. 3d 1374 (N.D. Ga. 2015)

Judge TOTENBERG delivered the opinion of the United States District Court, Northern District of Georgia.

On June 15, 2012 Georgia Aquarium submitted an application to the National Marine Fisheries Service ("NMFS" or "the Agency") under the Marine Mammal Protection Act ("MMPA"), for a permit to import eighteen beluga whales from Russia for public display. Georgia Aquarium sought to import the beluga whales "to enhance the North American beluga breeding cooperative by increasing the population base of captive belugas to a self-sustaining level and to promote conservation and education." The whales were previously captured and collected in the Sakhalin Bay of the Sea of Okhotsk in 2006, 2010, and 2011 by a team led by Dr. Lev Mukhametov, Director of Utrish Dolphinarium, Ltd. Since their capture, the whales have been held at the Utrish Marine Mammal Research Station (UMMRS) on the Russian coast of the Black Sea. Upon arrival in the U.S., the whales would be distributed among six different aquaria facilities including the Georgia Aquarium in Atlanta, Sea World Orlando, Sea World San Antonio, Sea World San Diego, Mystic Aquarium, and Shedd Aquarium pursuant to breeding loans. Following a lengthy notice and comment period, Georgia Aquarium's hopes were sunk on August 5, 2013, when NMFS denied Georgia Aquarium's permit application. . . .

NMFS cited three reasons why Georgia Aquarium's application failed to satisfy the MMPA's permit issuance criteria. First, NMFS determined that Georgia Aquarium did not demonstrate that the proposed import "by itself or in combination with other activities, will not likely have a significant adverse impact on the species or stock" in accordance with 50 C.F.R. § 216.34(4):

We cannot discount the likelihood that total removals from this stock have exceeded the total net production on an annual basis resulting in a small, but steady and significant decline over the past two decades. Further, the ongoing live-capture trade since 1989 may have contributed to a cumulative decline over the past two decades, and we considered this in combination with other past, present, and foreseeable future actions. Therefore, we are unable to make the determination that the proposed activity, by itself or in combination with other activities, would not likely have had a significant adverse impact on the species or stock. (AR 8998 at 17440.)

Second, NMFS denied the permit application because Georgia Aquarium did not demonstrate that the proposed import would not likely result in the taking of marine mammals beyond those authorized by the proposed permit in accordance with 50 C.F.R. § 216.34(7):

We have determined that the requested import will likely result in the taking of marine mammals beyond those authorized by the permit. There are ongoing, legal marine mammal capture operations in Russia that are expected to continue, and we believe that issuance of this permit would contribute to the demand to capture belugas from this stock for the purpose of public display worldwide, resulting in the future taking of additional belugas from this stock.

Third, NMFS found that Georgia Aquarium did not demonstrate that some of the whales proposed for importation were not nursing at the time of taking in accordance with 16 U.S.C. § 1372(b)(2) and 50 C.F.R. § 216.12(c):

We have determined that five of the [18] beluga whales proposed for import, estimated to be approximately 1.5 years old at the time of capture, were potentially still nursing and not yet independent [of their mothers]. This would only result in the inability to import these five specific animals, if not for the other criteria that [Georgia Aquarium] did not meet.

On September 30, 2013, Georgia Aquarium filed this appeal, pursuant to the Administrative Procedures Act ("APA"), asserting that NMFS's permit denial was arbitrary, capricious, and not in accordance with the law. The parties have briefed the issues on appeal through cross-motions for summary judgment. . . .

I. Purpose of the MMPA

The MMPA was enacted to protect marine mammal species and population stocks in the wild that are or may be "in danger of extinction or depletion as a result of man's activities." The stated purposes of the MMPA are:

(a) to prevent marine mammals species and population stocks from "diminish[ing] beyond the point at which they cease to be a significant functioning element in the ecosystem of which they are a part, [and] below their optimum sustainable population," and

(b) to protect and encourage development of the species and stocks "to the greatest extent feasible commensurate with sound policies of resource management and that the primary objective of their management should be to maintain the health and stability of the marine ecosystem" with "the goal to obtain an optimum sustainable population . . . ."

16 U.S.C. § 1361(2) & (6).

"Optimum sustainable population" or OSP is "the number of animals which will result in the maximum productivity of the population or the species, keeping in mind the carrying capacity of the habitat and the health of the ecosystem of which they form a constituent element."

"The primary purpose of the MMPA is to protect marine mammals; the Act was not intended as a 'balancing act' between the interests of [] industry and the animals. The interests of the marine mammals come first under the statutory scheme, and the interests of the industry, important as they are, must be served only after protection of the animals is assured."

II. Marine Mammal Import Permits

In furtherance of these statutory goals and purposes, the MMPA imposes a moratorium on the taking and importation of marine mammals, subject to certain limited exceptions. However, the MMPA explicitly prohibits the import of any marine mammal that was — (1) pregnant at the time of taking; (2) nursing at the time of taking, or less than eight months old, whichever occurs later; (3) taken from a species or population stock which the Secretary has, by regulation, designated as depleted; or (4) taken in a manner deemed inhumane by the Secretary. 16 U.S.C. § 1372(b); 50 C.F.R. § 216.12(c).

Under Section 1374 of the MMPA, NMFS may issue permits for the taking or importation of marine mammals for scientific research, enhancing the survival or recovery of a species or stock, or public display, provided that certain requirements are met. Section 1374(d)(3) of the MMPA requires that the permit applicant "must demonstrate . . . that the taking or importation of any marine mammal under such permit will be consistent with the [Act] and the applicable regulations." Essential to this requirement of § 1374(d)(3) that a permit applicant demonstrate a proposed import 'will be consistent with the purposes of [the MMPA],' is the mandate that stocks 'should not be permitted to diminish below their optimum sustainable population[s] [OSP].'"

Pursuant to the Act, NMFS's regulations provide "issuance criteria" for such permits. 50 C.F.R. § 216.34. Under the relevant issuance criteria, "the applicant must demonstrate" that (a) "[t]he proposed activity by itself or in combination with other activities, will not likely have a significant adverse impact on the species or stock," and (b) "[a]ny requested import or export will not likely result in the taking of marine mammals or marine mammal parts beyond those authorized by the permit," (50 C.F.R. § 216.34(a)(7)). In addition, § 216.12(c)(2) requires an applicant to show that the animals it seeks to import were not "nursing at the time of taking."

III. Burden of Proof

As NMFS stated in its Decision Document denying Georgia Aquarium's permit application, "it is the [permit] applicant's responsibility, not that of NMFS, to demonstrate that the MMPA criteria have been met." See 16 U.S.C. § 1374(d)(3); 50 C.F.R. § 216.34 (stating "the applicant must demonstrate that" the issuance criteria are met). Section 1374 of the MMPA requires that an applicant for a permit for taking marine mammals must demonstrate that the taking "will be consistent with the purposes" of the Act.

Georgia Aquarium asserts that "[t]he Congressional policy behind the MMPA is central to this case," but instead focuses on the support for permits for the public display of marine mammals because of the educational importance of informing the public about "the esthetic, recreational, and economic significance of marine mammals and their role in the ocean system." Thus, according to Georgia Aquarium, NMFS's permit denial is "inconsistent with the Congressional policy to further the public display of marine mammals" and is a "setback to marine mammal conservation, research and education."

Georgia Aquarium's arguments on appeal cast a wide net, but haul in little of substance. As succinctly explained by another court faced with similar questions posed here:

> Congress foresaw the possibility that, in a given situation, there would be a lack of scientific information as to whether a proposed level of taking would be to the disadvantage of the marine mammals involved, and that might result in an inability to find whether the stock was at its optimum sustainable population. Before issuing any permit for the taking of a marine mammal, the Secretary must first have it proven to his satisfaction that any taking is consistent with the purposes and policies of the act—that is to say, that taking will not be to the disadvantage of the animals concerned. If he cannot make that finding, he cannot issue a permit. It is that simple.

The Agency followed the statutory mandate of the MMPA in its denial of the Aquarium's permit application. First, NMFS's determination that the Sakhalin-Amur stock is likely declining and is subject to adverse impacts beyond the ongoing live-capture operations cited by Georgia Aquarium complies with the primary purpose of the MMPA to prevent marine mammal species and population stocks from "diminish[ing] beyond the point at which they cease to be a significant functioning element in the ecosystem of which they are a part, [and] below their optimum sustainable population." Second, NMFS's interpretation of its regulation as requiring that Georgia Aquarium demonstrate that the permit would not result in any replacement takes of additional beluga whales by the Russian capture operation is consistent with the purpose of the MMPA to prevent the decline of this stock of whales below its optimum sustainable population. And third, NMFS's finding that some of the beluga whales proposed for import, estimated to be approximately 1.5 years old at the time of capture, were potentially still nursing and not yet independent of their mothers is based on unrebutted scientific literature that beluga whales are not likely fully independent and still rely to some extent on their mother's milk until 3 years of age.

For these reasons, set forth more fully below, the Court finds that NMFS's permit denial was consistent with the purposes and requirements of the MMPA, and therefore was not arbitrary and capricious.

points for discussion

1. *Captive audience.* SeaWorld, which has three parks featuring the display of marine mammals, agreed in 2016 to stop its captive breeding program of orcas, following the death of a trainer, and the movie *Blackfish*, which shed some unfavorable light on SeaWorld's practices in handling their orcas. Is the permitting of public display animals inconsistent with the goals of the MMPA? Or can it be argued that it furthers the goals of the MMPA?

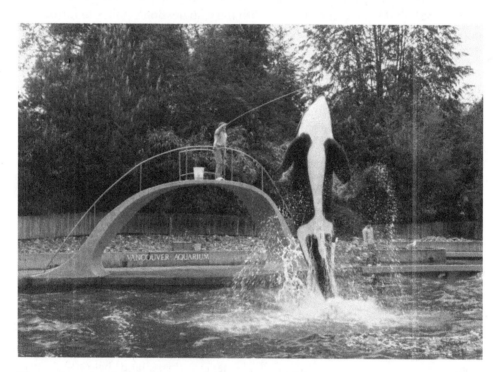

Figure 3-7. An Orca at the Vancouver Aquarium

2. *Market forces.* If the belugas had already been captured in another country, what is the harm from importing them? Does the MMPA contemplate global protection of marine mammals?
3. *Promoting conservation strategies.* Do you think that the Georgia Aquarium might have made a more forceful argument about how the public display and education value would outweigh the harm? What is the value of public display? What about research?

C. CHAPTER SUMMARY

1. **In general.** In addition to laws protecting the living organisms from over-harvest, two federal statutes provide a special set of especially powerful protections: the Endangered Species Act and the Marine Mammal Protection Act. Whereas the Endangered Species Act is oriented toward preventing species from becoming extinct, the Marine Mammal Protection Act is oriented toward the prevention of harm to mammals in the marine environment and possessing a greater sentience than fish. Having been passed less than a year apart, the statutes look superficially similar in terms of structure and language. Overlap exists in terms of the protection — some species are protected under both statutes.

2. **The Endangered Species Act (ESA).** The more ambitious of the two statutes imposes substantial duties on governments in addition to regulating private conduct with the potential to harm endangered species. The ESA mandates the keeping of a list of species "in danger of extinction throughout all or a significant portion of its range." Once listed, the federal government must "ensure" that its own actions — a fairly large range of actions — do not "jeopardize" the continued existence of the species, and do not adversely affect habitat for the species. Listed species also are prohibiting from harm stemming from private conduct on private land. The wide-ranging prohibition has led to the widespread use of permitting, such as the "incidental" taking of species while engaged in other lawful activities, such as fishing.

3. **The Marine Mammal Protection Act (MMPA).** Enacted more out of a concern for the cruelty of treatment of mammals in the marine environment, the MMPA also expresses the ambitious goal of completely eliminating the killing of marine mammals, the "zero mortality rate goal." Harm comes to marine mammals in many ways, so as with the case of the ESA, the MMPA permits fishing, as well as other activities deemed to be of either minimal harm or justified or privileged for other reasons. As with the case of the ESA, the MMPA has become a highly regulatory body of law.

D. SUGGESTED READING

Michael J. Bean, *Endangered Species, Endangered Act?*, 41 ENVT. 12 (1999).

Thomas P. Good et al., *Recovery Planning for Endangered Species Act–Listed Pacific Salmon: Using Science to Inform Goals and Strategies*, 32 FISHERIES 426 (2007).

Robert J. Hofman, *The Changing Focus of Marine Mammal Conservation*, 10 TRENDS ECOL. & EVOLUTION 462 (1995).

Kristin L. Laidre et al., *Arctic Marine Mammal Population Status, Sea Ice Habitat Loss, and Conservation Remedies for the 21st Century*, 29 Conserv. Bio. 724 (2015).

Andrew Metrick & Martin L. Weitzman, *Conflicts and Choices in Biodiversity Preservation*, 12 J. Econ. Persp. 21 (1998).

Martin F.J. Taylor et al., *The Effectiveness of the Endangered Species Act: A Quantitative Analysis*, 55 BioScience 360 (2005).

Edward O. Wilson, The Diversity of Life (1992).

chapter 4

Offshore Industrial Development

The oceans have not only living, but nonliving resources to offer in abundance. In addition to the harvesting of fish and other marine species, industrial societies have been extracting mineral resources — most prominently crude oil and natural gas — from the seabed for over a century. As thirst for oil and gas grew beyond the capacities of land-based sources of mineral energy, so too did the pressure to drill and extract from the seabed.

In his Pulitzer Prize–winning account, historian Jack Davis describes how oil was first found in the Gulf of Mexico seabed, in a small bay outside of Houston named Tabbs Bay. "It was inevitable that derricks would migrate from avian territory to marine territory," he writes. Driven in part by demand from a war effort, the Goose Creek oil field in Tabbs Bay flourished and eventually produced millions of barrels of oil every year, a substantial amount in the early twentieth century. Davis hastens to add, quoting actor James Stewart in the film *Thunder Bay*, "progress is not without fault, my friend."

The law of mineral leasing is the first, and still the largest, chapter in the history of offshore industrial development. But the nature of offshore industrial development is changing. The Deepwater Horizon tragedy in 2010, continuing issues with less catastrophic pollution, and climate change have increased pressure to make other, less polluting and less ecologically dangerous uses of our oceans. Renewable energy will continue to increase its share in energy production, and the oceans will figure prominently in that development. So too will legal developments in this area.

A. SEA AND SEABED FEDERALISM

In Chapter 1, we explored matters of jurisdiction over the oceans as between nation-states. But within the oceans governed by the United States, does state or federal law apply? Perhaps even more significantly, does the state or federal government hold title to the seabed? The stakes are significant, since the seabed may contain valuable mineral deposits. Moreover, the federal government and the states often have differing views on how shared or adjacent coastal and ocean resources should be used.

Questions of federalism and seabed ownership have their roots in the Constitution but have taken a meandering path to their present-day understandings. In *Martin v. Waddell*, 41 U.S. (16 Pet.) 367 (1842), the Supreme Court noted that each state was sovereign, and had jurisdiction over its internal and coastal waters, as well as title to riverbeds and the seabed beneath those waters. Along with ownership of the beds came ownership of any minerals or anything of value found in the soil and the power to regulate activities, such as fishing, in the water column above. At the time, the physical extent of national jurisdiction over adjacent seas was not entirely certain, but the United States regularly claimed ownership and control out to three nautical miles.

Just three years later, in *Pollard's Lessee v. Hagan*, 44 U.S. (3 How.) 212 (1845), the admission of Alabama into the United States raised the question of Alabama's rights, since it was not one of the original states and thus arguably not endowed with the same kind of sovereignty over rivers and ocean as the original 13 enjoyed. While the original 13 obtained their submerged lands directly and automatically from the King of England at the end of the Revolutionary War, the federal government was responsible for transferring submerged lands to later-admitted states, as Congress was carving them from territories. Prior to *Pollard*, it was not clear whether Congress was required to transfer submerged lands or could retain them in federal ownership post-statehood. But the Court held that Alabama was entitled to the same rights as the original 13:

> "When Alabama was admitted into the union, on an equal footing with the original States, she succeeded to all the rights of sovereignty, jurisdiction, and eminent domain which Georgia possessed at the date of the cession, except so far as this right was diminished by the public lands remaining in the possession and under the control of the United States." *Id.*, at 223.

The Court reiterated this "equal footing" principle in *Shively v. Bowlby*, 152 U.S. 1 (1894), a private dispute that nevertheless triggered examination of Oregon's jurisdiction and rights as a state. And again, the Court found that a latecomer like Oregon enjoyed the same rights as the original states (and Alabama). However, in contrast to the result in *Pollard*, the Court in *Shively* held that the United States was free to sell off submerged lands in the territorial period *before* statehood.

But because of uncertainty in international law, ownership of the seabed beyond the coast was unclear. Did it belong to coastal states or the federal government? If so, how far did ownership extend? In 1933, Interior Secretary Harold Ickes, responding to a query from a private individual, wrote that "[t]itle to the soil under the ocean within the 3-mile limit is in the State of California, and the land may not be appropriated except by authority of the State." The recipient of that letter, Olin Proctor of Long Beach, sought and was refused a federal mining permit in the seabed off the California coast; the letter explaining denial of his permit henceforth became known as the "Proctor letter," and was widely viewed as an accurate summation of the law. ERNEST R. BARTLEY, THE TIDELANDS OIL CONTROVERSY: A LEGAL AND HISTORICAL ANALYSIS 128-29 (1953). But as oil companies gained interest in the possibility of drilling for oil in the seabed, and as World War II began to take on greater global significance, the question of state jurisdiction was no longer in a vacuum; did the federal government not have rights in the seabed as well?

United States v. California, 332 U.S. 19 (1947), a bombshell of a case, provided a surprisingly blunt answer to that question. The Pacific Western Oil Company had a lease from the State of California to prospect for oil in its seabed. The United States challenged California's authority to enter into such a lease and, in an opinion authored by Justice Black, the Court held for the United States:

> None of the foregoing cases, nor others which we have decided, is sufficient to require us to extend the *Pollard* inland water rule so as to declare that California owns or has paramount rights in or power over the three-mile belt under the ocean. The question of who owned the bed of the sea only became of great potential importance at the beginning of this century, when oil was discovered there. As a consequence of this discovery, California passed an Act in 1921 authorizing the granting of permits to California residents to prospect for oil and gas on blocks of land off its coast under the ocean. . . . Now that the question is here, we decide for the reasons we have stated that California is not the owner of the three-mile marginal belt along its coast, and that the Federal Government, rather than the state, has paramount rights in and power over that belt, an incident to which is full dominion over the resources of the soil under that water area, including oil. 332 U.S. at 38-39.

Dissenting, Justice Frankfurter wrote:

> Of course, the United States has "paramount rights" in the sea belt of California — the rights that are implied by the power to regulate interstate and foreign commerce, the power of condemnation, the treaty-making power, the war power. We have not now before us the validity of the exercise of any of these paramount rights. Rights of ownership are here asserted — and rights of ownership are something else. Ownership implies acquisition in the various ways in which land is acquired — by conquest, by discovery and claim, by cession, by prescription, by purchase, by condemnation. When and how did the United States acquire this land?

The case turned on the question of what the original states had acquired from the King after the revolution; what did the international law of the late 1700s recognize as the limit of exclusive coastal nation jurisdiction? California argued that the law of the time was three miles; the United States contended international law did not recognize a three-mile limit until sometime in the nineteenth century. The Court agreed with the United States.

The outcome was driven not only by historical inquiry, but by the concept that the federal government had "paramount rights," even in state waters. The Court elaborated on this idea in *United States v. Louisiana*, 339 U.S. 699 (1950), that "[t]he marginal sea is a national, not a state concern. National interests, national responsibilities, national concerns are involved. The problems of commerce, national defense, relations with other powers, war and peace focus there. National rights must therefore be paramount in that area." *Id.* at 704. And in a twist of irony, the Court held in *United States v. Texas*, 339 U.S. 707, 717 (1950), that "equal footing" meant that Texas had no more rights than the original states, and thus could not claim ownership over the seabed more than three nautical miles from shore. Texas claimed that it owned nine miles because it had moved directly from a Spanish territory to statehood. Florida also made this claim with respect to its Gulf Coast.

This abrupt change in the law did not stand for long. A bill establishing state ownership of the seabed passed both chambers but was vetoed by President Truman. H.R.J. Res. 255, 79th Cong. (1946) (president's veto message 92 Cong. Rec. 10660 (1946)) (veto sustained 79 Cong. Rec. 10745 (1946)); S.J. Res. 20, 82nd Cong. (1952) (president's veto message S. Doc. No. 139, 98 Cong. Rec. 6251 (1952)). But a year later, President Eisenhower signed into law the Submerged Lands Act of 1953, which survives mostly intact to this day.

Submerged Lands Act of 1953

43 U.S.C. § 1301. Definitions

(a) The term "lands beneath navigable waters" means —

(1) all lands within the boundaries of each of the respective States which are covered by nontidal waters that were navigable under the laws of the United States at the time such State became a member of the Union, or acquired sovereignty over such lands and waters thereafter, up to the ordinary high-water mark as heretofore or hereafter modified by accretion, erosion, and reliction;

(2) all lands permanently or periodically covered by tidal waters up to but not above the line of mean high tide and seaward to a line three geographical miles distant from the coast line of each such State and to the boundary line of each such State where in any case such boundary as it existed at the time such State became a member of the Union, or as heretofore approved by Congress, extends seaward (or into the Gulf of Mexico) beyond three geographical miles, and

(3) all filled in, made, or reclaimed lands which formerly were lands beneath navigable waters, as hereinabove defined;

(b) The term "boundaries" includes the seaward boundaries of a State or its boundaries in the Gulf of Mexico or any of the Great Lakes as they existed at the time such State became a member of the Union, or as heretofore approved by the Congress, or as extended or confirmed pursuant to section 1312 of this title but in no event shall the term "boundaries" or the term "lands beneath navigable waters" be interpreted as extending from the coast line more than three geographical miles into the Atlantic Ocean or the Pacific Ocean, or more than three marine leagues into the Gulf of Mexico, except that any boundary between a State and the United States under this subchapter or subchapter II which has been or is hereafter fixed by coordinates under a final decree of the United States Supreme Court shall remain immobilized at the coordinates provided under such decree and shall not be ambulatory;

***

(c) The term "coast line" means the line of ordinary low water along that portion of the coast which is in direct contact with the open sea and the line marking the seaward limit of inland waters;

***

(e) The term "natural resources" includes, without limiting the generality thereof, oil, gas, and all other minerals, and fish, shrimp, oysters, clams, crabs, lobsters, sponges, kelp, and other marine animal and plant life but does not include water power, or the use of water for the production of power;

43 U.S.C. § 1311. Rights of States

(a) Confirmation and establishment of title and ownership of lands and resources; management, administration, leasing, development, and use

It is determined and declared to be in the public interest that (1) title to and ownership of the lands beneath navigable waters within the boundaries of the respective States, and the natural resources within such lands and waters, and (2) the right and power to manage, administer, lease, develop, and use the said lands and natural resources all in accordance with applicable State law be, and they are, subject to the provisions hereof, recognized, confirmed, established, and vested in and assigned to the respective States or the persons who were on June 5, 1950, entitled thereto under the law of the respective States in which the land is located, and the respective grantees, lessees, or successors in interest thereof;

(b) Release and relinquishment of title and claims of United States; payment to States of moneys paid under leases

(1) The United States releases and relinquishes unto said States and persons aforesaid, except as otherwise reserved herein, all right, title, and interest of the United States, if any it has, in and to all said lands, improvements, and natural resources. . . .

43 U.S.C. § 1312. Seaward boundaries of States

The seaward boundary of each original coastal State is approved and confirmed as a line three geographical miles distant from its coast line or, in the case of the Great Lakes, to the international boundary. Any State admitted subsequent to the formation of the Union which has not already done so may extend its seaward boundaries to a line three geographical miles distant from its coast line, or to the international boundaries of the United States in the Great Lakes or any other body of water traversed by such boundaries. Any claim heretofore or hereafter asserted either by constitutional provision, statute, or otherwise, indicating the intent of a State so to extend its boundaries is approved and confirmed, without prejudice to its claim, if any it has, that its boundaries extend beyond that line. Nothing in this section is to be construed as questioning or in any manner prejudicing the existence of any State's seaward boundary beyond three geographical miles if it was so provided by its constitution or laws prior to or at the time such State became a member of the Union, or if it has been heretofore approved by Congress.

43 U.S.C. § 1314. Rights and powers retained by United States; purchase of natural resources; condemnation of lands

(a) The United States retains all its navigational servitude and rights in and powers of regulation and control of said lands and navigable waters for the constitutional purposes of commerce, navigation, national defense, and international affairs, all of which shall be paramount to, but shall not be deemed to include, proprietary rights of ownership, or the rights of management, administration, leasing, use, and development of the lands and natural resources which are specifically recognized, confirmed, established, and vested in and assigned to the respective States and others by section 1311 of this title.

(b) In time of war or when necessary for national defense, and the Congress or the President shall so prescribe, the United States shall have the right of first refusal to purchase at the prevailing market price, all or any portion of the said natural resources, or to acquire and use any portion of said lands by proceeding in accordance with due process of law and paying just compensation therefor.

Note that the Submerged Lands Act not only addressed the legal status of the seabed, but in defining the "seaward boundary" of states, also established the extent of state territorial waters. That is to say, not only do states "own" the seabed and the mineral deposits therein up to three nautical miles, but also have jurisdiction over activities taking place in the water column over that same area. Note also the cryptic language in Section 1312: "Any claim heretofore or hereafter asserted either by constitutional provision, statute, or otherwise. . . ." This is meant to affirm some idiosyncratic but settled state seaward boundaries: Texas and Florida claim ownership and jurisdiction for up to three marine leagues — roughly nine nautical miles — off their Gulf Coasts. Florida's Atlantic Coast is as other normal seaward boundaries.

Note also that the Submerged Lands Act also clarified the federal role in the "marginal belt," what some courts have confusingly called the state territorial waters from the coast line to the three-nautical-mile line. Federal rights are "paramount" when invoked for commerce, navigation, national defense, and international affairs. During times of war, the federal government may acquire, as a right of first refusal, natural resources, and it retains the federal navigation servitude (discussed below).

points for discussion

1. *What ocean resources do the states own?* Consider the definition of "natural resources" in Section 1301. It includes oil and gas, and living resources, but not "water power, or the use of water for the production of power." What might that exclude?

2. *Baselines, again.* The seaward boundary is generally three nautical miles from what? Recall that for purposes of international law, the Exclusive Economic Zone, the Territorial Seas, and the Contiguous Zone are all defined as distances from a baseline, which is normally (excepting odd geographical features such as bays, coastal indentations, or reefs) the *mean low water line.* 33 C.F.R. § 2.20. The term "ordinary low water mark" was determined, by a Special Master appointed by the Court to make further adjudications in *United States v. California,* to be the "mean of all low waters," meaning the mean low water line, not the mean *lower* low water line, which would be an average of all of the *lower* of two low tides each day. 1 AARON SHALOWITZ, SHORE AND SEA BOUNDARIES 105 (1962). The baseline for purposes of the Submerged Lands Act, the "coast line," therefore conveniently coincides with the one used for international law purposes.

3. *Pollution regulation?* Does the federal paramount interest include the right to regulate pollution from activities in the state territorial waters or the state submerged lands? See below.

The Submerged Lands Act only put to rest the question of the seabed. It also settles the question of what constitutes the state territorial waters but leaves open questions of regulatory authority. Does the state have power to regulate activities in federal waters? Conversely, does the federal government have authority to regulate activities in state territorial waters? The following case demonstrates some of the legal complexities of negotiating federalism in the sea.

Figure 4-1. Container Ships at the Port of Long Beach, California

Pacific Merchant Shipping Ass'n v. Goldstene

639 F.3d 1154 (9th Cir. 2011)

Judge COWEN delivered the opinion of the Ninth Circuit Court of Appeals.

In this interlocutory appeal, Plaintiff Pacific Merchant Shipping Association ("PMSA") appeals from the District Court's denial of its motion for summary judgment in its action against Defendant James Goldstene, the Executive Officer of the California Air Resources Board ("CARB"). PMSA has challenged, on federal statutory and constitutional grounds, California fuel use regulations (known as the "Vessel Fuel Rules") insofar as they purport to apply to sea-going vessels located more than 3 miles from the California coast. We will affirm.

I.

On April 16, 2009, CARB transmitted the "Vessel Fuel Rules" to the California Secretary of state for filing pursuant to state law, and the regulations went into effect as planned on July 1, 2009. As the District Court noted, the express purpose of the Vessel Fuel Rules "is to reduce air pollutants affecting the state of California by requiring ocean-going vessels to use cleaner marine fuels." (ER24 (footnote added).) The regulations were adopted only after a lengthy process that included consultation with the public, state and local agencies, and the federal government.

The Vessel Fuel Rules mandate that vessel operators "use cleaner marine fuels in diesel and diesel-electric engines, main propulsion engines, and auxiliary boilers on vessels operating within twenty-four nautical miles off the California coastline." Specifically, the regulations apply to a geographical region known as "Regulated California Waters," which includes the waters within 24 nautical miles of the state's shoreline. Cal. Code Regs. tit. 13, § 2299.2(b); Cal. Code Regs. tit. 17, § 93118.2(b). This area evidently encompasses approximately 14,000 square miles of ocean beyond the 3-mile zone immediately adjacent to the coast. In general, the Vessel

Fuel Rules only cover vessels calling at a California port, and they accordingly contain an express exemption for vessels simply traveling through the region (known as "innocent passage"). . . . The regulations also require vessel owners and operators to keep detailed records, and non-compliance could subject such owners and operators to a wide range of sanctions, including fines, injunctive relief, and criminal prosecution. The Vessel Fuel Rules contain an express "sunset" clause, providing for their termination when CARB's Executive Officer makes a finding that the federal government has adopted and is enforcing requirements that will achieve equivalent emission reductions.

***

Initially, the ports of Long Beach and Los Angeles collectively constitute the largest port in the United States, with some 40% of all national imports entering the country through these two huge facilities. In 2006 alone, there were approximately 11,000 vessel "calls" at California ports, and this number is expected to increase significantly in the future.

CARB estimated that compliance with the Vessel Fuel Rules would cost ship operators $30,000 per California port "call," amounting to an industry-wide aggregate incremental cost of approximately $360 million annually and $1.5 billion through the end of 2014. On the other hand, it does not appear that such compliance would be technically impossible or even especially challenging. As the District Court emphasized in its decision, "any increased cost associated with compliance is less than one percent of the typical cost of a trans-Pacific voyage." . . . "That cost has been estimated by CARB to amount to only a $6.00 increase per 20-foot shipping container, a sum that would equate to only an extra 12.5 cents in the cost of a plasma TV" or about 0.14 cents for a pair of athletic shoes.

It appears uncontested that ocean-going vessels have long been a leading source of air pollution in California, due in large part to the widespread use of low-grade bunker fuel. Bunker fuel consists primarily of a thick and tar-like residual

Ships emit pollution in the form of sulfur dioxide (SO_2), oxides of nitrogen (NOx), and fine particulate matter ($PM_{2.5}$). These air pollutants emitted from power plants cause tens of thousands of premature deaths in the United States each year. In Europe alone, the pollution just from ships has been estimated to cause 50,000 premature deaths per year. Because ships are mobile and are a crucial part of interstate and international commerce, regulating their emissions has been legally difficult. California has often been on the forefront of air pollution regulation because its geography and climate render its air pollution problems particularly harmful to human health. Reducing emissions from ships visiting California, which is home to the busiest, second-busiest, and the sixth-busiest ports in the United States, has been a California priority for years. Tension between California's prerogative to protect its residents from air pollution and the interests of interstate and international commerce are ever-present.

formulated from the residues remaining after primary fuel distillation. Because of its high viscosity, this fuel has to be heated before it can be pumped and injected into an engine. It contains an average of approximately 25,000 parts per million ("ppm") of sulfur. In contrast, the diesel fuel used for trucks and other motor vehicles is limited to just 15 ppm of sulfur.

2006 data from CARB indicated that ocean-going vessels traveling within 24 nautical miles of the California coast generate per day approximately 15 tons of diesel particulate matter ("PM"), 157 tons of nitrogen oxides ("NOx"), and 117 tons of sulfur oxides ("SOx"). In fact, their emissions constitute the single largest source of SOx emissions in the state, responsible for 40% of all such emissions. Furthermore, both NOx and SOx are precursors to PM2.5, or fine particulate pollution. It was estimated that the vessels' daily PM emissions represent the equivalent of approximately 150,000 big rig trucks traveling 125 miles per day. It appears that emissions are likely to be blown onshore from beyond the geographical area actually covered by the Vessel Fuel Rules.

It is likewise undisputed that 27 million Californians (80% of the state's population) are exposed to emissions from ocean-going vessels and that these emissions have a number of harmful effects. In particular, diesel emissions are known to cause cancer and respiratory illnesses like aggravated asthma as well as to increase the risk of heart disease. CARB specifically estimated that the vessels' direct PM emissions cause 300 premature deaths across the state every single year, even after excluding cancer effects.

***

Implementation of the Vessel Fuel Rules should reduce PM emissions by approximately 13 tons per day, NOx emissions by 10 tons per day, and SOx emissions by 109 tons per day. Upon full implementation, the amount of SOx in the air should be cut by approximately 90%. In addition to anticipated health care savings and similar financial benefits, research indicated that the Vessel Fuel Rules should prevent, between 2009 and 2015, approximately 3,500 premature deaths and nearly 100,000 asthma attacks as well as reduce cancer risks.

***

PMSA is a California mutual benefit corporation whose members own and operate both United States and foreign-flagged ocean-going vessels. It filed its complaint in the United States District Court for the Eastern District of California on April 27, 2009, naming Goldstene (acting in his official capacity) as the sole Defendant. The pleading contained a single claim for relief with the heading: "[For Declaratory And Injunctive Relief Based On Preemption By The Submerged Lands Act,]" PMSA specifically alleged, inter alia, that it "is entitled to a judgment that enjoins defendant Goldstene from giving effect or enforcing [the Vessel Fuel Rules] seaward of California's boundary as established by the Submerged Lands Act and declares these regulations preempted by the Commerce Clause of the United States Constitution, and contrary to the Supremacy Clause of the United States Constitution." PMSA accordingly sought a declaration to the effect "that, insofar as they regulate conduct seaward of California's three-mile boundary," the Vessel Fuel Rules are preempted by the SLA and otherwise "impermissibly regulate navigation and foreign and domestic commerce as delegated to the United States Congress by Article I, Section 8, Clause 3 of the Constitution." PMSA further sought a permanent injunction barring the implementation or enforcement of the Vessel Fuel Rules as to conduct seaward of California's 3-mile boundary.

. . . PMSA moved for summary judgment. In a memorandum and order filed on June 30, 2009, the District Court denied PMSA's summary judgment motion. . . .

III.

This appeal presents the Court with a highly unusual and challenging set of circumstances. Given the circumstances, we do believe that the regulatory scheme at issue here pushes a state's legal authority to its very limits, although the state had clear justifications for doing so. More generally, we must take into account such fundamental considerations as, on the one hand, the supremacy of federal law, the various limitations on state regulations arising out of the dormant Commerce Clause and general maritime law preemption doctrines, and the federal government's unquestioned authority over this nation's relations with foreign countries, and, on the other hand, the sovereign police powers retained by California allowing the state to adopt a wide range of laws in order to protect the health, safety, and welfare of its own residents.

Having fully considered the numerous arguments raised by the parties, the record on appeal, the District Court's own reasoning, and the governing legal principles, we ultimately determine that the District Court properly denied PMSA's motion for summary judgment. In particular, PMSA fails to establish that the Vessel Fuel Rules are preempted by the SLA. PMSA also fails to show that it is entitled to summary judgment on the basis that the Vessel Fuel Rules "are otherwise 'unlawful and impermissibly regulate navigation and foreign and domestic commerce as delegated to the United States Congress.'"

A. Statutory Preemption Under the SLA

The SLA arose out of a number of rulings by the United States Supreme Court primarily deciding who owns the submerged lands (and the oil and other natural resources contained in these lands) off the coasts of the United States. In particular, the Supreme Court held in *United States v. California*, 332 U.S. 19 (1947), that "California is not the owner of the three-mile marginal belt along its coast, and that the Federal Government rather than the state has paramount rights in and power over that belt, an incident to which is full dominion over the resources of the soil under that water area, including oil. . . ."

"The Submerged Lands Act, passed May 22, 1953, came in response to these rulings." *United States v. Louisiana*, 446 U.S. 253 (1980). "By that statute, the United States released to the coastal States its rights in the submerged lands within state limits and confirmed its own rights therein seaward of those limits." The Supreme Court upheld this legislation as a constitutional exercise of Congress's power to dispose of federal property under Article IV, Section 3, Clause 2 of the Constitution. . . .

1. The Doctrine of Implicit Field Preemption and the General Presumption Against Preemption

***

PMSA contends that the 3-mile boundary purportedly established by the SLA constitutes a component of a comprehensive federal scheme and that the SLA "statutorily demarcates the territorial boundaries of the states for purposes of federal law." In other words, the powers of the states are subordinated even within their respective territorial boundaries, and they, in turn, lack any powers whatsoever (with a few possible narrow exceptions) beyond such boundaries in waters in which the federal government's own powers are "exclusive." According to PMSA, Congress purportedly legislated on a matter in which the federal interest is so dominant that it must be assumed that enforcement of state law on the same subject is precluded. PMSA goes on to argue that the Vessel Fuel Rules "assert the territorial dominion of California out to 24 miles" and thereby venture into a field comprehensively settled by Congress in the SLA — "the definition of a state's territorial seas."

In conducting its preemption analysis, the District Court expressly relied on the general presumption against preemption. It recognized that "a presumption applies to protect a state's historic police power in protecting the health and safety of its citizenry, unless the clear and manifest purpose of Congress dictates otherwise."

***

While PMSA contends that the Vessel Fuel Rules operate in fields historically occupied by the federal government (e.g., maritime commerce, conduct at sea outside of state boundaries, and the definition of state boundaries), we agree with the District Court that these state regulations ultimately implicate the prevention and control of air pollution. States have long sought to protect their own residents from the undisputedly harmful effects of air pollution and other forms of environmental harms. In its 1960 ruling in *Huron Portland Cement Co. v. City of Detroit*, 362 U.S. 440 (1960), the Supreme Court observed that "[l]egislation designed to free from pollution the very air that people breathe clearly falls within the exercise of even the most traditional concept of what is compendiously known as the police power. . . ." Likewise, this Court more recently stated that "[a]ir pollution prevention falls under the broad police powers of the states, which include the power to protect the health of citizens in the state" and that "[e]nvironmental regulation traditionally has been a matter of state authority." *Citations omitted.* Congress itself contemplated that the states would retain leading roles in regulating air quality when it passed the Clean Air Act. . . .

Given the "historic presence of state law" in the area of air pollution, we apply the well-established presumption or assumption against preemption in the current appeal. . . .

2. The SLA Does Not Preempt the Vessel Fuel Rules

Especially in light of this applicable presumption, we believe that the District Court properly rejected PMSA's whole theory of implied preemption. Simply put, PMSA reads too much into the SLA itself and what Congress itself intended to achieve in 1953. We instead conclude that, at the very least, a state law regulating extraterritorial conduct in the high seas immediately adjacent to the state's territorial waters satisfying the well-established effects test should generally be sustained. . . .

Initially, we reject PMSA's unfounded characterization of the Vessel Fuel Rules as amounting to some sort of territorial claim on the part of California. While the regulations do use, inter alia, the term "Regulated California Waters" and thereby set out precise geographical coordinates and descriptions (understandably so given that vessel owners and operators need to know when they must comply with the fuel use requirements), CARB, as a mere state administrative agency, does not actually purport to extend the borders of California. It merely seeks to regulate conduct beyond the state's territorial boundaries because of the serious harmful effects of this conduct on the state and its residents. It therefore does not invade or interfere with either Congress's power to set state territorial boundaries for domestic purposes or the President's power "to determine how far this country will claim territorial rights . . . as against other nations."

Turning specifically to the SLA itself, we must approach this legislation in light of the line of Supreme Court cases beginning with *California I*.

On the one hand, we do acknowledge that the initial holding in *California I* was premised on the fundamental principle that the federal government possesses paramount rights over the marginal seas. For instance, the *California I* Court noted that the "protection and control of [the 3-mile belt] has been and is a function of national external sovereignty" and that a national government "must have powers of dominion and regulation in the interests of its revenues, its health, and the security of its people from [war] waged on or too near its coasts." In *Barber v. Hawai'i*, 42 F.3d 1185 (1994), we stated that the *California I* Court thereby recognized the federal government as the exclusive owner of submerged lands and the waters above them within the 3-mile belt and that, "[c]onsequently, before the Submerged Lands Act, the states' jurisdiction ended at the low-tide mark of their tidal shores. . . ." The SLA, in turn, expressly reserves to the United States concurrent jurisdiction over the waters within this belt for purposes of commerce, navigation, national defense, and international affairs.

***

In fact, the *California I* Court itself indicated that a state's possession of police powers over the 3-mile belt had no bearing on the determination of whether the state or the federal government owned the lands in dispute. "Conceding that the state has been authorized to exercise local police power functions in the part of the marginal belt within its declared boundaries, these do not detract from the Federal Government's paramount rights in and power over this area." It went on to distinguish a number of prior Supreme Court cases upholding state regulation of conduct within the states' territorial waters. . . .

***

According to PMSA, the Supreme Court itself "has never been called upon to determine the effect of the SLA's boundary provisions on a state's exercise of jurisdiction over maritime conduct beyond the three-mile limit." We further note that PMSA does not cite to any judicial ruling actually striking down a state or local regulatory scheme on the basis of the SLA. On the contrary, the general weight of the case law clearly indicates that the federal legislation does not have the preemptive effect advanced by PMSA. We further conclude that the District Court's application of the effects test is consistent with the relevant case law. Pursuant to this test, California may enact reasonable regulations to monitor and control extraterritorial conduct substantially affecting its territory.

***

Furthermore, we conclude that the District Court quite properly relied on two circuit court decisions expressly considering the SLA and its bearing on a state's power to regulate extraterritorial conduct. Both of these decisions provide yet further support for the District Court's preemption ruling.

In *Warner v. Dunlap*, 532 F.2d 767 (1st Cir. 1976), the First Circuit specifically addressed the question of whether a Rhode Island statute, requiring every foreign vessel and every American vessel registered for foreign trade traversing Block Island Sound to take on a Rhode Island-licensed pilot, falls under the scope of the federal pilotage statute. . . . This federal provision, already mentioned in connection with our brief discussion of *Maine II*, provides for the state regulation of pilots in bays, inlets, rivers, harbors, and ports. Considering a challenge filed by Connecticut pilots, the federal appellate court ultimately upheld the state requirement, finding that the waters in question constituted a "bay." In the process, it specifically rejected the Connecticut pilots' theory that Rhode Island could not regulate their activities on the grounds that the routes they used were more than 3 miles off of the Rhode Island shore and that, pursuant to the SLA, the state only has territorial jurisdiction over this 3-mile zone. . . .

The Fifth Circuit considered a similar challenge in *Gillis v. Louisiana*, 294 F.3d 755 (5th Cir. 2002). Pilots claimed that Louisiana lacked the authority to regulate their activities on the portion of the Calcasieu Ship Channel lying more than 3 miles from the state's coastline. The Fifth Circuit rejected this claim, noting, inter alia, that Congress has traditionally left the regulation of pilotage largely to the states. With respect to the pilots' argument that Congress's enactment of § 1312 limited the ability of the states to regulate pilotage beyond their respective seaward boundaries, the *Gillis* court stated that:

> First, we disagree with the Pilots' premise that Congress implicitly limited state authority to regulate pilotage to bodies of water within their territorial boundaries when it enacted 43 U.S.C. § 1312. Section 1312, which is part of the Submerged Lands Act, addresses only who retains title to submerged lands both within and

beyond the three-mile line, with particular reference to ownership and exploration of natural resources in the seabed and subsoil. It does not address the regulation of pilotage on the waters above.

***

Accordingly, we believe that PMSA simply reads too much into the SLA itself. Congress, responding to such cases as *California I*, was primarily concerned with the distinct question of who owned the "submerged lands" and their valuable natural resources and accordingly adopted legislation that, to a great extent, was essentially a kind of real estate conveyance. Even if the statute does set out state territorial boundaries, it does not really address the separate question of whether the states are totally precluded from regulating any conduct beyond their seaward boundaries, even if such conduct clearly harms the state, its residents, and its interests. While the location of a state's territorial boundaries remains a critical consideration, it does not appear that Congress ever intended to create some sort of absolute (or near-absolute) rule under which otherwise sovereign states are precluded from exercising their expansive police powers with respect to extraterritorial conduct even if such an exercise is more than amply justified and does not interfere or conflict with any specific federal statute. In other words, PMSA is wrong to suggest that the SLA creates a territorial zone in which federal authority is not only paramount but always (or almost always) exclusive. . . .

B. The Dormant Commerce Clause and General Maritime Law Preemption

The Commerce Clause of the United States Constitution gives Congress the power "[t]o regulate Commerce with foreign Nations, and among the several States." . . . Under the dormant Commerce Clause doctrine, state legislation may be unconstitutional because of its effect on national or foreign commerce even in the absence of Congressional action. . . .

[T]here are two broad categories of state regulations burdening interstate commerce: (1) those that directly burden interstate commerce or otherwise discriminate against out-of-state interests; and (2) those that incidentally burden commerce. Regulations falling under the first category are generally struck down, while those in the second group are reviewed under a balancing test. Under this balancing test, regulations may violate the Commerce Clause if the burdens they impose so outweigh the putative benefits so as to render the regulations unreasonable or irrational. In turn, this Court previously explained that "[i]t is clear, however, that the Supreme Court used the term 'direct' to refer to regulations whose central purpose is to regulate commerce, usually in order to benefit local interests."

***

Initially, the regulatory scheme at issue here clearly does not fall under the "direct" category of state regulations because the central purpose of the Vessel Fuel Rules is to protect the health and well-being of the state's residents from the harmful effects of the fuel used by ocean-going vessels. The otherwise even-handed and generally applicable Vessel Fuel Rules also do not appear to discriminate against any out-of-state interests. We therefore are not presented with an example of state economic protectionism or favoritism. We are instead faced with an environmental regulatory scheme having only an incidental or indirect effect on commerce. . . .

The Court therefore must turn to a balancing test with respect to both the dormant Commerce Clause and general maritime law preemption claims.

We recognize the importance of uniformity as well as the unique role of the federal government in matters of foreign relations and international trade. . . . We further observe that we have emphasized that the notion of uniformity takes on special importance with respect to environmental regulation on the high seas. . . .

. . . [T]he state of California clearly has an especially powerful interest in controlling the harmful effects of air pollution resulting from the fuel used by ocean-going vessels while they are within 24 miles of the state's coast. In Section III.A.2., supra, we discussed in some detail the undisputed evidence regarding the highly damaging and even life-threatening effects of this air pollution on the people of California as well as the clear benefits resulting from the regulations adopted by CARB. The protection of our environment has repeatedly been recognized as a legitimate and important state interest. Based on the record before us, the exceptionally powerful state interest at issue here far outweighs any countervailing federal interests. . . .

For the foregoing reasons, we will affirm the District Court's denial of PMSA's motion for summary judgment.

points for discussion

1. *A prologue.* The Pacific Merchant Shipping Association tangled with the California Air Resources Board (CARB), and James Goldstene personally, previously. In *PMSA v. Goldstene*, 517 F.3d 1108 (9th Cir. 2008), the court struck down a CARB rule that set emissions standards for ocean-going vessels traveling within 24 miles of the California coast. Those rules, the "Merchant Vessel Rules," were held to have been preempted by the federal Clean Air Act, which does in fact set emissions standards for a wide variety of air pollution sources, including ocean-going vessels. This next iteration by the CARB, the Vessel Fuel Rules, were drafted precisely, in the words of Judge Cowen, to "correct the deficiency we identified in [the earlier case]." What if the federal Clean Air Act set fuel standards for ocean-going vessels? What if they were too weak to protect California's fragile air quality?

2. *Environmental federalism.* What if the situation were reversed — the federal government wished to impose air pollution standards that the coastal state found too onerous? The answer appears to be well settled, at least with

respect to most existing federal statutes, at least those predicated on federal Commerce Clause jurisdiction. The Clean Water Act, 33 U.S.C. §§ 1311 *et seq.*, clearly vests authority in the U.S. Army Corps of Engineers to regulate the "discharge of any pollutant into waters of the United States," which manifestly include state territorial waters. Moreover, Section 10 of the Rivers and Harbors Act, 33 U.S.C. §§ 403 *et seq.,* authorizes the Corps to protect navigable waters by regulating any obstruction or alteration of any navigable water of the United States. Again, that would encompass a state's three-nautical-mile belt of sea adjoining its coast. These would appear to be "paramount" interests of the United States. How does that compare, if at all, with the state interest in regulating under the guise of its police power? How would a state fare under a Dormant Commerce Clause challenge if, for example, it sought to impose more stringent rules for something like water pollution affecting its population? *See Wyeth v. Levine*, 555 U.S. 555 (2009). Do states have as much power to choose what happens in their territorial seas as the federal government?

Problem Exercise

Enter again the Fish-doo Corporation, the business entity we met in the problem exercise in the previous chapter. Recall that Fish-doo proposes to build a salmon fish farm in the state waters of Washington, about half a mile off the shore of the Olympic Peninsula, in the 17-mile-wide Juan de Fuca Strait passageway between Canada and the United States. Recall also that Fish-doo proposes to build unusually large salmon pens, three times the average size, or 12 football fields, to raise as much salmon as possible. It turns out, in addition to fish excrement and navigation, salmon farms pose other threats to fish and wildlife.

Advise Fish-doo as to which agencies they would need to deal with in order to operate their salmon farm.

B. OFFSHORE OIL AND GAS DEVELOPMENT

The United States is one of the largest crude oil *and* natural gas producers in the world. Much of the country's crude oil is extracted from offshore deposits: in 2017, about 18 percent, almost all of it from the Gulf of Mexico. By comparison, in 2017 only about 5 percent of natural gas produced in the United States was produced offshore; again, almost all of that from the Gulf of Mexico. Extracting oil and gas from offshore deposits is much more complicated and expensive than extraction from land, so it is only profitable to do so under certain circumstances. High crude oil prices in the 2000s drove offshore oil drilling to high levels, accounting for more than 25 percent of domestic production. By comparison, offshore natural gas production has plummeted. The advent of hydraulic fracturing made the extraction of natural gas from land extremely inexpensive. Natural gas wells on land proliferated, making the United States a gas-producing powerhouse, and drove natural gas prices down. The relatively expensive proposition of drilling for gas offshore became less attractive.

Offshore oil and gas extraction beyond three miles is governed by the Outer Continental Shelf Lands Act of 1953 (OCLSA), 43 U.S.C. §§ 1331-1356a. Recall from the previous chapter that the 1945 Truman Declaration staked a U.S. claim to the seabed as "naturally appurtenant" to U.S. land, and therefore under the jurisdiction and ownership of the United States. The most obvious implication is that mineral resources resident in that "naturally appurtenant" subsoil belong to the United States. The OCLSA is not only the congressional affirmation of that claim, but the governance structure for extracting mineral deposits.

Political support for oil and gas extraction from the continental shelf has waxed and waned since congressional passage. A disastrous oil rig accident in 1969 that washed oil ashore the tony beaches of Santa Barbara, California, galvanized opposition to offshore oil and gas production. But the oil embargo of 1973, and the subsequent lurch toward achieving "energy independence" helped bring offshore oil and gas back into the fold of federal energy policy. The OCLSA was amended in 1978 to include a mandate that offshore resources undergo an "expeditious and orderly development." 43 U.S.C. § 1332(3). High oil prices in the early 2000s drove a new spurt of offshore production, but this slowed a bit following the 2010 Deepwater Horizon oil rig explosion, which killed 11 oil rig workers and injured 17, and which poured nearly 134 million gallons of crude into the Gulf of Mexico, over *12 times* that of the Exxon Valdez oil spill of 1989. A competitive international energy environment and the prospect of drastically reducing the American oil trade deficit has nevertheless kept offshore oil production alive and well.

Before the 2010 Deepwater Horizon disaster, the federal agency charged with administering offshore oil leases was the Department of the Interior Minerals Management Service (MMS). The MMS administered the leasing process for firms wishing to drill for oil and gas on federal submerged lands, collected the royalty payments under those leases, and implemented and enforced the environmental and safety regulations. The Deepwater Horizon disaster had many causes, but substantial blame was laid upon the MMS. Some believed that housing both the leasing function and the safety and environmental enforcement function under the MMS compromised the latter's ability to police violations. The National Commission on the BP Deepwater Horizon Oil Spill and Offshore Drilling, convened by President Obama following the disaster, recommended separating the lease administration function from safety and environmental functions, giving the latter some independence to conduct more rigorous and demanding safety and environmental inspections, and to levy penalties. Leasing program administration is now carried out by the new Bureau of Ocean Energy Management (BOEM), and safety and environmental functions by the Bureau

Figure 4-2. The First Offshore Oil Wells, Off the Coast of Santa Barbara County

of Safety and Environmental Enforcement (BSEE). Both are resident in the Department of the Interior.

1. An Overview of the Mineral Leasing Process

OCLSA leasing is carried out for 26 "planning areas," in which proposed leases are considered together. The leasing process under OCLSA occurs in four stages: (1) development by BOEM of a five-year program for each of the planning areas, (2) specific leases are awarded, (3) exploration, and (4) development and production. It is a bit of an oversimplification to break down the leasing process into these four stages, as each stage encompasses a great deal of activity. But each stage constitutes a discrete federal action, with legal implications, and for which review requirements may exist under the National Environmental Policy Act (NEPA), the Coastal Zone Management Act (CZMA), and the Endangered Species Act (ESA).

Stage One: The Five-Year Plan. The Secretary is required to prepare a leasing program for five-year periods, setting for the schedule of lease sales, including information about size, timing, and location of leasing activity. 43 U.S.C. § 1344(a). The plan must reflect management that "considers economic, social, and environmental values of the renewable and nonrenewable resources contained in the outer Continental Shelf, and the potential impact of oil and gas exploration on other resource values . . . and the marine, coastal and human environments."

43 U.S.C. § 1344(a)(1). The Secretary, viz. BOEM, may not lease any area that was not included in the five-year plan.

At this stage, NEPA requires that BOEM prepare a *Programmatic* Environmental Impact Statement (PEIS), which is an environmental impact statement that evaluates broadly the environmental impacts of a proposed agency program, bearing in mind that the specifics of individual actions within the program cannot be assessed. At this stage, environmental impact analysis must necessarily focus on the effects of a level of leasing activity, and the cumulative impacts of having multiple geological activities in specific areas. As the five-year plan includes specific leasing areas, it is possible to at least state with some specificity the impacts of the program, should it be carried out to its fullest extent.

Stage Two: Lease Sale. The lease sale stage actually involves a series of steps to elicit, entertain, and accept or reject bids for leases. BOEM initiates the process by issuing a "Call for Information." This initiates a process of consultation with oil companies on where they would be likely to bid for a lease, but also with governments on a variety of factors, including environmental impacts. Following the consultation, BOEM defines the sale areas it will put up for leasing. That sale proposal triggers NEPA, and a requirement for a comprehensive environmental impact statement. Environmental analysis at this stage is more location-specific than at the five-year plan stage, and should consider geologic conditions, as well as wildlife for the lease sale areas. That said, many leased areas within a planning area are highly similar, so BOEM sometimes performs a multi-lease environmental impact statement, aggregating multiple sale areas that might be taken up by multiple lessees.

Once the environmental impact statement is completed and published, and a CZMA consistency determination is made (see Chapter 9), a Final Notice of Sale is published. The notice must appear in the Federal Register 30 days before a scheduled lease sale, and announce the process for submitting bids, required conditions for bids, and the time and date on which bids will be opened. Once bids are opened, BOEM will generally select the highest conforming bid for each tract in the area put up for sale. Acceptance of the bid is still subject to market value analysis, which may still render a bid unacceptable if BOEM deems the bid to be less than what is required for the bidder to make a normal rate of return.

Stage Three: Exploration. Although oil companies are extremely sophisticated and knowledgeable about the abundance of offshore mineral reserves, some further investigation is required. At the exploration stage, a lessee submits an exploration plan for approval by BOEM. In fact, post-lease, the exploration stage is where the drilling actually begins, as oil and gas companies drill test wells before actually deciding where to settle in and ramp up production. As such, an exploration plan must set forth information about drilling equipment and vessels, impacts on archaeological resources and wildlife, oil spill response, and other environmental and safety considerations. NEPA is again triggered, as is CZMA consistency review.

OCS Oil and Gas Leasing, Exploration, and Development Process

Figure 4-3. The Offshore Leasing Process

If, as is usually the case, endangered or threatened species may be impacted, consultation under the ESA is carried out. The risks are not smaller at this stage just because the drilling is exploratory; the Deepwater Horizon rig was conducting an exploratory drill when it exploded.

Stage Four: Development and Production. At last, once a company has bid upon and been awarded a lease, once all of the NEPA, CZMA, and ESA reviews have been completed, once the exploration plan has been approved, and once the exploration has itself been carried out, the development and production stage begins. The process is much like the exploration stage: The lessee submits a development and production plan, NEPA, ESA, and CZMA review is conducted, and once the plan is approved, the lessee must submit an Application for Permit to Drill (APD). Once that is granted, the company can begin full-scale production.

Leasing the continental shelf for oil or gas extraction is a deceptively complex process, with large benefits but also large risks. These different stages of the leasing process were intended to ensure that adequate attention is paid to the different considerations at different scales, and different stages of learning. Depending on the results of the exploration stage, different equipment might be needed for the development and production stage.

2. The Five-Year Plan

As the first of the four stages of leasing, the five-year planning stage is the broadest and the least detailed. But OCSLA does require a certain level of specificity, and that attention be paid to stated congressional priorities. The plan must set forth specific areas, or "tracts," in the planning areas to be identified in a five-year leasing plan. Consultation with stakeholders is required. The following case was one of the first to challenge the development of a five-year plan, following the 1978 Amendments.

California v. Watt

668 F.2d 1290 (D.C. Cir. 1981)

PER CURIAM, United States Court of Appeals, District of Columbia.

Congress enacted the Outer Continental Shelf Lands Act in 1953 to extend

As Secretary of the Interior, James Watt was one of President Ronald Reagan's most controversial cabinet appointees. Watt served as Deputy Assistant Secretary of Water and Power in the Interior Department under President Nixon, and later president of the Mountain States Legal Foundation, an advocacy group and public interest law firm dedicated to challenging government regulations. Once appointed, Watt made sure that the Interior Department did as little as possible, eliminating many regulations on the extraction of minerals and the logging of trees from public lands; minimized application of the ESA; and even refused private donations of land for conservation purposes. He once refused a permit for the musical group the Beach Boys to perform on the National Mall on Independence Day, stating that he felt that the group "attracted the wrong element," while granting singer Wayne Newton, a Republican supporter of the President, permission to perform on the Mall. Watt resigned over controversial remarks he made about affirmative action, stating about his coal leasing panel: "I have a black, a woman, two Jews and a cripple." Later after leaving office, he was convicted for withholding documents from a federal grand jury investigation in the Department of Housing and Urban Redevelopment, where he lobbied on behalf of a client.

"[t]he Constitution and laws and civil and political jurisdiction of the United States . . . to the subsoil and seabed of the Outer Continental Shelf." The 1953 Act authorized the Secretary of Interior to grant leases by competitive bidding in order to explore and develop the oil and gas deposits of the shelf's submerged lands, and empowered him to promulgate regulations to administer the provisions of the Act. . . .

Exploitation of [Outer Continental Shelf] ("OCS") resources under the 1953 Act proceeded at first at a relatively slow pace. . . . OCS activities were localized in impact and received little national scrutiny.

Two major events, however, changed all that and moved OCS development into the forefront of the national consciousness. The first was the blowout of an OCS drilling project in the Santa Barbara Channel on January 28, 1969, resulting in the "largest oil spill in U.S. history," and highlighting the environmental dangers associated with OCS exploitation. The second was the Arab oil embargo of 1973, which dramatically underscored the nation's dependence on foreign sources of oil. In response to the latter, President Nixon directed on January 23, 1974, that 10 million acres of the OCS be leased in 1975. . . . The announcement crystallized growing concern over the impact of OCS activities and the adequacy of the 1953 Act. Although the need to develop national energy independence was clear, state and local governments feared damaging impacts to their coastlines from oil spills and the onshore development which accompanies offshore drilling. Commercial and recreational fishing interests expressed concern over the possible effects on their livelihoods and leisure activities, while environmental and citizens groups raised questions about the effect of OCS activities on the ecology. These interests accordingly sought a role in the offshore leasing policy decisions which had previously been committed to the virtually unlimited discretion of the Secretary.

These pressures led to the introduction of legislation in 1974 to overhaul the 1953 Act, and culminated four years later in the passage of the Outer Continental Shelf Lands Act Amendments of 1978. The 1978 Amendments were intended to provide a comprehensive framework for the expeditious and orderly development (of the OCS), subject to environmental safeguards, in a manner which is consistent with the maintenance of competition and other national needs. . . .

To achieve the expeditious but orderly development of OCS resources, the 1978 Amendments provide structure for every conceivable step to be taken on this path, from promulgation of a five-year leasing program, to the lease sale stage, to the exploration process, to development and production, to sale of recovered minerals, to ensure that the Secretary takes into account all relevant policy considerations and the views of all interested persons, the 1978 Amendments provide for participation in the OCS process by Congress, affected state and local governments, relevant federal agencies, and the public.

A. An Overview of Section 18

As is apparent from the foregoing brief summary, the procedures embodied in the 1978 Amendments are pyramidic in structure, proceeding from broad-based planning to an increasingly narrower focus as actual development grows more imminent. The first important step in this process is the one with which we are primarily concerned today — preparation of the five-year leasing program pursuant to section 18.

Section 18 "establishes a process which will permit the Secretary of Interior to weigh energy potential, and other benefits against environmental and other risks in determining how, when and where oil and gas should be made available from the various Outer Continental Shelf areas to meet national energy needs." It requires the Secretary to prepare, maintain and periodically revise a leasing program consisting of a schedule of proposed sales, indicating, "as precisely as possible, the size, timing and location of leasing activity which he determines will best meet national energy needs for the five-year period following its approval or reapproval." The Secretary must prepare and maintain the program consistent with four basic principles:

(1) Management of the outer Continental Shelf shall be conducted in a manner which considers economic, social, and environmental values of the renewable and nonrenewable resources contained in the outer Continental Shelf, and the potential impact of oil and gas exploration on other resource values of the outer Continental Shelf and the marine, coastal, and human environments.

(2) Timing and location of exploration, development, and production of oil and gas among the oil- and gas-bearing physiographic regions of the outer Continental Shelf shall be based on a consideration of —

(A) existing information concerning the geographical, geological, and ecological characteristics of such regions;

(B) an equitable sharing of developmental benefits and environmental risks among the various regions;

(C) the location of such regions with respect to, and the relative needs of, regional and national energy markets;

(D) the location of such regions with respect to other uses of the sea and seabed, including fisheries, navigation, existing or proposed sea lanes, potential sites of deepwater ports, and other anticipated uses of the resources and space of the outer Continental Shelf;

(E) the interest of potential oil and gas producers in the development of oil and gas resources as indicated by exploration or nomination;

(F) laws, goals, and policies of affected States which have been specifically identified by the Governors of such States as relevant matters for the Secretary's consideration;

(G) the relative environmental sensitivity and marine productivity of different areas of the outer Continental Shelf; and

(H) relevant environmental and predictive information for different areas of the outer Continental Shelf.

(3) The Secretary shall select the timing and location of leasing, to the maximum extent practicable, so as to obtain a proper balance between the potential for environmental damage, the potential for the discovery of oil and gas, and the potential for adverse impact on the coastal zone.

(4) Leasing activities shall be conducted to assure receipt of fair market value for the lands leased and the rights conveyed by the Federal Government.

Section 18 also establishes a mechanism whereby state governments, among others, are authorized to offer suggestions and comments on the development of the leasing program. Under section 18(c), the Secretary is required, when preparing a proposed leasing program, to "invite and consider suggestions for such program" from the Governors of any state which might be affected thereby. The Secretary is also obliged, after he has drawn up the proposed program and at least sixty days before he publishes it in the Federal Register, to submit it to the Governor of each affected state for review and comment. If any such Governor submits timely comments requesting modification of the proposed program, the Secretary must reply in writing, granting or denying the request in whole or in part, "and stating his reasons therefor." . . . . The Secretary must then submit the proposed program and any comments received thereon to the Congress and the President at least sixty days before he approves it, indicating why any specific recommendation of a state government was not accepted.

Once the Secretary approves the leasing program, it achieves important practical and legal significance. No lease may be issued for any area unless the area is included in the approved leasing program and unless the lease contains provisions consistent with the approved program. The approved program also becomes the basis for future planning by all affected entities, from federal, state and local governments to the oil industry itself. Compliance with the mandates of section 18, therefore, is extremely important to the expeditious but orderly exploitation of OCS resources.

***

IV. Did the Secretary Comply with Section 18 in Preparing the Leasing Program?

Petitioners argue that the Secretary's compliance with section 18 was flawed in several respects. . . . [T]hey contend that the leasing program is not consistent with the principles set forth in sections 18(a)(2) and (a)(3), in that the Secretary 1) either misinterpreted or failed to consider certain factors enumerated in section 18(a)(2); 2) failed to actually base the leasing program upon the section 18(a)(2) factors; and 3) failed to select the timing and location of the proposed lease sales so as to achieve a proper balance among the potential for discovery of oil and gas, environmental damage, and adverse impact on the coastal zone as required by section 18(a)(3). . . .

B. Consistency with the Principle of Sections 18(a)(2)

. . . Petitioners argue that [the] language [of section 18] poses two related duties upon the Secretary in developing a leasing program; first, he must fully consider the eight factors listed in section 18(a)(2), and second, he must actually base the leasing program on the result of his consideration of these factors. In other words, the factors listed in section 18(a)(2) are matters which the Secretary must address at the leasing program stage, and are matters which the Secretary must factor into his decision-making process when drawing up the leasing program.

The Secretary takes a different view of section 18(a)(2)'s relevance at the program stage. He notes that section 18(a)(2) speaks of the timing and location of "exploration, development, and production," and not the timing and location of proposed lease sales. Exploration, development, and production, the Secretary points out, are activities which occur during future stages of OCS exploitation, after a leasing program has been developed. Since section 18 only requires that the leasing program be prepared in a manner "consistent with" the principle that these future activities be based upon consideration of the factors enumerated in section 18(a)(2), the Secretary concludes that he has an obligation, at the program stage, only to consider all of the factors enumerated in Section 18(a), to the extent that probative information exists now. Many of the elements, however, have viability only in connection with later stages of OCS activities. Thus his obligation now is to assure that his leasing program permits sufficient and proper consideration of those factors at their appropriate time in the future. At the time of the leasing schedule, therefore, it is important to identify and consider the enumerated issues. This enables the Secretary to determine which, if any, factors present an absolute impediment to scheduling an area; which, if any, require particular studies or adjustments that would warrant placement of the area on the schedule later; and which, if any, depend on highly variable or speculative matters which are best addressed at a specific future time.

We conclude that Congress intended the Secretary to consider all factors listed in section 18(a)(2) in developing the leasing program, and did not envision the deferral thereof until some later date. We also conclude that the Secretary must base the leasing program upon the result of his consideration of these factors.

***

We fully recognize that at the leasing program stage, much of the information culled from an assessment of the section 18(a)(2) factors may be predictive or speculative in nature. This does not mean, however, that consideration of any particular factor may be deferred until some later date. The Secretary's authority is to consider all regions and act on the basis of "existing information." Although the continual collection and assimilation of pertinent information must of course continue throughout the OCS process, and although the speculative nature of any information may well affect the weight the Secretary attaches thereto in drawing up the leasing program, section 18(a)(2) nonetheless requires the Secretary at the program stage to consider, each factor listed therein on the basis of the best information available, and to base the leasing program upon the information thereby obtained.

(1) Did the Secretary Misinterpret or Fail to Consider the
Factors Enumerated in Section 18(a)(2)?

Petitioners contend that the Secretary misinterpreted the directive of section 18(a)(2)(B) that, in developing the leasing program, he consider "an equitable sharing of developmental benefits and environmental risks among the various regions." The Secretary interpreted this factor as follows:

> Subpart (2)(B) . . . supports the contention that no one region is to bear the burden of supplying our nation with energy supplies, and that all regions should contribute to energy supplies unless the environmental risks are too high. The directive to share developmental benefits and environmental risks requires the Department to ensure that all regions of the country with economically recoverable deposits of hydrocarbons participate in the leasing program to the extent that environmental risks are not too high. This mandate addresses the historical inequity which has resulted from over-reliance on the Gulf of Mexico.

According to the Secretary, the primary "environmental risk" to be considered here was the risk of occurrence of a major oil spill. Considering this factor, the Secretary found that the probability of an oil spill related most directly to the quantity of oil likely to be produced in an area, and did not vary significantly on the basis of geography, weather, or geohazards. The Secretary therefore argues that the risk of an environmentally damaging incident is largely equal nationwide.

Petitioners argue that the Secretary defined "environmental risks" in an unduly narrow fashion. They assert that the environmental risks OCS activities pose to any region depend not only on the likelihood of an oil spill but also on an assessment of the damage such an oil spill would inflict. The amount of damage that would befall an area, according to petitioners, is a product of the area's environmental sensitivity. Thus, to determine the environmental risks posed to an area, petitioners argue that the Secretary must consider the likelihood of an oil spill, the environmental sensitivity of the area, and the damage which would result to that area if an oil spill occurred. Petitioners further contend that "an equitable sharing" of the environmental risks can only be brought about if the Secretary considers the relative environmental sensitivity of the various OCS regions. Petitioners claim, however, that because the Secretary failed to consider the relative environmental sensitivity of the various OCS regions under section 18(a)(2)(G), he was unable to consider an equitable sharing of environmental risks.

We find ourselves in essential agreement with petitioners. We note initially that the Secretary's conclusion does not follow from his premises; that is, it does not follow from the fact that the likelihood of an oil spill is related to the quantity of oil present in a region that the risk of an oil spill is equal nationwide. Rather, it follows that the risk of an oil spill is greatest where the most oil is to be found, and we have been directed to nothing in the record which indicates that the amount of oil to be found in the various regions is approximately the same. Be that as it may, we must also conclude that the Secretary's interpretation of "environmental risks" is at odds with the plain meaning of the statutory language. A risk is commonly understood to mean the "exposure to the chance of injury or loss." Injury or loss to the environment from an oil spill, however, does not flow from the mere mathematical possibility that the spill might occur; it depends upon both the likelihood of a spill and the amount of damage the spill would inflict. . . . Since the Secretary interpreted the term "environmental risk" contrary to the plain meaning of the statute, his consideration of this factor was flawed. Similarly, since the Secretary failed to consider the relative environmental sensitivity of the various OCS regions as required by section 18(a)(2)(G), it follows that he failed to give proper consideration to the mandate of section 18(a)(2)(B) that environmental risks be "equitabl(y) shar(ed)" among the various OCS regions.

***

C. Consistency with the Principle of Sections 18(a)(3)

The Secretary [] recognized . . . that both the selection of the areas to be leased (location) and the priority in the schedule given to leasing those areas (timing), must strike a proper balance between the three elements of section 18(a)(3). [T]he Secretary determined that . . . if the anticipated benefits outweigh the anticipated costs for an area, then the "proper balance between the potential for environmental damage, the potential for the discovery of oil and gas, and the potential for adverse impact on the coastal zone" . . . is to schedule the area for leasing consideration. . . .

We endorse [the Secretary's] interpretation of section 18(a)(3). It is reasonable to conclude that within the section's "proper balance" there is some notion of "costs" and "benefits," recognizing that "costs" in this context must be a term of uncertain content to the extent it is meant to stand for environmental and social costs. . . .

However reasonable we think the Secretary's interpretation of section 18(a)(3) is as a general matter, the record compels the conclusion that it was not completely implemented. First and foremost, of course, is the Secretary's failure to consider and factor in all aspects of section 18(a)(2). This omission precluded him from meeting the requirement of section 18(a)(3) to obtain a proper balance to the max- imum extent practicable. That fact is evident in the Secretary's explanation of how he timed the areas for leasing, which we have quoted above. In relying solely upon industry interest, resource potential, and administrative convenience, the Secretary did not fully comply with all the statutory standards.

***

Remaining unexplained [] is the failure to evaluate the quantifiable impact of an oil spill upon fishing, tourism and other OCS-related enterprises. Estimates of damage to these activities, like estimates of potential oil and gas production, are necessarily speculative to a considerable degree. But, unlike some environmental costs, damage to tourism, fishing, and the like is not inherently insusceptible of quantitative analysis. No reason appears why such estimates cannot be made, and the Secretary offers no satisfactory excuse for the failure to make them.

***

Pursuant to the broad equity powers vested in us pursuant to section 23(c)(6), we grant the relief requested. Although we do not vacate the program, thereby allowing the proposed lease sales scheduled thereon to proceed, we remand the program under review and the record thereof to the Secretary for revision in accor- dance with the Act. We retain jurisdiction over this case until the Secretary has revised and reapproved the program presently under review.

points for discussion

1. *On remand.* . . . This case was remanded to the MMS, which revised the five- year plan. Appeal was again taken, but this time the court of appeals held that the Secretary had succeeded in rectifying its earlier errors, and that the plan conformed to the requirements of OCSLA. *California v. Watt,* 712 F.2d 584 (D.C. Cir. 1983). With just a little more specificity and analysis, the

substance of the original five-year plan was upheld on appeal. In general, as long as the requisite specificity and analysis is undertaken, courts will generally defer to the policy determinations made by the Secretary. Litigation has been relatively rare. Only once has a five-year plan been completely canceled as a result of litigation, in *Conservation Law Foundation v. Watt*, 560 F. Supp. 561 (D. Mass. 1983), *aff'd, Massachusetts v. Watt*, 716 F.2d 946 (1st Cir. 1983).

2. *Standard of review*. Because of the mixed questions of law and fact, the standard of review is somewhat confusing. The court stated that "[W]e think the standard of review may be fairly summarized as follows. When reviewing findings of ascertainable fact made by the Secretary, the substantial evidence test guides our inquiry. When reviewing the policy judgments made by the Secretary, including those predictive and difficult judgmental calls the Secretary is called upon to make, we will subject them to searching scrutiny to ensure that they are neither arbitrary nor irrational — in other words, we must determine whether 'the decision is based on a consideration of the relevant factors and whether there has been a clear error of judgment.'" *California v. Watt*, 668 F.2d at 1302.

3. *Environmentally speaking*. Why do you think that the environmental sensitivity of the drilling area should figure so prominently in the five-year plan? The Secretary had noted in its five-year plan and the court noticed, that historically, there has been an "over-reliance" on oil resources in the Gulf of Mexico. Do you think that analysis of the environmental sensitivity of the Gulf might cure that over-reliance? What would it be compared to?

   The Gulf of Mexico is unusually hospitable to offshore oil and gas drilling, as almost half of its 615,000 square miles is shallow continental shelf. Moreover, it is near the energy capital of the country, Houston, and close to much of the country's refineries. The economic advantages of drilling in the Gulf are enormous. How would you go about evaluating the environmental disadvantages?

4. *A value for nature*. The court "endorsed" the Secretary's interpretation of § 18(a)(3) (43 U.S.C. § 1344(a)(3)), requiring a "proper balance" between environment, mineral value, and coastal impact, as calling for a cost-benefit analysis, but then found that it had not been done satisfactorily. The court was particularly concerned with the failure to estimate the impact of an oil spill to tourism and recreation industries. On remand, the Secretary set out in the revised five-year plan an estimate of each planning area's "external costs," those "environmental and socio-economic costs which are not normally included in the costs of operations. . . ." The petitioners did not challenge the formula used by the Secretary. Historically, environmental organizations have not engaged in the exercise of cost-benefit analysis, in part because environmental values are very hard to calculate, and in part because they have rarely had the staffing to undertake or challenge economic analysis. Would you seek to challenge the cost-benefit analysis on its own terms, or do you think it

Figure 4-4. An Offshore Oil Rig in the Gulf of Mexico

would be a mistake to go along with the monetization of environmental and ecological resources? *See* Shi-Ling Hsu & John Loomis, *A Defense of Cost-Benefit Analysis for Natural Resource Policy*, 32 ENVTL. L. REP. 10239 (2002). What do you think are the pitfalls of using a cost-benefit analysis to make siting and planning decisions? The advantages?

3. Lease Sales

The second stage of the oil and gas leasing process concerns the *sale* of a lease: the payment of an oil and gas company to lease a part of the federal submerged lands, *provided* that it meets (and provided that the federal government carries out) all obligations under OCSLA, the ESA, NEPA, and other statutory and regulatory requirements. *Sale* is perhaps not the most accurate way to describe this stage: Like other government contracts, oil and gas companies submit *bids* on specific areas available for leasing. Bids are required to contain many provisions, some of which are boilerplate, some of which are time- and area-specific.

This stage, specifying as it does the areas and times for drilling, involves a different scale of review. The Bureau of Ocean Energy Management (BOEM) must evaluate the economics of the lease and decide whether the payment is enough to justify a private occupation of public property, and extraction of publicly owned mineral deposits. BOEM must also evaluate a variety of environmental, economic, and social implications of a particular proposed lease (a bid).

The following case addresses the question as to BOEM's obligations under the Coastal Zone Management Act (CZMA) at the lease sale stage.

Secretary of the Interior v. California

464 U.S. 312 (1984)

Justice O'CONNOR delivered the opinion of the Court.

OCS lease sales are conducted by the Department of the Interior (Interior). Oil and gas companies submit bids and the high bidders receive priority in the eventual exploration and development of oil and gas resources situated in the submerged lands on the OCS. A lessee does not, however, acquire an immediate or absolute right to explore for, develop, or produce oil or gas on the OCS; those activities require separate, subsequent federal authorization.

In 1977, the Department of Commerce approved the California Coastal Management Plan. The same year, Interior began preparing Lease Sale No. 53 — a sale of OCS leases off the California coast near Santa Barbara. Interior first asked several state and federal agencies to report on potential oil and gas resources in this area. The Agency then requested bidders, federal and state agencies, environmental organizations, and the public, to identify which of 2036 tracts in the area should be offered for lease. In October 1978, Interior announced the tentative selection of 243 tracts, including 115 tracts situated in the Santa Maria Basin located off western Santa Barbara. Various meetings were then held with state agencies. Consultations with other federal agencies were also initiated. Interior issued a Draft Environmental Impact Statement in April, 1980.

On July 8, 1980 the California Coastal Commission informed Interior that it had determined Lease Sale No. 53 to be an activity "directly affecting" the California coastal zone. . . . The commission expressed its concern that oil spills on the OCS could threaten the southern sea otter, whose range was within 12 miles of the 31 challenged tracts. The commission explained that it "has been consistent in objecting to proposed offshore oil development within specific buffer zones around special sensitive marine mammal and seabird breeding areas. . . ." The commission concluded that 31 [] tracts should be removed from the sale because "leasing within 12 miles of the Sea Otter Range in Santa Maria Basin would not be consistent" with the California Coastal Management Program. . . .

Interior rejected the State's demands. In the Secretary's view, no consistency review was required because the lease sale did not engage CZMA § 307(c)(1), and the Governor's request was not binding because it failed to strike a reasonable balance between the national and local interests. On April 10, 1981, Interior announced that the lease sale of the 115 tracts would go forward, and on April 27 issued a final notice of sale.

Respondents filed two substantially similar suits in federal district court to enjoin the sale of 29 tracts situated within 12 miles of the Sea Otter range. Both complaints alleged, *inter alia,* Interior's violation of § 307(c)(1) of CZMA. They argued that leasing sets in motion a chain of events that culminates in oil and gas development, and that leasing therefore "directly affects" the coastal zone within the meaning of § 307(c)(1).

The district court entered a summary judgment for respondents on the CZMA claim. The Court of Appeals for the Ninth Circuit affirmed that portion of the district court judgment that required a consistency determination before the sale. We granted certiorari, and we now reverse.

Whether the sale of leases on the OCS is an activity "directly affecting" the coastal zone is not self-evident. As already noted, OCS leases involve submerged lands outside the coastal zone, and as we shall discuss, an OCS lease authorizes the holder to engage only in preliminary exploration; further administrative approval is required before full exploration or development may begin. . . .

We turn [] to the legislative history. [We are persuaded] that Congress did not intend OCS lease sales to fall within the ambit of CZMA § 307(c)(1). . . . [T]he "directly affecting" language in § 307(c)(1) was, by all appearances, only a modest compromise, designed to offset in part the narrower definition of the coastal zone favored by the Senate and adopted by the Conference Committee. Section 307(c)(1)'s "directly affecting" language was aimed at activities conducted or supported by federal agencies on federal lands physically situated in the coastal zone but excluded from the zone as formally defined by the Act. Consistent with this view, the same Conference Committee that wrote the "directly affecting" language rejected two provisions in the House bill that would have required precisely what respondents seek here — coordination of federally sponsored OCS activities with state coastal management and conservation programs. In light of the Conference Committee's further, systematic rejection of every other attempt to extend the reach of CZMA to the OCS, we are impelled to conclude that the 1972 Congress did not intend § 307(c)(1) to reach OCS lease sales.

***

Since 1978 there have been four distinct statutory stages to developing an offshore oil well: (1) formulation of a 5-year leasing plan by the Department of the Interior; (2) lease sales; (3) exploration by the lessees; (4) development and production. Each stage involves separate regulatory review that may, but need not, conclude in the transfer to lease purchasers of rights to conduct additional activities on the OCS. And each stage includes specific requirements for consultation with Congress, between federal agencies, or with the States. Formal review of consistency with state coastal management plans is expressly reserved for the last two stages.

(1) Preparation of a leasing program. The first stage of OCS planning is the creation of a leasing program. Interior is required to prepare a 5-year schedule of proposed OCS lease sales. During the preparation of that program Interior must solicit comments from interested federal agencies and the governors of affected states, and must respond in writing to all comments or requests received from the state governors. The proposed leasing program is then submitted to the President and Congress, together with comments received by the Secretary from the governor of the affected state. Plainly, prospective lease purchasers acquire no rights to

explore, produce, or develop at this first stage of OCSLA planning, and consistency review provisions of CZMA § 307(c)(3)(B) are therefore not engaged. . . .

(2) Lease sales. The second stage of OCS planning — the stage in dispute here — involves the solicitation of bids and the issuance of offshore leases. Requirements of the National Environmental Protection Act and the Endangered Species Act must be met first. The governor of any affected state is given a formal opportunity to submit recommendations regarding the "size, timing, or location" of a proposed lease sale. Interior is required to accept these recommendations if it determines they strike a reasonable balance between the national interest and the well-being of the citizens of the affected state. Local governments are also permitted to submit recommendations, and the Secretary "may" accept these. . . . Lease purchasers acquire the right to conduct only limited "preliminary" activities on the OCS — geophysical and other surveys that do not involve seabed penetrations greater than 300 feet and that do not result in any significant environmental impacts.

Again, there is no suggestion that these activities in themselves "directly affect" the coastal zone. But by purchasing a lease, lessees acquire no right to do anything more. Under the plain language of OCSLA, the purchase of a lease entails no right to proceed with full exploration, development, or production that might trigger CZMA § 307(c)(3)(B); the lessee acquires only a priority in submitting plans to conduct those activities. If these plans, when ultimately submitted, are disapproved, no further exploration or development is permitted.

(3) Exploration. The third stage of OCS planning involves review of more extensive exploration plans submitted to Interior by lessees. . . . Exploration may not proceed until an exploration plan has been approved. A lessee's plan must include a certification that the proposed activities comply with any applicable state management program developed under CZMA. OCSLA expressly provides for federal disapproval of a plan that is not consistent with an applicable state management plan unless the Secretary of Commerce finds that the plan is consistent with CZMA goals or in the interest of national security. The plan must also be disapproved if it would "probably cause serious harm or damage . . . to the marine, coastal, or human environment. . . ." If a plan is disapproved for the latter reason, the Secretary may "cancel such lease and the lessee shall be entitled to compensation. . . ."

There is, of course, no question that CZMA consistency review requirements operate here. CZMA § 307(c)(3)(B) expressly applies, and as noted, OCSLA itself refers to the applicable CZMA provision.

(4) Development and production. The fourth and final stage is development and production. The lessee must submit another plan to Interior. The Secretary must forward the plan to the governor of any affected state and, on request, to the local governments of affected states, for comment and review. Again, the governor's recommendations must be accepted, and the local governments' may be accepted, if they strike a reasonable balance between local and national interests. Reasons for accepting or rejecting a governor's recommendations must be communicated in writing to the governor. In addition, the development and production plan must

be consistent with the applicable state coastal management program. The State can veto the plan as "inconsistent," and the veto can be overridden only by the Secretary of Commerce. A plan may also be disapproved if it would "probably cause serious harm or damage . . . to the marine, coastal or human environments." If a plan is disapproved for the latter reason, the lease may again be cancelled and the lessee is entitled to compensation.

Once again, the applicability of CZMA to this fourth stage of OCS planning is not in doubt. CZMA § 307(c)(3)(B) applies by its own terms, and is also expressly invoked by OCSLA.

Congress has thus taken pains to separate the various federal decisions involved in formulating a leasing program, conducting lease sales, authorizing exploration, and allowing development and production. Since 1978, the purchase of an OCS lease, standing alone, entails no right to explore, develop, or produce oil and gas resources on the OCS. The first two stages are not subject to consistency review; instead, input from State governors and local governments is solicited by the Secretary of Interior. The last two stages invite further input for governors or local governments, but also require formal consistency review. States with approved CZMA plans retain considerable authority to veto inconsistent exploration or development and production plans put forward in those latter stages. The stated reason for this four-part division was to forestall premature litigation regarding adverse environmental effects that all agree will flow, if at all, only from the latter stages of OCS exploration and production.

As we have noted, the logical paragraph to examine in connection with a lease sale is not 307(c)(1), but 307(c)(3). Nevertheless, even if OCS lease sales are viewed as involving an OCS activity "conduct[ed]" or "support[ed]" by a federal agency, lease sales can no longer aptly be characterized as "directly affecting" the coastal zone. Since 1978 the sale of a lease grants the lessee the right to conduct only very limited, "preliminary activities" on the OCS. It does not authorize full scale exploration, development, or production. Those activities may not begin until separate federal approval has been obtained, and approval may be denied on several grounds. If approval is denied, the lease may then be cancelled, with or without the payment of compensation to the lessee. In these circumstances, the possible effects on the coastal zone that may eventually result from the sale of a lease cannot be termed "direct."

It is argued, nonetheless, that a lease sale is a crucial step. Large sums of money change hands, and the sale may therefore generate momentum that makes eventual exploration, development, and production inevitable. On the other side, it is argued that consistency review at the lease sale stage is at best inefficient, and at worst impossible: Leases are sold before it is certain if, where, or how exploration will actually occur.

The choice between these two policy arguments is not ours to make; it has already been made by Congress. In the 1978 OCSLA amendments Congress decided that the better course is to postpone consistency review until the two later stages of OCS planning, and to rely on less formal input from State governors and local governments in the two earlier ones. . . .

points for discussion

1. *Congress overrules the Court.* Congress amended the CZMA to overturn this case. Justice O'Connor's argument had two parts: (i) an OCSLA lease sale was not a federal agency activity that "directly affected" the coastal zone; and (ii) the CZMA by its terms explicitly required CZMA consistency review for the last two stages, exploration and production, and did not do so for the first two stages. Given that nothing physical actually happens until the exploration stage, there was some intuitive appeal to this interpretation, though not shared by the four dissenting justices.

   In response, Congress made several changes, to not only change the process, but broaden the reach of the CZMA. First, the words "directly affected" were removed from § 307(c)(1). Second, "federal agency activities" that require CZMA consistency determinations may take place "within or outside the coastal zone," making it clear that review is required for a broader range of activities. It now provides:

   > **(c) Consistency of Federal activities with State management programs; Presidential exemption; certification**
   >
   > > **(1) (A)** Each Federal agency activity within or outside the coastal zone that affects any land or water use or natural resource of the coastal zone shall be carried out in a manner which is consistent to the maximum extent practicable with the enforceable policies of approved State management programs. A Federal agency activity shall be subject to this paragraph unless it is subject to paragraph (2) or (3).

   16 U.S.C. § 1456(c).

   "Federal agency activity" is not defined in the statute, but by regulation, "[l]ease sales conducted by a Federal agency are Federal agency activities. . . ." C.F.R. § 930.51.

   CZMA § 307(c)(3)(B), which Justice O'Connor cites in concluding that CZMA consistency determinations apply at the latter two stages, provides:

   > **(B)** After the management program of any coastal state has been approved by the Secretary under section 1455 of this title, any person who submits to the Secretary of the Interior any plan for the exploration or development of, or production from, any area which has been leased under the Outer Continental Shelf Lands Act (43 U.S.C. 1331 et seq.) and regulations under such Act shall, with respect to any exploration, development, or production described in such plan and affecting any land or water use or natural resource of the coastal zone of such state, attach to such plan a certification that each activity which is described in detail in such plan complies with the enforceable policies of such state's approved management program and will be carried out in a manner consistent with such program. No Federal official or agency shall grant such person any license or permit for any activity described in detail in such plan until such state or its designated agency receives a copy of such certification and plan, together with any other necessary data and information. . . .

2. *The net result.* In amending the CZMA in response to this case, Congress explicitly provided that any "federal agency activity" shall be subject to a CZMA consistency determination. Does this go beyond ensuring that lease sales require CZMA consistency review? What other activities might now be covered because they "affect[] any land or water use or natural resource of the coastal zone"?

3. *Sunk costs.* Justice O'Connor acknowledges the argument that the "lease sale is a crucial step. Large sums of money changes hands. . . ." Too much? Does a lease sale represent a point of no return?

The following case also takes place at the lease sale stage but occurs in the wake of the 2010 Deepwater Horizon tragedy. The tensions created by the tragedy are evident: On the one hand, the impulse to halt all drilling was tempting; the possibility of a second spill was unthinkable. On the other hand, the legal significance of the tragedy on future leases was unclear. This case illustrates some of the legal struggles with this tension.

Oceana v. Bureau of Ocean Energy Management

37 F. Supp. 3d 147 (D.D.C. 2014)

Judge CONTRERAS delivered the opinion of the United States District Court, District of Columbia.

On April 20, 2010, the *Deepwater Horizon*, a deep-water exploratory oil rig, exploded, caught fire, and sank in the Gulf of Mexico, resulting in the largest oil spill in the United States in modern history. Less than two years later, the Bureau of Ocean Energy Management ("BOEM"), approved two lease sales in the area where the *Deepwater Horizon* spill occurred. The plaintiffs bring this action challenging BOEM's approval of those lease sales under the National Environmental Policy Act, the Administrative Procedure Act, and the Endangered Species Act. The plaintiffs also bring suit against the National Marine Fisheries Service ("NMFS") for failing to issue a Biological Opinion in the wake of the oil spill in violation of the Administrative Procedure Act. All parties moved for summary judgment. For the reasons that follow, the Court will grant all the defendants' motions for summary judgment, and deny the plaintiffs' motion for summary judgment.

***

Lease Sales in the Gulf of Mexico

The Gulf of Mexico ("GOM") is a unique and important part of the American landscape and economy. It "includes one of the most extensive estuary systems in the world," "produces more than one-third of the nation's domestic seafood supply," and is home to many endangered species, such as the sperm whale, the West Indian manatee, several species of sea turtles, beach mice, the whooping crane, and the gulf sturgeon. At the same time, the OCS of the Gulf of Mexico is responsible for 20% of total U.S. crude oil production.

***

As of the *Deepwater Horizon* oil spill in 2010, there were two lease sales remaining in the Gulf under the 2007 Multisale [Environmental Impact Statement]: Lease Sale 218 and Lease Sale 222 (which was combined with Lease Sale 216 in 2012). In light of the spill, on November 10, 2010, BOEM issued a notice of intent to prepare a Supplemental [Environmental Impact Statement] ("SEIS") for Lease Sale 216/222 and Lease Sale 218. The purpose of undertaking the SEIS was "to consider new circumstances and information arising, among other things, from the Deepwater Horizon blowout and spill." BOEM explained that the focus of the SEIS would be "on updating the baseline conditions and potential environmental effects of oil and natural gas leasing, exploration, development, and production in the WPA and CPA."

On July 1, 2011, BOEM issued a Draft SEIS for Lease Sale 216/222. Meanwhile, on December 14, 2011, BOEM held the first lease sale since the *Deepwater Horizon* explosion in the Gulf of Mexico — for Lease Sale 218. On January 20, 2012, BOEM issued the final SEIS for Lease Sale 216/222 ("2012 SEIS"). This 2012 SEIS concluded that "[n]o substantial new information, with the exception of archeological resources, was found that would alter the impact conclusions as presented in the Multisale EIS and the 2009-2012 Supplemental EIS for a CPA lease sale." BOEM also explained that "[i]t is important to note that, barring another catastrophic oil spill, which is a low probability accidental event, the adverse impacts associated with the proposed CPA lease sale are small, even in light of the DWH event."

Lease Sale 216 had been scheduled to take place in 2011 and Lease Sale 222 had been scheduled for 2012. Following the *Deepwater Horizon* incident, BOEM decided to postpone proposed Lease Sale 216 and combine it with proposed Lease Sale 222. After the 2012 SEIS was published, BOEM held Lease Sale 216/222 in June 2012.

Endangered Species Act Consultation

In 2007, the NMFS completed a Biological Opinion ("BO") for five Gulf of Mexico lease sales, including Lease Sale 218 and Lease Sale 216/222. In response to the *Deepwater Horizon* spill, on July 30, 2010, the BOEM reinitiated consultation with the FWS and the NMFS because BOEM explained that "the spill volumes and scenarios used in the analysis for the existing NMFS BO need to be readdressed given the 'rare event' of a spill exceeding 420,000 gallons as referenced in the current NMFS BO. . . ." BOEM noted that as a result, the "affects to and the status of some listed species or designated critical habitats may have been altered as a result of the DWH incident and therefore require further consideration."

To date, the consultation has not yet been completed. However, BOEM and NMFS have developed an interim consultation process until the new Biological

Opinion is issued. "That process gives NMFS the opportunity to review and comment on certain-post lease activities (such as exploration plans)."

***

B. NEPA Claims

The plaintiffs [] argue that BOEM failed to adequately consider new information about the risks of future oil spills. Specifically, the plaintiffs argue that BOEM (1) failed to incorporate critical information from its new spill risk analysis prior to the completion of the SEIS, (2) significantly downplayed the Gulf spill in the analysis it did perform, and (3) failed to conduct new modeling in light of the spill and its new analysis.

***

The plaintiffs first argue that BOEM completed an updated risk analysis in light of the *Deepwater Horizon* spill — the Draft Report — and yet did not provide data from that new analysis in the 2012 SEIS. . . . The plaintiffs take issue with Table 3-5's exclusion of the ≥ 10,000 bbl category from the table's body itself. . . . In these prior iterations, the tables provided a category for oil spills ≥ 10,000 bbl. In addition, the SEIS for Lease Sale 218 as well as the Draft SEIS for Lease Sale 216/222 include a table that includes a ≥ 10,000 bbl category. Essentially, of all the EISs or SEISs performed in the Gulf of Mexico CPA and WPA for the 2007-2012 leasing period, the 2012 SEIS is the only one that excludes a ≥ 10,000 bbl category in the table *body* estimating mean number and sizes of oil spills. Instead, in the notes section directly under the table, BOEM states "[a] spill size group for ≥ 10,000 bbl was not included in the table, because the catastrophic Deepwater Horizon oil spill (4.9 million bbl) was the only spill this size range during 1996-2010, and thus meaningful statistics (such as median spill size) could not be calculated." In the Draft Report, BOEM gave the following explanation for its treatment of the ≥ 10,000 bbl category:

> In the case of OCS Platform spills, spill size averages and medians were calculated *through to 2009 rather than 2010.* [sic] because the Macondo spill size overwhelms the rest of the record in any calculation using spill volume. The Macondo well spilled an estimated 4.9 million barrels in the Gulf of Mexico — about 8.5 times the roughly 750,000 bbl of petroleum previously spilled (spills ≥ 1 bbl) between 1964 and 2009 from OCS oil and gas activities. Unfortunately, the Macondo spill was a "worst case" spill — a complete loss of well control due to multiple failures on a well with a very large reservoir under very high pressures that released uncontrolled for months. Few wells would be capable of this size release even under the worst of circumstances. *It is appropriate to count the Macondo spill in the spill rates for spills of 1,000 and 10,000 bbl or greater.* Means (averages) and medians are statistical measures that are frequently used to characterize a "typical" event. *In the interest of characterizing the size of a "typical" or "representative" OCS spill it would be best to exclude the Macondo spill volume in the calculation of mean (average) or median spill size.*

***

The plaintiffs' concern with this category's exclusion from the body of the table is understandable. Given that every prior version of the table includes the ≥ 10,000 bbl category, the Court is puzzled as to why BOEM decided in the 2012 SEIS — which was only undertaken to account for changes in light of the *Deepwater Horizon* spill (a spill ≥ 10,000 bbl) — to exclude that figure from the table body itself. While the Court likely would not have relegated that category to the "Notes" section of the table, and, for the sake of consistency, have kept the category in the table as it appeared in the Draft SEIS, the Court cannot say that BOEM excluded the category from consideration in the 2012 SEIS altogether, as the plaintiffs would have the Court find. Even if the body of Table 3-5 itself does not provide statistics for a ≥ 10,000 bbl category spill occurring, *the 2012 SEIS still does.*

Though BOEM did not necessarily create a table and conduct its analysis the way the Court might have, it still took a "hard look" at the ≥ 10,000 bbl category, and in turn the *Deepwater Horizon* spill in the 2012 SEIS generally. As such, BOEM was not arbitrary and capricious in excluding the ≥ 10,000 bbl category from the body of the table itself — a single table within an SEIS of over 1,100 pages in length.

***

In sum, BOEM did not violate NEPA. It complied with 40 C.F.R. § 1502.22, incorporated all the new data it had into the 2012 SEIS, considered the effects of deepwater drilling, ran a special OSRA model run to account for impacts of an assumed catastrophic oil spill, and considered a true no action alterative. Though the Court may have done things a little differently with respect to Table 3-5, BOEM still considered the ≥ 10,000 bbl category in its analysis, and therefore took a "hard look" at the effects of the *Deepwater Horizon* spill in the 2012 SEIS.

C. ESA Claims

The plaintiffs also bring claims under the ESA. They argue that BOEM did not comply with the ESA's requirement to insure against the jeopardy of endangered species by approving the lease sales without the benefit of a Biological Opinion assessing important new information. Plaintiffs argue (1) that BOEM had to complete consultation with NMFS, not just re-initiate it. . . . The defendants counter that BOEM did not need to complete consultation because of section 7(d) of the ESA, which allows agencies to proceed with agency action so long as it does not constitute an irreversible or irretrievable commitment of resources. . . .

The first ESA issue is whether BOEM violated the ESA by failing to *complete* consultation with the NMFS before proceeding with Lease Sales 216/222 and 218. Section 7(a) of the ESA requires that "[e]ach federal agency shall, *in consultation* with and with the assistance of the Secretary, *insure* that any action authorized, funded, or carried out by such *agency is not likely to jeopardize the continued existence of any endangered species* or threatened species or result in the destruction or adverse modification of habitat of such species . . . ." Section 7(a)(2) "imposes two obligations upon federal agencies. The first is procedural and requires that agencies consult with the FWS [or NMFS] to determine the effects of their actions on endangered or threatened species and their critical habitat. The second is substantive and requires that agencies insure that their actions not jeopardize endangered or threatened species or their critical habitat." With respect to the procedural requirement, 50 C.F.R. § 402.14(a) provides that "[e]ach Federal agency shall review its actions at the earliest possible time to determine whether any action may affect listed species or critical habitat. If such a determination is made, formal consultation is required."

In this case, BOEM and the NMFS engaged in a formal consultation during the 2007 Multisale EIS phase that resulted in the 2007 Biological Opinion issued by the NMFS. That BO concluded that the proposed action in the 2007 Multisale "will not appreciably reduce the likelihood of survival and recovery of the listed species considered in this biological opinion." On July 30, 2010, in the wake of the *Deepwater Horizon* event, BOEM contacted the NMFS to reinitiate consultation. Since then, the agencies have been working closely to issue a new BO. Thus, the procedural aspect of section 7(a)(2) has been met. The BO, however, has not yet been issued, and NMFS anticipates a March 2015 date of completion.

While the plaintiffs argue that under the ESA, BOEM had to *complete* its consultation with the NMFS before it issued its Record of Decision for Lease Sales 216/222 and 218, neither the ESA nor the case law interpreting the ESA require completion of a BO before action in all instances. Section 7(d) of the ESA allows agencies to take action during the reinitiated consultation, so long as that action does not constitute an "irreversible or irretrievable commitment of resources." Section 7(d) provides that "*after initiation of consultation* required under subsection (a)(2) of this section, the Federal agency and the permit or license applicant shall not make any irreversible or irretrievable commitment of resources with respect to the agency action which has the effect of foreclosing the formulation or implementation of any reasonable and prudent alternative measures. . . ." As one court has helpfully explained, "under § 7(d), an agency is not forbidden from taking *all* action while consultation is underway, but is simply barred from irreversibly or irretrievably committing resources during that interval. The purpose of § 7(d) is to ensure that the status quo is maintained during consultation, so as to avoid a circumstance in which a large-scale commitment of resources is made during the consultation process, which resources cannot be diverted or redirected to other productive uses if the outcome of consultation is that the project would violate the 'no jeopardy' requirement of § 7(a)."

All courts considering lease sales under the OCSLA have concluded that "lease sales do not constitute an 'irreversible or irretrievable commitment of resources' within the meaning of section 7(d)." . . . This conclusion is due primarily to the structure of the OCSLA, which provides for ESA review at each stage of the process. *See Village of False Pass*, 733 F.2d at 609 ("it is clear that OCSLA prescribes three distinct stages for offshore oil and gas activities: leasing, exploration, and development and production. ESA appears to apply equally to each stage of its own force and effect."). And, as BOEM notes in its brief, the Department of Interior retains "strict control" over all operations conducted under leases, and the OCSLA expressly authorizes the Department to suspend any operation or activity conducted under the lease sales if there is a threat to any marine life or the surrounding environment. . . .

***

The Court notes, however, that by the time NMFS produces its Biological Opinion in 2015, the *Deepwater Horizon* oil spill will be five years behind it. The Court, though, does not question the holistic approach the agencies are taking in ambitiously assessing the environmental impact of oil and gas exploration and production on endangered and threatened species and their designated critical habitats throughout the Gulf of Mexico, rather than assessing each lease sale separately. This approach seems sensible, even preferable. But, of course, such an ambitious endeavor takes time. And the time expended to date seems to have been reasonably spent. The APA requires no more.

For the foregoing reasons, the federal-defendants' and intervenor-defendants' motions for summary judgment are GRANTED, and the plaintiffs' motion for summary judgment is DENIED. An order consistent with this Memorandum Opinion is separately and contemporaneously issued.

points for discussion

1. *Oil spill realism.* The court was concerned that BOEM had previously treated a spill of greater than 10,000 barrels as one of the scenarios to be analyzed as a matter of course but then, for the 2012 Supplemental EIS, suddenly relegated that scenario to a footnote. BOEM's explanation was that Deepwater Horizon was so large that it would have skewed the spill *rate* calculation. After expressing some skepticism, the court ultimately held that BOEM had taken the requisite "hard look" under NEPA. Do you agree? How would you have drafted a Supplemental EIS after the Deepwater Horizon tragedy? What new relevant information does the tragedy provide?

2. *Seriously skewed.* Analysis of "worst case" scenarios are not required under NEPA. *Robertson v. Methow Valley Citizens Council*, 490 U.S. 332, 355-56 (1989). BOEM asserted in its SEIS that "another catastrophic oil spill, which is a low probability accidental event, the adverse impacts associated with the proposed CPA lease sale are small, even in light of the DWH event." What are the difficulties with considering the Deepwater Horizon tragedy with current and future lease sales? For an argument in favor of reinstituting some worst-case analysis, see Oliver A. Houck, *There Ought to Be a Law*, 24 TUL. ENVTL. L.J. 1 (2010).

3. *Assessing the consultation.* If, as the court says, Section 7 of the ESA has a procedural part and a substantive part, do you agree that the substantive obligation has been fulfilled? Was the 2007 Biological Opinion sufficient?

4. *Prudent alternative?* The "Framework" Biological Opinion triggered by the Deepwater Horizon spill was published in February 2016. Memorandum from Dr. Roy E. Crabtree, Nat'l Marine Fisheries Serv., to Christopher D. Doley, Framework Biological Opinion, On *Deepwater Horizon* Oil Spill

Final Programmatic Damage Assessment and Restoration Plan and Final Programmatic Environmental Impact Statement (SER-2015-17459), http://sero.nmfs.noaa.gov/protected_resources/section_7/freq_biop/documents/DWH_bo/dwh_biop_2016.pdf. It is 414 pages long, not including the Appendix.

Do you agree that the lease sale does not constitute "an irretrievable commitment of resources," such that consultation is not required? If so, why bother with the re-initiation? What exactly does Deepwater Horizon change? Does the structure of the OCSLA offer some assurance that ultimately, species listed under the ESA can be protected administratively with subsequent regulation?

4. Exploration Plans

The third stage is when the first drilling activity actually takes place. An approved exploration plan is required of all lessees, and must contain, at least, a schedule of exploration activities, a description of equipment, the general location of each drilled well, and other information set forth by regulation. 43 U.S.C. § 1340(c)(3). Exploration plans will be approved if the Secretary determines that: (i) the applicant is qualified; (ii) the exploration will not interfere or endanger other leasing activity; and (iii) the exploration "will not be unduly harmful to aquatic life in the area, result in pollution, create hazardous or unsafe conditions, unreasonably interfere with other uses of the area, or disturb any site, structure, or object of historical or archeological significance." 43 U.S.C. § 1340(g)(3). OCSLA provides that the Secretary *may* require by regulation a drilling permit before drilling, 43 U.S.C. § 1340(d), which BOEM currently does, 30 C.F.R. § 251.7, known as an Application for Permit to Drill.

This stage requires information even more specific than at the lease sale stage, as specific times and more exact locations are required, and most importantly, the type of rig and drilling equipment to be used, along with an environmental report that includes details about the exploratory drilling and site-specific information about the geology, oceanography, flora and fauna, environmental monitoring systems, and other unusual or unique characteristics that may be affected by the drilling activity, and "any unavoidable or irreversible adverse effects on the environment that could occur." 30 C.F.R. § 251.7(b).

At this stage at least some NEPA analysis has been done, and ESA consultations begun. The question is whether earlier work can be applied to requirements at this stage. The following case illustrates some of the issues raised in this context.

Defenders of Wildlife v. Bureau of Ocean Energy Management

684 F.3d 1242 (11th Cir. 2012)

Judge DUBINA delivered the opinion of the Eleventh Circuit Court of Appeals.

This case concerns a challenge to an exploratory drilling plan under the Outer Continental Shelf Lands Act ("OCSLA"). The Bureau of Ocean Energy Management

("BOEM") approved the Shell Exploration Plan S-7444 ("Shell EP") to conduct drilling in the Gulf of Mexico. The Shell EP covers ten exploratory wells on off-shore Alabama leases in the Central Gulf of Mexico between 7,100 and 7,300 feet deep. This case is a consolidated appeal in which Petitioners, Defenders of Wildlife, *et al.* and Gulf Restoration Network, *et al.* ("Petitioners"), filed comments on the Shell EP, participated in the administrative proceeding below, and filed this petition for review. The only issues on petition for review are whether the Shell EP violates the National Environmental Policy Act ("NEPA"), and the Endangered Species Act ("ESA"). After reviewing the record, reading the parties' briefs, and having the benefit of oral argument, we deny the petition for review.

A leaseholder must submit an exploration plan for approval by BOEM. BOEM is required to approve, approve with modifications, or deny a plan within 30 days of submission. BOEM may allow exploration to proceed and issue a permit for drilling if the lessee's plan "will not be unduly harmful to aquatic life in the area, result in pollution, create hazardous or unsafe conditions, unreasonably interfere with other uses of the area, or disturb any site, structure, or object of historical or archeological significance." 43 U.S.C. § 1340(g)(3). The exploration plan must also comply with all other applicable laws, including NEPA and ESA.

(1) Compliance with NEPA

NEPA requires all federal agencies to prepare an environmental assessment ("EA") and [Environmental Impact Statement] on the environmental effects of proposed federal agency actions. All major Federal actions [that] significantly affect [] the quality of the human environment" require an EIS. A less exhaustive EA can be used to determine whether the proposed action may significantly affect the environment and whether an EIS is required. An EIS is not required if the agency makes a finding of no significant impact ("FONSI") that identifies reasons why the proposed action will not have a significant impact on the environment.

BOEM applies NEPA procedures using a tiered process encouraged by the Council on Environmental Quality's ("CEQ") regulations implementing NEPA. The CEQ regulations seek to avoid repetitive discussions and urge that:

> Whenever a broad environmental impact statement has been prepared (such as a program or policy statement) and a subsequent statement or environmental assessment is then prepared on an action included within the entire program or policy (such as a site specific action) the subsequent statement or environmental assessment need only summarize the issues discussed in the broader statement and incorporate discussions from the broader statement by reference and shall concentrate on the issues specific to the subsequent action.

40 C.F.R. § 1502.20. The Shell EA "tiers" from two prior EIS's: the 2007 Multisale EIS covering eleven Gulf lease sales in the 2007-2012 Multisale and the 2009 supplemental EIS for seven remaining lease sales in the 2007-2012 Multisale. In 2007, MMS, BOEM's predecessor, finalized an EIS covering the Western and Central Gulf areas. The 2007 EIS analyzed expected impacts of oil and gas exploration, including possible oil spills. It found large oil spills to be low-probability events and determined that environmental impacts would not be catastrophic to the region,

animal populations, and ecosystems. The 2009 supplemental EIS found that relevant new information did not change the conclusions from the 2007 multisale EIS.

In response to the April 2010 *Deepwater Horizon* disaster, BOEM commenced the process to prepare a supplemental EIS for the remaining lease sales in the Gulf under the 2007-2012 Multisale. The final supplemental EIS was issued on January 20, 2012. BOEM concluded that "[n]o substantial new information, with the exception of archaeological resources [related to historic shipwrecks], was found that would alter the impact conclusions as presented in the Multisale EIS and the 2009-2012 Supplemental EIS. . . ."

Prior to the *Deepwater Horizon* disaster, BOEM generally did not prepare EA's when approving exploration plans in the Western and Central Gulf of Mexico under leases studied in previous EIS's. After the spill, the Director of BOEM instructed the agency to restrict its use of categorical exclusions for exploration plans that proposed activity that would require approval of an application for a permit to drill and involve the use of a subsea Blow Out Preventer ("BOP") or surface BOP. Categorical exclusions are "a category of actions which do not individually or cumulatively have a significant effect on the human environment . . . and for which, therefore, neither an environmental assessment nor an environmental impact statement is required." 40 C.F.R. § 1508.4. Accordingly, BOEM prepared a site-specific EA for the Shell EP.

(2) Compliance with ESA

BOEM consulted with NMFS and FWS in 2007 regarding Gulf of Mexico lease sales under the 2007-2012 Multisale program. NMFS issued an opinion concluding that exploration, development, and production was not likely to jeopardize threatened or endangered species. FWS issued a similar memorandum. In September 2010, BOEM requested to reinitiate consultation with NMFS and FWS to consider new information as a result of the *Deepwater Horizon* disaster, and that consultation is ongoing.

On March 31, 2011, BOEM deemed the Shell EP submitted. BOEM conducted a review of whether the Shell EP significantly affected the quality of the environment, considering impacts of Shell's proposed effect on the environment from routine operations and unexpected accidents. Appendix A of the EA analyzes risks, characteristics, and impacts of possible major spills in light of information from the *Deepwater Horizon* disaster. Appendix B presents a detailed "Catastrophic Spill Event Analysis" on all relevant resources in the Gulf of Mexico, based on the 2010 *Deepwater Horizon* spill and 1979 Ixtoc spill. Based on this analysis and information in the record, BOEM found no indication that the proposed action would significantly affect the quality of the human environment within the meaning of NEPA. The plan was approved by BOEM and the United States Department of the Interior on May 10, 2011, after a FONSI. Thus, BOEM determined an EIS was unnecessary. Petition for review of the Shell EP was filed on June 9, 2011. Petitioners Gulf Restoration Network, *et al.* seek remand for further agency consideration and Petitioners Defenders of Wildlife, *et al.* seek both vacatur and remand.

NEPA Claim

BOEM conducted an EA for the Shell EP to determine whether the proposed activity would significantly affect the environment and found that an EIS was unnecessary. Petitioners argue that the EA is only a general summary of the environmental impact of the Shell EP and fails to include site-specific information. Thus, Petitioners insist, BOEM's decision not to prepare an EIS and its subsequent FONSI is a violation of NEPA. Yet, Petitioners simply cannot overcome our extremely deferential "arbitrary or capricious" standard of review.

(1) Site-Specific Analysis

Before concluding that an EIS is unnecessary, the agency must "accurately identif[y] the relevant environmental concern" and take a "hard look" at the problem. If a FONSI is made, the agency "must be able to make a convincing case for its finding." Contrary to Petitioners' claims, the EA contains a plethora of site-specific information on the potential impacts from Shell's proposed exploratory drilling. For example, the EA describes site-specific atmospheric conditions, water quality characteristics, likely impact on water quality, possible impact on deepwater coral and marine mammals including specific species of sea turtles, and effects of accidental events. Petitioners complain that the Shell EA is too similar to Shell EP S-7445, an EA prepared for a separate but similar exploration plan in a different area in the Gulf of Mexico. Shell EP S-7445 is 130 miles from shore with proposed drilling at 2,721 feet. The difference in location and water depth between the two EAs does not necessarily mean that there are significant differences in resources present and environmental impact because both wells are far from shore and in deep water. BOEM's reliance on and comparison to Shell EP S-7445 is consistent with its requirements under NEPA that it take a hard look at the environmental impacts of the proposed exploration. NEPA does not prohibit an agency from creating an EA that resembles another EA in a similar environment.

Next, Petitioners argue that BOEM failed to include a site-specific analysis of potential catastrophic spills and underestimated the likelihood of a spill. To the contrary, the EA extensively analyzes the risks and consequences of such an event. Appendix B of the EA, "Catastrophic Spill Event Analysis," evaluates the impact of a low-probability catastrophic spill. After taking into account regulations put into effect after the *Deepwater Horizon* disaster, BOEM determined that the risk of another spill was low. While this analysis is derived from a generalized scenario, it is based on the only two large spill disasters in the Gulf of Mexico—the 1979 Ixtoc blowout in the Bay of Campeche Mexico and the 2010 *Deepwater Horizon* disaster. An oil spill is an unexpected event, and its parameters cannot be precisely known in advance. Thus, it is appropriate for BOEM to summarize potential impacts resulting from a hypothetical oil spill.

***

(4) BOEM's Reliance on Prior EISs

Petitioners argue that BOEM cannot rely on tiering from the 2007 Multisale EIS and 2009 Supplemental EIS because those studies are outdated after the *Deepwater Horizon* disaster. Petitioners contend that because BOEM issued a notice of intent to prepare a supplemental EIS for the 2007-2012 Multisale, which covers the areas where the *Deepwater Horizon* disaster occurred and Shell proposes to drill, BOEM cannot rely on the prior EIS's in the current Shell EP. BOEM recognizes that this supplemental EIS is needed "to consider new circumstances and information arising from the *Deepwater Horizon* blowout and spill." The purpose of the supplemental EIS is to update baseline conditions and environmental impacts in the Gulf.

The purpose of OCSLA is the "expedited exploration and development of the Outer Continental Shelf in order to achieve national economic and energy policy goals, assure national security, reduce dependence on foreign sources, and maintain a favorable balance of payments in world trade." BOEM has a responsibility to balance the needs under OCSLA with the requirements of NEPA. Absent unique site-specific characteristics, BOEM is entitled to rely on broader prior analyses and tiering is specifically encouraged by NEPA regulations. Tiering allows BOEM to rely on prior work to inform a decision on a current lease. BOEM validly relied on the prior EIS's, but also evaluated mitigation measures adopted after the *Deepwater Horizon* disaster as factors to consider in determining the current risk of an oil spill. The agency's reliance on previous studies was not arbitrary or capricious because (1) BOEM included all known information about the spill in the Shell EP and (2) on January 20, 2012, BOEM reported that the conclusions from the most recent supplemental EIS would not alter any conclusions presented in the 2007 and 2009 EIS's. We conclude that BOEM's reliance on the 2007 Multisale EIS and 2009 Supplemental EIS was not arbitrary or capricious.

(B) ESA Claim

We next turn to Petitioners' claim that BOEM's request to reinitiate consultation conceded the inadequacy of prior consultations and effectively barred BOEM from approving the Shell EP until consultation was complete. If a federal agency determines that a proposed action will likely affect a species protected under the ESA, it must consult with either NMFS or FWS. Following the *Deepwater Horizon* disaster, BOEM reinitiated consultation with both NMFS and FWS, and those consultations are still ongoing.

Section 7(a)(2) of the ESA requires BOEM to insure that its action "is not likely to jeopardize" any endangered or threatened species or destroy or adversely modify such species' habitat. NMFS and FWS regulations define "jeopardize the continued existence of" as "to engage in an action that reasonably would be expected, directly or indirectly, to reduce appreciably the likelihood of both the survival and recovery of a listed species in the wild by reducing the reproduction, numbers, or distribution of that species." Because BOEM acknowledged that the environmental effects from the *Deepwater Horizon* disaster may have altered some species or habitats, it reinitiated consultation with NMFS and FWS. However, BOEM's reliance on conclusions by NMFS and FWS from 2007 does not necessarily jeopardize the continued existence of any species or adversely modify a critical habitat under the Shell EP. Petitioners have no proof that endangered species are in jeopardy, but instead argue that the prior consultations are inadequate because BOEM reinitiated consultation.

There is no precedent in our circuit to support Petitioners' argument that BOEM's choice to reinitiate consultation with NMFS and FWS automatically renders the former biological opinions invalid. The biological opinions of NMFS and FWS were reconfirmed in 2008 and 2009, and have not been withdrawn despite reinitiation of consultations. . . . [U]nder the facts of this case that decision is not arbitrary and capricious. . . .

For the reasons stated above, we conclude that BOEM's decision to approve the Shell EP was not arbitrary or capricious and instead reflects the agency's balance of environmental concerns with the expeditious and orderly exploration of resources in the Gulf of Mexico.

points for discussion

1. *Iterations.* This case, like the previous case, addressed the ESA claim that re-initiation of the Section 7 consultation, in light of the Deepwater Horizon spill, casts into doubt the validity of the 2007 Biological Opinion on endan-gered and threatened species in the Gulf. The notes to the previous case posed the question of whether the Deepwater Horizon spill, and the re-initiation of consultation, should have changed the status of that Biological Opinion. This case, although two years earlier than *Oceana v. BOEM*, addresses decision-making at a later stage — exploration. Does that make ESA consultation more necessary? Was there some reliance in *Oceana v. BOEM* on prospective regulation at later stages to protect listed species?

2. *Categorical exclusions.* This opinion mentioned in passing that "[p]rior to the *Deepwater Horizon* disaster, BOEM generally did not prepare EA's when approving exploration plans in the Western and Central Gulf of Mexico under leases studied in previous EIS's." Indeed, exploration plans for the Gulf of Mexico were generally covered by categorical exclusions, "which do not individually or cumulatively have a significant effect on the human environment and which have been found to have no such effect in pro-cedures adopted by a Federal agency in implementation of these regula-tions . . . and for which, therefore, neither an environmental assessment nor an environmental impact statement is required." Note that not only does the agency have to be able to argue that the action does not "individually or cumulatively have a significant effect," but it must have been found, in pre-vious actions, to have no significant impact. For example, personnel actions and investigations, internal organizational changes, and routine financial transactions are major federal agency actions that nevertheless have no sig-nificant environmental impact. The Deepwater Horizon exploration plan

was thought to be covered by a categorical exclusion. In fact, consistent with OCSLA, lease sales, exploration or development and production plans in the western Gulf of Mexico generally did not trigger the need for any environmental analysis under NEPA, unless certain circumstances were present. The existence of those circumstances has driven litigation over NEPA requirements in the Gulf of Mexico.

A federal agency that retains the authority to conduct an EA or EIS even if its action is covered by a categorical exclusion may also have "extraordinary circumstances" associated with categorical exclusions, which throw the action back into the realm in which an EA or EIS is required after all. Extraordinary circumstances essentially override the categorical exclusion. Extraordinary circumstances are actions that, despite being covered by a categorical exclusion, may:

> (a) Have significant impacts on public health or safety.
> (b) Have significant impacts on such natural resources and unique geographic characteristics as historic or cultural resources; park, recreation or refuge lands; wilderness areas; wild or scenic rivers; national natural landmarks; sole or principal drinking water aquifers; prime farmlands; wetlands; floodplains; national monuments; migratory birds; and other ecologically significant or critical areas.
> (c) Have highly controversial environmental effects or involve unresolved conflicts concerning alternative uses of available resources [NEPA § 102(2)(E)].
> (d) Have highly uncertain and potentially significant environmental effects or involve unique or unknown environmental risks.

> * * *

> (h) Have significant impacts on species listed, or proposed to be listed, on the List of Endangered or Threatened Species or have significant impacts on designated Critical Habitat for these species.

43 C.F.R. § 46.215. The MMS, the pre-Deepwater Horizon offshore leasing agency, set forth a categorical exclusion for lease sales, exploration plans, and development and production plans, but also *de facto* extraordinary circumstances that would necessitate an EA or EIS after all:

> (1) In areas of high seismic risk or seismicity, relatively untested deep water or remote areas, or
> (2) within the boundary of a proposed or established marine sanctuary, and/or within or near the boundary of a proposed or established wildlife refuge or areas of high biological sensitivity; or
> (3) on areas of hazardous natural bottom conditions; or
> (4) utilizing new or unusual technology.

Of these, several arguably applied to Deepwater Horizon. Environmental organizations took the position that the deepwater drilling was "relatively untested," and represented "new or unusual technology." *The Minerals Management Service: Bad Science in the Name of Private Interests*, UNION

OF CONCERNED SCIENTISTS (2010), https://www.ucsusa.org/center-for-science-and-democracy/scientific_integrity/abuses_of_science/a-to-z/mms-badscience.html#.Wx_s-EgvyM8. The MMS had concluded as early as 2000 that "most deepwater operations and activities are substantially the same as those associated with conventional operations and activities on the continental shelf." U.S. DEPARTMENT OF THE INTERIOR, MINERALS MANAGEMENT SERVICE, GULF OF MEXICO DEEPWATER OPERATIONS AND ACTIVITIES, ENVIRONMENTAL ASSESSMENT iv (2000), https://www.boem.gov/BOEM-Newsroom/Library/Publications/2000/2000-001.aspx. Is this an example of how, if hindsight were foresight, we'd all be billionaires? Or was MMS too complacent with a technology that it did not fully understand? The EA runs 248 pages.

3. *Action within an action.* The multiple stages of leasing, and the multiple scales of environmental review, are made more manageable by the practice of "tiering," which was a central point of contention in this case. Council on Environmental Quality (CEQ) regulations provide that "[a]gencies are encouraged to tier their environmental impact statements to eliminate repetitive discussions of the same issues and to focus on the actual issues ripe for decision at each level of environmental review." 40 C.F.R. § 1502.20. After a programmatic EIS at the five-year planning stage, subsequent NEPA analysis is only required to summarize the issues from the earlier EIS and incorporate it by reference. In theory, this means that subsequent NEPA analysis can just focus on the environmental impacts of the distinct actions at each stage. *Id.* The CEQ, however, recommended to the BOEM that for the Gulf of Mexico leasing it nevertheless "perform careful and comprehensive NEPA review of individual deepwater exploration, operation, development, production, and decommissioning activities, including site-specific information where appropriate." COUNCIL ON ENVIRONMENTAL QUALITY, REPORT REGARDING THE MINERALS MANAGEMENT SERVICE'S NATIONAL ENVIRONMENTAL POLICY ACT POLICIES, PRACTICES, AND PROCEDURES AS THEY RELATE TO OUTER CONTINENTAL SHELF OIL AND GAS EXPLORATION AND DEVELOPMENT (Aug. 16, 2010), https://obamawhitehouse.archives.gov/sites/default/files/microsites/ceq/20100816-ceq-mms-ocs-nepa.pdf. With tiering, is the categorical exclusion necessary?

5. Development and Production Stage

Finally, after exploration is complete, the lessee can begin full-scale production. A development and production plan must be submitted and approved, which must set forth: (i) the specific work to be performed; (ii) a description of all facilities and operations, location and size of facilities and operations, and the land, labor, material, and energy requirements associated with such facilities and operations; (iii) environmental safeguards to be implemented; (iv) how all safety standards are to be met; (v) the expected rate of production; and (vi) such other relevant information as the Secretary may require. 43 U.S.C. § 1351(c). If the Secretary determines that: (i) the plan "would probably cause serious harm or damage . . . to the marine, coastal or human environments," (ii) the threat of harm will not decrease over time, and (iii) "the advantages of disapproving the plan outweigh the advantages of development and production," he or she shall disapprove the plan. 43 U.S.C. § 1351(h)(1)(D)(i).

Any reversals at this late stage are rare, however, as the lessee would have expended a fair amount of effort already. The following case shows how sensitive some companies can be with respect to their development and production plans.

Mobil Oil Exploration & Producing Southeast, Inc. v. United States

530 U.S. 604 (2000)

Justice BREYER delivered the opinion of the Court.

Two oil companies, petitioners here, seek restitution of $156 million they paid the Government in return for lease contracts giving them rights to explore for and develop oil off the North Carolina coast. The rights were not absolute, but were conditioned on the companies' obtaining a set of further governmental permissions. The companies claim that the Government repudiated the contracts when it denied them certain elements of the permission-seeking opportunities that the contracts had promised. We agree that the Government broke its promise; it repudiated the contracts; and it must give the companies their money back.

I

A

A description at the outset of the few basic contract law principles applicable to this action will help the reader understand the significance of the complex factual circumstances that follow. "When the United States enters into contract relations, its rights and duties therein are governed generally by the law applicable to contracts between private individuals." *United States v. Winstar Corp.,* 518 U.S. 839, 895. The Restatement of Contracts reflects many of the principles of contract law that are applicable to this action. As set forth in the Restatement of Contracts, the relevant principles specify that, when one party to a contract repudiates that contract, the other party "is entitled to restitution for any benefit that he has conferred on" the repudiating party "by way of part performance or reliance." Restatement (Second) of Contracts § 373 (1979) (hereinafter Restatement). The Restatement explains that "repudiation" is a "statement by the obligor to the obligee indicating that the obligor will commit a breach that would of itself give the obligee a claim for damages for total breach." And "total breach" is a breach that "so substantially impairs the value of the contract to the injured party at the time of the breach that it is just in the circumstances to allow him to recover damages based on all his remaining rights to performance."

As applied to this action, these principles amount to the following: If the Government said it would break, or did break, an important contractual promise, thereby "substantially impair[ing] the value of the contract[s]" to the companies, ibid., then (unless the companies waived their rights to restitution) the Government must give the companies their money back. And it must do so whether the contracts would, or would not, ultimately have proved financially beneficial to the companies. The Restatement illustrates this point as follows:

> "A contracts to sell a tract of land to B for $100,000. After B has made a part payment of $20,000, A wrongfully refuses to transfer title. B can recover the $20,000 in restitution. The result is the same even if the market price of the land is only $70,000, so that performance would have been disadvantageous to B." Id., § 373, Comment a, Illustration 1.

B

In 1981, in return for up-front "bonus" payments to the United States of about $156 million (plus annual rental payments), the companies received 10-year renewable lease contracts with the United States. In these contracts, the United States promised the companies, among other things, that they could explore for oil off the North Carolina coast and develop any oil that they found (subject to further royalty payments) provided that the companies received exploration and development permissions in accordance with various statutes and regulations to which the lease contracts were made "subject."

The statutes and regulations, the terms of which in effect were incorporated into the contracts, made clear that obtaining the necessary permissions might not be an easy matter. In particular, the Outer Continental Shelf Lands Act (OCSLA), as amended, and the Coastal Zone Management Act of 1972 (CZMA), specify that leaseholding companies wishing to explore and drill must successfully complete the following four procedures.

First, a company must prepare and obtain Department of the Interior approval for a Plan of Exploration (Exploration Plan or Plan). Interior must approve a submitted Exploration Plan unless it finds, after "consider[ing] available relevant environmental information," § 1346(d), that the proposed exploration

> "would probably cause serious harm or damage to life (including fish and other aquatic life), to property, to any mineral . . . , to the national security or defense, or to the marine, coastal, or human environment." § 1334(a)(2)(A)(i).

Where approval is warranted, Interior must act quickly — within "thirty days" of the company's submission of a proposed Plan. § 1340(c)(1).

Second, the company must obtain an exploratory well drilling permit. To do so, it must certify (under CZMA) that its Exploration Plan is consistent with the coastal zone management program of each affected State. If a State objects, the certification fails, unless the Secretary of Commerce overrides the State's objection. If Commerce rules against the State, then Interior may grant the permit.

Third, where waste discharge into ocean waters is at issue, the company must obtain a National Pollutant Discharge Elimination System permit from the Environmental Protection Agency. 33 U.S.C. § 1311(a), 1342(a). It can obtain this permit only if affected States agree that its Exploration Plan is consistent with the state coastal zone management programs or (as just explained) the Secretary of Commerce overrides the state objections. 16 U.S.C. § 1456.

Fourth, if exploration is successful, the company must prepare, and obtain Interior approval for, a Development and Production Plan — a Plan that describes the proposed drilling and related environmental safeguards. Again, Interior's approval is conditioned upon certification that the Plan is consistent with state coastal zone management plans — a certification to which States can object, subject to Commerce Department override. § 1351(a)(3).

C

The events at issue here concern the first two steps of the process just described — Interior's consideration of a submitted Exploration Plan and the companies' submission of the CZMA "consistency certification" necessary to obtain an exploratory well drilling permit. The relevant circumstances are the following:

1. In 1981, the companies and the Government entered into the lease contracts. The companies paid the Government $156 million in up-front cash "bonus" payments.
2. In 1989, the companies, Interior, and North Carolina entered into a memorandum of understanding. In that memorandum, the companies promised that they would submit an initial draft Exploration Plan to North Carolina before they submitted their final Exploration Plan to Interior. Interior promised that it would prepare an environmental report on the initial draft. It also agreed to suspend the companies' annual lease payments (about $250,000 per year) while the companies prepared the initial draft and while any state objections to the companies' CZMA consistency certifications were being worked out, with the life of each lease being extended accordingly.
3. In September 1989, the companies submitted their initial draft Exploration Plan to North Carolina. Ten months later, Interior issued the promised ("informal" pre-submission) environmental report, after a review which all parties concede was "extensive and intensive." Interior concluded that the proposed exploration would not "significantly affec[t]" the marine environment or "the quality of the human environment."
4. On August 20, 1990, the companies submitted both their final Exploration Plan and their CZMA "consistency certification" to Interior.
5. Just two days earlier, on August 18, 1990, a new law, the Outer Banks Protection Act (OBPA), § 6003, 104 Stat. 555, had come into effect. That law prohibited the Secretary of the Interior from approving any Exploration Plan or Development and Production Plan or to award any

drilling permit until (a) a new OBPA-created Environmental Sciences Review Panel had reported to the Secretary, (b) the Secretary had certified to Congress that he had sufficient information to make these OCSLA-required approval decisions, and (c) Congress had been in session an additional 45 days, but (d) in no event could he issue an approval or permit for the next 13 months (until October 1991). § 6003(c)(3). OBPA also required the Secretary, in his certification, to explain and justify in detail any differences between his own certified conclusions and the new Panel's recommendations. § 6003(c)(3)(A)(ii)(II).

6. About five weeks later, and in light of the new statute, Interior wrote a letter to the Governor of North Carolina with a copy to petitioner Mobil. It said that the final submitted Exploration Plan "is deemed to be approvable in all respects." It added:

> "[W]e are required to approve an Exploration Plan unless it is inconsistent with applicable law or because it would result in serious harm to the environment. Because we have found that Mobil's Plan fully complies with the law and will have only negligible effect on the environment, we are not authorized to disapprove the Plan or require its modification."

But, it noted, the new law, the "Outer Banks Protection Act (OBPA) of 1990 . . . prohibits the approval of any Exploration Plan at this time." It concluded, "because we are currently prohibited from approving it, the Plan will remain on file until the requirements of the OBPA are met." In the meantime a "suspension has been granted to all leases offshore the State of North Carolina."

About 18 months later, the Secretary of the Interior, after receiving the new Panel's report, certified to Congress that he had enough information to consider the companies' Exploration Plan. He added, however, that he would not consider the Plan until he received certain further studies that the new Panel had recommended.

7. In November 1990, North Carolina objected to the companies' CZMA consistency certification on the ground that Mobil had not provided sufficient information about possible environmental impact. A month later, the companies asked the Secretary of Commerce to override North Carolina's objection.

8. In 1994, the Secretary of Commerce rejected the companies' override request, relying in large part on the fact that the new Panel had found a lack of adequate information in respect to certain environmental issues.

9. In 1996, Congress repealed OBPA. § 109, 110 Stat. 1321-177.

D

In October 1992, after all but the two last-mentioned events had taken place, petitioners joined a breach-of-contract lawsuit brought in the Court of Federal Claims. On motions for summary judgment, the court found that the United States had broken its contractual promise to follow OCSLA's provisions, in particular the provision requiring Interior to approve an Exploration Plan that satisfied OCSLA's requirements within 30 days of its submission to Interior. The United States thereby repudiated the contracts. And that repudiation entitled the companies to restitution of the up-front cash "bonus" payments they had made.

A panel of the Court of Appeals for the Federal Circuit reversed, one judge dissenting. The panel held that the Government's refusal to consider the companies' final Exploration Plan was not the "operative cause" of any failure to carry out the contracts' terms because the State's objection to the companies' CZMA "consistency statement" would have prevented the companies from exploring regardless.

We granted certiorari to review the Federal Circuit's decision.

II

The record makes clear (1) that OCSLA required Interior to approve "within thirty days" a submitted Exploration Plan that satisfies OCSLA's requirements, (2) that Interior told Mobil the companies' submitted Plan met those requirements, (3) that Interior told Mobil it would not approve the companies' submitted Plan for at least 13 months, and likely longer, and (4) that Interior did not approve (or disapprove) the Plan, ever. The Government does not deny that the contracts, made "pursuant to" and "subject to" OCSLA, incorporated OCSLA provisions as promises. The Government further concedes, as it must, that relevant contract law entitles a contracting party to restitution if the other party "substantially" breached a contract or communicated its intent to do so. Yet the Government denies that it must refund the companies' money.

This is because, in the Government's view, it did not breach the contracts or communicate its intent to do so; any breach was not "substantial"; and the companies waived their rights to restitution regardless. We shall consider each of these arguments in turn.

A

The Government's "no breach" arguments depend upon the contract provisions that "subject" the contracts to various statutes and regulations. Those provisions state that the contracts are "subject to" (1) OCSLA, (2) "Sections 302 and 303 of the Department of Energy Organization Act," (3) "all regulations issued pursuant to such statutes and in existence upon the effective date of" the contracts, (4) "all regulations issued pursuant to such statutes in the future which provide for the prevention of waste and the conservation" of Outer Continental Shelf resources, and (5) "all other applicable statutes and regulations." The Government says that these provisions incorporate into the contracts, not only the OCSLA provisions we have mentioned, but also certain other statutory provisions and regulations that, in the Government's view, granted Interior the legal authority to refuse to approve the submitted Exploration Plan, while suspending the leases instead.

First, the Government refers to 43 U.S.C. § 1334(a)(1)(A), an OCSLA provision that authorizes the Secretary to promulgate regulations providing for "the suspension . . . of any operation or activity . . . at the request of a lessee, in the national interest, to facilitate proper development of a lease." This provision, as the emphasized terms show, requires "the request of a lessee," i.e., the companies. The Government does not explain how this requirement was satisfied here. Hence, the Government cannot rely upon the provision.

Second, the Government refers to 30 CFR § 250.110(b)(4) (1999), formerly codified at 30 CFR § 250.10(b)(4) (1997), a regulation stating that "[t]he Regional Supervisor may . . . direct . . . a suspension of any operation or activity . . . [when the] suspension is necessary for the implementation of the requirements of the National Environmental Policy Act or to conduct an environmental analysis." The Government says that this regulation permitted the Secretary of the Interior to suspend the companies' leases because that suspension was "necessary . . . to conduct an environmental analysis," namely, the analysis demanded by the new statute, OBPA.

The "environmental analysis" referred to, however, is an analysis the need for which was created by OBPA, a later enacted statute. The lease contracts say that they are subject to then-existing regulations and to certain future regulations, those issued pursuant to OCSLA and § 302 and 303 of the Department of Energy Organization Act. This explicit reference to future regulations makes it clear that the catchall provision that references "all other applicable . . . regulations," supra this page, must include only statutes and regulations already existing at the time of the contract, a conclusion not questioned here by the Government. Hence, these provisions mean that the contracts are not subject to future regulations promulgated under other statutes, such as new statutes like OBPA. Without some such contractual provision limiting the Government's power to impose new and different requirements, the companies would have spent $156 million to buy next to nothing. In any event, the Court of Claims so interpreted the lease; the Federal Circuit did not disagree with that interpretation; nor does the Government here dispute it.

Instead, the Government points out that the regulation in question—the regulation authorizing a governmental suspension in order to conduct "an environmental analysis"—was not itself a future regulation. Rather, a similar regulation existed at the time the parties signed the contracts, 30 CFR § 250.12(a)(iv) (1981), and, in any event, it was promulgated under OCSLA, a statute exempted from the contracts' temporal restriction. But that fact, while true, is not sufficient to produce the incorporation of future statutory requirements, which is what the Government needs to prevail. If the pre-existing regulation's words, "an environmental analysis," were to apply to analyses mandated by future statutes, then they would make the companies subject to the same unknown future requirements that the contracts' specific temporal restrictions were intended to avoid. Consequently, whatever the regulation's words might mean in other contexts, we believe the contracts before us must be interpreted as excluding the words "environmental analysis" insofar as those words would incorporate the requirements of future statutes and future regulations excluded by the contracts' provisions. Hence, they would not incorporate into the contracts requirements imposed by a new statute such as OBPA.

Third, the Government refers to OCSLA, 43 U.S.C. § 1334(a)(1), which, after granting Interior rulemaking authority, says that Interior's

> "regulations . . . shall include . . . provisions . . . for the suspension . . . of any operation . . . pursuant to any lease . . . if there is a threat of serious, irreparable, or immediate harm or damage to life . . . , to property, to any mineral deposits . . . , or to the marine, coastal, or human environment." (Emphasis added.)

The Government points to the OBPA Conference Report, which says that any OBPA-caused delay is "related to . . . environmental protection" and to the need "for the collection and analysis of crucial oceanographic, ecological, and socioeconomic data," to "prevent a public harm." H.R. Conf. Rep. No. 101-653, p. 163 (1990). . . . At oral argument, the Government noted that the OBPA mentions "tourism" in North Carolina as a "major industry . . . which is subject to potentially significant disruption by offshore oil or gas development." § 6003(b)(3). From this, the Government infers that the pre-existing OCSLA provision authorized the suspension in light of a "threat of . . . serious harm" to a "human environment."

The fatal flaw in this argument, however, arises out of the Interior Department's own statement—a statement made when citing OBPA to explain its approval delay. Interior then said that the Exploration Plan "fully complies" with current legal requirements. And the OCSLA statutory provision quoted above was the most pertinent of those current requirements. The Government did not deny the accuracy of Interior's statement, either in its brief filed here or its brief filed in the Court of Appeals. Insofar as the Government means to suggest that the new statute, OBPA, changed the relevant OCSLA standard (or that OBPA language and history somehow constitute findings Interior must incorporate by reference), it must mean that OBPA in effect created a new requirement. For the reasons set out supra, . . . , however, any such new requirement would not be incorporated into the contracts.

Finally, we note that Interior itself, when imposing the lengthy approval delay, did not rely upon any of the regulations to which the Government now refers. Rather, it relied upon, and cited, a different regulation, 30 CFR § 250.110(b)(7) (1999), which gives Interior the power to suspend leases when "necessary to comply with judicial decrees prohibiting production or any other operation or activity." The Government concedes that no judicial decree was involved in this action and does not rely upon this regulation here.

We conclude, for these reasons, that the Government violated the contracts. Indeed, as Interior pointed out in its letter to North Carolina, the new statute, OBPA, required Interior to impose the contract-violating delay. It therefore made clear to Interior and to the companies that the United States had to violate the contracts' terms and would continue to do so.

Moreover, OBPA changed pre-existing contract-incorporated requirements in several ways. It delayed approval, not only of an Exploration Plan but also of Development and Production Plans; and it delayed the issuance of drilling permits as well. It created a new type of Interior Department environmental review that had not previously existed, conducted by the newly created Environmental Sciences

Review Panel; and, by insisting that the Secretary explain in detail any differences between the Secretary's findings and those of the Panel, it created a kind of presumption in favor of the new Panel's findings.

* * *

We do not say that the changes made by the statute were unjustified. We say only that they were changes of a kind that the contracts did not foresee. They were changes in those approval procedures and standards that the contracts had incorporated through cross-reference. The Government has not convinced us that Interior's actions were authorized by any other contractually cross-referenced provision. Hence, in communicating to the companies its intent to follow OBPA, the United States was communicating its intent to violate the contracts.

B

The Government next argues that any violation of the contracts' terms was not significant; hence there was no "substantial" or "material" breach that could have amounted to a "repudiation." In particular, it says that OCSLA's 30-day approval period "does not function as the 'essence' of these agreements." Brief for United States 37. The Court of Claims concluded, however, that timely and fair consideration of a submitted Exploration Plan was a "necessary reciprocal obligation," indeed, that any "contrary interpretation would render the bargain illusory." We agree.

We recognize that the lease contracts gave the companies more than rights to obtain approvals. They also gave the companies rights to explore for, and to develop, oil. But the need to obtain Government approvals so qualified the likely future enjoyment of the exploration and development rights that the contract, in practice, amounted primarily to an opportunity to try to obtain exploration and development rights in accordance with the procedures and under the standards specified in the cross-referenced statutes and regulations. Under these circumstances, if the companies did not at least buy a promise that the Government would not deviate significantly from those procedures and standards, then what did they buy?

The Government's modification of the contract-incorporated processes was not technical or insubstantial. It did not announce an (OBPA-required) approval delay of a few days or weeks, but of 13 months minimum, and likely much longer. The delay turned out to be at least four years. And lengthy delays matter, particularly where several successive agency approvals are at stake. Whether an applicant approaches Commerce with an Interior Department approval already in hand can make a difference (as can failure to have obtained that earlier approval). Moreover, as we have pointed out, OBPA changed the contract-referenced procedures in several other ways as well. Supra, at 2435.

The upshot is that, under the contracts, the incorporated procedures and standards amounted to a gateway to the companies' enjoyment of all other rights. To significantly narrow that gateway violated material conditions in the contracts. The breach was "substantia[l]," depriving the companies of the benefit of their bargain. And the Government's communication of its intent to commit that breach amounted to a repudiation of the contracts.

***

III

Contract law expresses no view about the wisdom of OBPA. We have examined only that statute's consistency with the promises that the earlier contracts contained. We find that the oil companies gave the United States $156 million in return for a contractual promise to follow the terms of pre-existing statutes and regulations. The new statute prevented the Government from keeping that promise. The breach "substantially impair[ed] the value of the contract[s]." Id., § 243. And therefore the Government must give the companies their money back.

For these reasons, the judgment of the Federal Circuit is reversed. We remand the cases for further proceedings consistent with this opinion.

It is so ordered.

points for discussion

1. *Special rules for the Gulf of Mexico: DOCDs and APDs.* 43 U.S.C. § 1351(a)(1) provides:

   > Prior to development and production pursuant to an oil and gas lease issued after September 18, 1978, in any area of the outer Continental Shelf, other than the Gulf of Mexico, or issued or maintained prior to September 18, 1978, in any area of the outer Continental Shelf, other than the Gulf of Mexico, with respect to which no oil or gas has been discovered in paying quantities prior to September 18, 1978, the lessee shall submit a development and production plan (hereinafter in this section referred to as a "plan") to the Secretary, for approval pursuant to this section.

   As the Court notes, the Secretary is still authorized to promulgate such "necessary and proper" regulations as to carry out the purposes of the OCSLA, among them regulations requiring Development Operations Coordination Documents (DOCDs), and applications for permits to drill (APDs). Does the DOCD indeed seem like an end-around on Congress's explicit exclusion?

2. *Revamping regulation.* Following the Deepwater Horizon tragedy (discussed in detail later in this chapter), the Department of the Interior not only broke up Minerals Management Service into the Bureau of Ocean Energy Management and the Bureau of Safety and Environmental Enforcement but promulgated new safety rules for offshore rigs. The new regulations established new installation precautions for the well casing — the pipe from which oil is extracted — and an important component that failed on the Deepwater Horizon, the blowout preventer, a complicated mechanism to prevent high pressure "blowouts," in which oil or gas rushes up the casing uncontrolled and ultimately causes an explosion. Third-party testing and

verification was required for casing, blowout preventers, and other critical components. Oil and Gas Sulphur Operations in the Outer Continental Shelf — Increased Safety Measures for Energy Development on the Outer Continental Shelf, 75 Fed. Reg. 63,346 (2010).

C. RENEWABLE ENERGY DEVELOPMENT

Development of the outer continental shelf for energy resources has clearly centered upon oil and gas resources. As you saw from the foregoing materials, disputes over ownership of the seabed were animated by the oil and gas resources that lay within. Climate change, however, has re-oriented some (not nearly all) of the energy industry, as some energy companies have sought to develop renewable energy sources. Offshore energy development has become a forum for that transition. Repurposing the outer continental shelf for siting renewable energy sources is a trend that is growing in importance, if haltingly. Renewable energy sources often raise land use concerns, which are generally less pronounced if developed out in the ocean, the Cape Wind project being a prominent exception.

Different types of renewable energy technology have either been deployed or are under consideration for deployment on a large scale on the continental shelf.

Offshore Wind Energy.   Wind turbines are now familiar sites throughout the United States, the most electricity generating capacity being installed in Texas, Iowa, and Oklahoma. Wind energy, though becoming more practical and economical, suffers from three important drawbacks. First, the strongest winds blow in sparsely populated areas, making transmission a major cost and logistical challenge. Second, placing wind turbines closer to population centers raises land use

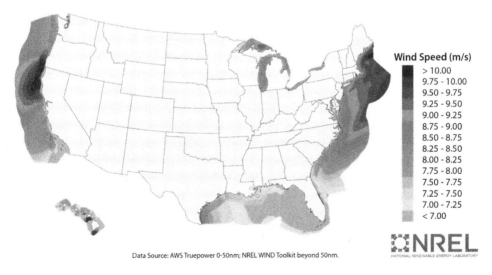

Data Source: AWS Truepower 0-50nm; NREL WIND Toolkit beyond 50nm.

Figure 4-5. **Wind Potential in Offshore Areas**

concerns, as people often object to being close to wind turbines. Third, winds are sporadic, making them less reliable for purposes of generating electricity. All three of these concerns are potentially alleviated by siting wind turbines offshore, on the continental shelf. As Figure 4-5 shows, some of the strongest winds are near population centers in the Northeast, West Coast, and coastal Texas. Second, siting turbines offshore avoids some of the aesthetic concerns that people raise (Cape Wind again, being a notorious exception). For that reason, offshore turbines can be taller than they are on land. Finally, winds over ocean waters blow more regularly and strongly, unimpeded by mountains and buildings, creating potentially stronger wind resources. Offshore winds provide the potential to satisfy double the current U.S. electricity demand.

The most familiar offshore wind turbines are installed much like they would be on land: fixing a turbine on a platform that is embedded in the seabed, with the turbine extending out well over the surface of the water. Countries such as Denmark, an offshore wind leader, already derive more than a third of their electricity from wind turbines, and about a third of that offshore.

The electricity generated by offshore wind turbines is transmitted to the mainland via cables that are embedded in the seabed. Since that cable must necessarily pass through the submerged lands belonging to a state, state permitting is required even if the turbines themselves are located in federal waters. As Cape Wind withdrew its permit application, another project nearby off the shores of Rhode Island, Deepwater Wind, was nearing completion as the first U.S. commercial offshore wind installation and is now generating up to 30 megawatts of power. More projects are planned off the coasts of New Jersey and Virginia.

Marine Hydrokinetic Energy.   Rather than harnessing winds, marine hydrokinetic seeks to harness the energy of ocean tides and currents, a more regular source of energy. Marine hydrokinetic turbines are submerged underwater, spun by movement of ocean currents and tides. Alternatively, floating buoys can bounce up and down with ocean currents, their vertical movement captured as energy. Several marine hydrokinetic techniques seek to translate the movement of water into energy. Like offshore wind, the resulting electricity must be transmitted to mainland electricity consumers via underwater cables buried in the seabed.

Offshore Solar.   Like offshore wind, offshore solar addresses some of the problems of solar power on land: intermittency, a large footprint, and land use objections. Many photovoltaic solar cells are arranged in a large array, like they are on land, and made to float on the ocean surface. Large offshore solar has not been deployed commercially in the United States, but countries such as China have begun to experiment, assembling much larger arrays of solar cells than would be practical on land.

Transmission Capacity.   In addition to these three technologies for generating electricity, the seabed is also a potential place to site transmission lines, to carry electricity from one place to another. To sound a familiar theme, siting transmission lines on land is notoriously difficult. Transmission lines are unsightly and carry a stigma that galvanizes local opposition. This land use intractability is exactly what motivated the development of the Atlantic Wind Connection, an undersea transmission line that will ultimately run from northern New Jersey to southern Virginia, a corridor that is chronically and severely lacking in electricity grid connectivity. And, as long as an undersea transmission line is being built, the Atlantic Wind Connection project will also site offshore wind turbines that will offload electricity onto the transmission line. The plan calls for a total of 6 gigawatts of capacity, enough to power 2 million homes.

1. Jurisdiction

Remember that the seabed out to three nautical miles from the coastline generally belongs to the states,[1] so primary permitting authority in that band generally lies with the coastal state. However, permitting an offshore wind turbine or marine hydrokinetic device in state waters also requires a Section 404 permit from the U.S. Army Corps of Engineers for any dredging and filling, which must inevitably occur when installing a structure on the seabed. In addition, the Rivers and Harbors Act of 1899 requires a permit for any structure that may interfere with navigation, such as offshore wind turbines.

In addition, remember this provision from the 1953 Submerged Lands Act:

(e) The term "natural resources" includes, without limiting the generality thereof, oil, gas, and all other minerals, and fish, shrimp, oysters, clams, crabs, lobsters, sponges, kelp, and other marine animal and plant life but does not include water power, or the use of water for the production of power.

43 U.S.C. § 1301.

Under that provision, states own the listed "natural resources," with the exception of water power. Marine hydrokinetic clearly falls within that exception, so electricity generated by undersea turbines belongs to the federal government. The 1920 Federal Power Act confers upon the Federal Energy Regulatory Commission authority to license hydropower projects, including marine hydrokinetic projects.

The interesting question comes up in federal waters. The Federal Energy Regulatory Commission still has jurisdiction to license hydropower projects. But thanks to the 2005 Energy Policy Act, the Bureau of Ocean Energy Management has jurisdiction over renewable energy development on the outer continental shelf! The two agencies resolved it with a Memorandum of Understanding in 2012 that divided up permitting duties, and ultimately produced a joint guidance document. Marine hydrokinetic developers still, however, have two permitting agencies.

But even with a relatively clear and stable statement of the law, and a clear delineation — state jurisdiction and ownership up to three nautical miles from the coast, federal beyond that — questions of jurisdiction and conflicts of laws persist. The Submerged Lands Act did not dispense with litigation over the seabed or state territorial waters, as the following case demonstrates. Perhaps even more than

---

1. Florida and Texas have a nine-nautical-mile boundary for their respective Gulf Coasts.

Figure 4-6. An Offshore Wind Turbine

raising jurisdictional questions, the following case is a showcase for local opposition to large projects, even otherwise desirable renewable energy projects.

Ten Taxpayer Citizens Group v. Cape Wind Associates

373 F.3d 183 (1st Cir. 2004)

Judge LYNCH delivered the opinion of the First Circuit Court of Appeals.

Cape Wind is a limited liability corporation based in South Yarmouth, Massachusetts. Its goal is to construct a commercial windmill farm on Horseshoe Shoals, a shallow area of Nantucket Sound more than three miles offshore. The proposed windmill farm includes at least 130 industrial wind turbines, each 470 feet tall. If it is completed as presently envisioned, the facility will spread across 28 square miles of Nantucket Sound and will be visible from shore. The project is the first of its kind in North America.

To construct the wind farm, Cape Wind needs extensive meteorological and oceanographic data concerning conditions on Horseshoe Shoals. For that purpose, Cape Wind in late 2001 announced plans to build a "scientific measurement device station" (SMDS) on Horseshoe Shoals. Intended as a temporary facility, the SMDS was designed to collect data for five years. It would consist of a data tower rising approximately 200 feet in the air, supported by three steel pilings driven 100 feet into the seabed. Together with its tripodal support structure, the tower would occupy about 900 square feet of ocean surface.

On August 19, 2002, the United States Army Corps of Engineers issued a permit to Cape Wind under § 10 of the Rivers and Harbors Act of 1899, for construction of the SMDS. Cape Wind neither sought nor obtained permits for the SMDS project under Massachusetts law. . . .

Ten Taxpayer filed this action . . . shortly before construction of the data tower began. In its complaint, Ten Taxpayer acknowledged that the SMDS site is more than three miles from the nearest Massachusetts shoreline and that, accordingly, the location falls under the jurisdiction of the federal government. Nevertheless, Ten Taxpayer contended, Cape Wind could not build the SMDS without regulatory approval from Massachusetts because Congress has ceded to Massachusetts the power to regulate any activity affecting fishing in Nantucket Sound. Under the Massachusetts laws regulating fisheries and fish habitats, administrative approval is required for structures erected on the seabed. Because Cape Wind did not obtain such approval, Ten Taxpayer alleged, the SMDS project was in violation of Massachusetts law. Ten Taxpayer sought an injunction blocking construction of the SMDS or, if the court would not enjoin construction, a $25,000 fine for every day that the SMDS remained on Horseshoe Shoals.

***

. . . Cape Wind filed a motion in federal court to dismiss Ten Taxpayer's complaint. Cape Wind attached to its motion two letters from the Massachusetts Department of Environmental Management indicating that, at least under Mass. Gen. Laws ch. 132A, Massachusetts does *not* claim regulatory authority over activities on Horseshoe Shoals. Cape Wind also argued that Ten Taxpayer lacks standing to assert the Commonwealth's regulatory interest in offshore lands.

On August 19, 2003, the district court granted Cape Wind's motion to dismiss. The court concluded that although Congress did delegate to Massachusetts the power to regulate fishing in Nantucket Sound, that grant did not confer on the Commonwealth a general warrant to "polic[e] the entire Nantucket Sound for environmental disturbances that could impact fishing." Massachusetts had no authority over the construction of the SMDS, and thus no state permits were required.

Ten Taxpayer filed this timely appeal. . . .

A. Regulation of the Seabed and Attached Structures

As a general rule, "paramount rights to the offshore seabed inhere in the Federal Government as an incident of national sovereignty." In a series of cases beginning in 1947, the Supreme Court established that the United States enjoys exclusive title in the lands underlying the sea, regardless of a state's historical claims to the waters off its coast [citing *United States v. Texas, United States v. Louisiana,* and *United States v. California*]. Together, those cases established that the "control and disposition" of the seabed is "the business of the Federal Government rather than the States."

That background rule, however, has been modified by Congress in several significant respects. Most importantly, Congress in 1953 passed the Submerged Lands

Act (SLA), which grants to the states full title to the seabed within three geograph-ical miles of their shores. Moreover, Congress expressly recognized that three-mile line as the official seaward boundary of the coastal states. *Id.* § 1312.

Shortly thereafter, however, Congress enacted the Outer Continental Shelf Lands Act of 1953 (OCSLA), A major purpose of the OCSLA was to specify that federal law governs on the "outer Continental Shelf" — defined as all submerged lands under U.S. sovereign control lying seaward of the three-mile boundary — and on any fixed structures attached to the outer Continental Shelf. The OCSLA makes the Constitution, laws, and civil and political jurisdiction of the United States fully applicable to the outer Continental Shelf. It also establishes nationwide rules for the leasing and development of natural resources in the seabed outside of state territory. Further, the OCSLA provides a federal cause of action for any person aggrieved by a violation of those rules, and grants the federal district courts juris-diction to hear such cases. It is, in short, a sweeping assertion of federal supremacy over the submerged lands outside of the three-mile SLA boundary.

***

B. Regulation of Fishing and Marine Fisheries

With the framework for regulating the seabed thus settled, Congress in 1976 enacted the Magnuson (now Magnuson-Stevens) Fishery Conservation and Management Act.

Like the OCSLA, the Magnuson-Stevens Act asserts federal control over the waters outside of the three-mile limit of state jurisdiction. The Act creates a "national framework for conserving and managing marine fisheries." It claims for the federal government "exclusive fishery management authority" in outer Continental Shelf waters within and beyond the United States's "exclusive economic zone," which extends approximately 197 nautical miles seaward from the three-mile boundary of state jurisdiction. Within that exclusive economic zone, the Act further claims for the United States "sovereign rights . . . over all fish, and all Continental Shelf fishery resources."

At the same time, the Magnuson-Stevens Act establishes that the states enjoy the power to regulate fishing activities *within* their borders, including within the three-mile SLA boundary: "[N]othing in this chapter shall be construed as extend-ing or diminishing the jurisdiction or authority of any State within its boundar-ies." By so providing, Congress "confirmed state jurisdiction over fisheries within a State's internal waters and, for coastal states, out to the three-mile limit."

C. Federal v. State Jurisdiction in Nantucket Sound

Nantucket Sound, where the disputed tower has been built, presents special dif-ficulties in distinguishing the respective spheres of state and federal jurisdiction. Nantucket Sound is almost completely enclosed by Massachusetts's territorial sea; only at the extreme eastern end of the Sound does a channel of federal water approximately one mile wide connect it to the open ocean. But the Sound is a large body of water, and its center portion — including the site of Cape Wind's data tower on Horseshoe Shoals — is more than three miles from any coast.

Despite that fact, Massachusetts in the early 1970s took the position that *all* of Nantucket Sound, including Horseshoe Shoals, is within Massachusetts's territorial jurisdiction under the doctrine of "ancient title." The Supreme Court rejected that claim in *United States v. Maine* (*Maine II*), 475 U.S. 89, 106 S. Ct. 951, 89 L. Ed. 2d 68 (1986), holding that the Commonwealth did not inherit title to the Sound from the British Crown. After *Maine II*, it is incontrovertible that Cape Wind's data tower is located on the outer Continental Shelf, outside of Massachusetts's territorial jurisdiction.

But there is a complication. In 1984 — while the *Maine II* litigation was pending — Congress passed a bill defining all of Nantucket Sound to be within the "jurisdiction and authority" of Massachusetts "[f]or the purposes of" the Magnuson-Stevens Act. In *Davrod Corp. v. Coates, supra,* this court held that § 1856(a)(2)(B) "expressly confirms" Massachusetts's power to regulate the length of fishing vessels in Nantucket Sound. In this case, Ten Taxpayer contends that the same provision authorizes Massachusetts to regulate the construction of Cape Wind's data tower, which Ten Taxpayer claims has the potential to affect fishing and fish habitats.

∗∗∗

The district court dismissed the complaint on the ground that the Magnuson-Stevens Act did not grant to the Commonwealth sufficiently broad authority to regulate the construction of a tower in federal waters in Nantucket Sound. *See Ten Taxpayers,* 278 F. Supp. 2d at 100-01 ("Congress did not delegate its complete sovereign authority over the pocket of federal waters in Nantucket Sound to the Commonwealth, but only that part necessary to establish consistent fishing regulations throughout the Sound."). On appeal, the parties devote considerable attention to the same question. Ten Taxpayer says that by placing Nantucket Sound under the "jurisdiction and authority" of Massachusetts "for the purposes of" the Magnuson-Stevens Act, Congress must have intended to empower the Commonwealth to regulate activities on the seabed of Nantucket Sound that, like the SMDS, have the potential to affect fishing. Cape Wind responds, *inter alia,* that the "purposes" of the Magnuson-Stevens Act do not include regulation of structures attached to the seabed.

∗∗∗

[W]e are extremely doubtful that the Massachusetts statutes on which Ten Taxpayer relies apply to the SMDS site. Obviously, no permit was required for the SMDS if Massachusetts has not purported to regulate activities on that site. Ten Taxpayer asserts claims under three Massachusetts statutes: Mass. Gen. Laws chapters 91, 130, and 132A. On our reading of Massachusetts law, none of those statutes applies to the erection of a tower on Horseshoe Shoals.

∗∗∗

In our view, the OCSLA leaves no room for states to require licenses or permits for the erection of structures on the seabed on the outer Continental Shelf. Congress retained for the federal government the exclusive power to authorize or prohibit specific uses of the seabed beyond three miles from shore. *See* § 1333(a)(3) ("The provisions of this section for adoption of State law as the law of the United States shall never be interpreted as a basis for claiming any interest in or jurisdiction on behalf of any State for any purpose over the seabed and subsoil of the outer Continental Shelf. . . ."). If adopted and enforced on the outer Continental Shelf, statutes like Mass. Gen. Laws chs. 91 and 132A, which require the approval of state agencies prior to construction, would effectively grant state governments a veto power over the disposition of the national seabed. That result is fundamentally inconsistent with the OCSLA.

Ten Taxpayer contends that the Magnuson-Stevens Act, which was enacted after the OCSLA, changed this calculus by defining the "body of water commonly known as Nantucket Sound" to be within the "jurisdiction and authority" of Massachusetts. Yet nothing in the Magnuson-Stevens Act purports to repeal or amend the OCSLA. On the contrary, the two statutes can readily coexist: the Magnuson-Stevens Act authorizes Massachusetts to regulate fishing-related conduct throughout Nantucket Sound, but "the subsoil and seabed of the outer Continental Shelf, and artificial islands and fixed structures erected thereon," remain the exclusive province of the federal government. Congress was perfectly clear in the Magnuson-Stevens Act that it did not intend to alter the rights of the United States in the outer Continental Shelf.

We conclude that any Massachusetts permit requirement that might apply to the SMDS project is inconsistent with federal law and thus inapplicable on Horseshoe Shoals under the OCSLA. The district court did not err in dismissing Ten Taxpayer's complaint.

The judgment of the district court is ***affirmed.*** Costs are awarded to Cape Wind.

points for discussion

1. *Fisheries regulation authority.* The court commented that the parties on appeal devoted "considerable attention" to briefing the issue of whether Congress's delegation over fishing authority over Nantucket Sound extended to the construction of the tower. What would be the Massachusetts argument (if it wanted to make it) that construction of the tower somehow implicates its authority to manage fisheries? Are there any particular fisheries that might be affected?

2. *The "tidelands."* The court dismisses Ten Taxpayer's claim that construction of the data tower implicates Massachusetts "tidelands," which do not extend out to Horseshoe Shoals. But is that the end of the matter? The offshore wind turbines generate electricity, but how will that electricity get to market? The following case, also one involving Cape Wind, provides some answers. For facilities in federal waters it is also important to remember that

transmission lines, even if buried in the seabed, must necessarily cross over state submerged lands. As such, states exercise permitting authority for that stretch of transmission cable.

Alliance to Protect Nantucket Sound v. Energy Facilities Siting Board

932 N.E.2d 787 (Mass. 2010)

Justice BOTSFORD delivered the opinion of the Supreme Judicial Court of Massachusetts.

[The facts of this case are contained in the earlier excerpt of *Ten Taxpayer Citizens Group v. Cape Wind Associates*, presented above.]

The Alliance, joined by Barnstable, claims that § 69K does not authorize the siting board to include in a certificate granted under that section any type of license relating to the Commonwealth's tidelands. The argument is that these tidelands are both owned and held in trust by the Commonwealth to protect the public's rights in them, and that no one — including a State agency such as the siting board — may claim authority to act in connection with the tidelands unless granted express legislative authority to do so. The Alliance contends that § 69K contains no language of delegation or even mention of the tidelands or the public trust with which they are imbued, and therefore, the siting board cannot grant a certificate that incorporates, in effect, a c. 91 tidelands license.

The public trust doctrine expresses the government's long-standing and firmly established obligation to protect the public's interest in the tidelands and, in particular, to protect the public's right to use the tidelands "for, traditionally, fishing, fowling, and navigation." [citations omitted] There is no question that the Commonwealth tidelands through which Cape Wind's transmission lines will pass are held in the public trust to which the Alliance refers. We also agree with the Alliance that under the public trust doctrine, "only the Commonwealth, or an entity to which the Legislature properly has delegated authority, may administer public trust rights." [citations omitted] The question, then, is whether the Legislature in § 69K "properly has delegated authority" to the siting board to exercise public trust rights. The answer requires examination of c. 91, the waterways statute administered by DEP, § 69K, and the statutory scheme of which § 69K is a part.

The Legislature has delegated to [the Department of Environmental Protection] ("DEP") the authority to license "structures" in the Commonwealth's tidelands, provided that they "serve a proper public purpose and that said purpose shall provide a greater public benefit than public detriment to the rights of the public in said lands." In doing so, DEP is to "protect the interests of the Commonwealth" in the tidelands. Section 69K, in turn, grants authority to the siting board to issue a certificate in accordance with § 69K-69O, which

> "shall be in the form of a composite of *all* individual permits, approvals or authorizations which would otherwise be necessary for the construction and operation

of the facility and that portion of the certificate which relates to subject matters within the jurisdiction of a state or local agency shall be enforced by said agency under the applicable laws of the commonwealth as if it had been directly granted by the said agency" (emphasis added).

We read the quoted provision in § 69K as an express legislative directive to the siting board to stand in the shoes of any and all State and local agencies with permitting authority over a proposed "facility" — that is, a directive to assume all the powers and obligations of such an agency with respect to the decision whether to grant the authorization that is within the agency's jurisdiction, with regulatory enforcement thereafter returned to that agency. DEP, as a State agency, is by definition included within the broad coverage of § 69K. There is no mention of public trust rights or obligations in § 69K, but there does not need to be. The Legislature has designated DEP as the agency charged with responsibility for protecting public trust rights in tidelands through the c. 91 licensing program, and where a tidelands license is necessary for a proposed facility, the Legislature has, in § 69K, expressly vested authority in the siting board to act in DEP's stead with respect to the initial permitting decision. Accordingly, an evaluation of § 69K's relationship to the public trust doctrine must take into account the fact that in a case such as this, § 69K operates as an overlay of c. 91.

***

In sum, we find in § 69K a sufficiently articulated legislative delegation of authority to the siting board to act in the place of DEP, and to administer the public trust rights within DEP's jurisdiction in the limited context of deciding whether to approve the equivalent of a c. 91 tidelands license. . . .[29, 30] Accordingly, the siting board in this case did not exceed its authority by including the equivalent of a c. 91 tidelands license in the certificate it granted Cape Wind.

***

29. While not directly bearing on the delegation question discussed in the text, additional sections of the siting board statute reflect the Legislature's interest in having DEP, the agency to which the Legislature generally has granted authority to issue such licenses, play a role in the siting board's decision where a c. 91 tidelands license is in issue. Thus, G.L. c. 164, § 69L and 69N, read together, define the "parties in interest" in any certificate proceeding to include, among others, any person or entity that the siting board permits to intervene. In the present case, DEP was an intervener in the § 69K proceeding concerning Cape Wind, and fully participated in that proceeding. . . .

30. In *Moot I*, 448 Mass. at 347, 352-353, 861 N.E.2d 410, we held that DEP exceeded its authority under G.L. c. 91, § 18, by promulgating a regulation exempting filled landlocked tidelands from c. 91's licensing requirements. "By exempting filled 'landlocked' tidelands from the statute's licensing requirements, [DEP was] relinquishing all control over the use of the filled land . . . without legislative authorization, effectively relinquishing all public rights that the Legislature has mandated be preserved through the licensing requirements." . . . Here, there has been no relinquishment or extinguishment of the public's rights in the tidelands at issue.

We agree with the Chief Justice that an express statement from the Legislature is necessary both to relinquish public rights in tidelands and to delegate authority to administer public trust rights and duties. The decisions of this court, however, have recognized a difference between a legislative

We accord substantial discretion to an agency to interpret the statute it is charged with enforcing, especially where, as here, the Legislature has authorized the agency to promulgate regulations. The siting board's interpretation of the "except" clause treats it as limiting only the types of permit denials that can serve as a basis for a company to petition for a § 69K certificate, but not as a limitation on the siting board's authority to review and potentially override that permit denial, if the company has an independent basis on which to file a certificate petition. . . .

***

Conclusion. Case no. SJC-10596 is remanded to the county court. Judgment is to enter affirming the decision of the Energy Facilities Siting Board and declaring that 310 Code Mass. Regs. § 9.12(2)(b)(10) is a valid regulation. In case no. SJC-10578, the judgment of dismissal is affirmed.

So ordered.

MARSHALL, C.J. (concurring in part and dissenting in part, with whom SPINA, J., joins).

The development of clean energy resources is an important national and State policy. The offshore wind-powered energy generating facility (wind farm) that Cape Wind, LLC (Cape Wind), proposes to construct in Nantucket Sound may further that policy by providing clean energy for the Commonwealth. It is not our role, however, to evaluate whether as a matter of sound policy the project should be constructed. Rather, we must determine whether the approval process of the Cape Wind project comports with the laws of the Commonwealth. It does not. Today's decision that the "certificate of environmental impact and public interest" (certificate), G.L. c. 164, § 69K (§ 69K), issued by the Energy Facilities Siting Board (siting board) was proper is contrary to existing law and seriously undermines the public trust doctrine, which for centuries has protected the rights of the people of Massachusetts in Commonwealth tidelands.

The court concludes that the *Commonwealth* has fulfilled its fiduciary obligation to the people of Massachusetts because the *siting board* has issued a certificate to Cape Wind under § 69K authorizing transmission cables to traverse Commonwealth tidelands. The siting board, however, does not have, and was not

delegation of authority to administer public trust rights and duties through regulation or use of tidelands subject to conditions, and a permanent relinquishment of the public's rights in tidelands. The latter can only happen where the Legislature has undertaken specific steps and made explicit findings to signal its intent to relinquish. [citations omitted] While it is clear from our case law what steps the Legislature must take to relinquish the public's rights in tidelands, our cases addressing delegation of authority to regulate tidelands, and in doing so to administer public trust rights and duties, have said only that such delegation must be express. . . . As we have discussed, our view is that in § 69K, the Legislature has expressly delegated to the siting board the authority to grant a revocable c. 91 license to use the tidelands at issue, and encompassed in that delegation is the authority, and obligation, to administer public trust rights and duties.

intended by the Legislature to have, the right to act as fiduciary on behalf of the people with regard to Commonwealth tidelands or to approve energy projects up and down the coastline of Massachusetts in Commonwealth tidelands. It may be that the Legislature or the Legislature's expressly authorized designee, exercising its responsibility as fiduciary, would conclude that transmission cables stretching across Commonwealth tidelands from the shore to the Commonwealth's seaward boundary should be approved. But that authorization has not occurred. The court's ruling to the contrary establishes a dangerous and unwise precedent, which has far-reaching consequences. A wind farm today may be a drilling rig or nuclear power plant tomorrow.

The court also concludes that the siting board acted appropriately by granting the certificate without considering *any* of the in-State impacts of the wind farm. Centuries of legislation and jurisprudence concerning the paramount rights of the people of the Commonwealth to the use of the sea and shore lead me to disagree. The stakes are high. As we have recently seen in the Gulf of Mexico, the failure to take into account in-State consequences of federally authorized energy projects in Federal waters can have catastrophic effects on State tidelands and coastal areas, and on all who depend on them.

The public trust doctrine stands as a covenant between the people of the Commonwealth and their government, a covenant to safeguard our tidelands for all generations for the use of the people, traditionally for fishing, fowling, and navigation. [citations omitted] The doctrine, and with it the public's trust in government, once undermined is not easily restored. The court's judgment, I fear, is a step in the wrong direction. I respectfully dissent.

The court acknowledges, as it must, that only the Commonwealth, or an entity to which the Legislature "properly has delegated authority," may administer public trust rights. I cannot agree with the court's conclusion that the Legislature has delegated such authority to the siting board. In *Fafard, supra* at 197, 733 N.E.2d 66, we once again made clear that only the Commonwealth or an "entity to which the Commonwealth has delegated authority *expressly*" may administer public trust rights (emphasis added). Accord *Moot I, supra* at 347, 861 N.E.2d 410 (same). See *Commonwealth v. Charlestown,* 18 Mass. 180, 1 Pick. 180, 185 (1822) (Legislature may "delegate" power under public trust doctrine to authorize construction of bridge over navigable waterway, "but, until they have made such delegation in *express* terms, it is a branch of sovereign power to be exercised by the [L]egislature alone" [emphasis added]). The siting board's enabling legislation provides for no such express delegation.

The requirement that any delegation by the Legislature of authority to administer public trust rights be "express" is rooted in the "history of the origins of the Commonwealth's public trust obligations and authority, as well as jurisprudence and legislation spanning two centuries." *Fafard, supra* at 199, 733 N.E.2d 66. That history, jurisprudence, and legislation has been recounted frequently and at length elsewhere. [citations omitted] Briefly, as protector of the public trust, the Commonwealth sits "in a fiduciary relation" to the people. *Commonwealth v. Roxbury,* 75 Mass. 451, 9 Gray 451, 492 (1857). Commonwealth tidelands are "impressed with a public trust, which gives the public's representatives an interest and responsibility" in their development. [citations omitted]

The Commonwealth may delegate, and of course has delegated, the responsibility, or some of it, to administer its tidelands to a State agency. See *Moot I, supra,* and cases cited. As noted, that delegation, when it occurs, must be explicit. Thus, pursuant to G.L. c. 91, the Department of Environmental Protection (DEP) may issue licenses for the construction of structures "in or over tide water" or cables "under tide water." *Id.* at § 14. See *id.* at § 18 (such licenses are "revocable"). The Legislature has been unmistakably clear that in granting such licenses DEP "shall protect the interests of the commonwealth" and its inhabitants in "lands, rights in lands, flats, shores," "rights in tide waters," and "tidelands" within the Commonwealth. See *Moot I, supra* at 342-343, 861 N.E.2d 410 ("obligation to preserve the public trust" has been expressly delegated by Legislature to DEP).

The court reasons that because the Legislature has expressly delegated authority to administer public trust rights to DEP, and because § 69K, in the court's view, directs the siting board to "stand in the shoes" of DEP, § 69K provides a "sufficiently articulated legislative delegation of authority" to the siting board to administer public trust rights. I cannot agree. The siting board cannot "stand in the shoes" of DEP with respect to the administration of public trust rights unless the Legislature has expressly authorized it to do so. Such an express authorization is the only "articulation" that is "sufficient" to delegate fiduciary responsibilities.

The court supports its conclusion by pointing to language in § 69K authorizing the siting board, in certain circumstances, to issue a certificate with respect to a proposed energy facility that "shall be in the form of a composite of all individual permits, approvals or authorizations which would otherwise be necessary for the construction or operation of the facility." That language, as does the rest of § 69K, makes no reference to tidelands and lacks any recognition of public trust rights, and, contrary to the court's conclusion, the Legislature has *not* "expressly vested authority" in the siting board to act with respect to public trust rights. The court cites no precedent supporting its "reading" of the statute, and there is none. Rather, the court's "reading" of the statute is at odds with our prior public trust jurisprudence, both ancient and contemporary.

* * *

Were the siting board statute itself and the case law not sufficiently clear to require a different outcome of this case, and they are, the legislative history of the creation of the siting board confirms that the Legislature did *not* in fact delegate authority to the siting board to administer public trust rights. In 1971, in the face of a looming energy crisis of proportion equal to any today, the Legislature created an Electric Power Plant Siting Commission (commission) to make "an investigation and study of the *regulatory procedures* employed by the commonwealth and by its political subdivisions relative to the location and operation of electric utility generation and transmission facilities" (emphasis added). The Legislature directed the commission to consider "the adequacy of existing state and municipal *regulatory procedures* to permit the furnishing of a sufficient supply of electric energy while, at the same time, preserving and protecting land, air and water resources" (emphasis added). In particular, the commission was directed to consider the "feasibility of a comprehensive state *regulatory* jurisdiction over the siting of electric generating plants and routing of major transmission facilities" (emphasis added). Nowhere in the commission's charge did the Legislature address expressly, or by implication, public trust rights in the Commonwealth's tidelands.

***

The commission's reports make clear that, in creating the siting board, the Legislature's intent was to ensure that "state and municipal *regulatory procedures*" (emphasis added), balance the need for sufficient electric energy with "environmental protection, public health and public safety." Third Report, *supra* at 24, 41. See First Report, *supra* at 8 (discussing need for one agency to have power "to resolve the conflicts, such as between the utilities and environmentalists" and stating "[p]ower plant siting is primarily a question of land-use"). The extensive legislative history, including three commission reports, multiple drafts of the legislation, amendments in both houses, and memoranda to the Governor from various executive agencies, contains *no* reference to tidelands, tidewaters, tidal flats, land under coastal waters, the public trust, or the traditional rights of navigation, fishing, and fowling. The silence is deafening.

***

The Legislature's decision expressly to exempt issues concerning "offshore energy resources activities and offshore facilities" from its expansion of the commission's scope of study reflects an understanding within the Legislature that concerns relating to offshore facilities were *not* part of the commission's scope of inquiry. This singular indication of the Legislature's consideration of issues potentially relevant to public trust rights in relation to the creation of the siting board suggests that the Legislature understood that the creation of the siting board would not implicate those rights.

The siting board's authority to grant a composite certificate is broad, but nothing in the statutory language, or its legislative history, indicates that such authority encompasses the power to act with respect to public trust rights. I would reverse on this ground alone.[10]

***

10. The court notes that DEP participated as an intervener in the § 69K proceeding concerning the Cape Wind, LLC (Cape Wind), project and that the commissioner of DEP sits on the siting board. Ante at n. 29. The court also points out that the siting board incorporated DEP's findings into its certificate decision without DEP's objection. As the court recognizes, none of these facts is sufficient to constitute the "express" delegation our cases require. Nevertheless, by approving of the certificate issued by the siting board, the court effectively sanctions DEP's abdication of DEP's fiduciary duties. Cape Wind and the Attorney General are simply wrong to assert that the siting board did not "usurp" DEP's role in deciding whether to issue a G.L. c. 91 tidelands license and that the substantive and procedural requirements of G.L. c. 91 have been satisfied.

The public trust doctrine and government energy policy are not at odds. Indeed, they are complementary. Both express the people's paramount interest in the wise and fruitful use of natural resources. Today's opinion, however, casts these two allies in opposition, and exalts regulatory expediency at the cost of fiduciary obligation. By issuing a certificate pursuant to G.L. c. 164, § 69K, which purports to include the "equivalent" of a G.L. c. 91 tidelands license, the siting board has purported to act as the protector of the public's long-standing rights under the public trust doctrine without the necessary express legislative authority to do so. Its usurpation of the Commonwealth's fiduciary responsibility to the people, and DEP's complicit agreement with that usurpation, should not be condoned. Moreover, even if the siting board had the authority to act, it has failed to exercise its role of fiduciary on behalf of the public because it failed to consider the in-State impacts of the wind farm. For these reasons, I respectfully dissent.

points for discussion

1. *The public trust.* The public trust doctrine, explored more fully in Chapter 7, is the duty of any government — most prominently states, but also the federal government — to retain certain public rights in things that are considered to be "inherently public." Those have historically featured waterways, which were vitally important to commerce, such that removal from the public realm would have a deleterious effect on trade and commerce. That principle is most famously captured in the 1890 case *Illinois Central Railroad Co. v. Illinois*, discussed in Chapter 6, *infra*, but has been applied in a number of cases since then, many of them involving tidelands. As a formal matter, there is no controversy that states such as the Commonwealth of Massachusetts have a public trust duty not to alienate the tidelands — submerged lands under its state territorial waters — but what "alienation" means is a fairly complex matter. Moreover, the public trust doctrine in some states allows alienation under some conditions, such as the existence of a clear public benefit. A *de facto* alienation of a public trust asset is also best done by a state legislature, rather than administratively, as a legislative body is best situated to make a disposition of public assets. The present case is an example. It illustrates one avenue of challenge that local opponents of offshore renewable energy sources might take to stop or, in the case of Cape Wind, slow down development until the developers finally give up.

2. One might be surprised to learn that the Cape Wind project, a $2.6 billion offshore wind energy project in the State of Massachusetts, was one of the most heavily litigated energy projects in history. Cape Wind, which would have supplied electricity to about 200,000 homes, also took place against the backdrop of Massachusetts having the third most expensive retail electricity rates in the United States (after only Hawai'i and Connecticut). However, Horseshoe Shoals is also almost entirely surrounded by the territorial waters of the State of Massachusetts, making it an island of federal waters

surrounded by state waters. Those waters are also adjacent to the highly affluent island enclaves of Martha's Vineyard and Nantucket. Cape Wind was opposed by many local residents of the islands, who were concerned that the 417-foot-high wind turbines would spoil the view from their properties. These included Robert F. Kennedy, Jr., an environmental advocate who has championed other environmental actions. The Kennedy family has long resided in the general area (the Kennedy family compound at Hyannis Port is on the mainland), and Martha's Vineyard is home to the 276-acre Kennedy family home acquired by the late Jaqueline Kennedy Onassis in 1981.

The Alliance to Protect Nantucket Sound, formed to stop Cape Wind, litigated and benefited from prominent legal firepower. It is unclear how much the litigation held up the project and contributed to its ultimate demise, but in the end, missed milestones and canceled power contracts led Cape Wind's founder, Jim Gordon, to cancel his lease in 2017.

2. BOEM Permitting

For offshore wind in federal waters, the permitting process should appear familiar. For the Bureau of Ocean Energy Management (BOEM), at least, renewable energy leasing occurs in four stages: (1) Planning and Analysis, (2) Leasing, (3) Site Assessment, and (4) Construction and Operations. These four stages are analogous to the four stages of oil and gas leasing: BOEM's five-year plan, lease sales, exploration, and development and production.

The first Planning and Analysis phase is undertaken by BOEM, which identifies "Priority Wind Energy Areas," areas most suitable for offshore wind development: windy, close to population centers, but not likely to be a visual blight. Environmental impact statements are prepared at this stage. BOEM may receive unsolicited applications for an offshore wind lease, in which case this initial stage is when it processes the application and prepares the environmental impact statement.

The second stage, Leasing, is like the leasing stage in oil and gas development, except that in most cases so far, there has not been competitive interest in offshore renewable energy leases, and so the competitive bidding process is moot. In the third stage, Site Assessment, the lessee must prepare a site assessment plan, in which it studies and evaluates the suitability of the proposed site for offshore renewable energy development, and files the plan with BOEM. BOEM can then approve, disapprove, or approve with modification. Oil and gas operations would do exploratory drilling to evaluate the mineral potential; a renewable energy developer might install a data tower to measure wind speeds, or a buoy to evaluate hydrokinetic potential. Environmental analysis is conducted at this stage as well, and the impacts are not trivial. Offshore wind projects must evaluate the mortality of spinning turbines on waterfowl. Marine hydrokinetic projects must evaluate the effects of having a great spinning turbine alongside many forms of sea life. Finally, analogous to the final stage of oil production, the development and production stage, the final stage of renewable energy production is the Construction and Operations stage. The lessee must submit a construction and operations plan, which BOEM can approve, disapprove, or approve with modifications. Upon approval, the lessee can begin construction.

D. HARM TO RESOURCES

1. Liability for Oil Spills

Offshore extraction of minerals, most prominently oil and gas, has always posed environmental and economic risks. The engineering of reaching down thousands of feet to the ocean floor and drilling several thousands of feet more to extract oil or gas, in astonishingly large quantities, is mind-boggling. Progress on both the productivity and safety fronts has been substantial. But it has by no means eradicated the possibility of accidents that cause severe harms to resources.

OCSLA, along with its 1978 amendments, set forth a comprehensive planning, permitting, and review scheme that was intended to authorize drilling on the continental shelf, but also provide safeguards that would hopefully minimize reoccurrences of the 1969 Santa Barbara oil spill. Congress could not have hoped to eliminate them entirely. But developing a legal framework to strictly regulate such activities *ex ante*, and also compensate those harmed *ex post*, would have to wait until something catastrophic made it politically unacceptable to be inert. That something would be the 1989 Exxon Valdez oil spill.

Robert E. Jenkins & Jill Watry Kastner, Running Aground in a Sea of Complex Litigation: A Case Comment on the *Exxon Valdez* Litigation

18 UCLA J. Envtl. L. & Pol'y 151 (1999)

On March 23, 1989, the supertanker Exxon Valdez slowly left Valdez, Alaska carrying 53 million gallons of crude oil. Its next planned stop was Long Beach, California. The ship traveled at a speed of no more than six knots during the first leg of its journey because there were small islands, reefs and, most likely, ice ahead. Captain Joseph Hazelwood stood on the bridge of the ship with the third mate Gregory Cousins. As the ship began making its way toward Prince William Sound, Hazelwood left to go to his office to do paperwork after telling Cousins to call if he needed anything. Exxon's manual dictated that the captain had to be on the bridge "whenever conditions present a potential threat to the vessel such as passing in the vicinity of shoals, rocks or other hazards presenting any threat to safe navigation."

A short time later, Hazelwood received a call that there was ice ahead and that they would need to maneuver around it. Hazelwood returned to the bridge, studied the ice reports, and ordered the helmsman to change course. Hazelwood then gave instructions to Cousins regarding the next turn the Exxon Valdez would need to make. Hazelwood left the bridge again and returned to his office down below. While Hazelwood did paperwork, Cousins went into the chart room to look at the map, leaving the helmsman alone on the bridge. Suddenly, the lookout sounded an alarm and cried that the flashing red buoy marking Bligh Reef could be seen off the starboard when it was supposed to be on the port side. Cousins quickly ordered a turn. However, the huge ship could not turn fast enough. Cousins called Hazelwood in his office and told the captain, "We're in serious trouble."

Just after midnight, the Exxon Valdez ran aground on Bligh Reef tearing open the hull of the ship. Bligh Reef was a well-known navigational hazard in Prince William Sound and clearly marked on the ship's navigating charts. The damage caused the ship to gush oil into the Sound at a rate of 200,000 gallons a minute. At the time, Prince William Sound was regarded as "one of the most pristine and diverse ecological systems in the world."

Chief Warrant Officer Mark Delozier of the Coast Guard was called out to the Exxon Valdez. When he arrived, he spoke to Hazelwood. While talking to Hazelwood, Delozier could smell the odor of alcohol. He ordered Hazelwood and some of the crewmembers to be tested for alcohol. It would later be discovered that Hazelwood spent much of the previous afternoon in a bar. Due to numerous delays, however, Hazelwood's blood sample was taken nearly eleven hours after the grounding. Although the authenticity of the samples was later challenged in trial, the test revealed that Hazelwood's blood alcohol level was .061 eleven hours after the accident. Federal law prohibits a crewmember from operating a vessel if his blood alcohol level is over .04. Exxon fired Captain Hazelwood immediately.

Eleven million gallons of oil from the damaged hull poured out and eventually spread over 2,592 miles of coastline. It has been called the worst environmental disaster in United States history. The oil spill caused the death of more wildlife than any other single human catastrophe. More than 250,000 seabirds, 3,500 otters and hundreds of bald eagles were killed. Additionally, the spill had an extensive impact on almost all levels of life in Alaska. Nearly 60,000 Alaskans claimed the oil spill impacted their lives. No one knows what the long-term effects of the oil spill will be. What is certain is that this spill sparked the beginning of one of America's "largest and most complex litigation in history" that would involve thousands of people, hundreds of lawyers and years of court battles.

Following the spill, thousands of plaintiffs filed hundreds of claims seeking compensation for their losses and punitive damages against Exxon. The plaintiffs included individuals, area businesses, environmental groups, and local, state and the federal governments. The plaintiffs filed individual claims and class actions in both state and federal court. . . .

The authors point out that many plaintiffs could recover from such a catastrophic accident, with so many effects. A patchwork of remedies under state and federal law, statutory and common law, provided some redress for those harmed by an oil spill.

State law. Tort remedies such as negligence, nuisance and strict liability have always provided some backstop of relief for those suffering environmental wrongs. As students who have successfully navigated a first-year course in tort law can appreciate, these common law causes of action (most of which have actually been codified in most states) have led to recovery in a variety of circumstances and for a variety of harms. Indeed, some lawsuits successfully invoking these causes of action seemed quite speculative at the outset. But the common law is by design a conservative institution, so abrupt changes in the law to redress environmental harms are rare. More recently, public trust law has been invoked in environmental causes of action, but the use of this body of law to right environmental wrongs remains an uncertain prospect.

General maritime law. The United States Constitution provides that "[T]he judicial power shall extend to all Cases . . . of admiralty and maritime jurisdiction." U.S. Const. art. III, § 2. The Judiciary Act of 1789 provided that "The district courts shall have original jurisdiction, exclusive of the courts of the States, of . . . Any civil case of admiralty or maritime jurisdiction. . . ." 28 U.S.C. § 1333. Jurisdiction over maritime claims is thus sometimes called "admiralty" jurisdiction. What has emerged over the past two centuries is a body of federal common law governing disputes arising from events "wholly on the navigable waters." *S. Port Marine LLC v. Gulf Oil Ltd.,* 234 F.3d 58, 64 (1st Cir. 2000). This general body of tort law tailored to redress harms incurred while at sea, grew to encompass a broader variety of events causing harm to a broader variety of parties. While most injuries to seamen during the course of employment became part of a much larger body of statutory law known as the Jones Act, newly-recognized injuries that had grown out of that narrower body survived. General maritime law grew to encompass claims over ship financing and liens, contractual claims, water pollution and, ultimately, oil spills.

Common maritime law causes of action include sometimes overlapping claims of negligence, gross negligence, strict liability, unseaworthiness, and wrongful death. The relationship between general maritime law — a federal concern — and state law remains incompletely settled. As recently as 1996, the U.S. Supreme Court had occasion to rule that a fatal accident taking place in state territorial waters could be governed by a state wrongful death statute, where general maritime law could not be interpreted as precluding it. *Yamaha Motor Corp. v. Calhoun,* 516 U.S. 199 (1996). In fact, the Deepwater Horizon litigation forms part of this body of law, still developing after 200 years. Importantly, general maritime law allows for punitive damages.

Federal Clean Water Act. The Clean Water Act provides for liability for the discharge of oil or other hazardous substances. 33 U.S.C. § 1321. The Act prohibits the "discharge of oil or hazardous substances (i) into or upon the navigable waters of the United States, adjoining shorelines, or into or upon waters of the contiguous zone, or (ii) in connection with activities under the Outer Continental Shelf Lands Act . . . in such quantities as may be harmful. . . ." 33 U.S.C. § 1321(b)(3). Administrative penalties and civil penalties are available, which were increased by the Oil Pollution Act of 1990, the central framework for liability for oil spills. But addressing harm to resources is not limited to compensation and penalties. Importantly, the Clean Water Act authorized the President to clean up oil spills, an authority that was strengthened by the Oil Pollution Act of 1990. 33 U.S.C. § 1321(c), *amended by* Oil Pollution Act of 1990, § 4201, Publ. L. No. 101-380, 104 Stat. 484 (1990).

While the facts of the accident could only engender hostility towards Exxon, the law as it stood at the time was much more sympathetic. Presiding over consolidated proceedings, District Court Judge Russel Holland ruled that Alaska state law was mostly preempted by federal law, because of a direct conflict. A public nuisance claim by Native Alaskans survived, but ultimately failed for wont of a special injury, different in kind and degree, as typically required for recovery under common law. *Adkins v. Trans-Alaska Pipeline Liability Fund*, 101 F.3d 86 (9th Cir. 1996). That left general maritime law and the Clean Water Act.

General maritime law, as a body of common law, has suffered fewer intrusions in the form of statutory law than the law of torts. It remains one of the few areas of modern law that truly looks like the common law as it existed hundreds of years ago. The greatest obstacle faced by plaintiffs seeking redress against Exxon was the principle set forth in *Robins Dry Dock & Repair Co. v. Flint*, 275 U.S. 303 (1927), which has been characterized as a principle barring damage recovery for "remote" injuries. *Venore Trans. Co. v. M/V Struma*, 583 F.2d 708 (4th Cir. 1978). Applied to the lawsuits emanating from the 1969 Santa Barbara oil spill, a Ninth Circuit decision held that the *Robins Dry Dock* rule limited recovery to "pure economic losses," unaccompanied by physical injury. *Union Oil. Co. v. Oppen*, 501 F.2d 558, 563-65 (1974). Put together, these two jurisprudential principles imputed to the *Robins Dry Dock* rule severely limits recovery for tortious actions at sea, but the *Union Oil* court did allow recovery for one class of plaintiffs: commercial fishers. Alaskans fishers would thus be compensated for loss of fishing income. So too, would Native Alaskans insofar as they suffered economically measurable fishing losses. As for the rest, a second exception to the *Robins Dry Dock* rule was provided by the Trans-Alaska Pipeline Authorization Act, Pub. L. 93-153, 87 Stat. 584 (1973), which provides for strict liability for oil spills, up to a ceiling of $100 million, and only for certain classes of plaintiffs. 43 U.S.C. § 1653(c). The Exxon payout under this provision was an insignificant $14 million. For the most part, these plaintiffs, who may have depended upon the fishing industry for their livelihood, including seafood wholesalers, fish processors, cannery workers, and taxidermists, were left out. So were those in the tourism and leisure industries, such as hotels, sport fishers, kayaking and boat rental businesses.

The Clean Water Act provided some compensation and imposed some penalties for the spill. As noted above, section 311 provides specifically for liability for oil spills, but is limited to some penalties that were deemed to be too modest for the *Exxon Valdez* case. The United States opted to pursue liability under section 301, which prohibits more generally the "discharge of any pollutant," 33 U.S.C. § 1311, and carries with it the threat of criminal penalties under section 309, 33 U.S.C.

§ 1319(c). Exxon pled guilty to four misdemeanor counts for a modest $125 million. Exxon also agreed to pay up to $1 billion over ten years for damages to natural resources, to be placed in a trust fund jointly administered by the U.S. and Alaska.

The most interesting part of the litigation pertained to punitive damages. Commercial and Native Alaskan fishers that could recover compensatory damages could also recover punitive damages under general maritime law. A jury found Exxon's behavior reckless, and in addition to awarding $287 million in compensatory damages, tacked on an additional $5 billion for punitive damages. This award was reduced to $4 billion, and then to $2.5 million, and finally, after *Exxon Shipping Company v. Baker*, 554 U.S. 571 (2008), to $507.5 million.

Although the punitive damages fiasco, playing out over the course of 15 tortuous years, post-dated the Oil Pollution Act, it was clear from the outset that the existing tools for preventing oil spills and providing compensation and imposing punishment were inadequate. It seemed particularly odd that on the one hand, maritime liability was confined to such a narrow class of plaintiffs, but that liability could be magnified by punitive damages. The Clean Water Act penalties were feckless. The Oil Pollution Act of 1990 was badly needed.

Oil Pollution Act of 1990

33 U.S.C. § 2701. Definitions

For the purposes of this Act, the term —

(1) "act of God" means an unanticipated grave natural disaster or other natural phenomenon of an exceptional, inevitable, and irresistible character the effects of which could not have been prevented or avoided by the exercise of due care or foresight;

***

(20) "natural resources" includes land, fish, wildlife, biota, air, water, ground water, drinking water supplies, and other such resources belonging to, managed by, held in trust by, appertaining to, or otherwise controlled by the United States (including the resources of the exclusive economic zone), any State or local government or Indian tribe, or any foreign government;

***

(30) "remove" or "removal" means containment and removal of oil or a hazardous substance from water and shorelines or the taking of other actions as may be necessary to minimize or mitigate damage to the public health or welfare, including, but not limited to, fish, shellfish, wildlife, and public and private property, shorelines, and beaches;

(31) "removal costs" means the costs of removal that are incurred after a discharge of oil has occurred or, in any case in which there is a substantial

threat of a discharge of oil, the costs to prevent, minimize, or mitigate oil pollution from such an incident;

(32) "responsible party" means the following:

(A) Vessels. —

In the case of a vessel, any person owning, operating, or demise chartering the vessel. In the case of a vessel, the term "responsible party" also includes the owner of oil being transported in a tank vessel with a single hull after December 31, 2010.

***

(C) Offshore facilities. —

In the case of an offshore facility . . . the lessee or permittee of the area in which the facility is located or the holder of a right of use and easement granted under applicable State law or the Outer Continental Shelf Lands Act . . . for the area in which the facility is located (if the holder is a different person than the lessee or permittee), except a Federal agency, State, municipality, commission, or political subdivision of a State, or any interstate body, that as owner transfers possession and right to use the property to another person by lease, assignment, or permit.

***

33 U.S.C. § 2702. Elements of Liability

(a) In general

Notwithstanding any other provision or rule of law, and subject to the provisions of this Act, each responsible party for a vessel or a facility from which oil is discharged, or which poses the substantial threat of a discharge of oil, into or upon the navigable waters or adjoining shorelines or the exclusive economic zone is liable for the removal costs and damages specified in subsection (b) that result from such incident.

(b) Covered removal costs and damages

(1) Removal costs

The removal costs referred to in subsection (a) are —

(A) all removal costs incurred by the United States, a State, or an Indian tribe. . . .

(B) any removal costs incurred by any person for acts taken by the person which are consistent with the National Contingency Plan.

(2) Damages

The damages referred to in subsection (a) are the following:

(A) Natural resources

Damages for injury to, destruction of, loss of, or loss of use of, natural resources, including the reasonable costs of assessing the damage, which shall be recoverable by a United States trustee, a State trustee, an Indian tribe trustee, or a foreign trustee.

(B) Real or personal property

Damages for injury to, or economic losses resulting from destruction of, real or personal property, which shall be recoverable by a claimant who owns or leases that property.

(C) Subsistence use

Damages for loss of subsistence use of natural resources, which shall be recoverable by any claimant who so uses natural resources which have been injured, destroyed, or lost, without regard to the ownership or management of the resources.

(D) Revenues

Damages equal to the net loss of taxes, royalties, rents, fees, or net profit shares due to the injury, destruction, or loss of real property, personal property, or natural resources, which shall be recoverable by the Government of the United States, a State or a political subdivision thereof.

(E) Profits and earning capacity

Damages equal to the loss of profits or impairment of earning capacity due to the injury, destruction, or loss of real property, personal property, or natural resources, which shall be recoverable by any claimant.

(F) Public services

Damages for net costs of providing increased or additional public services during or after removal activities, including protection from fire, safety, or health hazards, caused by a discharge of oil, which shall be recoverable by a State, or a political subdivision of a State.

33 U.S.C. § 2704. Limits on Liability

(a) General rule

Except as otherwise provided in this section, the total of the liability of a responsible party under section 2702 of this title and any removal costs incurred by, or on behalf of, the responsible party, with respect to each incident shall not exceed —

(1) for a tank vessel the greater of —

(A) with respect to a single-hull vessel, including a single-hull vessel fitted with double sides only or a double bottom only, $3,000 per gross ton;

(B) with respect to a vessel other than a vessel referred to in subparagraph (A), $1,900 per gross ton; or

(C)(i) with respect to a vessel greater than 3,000 gross tons that is —

(I) a vessel described in subparagraph (A), $22,000,000; or

(II) a vessel described in subparagraph (B), $16,000,000; or

(ii) with respect to a vessel of 3,000 gross tons or less that is —

(I) a vessel described in subparagraph (A), $6,000,000; or

(II) a vessel described in subparagraph (B), $4,000,000;

(2) for any other vessel, $950 per gross ton or $800,000, whichever is greater;

***

(c) Exceptions

(1) Acts of responsible party

Subsection (a) does not apply if the incident was proximately caused by —

(A) gross negligence or willful misconduct of, or

(B) the violation of an applicable Federal safety, construction, or operating regulation by the responsible party, an agent or employee of the responsible party, or a person acting pursuant to a contractual relationship with the responsible party (except where the sole contractual arrangement arises in connection with carriage by a common carrier by rail).

33 U.S.C. § 2718. Relationship to Other Law

(a) Preservation of State authorities; Solid Waste Disposal Act

Nothing in this Act . . . shall —

(1) affect, or be construed or interpreted as preempting, the authority of any State or political subdivision thereof from imposing any additional liability or requirements with respect to —

(A) the discharge of oil or other pollution by oil within such State; or

(B) any removal activities in connection with such a discharge; or

(2) affect, or be construed or interpreted to affect or modify in any way the obligations or liabilities of any person under the Solid Waste Disposal Act . . . or State law, including common law.

(c) Additional requirements and liabilities; penalties

Nothing in this Act . . . shall in any way affect, or be construed to affect, the authority of the United States or any State or political subdivision thereof —

(1) to impose additional liability or additional requirements; or

(2) to impose, or to determine the amount of, any fine or penalty (whether criminal or civil in nature) for any violation of law, relating to the discharge, or substantial threat of a discharge, of oil.

Figure 4-7. The Fire Aboard the Deepwater Horizon

point for discussion

1. *Lost profits.* Should fishermen be allowed only to recover for next year's lost profits? How likely is it that a fishery can rebound quickly? If the time horizon for damages to commercial fishers is long, how long should it be?

a. Liable Parties

The events leading up to the catastrophic blowout, on April 20, 2010, of the Macondo Well and the resulting destruction of the Deepwater Horizon oil rig (DWH) were deeply woven into the intricate technology of "deepwater" drilling for oil. A series of serious errors were made by a number of different parties, and it was not entirely clear which ones were the critical ones; it is still not completely certain which technologies failed when, and why. District Court Judge Carl Barbier's 90-page opinion in *In re Oil Spill by the Oilrig "Deepwater Horizon" in the Gulf of Mexico, on April 20, 2010,* 21 F. Supp. 3d 657 (E.D. La. 2014), does an admirable job of describing the accident and laying out just enough of the technological knowledge he and his clerks were required to acquire as a part of adjudicating one of the most complex environmental cases ever. Complicating the legal proceedings was the sheer number of parties, and potential parties at fault. They included the defendant oil company BP, of course, which leased DWH and has primary responsibilities for drilling and safety decisions; Transocean, which chartered and operated DWH; and Triton, which owned DWH. The rig itself is staffed mostly by Transocean employees, but also BP employees, most notably supervisory staff making critical production and safety decisions.

An oil rig is a floating platform that extends a long, segmented tube, typically known as the riser, down thousands of feet, drills into bedrock, and extracts oil embedded in the bedrock. Oil rigs are highly specialized, expensive pieces of equipment. DWH, a 400-by-250-foot floating platform, cost $3 billion to build, and was designed specifically for *exploratory* drilling; once DWH pierced the bedrock and reached an oil reservoir, it would temporarily cap the well and make way for a production rig, moving onto other projects. DWH, which entered service in 2001, had done this successfully over 50 times before. But the "Macondo Well," located about 50 miles south of the Louisiana coast, known by the DWH crew as the "well from hell," was horribly different. Another production rig, the *Marianas*, had already started exploratory drilling, reaching 8,970 feet when it experienced a "kick," the sudden and violent (but not necessarily disastrous) expulsion of oil into the well, and possibly up the riser. Left unchecked, a kick can develop into a blowout, in which oil flows uncontrolled up onto the rig, igniting and flowing out onto the ocean. *Marianas* abandoned Macondo and made way for DWH. By the time DWH reached Macondo, the project was $54 million behind schedule, and losing $1 million per day.

Offshore drilling, particularly deepwater drilling, is a delicate task. Water pressures are extremely high at great depths, and the pressure from oil reservoirs can be extremely high as well, so when the drilling tube — the "drill pipe," which fits inside the riser — drills downward, it must carry with it mud or other fluids to keep the tube from collapsing, or to keep oil from spurting upward in a kick or blowout. At the same time, too much pressure being forced out the end of the drill pipe can fracture the bedrock, and again, cause the uncontrolled release of oil into the riser and into the ocean. Pressure must be not-too-great and not-too-small, staying within a "safe drilling margin." Mind you, this is all maintained by a floating platform that is kept in place by a series of motors that can maneuver the vessel and keep it on top of the well.

BP, having resumed drilling at Macondo with DWH as a substitute for *Marianas*, experienced a number of additional kicks, but kept drilling. At one critical point, BP had reached the oil reservoir — at 18,260 feet — but lost all of its drilling mud through fractures in the fragile and porous bedrock. At that point, it had to repair the bedrock. BP also still needed an extra 100 feet in order to be able to conduct testing and to complete the well for later production. BP made the extremely risky decision to keep drilling. An expert witness at trial said it was "one of the most dangerous things [he] had ever seen in [his] 20 years' experience" and "totally unsafe," as the fragile bedrock left BP with virtually no drilling margin at all. BP succeeded in extending the well another 100 feet, but in so doing, generated much debris, which accumulated in the well and later may have led to equipment failure and the blowout.

At this point, BP thought it was ready for "temporary abandonment," or capping the well for a production rig to come along and start extracting oil. Before that can take place, it is critical to adequately set a cement plug on the well to contain the oil, and through which the production rig would drill. A complicated process is undertaken to pump cement down a drill pipe to allow it to set. This requires deployment of a small device called a "float collar," a small tube that holds open a two-way valve, and is ejected from the drill pipe to a converted two-way valve into a one-way valve; cement can pump out, but nothing comes back in. While the facts were in dispute, Judge Barbier made a specific factual finding that the float collar did not eject, and the cement did not seal the bottom of the drill pipe.

Had the cement been properly pumped and placed down a properly set wellbore, the following sequence of events would have been uneventful. A rig that prepares to temporarily abandon a well pumps mud and seawater down the drill pipe. Before it does that, it must conduct a series of tests to make sure that the cement is properly set, and that the rig can safely leave the well. Most important of these is a "negative pressure" test, which is intended to simulate what happens after the rig leaves the well and surrenders any artificial pressures or controls over the well. BP had Transocean crew conduct the negative pressure test, which yielded troubling, but puzzling results. BP supervisor Donald Vidrine, who had also presided over earlier fateful decisions, and who was later charged criminally (along with another BP supervisor, Robert Kaluza), offered up the theory that something was clogging the drill pipe near the sensor, which would generate anomalous results. When Vidrine proposed this theory to BP supervisors onshore he got this email response: "???????" However, onshore supervisors at BP did not halt operations. Vidrine ordered the test be conducted on another line, declared that test to be a success, and ordered the abandonment procedure to begin.

The conduct of the tests, the interpretation of the results, Vidrine's failure to consider the possibility that the cement had failed to set, BP's organizational failure to take control of an operation in dangerous territory, and Transocean's failure to countermand BP's decisions, were all complicated affairs. A number of competing explanations were offered before the tragedy, and also at trial, and approximately 100 paragraphs of Judge Barbier's findings of fact were devoted to a nuanced interpretation of what likely happened. The series of blunders was compounded by BP's failure to conduct a routine cement test beforehand, which might have alerted them to the problems with the cement. Once BP commenced the filling of the wellbore with seawater and mud, it became tragically apparent that the well was not at all securely plugged.

At 9:01 P.M., the first anomalous pressure readings from the drill pipe appeared. Pressure should have been decreasing, but it was increasing. Judge Barbier found that during the first seven minutes, it was reasonable for Transocean crew to fail to notice this gradual increase. However, between 9:08 and 9:14—a short six minutes—several other worrisome signs emerged. Pressure increased rapidly in the drill pipe. Judge Barbier found that failure to notice and respond to those new signs was unreasonable and reckless. BP supervisors Donald Vidrine and

Robert Kaluza, who had also presided over earlier fateful decisions, including failure to perform the cement check, and whom were both later charged criminally, made crucial decisions to proceed with the abandonment procedure. At 9:31, another routine test was skipped while the crew attempted to diagnose the anomalies. Given the troubling test results, and given the emerging signs of trouble, BP supervisors and Transocean crew should have immediately shut in the well. This could have been done by activating the blowout preventer, which creates a seal around the drill pipe. Instead, Transocean's captain of DWH, Kurt Kuchta, waited to get authorization. By 9:41, mud began to spill out onto the DWH floor. At 9:43, mud erupted from the drill pipe, smashing windows and hurling Transocean crew members across the room. At 9:46, a loud hissing noise signaled something ominously deadly: Gas was venting onto the rig. It was only then that the Transocean crew deployed the blowout preventer. Unfortunately, the blowout preventer failed. It could have been debris in the drill pipe, it could have been that the drill pipe buckled, it could have been the failure of a simple 27-volt battery that Transocean hadn't replaced in years, or it could have been a combination of these and other possible factors. But it was undisputed that the blowout preventer failed. At 9:48 P.M., DWH exploded into flames.

It was ironic that the DWH tragedy occurred on Earth Day, of all days. Eleven people were killed in the explosion, and 17 others were injured. Once DWH exploded into flames, it began to break apart. On April 22, DWH sank, and the 5,000-foot riser connecting DWH to the reservoir snapped. Over the next 87 days, the well would spill over 3 million barrels of crude oil into the Gulf of Mexico. If the Gulf waters did not circulate and flush the oil, that amount would have been enough to render the *entire Gulf of Mexico* 0.02 percent crude oil, or one out of every 4,924 gallons of water.

Apart from the complexity of what happened, there was the legal complexity of sorting out rights and liabilities among numerous parties — over 100,000 parties filed approximately 3,000 claims in state and federal courts. Claimants included commercial fishers, recreational and commercial businesses, recreation plaintiffs, plant and dock workers, property owners, tourism businesses and property owners who are dependent upon tourism, banking and retail businesses, subsistence fishers, and other vessels unable to travel because of the moratorium imposed after the explosion, to name just a few(!). And of course, plaintiffs included the United States government and the affected Gulf states — Texas, Louisiana, Mississippi, Alabama, and Florida.

Defendants included: **BP itself**, which leased DWH from **Transocean**, the operator of DWH; **Triton**, the owner of DWH; **QBE**, Transocean's underwriter; **Halliburton**, the maker of the cement and cement advisor to BP; **Cameron International**, maker of the blowout preventer; **M-I**, supplier of drilling fluids to BP; and **Weatherford**, maker of the float collar.

Judge Barbier's complicated adjudication of the claims notes that there were so many claimants, and so many different types of claims, that cases were separated out into "pleading bundles." In addition to the B1 bundle, essentially all private claims for economic loss and property damages, a separate pleading bundle, B3, pertained to liability stemming from post-explosion cleanup. This subsection pertains to the B1 bundle, while the next includes a case from the B3 bundle.

As you read through this excerpt of Judge Barbier's opinion, keep in mind: (i) which plaintiffs can sue, (ii) which defendants, and (iii) under which causes of action.

In re Oil Spill by the Oilrig Deepwater Horizon in the Gulf of Mexico, on April 20, 2010

808 F. Supp. 2d 943 (E.D. La. 2011)

Judge BARBIER delivered the opinion of the United States District Court, Eastern District of Louisiana.

This multi-district litigation ("MDL") consists of hundreds of consolidated cases, with thousands of claimants, pending before this Court. These cases arise from the April 20, 2010 explosion, fire, and sinking of the DEEPWATER HORIZON mobile offshore drilling unit ("MODU").... The consolidated cases include claims for the death of eleven individuals, numerous claims for personal injury, and various claims for environmental and economic damages.

In order to efficiently manage this complex MDL, the Court consolidated and organized the various types of claims into several "pleading bundles." The "B1" pleading bundle includes all claims for private or "non-governmental economic loss and property damages." There are in excess of 100,000 individual claims encompassed within the B1 bundle.

I. Procedural History

In the B1 Master Complaint, the PSC identifies a number of categories of claimants seeking various types of economic damages, including Commercial Fishermen Plaintiffs, Processing and Distributing Plaintiffs, Recreational Business Plaintiffs, Commercial Business Plaintiffs, Recreation Plaintiffs, Plant and Dock Worker Plaintiffs, Vessel of Opportunity ("VoO") Plaintiffs, Real Property Plaintiffs, Real Property/Tourism Plaintiffs, Banking/Retail Business Plaintiffs, Subsistence Plaintiffs, Moratorium Plaintiffs, and Dealer Claimants.

***

Plaintiffs allege claims under general maritime law, the Oil Pollution Act of 1990 ("OPA"), 33 U.S.C. § 2701 et seq., and various state laws. Under general maritime law, Plaintiffs allege claims for negligence, gross negligence, and strict liability for manufacturing and/or design defect. Under various state laws, Plaintiffs allege claims for nuisance, trespass, and fraudulent concealment, and they also allege a claim for strict liability under the Florida Pollutant Discharge Prevention and Control Act, Fla. Stat. § 376.011 et seq. Additionally, Plaintiffs seek punitive damages under all claims and request declaratory relief regarding any settlement provisions that purport to affect the calculation of punitive damages.

***

III. Parties' Arguments and Discussion

The subject Motions to Dismiss go to the heart of Plaintiffs' claims in this case. . . . [A]ll Defendants seek dismissal of all non-OPA claims for purely economic damages resulting from the oil spill. Essentially, Defendants move to dismiss all claims brought pursuant to either general maritime law or state law. . . . The Defendants' Motions raise a number of issues involving choice of law, and especially the interplay among admiralty, the Outer Continental Shelf Lands Act ("OCSLA"), 43 U.S.C. § 1301 et seq., OPA, and various state laws.

A. Vessel Status

. . . Plaintiffs and all other Defendants agree that the DEEPWATER HORIZON MODU was at all material times a "vessel" as that term is defined and understood in general maritime law. Cameron argues that although the DEEPWATER HORIZON may have been a vessel during the times it was moved from one drilling location to another, at the time of the casualty it was stationary and physically attached to the seabed by means of 5,000 feet of drill pipe. . . . The Court is not persuaded by Cameron's arguments. Under clearly established law, the DEEPWATER HORIZON was a vessel, not a fixed platform. Cameron's arguments run counter to longstanding case law which establishes conclusively that the Deepwater Horizon, a *mobile* offshore drilling unit, was a vessel.

***

C. Admiralty Jurisdiction

The test for whether admiralty jurisdiction exists in tort cases was outlined by the Supreme Court in *Grubart, Inc v. Great Lakes Dredge & Dock Co.*:

> [A] party seeking to invoke federal admiralty jurisdiction pursuant to 28 U.S.C. § 1333(1) over a tort claim must satisfy conditions both of location and of connection with maritime activity. A court applying the location test must determine whether the tort occurred on navigable water. The connection test raises two issues. A court, first, must assess the general features of the type of incident involved to determine whether the incident has a potentially disruptive impact on maritime commerce. Second, a court must determine whether the general character of the activity giving rise of the incident shows a substantial relationship to traditional maritime activity.

513 U.S. 527, 534, 115 S. Ct. 1043, 130 L. Ed. 2d 1024 (1995).

The location test, which is satisfied when the tort occurs on navigable water, is readily satisfied here. The B1 Master Complaint alleges that the blowout, explosions, fire, and subsequent discharge of oil, occurred on or from the DEEPWATER HORIZON and its appurtenances, which was operating on waters overlying the Outer Continental Shelf; i.e., navigable waters. The connection test is also met.

First, there is no question that the explosion and resulting spill caused a disruption of maritime commerce, which exceeds the "potentially disruptive" threshold established in *Grubart*. Second, the operations of the DEEPWATER HORIZON bore a substantial relationship to traditional maritime activity. Further, injuries incurred on land (or in the seabed) are cognizable in admiralty under the Admiralty Extension Act, 46 U.S.C. § 30101.

This case falls within the Court's admiralty jurisdiction. With admiralty jurisdiction comes the "application of substantive admiralty law." *Grubart*, 513 U.S. at 545, 115 S. Ct. 1043. "[W]here OCSLA and general maritime law both could apply, the case is to be governed by maritime law." *Tenn. Gas Pipeline v. Houston Cas. Ins. Co.*, 87 F.3d 150, 154 (5th Cir. 1996).

D. Plaintiffs' State Law Claims

Plaintiffs designated their B1 Master Complaint as "an admiralty or maritime case" under Rule 9(h) of the Federal Rules of Civil Procedure. Although Plaintiffs acknowledge that admiralty jurisdiction applies to this case, they insist that substantive maritime law does not preempt their state-law claims because state law can "supplement" general maritime law, either where there is a substantive gap in maritime law or where there is no conflict with maritime law. Plaintiffs also argue that OPA contains a state-law savings provision, which preserves these claims. . . .

The focus turns . . . to the relationship between federal maritime law and state law. As mentioned, with the admiralty jurisdiction comes substantive maritime law. This means that general maritime law — an amalgam of traditional common law rules, modifications of those rules, and newly created rules — applies to this matter to the extent it is not displaced by federal statute. This framework, established by the Constitution, intends that a consistent, uniform system will govern maritime commerce. *See The Lottawanna*, 88 U.S. 558, 575, 21 Wall. 558, 22 L. Ed. 654 (1874) ("It certainly could not have been the intention to place the rules and limits of maritime law under the disposal and regulation of the several States, as that would have defeated the uniformity and consistency at which the Constitution aimed on all subjects of a commercial character affecting the intercourse of the States with each other or with foreign states."). Admiralty does not entirely exclude state law, however, and States may "create rights and liabilities with respect to ***conduct within their borders,*** when the state action does not run counter to federal laws or the essential features of an exclusive federal jurisdiction." *Romero v. Int'l Terminal Operating Co.,* 358 U.S. 354, 375 n. 42, 79 S. Ct. 468, 3 L. Ed. 2d 368 (1959). . . .

But this case does not concern conduct within state borders (waters). This casualty occurred over the Outer Continental Shelf — an area of "exclusive federal jurisdiction" — on waters deemed to be the "high seas." The Admiralty Extension Act, though not itself a grant of exclusive jurisdiction, nevertheless ensures that damages incurred on land are cognizable in admiralty. Citizens from multiple states have alleged damage, and multiple states' laws are asserted. While it is recognized that States have an interest to protect their citizens, property, and resources from oil pollution, to subject a discharger to the varying laws of each state into which its oil has flowed would contravene a fundamental purpose of maritime law: "[t]o preserve adequate harmony and appropriate uniform rules relating to maritime matters." Thus, to the extent state law could apply to conduct outside state waters, in this case it must "yield to the needs of a uniform federal maritime law." *Romero,* 358 U.S. at 373, 79 S. Ct. 468. . . .

Plaintiffs argue that state law is not preempted in this instance because state law can supplement maritime law. Plaintiffs rely heavily on *Yamaha Motor Corp. v. Calhoun,* which involved a young girl killed in a jet ski accident in state territorial waters, where there is no federal statute providing a remedy for wrongful death. . . . The decedent's parents attempted to sue under the state wrongful death statute. The question in *Yamaha* was whether general maritime law's wrongful death action, often called the "*Moragne* action" (named for the case that created it, *Moragne v. States Marine Lines, Inc.,* 398 U.S. 375, (1970)), preempted state law.

The Court held that state law was not preempted. The *Yamaha* Court noted that before the *Moragne* action was created in 1970, courts permitted state wrongful death statutes to fill the substantive gap in the law. It also noted that the *Moragne* Court was focused on curing an anomaly that existed for seafarers (generally speaking, seamen and longshoremen): When killed outside territorial waters, seafarers could base a wrongful death claim on unseaworthiness (because the Death on the High Seas Act ("DOHSA") incorporates unseaworthiness for seafarers), but not when killed within state waters (because DOHSA does not apply there; thus seafarers could only use state law, which was negligence-based). Although *Moragne* ended this anomaly, it specifically left in place the seafarer's **pre-existing** ability to bring a wrongful death action under state law. Thus, the *Moragne* action was "in many respects a gap-filling measure to ensure that seamen (and their survivors) would all be treated alike," irrespective of whether death occurred within or beyond state waters, and "showed no hostility to concurrent application of state wrongful death statutes." Accordingly, *Yamaha* does not support using state law to supplement maritime law in this case, since there is no substantive gap for state law to fill (as contrasted with the situation in state waters before the creation of the *Moragne* action); remedies are available under both OPA and general maritime law. Also significant is the *Yamaha* Court's observation that maritime law had long accommodated States' interests in regulating maritime affairs that occurred **within their territorial waters.** Again, this casualty occurred beyond state waters, so *Yamaha* is also distinguishable for this reason.

***

Plaintiffs' contention that OPA's savings provisions preserves its state-law claims is also unavailing. These provisions state:

> (a) Preservation of State authorities; Solid Waste Disposal Act
>> Nothing in this Act or the Act of March 3, 1851 shall —
>>> (1) affect, or be construed or interpreted as preempting, the authority of any State or political subdivision thereof from imposing any additional liability or requirements with respect to —

(A) the discharge of oil or other pollution by oil within such State; or

(B) any removal activities in connection with such a discharge. . . .

***

These provisions evince Congress' intent to preserve the States' police power to govern pollution discharges within their territorial waters. The Court does not read as them giving States the power to govern out-of-state conduct affecting multiple states. "The usual function of a saving clause is to preserve something from immediate interference — not to create; and the rule is that expression by the Legislature of an erroneous opinion concerning the law does not alter it." *Knickerbocker Ice,* 253 U.S. at 162, 40 S. Ct. 438. In other words, although Congress has expressed its intent to not preempt state law, this intent does not delegate to the States a power that the Constitution vested in the federal government.

***

Accordingly, Plaintiffs' state common-law claims for nuisance, trespass, and fraudulent concealment, as well as Plaintiffs' FPDPCA claims are dismissed. Because the Court finds that state law is inapplicable to this case, Plaintiffs' arguments regarding the economic-loss doctrines of various states are moot.

E. General Maritime Law Claims

Defendants seek to dismiss all general maritime claims, contending that when Congress enacted OPA, it displaced pre-existing federal common law, including general maritime law, for claims covered by OPA. Defendants argue that OPA provides the sole remedy for private, non-governmental entities asserting economic loss and property damage claims. They urge that when Congress enacts a comprehensive statute on a subject previously controlled by federal common law, the federal statute controls and displaces the federal common law. Defendants further argue that under OPA, Plaintiffs are allowed to pursue their claims for economic damages solely against the designated "Responsible Party" and that OPA does not allow claims directly against non-Responsible Parties.

Prior to the enactment of OPA in 1990, a general maritime negligence cause of action was available to persons who suffered physical damage and resulting economic loss resulting from an oil spill. General maritime law also provided for recovery of punitive damages in the case of gross negligence, and strict product liability for defective products. However, claims for purely economic losses unaccompanied by physical damage to a proprietary interest were precluded under *Robins Dry Dock & Repair Co. v. Flint,* 275 U.S. 303, 48 S. Ct. 134, 72 L. Ed. 290 (1927). The Fifth Circuit has continuously reaffirmed the straightforward application of the *Robins Dry Dock* rule, explaining that "although eloquently criticized for its rigidity, the rule has persisted because it offers a bright-line application in an otherwise murky area."

One relevant exception to the *Robins Dry Dock* rule applies in the case of commercial fishermen. *See Louisiana v. M/V Testbank,* 524 F. Supp. 1170, 1173 (E.D. La. 1981) ("claims for [purely] economic loss [resulting from an oil spill and subsequent river closure] asserted by the commercial oystermen, shrimpers, crabbers, and fishermen raise unique considerations requiring separate attention . . . seamen have been recognized as favored in admiralty and their economic interests require the fullest possible legal protection."). A number of other courts have recognized that claims of commercial fishermen are sui generis because of their unique relationship to the seas and fisheries, treating these fishermen as akin to seamen under general maritime law.

Accordingly, long before the enactment of OPA, this was the state of general maritime law. Persons who suffered physical damage to their property as well as commercial fisherman had a cause of action under general maritime law to recover losses resulting from unintentional maritime torts. In the case of gross negligence or malicious, intentional conduct, general maritime law provided a claim for punitive or exemplary damages. And, in the case of a defective product involved in a maritime casualty, maritime law imposed strict liability.

In the wake of the EXXON VALDEZ spill in 1989, there were large numbers of persons who suffered actual economic losses but were precluded from any recovery by virtue of the *Robins Dry Dock* rule. At that time, an oil spill caused by a vessel on navigable water was governed by a web of different laws, including general maritime law, the CWA, and the laws of states affected by the spill in question. Various efforts had been made in the past to enact comprehensive federal legislation dealing with pollution from oil spills. With impetus from the EXXON VALDEZ incident, Congress finally enacted OPA in 1990.

OPA is a comprehensive statute addressing responsibility for oil spills, including the cost of clean up, liability for civil penalties, as well as economic damages incurred by private parties and public entities. Indeed, the Senate Report provides that the Act "builds upon section 311 of the Clean Water Act to create a single Federal law providing cleanup authority, penalties, and liability for oil pollution." S. Rep. 101-94 (1989). One significant part of OPA broadened the scope of private persons who are allowed to recover for economic losses resulting from an oil spill. OPA allows recovery for economic losses "resulting from" or "due to" the oil spill, regardless of whether the claimant sustained physical damage to a proprietary interest. OPA allows recovery for "[d]amages equal to the loss of profits or impairment of earning capacity due to the injury, destruction, or loss of real property, or natural resources, which shall be recoverable by *any claimant.*" 33 U.S.C. § 2702(b)(2)(E) (emphasis added). Furthermore, the House Report noted that "[t]he claimant need not be the owner of the damaged property or resources to recover for lost profits or income." H.R. Conf. Rep. 101-653 (1990).

Clearly, one major remedial purpose of OPA was to allow a broader class of claimants to recover for economic losses than allowed under general maritime law. Congress was apparently moved by the experience of the Alaskan claimants whose actual losses were not recoverable under existing law. Another obvious purpose of OPA was to set up a scheme by which a "Responsible Party" (typically the vessel or facility owner) was designated and made strictly liable (in most instances) for clean up costs and resulting economic damages. The intent is to encourage settlement and reduce the need for litigation. Claimants present their claims to the Responsible Party, who pays the claims and is then allowed to seek contribution from other allegedly liable parties. 33 U.S.C. § 2709, 2710, 2713. . . . The question arises in this case as to whether, or to what extent, OPA has displaced any claims previously existing under general maritime law, including claims for punitive damages.

Only a handful of courts have had the opportunity to address whether OPA displaces general maritime law. For example, the First Circuit in *South Port Marine, LLC v. Gulf Oil Limited Partnership,* 234 F.3d 58 (1st Cir. 2000), held that punitive damages were not available under OPA. The First Circuit began by noting that in enacting OPA "Congress established a comprehensive federal scheme for oil pollution liability" and "set[ ] forth a comprehensive list of recoverable damages." *Id.* at 64. "Absent from that list of recoverable damages is any mention of punitive damages." *Id.*

***

In [*Exxon Shipping Co. v.*] *Baker* [554 U.S. 471 (2008)], the Court employed a three-part analysis to determine if a statute preempts or displaces federal common law. First, is there a clear indication that Congress intended to occupy the entire field? Second, does the statute speak directly to the question addressed by the common law? Third, will application of common law have a frustrating effect on the statutory remedial scheme? The question presented in *Baker* was whether the CWA preempted or displaced general maritime punitive damages for economic loss. The Court first stated that it saw no clear indication of congressional intent to occupy the entire field of pollution remedies. Next, the Court noted that the CWA made no mention of punitive damages, and that "[i]n order to abrogate a common-law principle, the statute must speak directly to the question addressed by the common law." Finally, the Court did not perceive that punitive damages for private harms would have any frustrating effect on the CWA remedial scheme. Accordingly, the Court concluded that the CWA did not preempt punitive damages under general maritime law.

***

The B1 Master Complaint alleges economic loss claims on behalf of various categories of claimants, many of whom have not alleged physical injury to their property or other proprietary interest. Pre-OPA, these claimants, with the exception of commercial fishermen, would not have had a viable cause of action and would be precluded from any recovery by virtue of *Robins Dry Dock.* Accordingly, claims under general maritime law asserted by such claimants are not plausible and must be dismissed.

However, the Court finds that the B1 Master Complaint states a viable cause of action against the non-Responsible Parties under general maritime law on behalf of claimants who either allege physical damage to a proprietary interest and/or qualify for the commercial fishermen exception to *Robins Dry Dock*. In brief, these claims are saved and not displaced by OPA for the following reasons.

First, when reading OPA and its legislative history, it does not appear that Congress intended to occupy the entire field governing liability for oil spills, as it included two savings provisions — one that preserved the application of general maritime law and another that preserved a State's authority with respect to discharges of oil or pollution within the state. 33 U.S.C. § 2718, 2751.

Second, OPA does not directly address or speak to the liability of non-Responsible Parties to persons who suffer covered losses. Although OPA contains provisions regarding the Responsible Party's ability to seek contribution and indemnification, *Id.* § 2709, 2710, it is silent as to whether a claimant can seek redress directly from non-Responsible Parties. Prior to OPA's enactment, commercial fisherman and those who suffered physical damage had a general maritime law cause of action against these individuals.

Third, there is nothing to indicate that allowing a general maritime remedy against the non-Responsible Parties will somehow frustrate Congress' intent when it enacted OPA. Under OPA, a claimant is required to first present a claim to the Responsible Party. If the claim is not paid within ninety days, the claimant may file suit or file a claim against the Oil Spill Liability Trust Fund. A Responsible Party is strictly liable and damages are capped unless there is gross negligence or violation of a safety statute or regulation that proximately caused the discharge. To allow a general maritime claim against the Responsible Party would serve to frustrate and circumvent the remedial scheme in OPA.

Thus, claimants' maritime causes of action against a Responsible Party are displaced by OPA, such that all claims against a Responsible Party for damages covered by OPA must comply with OPA's presentment procedure. However, as to the non-Responsible Parties, there is nothing in OPA to indicate that Congress intended such parties to be immune from direct liability to persons who either suffered physical damage to a proprietary interest and/or qualify for the commercial fishermen exception. Therefore, general maritime law claims that existed before OPA may be brought directly against non-Responsible parties.

F. Claims for Punitive Damages

OPA is also silent as to the availability of punitive damages. Plaintiffs who could assert general maritime claims pre-OPA enactment may plausibly allege punitive damages under general maritime for several reasons. First, "[p]unitive damages have long been available at common law" and "the common-law tradition of punitive damages extends to maritime claims." *Townsend*, 129 S. Ct. at 2569. Congress has not occupied the entire field of oil spill liability in light of the OPA provision preserving admiralty and maritime law, "[e]xcept as otherwise provided." OPA does not mention punitive damages; thus, while punitive damages are not available under OPA, the Court does not read OPA's silence as meaning that punitive damages are precluded under general maritime law. Congress knows how to proscribe punitive damages when it intends to, as it did in the commercial aviation exception under the Death on the High Seas Act. . . .

There is also nothing to indicate that allowing a claim for punitive damages in this context would frustrate the OPA liability scheme. As stated above, claims against the Responsible Party must comply with OPA's procedure, regardless of whether there is also cause of action against the Responsible Party under general maritime law. However, the behavior that would give rise to punitive damages under general maritime law—gross negligence—would also break OPA's limit of liability. Thus, the imposition of punitive damages under general maritime law would not circumvent OPA's limitation of liability.

***

Thus, OPA does not displace general maritime law claims for those Plaintiffs who would have been able to bring such claims prior to OPA's enactment. These Plaintiffs assert plausible claims for punitive damages against Responsible and non-Responsible parties.

***

I. Vessel of Opportunity and Moratorium Claims

The parties disagree as to whether the Vessel of Opportunity ("VoO") and Moratorium Plaintiffs have stated plausible B1 claims. Plaintiffs argue that OPA may apply to some of the claims presented by VoO claimants because OPA provides for liability on the part of Responsible Parties for damages that "*result from*" discharges of oil. At least some of the VoO claimants allege property damage to their vessels. Moratorium Plaintiffs argue that they have stated a viable OPA claim because there are some losses that would have been incurred regardless of the Moratorium and further because the Moratorium was a foreseeable response to the spill. Defendants counter that OPA does not apply to claims alleged by VoO Plaintiffs because their injuries occurred as a result of their participation in the VoO program, not as a result of the spill. Defendants also argue that Moratorium claims must be dismissed for failure to state an OPA claim because the imposition of the Moratorium was an intervening or superseding cause of damage that could not reasonably have been anticipated.

Few courts have had occasion to address the question of OPA causation. See, e.g., *Gatlin Oil Co. v. United States*, 169 F.3d 207 (4th Cir. 1999) (holding that a plaintiff could not recover for fire damage because the evidence did not show that the fire caused the discharge of oil into navigable waters); *In re Settoon Towing LLC*, 2009 WL 4730969 (E.D. La. Dec. 4, 2009) (explaining that it was potentially possible for an injured party to recover for damages incurred as the result of a shutdown of the Gulf Intracoastal Waterway in the wake of a spill). The parties acknowledge that these claims are fact specific and present a more attenuated causation analysis than the other claims for economic loss, and they compare and contrast the instant

Moratorium claims and VoO claims with the facts in the few cases that have been decided.

The Court reminds the parties that the issue before the Court on a Motion to Dismiss is simply whether Plaintiffs have stated a plausible claim for relief. A claim is facially plausible when the plaintiff pleads facts that allow the court to "draw the reasonable inference that the defendant is liable for the misconduct alleged." *Iqbal*, 129 S. Ct. at 1949. A court "must . . . accept all factual allegations in the complaint as true" and "must draw all reasonable inferences in the plaintiff's favor." *Lormand*, 565 F.3d at 232.

The Court notes that OPA does not expressly require "proximate cause," but rather only that the loss is "due to" or "resulting from" the oil spill. While the Court need not define the precise contours of OPA causation at this time, it is worth noting that during oral argument both counsel for BP and the PSC conceded that OPA causation may lie somewhere between traditional "proximate cause" and simple "but for" causation. . . .

The Court need not define causation under OPA — necessarily a highly factual analysis — at this stage of the pleadings. The Court is satisfied that the VoO and Moratorium Plaintiffs have alleged sufficient facts to state plausible claims in the B1 bundle.

IV. Summary

In summary, the Court finds as follows:

1. The DEEPWATER HORIZON was at all material times a vessel in navigation.
2. Admiralty jurisdiction is present because the alleged tort occurred upon navigable waters of the Gulf of Mexico, disrupted maritime commerce, and the operations of the vessel bore a substantial relationship to traditional maritime activity. With admiralty jurisdiction comes the application of substantive maritime law.

***

4. The law of the adjacent state is not adopted as surrogate federal law under OCSLA, 43 U.S.C. § 1333(a)(2)(A).
5. State law, both statutory and common, is preempted by maritime law, notwithstanding OPA's savings provisions. All claims brought under state law are dismissed.
6. General maritime law claims that do not allege physical damage to a proprietary interest are dismissed under the *Robins Dry Dock* rule, unless the claim falls into the commercial fishermen exception. OPA claims for economic loss need not allege physical damage to a proprietary interest.
7. OPA does not displace general maritime law claims against non-Responsible parties. As to Responsible Parties, OPA does displace general maritime law

claims against Responsible Parties, but only with regard to procedure (i.e., OPA's presentment requirement).

***

10. Claims for punitive damages are available for general maritime law claimants against Responsible Parties (provided OPA's presentment procedure is satisfied) and non-Responsible Parties.

***

12. Plaintiffs have plausibly alleged OPA claims for VoO claimants and Moratorium claimants.

***

points for discussion

1. *Sailing away.* Cameron, the maker of the blowout preventer, tried fruitlessly to argue that DWH was not a "vessel," to avoid admiralty jurisdiction and therefore general maritime law. Why did Cameron want to fight admiralty jurisdiction?
2. *A state law matter?* The court held that plaintiffs' state law claims were preempted by both general maritime law and the OPA because the preempted DWH exploded outside of state territorial waters. What if DWH had happened within three nautical miles of the coast of Louisiana?
3. *Levels of jurisdiction.* Judge Barbier held that state law was preempted by both admiralty law and the OPA. As a policy matter, does that make sense? Should a state have a say over what happens just outside of its boundary three nautical miles from shore? What would be the drawback if it did?

Problem Exercise

Make a table with three columns: one with all of the possible plaintiffs in this case, one with all of the possible defendants (listed for your convenience before this case), and between those two columns, all of the different types of damages suffered. Then, for each possible cause of action, draw a line around the possible plaintiffs, the possible defendants, and the recoverable damages. For example, general maritime law apparently allows commercial fishers to recover "purely economic losses *or* physical damage to property under one of the exceptions to the *Robins Dry Dock* rule, and certainly. So:

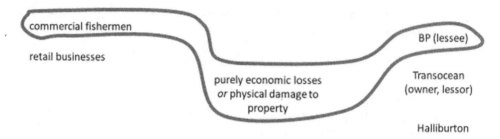

Figure 4-8. Example of Possible Cause of Action with Plaintiff(s) and Defendant(s)

What other defendants in addition to BP could also be liable? Graphically depict the other actions that survive this opinion.

Litigation from Deepwater Horizon was not nearly over. In some ways, it was just getting going. In addition to questions of liable parties, there is the question of apportionment of fault. This next ruling by Judge Barbier grapples with questions of culpability in a complex case.

In re Oil Spill by the Oilrig Deepwater Horizon in the Gulf of Mexico, on April 20, 2010

21 F. Supp. 3d 657 (E.D. La. 2014)

Judge BARBIER delivered the opinion of the United States District Court, Eastern District of Louisiana.

B. Liability Under the Clean Water Act

477. The Court previously held that BPXP is liable for civil penalties under the CWA, as it was the "owner" of an "offshore facility" (the Macondo well) "from which oil discharged."

478. The Court's prior ruling did not determine the amount of the CWA penalty, and the Court does not do so today. What is decided here is whether or not the discharge "was the result of gross negligence or willful misconduct," which determines the maximum amount of the penalty.

479. In the absence of gross negligence or willful misconduct (i.e., if the defendant acted with ordinary negligence or was not negligent), the maximum amount of the CWA civil penalty is $1,100 per barrel of oil discharged. However, the maximum amount per barrel is nearly quadrupled when the discharge results from gross negligence or willful misconduct.

499. Based on the Court's findings and as further explained below, the Court concludes that the discharge of oil "was the result of gross negligence or willful misconduct" by BPXP under the CWA, 33 U.S.C. § 1321(b)(7)(D). The Court finds that BPXP acted "recklessly"; therefore, regardless of whether the CWA's definition of "gross negligence" is the same as or lesser than "recklessness," that standard is met. Additionally, because it is undisputed that "willful misconduct" includes "reckless" conduct, that standard is also met.

500. The Court is mindful of the concept that "[a] greater degree of care is required when the circumstances present a greater apparent risk." A corollary here is that similar actions or omissions may be judged as meeting the standard of care, or falling just below the standard of care, or an extreme departure from the standard of care, depending on the context in which the action or omission occurred.

501. Turning to the case at bar, the industry and BP recognized that a blowout, explosion, and oil spill are potential harms associated with offshore drilling. Obviously, the magnitude of this potential harm is great in terms of severity, which in turn raises the standard of care.

502. The Macondo well was drilled in deepwater, which adds certain complexities not found in shallower waters or onshore. Furthermore, the high pressure and high temperature characteristics of the geological formation into which the Macondo well was drilled added complexity that is not present in all deepwater wells. These features increased the chance that a blowout, explosion, and oil spill would occur, which, in turn, further raises the standard of care.

503. This is not to say that every activity on a [Mobile Offshore Drilling Unit] or decision relating to a deepwater well is of a nature that any unreasonable act or decision is automatically treated as an extreme departure from the standard of care. The negative pressure test, however, was a particularly critical part of the temporary abandonment operation. As previously explained, the negative pressure test is a safety-critical test. Its purpose was to determine whether the cement and casing had successfully isolated the well from the reservoir, so that the heavy drilling mud — which otherwise prevented hydrocarbons from flowing into the well — could be safely removed. Therefore, the risk of foreseeable harm associated with misinterpreting a negative pressure test was great both in terms of severity and probability.

505. BP, as the operator, was ultimately responsible for interpreting the negative pressure test and declaring it a success or failure. Don Vidrine, the BP Well Site Leader on the rig, concluded the test was successful and instructed the Transocean rig crew to fully displace the well to seawater, despite the fact that he would later tell investigators that the results looked "squirrely" to him. All of the experts — even BP's — agree that Vidrine's interpretation was erroneous and that the test could not be deemed successful. A reasonable company man in Vidrine's situation would have concluded that the test was a failure and that it needed to be reconducted based on the anomalous pressure reading.

506. Moreover, about an hour after the test concluded, Mark Hafle, BP's senior drilling engineer in Houston, told Vidrine essentially that the test could not be considered a success given the inconsistent pressure readings. At this point, Vidrine should have been well-aware that the negative test had failed. Significantly, when that conversation ended at 9:02 p.m., there were approximately 36 minutes before the critical moment when hydrocarbons rose above the BOP — plenty of time for Vidrine or Hafle to halt the displacement and order a new negative pressure test.

511. Under the definition relied upon by the United States, "gross negligence" is an extreme departure from the care required under the circumstances or a failure to exercise even a slight care. For the reasons explained, the negative pressure test at the Macondo well demanded a level of care exceeding the "high" care typically required during such a test. There is no dispute that this negative pressure test

could not be considered a success. Vidrine should have understood this even before he spoke with Hafle. Hafle's comments to Vidrine should have confirmed what Vidrine should have already understood. Conducting a new negative pressure test is a precaution that imposed an extremely light burden compared to the foreseeable consequences that could, and did, result from the misinterpretation. Consequently, Vidrine's misinterpretation of the negative pressure test and subsequent failure to order a new one following his conversation with Hafle constitutes an extreme departure from the care required under the circumstances. For similar reasons, Hafle's failure to order a new negative pressure test, or pursue the issue further with Vidrine, or, at the very least, investigate the situation from his computer, also constitutes an extreme departure from the care required under the circumstances.

515. Accordingly, Hafle and Vidrine acted "recklessly" with respect to the negative pressure test, which satisfies both parties' definitions of "willful misconduct" as well as BP's definition of "gross negligence" under the CWA.

518. ... [T]he Court further finds and concludes that BPXP committed a series of negligent acts or omissions that resulted in the discharge of oil, which together amount to gross negligence and willful misconduct under the CWA. This is an additional and alternative grounds for finding BPXP's conduct amounted to gross negligence and willful misconduct.

519. BPXP's negligent acts that caused the blowout, explosion, and oil spill include: drilling the final 100 feet of the well with little or no margin, running the production casing with the float collar in unconverted mode *and* without a shoe filter, failing to verify whether the float collar converted by reverse circulating the well, not conducting a CBL, using LCM as a spacer for the displacement and negative pressure test, misinterpreting the negative pressure test, allowing simultaneous operations to occur during displacement, and failing to provide a displacement schedule to the Transocean drill crew. Notably, the decisions regarding drilling the final 100 feet, the CBL, and LCM-spacer were profit-driven decisions.

520. These instances of negligence, taken together, evince an extreme deviation from the standard of care and a conscious disregard of known risks.

521. BPXP was also negligent by pumping foamed cement without a successful stability test. Although cement instability did not cause the actual mode of failure (given the Court's conclusion that the cement was improperly placed through a breach in the shoe track), it is another instance of BP proceeding in the face of a known risk and therefore lends further support to the conclusion that BP's conduct was reckless.

531. ... [T]he Court [also] concludes that a corporation is vicariously liable under the CWA's enhanced penalty provision for the gross negligence and/or willful misconduct of its employees. Consequently, the Court need not determine whether BPXP authorized or ratified the conduct, or whether Vidrine and Hafle (or any other BP employee) were "managerial agents," or any other attribution standard that may apply under general maritime law, "traditional" common law, or any other law or jurisdiction.

C. Liability Under General Maritime Law

540. Here the Court determines under general maritime law the comparative fault of BP, Transocean, and Halliburton for the blowout, explosions, and oil spill.

The Court also determines whether any Defendant may be liable for punitive damages under general maritime law.

541. Here, "BP" refers to BP Exploration & Production Inc. and BP America Production Company, but not BP p.l.c. "Transocean" means Transocean Holdings LLC, Transocean Deepwater Inc., and Transocean Offshore Deepwater Drilling Inc., but not Transocean Ltd. or Triton Asset Leasing GmbH. "Halliburton" means Halliburton Energy Service, Inc. and Halliburton's Sperry division. BP, Transocean, and Halliburton are sometimes referred to collectively as "Defendants."

542. Based on the Court's findings and as further explained below, the Court concludes that each Defendant engaged in conduct that was negligent or worse and a legal cause of the blowout, explosion, and oil spill.

543. The Court further finds that BP's conduct was reckless. Transocean's conduct was negligent. Halliburton's conduct was also negligent.

544. The Court further concludes that the comparative fault of the Defendants, expressed as a percentage of total liability, is as follows:

BP: 67%
Transocean: 30%
Halliburton: 3%

545. Finally, the Court finds that the conduct of BP's employees was egregious enough that exemplary or punitive damages would be appropriate. However, in light of Fifth Circuit precedent, the Court concludes that BP is not liable for punitive damages.

549. As to Transocean, the Court has identified several instances where Transocean's conduct fell below the standard of care. This includes the drill crew's misinterpretation of the negative pressure test, the drill crew's failure to detect the pressure anomaly between 9:08 P.M. and 9:14 P.M., the drill crew's failure to perform a flow check followed by immediately shutting in the well at 9:31 P.M., the drill crew's failure to divert flow overboard, the master's failure to timely activate EDS, and Transocean's failure to properly maintain the BOP.

551. With respect to the misinterpretation of the negative pressure test, BP was ultimately responsible for its interpretation, not Transocean. It was BP's decision to use the left-over LCM as a spacer that caused the false reading on the kill line — a decision that was driven by its desire to save costs. BP instructed the Transocean drill crew to switch the negative pressure test from the drill crew's customary method, the drill pipe, to the kill line. The Court agrees with the view expressed by, among others, BP's expert Dr. Bourgoyne, that the negative pressure test would have been properly interpreted had the drill crew been permitted to continue the test on the drill pipe. Most importantly, the drill crew did not have the benefit of Mark Hafle's crucial observation about pressure anomalies, as did Don Vidrine.

552. Turning to the well monitoring and control issues, BP's acceptance of the negative pressure test likely created a misperception on the rig that any well-related issues were securely behind cemented pipe. Thus, the misinterpretation of the negative pressure test (for which BP bears most of the blame) contributed to the subsequent failures respecting well monitoring and control. BP's decision to permit simultaneous operations during displacement also contributed to the well control failures.

553. Furthermore, there is ample evidence that the drill crew was attentive and responsive to the well, such as when they reacted to the pressure spike at 9:17. Indeed, the drill crew noticed and reacted to the pressure anomaly between 9:27 and 9:30; while their response was incorrect, it hardly reflects a conscious disregard for a known risk or an extreme departure from the standard of care. The drill crew also noticed that the BOP's upper annular was not sealing the well and activated the variable bore rams, upon which they likely believed they had succeeded in stopping the blowout.

554. Another point about Transocean's well control failures is that they occurred in a relatively short time frame and in the context of a situation that escalated rapidly. The same can also be said about the master's failure to timely EDS. BP's misconduct, by contrast, was spread over a longer time frame. Thus, while Transocean had limited time to react properly, BP could consider its choices.

555. A related point is that BP's failures up to and including the negative pressure test created the catastrophic situation. Transocean's failures, by contrast, largely concern its inability (due in part to further failures by BP) to stop the catastrophe BP set in motion.

556. The Court also considers the proper actions taken by the marine crew following the explosions. BP's conduct, by contrast, lacks similar balance.

557. For these reasons, the Court concludes that Transocean's conduct was negligent and that Transocean's share of liability is considerably less than BP's.

558. As to Halliburton, it had two failures: one concerned cement and the other concerned well monitoring. With respect to the former, Halliburton's conduct is egregious. The Court refers not only to failures before the incident, but also to Halliburton's post-incident conduct involving "off the side" cement tests and destroyed computer simulations. Nevertheless, because the Court ultimately finds that the unstable foamed cement was not a cause of the blowout, no legal fault is allocated to Halliburton for these failures. Halliburton's failure concerning well monitoring was relatively small when compared to others' failures, and it was a failure shared by Transocean's drill crew.

559. Accordingly, to the extent claims against Halliburton were based on a strict products liability theory under maritime law, those claims fail in light of the finding that the cement, however defective, was not a cause of the blowout. This does not affect claims against Halliburton that sound in negligence, however.

560. The Court concludes that Halliburton's conduct was negligent and that Halliburton's share of liability is considerably less than both Transocean and BP.

561. Punitive damages may be imposed under general maritime law for reckless, willful, and wanton conduct.

562. Under the facts of this case, the Court finds that the conduct exhibited by BP's employees would make an award of punitive damages appropriate.

F. Liability Under the Oil Pollution Act of 1990

595. The Court previously held on summary judgment that BPXP is a "responsible party" under OPA with respect to the subsurface discharge of oil.

596. In the same ruling, the Court denied the United States' request for a finding that OPA's limits of liability did not apply based on the alleged violation of two federal regulations.

597. Although the point is perhaps moot with respect to BPXP, the Court believes it partially erred as to the latter ruling and corrects that mistake here.

598. OPA contains various liability caps for oil-spill related damages. These limits do not apply if

> the incident was proximately caused by . . . the violation of an applicable Federal safety, construction, or operating regulation by the responsible party, an agent or employee of the responsible party, or a person acting pursuant to a contractual relationship with the responsible party. . . .

599. The Government's argument was based in part on 30 C.F.R. § 250.420(a)(2), which in 2010 stated: "You must case and cement all wells. . . . Your casing and cementing programs must: . . . Prevent the direct or indirect release of fluids from any stratum through the wellbore into offshore waters."

600. The Government had argued that it was undisputed that the cement pumped into the Macondo well did not prevent the release of fluids from the formation through the wellbore and into offshore waters, therefore the OPA limits did not apply. The Court responded that the regulation was equivalent to a regulatory prohibition on oil spills, and therefore could not be relied upon to lift the liability cap as it would tend to circumvent the "proximate cause" requirement in OPA.

601. The Court has a far better understanding of the importance of cementing in offshore wells than it did in 2012, when it ruled on the Government's motion. Furthermore, the Court believes that a breach of 30 C.F.R. § 250.420(a)(2) can be a "proximate cause[ ]" of an "incident" for purposes of removing OPA's liability cap. The Court further finds that the cementing program at Macondo clearly did not prevent the direct or indirect release of fluids from a stratum, through the wellbore, and into offshore waters, and this failure was, in fact, a proximate cause of the incident.

602. Accordingly, the Court REVERSES IN PART its prior ruling of February 22, 2012.

603. The Court previously ruled that Transocean was not a "responsible party" with respect to the subsurface discharge of oil, and therefore was not liable for removal costs and damages under OPA's general liability provision, 33 U.S.C. § 2702. However, that ruling also noted that Transocean might be liable under another provision in OPA, 33 U.S.C. § 2704(c)(3), which makes an "owner or operator" (as opposed to a "responsible party") of an "Outer Continental Shelf ("OCS") facility" liable to government entities (as opposed to private parties) for all removal costs (as opposed to damages), without limit, when oil discharges from said facility.

608. . . . OPA uses "operator" in connection with vessels, onshore facilities, pipelines, and OCS facilities without any indication that the term carries a different or specific meaning when used in the OCS facility context. Furthermore, while the Court agrees that BP ultimately controlled and directed all operations at Macondo, the Court views Transocean as more than one who merely performed "mechanical

activation of pumps and valves." Instead, Transocean "conduct[ed] operations specifically related to pollution, that is operations having to do with the leakage or disposal of [oil]." For example, Transocean's drill crew did not need direction or approval from the BP Well Site Leader to activate the BOP and shut in the well. And, as the Court has found, the failure to do so timely actually resulted in oil pollution from the offshore facility.

609. Accordingly, the Court finds that "Transocean" (meaning Transocean Holdings LLC, Transocean Deepwater Inc., and Transocean Offshore Deepwater Drilling Inc., but not Transocean Ltd. or Triton Asset Leasing GmbH.) was an "operator" under 33 U.S.C. § 2704(c). The Court notes, however, that Transocean's liability to government entities for removal costs is ultimately shifted to BP by virtue of the contractual indemnity.

points for discussion

1. *A big case.* It is highly unusual for a district court to reverse its own previous ruling. It is a result of the complex, multi-phase nature of the case, in which determinations of liability occur at multiple stages, after multiple fact-findings.

2. *On punishment.* Omitted from this excerpt of Judge Barbier's long opinion is his ultimate ruling that punitive damages would *not* be available under general maritime law, despite his specific findings that BP engaged in "reckless, willful, and wanton conduct," and that "the conduct exhibited by BP's employees would make an award of punitive damages appropriate." The reason was that a Fifth Circuit court held that "operational recklessness or willful disregard is generally insufficient to visit punitive damages upon the employer. Rather, the

BP well supervisors Donald Vidrine and Robert Kaluza were later criminally charged with manslaughter for the deaths of the 11 DWH workers. Manslaughter charges against Vidrine were dropped after he agreed to testify against Kaluza. Vidrine, who had worked for 40 years in the oil industry, died in 2017 of cancer.

After a trial, Kaluza was acquitted. The prosecution theory was that Kaluza omitted important information from Vidrine as Vidrine took over the night shift from Kaluza. A *Forbes* article titled, "Two Years After Ruling, BP Engineer Still Carries Burden of Prosecution," was a sympathetic treatment of Kaluza's role in the disaster: "He knew that the situation was dire, but what he did not know was that he would be blamed for it." Walter Pavlo, *Two Years After Ruling, BP Engineer Still Carries Burden of Prosecution*, Forbes (Jan. 8, 2018). Others also expressed the notion that Vidrine and Kaluza were scapegoats, that they were being held to account for BP's culture of cost-cutting and risk-taking that allowed the tragedy to occur. Given the extent of damage, however, it is extraordinary that no single individual was sentenced to jail.

conduct must emanate from corporate policy or that a corporate official with policy-making authority participated in, approved of, or subsequently ratified the egregious conduct." 21 F. Supp. 3d at 749.

3. *Congressional settlement.* Congress actually passed legislation allocating settlement money from the case. The federal settlement under the Clean Water Act, the Oil Pollution Act, and the special legislation, the RESTORE Act, totaled $20.8 billion, settling all civil and criminal claims against BP, its partner Anadarko, Transocean and Halliburton, and all claims by the five Gulf states.

The RESTORE Act mandated that a certain percentage of all administrative and civil penalties, amounting to $5.3 billion, be allocated to a trust fund dedicated to restoring the Gulf of Mexico ecology and economy. In addition, BP will pay $8.8 billion for natural resource damages, assessed under 33 U.S.C. § 2702(b)(2)(A). In addition to the $20.8 billion settlement, BP funded $500 million in additional research, and ultimately paid out approximately $6 billion to over 220,000 private individual and business claimants.

Given Judge Barbier's account of the accident, it is challenging to find satisfaction in the civil and criminal penalties paid by BP and the other defendants, even as BP reported that its estimate of its cost, including its

Figure 4-9. The Map Shows the Extent of the Spill about Four Weeks after it Began

private business losses, exceeded $60 billion. In retrospect, the tragedy could have been avoided at so many points, not the least of which was the construction of a corporate culture of cost-cutting and risk-taking. The exercise of just routine diligence at any one of multiple points would have prevented the explosion and spill and the loss of life. But how much penalty is enough? Do you think that this case creates enough of an incentive for offshore oil operations to take better precautions against these sorts of incidents?

b. Oil Spill Cleanup

The Deepwater Horizon tragedy not only brought to the fore surprisingly complicated issues of proper plaintiffs, proper defendants, and proper damages, but also issues pertaining to cleanup procedures. The following case pertains to the motion for summary judgment by Nalco, the maker of a chemical dispersant used to try to clean up the 210 million gallons of spilled crude oil.

In re Oil Spill by the Oilrig "Deepwater Horizon" in the Gulf of Mexico, on April 20, 2010

2012 WL 5960192 (E.D. La. Nov. 28, 2012)

Judge BARBIER delivered the opinion of the United States District Court, Eastern District of Louisiana.

Before the Court is Defendant Nalco's Motion for Summary Judgment, and related briefing. Nalco's motion seeks to dismiss all claims asserted against it in the B3 Master Complaint. . . .

I. Factual and Procedural History

***

The oil spill instigated a massive response involving government entities and officials, BP and its contractors and subcontractors, and thousands of individuals. Responders attempted a number of countermeasures, including skimming, absorbing, burning, and — most relevant here — chemically dispersing oil. Dispersants "are chemical agents that emulsify, disperse, or solubilize oil into the water column or promote the surface spreading of oil slicks to facilitate dispersal of the oil into the water column." 40 C.F.R. § 300.5. The intended result is to reduce the risk of direct contact by wildlife and reduce the amount of oil impacting sensitive nearshore and shoreline areas. Furthermore, "microbial biodegradation of oil appears to be enhanced by dispersal because of the larger surface area available as compared to a surface slick." Approximately 1.8 million gallons of the dispersants Corexit EC9500A and Corexit EC9527A (collectively, "Corexit") were applied either to the water's surface or beneath the water's surface, near the source of the discharge. Nalco is the manufacturer of Corexit.

On August 10, 2010, the Judicial Panel on Multidistrict Litigation transferred cases arising from the DEEPWATER HORIZON/Macondo Well incident to this Court for consolidated or coordinated pretrial proceedings. . . . This Court organized the various types of claims into several "pleading bundles." Relevant here is the B3 bundle, which concerns claims relating to post-explosion clean-up efforts. . . .

The Plaintiffs' Steering Committee ("PSC") filed a B3 Master Complaint, which asserts, *inter alia,* claims under general maritime law and state law on behalf of individuals allegedly injured by exposure to oil, chemical dispersant, or a mixture of oil and dispersant. The B3 Plaintiffs include vessel captains and crew participating in clean-up activities, workers that decontaminated vessels soiled by oil and/or dispersants, workers that participated in onshore cleanup, and coastal residents and vacationers who claim exposure by virtue of proximity to coastal waters. The B3 Plaintiffs complain of a variety of exposure-related injuries, including headaches, nausea, respiratory problems, eye irritation, rashes, burns, and lesions. The B3 Master Complaint also alleges that the B3 Plaintiffs may have contracted latent illnesses that may take years to manifest and, accordingly, asserts a claim for medical monitoring costs. Named defendants include Nalco, the "Clean-Up Defendants" (private entities that sprayed Corexit), BP, and the other parties involved with the DEEPWATER HORIZON and Macondo Well (Transocean Ltd., Anadarko Petroleum Corp., MOEX Offshore 2007 LLC, et al.).

***

Nalco has now submitted its motion for summary judgment, memoranda in support, and reply briefs. The PSC and another plaintiff, Malcolm Coco (allegedly exposed to and injured by Corexit, *see* C.A. No. 11-946), filed oppositions. The Court has also received numerous letters from *pro se* individuals who are opposed to Nalco's motion. Briefing is also complete on the Clean-Up Defendants' motions for summary judgment, but those motions are not considered here.

***

III. Discussion

***

B. Statutory and Regulatory Background

Since it was enacted in 1972, Section 311 of the Clean Water Act ("CWA") has declared, "it is the policy of the United States that there should be no discharges of oil . . . into or upon the navigable waters of the United States. . . ." (codified at 33 U.S.C. § 1321(b)(1)). Consistent with this policy statement, the CWA established certain federal obligations and powers with respect to an oil spill. As detailed below, the Oil Pollution Act of 1990 ("OPA") made significant changes to these provisions. However, even before OPA's amendments the CWA authorized the President "to act to remove or arrange for the removal" of discharged oil, "unless he determines such removal will be done properly by the owner or operator of the vessel, onshore facility, or offshore facility from which the discharge occurs." 33 U.S.C. § 1321(c)(1) (1988). . . . In the case of a large discharge of oil that "created a substantial threat of a pollution hazard to the public health or welfare of the United States" (hereinafter, "Substantial Spill") the CWA permitted, but did not require, the federal government to "coordinate and direct" all public and private response efforts and "summarily remove, and, if necessary, destroy such vessel by whatever means are available without regard to any provisions of law governing the employment of personnel or the expenditure of appropriated funds." *Id.* § 1321(d) (1988).

OPA amended the CWA to, among other things, expand federal authority over, and responsibility for, oil spill responses. For all spills, regardless of size or character, the CWA now requires that "[t]he President shall, in accordance with the National Contingency Plan and any appropriate Area Contingency Plan, *ensure effective and immediate removal* of a discharge . . . of oil. . . ." 33 U.S.C. § 1321(c)(1)(A) (emphasis added). In the case of smaller spills, the President may choose from a variety of options when determining how to ensure effective and immediate removal: the President may remove or arrange for the removal of the discharge; direct removal actions; remove or destroy a vessel discharging oil "by whatever means are available"; or simply monitor removal efforts. However, when there is a Substantial Spill, the CWA deletes the option of monitoring removal efforts. Instead, "[t]he President *shall direct all Federal, State, and private actions* to remove" a Substantial Spill. *Id.* § 1321(c)(2)(A) (emphasis added). Legislative history states that this provision was "designed to eliminate the confusion evident in recent spills where the lack of clear delineation of command and management responsibility impeded prompt and effective response." H.R.Rep. No. 101-653, at 45 (1990) (Conf.Rep.), *reprinted in* 1990 U.S.C.C.A.N. 779, 825. When addressing a Substantial Spill, the President may remove the discharge, arrange for the removal of the discharge, or destroy a discharging vessel, as he could for smaller spills; however, to "facilitate emergency response," the President may perform these actions "without regard to any other provision of law governing contracting procedures or employment of personnel by the Federal Government." 33 U.S.C. § 1321(c)(2)(B). . . .

The CWA also required the President to prepare a National Contingency Plan ("NCP"), which "shall provide for efficient, coordinated, and effective action to minimize damage from oil . . . , including containment, dispersal, and removal . . . ," as well as a National Response System that is consistent with the NCP. *Id.* § 1321(d), (j). The National Response System establishes three levels of federal contingency plans: the NCP, Regional Contingency Plans, and Area Contingency Plans. 40 C.F.R. § 300.210.

The NCP mirrors the CWA's provision regarding federal authority and responsibility. Under the NCP, the Federal On-Scene Coordinator ("FOSC") "directs response efforts and coordinates all other efforts at the scene of the discharge or release." *Id.* § 300.120(a). When there is a Substantial Spill, "the [F]OSC must direct all response efforts" and "should declare as expeditiously as practicable to spill response participants that the federal government will control the response." *Id.* § 300.305(d)(2); *see also id.* § 300.322(b). The FOSC also may take additional response actions not explicitly provided in the NCP. *Id.* § 300.322(c)(3); *see also id.*

§ 300.324(a)(4) (permitting similar actions when there is a "worst case discharge"). If a spill "is so complex that it requires extraordinary coordination of federal, state, local, and responsible party resources to contain and clean up the discharge," the Coast Guard may declare a "spill of national significance" and name a National Incident Commander who will "assume the role of the [F]OSC in communicating with affected parties and the public, and coordinating federal, state, local, and international resources at the national level." *Id.* § 300.5, 300.323.

The CWA similarly states that each federal agency, State, or private party participating in an oil spill response under the CWA shall act in accordance with the NCP (or other response plan required by the CWA), unless directed otherwise by the President or the FOSC. 33 U.S.C. § 1321(c)(3); *see also id.* § 1321(d)(4) ("After publication of the [NCP], "the removal of oil . . . and actions to minimize damage from oil . . . shall, to the greatest extent possible, be in accordance with the [NCP]."). Furthermore, parties rendering care, assistance, or advice consistent with the NCP or as directed by the President are explicitly immunized from removal costs or damages that result from their actions or omissions. *Id.* § 1321(c)(4)(A). Legislative history states that this immunity is intended to encourage "immediate and effective responses" and that "[w]ithout such a provision the substantial financial risks and liability exposures associated with spill response could deter vessel operators, cleanup contractors, and cleanup cooperatives from prompt, aggressive response." H.R.Rep. No. 101-653, at 45. The CWA also immunizes the federal government "for any damages arising from its actions or omissions relating to any response plan required by [Section 311 of the CWA]. 33 U.S.C. § 1321(j)(8).

The CWA and the NCP contemplate that chemical dispersants may be used in response to an oil discharge. The CWA requires the NCP to contain, *inter alia*, "[p]rocedures and techniques to be employed in identifying, containing, ***dispersing,*** and removing oil . . . ," *id.* § 1321(d)(2)(F) (emphasis added), as well as:

A schedule, prepared in cooperation with the States, identifying —

(i) ***dispersants,*** other chemicals, and other spill mitigating devices and substances, if any, that may be used in carrying out the Plan,
(ii) the waters in which such ***dispersants,*** other chemicals, and other spill mitigating devices and substances may be used, and
(iii) the quantities of such ***dispersant,*** other chemicals, or other spill mitigating device or substance which can be used safely in such waters. . . .

Id. § 1321(d)(2)(G) (emphasis added); *see also id.* § 1321(j)(4) (requiring Area Contingency Plans to list available "dispersants or other mitigating substances and devices"). Furthermore, "in the case of any dispersant . . . not specifically identified in such schedule[,] . . . the President, or his delegate, may, on a case-by-case basis, identify the dispersants . . . which may be used, the waters in which they may be used, and the quantities which can be used safely in such waters." *Id.* § 1321(d)(2)(G).

Accordingly, the EPA prepared and maintains the NCP Product Schedule. 40 C.F.R. § 300.900(a), 300.905. If a dispersant is listed on the NCP Product Schedule, then the FOSC may authorize its use if the EPA (and sometimes other state representatives) concurs in such use and, when practicable, after consulting with certain natural resource trustees. *Id.* § 300.910(b). However, if a dispersant listed on the NCP Product Schedule is also "preauthorized" for use in specified circumstances under a Regional Contingency Plan or Area Contingency Plan, then the FOSC may authorize the use of that dispersant without the concurrence of, or consulting with, any other agency or officer. *Id.* § 300.910(a). The NCP also permits the FOSC to authorize the use of dispersants not listed on the NCP Product Schedule when it is necessary to prevent or substantially reduce a hazard to human life. *Id.* § 300.910(d).

To be included on the NCP Product Schedule, the manufacturer must submit certain data to the EPA. *See id.* § 300.905(2), 300.920(a). This includes special handling and worker precautions; shelf life; recommended application procedures, concentrations, and conditions for use depending on water salinity, water temperature, and types and ages of pollutants; results of certain effectiveness tests; results of certain toxicity tests; and component information. *Id.* § 300.915(a) & app. C. After reviewing the submission, the EPA determines whether to add the dispersant on the NCP Product Schedule. *Id.* § 300.920(a)(2). The EPA may also request further documentation or conduct its own testing on the product. The regulation notes, however, that "[t]he listing of a product on the NCP Product Schedule does not constitute approval of the product." *Id.* § 300.920(e).

C. The Use of Corexit During the DEEPWATER HORIZON/Macondo Well Oil Spill

Corexit EC9527A and Corexit EC9500A have been listed on the NCP Product Schedule since 1978 and 1994, respectively, and continue to be listed to this day. Both versions of Corexit also were preauthorized for use under the circumstances described in the Regional Response Plans for Region IV (covering Gulf waters adjacent to Mississippi, Alabama, Florida, and other areas) and Region VI (covering Gulf waters adjacent to Texas and Louisiana). Preauthorization under these plans generally permitted the FOSC to quickly authorize surface application of any dispersant on the NCP Product Schedule to waters either ten meters deep or three nautical miles from shore, whichever is farther from the shore.

The Commander of the Coast Guard's Marine Safety Unit at Morgan City, Louisiana became the first FOSC to direct the response to the DEEPWATER HORIZON/Macondo Well incident. On April 23, Rear Admiral Mary Landry succeeded as FOSC and established the Unified Area Command (discussed below). On April 29, the United States Coast Guard classified the spill as a "spill of national significance" pursuant to 40 C.F.R. § 300.323. . . .

The Unified Area Command included representatives from the Coast Guard, EPA, BP, and Transocean (owner of the DEEPWATER HORIZON). Each day, the FOSC and other members of the Unified Area Command would evaluate the risks posed by the oil spill, the tools available to minimize the damage, and otherwise manage the response. However, the FOSC exercised ultimate decision-making authority over response activities, including the use of dispersants.

On April 21, 2010, the FOSC determined that the use of dispersants would likely provide a net environmental benefit and authorized the first aerial application of Corexit under the preauthorization guidelines of the Regional Contingency Plan for Region VI. Between April 22 and July 19, the FOSC, with the appropriate concurrence of and/or consultation with other officials (when required), approved surface and subsea applications of Corexit on a daily basis. These authorizations included limits on when, where, and in what quantities Corexit could be applied. At times the FOSC authorized the use of dispersants outside the preauthorization zones (e.g., within three nautical miles of the shore) when it was deemed necessary to prevent or substantially reduce a hazard to human life. Nalco did not decide whether, when, where, how, or in what quantities Corexit was applied in response to the DEEPWATER HORIZON/Macondo Well oil spill.

D. Arguments and Law Regarding Preemption

***

The B3 Master Complaint alleged that Corexit was defective, unreasonably dangerous, and toxic under state tort law and general maritime law. . . . While Nalco disputes allegations that its products were defective, etc., it also contends that the B3 claims are preempted because they conflict with the FOSC's decisions to use Corexit and/or present an obstacle to the objectives of the CWA and NCP.

The PSC counters the preemption argument by asserting that its claims against Nalco sound in products liability, not that the government was wrong in its decision to use Corexit. According to the PSC, even if Corexit EC9527A and Corexit EC9500A were not considered unreasonably dangerous when they were initially listed on the NCP Product Schedule in 1978 and 1994, advancements in science since that time have raised the standard of care. Thus, Corexit was an unreasonably dangerous product when it was used in 2010, and tort law imposed a corresponding duty on Nalco to discontinue Corexit or change its formula. Citing *In re Methyl Tertiary Butyl Ether ("MTBE") Products Liability Litigation,* the PSC argues that no federal law required Nalco to submit Corexit for inclusion on the NCP Product Schedule; thus Nalco cannot assert that compliance with both federal law and state tort law was an impossibility. Furthermore, the PSC argues that the savings clauses in OPA and the CWA and the CWA's immunity provision for responders — which does not immunize personal injury claims — reflect Congress' intent to preserve these claims. The PSC also relies upon the NCP's disclaimer regarding dispersants listed on the NCP Product Schedule. Finally, the PSC and another Plaintiff, Malcolm Coco, argue that Nalco did not fulfill the NCP Product Schedule's submission requirements.

***

E. Analysis

A fundamental objective of the CWA is to "ensure effective and immediate removal of a discharge . . . of oil. . . ." 33 U.S.C. § 1321(c)(1)(A). Likewise, a goal of the NCP is to "provide for efficient, coordinated, and effective action to minimize damage from oil. . . ." *Id.* § 1321(d)(2). In the case of an oil spill as massive and dangerous as the one from the DEEPWATER HORIZON/Macondo Well (i.e., a Substantial Spill and a "spill of national significance"), Congress determined that these objectives are best achieved if the President directs all levels of the response — federal, state, and private. . . . The purpose was to eliminate confusion that impeded past oil spill responses by establishing a clear chain of command and responsibility. . . .

The CWA/NCP also expressly contemplated that dispersants may be used in response to an oil spill. *See* 33 C.F.R. § 1321(d)(2), (d)(2)(F), (d)(2)(G); 40 C.F.R. § 300.910. The NCP established procedures for submitting and listing a dispersant on the NCP Product Schedule, and empowered the FOSC (sometimes with the concurrence of the EPA, etc.) to determine when to use a dispersant. 40 C.F.R. § 300.910.

Although chemical dispersants have been used as an oil spill countermeasure for decades, it is clear that they are not without controversy. *See, e.g.,* Queale, *supra* note 3, at 66-67 (noting that dispersants have been used over 213 times since 1967 and explaining that "[i]t is the trade-off between effectiveness and toxicity that is at the heart of the dispersant controversy"). Likewise, the fact that the NCP Product Schedule requires the manufacturer to provide toxicity data and handling precautions suggests that the federal government has long been aware that there may be dangers or drawbacks associated with dispersants. . . . However, this also reflects that these dangers do not preclude the use of a dispersant — they are one of several factors to be considered by the FOSC. According to the EPA:

> EPA believes that the best approach to regulating dispersants is to . . . provide [F]OSCs, RRTs [Regional Response Teams], and Area Committees the toxicity data and *allow them to make decisions on dispersant use by weighing the toxicity data against other variables and the effectiveness data* for those dispersants that meet or exceed the effectiveness threshold.

59 Fed. Reg. 47,384, 47,410 (Sept. 15, 1994) (emphasis added). The documents provided to the Court similarly evince that the FOSC knew there were potential dangers associated with Corexit, but also that there may be significant negative consequences if Corexit was not used.

Thus, the design of the CWA/NCP is that the FOSC (and sometimes with the concurrence of the EPA, etc.), after weighing the pros and cons, will determine whether it is appropriate to use a particular dispersant. When this is considered with the fact that the CWA and NCP required the FOSC to direct all levels of this response, it follows that it would be improper for the Court to second guess the FOSC's decision to use (or not use) a particular dispersant — just as it would be improper for a State or private person to disobey the FOSC's direction during a response. This conclusion is clear even if the CWA did not expressly immunize the government from suit. The PSC essentially admits this point, but urges that the B3 claims are not preempted because they target the allegedly defective nature of Corexit, not the government's decision to use it. This distinction lacks significance, however, because — as further discussed below — the B3 claims would still create an obstacle to federal law. *Cf. Ouellette,* 479 U.S. at 497 ("This delineation of authority represents Congress' considered judgment as to the best method of serving the public interest and reconciling the often competing concerns of those affected by the pollution. ***It would be extraordinary for Congress, after devising an elaborate permit system that sets clear standards, to tolerate common-law suits that have the potential to undermine this regulatory structure.***" (emphasis added)).

The effect of state law, rather than its purpose, governs the preemption analysis. If the Court were to permit the B3 claims (and irrespective of whether Corexit is found to be defective or unreasonably dangerous), then, during the next Substantial Spill or "spill of national significance," the threat of liability might cause the manufacturer of dispersant X to refuse to provide its product, even though the FOSC determined that dispersant X should be used. Such a refusal, or perhaps even a hesitation by the manufacturer, would conflict with the statutory and regulatory design of placing the FOSC in charge of all levels of the response and empowering him or her to determine if, when, where, and how dispersants should be used. More importantly, this refusal would deprive the response of a tool expressly contemplated by federal law and, consequently, impede the FOSC's ability to "ensure effective and immediate removal" of oil and the "efficient, coordinated, and effective" response intended by the NCP. Thus, despite the fact that the B3 claims avoid a direct attack on the FOSC's decisions to use Corexit, they still stand as an obstacle to the accomplishment and execution of the full purposes and objectives of Congress. . . .

The savings clauses in OPA and the CWA, *supra* note 11, do not persuade the Court otherwise. The Supreme Court "has repeatedly decline[d] to give broad effect to saving clauses where doing so would upset the careful regulatory scheme established by federal law." *Geier,* 529 U.S. at 870. . . . (citations and quotations omitted); *see also AT & T Mobility LLC v. Concepcion,* ___U.S. ___, 131 S. Ct. 1740, 1748, 179 L. Ed. 2d 742 (2011) ("[A] federal statute's saving clause cannot in reason be construed as [allowing] a common law right, the continued existence of which would be absolutely inconsistent with the provisions of the act. In other words, the act cannot be held to destroy itself."). . . .

✳✳✳

The Court has also received numerous letters from *pro se* individuals who complain of the harmful effects of Corexit and, for this reason, oppose Nalco's motion. The issue before the Court is whether the claims against Nalco are, as a matter of law, preempted by the CWA and NCP. For clarity, the Court does not decide whether Corexit was toxic, defective, unreasonably dangerous, etc. While the Court is sympathetic to these complaints, they are irrelevant to the issue of preemption.

The Court also makes clear that today's decision is limited to Nalco. The Court does not address the pending motions by the Clean-Up Defendants, nor does this decision affect the liability of BP or any other defendants. On a related note, Nalco argued derivative immunity as an alternative defense to liability. Because resolution of the preemption issue is dispositive of Nalco's motion, the Court does not address derivative immunity.

IV. Conclusion

For the reasons explained above, the Court finds that the claims in the B3 Master Complaint asserted against Nalco, whether brought under state law or general maritime law, are preempted by the Clean Water Act and the National Contingency Plan. Accordingly,

IT IS ORDERED that Nalco's Motion for Summary Judgment, Rec. Doc. 6541, is **GRANTED** and the claims against Nalco in the B3 Master Complaint are **DISMISSED WITH PREJUDICE.**

point for discussion

1. *Lingering questions.* Why is it necessary, according to Judge Barbier, to consolidate control over cleanup efforts under the Federal On-site Coordinator? Why can't Louisiana take charge of cleanup over its own waters? Doesn't a state's police power allow it to protect its own citizens against products that are found to be harmful to human health?

   Corexit 9500A and 9527A were both listed on the National Contingency Plan Product Schedule. Curiously, neither Corexit 9500A and 9527A had been tested for exposure to humans. Because the old Toxic Substances Control Act effectively placed the burden of proof on the U.S. Environmental Protection Agency (EPA) to show an "unreasonable risk," EPA had no data on the toxicity of Corexit. EPA Administrator Lisa Jackson pressed Nalco to provide a list of ingredients, and it eventually revealed that one of the active ingredients is 2-butoxyethanol, a chemical that can cause liver and kidney damage if ingested.

   The Toxic Substances Control Act was amended in 2016, by the Frank R. Lautenberg Chemical Safety Act, named posthumously for the U.S. Senator from New Jersey who spearheaded the bipartisan efforts to reform regulation of toxic chemicals. But a large number of chemicals remaining on the National Contingency Plan Product Schedule still await testing. Could a products liability lawsuit be preempted by the Clean Water Act under these circumstances?

2. Natural Resource Damages

Teri Schure, Exxon Valdez Oil Spill: 21 Years Later

http://www.worldpress.org (June 15, 2010)

Four minutes after midnight on March 24, 1989, the Exxon Valdez ran aground on Bligh Reef in Alaska's Prince William Sound. Eleven million gallons of oil spewed into one of the most bountiful marine ecosystems in the world. It killed birds, marine mammals and fish and devastated the ecosystem in the oil's path. North

Slope crude spoiled lands and waters that had sustained Alaska native people for millennia.

Within a week, currents and winds pushed the slick 90 miles from the site of the tanker, out of Prince William Sound into the Gulf of Alaska. It eventually reached nearly 600 miles away from the wreck contaminating 1,500 miles of shoreline — about the length of California's coast — and was described as the "largest oil spill to date in U.S. waters."

As many as half a million birds died. Over 30,000 carcasses of 90 species of birds were plucked from the beaches, but this was only a fraction of the actual mortality, and harm to birds from chronic effects and decreased reproduction continues today.

Some fish died, but the most serious damage was to their critical spawning and rearing habitats. Salmon spawn in the intertidal zone, herring in the sub-tidal zone on kelp, and Dolly Varden and cutthroat trout feed in shallow water. Over 100 salmon streams were oiled.

Shoreline cleanup began in April of 1989 and continued until September of 1989 for the first year of the response. The response effort continued in 1990 and 1991 with cleanup in the summer months and limited shoreline monitoring in the winter months. Fate and effects monitoring by state and federal agencies are ongoing.

BP in Perspective

In an NBC News report on June 11, scientists claimed that the amount of oil being spilled in the Gulf of Mexico [as a result of the British Petroleum Deepwater Horizon explosion] was the equivalent of "one Exxon Valdez spill every one to 10 days."

To understand the devastating ramifications of the BP oil spill, it is imperative to review how the Exxon oil spill affected Prince William Sound from April of 1989 to today — 21 years later.

An Exxon Valdez Oil Spill Trustee Council was formed to oversee restoration of the injured ecosystem. The Council consists of three state and three federal trustees (or their designees). The Council is advised by members of the public and by members of the scientific community. Meetings are open to the public.

"Following the oil and its impacts over the past 20 years has changed our understanding of the long-term damage from an oil spill," the council stated.

"We know that risk assessment for future spills must consider what the total damages will be over a longer period of time, rather than only the acute damages in the days and weeks following a spill."

One of the lessons learned is that a spill's impacts can last a long time in a habitat with calm, cold waters like Prince William Sound, the council said.

None of that was expected "at the time of the spill or even 10 years later," it added. "In 1999, beaches in the sound appeared clean on the surface. Some subsurface oil had been reported in a few places, but it was expected to decrease over time and, most importantly, to have lost its toxicity due to weathering. A few species were not recovering at the expected rate in some areas, but continuing exposure to oil was not suspected as the primary cause."

It turns out that oil often got trapped in semi-enclosed bays for weeks, going up and down with the tide and some of it being pulled down into the sediment below the seabed.

"The cleanup efforts and natural processes, particularly in the winter, cleaned the oil out of the top 2-3 inches, where oxygen and water can flow," the council said, "but did little to affect the large patches of oil farther below the surface."

The group cited a faster transition to double-hulled oil tankers as the best protection for wildlife. Single-hulled tankers are still allowed in U.S. waters until 2015.

Status of Restoration

To the naked eye, Prince William Sound may appear "normal." Visitors can see spectacular, unspoiled vistas of islands surrounded by blue-green waters and mountain-rimmed fjords. But if you look beneath the surface, oil continues to contaminate beaches, national parks and designated wilderness. In fact, the Office of Technology Assessment estimated beach cleanup and oil skinning recovered only 3-4 percent of the Exxon Valdez oil, and studies by government scientists estimated that only 14 percent of the oil was removed during cleanup operations.

Pockets of oil — an estimated 16,000 gallons, according to federal researchers — remain buried in small portions of the intertidal zone hard hit by the spill. Moreover, surveys "have documented lingering oil also on the Kenai Peninsula and the Katmai coast, over 450 miles away," according to the council.

Twenty years after the oil spill, the ecosystem is still suffering. Substantial contamination of mussel beds persists, and this remarkably unweathered oil is a continuing source of toxic hydrocarbons. Sea otters, river otters, Barrow's goldeneyes and harlequin ducks have showed evidence of continued hydrocarbon exposure.

The depressed population of Pacific herring—a critical source of food for over 40 predators including seabirds, harbor seals and Steller sea lions — is having severe impacts up the food chain. Wildlife population declines continue for harbor seal, killer whales, harlequin ducks, common loon, pigeon guillemot, and pelagic red-faced cormorants and double-crested cormorants.

The Exxon oil spill resulted in profound physiological effects to fish and wildlife. These included reproductive failure, genetic damage, curved spines, lowered growth and body weights, altered feeding habits, reduced egg volume, liver damage, eye tumors and debilitating brain lesions.

In its 20th anniversary *Status Report*, the Exxon Valdez Oil Spill Trustee Council lists only 10 of the 31 injured resources and services they monitor as "recovered" (which includes bald eagles and river otters). Ten more, including killer whales and sea otters are listed as "recovering." Populations of Pacific herring and pigeon guillemots are listed as "not recovering."

***

Twenty years after the Exxon Valdez spilled 11 million gallons of crude oil in Alaska's Prince William Sound, oil persists in the region and, in some places, "is nearly as toxic as it was the first few weeks after the spill," according to the council overseeing restoration efforts.

"This Exxon Valdez oil is decreasing at a rate of 0-4 percent per year," the Exxon Valdez Oil Spill Trustee Council stated. "At this rate, the remaining oil will take decades and possibly centuries to disappear entirely."

The Oil Pollution Act specifies natural resource damages as a category of compensatory damages to be paid by a responsible party. Natural resource restoration occurs in three stages: pre-assessment, injury assessment and restoration planning, and restoration implementation. Injury occurs if "[a]n observable or measurable adverse change in a natural resource or impairment of a natural resource service." 15 C.F.R. § 990.30. An injury may be direct or indirect, and may involve destruction of a resource or its loss of use or service. *Id.* Injury includes adverse effects on survival, growth and reproduction; health physiology and biological condition; behavior; community composition; ecological processes and services; physical and chemical habitat quality or structure; or public services such as recreation. The categories of natural resources that were assessed for damages include: (i) recreational use, (ii) nearshore marine ecosystems, (iii) birds, (iv) sea turtles, (v) beach habitat, (vi) water column species, (vii) marine mammals, and (viii) benthic resources.

James W. Boyd, Lost Ecosystem Goods and Services as a Measure of Marine Oil Pollution Damages

Resources for the Future Discussion Paper 10-31 (2010)

Marine vessel, terminal, and harbour operations can generate a range of legal damages arising from liability for response and cleanup costs, damages to private property, and damages to public natural resources, the focus here. Public resources that can be affected include water quality, beach and other coastal recreational resources, coral reefs, commercial and recreational fisheries, sea grass beds, and habitats for bird and other animal populations. They are in the public domain, neither owned nor traded, but nonetheless clearly economically and socially valuable.

Liability for lost public goods and services is an established legal principle. In U.S. waters, for example, owners and operators are liable for natural resource damages (NRDs). NRD liability serves an important deterrence and compensation function by forcing owner operators to pay the costs of damages to valuable public resources. The goal of U.S. NRD liability law is to "make the environment and public whole" following a pollution event. In economic terms, this means calculating monetary damages equivalent to the social benefit lost as a result of a release, grounding, or other marine event.

At this writing, the full scope of damages arising from the April 20 explosion of the BP *Deepwater Horizon* oil rig in the Gulf of Mexico — and the subsequent massive oil spill — are not yet known, but predicted to exceed those from 1989's *Exxon Valdez* incident.

At a conceptual level, NRDs require us to measure lost ecological wealth. Doing so requires knowing two things: how natural systems produce valuable biophysical goods and services and what the value of those goods and service is.

Within ecology and economics, *assessment of ecosystem goods and services* is a growing area of inquiry. Broadly put, ecosystem services refers to the dependence of economic wealth and human wellbeing on natural systems. While the promise of a cohesive framework for assessing all types of damages is not yet realized, many scholars are working toward this goal through more rigorous conceptualization and communication of the links between changes in natural systems and effects on human welfare.

Such a framework would be a powerful tool for calculating natural resource damages (and marine damages specifically). Lost ecosystem goods and services are the right metric to internalize social costs and make the public whole following a marine pollution or damage incident. Given this equivalence between damages and lost goods and services, the calculation of marine damages can and will hinge on the degree to which ecosystem goods and services can be understood and valued.

NRD assessment is seen as controversial because there is widespread confusion over how to account for ecosystem goods and services that are lost or gained. Complex natural systems stymie the search for clear causal relationships between a spill and many of the damages they cause. This leads to legitimate disagreement over the magnitude of legal liability. Much more needs to be done by ecologists and economists in order to calculate damages with accuracy. But just because a damage is difficult to precisely quantify does not mean that it isn't real and economically significant. The discipline of treating natural systems as sources of wealth provides a guide to the kinds of information and analysis necessary to establish ecologically and economically defensible damages.

Natural resource damages are physical damages to land, fish, wildlife, biota, air, water, and groundwater. They typically relate to adverse changes in the health of a habitat or species population and in the underlying ecological processes on which they rely. The analytical challenge is to convert these physical damages into the economic consequences of that damage. To do so requires understanding of the larger biophysical system of which the damaged resource is a part.

Liability for events that damage resources is established in the United States under the Comprehensive Environmental Response, Compensation, and Liability Act (CERCLA), the Oil Pollution Act (OPA), and the National Marine Sanctuaries Act (NMSA). Earlier, the Deepwater Port Act of 1974 and the Clean Water Act amendments of 1977 introduced NRD liability to U.S. federal law. The statutes create a compensable monetary liability for damage, which in turn requires calculation of the monetary value of the damage. The principle behind natural resource damages is well-established in U.S. law.

By their nature, NRDs acknowledge that natural resources produce a collective social benefit. This means that the value of NRD-related ecological benefits is the value arising from public goods, not goods traded and priced by markets. Instead, government trustees must somehow calculate the lost social value in the absence of the data that we take for granted in the case of market-oriented damages, such as lost profits, revenues, or wages.

Restoration, assessment, and settlement of NRD damage claims are undertaken by federal, state, and tribal trustees. Only governmental trustees can seek natural resource damages, though private plaintiffs — if they can show a concrete harm to a legally protected, collective interest in a resource — can compel action on the part of these trustees. Injury to a natural resource alone is insufficient to establish liability.

For example, under the U.S. Oil Pollution Act, the National Oceanic and Atmospheric Administration (NOAA) is the federal trustee for claims arising from marine injuries, while the U.S. Department of Interior is responsible for claims arising under CERCLA. Rules guide the agencies' respective NRD assessment procedures and act as a blueprint for the determination of appropriate restoration actions and damages.

In practice, the calculation of natural resource damages has proved difficult and controversial. When economic value is lost in a market setting, damages can be based on production, inputs, inventories, sales, and price data. Pertinent economic data already collected by both private firms and governments is available as a basis for the damage calculation. NRDs, by definition, are damages to public goods for which market data are not available. A further, and more serious, complication is the need to understand how physical damages to a given resource damage other parts of the biophysical system. For example, groundings that damage sea grass beds also damage the species that rely on sea grass for habitat. Similarly, oil spills don't just create oily beaches, they can disrupt a broader range of ecological processes that ultimately can affect wetlands, commercial fisheries, recreation, and species abundance for years to come as news reports about the ruptured BP oil well in the Gulf of Mexico attest.

Let's focus on one of the earliest likely consequences from an oil spill: public resource damages to coastal wetlands that provide necessary habitat to marine species that are commercially, recreationally, or ethically valuable. What is the relationship between wetland damages and the population dynamics (breeding, foraging, and migration) of these species? Wetlands may also buffer inland groundwater supplies from the intrusion of salt water and thus help provide potable water to coastal communities. They can also protect against storm surges and flooding. If damaged, they may no longer provide this buffering and communities may be exposed to flood damages.

As this example suggests, the damage assessment problem is two-fold: First, what are the broader biophysical consequences arising from the incident (e.g., the spill, grounding, or other accident)? Second, what is the economic loss associated with that range of biophysical consequences? These two issues push ecology and economics to their analytical limits. The physical questions demand a sophisticated understanding of a complex and interconnected natural system where changes are difficult to observe and can arise over large scales (both geographic and temporal).

The economic questions require the application of non-market valuation tools because the goods and services damaged are public, neither owned nor traded in markets. Not only that, but the two forms of analysis must somehow be integrated, so that biophysical damage measures can be translated into economic costs.

In practice, government trustees understandably have found it difficult to measure lost ecosystem goods and services. As an alternative, agencies have focused on a more practical route to damages: namely reliance on resource *replacement cost* as the measure of damages. In the 1989 case, *Ohio v. Department of Interior*[, 880 F.2d 432 (D.C. Cir. 1989),] the court strongly favored the use of restoration costs as a basis for damages even if restoration is more expensive than available monetary estimates of lost value.[11] In 1996, NOAA followed the 1994 DOI rules with rules of its own, to be applied to assessments authorized under OPA. For example, if an oil spill damages sea grass the objective is to replace the sea grass. What does it cost to replace the sea grass? That "procurement cost" becomes the measure of damages. Superficially, this strategy avoids the need to measure lost social wealth, since the point is to simply "replace the wealth" via restoration. And clearly it is much easier to solicit restoration bids and use those monetary costs as a concrete focus in damage negotiations (as opposed to conducting a broad ecological and economic assessment of lost goods and services).

There are drawbacks to the replacement cost approach to damage assessment, however. The most obvious is that replacement costs have nothing to do with the actual social damage that has occurred (the benefits of goods and services foregone). In some cases, replacement costs may vastly exceed the social damages they are meant to repair. This is particularly true if the replacement activity is taken seriously, monitored over time, and guarantees a successful restoration outcome. In other cases, replacement costs may vastly under-represent the social damages caused by the proximate injury.

A damaged sea grass bed or coral reef may be restorable at an estimable cost. But it is possible that the bulk of social costs arise from damages to *other* resources dependent on the sea grass or coral reef. If these resources are not replaced — as they are generally not — replacement costs may fall significantly short of the real social damage. In either case, replacement cost as the damage measure fails to achieve the main legal and economic principle in play: the desire to have polluters internalize the full costs of their behavior. Economically, basing penalties on the lost social benefits is the correct and most precise way to make the public whole.

A related drawback is that restoration-costs-as-damages (by design) over-simplify the government trustee's analytical problem. By removing the need to analyze ecological and economic effects more comprehensively, the government is able to under-invest in the analytical capability required to measure real damages. For environmentalists and economists concerned about real measures of natural

11. The NRDA rules' current focus on the replacement cost of resources, rather than their estimated market value, is a direct outgrowth of these cases. H.R. Conf. Rep. No. 653, 101st Cong., 2d Sess. 108 (1990)....

wealth lost and gained, reliance on replacement cost has been a barrier to scientific progress.

The deterrent and compensatory functions of maritime accident law thus demand continued development of methods to measure real social damages that take into account biophysical causation and subsequent economic impacts. This is the goal of ecosystem services assessment generally. To the extent ecosystem services assessment becomes more practical, there may be important implications for the marine commercial and governmental sectors. The OPA does not limit damages to those that can be directly measured in markets or that are based on observable resource uses. As long as the agencies' own damage assessment rules are adhered to, there is a "rebuttable presumption" of the analyses' correctness and legal validity. This presumption provides agencies with considerable latitude in their choice of damage assessment methods. At least in the United States, where natural resource damages based on lost economic wealth are well-established in theory, there is a firm legal rationale for using lost ecosystem services benefits as the measure of damages, particularly as assessment methods improve.

Ecosystem services are the benefits of nature to households, communities, and economies. The term is interpreted in a variety of ways, but conveys an important idea: ecosystems are a tangible source of economic wealth. This is intuitively obvious and consistent with the entire concept of resources in the public trust. What is less obvious is how that wealth is to be measured. Because environmental goods and services are often public goods not traded in markets, economists lack information on the prices paid for those goods and services — we don't explicitly pay a price for the glorious view. Of course, just because something doesn't have a price, doesn't mean it is not valuable. The challenge, then, is to get people to reveal the values they place on goods and services that are un-priced.

Broadly, there are two ways to value un-priced goods and services. First, we can get people to state their preferences by asking them questions designed to elicit value. Second, we can look to people's behavior and infer natural resource benefits from that behavior. Houses near beautiful scenery sell for more than houses without scenery, for example. When people spend time and money traveling to enjoy natural resources, they signal the value of those resources, what are called revealed preferences. The definition of environmental *commodities* is central to both methods.

One of the nice things about markets is that they not only tell us the prices people pay for things, but also about the units (the quantities) people place value on. A grocery store is full of cans, boxes, loaves, and bunches; the number of these units bought yields a set of quantity measures to which prices can be attached. But public, non-market environmental goods and services don't come in convenient quantity units. Put another way, what are the *physical* damages that give rise and can be attached to economic losses?

In conventional markets, we take the difference between physical quantities and the price or value of those commodities for granted. At the store, we are presented with rows and rows of quantity units (the goods and services we buy) and we pay their price at checkout. For public, non-market goods, however, the distinction between quantities and their value is not obvious.

Ecosystem services analysis explicitly demands a linkage between ecological outcomes and economic consequences. It is important to get the units right — or at least be able to clarify why we use the units we do. The challenge lies in disentangling complex natural systems into more discrete commodity units so that natural scientists and economists can use the same terms to describe ecological changes in the same way. . . .

In the recent words of Alaskan trustees working on the aftermath of the *Exxon Valdez* spill: "Through hundreds of studies conducted over the past 20 years, we have come to understand that the Prince William Sound ecosystem is incredibly complex and the interactions between a changing environment and the injured resources and services are only beginning to be understood."

It is worth reflecting on why this is true. First, many marine accidents result in damages over a wide geographic area (in the *Valdez*'s case, 200 miles of shoreline were obviously affected, but measurable biological effects have been found over 1,300 miles of coastline) and over long time periods (20 years after the spill, fewer than half the species affected have recovered to pre-spill levels). The effect on water quality of such a spill can have a range of side effects that develop over a period of years or decades. In the short term, oil spills will deplete herring and other cornerstones of the marine food chain. In turn, this effect on food stocks affects the viability of species dependent on them, such as certain bird species. These biological effects can take years to play out and in turn, human uses dependent on these ecological endpoints may be affected for years as well.

Consider damages to habitat. Habitat can be thought of as a natural asset, where restoration represents investment in the asset and damage represents divestment. Similar to man-made capital assets, habitats are durable, implying that changes today affect physical and economic rates of return in the future. Damages (and restoration) therefore are inter-temporal phenomena in both physical and economic terms. Habitat regeneration takes time. Often restoration projects replicate natural system functions only after a period of years. And even if full replication of a more natural system is assured, there are damages associated with the interim loss in the ecological asset's function.

***

Maritime law often allows for the measurement and assignment of damages arising from lost public natural resources. Damaged environmental resources, even if they are public goods, can trigger subsequent economic damages to individuals, businesses, and communities. Given the goal of liability laws to "make the public whole" the natural resource damages question boils down to this: how do physical damages propagate through physical ecosystems and thereby create subsequent biophysical damages that reduce human welfare? Courts must understand biophysical damages that can take years to develop and may arise over broad geographic scales. They must also be able to translate those biophysical damages into economic terms.

In the United States, where NRD law is well-established and applicable to marine incidents, linked ecological and economic assessment has not yet been able to fully meet this aspiration for damage assessment. Instead, government trustees have relied on more practical — and thus entirely defensible — alternatives to the calculation of the actual social costs of pollution: namely restoration costs. The focus on restoration of resources that are obviously damaged is a natural first step and yields concrete damage estimates based on the costs of restoration.

Measuring ecosystem goods and services analysis is not easy and it is often not practical except where funding for large-scale monitoring and statistical assessment is possible. However, development of these methods is proceeding. When the physical and social science of ecosystem good and service evaluation develops into a more mature phase, the implications for marine liability damages will be direct and material to plaintiffs, trustees, and courts.

But it deserves emphasis that the ecological and economic damage caused by the BP *Deepwater Horizon* spill is likely to be very significant and far reaching, even if it is difficult to calculate with precision. This leaves us with a knotty question for public policy and the courts: how do we appropriately penalize a polluter when we may never actually know the damage they caused? A meaningful penalty is surely called for. But given current scientific and economic knowledge, the scale of that penalty is more likely to be resolved through political judgment than technical calculation.

points for discussion

1. *Damages versus restoration costs.* Under the Oil Pollution Act, trustees are limited to recovering the cost of restoring injured resources. In practice, this has meant that damages are limited to the cost of feasible restoration projects that the trustee can identify. Can you see why this approach might not make the public whole, say, from the damage caused by the Deepwater Horizon spill?

2. *Pros and cons of the ecosystem services approach.* In the context of the Oil Pollution Act, that is, given the emphasis on restoration projects, what are the benefits and drawbacks of focusing on ecosystem services rather than on the natural resources themselves?

3. *Boyd's last thought.* Boyd says that "the scale of the penalty" will be a "political judgment." What exactly does this mean? Will the amount extracted from a responsible party be a function of what is acceptable to the public and what won't destroy the responsible party's ability to pay (its continuing existence as a functioning corporation)? How could such a number be defended in court? Is this why most NRDAs are ultimately settled? If so, what accountability measures exist?

E. CHAPTER SUMMARY

1. **Sea and seabed federalism.** In the United States, the ocean and seabed are divided into areas of state and federal primary jurisdiction. Along with jurisdiction is ownership of the minerals in the seabed. The Submerged Lands Act of 1953 was only the most recent congressional declaration of what is the domain of states and the federal government.

2. **Oil and gas development.** Oil and gas leasing have been important and controversial activities of the seabed. While states may claim mineral resources for up to three nautical miles, most oil and gas leasing activity takes place in federal waters, under the direction of the Bureau of Ocean Energy Management, and pursuant to the Outer Continental Shelf Lands Act, but in conjunction with the Coastal Zone Management Act and the National Environmental Policy Act. The mineral leasing process takes place in four stages, each with unique procedural requirements.

3. **Renewable energy development.** Oil and gas leasing in the seabed continues but climate change, the 2010 Deepwater Horizon disaster, and other pollution have caused energy production to shift to renewable sources of energy. Like oil and gas, producing energy from renewable energy sources has expanded from land to sea to take advantage of a less-fraught legal environment, and favorable geographic conditions, like high and steady winds. The renewable energy leasing process mirrors the four-stage mineral leasing process and is also administered by the Bureau of Ocean Energy Management.

4. **Harm to ocean resources.** Extraction of oil and gas from the marine environment and its transport has produced some of the most ecologically catastrophic accidents in human history. Following the Exxon Valdez disaster, the Oil Pollution Act was passed to complement remedies available under the Clean Water Act, under state law, and under general maritime law. The result has been a complicated suite of laws designed to deter careless behavior leading to ecological tragedy, and to provide remedies for harms to ocean resources and people resulting from oil and gas activity at sea.

F. SUGGESTED READING

Michael Barsa & David A. Dana, *Reconceptualizing NEPA to Avoid the Next Preventable Disaster*, 38 B.C. ENVTL. AFF. L. REV. 219 (2011).

JACK E. DAVIS, THE GULF: THE MAKING OF AN AMERICAN SEA (2017).

Thomas A. Grigalunas et al., *Liability for Oil Spills: Issues, Methods, and Examples*, 26 COASTAL MGMT. 61 (1997).

Oliver A. Houck, *Worst Case and the Deepwater Horizon Blowout: There Ought to Be a Law*, 24 TUL. ENVTL. L.J. 1 (2010).

Samantha B. Joye, *Deepwater Horizon, 5 Years On*, 349 SCI. 592 (2015).

Sam Kalen, *Cruise Control and Speed Bumps: Energy Policy and Limits for Outer Continental Shelf Leasing*, 7 ENVTL. & ENERGY L. & POL'Y J. 155 (2012).

WENDY WILLIAMS & ROBERT WHITCOMB, CAPE WIND: MONEY, CELEBRITY, CLASS, POLITICS, AND THE BATTLE FOR OUR ENERGY FUTURE (2007).

chapter 5

The Coastal Law Context: Uplands, Shoreline, Water

While ocean law is concerned with management of publicly owned (or unowned) resources, the role of coastal law is to resolve and preempt conflicts among individuals, groups, and businesses who are interested in using coastal land, much of which is privately owned. This part of the book explores the ways in which coastal-specific common law, statutes, and constitutional law mediate between competing interests, both public and private. Although it is possible to classify some of these rules as property law or environmental law, we will group them together under a more place-based and descriptive title: "coastal law."

Disputes concerning the use of land and natural resources, and rules meant to address them, obviously are not limited to coastal areas. In your property law course, for example, you probably learned about conflicts between neighbors, and the ways in which nuisance law and municipal zoning law attempt to resolve and preempt those disputes. If you have taken an environmental or natural resources law course, you may have covered public lands law, a group of federal statutes that establish procedures and standards by which agencies allocate natural resources, such as forests, among competing interest groups, such as the timber industry and conservationists.

In some ways, the kinds of disputes that arise in coastal areas are no different than these; they involve competing claims to the use of private property and public resources. The unique features of coastal areas, however, have given rise to unique legal rules. As a prelude to our exploration of those rules, this chapter provides an introduction to what it is that makes the coast special and thus deserving of its own legal framework. The first part of the chapter covers some basic coastal geology, ecology, and geography. The second part examines our relationship with the coast, focusing on why people value, and thus compete for, its many resources.

A. INTRODUCTION TO COASTAL SYSTEMS AND PROCESSES

While in-depth study of coastal science is beyond the scope of a law school course, it is important to understand those features of coastal lands and resources that have been most influential in shaping coastal law. Those key features include continuous physical change; unusual ecological systems at the intersection of land and water; and a sea-level location, which renders coastal areas vulnerable both to storms and flooding and to waterborne pollution flowing to the sea.

1. The Geology of Instability

Coastal lands, more than other kinds of lands, are constantly in flux. Although rocky shores can be more stable than sandy beaches, all types of coastal land are prone to both short- and long-term physical change.

As the British physical geographer Peter French explains:

> Coastal landforms are not permanent features, they are transient features which accrete and erode subject to the environmental conditions at the time. Coasts and estuaries are highly dynamic environments, and constantly change in response to natural forces on a variety of time scales. For example, sediment grains can be moved on a beach or a mudflat whenever waves lap against the shore; a storm can change the profile of a beach in a few hours; a winter's rough seas can modify a soft cliff profile over a couple of months; or sea level can rise and fall over thousands of years. Thus it is important to keep in mind that the coast which we see today is not static and frozen in time, and that there is no reason why what we observe today will always be the same.

PETER W. FRENCH, COASTAL AND ESTUARINE MANAGEMENT 8-9 (1997).

The following excerpt vividly illustrates the volatile nature of the coast. The events described are typical of sandy shorelines, which make up a significant percentage of the United States' coastline, particularly along the Atlantic Ocean and the Gulf of Mexico.

Larry G. Ward et al., Living with the Chesapeake Bay and Virginia's Ocean Shores

1-4, 21-24 (1989)

The placid nature of Chesapeake Bay has been heralded since Captain John Smith first arrived in 1607, but its calmness, beauty, and serenity can be deceiving. The Bay's shoreline is strikingly dynamic. If Captain Smith could visit Chesapeake Bay once again, he probably would recognize very little — not because of the development, but because much of the shoreline he mapped is no longer there! Many of today's beaches are 200 to 2,000 feet landward of the shore that he saw. The settlements he knew on the shore are under water today.

***

The shores that John Smith knew are lost without record, but more recent shores that are now missing should not be forgotten. Older Eastern Shore watermen know the shoal off the mouth of the Choptank River was once Sharps Island, but few know the stories of the island's days as a resort. At the turn of this century the island was a favorite spot for hunting, and an artesian well supplied water for the resort's hotel. By 1910 the hotel stood abandoned on only 53 acres of island, and the well site was in the waters of the Chesapeake Bay. In a 1914 study, J. F. Hunter predicted that the island would be gone by 1951. His prediction was fairly accurate as the 1965 charts show no remnants of the island! The 438-acre island had disappeared in a little over a century, along with its forest, its buildings, its well, and most of its memories.

. . . Sharps Island is not alone in the pattern of its shrinking. Poplar Island is now only a set of islets, the dissected remains of a much larger island shown on an 1847 map. This island's shore eroded at a rate of nine feet per year over a 116-year period of record. Tilghman Island consisted of 2,015 acres in 1848, but had reduced to 1,686 acres by 1901. Today the south end of the island is nearly separated from the main body by a new strait. James Island consisted of 976 acres in 1848, 555 acres in 1901, and 490 acres in 1910.

***

Photo: Baldeagle Bluff/Wikimedia Commons

Figure 5-1. Holland Island House
A house on Holland Island in the Chesapeake Bay remained above the water in 2009. It disappeared into the bay a year later.

In 1866, after the Civil War had ceased to change the landscape of Virginia, a large stand of pines along the Eastern Shore felt the effects of a quieter battle. This confrontation was waged not by the destructive weapons of man, but rather by the competing forces of Mother Nature. The pines stood on a peninsula of land appropriately named Savage Neck. They faced the winds and waves of Chesapeake Bay, which were ceaselessly changing the geography of Northampton County. Each tree became a temporary monument to this conflict, standing briefly at the water's edge before yielding to the Bay.

Around the turn of the century, by some accounts, Savage Neck's beautiful vista attracted a group of investors. Taking advantage of the remaining trees, beach, and Bay, they constructed a modest hotel in a location with the choicest view. The venture was quite successful. The investors were not oblivious to the changes in the shoreline, but they felt little concern — a substantial fastland remained between the hotel and the beach.

Later, after air travel had emerged as a major mode of transportation and national defense, the need arose for a strategically located air-navigation facility. Such a facility had very specific siting requirements. One of the primary concerns in site selection was a lack of physical obstructions, including trees. After proper deliberation, the Federal Aviation Administration chose an open field on Savage Neck facing Chesapeake Bay and constructed the facility called a VOR. [VOR stands for Very High Frequency Omni-Directional Range. It is a ground-based system for aiding in air traffic control. — Eds.]

Before and after the VOR came into existence, private individuals were attracted to the sandy beaches and spectacular Bay view at Savage Neck. Over time summer cottages were built and those who occupied the cottages used the unobstructed beach for all forms of recreation including long walks. Many of these beachcombers were attracted to a section of the beach down by the VOR.

***

Each spring the cottage owners faced the realities of change when they inspected the winter storm damage. Usually the change was recorded with the loss of a favorite bush or the steps to the beach. Occasionally, there was a reverse trend with a significant gain in the width of the beach. Sometimes the loss of the beach was alarming. The only common denominator was that all experienced change.

> **What Is "Fastland"?**
>
> In Chapter 89 of Herman Melville's *Moby Dick*, entitled "Fast-Fish and Loose-Fish," the author explains that "[a]live or dead a fish is technically fast, when it is connected with an occupied ship or boat, by any medium at all controllable by the occupant or occupants, — a mast, an oar, a nine-inch cable, a telegraph wire, or a strand of cobweb, it is all the same." "Fastland" is another word for dry land, or upland. It has the same root as "fasten": the idea is that, unlike the wet sand beach, fastland is relatively stable or fixed. As the excerpt illustrates, the term should be used with caution.

With time the loss of fastland mounted and there was considerable discussion as to how to combat the problem. In the end the only feasible solution was to move the cottages landward a "safe" distance. Safe was considered to be 300 feet. Afterward the shoreline remained relatively stable for a time, discounting minor annual losses. But this apparent lull in shoreline retreat was dramatically broken with the "Ash Wednesday" storm of March 1962. Over three frightening days the unprotected bank yielded 40 to 60 feet to the Bay. Afterward the shoreline seemed to become more unstable and the annual rate of loss increased to over 10 feet per year. It became apparent that some measure of protection was necessary.

Photo: K. Duhring/Center for Coastal Resources Management/Virginia Institute for Marine Science

Figure 5-2. Breakwaters and Perched Beaches

The decision was made to stop the erosion of the shore. A number of efforts were tried, including a concrete seawall, a groin field, and concrete rubble. [For descriptions and illustrations of various beach stabilization structures, including seawalls, groins, rip-rap (rubble), breakwaters, and sills, see the website of the U.S. Army Corps of Engineers, http://chl.erdc.usace.army.mil/coastalstructures. — Eds.] Despite these efforts (and expenses) the shore continued to retreat, and one home that could not be moved was lost. Subsequently, an experimental structure was built with large sand-filled PVC-coated nylon bags. The bags were installed off the seaward end of the previously installed groins in a low, single-layer row running parallel to the shore before abutting the toe of the bank. The purpose of the structure (called a sill) was to "perch" the beach by serving as a low miniature breakwater, reducing the wave energy in the lee of the structure, and increasing the residence time of the sand. Under the right conditions, the incoming waves would push the sand to a higher elevation at the toe of the bank, thus preventing storm waves from reaching the bank. The sill experiment was a partial success. It perched two to four feet of sand above the normal backshore elevation. [The meaning of the term "backshore," and other coastal terms, is illustrated in Figure 5-3. — Eds.] As a result, the cliff remained untouched by storm waves for nearly five years. A small vegetated dune formed at the base of the cliff.

Unfortunately, beginning with a modest nor'easter in 1977, storm waves overtopped the small dune and again began carrying bank material into the Bay. The sill had slowed the erosion rate, but it was only a matter of time before it became ineffective. Once the waves eroded an additional 20 feet of bank, the sill was completely unable to perch a beach. Adding to the problem was the deterioration of the bags themselves. Sand abrasion wore off the PVC-coating, exposing the nylon to degradation by sunlight. Debris carried by waves could then damage the bags.

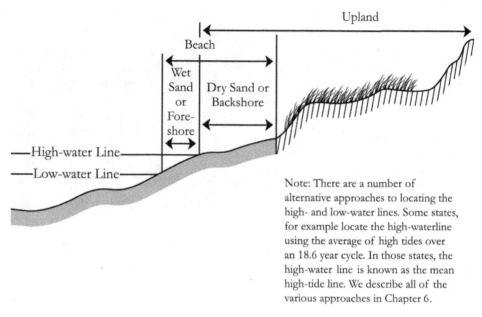

Note: There are a number of alternative approaches to locating the high- and low-water lines. Some states, for example locate the high-waterline using the average of high tides over an 18.6 year cycle. In those states, the high-water line is known as the mean high-tide line. We describe all of the various approaches in Chapter 6.

Adapted from U.S. Army Corps of Engineers Shore Protection Manual (1984)

Figure 5-3. Basic Coastal Terminology

Over a 13-year span various kinds of shore-protection schemes were tried. Although the sill was partially successful, it could not provide protection in the face of storm surges exceeding four feet. The net result was that the landowners once again faced the potential loss of their homes. After initial discouragement, they realized that their best choice was to move the houses once again. Today, the once-lucrative hotel on Savage Neck is a disappearing pile of debris in the [foreshore] and the VOR is under siege by the Bay. Its useful life may coincide with the arrival of the shoreline at its front door.

It is important to be aware that erosion and accretion are part of a larger process known as "sediment transport." In other words, sand grains do not magically vanish from or appear on a beach; rather, they are going to, or coming from, somewhere else along the coast. The following passage describes sediment transport in California.

Gary Griggs et al., Understanding the Shoreline

In Gary Griggs et al., Living with the Changing California Coast 38-74 (2005)

With thousands of waves breaking on the beach every day, the net result is a slowly moving current of water and beach sand that flows down coast and parallel to the shoreline, known as a longshore current. Longshore currents exist along most of California's beaches, are driven by waves breaking on the beach at an angle, and are very important in transporting sand along the shoreline. This alongshore transport of sand is known as littoral drift and can be thought of as a river of sand moving parallel to the coast. Hundreds of thousands of cubic yards of sand may travel as littoral drift each year along California's shoreline. The amount of sand moving along the shore is related to the amount of wave energy and the angle at which waves approach the shoreline with waves breaking parallel to the beach transporting almost no sand and those breaking at a greater angle transporting more sand.

***

Where Does the Beach Sand Come From?

Along the California coast, most of the beach sand comes from river and stream runoff, with a lesser amount resulting from the erosion of coastal cliffs and bluffs. Measurements of sediment transport in rivers indicate that coastal streams, particularly during times of flood flow, are the major suppliers of sand to the beaches. Along most of the California coast, estimates indicate that 80 percent to over 95 percent of the beach sand was originally stream derived. Physical and chemical weathering slowly break down rocks in the coastal mountains or watersheds into smaller fragments or into their constituent minerals or grains. Rainfall, runoff, and slope failures such as landslides begin to move the gravel, sand, silt, and clay downslope into the creeks, where it is gradually sorted out and transported downstream into

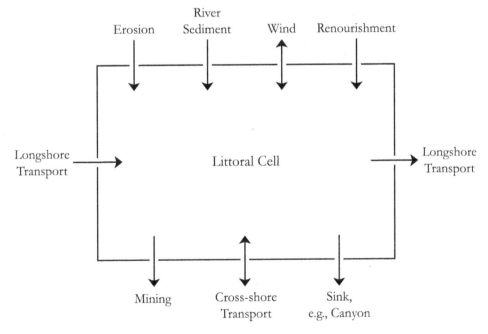

[Diagram added. — EDS.]

Figure 5-4. Model of Sediment Budget for Littoral Cell

the larger rivers. After many months and miles of abrasion and sorting, the smaller particles ultimately reach the shoreline while the larger boulders and cobbles are left behind in the streambeds. The sand and gravel end up on the beach; the silt and clay are carried offshore in suspension by coastal and offshore currents and are ultimately deposited on the sea floor somewhere a few miles to hundreds of miles offshore.

California is fortunate to have many relatively large rivers that deliver great volumes of sand to the coastline to nourish the beaches. The Eel, Russian, Santa Maria, Ventura, and Santa Clara rivers are all important sand suppliers. Beaches have often been observed to be much wider in the summers following winters with high rainfall because of the delivery of large amounts of sand to the local beaches by high stream flow or flood events. [S]ediment discharge during a single year of extreme flood conditions may exceed decades of low or normal stream flow. A recent study of major rivers in central and southern California has shown that sediment discharge during flood years such as 1964, 1969, 1983, and 1998 averages 27 times that during drier years. In 1969, over 100 million tons of sediment (about 7.5 million dumptruck loads) was flushed out of the Santa Ynez Mountains, more than during the previous 25 years combined.

The Beach — A River of Sand

Once sand arrives at the shoreline, waves and wave-induced currents provide the energy necessary to sort out sediments, push the sand up on the shoreline to form a beach, and then gradually move the sand along the coast. The direction of this alongshore movement of sand or littoral drift is determined by the dominant angle of wave approach. For example, along nearly the entire central and southern California coast, waves from the northwest drive littoral drift southward along the beaches. North of Cape Mendocino and between San Diego and the Mexican border, the flow of sand is often northward, or sand may move to the north and to the south at different times of the year depending on the dominant direction of wave approach.

It is very important to know something about the rate and direction of littoral drift prior to any human intervention in the nearshore system. The planning and design of coastal engineering structures to prevent erosion, the construction of harbors and channel entrances with their associated jetties and breakwaters, and questions of beach nourishment and long-term stability of beach material are all tied to the littoral drift system. As with the construction of a dam or reservoir on a stream, virtually anything we insert into this river of sand is going to disrupt the sand's natural flow. The number of past instances where littoral drift rates were either not well understood or not considered prior to construction of large engineering structures is unfortunately quite large in California. The consequences quickly became apparent, and the resulting dredging, down-coast cliff or beach erosion, associated loss of property, and subsequent armor emplacement have cost hundreds of millions of dollars. Today, however, as a result of about a hundred years of experience and coastal engineering projects, we are aware of these systems and structures. We have a reasonably good understanding of littoral drift directions and rates for most areas, so there is no longer any reason for repeating the mistakes of the past or planning projects without a full awareness of the long-term costs of littoral drift disruption.

Average yearly littoral drift rates along California's coast show a considerable range, from about 30,000 cubic yards at Redondo Beach to nearly 1 million cubic yards at Ventura. One million cubic yards is equivalent to about 100,000 dumptruck loads each year. If transported evenly through the year, this would require 275 dumptrucks full of sand moving along the beach each day, or about one every 5 minutes, 24 hours a day. Disrupting or blocking this amount of sand every year can have massive and devastating impacts. Imagine the size of a pile of sand that would be formed if a constant stream of dumptrucks dropped their loads every 5 minutes for a year, and how long it would take to move the resulting pile. This is the scenario faced by many of California's harbors.

Between 1970 and 2001, for example, over 10 million cubic yards of sand were dredged from the Santa Barbara Harbor, nearly 20 million cubic yards were dredged from the Ventura Harbor, and roughly 28 million cubic yards of sand were dredged from the Channel Islands Harbor, at a cost of tens of millions of dollars. Dredging from just these three harbors totaled over 58 million cubic yards or 5.8 million dumptruck loads of sand over this 31-year period. These are just a few of many large sand traps that exist along the coast of California, where annual dredging is a way of life.

Where Does the Sand Go?

We now know that beaches in most places along the coast are continually supplied with sand (although in decreasing amounts in southern California) and that longshore drift is constantly moving this material down coast. Where, then, is all of this sand going, and why aren't the beaches growing wider and wider as you move down coast? If we follow the paths of typical sand grains, we observe several possible routes by which sand may leave the beach permanently as it moves down the shoreline by wave action.

Sand Dunes

Dunes occur inland from beaches at many locations along the coast of California and can act as sinks where beach sand may be temporarily or permanently lost from the shoreline. As a beach widens and the area of dry sand on the back beach expands, inland transport by wind may occur. Generally, dunes form wherever ample dry sand is available, wind blows in a persistent onshore direction, and a low-lying or low-relief area exists landward of the beach where the sand can accumulate. If high cliffs or bluffs back the beach, dunes will have nowhere to migrate and will not develop to a significant size. If the wind direction is steady enough, sand will move, grain by grain, over the dune's surface, resulting in a downwind migration of the dune. Much of this sand is permanently lost from the beach. It has been estimated, for example, that 200,000 cubic yards of sand are blown inland each year along the 35-mile coastline from Pismo Beach to Point Arguello. Other major California sand dunes occur just north of Crescent City, at Humboldt Bay, at Point Reyes, at the Ocean Beach area of San Francisco, in southern Monterey Bay between Marina and Monterey, at Morro Bay, at the Oxnard Plain, from Santa Monica to El Segundo, and from San Diego to the Mexican border.

Dunes serve as important coastal buffers because they are flexible barriers to storm waves and provide protection to the lower-lying back dune areas. In fact, wherever dunes can be created and stabilized, they often work better than sea-walls. Dunes also maintain a large stockpile of sand that feeds the beach during severe storms or prolonged periods of wave attack. Under storm assault, the beach is first cut back, and if wave erosion continues, portions of the frontal dune may be eroded. This sand is moved offshore, where it is stored in sand bars that tend to reduce the wave energy impinging on the shoreline, because the waves will break farther offshore. As the winter storms subside, smaller spring and summer waves transport sand back onto the beach, which will ultimately be rebuilt. With time or the absence of large storms, the excess sand will be moved onshore by wind and will rebuild the dunes. The process of natural dune rebuilding may take several years, however. Dune erosion, either during storms or because of a reduction in sand supply, can be destructive to any structures built on the dunes.

Sand dunes must be seen as ephemeral or temporary landforms. Storms will recur; sandbars will shift; and dunes will erode, rebuild, and migrate. In addition, dune instability may result from human impacts in the form of construction or recreation. The primary, frontal, or fore dune is particularly prone to change, as has been discovered in recent years by owners of new condominiums and houses perched on active sand dunes. After many years of observations, landscape architect Ian McHarg suggests in his classic book *Design with Nature* that no development, recreation, or human activity of any type occur on the primary or secondary dunes, which are the least stable and contain the most fragile vegetation. This principle was widely violated along the California coast in the past, with costly consequences. Development, if it is to occur at all, should take place in the back dune area, which has the advantage of protection from winter storms. Limited cluster development might also occur in the trough between dunes, provided groundwater withdrawals will not adversely affect dune vegetation, and the dunes themselves are not breached by roads, utilities, or human trampling.

Recreational impact in sand dune areas has historically been widespread and comes in the form of pedestrian traffic and off-road vehicle use. Most foot traffic impacts come from uncontrolled crossings from the back dune area to the beach. Large numbers of crossings result in dissection of the dune field with numerous paths and the consequent development of large barren areas, the creation of blow-outs, decreased dune growth, and nondevelopment of new dunes. Heavy foot traffic has been shown to decrease the amount of vegetation, which in turn accelerates dune destabilization. Offroad vehicle traffic, which is a common recreational practice in some dune areas, has the same effects — loss of vegetation and destabilization of the dunes, which are difficult to repair. The fragile nature of sand dunes is now more widely appreciated, and more attention is paid to proposals that would remove vegetation, lower groundwater levels, or breach the dunes themselves.

Restricted and fenced pathways, boardwalks and revegetation are paying off by protecting vegetation and thereby aiding dune stabilization.

Sand Mining

In addition to the natural processes of sand loss through onshore winds, sand has historically been mined directly from some California beaches and dunes. Three major sand-mining companies removed sand directly from the beach face in southern Monterey Bay for nearly 90 years. The high-purity quartz sand was in great demand for many industrial uses, including water filtration, abrasives, and various coatings. Concern, however, as to whether the approximately 300,000 to 400,000 cubic yards of sand being removed each year exceeded the volume entering the area naturally and whether the mining was a significant factor in the regular retreat of the shoreline led to termination of [most — EDS.] beach sand mining in the 1980s. If the average volume of sand removal through direct mining each year is greater than that added by natural sources, shoreline retreat will take place. Although extensive sand and gravel mining operations still take place along streambeds in a number of locations in California, direct sand removal from beaches has been almost completely terminated.

Submarine Canyons

The greatest, but also the least visible, loss of sand from California's beaches takes place through the many submarine canyons along California's continental shelf. Where these canyons extend close to shore, which they do in many places, they intercept the littoral drift and funnel it away from the beach into deep offshore basins. The canyons of southern California have been recognized for over 70 years and are the ultimate sinks for most of southern California's beach sand. Every year, for example, the Scripps and La Jolla submarine canyons at La Jolla swallow an estimated 350,000 cubic yards of sand, enough to form a beach 10 feet deep, 90 feet wide, and 2 miles long.

points for discussion

1. *Reasons for change.* Beyond erosion and accretion, there are other reasons why the land-water interface, a line representing the place where the water meets the land, might move landward or seaward. First, dry land can change in elevation, that is, rise or subside, over time, even in the absence of erosion or accretion. Land can subside, for example, due to excessive pumping of ground water from beneath the property. Although land rarely rises, this has recently happened in Juneau, Alaska, where coastal lands rose in elevation as a result of glacial melt. (Smaller glaciers weigh less than bigger ones!) *See* Cornelia Dean, *As Alaska's Glaciers Melt, It's Land That's Rising*, N.Y. TIMES, May 18, 2009, at A1. Second, the level of the adjacent water body can drop, leading to an increase in the amount of dry land (this is known

as *reliction* or, sometimes, *dereliction*), or it can rise. There is no standard term describing the phenomenon of land lost to sea rise, but we will soon need one. (We will use the term "submergence.") Climate scientists believe that sea levels may rise by as much as 37 inches by the year 2100. (We will consider the implications of climate change for coastal law both later in this section and in Chapter 10.) If the elevation of the shore increases, the land-water interface will move seaward; the opposite is true if the elevation of coastal land decreases. Do you see why?[1]

Table 1. The Terminology of Change

Land/water boundary shifts seaward	Land/water boundary shifts landward
Accretion (material added to shore)	Erosion (material removed from shore)
Reliction or dereliction (water level falls)	Submergence (water level rises)
Uplift (land elevation increases)	Subsidence (land elevation decreases)

2. *Volatile property law.* The fact that land along the coast is in constant flux plays a central role in coastal conflicts. Most obviously, the basic rules of real property ownership are challenged when the shape of the "dry" portion of the land parcel, or "upland," is continuously changing. Can you think of other examples of "volatile property"? How does the law assign or reassign ownership rights after physical change to property occurs? For example, if your backyard slides away during a mudslide, do you have a right to the dirt now located at the bottom of the neighborhood? If lava flows increase the size of your oceanfront lot, do you own the newly created land? *See State by Kobayashi v. Zimring*, 566 P.2d 725 (Haw. 1977). If your cow becomes pregnant by another rancher's bull, who owns the calf? *See* Thomas W. Merrill, *Accession and Original Ownership*, 1 J. Legal Analysis 459, 466 (2009).

3. *Rules for change.* How should the law address ownership issues in the aftermath of change? The law could simply establish property boundaries using a fixed measurement system, such as latitude and longitude coordinates. For example, after an episode of erosion, the landowner would own the same sized parcel, although part of it would be under water. If the parcel grew in

---

1. *An important note on terminology:* Coastal areas include a wide variety of water bodies, including not only the sea, but bays, sounds, rivers, estuaries, and so forth. As it is used throughout this book, the word "seaward" means "toward the adjacent waterbody." Also, coastal uplands include not only the mainland, but islands and other "fastland" features as well. As it is used in this book, "landward" does not mean "in the direction of the mainland," but, rather, "in the direction of the adjacent upland."

size due to accretion, then the state (as owner of the previously "submerged lands" now filled by the accretion) would own the accretion. What would be the advantages and disadvantages of fixed-boundary rules?

Along the same lines, the law might recognize indelible rights in the physical components of the real property, such as the sand and other materials of which it is comprised. So, if sand migrated from *A*'s parcel to *B*'s parcel, *A* would continue to own it. *A* would be entitled to a court order allowing him to retrieve his sand from *B*'s parcel. In the alternative, we might see the increase and decrease of dry land as analogous to the increase and decrease in value of, say, shares in a corporation. Under this approach, the landowner would bear the risk of change, that is, would have no recourse where the amount of upland was diminished, but would be entitled to any upland added through sediment transport. As we will see, this is — with a few exceptions — the approach currently embodied in the law.

4. *Does property fit?* Why do we allow anyone to own property that is capable of erosion? Wouldn't we reasonably anticipate that the societal costs of managing property rights in "fluctuating land" would be extremely high? (Those costs would include, for example, moneys spent on litigating property disputes between parties. It is easy to see how the number of such disputes would increase — up to a point — relative to the volatility of the property.) One commentator has suggested that states cease to recognize private property rights in barrier islands, which are characterized by high rates of erosion and accretion. Under the approach she proposes, this kind of land would be treated similarly to water, which is owned by the state. Private individuals could possess rights to use and enjoy the land that were superior to other individuals, but subordinate to those held by the state. Amy H. Moorman, *Let's Roll: Applying Land-Based Notions of Property to the Migrating Barrier Islands*, 31 WM. & MARY ENVTL. L. & POL'Y REV. 459 (2007).

5. *Not going with the flow.* Another source of conflict arises from the phenomenon of sediment transport. There are a variety of ways in which a landowner can trap sediment such as sand, that is, keep it from being transported away by natural forces. Examples of these kinds of "stabilization" structures include breakwaters and groins. While stabilization may benefit the landowner who installs such a structure, it inevitably deprives other landowners of sediment that otherwise would have flowed to their property. *See* Figure 5-5. If the property of these other landowners is experiencing erosive forces, the deprivation of sand will mean that their upland will shrink at an increased rate. Can you think of a cause of action that one landowner, or a member of the public, might bring against a person who has built a harmful stabilization structure?

6. *Adding to the budget.* One alternative to the stabilization methods described above is "soft stabilization," otherwise known as beach renourishment. In beach renourishment, sand from another source is trucked, shipped, or

piped in to the eroding beach, and is used to build an artificial beach. Advocates of beach renourishment claim that it is superior to hard stabilization because it does not have harmful effects on down-current owners or the public. Can you think of some reasons why this might not always be true? (If not, proceed to the next note.)

7. *Or not?* Mining sand needed for renourishment can interfere with sediment transport to the detriment of would-be sediment recipients. Even though the sand used in renourishment might be mined from a spot on the ocean bottom far from land, that spot could easily be a sand "bank" from which sand would ultimately flow to naturally renourish other beaches along the coast. In short, "sediment budgets" are limited, and nearly every intentional or unintentional re-allocation of sediment by human action will have repercussions of some kind.

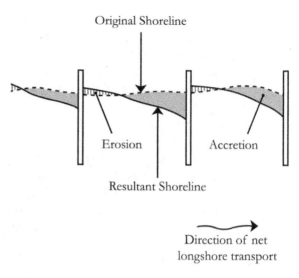

Adapted from N.C. Dept. of Envt. and Nat. Res. drawing

Figure 5-5.   Effect of Groins
Effect of groins on sediment transport.

2. Border Ecology

From your own experience, you have probably seen first-hand how coastal ecosystems are different from inland systems. Coastal systems, for example, are generally characterized by the presence of large quantities of water — marine, fresh, and brackish (a mixture of salty ocean water and the fresh water that flows to the coast from inland areas). The plants and wildlife in these systems, such as crabs, oysters, seagulls, and seals, are endemic to coastal areas.

This section introduces you to coastal ecology. There are two main points. First, the "wet" coastal environment, that is, those areas just seaward of the coastline, are extremely diverse, both within and among geographic regions. For example, the coast of southern California features sandy shorelines, rocky cliffs, and kelp forests, each of which can be characterized as a different habitat and is home to a different community of plants and wildlife. Second, wet habitats do not exist in a vacuum, but rather are ecologically connected both to the upland habitats landward of the coastline, and to the ocean habitats farther offshore. Because this course is focused on the coast, we will not delve too far into the ecology of the open ocean. (Just so you know, this is known as the pelagic environment.) However, we will need to think about upland ecology because uplands are where the natural environment and development directly meet.

a. Near-Shore Ecology

Ecologists divide the "wet" coastal environment into a number of ecosystem types. The following passage briefly describes these systems and their resident plants and wildlife. As you read the following passage, think about the ways in which people might be interested in using (or not using) these resources. Also, give some thought to the linkages between these systems and the ecological world beyond them. If you are interested in seeing photographs of these environments as you read about them, go to the National Park Service's excellent website at https:// www.nps.gov/subjects/geology/coastal-landforms.htm.

Geoffrey Waller (ed.), Sealife: A Complete Guide to the Marine Environment

70-91 (1996)

Shoreline Environments

The influence of the sea extends well above the high tide mark and in many areas its effect is felt some considerable distance inland. The shoreline provides many diverse breeding sites for seabirds, shorebirds and terrestrial animals.

***

The Strandline

The strandline often looks like a wavy band of debris which snakes its way along the beach at the high tide mark. The position of the strandline will oscillate with the levels of high water and will be pushed furthest up the beach after storms and the spring equinox tides of spring and autumn. The debris which is referred to as "flotsam and jetsam" is a mixture of dead plant material, dead animal remains and rubbish of human origin.

***

The strandline is an area where weak or dying animals may come to rest, especially after storms or during the breeding season. . . . In many regions of the world the strandline is home to the scavenging sandhopper and many land-dwelling insects including flies and beetles which feed on the dead organic debris. Although these animals provide an excellent clean-up service they can be a nuisance to anyone sitting near the strandline during the summer months.

Sea Cliffs

Cliffs provide suitable nesting sites for many species of seabirds such as fulmars, gulls and auks. Cliff ledges give freedom from human interference and protection from predators and other scavenging animals. High cliff areas also provide an assisted take off from the updraughts of air passing up and over the cliff face. . . . Sea cliff areas provide habitats for other animal species including reptiles and a variety of plants which are tolerant to salt spray. Bird excretion results in high concentration of nutrients which enrich the soils on the ledges. The nutrients are then available to the plants which flourish here and these plants help to bind the soil, thus reducing erosion.

***

Sand-dunes and Sandbanks

Sand-dunes are formed by sand blown up on the beach by the wind. Large systems of dunes can form in river deltas to create a complex pattern of freshwater, brackish water and seawater marshes. The areas then develop into important habitats for shorebirds, wildfowl, seabirds, herons, cranes, and even flamingos. Provided that the sand removed from the beach at low tide is being replaced by new supplies, the dunes can continue to grow in height. . . .

Sand-dune areas are inhospitable places for organisms. Strong winds, salty spray, hot sun, drifting sand, little water and poor nutrient retention make it a difficult place for plant and animal colonization. However, certain plants including the beach grasses are able to capture and hold large quantities of sand in their extensive root systems. . . . The grasses can withstand high winds, drought conditions and large temperature fluctuations. . . . Once dunes have become colonized by the "pioneer" plants, other shrubs and low-level plants take hold. . . . Eventually, evergreen shrubs will become established and this will be followed by coniferous plants. The last stage of dune colonization is the establishment of broad-leaved trees and their associated woodland communities.

Lagoons may also form behind areas of sand-dunes and these areas become "safehavens" for many rarer reptiles, amphibians, insects and birds. Freshwater ponds that form in these areas become magnets for local wildlife and amphibians which require freshwater for reproductive purposes breed here. Sandbanks can form offshore on the seaward side of dune systems and provide important front line protection against severe weather. Coastal seawater lagoons develop between these banks and the main shoreline. Within their shallow protected lagoons, many young fish and shellfish take refuge from the harsher conditions of the shoreline.

Intertidal Environments

The "intertidal" or "littoral" environments include those that are periodically exposed to the air by the cyclic rise (flood) and fall (ebb) of the tides. The extent of the tidal range varies enormously with location, the seasons and time of the month. "Spring" tides occur twice each month, two days after the "full" and "new" moons when the combined gravitational pull of the moon and sun are in a straight line. The "neap" tides occur between spring tides after the first and third quarters of the moon, when the direction of the moon's pull is at right angles. One tidal cycle (the time between successive high or low waters) may only occur once a day (diurnal) or, more commonly, twice a day (semi-diurnal).

***

Tidal action and wave action have major influences on intertidal habitats. Tidal currents can transport large quantities of sediments and loose materials. The scouring action of water and loose material causes abrasion and mechanical battering of any protruding bottom substrate. Wave and tidal actions also stir the loose sediment into a suspension and the water becomes turbid and dark. The reduction of light through turbidity is not beneficial to plants but essential nutrients can be released through the disturbance of the seabed.

***

On exposed rocky coastlines wave action will be the key factor influencing organisms in this habitat. On more sheltered shores with less wave action, there may be little gap between the marine and terrestrial environments. Here the brown luxuriant algal growth may be only centimeters below saltmarsh grassland. By comparison, on the wave-swept shores algal growth will be stunted and the terrestrial zone separated from the marine habitat by a broad band of bare rock. The shore communities on exposed rocky areas will be characterized by the key species of mussels and red algae which can withstand severe wave action. Where some shelter can be found from the pounding waves, barnacles will be present in large numbers. Sand and shingle shores exposed to heavy waves and surf are generally unstable and support little life except perhaps at the microscopic level. On the more sheltered shore where mud and sand are stable, a rich diversity of animals will be found living in the soft substrate. . . .

Intertidal areas have the largest fluctuations of environmental conditions, when compared to any other marine habitat. Organisms living in intertidal areas have to endure periods of exposure to air, water currents, wave action, and fluctuations of temperature, salinity, oxygen, and pH. . . . To cope with these changes intertidal plants and animals have evolved a diverse variety of behavioral and physical adaptations in these harsh conditions. In soft sediments most of the organisms adapt to a burrowing lifestyle for protection against predation and exposure. . . . On hard, rocky shores it is not possible to burrow for protection. Therefore, the organisms are biologically designed to a tougher specification to endure the harsh environmental conditions. One of the most successful adaptations is the development of a thick, hard and impervious shell. . . . The shape of these shells is low with streamlined profiles and this helps to reduce the impact of the waves. . . .

An animal surviving on exposed rocky areas must be able to attach itself firmly to the surface. . . . There is also protection in large numbers and many mussels and barnacles become tightly packed to reduce the likelihood of being washed off by wave action. . . . Many of the more mobile or delicate animals such as shrimps, crabs and isopods take refuge in rock pools, cracks, crevices and underneath rocks where wave action is reduced.

***

Estuaries and Saltmarshes

Estuaries are semi-enclosed coastal areas in which the seawater is significantly diluted by freshwater from streams and rivers feeding the estuaries. Many bays, inlets, sounds and gulfs can be considered estuaries on the basis of their physical structures. Freshwater from land run-off is nutrient rich, and when it mixes with salt water at the mouths of estuaries, plankton blooms often occur on the seaward side. Water flow decreases as the estuary widens and becomes shallower, and the sediment "load" of the river settles out to be deposited as mud or sandbanks. Where large rivers or river systems converge, offshore deltas of mud and sand may form. In temperate latitudes, mudflats may subsequently rise above the normal levels of high tide through sediment and soil accumulations from river floodings. Colonization of mudflats by marsh grasses will lead to permanent saltmarshes. In subtropical and tropical regions, saltmarshes are often replaced by areas of "mangroves" which occupy a similar habitat.

Estuaries

The salinity of estuaries fluctuates and repeated changes in salinity increase stress levels in marine organisms. . . . In some estuarine areas, the abundance of animals such as the oyster, crab, shrimp, ragworm, tubifix worm and Hydrobia snail can be high. Food webs within estuaries are complex and are not fully understood. . . .

***

Some benthic fish species such as the flounder and the young of a few other coastal species also inhabit the brackish waters of estuaries. Other species including the European eel, the Atlantic salmon, and the sea trout, will acclimatize in estuaries during their migration between freshwater and saltwater.

Mudflat areas are exposed at low tide and may extend to many square kilometers. Mudflats which are adjacent to saltmarsh areas provide important feeding grounds for many shorebirds and seabirds. . . .

Shorebirds have bills which are adapted for shoreline feeding, and different species of birds are able to take a variety of prey from different depths in the soft sediment. Large flocks of shorebirds can often be seen probing the mud near the water's edge, foraging for prey and looking for the telltale signs of burrowing animals. . . . The

> **Primary Production**
>
> Primary production is the "amount of organic matter synthesized by organisms from inorganic substances in unit time in unit volume of water. . . ." DAVID F. TVER, OCEAN AND MARINE DICTIONARY 244 (1979). It is a measure of the richness of food availability at the bottom of the food web.

diversity and numbers of seabirds, shorebirds and wildfowl found on estuaries and their associated wetlands reflect the enormous productivity of marshlands and mudflats. These areas afford the ornithologist with some of the best bird-watching sites. . . .

Saltmarshes

Saltmarshes are biologically important areas with high primary production. The marsh grasses hold sediment from the occasional river floodings which increases the richness of the developing soils. . . .

Saltmarshes form important habitats for many terrestrial animals including rats, snakes, insects and birds. Saltmarshes and their adjacent mudflats are important breeding and feeding grounds for many shorebirds, seabirds and wildfowl. The marshes may be used as "staging posts" along migratory routes for some bird species, or overwintering grounds and summer feeding areas for others.

Mangroves

The swampy intertidal areas of coastlines and estuaries are replaced by "mangrove forests" in the subtropical and tropical regions of the world. . . . [In the United States, this would include areas along the Gulf of Mexico, Florida, southeastern states such as Georgia and South Carolina, the Caribbean territories of Puerto Rico and the U.S. Virgin Islands, and Pacific territories such as Guam and the Solomon Islands. — Eds.]

Mangroves consist of a number of trees or tree-like shrubs that are tolerant to both saltwater and brackish water conditions. . . . They have extensive root systems which anchor them firmly in the soft substrate and some have specially adapted root systems to take in oxygen. . . .

***

The intertidal mangrove forests provide a number of different habitats which include the muddy sediments, the surface of the mud, the surface of trunks and roots of the trees, and, above the waterline, the canopy of the forest. Sessile animals including barnacles, tunicates, oysters and sponges attach themselves to the tree roots which are free of the clogging mud. . . .

***

In the subtidal areas of mangroves that are permanently covered by water, a high diversity of sealife is crowded together on the mangrove roots. Predominantly marine subtidal areas of mangroves also provide suitable nursery grounds for the juvenile stages of many important species of offshore fish. Rich populations of nearshore fish, shrimps, crabs, lobsters and shellfish are common in the saltwater shallows of mangrove forests. The forest canopy also provides a good habitat for many nesting birds and bats, including the world's largest species, the fruit bats or flying foxes.

Kelp Forests

In cold temperate and polar regions, the intertidal rocky shore communities merge subtidally into sublittoral macroalgal "kelp forests." The kelp forests prefer moderately exposed areas where there is reasonable water circulation. . . . On gentle underwater gradients, the kelp forests may extend for several kilometers offshore.

Kelp occurs in many cold areas of the world with rocky coastlines. It is found along the western coasts of North and South America and reaches into the subtropical latitudes where cooler "upwelling" waters may be found. . . . Alginates are extracted from kelp and the products are used extensively in the food, cosmetics and medical industries. . . .

***

Macroalgae [such as kelp] are highly productive plants and under ideal conditions some of the largest species can grow as much as 60 cm per day. However, the normal rate of daily growth is between 5 and 25 cm.

***

Kelp forests are similar to terrestrial forests in that they have diverse communities of [vertebrate and invertebrate] animals associated with them. The large fronds of many species provide a platform for sessile communities of smaller algae, diatoms, bryozoans and hydroids. Worms, crustaceans and mollusks are found wandering over the algal fronds. . . . Kelp forests are . . . home for many juvenile stages of commercially important offshore fish species that use the kelp as nursery areas.

Seagrass Meadows

Seagrasses are the only true marine vascular plants and they have a distribution that covers a wide range of latitudes worldwide. Some species occupy the lower levels of the intertidal zone, but the most abundant areas of seagrass are found just below the tidal level, and they can occur down to a depth of about 50m. Seagrasses are found in clear, sheltered waters with a sandy bottom, but they also grow on fine sediments in turbid waters with lost light intensities. Characteristically, they inhabit enclosed and sheltered bays, lagoons, lees of islands and offshore barriers.

***

Seagrass meadows are productive areas with quick growth and fast turnover of dead organic matter. This quick turnover releases nutrients for other users including bacteria, and other microbial organisms and detritus feeders; therefore, seagrass meadows are considered to be amongst the most productive areas of all shallow, sandy environments. The seagrasses provide shelter for diverse communities of invertebrate nematode worms, small epiphytic algae and sessile filter feeders. . . . Among the leaves, snails, bivalves, polychaete worms and various large crustacean including lobsters and crayfish can be found. Many vertebrate fish species are attracted to the seagrass areas to feed and spawn. The seagrasses are used as nursery grounds for many young fish which will later leave for adult feeding grounds elsewhere. Large animals that consume seagrass include some herbivorous fish, some marine turtles and the sirenians (dugong and manatees).

Coral Reefs

Coral reefs are well known for their underwater splendor, vivid colors and rich species diversity. . . . Most of the true coral reef builders belong to only one phylum, the Cnidaria, which includes, among others, the hydras, jellyfish and sea anemones. Reef-building corals are colonies of tiny individual animals called "polyps." Each polyp secretes a calcium carbonate exoskeleton . . . which protects the soft, sack-like body inside.

Coral reef areas at low latitudes exhibit a high rate of growth, even though the surrounding waters may be low in food and nutrients. This is possible as much of the food for many coral species is provided by microscopic green algae called zooxanthellae. These microscopic plants live inside the cells of the polyp's tissues. . . . [Zooxanthellae] do not harm the animal but live with it in partnership (mutualism). The coral polyp provides protection, living space and nutrients for the zooxanthellae. The zooxanthellae provide food and oxygen for the living coral by recycling waste products and carrying out photosynthesis. . . . [Some coral species do not have zooxanthellae and] are not confined to the shallow surface as they do not require sunlight. Therefore they are found in all areas of the world from the tropics to the polar regions and a wide range of seabed depths.

***

. . . Turbid waters cut down on the amount of sunlight available for zooxanthellae photosynthesis and large amounts of sediment suspended in the turbid water can "blanket" and choke a reef. Coral reefs are not present in coastal areas with substantial river estuaries or deltas, as many corals have low tolerance to fresh water.

. . . The species diversity of the associated reef communities is probably the highest of all biological habitats in the sea. A single reef may have as many as 3,000 animal species living in or on it. . . . As coral reefs have such large diversities of organisms, it is not surprising that the food webs are also some of the most complex in the animal world.

b. Upland Ecology

While the common law focused primarily on use of coastal areas located directly at or seaward of the coastline, the geographic reach of modern, statutory coastal law is much broader. In some states, such as South Carolina, state coastal statutes apply to all coastal counties, which means that "coastal" law applies to land located nearly 100 miles inland. Laws in Delaware, Florida, and Hawai'i define all the land in those states as "coastal"! There are two arguments for the proposition that broader jurisdiction, specifically, regulatory power over both wet and upland areas, reflects good environmental policy. First, there are obvious connections between impacts to upland systems and effects on the "wet" systems along the shore. Thus, if the goal is to conserve shoreline systems, we need to conserve upland systems as well in order to achieve that goal. Second, there are reasons to care about upland systems for their own sake: They support many populations of sometimes rare plants and animals, and they provide a healthy, attractive setting for many thousands of human communities.

As compared to "wet" ecosystems, it is difficult to divide upland systems into a small number of general categories. There are, however, some features that many of these systems share:

Photo: Mdf/Wikimedia Commons

Figure 5-6. Piping Plover
An endangered coastal species: the piping plover.

- *A moderated climate.* The temperature of large water bodies, such as oceans, gulfs, and seas, does not change as rapidly as air temperature. Temperature ranges of upland habitats are often moderated by the more constant temperatures of nearby marine waters. So, for example, temperatures in places like Martha's Vineyard, Massachusetts are not as extreme as temperatures in locations along the same latitude in western Massachusetts.
- *Greater likelihood that riparian features are present.* Because surface waters, such as rivers and creeks, run to the sea, upland habitats are more likely to include rivers and creeks than habitats farther inland. Low elevations, such as those near coastlines, act as a magnet for surface water. Conservation of riparian habitats gives rise to a host of unique concerns.
- *Salt- and storm-tolerant plant communities.* Upland plants are often exposed to salt that is carried inland by the wind or in marine fogs. In addition, these plants are evolved to withstand more frequent storms that can bring high winds and occasional flooding.
- *Rarity.* Upland ecosystem types, such as longleaf pine forests, tend to be rarer than either "wet" systems or systems farther inland. Of the 25 most endangered ecosystems (less than 2 percent of original amount remaining) in the United States, 11 of them are coastal, terrestrial (upland) systems. REED F. NOSS, EDWARD T. LAROE III & J. MICHAEL SCOTT, ENDANGERED ECOSYSTEMS OF THE UNITED STATES (1995), http://biology.usgs.gov/pubs/ecosys.htm. Rarity is a function of several factors. First, as a matter of simple math (if there is such a thing), there are fewer acres of land within, say, 20 miles of the coast, than there are in the rest of the United States. Second, the ecology of coastal uplands is shaped by a unique combination of forces, such as the aforementioned salt and storms, as well as characteristic soils. Perhaps most important, rarity is a function of direct competition with land development. As you will learn later in this chapter, coastal areas feature some of

the highest population densities in the United States. And, of course, there is very little home building (at least human home building) taking place in coral reefs or kelp forests!

As you will see throughout the course, these features shape coastal law. For example, rules governing the development of coastal uplands tend to be more stringent than rules governing development in areas farther inland.

points for discussion

1. *Why we might care.* What are the rationales for conserving biodiversity and ecosystems generally? Are any rationales particularly supportive of the argument that we ought to conserve coastal biodiversity and habitats? As between "wet" and upland systems, can or should we prioritize conservation efforts? On what basis?
2. *Getting the balance right.* If we can agree that there are good reasons for conserving biodiversity and ecosystems, we next get to the truly hard question: What is the appropriate level of conservation? In other words, how do we strike an appropriate balance between conservation and development across a particular coastal region? Should the approach depend on how rare the systems at risk are? What other criteria should be used to determine how much conservation is appropriate? What, if anything, should happen when more than 98 percent of an ecosystem has been lost?
3. *Cost-benefit analysis.* There are a variety of approaches that are used in other contexts for determining "the appropriate level" of environmental protection. Since the mid-1980s, one of the most commonly used approaches is cost-benefit analysis. As its name would suggest, cost-benefit analysis entails measuring the costs and benefits to society of a proposed action; so, for a proposed residential development in a previously undeveloped coastal area, one would measure the economic benefits provided by the development, such as consumer surplus, construction employment, and enhanced tax base, against the economic cost of losing the upland habitat. What are the strengths and weaknesses of this approach? How does one measure environmental costs? Can you think of another way to find an appropriate balance between conservation and development?
4. *A sustainable approach.* Rather than seeking to balance conservation and development, one might decide that the best way to ensure sustainability over the long run is to establish a conservation floor. The idea is that without baseline healthy ecosystems, there can be no healthy human populations or economies. But how would we determine what these baselines would be? One approach would be to ensure that we maintained healthy populations of all native plant and animal populations. If monitoring detected that populations were falling below healthy levels, then further activities potentially impacting those particular resources would be prohibited.

Another approach would be to use a metric based on what are known as "ecosystem services." Ecosystem services are useful and valuable services, such as flood control and water purification, provided to humans by natural systems. (You will find more information on the full range of ecosystem services provided by coastal systems later in this chapter.) We could make decisions about development based on its impact on provision of those services. If a particular action would significantly reduce a system's ability to provide one or more services, then that action would be prohibited. Do either of these baseline approaches seem desirable to you? Should values to humans be the only ones worth considering? Do you see any practical problems in their implementation? What kinds of information would you need in order to implement them?

5. *Preservation versus conservation.* Preservation implies that certain lands or resources ought to be maintained in their current condition, or as close to their current condition as possible. Conservation refers to the type of balancing described above, that is, using resources in some kind of optimal way. Are these two objectives really different? If so, why might we sometimes choose preservation over conservation? Can they be used together? How would one or both be applied across a dynamic land- or coast-scape over time?

6. *You're not from around here, are you?* In addition to land development and run-off (discussed below), one of the major threats to coastal systems comes in the form of invasive species, also known as exotic species. Because of transportation features such as ports, coastal areas are particularly subject to invasions. Animals and plants from other parts of the world arrive as "stowaways" aboard or affixed to boats and planes, then gain footholds by outcompeting native flora and fauna. In addition to threatening the health of native systems, invasives can impose other substantial costs on society. *See* David Pimentel, Rodolfo Zuniga & Doug Morrison, *Update on the Environmental and Economic Costs Associated with Alien-Invasive Species in the United States*, 52 ECOLOGICAL ECON. 273 (2005).

7. *Why coastal lawyers might care.* For lawyers who work in coastal law, for example, representing developers or coastal conservation organizations, ecology and geology matter because they play key roles in both the design and implementation of the law. As you will learn, attorneys for would-be developers are responsible for obtaining a variety of permits from government agencies before a project can commence. Writing the applications for these permits will usually involve consulting with experts on coastal geology and ecology. A good coastal lawyer should not only be able to identify when a permit is needed, but also when to bring in an expert; it also helps to be able to understand what it is the expert is saying!

3. Natural Disasters and Vulnerability

As compared to other places people choose to live, coastal areas are more prone to storms and the catastrophic damage that can be caused by high winds and flooding. In addition to the fact that the largest kinds of storms, i.e., hurricanes, monsoons, and typhoons, originate at sea and thus make contact with land along the coast, coastal areas are characterized by low elevations. Along the Atlantic seaboard and Gulf Coast, these storms — think Katrina, Sandy, Harvey, and Florence — can cause extreme damage and enormous economic impacts. Human activities, such as the destruction of coastal wetlands and the destabilization of dune structures, decrease natural barriers to storm surges. In addition, greater population densities result in higher numbers of deaths and injuries, as well as greater financial impacts.

On the Pacific Coast, the damage from large storm events is most often in the form of flooding caused by rainfall. Flash floods and mudslides can result in death and extensive damage to private property and public assets such as roads and bridges. The likelihood and degree of damage are increased by land use changes. Removal of natural vegetation and the presence of impermeable, paved surfaces increase the speed with which water flows downhill, thereby magnifying the power and destructiveness of floods.

Another potential, but rarer, cause of catastrophic flooding is tsunamis. Set in motion by earthquakes, tsunamis are capable of causing massive destruction. All of us remember the terrible devastation caused by the massive tsunamis of December 2004 (Indonesia, Thailand, and Sri Lanka) and March 2011 (Japan).

Photo: NOAA

Figure 5-7. Kodiak Tsunami
After a tsunami hit Kodiak, Alaska in 1964.

In 1960 and 1964, large tsunami waves struck the United States. The 1960 tsunami, which was caused by an earthquake off the coast of Chile, killed 61 people in Hawai'i. The 1964 tsunami generated waves of more than 30 feet, killing more than 100 in Alaska and 12 in California. Due to seismic patterns, the areas of the United States most vulnerable to tsunamis include the coasts of Alaska, Hawai'i, Washington, Oregon, California, Puerto Rico, and the Virgin Islands. Other areas are also vulnerable, although the probability of an occurrence is lower.

As the following excerpt explains, global climate change represents another kind of potential threat to coastal ecosystems and communities.

John C. Field et al., Potential Consequences of Climate Variability and Change on Coastal Areas and Marine Resources

In National Assessment Synthesis Team, US Global Change Research Program, Climate Change Impacts on the United States (2000)

The US has over 95,000 miles of coastline and over 3.4 million square miles of ocean within its territorial waters. These areas provide a wide range of essential goods and services to society. Some 53% of the total U.S. population live on the 17% of land in the coastal zone, and these areas become more crowded every year. Because of this growth, as well as increased wealth and affluence, demands on coastal and marine resources for both aesthetic enjoyment and economic benefits are rapidly increasing.

Coastal and marine environments are intrinsically linked to climate in many ways. The ocean is an important distributor of the planet's heat, with major ocean currents moving heat toward the poles from the equator. There is some chance that this distribution of heat through the ocean's "conveyor belt" circulation would be strongly influenced by the changes projected in many global climate models. Sea-level rise is another climate-related phenomenon with a major influence on coastlines. Global sea level has already risen by 4 to 8 inches (10-20 cm) in the past century and models suggest this rise is very likely to accelerate. The best estimate is that sea level will rise by an additional 19 inches (48 cm) by 2100, with an uncertainty range of 5 to 37 inches (13-95 cm). Geological forces (such as subsidence, in which the land falls relative to sea level) play a prominent role in regional sea-level change. Accelerated global sea-level rise is expected to have dramatic impacts in those regions where subsidence and erosion problems already exist.

Shoreline Erosion and Human Communities

Coastal erosion is already a widespread problem in much of the country and has significant impacts on undeveloped shorelines as well as on coastal development and infrastructure. Along the Pacific Coast, cycles of beach and cliff erosion have been linked to El Niño events that raise average sea levels over the short term and alter storm tracks that affect the coastline. For example, during the 1982-83 El Niño and the 1997-98 El Niño, erosion damage was widespread along the Pacific Coastline. If increases in the frequency or intensity of El Niño events occur, they would likely combine with long-term sea-level rise to exacerbate these impacts.

Atlantic and Gulf Coast shorelines are especially vulnerable to long term sea-level rise as well as any increase in the frequency of storm surges or hurricanes. Most erosion events on these coasts are the result of storms, and the slope of these areas is so gentle that a small rise in sea level produces a large inland shift of the shoreline. When buildings, roads, and seawalls block this natural shift, the beaches and shorelines erode, especially during storm events. This increases the threats to coastal development, transportation infrastructure, tourism, freshwater aquifers, and fisheries (which are already stressed by human activities). Coastal cities and towns, especially those in storm-prone regions such as the Southeast, are particularly vulnerable to extreme events. Intensive residential and commercial development in such regions puts life and property at risk.

Threats to Estuarine Health

Estuaries are extremely productive ecosystems that are affected in numerous ways by climate. Winter temperatures are projected to continue to increase more than summer temperatures, resulting in a narrowing of the annual water temperature range of many estuaries. This is likely to cause species' ranges to shift and increase the vulnerability of some estuaries to non-native invasive species. Either increases or decreases in runoff would very likely create impacts to estuaries. Increased runoff would likely deliver increased amounts of nutrients such as nitrogen and phosphorous to estuaries, while simultaneously increasing the stratification between freshwater runoff and marine waters. Both nutrient additions and increased stratification would increase the potential for blooms of algae that deplete the water of oxygen, increasing stresses on sea grasses, fish, shellfish, and other living things on the bottom of lakes, streams, and oceans. Decreased runoff would likely reduce flushing, decrease the size of estuarine nursery zones, and allow predators and pathogens of shellfish to penetrate further into the estuary.

Coastal Wetland Survival

Coastal wetlands (marshes and mangroves) are highly productive ecosystems that are strongly linked to fisheries productivity. They provide important nursery and habitat functions to many commercially important fish and shellfish populations. Dramatic losses of coastal wetlands have already occurred on the Gulf Coast due to subsidence, changes caused by dams and levees that alter flow and reduce sediment supply, dredge and fill activities, and sea-level rise. Louisiana alone has been losing coastal wetlands at rates between 24 and 40 square miles per year during the last 40 years, accounting for as much as 80% of the total US coastal wetland loss.

In general, coastal wetlands will survive if soil buildup equals the rate of relative sea-level rise or if the wetland is able to migrate inland. However, if soil accumulation is unable to keep pace with high rates of sea-level rise, or if wetland migration is blocked by bluffs, coastal development, or shoreline protective structures (such as dikes, sea walls, and jetties), the wetland will be excessively inundated and eventually lost. The projected increase in the current rate of sea-level rise will very likely exacerbate coastal wetland losses nationwide, although the extent of impacts will vary among regions.

Coral Reef Die-offs

Coral reefs play a major role in the environment and economies of two states (Florida and Hawaii) as well as most US territories in the Caribbean and Pacific. Coral reefs are valuable economic resources for fisheries, recreation, tourism, and coastal protection. In addition, reefs are one of the largest global storehouses of marine biodiversity, with untapped genetic resources. Some estimates of the global cost of losing coral reefs run in the hundreds of billions of dollars each year. The demise or continued deterioration of reefs could have profound implications for the US.

The last few years have seen unprecedented declines in the health of coral reefs. The 1998 El Niño was associated with record sea-surface temperatures and associated coral bleaching (when coral expel the algae that live within them and are necessary to their survival); in some regions, as much as 70% of the coral may have died in a single season. There has also been an upsurge in the variety, incidence, and virulence of coral diseases in recent years, with major die-offs in Florida and much of the Caribbean region. In addition, increasing atmospheric CO_2 concentrations could possibly decrease the calcification rates of the reef-building corals, resulting in weaker skeletons, reduced growth rates and increased vulnerability to erosion. Model results suggest that these effects would likely be most severe at the current margins of coral reef distribution.

4. Water-Dependent and Downstream of Everywhere

As noted, coastal areas — due to their low elevation — attract surface water flows from higher elevation, inland areas. Most of the fresh water carried by rivers, and much of the rain that falls across the country, will ultimately make its way through the "coastal band" and into estuaries, bays, and oceans. While freshwater supply can be a boon to human populations and is obviously critical to the ecological health of coastal and riparian ecosystems, water flows bring with them chemicals and other pollutants that have entered the water over vast expanses. While some amount of this "land-based run-off" may be removed, evaporate, or settle as rivers travel to the coast, everything that is left reaches the coast.

Run-off that originates in coastal areas is particularly harmful to the coastal environment because it has little chance to evaporate, settle, or otherwise be filtered through the natural environment. Aside from the physical proximity of the source, there are two key determinants of the extent to which harmful run-off impacts coastal waters. Most obviously, population density (usually a proxy for the amount of pollutants released into the environment) is an important factor. Less obviously, the extent to which released pollutants enter rivers, streams, and coastal waters is a function of "watershed permeability."

Chester L. Arnold & C. James Gibbons, Impervious Surface Coverage: The Emergence of a Key Environmental Indicator

62 J. Am. Plan. Ass'n 243-58 (1996)

Water resource protection at the local level is getting more complicated, largely due to the recognition of nonpoint source pollution, or polluted runoff, as a major problem. This diffuse form of pollution, now the nation's leading threat to water quality . . . , is derived from contaminants washed off the surface of the land by stormwater runoff, and carried either directly or indirectly into waterways or groundwater. As programs directed at nonpoint source control cascade down from federal to state to local governments, the technical complexities involved with such control are further complicated by regulatory and management considerations.

Stormwater runoff problems are nothing new to local land-use decision-makers. However, the principal concern about runoff has always been safety, with the focus on directing and draining water off of paved surfaces as quickly and efficiently as possible. Once off the road and out of sight, stormwater has been largely out of mind — downstream consequences be damned (or dammed). Regulations have been expanded in recent years to include consideration of flooding and erosion, yet these factors fall far short of a comprehensive and effective approach to mitigating the water quality impacts of development.

How do planners and other local officials get a handle on protecting their local water resources? While no magic bullet exists to simplify all the complexities involved, an indicator is emerging from the scientific literature that appears to have all the earmarks of a useful tool for local planners — the amount of impervious, or impenetrable, surface. . . .

People, Pavement and Pollution

Impervious surfaces can be defined as any material that prevents the infiltration of water into the soil. While roads and rooftops are the most prevalent and easily identified types of impervious surface, other types include sidewalks, patios, bedrock outcrops, and compacted soil. As development alters the natural landscape, the percentage of the land covered by impervious surfaces increases.

Roofs and roads have been around for a long time, but the ubiquitous and impervious pavement we take for granted today is a relatively recent phenomenon. A nationwide road census showed that in 1904, 93 percent of the roads in America were unpaved. . . . This changed with the early twentieth century ascendancy of the automobile over the railways, capped by the mid-century massive construction of the interstate highway system, which served to both stimulate and facilitate the growth of suburbia. From that point on, imperviousness became synonymous with human presence — to the point that studies have shown that an area's population density is correlated with its percentage of impervious cover. . . .

Impervious surfaces not only indicate urbanization, but also are major contributors to the environmental impacts of urbanization. As the natural landscape is paved over, a chain of events is initiated that typically ends in degraded water resources. This chain begins with alterations in the hydrologic cycle, the way that water is transported and stored.

These changes . . . have long been understood by geologists and hydrologists. As impervious coverage increases, the velocity and volume of surface runoff increase, and there is a corresponding decrease in infiltration. The larger volume of runoff and the increased efficiency of water conveyance through pipes, gutters, and artificially straightened channels result in increased severity of flooding, with storm flows that are greater in volume and peak more rapidly than is the case in rural areas. . . . The shift away from infiltration reduces groundwater recharge, lowering water tables. This both threatens water supplies and reduces the groundwater contribution to stream flow, which can result in intermittent or dry stream beds during low flow periods. . . .

Hydrologic disruption gives rise to physical and ecological impacts. Enhanced runoff causes increased erosion from construction sites, downstream areas and stream banks. The increased volume of water and sediment, combined with the "flashiness" of these peak discharges, result in wider and straighter stream channels. . . . Loss of tree cover leads to greater water temperature fluctuations, making the water warmer in the summer and colder in the winter. . . . There is substantial loss of both streamside (riparian) habitat through erosion, and in-stream habitat as the varied natural stream bed of pebbles, rock ledges, and deep pools is covered by a uniform blanket of eroded sand and silt. . . . Engineered responses to flooding like stream diversion, channelization, damming, and piping further destroy stream beds and related habitats like ponds and wetlands. Finally, with more intensive land uses comes a corresponding increase in the generation of pollutants. Increased runoff serves to transport these pollutants directly into waterways, creating nonpoint source pollution, or polluted runoff.

Major categories of nonpoint source pollutants include pathogens (disease-causing microorganisms), nutrients, toxic contaminants, and debris. Pathogen contamination indicates possible health hazards, resulting in closed beaches and shellfish beds. Over-abundance of nutrients such as nitrogen and phosphorous can threaten well water supplies, and in surface waters can lead to algal "blooms" that, upon decaying, rob the waters of life-sustaining oxygen. Toxic contaminants like heavy metals and pesticides pose threats to the health of aquatic organisms and their human consumers, and are often persistent in the environment. Debris, particularly plastic, can be hazardous to animal and human alike, and is an aesthetic concern. Sediment is also a major nonpoint source pollutant, both for its effects on aquatic ecology and because of the fact that many of the other pollutants tend to adhere to eroded soil particles. . . .

The results of polluted runoff are evident in every corner of the United States. According to the Environmental Protection Agency (1994), nonpoint source pollution is now the number one cause of water quality impairment in the United States, accounting for the pollution of about 40% of all waters surveyed across the nation. The effects of nonpoint source pollution on coastal waters and their living resources have been of particular concern. . . . Urban runoff alone ranks as the second most common source of water pollution for lakes and estuaries nationwide, and the third most common source for rivers. . . .

As point source pollution is increasingly brought under control, the true impact of urban nonpoint source pollution is being recognized. For instance, even in an urbanized estuary like Long Island Sound, where the major environmental problems have been strongly linked to point source discharges from sewage treatment plants, an estimated 47% of the pathogen contamination is from urban runoff. . . .

Imperviousness as an Environmental Indicator

***

. . . Although impervious surfaces do not generate pollution, they: (1) are a critical contributor to the hydrologic changes that degrade waterways; (2) are a major component of the intensive land uses that do generate pollution; (3) prevent natural pollutant processing in the soil by preventing percolation; and (4) serve as an efficient conveyance system transporting pollutants into the waterways. It is not surprising, then, that research from the past 15 years consistently shows a strong correlation between the imperviousness of a drainage basin and the health of its receiving stream. . . .

***

Thresholds are always controversial and subject to change, yet it is important to note that to date, the threshold of initial degradation in particular seems to be remarkably consistent. The scientific literature includes studies evaluating stream health using many different criteria — pollutant loads, habitat quality, aquatic species diversity and abundance, and other factors. In a recent review of these studies, Schueler (1994a) concludes that "this research, conducted in many geographic areas, concentrating on many different variables, and employing widely different methods, has yielded a surprisingly similar conclusion — stream degradation occurs at relatively low levels of imperviousness (10-20%)" (100). Recent studies also suggest that this threshold applies to wetlands health. Hicks (1995) found a well-defined inverse relationship between freshwater wetland habitat quality and impervious surface area, with wetlands suffering impairment once the imperviousness of their local drainage basin exceeded 10%. Impervious coverage, then, is both a reliable and integrative indicator of the impact of development on water resources.

***

Adapted from U.S. Dept. of Ag. drawing

Figure 5-8. Permeable Surface
Creating a permeable surface.

points for discussion

1. *An important question.* If coastal areas are so dangerous, why do so many people choose to live there? How might laws affect these choices?

2. *Expecting the expected.* What are the implications of natural disasters for coastal law and policy? Some of the specific issues that are raised include emergency planning, rebuilding after disasters, and insurance covering damage to structures. These issues are covered in Chapter 10.

3. *A slow-moving disaster?* In recent decades, the Intergovernmental Panel on Climate Change has assembled a large number of reports synthesizing the science of climate change and its potential impacts. These reports, including many that are focused on coastal issues, can be found at http://www .ipcc.ch/. Chapter 10 addresses current and possible future legal approaches to avoiding, planning for, and mitigating climate change impacts.

4. *Is everything on the coast?* Because the coasts are "downstream of everywhere," they are magnets for water-borne pollution. Run-off enters rivers and streams across vast watersheds; these rivers and streams tend to converge at the coast. One of the best-known examples of this phenomenon, on a grand scale, is the "dead zone" in the Gulf of Mexico. Fertilizer run-off from as far away as Minnesota flows down the Mississippi River into the Gulf. Once in the Gulf, these chemicals induce large algal blooms, and when the algae dies, the bacteria that consume the remnants also consume oxygen from Gulf waters. Low oxygen levels result in a toxic environment for other marine organisms, including fish. What kinds of implications does this have for the geographic scope of coastal law? What incentive would farmers in Minnesota have to reduce their use of fertilizers or to take steps to reduce run-off?

5. *More localized problems.* Even in a more localized context, addressing run-off issues can be difficult. In Los Angeles, rains carry chemicals from yards, streets, and parking lots into the Santa Monica Bay. If the goal were to reduce this run-off in order to protect near-shore habitats, swimmers, surfers, and tourism, what kinds of laws might be needed?

B. CONFLICT AMONG PRIVATE AND PUBLIC INTERESTS

Of course, it is not land or resources that precipitate the conflicts that coastal law is meant to prevent or resolve: Rather, the source of conflicts is people, and in particular, the different ways that people want coastal lands and resources to be used.

1. The Roots of Conflict

This section is organized around the following hypothesis: *In order for a property dispute to arise between two parties, A's use of her property must interfere with B's ability to use his property in the way that B wants.*

If this hypothesis is correct, then we would expect to find high rates of conflict in several circumstances. First, conflict should be more likely in densely populated areas than in less crowded areas. In other words, if there are more *A*'s and *B*'s, there will be more opportunities for interference. Second, conflict should be more likely in places where property owners have high expectations as to what they should be able to do with, or prevent others from doing to, their property. Neither *A* nor *B* will be willing to expend the financial and emotional costs involved in raising an issue with the other where the costs of the interference are lower than those costs.

As illustrated below, each of these circumstances exists in coastal areas. There are plenty of *A*'s and *B*'s, and the number is growing. And, *A*'s and *B*'s have high expectations about what they ought to be able to do with both their upland property and in the mostly public areas seaward of the high-water line.

a. Population Density Along the Coast

From the time that Europeans first began to settle what is now the United States, coastal areas have been more heavily populated, per square mile, than other parts of the continent. In the 1800s, relatively higher coastal population density was primarily attributable to two facts. First, immigrants arrived by sea and disembarked at sea ports on the coast. It was difficult for these early Americans to travel farther inland, especially in the era before train travel. Second, sea ports were (and continue to be) at the center of much of the nation's commercial activity. This commerce created jobs and, thus, attracted workers. In 1880, ocean counties had a population density more than 2.5 times greater than inland counties. Jordan Rappaport & Jeffrey D. Sachs, *The United States as a Coastal Nation*, 8 J. ECON. GROWTH 5 (2003).

Prior to the 1940s, people lived on or near the coast because it was where the big industrial cities (and the jobs) were. Coastal areas at a distance from ports and cities were relatively undesirable places to live because of the lack of commercial agricultural potential, the high occurrence of lowland diseases such as malaria and cholera, and the challenge of building structures resistant to the harsh, storm-prone environment.

In the decades after World War II, however, these parts of the coast began to attract permanent residents and businesses. The forces driving this population growth included improvements in construction, a reduction in disease outbreaks, the implementation of a subsidized federal flood insurance program, an aging population, and the growing popularity of beach culture in American life. By the year 2000, coastal counties had more than four times the population density of inland counties. Rappaport and Sachs suggest that a large part of the post-1940 increase in coastal population was, unlike prior increases, due mainly to quality-of-life factors, such as "ocean vistas, pleasant weather, and low crime." In 2003, more than half of all U.S. citizens—153 million people—lived in the nation's 673 coastal counties, though population density is spread unevenly along the coast. Regions with particularly high density include much of the Atlantic seaboard, the Gulf Coast, and southern and central California. Kristen M. Crossett et al., *Population Trends Along the Coastal United States: 1980-2008*, Nat'l Oceanic & Atmospheric Admin. (2004).

Quality-of-life factors are also responsible for relatively recent increases in seasonal population fluctuations, which are tied to coastal tourism or to second-home ownership. Ocean City, Maryland, for example, has a year-round population of about 8,000 people, but hosts nearly 4 million visitors in the course of an average summer! (Ocean City is located within a three-hour drive of Philadelphia, Baltimore, and Washington, D.C.) In 2005, there were more than 1 million vacation homes sold in the United States (representing about 12 percent of all home sales); 40 percent of second-home buyers indicated that their primary reason for purchasing was the proximity of the home to the ocean, a lake, or a river. Nat'l Ass'n of Realtors, 2006 Profile of Second Home Owners (2006).

The dense populations along the coast provide part of the explanation for the rapid development of coastal law over the past 40 years. Private land uses are more likely to conflict when people live closer to one another. In addition, private land uses are likely to conflict with use of public coastal areas in regions with dense residential populations because density leads to congestion and the proliferation of competing uses.

b. Expectations and Interests

While population density makes it more likely that one landowner's land use will interfere with another's, those "interferences" will only require conflict resolution to the extent that the affected owner — public or private — feels aggrieved. The reasonable owner will feel aggrieved only if the interference is contrary to her expectations about what she is entitled to do with her property.

What gives rise to property owners' "expectations"? First, someone who has paid a high price for his land because it has certain valuable features will expect that he can take advantage of those features. So, if he knowingly bought an unzoned piece of land, and paid more for it than he would have paid for a physically similar but restricted parcel, it is reasonable to assume that he would expect to be able to build whatever he liked (so long as it did not create a nuisance). This is what the U.S. Supreme Court termed "distinct investment-backed expectations." *Penn Central Transp. Co. v. New York City*, 438 U.S. 104, 124 (1978). Second, expectations are strongly connected to tradition; if certain land uses have been allowed in a particular place in the past, a person is likely to believe that she will be able to use her land in that way in the future.

The remainder of this section explores the nature of private and public expectations in coastal lands and resources, that is, the ways in which private landowners and the public are interested in exercising their rights. We also explore some of the reasons that those expectations are particularly high in coastal areas.

2. Landward of the Coastline

From a macro perspective, consider that the insured value of property in coastal counties of the 16 Atlantic and Gulf states (about $7 trillion) represents 16 percent of the insured value of all property in the United States. (These counties make up only about 7 percent of the United States by area.) AIR WORLDWIDE, THE COASTLINE AT RISK: ESTIMATED INSURED VALUE OF COASTAL PROPERTIES (2005), www.air-worldwide.com (last visited Feb. 25, 2019). Coastal property owners have a significant financial stake in coastal lands and structures.

a. Expectations and Interests: Individual Landowners

Purchasers of coastal homes pay a significant premium for their property. A 2004 study on property in coastal Delaware found that a home 500 feet from the beach was worth 38 percent more than a similar home located just two-thirds of a mile from the beach, and that an oceanfront location added an additional 60 percent to the price! George R. Parsons & Joelle Noailly, *A Value Capture Property Tax for Financing Beach Nourishment Projects*, 47 OCEAN & COASTAL MANAGEMENT 49 (2004).

This premium represents what economists call the hedonic value component of the property. In other words, it is the portion of the price that homebuyers are willing to pay for the amenities associated with living on or near the coast. These amenities include things like easy access to the beach or to coastal waters, to views of the ocean, marshes, and wildlife, and to breezes and the smell of salt air, etc.

Consistent with our above-stated hypothesis about the sources of conflict, we would anticipate that coastal landowners would be particularly sensitive to infringements on their ability to enjoy the amenity components of their property. In other words, they will have high expectations that neither the public nor other private owners will infringe on access, views, or anything else for which they have paid. In addition, it is reasonable to expect that some private landowners will believe they are more entitled to enjoy these amenities than the general public; after all, while the coastal landowner has paid for easy access, the daytripper has not. To the private landowner, these expectations are more than a psychic matter. If the actions of others reduce the amenities of her property, they are cutting into not only her enjoyment but also her investment.

In addition to "amenity-seekers," coastal areas also include traditional and indigenous landowners. For example, there are still some barrier islands in South Carolina and Georgia, such as St. Helena Island, where descendants of slaves own a significant amount of land. In some New England towns, commercial fishing has been the center of the culture for more than 300 years. Like more recent in-migrants, indigenous and traditional landowners also value (and depend upon) access to coastal natural resources. Moreover, many traditional and indigenous landowners care deeply about preserving the landscape and cultural integrity of their communities. These objectives can be threatened by the many changes wrought by land development. Consider the following passage, describing issues affecting coastal Gullah communities in South Carolina and Georgia.

Lisa V. Faulkenberry et al., A Culture of Servitude: The Impact of Tourism and Development on South Carolina's Coast

59 Hum. Org. 86, 89-90 (2000)

The general benefits of tourism development are apparent to virtually all residents, but most also recognize the potential dangers. "What is tourism selling?" Richard Farr, a county official asked. "It's really selling amenities and a beautiful landscape, sea, and open space." Yet if uncontrolled growth continues, he added, "you will have plucked the flower and it will wilt in your hand." "I would venture to say," Emily Broom noted, "that if you asked the people of this island [St. Helena] to choose, would they sacrifice the quality of their life here for the money that will come in as a result of developing this, they would say, 'We don't want the money.' " Yet, stopping development is virtually impossible, as Wallace Porter described:

> Here you got a lot of people — they're considered poor people. . . . You get some of the people from up North who want a piece of this coast, . . . they're gonna shell that money out. And those [local] people never seen that kind of money before. They're gonna sell.

As development continues, local governments encourage tourism, believing it will bring prosperity. The issue then becomes managing tourism growth to maximize the benefits of the industry while minimizing the drawbacks — sustainable development. "The whole atmosphere is one of, not so much in the sense of wanting to grow, as in the sense of wanting to do what we do well," Sue Dunbar explained. "Quality," Richard Farr insisted, "is in everybody's interest." As a result, governments seek to regulate various activities to establish a standard for future development.

Zoning becomes a primary means to regulate growth, yet sentiments vary regarding zoning restrictions. Some residents, like Charles Gambrell, prefer freer regulations to enable those with private property to utilize it any way they wish. On the other hand, residents of retirement and gated communities (typically called "plantations") greatly enjoy the tight covenants and restrictions that keep private areas looking neatly trimmed, uniformly maintained, clean, and crime-free. However, as unzoned farms on outlying areas (largely owned by African Americans) increasingly abut these plantations and assail residents with the smells and sounds of working farms, newcomers complain and secure government intervention to eliminate these primarily black-owned enterprises. This zoned exclusion, of course, further alienates African American residents. "Whoever got the most money, that's who normally win the case," a frustrated black business owner exclaimed.

African American informants describe a gradual and subtle loss of their political power. "They [government] try to intimidate you. They want to come in and make you look like you're stupid," Chad Allgood commented. With sarcasm, Philip Olsen wondered, "how did we . . . stumble through life, being as ignorant as we are, . . . and end up with exactly what you [newcomers and tourists] want?"

As long-term residents lose power over political decisions, they also lose control over their land. Historically, land in the Sea Islands was passed down through the generations within the family. Each time land ownership changed, names of most or all of the surviving family members were included on the deed to the property. This means that today, one parcel of land may be legally owned by hundreds of people, tremendously complicating the deed process and creating difficulties for those interested in acquiring local land. Thus, to buy even a tiny parcel of land, Richard Farr explained, "you have to talk to a thousand people. It's hopeless almost."

Yet, not all residents feel the obstacles involved in obtaining land are necessarily detrimental. Angela Holcombe suggested that: the smartest thing they've [Hilton Head blacks] done is . . . will down [land] through so many years. . . . So, when you go to develop it, you're coming up against so many people who have a right to this land. Somebody can't come in really fast and sweep it away from them. [Neither Mr. Farr nor Mrs. Holcombe appear to understand the law of partition. See point 4, following excerpt.—EDS.]

As land values and zoning restrictions increase, traditional subsistence practices disappear. "Even the land I used to farm," Wallace Porter remarked; "there's houses being built or mobile homes being put there. . . . Pretty soon there'll be no more farm land in this area." This would be a tragedy, Emily Broome contended, "because nothing will buy back the quality of life we have here if we lose it." Many community members recognize that increasing taxes are necessary to maintain the quality of life. Mary Spencer noted: "Part of the reason [for increasing taxes] is when you have increased growth and they're more people moving down here, it puts a real strain on the services the county can provide. Therefore, . . . the money's got to come from somewhere" to fund those services, she concluded.

For many other residents, however, increasing property taxes generates concerns, because "they have a piece of property and eventually they want to build on it and every year . . . you have taxes going up," Mary Spencer explained. "It makes it harder and harder to develop that land." "At one time they were going to develop Fripp Plantation," Emma Burch observed. "We would've been sandwiched in between golf courses which would've made the land taxes go up to the point where you couldn't farm it anymore." Thus, the discrepancy between the ability of outside, capital-rich developers to transform the environment into extravagant plantations and mansions and the relative inability of natives to do the same is exacerbated.

Informants suggest that simply continuing to own their land becomes an economic struggle. "As more people [tourists/retirees] come, the property values rise," Tony Watson explained; "so in relation to taxes and income, the poor people are now pushed and stretched [and struggle] to even continue to own their land." "When we first came over here [St. Helena]," Chad Allgood commented, "land wasn't worth a hundred dollars an acre. Now it's worth ten or fifteen thousand dollars an acre." "Every year we pay more [property] tax than the place was worth when we built it," Philip Olsen lamented. "We've paid for the house again." Those unable to pay the increasing tax burden face an inevitable but painful decision — sell their land. "People are frightened, especially after the taxes started going up," David Jones explained. "There's a conspiracy [by developers] to take our land." As a result, many locals have lost their land from increasing taxes that they were unable to pay. "They end up in places like the Bluffton area, miserable," Jones observed; "this was home and they didn't want to leave it."

points for discussion

1. *Why we might care.* Why might we want to use the law to protect indigenous and traditional coastal residents? Before you answer this question, you might ask from whom and what are we protecting them? Why do we need to interfere with the functioning of the market in land? Is there anything we can do to stop the forces of modernity?

2. *Museumism.* Is there something paternalistic about protecting traditional and indigenous coastal dwellers? Would we be doing it for our own sake (as outsiders) because we enjoy the idea of having some traditional cultures to observe and discuss? Or, would we be protecting those cultures for the benefit of those who are part of them?

3. *Cultural conceptions of culture.* At what point does a culture become traditional? Is there an age at which a culture graduates to traditional stature and thus is entitled to special consideration? Are, for example, 50-year-old surf bungalows in Redondo Beach, Los Angeles remnants of an important cultural tradition that ought to be protected from development pressures? What about a collection of seaside cottages from the 1930s used for a Hollywood movie set (Crystal Cove, Newport Beach, California)?

4. *Legal approaches to cultural preservation.* Another threat to the sustainability of traditional culture along the South Carolina coast is what is known as the "heirs property" problem. This problem arises when property has passed from generation to generation over long periods of time through the laws of intestate succession. Eventually, there may be hundreds of co-tenants, even though there is only one individual or family who resides on the property. The tenant-in-possession may not be interested in selling the property for development; a developer who wishes to purchase the property may, however, force a sale by purchasing the ownership share of a co-tenant and filing a partition action with the court. At the auction, the developer will

likely be able to outbid the land-rich but cash-poor tenant-in-possession. The result of this process, spread across the landscape, is the conversion of farmland and traditional communities to subdivisions and shopping centers. How might the law of co-tenancy be changed in order to provide more protection for tenants-in-possession, who may have been paying taxes and maintenance costs for many years? What other options might be available? For more information, see C. Scott Graber, *Heirs Property: The Problems and Possible Solutions*, 12 CLEARINGHOUSE REVIEW 273 (1978).

5. *Your coast.* Can you think of communities, in the coastal areas with which you are most familiar, who might face some of the same issues as the Gullah people of South Carolina and Georgia?

b. Expectations and Interests: Commercial Landowners

Because prices are higher for coastal land, most commercial land in coastal areas is either held for investment or used for coastal-dependent activities. The concept here is similar to that outlined above with respect to individual property owners: When a commercial interest purchases coastal land, it will be willing to pay a higher price because the property includes significant economic benefits attached to its location.

The uses that take advantage of these benefits are known as coastal-dependent (or water-dependent) uses. There are two principal types of coastal-dependent uses. The first includes tourism and land development, two enterprises that capitalize on the amenity-seeking individuals described above. The second includes industrial and resource extraction endeavors that can only be conducted (or can be conducted most profitably) in coastal areas. Examples of industrial coastal-dependent uses would be power plants, which require substantial amounts of cheap water for cooling, and ports. Fishing and certain kinds of mining, for example, sand and gravel mining, are examples of coastal-dependent resource extraction enterprises.

The interests of developers and tourism entrepreneurs often overlap with the interests of the population they serve. So, for instance, both would be interested (to some extent) in preserving the natural coastal environment: Who would want to take a vacation to, buy a second home in, or retire to an ugly, polluted place? However, entrepreneurs' interest in cost-competitiveness can conflict with the interest in environmental quality; it might be cheaper, for example, simply to fill in wetlands rather than to delicately construct a development around them. There are, as we will see later in the course, ways to try to balance environmentally sensitive construction (or resort management) and cost concerns. The important point is that residential development and tourism simultaneously depend upon and impact the coastal environment. Achieving the optimum amount and rate of development is a challenge both for government and for businesspeople.

Owners of land intended for other types of coastal-dependent uses, such as power-generating facilities, commercial fishing harbors, oyster farms, or sand mines, expect, of course, to be able to pursue their enterprises profitably. In a perfect world, they would like to have uninterrupted and uncontested access to the natural resources they need for their businesses. However, these resources are often publicly owned or located in public areas. For this reason, resource-dependent entrepreneurs in coastal areas must expect to encounter extensive regulation of, and public involvement in, their activities.

The following excerpt provides an example of conflict between commercial uses of coastal lands and resources, examining the growing conflict between development and a traditional fishing community in Rhode Island.

Arthur Gregg Sulzberger, Galilee in Conflict

Providence Journal, Aug. 28, 2005, at A-1

On warm summer days, smells and sounds clash along the oil-stained streets of Galilee.

The rich sweet scent of fried seafood mixes with the acrid odor of rotting fish; the squawks of the seagulls punctuate the deep baritones of foghorns.

Pickup trucks and tractor-trailers clank along, hauling catches out of the village and supplies into the bait shops, fish wholesalers and boat mechanics that help keep the local fishing fleet, one of the country's sturdiest, afloat.

Photo: William B. Flosom/NOAA

Figure 5-9. Lobster Boat Leaving Galilee

Tourists lap the tiny village in a frustrated search for free parking. Hundreds of other cars already soak up the sun in the pay lots as their passengers crowd onto the Block Island Ferry.

Visitors line the breakwater, casting off the rocks and waving to the boats as they pass in and out of Point Judith Pond. And on the creaky wooden deck of George's of Galilee, business, as always, is booming.

Richard Durfee watches the action from outside his wind-whipped, gray-shingled restaurant, which his family has owned for going on six decades.

"Tourism has always been here, and fishing has always been here, and they've always gotten along. It's what makes Galilee very special and very strong," says Durfee, 63.

"Galilee is special — it's probably the best economic use, per square inch, of any community I've ever seen. It works, and it works well."

And so it has. But a series of plans, some under way, others just abstractions, has the fishermen nervous about the future of the port and their role in it.

In the face of growing regulation, soaring insurance and declining catches, their industry appears increasingly vulnerable, particularly given the rising value of waterfront property.

These men — for they are mostly men, and, in many cases, the sons and grand-sons of those who turned this sliver of land into an engine of the local economy — fear that efforts to encourage tourism will alter the character of Galilee, much as vacationers and tourists redefined once-vibrant fishing communities such as Newport, Provincetown and Kennebunkport.

It matters because there aren't many places like it left. Galilee is the last self-sufficient fishing community in Rhode Island and one of a dwindling few in New England, along with New Bedford, Gloucester and Portland.

Sure, there are other places where fishermen dock boats, drop nets, or unload catches, but with ice venders, fish processors and boat mechanics, Galilee has everything it needs to bring fish, mollusk and crustacean from sea to plate.

In 2003 Galilee ranked as the 16th most productive fishing port in the nation, hauling in 44 million pounds of fish worth about $32.4 million.

***

Over the years the port grew — and George's grew with it. The restaurant became one of Narragansett's largest employers and Galilee's mini-chamber of commerce, fielding phone calls about the weather and ferry schedules.

As the restaurant was handed from father to son, the customer base began to shift. One day Richard Durfee stopped opening the restaurant early enough for fishermen to grab a cup of coffee before work.

Durfee and his family also own property around their restaurant — including a crafts shop and a candy shop — making them the largest private landowner in Galilee.

Just east of the restaurant, where four cottages (shacks really) once stood, four large beach houses are under construction, each being marketed at $1.75 million to $2.25 million. Each house includes a fourth-story cupola, which a spokesman for the project says is a good place to sip martinis.

"This is going to be a New York, Connecticut market," Ned Caswell said. "These will be beach cottages. These will be second homes."

In addition, the gated Village at Sand Hill Cove will include a strip of street-front businesses topped with two stories of condominiums. Durfee also plans to rebuild George's at its current location in a modern building topped with more apartments.

T. Brian Handrigan, a longtime Town Council member and owner of Champlin's Fish Market, has similar plans. Last December Handrigan purchased the 1.4-acre parking lot across the street from the Durfee development for just under $1 million.

He wants to replace the cars and trailers that fill the lot in the summer with new commercial space and condominiums.

"People complain about the parking lot . . . , about all the trailers; they want to see it gone, but what do they want in its place?" says Handrigan, shaking his head with frustration.

"If things are kept the way they are, a quaint fishing village, what does that mean?"

Outsiders have taken an interest in the community too. Paolino Properties — owned by Joseph R. Paolino Jr., a developer and former mayor of Providence, and his father — recently purchased the long-struggling Lighthouse Inn, which they renovated and reopened in time for summer.

Paolino says he is planning additional renovations on the 100-room hotel, the only one in the port. Another Providence man, Sean Mahoney, who owns the upscale bar and dessert cafe, L'Elizabeth, in Providence, just purchased Finbacks, a rough-and-tumble watering hole and fishermen's hangout.

He says fishermen are still welcome, so long as they adhere to his new policy — no swearing at the bar.

But not all property owners are interested in change. Joseph Pearce, owner of Galilee Parking and the second-largest landowner in Galilee says he has no interest in developing his 4.1 acres. Pearce is content collecting $10 bills for day parking on the property, which is also home to a handful of rickety summer cottages.

"I like things the way they are in Galilee."

Clarkson A. Collins, who recently retired as Narragansett's director of community development after 20 years, says Galilee could be at a turning point.

"It has been a very functional port, which is exactly what the fishing industry needs and wants, but on the other hand the area around it really hasn't reached its potential. There's no real invitation there to go and enjoy the area.

"But it will be a change. People will probably remember with fondness the sort of funky atmosphere that's there now."

***

Large-scale development in Galilee didn't occur until 1935, when the state dredged a 35-acre anchorage basin in Point Judith Pond and erected piers allowing vessels to dock in its protected waters. By then annual landings had increased to about 3,000 tons, up from just 300 at the turn of the century. (Within the year fishermen were already complaining that the place was being ruined by tourists.)

Galilee began to acquire its modern flavor in the 1970s. Fishermen were hauling in 60 million pounds of fish annually at the start of the decade. And with new regulations limiting foreign access to the fishing grounds used by Rhode Island's fishing fleet, Galilee was poised to take off as one of the most important fishing ports in the country.

Historical Note

Congress passed the Magnuson-Stevens Act, originally known as the Fishery Conservation and Management Act, in 1976. Its primary purpose was the "Americanization" of marine fisheries off the coasts of the United States. One of the ways it did this was to reserve exclusive use of waters within 200 nautical miles of U.S. shore to U.S. fishing boats.

For American fishermen, and fishing communities like Galilee, this law represented an enormous financial boon. Other American businesses were not as well served. Many businesses, such as uniform laundry services, that had developed to serve the large foreign vessels that the law excluded, were destroyed by the new rules.

The state was eager to encourage that development, restricting use of the state piers to commercial fishermen, despite the outcry of pleasure boat owners.

By 1974, the catch had risen to 77.1 million pounds.

Others argued that — regardless of the productivity of the fishing industry — more effort and energy needed to be invested to attract tourism. A 100-room hotel, the Dutch Inn, opened off the revamped Escape Road, and calls were made for the development of year-round housing to balance the economy.

Tourism proponents argued that Galilee needed to do more to capitalize on its ferry connection to Block Island, now one of the top tourist draws in the state. Visitors tended to park their cars in the port's 3,800 parking spaces (roughly 12 acres' worth) and head straight for the ferry. A 1997 study estimated that each Block Island visitor spent an average of $6 in Galilee and $87 on Block Island.

In 1997, the state announced a range of plans to turn Galilee into a center of tourism at a cost of $21.8 million to $65.7 million. Then-Gov. Lincoln Almond lobbied to pass control of the port from the Department of Environmental Management to the Economic Development Corporation, which wanted to build a second hotel, retail shops and restaurants and, possibly, an aquarium.

Almond shared his vision for the port in 1998: "I want to see a Galilee with scores of tourists, visitors and residents alike strolling the streets, shopping at boutiques and dining in fine restaurants. I want to see a Galilee with a new upscale hotel."

The proposal proved incendiary in Galilee.

Some critics mocked the EDC's recommendation for building a second hotel at a time when the first, a seasonal operation, was struggling to stay afloat and the owner was seeking approval to raze the structure and turn the property into a large parking lot.

Others said, waterfront view or not, Galilee can be a grim place: dirty, smelly and dangerous.

"A lot of people are attracted to the working waterfront because they think it's quaint," says Madeleine Hall-Arber, a professor at the Massachusetts Institute of Technology's Center for Marine Social Sciences, who has studied the gentrification of New England fishing ports for MIT's Sea Grant program.

"But suddenly if they move there and the boats start up at 4 in the morning and they start to notice the noise and the diesel fumes and all the activity, it's not so quaint."

A recent MIT report concluded that a growing coastal population, combined with increasing regulatory and financial pressures on the fishing industry, was accelerating the gentrification, threatening the fishing industry and culture that have long dominated the New England fishing communities.

The report points squarely at Provincetown and the trendy Cape Cod town's evolution from a "thriving fishing village" to a "summer art colony with a tourist shop and restaurant center that attracts thousands of weekend and summer visitors."

But in Galilee in 2002, the fishermen won. The Town Council passed a watered-down plan that encouraged tourist-related development, but kept control of the port squarely in the hands of DEM and the fishing industry.

***

Durfee, 36, who has been overseeing the Sand Hill Cove development project, says DEM and the state should get out of Galilee, sell the land and let the market decide the future of the port.

points for discussion

1. *Culturally significant businesses or economically important cultures?* Are the issues that arise in a discussion about the preservation of traditional businesses different from the issues surrounding the preservation of traditional cultures raised in the previous section? In other words, what counts as a "culture"?

2. *When government ought to intervene.* Should there be a policy debate about whether or not Galilee's buildings and infrastructure are best suited for commercial fishing or tourism, or is this simply an issue that is best resolved by the market? In other words, if land is more profitable when used to promote tourism than to service the fishing industry, isn't it more efficient to allow that land to be used for tourism?

3. *The costs of transition.* Who really loses when the owner of a fishing dock sells it to someone who wishes to convert it to a restaurant for tourists? After all, basic economics dictate that the seller would not sell unless he would be better off after the transaction.

4. *Once again, getting the balance right.* Once some amount of land has been devoted to the promotion of tourism, an interesting tension emerges. The success of coastal tourism depends upon the preservation of coastal resources. At the same time, the construction of hotels, motels, developments, marinas, boardwalks, restaurants, etc., can diminish the quantity and quality of those coastal resources that attracted tourists in the first place. Do tourism entrepreneurs realize that this is true and develop their property accordingly, that is, with a healthy mixture of construction and conservation? If you think not, try to lay out some ideas for how we as a society might encourage an appropriate mixture (or discourage an inappropriate mixture).

3. Seaward of the Coastline

Individual members of the public tend to have strong, intensely held personal connections to, and high expectations for, protection of coastal lands. For example, a 2006 poll by the Public Policy Institute of California found that nine in ten

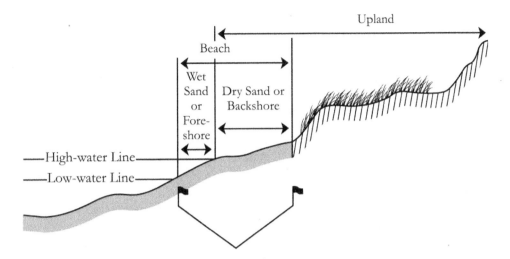

Figure 5-10. Legal Coastline
Depending on the legal jurisdiction, the legal coastline is located somewhere between the flags.

Californians said the quality of the beach and ocean was as important to them personally as it was for the overall quality of life and economy in the state. According to the poll, Californians said that the condition of the coast was "very important (61%)... on a personal level, very important (70%)... to the state's quality of life, and very important (63%) . . . to the economy." MARK BALDASSARE, PPIC STATEWIDE SURVEY: CALIFORNIANS AND THE ENVIRONMENT, FEBRUARY 2006 (2006).

Public expectations regarding coastal lands are shaped in large part by history and tradition. Over the course of millennia, many societies have mutually reached the conclusion that coastal areas ought to be governed in a special way. Those sentiments were reflected in legal systems, including several systems from which our own is derived: the influence of Roman, British, Spanish, and French law can be found throughout modern American law. As you will see, the influence of ancient coastal law is a cultural precedent. While we are obviously not bound by prior cultures' laws, our laws are a product of inherited social agreements about how coastal lands and resources ought to be used.

a. The Legal Coastline and "Public Trust" Lands

The two most important cultural precedents in coastal law are an invisible line that we will call "the legal coastline" and the concept that members of the public have certain rights in "public trust" areas seaward of that line.[2] The legal coastline is

---

2. Public trust lands seaward of the legal coastline are either always submerged, or sometimes submerged, i.e., when covered by the tide. Sometimes-submerged lands are referred to as "tidelands." For the sake of brevity, this book will hereinafter refer to public trust tidelands and submerged lands as "submerged lands" unless the distinction is relevant.

not the same as the one you might see drawn on a map of the United States, boldly separating yellow and pink coastal states from blue oceans, gulfs, and seas. Nor is it the line you would follow as you walked along the beach, trying to keep your old running shoes safe from the advancing and retreating wash of the waves.

Rather, the legal coastline is a rule that establishes the boundary separating dry upland parcels of real estate from public trust areas, that is, public waterways and the submerged lands that lay beneath them. It is a remnant of ancient law, at least as old as the Roman Empire, and probably older than that. It exists today in one of several forms in each of the 30 coastal states, embodied in state constitutions, statutes, or common law. Jurisdictions locate the legal coastline in different ways; a few locate it near the low-water line and, at the other extreme, a few locate it at the place where terrestrial vegetation begins. Most place it near the high-water line. (We will cover the specific rules in Chapter 6.)

The roots of the legal coastline can be traced to Roman, British, and other European versions of what today is known as the "public trust doctrine," one of the key concepts in coastal law. (You will study aspects of the doctrine in Chapters 6, 7, and 8.) At the core of the doctrine is the idea that the law should treat public waterways and submerged lands differently from the way it treats other lands and waters.

Ancient legal scholars, and the cultures in which they lived, based their distinct legal treatment of public waterways and submerged lands mostly on a rationale that could be called "public necessity" or, in more modern terminology, "antitrust." Public waterways, such as seas and rivers, were crucial to important commercial and subsistence activities such as the transport of goods and people and the harvest of fish and other marine life. The importance of these areas was such that it would be unjust, inefficient, and perhaps even dangerous to allow them to be controlled or blocked by individuals or private entities. Instead, the law provided that neither public waterways nor submerged lands could be owned like ordinary lands, but rather, they were to remain available for use by all members of the public.

In addition to conflicts arising from the private-public interface at the legal coastline, public trust areas themselves are the source of many potential conflicts. The core idea of public trust areas is open access, that is, these areas are to be open to use by all members of the public. While there are many benefits to open access, there are also some downsides. First, making each citizen a co-tenant, or co-beneficiary, in the property held by the trust leads to the same kinds of problems that might arise in any co-tenancy scenario. Where each co-tenant has the right to use and enjoy the whole, conflicts are inevitable. Consider, for example, hunting and wildlife watching; while these might be compatible if located in different areas, they cannot co-exist at the same time in the same place. Another problem that arises from open access is the well-known "tragedy of the commons." If every member of the public has the right to use public trust areas, and there is no cost to doing so, these areas can easily become congested and over-used, to the point that no one can enjoy them. As trustees of public trust areas, governments must intervene to prevent the tragedy; however, the greater the amount of regulation, the less true open access exists. Balancing these tensions, that is, preserving both open access and the environmental quality of public trust areas, can be a difficult and contentious task for government agencies.

b. Expectations and Interests

This section describes competing uses of public trust areas seaward of the legal coastline. In the first part, we explore "ecosystem services," which represent passive public use of coastal resources. The second part of this section describes active uses, such as going to the beach, fishing, or drilling for oil. The latter uses are considered active because they require that an individual take an action in order to acquire a benefit; if you want to catch a fish, you have to go fishing. Passive public uses, however, are provided by the actions (or processes) of ecosystems.

i. Ecosystem Services

The concept of ecosystem services, or at least the terminology, is relatively recent. In a series of interdisciplinary studies, researchers have made the case that (1) ecosystems provide certain valuable services to human society, and (2) these services can be valued by estimating the amount of money we would have to spend to generate them in some other way. For example, rainwater that makes its way through a freshwater wetland emerges in a cleaner form; the wetland plants both slow the rate of water flow and filter out some of the harmful chemicals from the water. If we were to pave over that wetland, we could replace it with a manmade filtration system that would clean the rainwater to a similar degree. We can estimate the economic value of the wetland's filtration service as the cost of the manmade filtration system.

This information would be a critical input into a government decision about whether or not to allow the wetland in question to be filled in so that an industrial park could be built in its place. Economic information allows decision-makers to make "apples-to-apples" comparisons and maximize social welfare. In addition, valuing ecosystem services could also facilitate market transactions in those services. Currently, a landowner who owns wetland property might have very little economic incentive to preserve the wetlands in an intact state. On the other hand, if the wetland is providing valuable filtration services to downstream water users, then it is possible that the property owner could charge those users a fee in return for keeping the wetland intact. So long as this fee is less than the amount a downstream user would have to pay for water purification, then the transaction should occur.

The reason that these transactions do not occur on a regular basis is an interesting question whose answer lies beyond the scope of this course. For more on this subject, you might want to read through Volume 20 of the STANFORD ENVIRONMENTAL LAW JOURNAL (2001), which contains a series of articles on ecosystem services. You might also try Barton H. Thompson, Jr., *Ecosystem Services & Natural Capital: Reconceiving Environmental Management*, 17 N.Y.U. ENVTL. L.J. 460 (2008).

Notwithstanding obstacles to a market in ecosystem services, consideration of these services plays an implicit role in coastal law and will likely — based on experiences such as Hurricane Katrina, where wetland loss was a key factor in amplifying storm surges — play a greater role in the future. In a recent paper, a group of economists conducted a literature review — a survey of other economists' attempts to measure the value of various goods and services provided by coastal ecosystems. The following excerpt from that paper helps to illustrate not only the range of coastal goods and services, but gives a sense of their economic value, as well as the difficulties inherent in measuring that value.

Matthew A. Wilson et al., Integrated Assessment and Valuation of Ecosystem Goods and Services Provided by Coastal Systems, Biology and the Environment: Proceedings of the Royal Irish Academy

In James G. Wilson (ed.), The Intertidal Ecosystem: The Value of Ireland's Shores 1-24 (2005)

Empirical valuation data for coastal ecosystems often appears scattered throughout the scientific literature and is uneven in quality. Despite this unevenness, below we present a brief review of existing valuation literature in order to provide useful insights for further research in the area. Such an exercise provides scientists and coastal managers alike with a sense of where the science of coastal ecosystem valuation has come from, and where it might go in the future. To accomplish this goal, below we have synthesized peer-reviewed economic data on coastal ecosystems . . . and delineated a few key examples from the literature for extended discussion. In so doing, we hope to elucidate major findings and gaps in the literature.

All information presented below was obtained

> ### Contingent Valuation and the "Travel Cost Method"
>
> " 'Contingent valuation' and the 'travel cost method' are two tools that economists use to estimate the monetary value of goods that are not traded in markets.
>
> ***
>
> "The contingent valuation method involves the use of sample surveys (questionnaires) to elicit the willingness of respondents to pay for (generally) hypothetical projects or programs. The name of the method refers to the fact that the values revealed by respondents are contingent upon the constructed or simulated market presented in the survey.
>
> "The [hypothesis behind the travel cost method] is that the 'price' for visiting a park or other recreational area (even one for which entry is free) will vary according to the travel costs of visitors coming from different places. Thus, a natural experiment exists where one can measure the quantity of visits to the park demanded by people at a range of prices (that is, coming from different distances) and estimate a demand curve, consumer surplus, and so on." Paul Portney, *The Contingent Valuation Debate: Why Economists Should Care*, 8(4) J. ECON. PERSP. 3, 3-4 (1994).

from studies that were published between 1978 and 2002. They deal explicitly with market and non-market coastal ecosystem goods and services measured throughout the world. To maintain consistency in data quality and findings, only peer-reviewed journal articles were included in this review.

***

Ecosystem Services

In addition to marketable goods and products, our analysis of the literature reveals that landscape features and habitats in the coastal zone also provide critical natural services that contribute to human welfare and thus, have significant economic value. . . . [M]uch of what people value in the coastal zone — natural amenities (open spaces, attractive views), good beaches for recreation, high levels of water quality, protection from storm surges, and waste assimilation/nutrient cycling — are provided by coastal systems. Below, we review a select published group of these economic value estimates.

Recreation and Nutrient Regulation

Stretches of beach, rocky cliffs, estuarine and coastal marine waterways, and coral reefs provide numerous recreational and scenic opportunities for humans. Boating, fishing, swimming, walking, beachcombing, scuba diving, and sunbathing are among the numerous leisure activities that people enjoy worldwide and thus represent significant economic value. Both travel cost (TC) and Contingent Valuation (CV) methods are commonly used to estimate this value. For example, the Chesapeake Bay estuary on the eastern seaboard of the United States has been the focus of an impressive amount of research on nonmarket recreational values associated with coastal systems. When attempting to estimate the monetary worth of water quality improvements in Chesapeake Bay, Bocksteal et al. (1989) focused on recreational benefits because it was assumed that most of the increase in well-being associated with such improvements would accrue to recreationists. The authors estimated the average increases in economic value for beach use, boating, swimming, and fishing with a 20% reduction in total nitrogen and phosphorous introduced into the estuary. Using a combination of CV and TC methods, the annual aggregate willingness to pay for a moderate improvement in the Chesapeake Bay's water quality was estimated to be in the range of $10 to $100 million in 1984 dollars. In a similar study, Kawabe and Oka (1996) used TC to estimate the aggregate recreational benefit (viewing the bay, clam digging, bathing, sailing, bathing, snorkeling and surfing) from improving organic contamination of Tokyo Bay by nitrogen at 53.2 billion yen. Using the CV method, the authors also estimated the aggregate value of improving chemical oxygen demand to reduce the reddish-brown color of the bay at 458.3 billion yen.

Aesthetic Information

Open space, proximity to clean water, and scenic vistas are often cited as a primary attractor of residents who own property and live within the coastal fringe. Hedonic pricing (HP) techniques have thus been used to show that the price of coastal housing units vary with respect to characteristics such as ambient environmental quality (i.e., proximity to shoreline, water quality) because buyers will bid up the price of units with more of a desirable attribute. For example, Leggett and Bockstael (2000) use hedonic techniques to show that water quality has a significant effect on property values along the Chesapeake Bay, USA. The authors use a measure of water quality — fecal coliform bacteria counts — that has serious human health implications and for which detailed, spatially explicit information from monitoring is available. The data used in this hedonic analysis consists of sales of waterfront property on the western shore of the Chesapeake Bay that occurred between 1993 and 1997. The authors consider the effect of a hypothetical localized improvement in observed fecal coliform counts — 100 counts per 100ml — on a set of 41 residential parcels. The projected increase in property values due to the hypothetical reduction total approximately $230,000. Extending the analysis to calculate an upper bound benefit for 494 properties, the authors estimate the benefits of improving water quality at all sites at $12.145 million.

Disturbance Prevention

A critically important service provided by coastal landscapes such as barrier islands, inland wetlands areas, beaches and tidal plains is disturbance prevention. Significant property damages have been attributed to flooding from tidal surges and rainfall as well as wind damage associated with major storm events. For example, Farber (1987) has described an "Avoided Cost" method for measuring the hurricane protection value of wetlands against wind damage to property in coastal Louisiana, USA. Using historical probabilities for storms and wind damage estimates in Louisiana, an expected wind damage function was derived and from this, expected reductions in wind damage from the loss of one mile of wetlands were estimated. Based on 1983 US dollars, the expected incremental annual damage from a loss of one mile of wetlands along the Louisiana coastline was $69,857 which, when extrapolated to a per-acre estimate, amounts to $.44 per acre).

***

Habitat and Nursery Functions

[T]he coastal zone is one of the most productive ecological habitats in the world. Eelgrass, salt marsh and intertidal mud flats all provide a variety of services to the public associated with their nursery and habitat functions. As we have already reported, improvements in the ecological integrity of these habitats may ultimately lead to measurable increases in the production of market goods such as fish, birds and wood products. In other cases, however, ecological productivity itself can represent a unique class of values not captured by traditional market-based valuation methods. Instead, these values represent an increase in the production of higher trophic levels brought about by the increased availability of habitat. Here, it is critical to realize that one may not, in general, add productivity value estimates to use values estimated using other market-related methodologies (i.e., hedonic and travel cost) because to do so would risk double counting some aspects of value, or measuring the same benefits twice.

In an example of coastal wetland productivity analysis, Johnston et al. (2002) use a simulation model based on biological functions that contribute to the overall productivity of the food web in the Peconic Estuary System (PES) in Suffolk County NY, USA. Based on habitat values for fin and shellfish, birds and waterfowl, an average annual abundance per unit area of wetland habitat in the PES is estimated by summing all relevant food web values and habitat values for a year. The value of fish and shellfish is based on commercial harvest values. The marginal value of bird species' usage of the habitat is based on the benefits human receive from viewing or hunting waterfowl. Using these values as input data, the simulation model result in annual marginal asset values for three wetland types: Eelgrass ($1,065 per acre/year); Saltmarsh ($338 per acre/year); and Inter-tidal mud flat ($67 per acre/year).

In an earlier study, Farber and Costanza (1987) estimated the marginal productivity of a coastal system in Terrebonne Parrish, Louisiana, USA by attributing commercial values for several species to the net biomass, habitat, and waste treatment of the wetland ecosystem. Arguing that the annual harvest from an ecosystem is a function of the level of environmental quality, the authors chose to focus on the commercial harvest data for five different native species — shrimp, blue crab, oyster, menhaden, and muskrat — to estimate the marginal productivity of wetlands. The annual economic value (marginal product) of each species was estimated in 1983 dollars: shrimp $10.86/acre; blue crab $.67/acre; Oyster $8.04/acre; Menhaden $5.80/acre; and muskrat pelts $12.09/acre. Taken together, the total value marginal productivity of wetlands in Terrebonne Parrish, Louisiana was estimated at $37.46 per acre.

points for discussion

1. *Services and decisions.* Do you think that policymakers, for example, legislators or agency officials, regularly use this kind of economic information about ecosystem services in making decisions about the use of coastal lands and resources? If not, why not? Assuming that we had very good, but not perfect, information about the value of ecosystem services, would that information ensure that policymakers acted to protect those services? What about the situation where destroying the service would provide a net gain to society, because the activity that destroyed the service was more valuable? What about the situation where the cost of alternative means of preventing floods, say, the construction of dikes, was less than the opportunity cost of leaving wetlands in place? What about wetlands, such as oyster reefs, that provide multiple services, (e.g., flood protection, food provisioning)?

Should a manmade flood control project be required to provide all services lost when the wetland it replaces is destroyed?

2. *The importance of what we don't know.* Again assuming very good information, policymakers still have to address questions of certainty in employing an ecosystem services approach. Let's say that an area of wetlands provides X dollars of ecosystem service benefit to society. Let's also say that developer Jim applies for a permit to destroy some of those wetlands in the course of building his residential development. A scientific study reveals uncertainty about the exact relationship between the current physical structure of the wetlands and the amount of flood prevention it provides. World famous scientist Fred believes that destroying just a few acres of the wetlands will drastically reduce the services it provides, while world famous scientist Ethel believes that the wetlands could provide similar services at half the size. If you were advising a government official making a decision on Jim's application for a permit to destroy a quarter of the wetlands, how would you advise? Notice that deciding whether to follow Fred's or Ethel's advice is not a scientific decision, because they are both world famous and thus each has an equally valid opinion. What kind of decision is it? (Hint: If you asked an economist whether you should invest your savings in stocks or municipal bonds, how do think she would reply?)

3. *Reconceptualizing the environment.* Can you think of other valuable applications for the kind of economic data reported in the Wilson et al. excerpt? Does it change the way you think about the natural environment?

ii. Active Uses

Individuals, companies, and the government seek to use public trust lands and resources in a variety of ways. It is tempting, for purposes of organization, to want to categorize these uses. For example, one might categorize uses as "recreational" or "commercial," or as "consumptive" or "non-consumptive." The problem is that every use arguably spans any possible division.

To illustrate, let's consider what might appear to be the most purely recreational, purely non-consumptive use, that is, going to the beach. On the one hand, people who go to the beach do not gain financially from doing so. If anything, they will go home with less money in their pockets, having enjoyed a frozen yogurt or a game of skeeball at the boardwalk. Going to the beach not only seems to be a nonprofit activity (nonprofit being one way to define recreation), but also a non-consumptive one. In other words, unlike catching a fish and selling it to a restaurant, users of the beach hopefully leave it exactly as they found it, capable of being used by another person on the following day.

But is going to the beach really non-commercial? First, economists would argue that economic value is not the same thing as monetary value: While you won't make money from going to the beach, it is worth something to you. Economists will prove this by pointing to the money you spent on, for example, your hotel room. The amount you spent provides some evidence of the value to you, in dollar terms, of visiting the beach. Perhaps more important, entire industries are driven by the fact that people like to go to the beach and are willing to pay — for hotels, restaurants, parking, etc. — in order to do that. These businesses provide jobs, reducing unemployment and affiliated public expenses; and they pay taxes, funding a variety of state and local programs, including schools and roads. Thus, it seems accurate to say that, at best, going to the beach is only partially recreational in nature. As a use of public trust lands, it generates a significant amount of revenue.

We can also make a pretty strong case for the proposition that going to the beach is both consumptive and Consumptive. Going to the beach represents a small "c" consumptive use because there are a limited number who can enjoy a particular beach at any given time. In other words, beaches are subject to what economists call "congestion." Going to the beach also represents a big "C" consumptive use. To the extent that a particular area of public trust land is devoted to "recreational" beach-going, many other uses will be precluded. While it might still be possible to allow compatible uses, such as surfing or wind-surfing, in the same area, it will not be possible (or a good idea) to use that same place as a commercial port or for oil drilling.

Along these same lines, it is difficult to categorize uses as either "ocean" or "coastal" uses. For one thing, it is difficult (in fact, it would be arbitrary) to draw a line that would divide marine waters into "ocean" or "coastal" waters. The reach of this book is generally limited to rules applicable within three nautical miles of the shore. (Three nautical miles is, in most cases, the geographic extent of individual states' jurisdiction over ocean uses.) However, this leaves us with still another problem: While there are some coastal uses, such as going to the beach, that do not impact the viability of ocean uses, there are no ocean uses that do not impact use of the coast. So, for example, "ocean uses" such as commercial fishing or the construction of offshore oil rigs require the dedication of coastal land, in the form of, respectively, ports to land fish and refineries to process oil. The use of one coastal area for a refinery precludes its use as something else, such as a recreation area. Moreover, by virtue of these onshore facilities, and because fishermen and oil workers have to live somewhere when they are not working, these "ocean" activities contribute significantly to coastal economies.

In light of all of these overlaps and complexities, the remainder of the chapter simply lists

Photo: Library of Congress

Figure 5-11. Duke Kahanamoku

and describes some of the most popular and economically important coastal and coastal ocean uses. Later in the course we will visit the difficult issues, such as how we might decide whether a particular area should be used as a beach, a refinery, or a wildlife refuge.

1. The Beach

The beach has become an integral part of American culture. Beginning in the early 1900s, real estate developers and resort owners in southern California began to incorporate images of surfers in their marketing materials. Surfer and sometime movie star Duke Kahanamoku, who moved from Hawai'i to southern California in 1922 and won gold medals swimming in the 1912 and 1920 Olympics, was an enormously popular figure who linked images of surfing, beaches, health, good looks, and glamour. Although "the Duke" succeeded in capturing the public's imagination, it was not until the late 1950s that beaches and surf culture became part of mainstream American culture.

In 1959, the film version of Frederick Kohner's novel *Gidget*, together with technical innovations in boards and wetsuits, began the evolution of surfing from a fringe lifestyle into a centerpiece of the young American ideal. *Gidget* spawned more than a decade of beach-centered popular culture, ranging from the Avalon and Funicello movies, such as *Beach Party*, to music stars such as the Beach Boys, Dick Dale, and Jan and Dean. DREW KAMPION, STOKED: A HISTORY OF SURF CULTURE (2003). Today, it is possible to find surf-themed and Hawai'ian print shirts in every Walmart and Target in the United States.

This cultural phenomenon is reflected in Americans' behavior. Beaches are today among the most heavily used recreational venues in America. In a survey conducted as part of the U.S. Census in 2007, "going to the beach" was the fourth most popular leisure activity in the United States, trailing only dining out, entertaining friends at home, and reading. More than 52 million Americans reported that they had been to the beach at least once in the past 12 months.

The beach is more than just recreation. As Professor Carol Rose explains, beaches — like parks and other places where people of all types can interact — play a valuable social and democratic role.

Photo: Courtesy TV Guide

Figure 5-12. Gidget
Gidget eventually made it to the small screen as well, and to the cover of a 1966 TV Guide magazine.

Carol Rose, The Comedy of the Commons: Custom, Commerce, and Inherently Public Property

53 U. Chi. L. Rev. 711, 779-81 (1986)

But what about recreation, and specifically, what about the beach cases . . . ? Certainly, the role of recreation is a striking example of historic change in public property doctrine. If recreation now seems to support the "publicness" of some property, this undoubtedly reflects a change in our attitudes toward recreation. We might suspect that this changed attitude relates to an increasing perception of recreation as having something analogous to scale returns, and as a socializing institution.

Recreation is often carried on in a social setting, and therefore it clearly improves with scale to some degree: one must have a partner for chess, two teams for baseball, etc. But in the mid-nineteenth century, Frederick Law Olmsted argued that recreation had scale returns in a much more expansive sense: recreation can be a socializing and educative influence, particularly helpful for democratic values. Thus, rich and poor would mingle in parks, and learn to treat each other as neighbors. Parks would enhance public mental health, with ultimate benefits to sociability; all could revive from the antisocial characteristics of urban life under the refining influence of the park's soothing landscape. Later recreation and park advocates, though moving away from Olmsted's more contemplative ethic, also stressed the democratic education that comes with sports and team play.

Insofar as recreation educates and socializes us, it acts as a "social glue" for everyone, not just those immediately engaged; and of course, the more people involved in any socializing activity, the better.

***

The contemplation of nature elevates our minds above the workaday world, and thus helps us to cope with that very world; recreational play trains us in the democratic give-and-take that makes our regime function. If these arguments are true, we should not worry that people engage in too much recreation, but too little.

***

The public's recreational use arguably is the most valuable use of this property and requires an entire expanse of beach (for unobstructed walking, viewing, contemplation) which could otherwise be blocked and "held up" by private owners. But are these beach recreation areas really comparable to town squares, or to the Gettysburg monument—not to speak of commercial transportation routes? Do they serve a democratizing and socializing function that can be compared to commerce or speech, that becomes ever more valuable as more people are involved? Do people using the beach really become more civil, or acquire the mental habits of democracy? . . .

Attractive as this Olmstedian view may seem, these are not always easy arguments to support, and are extraordinarily difficult to prove. The argument that recreation or the contemplation of nature makes us more civilized and sociable has a very long pedigree in Western thought. . . . [W]hether or not one accepts these arguments in the modern beach debate, older doctrine suggests that the "scale returns" of socialization, taken together with the possibility of private holdout, will underlie any arguments for the inherent publicness of property.

Perhaps the chief lesson from the nineteenth-century doctrines of "inherently public property," then, is that while we may change our minds about which activities are socializing, we always accept that the public requires access to some physical locations for some of these activities. Our law consistently allocates that access to the public, because public access to those locations is as important as the general privatization of property in other spheres of our law. In the absence of the socializing activities that take place on "inherently public property," the public is a shapeless mob, whose members neither trade nor converse nor play, but only fight, in a setting where life is, in Hobbes' all too famous phrase, solitary, poor, nasty, brutish, and short.

points for discussion

1. *What really happens at the beach?* How would you respond to Professor Rose's questions: "Are . . . beach recreation areas . . . comparable to town squares, or to the Gettysburg monument? . . . Do people using the beach . . . become more civil, or acquire the mental habits of democracy?"
2. *When government ought to intervene.* Is there any reason to believe that the private market will undersupply dry sand beach to the public?

2. Recreational Fishing, Boating, and Hunting

Recreational fishing, boating, and hunting are popular activities within public trust areas. All fishing and boating takes place within public trust areas, i.e., above submerged lands, although there are important land connections to both of these activities. Supply stores, hotels, marinas, and other facilities needed to service fishermen and vessels are generally located on the "private side" of the coast. In addition, land uses upstream of coastal waters impact water quality, which is an important factor in the health of marine, anadromous, and catadromous fish populations, as well as in the

> **"Anadromous" and "Catadromous" Fish**
>
> Anadromous fish, such as salmon, are fish that are spawned and spend their juvenile lives in freshwater, then migrate to saltwater for the remainder of their life-cycle. Catadromous fish, such as the American eel, do the opposite, that is, spawn in the sea then spend their adult lives in freshwater.

enjoyment of recreational boating. Coastal hunting, mostly for waterfowl such as ducks and geese, is popular on both private and public property. In addition to its economic impacts, hunting has proven to be a primary political and economic driver in efforts to conserve coastal wetlands.

According to the U.S. Coast Guard, of the approximately 12 million registered recreational boats in the United States, about 7 million are registered in coastal states or territories. Coast Guard statistics, however, do not distinguish between saltwater and freshwater vessels. The Recreational Boating and Fishing Foundation estimates that there are approximately 13 million "pure boaters" — people who boat but don't fish — in the United States. Again, though, we cannot tell what percentage represents saltwater boating. What we can say, and what is certainly enough for the purposes of this course, is that while recreational saltwater boating is not a major factor in the U.S. economy, it is very important in certain local economies, in areas such as the Gulf Coast, the southeastern United States, Puget Sound, and southern California.

In addition to its economic impacts, or perhaps because of them, recreational boating does raise public trust and land use planning issues. As you will later learn, the public trust doctrine — under every competing interpretation — requires that state governments ensure meaningful access to public trust areas and resources. In the case of boating, does this mean that governments must supply marinas and other facilities? The demand for coastal-dependent uses such as marinas highlights the need for long-term thinking and laws that incorporate comprehensive planning as opposed to ad hoc decision-making. In non-coastal areas, there will almost always be room for the new library or shopping center that we might need in 20 years. Where the land use is water-dependent, however, this is not the case.

Data on marine recreational fishing, another activity that relies on marinas, are better than those on pure boating. The following excerpt from a government report makes it clear that, although there are only approximately 8 million saltwater anglers in the United States, and although the overall impact on the nation's economy is small, the economic impacts of fishing resonate throughout many coastal economies.

U.S. Department of Commerce, National Marine Fisheries Service, The Economic Importance of Marine Angler Expenditures in the United States

7 (2004)

The $14.6 billion in retail purchases by saltwater anglers in the U.S. in 2000 generated a total of $30.5 billion in sales. . . . Angler expenditures in the U.S. also generated a total of $12.0 billion in personal income and supported approximately 349,119 jobs.

Approximately 11% of the angler dollars spent in the U.S. impacted the economies of other countries. Of the $14.6 billion spent by residents of the U.S. on retail goods and services, $13.0 billion (89%) directly affected the U.S. economy; $1.6 billion in goods and services were imported into the U.S. in response to angler demands. Thus, on average, about 89 cents of every dollar spent in the U.S. by recreational fishermen remained in the country in 2000.

***

Boat maintenance/expenses was the single most important angler expense category in generating sales, income, and jobs in the U.S. Nationwide, expenditures on boat maintenance/expenses generated over $7.1 billion in sales, $3.4 billion in income, and supported approximately 91,000 jobs. Boat purchases also contributed significant sales, income, and employment impacts to all of the states, as did new fishing vehicles, rods and reels, and lodging expenditures. The impacts created by anglers fishing from private boats and from the shore were higher than those produced from party/charter boat fishing in the U.S.

Federal taxes generated by angler purchases were approximately $3.1 billion. Revenues received by state/local governments were approximately $1.8 billion. In total, angler expenditures in the U.S. generated tax revenues of $4.9 billion in 2000.

***

To place the study results in context relative to the total income and employment generated in the U.S. in 2000, marine recreational fishing expenditures accounted for less than 0.2% of the total income and employment that existed in the nation.

Coastal lands, wetlands and marshes in particular, are an extremely popular place to hunt waterfowl such as ducks and geese. Although the economic impact of coastal hunting is not nearly as great as that of coastal fishing, it is still significant, representing more than $1 billion of activity nationwide. U.S. Fish & Wildlife Service, Economic Impact of Waterfowl Hunting in the United States (2008).

Perhaps the most important impact of public interest in coastal waterfowl hunting is in the area of wetlands conservation. Nonprofit organizations such as Ducks Unlimited, whose objective is to protect waterfowl habitat, concentrate their efforts on coastal wetlands. These areas are crucial components of the so-called flyways on which birds travel in their annual migrations. Of the 325,000 acres of land on which Ducks Unlimited holds conservation easements, most are located in the Lowcountry of South Carolina and in the Mississippi River delta. Ducks Unlimited, Conservation Fact Sheet (2009).

In addition to hunting, there are many Americans who derive pleasure from simply viewing or photographing wildlife. For the same reasons that coastal areas attract bird hunters, they also bring in millions of birdwatchers and the economic boost that comes with them. In terms of numbers of participants, birdwatching ranks behind beach-going as the second most popular coastal recreational activity, with some 15 million Americans actively involved. Other wildlife viewing activities include whale watching, scuba diving, and snorkeling.

3. *Commercial Fishing and Coastal Land Use*

The commercial fishing industry is one of the oldest industries in the United States. In the early years of the nation's history, it was also one of the most important industries, as catches from abundant fisheries off the northeast Atlantic Coast were salted and exported to Europe. In more recent times, catches in many regions have declined dramatically, for example, in California:

- Between 1982 and 1999, California's fishing fleet declined by an estimated 4,000 vessels, from approximately 6,700 to 2,700 boats.
- In 1976, California's fleet landed a peak of 1.3 billion pounds of fish and invertebrates, compared to landings of 650 million pounds in 2000.
- In 1980, the California fleet, at a peak since 1970, brought in more than $300 million in landed value, compared to $142 million in 2000 and $91 million in 2002.
- California's share of the U.S. total commercial landings fell from approximately 19 percent in 1970 to about 7.1 percent of the U.S. total, and 3.9 percent of total landed value in 2000.
- Between 1970 to 1990, total finfish and shellfish landings in California declined by more than half, while total U.S. landings almost doubled. California experienced a dramatic drop in landings of tuna, ground fish, urchin, shark, swordfish, salmon, and abalone.

NAT'L OCEANS ECON. PROGRAM, CALIFORNIA'S OCEAN ECONOMY 34 (2005).

Today, although the industry no longer makes a substantial contribution to the nation's economy as a whole, it is an extremely important source of jobs and revenue in certain towns and cities, particularly those where there are few other sources of employment. For example, commercial fishing represents a major economic activity in the State of Alaska, in places like Homer, Petersburg, and Bristol Bay. On a smaller scale, it is also economically important in some towns and cities in New England, the Gulf of Mexico, and the Pacific Northwest.

Like the oil and gas industry, commercial fishing operates both within and outside of state coastal waters. Some fisheries, like the Chesapeake Bay blue crab fishery, are exclusively "nearshore," while others, like the New England lobster fishery, occur in both state and federal waters. Other fisheries occur only in federal or, sometimes, international waters beyond 200 miles from shore. Regardless of where the fish are caught, however, most of them have to be landed at coastal ports and processed (filleted, canned, or frozen) at coastal plants. (Some fish are processed at sea, in large "factory" vessels.)

points for discussion

1. *Beginning to think about access.* As uses of public trust areas, are hunting and fishing qualitatively different from beach-going and (non-consumptive) boating? Recall that the core idea of the public trust doctrine is access. Access to what? Access for what?

2. *The myth of inexhaustibility.* As we will later learn, one alternate, historical rationale for the public trust doctrine was that private ownership of coastal waters was not necessary because resources, such as fish and wildlife, were inexhaustible. In other words, the belief for many centuries was that man was incapable of catching all the fish in the sea. Unfortunately, the combination of open access and this mistaken understanding of nature's productivity led to the widespread depletion of marine-life populations. In *Sea of Slaughter,* Farley Mowat describes in detail how 500 years of intensive hunting and fishing resulted in the near-eradication of many kinds of fish, birds, and marine mammals along the Atlantic Coast. Can you think of some ways to mesh the idea of open access with the conservation of fish and wildlife?

4. Oil and Gas Exploration and Development

We covered the law of offshore oil and gas in Chapter 4. While exploration and drilling occur in the ocean, those activities can have a significant impact on coastal lands and resources. Offshore operations require onshore support facilities, including businesses that provide housing and maintenance services. In some places, like Louisiana, offshore oil and gas development has given rise to coastal land uses such as refineries and other chemical processing plants. Finally, oil spills can have severe impacts on coastal as well as ocean ecosystems.

Louisiana's wetlands have been impacted both by spills and by the construction of thousands of miles of canals used by the petroleum industry to move equipment and products. The canals not only replace marsh but cause remaining wetlands to erode more quickly; many scientists believe that the canals are the driving force behind the dramatic loss of wetlands in Louisiana over the past century. John Carey, *Louisiana Wetlands Tattered by Industrial Canals, Not Just River Levees*, Sci. Am., Dec. 1, 2013.

5. Ports

Ports are one of the oldest uses of coastal areas. As the following excerpt describes, ports play a central role in local, regional, and national economic activity.

American Association of Port Authorities, The Local and Regional Economic Impacts of the U.S. Deepwater Port System 2006

(2007)

[T]he international and domestic cargo handled at the US deepwater seaports created the following economic impacts in 2006.

- 8.4 million jobs are related to the cargo moving via the nation's deepwater seaports.

- Of the 8.4 million jobs, 507,448 direct jobs are generated by the marine cargo and vessel activity.
- As the result of local and regional purchases by those 507,448 individuals holding the direct jobs, an additional 630,913 induced jobs are supported in the national economy.
- 306,289 indirect jobs were supported by $26.3 billion of local purchases by businesses supplying services at the marine terminals and by businesses dependent upon the cargo and vessel activity.
- 6.9 million jobs are with exporters/importers and users of the nation's deep-water seaports.

In 2006, marine cargo activity generated a total of $1,976 billion of total economic activity.

Of the $1,976 billion, $71 billion is the direct business revenue received by the firms directly dependent upon the nation's ports and providing maritime services and inland transportation services to the cargo handled at the marine terminals and the vessels calling the port, as well as ship and rig repair and maintenance services. An additional $26 billion is used for local purchases. The remaining $1,879 billion represents the value of the output to the national economy that is created due to the cargo moving via the deepwater ports. This includes the value added at each stage of producing an export cargo, as well as the value added at each stage of

Photo: Hobvias Sudoneighm/Wikimedia Commons

Figure 5-13. Port of Seattle
The Port of Seattle exemplifies the scale of the modern port facility.

production for the firms using imported raw materials and intermediate products that flow via the marine terminals and are consumed within the state.

Marine activity supported nearly $314 billion of total personal wage and salary income and local consumption expenditures for US residents. This includes $107 billion of direct, indirect, induced and local consumption expenditures, while the remaining $207 billion was received by the related port users and exporters and importers. The 507,448 direct job holders received $25 billion of direct wage and salary income, for an annual average salary of nearly $50,000.

A total of $102 billion of total federal, state, and local taxes were generated by maritime activity at the deepwater port including $35 billion of direct, induced and indirect federal, state and local tax revenue, and $67 billion of federal state and local tax revenue were created due to the economic activity of the related users and exporters and importers of the nation's port system.

The scale of port operations raises a host of environmental concerns. The following excerpt, from a report prepared by an environmental advocacy group, describes some of these issues.

Natural Resources Defense Council, Harboring Pollution

1-7 (2004)

Air Pollution from Port Operations

The diesel engines at ports, which power ships, trucks, trains, and cargo-handling equipment, create vast amounts of air pollution affecting the health of workers and people living in nearby communities, as well as contributing significantly to regional air pollution. More than 30 human epidemiological studies have found that diesel exhaust increases cancer risks, and a 1999 California study found that diesel exhaust is responsible for 71 percent of the cancer risk from air pollution. More recent studies have linked diesel exhaust with asthma. Major air pollutants from diesel engines at ports that can affect human health include particulate matter, volatile organic compounds, nitrogen oxides (NOx), ozone, and sulfur oxides (SOx).

***

The Effect of Port-Related Air Pollution on Human Health

The health effects of pollution from ports may include asthma, other respiratory diseases, cardiovascular disease, lung cancer, and premature death. In children, these pollutants have been linked with asthma and bronchitis, and high levels of the pollutants have been associated with increased school absenteeism and emergency room visits. In fact, numerous studies have shown that children living near busy diesel trucking routes are more likely to suffer from decreased lung function, wheezing, bronchitis, and allergies.

Many major ports operate virtually next door to residential neighborhoods, schools, and playgrounds. Due to close proximity to port pollution, nearby communities face extraordinarily high health risks from port air pollutants. Many of these areas are low-income communities of color, raising environmental justice concerns. In the Los Angeles area, oceangoing ships, harbor tugs, and commercial boats such as passenger ferries emit many times more smog-forming pollutants than all power plants in the Southern California region combined. . . .

Water Pollution from Port Operations

Port operations, including waste from ships that is either dumped directly or leached into water, can cause significant damage to water quality — and subsequently to marine life and ecosystems and human health. These effects may include bacterial and viral contamination of commercial fish and shellfish, depletion of oxygen in water, and bioaccumulation of certain toxins in fish.

Primary Threats to Water Quality

Bilge is water collected at the bottom of the hull of a ship — water that is often contaminated with oil leaking from machinery. Bilge water must be emptied periodically to maintain a ship's stability and to prevent the accumulation of hazardous vapors.

This oily wastewater, combined with other ship wastes such as sewage and wastewater from other onboard uses, is a serious threat to marine life. Antifouling additives are often added to the paint used on ships to prevent the growth of barnacles and other marine organisms on ship surfaces. Some of these additives contain tributyltin (TBT), a toxic chemical that can leach into water.

Stormwater runoff is precipitation that travels across paved surfaces. It can accumulate deposits of air pollution, automotive fluids, sediments, nutrients, pesticides, metals, and other pollutants. In fact, urban stormwater runoff from all sources, including marine ports, is the largest source of impairment in U.S. coastal waters and the second-largest source of water pollution in U.S. estuaries. Virtually all of the land at a port terminal is paved, and therefore impervious to water.

When water bodies are overloaded with nitrogen, algae and plankton can rapidly increase in numbers, forming "blooms" which are sometimes called red or brown tides. This process, called eutrophication, has been identified by the National Research Council as the most serious pollution problem facing estuaries in the United States. As major sources of NOx, ports are major contributors to eutrophication. In the year 2000, 8,354 oil spills were reported in U.S. waters, accounting for more than 1.4 million gallons of spilled oil. The majority of these spills occurred in internal and headlands waters, including the harbors and waterways upon which ports rely. A large share of oil contamination is the result of "chronic" pollution from such sources as port runoff, unloading and loading of oil tankers, and the removal of bilge water — resulting in up to three times as much oil contamination as tanker accidents. However, large, "catastrophic" spills also have a significant impact.

Dredging is a routine activity of ports to remove sediment that builds up in ship channels from erosion and silt deposition. Dredging also creates new channels and deepens existing ones. Each year, more than 300 million cubic yards of sediment in waterways and harbors are dredged to allow ships to pass through. About five to 10 percent of dredged sediment is contaminated with toxic chemicals, including polychlorinated biphenyls (PCBs), mercury and other heavy metals, polycyclic aromatic hydrocarbons (PAHs), and pesticides — all of which can cause water contamination and complicate sediment disposal. Dredging may also increase water turbidity (cloudiness), harm habitat, and disturb or kill threatened and endangered species. It may also risk stirring up and releasing buried contaminants.

These various forms of water pollution cause a broad range of environmental problems, including loss of critical wetlands areas, water sedimentation that harms important habitat (seagrass beds, in particular), collisions involving boats and marine mammals, and marine life exposure to debris, including plastic bags, netting, and plastic pellets.

Land Use Problems at Ports

The highly industrialized operations at ports are often in close proximity to residential areas, creating nuisances and hazards for nearby communities. Ports have several available options to avoid developing new terminals near residential areas.

They can develop property previously used in an industrial capacity, or they can increase efficiency of land use at existing terminals. The land use patterns at U.S. ports suggest much room for efficiency improvements. Of the 10 largest U.S. ports, even those that are most efficient in terms of land use, Long Beach and Houston, are four times less efficient than the Port of Singapore, a model of land-use efficiency.

One positive approach to land use is for ports to focus their expansion efforts on brownfields, or tracts of land that have been developed for industrial purposes, polluted, and then abandoned. The potential costs of cleaning up brownfield sites makes them less appealing to companies looking to locate or expand, and as a result, new industrial operations are often sited on pristine, undeveloped "greenfield" land. This often leads to a loss of habitat and wildlife, increases in air and water pollution, and urbanization of open space valuable for its recreational and aesthetic qualities.

However, developing brownfields offers many advantages to business, communities, and the environment. Businesses benefit from locating on sites near existing transportation infrastructure, and with a utility infrastructure already in place, while cleaning up contamination that poses a danger to both the community and the environment.

Port-Community Relations

Ports can be very bad neighbors. In addition to the air and water pollution problems they create, they can be loud, ugly, brightly lit at night, and a cause of traffic jams. These problems can go beyond simple annoyance to cause serious negative health effects. For example, noise pollution has been linked to hearing impairment, hypertension (high blood pressure), sleep deprivation, reduced performance, and even aggressive behavior. At ports bordering residential neighborhoods, bright lights at night and the flashing lights of straddle carriers and forklifts can affect nearby residents, disrupting biological rhythms and causing stress and annoyance. In addition to the negative effects experienced by people, noise from ship engines may disturb marine mammal hearing and behavior patterns, as well as bird feeding and nesting sites. Similarly, artificial lights at ports, sometimes burning 24 hours a day, can have negative effects on wildlife, including disorientation, confusion of biological rhythms that are adapted to a day/night alternation, and a general degradation of habitat quality. This pollution can cause high mortality in animal populations, particularly to birds attracted to brightly lit buildings and towers and that circle these structures until they die of exhaustion or run head on into them.

points for discussion

1. *Co-dependent relationships.* Ports represent one of the most vivid examples of a water-dependent land use. One can't have a port anywhere but on the water. How might society's need for certain water-dependent activities shape coastal law? In other words, what types of special provisions might we expect to see in an ideal set of rules and regulations if our goal is to ensure that there is always room on the coast for the water-dependent uses we need?
2. *Once again, getting the balance right.* How might the law help ports function as good neighbors while ensuring that they remain viable industrial hubs?

6. Sand and Gravel Mining

Sand and gravel are mined both on land and from submerged public trust lands, for a variety of purposes. Both are key ingredients in concrete. Sand is used in the manufacture of glass and for high-end industrial processes. And, as noted above, sand has more recently been mined for use in beach renourishment.

Over the past several decades, prices for sand and gravel have risen as land-based sources have either been depleted or rejected as incompatible with other nearby uses. During this time, demand has increased due to population and the development of new uses, such as renourishment. As a result, mining activity in the marine environment has increased around the globe.

Environmental concerns associated with sand and gravel mining include the destruction of benthic (ocean bottom) habitats, unpredictable impacts associated with disruption of sediment transport patterns, and localized erosion.

7. Aquaculture

Finally, it is worth noting that aquaculture, that is, the farming or ranching of fish and shellfish, is likely to become a bigger industry over the next few decades. While commercial fisheries have declined or remained stable, demand for seafood has continued to grow. Shellfish aquaculture, for example, the production of oysters or clams, has been taking place along America's coasts for many decades. Recently developed technologies make it possible to spawn and raise other kinds of fish, such as salmon or black cod, in captivity. The combination of demand and technology has created a business opportunity for entrepreneurs who wish to replicate the model used to raise fowl and livestock on land for hundreds of years.

Photo: Richard Dorell/Wikimedia Commons

Figure 5-14. Salmon Farms

From the entrepreneurs' perspective, coastal areas often represent the cheapest place to run an aquaculture operation. Rather than re-create the animals' natural environment somewhere else, it is easiest simply to build a "net pen" next to the shore and use the existing natural environment. Because these facilities are close to shore, feeding and maintenance are inexpensive.

At the same time, building fish farms close to shore raises a number of issues. First, farms can interfere with other uses of the particular area, such as fishing or navigation. Farms are also sometimes unsightly and, as such, can interfere with the "viewshed." Second, fish farms are a source of several different kinds of marine pollution. Chemicals used to treat sick fish can leach out into the marine environment; fish produce significant quantities of fecal matter; farmed fish can serve as disease vectors for local stocks; and, escaped fish can represent a form of biological pollution as invasive species.

point for discussion

At the end of the chapter, a very big question. Given that there is a limited amount of public trust space, how should space be allocated among competing uses? One can imagine a number of very different alternative approaches, including first-come-first-served, highest bidder, and popular referendum. What are some of the other principles that society could employ in allocating coastal space (and resources)? What are the strengths and weaknesses of various institutions, for example, courts, legislatures, direct democracy, and markets?

C. CHAPTER SUMMARY

1. **Geology.** Coastal geology is characterized by predictable and unpredictable change. A variety of forces continually reshape coastal lands. At the same time, people want to live near the coast. Traditional concepts of property law do not easily mesh with the physical reality of coastal geology.

2. **Ecology.** Coastal ecology is complex, in large part because the coast is the boundary between marine and terrestrial systems. The "wet parts" of coastal systems are affected by direct use as well as by use of upland areas. Upland areas are ecologically sensitive and are often characterized by rare habitats and species. Using coastal ecosystems while ensuring that they continue to support human life and valuable activities is a delicate balancing act.

3. **Geography.** Because of their location, coastal areas are vulnerable to natural disasters and "attract" pollution generated in upland areas. These unique features of coastal areas have broad implications for coastal (and upland) policy.

4. **Upland interests.** Coastal property is expensive for a reason: There are many benefits generated by living or owning a business near the water. Economic and psychological investment in coastal property creates expectations about the ways in which that property should be used and regulated.

5. **Public trust interests.** Due to a long history of access, members of the public have strong expectations about what they should be able to do at the beach, in wetlands, and on the water. Sectors of the public have expectations that conflict; moreover, public expectations often conflict with the expectations of upland owners.

D. SUGGESTED READING

Eric Bird, Coastal Geomorphology: An Introduction (1999).

Robert García & Erica Flores Baltodano, *Free the Beach! Public Access, Equal Justice, and the California Coast*, 2 Stan. J. C.R. & C.L. Liberties 142 (2005).

Curry L. Hagerty & Jonathan L. Ramseur, Congressional Research Service, R41262, Deepwater Horizon Oil Spill: Selected Issues for Congress (July 30, 2010), https://fas.org/sgp/crs/misc/R41262.pdf.

Daniel S. Holland et al., Economic Analysis for Ecosystem-Based Management: Applications to Marine and Coastal Environments (2009).

Lena Lencek & Gideon Bosker, The Beach: The History of Paradise on Earth (1999).

Kenneth H. Mann, Ecology of Coastal Waters: With Implications for Management (2d ed. 2000).

chapter 6

The Legal Geography of the Coast

Coastal law includes pieces of federal constitutional and statutory law, but most coastal law is state law. There are 30 coastal states within which coastal law is an amalgam of each state's constitutional, statutory, and common law. These laws are administered by state agencies, attorneys general, courts, or some combination thereof.

In our description of the legal geography of the coast, we will focus on the most important components of coastal law, within a roughly chronological framework. In Section A, we will learn about the oldest sources of American coastal law: the rules that state courts inherited from the English common law tradition. Section B covers federal jurisdiction: Congress's power to regulate use of coastal lands and resources. Section C explains how and why states have, in the last 30 years, expanded the geographic reach of state coastal law through state coastal statutes. The fourth and final section of this chapter focuses on constitutional limits to state and federal coastal jurisdiction.

A. LEGAL GEOGRAPHY AND THE COMMON LAW

Despite the dramatic break from English rule that was the American Revolution, courts in the new United States generally applied English common law to the cases brought before them. American common law incorporated two kinds of coastal law from the English legal tradition. First, courts adopted property rules defining legal ownership of riparian and littoral land, that is, land directly bordering public waterways. You can think of these *riparian and littoral rights* as supplements to the ordinary rights associated with ownership of real property, such as the right to exclude, the right to use and enjoy, and the right to alienate. Second, courts also borrowed from English law to develop what eventually became known as *the public trust doctrine.* The doctrine defines the public's rights in, and government responsibilities with respect to, public waterways and the submerged lands beneath them. As you will learn, American courts' adoption of the public trust doctrine was not as straightforward as the adoption of riparian and littoral rights. This was in large part because the legal owner of public trust property in England was the King or Queen; the doctrine did not transfer seamlessly to monarchy-free America. These two strains of the common law represented the bulk of coastal law in the United States for nearly 200 years and continue to provide both the legal and philosophical basis for the statutes and state constitutional provisions that now supplement them.

In reading through the follow-

What do "Riparian" and "Littoral" Mean?

The word "riparian" in the context of the legal term "riparian rights" refers to a parcel of land that borders on a river or stream. The word "littoral" refers to a parcel of land located directly on the shore of a lake or the sea. In coastal law, the term "littoral property" is usually used to refer to oceanfront land. In many coastal areas, rivers flow into estuaries, marshes, and other types of brackish waters. Even where rivers flow directly into the sea, the river mouth or delta will have some features in common with the sea, such as salinity and tidal influence. Drawing a line at the point where a river ends, and the ocean begins, that is, where riparian property ends, and littoral property begins, is necessarily a somewhat arbitrary exercise.

---

ing materials, there are two points to keep in mind. First, the jurisdictional reach of riparian and littoral rights and the public trust doctrine has changed over time, as American courts have modified hoary English rules to suit modern American circumstances. Second, most of those modifications have resulted from courts' re-conception of "public waterways." As noted above, both riparian and littoral rights and the public trust doctrine are anchored to the legal definition of that concept.

1. Tidal Influence and Navigability

In English common law, public waterways are defined as waters influenced by the tides; all other waters are considered to be compatible with the institution of private property. As the following decisions illustrate, American courts have altered or amended the "tidal influence test."

The first decision, *Illinois Central,* is one of the seminal opinions on the American public trust doctrine. The case pitted the State of Illinois against the Illinois Central Railroad Company. The state filed the suit in attempt to void an earlier transfer by the Illinois Legislature of submerged lands along the Chicago lakefront to the company. In Chapter 7, where we will study the rules that govern states' use and management of public trust resources, we will learn the outcome of the case. For now, we are only concerned with the jurisdictional scope of the doctrine, that is, the identity of the resources found within the corpus of the public trust. One of the preliminary issues that the U.S. Supreme Court had to address was whether or not the public trust doctrine was relevant to submerged lands beneath waters that were not influenced by the ebb and flow of the tide, specifically, the waters of Lake Michigan.

Illinois Central Railroad Co. v. Illinois

146 U.S. 387, 435-37 (1892)

Justice FIELD delivered the opinion of the United States Supreme Court.

***

It is the settled law of this country that the ownership of and dominion and sovereignty over lands covered by tide waters, within the limits of the several States, belong to the respective States within which they are found. . . . This doctrine has been often announced by this court. . . .

The same doctrine is in this country held to be applicable to lands covered by fresh water in the Great Lakes over which is conducted an extended commerce with different States and foreign nations. These lakes possess all the general characteristics of open seas, except in the freshness of their waters, and in the absence of the ebb and flow of the tide. In other respects they are inland seas, and there is no reason or principle for the assertion of dominion and sovereignty over and ownership by the State of lands covered by tide waters that is not equally applicable to its ownership of and dominion and sovereignty over lands covered by the fresh waters of these lakes. At one time the existence of tide waters was deemed essential in determining the admiralty jurisdiction of courts in England. That doctrine is now repudiated in this country as wholly inapplicable to our condition. In England the ebb and flow of the tide constitute the legal test of the navigability of waters. There no waters are navigable in fact, at least to any great extent, which are not subject to the tide. There, as said in the case of *The Propeller Genesee Chief v. Fitzhugh*, 12 How. 443, 455 (1852), "tide water and navigable water are synonymous terms, and tide water, with a few small and unimportant exceptions, meant nothing more than public rivers, as contradistinguished from private ones"; and writers on the subject of admiralty jurisdiction "took the ebb and flow of the tide as the test because it was a convenient one, and more easily determined the character of the river. Hence the established doctrine in England, that the admiralty jurisdiction is confined to the ebb and flow of the tide. In other words, it is confined to public navigable waters."

But in this country the case is different. Some of our rivers are navigable for great distances above the flow of the tide; indeed, for hundreds of miles, by the largest vessels used in commerce. As said in the case cited: "There is certainly nothing in the ebb and flow of the tide that makes the waters peculiarly suitable for admiralty jurisdiction, nor anything in the absence of a tide that renders it unfit. If it is a public navigable water, on which commerce is carried on between different States or nations, the reason for the jurisdiction is precisely the same. And if a distinction is made on that account, it is merely arbitrary, without any foundation in reason; and, indeed, would seem to be inconsistent with it."

Photo: Library of Congress

Figure 6-1. Railways Along Lake Michigan in Chicago, Illinois, 1901

The Great Lakes are not in any appreciable respect affected by the tide, and yet on their waters, as said above, a large commerce is carried on, exceeding in many instances the entire commerce of States on the borders of the sea. When the reason of the limitation of admiralty jurisdiction in England was found inapplicable to the condition of navigable waters in this country, the limitation and all its incidents were discarded. So also, by the common law, the doctrine of the dominion over and ownership by the crown of lands within the realm under tide waters is not founded upon the existence of the tide over the lands, but upon the fact that the waters are navigable, tide waters and navigable waters, as already said, being used as synonymous terms in England. The public being interested in the use of such waters, the possession by private individuals of lands under them could not be permitted except by license of the crown, which could alone exercise such dominion over the waters as would insure freedom in their use so far as consistent with the public interest. The doctrine is founded upon the necessity of preserving to the public the use of navigable waters from private interruption and encroachment, a reason as applicable to navigable fresh waters as to waters moved by the tide. We hold, therefore, that the same doctrine as to the dominion and sovereignty over and ownership of lands under the navigable waters of the Great Lakes applies, which obtains at the common law as to the dominion and sovereignty over and ownership of lands under tide waters on the borders of the sea, and that the lands are held by the same right in the one case as in the other. . . .

You might be wondering: Why it is called the public *trust* doctrine? As noted, we will explore the complex substance of the doctrine in the next chapter. For now, here is a brief answer to the question. The word "trust" refers to the relationship between each state and its citizens. Each state is said to hold certain assets, such as submerged lands, in trust for the benefits of its citizens. Who created this trust? As the following decision indicates, one answer is that — at least with respect to states established after the original 13 — the federal government did.

The following case involved a dispute between the Phillips Petroleum Company and the State of Mississippi. The oil company had leased some marshlands, intending to drill for oil, from a private party that claimed to own those marshlands. The state objected to the leases, asserting that the lands in question were subject to the public trust doctrine and thus belonged to the state. In order to resolve the question of who owned the marshlands, the Supreme Court was required to identify which assets — waters and submerged lands — the United States had put into trust for the people of Mississippi when Mississippi became a state.

Phillips Petroleum Co. v. Mississippi

484 U.S. 469 (1988)

Justice WHITE delivered the opinion of the United States Supreme Court.

The issue here is whether the State of Mississippi, when it entered the Union in 1817, took title to lands lying under waters that were influenced by the tide running in the Gulf of Mexico, but were not navigable in fact.

I.

As the Mississippi Supreme Court eloquently put it: "Though great public interests and neither insignificant nor illegitimate private interests are present and in conflict, this in the end is a title suit." *Cinque Bambini Partnership v. State*, 491 So. 2d 508, 510 (1986). More specifically, in question here is ownership of 42 acres of land underlying the north branch of Bayou LaCroix and 11 small drainage streams in southwestern Mississippi; the disputed tracts range from under one-half acre to almost 10 acres in size. Although the waters over these lands lie several miles north of the Mississippi Gulf Coast and are not navigable, they are nonetheless influenced by the tide, because they are adjacent and tributary to the Jourdan River, a navigable stream flowing into the Gulf. The Jourdan, in the area involved here, is affected by the ebb and flow of the tide. Record title

> **What Is the "Equal Footing Doctrine"?**
>
> The *equal footing doctrine* is, as the Court states later in the case, a federal doctrine that guarantees each state admitted after the original 13 "all the [same] rights of sovereignty, jurisdiction, and eminent domain." *Pollard's Lessee v. Hagan*, 44 U.S. 212, 223 (1845). While the term can be found in the Northwest Ordinance of 1787 and in Acts of Congress creating the new states, it was left to the Supreme Court to determine the meaning of "equal footing" in various contexts.

to these tracts of land is held by petitioners, who trace their claims back to prestatehood Spanish land grants.

The State of Mississippi, however, claiming that by virtue of the "equal-footing doctrine" it acquired at the time of statehood and held in public trust all land lying under any waters influenced by the tide, whether navigable or not, issued oil and gas leases that included the property at issue. This quiet title suit, brought by petitioners, ensued.

The Mississippi Supreme Court, affirming the Chancery Court with respect to the lands at issue here, held that by virtue of becoming a State, Mississippi acquired "fee simple title to all lands naturally subject to tidal influence, inland to today's mean high-water mark. . . ." *Ibid.* Petitioners' submission that the State acquired title to only lands under navigable waters was rejected.[1]

> **Some History . . .**
>
> Before Mississippi was a state, it was part of the Mississippi Territory, which the United States acquired from Spain in 1795 through the Treaty of San Lorenzo. When the United States acquired territory in this way, Congress later "assured confirmation of all land claims for which there existed any actual proof of ownership, residence, and improvement." Paul Wallace Gates, *Private Land Claims in the South*, 22 J. SOUTH. HIST. 183, 184 (1956). *See also Forsyth v. Reynolds*, 56 U.S. 358 (1853). So, why didn't the petitioners' Spanish land grants give them good title? For the answer, see *Cinque Bambini Partnership v. State*, 491 So. 2d 508, 518 (1986).

II.

We granted certiorari to review the Mississippi Supreme Court's decision . . . and now affirm the judgment below.

As petitioners recognize, the "seminal case in American public trust jurisprudence is *Shively v. Bowlby*, 152 U.S. 1 (1894)." The issue in *Shively v. Bowlby*, 152 U.S. 1 (1894), was whether the State of Oregon or a prestatehood grantee from the United States of riparian lands near the mouth of the Columbia River at Astoria, Oregon, owned the soil below the high-water mark. Following an extensive survey of this Court's prior cases, the English common law, and various cases from the state courts, the Court concluded:

> *Shively v. Bowlby*
>
> In *Shively v. Bowlby*, 152 U.S. 1, 18-26 (1894), the Supreme Court laid out the manner in which the original 13 states defined the geographic scope of their public trust doctrines. There are three points worth noting. First, each state did it differently. Second, in some cases, the definition was based on customary use during the Colonial era. And, third, the definitions are intimately interwoven with state definitions of riparian and littoral rights.

1. The Chancery Court had held that 140 acres of the lands claimed by petitioners were public trust lands. The Mississippi Supreme Court reversed with respect to 98 of these 140 acres, finding that these tracts were artificially created tidelands (caused by road construction), and therefore were

"At common law, the title and dominion in lands flowed by the tide water were in the King for the benefit of the nation. . . . Upon the American Revolution, these rights, charged with a like trust, were vested in the original States within their respective borders, subject to the rights surrendered by the Constitution of the United States.

***

"The new States admitted into the Union since the adoption of the Constitution have the same rights as the original States in the tide waters, and in the lands under them, within their respective jurisdictions." *Id.*, at 57.

Shively rested on prior decisions of this Court, which had included similar, sweeping statements of States' dominion over lands beneath tidal waters. *Knight v. United States Land Association*, 142 U.S. 161, 183 (1891), for example, had stated that "[i]t is the settled rule of law in this court that absolute property in, and dominion and sovereignty over, the soils under the tide waters in the original States were reserved to the several States, and that the new States since admitted have the same rights, sovereignty and jurisdiction in that behalf as the original States possess within their respective borders." On many occasions, before and since, this Court has stated or restated these words from *Knight* and *Shively*.

Against this array of cases, it is not surprising that Mississippi claims ownership of all of the tidelands in the State. Other States have done as much. The 13 original States, joined by the Coastal States Organization (representing all coastal States), have filed a brief in support of Mississippi, insisting that ownership of thousands of acres of tidelands under nonnavigable waters would not be disturbed if the judgment below were affirmed, as it would be if petitioners' navigability-in-fact test were adopted. . . .

Petitioners rely on early state cases to indicate that the original States did not claim title to nonnavigable tidal waters. But it has been long established that the individual States have the authority to define the limits of the lands held in public trust and to recognize private rights in such lands as they see fit. Some of the original States [Massachusetts, for example] did recognize more private interests in tidelands than did others of the 13 — more private interests than were recognized at common law, or in the dictates of our public trusts cases. Because some of the cases which petitioners cite come from such States (*i.e.*, from States which abandoned the common law with respect to tidelands), they are of only limited value in understanding the public trust doctrine and its scope in those States which have not relinquished their claims to all lands beneath tidal waters.

Finally, we note that several of our prior decisions have recognized that the States have interests in lands beneath tidal waters which have nothing to do with navigation. For example, this Court has previously observed that public trust lands

---

not part of the public trust created in 1817. Since these lands were neither tidelands in 1817, nor were they added to the tidelands by virtue of natural forces of accretion, they belonged to their record title-holders. [Citation omitted.] Because the State did not cross-petition, this portion of the Mississippi Supreme Court's decision is not before us. The only issue presented here is title to the 42 acres which the Mississippi Supreme Court found to be public trust lands.

may be used for fishing—for both "shell-fish [and] floating fish." *See, e.g., Smith v. Maryland*, 18 How. 71, 75 (1855). On several occasions the Court has recognized that lands beneath tidal waters may be reclaimed to create land for urban expansion. Because of the State's ownership of tidelands, restrictions on the planting and harvesting of oysters there have been upheld. It would be odd to acknowledge such diverse uses of public trust tidelands, and then suggest that the sole measure of the expanse of such lands is the navigability of the waters over them.

Consequently, we reaffirm our longstanding precedents which hold that the States, upon entry into the Union, received ownership of all lands under waters subject to the ebb and flow of the tide. Under the well-established principles of our cases, the decision of the Mississippi Supreme Court is clearly correct: the lands at issue here are "under tidewaters," and therefore passed to the State of Mississippi upon its entrance into the Union.

III.

Petitioners do not deny that broad statements of public trust dominion over tidelands have been included in this Court's opinions since the early 19th century. Rather, they advance two reasons why these previous statements of the public trust doctrine should not be given their apparent application in this case.

A.

First, petitioners contend that these sweeping statements of state dominion over tidelands arise from an oddity of the common law, or more specifically, of English geography. Petitioners submit that in England practically all navigable rivers are influenced by the tide. . . . Thus, "tidewater" and "navigability" were synonyms at common law. Consequently, in petitioners' view, the Crown's ownership of lands beneath tidewaters actually rested on the navigability of those waters rather than the ebb and flow of the tide. . . . English authority and commentators are cited to show that the Crown did not own the soil under any nonnavigable waters. Petitioners also cite for support statements from this Court's opinions, such as *The Propeller Genesee Chief v. Fitzhugh*, 53 U.S. 443 (1852) . . . and *Martin v. Waddell*, 41 U.S. 367, 413-414 (1842), which observed that it was "the *navigable* waters of England, and the soils under them, [which were] held by the Crown" at common law (emphasis added).

The cases relied on by petitioners, however, did not deal with tidal, nonnavigable waters. And we will not now enter the debate on what the English law *was* with respect to the land under such waters, for it is perfectly clear how this Court understood the common law of royal ownership, and what the Court considered the rights of the original and the later entering States to be. As we discuss above, this Court has consistently interpreted the common law as providing that the lands beneath waters under tidal influence were given to States upon their admission into the Union. . . . It is true that none of these cases actually dealt with lands such as those involved in this case, but it has never been suggested in any of this Court's prior decisions that the many statements included therein—to the effect that the

States owned all the soil beneath waters affected by the tide — were anything less than an accurate description of the governing law.

B.

Petitioners, in a related argument, contend that even if the common law does not support their position, subsequent cases from this Court developing the *American* public trust doctrine make it clear that navigability — and not tidal influence — has become the *sine qua non* of the public trust interest in tidelands in this country.

It is true that *The Genesee Chief, supra* at 456-457, overruled prior cases of this Court which had limited admiralty jurisdiction to waters subject to tidal influence. . . . The Court did sharply criticize the "ebb and flow" measure of admiralty inherited from England in *The Genesee Chief*, and instead insisted quite emphatically that the different topography of America — in particular, our "thousands of miles of public navigable water[s] . . . in which there is no tide" — required that "jurisdiction [be] made to depend upon the navigable character of the water, and not upon the ebb and flow of the tide" [citation omitted]. Later, it came to be recognized as the "settled law of this country" that the lands under navigable freshwater lakes and rivers were within the public trust given the new States upon their entry into the Union, subject to the federal navigation easement and the power of Congress to control navigation on those streams under the Commerce Clause.

That States own freshwater river bottoms as far as the rivers are navigable, however, does not indicate that navigability is or was the prevailing test for state dominion over tidelands. Rather, this rule represents the American decision to depart from what it understood to be the English rule limiting Crown ownership to the soil under tidal waters. In *Oregon ex rel. State Land Board v. Corvallis Sand & Gravel Co.*, 429 U.S. 363, 374 (1977), after recognizing the accepted doctrine that States coming into the Union had title to all lands under the tidewaters, the Court stated that *Barney v. Keokuk*, 94 U.S. 324 (1876), had "extended the doctrine to waters which were nontidal but nevertheless navigable, consistent with [the Court's] earlier extension of admiralty jurisdiction."

This Court's decisions in *The Genesee Chief* and *Barney v. Keokuk* extended admiralty jurisdiction and public trust doctrine to navigable freshwaters and the lands beneath them. But we do not read those cases as simultaneously withdrawing from public trust coverage those lands which had been consistently recognized in this Court's cases as being within that doctrine's scope: *all* lands beneath waters influenced by the ebb and flow of the tide.

C.

Finally, we observe that not the least of the difficulties with petitioners' position is their concession that the States own the tidelands bordering the oceans, bays, and estuaries — even where these areas by no means could be considered navigable, as is always the case near the shore. It is obvious that these waters are part of the sea, and the lands beneath them are state property; ultimately, though, the only proof of this fact can be that the waters are influenced by the ebb and flow of the tide. This is undoubtedly why the ebb-and-flow test has been the measure of public ownership of tidelands for so long.

Admittedly, there is a difference in degree between the waters in this case, and nonnavigable waters on the seashore that are affected by the tide. But there is no difference in kind. For in the end, all tidewaters are connected to the sea: the waters in this case, for example, by a navigable, tidal river. Perhaps the lands at issue here differ in some ways from tidelands directly adjacent to the sea; nonetheless, they still share those "geographical, chemical and environmental" qualities that make lands beneath tidal waters unique.

Indeed, we find the various alternatives for delineating the boundaries of public trust tidelands offered by petitioners and their supporting *amici* to be unpersuasive and unsatisfactory. As the State suggested at argument, . . . and as recognized on several previous occasions, the ebb-and-flow rule has the benefit of "uniformity and certainty, and . . . eas[e] of application." *See, e.g., Cobb v. Davenport,* 32 N. J. L. 369, 379 (1867). We are unwilling, after its lengthy history at common law, in this Court, and in many state courts, to abandon the ebb-and-flow rule now, and seek to fashion a new test to govern the limits of public trust tidelands. Consequently, we hold that the lands at issue in this case were those given to Mississippi when the State was admitted to within the Union.

***

point for discussion

Connecting the physical reach of the public trust doctrine with its purpose. In this chapter, we are primarily concerned with the legal definition of the word "coastal," that is, the physical bounds of coastal law. In Chapter 7, we will learn about the rationales underlying the public trust doctrine and the purposes that it is meant to serve. Among other things, we will examine what the word "access" means, in the context of the doctrine, in great detail. Given the Court's language in *Phillips* (e.g., indicating that Mississippi courts have recognized "diverse uses of public trust tidelands"), you might begin to think about two questions to which we will return later: How much leeway do courts (or state legislatures) have in interpreting or evolving the public trust doctrine to satisfy changing public demands for access? How should those demands be balanced against the interests of riparian and littoral landowners?

As the Supreme Court stated in *Phillips,* "the individual States have the authority to define the limits of the lands held in public trust and to recognize private rights in such lands as they see fit." Mississippi obviously chose to define the geographic scope of the doctrine as broadly as possible. Not all state courts have followed this route. In the following case, one of the issues was whether non-navigable marshlands were covered by North Carolina's public trust doctrine.

Gwathmey v. State of North Carolina

464 S.E.2d 674 (N.C. 1995)

Chief Justice MITCHELL delivered the opinion of the Supreme Court of North Carolina.

***

This Court has long recognized that after the Revolutionary War, the State became the owner of lands beneath navigable waters. . . .

***

. . . The issue of navigability is controlling because the public trust doctrine is not an issue in cases where the land involved is above water or where the body of water regularly covering the land involved is not navigable in law. . . .

***

. . . By an assignment of error, defendant, the State of North Carolina, contends that the trial court erred in concluding that no public trust rights exist in the lands claimed by the plaintiffs. The State says this is so because those lands were not covered by waters "navigable in fact." More specifically, the State contends that the proper test for determining navigability in law where tidal waters are concerned is the "lunar tides" test, also known as the "ebb and flow" test. Under this test, "navigable waters are distinguished from others, by the ebbing and flowing of the tides." *Wilson v. Forbes*, 13 N.C. 30, 34 (1828) (Henderson, J.). We do not agree.

The evidence adduced at trial tended to show that the marshlands claimed by the plaintiffs are located in the Middle Sound area. The waters of Middle Sound are subject to the ebb and flow of the lunar tide. The marshlands in question are covered by the waters of the sound at certain stages of the tides. The depth of the water over any specific portion of the marshlands claimed by the plaintiffs varies according to the level of the tide in the sound. The State argues that because the marshlands are covered at regular intervals by waters subject to the ebb and flow of the tides, they are covered by navigable waters under the lunar tides test and are not subject to private appropriation. Based on an extensive review of the law of this State regarding the test for "navigability in law" as that term applies to the public trust doctrine, we conclude that the State's argument must fail because it is premised on the applicability of the lunar tides test.

Under the common law as applied in England, the navigability of waters was determined by whether they were subject to the ebb and flow of the tides. This common law rule "developed from the fact that England does not have to any great extent nontidal waters which are navigable." *Home Real Estate Loan & Ins. Co. v. Parmele*, 214 N.C. 63, 68 (1938).

In one of this Court's earliest decisions dealing with the test to be applied for determining navigability in law, however, we expressly stated:

> It is clear that by the [lunar tides] rule adopted in England, navigable waters are distinguished from others, by the ebbing and flowing of the tides. But this rule is entirely inapplicable to our situation, arising both from the great length of our rivers, extending far into the interior, and the sand-bars and other obstructions at their mouths. By that rule Albemarle and Pamlico sounds, which are inland seas, would not be deemed navigable waters, and would be the subject of private property.

Wilson v. Forbes, 13 N.C. at 34-35. Justice Hall concurred in a separate opinion, stating:

> I think that part [the lunar tides test] of the English law is not applicable to the waters and streams of this State. But few of them could be marked by such a distinction. There can be no essential difference for the purposes of navigation, whether the water be salt or fresh, or whether the tides regularly flow and ebb or not. . . .

13 N.C. at 38 (Hall, J.).

***

In *Wilson*, this Court made it clear that the lunar tides test had never been part of the English common law applied in this State before or after the Revolution. *Wilson*, 13 N.C. 30. Therefore, it is not a part of the common law to be applied in North Carolina. Additionally, we indicated in *Wilson* that the lunar tides test was "obsolete," as it was inapplicable to the conditions of the waters within this State. *Id.* For both of these reasons, the lunar tides test is not a part of the common law as it applies in North Carolina. *See* N.C.G.S. § 4-1.

In *Collins v. Benbury*, 25 N.C. 277 (1842), this Court emphasized that "whether there was any tide or not in the [Albemarle] Sound, when this patent issued, we do not think material; for we concur in the opinion of his Honor that this is 'a navigable water,' in the sense of our [entry] statutes." *Id.* at 282. Thus, this Court reaffirmed its earlier conclusion in *Wilson* that the lunar tides test does not control when determining the navigability of waters in this State for purposes of applying the public trust doctrine.

***

. . . [A]lthough the State has acknowledged this Court's clear rejection of the English lunar tides test in *Wilson* and in *Collins*, the State nevertheless argues that our summary of North Carolina law in *State v. Glen*, 52 N.C. 321 (1859), established a dual test for determining navigability in law in North Carolina. Its argument is based on the following language from *Glen*:

> *All the bays and inlets on our coast, where the tide from the sea ebbs and flows,* and *all other waters, whether sounds, rivers, or creeks, which can be navigated by sea vessels,* are called navigable, in a technical sense, are altogether *publici juris,* and the soil under them cannot be entered and a grant taken for it under the entry law. In them, too, the right of fishing is free. . . .

Glen, 52 N.C. at 333 (emphasis added). The State essentially argues that by using the words "where the sea ebbs and flows" to describe "all the bays and inlets on our coast," this Court indicated in *Glen* that the lunar tides test was a proper test for determining navigability, but not the sole and exclusive test. The State reads the remainder of the italicized language in the above quotation to mean that only the issue of the navigability of waters which are unaffected by the lunar tides is to be determined by whether they are navigable in fact. Accordingly, the State would have us hold that waters which meet either the test of navigability in fact or the lunar tides test are navigable in law. However, we are convinced that the language in *Glen* that refers to the ebb and flow of the tides is merely a phrase descriptive of all of the bays and inlets of the open ocean along our coast and has no independent legal significance.

The portion of the *Glen* opinion from which the above quotation was taken is but a summarization of cases previously reviewed in that opinion. Earlier in *Glen*, this Court stated that in England, navigability in law was ascertained by the ebb and flow of the tide. *Id.* at 325. We then said that the lunar tides or ebb and flow test

> has been held by our courts not to be applicable to the watercourses of North Carolina, and has been long since repudiated. We *hold* that *any waters*, whether sounds, bays, rivers, or creeks, which are wide enough and deep enough for the navigation of sea vessels, are navigable waters, the soil under which is not the subject of entry and grant under our entry law, and the rights of fishing in which are, under our common and statute law, open and common to all the citizens of the State.

Id. (emphasis added). *Glen* is not to be read to mean that there is a dual test for navigability which includes the lunar tides test when, in that opinion, this Court so clearly rejected the lunar tides test and expressly held that the test of navigability in fact controls in North Carolina. Additionally, in cases subsequent to this Court's decision in *Glen*, the lunar tides test was clearly rejected as an anachronistic tool, inapplicable to North Carolina's waters. . . .

points for discussion

1. *Equal footing and the public trust doctrine.* Although the Court in *Illinois Central* explains the expansion of the definition of public waterways by American courts to include navigable waters as based on the public need for avenues of commerce, there is another equally powerful explanation. As the Supreme Court of Mississippi tells the story in the decision upheld by the U.S. Supreme Court in *Phillips*:

   > Originally, "tidewaters," "ebb and flow of the tide," and similar language dominated discussions of the trust. It soon became apparent, however, that many of the new states had no coastline and hence had no lands within the ebb and flow of the tide. If the equal footing doctrine was to have meaning

in those inland states, something had to be done to the theretofore restrictive delineation of the trust lands.

Cinque Bambini Partnership v. State, 491 So. 2d 508, 514 (Miss. 1986).

Pursuant to this logic, what would happen if an admitted state were land-locked and had no navigable waterways? Another way to apply the equal footing doctrine would be to say that the 37 states admitted after the original 13 received exactly what the original 13 received, that is, the kind of property held in trust by the King prior to 1776. Under this approach, the 37 other states would only be entitled to waters influenced by the ebb and flow of the tide; inland states would be entitled to nothing. Which approach is more logical? Which is fairer?

2. *The exact meaning of tidal influence.* How do we know which bodies of water are "influenced by the ebb and flow of the tide"? All bodies of water, including small lakes and even swimming pools, as well as the surface of the earth itself, shift in response to the combined gravitational pull of the moon and the sun. (Some people believe that the human brain is influenced by these same forces, hence the word "lunatic.") The smaller the body of water, the smaller the tidal response, and the more difficult it is to measure that response. In the eighteenth century, "influenced by the ebb and flow of the tide" probably meant "visibly influenced" by the tide. In *Cinque Bambini*, the court seemed less concerned with whether water in the marshlands moved significantly due to tidal influence than with the fact that there was a hydrological connection between the Gulf of Mexico and the marshlands:

> What emerges is that the legal boundaries of navigable tidewaters are conceptually and functionally the same as those for navigable freshwaters. The high-water mark concept is used in both instances. That sophisticated geophysical study by reference to the tidal epoch and the like may customarily be employed in the establishment of mean high tide, while simpler processes are used with navigable rivers, is of no moment. Recognition of the conceptual equivalence of these two approaches to the establishing of certain boundaries for present purposes serves to make clear that the navigable waters test was no new test but the removal of an arbitrary and irrational limitation on the old ebb and flow test. In each instance — freshwaters or tidewaters — the central focus is upon navigable waters, but no one has ever suggested that the boundaries of that granted in trust were the contours of the navigable channel. The boundary of each waterway navigable in fact is that point where mean high-water mark (variously determined) strikes land. Within that surveyable, territorial boundary (and outside the navigable channel/area) will always be some non-navigable areas. *Yet so long as by unbroken water course — when the level of the waters is at mean high-water mark — one may hoist a sail upon a toothpick and without interruption navigate from the navigable channel/area to land, always afloat, the waters traversed and the lands beneath them are within the inland boundaries we consider the United States set for the properties granted the State in trust.*

Cinque Bambini Partnership v. State, 491 So. 2d 508, 515 (Miss. 1986) (emphasis added).

3. *Navigability in fact and navigability in law.* Wait a minute: What does a sailing toothpick have to do with navigation? As with many words, the legal definition of the word "navigable" is not always the same as the ordinary definition. In *Illinois Central*, the Court implies that the test of navigability is whether the waterway in question is suitable for use by commercial vessels. In another part of the *Gwathmey* decision, the Supreme Court of North Carolina explains that:

> The controlling law of navigability as it relates to the public trust doctrine in North Carolina is as follows: "'If water is navigable for pleasure boating it must be regarded as navigable water, though no craft has ever been put upon it for the purpose of trade or agriculture. The purpose of navigation is not the subject of inquiry, but the fact of the capacity of the water for use in navigation.'"

136 N.C. at 608-09 (quoting *Attorney General v. Woods*, 108 Mass. 436, 440 (1871)). In other words, if a body of water in its natural condition can be navigated by watercraft, it is navigable in fact and, therefore, navigable in law, even if it has not been used for such purpose. Lands lying beneath such waters that are navigable in law are the subject of the public trust doctrine.

Photo: Clinton Steeds

Figure 6-2. Mulberry River, Arkansas

In a 1980 decision, the Supreme Court of Arkansas broke from its prior commercial navigability test and held that a segment of the Mulberry River that was usable by canoes during six months of the year was "navigable in law" and thus part of the public trust. The court explained its rationale as follows:

> Determining the navigability of a stream is essentially a matter of deciding if it is public or private property. . . . Navigation in fact is the standard modern test of navigability, and, as embroidered by the federal courts, controls when navigation must be defined for federal purposes — maritime jurisdiction,

regulation under the Commerce Clause, and title disputes between the state and federal governments. . . . Otherwise, the states may adopt their own definitions of navigability.

While navigation in fact is widely regarded as the proper test of navigability . . . , it is a test which should not be applied too literally. For example, it has been said a stream need not be navigable at all its points or for the entire year to be navigable. . . . The real issue in these cases is the definition of navigation in fact.

***

Arkansas, as most states in their infancy, was mostly concerned with river traffic by steamboats or barges. . . . We have had no case regarding recreational use of waters such as the Mulberry. It may be that our [earlier] decisions did or did not anticipate such use of streams which are suitable, as the Mulberry is, for recreational use. Such use would include flatbottomed boats for fishing and canoes for floating—or both. There is no doubt that the segment of the Mulberry River that is involved in this lawsuit can be used for a substantial portion of the year for recreational purposes. Consequently, we hold that it is navigable at that place with all the incidental rights of that determination.

Arkansas v. McIlroy, 595 S.W.2d 659, 663 (Ark. 1980).

4. *Private waters.* All waterways that are not public are private. Or are they? States differ on the extent to which they recognize private ownership. In general, landowners on either side of a private stream own the stream bottom to the "thread" or center of the channel. In most states, the same is true for private lakes: A littoral owner owns the bottom of the lake from the two points at either end of his or her shoreline to a point in the middle of the lake. The two areas in which state law varies relate to the rights of private owners to control access to, and use of, the overlying water. In some states, such as Arkansas (hence McIlroy's lawsuit!), the owner has a right to prevent others from entering waters above privately owned submerged land. But in other states, such waters are open to the public, provided there is a legal way to enter the area. (In some cases, members of the public might have a right to cross private property to get to the water, e.g., where a public easement exists; without an established right of some kind, the public cannot lawfully walk across private land to get to the water.) The question of rights to consumptive use of the water is more complicated and is better saved for a course on water law.

2. Locating the Exact Boundary Separating Uplands from Public Waterways: More on the Legal Coastline

Just as states have some freedom in defining public waterways, they also have some discretion in locating the legal coastline that separates those waterways from private uplands. There are two categories of rules that states use to locate this line. Most states set the legal coastline at the high-water mark. Some of these states have statutes that specifically define "high water," while others — as you will see below — have left that chore to the courts. Seven states — Delaware, Maine, Massachusetts,

New Hampshire, Pennsylvania, Virginia, and Wisconsin — extend the area capable of ordinary private ownership to the low-water mark.

Both types of rules deviate from general rules regarding real property insofar as, in all states, the location of legal coastline can change over time. We will learn about the specifics of change, that is, how and why the boundary moves, in Chapter 8. In reading through the following cases, think about why Hawai'i and Rhode Island have adopted the rules they have. What are the advantages and disadvantages of alternative rules?

In re Ashford

440 P.2d 76 (Haw. 1968)

Justice RICHARDSON delivered the opinion of the Supreme Court of Hawai'i.

On August 22, 1963, Clinton R. Ashford and Joan B. S. Ashford, the appellees, petitioned the land court to register title to certain land situated on the Island of Molokai. The lands are the makai (seaward) portions of Royal Patent 3004 to Kamakaheki and Royal Patent 3005 to Kahiko, both issued on February 22, 1866.

The question before this court is the location of the makai boundaries of both parcels of land, which are described in the royal patents as running "ma ke kai" (along the sea). The appellees contend that the phrase describes the boundaries at mean high water which is represented by the contour traced by the intersection of the shore and the horizontal plane of mean high water based on publications of the U.S. Coast and Geodetic Survey. To support their position, appellees called a surveyor in private practice who surveyed the parcels on September 19, 1962. Basing his survey on publications of the U.S. Coast and Geodetic Survey, appellees' surveyor described the process which he used in delineating the boundaries at mean high water.

The State of Hawaii, appellant, denies that the makai boundaries of the two lots are correctly designated by the appellee, and claims that "ma ke kai" is approximately 20 to 30 feet above the line claimed by the appellee. The State contends in this case that "ma ke kai" is the high-water mark that is along the edge of vegetation or the line of debris left by the wash of waves during ordinary high tide.[1] In the trial court, the State presented kamaaina witnesses[2] for the purpose of establishing, by reputation evidence, the location of "ma ke kai" and also the location of public and private boundaries along the seashore in accordance with tradition, custom and usage in old Hawaii. The questions posed to the witnesses along this line were objected to and sustained by the court. However, the court allowed the witnesses to answer the questions, subject to the objections, to preserve the record for the purpose of appeal to this court.

---

1. The description excludes any line caused by extraordinary phenomena such as storms and tidal waves.

2. "We use the word 'kamaaina' above without translation in our investigation of ancient boundaries, water rights, etc. A good definition of it would be to say that it indicates such a person as the above witness described himself to be, a person familiar from childhood with any locality." *In re Boundaries of Pulehunui*, 4 Haw. 239, 245.

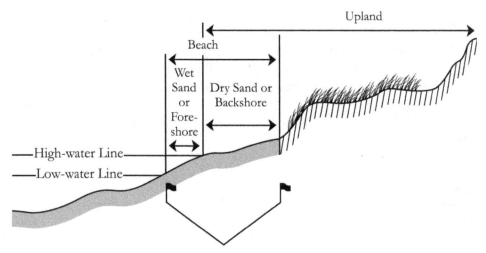

Depending on the legal jurisdiction, the legal
coastline is located somewhere between the flags.

Figure 6-3. *Ashford*
Where do the two parties in *Ashford* argue the legal coastline should be located?

We are of the opinion that "ma ke kai" is along the upper reaches of the wash
of waves, usually evidenced by the edge of vegetation or by the line of debris left by
the wash of waves, and that the trial court erred in finding that it is the intersection
of the shore with the horizontal plane of mean high water.

The trial court erred in sustaining the objections by the appellees to certain
questions put to kamaaina witnesses involving the location of "ma ke kai."

The Great Mahele

"The first major land reform [in Hawai'i] took place in the early 19th century in what
is known as the Great Mahele (division). Prior to this time all land was owned by the
king under a feudal system with the chiefs holding in fief on condition of tribute and
military service and the commoners as serfs who tilled the soil and performed other
services. Under the Mahele one third of the land was allocated to the chiefs, one
third to the commoners and one third was retained by [King Kamehameha V]. Of
the portion retained by the king about two-thirds was set aside for the government
and designated Government Lands and the remainder was reserved to the king as
his private estate and was called Crown Land. This change from a feudal system
to ownership in fee was an out-growth of the influence of white man who started
coming to the Islands about 1800 with the arrival of the first missionaries from New
England in 1820. Although the native Hawaiians adopted the principle of fee ownership of land in 1848 with the Mahele, as a practical matter it had no significance
for them. As long as they could occupy the land, raise their taro and catch their fish
they were happy. Consequently, it was a rather simple matter for the white man to
acquire the fee title to lands in Hawaii. As a result in mid 1956 twelve owners owned
52.08% of the private lands of the Territory. Sixty owners held 80.3% of the private
lands." John J. Hulten, *Land Reform in Hawaii*, 42 LAND ECON. 235, 235-36 (1966).

When the royal patents were issued in 1866 by King Kamehameha V, the sovereign, not having any knowledge of the data contained in the publications of the U.S. Coast and Geodetic Survey, did not intend to and did not grant title to the land along the ocean boundary as claimed by the appellees. Hawaii's land laws are unique in that they are based on ancient tradition, custom, practice and usage. . . . The method of locating the seaward boundaries was by reputation evidence from kamaainas and by the custom and practice of the government's survey office. It is not solely a question for a modern-day surveyor to determine boundaries in a manner completely oblivious to the knowledge and intention of the king and old-time kamaainas who knew the history and names of various lands and the monuments thereof.

In this jurisdiction, it has long been the rule, based on necessity, to allow reputation evidence by kamaaina witnesses in land disputes. . . . The rule also has a historical basis unique to Hawaiian land law. It was the custom of the ancient Hawaiians to name each division of land and the boundaries of each division were known to the people living thereon or in the neighborhood. "Some persons were specially taught and made repositories of this knowledge, and it was carefully delivered from father to son." . . . With the Great Mahele in 1848, these kamaainas, who knew and lived in the area, went on the land with the government surveyors and pointed out the boundaries to the various divisions of land. In land disputes following the Great Mahele, the early opinions of this court show that the testimony of kamaaina witnesses were permitted into evidence. In some cases, the outcome of decisions turned on such testimony. . . .

Two kamaaina witnesses, living in the area of appellees' land, testified, over appellees' objections, that according to ancient tradition, custom and usage, the location of a public and private boundary dividing private land and public beaches was along the upper reaches of the waves as represented by the edge of vegetation or the line of debris. In ancient Hawaii, the line of growth of a certain kind of tree, herb or grass sometimes made up a boundary. . . .

Cases cited from other jurisdictions cannot be used in determining the intention of the King in 1866. We do not find that data or information published and contained in the publications of the U.S. Coast and Geodetic Survey were relied upon by the kamaainas for the purpose of locating seaward boundaries in Hawaii. All of the matters contained in such publications were unknown to the ancient Hawaiians and foreign to the determination of boundaries in Hawaii. Property rights are determined by the law in existence at the time such rights are vested. . . .

We find no reference concerning the location of boundaries in Hawaii, prior to 1866, to data contained in the U.S. Coast and Geodetic Survey or to high-water mark as the intersection of the seashore with the horizontal plane of mean high water, or .7 or .9 of a foot above sea level. The trial court erred in holding that this was an area solely for the expert testimony of a surveyor to determine from data contained in publications of the U.S. Coast and Geodetic Survey.

Reversed and remanded for further proceedings consistent with this opinion.

What is the connection between the kamaaina testimony and the intent of King Kamehameha V? Could that testimony be used to provide support for a prescriptive public easement claim? In the next case, the upland owner may have been attempting to thwart the creation of such an easement.

State v. Ibbison

448 A.2d 728 (R.I. 1982)

Justice SHEA delivered the opinion of the Supreme Court of Rhode Island.

In this case we consider a question involving the interpretation of a provision of our state constitution. Article I, section 17 of the Rhode Island Constitution, as amended by Art. XXXVII, secs. 1-2, provides that the people of the state "shall continue to enjoy and freely exercise all the rights of fishery, and the privileges of the shore, to which they have been heretofore entitled under the charter and usages of this state." The question raised is this: To what point does the shore extend on its landward boundary? The setting of this boundary will fix the point at which the land held in trust by the state for the enjoyment of all its people ends and private property belonging to littoral owners begins.

The defendants in this case, James Ibbison III, Don E. Morris, Allen E. Zumwalt, James W. Sminkey, Miles R. Stray, and William S. Gavitt were convicted in the Fourth Division District Court on February 2, 1979, of criminal trespass in violation of § 19-17 of the Westerly Code. This section of the code prohibits a person from knowingly entering upon the land of another without having been requested or invited to do so by the owner or occupant of the land. The defendants were each fined $10 plus costs. They appealed their convictions to the Superior Court. On December 9, 1980, a justice of the Superior Court granted defendants' motion to dismiss the charges. The District and Superior Court justices reached different conclusions based on their fixing the boundary between the shore and littoral owners at different points. The state has appealed the dismissals.

Since this case is not before us after a trial in the Superior Court and we have no transcript of the District Court proceedings, there is no record of the facts other than the assertions of counsel. Fortunately, a lengthy recitation of facts is not necessary because the key fact needed for the resolution of this appeal has been stipulated to by the parties.

This dispute arose as defendants were engaged in a beach-clean-up operation in Westerly. As defendants traveled along the beach, they were stopped by Wilfred Kay, a littoral owner, and Patrolman Byron Brown of the Westerly police department. Kay, believing his private property extended to the mean-high-water line, had staked out that line previously. He informed defendants that they were

Photo: Waffries/Wikimedia Commons

Figure 6-4. The Beach in Westerly, Rhode Island

not permitted to cross the landward side of it. The defendants, on the other hand, believed that their right to traverse the shore extended to the high-water mark. This line was defined by defendants in the Superior Court as a visible line on the shore indicated by the reach of an average high tide and further indicated by drifts and seaweed along the shore. It has been stipulated by the parties that defendants had crossed the mean-high-tide line but were below the high-water mark at the time of their arrest. Also, at the time of the arrest, the mean-high-tide line was under water.

We have referred to the term "high-water mark" as used by defendants and accepted by the Superior Court. We shall now discuss the term "mean high tide line." This line is relied upon by the state as the proper boundary, and it is the line accepted by the District Court. The mean high tide is the arithmetic average of high-water heights observed over an 18.6-year Metonic cycle.[2] It is the line that is formed by the intersection of the tidal plane of mean high tide with the shore.

The issue before us is in reality very narrow because the prior decided cases of this court have consistently recognized that the shore lies between high and low water. For example, the shore has been designated as "land below high-water mark," *Armour & Co. v. City of Newport*, 43 R.I. 211, 213 (1920); "land below ordinary high-water mark," *Narragansett Real Estate Co. v. MacKenzie*, 34 R.I. 103, 112 (1912); "lands covered by tide waters," *City of Providence v. Comstock*, 27 R.I. 537, 542 (1906); "all land below high-water mark," *Rhode Island Motor Co. v. City of Providence*, 55 A. 696 (R.I. 1903); "the space between high and low-water mark," *Clark v. Peckham*, 10 R.I. 35, 38 (1871).

The problem we face is that none of these cases have defined how the high-water line is to be calculated. Although no prior Rhode Island case explicitly resolves the question before us, there are two cases, however, that are somewhat helpful. In *Allen v. Allen*, 19 R.I. 114 (1895), this court stated that "the State holds the legal fee of all lands below high-water mark *as at common law.*" (emphasis added.) Next, in *Jackvony v. Powel*, 67 R.I. 218 (1941), the court held unconstitutional under Art. I, sec. 17 a statute that would have permitted the city of Newport to erect a fence at Easton's Beach between the high- and low-water marks. *Id.* at 219.

At various times in the *Jackvony* case, the court referred to the high-water line or mark, and at other times it referred to the mean high tide. Specifically, with regard to the privileges of the people in the shore, the court referred to the shores as "bordering on tidewaters and lying between the lines of mean high tide and mean low tide." *Id.* at 225. We find that the *Jackvony* court used the two terms interchangeably.

The interesting point about the *Allen* case is the court's reliance on the common law in finding that the state holds title to all lands below the high-water mark, *Allen v. Allen*, 19 R.I. at 115, because at common law the boundary was the mean-high-tide-line. Here again, we believe that the *Allen* court uses these terms interchangeably.

It is difficult to discern any real difference between the two positions argued here. By definition, the mean high tide is, in reality, an average high

---

2. This cycle begins and ends when a new moon occurs on the same day of the year as it did at the beginning of the last cycle; that is, at the end of a metonic cycle the phases of the moon recur in the same order and on the same days as in the preceding cycle.

tide. Similarly, defendants have defined the high-water mark in terms of an average. The defendants contend that their high-water mark is such, however, that it is readily observable because of drifts and the presence of seaweed. Our difficulty in accepting this position is that we have absolutely no evidence before us from which we could determine that this is generally true. As noted previously, we are handicapped by the absence of a record in this case. For this reason the only permissible action for us to take is to affix the boundary as was done at common law and which this court in *Allen* declared to be the settled policy of this state.

The common-law background of this issue can be traced back several hundred years. Originally, land titles in England came from a grant from the Crown beginning back during the reign of King John which ended in 1216. These early grants were imprecise, however, especially because of the lack of definition of the seaward boundary of coastal grants. . . . The grantees, however, no doubt viewed their property as extending to the sea.

In 1568-1569, Thomas Digges, a mathematician, engineer, astronomer, and lawyer, wrote a short treatise in which he concluded that the tidelands had not been included in the grants of the seacoasts by the Crown. *Id.* This work went largely unnoticed until 1670 when Sir Matthew Hale incorporated Digges' theory into his very influential treatise *De Jure Maris*. In this work Hale defined the shore as follows:

> "The shore is that ground that is between the ordinary high-water and low-water mark. This doth prima facie and of common right belong to the king, both in the shore of the sea and the shore of the arms of the sea." 1 Clark, *supra* at 191 n. 54 (quoting *De Jure Maris*, ch. IV, p. 378, reprinted in Moore, *A History of the Foreshore*, at p. 370.)

After this time, the burden of proof was placed on landowners to show that their particular property extended to the low-water mark, and not the high-water mark. The burden placed this way made it very difficult for landowners to overcome. . . .

This was the state of development of the law in England at the time of the colonization of the eastern shoreline of North America. *Id.* After the Revolutionary War and the formation of our Republic, the individual states retained their own tidelands as they had previously. . . . In a series of United States Supreme Court decisions beginning with *Martin v. Waddell*, 41 U.S. 367 (1842), and culminating with *Borax Consolidated Ltd. v. City of Los Angeles*, 296 U.S. 10 (1935), the Court confirmed individual state ownership of the tidelands.

There had been some uncertainty in the United States regarding whether the boundary was properly at the point of the mean high tide or the mean low tide, but this uncertainty was largely removed in 1935 when it was held in *Borax Consolidated, supra*, that the common-law rule put the boundary between littoral owners and the state at the line of the mean high tide. . . .

In *Borax Consolidated* the Court reviewed a Court of Appeals decision setting the boundary between land claimed by the plaintiff under a federal preemption patent and the State of California at the mean-high-tide line. The Court analyzed this issue's common-law history in depth including the writings of Sir Matthew

Hale and also an influential English decision, *Attorney General v. Chambers*, 4 De G.M. & G. 206. In affirming the Court of Appeals, the Court concluded as follows:

> "The tideland extends to the high-water mark. This does not mean, as petitioners contend, a physical mark made upon the ground by the waters; it means the line of high water as determined by the course of the tides. By the civil law, the shore extends as far as the highest waves reach in winter. But by the common law, the shore 'is confined to the flux and reflux of the sea at ordinary tides.' It is the land 'between ordinary high and low-water mark, the land over which the daily tides ebb and flow. When, therefore, the sea, or a bay, is named as a boundary, the line of ordinary high-water mark is always intended where the common law prevails.'" [Citations omitted.] *Borax Consolidated Ltd. v. City of Los Angeles*, 296 U.S. at 22-23.

Having identified the common-law boundary of the shore as the land between the "ordinary high and low-water mark," the Court described how the line is to be determined since the range of the tide at any given place varies from day to day. At a new moon and a full moon, the range of tides is greater than average because at these particular times, high water rises higher and low water falls lower than usual. The tides at such times are called spring tides. Correspondingly, when the moon is in its first and third quarters, the tide does not rise as high or fall as low as on the average. During these times, the tides are called neap tides. . . .

The Court noted that at common law the spring tides, the highest tides of the month, were excluded as the landward boundary of the shore since for the most part this land was dry and not reached by the tides. . . . Presumably, the point reached by the spring tides is the same point as that argued by defendants as being the high-water mark evidenced by drifts and seaweed.

Recognizing the monthly changes of the tides, the Court recited the following formula, used by the Court of Appeals, for finding the mean-high-tide line:

> "In view of the definition of the mean high tide, as given by the United States Coast and Geodetic Survey, that 'mean high water at any place is the average height of all the high waters at that place over a considerable period of time,' and the further observation that 'from theoretical considerations of an astronomical character' there should be a 'periodic variation in the rise of water above sea level having a period of 18.6 years' the Court of Appeals directed that in order to ascertain the mean high tide line with requisite certainty in fixing the boundary of valuable tidelands, such as those here in question appear to be, 'an average of 18.6 years should be determined as near as possible.' We find no error in that instruction." *Id.* at 26-27.

We concur in this analysis and apply the mean-high-tide line as the landward boundary of the shore for the purposes of the privileges guaranteed to the people of this state by our constitution. This court has held that the common law governs the rights and obligations of the people of the state unless that law has been modified by our General Assembly. . . . Here we apply the common law to govern the interpretation of a constitutional provision.

In fixing the landward boundary of the shore at the mean-high-tide line, we are mindful that there is a disadvantage in that this point is not readily identifiable by the casual observer. We doubt, however, that any boundary could be set that would be readily apparent to an observer when we consider the varied topography of our shoreline. The mean-high-tide line represents the point that can be determined scientifically with the greatest certainty. Clearly, a line determined over a period of years using modern scientific techniques is more precise than a mark made by the changing tides driven by the varying forces of nature. In *Luttes v. State*, 159 Tex. 500, 519 (1958) the Texas court concluded that "common sense suggests a line based on a long term average of daily highest water levels, rather than a line based on some theory of occasional or sporadic highest waters."

Additionally, we feel that our decision best balances the interests between littoral owners and all the people of the state. Setting the boundary at the point where the spring tides reach would unfairly take from littoral owners land that is dry for most of the month. Similarly, setting the boundary below the mean-high-tide line at the line of the mean low tide would so restrict the size of the shore as to render it practically nonexistent.

Finally, setting the boundary as we have done brings us in accord with many of the other states. *People v. William Kent Estate Co.*, 242 Cal. App. 2d 156 (1966); *Shorefront Park Improvement Association v. King*, 157 Conn. 249 (1968); *Wicks v. Howard*, 40 Md. App. 135 (1978); *Harrison County v. Guice*, 244 Miss. 95 (1962); *O'Neill v. State Highway Department*, 50 N.J. 307 (1967); *Carolina Beach Fishing Pier, Inc. v. Town of Carolina Beach*, 277 N.C. 297 (1970); *Luttes v. State, supra; Wilson v. Howard*, 5 Wash. App. 169 (1971). We note that in a couple of these cases the term "high-water mark" is used in place of "mean high tide line." However, this is inconsequential as each state defines the phrase in terms of the mean high tide.

This brings us to the actual disposition of this matter. In view of the lack of clarity in early decisions of this court regarding whether the landward boundary of the shoreline was to be computed as a mean or as an absolute high-water mark, we shall affirm the dismissals of the charges by the Superior Court justice but for different reasons. It is well settled that this court may sustain judgments entered below even though we do not accept that court's reasoning. . . .

We affirm the dismissals since basic due process provides that no man shall be held criminally responsible for conduct that he could not reasonably understand to be proscribed. . . . Although this situation most often occurs when statutes are challenged for vagueness, we find that the facts of this case are such that these defendants are entitled to similar protection.

In the future, any municipality that intends to impose criminal penalties for trespass on waterfront property above the mean-high-tide line must prove beyond reasonable doubt that the defendant knew the location of the boundary line and intentionally trespassed across it.

For the reasons stated, the appeal is denied and dismissed, the granting of the motion to dismiss is affirmed, and the papers of the case are remanded to the Superior Court.

points for discussion

1. *High water versus low water.* Why do you think some states recognize private property ownership to the low-water mark? What historic facts or conditions might have justified the original adoption of this position? Does a rule setting the legal coastline at "low water" mean that access to public trust areas can be gained only by vessel? Given that the roots of the public trust are in navigability, why would any state have chosen to set the line at the high-water mark?

2. *Practically speaking.* In *Ibbison*, the court finds that the defendants were walking on private land but were not trespassing. What will the beach in Rhode Island look like after *Ibbison*, given that "any municipality that intends to impose criminal penalties for trespass on waterfront property above the mean-high-tide line must prove beyond reasonable doubt that the defendant knew the location of the boundary line and intentionally trespassed across it"? In order to answer this question, you need to know why it is essentially impossible for anyone to be able to locate the state/private beach boundary in real time. As the Rhode Island court summarized criminal trespass law: The state must first prove that "the defendant knew the location of the boundary line." In a law review article, one of your casebook authors has explained why real-time line location of a datum-based line, like the mean-high-tide line, is difficult, and why real-time location of the property boundary (which may be in a different location from the datum-based line) is impossible. Josh Eagle, *Are Beach Boundaries Enforceable? Real-Time Locational Uncertainty and the Right to Exclude*, 93 WASH. L. REV. 1181 (2018). If the boundary can't be known in real time, then it is logical that trespass law, at least criminal trespass law, is of no use to a landowner wishing to exclude the public. What makes real-time location impossible?

> The first problem in enforcing the ocean-side boundary arises from the fact that the mean higher-high-water line is, in part, a product of the dynamic topography of the beach. [Some states, such as Texas, use mean higher high water instead of mean high tide as the datum-basis for setting the property line. While mean high tide averages the height all high tides, mean higher high water averages the height of each day's highest high tide.] The mean higher-high-water plane remains fixed for the entirety of each 19-year tidal epoch; the beach profile, however, is unstable. Waves, tides, wind, and other forces constantly rearrange sand on beaches. As sand moves, the shape of the beach changes, and the result is a new mean higher-high-water line. [It is not atypical for this movement to occur daily: in Texas, the mean higher-high-water line moves 8 to 45 feet each day on average.]

> ***

> [A second problem] is that surveys used to determine tidal datums like mean higher-high-water are inherently inaccurate. Inaccuracy in line-drawing results from irreducible error in, among other things, the measurement of the height of tides. Studies have estimated that this error in vertical measurement translates to uncertainty in the range of three to nine meters horizontally. In other words, the true higher-high-water line may be thirty feet higher or lower on the beach — further away from or closer to the ocean — than the real-time surveyed line.

> ***

> [But, the actual impossibility of locating the line is due to common law rules for locating the boundary after change occurs. This is something you will learn a lot about in Chapter 8.] Under the common law, certain kinds of beach change — namely change that is rapid or artificially caused — result in a property boundary that is in a different place from the datum-based line: because of these rules, finding the mean higher-high-water line would

[require a quiet title action, so that the line location on January 1, 2018 can't be known until the case is resolved, maybe in 2019.]

Eagle, *supra*, at 1191-94.

3. *The* Borax Consolidated *decision.* The Supreme Court of Rhode Island cites the U.S. Supreme Court's decision in *Borax Consolidated* in support of its own holding that, henceforth in Rhode Island, the location of the high-water boundary will be determined by reference to the mean-high-tide line. Why wasn't the *Borax Consolidated* decision binding on the Rhode Island court? The *Borax* case involved federal common law because, as the court notes, the plaintiff claimed the uplands "under a federal preemption patent." In other words, the federal government had owned the uplands at one point in time, before transferring them to plaintiff's predecessor in interest. Distinguishing the case from prior cases in which uplands had been acquired from Mexico by private owners prior to California statehood, the U.S. Supreme Court noted that:

> There is no question that the United States was free to convey the upland, and the patent affords no ground for holding that it did not convey all the title the United States had in the premises. The question as to the extent of this federal grant, that is, as to the limit of the land conveyed, or the boundary between the upland and the tideland, is necessarily a federal question.

296 U.S. at 22. The holding in *Borax* would not be binding in cases involving land in any of the original thirteen states, including Rhode Island.

4. *High water versus mean high tide.* Which of the various measures of high water — vegetation, drift line, and mean high tide — are most consistent with the primary purpose of the public trust doctrine, that is, public access? Are there other reasons for choosing one rule over another? Why do you think the Hawai'i court chose a different rule than the Rhode Island court did?

5. *The case-by-case nature of the common law.* Rhode Island became a state in 1790. What was the boundary between uplands and tidelands in Rhode Island between 1790 and 1982, when *Ibbison* was decided? Is the court in *Ibbison* changing the definition of high water or simply clarifying it?

What Percentage of Coastal Upland Has Its Origin in a Federal Patent?

We don't know. We do know that the federal government owned a significant amount of the coastal uplands in the federal territories from which Congress ultimately carved many states. Title that does not derive from a federal patent has its roots in pre-territorial transfers by the nations, or agents of the nations, who owned the land at that time. For example, Mexico and Spain had transferred much of the coastal upland in California to private parties before the United States acquired California from Mexico in 1848. *See* Note, *Federal Rule of Accretion and California Coastal Protection*, 48 S. CAL. L. REV. 1457, 1469-70 (1975).

6. *More on the Hawai'i rule.* In Hawai'i, the legislature ultimately passed several statutes defining the legal coastline. The current version, effective in 2006, defines "shoreline" as:

> [T]he upper reaches of the wash of the waves, other than storm and seismic waves, at high tide during the season of the year in which the highest wash of the waves occurs, usually evidenced by the edge of vegetation growth, or the upper limit of debris left by the wash of the waves.

HAW. REV. STAT. § 205A-1.

7. *Landowner incentives.* The use of the vegetation line as the high-water mark in Hawai'i has a number of implications for the public and for private owners. For the public, it means that part of the dry sand beach is open for public use. For private landowners, it creates an incentive to maintain vegetation. A recent newspaper article noted that

> beachfront landowners continue to run irrigation lines to the edge of the shoreline to promote vegetation growth that reduces the size of the public beach. The irrigation, along with north Kaua'i's plentiful rainfall, can keep greenery growing well seaward of where waves wash in winter. . . .
>
> . . . [T]he naupaka, heliotropes, palms and other plants grown in this way limit the size of the public beach, and prevent the beach from expanding and contracting normally with the seasons.
>
> "They are de facto vegetative seawalls. In times of high tides, you can't walk the beach any more," said [one coastal activist].
>
> [Another Hawai'ian], whose foundation normally supports the rights of property owners, said the process of watering the public shoreline is unacceptable. "We're not supporting anybody who's inducing vegetation. That's just encroaching," [he] said.

Shoreline Owners Just Keep Building, HONOLULU ADVERTISER (Hawai'i), Sept. 18, 2006, at 1A.

> Is this irrigated vegetation natural or artificial? Should the Hawai'i legislature consider a measure to ban shoreline irrigation?

3. The Seaward End of Public Waterways

How far out to sea do "public waterways," that is, waters subject to a state's public trust doctrine, extend? As you learned in Chapter 5, the Submerged Lands Act gives states ownership of resources (subject to federal regulation, of course) out to three nautical miles from shore. Is the ownership granted by the Act trust ownership or ordinary ownership? The difference matters, as you will see in the next chapter. Opinions vary on the answer to the question. Based on the Supreme Court's holding in *United States v. California,* can you make the arguments for and against inclusion of three-mile band resources in the trust corpus?

4. Beyond Public Waterways

From cases such as *Illinois Central*, *Phillips*, and *McIlroy*, we might reasonably conclude that, in identifying public waterways, courts sometimes pay less attention to history than to whether the public has an important interest in the waterway in question. The focus of all those cases, though, was on some form of navigation, whether commercial or recreational.

In a few states, courts have used the public importance rationale to expand the geographic scope of the public trust beyond the boundaries of public waterways. In the first case below, the Supreme Court of New Jersey expands the scope of the public trust doctrine so as to include some use of adjacent dry sand beaches. In the second case, the Supreme Court of Oregon accomplishes the same end, but through slightly different means.

> ### The Historical Context of *Avon*
>
> "Where beaches were municipally owned, as in parts of Connecticut and New Jersey, the shore municipalities often limited beach use to a town's residents, or put beach fees or other barriers in the way of nonresidents' use of town beaches. Tactics of indirect exclusion included charging much more for nonresident beach passes, making cheap seasonal passes difficult or impossible for nonresidents to get, limiting parking near the beach and/or banning on-street parking altogether, making beach access contingent on membership in a beach club which, in turn, would be available only to residents of the community, barring disrobing and wearing swimwear on the streets (which effectively meant one had to belong to a beach club), and banning eating on the beach (which discouraged day trippers with picnics). Such private and municipal actions limiting access to a beach often were motivated not just by a desire to prevent overcrowding or to preserve privacy, but were undertaken to keep out 'those people' — that is, people of color, the poor, people from the inner cities, hippies, and so on. Thus, restrictions on beach access, particularly through governmentally imposed policies that favored residents only, sometimes took on the dimensions of a type of exclusionary zoning." Marc Poirier, *Environmental Justice and the Beach Access Movements of the 1970s in Connecticut and New Jersey: Stories of Property and Civil Rights*, 28 CONN. L. REV. 719, 743-44 (1996).

Matthews v. Bay Head Improvement Association

471 A.2d 355 (N.J. 1984)

Justice SCHREIBER delivered the opinion of the unanimous Supreme Court of New Jersey.

The public trust doctrine acknowledges that the ownership, dominion and sovereignty over land flowed by tidal waters, which extend to the mean high-water mark, is vested in the State in trust for the people. The public's right to use the tidal lands and water encompasses navigation, fishing and recreational uses, including bathing, swimming and other shore activities. *Borough of Neptune City v. Borough of Avon-by-the-Sea*, 61 N.J. 296, 309 (1972*).* In *Avon* we held that the public trust applied to the municipally-owned dry sand beach immediately landward of the high-water mark. The major issue in this case is whether, ancillary to the public's right to enjoy the tidal lands, the public has a right to gain access through and to use the dry sand area not owned by a municipality but by a quasi-public body.

The Borough of Point Pleasant instituted this suit against the Borough of Bay Head and the Bay Head Improvement Association (Association), generally asserting that the defendants prevented Point Pleasant inhabitants from gaining access to the Atlantic Ocean and the beachfront in Bay Head. The proceeding was dismissed as to the Borough of Bay Head because it did not own or control the beach. Subsequently, Virginia Matthews, a resident of Point Pleasant who desired to swim and bathe at the Bay Head beach, joined as a party plaintiff, and Stanley Van Ness, as Public Advocate, joined as plaintiff-intervenor. When the Borough of Point Pleasant ceased pursuing the litigation, the Public Advocate became the primary moving party. The Public Advocate asserted that the defendants had denied the general public its right of access during the summer bathing season to public trust lands along the beaches in Bay Head and its right to use private property fronting on the ocean incidental to the public's right under the public trust doctrine. . . .

Both sides moved for summary judgment. The trial court granted the defendants' motions except with respect to the plaintiff's claim that the public had acquired rights in the dry sand beach resulting from an implied dedication or prescriptive easement prior to 1932. When the plaintiff abandoned these claims, the trial court entered a final judgment in favor of the defendants. Upon plaintiff's appeal, the Appellate Division affirmed, one judge dissenting. . . .

***

I. Facts

The Borough of Bay Head (Bay Head) borders the Atlantic Ocean. Adjacent to it on the north is the Borough of Point Pleasant Beach, on the south the Borough of Mantoloking, and on the west Barnegat Bay. Bay Head consists of a fairly narrow strip of land, 6,667 feet long (about 1 1/4 miles). A beach runs along its entire length adjacent to the Atlantic Ocean. There are 76 separate parcels of land that border the beach. All except six are owned by private individuals. Title to those six is vested in the Association.

The Association was founded in 1910 and incorporated as a nonprofit corporation in 1932. Its certificate of incorporation states that its purposes are

> the improving and beautifying of the Borough of Bay Head, New Jersey, cleaning, policing and otherwise making attractive and safe the bathing beaches in said Borough, and the doing of any act which may be found necessary or desirable for the greater convenience, comfort and enjoyment of the residents.

Its constitution delineates the Association's object to promote the best interests of the Borough and "in so doing to own property, operate bathing beaches, hire life guards, beach cleaners and policemen. . . ."

Nine streets in the Borough, which are perpendicular to the beach, end at the dry sand. The Association owns the land commencing at the end of seven of these streets for the width of each street and extending through the upper dry sand to the mean high water line, the beginning of the wet sand area or foreshore. In addition, the Association owns the fee in six shore front properties, three of which are contiguous and have a frontage aggregating 310 feet. Many owners of beachfront property executed and delivered to the Association leases of the upper dry sand area. These leases are revocable by either party to the lease on thirty days' notice. Some owners have not executed such leases and have not permitted the Association to use their beaches. Some also have acquired riparian grants from the State extending approximately 1,000 feet east of the high water line.

The Association controls and supervises its beach property between the third week in June and Labor Day. It engages about 40 employees, who serve as lifeguards, beach police and beach cleaners. . . .

Membership is generally limited to residents of Bay Head. Class A members are property owners. Class B are non-owners. Large families (six or more) pay $90 per year and small families pay $60 per year. Upon application residents are routinely accepted. Membership is evidenced by badges that signify permission to use the beaches. Members, which include local hotels, motels and inns, can also acquire badges for guests. The charge for each guest badge is $12. Members of the Bay Head Fire Company, Bay Head Borough employees, and teachers in the municipality's school system have been issued beach badges irrespective of residency.

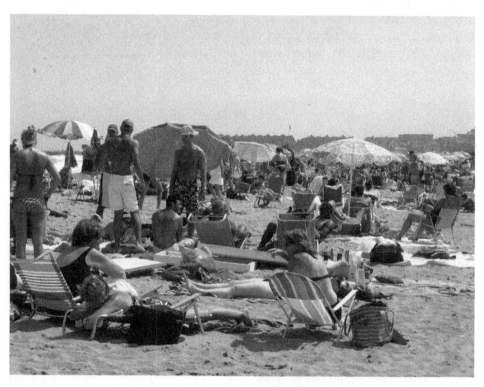

Photo: Nightscream/Wikimedia Commons

Figure 6-5. Manasquan Beach, New Jersey, Near Point Pleasant Beach

Except for fishermen, who are permitted to walk through the upper dry sand area to the foreshore, only the membership may use the beach between 10:00 A.M. and 5:30 P.M. during the summer season. The public is permitted to use the Association's beach from 5:30 P.M. to 10:00 A.M. during the summer and, with no hourly restrictions, between Labor Day and mid-June.

No attempt has ever been made to stop anyone from occupying the terrain east of the high-water mark. During certain parts of the day, when the tide is low, the foreshore could consist of about 50 feet of sand not being flowed by the water. The public could gain access to the foreshore by coming from the Borough of Point Pleasant Beach on the north or from the Borough of Mantoloking on the south.

Association membership totals between 4,800 to 5,000. The Association President testified during depositions that its restrictive policy, in existence since 1932, was due to limited parking facilities and to the overcrowding of the beaches. The Association's avowed purpose was to provide the beach for the residents of Bay Head.

There is also a public boardwalk, about one-third of a mile long, parallel to the ocean on the westerly side of the dry sand area. The boardwalk is owned and maintained by the municipality.

The trial court held that the Association was not an arm of the Borough of Bay Head, that the Association was not a municipal agency, and that nothing in the record justified a finding that public privileges could attach to the private properties owned or leased by the Association. A divided Appellate Division affirmed. The majority agreed with the trial court that the Association was not a public agency or a public entity and that the action of the private owners through the Association established no general right in the public to the use of the beaches.

Judge Greenberg dissented. He argued that the Association's beaches are de facto public to a limited extent, being public to residents and visitors who stay in hotels. They are private to everyone else. He reasoned that Bay Head residents have the advantage of living in a municipality with public beaches, but are not troubled by having their beaches made available to outsiders. Judge Greenberg concluded that the Association's beaches must be open to all members of the public. However, he would not preclude any lessor from terminating his lease with the Association and thereby eliminating the public right of access to that part of the beach.

II. The Public Trust

In *Borough of Neptune City v. Borough of Avon-by-the-Sea*, 61 N.J. 296, 303 (1972), Justice Hall alluded to the ancient principle "that land covered by tidal waters belonged to the sovereign, but for the common use of all the people." The genesis of this principle is found in Roman jurisprudence, which held that "[b]y the law of nature" "the air, running water, the sea, and consequently the shores of the sea" were "common to mankind." Justinian, *Institutes* 2.1.1 (T. Sandars trans. 1st Am. ed. 1876). No one was forbidden access to the sea, and everyone could use the seashore[3] "to dry his nets there, and haul them from the sea. . . ." *Id.*, 2.1.5. The seashore

___

3. The seashore extended to the limit of the highest winter flood, Justinian, *supra*, 2.1.3, and not the mean high-water mark.

was not private property, but "subject to the same law as the sea itself, and the sand or ground beneath it." *Id.* This underlying concept was applied in New Jersey in *Arnold v. Mundy*, 6 N.J.L. 1 (Sup. Ct. 1821).

***

In *Avon*, Justice Hall reaffirmed the public's right to use the waterfront as announced in *Arnold v. Mundy*. He observed that the public has a right to use the land below the mean average high-water mark where the tide ebbs and flows. These uses have historically included navigation and fishing. In *Avon* the public's rights were extended "to recreational uses, including bathing, swimming and other shore activities." 61 N.J. at 309. *Compare Blundell v. Catterall*, 106 Eng. Rep. 1190 (K.B. 1821) (holding no right to swim in common property) *with Martin v. Waddell's Lessee*, 41 U.S. 367 (1842) (indicating right to bathe in navigable waters). The Florida Supreme Court has held:

> The constant enjoyment of this privilege [bathing in salt waters] of thus using the ocean and its fore-shore for ages without dispute should prove sufficient to establish it as an American common law right, similar to that of fishing in the sea, even if this right had not come down to us as a part of the English common law, which it undoubtedly has. [*White v. Hughes*, 139 Fla. 54, 59 (1939).]

It has been said that "[h]ealth, recreation and sports are encompassed in and intimately related to the general welfare of a well-balanced state." *N.J. Sports & Exposition Authority v. McCrane*, 119 N.J. Super. 457, 488 (Law Div. 1971), aff'd, 61 N.J. 1, appeal dismissed *sub nom. Borough of East Rutherford v. N.J. Sports & Exposition Authority*, 409 U.S. 943 (1972). Extension of the public trust doctrine to include bathing, swimming and other shore activities is consonant with and furthers the general welfare. The public's right to enjoy these privileges must be respected.

In order to exercise these rights guaranteed by the public trust doctrine, the public must have access to municipally-owned dry sand areas as well as the foreshore. The extension of the public trust doctrine to include municipally-owned dry sand areas was necessitated by our conclusion that enjoyment of rights in the foreshore is inseparable from use of dry sand beaches. *See Lusardi v. Curtis Point Property Owners Ass'n,* 86 N.J. 217, 228 (1981). In *Avon* we struck down a municipal ordinance that required nonresidents to pay a higher fee than residents for the use of the beach. We held that where a municipal beach is dedicated to public use, the public trust doctrine "dictates that the beach and the ocean waters must be open to all on equal terms and without preference and that any contrary state or municipal action is impermissible." 61 N.J. at 309. The Court was not relying on the legal theory of dedication, although dedication alone would have entitled the public to the full enjoyment of the dry sand. Instead the Court depended on the public trust doctrine, impliedly holding that full enjoyment of the foreshore necessitated some use of the upper sand, so that the latter came under the umbrella of the public trust.

***

III. Public Rights in Privately-Owned Dry Sand Beaches

In *Avon* and *Van Ness v. Borough of Deal*, 78 N.J. 389 (1978) our finding of public rights in dry sand areas was specifically and appropriately limited to those beaches owned by a municipality. We now address the extent of the public's interest in privately-owned dry sand beaches. This interest may take one of two forms. First, the public may have a right to cross privately owned dry sand beaches in order to gain access to the foreshore. Second, this interest may be of the sort enjoyed by the public in municipal beaches under *Avon* and *Deal*, namely, the right to sunbathe and generally enjoy recreational activities.

Beaches are a unique resource and are irreplaceable. The public demand for beaches has increased with the growth of population and improvement of transportation facilities. Furthermore, the projected demand for salt water swimming will not be met "unless the existing swimming capacities of the four coastal counties are expanded." Department of Environmental Protection, *Statewide Comprehensive Outdoor Recreation Plan* 200 (1977). The DEP estimates that, compared to 1976, the State's salt water swimming areas "must accommodate 764,812 more persons by 1985 and 1,021,112 persons by 1995." *Id.* . . .

Exercise of the public's right to swim and bathe below the mean high-water mark may depend upon a right to pass across the upland beach. Without some means of access the public right to use the foreshore would be meaningless. To say that the public trust doctrine entitles the public to swim in the ocean and to use the foreshore in connection therewith without assuring the public of a feasible access route would seriously impinge on, if not effectively eliminate, the rights of the public trust doctrine. This does not mean the public has an unrestricted right to cross at will over any and all property bordering on the common property. The public interest is satisfied so long as there is reasonable access to the sea.

Judge Best, in his dissent in *Blundell v. Catterall*, 5 B. & Ald. 268, 275 (K.B. 1821), stated that passage to the seashore was essential to the exercise of that right. He believed that bathing in the tidal waters was an essential right similar to that of navigation and served the general welfare by promoting health and the ability to swim. 5 B. & Ald. at 278-79 (Best, J., dissenting). Though respecting the interest of the private owner, Judge Best observed that the greatest part of the seashore had been barren and therefore had not become exclusive property. "It is useful only as a boundary and an approach to the sea; and therefore, ever has been, and ever should continue common to all who have occasion to resort to the sea." *Id.* at 283-84. Judge Best would have held on principles of public policy "that the interruption of free access to the sea is a public nuisance. . . . The principle of exclusive appropriation must not be carried beyond things capable of improvement by the industry of man. If it be extended so far as to touch the right of walking over these barren sands, it will take from the people what is essential to their welfare, whilst it will give to individuals only the hateful privilege of vexing their neighbours." *Id.* at 287.

The touchstone of Judge Best's reasoning is that the particular circumstances must be considered and examined before arriving at a solution that will accommodate the public's right and the private interests involved. Thus an undeveloped segment of the shore may have been available and used for access so as to establish a public right of way to the wet sand. Or there may be publicly-owned property, such as in *Avon*, which is suitable. Or, as in this case, the public streets and adjacent upland sand area might serve as a proper means of entry. The test is whether those means are reasonably satisfactory so that the public's right to use the beachfront can be satisfied.

The bather's right in the upland sands is not limited to passage. Reasonable enjoyment of the foreshore and the sea cannot be realized unless some enjoyment of the dry sand area is also allowed.[7] The complete pleasure of swimming must be accompanied by intermittent periods of rest and relaxation beyond the water's edge. . . . The unavailability of the physical situs for such rest and relaxation would seriously curtail and in many situations eliminate the right to the recreational use of the ocean. This was a principal reason why in *Avon* and *Deal* we held that municipally-owned dry sand beaches "must be open to all on equal terms. . . ." *Avon*, 61 N.J. at 308. We see no reason why rights under the public trust doctrine to use of the upland dry sand area should be limited to municipally-owned property. It is true that the private owner's interest in the upland dry sand area is not identical to that of a municipality. Nonetheless, where use of dry sand is essential or reasonably necessary for enjoyment of the ocean, the doctrine warrants the public's use of the upland dry sand area subject to an accommodation of the interests of the owner.

We perceive no need to attempt to apply notions of prescription, *City of Daytona Beach v. Tona-Rama, Inc.*, 294 So. 2d 73 (Fla. 1974), dedication, *Gion v. City of Santa Cruz*, 2 Cal. 3d 29 (1970), or custom, *State ex rel. Thornton v. Hay*, 254 Or. 584 (1969), as an alternative to application of the public trust doctrine. Archaic judicial responses are not an answer to a modern social problem. Rather, we perceive the public trust doctrine not to be "fixed or static," but one to "be molded and extended to meet changing conditions and needs of the public it was created to benefit." *Avon*, 61 N.J. at 309.

Precisely what privately-owned upland sand area will be available and required to satisfy the public's rights under the public trust doctrine will depend on the circumstances. Location of the dry sand area in relation to the foreshore, extent and availability of publicly-owned upland sand area, nature and extent of the public demand, and usage of the upland sand land by the owner are all factors to be weighed and considered in fixing the contours of the usage of the upper sand.

Today, recognizing the increasing demand for our State's beaches and the dynamic nature of the public trust doctrine, we find that the public must be given both access to and use of privately-owned dry sand areas as reasonably necessary. While the public's rights in private beaches are not co-extensive with the rights enjoyed in municipal beaches, private landowners may not in all instances prevent the public from exercising its rights under the public trust doctrine. The public

---

7. Some historical support for this proposition may be found in an analogous situation where fishermen, in exercising the right of public fishery in tidal waters, were permitted to draw nets on the beach above the ordinary high-water mark in the act of fishing. S. Moore & H. Moore, *The History and Law of Fisheries* 96 (1903).

must be afforded reasonable access to the foreshore as well as a suitable area for recreation on the dry sand.

V. The Beaches of Bay Head

The Bay Head Improvement Association, which services the needs of all residents of the Borough for swimming and bathing in the public trust property, owns the street-wide strip of dry sand area at the foot of seven public streets that extends to the mean high water line. It also owns the fee in six other upland sand properties connected or adjacent to the tracts it owns at the end of two streets. In addition, it holds leases to approximately 42 tracts of upland sand area. The question that we must address is whether the dry sand area that the Association owns or leases should be open to the public to satisfy the public's rights under the public trust doctrine. Our analysis turns upon whether the Association may restrict its membership to Bay Head residents and thereby preclude public use of the dry sand area.

. . . Ordinarily, a society or association may set its own membership qualifications and restrictions. However, that is not an inexorable rule. Where an organization is quasi-public, its power to exclude must be reasonably and lawfully exercised in furtherance of the public welfare related to its public characteristics. . . .

***

. . . When a nonprofit association rejects a membership application for reasons unrelated to its purposes and contrary to the general welfare, courts have "broad judicial authority to insure that exclusionary policies are lawful and are not applied arbitrarily or discriminately." *Greisman v. Newcomb Hospital*, 40 N.J. 389, 395 (1963). . . . That is the situation here.

Bay Head Improvement Association is a non-profit corporation whose primary purpose as stated in its certificate of incorporation is the "cleaning, policing and otherwise making attractive and safe the bathing beaches" in the Borough of Bay Head "and the doing of any act which may be found necessary or desirable for the greater convenience, comfort and enjoyment of the residents". . . .

***

. . . When viewed in its totality — its purposes, relationship with the municipality, communal characteristic, activities, and virtual monopoly over the Bay Head beachfront — the quasi-public nature of the Association is apparent. The Association makes available to the Bay Head public access to the common tidal property for swimming and bathing and to the upland dry sand area for use incidental thereto, preserving the residents' interests in a fashion similar to *Avon*.

There is no public beach in the Borough of Bay Head. If the residents of every municipality bordering the Jersey shore were to adopt the Bay Head policy, the public would be prevented from exercising its right to enjoy the foreshore. The Bay Head residents may not frustrate the public's right in this manner. By limiting membership only to residents and foreclosing the public, the Association is acting in conflict with the public good and contrary to the strong public policy "in favor of encouraging and expanding public access to and use of shoreline areas." *Gion v. City of Santa Cruz*, 2 Cal. 3d 29, 43 (1970). Indeed, the Association is frustrating the public's right under the public trust doctrine. It should not be permitted to do so.

Accordingly, membership in the Association must be open to the public at large. In this manner the public will be assured access to the common beach property during the hours of 10:00 A.M. to 5:30 P.M. between mid-June and September, where they may exercise their right to swim and bathe and to use the Association's dry sand area incidental to those activities. Although such membership rights to the use of the beach may be broader than the rights necessary for enjoyment of the public trust, opening the Association's membership to all, nonresidents and residents, should lead to a substantial satisfaction of the public trust doctrine. However, the Association shall also make available a reasonable quantity of daily as well as seasonal badges to the nonresident public. Its decision with respect to the number of daily and seasonal badges to be afforded to nonresidents should take into account all relevant matters, such as the public demand and the number of bathers and swimmers that may be safely and reasonably accommodated on the Association's property, whether owned or leased. The Association may continue to charge reasonable fees to cover its costs of lifeguards, beach cleaners, patrols, equipment, insurance, and administrative expenses. The fees fixed may not discriminate in any respect between residents and nonresidents. The Association may continue to enforce its regulations regarding cleanliness, safety, and other reasonable measures concerning the public use of the beach. In this connection, it would be entirely appropriate, in the formulation and adoption of such reasonable regulations concerning the public's use of the beaches, to encourage the participation and cooperation of all private beachfront property owners, regardless of their membership in or affiliation with the Association.

The Public Advocate has urged that all the privately-owned beachfront property likewise must be opened to the public. Nothing has been developed on this record to justify that conclusion. We have decided that the Association's membership and thereby its beach must be open to the public. That area might reasonably satisfy the public need at this time. We are aware that the Association possessed, as of the initiation of this litigation, about 42 upland sand lots under leases revocable on 30 days' notice. If any of these leases have been or are to be terminated, or if the Association were to sell all or part of its property, it may necessitate further adjudication of the public's claims in favor of the public trust on part or all of these or other privately-owned upland dry sand lands depending upon the circumstances. However, we see no necessity to have those issues resolved judicially at this time since the beach under the Association's control will be open to the public and may be adequate to satisfy the public trust interests. We believe that the Association and property owners will act in good faith and to the satisfaction of the Public Advocate. Indeed, we are of the opinion that all parties will benefit by our terminating this prolonged litigation at this time.

The record in this case makes it clear that a right of access to the beach is available over the quasi-public lands owned by the Association, as well as the right to use the Association's upland dry sand. It is not necessary for us to determine under what circumstances and to what extent there will be a need to use the dry sand of private owners who either now or in the future may have no leases with the Association. Resolution of the competing interests, private ownership and the public trust, may in some cases be simple, but in many it may be most complex. In any event, resolution would depend upon the specific facts in controversy.

None of the foregoing matters were fully argued or briefed, the disputes concerning rights in and to private beaches having been most general. All we decide here is that private land is not immune from a possible right of access to the foreshore for swimming or bathing purposes, nor is it immune from the possibility that some of the dry sand may be used by the public incidental to the right of bathing and swimming.

We realize that considerable uncertainty will continue to surround the question of the public's right to cross private land and to use a portion of the dry sand as discussed above. Where the parties are unable to agree as to the application of the principles enunciated herein, the claim of the private owner shall be honored until the contrary is established.

***

The judgment of the Appellate Division is reversed in part and affirmed in part.

In the *Matthews* decision, the Supreme Court of New Jersey stated that:

> The Court [in the earlier New Jersey *Avon* decision] was not relying on the legal theory of dedication, although dedication alone would have entitled the public to the full enjoyment of the dry sand. Instead the Court depended on the public trust doctrine, impliedly holding that full enjoyment of the foreshore necessitated some use of the upper sand, so that the latter came under the umbrella of the public trust....

In the following case, the Supreme Court of Oregon addresses the question of whether and how the public might acquire rights in private uplands through the doctrines of prescription or dedication. The Court concludes that each of these arguments might be viable, although it eventually rules in favor of the public on the alternate ground of "custom." In reading the decision, think about the various legal bases for expanding public trust rights landward: the public trust doctrine, prescription, custom, even moving the legal coastline landward. Which of these arguments is legally most robust? What are the policy considerations that lie behind each rationale? Does each theory ultimately produce a different result? If you were on a court considering a case brought by a plaintiff seeking upland access, and the facts supported any of the four approaches, which would you prefer and why?

State ex rel. Thornton v. Hay

462 P.2d 671 (Or. 1969)

Justice GOODWIN delivered the opinion of the Supreme Court of Oregon.

William and Georgianna Hay, the owners of a tourist facility at Cannon Beach, appeal from a decree which enjoins them from constructing fences or other improvements in the dry-sand area between the sixteen-foot elevation contour line and the ordinary hightide line of the Pacific Ocean.

The issue is whether the state has the power to prevent the defendant landowners from enclosing the dry-sand area contained within the legal description of their ocean-front property.

The state asserts two theories: (1) the landowners' record title to the disputed area is encumbered by a superior right in the public to go upon and enjoy the land for recreational purposes; and (2) if the disputed area is not encumbered by the asserted public easement, then the state has power to prevent construction under zoning regulations made pursuant to Oregon Revised Statutes (ORS) 390.640.

The defendant landowners concede that the State Highway Commission has standing to represent the rights of the public in this litigation . . . and that all tideland lying seaward of the ordinary, or mean high-tide line is a state recreation area. . . .

From the trial record, applicable statutes, and court decisions, certain terms and definitions have been extracted and will appear in this opinion. A short glossary follows:

ORS 390.720 refers to the "ordinary" high-tide line, while other sources refer to the "mean" high-tide line. For the purposes of this case the two lines will be considered to be the same. The mean high-tide line in Oregon is fixed by the 1947 Supplement to the 1929 United States Coast and Geodetic Survey data.

The land area in dispute will be called the dry-sand area. This will be assumed to be the land lying between the line of mean high tide and the visible line of vegetation.

The vegetation line is the seaward edge of vegetation where the upland supports vegetation. It falls generally in the vicinity of the sixteen-foot-elevation contour line, but is not at all points necessarily identical with that line. . . .

***

Below, or seaward of, the mean high-tide line, is the state-owned foreshore, or wet-sand area, in which the landowners in this case concede the public's paramount right, and concerning which there is no justiciable controversy.

The only issue in this case, as noted, is the power of the state to limit the record owner's use and enjoyment of the dry-sand area, by whatever boundaries the area may be described.

The trial court found that the public had acquired, over the years, an easement for recreational purposes to go upon and enjoy the dry-sand area, and that this easement was appurtenant to the wet-sand portion of the beach which is admittedly owned by the state and designated as a "state recreation area."

Because we hold that the trial court correctly found in favor of the state on the rights of the public in the dry-sand area, it follows that the state has an equitable right to protect the public in the enjoyment of those rights by causing the removal of fences and other obstacles.

It is not necessary, therefore, to consider whether ORS 390.640 would be constitutional if it were to be applied as a zoning regulation to lands upon which the public had not acquired an easement for recreational use.

In order to explain our reasons for affirming the trial court's decree, it is necessary to set out in some detail the historical facts which lead to our conclusion.

The dry-sand area in Oregon has been enjoyed by the general public as a recreational adjunct of the wet-sand or foreshore area since the beginning of the state's political history. The first European settlers on these shores found the aboriginal inhabitants using the foreshore for clam digging and the dry-sand area for their cooking fires. The newcomers continued these customs after statehood. Thus, from the time of the earliest settlement to the present day, the general public has assumed that the dry-sand area was a part of the public beach, and the public has used the dry-sand area for picnics, gathering wood, building warming fires, and generally as a headquarters from which to supervise children or to range out over the foreshore as the tides advance and recede. In the Cannon Beach vicinity, state and local officers have policed the dry sand, and municipal sanitary crews have attempted to keep the area reasonably free from man-made litter.

Perhaps one explanation for the evolution of the custom of the public to use the dry-sand area for recreational purposes is that the area could not be used conveniently by its owners for any other purpose. The dry-sand area is unstable in its seaward boundaries, unsafe during winter storms, and for the most part unfit for the construction of permanent structures. While the vegetation line remains relatively fixed, the western edge of the dry-sand area is subject to dramatic moves eastward or westward in response to erosion and accretion. For example, evidence in the trial below indicated that between April 1966 and August 1967 the seaward edge of the dry-sand area involved in this litigation moved westward 180 feet. At other points along the shore, the evidence showed, the seaward edge of the dry-sand area could move an equal distance to the east in a similar period of time.

Until very recently, no question concerning the right of the public to enjoy the dry-sand area appears to have been brought before the courts of this state. The public's assumption that the dry sand as well as the foreshore was "public property" had been reinforced by early judicial decisions. *See Shively v. Bowlby*, 152 U.S. 1 (1894), which affirmed *Bowlby v. Shively*, 22 Or. 410 (1892). These cases held that landowners claiming under federal patents owned seaward only to the "high-water" line, a line that was then assumed to be the vegetation line.

In 1935, the United States Supreme Court held that a federal patent conveyed title to land farther seaward, to the mean high-tide line. *Borax, Ltd. v. Los Angeles*, 296 U.S. 10 (1935). While this decision may have expanded seaward the record ownership of upland landowners, it was apparently little noticed by Oregonians. In any event, the *Borax* decision had no discernible effect on the actual practices of Oregon beachgoers and upland property owners.

Recently, however, the scarcity of ocean-front building sites has attracted substantial private investments in resort facilities. Resort owners like these defendants now desire to reserve for their paying guests the recreational advantages that accrue to the dry-sand portions of their deeded property. Consequently, in 1967, public debate and political activity resulted in legislative attempts to resolve conflicts between public and private interests in the dry-sand area:

ORS 390.610

(1) The Legislative Assembly hereby declares it is the public policy of the State of Oregon to forever preserve and maintain the sovereignty of the state heretofore existing over the seashore and ocean beaches of the state from the Columbia River on the North to the Oregon-California line on the South so that the public may have the free and uninterrupted use thereof.

(2) The Legislative Assembly recognizes that over the years the public has made frequent and uninterrupted use of lands abutting, adjacent and contiguous to the public highways and state recreation areas and recognizes, further, that where such use has been sufficient to create easements in the public through dedication, prescription, grant or otherwise, that it is in the public interest to protect and preserve such public easements as a permanent part of Oregon's recreational resources.

(3) Accordingly, the Legislative Assembly hereby declares that all public rights and easements in those lands described in subsection (2) of this section are confirmed and declared vested exclusively in the State of Oregon and shall be held and administered in the same manner as those lands described in ORS 390.720.

***

The state concedes that such legislation cannot divest a person of his rights in land, *Hughes v. Washington*, 389 U.S. 290 (1967), and that the defendants' record title, which includes the dry-sand area, extends seaward to the ordinary or mean high-tide line. . . .

The landowners likewise concede that since 1899 the public's rights in the foreshore have been confirmed by law as well as by custom and usage. Oregon Laws 1899, p. 3, provided:

> That the shore of the Pacific ocean, between ordinary high and extreme low tides, and from the Columbia river on the north to the south boundary line of Clatsop county on the south, is hereby declared a public highway, and shall forever remain open as such to the public.

The disputed area is *sui generis*. While the foreshore is "owned" by the state, and the upland is "owned" by the patentee or record-title holder, neither can be said to "own" the full bundle of rights normally connoted by the term "estate in fee simple." 1 Powell, Real Property § 163, at 661 (1949).

In addition to the *sui generis* nature of the land itself, a multitude of complex and sometimes overlapping precedents in the law confronted the trial court. Several early Oregon decisions generally support the trial court's decision, i.e., that the public can acquire easements in private land by long-continued use that is inconsistent with the owner's exclusive possession and enjoyment of his land. A citation of the cases could end the discussion at this point. But because the early cases do not agree on the legal theories by which the results are reached, and because this is an important case affecting valuable rights in land, it is appropriate to review some of the law applicable to this case.

One group of precedents relied upon in part by the state and by the trial court can be called the "implied-dedication" cases. The doctrine of implied dedication is well known to the law in this state and elsewhere. . . . Dedication, however, whether express or implied, rests upon an intent to dedicate.[4] In the case at bar, it is unlikely that the landowners thought they had anything to dedicate, until 1967, when the notoriety of legislative debates about the public's rights in the dry-sand area sent a number of ocean-front landowners to the offices of their legal advisers.

A second group of cases relied upon by the state, but rejected by the trial court, deals with the possibility of a landowner's losing the exclusive possession and enjoyment of his land through the development of prescriptive easements in the public.

In Oregon, as in most common-law jurisdictions, an easement can be created in favor of one person in the land of another by uninterrupted use and enjoyment of the land in a particular manner for the statutory period, so long as the user is open, adverse, under claim of right, but without authority of law or consent of the owner. . . . In Oregon, the prescriptive period is ten years. . . . The public use of the disputed land in the case at bar is admitted to be continuous for more than sixty years. There is no suggestion in the record that anyone's permission was sought or given; rather, the public used the land under a claim of right. Therefore, if the public can acquire an easement by prescription, the requirements for such an acquisition have been met in connection with the specific tract of land involved in this case.

The owners argue, however, that the general public, not being subject to actions in trespass and ejectment, cannot acquire rights by prescription, because the statute of limitations is irrelevant when an action does not lie.

While it may not be feasible for a landowner to sue the general public, it is nonetheless possible by means of signs and fences to prevent or minimize public invasions of private land for recreational purposes. In Oregon, moreover, the courts and the Legislative Assembly have both recognized that the public can acquire prescriptive easements in private land, at least for roads and highways. . . .

. . . [W]e conclude that the law in Oregon, regardless of the generalizations that may apply elsewhere,[5] does not preclude the creation of prescriptive easements in beach land for public recreational use.

Because many elements of prescription are present in this case, the state has relied upon the doctrine in support of the decree below. We believe, however, that there is a better legal basis for affirming the decree. The most cogent basis for the decision in this case is the English doctrine of custom. Strictly construed, prescription applies only to the specific tract of land before the court, and doubtful

4. Because of the elements of public interest and estoppel running through the cases, intent to dedicate is sometimes "presumed" instead of proven. But conceptually, at least, dedication is founded upon an intent to dedicate. . . .

5. *See, e.g., Sanchez v. Taylor,* 377 F.2d 733, 738 (10th Cir. 1967), holding that the general public cannot acquire grazing rights in unfenced land. Among other reasons assigned by authorities cited in *Sanchez v. Taylor* are these: prescription would violate the rule against perpetuities because no grantee could ever convey the land free of the easement; and prescription rests on the fiction of a "lost grant," which state of affairs cannot apply to the general public. The first argument can as well be made against the public's acquiring rights by express dedication; and the second argument applies equally to the fictional aspects of the doctrine of implied dedication. Both arguments are properly ignored in cases dealing with roads and highways, because the utility of roads and the public interest in keeping them open outweighs the policy favoring formal over informal transfers of interests in land.

prescription cases could fill the courts for years with tract-by-tract litigation. An established custom, on the other hand, can be proven with reference to a larger region. Ocean-front lands from the northern to the southern border of the state ought to be treated uniformly.

The other reason which commends the doctrine of custom over that of prescription as the principal basis for the decision in this case is the unique nature of the lands in question. This case deals solely with the dry-sand area along the Pacific shore, and this land has been used by the public as public recreational land according to an unbroken custom running back in time as long as the land has been inhabited.

A custom is defined in Bouvier's Law Dictionary as "such a usage as by common consent and uniform practice has become the law of the place, or of the subject matter to which it relates."

In 1 Blackstone, Commentaries 75-78, Sir William Blackstone set out the requisites of a particular custom.

Paraphrasing Blackstone, the first requirement of a custom, to be recognized as law, is that it must be ancient. It must have been used so long "that the memory of man runneth not to the contrary." Professor Cooley footnotes his edition of Blackstone with the comment that "long and general" usage is sufficient. In any event, the record in the case at bar satisfies the requirement of antiquity. So long as there has been an institutionalized system of land tenure in Oregon, the public has freely exercised the right to use the dry-sand area up and down the Oregon coast for the recreational purposes noted earlier in this opinion.

The second requirement is that the right be exercised without interruption. A customary right need not be exercised continuously, but it must be exercised without an interruption caused by anyone possessing a paramount right. In the case at bar, there was evidence that the public's use and enjoyment of the dry-sand area had never been interrupted by private landowners.

Blackstone's third requirement, that the customary use be peaceable and free from dispute, is satisfied by the evidence which related to the second requirement.

The fourth requirement, that of reasonableness, is satisfied by the evidence that the public has always made use of the land in a manner appropriate to the land and to the usages of the community. There is evidence in the record that when inappropriate uses have been detected, municipal police officers have intervened to preserve order.

The fifth requirement, certainty, is satisfied by the visible boundaries of the dry-sand area and by the character of the land, which limits the use thereof to recreational uses connected with the foreshore.

The sixth requirement is that a custom must be obligatory; that is, in the case at bar, not left to the option of each landowner whether or not he will recognize the public's right to go upon the dry-sand area for recreational purposes. The record shows that the dry-sand area in question has been used, as of right, uniformly with similarly situated lands elsewhere, and that the public's use has never been questioned by an upland owner so long as the public remained on the dry sand and refrained from trespassing upon the lands above the vegetation line.

Finally, a custom must not be repugnant, or inconsistent, with other customs or with other law. The custom under consideration violates no law, and is not repugnant.

Two arguments have been arrayed against the doctrine of custom as a basis for decision in Oregon. The first argument is that custom is unprecedented in this state, and has only scant adherence elsewhere in the United States. The second argument is that because of the relative brevity of our political history it is inappropriate to rely upon an English doctrine that requires greater antiquity than a newly-settled land can muster. Neither of these arguments is persuasive.

The custom of the people of Oregon to use the dry-sand area of the beaches for public recreational purposes meets every one of Blackstone's requisites. While it is not necessary to rely upon precedent from other states, we are not the first state to recognize custom as a source of law. *See Perley et ux'r v. Langley,* 7 N.H. 233 (1834).

***

... [I]n support of custom, the record shows that the custom of the inhabitants of Oregon and of visitors in the state to use the dry sand as a public recreation area is so notorious that notice of the custom on the part of persons buying land along the shore must be presumed. In the case at bar, the landowners conceded their actual knowledge of the public's longstanding use of the dry-sand area, and argued that the elements of consent present in the relationship between the landowners and the public precluded the application of the law of prescription. As noted, we are not resting this decision on prescription, and we leave open the effect upon prescription of the type of consent that may have been present in this case. Such elements of consent are, however, wholly consistent with the recognition of public rights derived from custom.

Because so much of our law is the product of legislation, we sometimes lose sight of the importance of custom as a source of law in our society. It seems particularly appropriate in the case at bar to look to an ancient and accepted custom in this state as the source of a rule of law. The rule in this case, based upon custom, is salutary in confirming a public right, and at the same time it takes from no man anything which he has had a legitimate reason to regard as exclusively his.

For the foregoing reasons, the decree of the trial court is affirmed.

points for discussion

1. *Access to access.* Although based on distinct legal theories, both *Matthews* and *Thornton* recognize that the public trust doctrine's promise of public access cannot be realized unless members of the public can physically reach public trust areas — the wet sand part of the beach. As we will see in Chapter 9, many states have instituted systematic plans for ensuring and increasing public access to trust areas, particularly beaches. States do this in a variety of ways, including the outright purchase of dry sand, the purchase of easements over dry sand, and requirements that beachfront landowners exchange easements for desired state permits.

2. *The chicken or the egg? Matthews*, like *Phillips*, highlights a fascinating and problematic feature of the common law. Because courts only address the specific issues that are before them, the law can remain murky for long periods of time. Lower courts may make decisions that never reach a state's highest court, or disputes bearing on the particular question may not arise. When a state's highest court does ultimately decide an issue — for example, whether the public trust doctrine guarantees the public some use of the dry sand beach — is the court making new law or revealing the law as it always has been? In *Matthews*, the court states that:

   > In order to exercise these rights guaranteed by the public trust doctrine, the public must have access to municipally-owned dry sand areas as well as the foreshore. The extension of the public trust doctrine to include municipally-owned dry sand areas was necessitated by our conclusion that enjoyment of rights in the foreshore is inseparable from use of dry sand beaches.

   Which language indicates that the court believes it is changing the doctrine? Unveiling it? Can you point to facts in the case that would support either of these conclusions? Why does it matter?

3. *States, cities, and nonprofit associations.* In *Avon*, the Supreme Court of New Jersey held that towns and cities could not limit access to dry sand beaches they owned to their own residents. The holding was based on the fact that all municipal power is a product of state delegation; municipalities must therefore act in a manner consistent with the best interest of all of a state's residents. The *Matthews* court makes a similar, but more tenuous, argument with respect to the owner of the dry sand in that case. Do you find it persuasive? For the next case in the line, see *Raleigh Ave. Beach Ass'n v. Atlantis Beach Club, Inc.*, 185 N.J. 40 (2005) (holding that the public has, under certain conditions, rights to access dry sand beaches owned by a for-profit corporation).

4. *The factors.* The *Matthews* court did not hold that the public has unlimited rights to access dry sand beaches owned by nonprofit associations. It also did not hold that the public has limited rights to every dry sand beach owned by a nonprofit association:

   > Location of the dry sand area in relation to the foreshore, extent and availability of publicly-owned upland sand area, nature and extent of the public demand, and usage of the upland sand land by the owner are all factors to be weighed and considered in fixing the contours of the usage of the upper sand.

   Why did the court adopt this approach rather than a blanket approach? How will this approach impact future behavior of both members of the public and beach owners?

5. *Custom versus prescription.* In *Thornton*, the Supreme Court of Oregon states that custom is "a better legal basis for affirming the [lower court's] decree" than prescription. Do you agree? Why do you think the court preferred custom to prescription?

6. *Widespread custom.* Applying Blackstone's seven elements of custom, would you conclude that the public is free to use all of the dry sand beaches in Oregon? In your state?

B. FEDERAL JURISDICTION . . .

So far, we have learned that state law defines "public waterways," and that public waterways both set the location of riparian and littoral property and (usually) establish the scope of the public trust doctrine. Although these are matters of state law, we have also learned that federal courts have played an important role in defining the bounds of state public trust doctrines. In addition, the federal government has its own, separate interests in coastal waterways and coastal uplands. This section describes these federal interests and the sources of the federal government's authority to constrain both state regulation and private use of waterways and uplands. In addition, the cases address the issue of federal agency authority under some important federal statutes written in less than crystal clear terms.

1. . . . And Navigable-in-Fact Waterways

The federal government is a government of enumerated powers. *McCulloch v. Maryland*, 17 U.S. 316 (1819). The power to restrict state or private activities affecting "navigable" waterways originates in the Commerce Clause. U.S. CONST. art. I, § 8. The Commerce Clause provides Congress with two flavors of authority. First, Congress can act as *regulator* of waterways that have a relationship to "Commerce with foreign Nations, and among the several States, and with the Indian Tribes." U.S. CONST. art. I, § 8. Second, Congress can act in order *to protect a form of property interest* it holds in those waterways: the federal "navigational servitude." These two federal roles are somewhat analogous to the states' roles in wielding the police power and implementing the public trust doctrine. (One difference is that, because of the enumerated powers doctrine, courts might be more stringent in interpreting the breadth of federal power.)

As the following case illustrates, the distinction between the federal government as regulator and the federal government as servitude holder mainly is important for one reason. A long line of Supreme Court cases establishes the principle that while the government qua regulator may have to pay when its rules or actions impact private property interests, the government qua holder of the servitude does not.

Kaiser Aetna v. United States

444 U.S. 164 (1979)

Justice REHNQUIST delivered the opinion of the United States Supreme Court.

The Hawaii Kai Marina was developed by the dredging and filling of Kuapa Pond, which was a shallow lagoon separated from Maunalua Bay and the Pacific Ocean by a barrier beach. Although under Hawaii law Kuapa Pond was private property, the Court of Appeals for the Ninth Circuit held that when petitioners converted the pond into a marina and thereby connected it to the bay, it became subject to the "navigational servitude" of the Federal Government. Thus, the public acquired a right of access to what was once petitioners' private pond. We granted

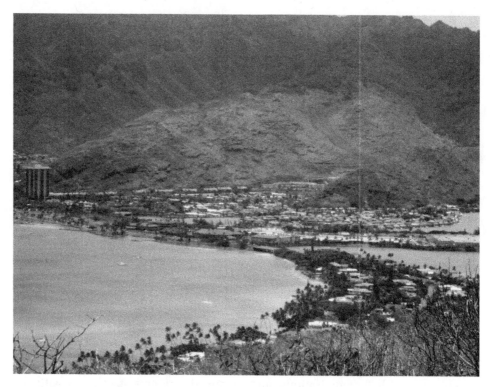

Photo: Cameron Freer

Figure 6-6. Hawai'i Kai Marina Today
The bridge mentioned in the opinion, below, separates the marina from the Pacific Ocean. Or does it?

certiorari because of the importance of the issue and a conflict concerning the scope and nature of the servitude. . . .

I.

Kuapa Pond was apparently created in the late Pleistocene Period, near the end of the ice age, when the rising sea level caused the shoreline to retreat, and partial erosion of the headlands adjacent to the bay formed sediment that accreted to form a barrier beach at the mouth of the pond, creating a lagoon. It covered 523 acres on the island of Oahu, Hawaii, and extended approximately two miles inland from Maunalua Bay and the Pacific Ocean. The pond was contiguous to the bay, which is a navigable waterway of the United States, but was separated from it by the barrier beach.

Early Hawaiians used the lagoon as a fishpond and reinforced the natural sandbar with stone walls. Prior to the annexation of Hawaii, there were two openings from the pond to Maunalua Bay. The fishpond's managers placed removable sluice gates in the stone walls across these openings. Water from the bay and ocean entered the pond through the gates during high tide, and during low tide the current flow reversed toward the ocean. The Hawaiians used the tidal action to raise and catch fish such as mullet.

Kuapa Pond, and other Hawaiian fishponds, have always been considered to be private property by landowners and by the Hawaiian government. Such ponds were once an integral part of the Hawaiian feudal system. And in 1848 they were allotted as parts of large land units, known as "ahupuaas," by King Kamehameha III during the Great Mahele or royal land division. Titles to the fishponds were recognized to the same extent and in the same manner as rights in more orthodox fast land. Kuapa Pond was part of an ahupuaa that eventually vested in Bernice Pauahi Bishop and on her death formed a part of the trust corpus of petitioner Bishop Estate, the present owner.

In 1961, Bishop Estate leased a 6,000-acre area, which included Kuapa Pond, to petitioner Kaiser Aetna for subdivision development. The development is now known as "Hawaii Kai." Kaiser Aetna dredged and filled parts of Kuapa Pond, erected retaining walls, and built bridges within the development to create the Hawaii Kai Marina. Kaiser Aetna increased the average depth of the channel from two to six feet. It also created accommodations for pleasure boats and eliminated the sluice gates.

When petitioners notified the Army Corps of Engineers of their plans in 1961, the Corps advised them they were not required to obtain permits for the development of and operations in Kuapa Pond. Kaiser Aetna subsequently informed the Corps that it planned to dredge an 8-foot-deep channel connecting Kuapa Pond to Maunalua Bay and the Pacific Ocean, and to increase the clearance of a bridge of the Kalanianaole Highway — which had been constructed during the early 1900's along the barrier beach separating Kuapa Pond from the bay and ocean — to a maximum of 13.5 feet over the mean sea level. These improvements were made in order to allow boats from the marina to enter into and return from the bay, as well as to provide better waters. The Corps acquiesced in the proposals, its chief of construction commenting only that the "deepening of the channel may cause erosion of the beach."

The Army Corps and Permitting

"The [Army Corps of Engineers] was created by Congress in 1802 to erect and maintain frontier forts and other defense facilities. Soon its activities expanded to coastal installations, and over the course of the nineteenth century the Corps' purposes expanded from fortification of defense facilities to making changes to rivers and harbors to promote navigation. Throughout this period, the draining and filling of wetlands for land 'reclamation' was national policy.

***

"[Toward the end of the nineteenth century, Congress enacted] the Rivers and Harbors Act of 1890, requiring the prior approval of the Secretary of War for all construction activities and other obstructions to navigation, and for depositing refuse into navigable waters."

Thomas Addison & Timothy Burns, *The Army Corps of Engineers and Nationwide Permit 26: Wetlands Protection or Swamp Reclamation?*, 18 ECOLOGY L.Q. 620, 623-24 (1991).

> ### The Army Corps and Permitting *(continued)*
>
> In 1972, Congress enacted the Clean Water Act. Section 404 of that Act requires Corps approval of discharges of dredged or fill materials into "navigable waters." As the Corps puts it:
>
> > Within its current regulatory program, the Corps of Engineers has authority over work on structures in navigable waterways under Section 10 of the Rivers and Harbors Act of 1899 and over the discharge of dredged or fill material under Section 404 of the [Clean Water Act]. This latter requirement applies to wetlands and other valuable aquatic areas throughout the United States. [The link to which the court cited no longer works. Instead, try: https://www.usace.army.mil/ About/History/Brief-History-of-the-Corps/Environmental-Activities/.—EDs.]
>
> There is little guidance in the Clean Water Act regarding the standards that the Corps must apply in deciding whether or not to grant a particular Section 404 permit. And, according to Professor William Rodgers, the language of the statute gives the Corps vast discretion and represents "an extreme example of open-ended 'balancing' under casual criteria." 2 WILLIAM H. RODGERS, JR., ENVIRONMENTAL LAW: AIR AND WATER § 4.12, at 182 (1986). The primary constraint on Corps' decision-making is the regulations that Congress authorized the Environmental Protection Agency to develop in Section 404(b)(1), known as "water quality regulations":
>
> > Section 230.10(a) [of the regulations] restricts the Corps's discretion by requiring that discharges *not* be permitted "if there is a practicable alternative . . . which would have less adverse impact on the aquatic ecosystem." Subsection (b) requires that permitted discharges not violate various other laws, including state water quality standards. Subsection (c) proscribes permitting of discharges "which will cause or contribute to significant degradation of the waters of the United States." Finally, subsection (d) precludes the granting of permits unless "appropriate and practicable steps have been taken which will minimize potential adverse impacts of the discharge on the aquatic ecosystem."
>
> Alyson C. Flournoy, *Supply, Demand, and Consequences: The Impact of Information Flow on Individual Permitting Decisions Under Section 404 of the Clean Water Act*, 83 IND. L.J. 537, 550 (2008).

At the time of trial, a marina-style community of approximately 22,000 persons surrounded Kuapa Pond. It included approximately 1,500 marina waterfront lot lessees. The waterfront lot lessees, along with at least 86 nonmarina lot lessees from Hawaii Kai and 56 boatowners who are not residents of Hawaii Kai, pay fees for maintenance of the pond and for patrol boats that remove floating debris, enforce boating regulations, and maintain the privacy and security of the pond. Kaiser Aetna controls access to and use of the marina. It has generally not permitted commercial use, except for a small vessel, the *Marina Queen*, which could carry 25 passengers and was used for about five years to promote sales of marina lots and for a brief period by marina shopping center merchants to attract people to their shopping facilities.

In 1972, a dispute arose between petitioners and the Corps concerning whether (1) petitioners were required to obtain authorization from the Corps, in accordance with § 10 of the Rivers and Harbors Appropriation Act of 1899, 33 U.S.C. § 403,[2] for future construction, excavation, or filling in the marina, and (2) petitioners were precluded from denying the public access to the pond because, as a result of the improvements, it had become a navigable water of the United States. The dispute foreseeably ripened into a lawsuit by the United States Government against petitioners in the United States District Court for the District of Hawaii. In examining the scope of Congress' regulatory authority under the Commerce Clause, the District Court held that the pond was "navigable water of the United States" and thus subject to regulation by the Corps under § 10 of the Rivers and Harbors Appropriation Act. . . . It further held, however, that the Government lacked the authority to open the now dredged pond to the public without payment of compensation to the owner. . . . In reaching this holding, the District Court reasoned that although the pond was navigable for the purpose of delimiting Congress' regulatory power, it was not navigable for the purpose of defining the scope of the federal "navigational servitude" imposed by the Commerce Clause. . . . Thus, the District Court denied the Corps' request for an injunction to require petitioners to allow public access and to notify the public of the fact of the pond's accessibility.

The Court of Appeals agreed with the District Court's conclusion that the pond fell within the scope of Congress' regulatory authority, but reversed the District Court's holding that the navigational servitude did not require petitioners to grant the public access to the pond. . . . The Court of Appeals reasoned that the "federal regulatory authority over navigable waters . . . and the right of public use cannot consistently be separated. It is the public right of navigational use that renders regulatory control necessary in the public interest" (citation omitted). The question before us is whether the Court of Appeals erred in holding that petitioners' improvements to Kuapa Pond caused its original character to be so altered that it became subject to an overriding federal navigational servitude, thus converting into a public aquatic park that which petitioners had invested millions of dollars in improving on the assumption that it was a privately owned pond leased to Kaiser Aetna.[3]

---

2. Title 33 U.S.C. § 403 provides:

The creation of any obstruction not affirmatively authorized by Congress, to the navigable capacity of any of the waters of the United States is prohibited; and it shall not be lawful to build or commence the building of any wharf, pier, dolphin, boom, weir, breakwater, bulkhead, jetty, or other structures in any port, roadstead, haven, harbor, canal, navigable river, or other water of the United States, outside established harbor lines, or where no harbor lines have been established, except on plans recommended by the Chief of Engineers and authorized by the Secretary of the Army; and it shall not be lawful to excavate or fill, or in any manner to alter or modify the course, location, condition, or capacity of, any port, roadstead, haven, harbor, canal, lake, harbor of refuge, or inclosure within the limits of any breakwater, or of the channel of any navigable water of the United States, unless the work has been recommended by the Chief of Engineers and authorized by the Secretary of the Army prior to beginning the same.

3. Petitioners do not challenge the Court of Appeals' holding that the Hawaii Kai Marina is within the scope of Congress' regulatory power and subject to regulation by the Army Corps of Engineers pursuant to its authority under § 10 of the Rivers and Harbors Appropriation Act, 33 U.S.C. § 403.

II.

The Government contends that petitioners may not exclude members of the public from the Hawaii Kai Marina because "[the] public enjoys a federally protected right of navigation over the navigable waters of the United States." Brief for United States 13. It claims the issue in dispute is whether Kuapa Pond is presently a "navigable water of the United States." *Ibid.* When petitioners dredged and improved Kuapa Pond, the Government continues, the pond — although it may once have qualified as fast land — became navigable water of the United States.[4] The public thereby acquired a right to use Kuapa Pond as a continuous highway for navigation, and the Corps of Engineers may consequently obtain an injunction to prevent petitioners from attempting to reserve the waterway to themselves.

The position advanced by the Government, and adopted by the Court of Appeals below, presumes that the concept of "navigable waters of the United States" has a fixed meaning that remains unchanged in whatever context it is being applied. While we do not fully agree with the reasoning of the District Court, we do agree with its conclusion that all of this Court's cases dealing with the authority of Congress to regulate navigation and the so-called "navigational servitude" cannot simply be lumped into one basket. . . . As the District Court aptly stated, "any reliance upon judicial precedent must be predicated upon careful appraisal of the *purpose* for which the concept of 'navigability' was invoked in a particular case."

It is true that Kuapa Pond may fit within definitions of "navigability" articulated in past decisions of this Court. But it must be recognized that the concept of navigability in these decisions was used for purposes other than to delimit the boundaries of the navigational servitude: for example, to define the scope of Congress' regulatory authority under the Interstate Commerce Clause . . . , to determine the extent of the authority of the Corps of Engineers under the Rivers and Harbors Appropriation Act of 1899,[6] and to establish the limits of the jurisdiction of federal courts conferred by Art. III, § 2, of the United States Constitution over admiralty

---

4. The Government further argues:

"The fact that the conversion was accomplished at private expense does not exempt Kuapa Pond from the navigable waters of the United States. To allow landowners to dredge their fast lands and reshape the navigable waters of the United States to more conveniently serve their land, and then to exclude the public from the navigable portions flowing over the site of former fast lands, would unduly burden navigation and commerce. The states lack the power under the Commerce Clause to sanction any such form of private property. . . ." Brief for United States 14-15.

6. *See, e.g., United States v. Republic Steel Corp.,* 362 U.S. 482 (1960) (deposit of industrial solids into river held to create an "obstruction" to the "navigable capacity" of the river forbidden by § 10 of the Rivers and Harbors Appropriation Act of 1899).

The Corps of Engineers has adopted the following general definition of "navigable waters":

Navigable waters of the United States are those waters that are subject to the ebb and flow of the tide and/or are presently used, or have been used in the past, or may be susceptible for use to transport interstate or foreign commerce. A determination of navigability, once made, applies laterally over the entire surface of the waterbody, and is not extinguished by later actions or events which impede or destroy navigable capacity. 33 CFR § 329.4 (1978).

and maritime cases.[7] Although the Government is clearly correct in maintaining that the now dredged Kuapa Pond falls within the definition of "navigable waters" as this Court has used that term in delimiting the boundaries of Congress' regulatory authority under the Commerce Clause . . . , this Court has never held that the navigational servitude creates a blanket exception to the Takings Clause whenever Congress exercises its Commerce Clause authority to promote navigation. Thus, while Kuapa Pond may be subject to regulation by the Corps of Engineers, acting under the authority delegated it by Congress in the Rivers and Harbors Appropriation Act, it does not follow that the pond is also subject to a public right of access.

A.

Reference to the navigability of a waterway adds little if anything to the breadth of Congress' regulatory power over interstate commerce. It has long been settled that Congress has extensive authority over this Nation's waters under the Commerce Clause. Early in our history this Court held that the power to regulate commerce necessarily includes power over navigation. . . . As stated in *Gilman v. Philadelphia*, 70 U.S. 713, 724-725 (1866):

> Commerce includes navigation. The power to regulate commerce comprehends the control for that purpose, and to the extent necessary, of all the navigable waters of the United States which are accessible from a State other than those in which they lie. For this purpose they are the public property of the nation, and subject to all the requisite legislation by Congress.

The pervasive nature of Congress' regulatory authority over national waters was more fully described in *United States v. Appalachian Power Co.*, 311 U.S. at 377, 426-427 (1940):

---

7. "Navigable water" subject to federal admiralty jurisdiction was defined as including waters that are navigable in fact in *The Propeller Genesee Chief v. Fitzhugh*, 12 How. 443 (1852). . . . And in *Ex parte Boyer*, 109 U.S. 629 (1884), this Court held that such jurisdiction extended to artificial bodies of water:

> Navigable water situated as this canal is, used for the purposes for which it is used, a highway for commerce between ports and places in different States, carried on by vessels such as those in question here, is public water of the United States, and within the legitimate scope of the admiralty jurisdiction conferred by the Constitution and statutes of the United States, even though the canal is wholly artificial, and is wholly within the body of a State, and subject to its ownership and control; and it makes no difference as to the jurisdiction of the district court that one or the other of the vessels was at the time of the collision on a voyage from one place in the State of Illinois to another place in that State. *Id.* at 632.

Congress, pursuant to its authority under the Necessary and Proper Clause of Art. I to enact laws carrying into execution the powers vested in other departments of the Federal Government, has also been recognized as having the power to legislate with regard to matters concerning admiralty and maritime cases. . . .

[It] cannot properly be said that the constitutional power of the United States over its waters is limited to control for navigation. . . . In truth the authority of the United States is the regulation of commerce on its waters. Navigability . . . is but a part of this whole. Flood protection, watershed development, recovery of the cost of improvements through utilization of power are likewise parts of commerce control. . . . [The] authority is as broad as the needs of commerce. . . . The point is that navigable waters are subject to national planning and control in the broad regulation of commerce granted the Federal Government.

Appalachian Power Co. indicates that congressional authority over the waters of this Nation does not depend on a stream's "navigability." And, as demonstrated by this Court's decisions . . . , a wide spectrum of economic activities "affect" interstate commerce and thus are susceptible of congressional regulation under the Commerce Clause irrespective of whether navigation, or, indeed, water, is involved. The cases that discuss Congress' paramount authority to regulate waters used in interstate commerce are consequently best understood when viewed in terms of more traditional Commerce Clause analysis than by reference to whether the stream in fact is capable of supporting navigation or may be characterized as "navigable water of the United States." With respect to the Hawaii Kai Marina, for example, there is no doubt that Congress may prescribe the rules of the road, define the conditions under which running lights shall be displayed, require the removal of obstructions to navigation, and exercise its authority for such other reason as may seem to it in the interest of furthering navigation or commerce.

[The Court explains that such regulations, if too onerous with respect to the rights of the Marina's owners, would constitute a taking of their property under the Fifth Amendment to the Constitution. In the case that a court found that such a taking had occurred, the government would have to pay the owners the value of the property taken by the regulation in question. The Court then goes on to explain why the government's exercise of rights it possesses as holder of the navigational servitude would not give rise to a viable takings claim.]

***

The navigational servitude is an expression of the notion that the determination whether a taking has occurred must take into consideration the important public interest in the flow of interstate waters that in their natural condition are in fact capable of supporting public navigation. . . .

***

. . . But this is . . . a case in which the owner of what was once a private pond, separated from concededly navigable water by a barrier beach and used for aquatic agriculture, has invested substantial amounts of money in making improvements. The Government contends that as a result of one of these improvements, the pond's connection to the navigable water in a manner approved by the Corps of Engineers, the owner has somehow lost one of the most essential sticks in the bundle of rights that are commonly characterized as property — the right to exclude others.

***

. . . The navigational servitude, which exists by virtue of the Commerce Clause in navigable streams, gives rise to an authority in the Government to assure that such streams retain their capacity to serve as continuous highways for the purpose of navigation in interstate commerce. . . .

***

More than one factor contributes [to a finding that the navigational servitude does not include the waters of Hawai'i Kai Marina]. It is clear that prior to its improvement, Kuapa Pond was incapable of being used as a continuous highway for the purpose of navigation in interstate commerce. Its maximum depth at high tide was a mere two feet, it was separated from the adjacent bay and ocean by a natural barrier beach, and its principal commercial value was limited to fishing.[10] It consequently is not the sort of "great navigable stream" that this Court has previously recognized as being "[incapable] of private ownership." *See, e.g., United States v. Chandler-Dunbar Co.,* 229 U.S. 53, 69 (1913). . . . And, as previously noted, Kuapa Pond has always been considered to be private property under Hawaiian law. . . .

***

Accordingly the judgment of the Court of Appeals is *Reversed.*

Mr. Justice BLACKMUN, with whom Mr. Justice BRENNAN and Mr. Justice MARSHALL join, dissenting.

The Court holds today that, absent compensation, the public may be denied a right of access to "navigable waters of the United States" that have been created or enhanced by private means. I find that conclusion neither supported in precedent nor wise in judicial policy, and I dissent.

***

I.

The first issue, in my view, is whether Kuapa Pond is "navigable water of the United States," and, if so, why. The Court begins by asking "whether . . . petitioners' improvements to Kuapa Pond caused its original character to be so altered that it became subject to an overriding federal navigational servitude." . . . It thus assumes that the only basis for extension of federal authority must have arisen *after* the pond was "developed" and transformed into a marina. This choice of starting point overlooks the Government's contention, advanced throughout this litigation,

---

10. While it was still a fishpond, a few flat-bottomed shallow draft boats were operated by the fishermen in their work. There is no evidence, however, that even these boats could acquire access to the adjacent bay and ocean from the pond.

Although Kuapa Pond clearly was not navigable in fact in its natural state, the dissent argues that the pond nevertheless was "navigable water of the United States" prior to its development because it was subject to the ebb and flow of the tide. . . . This Court has never held, however, that whenever a body of water satisfies this mechanical test, the Government may invoke the "navigational servitude" to avoid payment of just compensation irrespective of the private interests at stake.

that Kuapa Pond was navigable water in its natural state, long prior to petitioners' improvements, by virtue of its susceptibility to the ebb and flow of the tide.[1]

The Court concedes that precedent does not disclose a single criterion for identifying "navigable waters." I read our prior cases to establish three distinct tests: "navigability in fact," "navigable capacity," and "ebb and flow" of the tide. Navigability in fact has been used as a test for the scope of the dominant federal interest in navigation since *The Propeller Genesee Chief v. Fitzhugh*, 12 How. 443, 457 (1852), and *The Daniel Ball*, 10 Wall. 557, 563 (1871). The test of navigable capacity is of more recent origin; it hails from *United States v. Appalachian Power Co.*, 311 U.S. 377, 407-408 (1940), where it was used to support assertion of the federal navigational interest over a river nonnavigable in its natural state but capable of being rendered fit for navigation by "reasonable improvements." Ebb and flow is the oldest test of the three. It was inherited from England, where under common law it was used to define ownership of navigable waters by the Crown. In the early days of the Republic, it was regarded as the exclusive test of federal jurisdiction over the waterways of this country. *See The Thomas Jefferson*, 10 Wheat. 428, 429 (1825); *Waring* v. *Clarke*, 5 How. 441, 463-464 (1847).

Petitioners say that the ebb-and-flow test was abandoned in *The Propeller Genesee Chief* and *The Daniel Ball* in favor of navigability in fact. I do not agree with that interpretation. It is based upon language in those opinions suggesting that the test is "arbitrary," that it bears no relation to what is "suitable" for federal control, that it "has no application in this country," and indeed that it is not "any test at all." *See The Propeller Genesee Chief v. Fitzhugh*, 12 How., at 454; *The Daniel Ball*, 10 Wall., at 563. One may acknowledge the language without accepting petitioners' inference. *The Propeller Genesee Chief* and *The Daniel Ball* were concerned with *extending* federal power to accommodate the stark realities of fresh-water commerce. In the former the question was whether admiralty jurisdiction included the Great Lakes. In the latter the question was the scope of federal regulatory power over navigation on a river. In either case it is not surprising that the Court, contemplating the substantial interstate fresh-water commerce on our lakes and rivers, found a test developed in England, an island nation with no analogue to our rivers and lakes, unacceptable as a test for the extent of federal power over these inland waterways. *Cf. The Propeller Genesee Chief*, 12 How., at 454-457. But the inadequacy of the test for defining the interior reach of federal power over navigation does not mean that the test must be, or must have been, abandoned for determining the breadth of federal power on our coasts.

The ebb-and-flow test is neither arbitrary nor unsuitable when applied in a coastwise setting. The ebb and flow of the tide define the geographical, chemical, and environmental limits of the three oceans and the Gulf that wash our shores. Since those bodies of water in the main are navigable, they should be treated as navigable to the inner reach of their natural limits. Those natural limits encompass a water body such as Kuapa Pond, which is contiguous to Maunalua Bay, and which in its natural state must be regarded as an arm of the sea, subject to its tides and currents as much as the Bay itself.

---

1. The District Court found that "the Pacific tides ebbed and flowed over Kuapa Pond in its pre-marina state." 408 F. Supp. 42, 50 (D. Haw. 1976). The tide entered through two openings in the barrier beach; it also percolated through the barrier beach itself. *Id.*, at 46. Although "[large] areas of land at the inland end were completely exposed at low tide," the entire pond was inundated at high tide. *Ibid.*

I take it the Court must concede that, at least for regulatory purposes, the pond in its current condition is "navigable water" because it is now "navigable in fact." . . . I would add that the pond was "navigable water" prior to development of the present marina because it was subject to the ebb and flow of the tide. In view of the importance the Court attaches to the fact of private development, this alternative basis for navigability carries significant implications.

II.

A more serious parting of ways attends the question whether the navigational servitude extends to all "navigable waters of the United States," however the latter may be established. The Court holds that it does not, at least where navigability is in whole or in part the work of private hands. I disagree.

The Court notes that the tests of navigability I have set forth originated in cases involving questions of federal regulation rather than application of the navigational servitude. . . . It also notes that Congress has authority to regulate in aid of navigation far beyond the limitations of "navigability." . . . From these indisputable propositions the Court concludes that "navigable waters" for these other purposes need not be the same as the "navigable waters" to which the navigational servitude applies.

Preliminarily, it must be recognized that the issue is *not* whether the navigational servitude runs to every watercourse over which the Federal Government may exercise its regulatory power to promote navigation. Regulatory jurisdiction "in aid of" navigation extends beyond the navigational servitude, and indeed beyond navigable water itself. In *United States v. Rio Grande Dam & Irrig. Co.*, 174 U.S. 690, 707-710 (1899), for example, the Court confirmed the Federal Government's power to enjoin an irrigation project above the limits of navigable water on the Rio Grande River because that project threatened to destroy navigability below. But this is not such a case. Federal authority over Kuapa Pond does not stem solely from an effect on navigable water elsewhere, although this might be a sound alternative basis for regulatory jurisdiction. Instead, the authority arises because the pond itself is navigable water.

Nor does it advance analysis to suggest that we might decide to call certain waters "navigable" for some purposes, but "nonnavigable" for purposes of the navigational servitude. . . . To my knowledge, no case has ever so held. Although tests of navigability have originated in other contexts, prior cases have never attempted to limit any test of navigability to a single species of federal power. Indeed, often they have referred to "navigable" water as "public" water. *See, e.g., The Propeller Genesee Chief*, 12 How., at 455, 457; *The Daniel Ball*, 10 Wall., at 563. In any event, to say that Kuapa Pond is somehow "nonnavigable" for present purposes, and that it is not subject to the navigational servitude for this reason, is merely to substitute one conclusion for another. To sustain its holding today, I believe that the Court must prove the more difficult contention that the navigational servitude does not extend to waters that are clearly navigable and fully subject to use as a highway for interstate commerce.

The Court holds, in essence, that the extent of the servitude does not depend on whether a waterway is navigable under any of the tests, but on whether the navigable waterway is "natural" or privately developed. In view of the fact that Kuapa Pond originally was created by natural forces, and that its separation from the Bay has been maintained by the interaction of natural forces and human effort, neither characterization seems particularly apt in this case. One could accept the Court's approach, however, and still find that the servitude extends to Kuapa Pond, by virtue of its status prior to development under the ebb-and-flow test. Nevertheless, I think the Court's reasoning on this point is flawed. In my view, the power we describe by the term "navigational servitude" extends to the limits of interstate commerce by water; accordingly, I would hold that it is coextensive with the "navigable waters of the United States."

As the Court recognizes, . . . the navigational servitude symbolizes the dominant federal interest in navigation implanted in the Commerce Clause. *See Scranton v. Wheeler*, 179 U.S. 141, 159-163 (1900); *cf. Gibbons v. Ogden*, 9 Wheat. 1, 189-190 (1824). To preserve this interest, the National Government has been given the power not only to regulate interstate commerce by water, but also to control the waters themselves, and to maintain them as "common highways, . . . forever free." *See* the Act of Aug. 7, 1789, 1 Stat. 50, 52, n. (a) (navigable waters in Northwest Territory). . . . *See United States v. Chandler-Dunbar Co.*, 229 U.S. 53, 62-64 (1913); *Gilman v. Philadelphia*, 3 Wall. 713, 724-725 (1866). The National Government is guardian of a public right of access to navigable waters of the United States. The navigational servitude is the legal formula by which we recognize the paramount nature of this governmental responsibility.

The Court often has observed the breadth of federal power in this context. In *United States v. Twin City Power Co.*, 350 U.S. 222 (1956), for example, it stated:

> The interest of the United States in the flow of a navigable stream originates in the Commerce Clause. That Clause speaks in terms of power, not of property. But the power is a dominant one which can be asserted to the exclusion of any competing or conflicting one. The power is a privilege which we have called "a dominant servitude" or "a superior navigation easement." (Citations omitted.) *Id.*, at 224-225.

Perhaps with somewhat different emphasis, the Court also has stated, in cases involving navigable waters, that "the flow of the stream [is] in no sense private property," *United States v. Chandler-Dunbar Co.*, 229 U.S., at 66, and that the waters themselves "are the public property of the nation." *Gilman v. Philadelphia*, 3 Wall., at 725.

The Court in *Twin City Power Co.* recognized that what is at issue is a matter of power, not of property. The servitude, in order to safeguard the Federal Government's paramount control over waters used in interstate commerce, limits the power of the States to create conflicting interests based on local law. That control does not depend on the form of the water body or the manner in which it was created, but on the fact of navigability and the corresponding commercial significance the waterway attains. Wherever that commerce can occur, be it Kuapa Pond or Honolulu Harbor, the navigational servitude must extend.

* * *

IV.

I come, finally, to the question whether Kuapa Pond's status under state law ought to alter this conclusion drawn from federal law. The Court assumes, without much discussion, that Kuapa Pond is the equivalent of "fast land" for purposes of Hawaii property law. There is, to be sure, support for this assumption, and for present purposes I am prepared to follow the Court in making it. *See, e.g., In re Application of Kamakana*, 58 Haw. 632 (1978). Nonetheless, I think it clear that local law concerns rights of title and use between citizen and citizen, or between citizen and state, but does not affect the scope or effect of the federal navigational servitude.

The rights in Kuapa fisheries that have been part of Hawaii law since the Great Mahele are not unlike the right to the use of the floor of a bay that was at issue in *Lewis Blue Point Oyster [Cultivation] Co. v. Briggs*, 229 U.S. 82 (1913). There the Court found no entitlement to compensation for destruction of an oysterbed in the course of dredging a channel. The Court reasoned: "If the public right of navigation is the dominant right and if, as must be the case, the title of the owner of the bed of navigable waters holds subject absolutely to the public right of navigation, this dominant right must include the right to use the bed of the water for every purpose which is in aid of navigation." *Id.*, at 87. By similar logic, I do not think Hawaii or any other State is at liberty through local law to defeat the navigational servitude by transforming navigable water into "fast land." Instead, state-created interests in the waters or beds of such navigable water are secondary to the navigational servitude. Thus, I believe this case should be decided purely as a matter of federal law, in which state law cannot control the scope of federal prerogatives.

For all of the foregoing reasons, the judgment of the Court of Appeals was correct. I therefore dissent.

points for discussion

1. *The navigational servitude: A property interest?* One way to characterize the federal navigational servitude is as a form of public property. Under this view, it is, as the word "servitude" would suggest, a type of easement that both mirrors and trumps state public trust doctrines. How was this easement created? When, pursuant to the public trust and equal footing doctrines, the federal government granted title to submerged lands to the states, it retained — for all the country's citizens and by virtue of the Commerce Clause — the right to use navigable waterways. (A note of caution: In determining which waterways are subject to this easement, the word "navigable" is a matter of federal, not state, law.) In the case of *Silver Springs Paradise Co. v. Ray*, 50 F.2d 356 (5th Cir. 1931), Ray claimed that he had the exclusive right to navigate glass-bottomed boats loaded with tourists through the crystal-clear waters that pooled above Silver Springs. Ray's claim of exclusivity was based on the fact that he owned the submerged lands beneath the pool as well as all of the surrounding uplands. Ray's competitor-in-enterprise, Silver Springs Paradise Company, owned some land three-quarters of a mile away, on the shores of the river that flowed out of the pool. The Paradise Company would load tourists onto its glass-bottomed boats at this site, and then transport them upstream to the springs. The court applied federal law to this dispute (instead of Florida's public trust doctrine), owing to the fact that Ray's predecessor-in-interest had purchased the property from the federal government at a time when Florida was still a territory.

Photo: Library of Congress

Figure 6-7. Glass-Bottomed Boats at Silver Springs, Florida, 1951

In holding that Ray had no exclusive right, regardless of whether or not he owned the submerged land, the court said:

> The public right of navigation entitles the public generally to the reasonable use of navigable waters for all legitimate purposes of travel or transportation, for boating or sailing for pleasure, as well as for carrying persons of property gratuitously or for hire, and in any kind of water craft the use of which is consistent with others also enjoying the right possessed in common.

50 F.2d at 359. In addition to providing a public right of navigation, the servitude allows the federal government, as easement holder, to maintain or improve the navigability of waterways without compensating private citizens or states for damage that results from these actions. In *Lewis Blue Point Oyster Cultivation Co. v. Briggs*, 229 U.S. 82 (1913), cited by Justice Blackmun, the plaintiff had leased submerged lands from the State of New York for the purpose of planting and harvesting oysters. In order to improve navigability, the federal government hired a contractor to dredge the channel in which the plaintiff's oyster beds were located. Despite the fact that the dredging caused substantial damage to both the beds and plaintiff's business, the Supreme Court held that plaintiff was not entitled to any compensation. As the Court stated in a later case:

> The dominant power of the federal Government, as has been repeatedly held, extends to the entire bed of a stream, which includes the land below the ordinary high-water mark. The exercise of the power within these limits is not an invasion of any private property rights in such lands for which the United States must make compensation. The damage sustained results not from a taking of the riparian owner's property in the stream bed, but from the lawful exercise of a power to which that property has always been subject.

United States v. Chicago, 312 U.S. 592, 596-97 (1941), *modified*, 313 U.S. 543 (1941). Why exactly did the Court hold in *Kaiser Aetna* that the pond was not subject to the navigational servitude?

2. *The relationship between state public trust doctrines and the navigational servitude.* As described in point 1, the navigational servitude "mirrors and trumps" state public trust doctrines. What does this mean? Essentially, while both the servitude and the doctrines ensure public access to public waterways, they differ in two ways: first, the servitude traditionally protects only the public use of navigation, while the public trust doctrine (even its most traditional form) protects other uses, such as fishing. (For an argument that the servitude should be expanded to cover other uses, see Benjamin Longstreth, *Protecting "The Wastes of the Foreshore": The Federal Navigation Servitude and Its Origins in State Public Trust Doctrine*, 102 COLUM. L. REV. 471 (2002).) Second, at least according to the majority in *Kaiser Aetna*, the definition of public waterways is narrower in the context of the servitude, and generally speaking is "navigable-in-fact." The servitude "trumps" because the Commerce Clause allows the federal government to preempt state law. Courts do not always clearly distinguish between the servitude and public trust doctrines. For example, look at the references to *The Genesee Chief* in the pages of *Illinois Central* and *Phillips* that you read earlier. Did the Court invoke that case as analogy or precedent? Do you see why citing it in a public trust doctrine context might cause confusion?

3. *Commerce Clause authority.* The Commerce Clause provides Congress with the authority "[t]o regulate Commerce with foreign Nations, and among the several States, and with the Indian Tribes." U.S. CONST. art. I, § 8. In the view of the *Kaiser Aetna* majority, the navigational servitude is rooted in the Commerce Clause, but does not represent the entirety of Congress's Commerce Clause authority. So, for example, the Court notes that

> With respect to the Hawaii Kai Marina, for example, there is no doubt that Congress may prescribe the rules of the road, define the conditions under which running lights shall be displayed, require the removal of obstructions to navigation, and exercise its authority for such other reason as may seem to it in the interest of furthering navigation or commerce.

444 U.S. at 174. What interstate-commerce-related interest does the federal government have in prescribing "the rules of the road" for a private marina? How is an obstruction to navigation within a private waterway of any concern to the federal government? Operating a vessel without running lights?

2. . . . And Non-Navigable-in-Fact Waterways

The power to regulate the use of uplands comes primarily from the Commerce Clause, although other sources of legislative authority such as the Property Clause and the treaty power can also be used in the appropriate context. The Property Clause, U.S. CONST. art. IV, § 3, provides that "[t]he Congress shall have power to dispose of and make all needful Rules and Regulations respecting the Territory or other Property belonging to the United States. . . ." The treaty power is an implied power that derives from the President's ability, under art. II, § 2, to enter into treaties with foreign nations. The Supreme Court has concluded that, in order for the President's power to have meaning, Congress must have the authority to write laws necessary to fulfill the United States' treaty obligations. *Missouri v. Holland*, 252 U.S. 416 (1920).

The treaty power would come into play in the coastal arena where a treaty obliged the United States to protect coastal lands, waters, or wildlife. So, for example, Congress originally wrote the Migratory Bird Act to meet bird conservation duties arising from a treaty with Great Britain. The Property Clause could form the basis for coastal legislation that regulated the use of federal coastal lands, for example, a National Park, or state or private lands adjacent to federal lands. *See, e.g., Minnesota v. Block*, 660 F.2d 1240 (8th Cir. 1982).

The Commerce Clause is the most frequently used authority for federal laws that are particularly relevant to coastal uplands, namely environmental laws such as the Clean Water Act and the Endangered Species Act. In 2001, the Supreme Court decided a controversial and important case involving "isolated wetlands," features that are often found in coastal areas. "Isolated wetlands" is a term of art. As you will learn, the central question is: How isolated are they?

Solid Waste Agency of Northern Cook County v. United States Army Corps of Engineers

531 U.S. 159 (2001)

Chief Justice REHNQUIST delivered the opinion of the United States Supreme Court.

Section 404(a) of the Clean Water Act (CWA or Act), . . . 33 U.S.C. § 1344(a), regulates the discharge of dredged or fill material into "navigable waters." The United States Army Corps of Engineers (Corps), has interpreted § 404(a) to confer federal authority over an abandoned sand and gravel pit in northern Illinois which provides habitat for migratory birds. We are asked to decide whether the provisions of § 404(a) may be fairly extended to these waters, and, if so, whether Congress could exercise such authority consistent with the Commerce Clause, U.S. Const., Art. I, § 8, cl. 3. We answer the first question in the negative and therefore do not reach the second.

Petitioner, the Solid Waste Agency of Northern Cook County (SWANCC), is a consortium of 23 suburban Chicago cities and villages that united in an effort to locate and develop a disposal site for baled nonhazardous solid waste. The Chicago Gravel Company informed the municipalities of the availability of a 533-acre parcel, bestriding the Illinois counties Cook and Kane, which had been the site of a sand and gravel pit mining operation for three decades up until about 1960. Long since abandoned, the old mining site eventually gave way to a successional stage forest, with its remnant excavation trenches evolving into a scattering of permanent and seasonal ponds of varying size (from under one-tenth of an acre to several acres) and depth (from several inches to several feet).

The municipalities decided to purchase the site for disposal of their baled non-hazardous solid waste. By law, SWANCC was required to file for various permits from Cook County and the State of Illinois before it could begin operation of its balefill project. In addition, because the operation called for the filling of some of the permanent and seasonal ponds, SWANCC contacted federal respondents (hereinafter respondents), including the Corps, to determine if a federal landfill permit was required under § 404(a) of the CWA, 33 U.S.C. § 1344(a).

Section 404(a) grants the Corps authority to issue permits "for the discharge of dredged or fill material into the navigable waters at specified disposal sites." *Ibid.* The term "navigable waters" is defined under the Act as "the waters of the United States, including the territorial seas." § 1362(7). The Corps has issued regulations defining the term "waters of the United States" to include

> waters such as intrastate lakes, rivers, streams (including intermittent streams), mudflats, sandflats, wetlands, sloughs, prairie potholes, wet meadows, playa lakes, or natural ponds, the use, degradation or destruction of which could affect interstate or foreign commerce. . . . 33 CFR § 328.3(a)(3) (1999).

In 1986, in an attempt to "clarify" the reach of its jurisdiction, the Corps stated that § 404(a) extends to intrastate waters:

a. Which are or would be used as habitat by birds protected by Migratory Bird Treaties; or
b. Which are or would be used as habitat by other migratory birds which cross state lines; or
c. Which are or would be used as habitat for endangered species; or
d. Used to irrigate crops sold in interstate commerce.

51 Fed. Reg. 41217.

This last promulgation has been dubbed the "Migratory Bird Rule."

The Corps initially concluded that it had no jurisdiction over the site because it contained no "wetlands," or areas which support "vegetation typically adapted for life in saturated soil conditions," 33 CFR § 328.3(b) (1999). However, after the Illinois Nature Preserves Commission informed the Corps that a number of migratory bird species had been observed at the site, the Corps reconsidered and ultimately asserted jurisdiction over the balefill site pursuant to subpart (b) of the "Migratory Bird Rule." The Corps found that approximately 121 bird species had been observed at the site, including several known to depend upon aquatic environments for a significant portion of their life requirements. Thus, on November 16, 1987, the Corps formally "determined that the seasonally ponded, abandoned gravel mining depressions located on the project site, while not wetlands, did qualify as 'waters of the United States' . . . based upon the following criteria: (1) the proposed site had been abandoned as a gravel mining operation; (2) the water areas and spoil piles had developed a natural character; and (3) the water areas are used as habitat by migratory bird [sic] which cross state lines." U.S. Army Corps of Engineers, Chicago District, Dept. of Army Permit Evaluation and Decision Document. . . .

★★★

. . . [T]he Corps refused to issue a § 404(a) permit. The Corps found that SWANCC had not established that its proposal was the "least environmentally damaging, most practicable alternative" for disposal of nonhazardous solid waste; that SWANCC's failure to set aside sufficient funds to remediate leaks posed an "unacceptable risk to the public's drinking water supply"; and that the impact of the project upon area-sensitive species was "unmitigatable since a landfill surface cannot be redeveloped into a forested habitat." *Id.* at 87.

Petitioner filed suit . . . challenging both the Corps' jurisdiction over the site and the merits of its denial of the § 404(a) permit. The District Court granted summary judgment to respondents on the jurisdictional issue, and petitioner abandoned its challenge to the Corps' permit decision. On appeal to the Court of Appeals for the Seventh

> **Migratory Birds and Wetlands**
>
> Wetlands are literally "life requirements" for many species of migratory birds. Among the species that visited the balefill site at issue in the case, the arctic tern annually undertakes one of the most physically demanding migrations of any species on earth. These birds, no more than 12 inches from beak to tail, spend the Northern Hemisphere summer breeding in the Arctic, then travel to Antarctica to escape the North American winter. Throughout the course of this 25,000-mile round-trip journey, the arctic tern lives at the margin of survival, stopping only to feed. Migratory birds lose significant percentages of their body weight between stops, and can eat an amount equal to 20 percent of their body weight in 24 hours. Due to their high productivity, wetlands are among the most important types of stopover areas for refuelings.

Circuit, petitioner renewed its attack on respondents' use of the "Migratory Bird Rule" to assert jurisdiction over the site. Petitioner argued that respondents had exceeded their statutory authority in interpreting the CWA to cover nonnavigable, isolated, intrastate waters based upon the presence of migratory birds and, in the alternative, that Congress lacked the power under the Commerce Clause to grant such regulatory jurisdiction.

The Court of Appeals began its analysis with the constitutional question, holding that Congress has the authority to regulate such waters based upon "the cumulative impact doctrine, under which a single activity that itself has no discernible effect on interstate commerce may still be regulated if the aggregate effect of that class of activity has a substantial impact on interstate commerce." 191 F.3d 845, 850 (7th Cir. 1999). The aggregate effect of the "destruction of the natural habitat of migratory birds" on interstate commerce, the court held, was substantial because each year millions of Americans cross state lines and spend over a billion dollars to hunt and observe migratory birds. . . .[2] The Court of Appeals then turned to the

2. Relying upon its earlier decision in *Hoffman Homes, Inc. v. EPA*, 999 F.2d 256 (7th Cir. 1993), and a report from the United States Census Bureau, the Court of Appeals found that in 1996 approximately 3.1 million Americans spent $ 1.3 billion to hunt migratory birds (with 11 percent crossing state lines to do so) as another 17.7 million Americans observed migratory birds (with 9.5 million traveling for the purpose of observing shorebirds). See 191 F.3d at 850.

regulatory question. The court held that the CWA reaches as many waters as the Commerce Clause allows and, given its earlier Commerce Clause ruling, it therefore followed that respondents' "Migratory Bird Rule" was a reasonable interpretation of the Act. . . .

We granted certiorari, 529 U.S. 1129 (2000), and now reverse.

Congress passed the CWA for the stated purpose of "restoring and maintaining the chemical, physical, and biological integrity of the Nation's waters." 33 U.S.C. § 1251(a). In so doing, Congress chose to "recognize, preserve, and protect the primary responsibilities and rights of States to prevent, reduce, and eliminate pollution, to plan the development and use (including restoration, preservation, and enhancement) of land and water resources, and to consult with the Administrator in the exercise of his authority under this chapter." § 1251(b). Relevant here, § 404(a) authorizes respondents to regulate the discharge of fill material into "navigable waters," 33 U.S.C. § 1344(a), which the statute defines as "the waters of the United States, including the territorial seas," § 1362(7). Respondents have interpreted these words to cover the abandoned gravel pit at issue here because it is used as habitat for migratory birds. We conclude that the "Migratory Bird Rule" is not fairly supported by the CWA.

This is not the first time we have been called upon to evaluate the meaning of § 404(a). In *United States v. Riverside Bayview Homes, Inc.*, 474 U.S. 121 (1985), we held that the Corps had § 404(a) jurisdiction over wetlands that actually abutted on a navigable waterway. In so doing, we noted that the term "navigable" is of "limited import" and that Congress evidenced its intent to "regulate at least some waters that would not be deemed 'navigable' under the classical understanding of that term." *Id.* at 133. But our holding was based in large measure upon Congress' unequivocal acquiescence to, and approval of, the Corps' regulations interpreting the CWA to cover wetlands adjacent to navigable waters. . . . We found that Congress' concern for the protection of water quality and aquatic ecosystems indicated its intent to regulate wetlands "inseparably bound up with the 'waters' of the United States." 474 U.S. at 134.

It was the significant nexus between the wetlands and "navigable waters" that informed our reading of the CWA in *Riverside Bayview Homes.* Indeed, we did not "express any opinion" on the "question of the authority of the Corps to regulate discharges of fill material into wetlands that are not adjacent to bodies of open water. . . ." 474 U.S. at 131-132, n.8. In order to rule for respondents here, we would have to hold that the jurisdiction of the Corps extends to ponds that are *not* adjacent to open water. But we conclude that the text of the statute will not allow this.

Indeed, the Corps' *original* interpretation of the CWA, promulgated two years after its enactment, is inconsistent with that which it espouses here. Its 1974 regulations defined § 404(a)'s "navigable waters" to mean "those waters of the United States which are subject to the ebb and flow of the tide, and/or are presently, or have been in the past, or may be in the future susceptible for use for purposes of interstate or foreign commerce." 33 CFR § 209.120(d)(1). The Corps emphasized that "it is the water body's capability of use by the public for purposes of transportation or commerce which is the determinative factor." § 209.260(e)(1). Respondents put forward no persuasive evidence that the Corps mistook Congress' intent in 1974.

Respondents next contend that whatever its original aim in 1972, Congress charted a new course five years later when it approved the more expansive definition of "navigable waters" found in the Corps' 1977 regulations. In July 1977, the

Corps formally adopted 33 CFR § 323.2(a)(5) (1978), which defined "waters of the United States" to include "isolated wetlands and lakes, intermittent streams, prairie potholes, and other waters that are not part of a tributary system to interstate waters or to navigable waters of the United States, the degradation or destruction of which could affect interstate commerce." Respondents argue that Congress was aware of this more expansive interpretation during its 1977 amendments to the CWA. Specifically, respondents point to a failed House bill, H. R. 3199, that would have defined "navigable waters" as "all waters which are presently used, or are susceptible to use in their natural condition or by reasonable improvement as a means to transport interstate or foreign commerce." 123 Cong. Rec. 10420, 10434 (1977).[4] They also point to the passage in § 404(g)(1) that authorizes a State to apply to the Environmental Protection Agency for permission "to administer its own individual and general permit program for the discharge of dredged or fill material into the navigable waters (other than those waters which are presently used, or are susceptible to use in their natural condition or by reasonable improvement as a means to transport interstate or foreign commerce . . . including wetlands adjacent thereto) within its jurisdiction. . . ." 33 U.S.C. § 1344(g)(1). The failure to pass legislation that would have overturned the Corps' 1977 regulations and the extension of jurisdiction in § 404(g) to waters "other than" traditional "navigable waters," respondents submit, indicate that Congress recognized and accepted a broad definition of "navigable waters" that includes nonnavigable, isolated, intrastate waters.

Although we have recognized congressional acquiescence to administrative interpretations of a statute in some situations, we have done so with extreme care. "Failed legislative proposals are 'a particularly dangerous ground on which to rest an interpretation of a prior statute.'" *Central Bank of Denver, N. A. v. First Interstate Bank of Denver, N. A.*, 511 U.S. 164 (1994) (quoting *Pension Benefit Guaranty Corporation v. LTV Corp.*, 496 U.S. 633 (1990)). A bill can be proposed for any number of reasons, and it can be rejected for just as many others. The relationship between the actions and inactions of the 95th Congress and the intent of the 92d Congress in passing § 404(a) is also considerably attenuated. Because "subsequent history is less illuminating than the contemporaneous evidence," *Hagen v. Utah*, 510 U.S. 399, 420 (1994), respondents face a difficult task in overcoming the plain text and import of § 404(a).

We conclude that respondents have failed to make the necessary showing that the failure of the 1977 House bill demonstrates Congress' acquiescence to the Corps' regulations or the "Migratory Bird Rule," which, of course, did not first appear until 1986. Although respondents cite some legislative history showing Congress' recognition of the Corps' assertion of jurisdiction over "isolated waters," as we explained in *Riverside Bayview Homes*, "in both Chambers, debate on the proposals to narrow the definition of navigable waters centered largely on the issue of wetlands preservation." 474 U.S. at 136. Beyond Congress' desire to regulate wetlands adjacent to "navigable waters,"

---

4. While this bill passed in the House, a similarly worded amendment to a bill originating in the Senate, S. 1952, failed. See 123 Cong. Rec. 26710, 26728 (1977).

respondents point us to no persuasive evidence that the House bill was proposed in response to the Corps' claim of jurisdiction over nonnavigable, isolated, intrastate waters or that its failure indicated congressional acquiescence to such jurisdiction.

***

We thus decline respondents' invitation to take what they see as the next ineluctable step after *Riverside Bayview Homes*: holding that isolated ponds, some only seasonal, wholly located within two Illinois counties, fall under § 404(a)'s definition of "navigable waters" because they serve as habitat for migratory birds. As counsel for respondents conceded at oral argument, such a ruling would assume that "the use of the word navigable in the statute . . . does not have any independent significance." Tr. of Oral Arg. 28. We cannot agree that Congress' separate definitional use of the phrase "waters of the United States" constitutes a basis for reading the term "navigable waters" out of the statute. We said in *Riverside Bayview Homes* that the word "navigable" in the statute was of "limited effect" and went on to hold that § 404(a) extended to nonnavigable wetlands adjacent to open waters. But it is one thing to give a word limited effect and quite another to give it no effect whatever. The term "navigable" has at least the import of showing us what Congress had in mind as its authority for enacting the CWA: its traditional jurisdiction over waters that were or had been navigable in fact or which could reasonably be so made. . . .

Respondents — relying upon all of the arguments addressed above — contend that, at the very least, it must be said that Congress did not address the precise question of § 404(a)'s scope with regard to nonnavigable, isolated, intrastate waters, and that, therefore, we should give deference to the "Migratory Bird Rule." *See, e.g., Chevron U.S.A. Inc. v. Natural Resources Defense Council, Inc.*, 467 U.S. 837 (1984). We find § 404(a) to be clear, but even were we to agree with respondents, we would not extend *Chevron* deference here.

Where an administrative interpretation of a statute invokes the outer limits of Congress' power, we expect a clear indication that Congress intended that result. This requirement stems from our prudential desire not to needlessly reach constitutional issues and our assumption that Congress does not casually authorize administrative agencies to interpret a statute to push the limit of congressional authority. . . . This concern is heightened where the administrative interpretation alters the federal-state framework by permitting federal encroachment upon a traditional state power. . . . Thus, "where an otherwise acceptable construction of a statute would raise serious constitutional problems, the Court will construe the statute to avoid such problems unless such construction is plainly contrary to the intent of Congress" (citation omitted).

Twice in the past six years we have reaffirmed the proposition that the grant of authority to Congress under the Commerce Clause, though broad, is not unlimited. *See United States v. Morrison*, 529 U.S. 598 (2000); *United States v. Lopez*, 514 U.S. 549 (1995). Respondents argue that the "Migratory Bird Rule" falls within Congress' power to regulate intrastate activities that "substantially affect" interstate commerce. They note that the protection of migratory birds is a "national interest of very nearly the first magnitude," *Missouri v. Holland*, 252 U.S. 416 (1920), and that, as the Court of Appeals found, millions of people spend over a billion dollars annually on recreational pursuits relating to migratory birds. These arguments raise significant constitutional questions. For example, we would have to evaluate the precise object or activity that, in the aggregate, substantially affects interstate commerce. This is not clear, for although the Corps has claimed jurisdiction over petitioner's land because it contains water areas used as habitat by migratory birds, respondents now, *post litem motam*, focus upon the fact that the regulated activity is petitioner's municipal landfill, which is "plainly of a commercial nature." Brief for Federal Respondents 43. But this is a far cry, indeed, from the "navigable waters" and "waters of the United States" to which the statute by its terms extends.

These are significant constitutional questions raised by respondents' application of their regulations, and yet we find nothing approaching a clear statement from Congress that it intended § 404(a) to reach an abandoned sand and gravel pit such as we have here. Permitting respondents to claim federal jurisdiction over ponds and mudflats falling within the "Migratory Bird Rule" would result in a significant impingement of the States' traditional and primary power over land and water use. *See, e.g., Hess v. Port Authority Trans-Hudson Corporation*, 513 U.S. 30, 44 (1994) ("Regulation of land use [is] a function traditionally performed by local governments"). Rather than expressing a desire to readjust the federal-state balance in this manner, Congress chose to "recognize, preserve, and protect the primary responsibilities and rights of States . . . to plan the development and use . . . of land and water resources. . . ." 33 U.S.C. § 1251(b). We thus read the statute as written to avoid the significant constitutional and federalism questions raised by respondents' interpretation, and therefore reject the request for administrative deference.

We hold that 33 CFR § 328.3(a)(3) (1999), as clarified and applied to petitioner's balefill site pursuant to the "Migratory Bird Rule" . . . exceeds the authority granted to respondents under § 404(a) of the CWA. The judgment of the Court of Appeals for the Seventh Circuit is therefore

Reversed.

Justice STEVENS, with whom Justice SOUTER, Justice GINSBURG, and Justice BREYER join, dissenting.

In 1969, the Cuyahoga River in Cleveland, Ohio, coated with a slick of industrial waste, caught fire. Congress responded to that dramatic event, and to others like it, by enacting the Federal Water Pollution Control Act (FWPCA) Amendments of 1972 . . . commonly known as the Clean Water Act (Clean Water Act, CWA, or Act). The Act proclaimed the ambitious goal of ending water pollution by 1985. § 1251(a). The Court's past interpretations of the CWA have been fully consistent with that goal. Although Congress' vision of zero pollution remains unfulfilled, its pursuit has unquestionably retarded the destruction of the aquatic environment. Our Nation's waters no longer burn. Today, however, the Court takes an unfortunate step that needlessly weakens our principal safeguard against toxic water.

It is fair to characterize the Clean Water Act as "watershed" legislation. The statute endorsed fundamental changes in both the purpose and the scope of federal regulation of the Nation's waters. In § 13 of the Rivers and Harbors Appropriation Act of 1899 (RHA) . . . , Congress had assigned to the Army Corps of Engineers (Corps) the mission of regulating discharges into certain waters in order to protect their use as highways for the transportation of interstate and foreign commerce; the scope of the Corps' jurisdiction under the RHA accordingly extended only to waters that were "navigable." In the CWA, however, Congress broadened the Corps' mission to include the purpose of protecting the quality of our Nation's waters for esthetic, health, recreational, and environmental uses. The scope of its jurisdiction was therefore redefined to encompass all of "the waters of the United States, including the territorial seas." § 1362(7). That definition requires neither actual nor potential navigability.

The Court has previously held that the Corps' broadened jurisdiction under the CWA properly included an 80-acre parcel of low-lying marshy land that was not itself navigable, directly adjacent to navigable water, or even hydrologically connected to navigable water, but which was part of a larger area, characterized by poor drainage, that ultimately abutted a navigable creek. *United States v. Riverside Bayview Homes, Inc.*, 474 U.S. 121 (1985).[2] Our broad finding in *Riverside Bayview* that the 1977 Congress had acquiesced in the Corps' understanding of its jurisdiction applies equally to the 410-acre parcel at issue here. Moreover, once Congress crossed the legal watershed that separates navigable streams of commerce from marshes and inland lakes, there is no principled reason for limiting the statute's protection to those waters or wetlands that happen to lie near a navigable stream.

In its decision today, the Court draws a new jurisdictional line, one that invalidates the 1986 migratory bird regulation as well as the Corps' assertion of jurisdiction over all waters except for actually navigable waters, their tributaries, and wetlands adjacent to each. Its holding rests on two equally untenable premises: (1) that when Congress passed the 1972 CWA, it did not intend "to exert anything more than its commerce power over navigation" . . . ; and (2) that in 1972 Congress drew the boundary defining the Corps' jurisdiction at the odd line on which the Court today settles.

As I shall explain, the text of the 1972 amendments affords no support for the Court's holding, and amendments Congress adopted in 1977 do support the Corps'

---

2. . . . The District Court in *Riverside Bayview* found that there was no direct "hydrological" connection between the parcel at issue and any nearby navigable waters. . . . The wetlands characteristics of the parcel were due, not to a surface or groundwater connection to any actually navigable water, but to "poor drainage" resulting from "the Lamson soil that underlay the property." Brief for Respondent in *Riverside Bayview* 7. Nevertheless, this Court found occasional surface runoff from the property into nearby waters to constitute a meaningful connection. *Riverside Bayview*, 474 U.S. at 134. . . . Of course, the *ecological* connection between the wetlands and the nearby waters also played a central role in this Court's decision. *Riverside Bayview*, 474 U.S. at 134-135. Both types of connection are also present in many, and possibly most, "isolated" waters. . . . Indeed, although the majority and petitioner both refer to the waters on petitioner's site as "isolated" . . . , their role as habitat for migratory birds, birds that serve important functions in the ecosystems of other waters throughout North America, suggests that—ecologically speaking—the waters at issue in this case are anything but isolated.

present interpretation of its mission as extending to so-called "isolated" waters. Indeed, simple common sense cuts against the particular definition of the Corps' jurisdiction favored by the majority.

The significance of the FWPCA Amendments of 1972 is illuminated by a reference to the history of federal water regulation, a history that the majority largely ignores. Federal regulation of the Nation's waters began in the 19th century with efforts targeted exclusively at "promoting water transportation and commerce." Sam Kalen, *Commerce to Conservation: The Call for a National Water Policy and the Evolution of Federal Jurisdiction Over Wetlands*, 69 N.D. L. Rev. 873, 877 (1993). This goal was pursued through the various Rivers and Harbors Acts, the most comprehensive of which was the RHA of 1899. Section 13 of the 1899 RHA, commonly known as the Refuse Act, prohibited the discharge of "refuse" into any "navigable water" or its tributaries, as well as the deposit of "refuse" on the bank of a navigable water "whereby navigation shall or may be impeded or obstructed" without first obtaining a permit from the Secretary of the Army. 30 Stat. 1152.

During the middle of the 20th century, the goals of federal water regulation began to shift away from an exclusive focus on protecting navigability and toward a concern for preventing environmental degradation. . . . This awakening of interest in the use of federal power to protect the aquatic environment was helped along by efforts to reinterpret § 13 of the RHA in order to apply its permit requirement to industrial discharges into navigable waters, even when such discharges did nothing to impede navigability. . . . Seeds of this nascent concern with pollution control can also be found in the FWPCA, which was first enacted in 1948 and then incrementally expanded in the following years.

The shift in the focus of federal water regulation from protecting navigability toward environmental protection reached a dramatic climax in 1972, with the passage of the CWA. The Act, which was passed as an amendment to the existing FWPCA, was universally described by its supporters as the first truly comprehensive federal water pollution legislation. The "major purpose" of the CWA was "to establish a *comprehensive* long-range policy for the elimination of water pollution." S. Rep. No. 92-414, p. 95 (1971), reprinted in 2 Legislative History of the Water Pollution Control Act Amendments of 1972 (Committee Print compiled for the Senate Committee on Public Works by the Library of Congress), Ser. No. 93-1, p. 1511 (1971) (hereinafter Leg. Hist.) (emphasis added). And "no Congressman's remarks on the legislation were complete without reference to [its] 'comprehensive' nature . . . ." *Milwaukee v. Illinois*, 451 U.S. 304, 318 (1981) (Rehnquist, J.). A House sponsor described the bill as "the most comprehensive and far-reaching water pollution bill we have ever drafted," 1 Leg. Hist. 369 (Rep. Mizell), and Senator Randolph, Chairman of the Committee on Public Works, stated: "It is perhaps the most comprehensive legislation that the Congress of the United States has ever developed in this particular field of the environment." *Id.* at 1269. This Court was therefore undoubtedly correct when it described the 1972 amendments as establishing "a comprehensive program for controlling and abating water pollution." *Train v. City of New York*, 420 U.S. 35, 37 (1975).

Section 404 of the CWA resembles § 13 of the RHA, but, unlike the earlier statute, the primary purpose of which is the maintenance of navigability, § 404 was principally intended as a pollution control measure. A comparison of the contents of the RHA and the 1972 Act vividly illustrates the fundamental difference between the purposes of the two provisions. The earlier statute contains pages of detailed appropriations for improvements in specific navigation facilities . . . , for studies concerning the feasibility of a canal across the Isthmus of Panama . . . , and for surveys of the advisability of harbor improvements at numerous other locations. . . . Tellingly, § 13, which broadly prohibits the discharge of refuse into navigable waters, contains an exception for refuse "flowing from streets and sewers . . . in a liquid state". . . .

The 1972 Act, in contrast, appropriated large sums of money for research and related programs for water pollution control . . . , and for the construction of water treatment works. . . . Strikingly absent from its declaration of "goals and policy" is *any* reference to avoiding or removing obstructions to navigation. Instead, the principal objective of the Act, as stated by Congress in § 101, was "to restore and maintain the chemical, physical, and biological integrity of the Nation's waters." 33 U.S.C. § 1251. Congress therefore directed federal agencies in § 102 to "develop comprehensive programs for preventing, reducing, or eliminating the pollution of the navigable waters and ground waters and improving the sanitary condition of surface and underground waters." 33 U.S.C. § 1252. The CWA commands federal agencies to give "due regard," not to the interest of unobstructed navigation, but rather to "improvements which are necessary to conserve such waters for the protection and propagation of fish and aquatic life and wildlife [and] recreational purposes." *Ibid.*

Because of the statute's ambitious and comprehensive goals, it was, of course, necessary to expand its jurisdictional scope. Thus, although Congress opted to carry over the traditional jurisdictional term "navigable waters" from the RHA and prior versions of the FWPCA, it broadened the *definition* of that term to encompass all "waters of the United States." § 1362(7). Indeed, the 1972 conferees arrived at the final formulation by specifically deleting the word "navigable" from the definition that had originally appeared in the House version of the Act.[7] The majority today undoes that deletion.

---

7. The version adopted by the House of Representatives defined "navigable waters" as "the navigable waters of the United States, including the territorial seas." H. R. 11896, 92d Cong., 2d Sess., § 502(8) (1971), reprinted in 1 Leg. Hist. 1069. The CWA ultimately defined "navigable waters" simply as "the waters of the United States, including the territorial seas." 33 U.S.C. § 1362(7).

The Conference Report explained that the definition in § 502(7) was intended to "be given the broadest possible constitutional interpretation." S. Conf. Rep. No. 92-1236, p. 144 (1972), reprinted in 1 Leg. Hist. 327. The Court dismisses this clear assertion of legislative intent with the back of its hand. *Ante,* at 7, n. 3. The statement, it claims, "signifies that Congress intended to exert [nothing] more than its commerce power over navigation." *Ibid.*

The majority's reading drains all meaning from the conference amendment. By 1972, Congress' Commerce Clause power over "navigation" had long since been established.... Why should Congress intend that its assertion of federal jurisdiction be given the "broadest possible constitutional interpretation" if it did not intend to reach beyond the very heartland of its commerce power? The activities regulated by the CWA have nothing to do with Congress' "commerce power over navigation." Indeed, the goals of the 1972 statute have nothing to do with *navigation* at all.

As we recognized in *Riverside Bayview*, the interests served by the statute embrace the protection of "'significant natural biological functions, including food chain production, general habitat, and nesting, spawning, rearing and resting sites'" for various species of aquatic wildlife. 474 U.S. at 134-135. For wetlands and "isolated" inland lakes, that interest is equally powerful, regardless of the proximity of the swamp or the water to a navigable stream. Nothing in the text, the stated purposes, or the legislative history of the CWA supports the conclusion that in 1972 Congress contemplated — much less commanded — the odd jurisdictional line that the Court has drawn today.

The majority accuses respondents of reading the term "navigable" out of the statute.... But that was accomplished by Congress when it deleted the word from the § 502(7) definition. After all, it is the *definition* that is the appropriate focus of our attention.... Moreover, a proper understanding of the history of federal water pollution regulation makes clear that — even on respondents' broad reading — the presence of the word "navigable" in the statute is not inexplicable. The term was initially used in the various Rivers and Harbors Acts because (1) at the time those statutes were first enacted, Congress' power over the Nation's waters was viewed as extending only to "water bodies that were deemed 'navigable' and therefore suitable for moving goods to or from markets" [citation omitted]; and (2) those statutes had the primary purpose of protecting navigation. Congress' choice to employ the term "navigable waters" in the 1972 Clean Water Act simply continued nearly a century of usage. Viewed in light of the history of federal water regulation, the broad § 502(7) definition, and Congress' unambiguous instructions in the Conference Report, it is clear that the term "navigable waters" operates in the statute as a shorthand for "waters over which federal authority may properly be asserted."

II.

As the majority correctly notes . . . , when the Corps first promulgated regulations pursuant to § 404 of the 1972 Act, it construed its authority as being essentially the same as it had been under the 1899 RHA. The reaction to those regulations in the federal courts, in the Environmental Protection Agency (EPA), and in Congress, convinced the Corps that the statute required it "to protect water quality to the full extent of the Commerce Clause" and to extend federal regulation over discharges "to many areas that have never before been subject to Federal permits or to this form of water quality protection." 40 Fed. Reg. 31320 (1975).

In 1975, the Corps therefore adopted the interim regulations that we upheld in *Riverside Bayview*. As we noted in that case, the new regulations understood "the waters of the United States" to include, not only navigable waters and their tributaries, but also "nonnavigable intrastate waters whose use or misuse could affect interstate commerce." 474 U.S. at 123. The 1975 regulations provided that the new program would become effective in three phases: phase 1, which became effective immediately, encompassed the navigable waters covered by the 1974 regulation and the RHA; phase 2, effective after July 1, 1976, extended Corps jurisdiction to nonnavigable tributaries, freshwater wetlands adjacent to primary navigable waters, and lakes; and phase 3, effective after July 1, 1977, extended Corps jurisdiction to all other waters covered under the statute, including any waters not covered by phases 1 and 2 (such as "intermittent rivers, streams, tributaries, and perched wetlands that are not contiguous or adjacent to navigable waters") that "the District Engineer determines necessitate regulation for the protection of water quality." 40 Fed. Reg. 31325-31326 (1975). The final version of these regulations, adopted in 1977, made clear that the covered waters included "isolated lakes and wetlands, intermittent streams, prairie potholes, and other waters that are not part of a tributary system to interstate waters or to navigable waters of the United States, the degradation or destruction of which could affect interstate commerce."[12]

The Corps' broadened reading of its jurisdiction provoked opposition among some Members of Congress. As a result, in 1977, Congress considered a proposal that would have limited the Corps' jurisdiction under § 404 to waters that are used, or by reasonable improvement could be used, as a means to transport interstate or foreign commerce and their adjacent wetlands. . . . A bill embodying that proposal passed the House but was defeated in the Senate. The debates demonstrate that Congress was fully aware of the Corps' understanding of the scope of its jurisdiction under the 1972 Act. We summarized these debates in our opinion in *Riverside Bayview*:

> In both Chambers, debate on the proposals to narrow the definition of navigable waters centered largely on the issue of wetlands preservation. . . . Proponents of a more limited § 404 jurisdiction contended that the Corps' assertion of jurisdiction over wetlands and other nonnavigable "waters" had far exceeded what Congress had intended in enacting § 404. Opponents of the proposed changes argued that a narrower definition of "navigable waters" for purposes of § 404 would exclude vast stretches of crucial wetlands from the Corps' jurisdiction, with detrimental effects on wetlands ecosystems, water quality, and the aquatic environment generally. The debate, particularly in the Senate, was lengthy. In the House, the debate

---

12. 42 Fed. Reg. 37127 (1977), as amended, 33 CFR § 328.3(a)(3) (1977). The so-called "migratory bird" rule, upon which the Corps based its assertion of jurisdiction in this case, is merely a specific application of the more general jurisdictional definition first adopted in the 1975 and 1977 rules. The "rule," which operates as a rule of thumb for identifying the waters that fall within the Corps' jurisdiction over phase 3 waters, first appeared in the preamble to a 1986 repromulgation of the Corps' definition of "navigable waters." 51 Fed. Reg. 41217 (1986). As the Corps stated in the preamble, this repromulgation was not intended to alter its jurisdiction in any way. *Ibid.* Instead, the Corps indicated, the migratory bird rule was enacted simply to "clarify" the scope of existing jurisdictional regulations. *Ibid.*

ended with the adoption of a narrowed definition of "waters"; but in the Senate the limiting amendment was defeated and the old definition retained. The Conference Committee adopted the Senate's approach: efforts to narrow the definition of "waters" were abandoned; the legislation as ultimately passed, in the words of Senator Baker, "retained the comprehensive jurisdiction over the Nation's waters exercised in the 1972 Federal Water Pollution Control Act." 474 U.S. at 136-137.

The net result of that extensive debate was a congressional endorsement of the position that the Corps maintains today. We explained in *Riverside Bayview:*

> The scope of the Corps' asserted jurisdiction over wetlands was specifically brought to Congress' attention, and Congress rejected measures designed to curb the Corps' jurisdiction in large part because of its concern that protection of wetlands would be unduly hampered by a narrowed definition of "navigable waters." Although we are chary of attributing significance to Congress' failure to act, a refusal by Congress to overrule an agency's construction of legislation is at least some evidence of the reasonableness of that construction, particularly where the administrative construction has been brought to Congress' attention through legislation specifically designed to supplant it. *Id.* at 137.

Even if the majority were correct that Congress did not extend the Corps' jurisdiction in the 1972 CWA to reach beyond navigable waters and their nonnavigable tributaries, Congress' rejection of the House's efforts in 1977 to cut back on the Corps' 1975 assertion of jurisdiction clearly indicates congressional acquiescence in that assertion. Indeed, our broad determination in *Riverside Bayview* that the 1977 Congress acquiesced in the very regulations at issue in this case should foreclose petitioner's present urgings to the contrary. The majority's refusal in today's decision to acknowledge the scope of our prior decision is troubling. . . . Having already concluded that Congress acquiesced in the Corps' regulatory definition of its jurisdiction, the Court is wrong to reverse course today. . . .

***

Contrary to the Court's suggestion, the Corps' interpretation of the statute does not "encroach" upon "traditional state power" over land use. . . ." Land use planning in essence chooses particular uses for the land; environmental regulation, at its core, does not mandate particular uses of the land but requires only that, however the land is used, damage to the environment is kept within prescribed limits." *California Coastal Comm'n v. Granite Rock Co.*, 480 U.S. 572 (1987). The CWA is not a land-use code; it is a paradigm of environmental regulation. Such regulation is an accepted exercise of federal power. . . .

***

Because I would affirm the judgment of the Court of Appeals, I respectfully dissent.

points for discussion

1. *"Navigable" again!* Section 404 of the Clean Water Act provides that, before a person deposits dredged or fill materials into "navigable waters," he must

get a permit from the Army Corps of Engineers. But what does "navigable waters" mean in the context of the statute? The statute defines "navigable waters" as "waters of the United States." What exactly are waters of the United States? If Congress meant Section 404 to cover only navigable-in-fact waters, would it have defined the term at all? The language used in the statute required the Army Corps to issue interpretive regulations, so that both its officials and members of the public would know when a permit was needed. As the opinion indicates, courts will defer to such agency interpretations. The leading case in the area, *Chevron U.S.A. Inc. v. Natural Resources Defense Council, Inc.*, 467 U.S. 837 (1984), stands for the proposition that courts will uphold agency interpretations where (1) the language of the statute is ambiguous, and (2) the agency's interpretation is based on a permissible construction of the statute, that is, is consistent with the overall purpose of the law. Do you agree with the majority that the language of the statute is unambiguous? If not, is the "migratory bird rule" a permissible construction of "waters of the United States"?

2. *The end of the Commerce Clause.* Does the majority opinion say that Congress could not require citizens to obtain permits before depositing dredged or fill material into "isolated wetlands"? In other words, could Congress, pursuant to its Commerce Clause authority, incorporate the migratory bird rule into the statute?

3. *Into the void.* As the majority notes, striking the migratory bird rule does not leave isolated wetlands unprotected; so long as they can prove that doing so is in the public interest, states have the authority to regulate dumping into these waters. Why do you think environmental groups might be concerned about states having the lead role? (The Army Corps of Engineers historically has approved more than 99 percent of Section 404 permit applications. *See* Testimony of Michael Davis, Deputy Assistant Secretary of the Army for Civil Works, Before Senate Environment and Public Works Committee, Subcommittee on Air Quality, Wetlands, Private Property, and Nuclear Safety, March 28, 2000.)

4. *"Significant nexus" explained?* In the following excerpt, the authors describe development of the law since the follow-on case to *SWANCC*, *Rapanos v. United States*, 547 U.S. 715 (2006):

> [As of the end of 2010,] it has been more than four years since the U.S. Supreme Court issued its latest interpretation of the limits of the Clean Water Act (CWA), [in *Rapanos*]. . . . When the opinion was issued, it was hoped that some level of clarity would arise from the "significant nexus" test set forth in Justice Anthony M. Kennedy's concurring opinion. To date, however, the U.S. Army Corps of Engineers (the Corps), the U.S. Environmental Protection Agency (EPA), and the courts have struggled with finding meaning in this test.
>
> . . . *Rapanos* [and a companion case, *Carabell v. United States*] examined the geographical reach of federal jurisdiction; specifically, whether three wetlands linked by a hydrological connection to "navigable waters" more than 20 miles away . . . and a wetland separated by a berm from a drainage ditch that eventually drains into a navigable water . . . were subject to § 404 of the CWA. . . .

. . . Justice Kennedy provided the necessary fifth vote to reverse the [holding of the] U.S. Court of Appeals for the Sixth Circuit [that the wetlands in question were subject to § 404]. However, though Justice Kennedy sided with the plurality to vacate the Sixth Circuit's ruling and remand for additional fact-finding, his opinion did not embrace Justice Scalia's rationale [that the CWA applies only if "the adjacent channel contains a 'wate[r]' of the United States,' (i.e., a relatively permanent body of water connected to traditional interstate navigable waters)," and "that the wetland has a continuous surface connection with that water, making it difficult to determine where the 'water' ends and the 'wetland' begins."]. Justice Kennedy's test held that waters are jurisdictional only to the degree they have a significant nexus with navigable-in-fact water. This nexus is present when the waters in question, "alone or in combination with similarly situated lands in the region, significantly affect the chemical, physical, and biological integrity" of the navigable water.

. . . [I]n June 2007, the [U.S. Army Corps of Engineers issued a jurisdictional guidance document], essentially adopting both the Justice Scalia and Justice Kennedy tests. Yet, much of the guidance is focused on interpreting the significant nexus test. Hence, the agencies (and the courts when confronted by application of the guidance) will likely rely on this test as a foundation for jurisdictional determinations where the "waters of the United States" in question are not truly "navigable," permanent, or directly adjacent to a navigable water. Thus, the on-the-ground application of the significant nexus test is key to the scope of the agency's jurisdiction over a wide spectrum of waters that are not obviously navigable in fact.

The 2007 guidance, as revised in December 2008, strives to put Justice Kennedy's test into administrative action. [T]he guidance focuses on those water bodies and wetlands that would require application of the significant nexus test: "non-navigable tributaries that do not typically flow year-round or have continuous flow at least seasonally; wetlands adjacent to such tributaries; and wetlands adjacent to but that do not directly abut a relatively permanent, non-navigable tributary." The guidance's definition of significant nexus differs slightly from Justice Kennedy's: "A significant nexus exists if the tributary, in combination with all of its adjacent wetlands, has more than a speculative or an insubstantial effect on the chemical, physical, and/or biological integrity of a [traditionally navigable water]."

The guidance attempts to draw a clear line where it will assert jurisdiction over certain waters known to be jurisdictional. The following waters are considered by agencies always to be jurisdictional:

- [Traditionally Navigable Waters, or] TNWs;
- wetlands adjacent to traditional navigable waters;
- non-navigable tributaries to traditional navigable waters that have relatively permanent flow at least seasonally (i.e., typically three months); and
- wetlands that directly abut such tributaries.

***

A second category of waters is presumptively not regulated. The guidance states that the following waters are "presumed" by agencies not to be jurisdictional:

- swales and erosional features (e.g., gullies, small washes characterized by low volume, infrequent, or short duration flow);
- ditches (including roadside ditches) excavated wholly in and draining only uplands and that do not have a relatively permanent flow of water; and
- waters, including wetlands, deemed non-jurisdictional by SWANCC.

***

The third categorical determination made by the agencies is based on the significant nexus test. It is this "gray area" where the proximate causation/foreseeability principles will be the hardest to apply. The following waters are considered by agencies possibly to be jurisdictional, depending on the presence of a significant nexus:

- non-navigable tributaries that are not relatively permanent (e.g., ephemeral tributaries that flow only in response to precipitation and intermittent streams that do not typically flow year-round or have continuous flow at least seasonally);
- wetlands adjacent to non-navigable tributaries that are not relatively permanent; and
- wetlands adjacent to, but that do not directly abut, non-navigable tributaries that are relatively permanent (e.g., separated from it by uplands, a berm, dike, or similar feature).

***

Though the guidance provides no bright line, it is clear that the evidentiary burden increases with the distance between the water to be regulated and the traditional navigable water, as well as with the regularity of the flow (which would establish the requisite connection and effect on the navigable-in-fact water).

Lawrence R. Liebesman et al., Rapanos v. United States: *Searching for a Significant Nexus Using Proximate Causation and Foreseeability Principles*, 40 ELR 11242 (2010).

5. *The latest.* In a December 2018 report to Congress, the Congressional Research Service summarized the many developments in what is now regularly called the Waters of the United States (WOTUS) rule, that is, the regulation interpreting the term "water of the United States" in the CWA:

> . . . As explained in the 2015 Clean Water Rule's preamble, the Corps and EPA used Justice Kennedy's "significant nexus" standard in developing the rule as well as the plurality opinion (written by Justice Scalia) in establishing boundaries on the scope of jurisdiction.
>
> The 2015 Clean Water Rule identified categories of waters that are and are not jurisdictional as well as waters that require a case-specific

evaluation (see Figure [6-8]). Broad categories under the final rule include the following:

- **Jurisdictional by rule in all cases.** Traditional navigable waters, interstate waters, the territorial seas, and impoundments of these waters are jurisdictional by rule. All of these waters were also jurisdictional under pre-2015 rules.
- **Jurisdictional by rule, as defined.** Two additional categories — tributaries and adjacent waters — are jurisdictional by rule if they meet definitions established in the 2015 Clean Water Rule. According to the rule's preamble, the definitions ensure that the rule covers waters that meet the significant nexus standard. Tributaries, under pre-2015 rules, were jurisdictional by rule without qualification but lacked a regulatory definition. The 2015 Clean Water Rule newly defined tributaries. Tributaries that meet the new definition are jurisdictional by rule.

  Similarly, "adjacent waters" — including wetlands, ponds, lakes, oxbows, impoundments, and similar waters that are adjacent to traditional navigable waters, interstate waters, the territorial seas, jurisdictional tributaries, or impoundments of these waters — are jurisdictional by the 2015 Clean Water Rule if they meet the rule's established definition. Under the 2015 Clean Water Rule, adjacent means "bordering, contiguous, or neighboring" one of the aforementioned waters. The rule established a definition of neighboring that set new limits for the purposes of determining adjacency. Neighboring is defined to include waters (1) located within 100 feet of the ordinary high-water mark (OHWM) of a traditional navigable water, interstate water, the territorial seas, jurisdictional tributary, or impoundment of these waters; (2) located in the 100-year floodplain and within 1,500 feet of the OHWM of a traditional navigable water, interstate water, the territorial seas, jurisdictional tributary, or impoundment of these waters; or (3) located within 1,500 feet of the high tide line of a traditional navigable water or the territorial seas and waters located within 1,500 feet of the OHWM of the Great Lakes. Under pre-2015 rules, adjacent was defined to mean "bordering, contiguous, or neighboring" and did not include specific limits on "neighboring."

- **Waters requiring a case-specific evaluation.** Some types of waters — but fewer than under practices used prior to the 2015 Clean Water Rule — would remain subject to a case-specific evaluation of whether or not they meet the standards for federal jurisdiction. This case-specific evaluation examines whether the water has a significant nexus to traditional navigable waters, interstate waters or wetlands, or the territorial seas. Similarly situated waters (i.e., prairie potholes, Carolina bays and Delmarva bays, pocosins, western vernal pools, and Texas coastal prairie wetlands) are combined for the purposes of a significant nexus analysis. In addition, the 2015 Clean Water Rule provides that two other categories of waters are subject to case-specific significant nexus analysis: (1) waters within the 100-year floodplain of a traditional navigable water, interstate water, or the territorial seas; and (2) waters within 4,000 feet of the high tide line or the OHWM of a traditional navigable water, interstate water, the territorial seas, impoundments, or jurisdictional tributary.

(Not drawn to scale)

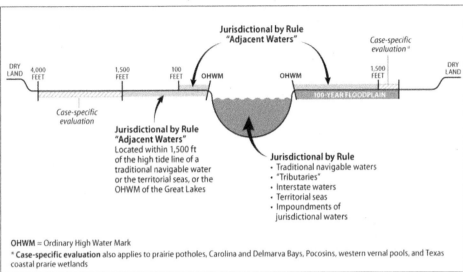

Source: Prepared by CRS, from Army Corps of Engineers and EPA, "Clean Water Rule: Definition of 'Waters of the United States'; Final Rule," 80 *Federal Register* 37054, June 29, 2015.

Figure 6-8. Jurisdictional Waters Under the 2015 Clean Water Rule

- **Exclusions.** Certain waters would be excluded from CWA jurisdiction. Some were restated exclusions under pre-2015 rules (e.g., prior converted cropland). Some have been excluded by practice and would be expressly excluded by rule for the first time (e.g., ground water and some ditches). Some were new in the final rule (e.g., stormwater management systems). The 2015 Clean Water Rule did not affect existing statutory exclusions — that is, exemptions for existing "normal farming, silviculture, and ranching activities" and for maintenance of drainage ditches (CWA § 404(f)(16)) as well as for agricultural stormwater discharges and irrigation return flows (CWA § 402(l) and CWA § 502(14)).

Issues and Controversy

Much of the controversy since the Supreme Court's rulings has centered on instances that have required CWA permit applicants to seek a case-specific analysis to determine if CWA jurisdiction applies to their activity. The Corps and EPA's stated intention in promulgating the Clean Water Rule was to clarify questions of CWA jurisdiction in view of the rulings while also reflecting their scientific and technical expertise. Specifically, they sought to articulate categories of waters that are and are not protected by the CWA, thus limiting the water types that require case-specific analysis.

Industries that are the primary applicants for CWA permits and agriculture groups raised concerns over how broadly the 2014 proposed rule would be interpreted. They contended that the proposed definitions were ambiguous and would enable agencies to assert broader CWA jurisdiction than is consistent with law and science.

The final 2015 Clean Water Rule added and defined key terms, such as tributary and significant nexus, and modified the proposal in an effort to improve clarity, but the concerns remained. Some local governments that own and maintain public infrastructure also criticized the 2014 proposed rule. They argued that it could increase the number of locally owned ditches under federal jurisdiction because it would define some ditches as WOTUS under certain conditions. Corps and EPA officials asserted that the proposed exclusion of most ditches would decrease federal jurisdiction, but the issue remained controversial. The final 2015 Clean Water Rule excluded most ditches and expressly excluded stormwater management systems and structures from jurisdiction. Some states supported a rule to clarify the scope of CWA jurisdiction, but there was no consensus on the 2014 proposed rule or the final 2015 Clean Water Rule.

Many states asserted that the changes would too broadly expand federal jurisdiction, some believed that the agencies did not adequately consult with states, and some were largely supportive. Environmental groups generally supported the agencies' efforts to protect waters and reduce uncertainty. Still, some argued that the scope of the 2014 proposed rule should be further expanded — for example, by designating additional categories of waters and wetlands (e.g., prairie potholes) as categorically jurisdictional. The final 2015 Clean Water Rule did not do so. Instead, such waters would require case-specific analysis to determine if jurisdiction applies. Corps and EPA officials under the Obama Administration defended the 2014 proposed rule but acknowledged that it raised questions they believed the final 2015 Clean Water Rule clarified. In their view, the 2015 Clean Water Rule did not protect any new types of waters that were not protected historically, did not exceed the CWA's authority, and would not enlarge jurisdiction beyond what is consistent with the Supreme Court's rulings as well as scientific understanding of significant connections between small and ephemeral streams and downstream waters. The agencies asserted that they had addressed criticisms of the 2014 proposed rule by, for example, defining tributaries more clearly, setting maximum distances from jurisdictional waters for the purposes of defining neighboring waters, and modifying the definition of WOTUS to make it clear that the rule preserves agricultural exclusions and exemptions.

Issuance of the final 2015 Clean Water Rule did not diminish concerns amongst stakeholders. Many groups contended that the rule did not provide needed clarity, that its expansive definitions made it difficult to identify any waters that would fall outside the boundary distances established in the rule, and that the threshold for determining "significant nexus" was set so low that virtually any water could be found to be jurisdictional. The 2015 Clean Water Rule would impose costs, critics said, but have little or no environmental benefit. Environmental groups were supportive but also faulted parts of the final rule. Some environmental groups believed the rule reduced the jurisdictional reach of the CWA and rolled back protections for certain waters, including minor tributaries and some ephemeral aquatic habitats.

Current Status of the 2015 Clean Water Rule

Currently, the 2015 Clean Water Rule is in effect in 22 states and enjoined in 28 states. In states where the 2015 Clean Water Rule is enjoined, regulations promulgated by the Corps and EPA in 1986 and 1988, respectively, are in effect. Since the 2015 Clean Water Rule was finalized, its implementation has been influenced both by the courts and administrative actions.

Court Actions

Following issuance of the 2015 Clean Water Rule, industry groups, more than half the states, and several environmental groups filed lawsuits challenging the rule in multiple federal district and appeals courts. By the time the 2015 Clean Water Rule entered into effect (August 28, 2015), a district court had already prevented its enforcement in 13 states. Specifically, on August 27, 2015, the U.S. District Court for the District of North Dakota issued a preliminary injunction on the 2015 Clean Water Rule in the 13 states challenging the rule in that court.

In October 2015, the U.S. Court of Appeals for the Sixth Circuit ordered a nationwide stay of the 2015 Clean Water Rule and later ruled (in February 2016) that it had jurisdiction to hear consolidated challenges to the rule. However, in January 2018, the Supreme Court unanimously held that federal district courts, rather than appellate courts, are the proper forum for filing challenges to the 2015 Clean Water Rule. Accordingly, on February 28, 2018, the appeals court vacated its nationwide stay.

On November 22, 2017, the Corps and EPA proposed to add an "applicability date" to the 2015 Clean Water Rule. The agencies finalized this rule on February 6, 2018, effectively delaying the implementation of the 2015 Clean Water Rule until February 6, 2020. According to the preamble of the 2018 Applicability Date Rule, the agencies' intention in adding an applicability date to the 2015 Clean Water Rule was to maintain the legal status quo and provide clarity and certainty for regulated entities, states, tribes, agency staff, and the public regarding the definition of waters of the United States while the agencies work on revising the 2015 Clean Water Rule. Environmental groups and states immediately filed lawsuits challenging the 2018 Applicability Date Rule, asserting that it violated the Administrative Procedures Act.

On August 16, 2018, the U.S. District Court for the District of South Carolina issued a nationwide injunction of the rule. As a result, the 2015 Clean Water Rule went into effect in the states where injunctions had not been issued. During the period between when the 2018 Applicability Date Rule was finalized and the district court issued a nationwide injunction of that rule, the U.S. District Court for the Southern District of Georgia enjoined the 2015 Clean Water Rule in 11 states. Since that time, two additional court actions have enjoined the 2015 Clean Water Rule in four additional states. The U.S. District Court for the Southern District of Texas enjoined the 2015 Clean Water Rule in three states on September 11, 2018. On September 18, 2018, the U.S. District Court for the District of North Dakota granted a request from the Governor of Iowa to clarify that the preliminary injunction applied to Iowa. Accordingly, the 2015 Clean Water Rule is currently in effect in 22 states and enjoined in 28 states.

Administrative Actions

The Administration has also taken steps to rescind and revise the 2015 Clean Water Rule. On February 28, 2017, President Trump issued an executive order directing the Corps and EPA to review and rescind or revise the rule and to consider interpreting the term *navigable waters* as defined in the CWA in a manner consistent with Justice Scalia's opinion in *Rapanos*. On July 27, 2017, the agencies proposed a rule that would "initiate the first step in a comprehensive, two-step process intended to review and revise the definition of 'waters of the United States' consistent with the Executive Order." The first step proposes to rescind the 2015 Clean Water Rule and re-codify the regulatory definition of WOTUS as it existed prior to the rule. On July 12, 2018, the Corps and EPA published a supplemental notice of proposed rulemaking to clarify, supplement, and seek additional comment on the agencies' proposed repeal. The public comment period closed on August 13, 2018. The agencies have not yet issued a final step-one rule.

On December 11, 2018, the Corps and EPA announced a proposed step-two rule that would revise the definition of WOTUS. The EPA press release states that the proposal is intended to clarify federal authority under the CWA and more clearly define "the difference between federally protected waterways and state protected waterways."

Actions in the 115th Congress

Considering the numerous court rulings, ongoing legal challenges, and issues that Administrations have faced in defining the scope of WOTUS, some stakeholders have urged Congress to define WOTUS through amendments to the CWA. In the 115th Congress, Members of Congress have shown continued interest in the 2015 Clean Water Rule and the scope of WOTUS. Some Members have introduced the following free-standing legislation and provisions within appropriations bills that would repeal the 2015 Clean Water Rule, allow the Corps and EPA to withdraw the rule without regard to the Administrative Procedures Act, or amend the CWA to add a narrower definition of *navigable waters*.

CONGRESSIONAL RESEARCH SERVICE, R45424, "WATERS OF THE UNITED STATES" (WOTUS): CURRENT STATUS OF THE 2015 CLEAN WATER RULE (Dec. 12, 2018).

C. STATE STATUTES AND THE EXPANSION OF TRADITIONAL COMMON LAW COVERAGE IN RESPONSE TO THE COASTAL ZONE MANAGEMENT ACT

While Congress has written a number of laws that can restrict activities on private land, such as the Clean Water Act and the Endangered Species Act, it has refrained from entering into the area of land use planning. As the majority in *SWANCC* noted, citing to an earlier case, "[r]egulation of land use [is] a function traditionally performed by local governments."

Planning — decision-making about where future uses should and should not be allowed — can reduce the costs of conflict and allow for more rational investment decisions. Planning theoretically allows for more efficient use of limited coastal resources. Planning requires that government acquire information about available resources and conduct studies about future needs. The planning process enables government officials, in consultation with experts and the public, to ensure that available resources will be used for their most socially beneficial purpose.

Consider, for example, a large parcel of undeveloped land adjacent to an existing port. At present, the port has sufficient capacity for handling incoming vessels and freight. Studies, however, predict that this will no longer be true ten years from now. A planning process would recognize this future need. Government would then be in a position to rationally regulate land use on the vacant parcel. Government might, for example, limit use of that land to port-expansion or, in the alternative, to low-investment uses that would facilitate future conversion of the parcel to port-related use. Why do you think the private market, that is, land use without such regulation, might result in less than efficient use of the vacant land?

The following statute illustrates that Congress believed both that planning is important and that it is a matter in which the states (or local government entities) should play the leading role. For purposes of this chapter, the key points are the extent to which Congress identified the special nature of coastal lands and waters, and the way in which the statute defines (or doesn't define) exactly what the word "coastal" means. (We will turn, in Chapter 9, to the question of how the statute operates.)

Coastal Zone Management Act

16 U.S.C. §§ 1452 and 1453

§ 1452. Congressional declaration of policy

The Congress finds and declares that it is the national policy —

(1) to preserve, protect, develop, and where possible, to restore or enhance, the resources of the Nation's coastal zone for this and succeeding generations;

(2) to encourage and assist the states to exercise effectively their responsibilities in the coastal zone through the development and implementation of management programs to achieve wise use of the land and water resources of the coastal zone, giving full consideration to ecological, cultural, historic, and esthetic values as well as the needs for compatible economic development, which programs should at least provide for —

(A) the protection of natural resources, including wetlands, floodplains, estuaries, beaches, dunes, barrier islands, coral reefs, and fish and wildlife and their habitat, within the coastal zone,

(B) the management of coastal development to minimize the loss of life and property caused by improper development in flood-prone, storm surge, geological hazard, and erosion-prone areas and in areas likely to be affected by or vulnerable to sea level rise, land subsidence, and saltwater intrusion, and by the destruction of natural protective features such as beaches, dunes, wetlands, and barrier islands,

(C) the management of coastal development to improve, safeguard, and restore the quality of coastal waters, and to protect natural resources and existing uses of those waters,

(D) priority consideration being given to coastal-dependent uses and orderly processes for siting major facilities related to national defense, energy, fisheries development, recreation, ports and transportation, and the location, to the maximum extent practicable, of new commercial and industrial developments in or adjacent to areas where such development already exists,

(E) public access to the coasts for recreation purposes,

(F) assistance in the redevelopment of deteriorating urban waterfronts and ports, and sensitive preservation and restoration of historic, cultural, and esthetic coastal features,

(G) the coordination and simplification of procedures in order to ensure expedited governmental decisionmaking for the management of coastal resources,

(H) continued consultation and coordination with, and the giving of adequate consideration to the views of, affected Federal agencies,

(I) the giving of timely and effective notification of, and opportunities for public and local government participation in, coastal management decisionmaking,

(J) assistance to support comprehensive planning, conservation, and management for living marine resources, including planning for the siting of pollution control and aquaculture facilities within the coastal zone, and improved coordination between State and Federal coastal zone management agencies and State and wildlife agencies, and

(K) the study and development, in any case in which the Secretary considers it to be appropriate, of plans for addressing the adverse effects upon the coastal zone of land subsidence and of sea level rise; and

(3) to encourage the preparation of special area management plans which provide for increased specificity in protecting significant natural resources, reasonable coastal-dependent economic growth, improved protection of life and property in hazardous areas, including those areas likely to be affected by land subsidence, sea level rise, or fluctuating water levels of the Great Lakes, and improved predictability in governmental decisionmaking;

(4) to encourage the participation and cooperation of the public, state and local governments, and interstate and other regional agencies, as well as of the Federal agencies having programs affecting the coastal zone, in carrying out the purposes of this title;

(5) to encourage coordination and cooperation with and among the appropriate Federal, State, and local agencies, and international organizations where appropriate, in collection, analysis, synthesis, and dissemination of coastal management information, research results, and technical assistance, to support State and Federal regulation of land use practices affecting the coastal and ocean resources of the United States; and

(6) to respond to changing circumstances affecting the coastal environment and coastal resource management by encouraging States to consider such issues as ocean uses potentially affecting the coastal zone.

§ 1453. Definitions

For the purposes of this title —

(1) The term "coastal zone" means the coastal waters (including the lands therein and thereunder) and the adjacent shorelands (including the waters therein and thereunder), strongly influenced by each other and in proximity to the shorelines of the several coastal states, and includes islands, transitional and intertidal areas, salt marshes, wetlands, and beaches. The zone extends, in Great Lakes waters, to the international boundary between the United States and Canada and, in other areas, seaward to the outer limit of State title and ownership under the Submerged Lands Act. . . . The zone extends inland from the shorelines only to the extent necessary to control shorelands, the uses of which have a direct and significant impact on the coastal waters, and to control those geographical areas which are likely to be affected by or vulnerable to sea level rise. Excluded from the coastal zone are lands the use of which is by law subject solely to the discretion of or which is held in trust by the Federal Government, its officers or agents.

(2) The term "coastal resource of national significance" means any coastal wetland, beach, dune, barrier island, reef, estuary, or fish and wildlife habitat, if any such area is determined by a coastal state to be of substantial biological or natural storm protective value.

(3) The term "coastal waters" means (A) in the Great Lakes area, the waters within the territorial jurisdiction of the United States consisting of the Great Lakes, their connecting waters, harbors, roadsteads, and estuary-type areas such as bays, shallows, and marshes and (B) in other areas, those waters, adjacent to the shorelines, which contain a measurable quantity or percentage of sea water, including, but not limited to, sounds, bays, lagoons, bayous, ponds, and estuaries.

(4) The term "coastal state" means a state of the United States in, or bordering on, the Atlantic, Pacific, or Arctic Ocean, the Gulf of Mexico, Long Island Sound, or one or more of the Great Lakes. For the purposes of this title, the term also includes Puerto Rico, the Virgin Islands, Guam, the Commonwealth of the Northern Mariana Islands, and the Trust Territories of the Pacific Islands, and American Samoa.

***

(7) The term "estuary" means that part of a river or stream or other body of water having unimpaired connection with the open sea, where the sea water is measurably diluted with fresh water derived from land drainage. The term includes estuary-type areas of the Great Lakes.

(8) The term "estuarine sanctuary" means a research area which may include any part or all of an estuary and any island, transitional area, and upland in, adjoining, or adjacent to such estuary, and which constitutes to the extent feasible a natural unit, set aside to provide scientists and students the opportunity to examine over a period of time the ecological relationships within the area.

While the CZMA gave states some incentives to develop new coastal law, it did not add to their existing jurisdictional powers. As we now know, states' common law public trust doctrines give them the power to regulate use of their public waterways and submerged lands. State legislatures have two sources of authority for regulating land use in *upland* areas. First, states can regulate upland land use as necessary to protect public trust property or public trust uses. So, for example, states might limit the kinds or amount of construction on uplands adjacent to public waterways on the ground that such construction would cause harm to those waterways or interfere with public use of them. In addition, states can also use their general police powers. Unlike the federal government, which by virtue of the U.S. Constitution is a government of enumerated powers, states have inherent, plenary power to protect the interests of their citizens. Courts have broadly defined the "police power" to include any measures necessary to ensure public "health, welfare, safety, and morals." States have delegated much of this power to local governments. Pursuant to the police power, a city might, for example, regulate the height of buildings constructed on coastal uplands. This might be done in order to protect public safety, given that such areas are prone to storms or erosion, or to promote the aesthetic quality of a beach community.

In a few cases, state courts and legislatures had expanded coastal law to include uplands prior to 1972. So, for example, in the *Borough of Neptune* case (cited in *Matthews*), the Supreme Court of New Jersey expanded the state's public trust doctrine to include limited public access to some dry sand beaches. Faced with a similar situation in the late 1950s, the Supreme Court of Texas refused to recognize public rights in dry sand beaches landward of the mean higher high tide line. *Luttes v. State*, 324 S.W.2d 167 (Tex. 1958). In response to this decision, in 1959, the Texas legislature passed the Texas Open Beaches Act, which facilitated judicial recognition of public access to dry sand beaches along the Gulf Coast. (We will learn more about Texas law in Chapter 9.)

Notwithstanding these earlier examples, most expansion of state coastal jurisdiction, and the most dramatic expansions, occurred after 1976 and the passage of the federal Coastal Zone Management Act. Look at the definition of "coastal zone" in Section 1453(1), above. There are a number of words in the definition that are open to interpretation, for example, "adjacent," "wetlands," "beaches," "control," "direct," "significant," and "likely." The following table, prepared in 2004 by the Coastal Services Center of the National Oceanic and Atmospheric Administration, the federal agency charged by Congress with implementing the CZMA, shows how states have interpreted these words — and relied on ecological, economic, and political considerations — in defining their own coastal zones.

Table 1

**National Oceanic and Atmospheric Administration,
State Coastal Zone Boundaries (2004)**

State	Definition of State's Coastal Zone
	(The seaward boundary of the Great Lake States is the U.S.-Canada International boundary, and for all other States is the 3 nautical mile territorial sea, except [where otherwise indicated].)
Alabama	Alabama's coastal zone extends inland to the continuous 10-foot elevation contour in Baldwin and Mobile Counties.
Alaska	Alaska's coastal zone is based on three zones based on biophysical relationships: (1) zone of direct interaction — the area where physical and biological processes are a direct function of contact between land and sea; (2) the zone of direct influence — the area closely affected and influenced by the close proximity of land and sea; and (3) the zone of indirect influence — the area beyond the zone of indirect influence to the limit of identifiable land/sea interaction. Local coastal programs may establish more specific boundaries.
California	California's coastal zone generally extends 1,000 yards inland from the mean high tide line. In significant coastal estuarine habitat and recreational areas it extends inland to the first major ridgeline or 5 miles from the mean high tide line, whichever is less. In developed urban areas, the boundary is generally less than 1,000 yards. The coastal zone for the San Francisco Bay Conservation and Development Commission (BCDC) includes the open water, marshes and mudflats of greater San Francisco Bay, and areas 100 feet inland from the line of highest tidal action. The boundary also includes: the Suisun marsh and buffer zone: managed wetlands diked off from the Bay; and open waters diked off from the Bay and used in salt production.

State	Definition of State's Coastal Zone
Connecticut	Connecticut's coastal zone has two tiers incorporated within the 36 coastal townships. The first tier is bounded by a continuous line delineated by a 1,000 foot linear setback measured from the mean high-water mark in coastal waters; or a 1,000 foot linear setback measured from the inland boundary of state regulated tidal wetlands; or the continuous interior contour elevation of the one hundred year frequency coastal flood zone; whichever is farthest inland. The second tier is the area between the inland boundary of the 36 coastal communities and the inland boundary of the first tier.
Delaware	Delaware's coastal zone includes the whole state.
Florida	Florida's coastal zone is the entire State, but has two tiers. Local governments eligible to receive coastal management funds are limited to those Gulf and Atlantic coastal cities and counties which include or are contiguous to state water bodies where marine species of vegetation constitute the dominant plant community. Florida's seaward boundary in the Gulf of Mexico is 3 marine leagues (9 nautical miles) and is 3 nautical miles in the Atlantic.
Georgia	Georgia's coastal zone includes the 11 counties that border tidally-influenced waters or have economies that are closely tied to coastal resources.
Hawai'i	Hawaii's coastal zone is the entire state.
Indiana	Indiana's coastal zone is based on watershed boundaries within coastal townships and the counties of Lake, Porter and LaPorte. To create an inland boundary that is identifiable in practical landmarks, the coastal zone boundary is described based on the U.S. Geological Survey Quadrangle maps and major roads for each county. The coastal zone boundary is located in the northern portions of Lake, Porter, and LaPorte Counties. At its widest extent, the boundary extends away from the shoreline 17 miles to the Crown Point area and at its narrowest point, less than 2 miles, just north of Hudson Lake in LaPorte County. *See* NOAA, *Indiana Lake Michigan Coastal Program and Final Environmental Impact Statement,* Appendix C (April 2002), to determine the precise coastal zone boundary in a particular area of the State.

State	Definition of State's Coastal Zone
Louisiana	Louisiana's coastal zone varies from 16 to 32 miles inland from the Gulf coast and generally follows the Intracoastal Waterway running from the Texas-Louisiana state line, then follows highways through Vermilion, Iberia, and St. Mary parishes, then dipping southward following the natural ridges below Houma, then turning northward to take in Lake Pontchartrain and ending at the Mississippi-Louisiana border.
Maine	Maine's coastal zone includes the inland line of coastal towns on tidewaters and all islands.
Maryland	Maryland's coastal zone extends to the inland boundary of the 16 counties bordering the Atlantic Ocean, the Chesapeake Bay, and the Potomac River (as far as the municipal limits of Washington, D.C.), and includes Baltimore City and all local jurisdictions within the counties.
Massachusetts	Massachusetts' coastal zone extends 100 feet inland of specified major roads, RR tracks, or other visible right of ways which are located within a half mile of coastal waters or salt marshes. The coastal zone includes all islands, transitional and intertidal areas, and coastal wetlands and beaches. In instances where the road boundary excludes significant resource areas, the boundary line may depart from the road to encompass.
Michigan	Michigan's coastal zone, generally, extends a minimum of 1,000 feet from the ordinary high-water mark. The boundary extends further inland in some locations to encompass coastal lakes, rivermouths, and bays; floodplains; wetlands; dune areas; urban areas; and public park, recreation, and natural areas.
Minnesota	Minnesota's coastal zone is divided into three areas. The first includes the area of the St. Louis River in Carlton County, south of Duluth. The second is the city of Duluth and surrounding areas of urban growth and expansion to the north and west. The third is the region between the Duluth city limits north to the Canadian border, also known as the North Shore, which includes portions of St. Louis, Lake, and Cook Counties. *See* NOAA, *Minnesota's Lake Superior Coastal Program Final Environmental Impact Statement*, Chapter One (May 1999), to determine the precise coastal zone boundary in a particular area of the State.
Mississippi	Mississippi's coastal zone includes the 3 counties adjacent to the coast. The coastal zone includes these counties, as well as all adjacent coastal waters. Included in this definition are the barrier islands of the coast.

State	Definition of State's Coastal Zone
New Hampshire	New Hampshire's coastal zone is the 17 coastal municipalities.
New Jersey	New Jersey's coastal zone recognizes four distinct regions of the State and treats them separately. From the New York border to the Raritan Bay, the boundary extends landward from mean high water to the first road or property line. From the Raritan Bay south along the Atlantic shoreline and up to the Delaware Memorial Bridge, the boundary extends from half a mile to 24 miles inland (1,376 square miles of land area).
	From the Delaware Memorial Bridge northward up the Delaware River to Trenton, the boundary extends landward to the first road inclusive of all wetlands. The fourth boundary serves a 31-mile square area in the northeast corner of the state bordering the Hudson river (New Jersey Meadowlands Commission).
New York	New York's coastal zone varies from region to region while incorporating the following conditions: The inland boundary is approximately 1,000 feet from the shoreline of the mainland. In urbanized and developed coastal locations the landward boundary is approximately 500 feet from the mainland's shoreline, or less than 500 feet where a roadway or railroad line runs parallel to the shoreline at a distance of under 500 feet and defines the boundary. In locations where major state-owned lands and facilities or electric power generating facilities abut the shoreline, the boundary extends inland to include them. In some areas, such as Long Island Sound and the Hudson River Valley, the boundary may extend inland up to 10,000 feet to encompass significant coastal resources, such as areas of exceptional scenic value, agricultural or recreational lands, and major tributaries and headlands.
North Carolina	North Carolina's coastal zone includes the 20 counties that in whole or in part are adjacent to, adjoining, intersected by or bounded by the Atlantic Ocean or any coastal sound(s). Within this boundary, there are two tiers. The first tier is comprised of Areas of Environmental Concern (AEC) and is subject to more thorough regulatory controls. AECs include: coastal wetlands, estuarine waters, public trust areas, estuarine shorelines, ocean beaches, frontal dunes, ocean erosion areas, inlet lands, small surface water supply watersheds, public water supply wellfields, and fragile natural resource areas. The second tier includes land uses which have potential to affect coastal waters even though they are not located in AECs.

State	Definition of State's Coastal Zone
Ohio	Ohio's coastal zone includes portions of 9 counties bordering Lake Erie and its tributaries and varies depending on biophysical characteristics of various coastal regions[:] in the western part of the coast the boundary extends inland up to 15 miles along certain low lying wetland and floodplain areas; in most of the eastern part of the State, areas with high bluffs, the boundary extends inland for only about an eighth of a mile, with the exception of the Mentor Marsh area.
Oregon	Oregon's coastal zone extends inland to the crest of the coastal range, except for the following: along the Umpqua River, where it extends upstream to Scottsburg; along the Rogue River, where it extends upstream to Agness; and except in the Columbia River Basin, where it extends upstream to the downstream end of Puget Island.
Pennsylvania	Pennsylvania's coastal zone along Lake Erie varies from 900 feet in urban areas to over 3 miles in more rural areas, and encompasses the floodplains of Lake Erie and tributary streams, bluff hazards recession areas, and coastal wetlands. The coastal zone along the Delaware River Estuary extends inland to 660 feet in urbanized areas, to 3.5 miles in rural areas, and includes floodplains of the Delaware and Schuykill Rivers and their tributaries to the upper limit of tidal influence, and tidal and freshwater wetlands.
Rhode Island	Rhode Island's coastal zone includes the whole state. However, the inland extent of the regulatory authority of the State's CZMA agency is 200 feet inland from any coastal feature, to watersheds, and to certain activities that occur anywhere within the State that include: power-generating plants; petroleum storage facilities; chemical or petroleum processing; minerals extraction; sewage treatment and disposal plants; solid waste disposal facilities; and, desalination plants.
South Carolina	South Carolina's coastal zone includes all lands and waters in the counties which contain any one or more of the critical areas (coastal waters, tidelands, beaches, and primary oceanfront sand dunes).
Texas	Texas' coastal zone is generally the area seaward of the Texas coastal facility designation line which roughly follows roads that are parallel to coastal waters and wetlands generally within one mile of tidal rivers. The boundary encompasses all or portions of 18 coastal counties. Texas' seaward boundary is 3 marine leagues (9 nautical miles).

State	Definition of State's Coastal Zone
Virginia	Virginia's coastal zone includes the 29 counties, 17 cities, and 42 incorporated towns of *Tidewater Virginia*, including the Atlantic Coast watershed and portions of the Chesapeake Bay and Albemarle-Pamlico Sound watersheds.
Washington	Washington's coastal zone is the 15 coastal counties that front saltwater.
Wisconsin	Wisconsin's coastal zone is the 15 counties that front Lake Superior, Lake Michigan, or Green Bay.

points for discussion

1. *Differences among state coastal zones.* What explains the differences among states' definitions of their "coastal zones"? Which states have been most expansive in defining their coastal zones? Why?

2. *Zones within zones.* Notice that states such as North Carolina and South Carolina have created subzones within their coastal zones, for example, "areas of environmental concern" and "critical areas." These designations allow states to apply more stringent regulation in unique or particularly sensitive places.

D. THE (ILLUSTRATED) LEGAL GEOGRAPHY OF THE COAST

Figure 6-9 represents a hypothetical coastal area. Who has jurisdiction to regulate what, where, and under which theory or theories?

E. LIMITS ON STATE AND FEDERAL EXERCISE OF REGULATORY POWER: INTRODUCTION TO "TAKINGS"

Thus far in the chapter, we have learned about the sources and reach of state and federal coastal regulatory authority. States can regulate use of public waterways and coastal uplands using either the police power or the "protecting the public trust" power. Congress can do the same via the Commerce Clause or the navigational servitude. (In certain circumstances, Congress can also make use of the Property Clause, art. IV, sec. 3, or the treaty power.)

There are, however, limits on the use of this authority. For one thing, there may be political or traditional limits on the exercise of government power. As we saw in the case of the Coastal Zone Management Act, Congress was hesitant to interfere

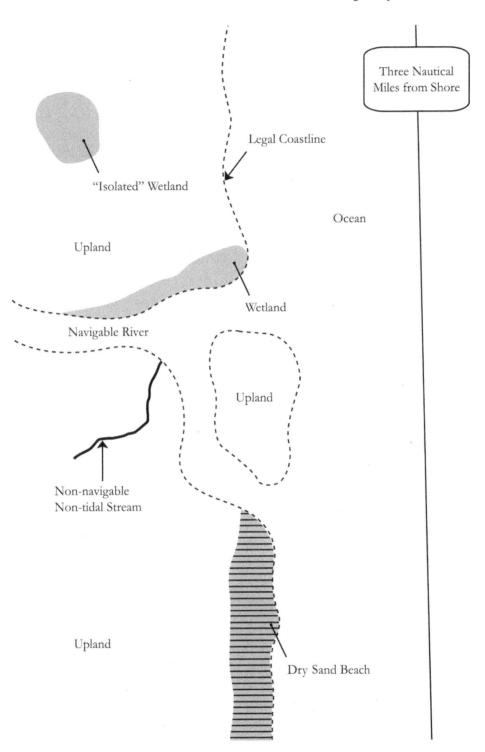

Figure 6-9. Hypothetical Coastal Area

with the traditional state role of land use planning and regulation, despite the fact that it probably could have used its Commerce Clause power to do just that.

There are also constitutional limits on the exercise of government power. For example, the U.S. Constitution prevents state governments from enforcing a law that infringes on the "privileges and immunities" guaranteed to citizens. Thus, a state law that barred members of a particular race from visiting state beaches would be unconstitutional. Especially with respect to privately owned uplands, one of the most frequently litigated constitutional claims is that rules limiting the use of property have effected a "regulatory taking." The following excerpt explains this claim.

Robert Meltz, Takings Law Today: A Primer for the Perplexed

34 Ecology L.Q. 307, 307-61 (2007)

. . . Takings law flows from eminent domain: the inherent power of the sovereign to take private property, as principally constrained by the "public use" and "just compensation" prerequisites of the Takings Clause. Until the late nineteenth century, eminent domain was invoked almost exclusively in the context of "direct condemnation" suits. In such actions, the government-plaintiff explicitly acknowledges it is using eminent domain against the property being taken, and the property owner typically disputes chiefly the amount of just compensation required. In the 1870s, however, the Supreme Court began to give systematic imprimatur to a very different kind of suit. When the sovereign brought about certain interferences with private property, the Court recognized that the property had been "taken" per the Takings Clause just as surely as if the sovereign had formally condemned. That being so, it concluded, the property owner had a right to sue the government, seeking recovery of the value of the property alleged to have been "taken." The owner could, in other words, assert an unacknowledged exercise of eminent domain. In these suits, in contrast with direct condemnations, there are typically two key issues: Was the property taken, and, if so, how much compensation should the property owner receive?

The owner-plaintiff in such a "taking" or "inverse condemnation" suit generally seeks compensation rather than invalidation of the government act, because the Takings Clause "does not prohibit the taking of private property, but instead places a condition on the exercise of that power" — namely, the payment of just compensation. Takings claims take two forms. As-applied claims contend that regardless of whether the government action effects a taking as to other property, it took the plaintiff's property owing to that property's particular circumstances. Facial claims, which are more difficult to prove, assert that the action took the property even without an inquiry into its circumstances, because under any conceivable scenario there was a taking. Plaintiffs may also assert either temporary or permanent takings.

Takings suits . . . are difficult to win, at least where none of the special-situation per se rules applies. The central demand of the Takings Clause — that the property be "taken" — is held unsatisfied by the overwhelming majority of government actions vis-à-vis private property. . . .

***

The Takings Clause is not implicated unless the government conduct affects "property" cognizable under the clause. Thus, whether the plaintiff has alleged a Takings Clause-recognized property interest is the key threshold substantive inquiry in a taking case. Unilateral expectations and abstract needs are not property entitled to protection. Merely because a government action ends an economically beneficial circumstance that plaintiff would like to continue does not mean that "property" has been affected.

Property interests are not created by the Constitution itself, "rather they are created and their dimensions defined by existing rules or understandings that stem from an independent source such as state law," or, less commonly, federal law. Concepts that define the bounds of a property interest — the sticks in the "bundle of rights" — include the law creating it, existing rules and understandings, and "background principles" of nuisance and property law existing when the property was acquired. In modern usage, the term "property" is said to refer to the rights inhering in the person's relationship to some thing, not the thing itself — though this principle is often honored in the breach by judicial references to a parcel of land as "the property."

The latitude that governments, including courts, have to shape and redefine property concepts is a recurring issue. If this discretion is left unrestrained, Takings Clause protections plainly would be vitiated. Thus, the "government's power to redefine . . . property [is] necessarily constrained by constitutional limits," and "a State, by ipse dixit, may not transform private property into public property without compensation." On the other hand, and key to the issue's complexity, notions of property obviously evolve over time. Thus, new environmental awareness "shapes our evolving understanding of property rights." Further complexity arises when it is unclear whether the government is merely clarifying what a property rule has always been, or is announcing a new rule.

> **Think Back**
>
> In *Phillips*, was the Supreme Court of Mississippi "merely clarifying what a property rule has always been, or . . . announcing a new rule"?

***

Until 1922, the Supreme Court recognized only two types of government actions that triggered, under the Takings Clause, a government duty to compensate: formal appropriation of property and physical invasion thereof. In that year, the notion of the "regulatory taking" was born. In *Pennsylvania Coal Co. v. Mahon*, 260 U.S. 393 (1922), the Court declared that when government regulation of property use goes "too far," a taking may result despite the absence of formal appropriation or physical invasion. Beginning in the late 1970s with the seminal *Penn Central*

Transportation Co. v. New York City, 438 U.S. 104 (1978), decision, the Court initiated an effort, continuing today, to articulate a coherent body of rules or guidelines for determining which government regulations require compensation under the Takings Clause and which do not. . . . [T]his jurisprudence is a mix of per se rules and balancing tests, with an ample amount of ambiguity thrown in.

1. *Lucas* "Total Taking" Rule

In *Lucas v. South Carolina Coastal Council*, 505 U.S. 1003 (1992), the Supreme Court held that government regulation completely eliminating the economic use (and seemingly value, too) of land is a per se "total taking." Though described by the Court as one of its two categorical takings rules, along with the *Loretto v. Teleprompter Manhattan CATV Corp.*, 458 U.S. 419 (1982), permanent physical occupation rule, this rule contains a big exception. Despite complete elimination of use and/or value, a restriction is not a taking if it merely duplicates what could have been achieved under "background principles of the State's law of property and nuisance" existing when the plaintiff acquired the land. Such background principles limit the rights that the plaintiff acquired in the property. Plainly, there can be no taking when a government restriction eliminates a right the landowner never had.

***

2. *Penn Central* "Partial Regulatory Taking" Test

When the *Lucas* test is inapplicable — that is, when the government interference falls short of completely eliminating use and/or value — courts use the test announced in *Penn Central*. Unlike the categorical *Lucas* rule, the *Penn Central* test involves multifactor balancing; to determine whether a partial regulatory taking has occurred, the court examines the government action for its (1) economic impact on the property owner, (2) degree of interference with the owner's reasonable investment-backed expectations, and (3) character. These factors are mere guideposts, with (so far) only modest content — as much an analytical framework as a "test." Nor are they necessarily exhaustive. The Court stresses that a partial regulatory taking analysis is not governed by "set formula," but rather is an "essentially ad hoc, factual inquiry" [citation omitted].

***

The *Penn Central* test has rarely been invoked successfully in the Supreme Court, except where a special feature of the challenged regulation, such as physical invasion, total taking, or interference with a fundamental property interest, triggered categorical analysis. This situation led some observers during the 1990s to suggest that only the Court's categorical takings tests — those for total takings and physical occupations — retained vitality. Since 2000, however, no fewer than three decisions of the Court have made clear that outside the "relatively narrow" per se rule situations, *Penn Central* reigns triumphant. Thus, when falling short of a *Lucas* total wipeout, a plaintiff still may have suffered a partial regulatory taking under *Penn Central.*

Notwithstanding the Court's recent reinvigoration of the *Penn Central* test, it has shed little light on the content of the test's three factors, or on how to balance them. Each factor raises "vexing subsidiary questions" [citation omitted]. Commentators on property owner and government sides alike have harshly criticized the lack of definition in the factors, particularly now that the Court has had more than a quarter-century to illuminate them. . . .

a. [*Penn Central* Factor 1:] Economic Impact

The *Penn Central* inquiry "turns in large part, albeit not exclusively" on the economic impact factor and the degree of interference with property interests.

i. Use or Value?

Penn Central stated no preference for whether economic impact is to be measured in terms of remaining economic use or remaining market value. Just as in the *Lucas* total takings analysis, many courts today focus on remaining economic use. . . .

ii. Degree of Loss Required

The Supreme Court has never given us definite numbers — it has never said that a value loss less than a specified percentage of pre-regulation value precludes a regulatory taking, or that one greater than some threshold (short of a total taking) points strongly toward a taking. The Court has said several things, however, indicating that the economic impact generally must be very substantial, or arguably severe, where the other *Penn Central* factors are not determinative.

Perhaps most cogent as to the need for substantial loss, the Court said in *Lingle v. Chevron USA*, 544 U.S. 528 (2005), that the regulatory taking inquiry asks at bottom whether the restriction is the functional equivalent of a physical occupation or appropriation of the land. It is difficult to argue that small to moderate economic impacts are the functional equivalents of appropriations or ousters. The functional equivalency standard of *Lingle* might be the most useful direction we have yet received from the Court as to the meaning of the economic impact and other *Penn Central* factors. Also pointing to a substantial-loss prerequisite, the Court remarked that land use regulation may "under extreme circumstances" result in a taking. Somewhat less useful as to the required degree of economic impact, the Court says that mere diminution in property value, short of a total wipeout, cannot by itself establish a taking, citing cases in which value diminutions upwards of 75 percent were upheld. Most broadly, the Court tells us that "government hardly could go on if to some extent values incident to property could not be diminished without paying for every such change in the general law." And that being deprived of a parcel's most profitable use ("highest and best use") is not, without more, a taking.

***

vii. Offsetting Direct Benefits

When regulatory programs provide benefits directly to the property owner, courts may offset them against the economic impact. In *Penn Central*, the Court held that transferable development rights conferred on the landowner "mitigate whatever financial burdens the law has imposed . . . and . . . are to be taken into account in considering the impact of regulation" [citation omitted]. Thus, it seems that direct benefits may offset economic impacts even though they do not relate to the remaining economic uses of the parcel on which the taking is alleged to have occurred.

The alternative to considering a direct benefit in the taking analysis would be to confine it to, at most, the calculation of compensation once a taking was found. The argument is that where benefits do not relate to the remaining uses of the parcel, they are outside the proper concern of the taking determination. Moreover, the argument continues, including benefits in the taking analysis allows the government to deflect takings claims on the cheap, since even a small direct benefit may confer enough economic value to result, under *Penn Central*, in a no-taking holding. . . .

b. [*Penn Central* Factor 2:] Reasonable Investment-Backed Expectations

This factor has been castigated by the property rights bar as introducing a psychological element into the extent of a constitutional protection, but the Supreme Court shows no sign of demoting it. The analysis is often seen as having two steps: (1) Did the claimant have actual investment-backed expectations? and (2) Were those expectations objectively reasonable? As to the second step, a reasonable investment-backed expectation must be more than a unilateral expectation or abstract need. . . . As introduced by *Penn Central*, this factor appeared to refer only to the property owner's expectations at the time of his investment. Later decisions indicate that post-investment events, including the owner's failure to seek development approval as new regulations came into being, may be relevant.

i. Pre-Acquisition Regulation ("Notice Rule")

During the 1990s, several state supreme courts and a few federal circuits adopted, at least arguably, an absolute notice rule. Under this rule, no regulatory taking claim could be entertained on the basis of a government land use restriction imposed pursuant to laws or regulations existing when the land was acquired by the plaintiff—or the adoption of which after acquisition was foreseeable. Courts based the rule on either the investment-backed expectations factor of *Penn Central* or the background principles concept of *Lucas*.

In 2001, the Supreme Court in *Palazzolo v. Rhode Island*, 533 U.S. 606 (2001), struck down the absolute version of the notice rule, but left undecided whether the preexisting regulatory regime still plays some less-than-dispositive role in the takings analysis. . . . Justice O'Connor's concurrence argued that it does have a role. . . . Her concurrence has proved influential: post-*Palazzolo* decisions, principally in the Federal Circuit, continue to give substantial weight to pre-acquisition regulatory schemes. These decisions often cite three factors: (1) Is it a highly regulated industry or activity? (2) Was plaintiff aware of the problem that spawned the regulation when the property was acquired? and (3) Could the regulation have been reasonably anticipated? A pre-acquisition regulatory scheme is a particular obstacle for takings plaintiffs, such as land developers, who have experience with the scheme prior to acquiring the property, on the theory that they are especially "on notice" [citation omitted].

ii. "Heavily Regulated Field"

Those who voluntarily enter a "heavily regulated field" find regulatory takings claims especially difficult to maintain. Such entities are said to lack a reasonable expectation that the legislature will not enact new requirements from time to time that buttress the regulatory scheme. The list of human activities labeled by courts as heavily regulated fields continues to grow. Since 2001 the Federal Circuit also has incorporated the "heavily regulated field" factor into its determination of the weight to be given pre-acquisition regulatory schemes. But not all expectations are unreasonable in a heavily regulated field; if the new law departs sufficiently from the pre-acquisition pattern of legislation, a taking may still be found. It appears that no court has yet said that land use generally is a heavily regulated field, with all that determination would entail for landowners seeking to establish takings.

iii. Buyer Knew, or Should Have Known, That Economic Prospects Were Particularly Uncertain

This factor plainly undermines the reasonable investment-backed expectations of the land buyer, cutting against a later regulatory taking claim. Examples include a person who acknowledges at the time of purchase that regulatory approvals will be hard to obtain, who is or should be aware at such time of government planning affecting economic prospects, or who pays substantially less for the parcel than its unregulated value.

iv. Initially Limited Intentions of Property Buyer

Those who buy land with limited economic intentions, and who keep the parcel in low-intensity use for years, may be barred from asserting a taking when later regulations thwart the owner's expanded development desires.

***

c. [*Penn Central* Factor 3:] Character of Government Action

This is the *Penn Central* test's most elastic factor. When first announced, the Court explained it only as meaning that takings "may more readily be found when the interference with property can be characterized as a physical invasion by government . . . than when interference arises from some public program adjusting the benefits and burdens of economic life to promote the common good" [citation omitted]. This physical/regulatory distinction remains the most important element of the character factor, though the Court has since added others.

***

ii. Benefit Creation Versus Harm Avoidance

According to a classic litmus test, a government restriction viewed as creating a public benefit (e.g., a park) is compensable, while a restriction seen as averting a public harm (e.g., pollution) is not. In 1992, *Lucas* criticized this benefit-creation/harm-avoidance dichotomy, branding it as value-laden and easily manipulated. But while less invoked by courts in situations susceptible to both characterizations, the distinction still appears to influence courts *sub silentio* in other contexts, and is even cited explicitly on occasion. As a result, exercises of the police power that directly protect public health and safety, such as preventing pollution of a community's water supply, remain unlikely to be a taking under *Penn Central*.

***

iv. Average Reciprocity of Advantage

This inquiry looks at whether a restriction not only burdens the landowner, but also benefits him indirectly by subjecting other similarly situated landowners to the same sort of restriction. The paradigmatic example is zoning: a homeowner is required to forego, say, commercial use of his property, but benefits from others in the area being restricted in the same way. . . .

***

ix. "Singling Out" Property Owner Versus General Application

The fact that a government action "singles out" the plaintiff from similarly situated landowners is often said to raise a taking (and equal protection) issue. The rationale appears to be that singling out offends "fairness and justice" and suggests bad faith, or points to an absence of average reciprocity of advantage. Similarly, when the government seeks to remedy a widespread social ill not attributable to any particular group, concentrating the remedial burden on such a group (particularly when there are alternatives) may tip the character factor toward supporting a taking.

3. Parcel-as-a-Whole Rule

Under *Penn Central*, a court must assess the economic loss to the property owner and the degree of interference with her expectations, and under *Lucas*, at least the former. Critically, this inquiry focuses on the proportionate rather than absolute size of the loss — that is, it compares what the government action took from the property owner with what the owner still has. To assess what the owner still has, the court must define the extent of the plaintiff's property to be included in the analysis.

This quantum of property is called the "parcel as a whole" or "relevant parcel." Not surprisingly, the property owner wants the relevant parcel defined narrowly so as to enhance the proportionate impact of the government action, while the government wants it defined broadly so as to diminish the proportionate impact. A court's determination of the parcel as a whole may easily decide the case. While state law is often key to defining which interests are afforded federal Takings Clause protection as property, it is federal law that determines how those interests are aggregated for purposes of determining the relevant parcel.

***

points for discussion

1. *A hotbed of takings cases.* Many takings cases involve coastal property. Why do you think this is? The takings cases in this book are not just important takings cases involving coastal property; they are important takings cases, period.
2. *Regulatory takings and judicial takings.* As a general matter, takings cases are based on the claim that a particular statute or regulation, that is, an action of the legislature or of an executive branch agency, has effected a taking of property. In a recent U.S. Supreme Court case, *Stop the Beach Renourishment v. Florida Department of Environmental Protection*, 560 U.S. 702 (2010), the plaintiff argued that a decision of the Supreme Court of Florida, specifically that court's definition of Florida law on littoral rights, had taken their property. (We will read parts of these two opinions in Chapter 8.) Although the Court found that no compensation was owed, a plurality — for the first time — recognized the potential viability of such a claim. This development is particularly relevant to coastal law because so much coastal law — like the littoral rights at issue in that case — is common law.
3. *Defenses to takings claims.* As Meltz notes, the threshold issue in proving a takings claim is establishing that the law, regulation, or judicial decision has impacted the value or usefulness of a property interest belonging to the plaintiff. Government defendants often focus their efforts on this issue because winning on that issue results in winning the case; if the government action did not "touch" plaintiff's property then the court's inquiry need not go any further.

   One of the classic "no property" arguments is that the government acted to prevent a public nuisance. *See, e.g., Hadacheck v. Sebastian,* 239 U.S. 394 (1915); *Mugler v. Kansas,* 123 U.S. 623 (1887). Let's say plaintiff had built a factory to produce bricks, and that plaintiff was not able to operate the brick-making factory without producing toxic dust that threatened public health. A law prohibiting brick-making would obviously have severe economic consequences for plaintiff; while she might be able to sell her equipment to a brick-maker elsewhere and use the real estate for some other purpose, she will be less well off than she was before passage of the law. In asserting the "public nuisance defense," the government is arguing that, because brick-making harms public health, the law merely prevented plaintiff from using the equipment and real property in a way that she was not entitled to do in the first place. In other words, the law did not affect any of the plaintiff's legitimate property rights. This defense raises some very difficult questions: Was brick-making a legitimate use of property prior to passage of the law? If so, shouldn't the public have to compensate for the plaintiff's loss of property? If not, how could plaintiff have known that she shouldn't have invested in brick-making? Should the government be free to edit the list of public nuisances as time goes by?

There are two other "no property" defenses that the government can use in coastal cases. As illustrated by *Kaiser Aetna*, the federal government can argue that property alleged to have been taken was subject to the navigation servitude. States can make a similar argument based on the public trust doctrine. In *McQueen v. South Carolina Coastal Council*, 354 S.C. 142 (2003), *cert. denied*, 540 U.S. 982 (2003), the State of South Carolina denied McQueen's application for a permit to build a bulkhead around, then fill in, a part of his property that had gradually eroded into the adjacent saltwater canal. Without the permit, and the bulkhead and fill, McQueen was not able to build a home on the property because the remaining upland area was of insufficient size. McQueen sued the state, claiming that the denial of the permit effected a *Lucas* taking of his property, that is, it rendered the land completely valueless. While it recognized the extent of the economic impact on the plaintiff, the Supreme Court of South Carolina denied his takings claim, holding that "[t]he tidelands included on McQueen's lots are public trust property subject to control of the State. McQueen's ownership rights do not include the right to backfill or place bulkheads on public trust land and the State need not compensate him for the denial of permits to do what he cannot otherwise do." *Id.* at 150. *See also Esplanade Props., LLC v. City of Seattle*, 307 F.3d 978 (9th Cir. 2002).

4. *What is the whole parcel?* The government might also focus its defense of a takings case on the first prong of *Penn Central*, "diminution in value." Specifically, the government can try to frame the property right(s) affected by the regulation as representing just one of many rights held by the owner in the property. As an example, consider the developer who purchases a ten-acre lot intending to build ten houses on acre lots. The developer builds and sells the first nine houses, but it turns out that the tenth lot is jurisdictional wetland under Section 404 of the Clean Water Act and that the Army Corps will not grant her a permit to fill. Given that the developer cannot build anything on the lot, what is the most accurate way to characterize the diminution in value she has suffered as a result of the Corps' decision? Is it 10 percent or 100 percent? Another way to put this is: What is the "denominator," the ten-acre parcel or the one-acre lot? *Cf. United States v. Riverside Bayview Homes*, 474 U.S. 121 (1985). The answer to this question would be

hugely important in determining the outcome in the case. In a recent decision, *Murr v. Wisconsin*, 137 S. Ct. 1933 (2017), the Court held that:

> . . . no single consideration can supply the exclusive test for determining the denominator. Instead, courts must consider a number of factors. These include the treatment of the land under state and local law; the physical characteristics of the land; and the prospective value of the regulated land. The endeavor should determine whether reasonable expectations about property ownership would lead a landowner to anticipate that his holdings would be treated as one parcel, or, instead, as separate tracts. The inquiry is objective, and the reasonable expectations at issue derive from background customs and the whole of our legal tradition.

Id. at 1945.

F. CHAPTER SUMMARY

1. **Geographic reach of state coastal common law such as the public trust doctrine and riparian and littoral rights.** Each state defines its public waterways for purposes of determining the dry and submerged lands to which common law applies.

2. **The legal coastline.** Similarly, except with respect to parcels for which ownership can be traced to a federal grant, each state has the power to determine the location of the boundary between uplands and public waterways. Most states use the high-water mark. Most high-water-mark states define "high water" as the mean-high-tide line.

3. **The three-mile boundary.** As a general matter, state jurisdiction extends three nautical miles seaward from the coast. It is unclear whether areas beyond the immediate coastline are covered by the public trust doctrine because such areas were not included in original public trust endowments.

4. **The expanding scope of the public trust doctrine.** Courts and legislatures can expand the scope of the public trust doctrine either explicitly or through new interpretations of old law. While a few states have been aggressive in expanding the geographic scope of the doctrine, it appears that most states hew to more traditional interpretations.

5. **Federal power.** Because of the close connection between the Commerce Clause and navigable waterways, the federal government has both a great deal of power with respect to, and strong interest in, coastal areas. Congress can exercise a lesser, but still significant, degree of Commerce Clause power in regulating activities affecting uplands or non-navigable waters.

6. **The Coastal Zone Management Act and state law.** Despite the obvious national interest in coastal land use, Congress refrained from taking a lead role in the area, deferring to the states. In response to the CZMA, states have expanded common law coastal jurisdiction beyond traditional public trust areas and riparian and littoral lands. Each state has defined its coastal zone differently.

7. **Takings.** Although government has a great deal of power to regulate use of coastal lands, this power is limited by the Takings Clause of the Fifth Amendment to the U.S. Constitution (and similar provisions in state constitutions). Both the federal navigational servitude and state public trust doctrines can be used as defenses to takings claims.

Chapter Review Questions

- Which upland owners are entitled to common law riparian and littoral rights?
- Which lands and natural resources are contained in the "public trust" corpus managed by the state? (We will learn about the trust rules, that is, rules related to use and alienation of public trust assets, in Chapter 7. For now, we will focus on simply identifying the nature of the assets in the trust.)
- How and why have some states enlarged the geographic scope of their public trust doctrines over time?
- Which enumerated powers of the U.S. Constitution provide the federal government with the authority to regulate state and private activities in coastal areas?
- What are some of the key political and constitutional limits on the power of state and federal government to regulate coastal land use?

G. SUGGESTED READING

Robin Kundis Craig, *Beyond* SWANCC: *The New Federalism and Clean Water Act Jurisdiction*, 33 ENVTL. L. 113 (2003).

Thomas E. McKnight, *Title to Lands in the Coastal Zone: Their Complexities and Impact on Real Estate Transactions*, 47 CAL. ST. B.J. 408 (1972).

Eva H. Morreale, *Federal Power in Western Waters: The Navigation Power and the Rule of No Compensation*, 3 NAT. RESOURCES J. 1, 21 (1963).

Joseph L. Sax, *Takings and the Police Power*, 74 YALE L.J. 36 (1964).

Barton H. Thompson, Jr., *Judicial Takings*, 76 VA. L. REV. 1449 (1990).

Charles F. Wilkinson, *The Headwaters of the Public Trust: Some Thoughts on the Source and Scope of the Traditional Doctrine*, 19 ENVTL. L. 425 (1989).

chapter 7

The Public Trust Doctrine

Although it has now been supplemented in many states by statutes or constitutional provisions, the common law public trust doctrine is the root of coastal law. Moreover, because it is more widely relevant in coastal areas than in other parts of the country, it is one of the reasons that coastal law is unique (and thus merits its own course).

While the term "public trust doctrine" did not appear in an American court decision until 1936,[1] the basic proposition of the doctrine — that *the public has the right to access and to use public waterways* — has been recognized for thousands of years by emperors, kings, queens, governors, scholars, and courts. Although the basic proposition is not disputed today, the doctrine is surrounded by substantial legal uncertainty. (As we saw in Chapter 6, even basic issues, such as the definition of "public waterways," are murky.) This chapter examines these gray areas by exploring such questions as:

- What, exactly, does "public trust" mean? If state governments literally hold submerged lands and public waterways in trust for the benefit of the public, what are the terms of the trust agreement? For example, can state governments sell, lease, or otherwise dispose of trust assets?
- Is the public trust doctrine best described as common law? How else might we describe it? Do state legislatures have the power to modify or eliminate it?
- What does it mean to say that the public has a right of access? Do state governments have an affirmative duty to ensure or enhance public access? To what extent can government regulate access? What happens when one member of the public's use of trust resources interferes with another's?
- Finally, does the doctrine impose an affirmative duty on government to manage submerged lands and other trust assets? In other words, does it require government to maintain environmental quality within trust areas?

---

1. The exact phrase first appears in a case entitled *Ne-Bo-Shone Ass'n, Inc. v. Hogarth*, 81 F.2d 70 (6th Cir. 1936).

We start with a brief look at two historical sources to which American courts frequently cite: the *Institutes* of Justinian and the Magna Carta. These sources highlight the rationales for treating public waterways and submerged lands differently from other things owned by the government. Moreover, they illustrate the very long tradition behind the modern public trust doctrine.

A. HISTORICAL ROOTS OF THE DOCTRINE

Many ancient cultures either recognized public rights in or, to the same effect, did not recognize private rights in, certain natural resources. American courts, though, have drawn primarily on Roman and British law in shaping the American version of the doctrine. (If you recall, the *Matthews* decision is a good example of this.)

1. Roman Law

After Justinian became Roman emperor in 527 A.D., he convened experts known as "jurisconsults" from throughout the empire to produce a digest of Roman law as well as a textbook, the *Institutes*. In the following excerpt, the author describes the state of coastal law in Rome, circa 530 A.D.

As you read these passages, try to visualize the world in which these concepts and rules arose: The sea and rivers were equivalent to our interstate highways and train lines in terms of their importance to transportation and commerce; most people lived subsistence existences, and to the extent that they lived near rivers or the sea, were likely to derive a significant percentage of the protein in their diets from fish; and people knew relatively little about the sea other than that it was sometimes dangerous and provided what appeared to be endless supplies of fish.

Richard Perruso, The Development of the Doctrine of *Res Communes* in Medieval and Early Modern Europe

70 L. Hist. Rev. 69, 70-75 (2002)

Common Property in the Digest

The treatment of the sea and shore in the *Institutes* of Justinian appears to reflect the synthesis of three separate legal principles articulated in the opinions of the Digest: 1) a mandated public access to seas, shores, rivers and river banks for commercial purposes; 2) the application of the doctrine of *occupatio*, or acquisition by a first taker, to sea and shore property; 3) an idea, based on non-legal literature and reflected only in the opinion attributed to the jurist Marcian, that air, flowing water, the seas and the shores were "common to all men."

1. *Public Access.* It was widely held among the Roman jurisconsults that the sea and the shores, as well as most rivers and riverbanks, served certain important public functions, such as fishing and navigation, and that public access to these areas ought to be protected. This public right of access is not to be confused with public, i.e. state, ownership. Not all state-owned property involved public access, and riverbanks enjoyed public access even though the property was private and belonged to the owner of the neighboring estate.

Thus no one could interfere with another's lawful use of the sea, shore, rivers or riverbanks. Someone who was prevented from fishing in the sea or carrying on some other kind of lawful activity could obtain an *actio iniuriarum* against the person who prevented him, just as he could if he were prevented from taking a seat at the theater or a public bath. This was considered a personal action, not a property action; the individual who was prevented from fishing in the sea could not bring a property action (such as an interdict) because he was deemed to have no property interest in the sea.

> **Quick Question**
>
> Does a similar kind of "personal action" exist in modern American law?

2. *Occupatio.* Under Roman law, wild animals and birds were *res nullius*, i.e., things belonging to no one, and became the property of the first person to reduce them to possession. Gaius says that wild animals are conceded to the possessor by natural reason (*id ratione naturali occupanti conceditur*). If the animal escaped, however, it again became a *res nullius*, and subject to ownership by any other person who subsequently reduced it to possession. This means of acquiring ownership was called *occupatio.* Florentinus applied the doctrine of *occupatio* to pebbles and gems found on the shore.

Roman law permitted building on the shore so long as public use of the shore was not inconvenienced. This was in itself a departure from the ordinary rules concerning public property, which forbade private construction in public places. In addition, Neratius said that the builder became the owner of the shore property itself so long as the building remained standing. The shore ground was thus acquired by *occupatio.* However, if the building came down, the shore property reverted to its original state. This was consistent with the treatment of wild animals. Pomponius applied this rule to buildings constructed on piles in the sea, and to buildings on islands arising in the sea. However, the rule did not apply to construction on riverbanks.

3. *Common Property*

* * *

[M]ost of the Digest opinions characterize all property that was set aside from private ownership and provided for the use of everyone as public, not common. This is consistent with the distinctions set out in the *Institutes* of Gaius.

* * *

Several distinct constellations of meanings for the word *communis* can be discerned in these works. In the *De Officiis*, Cicero admonishes that no one should deprive another of those things that cost nothing to give. . . .

* * *

As examples of these common things, Cicero gives flowing water (*aquaprofluens*), fire, and honest counsel. Cicero's argument is against hoarding things that can be shared without sacrifice. To prevent another from taking water from a flowing stream can only be an act of malice, since the owner is in no way impoverished by sharing.

While the *De Officiis* is primarily an ethical and philosophical work, the legal implication in the above passage is that legislatures have not assigned property rights to certain types of property because of their widespread availability. Flowing water, fire, and honest counsel are thus outside the established system of property rights.

* * *

A second and somewhat different idea is found in Seneca's *De Beneficiis*. Seneca, in the *De Beneficiis*, states that some types of property by their physical nature do not lend themselves to individual possession. . . . By their physical nature the sea and the wind are not capable of being monopolized, that is, of being effectively claimed as property.

Ovid also mentions common property. In his *Metamorphoses*, Ovid describes an Iron Age of history in which private property in land was created for the first time. . . . Ovid thus offers a historical context for common property by suggesting that prior to the invention of private property, all property was held in common. . . . Such ideas appear to have been responsible for the creation of a separate class of things that, at least in their entirety, were not subject to ownership by anyone. However, the question still remains how Marcian and the compilers of the *Corpus Iuris* intended the treatment of the common sea and shore to be different in practical terms from that of those areas (roads, rivers, etc.) designated as public.

* * *

When Marcian's opinion . . . is interpreted in the light of the literary and philosophical writings discussed above, it may be read to suggest that, unlike for public areas (many of which, like roads, might serve a particular government function) state jurisdiction was exercised over common areas only to ensure that everyone had access to them. Implicit in this is the idea that the state should also refrain from interfering with everyone's use of these areas.

This implication cannot be read as a juridical limitation on state authority. No legal remedy was available for interference by the Roman state; the *actio iniuriarum* was available only against private interferences. Nevertheless, Marcian's opinion . . . may be read to imply that the state, regardless of its authority, ought not to interfere with fishing or navigation on the sea. Thus Bonfante refers to "the international community of use" as an "ethical concept."

Common Property in the Institutes of Justinian

The approach of the Roman jurisconsults had largely been to formulate particular rules for particular types of property (e.g., shores, rivers, roads), rather than to attempt any systematic approach to property law. This reflects the pragmatic approach of classical jurists who typically illustrated a rule with a particular example and avoided becoming involved in theoretical discussion. As a result, they were willing to develop different rules for roads, rivers, and seas, even though most jurisconsults regarded all of these areas as "public." For example, building might be permitted on shores even though it was not permitted on other types of public property.

Book II, Title I of the *Institutes* of Justinian suggests a more systematic approach to property law by establishing four categories of non-private property: *res publica*, *res communes*, *res universitatis*, and *res nullius*. The text provides examples for each category. *Res publica*, public things, were the property of the state. *Res communes*, common things, were the property of all men. *Res universitatis*, communal things, were those things owned by a community other than the state, such as theaters and stadiums owned by a city. *Res nullius*, things of no one, included both those things that were *res sacra*, *i.e.*, religious property owned by God or the Christian church, and things which had never been acquired by anyone, such as wild animals.

De usu et proprietate littorum.

§ V. Littorum quoque usus publicus est, et juris gentium, sicut et ipsius maris; et ob id cuilibet liberum est casam ibi ponere, in quam se recipiat, sicut retia siccare, et ex mari deducere; proprietas autem eorum potest intelligi nullius esse: sed ejusdem juris esse, cujus et mare, et, quæ subjacet mari, terra vel arena.

§ 5. *The use of the sea-shore, as well as of the sea, is also public by the law of nations; and therefore any person may erect a cottage upon it, to which he may resort to dry his nets, and hawl them from the water; for the shores are not understood to be property in any man, but are compared to the sea itself, and to the sand or ground which is under the sea.*

Google Books

Figure 7-1. *Institutes* of Justinian
Book II, Title I, Section 5 of the *Institutes* of Justinian. From an 1812 translation by Thomas Cooper.

Under the *Institutes*, air, flowing water, the sea and seashores are "common under natural law." Rivers and ports are public, and the right to fish in rivers is open to all. It has been suggested that the author . . . originally may have intended for "*aqua profluens*," or "flowing water," to refer to rivers, and for rivers to be included as common property. In any case, the classification of rivers as public in the *Institutes* precluded this interpretation in the Middle Ages. Instead, the medieval glossators and commentators would typically equate *aqua profluens* with "*aqua de celo defluens*" or "*pluvia,*" *i.e.,* "water flowing from heaven," or "rain." Riverbanks under the *Institutes* are private, and belong to the riparian owners, as do the trees growing on them.

Certain ambiguities and inconsistencies in the *Institutes'* discussion of the shore and sea may reflect the haste of the compilation or may have resulted from the difficulties of integrating the various opinions of the jurisconsults into a single text. Thus, while the sea and shores are said to be common, the shores are also said to be *res nullius,* the property of no one. The use of the seashores and of the sea is said to be public by the *ius gentium,* the law of nations, as is the use of the riverbanks.

More importantly, while the *Institutes* establish a distinction between public and common property, they provide no explanation for why air, sea, shore and flowing water are classified as common, while rivers are classified as public. Nor is there any explanation of what practical consequences, if any, result from the classification of property as common, rather than public.

2. British Law

In addition to Roman law, one of the most powerful forces in shaping British common law, and thus American common law, was the Magna Carta, also sometimes known as the Magna Charta. As described by Professor Helmholz, a leading legal historian:

The [Magna Carta] is widely familiar among educated men and women as the most famous concession of legal rights made by the English king to his subjects. The events that led up to it are also widely known. By the latter part of his reign, King John had lost the confidence of the great men of his kingdom. Habitual indifference to accepted standards of justice, reckless assertion of regalian rights over the church, extravagant military expenditures with little to show for them, and loss of the bulk of his continental possessions to the king of France at the Battle of Bouvines in 1214 had

Joseph Martin Kronheim

Figure 7-2. King John Signs the Magna Carta

combined to sap their confidence in him. In the wake of this humiliating defeat and in the face of a rebellion coming from the north of England, Archbishop Stephen Langton, William Marshal, and a group of moderate barons sought to force John to establish rules that would set right what had been done wrong. They produced a list of grievances, some taken from a distant past, some seemingly based upon the Coronation Charter of Henry I, and some of more recent invention. At Runnymede in June 1215, they compelled John to put his seal to a long list of concessions that would, they hoped, remedy the abuses that had occurred. If the king could be made to abide by them, peace in the realm might return and respect for the law might be restored.

R.H. Helmholz, *Magna Carta and the Ius Commune*, 66 U. Chi. L. Rev. 297, 297-98 (1999).

Thus, the Magna Carta has for over 800 years been the primary source in British law of rules governing the legal relationship between the sovereign and citizens. As the following excerpt describes, one of the issues between King John and the barons related to the King's practice of granting private fishing rights in tidal rivers.

Note: The Public Trust in Tidal Areas: A Sometime Submerged Traditional Doctrine

79 Yale L.J. 762, 764-67 (1970)

The Dark Ages

As is well known, with the decline of the Roman Empire, Europe retrogressed in terms of commerce, navigation, and effective governmental administration. Public ownership of waterways and tidal areas frequently gave way to ownership by local powers and feudatories. Many continental princes, for example, came to claim that the right to fish was their personal property and required that all their fishermen be licensed for a fee. In the British Isles, then a thinly populated frontier, this process of decentralizing control was far advanced by the time of the Domesday Book [1086 A.D. — Eds.]. The English King's jurisdictional and sovereign claims to tidal areas became confused with a personal private property claim, a confusion handily furthered to this day by successors in interest to the King, notably the American states. The King claimed a private interest in tidal and riverbed soil, and consequently the private right to whatever could be found on or under the soil — be it sand, stones, minerals, seaweed and shells (for fertilizer), or deserted wrecks or flotsam that washed up onto the shore. He also claimed the right to "several fishery" (an exclusive private right to fish) in these areas. Since private ownership always entails the right to alienate, and since the King could not easily enjoy these interests everywhere directly, Saxon grants, confirmed and extended by the Norman kings, vested the largest portion of the English foreshore in particular subjects. Several especially anomalous aspects of this royal grab for property survived well into the modern age. In theory, the Crown had the exclusive right to certain types of fish, and it retained the right to take a net down many of the kingdom's rivers several times a year through all private fisheries. Between what the King claimed for himself and what the lords received by grant or took by prescription, the old common ownership in the public provided for in Roman law was seriously if unevenly eroded.

Magna Charta

This process of proliferating private ownership and control of tidal areas led to increasing public inconvenience. The Magna Charta, in part a reaction to these inconveniences, can be seen as a salient point at which the doctrinal trend began to shift back in the direction of protecting the public's interest, especially in the areas of navigation and fishery rights. The steps taken in this period, however, were insignificant when compared with those which have since been attributed to it. Every grain of public interest protection to be found in the Magna Charta was subsequently seized upon and developed to illogical and unhistorical lengths by a legal system struggling to adapt the law of the foreshore to new and more demanding economic and political conditions. In the process of developing ("interpreting") the terms of the contract made at Runnymede, the courts, while never abandoning the original Roman conception of a general common ownership in all the people, began to speak in terms of particular guaranteed rights. The resulting doctrinal ambiguity continues to this day, although the emphasis on particular public rights or easements has become dominant. By considering both what the Magna Charta actually provided and what has since been claimed for it, we can get a pretty clear idea of how far, and in what direction, the common law has moved over the centuries.

At the time of Magna Charta, river navigation was threatened by the large number of weirs (permanent fishing structures fixed to the bottom) and other such devices — so much so that Chapter 33 specifically prohibits them: "All kydells [weirs] for the future shall be removed altogether from Thames and Medway, and throughout all England, *except upon the seashore.*" [Emphasis added.]

The common law developed this simple provision a very great distance as it sought to broaden the public's interest. Although the provision in all versions of

Photo: Edward Sheriff Curtis/Library of Congress

Figure 7-3. Fish Weir
This photo of a Native American fish weir, taken in 1923, illustrates the potential impact on navigation.

the Charter prohibits weirs only, and then only in inland waters, the presumed general intent to insure unobstructed passage for navigation has been seized upon as a basis for repeated assertions that the super-sanction of Magna Charta prohibited *all* obstructions.

The exception made in the last four words of Chapter 33, "except upon the seashore" (*nisi per costeram maris*), seems to render this part of the Charter almost useless to those championing the public interest in tidal areas. If anything, it is harmful in that it has been interpreted by Lord Hale to imply that the seabed below the low water mark (where most weirs were located) might be alienable to private property holders. This chapter is the basis on which Magna Charta has been cited, with some considerable exaggeration, as grounds for a public easement in freely navigable waterways, but it cannot be stretched to cover what it specifically excepts.

This chapter of Magna Charta has also been interpreted to bar several fisheries by extrapolation from its banning one of their most effective tools. However, the protection of navigation provides a more convincing and complete rationale. Weirs are a much more likely impediment to navigation in rivers than in the sea. Moreover, it seems unlikely that the king would have allowed fishing monopolies in the sea and not in inland waters, where a larger proportion of the potential fishing areas were claimed by the riparian owners.

> **The King's Forest**
>
> "The word 'forest' had acquired an exact technical meaning, and was applied to certain wide districts, scattered irregularly throughout England, reserved to the Crown for purposes of sport. Here the wild boar and deer of various species found shelter, in which they were protected by the severe regulations of the 'Forest Law.' . . . A 'forest' was a district where this law prevailed to the exclusion of the common law which ruled outside." WILLIAM S. McKECHNIE, MAGNA CARTA: A COMMENTARY ON THE GREAT CHARTER OF KING JOHN 414-15, 424 (1914).
>
> Afforestation added to the boundaries of the forests by royal decree, and disafforestation removed the distinction of "forest" from lands.

The only other portion of Magna Charta faintly related to the public interest in waters or tidal areas is Chapter 47: "All forests that have been made such in our time shall forthwith be disafforested; and a similar course shall be followed with regard to river-banks that have been placed *'in defense'* by us in our time." [Emphasis added.] Although there is no specific exception of tidal areas here, there is also no mention of them.

points for discussion

1. *Natural law.* According to Perruso, "[u]nder the *Institutes*, air, flowing water, the sea and seashores are 'common under natural law.'" What is natural law? Based on your experience, does it have a place in the American legal system?

2. *Gray area.* While both the Digest and the *Institutes* provide support for the idea of public access, they do not leave us with a perfectly clear picture of what *public access* means, and more important, what it means for government to ensure that access. So, for example, while the Digest states that "no one could interfere with another's lawful use of the sea, shore, rivers or riverbanks," it also says that "Roman law permitted building on the shore so long as public use of the shore was not inconvenienced." Wouldn't a private building on the shore always interfere to some extent with another's lawful use of the shore, even if only that part of the shore located beneath the building? What does it mean to *inconvenience* public use? How might we distinguish between acceptable and unacceptable levels of private claims on the shore?

3. *The* Institutes *as source.* Try searching the phrase "Institutes of Justinian" in a Westlaw or LEXIS federal and state cases database. See if you can find examples of courts correctly or incorrectly citing to the original text. (You may have to add the search term "water" to narrow down the results.) For a complete version of the *Institutes*, see THOMAS COLLETT SANDARS, THE INSTITUTES OF JUSTINIAN WITH ENGLISH INTRODUCTION, TRANSLATION, AND NOTES (5th London ed. 1876).

4. *Conceptions of the trust.* Perhaps the most significant difference between the Roman and British law constructs of the public trust doctrine is that, under the British version, the King is presumed to own all property while, under the Roman version, certain property is deemed to be communally owned. As the author of the second excerpt points out, the fact of royal ownership creates the possibility of a trust analogy; in order to have a trust, there must be someone to hold legal title to the property, that is, a trustee. Who is the trustee in the Roman version? Is it different to say (1) that the government owns the property, or (2) that the government has a responsibility to ensure public access by, for example, refusing to recognize or enforce private claims? Which view do you think would provide greater security to the public? Why?

B. WHAT DOES THE DOCTRINE REQUIRE OF GOVERNMENT?

As noted, the most basic statement of the public trust doctrine is that *it ensures public access to public waterways.* Of course, the doctrine itself cannot ensure access; it must be enforced.

In this section, we examine government's public trust duties. Court decisions, and academic commentary on those cases, suggest that there are two actual duties and one potential duty. Note that all three of these duties derive from the basic premise of public access.

- *The duty not to dispose of public trust submerged lands.* In most states, courts (or state constitutions) have put limits on the ability of the legislative and executive branches of government to take property out of the trust corpus, that is, to transfer it to a private party "free of the trust." Courts enforce the duty not to dispose both literally and conceptually, placing limits on sales and on actions that impair recognized trust uses. The duty is inherently vague, thus leaving substantial room for judicial discretion. Moreover, courts have created significant exceptions to the general rule of inalienability.

- *The duty to protect basic public access to public waterways.* States must ensure that members of the public can make use of public waterways for traditional public trust uses such as navigation and fishing. Pursuant to this duty, a state would, for example, be required to force the creator of an obstruction that unreasonably impaired navigation to remove that obstruction.

- *The duty to provide meaningful access to public waterways?* There are two "prongs" of the duty to provide meaningful access. First, states might have a responsibility to facilitate public use of trust property, for example, by acquiring easements that allow members of the public to cross privately owned dry sand. Second, states might have a responsibility to ensure that public trust areas are managed in such a way that they support activities such as fishing and recreational wildlife watching. (This is an idea that some scholars have promoted,

> **Quick Question**
>
> Was the Supreme Court of New Jersey trying to fulfill or to establish this duty in *Matthews*?

but few courts have yet to adopt.) The idea here is that physical access for the purpose of fishing, for example, would be meaningless if the state had previously allowed fishermen to wipe out fish stocks.

1. The Duty Not to Dispose

The duty not to dispose is the most important of the three duties. After all, if a state sold all of its public trust assets into private hands, it would no longer be able to ensure public access to them. As you will see in the following cases, the duty not to dispose is confusing for several reasons.

First, there is confusion as to what it is that the state cannot alienate. Like all property, trust property is most accurately viewed as a set of rights. The potential alienation of, say, 50 acres of submerged lands would not only eliminate the public's right to use those submerged lands; it might also impair the public's right to use the waters above those lands for a trust use such as navigation. Should courts focus on the former or the latter?

Second, the duty not to dispose is, in most states, a question of degree. As we will see in the first two cases below, states can dispose of some, but not too much, submerged land. While all states allow the transfer of at least small amounts of submerged lands, only a few appear to permit transfers that would result in the transferee's ability to exclude the public from large areas of what were previously public waterways. There is no bright-line test that can be used to identify the point at which "some" becomes "too much."

Third, while in some states the duty not to dispose is incorporated in statutes or constitutions, in others it is simply part of the common law tradition. In this latter category of states, courts treat the duty not to dispose (and indeed the entire public trust doctrine) in two distinct ways. Some states treat the doctrine as ordinary common law; that is, courts can modify or eliminate the duty as they might other common law rules or doctrines. Fascinatingly, other courts have treated the duty (and the doctrine) as a kind of "super law," immune not only from later court decisions, but also from legislative preemption.

a. The Sovereignty Rationale

In the last chapter, we read a short excerpt of the Supreme Court's decision in *Illinois Central.* As you recall, the Court explained why American courts had, over the course of the nineteenth century, expanded the geographic scope of English common law regarding ownership of submerged lands. While English law had limited royal ownership to "lands covered by tide waters," in America "the same doctrine . . . [is] applicable to . . . 'public navigable water[s], on which commerce is carried on between different states of nations.'" 146 U.S. at 435-37.

In several earlier cases, the Supreme Court had established that, at the founding of the nation, the states had stepped into the shoes of the King, becoming the legal owner of submerged lands within their borders. In the following excerpt from *Illinois Central,* the Court explores the implications of state ownership. Do the states hold title to submerged lands in the same way that a private landowner would hold title to a piece of ordinary property? Do states, in other words, have the right to exclude, to use and enjoy, and to alienate submerged lands?

Illinois Central Railroad Co. v. Illinois

146 U.S. 387 (1892)

Mr. Justice FIELD delivered the opinion of the Court.

***

This suit was commenced on the 1st of March, 1883, in a Circuit Court of Illinois, by an information or bill in equity, filed by the Attorney General of the State, in the name of its people against the Illinois Central Railroad Company, a corporation created under its laws, and against the city of Chicago. . . . [U]pon . . . petition the case was removed to the Circuit Court of the United States for the Northern District of Illinois.

The object of the suit is to obtain a judicial determination of the title of certain lands on the east or lake front of the city of Chicago, situated between the Chicago River and Sixteenth street, which have been reclaimed from the waters of the lake, and are occupied by the tracks, depots, warehouses, piers and other structures used by the railroad company in its business; and also of the title claimed by the company to the submerged lands, constituting the bed of the lake, lying east of its tracks, within the corporate limits of the city, for the distance of a mile, and between the south line of the south pier near Chicago River extended eastwardly, and a line extended, in the same direction, from the south line of lot 21 near the company's round-house and machine shops. The determination of the title of the company will involve a consideration of its right to construct, for its own business, as well as for public convenience, wharves, piers and docks in the harbor.

***

The State of Illinois was admitted into the Union in 1818 on an equal footing with the original States in all respects. Such was one of the conditions of the cession from Virginia of the territory northwest of the Ohio River, out of which the State was formed. But the equality prescribed would have existed if it had not been thus stipulated. There can be no distinction between the several States of the Union in the character of the jurisdiction, sovereignty and dominion which they may possess and exercise over persons and subjects within their respective limits. . . .

It is the settled law of this country that the ownership of and dominion and sovereignty over lands covered by tide waters, within the limits of the several States, belong to the respective States within which they are found, with the consequent right to use or dispose of any portion thereof, when that can be done without substantial impairment of the interest of the public in the waters, and subject always to the paramount right of Congress to control their navigation so far as may be necessary for the regulation of commerce with foreign nations and among the States. This doctrine has been often announced by this court, and is not questioned by counsel of any of the parties. *Pollard's Lessee v. Hagan*, 44 U.S. 212 (1845). . . .

***

. . . [W]e shall examine how far such dominion, sovereignty and proprietary right have been encroached upon by the railroad company, and how far that company had, at the time, the assent of the State to such encroachment, and also the validity of the claim which the company asserts of a right to make further encroachments thereon by virtue of a grant from the State in April, 1869.

The city of Chicago is situated upon the south western shore of Lake Michigan. . . . For a long time after the organization of the city its harbor was the Chicago River, a small, narrow stream opening into the lake . . . , and in it the shipping arriving from other ports of the lake and navigable waters was moored or anchored, and along it were docks and wharves. The growth of the city in subsequent years in population, business and commerce required a larger and more convenient harbor, and the United States, in view of such expansion and growth, commenced the construction of a system of breakwaters and other harbor protections in the waters of the lake. . . . In the prosecution of this work there was constructed a line of breakwaters or cribs of wood and stone covering the front of the city between the Chicago River and Twelfth street, with openings in the piers or lines of cribs for the entrance and departure of vessels, thus enclosing a large part of the lake for the uses of shipping and commerce, and creating an outer harbor for

Chicago. It comprises a space about one mile and one-half in length from north to south, and is of a width from east to west varying from one thousand to four thousand feet. As commerce and shipping expand, the harbor will be further extended towards the south, and, as alleged by the amended bill, it is expected that the necessities of commerce will soon require its enlargement so as to include a great part of the entire lake front of the city. It is stated, and not denied, that the authorities of the United States have in a general way indicated a plan for the improvement and use of the harbor which has been enclosed as mentioned, by which a portion is devoted as a harbor of refuge where ships may ride at anchor with security and within protecting walls, and another portion of such enclosure nearer the shore of the lake may be devoted to wharves and piers, alongside of which ships may load and unload and upon which warehouses may be constructed and other structures erected for the convenience of lake commerce.

The case proceeds upon the theory and allegation that the defendant, the Illinois Central Railroad Company, has, without lawful authority, encroached, and continues to encroach, upon the domain of the State, and its original ownership and control of the waters of the harbor and of the lands thereunder, upon a claim of rights acquired under a grant from the State and ordinance of the city to enter the city and appropriate land and water two hundred feet wide in order to construct a track for a railway, and to erect thereon warehouses, piers and other structures in front of the city, and upon a claim of riparian rights acquired by virtue of ownership of lands originally bordering on the lake in front of the city. It also proceeds against the claim asserted by the railroad company of a grant by the State, in 1869, of its right and title to the submerged lands, constituting the bed of Lake Michigan lying east of the tracks and breakwater of the company, for the distance of one mile, and between the south line of the south pier extended eastwardly and a line extended in the same direction from the south line of lot twenty-one south of and near the machine shops and round-house of the company; and of a right thereby to construct at its pleasure, in the harbor, wharves, piers and other works for its use.

The State prays a decree establishing and confirming its title to the bed of Lake Michigan and exclusive right to develop and improve the harbor of Chicago by the construction of docks, wharves, piers and other improvements, against the claim of the railroad company, that it has an absolute title to such submerged lands by the act of 1869, and the right, subject only to the paramount authority of the United States in the regulation of commerce, to fill all the bed of the lake within the limits above stated, for the purpose of its business; and the right, by the construction and maintenance of wharves, docks and piers, to improve the shore of the lake for the promotion generally of commerce and navigation. And the State, insisting that the company has, without right, erected and proposes to continue to erect wharves and piers upon its domain, asks that such alleged unlawful structures may be ordered to be removed, and the company be enjoined from erecting further structures of any kind.

***

We proceed to consider the claim of the railroad company to the ownership of submerged lands in the harbor, and the right to construct such wharves, piers, docks and other works therein as it may deem proper for its interest and business. The claim is founded upon the third section of the act of the legislature of the State passed on the 16th of April, 1869. . . .

***

The act, of which this section is a part, was accepted by a resolution of the board of directors of the company at its office in the city of New York, July 6, 1870; but the acceptance was not communicated to the State until the 18th of November, 1870. A copy of the resolution was on that day forwarded to the Secretary of State, and filed and recorded by him in the records of his office. On the 15th of April, 1873, the legislature of Illinois repealed the act. The questions presented relate to the validity of the section cited of the act and the effect of the repeal upon its operation.

. . . [One object of this section of the Act] was to grant to the railroad company submerged lands in the harbor.

***

As to th[is] grant . . . , the act declares that all the right and title of the State in and to the submerged lands, constituting the bed of Lake Michigan, and lying east of the tracks and breakwater of the company for the distance of one mile, and between the south line of the south pier extended eastwardly and a line extended eastwardly from the south line of lot twenty-one, south of and near to the round-house and machine shops of the company "are granted in fee to the railroad company, its successors and assigns." The grant is accompanied with a proviso that the fee of the lands shall be held by the company in perpetuity, and that it shall not have the power to grant, sell or convey the fee thereof. It also declares that nothing therein shall authorize obstructions to the harbor or impair the public right of navigation, or be construed to exempt the company from any act regulating the rates of wharfage and dockage to be charged in the harbor.

This clause is treated by the counsel of the company as an absolute conveyance to it of title to the submerged lands, giving it as full and complete power to use and dispose of the same, except in the technical transfer of the fee, in any manner it may choose, as if they were uplands, in no respect covered or affected by navigable waters, and not as a license to use the lands subject to revocation by the State. Treating it as such a conveyance, its validity must be determined by the consideration whether the legislature was competent to make a grant of the kind.

The act, if valid and operative to the extent claimed, placed under the control of the railroad company nearly the whole of the submerged lands of the harbor, subject only to the limitations that it should not authorize obstructions to the harbor or impair the public right of navigation, or exclude the legislature from regulating the rates of wharfage or dockage to be charged. With these limitations the act put it in the power of the company to delay indefinitely the improvement of the harbor, or to construct as many docks, piers and wharves and other works as it might choose, and at such positions in the harbor as might suit its purposes, and permit any kind of business to be conducted thereon, and to lease them out on its own terms, for indefinite periods. The inhibition against the technical transfer of the fee of any portion of the submerged lands was of little consequence when it could make a lease for any period and renew it at its pleasure. And the inhibitions against authorizing obstructions to the harbor and impairing the public right of navigation placed no impediments upon the action of the railroad company which did not previously exist. A corporation created for one purpose, the construction and operation of a railroad between designated points, is, by the act, converted into a corporation to manage and practically control the harbor of Chicago, not simply for its own purpose as a railroad corporation, but for its own profit generally.

The circumstances attending the passage of the act through the legislature were on the hearing the subject of much criticism. As originally introduced, the purpose of the act was to enable the city of Chicago to enlarge its harbor and to grant to it the title and interest of the State to certain lands adjacent to the shore of Lake Michigan on the eastern front of the city, and place the harbor under its control, giving it all the necessary powers for its wise management. But during the passage of the act its purport was changed. Instead of providing for the cession of the submerged lands to the city, it provided for a cession of them to the railroad company. It was urged that the title of the act was not changed to correspond with its changed purpose, and an objection was taken to its validity on that account. But the majority of the court were of opinion that the evidence was insufficient to show that the requirement of the constitution of the State, in its passage, was not complied with.

The question, therefore, to be considered is whether the legislature was competent to thus deprive the State of its ownership of the submerged lands in the harbor of Chicago, and of the consequent control of its waters; or, in other words, whether the railroad corporation can hold the lands and control the waters by the grant, against any future exercise of power over them by the State.

That the State holds the title to the lands under the navigable waters of Lake Michigan, within its limits, in the same manner that the State holds title to soils under tide water, by the common law, we have already shown, and that title necessarily carries with it control over the waters above them whenever the lands are subjected to use. But it is a title different in character from that which the State holds in lands intended for sale. It is different from the title which the United States hold in the public lands which are open to preemption and sale. It is a title held in trust for the people of the State that they may enjoy the navigation of the waters, carry on commerce over them, and have liberty of fishing therein freed from the obstruction or interference of private parties. The interest of the people in the navigation of the waters and in commerce over them may be improved in many instances by the erection of wharves, docks and piers therein, for which purpose the State may grant parcels of the submerged lands; and, so long as their disposition is made for such purpose, no valid objections can be made to the grants. It is grants of parcels of lands under navigable waters, that may afford foundation for wharves, piers, docks and other structures in aid of commerce, and grants of parcels which, being occupied, do not substantially impair the public interest in the lands and waters remaining, that are chiefly considered and sustained in the adjudged cases as a valid exercise of legislative power consistently with the trust to the public upon which such lands are held by the State. But that is a very different doctrine from the one which would sanction the abdication of the general control of the State over lands under the navigable waters of an entire harbor or bay, or of a sea or lake. Such abdication is not consistent with the exercise of that trust which requires the government of the State to preserve such waters for the use of the public. The trust devolving upon the State for the public, and which can only be discharged by the management and control of property in which the public has an interest, cannot be relinquished by a transfer of the property. The control of the State for the purposes of the trust can never be lost, except as to such parcels as are used in promoting the interests of the public therein, or can be disposed of without any substantial impairment of the public interest in the lands and waters remaining. It is only by observing the distinction between a grant of such parcels for the improvement of the public interest, or which when occupied do not substantially impair the public interest in the lands and waters remaining, and a grant of the whole property in which the public is interested, that the language of the adjudged cases can be reconciled. General language sometimes found in opinions of the courts, expressive of absolute ownership and control by the State of lands under navigable waters, irrespective of any trust as to their use and disposition, must be read and construed with reference to the special facts of the particular cases. A grant of all the lands under the navigable waters of a State has never been adjudged to be within the legislative power; and any attempted grant of the kind would be held, if not absolutely void on its face, as subject to revocation. The State can no more abdicate its trust over property in which the whole people are interested, like navigable waters and soils under them, so as to leave them entirely under the use and control of private parties, except in the instance of parcels mentioned for the improvement of the navigation and use of the waters, or when parcels can be disposed of without impairment of the public interest in what remains, than it can abdicate its police powers in the administration of government and the preservation of the peace.

> **Quick Question**
>
> So, the State *can* make transfers? Why wouldn't the public interest be better served by a total ban on transfers?

In the administration of government the use of such powers may for a limited period be delegated to a municipality or other body, but there always remains with the State the right to revoke those powers and exercise them in a more direct manner, and one more conformable to its wishes. So with trusts connected with public property, or property of a special character, like lands under navigable waters, they cannot be placed entirely beyond the direction and control of the State.

The harbor of Chicago is of immense value to the people of the State of Illinois in the facilities it affords to its vast and constantly increasing commerce; and the idea that its legislature can deprive the State of control over its bed and waters and place the same in the hands of a private corporation created for a different purpose, one limited to transportation of passengers and freight between distant points and the city, is a proposition that cannot be defended.

The area of the submerged lands proposed to be ceded by the act in question to the railroad company embraces something more than a thousand acres, being, as stated by counsel, more than three times the area of the outer harbor, and not only including all of that harbor but embracing adjoining submerged lands which will, in all probability, be hereafter included in the harbor. It is as large as that embraced by all the merchandise docks along the Thames at London; is much larger than that included in the famous docks and basins at Liverpool; is twice that of the port of Marseilles, and nearly if not quite equal to the pier area along the water front of the city of New York. And the arrivals and clearings of vessels at the port exceed in number those of New York, and are equal to those of New York and Boston combined. Chicago has nearly twenty-five per cent of the lake carrying trade as compared with the arrivals and clearings of all the leading ports of our great inland seas. In the year ending June 30, 1886, the joint arrivals and clearances of vessels at that port amounted to twenty-two thousand and ninety-six, with a tonnage of over seven millions; and in 1890 the tonnage of the vessels reached nearly nine millions. As stated by counsel, since the passage of the Lake Front Act, in 1869, the population of the city has increased nearly a million souls, and the increase of commerce has kept pace with it. It is hardly conceivable that the legislature can divest the State of the control and management of this harbor and vest it absolutely in a private corporation. Surely an act of the legislature transferring the title to its submerged lands and the power claimed by the railroad company, to a foreign State or nation would be repudiated, without hesitation, as a gross perversion of the trust over the property under which it is held. So would a similar transfer to a corporation of another State. It would not be listened to that the control and management of the harbor of that great city — a subject of concern to the whole people of the State — should thus be placed elsewhere than in the State itself. All the objections which can be urged to such attempted transfer may be urged to a transfer to a private corporation like the railroad company in this case.

Any grant of the kind is necessarily revocable, and the exercise of the trust by which the property was held by the State can be resumed at any time. Undoubtedly there may be expenses incurred in improvements made under such a grant which the State ought to pay; but, be that as it may, the power to resume the trust whenever the State judges best is, we think, incontrovertible. The position advanced by the railroad company in support of its claim to the ownership of the submerged lands and the right to the erection of wharves, piers and docks at its pleasure, or for its business in the harbor of Chicago, would place every harbor in the country at the mercy of a majority of the legislature of the State in which the harbor is situated.

We cannot, it is true, cite any authority where a grant of this kind has been held invalid, for we believe that no instance exists where the harbor of a great city and its commerce have been allowed to pass into the control of any private corporation. But the decisions are numerous which declare that such property is held by the State, by virtue of its sovereignty, in trust for the public. The ownership of the navigable waters of the harbor and of the lands under them is a subject of public concern to the whole people of the State. The trust with which they are held, therefore, is governmental and cannot be alienated, except in those instances mentioned of parcels used in the improvement of the interest thus held, or when parcels can be disposed of without detriment to the public interest in the lands and waters remaining.

This follows necessarily from the public character of the property, being held by the whole people for purposes in which the whole people are interested. As said by Chief Justice Taney, in *Martin v. Waddell*, 16 Pet. 367, 410 (1842):

> When the Revolution took place the people of each State became themselves sovereign, and in that character hold the absolute right to all their navigable waters, and the soils under them, for their own common use, subject only to the rights since surrendered by the Constitution to the general government.

In *Arnold v. Mundy*, 56 U.S. 426 (1854) . . . which is cited by this court in *Martin v. Waddell*, . . . and spoken of by Chief Justice Taney as entitled to great weight, and in which the decision was made "with great deliberation and research," the Supreme Court of New Jersey comments upon the rights of the State in the bed of navigable waters, and, after observing that the power exercised by the State over the lands and waters is nothing more than what is called the *jus regium*, the right of regulating, improving and securing them for the benefit of every individual citizen, adds:

> The sovereign power, itself, therefore, cannot consistently with the principles of the law of nature and the constitution of a well-ordered society, make a direct and absolute grant of the waters of the State, divesting all the citizens of their common right. It would be a grievance which never could be long borne by a free people. [Citation omitted.]

Necessarily must the control of the waters of a State over all lands under them pass when the lands are conveyed in fee to private parties, and are by them subjected to use.

In the case of *Stockton v. Baltimore and New York Railroad Company*, 32 Fed. 9 (1887) . . . which involved a consideration by Mr. Justice Bradley, late of this court, of the nature of the ownership by the State of lands under the navigable waters of the United States, he said:

> It is insisted that the property of the State in lands under its navigable waters is private property, and comes strictly within the constitutional provision. It is significantly asked, can the United States take the state house at Trenton, and the surrounding grounds belonging to the State, and appropriate them to the purposes of a railroad depot, or to any other use of the general government, without compensation? We do not apprehend that the decision of the present case involves or requires a serious answer to this question. The cases are clearly not parallel. The character of the title or ownership by which the State holds the state house is quite different from that by which it holds the land under the navigable waters in and around its territory. The information rightly states that, prior to the Revolution, the shore and lands under water of the navigable streams and waters of the province of New Jersey belonged to the King of Great Britain as part of the *jura regalia* of the crown, and devolved to the State by right of conquest. The information does

not state, however, what is equally true, that, after the conquest, the said lands were held by the State, as they were by the king, in trust for the public uses of navigation and fishery, and the erection thereon of wharves, piers, light-houses, beacons and other facilities of navigation and commerce. Being subject to this trust, they were *publici juris*; in other words, they were held for the use of the people at large. It is true that to utilize the fisheries, especially those of shell fish, it was necessary to parcel them out to particular operators, and employ the rent or consideration for the benefit of the whole people; but this did not alter the character of the title. The land remained subject to all other public uses as before, especially to those of navigation and commerce, which are always paramount to those of public fisheries. It is also true that portions of the submerged shoals and flats, which really interfered with navigation, and could better subserve the purposes of commerce by being filled up and reclaimed, were disposed of to individuals for that purpose. But neither did these dispositions of useless parts affect the character of the title to the remainder.

***

The legislature could not give away nor sell the discretion of its successors in respect to matters, the government of which, from the very nature of things, must vary with varying circumstances. The legislation which may be needed one day for the harbor may be different from the legislation that may be required at another day. Every legislature must, at the time of its existence, exercise the power of the State in the execution of the trust devolved upon it. We hold, therefore, that any attempted cession of the ownership and control of the State in and over the submerged lands in Lake Michigan, by the act of April 16, 1869, was inoperative to affect, modify or in any respect to control the sovereignty and dominion of the State over the lands, or its ownership thereof, and that any such attempted operation of the act was annulled by the repealing act of April 15, 1873, which to that extent was valid and effective. There can be no irrepealable contract in a conveyance of property by a grantor in disregard of a public trust, under which he was bound to hold and manage it.

***

If the act in question be treated as a mere license to the company to make the improvement in the harbor contemplated as an agency of the State, then we think the right to cancel the agency and revoke its power is unquestionable.

It follows from the views expressed, and it is so declared and adjudged, that the State of Illinois is the owner in fee of the submerged lands constituting the bed of Lake Michigan, which the third section of the act of April 16, 1869, purported to grant to the Illinois Central Railroad Company, and that the act of April 15, 1873, repealing the same is valid and effective for the purpose of restoring to the State the same control, dominion and ownership of said lands that it had prior to the passage of the act of April 16, 1869.

Mr. Justice SHIRAS, with whom concurred Mr. Justice GRAY and Mr. Justice BROWN, dissenting.

That the ownership of a State in the lands underlying its navigable waters is as complete, and its power to make them the subject of conveyance and grant is as full, as such ownership and power to grant in the case of the other public lands of the State, I have supposed to be well settled.

Thus it was said in *Weber v. Harbor Commissioners*, 85 U.S. 57, 65 (1853), that

> upon the admission of California into the Union upon equal footing with the original States, absolute property in, and dominion and sovereignty over, all soils under the tide waters within her limits passed to the State, with the consequent right to dispose of the title to any part of said soils in such manner as she might deem proper, subject only to the paramount right of navigation over the waters, so far as such navigation might be required by the necessities of commerce with foreign nations or among the several States, the regulation of which was vested in the general government.

In *Hoboken v. Pennsylvania Railroad*, 124 U.S. 656, 657 (1888) — a case in many respects like the present — it was said:

> Lands below high-water mark on navigable waters are the absolute property of the State, subject only to the power conferred upon Congress to regulate foreign commerce and commerce between the States, and they may be granted by the State, either to the riparian proprietors or to a stranger, as the State may see fit,

and, accordingly, it was held,

> that the grant by the State of New Jersey to the United Companies by the act of March 31, 1869, was intended to secure, and does secure, to the respective grantees the whole beneficial interest in their respective properties, for their exclusive use for the purposes expressed in the grants.

In *Stevens v. Paterson & Newark Railroad*, 34 N.J. Law 532, 549 (1870), it was declared by the Court of Errors and Appeals of New Jersey that it was competent for the State to grant to a stranger lands constituting the shore of a navigable river under tide water below the tide-water mark, to be occupied and used with structures and improvements.

Langdon v. New York City, 93 N.Y. 129 (1883), was a case in which it was said by the Court of Appeals of New York:

> From the earliest times in England the law has vested the title to, and the control over, the navigable waters therein, in the crown and parliament. A distinction was taken between the mere ownership of the soil under water and the control over it for public purposes. The ownership of the soil, analogous to the ownership of dry land, was regarded as *jus privatum*, and was vested in the crown. But the right to use and control both the land and water was deemed a *jus publicum*, and was vested in parliament. The crown could convey the soil under water so as to give private rights therein, but the dominion and control over the waters, in the interest of commerce and navigation, for the benefit of all the subjects of the kingdom, could be exercised only by Parliament. . . . In this country, the State has succeeded to all the rights of both crown and parliament in the navigable waters and the soil under them, and here the *jus privatum* and the *jus publicum* are both vested in the State.

These citations might be indefinitely multiplied from authorities both Federal and State.

This State of Illinois, by her information or bill of complaint in this case, alleges that "the claims of the defendants are a great and irreparable injury to the State of Illinois as a proprietor and owner of the bed of the lake, throwing doubts and clouds upon its title thereto, and preventing an advantageous sale or other disposition thereof"; and in the prayer for relief the State asks that "its title may be established and confirmed, that the claims made by the railroad company may be declared to be unfounded, and that the State of Illinois may be declared to have the sole and exclusive right to develop the harbor of Chicago by the construction of docks, wharves, etc., and to dispose of such rights at its pleasure."

Indeed, the logic of the State's case, as well as her pleadings, attributes to the State entire power to hold and dispose of, by grant or lease, the lands in question; and her case is put upon the alleged invalidity of the title of the railroad company, arising out of the asserted unconstitutionality of the act of 1869, which act made the grant, by reason of certain irregularities in its passage and title, or, that ground failing, upon the right of the State to arbitrarily revoke the grant, as a mere license, and which right she claims to have duly exercised by the passage of the act of 1873.

The opinion of the majority, if I rightly apprehend it, likewise concedes that a State does possess the power to grant the rights of property and possession in such lands to private parties, but the power is stated to be, in some way restricted to "small parcels, or where such parcels can be disposed of without detriment to the public interests in the lands and waters remaining." But it is difficult to see how the validity of the exercise of the power, if the power exists, can depend upon the size of the parcel granted, or how, if it be possible to imagine that the power is subject to such a limitation, the present case would be affected, as the grant in question, though doubtless a large and valuable one, is, relatively to the remaining soil and waters, if not insignificant, yet certainly, in view of the purposes to be effected, not unreasonable. It is matter of common knowledge that a great railroad system, like that of the Illinois Central Railroad Company, requires an extensive and constantly increasing territory for its terminal facilities.

It would seem to be plain that, if the State of Illinois has the power, by her legislature, to grant private rights and interests in parcels of soil under her navigable waters, the extent of such a grant and its effect upon the public interests in the lands and waters remaining are matters of legislative discretion.

***

points for discussion

1. *The real facts of* Illinois Central. *Illinois Central* has been the subject of a great deal of scholarship over the years. In 2004, Professors Kearney and Merrill published a fascinating historical study of the case, entitled *The Origins of the American Public Trust Doctrine, or What Really Happened in*

Illinois Central, 71 U. Chi. L. Rev. 800 (2004), that is well worth reading. In addition to excellent legal analysis of the case, it provides fascinating historical detail, particularly regarding the circumstances surrounding passage of the initial legislation.

2. *The sovereignty rationale.* The idea behind the duty not to dispose is, as the Court says, that

> [t]he State can no more abdicate its trust over property in which the whole people are interested, like navigable waters and soils under them, so as to leave them entirely under the use and control of private parties . . . than it can abdicate its police powers in the administration of government and the preservation of the peace. In the administration of government the use of such powers may for a limited period be delegated to a municipality or other body, but there always remains with the State the right to revoke those powers and exercise them in a more direct manner, and one more conformable to its wishes.

In an earlier decision, *Pollards Lessee v. Hagan*, 44 U.S. (3 How.) 212 (1845), the Court included the power over public waterways within the state's eminent domain power. (The Court used the term "eminent domain" in its more archaic, broader meaning, that is, "[t]he right which belongs to the society, or to the sovereign, of disposing, in case of necessity, and for the public safety, of all the wealth contained in the state. . . ." *Id.* at 222.) In the *Pollard* opinion, the Court makes the argument that a state cannot be a sovereign entity unless it possesses the eminent domain power and, thus, ownership and control of its public waterways. Why would ownership and control of public waterways be fundamental to sovereignty? In other contexts, for example, the use of the eminent domain power to condemn private property for a public purpose, the state can delegate the power to municipalities and even to private entities, but must do so with recourse and the right to revoke the delegation.

3. *Categorizing the public trust doctrine.* The decision in *Illinois Central* begs many questions. Among them is "what kind of law is the 'public trust doctrine'"? One way to read decisions like *Illinois Central* is that states have sovereign responsibilities — including the obligation to hold title to submerged lands — that they can neither shirk nor delegate to private parties. This view is consistent with Roman and British law conceptions of submerged lands and navigable waters as immutably public. If we accept this reading as correct, then it means that neither courts nor legislatures can eliminate or qualify those obligations. Could a state amend its constitution to provide that the public trust doctrine no longer applies in that state?

4. *The substantive rule in* Illinois Central. The central rule in *Illinois Central*, that is, the "duty not to dispose," is a direct, albeit expanded version of the restriction on the sovereign's right to alienate found in Chapter 33 of the Magna Carta: The state cannot transfer ownership of trust lands into private hands in a way that interferes with the public's ability to use areas above

those lands ("trust areas") for trust purposes. The Supreme Court recognizes what appear to be two exceptions to the duty not to dispose. First, the state can make a transfer if the transferee will put the submerged lands to a use that "promot[es] the interest of the public." *Illinois Central*, 146 U.S. at 453. Second, the state can make transfers that result in no "substantial impairment of the public interest in the lands and waters remaining." *Id.*

Each of these two kinds of transfers — sometimes called "in furtherance" and "*de minimis*" transfers, respectively — are permissible because they do not significantly reduce the aggregate value to the public of trust uses. (For trust purposes, the submerged lands themselves are not valuable to the public; rather, the public benefits from using overlying areas for navigation, commerce, fishing, and recreation.) Here is how to analyze a transfer to determine whether it fits within the exceptions: Let's say a state owns 100 acres of submerged lands. Further suppose that the state gives a company the right to build a wharf that will occupy one acre. This one-acre disposal is a lawful "in furtherance" disposal if the use-value of the remaining 99 acres will be higher than the use-value of the 100 acres prior to the disposal. Q: How could 99 acres be more valuable than 100? A: When those 99 acres are combined with a wharf: A wharf can potentially make a waterway more valuable because it makes the waterway more useful by facilitating navigation and commerce. The *de minimis* exception would come into play where the proposed wharf would do more harm than good, e.g., by destroying critical fish habitat, or where the transferee intended to use the submerged land for something with no trust benefits, e.g., filling it in and building a house. Here, the transfer would be lawful if it resulted in *not too much* reduction in use-value, in the eyes of the reviewing court. This is obviously a subjective determination.

Two other points are worth noting. First, the Court seems to suggest that there are two problematic aspects of the transfer in *Illinois Central*: its impact (it would give the company complete control of commerce in the harbor) and its duration (the transfer is in the form of a fee simple interest in the submerged lands). Would the transfer have been valid if it were for a period of 50 years? If it were in the form of a revocable license? Second, some states have attempted to eliminate the potential for harm to the public by mandating that all transfers of submerged land be made "subject to the trust." In other words, the transferee cannot prevent the public from navigating on or fishing in the trust area. This approach allows the transferee to use the submerged lands for activities like shellfish cultivation (shellfish are generally not subject to the trust because they are attached to the bottom!), and the mineral estate beneath the submerged lands for mining and oil production. Would a transfer "subject to the trust" allow the transferee to construct a wharf?

5. *Actual and constructive disposal.* It is easy to see how a transfer of submerged land might physically interfere with the public's ability to enjoy trust uses. If I can't go into the area, I can't navigate or fish there. In *Illinois Central*, the

transfer would *not* have interfered with physical use of the trust area above the 1,000 transferred acres: The terms of the 1869 legislation prohibited the company from "impair[ing] the public right of navigation." The Court was concerned with interference with the trust use of *commerce*. The problem was physical only in the sense that, as a result of the transfer, neither the state nor any other party could build a wharf in the harbor: This would interfere with the public's ability to use the harbor for commerce by giving the company monopoly ownership of the land/water interface. The rate-setting provisions in the original legislation were not enough to convince the Court that transfer would not result in harmful pricing; in addition, the Court was concerned that the company might not develop the harbor at a rate consistent with the public interest.

Because public trust claims vest courts with substantial discretion, trust claims can have more traction than other theories, such as alleged violation of the police power, upon which challenges to state action might be based. Thus, during the last half-century, plaintiffs' attorneys have developed *Illinois Central*–based causes of action that push the notion of interference even further, toward a "constructive disposal" theory. In constructive disposal cases, plaintiffs correctly emphasize the fact that the state holds title to submerged lands *only* in order to protect the public's right to use trust areas for trust purposes. Viewed through this lens, the duty not to dispose can be stated as follows:

> The state cannot dispose of trust property (or, adopt a rule that gives one citizen or a subset of citizens special use-rights that interfere with the remaining public's use-rights), unless the disposal (rule) would result in a net gain to the public in terms of overall use-value (the "in furtherance" exception) or would not substantially diminish overall use-value (the *de minimis* exception).

This is not too much of a stretch. One could get to the same result by arguing that the state's right to use and enjoy trust property, that is, to use it or *to regulate its use*, is subject to the same restrictions as the state's right to alienate. This has to be true; otherwise, the state could fill in submerged lands, build some houses on the filled-in land, then sell the property to a private party and argue that the sale itself had a *de minimis* impact on trust uses (because the lands had already been filled!).

Here is an example of a constructive disposal claim: Pursuant to a state water pollution statute, a state agency grants a company a permit to discharge pollutants into a public stream. This pollution kills off the fish in the stream. The duty not to dispose framing is: In issuing the permit, the state has given the company special "fishing" rights, and the exercise of these rights interferes with the general public's ability to engage in a trust use (fishing); this "disposal" does not result in a net gain to the public in terms of overall use-value and, in fact, it substantially diminishes use-value.

Helpful hint: The last three cases in this chapter—*Vogt, Weden,* and *National Audubon*—fit this model. After you read each of these cases, be sure to try to write out the claim in terms of the "duty not to constructively dispose."

6. *The procedural version of* Illinois Central. Another way to describe the holding in *Illinois Central* is to say that the public trust doctrine requires a special judicial standard of review, one that applies only in those instances where legislatures or agencies act in such a way as to affect the public's rights in trust resources. Under this view, courts would examine those actions, and could invalidate them, if there is no evidence that the legislature or agency carefully considered the public's rights when making its decision. The reason for reading *Illinois Central* this way is that the "rule" of the case ultimately requires a subjective determination by a court: Has a legislature given away too much? *See, e.g.,* 1 W. RODGERS, JR., ENVIRONMENTAL LAW: AIR AND WATER § 2.20, at 162 (1986). In other words, the doctrine is mainly a rule of procedure.

7. *The dissent.* The dissent in *Illinois Central* struggles with the technicalities of converting the English trust to the American system. The English doctrine represented a compromise between the King and his subjects. Why is the doctrine necessary in a democracy? For an argument that it is not, see James L. Huffman, *A Fish Out of Water: The Public Trust Doctrine in a Constitutional Democracy,* 19 ENVTL. L. 527 (1989). For a different perspective, see Barton H. Thompson, Jr., *The Public Trust Doctrine: A Conservative Reconstruction & Defense,* 15 SOUTHEASTERN ENVTL. L.J. 47 (2006).

b. Applying *Illinois Central*

Illinois Central stands for the proposition that a state retains the right to rescind large-scale, private-purpose transfers. As noted above, the opinion also creates two exceptions. The cases below provide examples of how courts determine whether transfers of submerged lands fit within these exceptions.

CWC Fisheries, Inc. v. Bunker

755 P.2d 1115 (Alaska 1988)

Justice BURKE delivered the opinion of the Supreme Court of Alaska.

This appeal presents the question of whether tidelands conveyed pursuant to class I tideland preference rights under AS 38.05.820 were conveyed subject to the public's right to fish the waters above those tidelands. We conclude that they were, and we therefore affirm the judgment of the superior court dismissing CWC Fisheries' trespass claim against Dean Bunker.

Shortly after statehood, as part of the Alaska Land Act, the legislature enacted Alaska Statutes (AS) 38.05.820. . . . Under this provision, [certain] occupants of tideland tracts, . . . who had erected substantial permanent improvements on their property prior to statehood, were given a "class I preference right" to their property. AS 38.05.820(c), (d)(5). A class I preference right entitled the occupant to obtain title to the occupied tideland tract from the state for a nominal fee. . . .

I.

On October 3, 1963, Snug Harbor Packing Company applied for a class I preference right to an area of tideland fronting its fish cannery on the southwestern shore of Chisik Island in the Tuxedni Channel. The Department of Natural Resources (DNR) granted the application, and issued a patent to Snug Harbor on March 20, 1972. The patent granted Snug Harbor the tideland lot "to have and to hold . . . with the appurtenances thereof unto the said Grantee and their heirs and assigns forever," subject to the State of Alaska's express reservation of mineral rights, and an express prohibition on the taking of herring spawn at the site. The lot, known as ATS 360, was used by the company primarily in its canning and processing operations throughout the period of Snug Harbor's ownership.

In August, 1964, Dean Bunker, a commercial fisherman operating salmon set nets in the Tuxedni Channel, applied for a shore fishery lease on a tract of tideland encompassing the present ATS 360 location. The DNR informed Bunker that he could not lease the ATS 360 site because Snug Harbor had already applied for a class I preference right on that site. However, the Department told Bunker that he could continue to fish the site under a reservation of fishing rights which would be placed in the patent issued to Snug Harbor. The reservation promised by the DNR was never placed in the patent issued to Snug Harbor. Nonetheless, Bunker claims to have regularly fished the waters above ATS 360 from 1964 to 1985.

In 1980, CWC Fisheries, Inc. (CWC) bought Snug Harbor's operation and took over the premises. Since the acquisition, CWC has gradually phased out cannery and fleet operations at ATS 360. The site now serves only as a refueling and support facility for CWC's fishing operations.

The present dispute arose in 1985, when CWC granted set net fishing rights at ATS 360 to Eric Randall, as part of an agreement to employ Randall as winter caretaker and summer superintendent

Photo: National Archives

Figure 7-4. Set Net
The 1891 version of a fixed gillnet, or set net.

at the site. Since fish and game regulations prohibit any two parties from set net fishing concurrently on a lot the size of ATS 360, the CWC/Randall agreement has, apparently for the first time, placed CWC's use of ATS 360 in direct conflict with Bunker's.

CWC and Randall filed suit against Bunker, alleging trespass and requesting damages and injunctive relief. Bunker denied CWC's claims of trespass, and argued that the State's conveyance of ATS 360 was made subject to the right of the general public to enter those tidelands for purposes of navigation, commerce, and fishery under the "public trust" doctrine established by the United States Supreme Court in *Illinois Central Railroad Co. v. Illinois*, 146 U.S. 387 (1892).[6]

On September 24, 1986, the superior court granted summary judgment for Bunker, holding that CWC held title to ATS 360 subject to the public trust, and that neither CWC nor its assignee could rightfully exclude Bunker from the site. Accordingly, the court dismissed CWC's trespass claim against Bunker. CWC appeals the dismissal.

II.

The public trust doctrine was first advanced by the United States Supreme Court in *Illinois Central Railroad Co. v. Illinois*, 146 U.S. 387 (1892). In that case, the Court held that the State of Illinois was free to revoke a prior state grant of 1,000 acres of submerged land beneath the waters of Lake Michigan, because it had possessed no power to validly convey such land in the first place. The Court held that when a state receives title to tidelands and lands beneath navigable waterways within its

> **Quick Question**
>
> Is this an accurate description of the U.S. Supreme Court's holding in *Illinois Central*?

borders at the time of its admission to the Union, it receives such land "in trust for the people of the State that they may enjoy the navigation of the waters, carry on commerce over them, and have liberty of fishing therein freed from the obstruction or interference of private parties." *Id.* at 452. The Court noted that the state is entitled to convey such lands to private parties, free of the public trust, only under very limited circumstances. It stated:

> The control of the State for the purposes of the trust can never be lost, except as to such parcels as are used in promoting the interests of the public therein, or can be disposed of without any substantial impairment of the public interest in the lands and waters remaining. *Id.* at 453.

In all other instances, the Court held, the state is prohibited from "abdicat[ing] its trust over [the] property" by absolute conveyance to private parties. *Id.* at 453.

Illinois Central remains the leading case regarding public rights in tide and submerged lands conveyed by the state. . . . While we have never had prior occasion to

---

6. Bunker also counterclaimed, arguing that he had acquired the site by adverse possession, and filed a third-party claim against the DNR for negligent misrepresentation with regard to the fishery reservation which was never placed in Snug Harbor's patent. These claims have since been dismissed, and are not at issue here.

apply the public trust doctrine to tidelands in Alaska, those modern courts which have considered its application have generally held that any attempted conveyance of tidelands by the state which fails to meet the *Illinois Central* criteria for passing title free of the public trust will pass only "naked title to the soil," subject to continuing public trust "easements" for purposes of navigation, commerce, and fishery. . . .[8] The grantee may "assert a vested right to the servient estate (the right of use subject to the trust)," *National Audubon Society v. Superior Court*, 33 Cal. 3d 419 (1983), but may not enjoin any member of the public from utilizing the property for public trust purposes. . . .

We adopt the approach employed by our sister states on this question, and hold that any state tideland conveyance which fails to satisfy the requirements of *Illinois Central* will be viewed as a valid conveyance of title subject to continuing public easements for purposes of navigation, commerce, and fishery.

In determining whether a state conveyance has passed title to a parcel of tideland free of any trust obligations under *Illinois Central*, we must ask, first, whether the conveyance was made in furtherance of some specific public trust purpose and, second, whether the conveyance can be made without substantial impairment of the public's interest in state tidelands. . . . If either of these questions can be answered in the affirmative, conveyance free of the public trust would be permissible. *See Illinois Central*, 146 U.S. at 453.

Initially, CWC argues that the conveyance of ATS 360 was a grant "in aid of navigation and commerce." It notes that the property was originally used by Snug Harbor in its commercial canning and processing operations, and that the site's wharfage and docking facilities were, and are, utilized by commercial fishermen in Cook Inlet. Further, CWC points to the "substantial permanent improvements" language of AS 38.05.820, which, it maintains, constitutes clear evidence of the state's intent to further commerce and navigation through its tideland allocations under the Alaska Land Act. . . . We are not persuaded by CWC's argument.

Before any tideland grant may be found to be free of the public trust under the "public trust purposes" theory, the legislature's intent to so convey it must be clearly expressed or necessarily implied in the legislation authorizing the transfer. . . . If any interpretation of the statute which would retain the public's interest in the tidelands is reasonably possible, we must give the statute such an interpretation. . . . Here, the operative language of AS 38.05.820 reads simply:

> (a) It is the policy of the state to allow preference rights for the acquisition of tide and submerged land occupied or developed for municipal business, residential or other beneficial purposes on or before the date of admission of Alaska into the Union.

∗∗∗

8. Some courts have expanded the public trust doctrine to include additional public uses, such as boating, swimming, water skiing, and other recreational or scientific activities for which the waters might be utilized. *See, e.g., Marks v. Whitney*, 491 P.2d 374, 380 (Cal. 1971); *Orion Corp. v. State*, 747 P.2d 1062, 1073 (Wash. 1987); *Menzer v. Village of Elkhart Lake*, 186 N.W.2d 290, 296 (Wis. 1971); *see also* ch. 82, § 1(c), SLA 1985 (Alaska Statutes, Temporary and Special Acts and Resolves 1985) (refers to trust as including "recreational purposes or any other public purpose for which the water is used or capable of being used"). We are concerned in this case only with the traditionally recognized fishery interest.

(c) An occupant of tide or submerged land which is not seaward of a municipal corporation, who occupied or developed it on and prior to September 7, 1957, has a class I preference right to the land from the state. . . .

(d) For the purposes of this section, unless the context otherwise requires,

***

(5) "occupant" means a person or the successor in interest of a person, who actually occupied for business, residential or other beneficial purpose, tideland, or tide and submerged land contiguous to tideland, in the state, on and before January 3, 1959, with substantial permanent improvements. *Id.*

The statute does not expressly state that the preference rights were given in aid of navigation and commerce, nor does it state that the lands in question would be conveyed free of the public trust. While it is true that the statute conditions the preference right upon the existence of "substantial permanent improvements" on the property, such a requirement can hardly be interpreted as an expression of the state's intent to abdicate its trust responsibilities. As we noted in *City of Homer v. State, Department of Natural Resources*, 566 P.2d 1314, 1316 (Alaska 1977), at least one purpose of the Alaska Land Act was "to establish equitable methods of disposing of certain tidelands." The "substantial permanent improvements" requirement simply serves as an additional factor in determining equitable distribution as between occupants. We find nothing in the language of AS 38.05.820 that expresses a clear legislative intent to convey state tidelands free of the public trust.

Likewise, we do not think such intent is "necessarily implied" by the surrounding circumstances. Indeed, Article VIII, Section 3 of the Alaska Constitution, which was in effect at the time AS 38.05.820 was enacted, explicitly provides that "wherever occurring in their natural state, fish, wildlife, and waters are reserved to the people for common use."

At least in the absence of some clear evidence to the contrary, we will not presume that the legislature intended to take action which would, on its face, appear inconsistent with the plain wording of this constitutional mandate.[10] In sum, we are not persuaded that this conveyance was made "in furtherance of trust purposes" such as would free the property from any continuing public trust obligations.

Next, we turn to the "substantial impairment" aspect of the *Illinois Central* test. CWC argues that ATS 360 is a small, rather remote, parcel of tideland, one which can hardly be considered to involve the degree of impairment suggested by the public trust cases. Moreover, CWC notes that, under existing law, only one person is permitted to set net fish on the site at any one time. To vest such fishing privilege in the patent holder, CWC maintains, would no more impair the public's interest in the tidelands than does the state's shore fishery leasing program, under which particular individuals are granted exclusive fishing privileges at specified sites. . . .

Again, we disagree. Even if we were to accept CWC's suggestion that size and location might, by themselves, be decisive factors in determining whether a given

---

10. We need not decide at this time whether a fee simple tideland conveyance which satisfied the strictures of *Illinois Central* would nonetheless run afoul of article VIII, section 3.

legislative conveyance amounts to a substantial impairment of the public's interest in state tidelands, these tidelands would still fail to meet the test. This case does not involve a mere isolated conveyance of a remote piece of tideland. The statute at issue here made available for private ownership virtually all Alaska tidelands occupied and developed prior to statehood. . . . To hold that persons receiving title under that statute hold the fee free of any public trust obligations would, we believe, amount to a substantial impairment of the public's interest in state tidelands as a whole.[12]

Finally, we fail to see how the state's shore fisheries leasing program can be said to bear any reasonable resemblance to the proposition urged upon us by CWC. Lessees under that program do not exercise their fishing privileges as an incident of title to the tidelands. They do not hold or enjoy such privileges in perpetuity. Rather, they are granted a limited fishing privilege on specified tracts of state-owned tideland for a period of reasonable, but finite, duration. Whatever the validity of the state's shore fisheries leasing program under the public trust doctrine, we are satisfied that the fee simple ownership claimed by CWC in this case goes far beyond any impairment created under that state-administered regulatory scheme.[14]

We hold that tidelands conveyed to private parties pursuant to class I preference rights under AS 38.05.820 were conveyed subject to the public's right to utilize those tidelands for purposes of navigation, commerce and fishery. While patent holders are free to make such use of their property as will not unreasonably interfere with these continuing public easements, they are prohibited from any general attempt to exclude the public from the property by virtue of their title.

In the instant case, CWC and Randall are entitled to make use of the fisheries at ATS 360, but they are prohibited from excluding other members of the public who seek to do the same.[15] Here, state regulations limit the number of individuals who may fish this tract at any one time; therefore, the parties must look to relevant provisions of state law in determining their respective priority rights. For the reasons discussed above, however, CWC's trespass action must fail.

Accordingly, the judgment of the superior court is affirmed.

---

12. We note in this regard that, under present state law, explicit easements protecting public access to navigable waters must be reserved by the state before *any* interest in state land may be transferred. AS 38.05.127. While this statute was not in effect at the time of the conveyance at issue here, it nonetheless serves as a clear indication of the public's concern for the preservation of public access rights to all navigable waters. The "substantial impairment" requirement must be viewed in this context.

14. In addition to the arguments discussed above, CWC argues at some length that, even if ATS 360 were conveyed subject to the public trust, Bunker may not invoke that doctrine because he is seeking to use the property for private commercial purposes. This argument merits little discussion. Even commercial fishermen are members of the public, and, as such, are entitled to use those waters reserved to the public under the public trust doctrine, provided they comply with all relevant statutes and regulations concerning their intended use. *Illinois Central* suggests nothing less.

15. This case does not involve a situation in which one public trust use is directly in conflict with another (*e.g.*, fisheries versus navigation). We note, however, that in such cases, the legislature will generally be afforded broad authority to make policy choices favoring one trust use over another. . . .

Pursuant to the logic of *CWC Fisheries*, the common law doctrine allows the state to make public interest and *de minimis* transfers not only in perpetuity, but also free of the public easement. (The public would retain the right to use some of these waters for navigation by virtue of the federal servitude.) Notice that Alaska, like many states, has modified the common law to prohibit the elimination of the public easement by some or all transfers in these categories. *See* footnote 12, above. The following case interprets a constitutional provision that modifies the doctrine with respect to a subcategory of California's public trust lands. Although the case does not deal directly with the common law public trust doctrine, it does provide an example of how to answer the question: "What does *de minimis* mean"?

County of Orange v. Heim

30 Cal. App. 3d 694 (1973)

Judge KAUFMAN of the Court of Appeal of California, Fourth Appellate District, Division Two, delivered the opinion of the court.

The Case

This proceeding was commenced . . . to establish the validity of a land exchange agreement and accompanying dredging and landfill agreement made between the County of Orange (County) and The Irvine Company (Irvine) in connection with a plan (hereinafter the Plan) for the development of Upper Newport Bay (UNB) as a harbor. It has developed into a truly adversary litigation of substantial proportions.

***

Following a trial to the court of some 28 trial days, during which the court heard testimony of some 20 witnesses and received more than 100 exhibits and made 2 inspections of UNB, one by boat and one by automobile, the court rendered a thoughtful memorandum opinion (later modified), made extensive findings of fact and conclusions of law and, on February 11, 1971 [issued an order that, among other things, held the proposed land exchange valid. Opponents of the exchange, including local citizens' groups, have appealed that decision.]

Pertinent Facts

UNB is a portion of a single bay known as Newport Harbor or Newport Bay. It is that portion of the greater harbor which extends north of the Pacific Coast Highway and it and its tidelands are now located entirely within the limits of the City of Newport Beach and within the area encompassed by Harbor District.

In 1901, James Irvine, predecessor in interest to Irvine Company, received from the State of California a tidelands patent to some 243 acres of tidelands lying at the upper end of UNB (hereinafter the patented tidelands). Irvine is the fee owner of

Figure 7-5. 1908 Map of Newport Bay
The three islands and the patented tidelands described in the opinion are in the rectangles.

these patented tidelands, but its fee ownership is subject to a public easement and right generally referred to as the public easement or trust for navigation, commerce and fishing. . . . Irvine also claims to be the fee owner of three islands, comprising 103.3 acres of uplands, lying astride the channel of UNB as well as substantially all of the uplands contiguous to UNB and its tidelands.

By chapter 526, Statutes of 1919 as amended by chapter 575, Statutes of 1929 (the granting statutes) the State granted to County, in trust, the tidelands and submerged lands bordering upon and under UNB then outside the city limits of Newport Beach. These lands, although technically a combination of tidelands and submerged lands . . ., will hereinafter be referred to as the granted tidelands or the County tidelands. They comprise some 403.7 acres.

***

Over the past 45 years, commencing in 1925, a number of studies have been made concerning the development of UNB as a harbor. Each study acknowledged the necessity of dredging away the Irvine-owned islands to widen the existing channel. Most, if not all, of the studies envisioned an alienation or exchange of granted tidelands for the Irvine-owned islands and portions of the contiguous uplands.

***

[In the 1950s], County, Harbor District and Irvine proceeded to attempt to devise a final plan for the development of an improved harbor in the UNB. After many public hearings, consultation with recognized experts and affected public agencies and after consideration of all the prior planning and modification of several proposed plans, County, Harbor District and Irvine finally settled on the Plan entitled "Upper Newport Bay Land Exchange Plan," dated March 31, 1964. Pursuant to the Plan, on January 13, 1965, County, Harbor District and Irvine entered into the land exchange agreement and the dredging and landfill agreement challenged in this proceeding.

The Plan envisions the creation of a navigable waterway averaging 800 feet in width extending about 2.5 miles north from the Pacific Coast Highway bridge, which is to be reconstructed at a higher level. At the north end of the granted (County) tidelands, the waterway would widen into a turning basin. Beyond this, mainly on what are now patented (Irvine) tidelands, there would be a mile-long rowing course and a marine stadium separated by a long, somewhat narrow arm of public park land fronted by a swimming beach. To the north of the marine stadium, the general use diagram attached as appendix VIII to the Plan depicts additional public park land with boat launching facilities. About halfway between the north and south ends of the new waterway on the east side there is depicted a public park of approximately 67 acres having about 1,600 feet of channel frontage. On the west side of the new waterway the only public ownership indicated consists of two small parks, each less than five acres, both having beaches along their 400 to 600 feet of water frontage. On the southeast side of the waterway there is depicted a public park with a swimming lagoon and boat launching facilities comprising approximately 70 acres, but this property is already in public ownership. All of the remaining land contiguous to the new waterway would be owned by Irvine and, according to the general use diagram would be used in various parts for low-density housing, medium-density housing, aquatic commercial uses and private boat basins.

To accomplish this, portions of the three islands owned by Irvine together with certain portions of Irvine's contiguous fee-owned uplands are to be dredged away to create the waterway and, in effect, moved to the sides of the waterway. Portions of the filled areas to the sides of the waterway are to be conveyed to Irvine in exchange for the Irvine properties to be dredged away. In addition, Irvine is to convey to County a total of 120 acres of fee-owned uplands contiguous to UNB which, according to the general use diagram, are to be utilized by County for access and public park lands as described in the foregoing paragraph. Finally, Irvine is to convey to County its fee ownership of a portion of the patented tidelands, and County is to release the remaining portions of the patented tidelands from the easement and public trust for navigation, commerce and fishing.

***

Contentions, Issues and Disposition

From our viewpoint, the case and the contentions of the parties raise not only the ultimate question of the validity of the land exchange agreement but also grave questions relating to the proper operation of our tripartite system of constitutional government, specifically the proper function of the judiciary vis-à-vis the Legislature and the [state lands commission] exercising quasi-legislative functions. . . . These fundamental questions are made more complex by the fact that the tidelands trust with which we are dealing in this case is embodied in the California Constitution. . . . Moreover, in resolving these problems we, as an intermediate appellate court, are not entirely free. We are bound by pertinent decisions of the California Supreme Court. . . . With some misgivings, we have concluded that the land exchange agreement and the action of the [state lands commission] purporting to free from the constitutional tidelands trust the lands to be conveyed to Irvine are violative of the prohibition against alienation of tidelands into private ownership found in Article XV, Section 3 of the California Constitution as interpreted and applied in *City of Long Beach v. Mansell*, 3 Cal. 3d 462, 482-486 (1970). This conclusion makes unnecessary our consideration of a number of contentions of the parties, but the fundamental nature of the questions presented and the interrelation of several of the issues require considerable exposition.

***

We turn now to the dispositive issues.

Article XV, Section 3 of the California Constitution provides in pertinent part: "All tidelands within two miles of any incorporated city, city and county, or town in this State, and fronting on the water of any harbor, estuary, bay or inlet used for the purposes of navigation, shall be withheld from grant or sale to private persons, partnerships or corporations; . . ." This constitutional provision (sometimes hereinafter referred to as the constitutional tidelands trust) was recently interpreted and applied by the California Supreme Court in *City of Long Beach v. Mansell, supra*. Distinguishing the common law tidelands trust doctrine, the court in *Mansell* specifically recognized the flat prohibition in Article XV, Section 3 of the California Constitution against alienation of tidelands within two miles of an incorporated city but, nevertheless, delineated three situations in which the prohibition did not apply: (1) the settlement of a genuine boundary dispute . . .; (2) a situation in which the circumstances are such as to create an equitable estoppel . . .; and (3) under the particular, limited circumstances there involved, a small, beneficial land exchange. Neither a boundary dispute nor equitable estoppel are involved in the case at bench. Respondents contend and the trial court found, however, the land exchange agreement here in question to be constitutional under the principles explicated in *Mansell* relating to the land exchange in that case.

***

The land exchange proposed in *Mansell* may be summarized as follows. Some five acres of tidelands had been filled and reclaimed in the course of a public program of harbor development which resulted in the creation of marine stadium in Long Beach. These five acres were to be conveyed to the McGrath Testamentary Trust in exchange for 8.5 acres of McGrath lands abutting either Long Beach Harbor or existing public trust facilities. The 8.5-acre parcel was said to be of such a configuration that it could be used more effectively by the city and state in furtherance of the public trust purposes than the 5 acres to be exchanged therefor. Moreover, the exchange itself was sought to be made in furtherance of an existing and on-going program of harbor development. . . .

In upholding this exchange, the court stated:

> However the language in *Atwood v. Hammond*, 4 Cal. 2d 31, 41-43 (1935) may be characterized in terms of its value as precedent, we think that it represents a clear statement of this court that Article XV, Section 3, does not forbid alienation of lands within two miles of an incorporated city which have been reclaimed "as the result of a highly beneficial program of harbor development," are relatively small in area, and have been freed of the public trust by legislative act. . . . Secondly, we consider that the principle of the *Atwood* case is wholly consistent with the purposes of the framers of the Constitution. The debates at the Constitutional Convention, to which we have adverted above, reveal a general intention to retain tidelands within two miles of incorporated cities in order that such tidelands might be utilized in the public interest for navigational and related purposes rather than in the interest of private persons to whom they might be granted. Surely if in the course of, and for the purpose of carrying out, a comprehensive public program of harbor development certain portions of tidelands are filled under circumstances clearly showing that, in the light of the relatively minor area involved and the manner of reclamation in relation to the program as a whole, such reclamation is merely a reasonably necessary incident of the program and of the promotion of its public objective, and if thereafter such filled areas are declared by the Legislature to be of no value for navigational and related purposes, then we think that a sale and transfer into private ownership of such filled-in areas might be found to be entirely consistent with the intention and objective of the framers of the Constitution. But we emphasize that the circumstances under which this may occur are of necessity unique, that the conditions sanctioning its approval must be scrupulously observed and satisfied, and that generally speaking the reclaimed area alleged to be free from both the public trust and the constitutional restriction against alienation into private ownership must be, as it were, a residual product of the larger program — a "relatively small parcel" to use the language of *Atwood* (4 Cal. 2d at p. 43) — determined by the Legislature to have no further value for the purposes of the public easement.
>
> To reiterate, we conclude that when lands within two miles of an incorporated city or town which were subject to the ebb and flow of the tide at the date of the adoption of the Constitution — and which therefore are "tidelands" within the meaning of Article XV, Section 3 — (1) have been found and determined by the Legislature to be valueless for trust purposes and are freed from the public trust [reference to prior footnote omitted] and (2) have been or are to be reclaimed pursuant to and in the course of a highly beneficial public program of harbor development, such lands — if they constitute a relatively small parcel of the total acreage involved — thereupon cease to be "tidelands" within the meaning of the

constitutional provision and are subject to alienation into absolute private ownership. [Fn. omitted.] 3 Cal. 3d at pp. 484, 485-486.

Our task is to determine whether the land exchange agreement in the case at bench "scrupulously satisfies" the several conditions with which the court in *Mansell* so carefully circumscribed the permissible conveyance of Article XV, Section 3 tidelands into private ownership as part of a beneficial land exchange.

∗∗∗

We [now] come . . . to what we view as the controlling issue. It will be remembered that one of the conditions set forth in *Mansell* as a prerequisite to a permissible exchange of Article XV, Section 3 tidelands was that the tidelands to be exchanged constitute "a relatively small parcel." 3 Cal. 3d at pp. 485, 486. The trial court adopted both a finding of fact and a conclusion of law that the lands to be conveyed to Irvine in the exchange constitute a "relatively small parcel" within the meaning of *Mansell*. The acreages and lineal feet of water-frontage involved, of course, are factual determinations by which we are bound if founded on substantial evidence. Whether these areas and distances constitute a "relatively small parcel" within the meaning of *Mansell*, however, is properly a conclusion of law subject to our determination. We have concluded that the lands to be conveyed to Irvine under the land exchange agreement do not constitute a "relatively small parcel" within the meaning of *Mansell*.

The following acreage and percentage figures are taken from the trial court's findings. [For help understanding the math in the remainder of the opinion, see Table 1 after the decision. — Eds.] County presently owns the granted tidelands comprising 403.7 acres together with the easement for public trust purposes over Irvine's patented tidelands comprising 243 acres. From the granted tidelands (403.7 acres) County is to convey to Irvine 97.9 acres, equivalent to 24 percent of the original granted tidelands. Of Irvine's patented tidelands, encumbered with the easement for public trust purposes (243 acres), Irvine is to convey to County the fee interest in 183.8 acres and County is to release from the easement for public trust purposes 59.2 acres, equivalent to 24 percent of the patented tidelands. On the other hand, Irvine is to convey to County to be dredged and become part of the channel contiguous uplands and portions of its three islands, totaling 146.5 acres. In addition, Irvine is to convey to County an additional 120 acres of its fee-owned uplands, primarily for parks and access.

In finding and concluding that the tidelands to be conveyed to Irvine constitute a relatively small parcel, the court computed the net acreage of the granted (County) tidelands to be conveyed to Irvine and the easement over the patented (Irvine) tidelands to be released to Irvine to be 10.6 acres, equivalent to 1.6 percent of the total combined acreage of the granted tidelands and the patented tidelands. In so doing, it offset against the 97.9 acres of granted (County) tidelands to be conveyed to Irvine and the 59.2 acres of patented (Irvine) tidelands as to which the easement is to be released, the 146.5 acres of uplands (consisting of contiguous uplands and portions of Irvine's three islands) to be conveyed by Irvine to County and to be dredged away to form the channel. In other words, the court subtracted from the total acreage to be conveyed to Irvine only the acreage of the lands being conveyed by Irvine to County that are to be dredged and become part of the harbor. The court did not subtract the additional

Quick Question

Why did the lower court exclude these two figures from its calculation?

120 acres of uplands contiguous to UNB to be conveyed by Irvine to County nor the fee title to the 183.8 acres of patented tidelands (encumbered by the easement for public trust purposes) to be conveyed by Irvine to County.

Appellants [opponents of the exchange — EDS.] contend that the subtraction process utilized by the trial court was not contemplated by and is impermissible under *Mansell*. They correctly point out that the language "relatively small parcel" was borrowed by the *Mansell* court from *Atwood v. Hammond, supra*, 4 Cal. 2d at page 43. . . . They urge that this terminology was used in *Atwood* to mean a small part of the original grant by the State to the subordinate public agency. (See *Atwood v. Hammond, supra*, 4 Cal. 2d at p. 41: "it was competent for the state by legislative action to terminate this public trust as to the 18-acre parcel, which constitutes but a *small part of the area granted to the city*." [Italics supplied.]) They urge that the proposed land exchange calls for conveyance to Irvine of 24 percent of the granted tidelands and, coincidentally, release of the public easement over the patented tidelands of 24 percent, and that such conveyance and release, involving 157.1 acres of Article XV, Section 3 tidelands cannot be considered a "relatively small parcel" within the meaning of *Mansell*. They further point out that the *Mansell* court did not employ any subtracting process such as is advocated in the case at bench. As previously pointed out, the exchange approved in *Mansell* involved 5 acres of filled, reclaimed tidelands for 8.5 acres of McGrath lands. Had the *Mansell* court employed a subtraction process, the result would have been a net gain to the public agencies of 3.5 acres. In this connection, appellants point out the restrictive language in the *Mansell* opinion: "But we emphasize that the circumstances under which this may occur are of necessity unique, that the conditions sanctioning its approval must be scrupulously observed and satisfied, and that generally speaking the reclaimed area alleged to be free from both the public trust and the constitutional restriction against alienation into private ownership must be, as it were, a residual product of the larger program — a 'relatively small parcel' to use the language of *Atwood* . . . — determined by the Legislature to have no further value for the purposes of the public easement." 3 Cal. 3d at p. 485.

Respondents, on the other hand, point out that in its reiteration of its holding, the *Mansell* court used the language "if they [the tidelands to be conveyed] constitute a relatively *small parcel of the total acreage involved*" (3 Cal. 3d at p. 486; italics supplied) and urge that this language supports the "net result" approach advocated by respondents. Respondents suggest that one explanation for the *Mansell* court's not employing any subtraction process might be that the 8.5 acres of McGrath lands were not themselves filled tidelands and that any subtraction process would, therefore, have been inappropriate in *Mansell*. We cannot be certain whether the 8.5 acres of McGrath lands to be received by the public agencies in *Mansell* were filled tidelands, but the implication in the opinion is that they were. They were identified in the opinion as a portion of the "section 2(b)" lands, which were filled, reclaimed tidelands . . . and it was noted that they "abut either water or existing public trust facilities." 3 Cal. 3d at p. 477.

More persuasively, however, respondents appeal to reason. They emphasize that the trial court deducted only the acreage of those parcels which were to be conveyed by Irvine to County to be dredged away to form part of the channel. When so dredged these lands would be in fact submerged lands and, thus, become subject to the public trust for navigation, commerce and fishing. . . . While, technically, we might be on firm ground in rejecting outright this subtraction process, for we do not believe any such process was envisioned in *Mansell*, nevertheless, we are reluctant to do so, for where, as here, the subtracted lands will themselves be tidelands or submerged lands, the appeal to logic is irresistible, and we can envision other situations in which such a subtraction process might prove a useful judicial tool.

Even if we accept the advocated subtraction process, however, we think there is another dimension to the "relatively small parcel" criterion that precludes classifying the lands to be conveyed to Irvine in the proposed exchange as a "relatively small parcel" within the meaning of *Mansell*. That dimension relates to the shoreline. At the present time through County's ownership in trust of the granted tidelands and its control over the public easement in the patented tidelands, the public has control of all of the shoreline of UNB. We recognize that, at present, access to the shoreline is limited and that the shoreline is in many places covered and uncovered by the ebb and flow of the tide limiting its utility. Nevertheless, the public does presently control the entire shoreline, and as a result of the exchange it would be relinquishing two-thirds of the shoreline to be conveyed into private ownership. We do not believe that in formulating the "relatively small parcel" criterion, the *Mansell* court meant to countenance public relinquishment of two-thirds of the shoreline of an entire bay. We fully recognize that the trial court found the public benefits to outweigh this detriment, but it must ever be borne in mind that in dealing with the conveyance of Article XV, Section 3 tidelands, it is not benefit with which we are concerned; it is constitutionality.

* * *

The judgment is reversed. . . .

points for discussion

1. *The state as grantor and clear intent.* In *CWC Fisheries*, the Supreme Court of Alaska states that:

> Before any tideland grant may be found to be free of the public trust under the "public trust purposes" theory, the legislature's intent to so convey it must be clearly expressed or necessarily implied in the legislation authorizing the transfer. . . . If any interpretation of the statute which would retain the public's interest in the tidelands is reasonably possible, we must give the statute such an interpretation. . . .

Table 1. Framing the Exchange in *Heim*

Details of Proposed Land Exchange	
Before	
Orange County owns	**Irvine Company owns**
403.7 acres of granted tidelands	243 acres of patented tidelands (subject to public easement)
243 acres of public easement over Irvine Company patented tidelands	146.5 acres of upland (three islands)
	120 acres of upland (adjacent to UNB)
After	
Orange County owns	**Irvine Company owns**
305.8 acres of granted tidelands (fee simple)	97.9 acres of granted tidelands (fee simple)
183.8 acres of patented tidelands (fee simple)	59.2 acres of patented tidelands (fee simple)
120 acres of upland (adjacent to UNB)	
146.5 acres of upland (three islands)	
Trial Court's Calculation	
Public tidelands before exchange	**Public tidelands after exchange**
403.7 acres of granted tidelands	305.8 acres of granted tidelands (fee simple)
243 acres of public easement (over Irvine Company patented tidelands)	183.8 acres of patented tidelands (fee simple)
	146.5 acres where islands had been
Net change in public tidelands: 646.7 acres (before) − 636.1 acres (after) = 10.6 acres	
Plan Opponents' Calculation	
Public gives up	
97.9 acres of granted tidelands	
Easement over 59.2 acres of patented tidelands	
Total amount of public access to tidelands conveyed: 157.1 acres	
Court of Appeals' Calculation	
Percent of shoreline tidelands open to public access before exchange	**Percent of shoreline tidelands open to public access after exchange**
100	33
Net change in percentage of shoreline tidelands open to public access: 100 − 33 = 67% reduction	

This rule of strict construction is an extension of the general rule that, when a state is the grantor in a property transaction, the grant is to be read as narrowly as possible:

> ... [I]n construing this grant, the State is entitled to the benefit of certain well-settled canons of construction that pertain to grants by the State to private persons or corporations, as, for instance, that if there is any ambiguity or uncertainty in the act that interpretation must be put upon it which is most favorable to the State; that the words of the grant, being attributable to the party procuring the legislation, are to receive a strict construction as against the grantee. ...

Illinois Central, 146 U.S. at 468.

Courts will read state grants even more narrowly where the grant, like a grant that affects public trust property, is "in derogation of sovereignty." *United States v. 2899.17 Acres of Land*, 269 F. Supp. 903, 909 (M.D. Fla. 1967). Is this another "version" of the public trust doctrine? In *CWC Fisheries*, the court applies the rule of strict construction to find that transfers made pursuant to the class 1 preference provisions do not fit into either of the public purpose or *de minimis* categories established in *Illinois Central*. How might a court apply the rule of strict construction in interpreting the terms of a public purpose or *de minimis* grant?

2. *The meaning of "no substantial impairment" or "relatively small parcel."* Given the obviously vague language found in *Illinois Central* and *Mansell*, cited in *Heim*, how should courts go about determining whether a given transfer is small enough to be "freed from the public trust"? Is size the only important consideration, or should a court also look into the use-value lost due to the transfer or exchange?

3. *Changes in use.* Suppose that a state transfers submerged lands in fee simple to a private party so that the private party can then develop a marina. Assume that such a transfer fits within the public purpose category, that is, it is permanent and freed from public trust limitations. Many decades later, the private owner decides to close the marina and build an apartment building on the pilings. Does the state have the power (or the obligation) to reclaim the property? *See Boston Waterfront Dev. Corp. v. Commonwealth*, 393 N.E.2d 356 (Mass. 1979) (implied condition subsequent that transferred lands always be used for a public purpose).

4. *The fate of Upper Newport Bay.* According to the Newport Bay Naturalists and Friends organization:

> ... In the 1950's and 1960's the Irvine Company and the County of Orange were planning an exchange of property in/around the Bay that would have resulted in hotels and marinas being built along its shoreline.
>
> In 1969 a lawsuit was filed by the County Auditor, Fran and Frank Robinson, and others to resolve the constitutional issues surrounding the land swap. At about the same time the Friends of Newport Bay was formed to press for public ownership of the entire Upper Bay. As a result of the

determined efforts of the Robinsons and others, 572 acres was purchased from the Irvine Company by the State and another 214 acres was transferred from the County and Upper Newport Bay Ecological Reserve was created.

The Ecological Reserve was dedicated on April 11, 1975 with the following words, "In the name of the people of the State of California, so that this and future generations may continue to have, to use and enjoy the priceless heritage of the wildlife resources, the Upper Newport Bay Ecological Reserve is hereby dedicated."

c. Disposing with the Duty Not to Dispose

In *Illinois Central*, the Supreme Court held that the Illinois legislature did not have the power to transfer substantial amounts of public trust property into private hands. This holding implies that the public trust doctrine is something more than common law, because statutes enacted by a legislature (and signed by a governor or the President) generally trump court-created rules. Specifically, *Illinois Central* can be read as casting the public trust doctrine as implied and immutable "super law." (*Heim*, of course, presents a different scenario because, in California, the doctrine has been incorporated into the state's constitution.)

As mentioned in the notes following *Illinois Central*, there are those who would argue that this is inconsistent with the notion that the legislature is the most democratic branch of government. Moreover, pondering the duty not to dispose inevitably leads to a paradox: On the one hand, disposal is seen to be contrary to the public interest; on the other hand, there are cases in which disposal would be in the public interest. *Illinois Central*'s limitation on the duty not to dispose represents one approach to mediating this tension; here is another.

Gwathmey v. State of North Carolina

464 S.E.2d 674 (N.C. 1995)

Chief Justice MITCHELL delivered the opinion of the Supreme Court of North Carolina.

The parties stipulated at trial that the lands claimed by each of the plaintiffs that comprise the subject of this litigation are marshlands located between the high and low water marks in the Middle Sound area of New Hanover County. Title to the lands in question was conveyed by the State Board of Education (SBE) to the original purchasers of the marshlands between 1926 and 1945. Each of the deeds from the SBE to the original purchasers purports to convey a tract of "marshland" in the "Middle Sound" area to the purchasers, their "heirs and assigns in fee simple forever."

***

In 1965, the General Assembly enacted N.C.G.S. § 113-205, which required individuals who claimed any part of the bed lying beneath navigable waters of any coastal county to register their claims with the Secretary of the Department of Natural Resources by 1 January 1970, or their claims would be null and void. The plaintiffs in this case, or their predecessors in interest, registered their claims in compliance with this statute. The parties stipulated that the plaintiffs' submerged lands claims,

Photo: Gerry Dincher/Wikimedia Commons

Figure 7-6. Salt Marsh in North Carolina

as originally filed, included both marshlands lying between the mean high and mean low water marks of Middle Sound and lands beyond the mean low water mark that lie beneath the open waters of Middle Sound or Howe Creek. In 1987, the Submerged Lands Program, which was established to assess the validity of the claims of title previously registered pursuant to N.C.G.S. § 113-205, came under the administration of the Division of Marine Fisheries. In assessing the plaintiffs' claims, the Division of Marine Fisheries issued resolution letters concluding that the plaintiffs had valid titles to the marshlands between the mean high and mean low water marks. However, pursuant to N.C.G.S. § 146-20.1(b), the resolution letters purporting to validate the plaintiffs' titles to the marshlands were accompanied in each case by a purported reservation of public trust rights in those same marshlands. The plaintiffs responded by filing separate complaints against the State between 26 February 1991 and 31 May 1991, in Superior Court, New Hanover County, seeking a determination of the quality of their titles to the marshlands and other relief. The plaintiffs' actions were consolidated by consent of all the parties following filing of the State's answer.

***

Based upon its findings and conclusions, the trial court ordered, adjudged, and decreed that the plaintiffs were owners in fee simple absolute without any reservation of public trust rights of the "certain tract of marshlands described" in each of their deeds. With regard to the claims of the plaintiffs Richard and Gwendolyn Gwathmey, however, the trial court adjudged and decreed that "those areas of deeded bottom lying beneath the open waters of Howe Creek and within the boundaries of Plaintiffs' [Gwathmey] deed are owned in fee simple subject to the public trust."

The defendant State of North Carolina gave notice of appeal. On 7 April 1994, this Court allowed the defendant's petition for discretionary review prior to a determination by the Court of Appeals.

Before addressing the specific issues raised on this appeal, we will briefly discuss the public trust doctrine and the operation of the entry laws in North Carolina. A brief introductory review of these two areas of the law at this point will facilitate an understanding of the issues raised on this appeal.

This Court has long recognized that after the Revolutionary War, the State became the owner of lands beneath navigable waters but that the General Assembly has the power to dispose of such lands if it does so expressly by special grant. . . . However, "looming over any discussion of the ownership of estuarine marshes is the 'public trust' doctrine — a tool for judicial review of state action affecting State-owned submerged land underlying navigable waters, including estuarine marshland, and a concept embracing asserted inherent public rights in these lands and waters." Monica Kivel Kalo & Joseph J. Kalo, *The Battle to Preserve North Carolina's Estuarine Marshes: The 1985 Legislation, Private Claims to Estuarine Marshes, Denial of Permits to Fill, and the Public Trust*, 64 N.C. L. REV. 565, 572 (1986).

In *Tatum v. Sawyer*, 9 N.C. 226 (1822), this Court recognized the importance of navigable waters as common highways and held: "Lands covered by navigable waters are not subject to entry under the entry law of 1777, not by any express prohibition in that act, but, being necessary for public purposes as common highways for the convenience of all, they are fairly presumed not to have been within the intention of the Legislature." . . . Thus, this Court has recognized the public interests inherent in navigable waters and qualified the State's ability to part with title to lands submerged by navigable waters with a presumption that legislative enactments do not indicate a legislative intent to authorize the conveyance of lands beneath navigable waters. . . . The practical significance of this presumption under the public trust doctrine is that it can operate to invalidate claims to lands submerged by navigable waters.

***

This Court's discussions of navigability have arisen most often in cases where the parties claimed title to contested lands under grants obtained pursuant to the general entry laws. In 1777, the General Assembly enacted the entry laws, also known as the "general entry laws." These laws established a system whereby the people of North Carolina could acquire the State's unappropriated vacant lands. The entry laws provided for the election of "entry-takers" and surveyors in every county. An individual who wished to acquire State land was first required to pay the statutory amount set for the quantity of land purchased in addition to the fees authorized by the laws. Subsequently, the surveyor was required to enter the lands claimed and survey them. The entry laws also provided that if part of the survey was made on any navigable water, the water was to form one boundary of the land surveyed. The law prescribed the manner in which the individual received a grant from the State for the land surveyed and in which that grant would be registered in the county in which the land was located.

***

The State's argument that the public trust doctrine prevents the State from conveying lands beneath navigable waters without reserving public trust rights is based principally on two cases. The first is *Shepard's Point Land Co. v. Atlantic Hotel*, 132 N.C. 517 (1903), which involved competing claims to waterfront property in Morehead City based on general entry law grants. The defendant's property consisted of dry land on the shore of Bogue Sound. The land claimed by the plaintiff was submerged by the navigable waters of Bogue Sound and was located directly in front of the defendant's waterfront property. Before reaching its ultimate conclusion, this Court quoted the following language from a United States Supreme Court case: "'The control of the State for the purposes of the [public] trust can never be lost except as to such parcels as [1] are used in promoting the interests of the public therein or [2] can be disposed of without any substantial impairment of the public interest in the lands and waters remaining.'" *Id.* at 527 (quoting *Illinois Cent. R. Co. v. Illinois*, 146 U.S. 387, 453 (1892)).[5]

The State contends that the validity of any conveyance of land encumbered with the public trust must be judged with reference to the principles enunciated in *Shepard's Point Land Co.* That case is not controlling. The quoted statement was obiter dictum in *Shepard's Point Land Co.* because in that case the plaintiff's claim of title was based on the general entry laws. This Court based its decision to reject the plaintiff's claim on the well-established principle that lands submerged by navigable waters are not subject to entry under the general entry laws. We reject the above statement in *Shepard's Point Land Co.* to the extent that it implies that the public trust doctrine completely prohibits the General Assembly from conveying lands beneath navigable waters to private parties without reserving public trust rights. That position is without authority in either our statutes or our Constitution.

In *State v. Twiford*, 136 N.C. 603, 48 S.E. 586 (1904), this Court said: "Navigable waters are free. They cannot be sold or monopolized. They can belong to no one but the public and are reserved for free and unrestricted use by the public for all time. Whatever monopoly may obtain on land, the waters are unbridled yet." *Id.* at 609. To the extent that this statement in *Twiford* can be read expansively to indicate that the General Assembly does not have the power to convey lands underlying navigable waters in fee, it too was mere obiter dictum, unsupported by our laws or our Constitution, and is hereby expressly disapproved.

In *State ex rel. Rohrer v. Credle*, 322 N.C. 522, 369 S.E.2d 825 (1988), this Court said:

> Navigable waters, then, are subject to the public trust doctrine, insofar as this Court has held that where the waters covering land are navigable in law, those lands are held in trust by the State for the benefit of the public. A land grant in fee embracing such submerged lands is void.

---

5. It is worth noting that the Supreme Court in *Illinois Central* admitted that no authority supported its position. *Illinois Cent. R. Co.*, 146 U.S. at 455. More importantly, that case did not involve North Carolina law.

Id. at 527 (citing *Shepard's Point Land Co.*, 132 N.C. 517, 44 S.E. 39). The first sentence is entirely consistent with our opinion in this case. The second sentence is true in the sense that a land grant in fee pursuant to the general entry laws and conveying such submerged lands is void. However, we hereby expressly reject any construction of the second sentence in the above quotation from *Credle* that would support the proposition that the General Assembly is powerless to convey lands lying beneath navigable waters free of public trust rights when it does so by special legislative grant. To construe the second sentence so broadly would conflict with the long-established rule of *Ward v. Willis*, 51 N.C. 183 (1858) (per curiam), that fee simple conveyances — without reserving rights to the people under the public trust doctrine — of lands beneath navigable waters pursuant to special legislative grants are valid. Further, our construction of the second sentence recognizes that in *Rohrer* this Court relied on cases involving grants under the general entry laws to support its statement in the second sentence. Thus, we are only limiting the statement there to the precedent established in those cases.

In *Credle*, we also quoted with approval dictum from our decision in *Twiford* to the effect that lands under navigable waters can never be conveyed in fee simple. . . . For reasons previously discussed in our analysis of *Twiford* in this opinion, we expressly disavow any such statements.

In *Martin v. N.C. Housing Corp.*, 277 N.C. 29 (1970), this Court restated the long-established principle that "'under our Constitution, the General Assembly, so far as that instrument is concerned, is possessed of full legislative powers unless restrained by express constitutional provision or necessary implication therefrom.'" . . . Similarly, in *State ex rel. Martin v. Preston*, 325 N.C. 438 473 (1989), we emphasized that "all power which is not expressly limited by the people in our State Constitution remains with the people, and an act of the people through their representatives in the legislature is valid unless prohibited by that Constitution". . . .

No constitutional provision throughout the history of our State has expressly or impliedly precluded the General Assembly from conveying lands beneath navigable waters by special grant in fee simple and free of any rights arising from the public trust doctrine. *See Battle to Preserve N.C.'s Estuarine Marshes*, 64 N.C. L. REV. at 576-77. The public trust doctrine is a common law doctrine. In the absence of a constitutional basis for the public trust doctrine, it cannot be used to invalidate acts of the legislature which are not proscribed by our Constitution. Thus, in North Carolina, the public trust doctrine operates as a rule of construction creating a presumption that the General Assembly did not intend to convey lands in a manner that would impair public trust rights. "Unless clear and specific words state otherwise, terms are to be construed so as to cause no interference with the public's dominant trust rights, for the presumption is that the sovereign did not intend to alienate such rights." *RJR Technical Co. v. Pratt*, 339 N.C. 588, 590 (1995). However, this presumption is overcome by a special grant from the General Assembly expressly conveying lands underlying navigable waters in fee simple and without reservation of any public trust rights. . . .

For the foregoing reasons, we conclude that the General Assembly is not prohibited by our laws or Constitution from conveying in fee simple lands underlying waters that are navigable in law without reserving public trust rights. The General Assembly has the power to convey such lands, but under the public trust doctrine it will be presumed not to have done so. That presumption is rebutted by a special grant of the General Assembly conveying the lands in question free of all public trust rights, but only if the special grant does so in the clearest and most express terms.

***

We imply no criticism here of the able trial court. As we have indicated throughout this opinion, the law involving the public trust doctrine has been recognized by this and other courts as having become unnecessarily complex and at times conflicting.

***

Judgment vacated and case remanded.

points for discussion

1. *Is the public trust doctrine state law or something else?* Go back and re-read footnote 5 in the *Gwathmey* opinion. Is the North Carolina Supreme Court correct in interpreting *Illinois Central* as resting on Illinois law? Could a state abandon its trust assets and its trust responsibilities altogether?

2. We saw in Chapter 6, in *Phillips*, that the Supreme Court believes that states have some power to define trust property and thus, the scope of the trust corpus: According to the Court's opinion in that case, "it has long been established that the individual States have the authority to define the limits of the lands held in public trust and to recognize private rights in such lands as they see fit." *Phillips Petroleum Co. v. Mississippi*, 484 U.S. 469, 475 (1988). Similar language can be found in a more recent case, *PPL Montana v. Montana*, 565 U.S. 576 (2012). In that case, Montana asserted ownership of riverbeds in three separate rivers and sought rents from a power company that had long before built dams on those riverbeds. The legal issue was essentially whether Montana could claim beds of entire rivers as trust property, even if some stretches of those rivers were non-navigable at the time Montana entered the Union. The Supreme Court of Montana held that the state could claim the entirety of such rivers as trust property, but the U.S. Supreme Court disagreed. The Court asserted that federal rules, part of the equal-footing doctrine, governed the initial trust holdings given to each new state (and that states were only entitled to claim ownership of riverbeds under navigable segments). At the same time, the Court said: "Under accepted principles of federalism, the States retain residual power to determine the scope of the public trust over waters within their borders, while federal law determines riverbed title under the equal-footing doctrine." *Id.* at 604. Given this language, would the Court agree that a state could dispose of all its equal-footing endowment, abandoning the public trust doctrine altogether?

3. *Any limits to the North Carolina legislature's power to dispose?* Does the holding in this case mean that if the North Carolina legislature passed a special law deeding title to the entire Pamlico Sound to a private party, then the courts would have no power to set that transaction aside? If the answer is "yes," would that mean that the public could not enter the sound?

4. *Constitutionalizing the doctrine.* The court in *Gwathmey* recognizes that it would reach a different result if the doctrine were enshrined in the state constitution. Some states have incorporated the doctrine (or provisions to similar effect) into their constitutions. California's constitution, as we saw in *Heim*, contains a very detailed provision:

> No individual, partnership, or corporation, claiming or possessing the frontage or tidal lands of a harbor, bay, inlet, estuary, or other navigable water in this State, shall be permitted to exclude the right of way to such water whenever it is required for any public purpose, nor to destroy or obstruct the free navigation of such water; and the Legislature shall enact such laws as will give the most liberal construction to this provision, so that access to the navigable waters of this State shall be always attainable for the people thereof.

CAL. CONST. art. 10, §§ 3-4 (2009).

Likewise, Florida's constitutional provision is modeled on the holding in *Illinois Central*, but contains a broader exception to the duty not to dispose:

> The title to lands under navigable waters, within the boundaries of the state, which have not been alienated, including beaches below mean high water lines, is held by the state, by virtue of its sovereignty, in trust for all the people. Sale of such lands may be authorized by law, but only when in the public interest. Private use of portions of such lands may be authorized by law, but only when not contrary to the public interest.

FLA. CONST. art. 10, § 11 (2008).

And Rhode Island's constitution lays out the privileges of its citizens and the duties of its government with respect to its public trust lands.

> The people shall continue to enjoy and freely exercise all the rights of fishery, and the privileges of the shore, to which they have been heretofore entitled under the charter and usages of this state, including but not limited to fishing from the shore, the gathering of seaweed, leaving the shore to swim in the sea and passage along the shore; and they shall be secure in their rights to the use and enjoyment of the natural resources of the state with due regard for the preservation of their values; and it shall be the duty of the general assembly to provide for the conservation of the air, land, water, plant, animal, mineral and other natural resources of the state, and to adopt all means necessary and proper by law to protect the natural environment of the people of the state by providing adequate resource planning for the control and regulation of the use of the natural resources of the state and for the preservation, regeneration and restoration of the natural environment of the state.

R.I. CONST. art. 1, § 17 (2009).

For a complete survey of these provisions, and the forms that they take, see Matthew Thor Kirsch, *Upholding the Public Trust in State Constitutions*, 46 DUKE L.J. 1169 (1997).

2. The Duty to Protect Public Access

As we know, the core of the public trust doctrine is public access. States have a responsibility to ensure that members of the public have an opportunity to make use of public waterways. This duty is obviously very similar to the duty not to dispose: The state must prevent individuals from establishing private claims that then interfere with the rights of others to use and enjoy trust areas. So, for example, the state is responsible for enforcing the removal of unlicensed obstructions to navigation such as bridges or dams. Thinking back to *Illinois Central*, does the legislation described in the following newspaper story make sense?

Dan Barry, A Quiet Escape on the Rivers, and an Endangered Species

N.Y. Times, July 8, 2007, at A-12

On the Little Pee Dee River, S.C.

The boat moves through the murky river waters while swallow-tailed kites stir the evening sky and a little blue heron poses beside the cypress-lined shore, as if for Audubon. But these natural wonders only distract from the expedition's purpose, which is to seek out a specific endangered species.

Shhh. There's one now.

Photo: Angel Franco/New York Times/Redux

Figure 7-7. South Carolina River Shack

"River shack!" Chris Crolley, the boat captain, says, his tone a mix of awe and disgust. "There you go."

His vessel gently sidles up to the specimen: a kind of raft made of planks and 55-gallon drums, some plastic, some rusting metal, and featuring two padlocked tool sheds made of plywood. The few homey touches include a foot-tall plastic picket fence, a small grill, a couple of buckets that might serve as toilets, and a ceramic frog or two. Keeping it moored is a long pole bolted to an ancient cypress.

Mr. Crolley and others on his bobbing boat examine the unoccupied structure the way a clutch of botanists might study an unusual plant. They marvel at both the cheap construction — "This is on the lower end of nice," someone says — and the audacity of its appearance here on the scenic, public Little Pee Dee River, a few miles from the small town of Hemingway.

But this particular shack defies easy classification because it has not one but two sheds. Mr. Crolley, 36, so familiar with these waters that he is sometimes called Aquaman, pauses in thought before looking up from under his floppy hat and giving name to the subspecies before him. "Duplex," he says triumphantly.

For who knows how long, people have plopped these river shacks into watery coves and curves along the South Carolina coast. They permanently anchor their shacks miles from the nearest landing and use them to fish, hunt or just get off the grid for a while. Some contraptions are so modest that to call them shacks is too kind, while others are so well appointed that they all but cry out for granite countertops and potpourri.

It all sounds so innocent, so idyllic — so American, in a Huck Finn kind of way. That is, until you consider that the river shack owners are essentially laying claim to public property without paying license fees, taxes or, in some cases, even respect. A few people use the river as their personal toilet; others abandon their shacks, leaving the structures to rot amid the natural splendor.

But environmentalists who see these shacks as an affront to the concept of resource management recently succeeded in lobbying for their extinction. This spring the state passed a law requiring owners to seek permits for the structures — recent surveys counted at least 170 on several rivers and Lake Marion — with the stipulation that in five years all shacks must be removed from the water.

The law has angered people like John Hilton, 21, a college student who has spent years building and refining a river shack on Lake Marion with a few friends. "There's 90 55-gallon drums floating it," he says. "It has a tin roof, screened-in porches, and is made with treated lumber."

True, he says, he and his friends do not own land or water rights. And true, their river shack is analogous to some buddies plunking down a Home Depot shed on a public beach and calling it their own. "But I don't see it fair to bring that concern up after all these years of them being legal," he says.

The issue even posed a dilemma for Gov. Mark Sanford, who ultimately decided to allow the river shack bill to pass into law without his signature. While he supports land preservation, he explained in a letter to legislators, he wonders about increasing gentrification, and "the idea that someone could tie a bunch of 55-gallon drums together and stake out a house on the waterway is representative of what I would consider the magic of 'old time South Carolina.'"

But Patrick Moore, a lawyer working for the Coastal Conservation League, which led the legislative fight against river shacks, sees no dilemma. "The idea that these shacks are some sort of entitlement of our natural heritage is, frankly, an insult to that very heritage," he says.

Mr. Moore, 28, peers from under his own floppy hat as he sits in the back of Mr. Crolley's 18-foot boat, now churning north in search of more specimens. Mr. Crolley is a naturalist whose company, Coastal Expeditions, explores and celebrates the South Carolina coast. He tends to call out the scientific classification for every animal and tree he sees, and, like Mr. Moore, he detests river shacks.

They come upon a cluster of river shacks with no one home, a kind of hamlet, really. Here is a cute white cottage on the water — literally. And here is a structure that appears to be the Versailles of river shacks, with electric lights, an air conditioner, a stainless steel grill large enough to cook a whole pig, a —

"Is that a satellite dish?" Mr. Crolley asks, incredulous. "Yes it is."

The boat moves on, its passengers struggling with mixed feelings of outrage and envy. Soon an abandoned river shack appears on the horizon, and then another, and then another, victims of the swampy environment and neglect. All that is left of one are some Styrofoam pontoons, looking like faux ice floes. Another is flipped upside down, its only visitor the river, streaming through two broken windows.

No human comment is necessary. A flock of white ibises glides past. A jumping fish makes a splash. And a river in old time South Carolina carries on.

While the duty to remove obstructions is easy to understand, access issues can become complicated. The following two cases illustrate that the public's right of access is not readily translated into a right that accrues to individual members of the public.

State v. Vogt

775 A.2d 551 (N.J. 2001)

Judge WELLS delivered the opinion of the Superior Court of New Jersey, Appellate Division.

Defendant, Arlene Vogt, appeals from her conviction of "nudity in a public place" in violation of Lower Township Ordinance 3-2.6 in its Municipal Court. Arlene was again convicted upon her *de novo* appeal to the Law Division, Atlantic County, pursuant to R. 3:23-1. She was sentenced to pay a fine of $500 of which $450 was suspended, together

Photo: Bert Filemyr

Figure 7-8. Higbee Beach, New Jersey Wildlife management area?

with $30 in costs. The conduct for which Vogt was convicted consisted essentially of appearing topless on a public bathing beach known as Higbee Beach in Lower Township, Cape May County.

∗∗∗

Ordinance 3-2.6, upon which Arlene was convicted, states:

Indecent or Nude Exposure. It shall be unlawful for any person to appear or travel on any street, avenue, highway, road, boardwalk, beach, beach front or waterway located in the Township of Lower, or to appear in any public place, store or business in said borough in a state of nudity or in an indecent or lewd dress or garment, or to make any indecent or unnecessary exposure of his or her person.

The evidence introduced before the municipal judge was neither complicated nor in dispute. The State's only witness at the municipal court trial was the arresting officer, Officer Martin Biersbach. According to his testimony, on August 7, 1999, at about 4:10 P.M., he was walking with binoculars on Higbee Beach, trying to find nude people to charge with violating the public-nudity ordinance. Through his binoculars he spotted what appeared to be two men in bathing suits, but as he approached he saw that one was a woman, defendant Arlene; the man with her was her husband, William. Also in the area was "a camera man from a news channel."

Seeing that Arlene was not wearing a top, Biersbach asked her for identification; after she identified herself, he advised her that she was in violation of the public-nudity ordinance. She asked for a summons because "she wanted to address it in court." He gave her a summons citing the number of the ordinance and describing the offense as "Nudity in Public Place." He did not cite William. Arlene was on the state-owned portion of Higbee Beach; in the companion appeal, William appeared nude on the federally owned portion.

Arlene chose not to testify. On her behalf William testified that when his wife was cited by Biersbach, she insisted that she was not "nude" because she was wearing a bathing suit bottom. William had been sunbathing nude on Higbee Beach since 1979. As the beach was well known as a destination for nudists, no one was ever alarmed at seeing nudity there. William examined pictures of men's breasts introduced into evidence by Arlene, opining that some men's breasts were larger than women's breasts. William admitted that Arlene was topless at the time and that she was aware of the ordinance. William professed that, in his opinion, the ordinance was vague.

When asked by the judge if she had anything to say before sentencing, Arlene responded: "It's my first offense, so I would ask that you be lenient, and it was done as a test case simply to try to get nudity back at Higbee's Beach, or at least a portion of it. And the police department was informed of the action I was going to take that day."

Because to some extent we plow old ground in this case, we pause briefly to set forth the historical and legal context in which the issues arise. Both the Municipal Judge and the Law Division relied extensively on this history in considering the issues raised by Vogt. Higbee Beach has historically been the situs of public nude sunbathing. In *Tri-State Metro Naturists v. Lower Tp.*, 219 N.J. Super. 103, 107-108 (Law Div. 1987), Judge Gibson described the beach:

> The site of the nude sunbathing is a portion of a state-owned wildlife preserve known as Higbee Beach. Higbee Beach consists of approximately 200 acres of generally undeveloped land bordering on Delaware Bay along the southerly most tip of Cape May County. That property was purchased by the State of New Jersey in 1978, following which a Management Plan was adopted by the Department of Environmental Protection and implemented through the Division of Fish, Game and Wildlife. The Management Plan reflects the "growing number of outdoor enthusiasts" that visit the area and the "increasing popularity with such tourists as a free beach and place of quiet solitude." Pursuant to N.J.S.A. 13:8A-25 regulations were promulgated covering a wide variety of subjects, the primary purpose of which was to preserve wildlife but which included the management of human conduct as well, including recreational activities. . . . The recreational activity covered by the regulations is extensive and includes birdwatching, picnicking and bathing. No prohibition exists, however, with respect to nude bathing or sunbathing. . . .
>
> [T]he area can clearly be labeled as secluded. There is only one road that leads into Higbee Beach and the area is not easily accessible through neighboring property. It is not a place that one would stumble upon by accident. On the other hand, it is clearly open to the public and is used by a large number of people. The fact that it is remote and secluded, therefore, does not mean that it is private or out of public view.

***

In the present case before the Municipal Court, the Law Division and here, Arlene raised four issues which we paraphrase: (1) The ordinance is unconstitutionally vague on its face and as applied to her; (2) the ordinance denies equal protection under the Fourteenth Amendment to the United States Constitution because it distinguishes legal and illegal conduct on the basis of gender; (3) the ordinance denies equal protection under Art. 1, Para. 1 of the State Constitution because the individual rights it affects outweigh the asserted governmental interests it serves; and (4) given the historical pedigree of nude sunbathing at Higbee Beach, the application of the ordinance violates the "public trust" doctrine.

***

In a comprehensive written opinion Judge Garofolo resolved each of these issues against Arlene.

***

Arlene argues that her prosecution should have been deemed foreclosed by the "public trust doctrine." The public trust doctrine derives from Roman law; its original application was to allow all citizens to have access to tidal waters and the seashore. . . . While the doctrine was first "limited to the ancient prerogatives of navigation and fishing," our courts have extended it "to recreational uses, including bathing, swimming and other shore activities." [citation omitted]. In so expanding the doctrine, our Supreme Court opined that the doctrine, "like all common law principles, should not be considered fixed or static, but should be molded and extended to meet changing conditions and needs of the public it was created to benefit." [citation omitted].

Arlene seizes upon the latter language, which she says "forbids Lower Township from prohibiting, by ordinance or otherwise, the long-established, long-accepted, unremarkable use of the area for topless or nude sunbathing," which use falls within the category of "other shore activities" protected by the doctrine.

Judge Garofolo refused to apply the doctrine, drawing a distinction between the right of access, which is what the doctrine protects, and the right to be free of restrictions on that access, which lies outside the doctrine's scope. He reasoned:

> However, the public trust doctrine has never been extended to apply to any principle other than keeping beaches and tidal waters open for public fishing, navigation, swimming and recreation. Thus, *Matthews* [*v. Bay Head,* see Chapter 6 — EDS.] held that a municipality could not exclude non-resident members of the public from its beaches. . . . [The trial court mistakenly cited to *Matthews,* which dealt with nonprofit associations, not municipalities. — EDS.] While Ms. Vogt had access to and a right to use Higbee Beach, it does not follow that she had a right to sunbathe nude there.

In New Jersey the doctrine has been enforced mainly in the context of disapproving municipal regulations that favored residents over non-residents with regard to access to and fees for using beaches and related facilities. . . .

But courts applying the doctrine have recognized that the doctrine does not prevent a municipality from imposing reasonable restrictions on that access and use. Thus, in *Van Ness v. Deal,* 78 N.J. 174, 179 (1978), the Court, while applying the doctrine to open a beach to non-residents, recognized that "the municipality, in the exercise of its police power and in the interest of the public health and safety, would have the right to adopt reasonable regulations as to the use and enjoyment of the beach area."

In *State v. Oliver,* 320 N.J. Super. 405, 415-16, *certif. denied,* 161 N.J. 332 (1999), the court denied that the public-trust doctrine prevented a borough from closing its beach to surfboarders during a storm. Judge Carchman reasoned:

> The right of the public to enjoy that property encompassed by the doctrine is not inconsistent with the right of the sovereign, as trustee, to protect those utilizing such property. This is the essence of the government's inherent authority, if not its obligation, to act in the interest of the public safety and welfare. . . . Such action may take the form of the legitimate exercise of police power, for example, to close beaches and preclude use of property, even that falling within the Public Trust Doctrine, when the public safety and welfare is threatened. [*Ibid.*]

And the judge noted that the power to impose such use restrictions was granted by various statutes, including N.J.S.A. 40:61-22.20, which confers on shore towns the power to, "by ordinance, make and enforce rules and regulations for the government and policing of such lands [beaches], boardwalks, bathing facilities."

Thus Judge Garofolo correctly declined to accept Arlene's theory that because Higbee Beach is held in trust for the public, she was free to bare her breasts. Her freedom was subject to the township's power to impose such limits as reasonably lay within its statutory and inherent police powers.

***

Affirmed.

Weden v. San Juan County

958 P.2d 273 (Wash. 1998)

Justice JOHNSON delivered the opinion of the Supreme Court of Washington.

In January 1996, San Juan County passed an ordinance that banned the use of motorized personal watercraft, subject to certain limited exceptions, on all marine waters and one lake in that county. We are asked to determine whether that ordinance is unconstitutional or violative of the public trust doctrine. We conclude that it is neither and, consequently, reverse the Whatcom County Superior Court's judgment that the ordinance is void and of no force and effect and remand for entry of an order granting San Juan County's motion for summary judgment.

> **Note**
>
> "Motorized personal watercraft" is a more technical-sounding term for a jet ski.

Facts

The Board of Commissioners of San Juan County (Board) held public meetings on September 18 and 19, 1995, for the purpose of discussing what some citizens had identified as a growing problem with the use of motorized personal watercraft (PWC) in San Juan County waters.[1] Following those meetings, the Board conducted a workshop with the San Juan County Prosecuting Attorney "regarding drafting of proposed regulations regarding the use of Personal Watercraft in San Juan County. . . ." . . . On January 23, 1996, the Board conducted a public meeting on a proposed ordinance that was developed at the workshop. One week later, the Board adopted Ordinance No. 3-1996 (the Ordinance). The Ordinance prohibits the operation of PWC on all marine waters of San Juan County, except:

> During such time that the Personal Water Craft is being used for or engaged in interstate or foreign commerce; and that during such use the Personal Water Craft is following the most direct route practicable;

---

1. The Board reported receiving a petition signed by 1,479 people requesting that PWC be banned or restricted.

During such time that Personal Water Craft are operating under a permit issued by San Juan County or a United States Coast Guard Permit;

For emergency purposes when there is a reasonable belief that such use is necessary to protect persons, animals or property.

. . . The Ordinance also banned the use of PWC outright on Sportsman Lake in San Juan County.

A personal watercraft is defined in the Ordinance as "a vessel of less than sixteen feet (16') in length that is propelled by machinery, commonly a jet pump, and which is designed to be operated by a person sitting, standing or kneeling on the vessel, rather tha[n] being operated by a person sitting or standing inside the vessel."

***

The Ordinance contained an extensive list of "legislative findings" regarding the nature of the marine environment in San Juan County and the characteristics of PWC. Regarding the marine environment, the Ordinance states:

The marine waters of San Juan County has many species of threatened and endangered species of marine mammals and birds as visitors, migrants or residents that are sensitive to vessel traffic in and among the San Juan Islands. . . .

***

The refuges and other protected areas offer habitat [where] birds nest and rest and seals rest and nurture their young. Birds disturbed or panicked by vessels trample eggs and chicks, knock chicks from nests onto waves and rocks, and expose vulnerable offspring to sun, rain, and predators. Newborn seal pups may become separated from their mothers, crushed by a herd of panicked adults or be forced into cold or swift water prematurely. If the disturbances are continued entire refuge areas may be abandoned by wildlife.

The Board also noted that tourism, which is a "major economic factor" in San Juan County, is "heavily dependent" on visitors who seek "tranquillity" [sic] and the opportunity "to view marine life and habitat." . . . It made no findings specifically relating to the use of PWC on Sportsman Lake.

The Board's findings in reference to PWC were as follows:

PWCs are capable of high speeds, up to 60 MPH, have a high degree of maneuverability. Operation typically includes rapid changes of direction, rare travel in straight lines, and frequent operation in multiple numbers in a confined area. Operators are expected [to] be in contact with the water either by spray or falling overboard. PWCs are small and have a shallow draft which allows them to be operated at high speeds close to shore.

The high speed of a PWC, the rapidity with which it can change direction and the waves and noise it produces cause disruption to other vessels, swimmers and divers and the natural environment. If the operators violate the law, they are almost impossible to apprehend because of the high speed and high maneuverability. Because they rarely travel in straight lines, the vessel speed cannot be easily determined.

The Ordinance enumerates multiple effects of PWC about which the Board was concerned:

> The noise from PWCs interferes with the historical and current uses and enjoyment of the shoreline property. Although unmodified PWC are no louder than other types of boats, modifications to PWCs are more common than other vessels. PWCs commonly operate with other PWCs close together for reasons of safety, fun and convenience. As a general rule, additional PWCs operated in the same area will cause the overall noise level to increase. PWC[s] frequently operate in a small area causing conflict with shoreline users. Finally, part of the fun of PWC use is rapid acceleration, deceleration and the jumping of wakes. These operations create an uneven noise, that is louder when the PWC is out of the water, that is objectionable and has been compared in pitch to the sound of a mosquito. These characteristics are not shared by other vessels operated to reach a destination.

Washington State Archives

Figure 7-9. Map of San Juan County
1926 map of San Juan County, Washington.

> The operational characteristics of PWCs make them hazardous and incompatible with destination commercial and recreational vessel traffic in and through San Juan County. The maneuverability and ability to travel close to shore of PWCs make them able to harass wildlife and bird life unlike destination power vessels. These attributes are also inconsistent with the protection and preservation of the wildlife which inhabit the waters and refuges of the County. These attributes are also inconsistent with the tranquil lifestyle quality desired by the tourists and residents of the County.

> The operation of PWCs is less safe and more damaging in San Juan County marine waterways than in other waters because of cold water temperatures, changeable and unpredictable currents, variable tidal heights exposing rocks at different times, floating deadheads, rocks and reefs, and populations of marine life.

> Accident statistics for PWCs is not yet available for San Juan County, largely because PWC use is only emerging. The evidence from other larger communities where PWC is more established is helpful, however. A report entitled "California Boating Accident Report for 1994" showed that Personal Water Craft made up 13.1 percent of the boating industry, but were involved in 36 percent of all reported

boating accidents, 46 percent of the injuries and 17.5 percent of the fatalities and 17 percent of the property damage.

***

The high-speed, high-pitched sound, and ability to operate close to shore are characteristics that are unique to PWCs. While the effect of such operation on marine life in San Juan County is unknown, it cannot be beneficial and appear [sic] most likely to be deleterious. Although most wildlife is believed to be quick enough to avoid collisions with powerboats, it is unknown whether all marine life of San Juan County can react quickly enough to avoid PWCs. Without additional evidence to support the safety of PWCs, and given the harmful impact that could result to the County from destruction of its marine life it is found that the best policy is one of "prudent avoidance" and prohibition of PWCs within San Juan County.

***

The Washington State Legislature has enacted regulations regarding the operation of PWCs, which are inadequate for the unique conditions in San Juan County. . . .

Although noise is regulated by RCW 88.12.085, that regulation does not address the cumulative noise of vessels operating in the same area, the annoying impact of vessels that are not destination-bound, and other noise characteristics unique to PWCs.

Shortly after the Board enacted the Ordinance, a group of PWC users, PWC rental and sales businesses, and a PWC industry association (Respondents), brought suit against San Juan County in Whatcom County Superior Court. In their suit they sought a declaratory judgment that "Ordinance 3-1996 is illegal, void and of no force or effect." They alleged that the Ordinance violates Article XI, Section 11 of the Washington Constitution because it conflicts with state vessel registration and safety laws, as well as various other general state laws. Respondents also alleged that the Ordinance violates their right to substantive due process, is unconstitutionally vague, and is violative of the public trust doctrine.

***

Analysis

***

Police Power

Article XI, section 11 of the Washington Constitution provides that "[a]ny county, city, town or township may make and enforce within its limits all such local police, sanitary and other regulations as are not in conflict with general laws." Regarding this "constitutional grant of authority," we stated in *Hass v. City of Kirkland*, 78 Wn. 2d 929 (1971):

This is a direct delegation of the police power as ample within its limits as that possessed by the legislature itself. It requires no legislative sanction for its exercise so long as the subject-matter is local, and the regulation reasonable and consistent with the general laws.... While there are limits to the police power, the use of police power by government allows the Legislature to enact laws in the interest of the people. As described in *Lawton v. Steele*, 152 U.S. 133 (1894), the police power is vast:

> The extent and limits of what is known as the police power have been a fruitful subject of discussion in the appellate courts of nearly every State in the Union. *It is universally conceded to include everything essential to the public safety, health, and morals*, and to justify the destruction or abatement, by summary proceedings, of whatever may be regarded as a public nuisance. Under this power it has been held that the State may order the destruction of a house falling to decay or otherwise endangering the lives of passers-by; the demolition of such as are in the path of a conflagration; the slaughter of diseased cattle; the destruction of decayed or unwholesome food; the prohibition of wooden buildings in cities; the regulation of railways and other means of public conveyance, and of interments in burial grounds; the restriction of objectionable trades to certain localities; the compulsory vaccination of children; the confinement of the insane or those afflicted with contagious diseases; the restraint of vagrants, beggars, and habitual drunkards; the suppression of obscene publications and houses of ill fame; and the prohibition of gambling houses and places where intoxicating liquors are sold. *Beyond this, however, the State may interfere wherever the public interests demand it, and in this particular a large discretion is necessarily vested in the legislature to determine, not only what the interests of the public require, but what measures are necessary for the protection of such interests.* To justify the State in thus interposing its authority in behalf of the public, it must appear, first, that the interests of the public generally, as distinguished from those of a particular class, require such interference; and, second, that the means are reasonably necessary for the accomplishment of the purpose, and not unduly oppressive upon individuals. The legislature may not, under the guise of protecting the public interests, arbitrarily interfere with private business, or impose unusual and unnecessary restrictions upon lawful occupations. In other words, its determination as to what is a proper exercise of its police powers is not final or conclusive, but is subject to the supervision of the courts. *Lawton*, 152 U.S. at 136-37 (emphasis added) (citations omitted).

The above quoted language was adopted by *City of Seattle v. Ford*, 144 Wash. 107, 111-12 (1927).

***

The police power is firmly rooted in the history of this state, and its scope has not declined. In *Covell v. City of Seattle*, 127 Wn. 2d 874 (1995), we reiterated, "[m]unicipal police power is as extensive as that of the legislature, so long as the subject matter is local and the regulation does not conflict with general laws. ... The scope of police power is broad, encompassing all those measures which bear a reasonable and substantial relation to promotion of the general welfare of the people." *Covell*, 127 Wn. 2d at 878.

[Public Trust Doctrine]

Since as early as 1821, the public trust doctrine has been applied throughout the United States "as a flexible method for judicial protection of public interests in coastal lands and waters." Ralph W. Johnson et al., *The Public Trust Doctrine and Coastal Zone Management in Washington State*, 67 Wash. L. Rev. 521, 524 (1992). The doctrine protects "public ownership interests in certain uses of navigable waters and underlying lands, including navigation, commerce, fisheries, recreation, and environmental quality." Johnson, *supra*, at 524. The doctrine reserves a public property interest, the *jus publicum*, in tidelands and the waters flowing over them, despite the sale of these lands into private ownership. Johnson, *supra*, at 524. "The state can no more convey or give away this *jus publicum* interest than it can 'abdicate its police powers in the administration of government and the preservation of the peace.'" *Caminiti v. Boyle*, 107 Wn. 2d 662, 669 (1987) (quoting *Illinois Cent. R.R. v. Illinois*, 146 U.S. 387, 453 (1892)). Due to the "universally recognized need to protect public access to and use of such unique resources as navigable waters, beds, and adjacent lands," courts review legislation under the public trust doctrine with a heightened degree of judicial scrutiny, "as if they were measuring that legislation against constitutional protections." Johnson, *supra*, at 525, 526-27.

This court did not expressly adopt the public trust doctrine until 1987, but indicated then that the doctrine has always existed in Washington law. . . . The doctrine in Washington "prohibits the State from disposing of its interest in the waters of the state in such a way that the public's right of access is substantially impaired, unless the action promotes the overall interests of the public." *Rettkowski v. Department of Ecology*, 122 Wn. 2d 219, 232 (1993).

The test of whether or not an exercise of legislative power with respect to tidelands and shorelands violates the "public trust doctrine" is found in the following language of the United States Supreme Court:

> The control of the State for the purposes of the trust can never be lost, except as to such parcels as are used in promoting the interests of the public therein, or can be disposed of without any substantial impairment of the public interest in the lands and waters remaining.

Accordingly, we must inquire as to: (1) whether the State, by the questioned legislation, has given up its right of control over the jus publicum and (2) if so, whether by so doing the State (a) has promoted the interests of the public in the jus publicum, or (b) has not substantially impaired it. . . . (citations omitted).

We have previously acknowledged that the *jus publicum* interest encompasses the "rights of fishing, boating, swimming, water skiing, *and other related recreational purposes* generally regarded as corollary to the right of navigation and the use of public waters." *Caminiti*, 107 Wn. 2d at 669 (emphasis added). . . . Nevertheless, we agree with the County that the Ordinance does not violate the public trust doctrine because the County has not given up its right of control over its waters. Although the Ordinance prohibits a particular form of recreation, the waters are open to access by the *entire* public, including owners of PWC who utilize some other method of recreation.

While the Ordinance governs activities more appropriate for general state legislation, the State has failed to act. The San Juan County Ordinance cannot conflict with state laws that do not exist. Further, the Ordinance is consistent with the goals of statewide environmental protection statutes. Finally, it would be an odd use of the public trust doctrine to sanction an activity that actually harms and damages the waters and wildlife of this state.

Reasonable Exercise of Police Power

The Ordinance must be a "reasonable" exercise of the County's police power in order to pass muster under Article XI, Section 11 of the state constitution. *City of Seattle v. Montana*, 129 Wn. 2d 583, 591 (1996). "A law is a reasonable regulation if it promotes public safety, health or welfare and bears a reasonable and substantial relation to accomplishing the purpose pursued." *Montana*, 129 Wn. 2d at 592. . . . "[T]he wisdom, necessity and expediency of the law are not for judicial determination," and an enactment may not be struck down as beyond the police power unless it "is shown to be clearly unreasonable, arbitrary or capricious." *Homes Unlimited, Inc. v. City of Seattle*, 90 Wn. 2d 154, 159 (1978).

In *State ex rel. Faulk v. CSG Job Ctr.*, 117 Wn. 2d 493 (1991), we announced a two-part test to be employed when determining the validity of a statute passed pursuant to the police power. First, the statute must promote the health, safety, peace, education, or welfare of the people. . . . Second, the requirements of the statute must bear some reasonable relationship to accomplishing the purpose underlying the statute. *Id.*

The Ordinance indicates the ban on PWC is intended to prevent "disruption to other vessels, swimmers and divers and the natural environment," prevent interference "with the historical and current uses and enjoyment of the shoreline property," ensure the safety of "destination commercial and recreational vessel traffic," protect "wildlife and bird life," and further the tourism-based economy. . . .

***

In light of the evidence supporting the Board's findings, albeit contested by Respondents and their experts, and the Board's determination that PWC possess characteristics not shared by other watercraft, we are satisfied that the Ordinance constitutes a means reasonably necessary to achieve a legitimate public purpose.

***

Conclusion

In sum, we conclude that the Ordinance does not conflict [with] . . . the public trust doctrine. The Ordinance is reasonably necessary to further the County's legitimate public purposes and not unduly oppressive; it is a reasonable exercise of the County's police power. . . .

***

Justice SANDERS dissents.

* * *

Discussing the public trust doctrine . . . , the majority correctly acknowledges the legal status of these waters as held in trust for *all* the people of the State, although it fails to draw the necessary legal conclusion that use of these waters, therefore, is of truly general, not merely local, concern. In this regard the majority itself recognizes the broad public interest and ownership associated with these waters by observing " '[t]he *state* can no more convey or give away this jus publicum interest than it can "abdicate its police powers in the administration of government and the preservation of the peace." ' " Majority at 698 (quoting *Caminiti v. Boyle*, 107 Wn. 2d 662, 669 (1987), *cert. denied*, 484 U.S. 1008, 108 S. Ct. 703, 98 L. Ed. 2d 654 (1988) (citations omitted) (emphasis added)). And the majority even quotes approvingly from precedent to the effect that the public trust doctrine " 'prohibits the *State* from disposing of its interest in the waters of the state in such a way that the public's right of access is substantially impaired. . . .' " Majority at 698-99 (quoting *Rettkowski v. Department of Ecology*, 122 Wn. 2d 219, 232 (1993)) (emphasis added) (citations omitted). Elsewhere it acknowledges the *jus publicum* interest encompasses the " 'rights of fishing, boating, swimming, water skiing, *and other related recreational purposes* generally regarded as corollary to the right of navigation and the use of public waters.' " Majority at 699 (quoting *Caminiti*, 107 Wn. 2d at 669). The *jus publicum* interest in these waters and their use is of statewide interest to all the people of this State, not just a purely local interest to island residents.

* * *

Perhaps the point would be illustrated if San Juan County were to ban *all* boating from its waters. The difference then between that scenario and this ordinance would be mere degree, not kind, with respect to issues of locality. Similarly, what if Pierce County closed the Narrows to pleasure boating — would the majority opine that to be a purely local interest as well — even though the county would have cut the Sound in half politically?

This court has no prerogative to ignore the public trust doctrine. . . .

* * *

points for discussion

1. *Public or publics?* Since the first chapter, we've used the word "public" as if it referred to one homogenous group of people, all of whom shared the same values and interests. Of course, this is a fiction, and various sectors of the public want access for different reasons. *Weden*, for example, pitted jetskiers against members of the public who wanted to use the lake for other, incompatible purposes such as quiet recreation or, perhaps, fishing. Can you think

of ways, besides banning personal watercraft, that the county could have resolved the use conflict, perhaps through zoning?

2. *Reasonable regulation and the choice among competing uses.* In many cases similar to these, courts have found that the state can restrict access to public trust areas or put conditions on that access, where it is reasonable to do so. Is this at odds with the history and rationale of the public trust doctrine, which provide support for the idea that the government should not recognize too many private rights in public trust assets? Isn't giving exclusive beach access to clothed persons akin to giving them greater rights in, or a greater share of, trust assets? Recall point 5 after *Illinois Central.* Can you frame *Vogt* and *Weden* as challenges to constructive disposals? Or, is the reality simply that some trust uses, e.g., topless beachgoing and "ordinary" beachgoing, are not compatible; the state must choose one. *See Carstens v. Cal. Coastal Comm'n,* 182 Cal. App. 3d 277 (1986) (The public trust doctrine does not prevent the state from preferring one trust use over another.).

3. *The alternative.* One of the fundamental assumptions underlying the ancient public trust doctrine, for example, the Roman version discussed at the beginning of the chapter, is that some resources do not need the protections offered by private property because they are inexhaustible. Until recently, for example, people believed that there was no need to regulate use of fisheries (or to sell them into private hands) because they perceived no limit to the productivity of fish stocks. If there was no limit, there was no purpose to regulation: Everyone could take as much as he or she wanted without harming the ability of others to catch fish. Beginning in the mid-twentieth century, we began to understand the fallacy of inexhaustibility, and Garrett Hardin, among others, began to write about how unlimited pursuit of limited resources inevitably led to waste and destruction of those resources. Garrett Hardin, *The Tragedy of the Commons*, 162 Sci. 1243 (1969). In response, governments began to develop and implement systems for regulating catch. Do you think that increased demand for access to public trust areas means that the public trust doctrine must eventually cede to some other principle of managed access? Or, is the doctrine compatible with the notion of restricted access?

4. *Snowmobiles in Yellowstone and all-terrain vehicles on public beaches.* Conflicts between the use of motorized vehicles and wildlife or less noisy forms of recreation are becoming more and more common. For a history of the long and convoluted battle over snowmobile use in Yellowstone National Park, see Daniel L. Dustin & Ingrid E. Schneider, *The Science of Politics/The Politics of Science: Examining the Snowmobile Controversy in Yellowstone National Park*, 34 Envtl. Mgmt. 761 (2005). These issues also arise in National Seashores, many of which have long traditions of allowing off-road vehicle use. For a description of the issues in one such case, see the Cape Hatteras National Seashore Draft Off-Road Vehicle Management Plan (Mar. 5, 2010), http://parkplanning.nps.gov/document .cfm?parkID=358&projectId=10641&documentID=32596.

5. *Special closures along California's coast.* The California Marine Life Protection Act requires the establishment of a network of marine protected areas in state waters to achieve more effective ecosystem, habitat, and species protection, to promote recovery of species, to enhance scientific research and education opportunities, and to ensure that the state's marine protected areas are designed and managed as a network. In the process of implementing the Act, it became clear that certain locations along the coast that habitually are used by seabirds or marine mammals for roosting, hauling out, and/or breeding should be off-limits for human contact during times that the animals are using those locations. The presence of humans in these areas disturbs the animals and potentially interrupts reproduction or endangers individual survival. Relying on its general authority under the California Public Resources Code, the state included several "special closure" areas (where human access is strictly prohibited) within the network of marine protected areas in order to protect animals' survival and ability to reproduce successfully. Is this permissible state action under the public trust doctrine? Does the breadth of the state's interpretation of the doctrine matter? In other words, would a California court likely render a different holding than a South Carolina or New Jersey court?

6. *The local role.* Note that *Weden* and *Vogt* involved county and municipal ordinances, respectively. In *Town of Nags Head v. Cherry, Inc.*, 723 S.E.2d 156 (N.C. 2012), the town sought removal of a private home that had, due to erosion, "moved" seaward of the legal coastline. The court held that the town did not have standing to enforce the public trust doctrine, holding that "[t]he state is the sole party able to seek non-individualized, or public, remedies for alleged harm to public waters." *Id.* at 159.

7. *Finally, an interesting story about surfing.* Economist and Nobel laureate Elinor Ostrom and others have identified many situations in which local resource users band together to prevent the kind of tragedy about which Hardin wrote. *See* ELINOR OSTROM, GOVERNING THE COMMONS: THE EVOLUTION OF INSTITUTIONS FOR COLLECTIVE ACTION (1990). A recent paper explores the relationship between the quality of particular surf breaks in southern California and the development of surf gangs who make informal property claims to those public trust areas. As one might expect, the better the surfing, the more likely it is that locals will organize to exclude outsiders. (Once a break becomes too crowded, it is no longer especially valuable to anyone who wants to surf it.) Daniel T. Kaffine, *Quality and the Commons: The Surf Gangs of California*, 52 J.L. & ECON. 727 (2009). If local surfers are in fact excluding "outsiders," how should the State of California respond?

3. A Duty to Ensure Meaningful Access?

There is no dispute that the public trust doctrine ensures the public physical access, subject only to reasonable regulations and the accommodation of competing uses. There are, however, two additional aspects of access.

One issue involves what could be called "access to access." The argument is that it is not enough for the government to ensure physical access *through* trust areas; in addition, it must ensure physical access *to* them. Court decisions promoting access to access through the common law public trust doctrine are relatively rare: New Jersey, in cases like the *Matthews v. Bay Head* decision we read in Chapter 6, is the only state whose courts have aggressively moved in this direction. (The court in *Matthews*, though, did not frame its decision explicitly as access to access; rather — as you recall — it framed its decision as one that simply expanded the geographic scope of the state's public trust doctrine.) As we will see in Chapter 9, though, many states have — through coastal statutes — incorporated access to access as a primary objective of coastal law.

The second "meaningful access" issue is subtler. Some courts and scholars have opined that the public trust doctrine goes beyond guaranteeing mere physical access and requires that government maintain the environmental quality of trust areas. (Although the term "environmental quality" is inherently vague, it refers to both levels of pollution and the health of fish and wildlife populations.) The primary basis for this argument is that the promise of physical access for recognized trust purposes, such as fishing and recreation, would not be worth much in heavily polluted waters or in the absence of fish and wildlife. What happens when courts expand public trust uses even further? In *Marks v. Whitney*, 6 Cal. 3d 251 (1971), the Supreme Court of California stated:

> The public uses to which tidelands are subject are sufficiently flexible to encompass changing public needs. . . . There is a growing public recognition that one of the most important public uses of the tidelands — a use encompassed within the tidelands trust — is the preservation of those lands in their natural state, so that they may serve as ecological units for scientific study, as open space, and as environments which provide food and habitat for birds and marine life, and which favorably affect the scenery and climate of the area.

Id. at 259-60.

The "duty to maintain environmental quality" is controversial because, as we will see, public trust–based regulation (unlike police power–based regulation) may be "immune" from Fifth Amendment takings claims. (Think back to the federal government's ability to use the navigational servitude as a defense to such claims.) Some commentators see an expanded notion of governmental public trust responsibilities as a threat to private property rights.

The following materials address two questions. First, does the common law public trust doctrine obligate states to maintain environmental quality in trust areas? And, if so, does the doctrine

---

NEPA

The National Environmental Policy Act (NEPA) is a federal statute that, among other things, requires federal agencies to consider the impact of proposed, major actions on the human environment. Under the statute, agencies are not required to avoid environmental impacts; rather, the purpose of the statute is to force agencies to consider the impacts and to make information concerning those impacts available to the public. *See* 42 U.S.C. §§ 4321 *et seq.*

itself—by virtue of, for example, its incorporation of trust principles—provide practical help to resource managers in making important day-to-day decisions? For example, given competing trust objectives, does the doctrine mandate that managers give maintenance of environmental quality absolute priority? If not, does the doctrine require that some baseline level of environmental quality be maintained? If the doctrine does not entail these kinds of substantive environmental goals, does it serve as a form of common law National Environmental Policy Act? That is, does it merely require states to consider the impact of their decisions on all possible uses of trust assets?

In our search for answers to these difficult questions, we begin with the case of *National Audubon Society v. The Superior Court of Alpine County.*

National Audubon Society v. The Superior Court of Alpine County

33 Cal. 3d 419 (1983)

Justice BROUSSARD delivered the opinion of the Supreme Court of California.

Mono Lake, the second largest lake in California, sits at the base of the Sierra Nevada escarpment near the eastern entrance to Yosemite National Park. The lake is saline; it contains no fish but supports a large population of brine shrimp which feed vast numbers of nesting and migratory birds. Islands in the lake protect a large breeding colony of California gulls, and the lake itself serves as a haven on the migration route for thousands of Northern Phalarope, Wilson's Phalarope, and Eared Grebe. Towers and spires of tufa on the north and south shores are matters of geological interest and a tourist attraction.

Although Mono Lake receives some water from rain and snow on the lake surface, historically most of its supply came from snowmelt in the Sierra Nevada. Five freshwater streams—Mill, Lee Vining, Walker, Parker and Rush Creeks—arise near the crest of the range and carry the annual runoff to the west shore of the lake. In 1940, however, the Division of Water Resources, the predecessor to the present California Water Resources Board, granted the Department of Water and Power of the City of Los Angeles (hereafter DWP) a permit to appropriate virtually the entire flow of four of the five streams flowing into the lake. DWP promptly constructed facilities to divert about half the flow of these streams into DWP's Owens Valley aqueduct. In 1970 DWP completed a second diversion tunnel, and since that time has taken virtually the entire flow of these streams.

As a result of these diversions, the level of the lake has dropped; the surface area has diminished by one-third; one of the two principal islands in the lake has become a peninsula, exposing the gull rookery there to coyotes and other predators and causing the gulls to abandon the former island. The ultimate effect of continued diversions is a matter of intense dispute, but there seems little doubt that both the scenic beauty and the ecological values of Mono Lake are imperiled.

Photo: Ron Reiring

Figure 7-10. Mono Lake
Mono Lake from the air.

Plaintiffs filed suit in superior court to enjoin the DWP diversions on the theory that the shores, bed and waters of Mono Lake are protected by a public trust. . . . The superior court . . . entered summary judgments against plaintiffs . . . , ruling that the public trust doctrine offered no independent basis for challenging the DWP diversions. . . . Plaintiffs petitioned us directly for writ of mandate to review that decision. . . .

This case brings together for the first time two systems of legal thought: the appropriative water rights system which since the days of the gold rush has dominated California water law, and the public trust doctrine which, after evolving as a shield for the protection of tidelands, now extends its protective scope to navigable lakes. Ever since we first recognized that the public trust protects environmental and recreational values (*Marks v. Whitney* (1971) 6 Cal. 3d 251 [98 Cal. Rptr. 790, 491 P.2d 374]), the two systems of legal thought have been on a collision course. . . . They meet in a unique and dramatic setting which highlights the clash of values. Mono Lake is a scenic and ecological treasure of national significance, imperiled by continued diversions of water; yet, the need of Los Angeles for water is apparent, its reliance on rights granted by the board evident, the cost of curtailing diversions substantial.

Attempting to integrate the teachings and values of both the public trust and the appropriative water rights system, we have arrived at certain conclusions which we briefly summarize here. In our opinion, the core of the public trust doctrine is the state's authority as sovereign to exercise a continuous supervision and control over the navigable waters of the state and the lands underlying those waters. This authority applies to the waters tributary to Mono Lake and bars DWP or any other party from claiming a vested right to divert waters once it becomes clear that such diversions harm the interests protected by the public trust. . . .

The water rights enjoyed by DWP were granted, the diversion was commenced, and has continued to the present without any consideration of the impact upon the public trust. An objective study and reconsideration of the water rights in the Mono Basin is long overdue. The water law of California — which we conceive to be an integration including both the public trust doctrine and the board-administered appropriative rights system — permits such a reconsideration; the values underlying that integration require it.

***

1. Background and History of the Mono Lake Litigation

DWP supplies water to the City of Los Angeles. Early in this century, it became clear that the city's anticipated needs would exceed the water available from local sources, and so in 1913 the city constructed an aqueduct to carry water from the Owens River 233 miles over the Antelope-Mojave plateau into the coastal plain and thirsty city.

The city's attempt to acquire rights to water needed by local farmers met with fierce, and at times violent, opposition. . . . But when the "Owens Valley War" was over, virtually all the waters of the Owens River and its tributaries flowed south to Los Angeles. Owens Lake was transformed into an alkali flat.

The city's rapid expansion soon strained this new supply, too, and prompted a search for water from other regions. The Mono Basin was a predictable object of this extension, since it lay within 50 miles of the natural origin of Owens River, and thus could easily be integrated into the existing aqueduct system.

After purchasing the riparian rights incident to Lee Vining, Walker, Parker and Rush Creeks, as well as the riparian rights pertaining to Mono Lake, the city applied to the Water Board in 1940 for permits to appropriate the waters of the four tributaries. At hearings before the board, various interested individuals protested that the city's proposed appropriations would lower the surface level of Mono Lake and thereby impair its commercial, recreational and scenic uses.

The board's primary authority to reject that application lay in a 1921 amendment to the Water Commission Act of 1913, which authorized the board to reject an application "when in its judgment the proposed appropriation would not best conserve the public interest." (Stats. 1921, ch. 329, § 1, p. 443, now codified as Wat. Code, § 1255.) The 1921 enactment, however, also "declared to be the established policy of this state that the use of water for domestic purposes is the highest use of water" . . . , and directed the Water Board to be guided by this declaration of policy. Since DWP sought water for domestic use, the board concluded that it had to grant the application notwithstanding the harm to public trust uses of Mono Lake.

***

The board's decision states that "[it] is indeed unfortunate that the City's proposed development will result in decreasing the aesthetic advantages of Mono Basin but *there is apparently nothing that this office can do to prevent it.* The use to which the City proposes to put the water under its Applications . . . is defined by the Water Commission Act as the highest to which water may be applied and to make available unappropriated water for this use the City has, by the condemnation proceedings described above, acquired the littoral and riparian rights on Mono Lake and its tributaries south of Mill Creek. This office therefore has *no alternative but to dismiss all protests based upon the possible lowering of the water level in Mono Lake and the effect that the diversion of water from these streams may have upon the aesthetic and recreational value of the Basin.*" (Div. Wat. Resources Dec. 7053, 7055, 8042 & 8043 (Apr. 11, 1940), at p. 26, italics added.)

By April of 1941, the city had completed the extension of its aqueduct system into the Mono Basin by construction of certain conduits, reservoirs at Grant and Crowley Lakes, and the Mono Craters Tunnel from the Mono Basin to the Owens River. In the 1950's, the city constructed hydroelectric power plants along the system to generate electricity from the energy of the appropriated water as it flowed downhill into the Owens Valley. Between 1940 and 1970, the city diverted an average of 57,067 acre-feet of water per year from the Mono Basin. The impact of these diversions on Mono Lake was clear and immediate: the lake's surface level receded at an average of 1.1 feet per year.

In June of 1970, the city completed a second aqueduct designed to increase the total flow into the aqueduct by 50 percent. Between 1970 and 1980, the city diverted an average of 99,580 acre-feet per year from the Mono Basin. By October of 1979, the lake had shrunk from its prediversion area of 85 square miles to an area of 60.3 square miles. Its surface level had dropped to 6,373 feet above sea level, 43 feet below the prediversion level.

No party seriously disputes the facts set forth above. However, the parties hotly dispute the projected effects of future diversions on the lake itself, as well as the indirect effects of past, present and future diversions on the Mono Basin environment.

DWP expects that its future diversions of about 100,000 acre-feet per year will lower the lake's surface level another 43 feet and reduce its surface area by about 22 square miles over the next 80 to 100 years, at which point the lake will gradually approach environmental equilibrium (the point at which inflow from precipitation, groundwater and nondiverted tributaries equals outflow by evaporation and other means). At this point, according to DWP, the lake will stabilize at a level 6,330 feet above the sea's, with a surface area of approximately 38 square miles. Thus, by DWP's own estimates, unabated diversions will ultimately produce a lake that is about 56 percent smaller on the surface and 42 percent shallower than its natural size.

Plaintiffs consider these projections unrealistically optimistic. They allege that, 50 years hence, the lake will be at least 50 feet shallower than it now is, and hold less than 20 percent of its natural volume. Further, plaintiffs fear that "the lake will not stabilize at this level," but "may continue to reduce in size until it is dried up." Moreover, unlike DWP, plaintiffs believe that the lake's gradual recession indirectly causes a host of adverse environmental impacts. Many of these alleged impacts are related to an increase in the lake's salinity, caused by the decrease in its water volume.

As noted above, Mono Lake has no outlets. The lake loses water only by evaporation and seepage. Natural salts do not evaporate with water, but are left behind. Prior to commencement of the DWP diversions, this naturally rising salinity was balanced by a constant and substantial supply of fresh water from the tributaries. Now, however, DWP diverts most of the fresh water inflow. The resultant imbalance between inflow and outflow not only diminishes the lake's size, but also drastically increases its salinity.

Plaintiffs predict that the lake's steadily increasing salinity, if unchecked, will wreck havoc throughout the local food chain. They contend that the lake's algae, and the brine shrimp and brine flies that feed on it, cannot survive the projected salinity increase. To support this assertion, plaintiffs point to a 50 percent reduction in the shrimp hatch for the spring of 1980 and a startling 95 percent reduction for the spring of 1981. These reductions affirm experimental evidence indicating that brine shrimp populations diminish as the salinity of the water surrounding them increases. . . . DWP admits these substantial reductions, but blames them on factors other than salinity.

DWP's diversions also present several threats to the millions of local and migratory birds using the lake. First, since many species of birds feed on the lake's brine shrimp, any reduction in shrimp population allegedly caused by rising salinity endangers a major avian food source. The Task Force Report[, a study of Mono Lake undertaken by several California agencies,] considered it "unlikely that any of Mono Lake's major bird species . . . will persist at the lake if populations of invertebrates disappear." (Task Force Report at p. 20.) Second, the increasing salinity makes it more difficult for the birds to maintain osmotic equilibrium with their environment.[10]

The California gull is especially endangered, both by the increase in salinity and by loss of nesting sites. Ninety-five percent of this state's gull population and 25 percent of the total species population nests at the lake. . . . Most of the gulls nest on islands in the lake. As the lake recedes, land between the shore and some of the islands has been exposed, offering such predators as the coyote easy access to the gull nests and chicks. In 1979, coyotes reached Negrit Island, once the most

---

10. In the face of rising salinity, birds can maintain such equilibrium only by increasing either their secretion of salts or their intake of fresh water. The former option is foreclosed, however, because Mono Lake is already so salty that the birds have reached their limit of salt secretion. Thus, the birds must drink more fresh water to maintain the osmotic equilibrium necessary to their survival. As the Task Force predicts, "[the] need for more time and energy to obtain fresh water will mean reduced energy and time for other vital activities such as feeding, nesting, etc. Birds attempting to breed at Mono Lake . . . are likely to suffer the most from direct salinity effects, since the adult birds must devote so much time to obtain fresh water that they may not be able to raise young successfully." (Task Force Report, at p. 19.)

popular nesting site, and the number of gull nests at the lake declined sharply. In 1981, 95 percent of the hatched chicks did not survive to maturity. Plaintiffs blame this decline and alarming mortality rate on the predator access created by the land bridges; DWP suggests numerous other causes, such as increased ambient temperatures and human activities, and claims that the joining of some islands with the mainland is offset by the emergence of new islands due to the lake's recession.

Plaintiffs allege that DWP's diversions adversely affect the human species and its activities as well. First, as the lake recedes, it has exposed more than 18,000 acres of lake bed composed of very fine silt which, once dry, easily becomes airborne in winds. This silt contains a high concentration of alkali and other minerals that irritate the mucous membranes and respiratory systems of humans and other animals. . . . While the precise extent of this threat to the public health has yet to be determined, such threat as exists can be expected to increase with the exposure of additional lake bed. DWP, however, claims that its diversions neither affect the air quality in Mono Basin nor present a hazard to human health.

Furthermore, the lake's recession obviously diminishes its value as an economic, recreational, and scenic resource. Of course, there will be less lake to use and enjoy. The declining shrimp hatch depresses a local shrimping industry. The rings of dry lake bed are difficult to traverse on foot, and thus impair human access to the lake, and reduce the lake's substantial scenic value. Mono Lake has long been treasured as a unique scenic, recreational and scientific resource . . ., but continued diversions threaten to turn it into a desert wasteland like the dry bed of Owens Lake.

***

Duties and Powers of the State as Trustee

In the following review of the authority and obligations of the state as administrator of the public trust, the dominant theme is the state's sovereign power and duty to exercise continued supervision over the trust. One consequence, of importance to this and many other cases, is that parties acquiring rights in trust property generally hold those rights subject to the trust, and can assert no vested right to use those rights in a manner harmful to the trust.

As we noted recently in *City of Berkeley v. Superior Court*, 26 Cal. 3d 515 (1980), the decision of the United States Supreme Court in *Illinois Central Railroad Company v. Illinois*, 146 U.S. 387 (1892), "remains the primary authority even today, almost nine decades after it was decided." (P. 521.) . . .

***

The California Supreme Court indorsed the *Illinois Central* principles in *People v. California Fish Co.*, 166 Cal. 576 (1913). *California Fish* concerned title to about 80,000 acres of tidelands conveyed by state commissioners pursuant to statutory authorization. The court first set out principles to govern the interpretation of statutes conveying that property: "[Statutes] purporting to authorize an abandonment of . . . public use will be carefully scanned to ascertain whether or not such was the legislative intention, and that intent must be clearly expressed or necessarily implied. It will not be implied if any other inference is reasonably possible. And if any interpretation of the statute is reasonably possible which would not involve a destruction of the public use or an intention to terminate it in violation of the trust, the courts will give the statute such interpretation." *Id.*, at p. 597. Applying these principles, the court held that because the statute in question and the grants pursuant thereto were not made for trust purposes, the grantees did not acquire absolute title; instead, the grantees "own the soil, subject to the easement of the public for the public uses of navigation and commerce, and to the right of the state, as administrator and controller of these public uses and the public trust therefor, to enter upon and possess the same for the preservation and advancement of the public uses and to make such changes and improvements as may be deemed advisable for those purposes." *Id.*, at pp. 598-599.

Finally, rejecting the claim of the tideland purchasers for compensation, the court stated they did not lose title, but retained it subject to the public trust. *See* pp. 599-601. While the state may not "retake the absolute title without compensation" (p. 599), it may without such payment erect improvements to further navigation and take other actions to promote the public trust.[20]

Boone v. Kingsbury, 206 Cal. 148 (1928), presents another aspect of this matter. The Legislature authorized the Surveyor-General to lease trust lands for oil drilling. Applying the principles of *Illinois Central*, the court upheld that statute on the ground that the derricks would not substantially interfere with the trust. Any licenses granted by the statute, moreover, remained subject to the trust: "The state may at any time remove [the] structures . . . , even though they have been erected with its license or consent, if it subsequently determines them to be purprestures or finds that they substantially interfere with navigation or commerce." *Id.*, at 192-193.[21]

----

20. In *Mallon v. City of Long Beach*, 44 Cal. 2d 199 (1955), the court held that revenues derived from the use of trust property ordinarily must be used for trust purposes. *Id.* at 205-206. . . . The Legislature could abandon the trust over the proceeds, the court said, absent evidence that the abandonment would impair the power of future legislatures to protect and promote trust uses. *Id.*, at 207. So long as the tidelands themselves remained subject to the trust, however, future legislatures would have the power to revoke the abandonment and reestablish a trust on the revenues. *Ibid.*

21. In *Colberg, Inc. v. State of California ex rel. Dept. Pub. Wks.*, 67 Cal. 2d 408 (1967), the state constructed a freeway bridge which partially impaired navigation in the Stockton Deep Water Ship Channel. Upstream shipyard owners . . . filed suit for damages on a theory of inverse condemnation. The opinion stated that "the state, as trustee for the benefit of the people, has power to deal with its navigable waters in any manner consistent with the improvement of commercial intercourse, whether navigational or otherwise." *Id.*, at 419. It then concluded that lands littoral to navigable waters are burdened by a navigational servitude in favor of the state and, absent an actual taking of those lands, the owners cannot claim damages when the state acts within its powers.

We agree with [Department of Water and Power of Los Angeles (DWP)] and the state that *Colberg* demonstrates the power of the state, as administrator of the public trust, to prefer one trust use over another. We cannot agree, however, with DWP's further contention that *Colberg* proves the power of a state agency to abrogate the public trust merely by authorizing a use inconsistent with the trust. Not only did plaintiffs in *Colberg* deliberately decline to assert public trust rights, but the decision rests on the power of the state to promote one trust purpose (commerce) over another (navigation), not on any power to grant rights free of the trust. . . .

Finally, in our recent decision in *City of Berkeley v. Superior Court, supra*, we considered whether deeds executed by the Board of Tidelands Commissioners pursuant to an 1870 act conferred title free of the trust. Applying the principles of earlier decisions, we held that the grantees' title was subject to the trust, both because the Legislature had not made clear its intention to authorize a conveyance free of the trust and because the 1870 act and the conveyances under it were not intended to further trust purposes.

Once again we rejected the claim that establishment of the public trust constituted a taking of property for which compensation was required: "We do not divest anyone of title to property; the consequence of our decision will be only that some landowners whose predecessors in interest acquired property under the 1870 act will, like the grantees in *California Fish*, hold it subject to the public trust." *Id.*, at 532.

In summary, the foregoing cases amply demonstrate the continuing power of the state as administrator of the public trust, a power which extends to the revocation of previously granted rights or to the enforcement of the trust against lands long thought free of the trust. . . . Except for those rare instances in which a grantee may acquire a right to use former trust property free of trust restrictions, the grantee holds subject to the trust, and while he may assert a vested right to the servient estate (the right of use subject to the trust) and to any improvements he erects, he can claim no vested right to bar recognition of the trust or state action to carry out its purposes.

Since the public trust doctrine does not prevent the state from choosing between trust uses . . . , the Attorney General of California, seeking to maximize state power under the trust, argues for a broad concept of trust uses. In his view, "trust uses" encompass all public uses, so that in practical effect the doctrine would impose no restrictions on the state's ability to allocate trust property. We know of no authority which supports this view of the public trust, except perhaps the dissenting opinion in *Illinois Central Railroad Co. v. Illinois, supra*. Most decisions and commentators assume that "trust uses" relate to uses and activities in the vicinity of the lake, stream, or tidal reach at issue. The tideland cases make this point clear; after *City of Berkeley v. Superior Court, supra*, no one could contend that the state could grant tidelands free of the trust merely because the grant served some public purpose, such as increasing tax revenues, or because the grantee might put the property to a commercial use.

Thus, the public trust is more than an affirmation of state power to use public property for public purposes. It is an affirmation of the duty of the state to protect the people's common heritage of streams, lakes, marshlands and tidelands, surrendering that right of protection only in rare cases when the abandonment of that right is consistent with the purposes of the trust.

***

[The decision then explains the history and substance of California water allocation law. Under California's "prior appropriation" allocation rules, water users — such as the Department of Water and Power of Los Angeles — can acquire rights to take fixed amounts of water from rivers, streams, and lakes by extracting the water and putting it to a "reasonable and beneficial use." The state agency responsible for overseeing water allocation is known as the Water Resources Control Board.]

***

Article X, section 2 (enacted in 1928 as art. XIV, § 3) [of the California Constitution] reads in pertinent part as follows:

> It is hereby declared that because of the conditions prevailing in this State the general welfare requires that the water resources of the State be put to beneficial use to the fullest extent of which they are capable, and that the waste or unreasonable use or unreasonable method of use of water be prevented, and that the conservation of such waters is to be exercised with a view to the reasonable and beneficial use thereof in the interest of the people and for the public welfare. The right to water or to the use or flow of water in or from any natural stream or water course in this State is and shall be limited to such water as shall be reasonably required for the beneficial use to be served, and such right does not and shall not extend to the waste or unreasonable use or unreasonable method of use or unreasonable method of diversion of water. . . . This section shall be self-executing, and the Legislature may also enact laws in the furtherance of the policy in this section contained.

[After this amendment was added], the Water Board . . . remained, under controlling judicial decisions, a ministerial body with the limited task of determining priorities between claimants seeking to appropriate unclaimed water. More recent statutory and judicial developments, however, have greatly enhanced the power of the Water Board to oversee the reasonable use of water and, in the process, made clear its authority to weigh and protect public trust values.

In 1955, the Legislature declared that in acting on appropriative applications, "the board shall consider the relative benefit to be derived from (1) all beneficial uses of the water concerned including, but not limited to, use for domestic, irrigation, municipal, industrial, preservation and enhancement of fish and wildlife, recreational, mining and power purposes. . . . The board may subject such appropriations to such terms and conditions as in its judgment will best develop, conserve, and utilize in the public interest, the water sought to be appropriated." Wat. Code, § 1257. In 1959 it stated that "[the] use of water for recreation and preservation and enhancement of fish and wildlife resources is a beneficial use of water." Wat. Code, § 1243. Finally in 1969 the Legislature instructed that "[in] determining the amount of water available for appropriation, the board shall take into account, whenever it is in the public interest, the amounts of water needed to remain in the source for protection of beneficial uses." Wat. Code, § 1243.5.

***

Thus, the function of the Water Board has steadily evolved from the narrow role of deciding priorities between competing appropriators to the charge of comprehensive planning and allocation of waters. This change necessarily affects the board's responsibility with respect to the public trust. The board of limited powers of 1913 [when the DWP constructed the aqueduct to bring water from the Owens Valley to Los Angeles] had neither the power nor duty to consider interests protected by the public trust; the present board, in undertaking planning and allocation of water resources, is required by statute to take those interests into account.

The Relationship Between the Public Trust Doctrine and the California Water Rights System

As we have seen, the public trust doctrine and the appropriative water rights system administered by the Water Board developed independently of each other. Each developed comprehensive rules and principles which, if applied to the full extent of their scope, would occupy the field of allocation of stream waters to the exclusion of any competing system of legal thought. Plaintiffs, for example, argue that the public trust is antecedent to and thus limits all appropriative water rights, an argument which implies that most appropriative water rights in California were acquired and are presently being used unlawfully. Defendant DWP, on the other hand, argues that the public trust doctrine as to stream waters has been "subsumed" into the appropriative water rights system and, absorbed by that body of law, quietly disappeared; according to DWP, the recipient of a board license enjoys a vested right in perpetuity to take water without concern for the consequences to the trust.

We are unable to accept either position. In our opinion, both the public trust doctrine and the water rights system embody important precepts which make the law more responsive to the diverse needs and interests involved in the planning and allocation of water resources. To embrace one system of thought and reject the other would lead to an unbalanced structure, one which would either decry as a breach of trust appropriations essential to the economic development of this state, or deny any duty to protect or even consider the values promoted by the public trust. Therefore, seeking an accommodation which will make use of the pertinent principles of both the public trust doctrine and the appropriative water rights system, and drawing upon the history of the public trust and the water rights system, the body of judicial precedent, and the views of expert commentators, we reach the following conclusions:

a. The state as sovereign retains continuing supervisory control over its navigable waters and the lands beneath those waters. This principle, fundamental to the concept of the public trust, applies to rights in flowing waters as well as to rights in tidelands and lakeshores; it prevents any party from acquiring a vested right to appropriate water in a manner harmful to the interests protected by the public trust.

b. As a matter of current and historical necessity, the Legislature, acting directly or through an authorized agency such as the Water Board, has the power to grant usufructuary licenses that will permit an appropriator to take water from flowing streams and use that water in a distant part of the state, even though this taking does not promote, and may unavoidably harm, the trust uses at the source stream. The population and economy of this state depend upon the appropriation of vast quantities of water for uses unrelated to in-stream trust values.[26] California's Constitution, its statutes, decisions, and commentators all emphasize the need to make efficient use of California's limited water resources: all recognize, at least implicitly, that efficient use requires diverting water from in-stream uses. Now that the economy and population centers of this state have developed in reliance upon appropriated water, it would be disingenuous to hold that such appropriations are and have always been improper to the extent that they harm public trust uses, and can be justified only upon theories of reliance or estoppel.

c. The state has an affirmative duty to take the public trust into account in the planning and allocation of water resources, and to protect public trust uses whenever feasible. Just as the history of this state shows that appropriation may be necessary for efficient use of water despite unavoidable harm to public trust values, it demonstrates that an appropriative water rights system administered without consideration of the public trust may cause unnecessary and unjustified harm to trust interests. . . . As a matter of practical necessity the state may have to approve appropriations despite foreseeable harm to public trust uses. In so doing, however, the state must bear in mind its duty as trustee to consider the effect of the taking on the public trust, and to preserve, so far as consistent with the public interest, the uses protected by the trust.

Once the state has approved an appropriation, the public trust imposes a duty of continuing supervision over the taking and use of the appropriated water. In exercising its sovereign power to allocate water resources in the public interest, the state is not confined by past allocation decisions which may be incorrect in light of current knowledge or inconsistent with current needs.

The state accordingly has the power to reconsider allocation decisions even though those decisions were made after due consideration of their effect on the public trust. The case for reconsidering a particular decision, however, is even stronger when that decision failed to weigh and consider public trust uses. In the case before us, the salient fact is that no responsible body has ever determined the impact of diverting the entire flow of the Mono Lake tributaries into the Los Angeles Aqueduct. This is not a case in which the Legislature, the Water Board, or any judicial body has determined that the needs of Los Angeles outweigh the needs of the Mono Basin, that the benefit gained is worth the price. Neither has any responsible body determined whether some lesser taking would better balance the diverse interests. Instead, DWP acquired rights to the entire flow in 1940 from a water board which believed it lacked both the power and the duty to protect the Mono Lake environment, and continues to exercise those rights in apparent

---

26. In contrast, the population and economy of this state does *not* depend on the conveyance of vast expanses of tidelands or other property underlying navigable waters. . . . Our opinion does not affect the restrictions imposed by the public trust doctrine upon transfer of such properties free of the trust.

disregard for the resulting damage to the scenery, ecology, and human uses of Mono Lake.

It is clear that some responsible body ought to reconsider the allocation of the waters of the Mono Basin. No vested rights bar such reconsideration. We recognize the substantial concerns voiced by Los Angeles — the city's need for water, its reliance upon the 1940 board decision, the cost both in terms of money and environmental impact of obtaining water elsewhere. Such concerns must enter into any allocation decision. We hold only that they do not preclude a reconsideration and reallocation which also takes into account the impact of water diversion on the Mono Lake environment.

points for discussion

1. *Back to scope, briefly.* What are the trust assets according to the court's decision in *National Audubon*? The choices: the submerged lands beneath Mono Lake, the water in Mono Lake, the water in the non-navigable streams flowing into Mono Lake, and the wildlife that uses Mono Lake. Look back at point 5 after *Illinois Central*. Is it easier to understand *National Audubon* if one thinks of the trust corpus not in terms of assets, but in terms of rights? We don't have to worry about whether the trust includes the water or the wildlife if we simply say that the diversions unreasonably interfered with the public's right to access the area above the submerged lands for recreation.

2. *A duty to engage in an informed decision-making process?* The court concludes by ordering the Water Board to reconsider water allocation decisions pertaining to the water flowing into Mono Lake from the five streams. Does the court's decision preclude the Water Board, after it reconsiders those decisions, taking into account their effect on public trust uses of Mono Lake, from allocating water in the same way it did before the lawsuit? If not, what are the benefits of a "procedural public trust doctrine"?

3. *Changed conditions.* In *National Audubon*, the California Supreme Court explains that "the public trust imposes a duty of continuous supervision" and "the State is not confined by past [] decisions which may be incorrect in light of current knowledge or inconsistent with current needs." Would climate-change-induced sea level rise and corresponding inundation of beachfront properties constitute the kind of changed conditions that should trigger removal of previously permitted seawalls and other shoreline armoring that functionally prevents or makes public access to and along the shoreline unsafe?

4. *Broad trust purposes.* Note that California seems to have a longer list of trust purposes than the traditional navigation, commerce, fishing, and recreation, including "preservation of . . . lands in their natural state . . . [for] study, . . . open space, and as environments which provide food and habitat for birds and marine life." How does broadening the range of allowable trust

purposes affect the potency of the public trust doctrine? Does it decrease the limits on state power that are at the core of the doctrine?

One impact of *National Audubon* has been an increased amount of attention on the use of the trust as a tool to increase environmental protection. The following excerpt explores one approach to moving in that direction.

Jack H. Archer et al., The Public Trust Doctrine and the Management of America's Coasts

30-44 (1994)

This section recognizes that there is limited statutory or case law prescribing the rights and obligations of the state or state agency which acts as trustee over public trust lands and resources. This section recommends that states examine the law of private and charitable trusts as an analogous body of law which can provide guidance in defining trusteeship responsibilities. Private and charitable trust law is, with little difficulty, adaptable to public trust issues. Thus this section discusses the various rights and obligations of private trustees and how such rights and obligations can inform decisions by state trustees exercising their authority under the public trust doctrine.

... [W]hat does it mean to hold this land "in trust" or to be a "trustee"? Despite its fundamental character, this question has not been addressed squarely by the courts. Although the United States Supreme Court has declared that states hold submerged and navigable lands subject to the trust, few courts have taken the next step and identified the actual "trustee" or defined with any specificity the trustee's duties and responsibilities.

Because few courts have answered these questions in the public trust context, this section recommends that state lawmakers and agencies should look to private and charitable trust law as a potentially useful source of analogous law for assistance in addressing issues of public trust implementation for which legislative and judicial precedents are lacking. The vast body of law and practical experience under general private and charitable trust law has yet to be tapped in formulating public trust principles. Specifically, if a state is a trustee over public trust lands and resources for the benefit of its people, then the imposition of the general rights and obligations of a private or charitable trustee establishes useful parameters and guidelines for state courts and agencies to use to evaluate the appropriate role of the state in protecting and using its trust property.

The private trust analogy also focuses on a number of serious policy questions, particularly the evident conflict between the interests and uses of the present-day beneficiaries and the interests and uses of future generations. While the analogy to private trust law does not necessarily provide a specific resolution of these issues, it can provide courts and agencies with guidance that may be applied in making difficult choices between current and future beneficiaries, as well as among current beneficiaries.

Another fruitful area of law and practical experience may be found by analogizing public trust obligations and responsibilities to the charitable trust. Charitable trusts are generally subject to the law governing private trusts. In addition, however, they have been adapted to meet the special requirements of charitable trusts, many of which are analogous to the public trust. A particular benefit of the use of this analogy is the potential for the imposition of the *cy pres* doctrine to public trust lands.

***

Identification of the Trustee

In private trust law, the trustee is named in the trust instrument. The source of confusion in identifying the trustee under the public trust doctrine stems from the English common law distinction between the Crown and the people. When the United States was formed, the states adopted the English common law. However, the sovereign in the United States is the embodiment of the people — their duly elected, representative government. The popularly elected legislature of each state is, in effect, both the sovereign and the public. Thus, although American courts have consistently held that either the state or the legislature holds title to submerged navigable lands which are subject to the public trust, it appears that the legislature (or its delegate, typically a natural resource or coastal management agency) fills the roles of both the sovereign and the public. In traditional trust terms, the legislature acts as both the trustee and the representative of the beneficiaries of the trust, the public.

Responsibilities and Obligations of the State as Trustee

Although many courts have ruled that the state holds public trust lands as a trustee, only a few decisions have addressed the actual duties and obligations of the state as trustee. Perhaps the most detailed and influential discussion of the duties and powers of the state as trustee is found in *Mono Lake* [*National Audubon* — EDS.], which quoted at length from *Illinois Central* and earlier California cases and concluded: "In summary, the foregoing cases amply demonstrate the continuing power of the state as administrator of the public trust, a power which extends to the revocation of previously granted rights or to the enforcement of the trust against lands long thought to be free of the trust." However, despite its lengthy discussion of specific examples of trust rights, even the *Mono Lake* decision fails to explain or define the rights and obligations of the trustee in a coherent, comprehensive fashion.

Analogies to Private Trust Law

Given the consensus that states hold public trust lands in trust for the benefit of the public, and the dearth of cases which have addressed the obligations and responsibilities of the state as trustee, it is both reasonable and instructive for states and coastal managers to look to private and charitable trust law for guidance in determining their rights and obligations as trustees. Analogies to private and charitable trust law suggest helpful approaches for managing public trust lands and resources and provide a framework within which to address difficult questions relating to the disposition of trust lands.

The fundamental premise in private and charitable trust law is that the trustee is in a fiduciary relationship to the beneficiaries of the trust — a relationship involving trust and confidence and the duty on the part of the fiduciary to act solely for the benefit of the other party as to matters within the scope of the relationship. In private trust law, the beneficiaries of the trust are readily identifiable as those persons set out in the trust instrument. However, in both charitable trusts and in the public trust context, the beneficiaries consist of a large group of people who are not specifically identified. Thus the trustee owes a fiduciary duty not to any specific person but to the community as a whole. The primary duties of private and charitable trustees to fulfill their fiduciary responsibilities are readily applicable to the public trustee. Each duty and the corresponding analogy to the public trust is addressed separately below.

***

c. Duty to Furnish Information. A private trustee is responsible to provide the beneficiaries with complete and accurate information as to the administration of the trust. The duty to provide information raises specific problems where there are multiple beneficiaries. Should each member of the public have a right to obtain full information concerning all trust lands? Should only members of the public who have a specific separate interest in the trust lands have access to the information? How does the right to information relate to the public's rights to enforce the trust? The problems created by the obligation to provide information to multiple beneficiaries may suggest that the state legislature or its delegate must act as both trustee and beneficiary. Thus the state legislature or its agency delegate must consider the interests of all its citizens in analyzing and reviewing information regarding public trust lands and resources. In addition to "freedom of information" and similar statutes that afford citizens access to public records in almost every state, many states in recent years have required that notice be published to the general public before any conveyance of public trust lands or change in the use of such lands. Such notice should be provided as part of the trustee's duty to disclose.

***

e. Duty to Preserve the Trust Property and Duty to Deal Impartially with Beneficiaries. A private trustee has a duty to the beneficiaries of the trust to use care and skill to preserve the trust property. Where the trust property consists of financial assets, this obligation requires preservation of the principal. Where the trust property is real property, the obligation primarily concerns the maintenance, repair, improvement, and upkeep of the real property, including payment of taxes, mortgages, and fees.

In the public trust context, the duty to preserve trust property might require considerably more diligence on the part of the public trustee in managing trust lands and resources than has yet been found necessary under the public trust doctrine. For example, the state could be required to adopt and enforce measures to provide environmental protection for trust lands and resources. Where public trust lands and resources are threatened by environmental degradation, pollution, or misuse, the trustee may have a duty to take action to protect and preserve those lands and resources.

The duty to deal impartially with beneficiaries arises between successive beneficiaries. In the private trust context, there is often a conflict of interest between the current beneficiaries and future beneficiaries or remaindermen, who will receive the trust property in the future. The current beneficiary has an interest in having the trustee invest the trust property to yield the highest current income. In contrast, the future beneficiary wants the trustee to exercise the utmost caution to preserve or expand the trust principal.

The private trustee is charged with the difficult task of managing the trust to benefit both current and future beneficiaries, while maintaining its impartiality. In the public trust context, the duty of impartiality toward beneficiaries raises a serious issue with respect to the state's obligation as trustee to preserve trust property for future beneficiaries, i.e., future generations. The analogy to the private trust duty to protect the interests of future beneficiaries, together with recent interest in the public trust doctrine as a means to preserve public trust land resources, provides the basis for an affirmative responsibility in the state to protect and preserve its public trust resources.

A conflict for the state as trustee arises between the use of public trust property today and its preservation for the future. The public trust doctrine was not originally developed to protect trust resources, but was intended rather to protect the public's rights to have access and to use such resources. In particular, the public trust doctrine was intended to ensure that the general public had access to trust lands for the purpose of fishing, commerce, and navigation. Each of these uses involved use and exploitation of trust resources by current beneficiaries. Rarely, until recently, was thought given to the potential spoliation of such resources by present public trust use. The state's challenge today is to balance uses by current beneficiaries against the goal of preservation of trust resources for continued use by future generations.

Precedent exists in historical public trust law and more recent court cases to assist states in resolving this conflict. Under the traditional public trust doctrine, restrictions on exploitation (such as limiting the size of a catch) were seen as reasonable to protect everyone's access to the resources. Furthermore, California courts have held that preservation is a protected public trust use. Thus, following this precedent and using the private trust analogy, states may claim authority to preserve public trust resources for use by future generations, even if preservation is challenged by proponents of what would otherwise be an appropriate public trust use. States have an obligation to balance present-day exploitation of resources against future use and an obligation to regulate present-day exploitation to ensure the reasonable preservation of resources for future use.

f. Duty to Enforce Claims. A private trustee has a duty to its beneficiaries to enforce claims related to the trust property. For example, a private trustee may be liable if it delays in bringing a lawsuit and the party obligated to the trust or the beneficiaries has become insolvent. A private trustee may also have a duty to bring an appeal if it should reasonably do so under the circumstances.

The duty to enforce claims raises the possibility in the public trust context that there is an affirmative obligation on the states to protect public trust interests in lands already in private ownership. States may be compelled to reassert public trust interests in lands long held by private parties. Where a state does not act to enforce the trust, the attorney general or private parties may be entitled to compel enforcement.

g. Duty to Make Trust Property Productive. A private trustee has a duty to invest trust funds so that they will be reasonably productive of income. Where the trust estate consists of real property, "productivity" often depends on the terms of the trust and the surrounding circumstances. For example, it may be the duty of the trustee to sell the land and invest the proceeds. Where the trustee is not directed or empowered to sell the real property, it generally has the power to lease the land in order to make it productive and to generate income. Alternatively, in the case of an agricultural property or otherwise productive property, the terms of the trust might authorize the trustee to manage the land and generate income from its produce.

The duty to make trust property productive might initially appear to raise difficult issues in the public trust context, since in the private trust context, productivity is typically measured by income generation. However, in the public trust context there is a serious issue whether productivity should be measured by income generation — i.e., development potential — rather than by the benefits to the public as beneficiaries — i.e., maximizing the availability of public trust lands for public trust uses. Given the modern trend toward preservation of natural resources, states can and should make a strong argument that "productivity" in the case of the public trust may be served by enhancing public access to and preserving trust resources for current and future generations.

Another requirement in both private and charitable trust law is the duty of the trustee to diversify the investments or holdings of the trust, in order to minimize risk. Diversification in the private or charitable trust context typically means diversification of investment instruments. For example, a trustee may be required to invest not more than a reasonable percentage of the trust assets in any one investment instrument, such as common stocks, corporate bonds, and governmental obligations, unless specifically instructed to do so under the terms of the trust.

The diversification requirement *may* not be directly applicable in the public trust context. However, the analogy may be used by states to support a decision by the legislature or its delegate to diversify the state's holdings in public trust land so as not to risk their destruction and the resultant inability of future generations to enjoy their use. This duty may imply an obligation of the state, as trustee, to maintain certain public trust lands and resources in a natural state for preservation, while developing other lands and resources for public uses.

Analogies to Charitable Trust Law

Charitable trusts are governed by essentially the same trust law as private trusts. However, special rules have been developed to address two important differences. The most obvious is that the beneficiaries of the charitable trust are numerous and not easily identifiable. By comparison, the beneficiaries of a private trust are typically listed in the trust instrument and are easily identified. The other key difference between charitable and private trusts is that charitable trusts may be unlimited in duration, as long as they are designed to accomplish goals that are beneficial to the community. Private trusts, by contrast, must in most states be of limited and defined duration, under an ancient property law doctrine known as the "rule against perpetuities" or its modern statutory equivalent.

Perhaps the most interesting special rule of charitable trust law with implications for the public trust doctrine is the *cy pres* doctrine. Under this doctrine, a court can change the terms of the trust in appropriate circumstances. Specifically, if the trustee is able to show that the purpose for which the charitable trust was created is either illegal or effectively impossible or substantially impracticable to carry out, courts have the authority to permit the trust to be applied to another related or similar purpose that would accomplish the general goals established under the trust.

Under British law, the authority to change the terms of a charitable trust lies with the Parliament. In the United States, however, legislatures are without authority to change gifts already made — this authority lies in the courts. The *cy pres* doctrine may be a tool to be used by states in expanding the range of public trust uses. As described earlier, the original uses under the public trust doctrine were fishing, commerce, and navigation, although many courts have expanded the list of uses over time. Courts have relied upon a variety of legal theories to increase the number of public trust uses. However, further expansion might be better grounded in an analogy to the *cy pres* doctrine. The reasoning is analogous — the historical purposes of the public trust may, in particular circumstances, have become outdated or the uses traditionally protected by the trust no longer fully serve the purposes for which the public trust doctrine was created. Thus, in a manner similar to the use of the *cy pres* doctrine, courts might well be convinced to allow the state as trustee to permit public trust lands and resources to be used for a broader spectrum of water-dependent or water-oriented uses reflecting the needs and interests of the contemporary public.

Under general trust law, the terms of the trust may be enforced either by a beneficiary or by one of the trustees. Charitable trusts, as stated above, usually have no specified beneficiaries. Therefore, a rule of law has been established giving the state attorney general the right to enforce charitable trusts as a representative of all beneficiaries. In addition, there are two other ways to enforce charitable trusts. First, an individual beneficiary may encourage the attorney general to bring an action where the individual is the "relator." In this situation, the attorney general brings the lawsuit based on a specific claim or complaint of a beneficiary. Second, any beneficiary with a "special interest" in the performance of the charitable trust has the right to bring a lawsuit to enforce it. However, such an individual must demonstrate that the interest is special in that it derives from some benefit under the trust that is different from the benefit generally available to all beneficiaries. Furthermore, even in such special interest cases, the attorney general is usually a necessary party to the action.

In the public trust context, enforcement of the trust becomes somewhat complex. If the attorney general is the party to bring the lawsuit on behalf of all beneficiaries and the lawsuit is brought against the trustee, then the attorney general would effectively be suing the state or its delegate, the administrative agency. Thus enforcement is more likely to be limited as a practical matter (unless a statute dictates otherwise) to beneficiaries who have "special interests" and are willing to bring an action against the state or agency. For example, a fisherman who can prove that he has consistently used a public dock over a very long period of time might have a special interest that would allow him to bring a lawsuit against a state agency which permitted the licensing of the dock for private use only or for "dockominiums." A limitation identified by this analysis is that of cost. Where the only enforcement mechanism available is a lawsuit brought by a private party with a "special interest," and where a court cannot award monetary damages, there may be little incentive for private parties to bring costly lawsuits to enforce the public trust — at least without the incentive of a statutory entitlement to an award of legal fees for the prevailing party.

Conclusion

The analogies to private and charitable trust law may be fruitful sources of legal and practical approaches to implementation of the public trust. However, the question remains whether courts could be persuaded to hold the state as a public trustee to the fiduciary responsibilities of a private or charitable trustee. The likely case to test this issue would involve a lawsuit by a private citizen as a special interest beneficiary of the trust against a state agency for breach of the state's fiduciary obligations. To date, few cases have been brought on a straight trust/fiduciary obligations theory. Thus it remains to be seen how successful such a theory could be.

Pending such cases, however, states and coastal managers may affirmatively use the private and charitable trust analogies to strengthen their control and enforcement over public trust lands. For example, states and their delegates may clothe themselves in the mantle of a trustee, in the traditional private and charitable trust sense, in order to assert greater control over the management and preservation of public trust resources for both current and future generations by explicitly incorporating private and charitable trust principles into regulations, using guidelines and other regulatory activity affecting public trust lands and resources.

In the following case, the Supreme Court of Alaska explores the role of the state as trustee and the potential application of private trust principles.

Brooks v. Wright

971 P.2d 1025 (Alaska 1999)

Justice FAVE delivered the opinion of the Supreme Court of Alaska.

Introduction

Various citizens and community organizations sought to remove from the ballot an initiative prohibiting use of snares to trap wolves. The superior court agreed to decertify the initiative, reasoning that the initiative process is "clearly inapplicable" to natural resource management . . . because the state's role as "trustee" over natural resources gives it exclusive law-making powers over natural resource issues. After concluding that the prohibition of wolf snare traps is an appropriate subject for initiative, we reversed the superior court's order and placed the initiative back on the November 1998 general election ballot, announcing that an opinion would follow. Voters rejected the initiative in the November 1998 general election.

> **Initiatives and Other Forms of "Direct Democracy"**
>
> "Direct democracy consists of several types of proposed laws (known as ballot measures, propositions, issues, or questions), which require voter approval for enactment. Once enacted, a ballot measure creates, changes, or repeals a law; however, some states only allow advisory ballot measures that carry no legal force. There are four kinds of ballot measures: initiatives, referenda, referrals, and recalls. Initiatives are citizen-created statutory changes or constitutional amendments that are placed on the ballot after collection of a set number of citizens' signatures. Direct initiatives, the most common type, bypass the legislature completely, while indirect initiatives must be submitted to the legislature for consideration first. As with initiatives, referenda proponents must gather a set number of citizens' signatures to place a referendum on the ballot, but referenda force statewide votes on laws passed by the legislature during its last session. Referrals are laws and amendments that the legislature itself places on the ballot, and which may only be passed with the electorate's support. Finally, a recall allows citizens to remove public officials from office directly, without resort to impeachment." Cody Hoesly, *Reforming Direct Democracy: Lessons from Oregon*, 93 CALIF. L. REV. 1191, 1194-95 (2005).

Facts and Proceedings

In October 1997 Lieutenant Governor Fran Ulmer certified a ballot initiative which, if passed, would criminalize both the use of snares to trap wolves and the possession, sale, or purchase of wolf pelts known to have been taken by snare. The initiative, titled "An Act Relating to the Use of Snares in Trapping Wolves," reads in full:

> BE IT ENACTED BY THE PEOPLE OF THE STATE OF ALASKA:
>   AS 16.05 is amended by adding a new section to read:
>   Section 16.05.784. PROHIBITED METHODS OF TRAPPING WOLVES.
>   (a) A person may not use a snare with the intent of trapping a wolf.
>   (b) A person may not possess, purchase, offer to purchase, sell, or offer to sell the skin of a wolf known by the person to have been caught with a snare.
>   (c) A person who violates this section is guilty of a Class A misdemeanor.

One month later, a group of two citizens and two community organizations (Wright) filed suit against the State challenging the constitutionality of the initiative. Wright argued that, by virtue of the state's role as trustee over Alaska's natural resources under Article VIII [of the Alaska Constitution], the legislature has exclusive law-making power with respect to wildlife management issues.

***

Discussion

***

Wright . . . argues that . . . the initiative process is "clearly inapplicable" to natural resource management decisions because of the state's role as trustee over wildlife and other natural resources.

***

Article VIII of the Alaska Constitution concerns the management of natural resources:

> SECTION 3. COMMON USE. Wherever occurring in their natural state, fish, wildlife, and waters are reserved to the people for common use.
> SECTION 4. SUSTAINED YIELD. Fish, forests, wildlife, grasslands, and all other replenishable resources belonging to the State shall be utilized, developed, and maintained on the sustained yield principle, subject to preferences among beneficial uses.

Wright argues that these clauses establish a "public trust" for management of the state's wildlife, with the State of Alaska as "trustee" and the people of Alaska as the intended beneficiaries. From this premise, Wright further claims that the state, as part of its fiduciary duty, retains exclusive law-making authority over natural resource issues. We disagree.

We have frequently compared the state's duties as set forth in Article VIII to a trust-like relationship in which the state holds natural resources such as fish, wildlife, and water in "trust" for the benefit of all Alaskans. Instead of recognizing the creation of a public trust in these clauses per se, we have noted that "the common use clause was intended to engraft in our constitution certain trust principles guaranteeing access to the fish, wildlife and water resources of the state."

We have applied the public trust doctrine to cases involving exclusive grants of natural resources by the state. In *CWC Fisheries, Inc. v. Bunker*, 755 P.2d 1115 (Alaska 1988), we held that a holder of a state-granted fee interest in tidelands takes the land subject to a public easement. We based our holding in part on the state's public trust responsibilities with respect to tideland conveyance, but did not address whether Article VIII creates a public trust per se or whether such responsibilities preclude public participation in natural resource management decisions. Furthermore, we suggested that expansion of the public trust doctrine to include all or most public uses merely because it has been applied to a particular public use would be inappropriate.

A few months after *CWC Fisheries*, we clarified in *Owsichek v. State Guide Licensing & Control Bd.*, 763 P.2d 488 (Alaska 1988) that the purpose of the public trust doctrine was not to *grant* the legislature ultimate authority over natural resource management, but rather to *prevent* the state from giving out "exclusive grants or special privilege as was so frequently the case in ancient royal tradition." [*Id.* at 493.] Hence, the State of Alaska acts as "trustee" over wolves and other wildlife not so much to avoid *public* misuse of these resources as to avoid the *state's* improvident use or conveyance of them.

Indeed, in *Owsichek*, after a discussion of the holding in *CWC Fisheries*, we emphasized that the state's duties with respect to natural resource management under Article VIII "[are] to be exercised like all other powers of government, . . . and not as a prerogative for the advantage of the government as distinct from the people."

Wright relies on a recent case, *Baxley v. State*, 958 P.2d 422 (Alaska 1998), to argue that we should apply basic principles of private trust law to the trust-like relationship described in Article VIII. In *Baxley*, we referred to the public trust doctrine in examining the propriety of four state oil leases in the Beaufort Sea:

> The public trust doctrine provides that the State holds certain resources (such as wildlife, minerals, and water rights) in trust for public use and that government owes a fiduciary duty to manage such resources for the common good of the public as beneficiary. [*Id.* at 434.]

***

We have since emphasized that the applicability of private trust law depends greatly on both the type of trust created and the intent of those creating the trust. In [a case involving public lands], we cautioned that "reliance [on principles of private trust law] does not imply that application of such principles yields the same result regardless of the nature of the trust at issue." *Weiss v. State*, 939 P.2d 380, 393 (Alaska 1997), *cert. denied*, 522 U.S. 948 (1997).

***

. . . [A]pplication of private trust principles may be counterproductive to the goals of the trust relationship in the context of natural resources. For instance, private trusts generally require the trustee to maximize economic yield from the trust property, using reasonable care and skill. *See* RESTATEMENT (SECOND) OF TRUSTS §§ 174, 176, 181 (1959). But Article VIII requires that natural resources be managed for the benefit of all people, under the assumption that both development and preservation may be necessary to provide for future generations, and that income generation is not the sole purpose of the trust relationship. And although trust law dictates that the acts of a trustee should be reviewed for abuse of discretion, we have held that grants of exclusive rights to harvest natural resources listed in the common use clause are subject to close scrutiny. Private trust law principles also provide no guidance as to when the public's right to common use of resources can be limited through means such as licensing requirements. Finally, exceptions do exist to the general principle that beneficiaries cannot dictate how to manage the trust property. For example, in some circumstances, the creator may provide for the beneficiary's participation in trust management, and the beneficiary of a trust may act as trustee.

Other jurisdictions have held that, while general principles of trust law do provide some guidance, they do not supercede the plain language of statutory and constitutional provisions when determining the scope of the state's fiduciary duty or authority.[54] One commentator notes that general trust law should not be applied to the public trust doctrine in a way that limits or destroys the democratic process: "It would be a strict violation of democratic principle for the original voters and legislators of a state to limit, through a trust, the choices of the voters and legislators of today." James L. Huffman, *A Fish Out of Water; The Public Trust Doctrine in a Constitutional Democracy*, 19 ENVTL. L. 527, 544 (1989).

We most recently visited the public trust doctrine in the natural resource context in *Pullen v. Ulmer*, 923 P.2d 54 (Alaska 1996). In that case, we decertified an initiative allowing subsistence, personal use, and sport fisheries to have preference over other fisheries with respect to the harvestable salmon surplus. We concluded that salmon should be considered "assets" of the state for purposes of carrying out the state's trust duties with respect to wildlife. Because state assets may not be appropriated by initiative pursuant to Article XI, and because we viewed the preferential treatment of certain fisheries over others as an appropriation, we removed the initiative from the ballot. We left open the question of whether the state's trust responsibilities under Article VIII give the legislature exclusive law-making control over wildlife management.

We find little support in the public trust line of cases for the proposition that the common use clause of Article VIII grants the legislature exclusive power to make laws dealing with natural resource management. Article VIII does not explicitly create a public trust; rather, we have used the analogy of a public trust to describe the nature of the state's duties with respect to wildlife and other natural

---

54. *See, e.g., Evans v. City of Johnstown*, 96 Misc. 2d 755, 410 N.Y.S.2d 199, 207-08 (N.Y. App. Div. 1978) ("While the use of the name 'public trust' may suggest duties similar to those under a private trust, that interpretation is not feasible."); *City of Coronado v. San Diego Unified Port Dist.*, 227 Cal. App. 2d 455, 38 Cal. Rptr. 834, 844 (Cal. Dist. App. 1964) ("Private trust principles cannot be called upon to nullify an act of the legislature or modify its duty. . . .").

resources meant for common use. Additionally, the wholesale application of private trust law principles to the trust-like relationship described in Article VIII is inappropriate and potentially antithetical to the goals of conservation and universal use. And in *Pullen*, the only case in which we discussed the initiative process, we declined to hold that the public trust doctrine gives the legislature exclusive law-making authority over the subject matter of Article VIII. We therefore reject Wright's argument to the contrary and decline to decertify the initiative on public trust grounds.

For these reasons, we conclude that the legislature does *not* have exclusive law-making powers over natural resources issues merely because of the state's management role over wildlife set forth in Article VIII of the Alaska Constitution. . . .

Conclusion

Pursuant to this court's August 17, 1998 order, the superior court's order on summary judgment is reversed and its injunction against placement of the proposed ballot measure, "An Act Relating to the Use of Snares in Trapping Wolves," on the general election ballot is vacated.

points for discussion

1. *The trust analogy.* How useful do you think the analogy to private trust law will be to government officials making decisions about whether and how to regulate use of trust assets? Go back to some of the examples of conflict about which we have already read, for example, Mono Lake or the waters of San Juan County. How would the trust analogy help (or not help) you sort out these problems?

2. *The public trust doctrine and the wildlife trust.* The public trust doctrine and the so-called wildlife trust have related, but distinct, historical roots. Today, as seen in *Brooks*, courts and scholars often wind the two together, claiming that government responsibilities with respect to the two categories of assets are essentially the same.

   Why might this be a problem? History provides one clue. In England, the sovereign was deemed legal owner of tidal and submerged lands; he or she also held legal title to wild birds, game, and fish. The sovereign held only the first category of assets in trust for the people. The people had no rights, equitable or otherwise, in fish or wildlife: With only a few exceptions, subjects could only take animals with permission of the King. In the United States, neither the states nor the federal government legally own wildlife; instead, they have the power to regulate use. With respect to this power, the words "public trust" refer not to an actual trust, but to the broader idea that government has a responsibility to act in the best interests of its citizens.

   How might this kind of "public trust" responsibility differ from government responsibility under the public trust doctrine? Think "access."

Government should have more leeway in regulating the take of fish and wildlife because there is no countervailing public right to access the resource. Mixing the two kinds of "trusts" could lead courts (and legislatures) to believe that government power to manage wildlife is constrained. Thus, for example, in the case of an endangered species, it is clear that the government has the power to eliminate the public right to take any animals of the species. Because of the "access" component of the public trust doctrine, the government would have a much more difficult time eliminating all access to a public waterway.

Despite this critical difference, management principles for both types of resource are similar. In the case of doctrine assets, the idea is to ensure that the public, today and tomorrow, has the ability to use those assets. Similarly, as to wildlife, the government should seek to maintain wildlife populations, and the ecosystems that support them, so that future generations will be able to use and enjoy them.

One final observation: To the extent that courts have expanded the range of public trust doctrine uses to include, say, recreational wildlife watching, the doctrine and the wildlife trust do begin to overlap. The application of the public trust doctrine to Mono Lake water, for example, means that the doctrine is being applied as a wildlife (or ecosystem) management tool. Do you see why?

Problem Exercise: Application of the Public Trust doctrine

To test your understanding of the public trust doctrine, complete the following exercise.

Facts

Atlantica is a state on the Eastern seaboard of the United States. The coastline of Atlantica consists of more than 300 miles of rocky shores, beaches, and estuaries along the Atlantic Ocean. In the 150 years that Atlantica has been a state, much of its coastline has been developed.

Recently, a group of concerned citizens named "Save Our Coasts" (SOC) has undertaken a study of the historic and current state of Atlantica's coastal public trust lands. As part of this study, SOC geographers pieced together a set of aerial photographs taken in 1935 of the southern third of the Atlantica coast and compared them to aerial photographs taken in 2003 of the same area. While the geographers could not reach definite conclusions about particular places, their report suggests that private landowners had engaged in "substantial filling of coastal wetlands between 1935 and 2003." The report estimates the total filled area to be somewhere between 100,000 and 300,000 acres. Some of these filled areas remained undeveloped in 2003; these undeveloped areas are now fields, forests, and sandy beaches. Also, according to the SOC geographers' report, "a significant percentage of filled areas" are now home to a variety of structures, including hotels, businesses, and private residences.

George Portly, a state legislator from one of Atlantica's most heavily developed coastal counties, learned about the SOC report and became concerned about what SOC will do with the information it has gathered. After reading the report, Portly drafted a bill, the Coastal Quiet Title Act of 2009. This bill contains the following provision:

> In order to protect private property owners, to provide certainty to the troubled real estate markets of Atlantica, and to stabilize coastal economies, the State of Atlantica hereby relinquishes any and all claims to formerly submerged lands that have been converted to uplands by intentional filling. This law applies only to those lands filled prior to the effective date of this statute.

The Atlantica legislature passed this bill on August 15, 2009, and the Governor signed it on September 1, 2009.

SOC filed suit against the Atlantica legislature on September 15, 2009, alleging that the CQTA violated the public trust doctrine. The case is now before the Atlantica Supreme Court. Atlantica courts have not decided any significant public trust doctrine cases since the early 1900s, when its Supreme Court ruled that "submerged lands of the state underlying certain waters are covered by the public trust doctrine."

Assignment

Write a majority *and* a dissenting opinion for the Atlantica Supreme Court. You should assume that SOC has standing to bring the case and that there are no jurisdictional problems. In other words, you should focus on the substantive issue of whether or not the CQTA violates the public trust doctrine.

C. CHAPTER SUMMARY

1. **History and evolution.** While the roots of the modern public trust doctrine are easily found in Roman and British law, the doctrine began to evolve from the very moment the United States became a nation. The doctrine has continued to evolve in various directions, with scholars pushing both in favor of and against change.
2. **The duty not to dispose.** This duty is not absolute, although it is real. In all states, government may dispose of trust assets, but there are limitations on disposition. In addition to limitations on size, the doctrine imposes limits on the purposes of the transfer and on the extent to which the state can extinguish public access rights over or through transferred lands.
3. **The duty to protect access.** Access is at the core of the public trust doctrine. States can limit access in order to benefit the public as a whole. Sometimes,

where two or more uses are incompatible with one another, states may have to prohibit certain uses. This does not eliminate access; it only eliminates access for a particular purpose.

4. **The duty to manage.** Thus far, courts have not held that the doctrine imposes affirmative management duties on states. It is possible, however, to imagine how a duty to provide meaningful access might emerge as courts begin to recognize ecological use as a valid trust purpose.

D. SUGGESTED READING

Joseph D. Kearney & Thomas W. Merrill, *Origins of the American Public Trust Doctrine: What Really Happened in* Illinois Central, 71 U. CHI. L. REV. 799 (2004).

Richard J. Lazarus, *Changing Conceptions of Property and Sovereignty in Natural Resources: Questioning the Public Trust Doctrine*, 71 IOWA L. REV. 631 (1985).

Dave Owen, *The Mono Lake Case, the Public Trust Doctrine, and the Administrative State*, 45 U.C. DAVIS L. REV. 1099 (2012).

Eric Pearson, Illinois Central *and the Public Trust Doctrine in State Law*, 15 VA. ENVTL. L.J. 713 (1995).

Joseph L. Sax, *The Public Trust Doctrine in Natural Resource Law: Effective Judicial Intervention*, 68 MICH. L. REV. 471 (1970).

Barton H. Thompson, Jr., *The Public Trust Doctrine: A Conservative Reconstruction and Defense*, 15 SOUTHEASTERN ENVTL. L.J. 47 (2006).

chapter **8**

Upland Owners' Rights

This chapter is concerned with property rights; in particular, the set of common law rights appurtenant to riparian and littoral land. Why did the common law develop these "riparian and littoral rights" as companions to the public trust doctrine?

The enforcement of rights is both fair and efficient. It is fair, because it protects investment; and it is efficient, because it promotes further investment. At the same time, too much or the wrong kind of private investment in upland property would result in inefficiencies as costs imposed on the public trust surpass benefits generated by private activity. Thus, upland owners' rights (like the public trust doctrine) serve as mechanisms for ensuring optimal use of both uplands and the neighboring public property. Because they function as optimality-seeking balancing mechanisms, upland owners' rights — like other property rights such as the right to use and enjoy — are qualified rights. The materials in this chapter illustrate various judicial approaches to getting the balance right.

A. INTRODUCTION TO UPLAND RIGHTS

As next-door neighbor to the sovereign, the upland owner is in a unique position in that the upland owner is not on equal footing with the sovereign. One can view riparian and littoral rights as the common law's effort to protect upland owners from the actions of a more powerful neighbor, the state sovereign, whose right to use and enjoy is grounded in the potent public trust doctrine. For example, a state legislature might be interested in filling its submerged lands and using the new dry land to build a marina. This would significantly alter the upland owner's view and ability to access the water, two things the owner has likely paid a premium for.

As a historical matter, the practice of upland owners developing their properties to take advantage of water-borne commerce, by building a dock, for example, began well before governments had the desire or wherewithal to undertake such projects. The ability of upland owners to use property in this way made uplands more expensive: Owners' investments enhanced their reasonable expectations. As we have seen in our brief examination of Fifth Amendment takings law, courts place great weight on protecting such expectations. The social benefits associated with protecting reasonable, investment-backed expectations include the fact that doing so builds trust in government, minimizing what some have called "demoralization costs." Frank I. Michelman, *Property, Utility, and Fairness: Comments on the Ethical Foundations of "Just Compensation" Law*, 80 Harv. L. Rev. 1165, 1214 (1967).

In addition to the rights that generally inhere in the title to real property (such as the right to exclude, the right to use and enjoy, and the right to alienate), the owner of a parcel of riparian or littoral land — the upland owner — possesses *riparian* and *littoral* rights that are specifically tailored to the waterside location of the property. Riparian and littoral rights are generally matters of state law, so the types of these rights and their legal strength vary from state to state. Moreover, each state's set of riparian rights can differ from its set of littoral rights. (For example, some states recognize a "right to wharf out" in riparian, but not littoral owners.)

To make matters more complicated, it is not always clear whether a particular parcel is, for legal purposes, riparian or littoral. Estuaries, for example, are places where rivers meet the sea; nature does not provide clear lines between freshwater and tidal systems. This book will use the term "upland owners' rights" to refer to both riparian and littoral rights, except, of course, where the difference matters.

Upland owners' rights, like the right to use and enjoy, can be defined only in the context of conflict, and not in a vacuum. Some conflicts pit private parties against one another. Cases between a private party and a state or the federal government are usually framed as alleged takings of property under the Fifth Amendment to the U.S. Constitution (or the state constitutional equivalent).

Because the sets of riparian and littoral rights differ from state to state, each case in this chapter illustrates the view of one particular state's courts. However, all states recognize upland owners' rights, and it is easy to make a list of rights usually found in those sets. For example, one treatise (Robert E. Beck, ed., Waters and Water Rights 1-6, at § 6.01 (2009)) identifies riparian rights as:

- The right to access the adjacent public waterway
- The right to wharf out (build a wharf, pier, or similar structure) to connect the upland with a navigable channel
- The right to accretions
- The right to non-consumptive use of the water, for example, the diversion of water to generate power for a mill
- The right to consume water (mainly relevant for properties bordering freshwater waterways)

B. THE RIGHT TO ACCESS THE ADJACENT PUBLIC WATERWAY

We know, from Chapter 7, that all members of the public have the right to access public waterways. The upland owner's right of access is best thought of as a special right of access, one that is unique to the upland owner; that is, not shared with the public at large. Specifically, it is the right to access the adjacent public waterway from the owner's upland property.

What does "access" mean? The common law recognizes different kinds or means of access:

- *Pure access.* Upland owners have the right to travel unabated from their property to the public waterway. Some state courts have also recognized direct visual access to the water, that is, a view, as a form of protected pure access.
- *Wharfing out.* Although the right to wharf out is, as the list above indicates, sometimes considered to be separate from the right of access, it is better conceived as derivative of that right. The right to wharf out allows the upland owner the opportunity to physically connect the upland property to a navigable-in-fact area, such as a channel, within the public waterway.

1. Pure Access

All pure access lawsuits have their origins in either (1) government use of submerged lands, or (2) the transfer of submerged lands (in fee or a lesser interest) to a private party. The state, as legal owner of submerged lands, has the right and duty to use (or not) those lands in furtherance of public trust purposes. In addition, the state may, so long as it does not violate the applicable "duty not to dispose," transfer title to submerged lands to private parties. Pure access cases arise when government or private use of submerged lands interferes with an upland owner's ability to access the adjacent public waterway.

Figure 8-1 illustrates such a scenario. Say, for example, the government decides to fill in public trust submerged lands (the gray area) directly seaward of Blackacre. The government plans to build a marina for recreational boats on the seaward

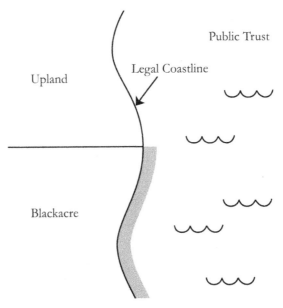

Figure 8-1. Pure Access Lawsuit
Facts giving rise to the "pure access" lawsuit.

side of the gray area, and some structures on the newly created land. Not only does this action interfere with the right of Fred (owner of Blackacre) to physically and visually access the public waterway; it also converts Blackacre from upland property to ordinary property: Blackacre no longer touches the water! Must the government compensate Fred for the loss of rights and value?

A similar controversy would arise if the government sold, leased, or granted an easement over the gray area to a private party (other than Fred). These kinds of transfers were very common (as we saw in *Illinois Central*) during the heyday of railroad construction. If the railroad company obtains fee title to the gray area, then fills it in and builds tracks on it, is it liable to Fred? What if the railroad company merely obtains an easement over the gray area, and instead of filling it in, builds an elevated track supported by pilings?

The first case below presents facts similar to those illustrated in Figure 8-1. In the second case, the allegations are slightly different, and represent an effort to expand the meaning of the term "access."

Rumsey v. The New York and New England Railroad Company

30 N.E. 654 (N.Y. 1892)

Judge O'BRIEN delivered the opinion of the Court of Appeals of New York.

. . . The plaintiffs are, and for more than twenty years have been, the owners of about forty acres of land on the east bank of the Hudson River at Fishkill, bounded on the west by the river, and covering about one thousand feet of the river front. It also appears that on the 3d of March, 1885, the state, pursuant to a resolution of the commissioners of the land office, granted to the plaintiffs the lands under water adjacent to and in front of the uplands, from high-water mark westerly to the channel bank of the river, excepting therefrom the rights of the New York Central and Hudson River Railroad Company. This railroad, it seems, was constructed across the water front prior to and about the year 1854, and since that time the plaintiffs and their grantors have used a strip of land leading from the uplands through a culvert under the Hudson River railroad to the channel of the river, for loading vessels with brick made on the premises, and for all purposes connected with the manufacture of brick on the premises, with the consent of the Hudson River railroad, until such use was obstructed by the building of the defendants' road-bed. This was built in the years 1880 and 1881, outside of and nearly parallel with the road-bed of the Hudson River road, in front of the culvert above described, and along the whole river front of plaintiffs'

> **Point of Clarification**
>
> It appears from this language that the resolution of the commissioners, or some other state entity, had prior to 1854 granted the railroad company an easement over the submerged lands. The terms of this easement apparently allowed the railroad company to construct a rail line and then a road-bed in the easement area.

land, without any right or authority from the plaintiffs or their grantors. The effect of this was to cut off the plaintiffs from access to the river from their lands. The plaintiffs' title to the uplands and the lands under water, where the defendant's road is built, has been determined in their favor by the decisions of this court.

***

In this action the plaintiffs seek to recover damages to their uplands, sustained by the act of the defendant in constructing its road-bed across the plaintiffs' water front, and thereby cutting off their access to the river, and such damages are claimed from the·time of the construction of the railroad to the commencement of the action. The court assessed the damages at $10,500. This result was reached upon the theory that the use of the plaintiffs' premises for the purpose of a

L.R. Burleigh/Library of Congress

Figure 8-2. Brickyards
Brickyard on the Hudson, circa 1889. Note landing used for shipping bricks

brick yard had been depreciated to that extent in consequence of the construction of the defendant's road. At the same time the court found that the culvert, as a passage-way, was discontinued about the year 1875, and the dock at the westerly end of the culvert was allowed to go to decay, as was also the cause-way which connected the dock with the brick yard. That the plaintiffs' lands had no buildings or machinery on them to fit them for use for brick-making purposes, and that they had been in this situation since the year 1875, and that the defendant had in no wise injured the plaintiffs' lands, except only to prevent or delay the sale of the clay thereon for brick-making purposes. It appears, therefore, from these findings, that the use of the premises for brick making or as a brick yard had been discontinued six years before the defendant's road was built. The plaintiffs asked to recover in this action only such damages as they have sustained up to the commencement of the action, by reason of the acts complained of. As a basis for the estimate the land must be taken as it was used during the time embraced in the action. It does not appear that the use of the premises as a brick yard was discontinued in consequence of the acts of the defendant, and that fact could not well be established, for it ceased to be used for such purpose long before the defendant's road was built. The proper measure of damages in such a case is the diminished rental or usable value of the property as it was, in consequence of the loss by defendant's acts, of access to the river, in the manner enjoyed by the owner prior to the construction of the embankment across the water front by the defendant. The plaintiffs cannot be permitted to prove or allowed to recover damages that they might have sustained if they had put the property to some other use or placed other structures upon it. . . .

The damages could not be based upon the rental or usable value of the property for a brickyard any more than they could be based upon their use for some other specific or particular purpose to which they were not in fact put by the owners. The question is what damages did the plaintiff in fact suffer by having the access to the river cut off, not what they might have suffered had the land been devoted to some particular use to which it was not put.

The proof of damages on the part of plaintiff consisted entirely of the opinions of witnesses as to the rental value of the land in the absence of the structure built by defendant. This proof was competent as far as it went, but it did not establish the legal measure of damages. It should also have been shown what was the rental or usable value of the premises as they were with the obstruction which interfered with the access to the river, as the difference in these two sums represented the actual loss caused by the defendants. The defendant offered to prove the additional cost of shipping brick to market upon the river rendered necessary by the construction of the embankment. This testimony was objected to by the plaintiffs and excluded by the court, to which the defendant excepted. This ruling was erroneous. The additional expense caused by the defendant's structure in the river of transporting brick, or any other product of the land, to market was an important element of the damages sustained, and the defendant should have been permitted to prove the fact in that regard, at least by way of answer to plaintiffs' theory of damages. The method adopted of establishing the plaintiffs' damages, therefore, demands a reversal of the judgment.

The plaintiffs were permitted to recover for more than four years prior to their grant of the land under water on the 3d of March, 1885. During this period the plaintiffs' rights were those of ordinary riparian owners on the banks of navigable rivers. They owned the uplands bounded by the river, and as such owners had the right, under the statute, to apply to the commissioners of the land office for a grant of the land under water in front of their premises. In this respect and on this branch of the case, the facts are identical with those in the case of *Gould v. Hudson River Railroad Company*, 6 N.Y. 522 (1852).

If that case is to be followed, the plaintiff cannot recover any damages prior to March 3, 1885. It was there held that the owner of lands on the Hudson river has no private right or property in the waters or the shore between high and low-water mark and, therefore, is not entitled to compensation from a railroad company which, in pursuance of a grant from the legislature, constructs a railroad along the shore, between

---

The *Gould* Case

The opinion goes on to discredit the holding in the *Gould* case. The *Gould* decision is notable because it established a rule to the effect that no upland owner could ever recover from the state, or a state transferee (like the railroad here), under any circumstances for a partial or complete loss of upland rights. The rationale was that the state, as owner of the submerged lands, was entitled to use them however it saw fit.

high and low-water mark, so as to cut off all communications between the land and the river otherwise than across the railroad. It is believed that this proposition is not supported by any other judicial decision in this state, and if we were dealing with the question now as an original one, it would not be difficult to show that the judgment in that case was a departure from precedent and contrary to reason and justice. It is no doubt true that even a single adjudication of this court, upon a question properly before it, is not to be questioned or disregarded except for the most cogent reasons, and then only in a case where it is plain that the judgment was the result of a mistaken view of the condition of the law applicable to the question. But the doctrine of *stare decisis*, like almost every other legal rule, is not without its exceptions. It does not apply to a case where it can be shown that the law has been misunderstood or misapplied, or where the former determination is evidently contrary to reason. The authorities are abundant to show that in such cases it is the duty of courts to re-examine the question. Chancellor Kent, commenting upon the rule of *stare decisis*, said that more than a thousand cases could then be pointed out, in the English and American reports, which had been overruled, doubted or limited in their application. He added that "it is probable that the records of many of the courts of this country are replete with hasty and crude decisions; and in such cases ought to be examined without fear, and revised without reluctance, rather than to have the character of our law impaired, and the beauty and harmony of the system destroyed by the perpetuity of error." [Citations omitted.]

The *Gould* case has been frequently criticised and questioned and it is believed has never been fully acquiesced in by the courts or the profession as a decisive authority or a correct exposition of the law respecting the rights of riparian owners. . . . The learned judge who gave the prevailing opinion in the case assumed, as the foundation of his argument, that the question was conclusively determined by the Supreme Court adverse to the plaintiff in [an earlier case] . . . . That case grew out of the construction of the canal basin at Albany, a public improvement to promote commerce and navigation, and the question was whether, as against such an improvement, the plaintiff's right to the use of his dock and water front, as he had enjoyed it before, was exclusive. It may be conceded that the sovereign power in a work for the improvement of the navigation of a public river may incidentally interfere with the enjoyment and use of the water front by riparian owners, but the power to grant a private individual or corporation the right to cut such owner off entirely from communication with the stream, without compensation, is quite another and different question. . . . [W]e are now concerned with but a single branch of an important and somewhat complicated subject, namely, the right of such owner, as against some other private interest, to have access to and enjoy the use of the highway.

It may be observed, however, that since the decision of the *Gould* case in 1852, this question and questions of a kindred nature have been elaborately examined, discussed and settled in this court, in our highest federal tribunal, in the court of last resort in England, and in the highest court of several of our sister states. The doctrine of that case has been repudiated or ignored in these decisions, and the rights of the proprietors of lands upon rivers and public highways determined upon principles more in accord with reason and justice. The long line of decisions in this court . . . hold that an owner of land abutting upon a public street has a property right in such street for the purposes of access, light and air, and that the state has no power to grant to a railroad the right to occupy the street when such occupation injuriously affects the enjoyment by the property owner of such rights, except by the exercise of the power of eminent domain, and when a street is thus used by the railroad, without condemnation proceedings or a grant from the property owner, it is responsible to him for any damages resulting therefrom.

> **Quick Questions**
>
> Is the analogy between property adjacent to highways and upland property a good one? In other words, should the rights held by each kind of owner be given similar levels of protection? Put differently, are the state's rights and obligations the same with respect to highways and public waterways?

Unless there is some distinction to be made between the rights which pertain to an owner of land upon a public river and one upon a public street, which is not perceived, then the principles sanctioned by this court in these cases virtually overrule the *Gould* case, as they are apparently irreconcilable.

The question respecting the rights of riparian owners in such a case was determined in the Supreme Court of the United States in *Yates v. Milwaukee*, 77 U.S. 497, 504 (1871). Mr. Justice Miller, in delivering the opinion of the court, stated the law clearly as determined by that court:

> But whether the title of the owner of such a lot extends beyond the dry land or not, he is certainly entitled to all the rights of a riparian proprietor whose land is bounded by a navigable stream, and among these rights are access to the navigable part of the river from the front of his lot, the right to make a landing, wharf or pier for his own use or for the use of the public, subject to such general rules and regulations as the legislature may see proper to impose for the protection of the rights of the public, whatever these may be. . . . This riparian right is property and is valuable, and though it must be enjoyed in due subjection to the rights of the public, it cannot be arbitrarily or capriciously destroyed or impaired. It is a right of which, when once vested, the owner can only be deprived in accordance with established law, and if necessary that it be taken for the public good upon due compensation.

In England it was held quite recently that the owner of an estate on the tidewaters of the Thames was entitled to compensation, not only for the land actually taken under the authority of a statute for the construction of a public road along the shore, which cut off the owner's access to the river, but also for the permanent damage to the whole estate in consequence of its change by the improvement from river side to road side property, including his individual and particular right to use the shore of the river. . . .

In nearly all of our sister states where the question has arisen the same or substantially similar rules have been adopted. [Citations omitted.]

***

It must now, we think, be regarded as the law in this state that an owner of land on a public river is entitled to such damages as he may have sustained against a railroad company that constructs its road across his water front and deprives him of access to the navigable part of the stream unless the owner has granted the right, or it has been obtained by the power of eminent domain. This principle cannot, of course, be extended so as to interfere with the right of the state to improve the navigation of the river or with the power of congress to regulate commerce under the provisions of the Federal Constitution. The plaintiffs were, therefore, entitled to recover such damages as they could prove to have been sustained by them prior to March 3, 1885, but on account of the erroneous rules adopted for determining the damages, above pointed out, the judgment should be reversed and a new trial granted, costs to abide the event.

Hayes v. Bowman

91 So. 2d 795 (Fla. 1957)

Justice THORNAL delivered the opinion of the Supreme Court of Florida.

Appellants Hayes and Abbott, who were plaintiffs below, seek reversal of a final decree of the Chancellor in a declaratory judgment proceeding involving alleged riparian rights of the parties in the tidal waters of Boca Ciega Bay.

Although many incidental questions are propounded, the determining point is whether a fill proposed by the appellees would, when constructed, encroach upon the common law riparian rights of appellants.

An understanding of the opposing contentions will be assisted by a drawing of the land and proposed fill, all of which is set out as follows:

Prior to the institution of this suit appellees and their predecessors were owners of a portion of the mainland on the western shore of Boca Ciega Bay. They acquired a parcel of submerged lands in the Bay from the Trustees of the Internal Improvement Fund. By dredging and filling they built a subdivision known as Brightwater Beach Estates shown in the foregoing drawing. The northern tier of lots comprising Block 4 is located on a narrow dredged-in peninsula approximately 1750 feet long in an easterly direction from the mainland

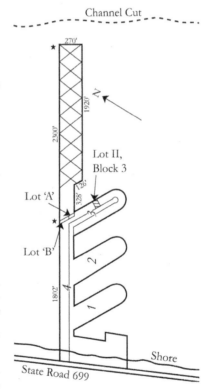

Figure 8-3. Facts in *Hayes*
A map from the court's opinion in *Hayes*. Does it capture the relevant facts?

toward the Channel. Lots A and B, Block 4, constitute a parcel of land across the eastern extremity of said Block 4. Blocks 1, 2 and 3 are dredged-in "fingers" or peninsulas constructed in a southeasterly direction from the southern boundary line of said Block 4. Block 3 is the easternmost of these three fingers. Appellants' property is Lot 11, Block 3. It is located on the easterly side of the Block. Consequently, the front of appellants' lot faces the waters and Channel of the Bay. The sidelines of appellants' lot run in a generally northeasterly-southwesterly direction.

Appellees own Lots A and B above mentioned. The south line of these lots is about 200 feet north of the northerly line of appellants' lot.

On October 22, 1954, appellees acquired from the Trustees of the Internal Improvement Fund an additional strip of submerged land 270 feet in width extending from the easterly edge of Lots A and B a distance of 2300 feet easterly toward the Channel. Appellees now propose to dredge and fill this newly acquired submerged land. Appellants filed a complaint to enjoin the proposed operation. The Chancellor entered a summary final decree for the appellees. Hence, this appeal seeking reversal of the decree.

It is the contention of the appellants that as upland owners of land bounded by navigable waters they enjoy certain common law riparian rights to an unobstructed view of the Bay, as well as a right of ingress and egress to and from their land over the waters of the Bay from and to the Channel. They contend that these rights exist in an area over the waters of the Bay to be determined by extending their side lot lines in a northeasterly direction to the Channel. They assert that appellees' proposed fill 2300 feet easterly of said Lots A and B toward the Channel would therefore completely bi-sect the corridor over and through which they are entitled to enjoy their riparian rights and reach the Channel. In other words, they contend that the common law riparian rights of an upland owner abutting navigable waters are exclusive against all interference in that area over the waters established by an extension of the side lines of the upland lot to the Channel.

It is the position of the appellees that when the Channel substantially parallels the shoreline the common law riparian rights of the upland owner are to be established in an area measured by lines drawn perpendicularly from the thread of the Channel to the corners of the property of the upland owner. By applying this rule they contend that the construction of the proposed fill would not in any way interfere with the area vouchsafed to appellants for the exercise of their common law rights.

A cautious analysis and a thorough understanding of the nature of the sovereign's proprietorship of submerged lands under tidal waters is suggested by this record. To paraphrase the language of Judge Learned Hand in *Jackson & Co. v. Royal Norwegian Government*, 2 Cir., 177 F.2d 694, 702 (1949), "out of the rivers of ink that have been written on this subject" certain fundamental principles have emerged which are entitled to careful examination and restatement. In our democracy the State's title is in the nature of the sovereign proprietorship as it existed at common law. We must at the same time understand and give due regard to the littoral and riparian rights of the upland owners. These are appurtenances to private property which are entitled to due recognition and protection. The vital aspect of the problem in Florida is acutely demonstrated when we look to our general coastline of 1197 statute miles and our detailed tidal shoreline, including bays, sounds and other bodies measured to the head of tidewater, which measures 8426 statute miles. . . . The expanding importance of the situation is underscored by the enactment of the so-called Submerged Lands Act of 1953 by the Congress of the United States. . . .

At common law, although admittedly there was some divergence of view, the title to all land under tidal waters below high-water mark belonged to the Crown. These waters and the lands which they covered were held by the king in trust for the use of all his subjects. The primary uses were navigation, bathing and fishing. Thus it was that the title, *jus privatum*, was held by the king as sovereign but the dominion, *jus publicum*, was vested in him for the benefit of the people. At least from the time of Sir Matthew Hale (1609-1676) this was the accepted rule, except in cases where an individual had acquired rights in the submerged lands by express grant which did not interfere with navigation, and other riparian rights such as fishing. Thus arose the doctrine of the so-called "inalienable trust" whereby the sovereign held the legal title for the equitable use of his subjects. . . .

With the colonization of the Western hemisphere this became the accepted doctrine among the thirteen original states and the territories. . . . The rule has been varied slightly in some states by statute.

Subject to certain statutory variations which we hereafter point out, it is well settled in Florida that the State holds title to lands under tidal navigable waters and the foreshore thereof (land between high and low water marks). As at common law, this title is held in trust for the people for purposes of navigation, fishing, bathing and similar uses. Such title is not held primarily for purposes of sale or conversion into money. Basically it is trust property and should be devoted to the fulfillment of the purposes of the trust, to wit: the service of the people.

However, consonant with the common law rule, the State may dispose of submerged lands under tidal waters to the extent that such disposition will not interfere with the public's right of navigation, swimming and like uses. Moreover, any person acquiring any such lands from the State must so use the land as not to interfere with the recognized common law riparian rights of upland owners (an unobstructed view, ingress and egress over the foreshore from and to the water). . . . Upland owners have been granted additional statutory riparian rights which must be recognized. These we mention hereafter.

This power of the State to dispose of submerged tidal lands has assumed important proportions in recent years. Valuable subdivisions have been built on dredged-in fill. Large areas have been leased to those who would speculate in drilling for oil. Increased interest in this type of land bears forebodings of even more complex problems in the future. These lands constitute tremendously valuable assets. Like any other fiduciary asset, however, they must be administered with due regard to the limitations of the trust with which they are impressed. . . .

The custodians of this trust are the Trustees of the Internal Improvement Fund. Prior to 1951 the Trustees were authorized to sell tidal lands upon which the waters were not more than three feet deep at high tide and which were separated from the mainland by a channel not less than five feet deep at high tide, and also certain sand bars and shallow banks along the mainland. . . . The submerged lands acquired by appellees for purposes of the proposed fill were purchased [from the Trustees]. . . .

The riparian rights of upland owners of lands bounded by tidal waters in Florida have been expanded by statute. . . . By Chapter 8537, Laws of 1921, the so-called Butler Bill (deriving its name from its sponsor Senator J. Turner Butler of Duval County), the right of an upland owner to dredge, bulkhead and fill in front of his land to the edge of the channel was provisionally granted to the owners of lands extending to the high-water mark instead of being limited to ownerships which extended to the low-water mark. The privilege did not apply over public bathing beaches. . . . It should be noted that no title is acquired until such submerged lands are actually filled in or permanently improved. . . . Before this was done, the State's offer to riparian owners for them to secure title by improving the foreshore could be withdrawn and the provisional rights then reverted to the State.

The so-called common law riparian rights of upland owners bordering upon navigable waters have now been expressly recognized by statute.

At the risk of repeating a number of rules heretofore settled we have herewith attempted to summarize the development of state ownership of submerged tidal lands, the power of disposition thereof and the co-relative riparian rights of upland owners. It remains to apply these rules to the case before us.

For purposes of this record we assume that appellants are "upland owners." No question is raised in that regard. It will be recalled that the lot owned by appellants is itself located on dredged-in fill. It is situated in Boca Ciega Bay on the dredged-in subdivision connected with the mainland by the peninsula designated as Block 4 of the subdivision. . . .

We harken back to the main points made by the parties. Appellants claim that they are entitled to an unobstructed view toward the Channel over a corridor measured by extending their northeasterly-southwesterly lot lines directly to the Channel. Appellees claim that this corridor is to be bounded by imaginary lines drawn at right angles from the thread of the Channel to the corners of appellants' lot. If appellants' contention is approved, the

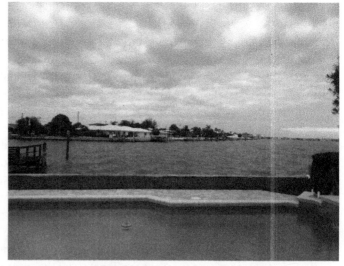

Photo: Allison Humen

Figure 8-4. View from Hayes Property circa 2011

proposed fill would obstruct their view. If appellees' position is adopted, there would be no obstruction.

It is absolutely impossible to formulate a mathematical or geometrical rule that can be applied to all situations of this nature. The angles (direction) of side lines of lots bordering navigable waters are limited only by the number of points on a compass rose. Seldom, if ever, is the thread of a channel exactly or even approximately parallel to the shoreline of the mainland. These two conditions make the mathematical or geometrical certainty implicit in the rules recommended by the contesting parties literally impossible. We must therefore search elsewhere for a solution to this admittedly difficult problem. We find our answer at least suggested by the language of Section 271.01, Florida Statutes . . . granting bulkheading privileges to upland owners "in the direction of the channel, or as near in the direction of the channel as practicable to equitably distribute the submerged lands. . . . " Added legislative support for this notion is contributed by the fact that Section 271.09, Florida Statutes . . . does not purport to define or delineate the exact area over which the so-called common law riparian rights are to be enjoyed.

We are therefore of the view and must hold that the common law riparian rights to an unobstructed view and access to the Channel over the foreshore across the waters toward the Channel must be recognized over an area as near "as practicable" in the direction of the Channel so as to distribute equitably the submerged lands between the upland and the Channel. This rule means that each case necessarily must turn on the factual circumstances there presented and no geometric theorem can be formulated to govern all cases. An upland owner must in all cases be permitted a direct, unobstructed view of the Channel and as well a direct, unobstructed means of ingress and egress over the foreshore and tidal waters to the Channel. If the exercise of these rights is prevented, the upland owner is entitled to relief.

In the instant case the Chancellor obviously held that the appellees had not encroached upon or threatened to encroach upon appellants' right of view or right of approach to the Channel of Boca Ciega Bay. We agree with the Chancellor. The appellants still have a direct, unobstructed view of the Bay "in the direction of the Channel" as well as a direct and unobstructed means of ingress and egress to the Channel of the Bay.

It is true as appellants allege that they will be deprived of a view of the "bright, white tower of Stetson Law School which shines as a beacon of learning on the eastern horizon." We are nonetheless impelled to the thought that a view of that splendid institution of learning, so ably headed now by a former member of this Court, is not a special riparian right guaranteed to appellants and those similarly conditioned.

In *Freed v. Miami Beach Pier Corporation*, 112 So. 841 (Fla. 1927), the late Justice Whitfield, who many times wrote the view of this Court on the subject at hand, pointed out that the shore line and the channel may not run in the same direction and the boundary lines of lands that extend to the shore line may not run at right angles with the shore line. He then added that these conditions tender questions as to rights of riparian owners that require the application of appropriate rules to particular facts in each case as it is presented for adjudication.

Riparian rights do not necessarily extend into the waters according to upland boundaries nor do such rights under all conditions extend at right angles to the shore line. Our own precedents are completely inconsistent with the appellees' view that such rights extend over an area measured by lines at right angles to the Channel. It should be borne in mind that littoral or riparian rights are appurtenances to ownership of the uplands. They are not founded on ownership of the submerged lands. It is for this reason, among others that we cannot define the area within which the rights are to be enjoyed with mathematical exactitude or by a metes and bounds description.

We therefore prescribe the rule that in any given case the riparian rights of an upland owner must be preserved over an area "as near as practicable" in the direction of the Channel so as to distribute equitably the submerged lands between the upland and the Channel. In making such "equitable distribution" the Court necessarily must give due consideration to the lay of the upland shore line, the direction of the Channel and the co-relative rights of adjoining upland owners.

We realize that such a rule, like many others in equity, invokes the conscience of the Chancellor in the application of broad principles to the factual situation presented by the particular case. Unlike John Seldon, however, we cannot agree that the standard for the exercise of the Chancellor's conscience is the length of "the Chancellor's foot." It is a judicial determination that he must make in each instance consistent with the rights of the parties presented by the record.

In the case before us the ruling of the Chancellor does no violence to the rights of appellants. They still may enjoy their riparian rights over the waters of Boca Ciega Bay in an area as "near as practicable" in the direction of the Channel with a resulting equitable distribution of the submerged lands and the waters and area above said lands between their upland and the edge of the Channel. It should be made clear that this holding is limited to the effect of the proposed filling of the particular submerged land adjacent to appellees' lots A and B, Block 4, mentioned in our summary of the facts. If the fill should be extended in a southerly direction so as to interrupt appellants' remaining view of or approach to the Channel, appellants might then have substantial grounds for complaint.

It appears to us that our position is strengthened when we take note of the fact that the Trustees of the Internal Improvement Fund are five constitutional officers of the executive branch of the government. If we are ever to apply the rule that public officials will be presumed to do their duty, it would appear to us to be most appropriate in this instance. Certainly we are not to assume that in the supervision and disposition of submerged lands the Trustees will knowingly ignore the rights of upland owners. It is to be assumed that they will exercise their judgment in a fashion that will give due regard to private rights as well as public rights. This Board would appear to be the most appropriate repository of the responsibility to be exercised in these matters in the first instance. The exercise of their judgment should not be subjected to adverse judicial scrutiny absent a clear showing of abuse of discretion or a violation of law. . . .

***

The decree of the Chancellor is Affirmed.

points for discussion

1. *The plaintiffs lost.* The aerial photograph illustrates what the property at issue in *Hayes* looked like in 1957.

2. *Access and expectations.* The unique feature of every piece of riparian or littoral land is that it abuts a public waterway. Think of a piece of riparian or littoral property with which you are familiar. If you bought that land, what would your expectations be with respect to use of the adjacent waterway? Would it depend on the exact location and features

Photo: University of FloridaDigital Collections

Figure 8-5. "Bowman's Peninsula" in 1957
It is three peninsulas down from the bridge. Notice the substantial amount of filled land in the bay.

of the property and the waterway? Do you think other buyers might have very different expectations? Given that one of the rationales for the existence of upland owners' rights is to protect reasonable, investment-backed expectations, it would seem imperative to develop a general sense of what constitute reasonable expectations. Is this possible? How can legal rules account for the fact that both private and public expectations are subject to change over time?

3. *Does a case-by-case, equitable approach to dispute resolution get the job done?* The suite of upland owners' rights is a judicial mechanism for resolving conflicts, helping courts balance the interests of upland owners with the state or public interest in the adjacent waterways. In addition to helping courts resolve disputes, these rights are also meant to provide needed certainty or, at least, a sense of predictability to those who invest in upland property. But, as you can see from both *Rumsey* and *Hayes*, courts actually resolve conflicts in a very fact-specific, case-by-case, equitable manner. Does this approach hinder optimal land use or generate unnecessary litigation? Is there a viable alternative? Consider the analogy of municipal zoning and nuisance law: One rationale for zoning was that it would reduce the unpredictability and inefficiencies of common law adjudication of land use disputes. Could a similar mechanism work in the coastal law context? *See Sarasota Cty. v. Barg*, 302 So. 2d 737 (Fla. 1974).

4. *The identity of the actor as a relevant fact.* In *Rumsey*, the court seems to consider it important that the interference with plaintiffs' access rights was caused by a private firm, the railroad company. But, of course, the railroad company would not have been able to do anything on the submerged lands without New York's grant of the easement. Should it matter who is causing the interference? Remember that the public trust doctrine shields the state from takings liability to the extent it acts to protect or enhance navigation or another trust purpose. Would the case have come out the same way if the state had transferred the land to a private company for the construction and operation of a marina? *See Scranton v. Wheeler*, 179 U.S. 141 (1900); *Newport Beach v. Fager*, 39 Cal. App. 2d 23 (1940). What if the state had constructed the rail line in order to service state-owned railroad cars? Does it depend how broadly the court construes the state's public trust powers? *See, e.g., Colberg, Inc. v. California*, 432 P.2d 3 (Cal. 1967) (state's construction of bridge cutting off upland owner's access to navigable water does not require state to compensate upland owner; "the spanning of navigable waters by a railroad bridge was an act within the trust purposes of 'commerce, navigation, and fisheries'").

5. *The waterfront takings test.* As stated in the prior point, the government can use the public trust doctrine as a defense when a waterfront landowner seeks compensation for state interference with her upland rights. *Rumsey* is an example of a typical nineteenth-century dispute between a state (or state transferee) and a waterfront owner. In those cases, courts developed a kind of takings test to determine when state action required compensation to the waterfront owner. The waterfront takings test "generally included three rules: If the state or its transferee used trust lands for trust purposes, no compensation was owed; if the use of trust lands was beyond the scope of the trust, compensation was owed for unreasonable interference with upland rights; along the same lines, the state was entitled to, without compensation, prevent upland owners from exercising upland rights if the exercise of those rights interfered with trust uses of public waterways." Josh Eagle, *Taking the Oceanfront Lot*, 91 IND. L.J. 851, 866 (2016). In *Rumsey*, the railroad's use became unreasonable when it fully eliminated Rumsey's ability to exercise his right of access. The railroad's previous, lesser interference, that is, in the years before it built its "road-bed," would not have given rise to liability. Is the waterfront takings test more or less favorable to property owners than *Penn Central*?

6. *Free-floating rights?* The government transfers submerged lands to a railroad company that intends to fill them, cutting off the upland owner's right of pure access and converting his property from upland property to ordinary property. Can the government avoid having to compensate the upland owner for the loss of rights and value by assigning him the upland rights that would otherwise belong to the railroad company (as the new upland owner)? *See Belvedere Dev. Corp. v. Dep't of Transp.*, 476 So. 2d 649 (Fla. 1985).

7. *Waterways and highways.* Many states have statutes or common law requiring government to compensate business owners when the state closes roads for repair, rendering business premises inaccessible. In a case with the narrowly tailored title of *State of Florida v. Suit City of Aventura*, 774 So. 2d 9 (Fla. 2000), the business owner argued that upland rights cases like *Hayes* and *Lee County v. Kiesel*, 705 So. 2d 1013 (Fla. 1998), supported its claim to compensation when a newly constructed road blocked visual access to his property. The court rejected this argument, holding that while Florida's upland owners did have a right to visual access, it was a right to see the water from the upland property, not vice versa. Moreover, the court emphasized that only upland owners — and not every property owner in Florida — held this right. Why shouldn't the law treat property owners who own property adjacent to public roads the same way it treats upland owners? Don't they have reasonable, investment-backed expectations as well?

2. Wharfing Out

Wharfing out is the act of filling submerged lands, dredging a channel, or constructing a dock, pier, or marina in order to reach the navigable part of the adjacent public waterway. Unlike the upland owner's enjoyment of pure access, wharfing out has the potential to interfere with public rights including, but not limited to, navigation. And because wharfing out involves the upland owner's permanent occupation of public trust submerged lands, it begins to feel like a disposition of those lands, thus subject to the public trust doctrine. At the same time, there may be greater societal benefits associated with wharfing out than with enjoyment of pure access. While the ability to enjoy pure access increases the value of the upland property, wharfing out may provide some public benefit insofar as it facilitates commerce or greater public access through, for example, the development of boating facilities.

Prior v. Swartz

25 A. 398 (Conn. 1892)

Judge SEYMOUR delivered the opinion of the Supreme Court of Errors of Connecticut, New Haven and Fairfield Counties.

It will not be necessary to state fully the finding in this case in order to understand the points involved.

The defendant, owning land adjoining that part of Long Island Sound known as Stamford Harbor, and within the navigable waters of this state, built a wharf opposite and contiguous to his land from the upland, above high-water mark, to low water mark, and thence, below low water mark, out towards the channel of the harbor; and, for the purpose of connecting the end of his wharf with the harbor channel, he dug a channel between the two, also a channel in front of and alongside the end of his wharf.

The wharf was built and the channels were dug to enable steamers and other vessels to receive and discharge passengers and freight to and from the defendant's adjoining upland, and in order that he might use the waters of Long Island Sound opposite and contiguous to his land for the purposes of navigation.

L.R. Burleigh/Library of Congress

Figure 8-6. Stamford Harbor in 1883

The plaintiff contends that, while it is the law of this state that the owner of the adjoining upland has the exclusive right of access to the water, over and upon the soil between high and low water marks, and the exclusive privilege of wharfing and erecting piers over the same, yet in no case has it been decided, and the law is not so, that he has a right to build his wharf below low water mark.

It is stated in Swift's System, vol. 1, chapter 22, page 341, that

> all rivers that are navigable, all navigable arms of the sea, and the ocean itself on our coast, may in a certain sense be considered as common, for all the citizens have a common right to their navigation. But all adjoining proprietors on navigable rivers and the ocean have a right to the soil covered with water as far as they can occupy it, that is, to the channel, and have the exclusive privilege of wharfing and erecting piers on the front of their land. . . . Nor may adjoining proprietors erect wharves, bridges or dams across navigable rivers so as to obstruct their navigation.

This statement of the law is quoted in the opinion in *East Haven v. Hemingway*, 7 Conn. 186, 202 (1828), with the suggestion that the court does not understand by it that the adjoining proprietors are seized of the soil covered by water, but that they have a right of occupation, properly termed a franchise. The controversy between the parties regarded the title to the soil, with the wharf and store standing thereon, between high and low water mark on the east side of Dragon River, which is an arm of the sea where the tide ebbs and flows, and was navigable adjoining the premises for large vessels.

That case decided that the proprietor of land adjoining a navigable river has an exclusive right to the soil between high and low water mark, for the purpose of erecting wharves and stores thereon. We do not recall any case in this state in which the precise point made in this case was in issue.

There are, however, expressions in the opinions in several cases which indicate the general views of at least the judges writing the respective opinions. Thus in *Simons v. French*, 25 Conn. 346, 352 (1856), Judge Storrs says:

> In Connecticut it is now settled . . . that the owner of the upland adjoining such [adjacent] flats becomes entitled, by virtue of his ownership of the upland, to the

exclusive right of wharfage out over them in front of said upland to the channel of an arm of the sea adjoining such flats.

In *Mather v. Chapman*, 40 Conn. 382, 395 (1873) the court says:

It is conceded that by the settled law of Connecticut the title of a riparian proprietor terminates at ordinary high-water mark. It is also conceded that, though his title in fee thus terminates, yet he has certain privileges in the adjoining waters. Among the most important of these privileges are — (1) that of access to the deep sea; (2) the right to extend his land into the water by means of wharves, subject to the qualification that he thereby does no injury to the free navigation of the water by the public.

. . . And in *New Haven Steamboat Co. v. Sargent*, 50 Conn. 199, 207 (1882), the right of a party, owner of the upland, to extend his wharf, if he desires, to the channel of the harbor, in that case some nine hundred feet below low water mark, is expressly stated, and the words "deep water" and "channel" are used as synonymous.

Aside from these references, the reason ordinarily stated for giving to riparian proprietors the right of wharfage, to wit, to facilitate commerce and the loading and unloading of ships, together with the common sense of the matter, clearly indicates that the right should not be restricted as claimed by the plaintiff unless there are positive decisions to that effect or imperative reasons for so doing.

If, in view of the opinions already quoted, the question is to be regarded as an open one in this state, we see no good reason why it should not be decided in accordance with the convenience of riparian proprietors, and for the encouragement of commerce, so long as there is no counterbalancing injury involved to others. Except in cases where navigability begins at low water mark, the right to wharf out to low water mark only would be no privilege to adjoining proprietors nor benefit to commerce.

It is significant that the word "wharf," as ordinarily defined, implies a structure in aid of navigation and to which vessels have access. This is well stated in *Langdon v. Mayor of City of New York*, 93 N.Y. 129, 151 (1883) thus:

A wharf is a structure on the margin of navigable waters, alongside of which vessels can be brought for the sake of being conveniently loaded or unloaded. . . . Hence water of sufficient depth to float vessels is an essential part of every wharf, a necessary incident thereof or appurtenance thereto, without which there can be no wharf and no wharfage. Indeed a wharf cannot be defined or conceived except in connection with adjacent navigable water.

It seems to us therefore that a proprietor of land adjoining Stamford Harbor, and waters of a like character in this state, has a right to connect himself with navigable water by means of wharves or channels extending from and adjacent to his uplands, so long as he does nothing to interfere with the free navigation of the waters.

The defendant claimed that the legislature had passed an act, which was recited in the finding, which directly authorized the erection of the wharf in question.

The grounds over part of which the wharf was built and the channels dug, were designated for the planting and cultivation of oysters by a committee of the town of

Stamford in accordance with the statutes. The plaintiff claimed that the defendant had no right to wharf out into said grounds or to dig said channels in the same, the same being situated below low water mark and within the navigable waters of this state; that the plaintiff having acquired his title to the grounds through original designations of a competent committee appointed for that purpose, his rights therein could not be affected by adjoining land-owners, as the rights of such land-owners, in contemplation of the statute, only extended to low water mark; that the statute gave the defendant no right to build a wharf or dig a channel below low water mark and no right to build any wharf, and that even if it did it gave him such right only as subservient to the plaintiff's right to plant and cultivate oysters, and the right to build such wharf could be exercised only by obtaining the plaintiff's consent so to do.

The court ruled adversely to the claims of the plaintiff and rendered judgment for the defendant. The view we have taken of the law makes it unnecessary for us to examine the act of the legislature referred to. If, as we hold, the owner of the uplands in question had a right, as incident to such ownership, to connect the same by means of wharves or channels with the navigable water of the harbor, nothing has been done, so far as appears, to legally deprive him of that right, and the designation of the grounds for the planting and cultivation of oysters under the terms of the statute . . . are ineffectual for that purpose.

There is no error in the judgment appealed from. In this opinion the other judges concurred.

Krieter v. Chiles

595 So. 2d 111 (Fla. Dist. Ct. App. 1992)

Judge LEVY delivered the opinion of the Court of Appeal of Florida, Third District.

This case involves a dispute over the construction of a private dock on submerged land held in title by the State of Florida in its sovereignty. The parties do not dispute that title to the submerged land in question is held by the state. This submerged tidal land is held in trust, by the Trustees, for the people of the state. . . . When Florida became a state in 1845, it took title to these submerged lands to hold in trust for the use and benefit of all the people of Florida. . . .

In 1967, Pennekamp Park was expanded to include the submerged land between its 1959 offshore boundary and Key Largo. This expanded territory of Pennekamp Park, like that of the older boundaries of Pennekamp Park, has always been held in title by the state in its sovereignty. This expansion of the state-created park into what is already sovereign submerged land does not change the situation that the submerged land in question has always been held in trust by the Trustees for the people of this state.

Marie M. Krieter is a trustee of the Marie M. Krieter Trust, which was created on November 15, 1989. As trustee, Krieter owns property ["Upland Property"] on Key Largo that fronts the Atlantic Ocean. The property contains 100 feet of ocean frontage. Approximately 220 yards from the Atlantic Ocean is an access road to the property. A resident of the upland property, Robert Krieter, submitted an application, on May 19, 1988, to the Florida Department of Environmental Regulation [D.E.R.] for the construction of a private single family dock on the property. D.E.R. reviewed the application and forwarded it to the Trustees as required. . . .

In their letter dated December 18, 1990, the Trustees denied Krieter's request for consent of use. The Trustees stated that they adopted a policy, on April 12, 1990, that no future authorizations would be granted to construct any new private docks in the waters of Pennekamp Park. Marie Krieter brought suit, as trustee of the Marie M. Krieter Trust, against the Trustees and alleged a taking of private property without compensation. . . . The Trustees moved to dismiss the complaint for failure to state a cause of action[, and the trial court granted this motion].

The appellant's upland property carries with it certain riparian rights. . . . Although the riparian right of ingress and egress is an appurtenance to the ownership of private upland property . . . , it is a qualified right which must give way to the rights of the state's people. . . . As a riparian owner, the appellant argues that the expansion of Pennekamp Park, and the Trustees' subsequent denial of her request for a consent of use to build a dock, denies her the right of ingress and egress, by wharfing out, from her upland property. The appellant argues this is a taking by the state for which she is entitled to compensation. We disagree.

Among other principles, the Public Trust Doctrine dictates that there be some impairment of a citizen's right to enjoy absolute freedom before allowing a citizen the use of public submerged land. . . . The appellant made no showing in the record of necessity or that ingress or egress to her property by means of water is the only method thereof. As she alleged in her complaint, her property is bounded on one side by a public road on which she can travel to and from her property. Ingress and egress by water, therefore, is not a necessity for which the appellant may claim a right superior to that of the public.

As a riparian owner, the appellant has no title, of any nature, to the sovereign lands that are held in trust by the Trustees for the people of Florida. . . . The Trustees have the authority to preclude the construction of private docks when it is in the public interest to do so. . . . This case is not a question of an expanding state marine park that encroaches upon the rights of a riparian owner. The appellant's riparian rights were subject to the state's ownership of the sovereign submerged lands long before Pennekamp Park was expanded to the shores of Key Largo. The appellant does not have the right to wharf out for purposes of ingress and egress. Ingress and egress is available from the property by land-based routes. Only in the absence of this modern-day alternative could the appellant argue a necessity of ingress and egress. In the absence of such a necessity, the appellant's riparian rights are subject to the public's interests.

Affirmed.

Lowcountry Open Land Trust v. State of South Carolina

552 S.E.2d 778 (S.C. 2001)

Judge SHULER of the South Carolina Court of Appeals delivered the opinion of the court.

In this quiet title action, James A. Atkins appeals the master-in-equity's ruling that Lowcountry Open Land Trust, as fee simple owner of tidelands adjoining the Ashley River, can bar Atkins from "wharfing out" over its land to obtain access to the river. We affirm.

Facts/Procedural History

By deed dated June 7, 1991, the Legare family donated 448.40 acres of marshland on the west bank of the Ashley River to Lowcountry Open Land Trust (LOLT).[1]

Two months later James Atkins purchased an adjacent upland lot. Thereafter, the South Carolina Department of Health and Environmental Control (DHEC) provisionally approved a permit authorizing Atkins to build a sixty-foot dock across LOLT's property to the Ashley River.

On June 3, 1996, LOLT filed a declaratory judgment action against the State of South Carolina . . . seeking a declaration of fee simple title to the 448.40-acre tidelands tract. The court permitted Atkins to intervene, and referred the case to the Master-in-Equity for Charleston County. . . .[3]

Photo: Brian Stansberry

Figure 8-7. Marshland along the Ashley River

The master held a trial on May 10, 1999 on partly-stipulated facts, including the following:

> LOLT is record owner of a 448.40 acre tract of marshland ("the 448 acre tract") located on the Ashley River in Charleston County. . . . By stipulating that LOLT is the record owner of the 448 acre tract, the State of South Carolina does not concede that LOLT owns the tidelands.

---

1. LOLT is a non-profit, charitable corporation formed to preserve and protect coastal areas in South Carolina by obtaining title to real property and conservation easements.

3. LOLT has appealed the dock construction permit and DHEC has withheld final approval pending resolution of this action.

Purported title to the tract derives from that certain Grant of the State of South Carolina dated March 7th, 1836, pursuant to an Act of the Legislature entitled "An Act for Establishing the Mode of Granting the Lands Now Vacant in This State, and for Allowing a Commutation to be Received for Some Lands That Have Been Granted" passed the 19th day of February, 1791, said Grant being executed by George McDuffie, Governor and Commander-in-Chief in and over the State of South Carolina, to Edward C. Peronneau. . . .

***

Such private title, if any, which exists in the intertidal marshes located on the 448 acre tract extends in an unbroken chain from the grant of the State of South Carolina. . . .

On September 28, 1999, the master issued an order confirming fee simple title in LOLT and finding Atkins could not build the dock without LOLT's permission. Both the State and Atkins filed motions to alter or amend the judgment; the master denied Atkins' motion, but granted the State's in part on an issue not relevant here. This appeal followed.

Law/Analysis

***

I. Tidelands Ownership

Atkins first argues the master erred in concluding the State granted the tidelands at issue to LOLT. We find no error.

The State of South Carolina holds presumptive title to all tidelands within its borders, which are held in trust for the benefit of the public. . . . The State may, however, grant private individuals an ownership interest in tidelands. . . .

Traditionally, South Carolina has granted private rights to tidelands through acts of the Legislature. . . . Because tidelands are held in public trust, a grant of private ownership must contain "specific language, either in the deed or on the plat, showing that [the grant] was intended to go below high-water mark . . . ." *Hobonny Club, Inc. v. McEachern*, 272 S.C. 392, 396 (1979). . . .

Atkins claims the 1836 grant from the State of South Carolina to Edward C. Peronneau is ambiguous, and therefore lacks the specificity required to demonstrate an intentional transfer of title. We disagree.

A grant from the State purporting to vest title to tidelands in a private party is construed strictly in favor of the government and against the grantee. . . . Consequently, the party asserting a transfer of title bears the burden of proving its own good title. . . .

To establish fee simple ownership of the marshland tract, therefore, LOLT must show (1) its predecessors in title possessed a valid grant, and (2) the grant's language was sufficient to convey the land below the high-water mark to Peronneau. . . . Since the parties stipulated to LOLT's unbroken chain of title flowing from the

State's grant, the only question remaining is whether the grant itself adequately conveyed the tideland acreage. . . . We believe the evidence overwhelmingly supports the master's finding that it did.

The grant to Peronneau describes the property transferred as:

> Eleven Hundred and Two Acres Surveyed for him this 14th day of January 1836, Situate in Charleston District, on the West side of Ashley River, Branch Waters of Charleston Harbour. . . .

In addition, the certification of James Kingman, who surveyed the property and prepared the plat on February 10, 1836, states:

> I do hereby Certify for Edward C. Peronneau a Tract of Marsh Land containing One Thousand One Hundred and Two Acres, Surveyed for him the 14th day of January 1836 Situate in Charleston District on the West Side of Ashley River, Branch Waters of Charleston Harbour, Bounded South Easterly by Lucas and Said Edward C. Peronneau and on all other Sides by Ashley River — And hath such form and Marks as the above Plat Represents —

Finally, the plat, incorporated into the grant, clearly depicts an area delineated as "1102 acres," bounded on one side by the land of Lucas and Edward C. Peronneau and on all other sides by the Ashley River, with "Marsh" appearing twice on its face. These facts convince us the master correctly ruled the grant from the State of South Carolina intended to convey fee simple title of the tidelands to Peronneau. . . .[6]

II. Atkins' Right to Wharf over the Tidelands

Atkins further asserts that even if LOLT owns the tidelands in fee, he retains an upland owner's riparian right to "wharf out" over LOLT's property to access the navigable waters of the Ashley River.[7] We disagree.

We first note that because Atkins' property adjoins a saltwater marsh, he has no truly "riparian" rights at all. A riparian owner is one whose land is traversed

---

6. The master found LOLT was the "sole owner in fee simple" of the 448-acre tract, "subject only to the public trust as administered by the State of South Carolina." As both parties correctly note, the public trust doctrine applies to "*all* lands beneath waters influenced by the ebb and flow of the tide." *Phillips Petroleum Co. v. Miss.*, 484 U.S. 469, 479-80 (1988). They further recognize, again accurately, that the doctrine differentiates between private, proprietary title (*jus privatum*), and public trust title (*jus publicum*). However, the master's conclusion that a grant of tidelands from the State of South Carolina can convey *only* the *jus privatum* interest is erroneous. Although some states disallow conveyance of the *jus publicum*, South Carolina does not. . . .

***

However, because LOLT does not appeal the master's finding in this regard, and furthermore argues that a tidelands grant from the State of South Carolina conveys only the *jus privatum* interest in such property, we decline to address the question of whether the grant in this case conveyed solely that interest subject to the public trust. . . .

7. An "upland" owner is one holding title to land bordering a body of water. Black's Law Dictionary 1540 (6th ed. 1990). "Wharfing out" describes the "exercise of [an upland owner's] right to construct or maintain a wharf," including "a pier, a dock, or a related structure[,] to permit effective access to and from the water." Waters and Water Rights, § 6.01(a)(2) (Robert E. Beck ed., 1991).

or bounded by a natural watercourse. . . . A "watercourse" is defined as running water flowing in a definite channel having a bed or banks, and includes streams, rivers, creeks, etc. . . . Modern usage, however, occasionally expands the definition to include lakes. . . .

Owners of riparian land possess rights "relating to the water, its use, [and the] ownership of soil under the [water]. . . . " Black's Law Dictionary 1327 (6th ed. 1990). . . . Under the common law, in addition to those rights of the public at large, a riparian owner possesses a property right incident to his ownership of the bank and bed to the thread of the watercourse. . . . This right guarantees access from the front of the owner's land to the navigable part of the stream, and, when not forbidden by public law, may include the construction of landings, wharves or piers to facilitate such access. . . .

Each state, however, is authorized to delineate the extent of riparian rights appurtenant to property within its borders. . . . South Carolina follows the common law rule regarding riparian rights. . . . Accordingly, a riparian owner, subject to certain conditions, may wharf over a navigable river or stream. . . .

Separate and apart from riparian rights, interests attached to property abutting an ocean, sea or lake are termed "littoral." *See* Black's Law Dictionary 1327 (6th ed. 1990) ("[Riparian] is sometimes used as relating to the shore of the sea or other tidal water, or of a lake or other considerable body of water not having the character of a watercourse. But this is not accurate. The proper word to be employed in such connections is 'littoral.' "); 78 Am. Jur. 2d § 260 ("Strictly speaking, a riparian owner is one whose land abuts upon a river and a littoral owner is one whose land abuts upon a lake or sea."). Consequently, if Atkins possesses any rights inherent in his upland property, they would be littoral rights, not riparian.

As with riparian rights, littoral rights are governed by the individual states. *See Oregon ex rel. State Land Bd. v. Corvallis Sand & Gravel Co.*, 429 U.S. 363, 378 (1977) ("Property ownership is not governed by a general federal law, but rather by the laws of the several States. . . . This principle applies to the banks and shores of waterways . . . .") (internal citation omitted) . . . . Prior to and at the time of the American Revolution, the British crown conveyed all lands under tide waters, along with governmental dominion over them, to the colonies and later states; each grant carried with it the attendant common law rights of a littoral landowner, except as modified by federal law or the "charters, constitutions, statutes, or usages of the several colonies and states." *Shively v. Bowlby*, 152 U.S. 1, 14 (1894).

While the common law of England afforded an owner of land fronting a navigable tidal river *access* from his land to the water, this right was "not a title in the soil below high-water mark, *nor a right to build thereon*, but a right of access only, analogous to that of an abutter upon a highway." *Id.* (emphasis added). Consequently, the crown as tidelands owner was empowered to deem any structure erected without license below high-water mark a purpresture that could be destroyed or seized and rented for the crown's benefit.[8] 152 U.S. at 13. Nevertheless, in an effort to foster

---

8. A purpresture is an encroachment by private use upon public rights and easements. See Black's Law Dictionary 1236 (6th ed. 1990).

navigation and commerce in the nascent American economy, several colonial and state governments granted littoral owners greater rights and privileges than were found in English common law, including the right to build wharves. 152 U.S. at 18. . . . South Carolina, however, was not among them.

The extent of littoral rights in this jurisdiction is an unanswered question.[9] Atkins presents no authority, and we are aware of none, outlining the scope of an upland owner's incidental property rights in tidelands. Accordingly, absent any showing of a legal enactment or demonstrated customary use of neighboring tidelands by littoral owners, we will apply the common law rule. As in historical England, therefore, we find an owner whose property abuts tidal waters possesses no littoral right to wharf out to a navigable stream, and therefore must obtain permission from the underlying landowner before erecting a dock, pier or comparable structure.[10]

Where wharfing out is not a littoral right and title to marshlands rests in the state, the requisite permission to erect a dock or similar structure by one not owning the underlying land usually is obtained through a regulatory licensing procedure. . . . A public permit, however, "does not displace the need to obtain the landowner's consent to wharf on land where title is in one other than the permitting authority." WATERS AND WATER RIGHTS, *supra*, § 6.01 (a)(2). To the contrary, if ownership vests in private hands, an adjacent landowner desiring to build on tidelands must obtain the express consent of the fee simple owner. *Id.* . . .

Because we agree with the master that LOLT owns the tidelands in fee, and find that in South Carolina the owner of adjacent upland property must gain permission from the fee owner to wharf across privately-owned tidelands to a navigable body of water, the decision of the master is AFFIRMED.[12]

9. Although the extent of these rights heretofore has not been defined, our state clearly treats land bordering tidal water differently from riparian land. *See, e.g., State ex rel. McLeod v. Sloan Constr. Co.*, 284 S.C. 491, 498-99 (Ct. App. 1985) ("The State's argument simply ignores the different common law rules for construing riparian grants along tidal and nontidal waters.").

10. We further note that, even in states where the scope of littoral rights includes the prerogative to wharf out to a tidal navigable stream, the general rule is that such rights reside solely in the tidelands owner. 78 AM. JUR. 2D WATERS § 277 (1975) ("When the state has conveyed or leased tidelands bordering on tidal waters, the [littoral] rights are lodged in the tidelands' owner or lessee."); *see, e.g., Hoboken v. Penn. R. Co.*, 124 U.S. 656, 690-91 (1888) ("The State [may] grant to a stranger lands constituting the shore of a navigable river under tide-water, below the high-water mark, to be occupied . . . in such a manner as to cut off the access of the riparian owner from his land to the water . . . . ") . . . Under these authorities, LOLT, as fee simple owner of the tidelands, now holds the littoral right of access to the adjacent Ashley River.

12. . . . [A]lthough Atkins asserts, correctly, that his "riparian rights" argument is not based on the public trust doctrine, he does claim at several points in his final and reply briefs that he should be allowed to build the dock because, under the doctrine, LOLT can exclude neither the public nor him from utilizing the tidelands. This assertion, however, is erroneous.

Under the common law, the public trust doctrine secured the right of the public to navigate and fish upon otherwise private property. . . . Nevertheless, several states, including South Carolina, have expanded the doctrine to cover a broad range of water-based activities. *See Sierra Club v. Kiawah Resort Assocs.*, 318 S.C. 119, 127-28 (1995) ("Under [the public trust doctrine], everyone has the inalienable right to breathe clean air; to drink safe water; to fish and sail, and recreate upon the high seas, territorial seas and navigable waters; as well as to land on the seashores and riverbanks."). . . .

Wicks v. Howard

388 A.2d 1250 (Md. Ct. Spec. App. 1978)

Judge LOWE delivered the opinion of the Court of Appeals of Maryland.

In Maryland, by common law rule, title to all navigable waters and to the soil below the mean high-water mark of those waters is vested in the State as successor to the Lord Proprietary who had received it by grant from the Crown; "and so it

Figure 8-8. *Wicks v. Howard* Map
Location of the Wicks and Howard properties.

Regardless of the scope of the doctrine in this state, and assuming, as we must, that LOLT owns fee title to the marshland bordering Atkins' property subject to the public trust, the doctrine affords no basis to claim a right to wharf out over another's private property.... *See generally Munninghoff v. Wis. Conservation Comm'n*, 255 Wis. 252 (Wis. 1949) (holding muskrat trapping is not included in the public trust doctrine as it "involves the exercise of a property right in the land or the bottom" of the waterway; court distinguished the activity from those covered under the doctrine such as walking on the bottom while fishing, boating, standing on the bottom while bathing, and propelling a small vessel by poling along the bottom); ... *Sheftel v. Lebel*, 689 N.E.2d 500, 505 n.9 (Mass. App. Ct. 1998) ("The public's rights with respect to fishing, fowling, and navigation on and over public trust lands do not encompass the right to affix any permanent structures to the soil of the tidal flats."); *State v. Longshore*, 5 P.3d 1256, 1263 (Wash. 2000) (finding that because clamming "requires a digging down into the soil, a contact with and disturbance of the land itself," the public trust doctrine does not encompass the right to gather naturally occurring shellfish on private property).

remains, unless it be included in some grant by the State, made prior to [March 3, 1862]." [Citation omitted.] Waters are deemed navigable for these purposes if, and only if, they are subject to the ebb and flow of tides. . . . This is still the law of Maryland, to the extent that it has not been modified or abrogated by statute. . . . In the absence of specific statutory authority to the contrary, therefore, the right to extend permanent improvements into the waters in front of one's land is not an inherent or common law riparian right. The inherent common law right is to the water's use, and that, of course, presupposes the concomitant right of access.

The right to extend improvements such as wharves and piers into the water is a statutory one, granted by the State as successor to the Lord Proprietary to enhance the right of riparian access to the waters. The original grant of the right to make and hold title to improvements in the waters in front of one's land gave title of such improvements, not necessarily to the adjacent landowner by virtue of his owner-ship, but rather to the "improvers, their heirs and assigns forever," as "an encour-agement for such improvers." Ch. 9, Acts of 1745 (repealed 1860). . . .

In 1862 the General Assembly enacted Ch. 129, because of the "[d]oubts enter-tained in regard to the extent of the rights of proprietors bounding on navigable waters. . . ."

The act subsequently codified as Md. Code, Art. 54, § 46 gave the "exclusive right" to make improvements into the waters in front of riparian land bounding on navigable waters to the "proprietor" of the land, and vested title to the improve-ments in the successive owners of the land as an incident of their ownership. No vested title either to the improvement or to the use of the submerged land upon which it was erected — or might rest — accrued to the riparian owner until the improvements had actually been completed. . . .

Similar principles of right to improve and ownership were carried over in the Wetlands Act of 1970. Md. Code, Nat. Res. Art., § 9-201 states in pertinent part that the owner of land bounding on navigable water

> . . . may make improvements into the water in front of his land to preserve his access to the navigable water or protect his shore against erosion. After an improvement has been constructed, it is the property of the owner of the land to which it is attached.

There is no reason to believe that this restatement of the 1862 law carries with it any implication of such an interest vesting before an improvement is completed.

In the case at bar, the appellants prepared to assert their statutory right to erect a wharf or pier in front of their relatively recently purchased riparian property. They did not seek to construct a wharf perpendicular to their shoreline, nor even within the framework of an imaginary extension of their property lines into the water. They contend that their (statutory) right to extend improvements into the water so as to enhance their common law right of access carries with it an implied right to have the wharf extend in a straight line to the nearest point where it would meet the channel perpendicularly, notwithstanding that the wharf would not be perpendicular to their shoreline, but would create an angle nearer 45 degrees.

Appellants complain that since 1959 (16 years before appellants took title to their lot in May, 1975) appellee has "encroached" upon the waters appurtenant to their lot, derogating their recently acquired riparian right to make improvements, by virtue of a dog-leg shaped wharf jutting out from the shoreline. Although constructed entirely in front of appellee's own property (and within an imaginary extension of his boundary lines), it lay between appellants' lot and the point on the river channel toward which they sought to aim their pier. Appellants would be unable to construct their wharf in a straight line for a sufficient distance to reach the channel without ramming appellee's existing pier, because to reach the channel perpendicularly with a straight wharf from appellants' lot, it must extend at an oblique angle with the shoreline, cross the imaginary extension of the boundary between the parties' lands, and terminate at the channel directly in front of appellee's land. . . .

Claiming a right to so construct a wharf, they asked the Circuit Court for Cecil County to compel the removal of appellee's pier or grant them money damages for having encroached upon their riparian "right."

The trial judge carefully set forth the evidence, his findings of fact and some of the guiding equitable principles persuasive to him in arriving at his conclusion.

[The trial judge concluded that:

It appears to this Court that Respondent's [Appellee's] pier is in front of his lot. [The record] indicates the pier to be 50 feet from the Wicks property line extended and at no point, in its entire length, toward navigable water, does it infringe on the Wicks' riparian rights.

It is also clear, to this Court, from . . . a plat done by [Appellants'] own witness . . . that Respondent's pier is in *front* of his own lot and *does not interfere* with Complainants [Appellants] in the least. This plat also makes it obvious that Complainants have ample room to construct a dock or pier in *front* of and from their property to *navigable* water — which is shown on the plat to be 12 to 15 feet in depth.

It is naturally the conclusion of the Court under the law and facts in this case that Complainants do have a right to access to the channel. They do not have a right to the channel across the Howard property riparian rights and dock . . . . The exhibits clearly show and so does the evidence, that, if they wish, they could build a pier *in front* of their property to navigable water and from there to the channel.

This Court, sitting in equity, must also consider the financial impact on Respondent if he were required to remove his dock, which it must be recalled was built some 50 feet from the adjoining property line, now Complainants' property. It is my opinion that the apparent benefits to Complainants are so disproportionate to the injury and expense Defendant would suffer that an Equity Court would not be justified to grant an injunction under the law and facts here before the Court.

***

Only if appellants could provide law holding that they have a right to construct a wharf in a direction from their land in such a way as to maximize their convenience in striking the channel perpendicularly, could we find error in the decision as a matter of law. But there is no such authority. That the trial judge was not persuaded by some evidence of appellants that such directions had been taken by others in the geographical vicinity does not constitute error as a matter of law.

As noted, the applicable statute (which establishes the construction rights of appellants) is in fact simply a legislative attempt to guarantee each riparian owner his well established common law right of access to navigable waters by granting to him the exclusive privilege of making improvements in State-owned waters abutting his property. It need hardly be noted that geographic variables preclude complete equality of access on a formula basis. The nature of the right is such that the landowner is protected against encroachments on this right of some access; but until the right is exercised, and the improvements actually completed, he has no vested interest in any particular imagined, proposed, or even partially finished construction project. . . . There is no rigid method of apportioning the statutory riparian rights to construct improvements, the governing principle being merely that the division must be equitable, not necessarily equal. . . . While it may be true that some courts in some cases have fashioned the remedy urged upon us by appellants (which cases, we note, have been few and far between), no court has ever held that such a method should always be applied as a matter of law. We unhesitatingly decline to be the first.

. . . [W]e find sufficient evidence in the record, or inferences legitimately drawable therefrom, to have permitted the chancellor to reach the conclusions he set forth. It is his judgment from which this appeal was taken (not his opinion) and we are convinced that his judgment was correct. We are additionally convinced that the factors he considered were proper under the circumstances, and that the result reached was eminently fair. As we are in accord with all of the reasons he ascribed, in affirming his judgments, we adopt his opinion as our own. . . .

Judgment affirmed. Costs to be paid by appellants.

points for discussion

1. *Measuring the strength of the right to wharf out.* Treatises simply state that upland owners have the right to wharf out. What judicially cognizable right, though, does an upland owner actually have? Are the limits on the right to wharf out, as explained in *Prior* and *Krieter*, consistent? Clearly, states and the federal government can prevent any construction that interferes with navigation. To the extent that courts interpret the public trust doctrine as protecting public rights other than navigation, for example, traditional rights such as fishing and evolving rights such as ecosystem health, states will have broader power to prevent wharves, docks, piers, and fill. (Wharfing out by means of fill is, as discussed in the next chapter, now also limited by Section 404 of the federal Clean Water Act.) In addition to government limits, both upland neighbors (*Wicks*) and private owners of submerged lands (*Lowcountry Open Land Trust*) can limit an upland owner's right to wharf out. *Wicks* indicates, as does *Hayes*, that when upland owners' rights collide, the court will seek an equitable resolution. We discuss some of the implications of *Lowcountry Open Land Trust* in points 2 and 3.

2. *The littoral right to wharf out.* The court in *Lowcountry Open Land Trust* states that "an owner whose property abuts tidal waters possesses no littoral

right to wharf out to a navigable stream, and therefore must obtain permission from the underlying landowner before erecting a dock, pier or comparable structure." This is probably an overstatement of riparian owners' rights and an understatement of littoral owners' rights. In both cases, the upland owner must obtain the permission of the owner of the submerged lands, usually the state, before wharfing out. It is true that, in most states, the state will be more likely to object to, and have a stronger basis for objecting to, wharfing out off the beachfront than off riparian or other kinds of littoral (lakefront) property. Why do you think this is? *See* Joseph J. Kalo, *North Carolina Oceanfront Property and Public Waters and Beaches: The Rights of Littoral Owners in the Twenty-first Century*, 83 N.C. L. Rev. 1427 (2005).

3. *Wharfing out over privately owned or leased submerged lands.* Both *Prior* and *Lowcountry Open Land Trust* involve wharfing out over submerged lands in which a private party holds a property interest. In *Prior*, the court held that the lessee of submerged lands took subject to the upland owner's right to wharf out. (Can you see a parallel with *Rumsey*?) In *Lowcountry Open Land Trust*, the court held that the owner of the submerged lands, stepping into the shoes of the state, could deny the upland owner a permit to build a structure across its property. Moreover, in footnote 7, the court went further, stating that the state's transfer of a fee interest in the submerged lands converted Atkins's property from littoral property to ordinary property, thus stripping him of all littoral rights. The court did not have to rule on the issue of whether the state retained a public easement when it transferred out the marsh. Do you think the case should be resolved differently if the state had retained such an easement? *See Lowcountry Open Land Trust v. State of S.C.*, 552 S.E.2d 778 n.8 (S.C. 2001); *Hayes v. Bowman*, 91 So. 2d 795, 799 (Fla. 1957) ("[A]ny person acquiring any such lands from the State must so use the land as not to interfere with the recognized common law riparian rights of upland owners (an unobstructed view, ingress and egress over the foreshore from and to the water)."); *Cobb v. Lincoln Park Comm'rs*, 67 N.E. 5 (Ill. 1903). Given that the transfer-out of marshland eliminated all of his littoral rights (and ignoring the statute of limitations), should Atkins have filed a "pure access" takings case against the state? If he won, would the state be prevented from transferring out any submerged lands in the future? How does this idea fit with the public trust doctrine's duty not to dispose?

4. *Subdividing the right to wharf out.* Some entrepreneurial upland owners have converted their right to wharf out into condominium property, then sold off the "dockominiums" to boat owners. Given that the dock rests on a permit or license from the state, how would you advise a client interested in purchasing a "dockominium"? *See ABKA v. Wis. Dep't of Nat. Res.*, 648 N.W.2d 854 (Wis. 2002). Could an upland owner achieve the same objective by selling off one-square-foot chunks of her upland parcel? *See* S.C. Code Ann. Regs. 30-12(A)(1)(o)(i) ("To be eligible for a private or commercial dock, a lot must have . . . 75 feet of frontage at the marsh edge").

5. *Between a rock and a hard place.* If upland owners' rights are truly property rights, then state action abrogating them entirely would give rise to a

fairly strong takings claim. Say, for example, a state legislature banned all future construction of wharves, docks, etc. What result? *See Franco-Am. Charolaise, Ltd. v. Okla. Water Res. Bd.*, 855 P.2d 568 (Okla. 1990). Why is this different from the denial of a permit application in a specific case?

C. THE RIGHT TO ACCRETIONS

The physical boundary between upland property and the adjacent public waterway is continually changing. As we read in Chapter 5, these changes are wrought by a variety of natural and manmade forces, including wave action, currents, and wind. The upland owner's right to accretions is part of a set of legal rules governing ownership along the land/water interface.

1. Gradual versus Sudden Change

The common law recognized four kinds of physical change:

- *Accretion.* Accretion occurs when the waterfront edge of the upland property imperceptibly moves toward the water due to the adhesion of new material, usually sand, to the existing land.
- *Erosion.* Erosion occurs when the waterfront edge of the upland property imperceptibly moves landward due to the out-migration of existing land.
- *Reliction (or dereliction).* Reliction occurs when the waterfront edge of the upland property imperceptibly moves toward the water due to a decline in water levels.
- *Avulsion.* Avulsion refers to *perceptible* accretion, erosion, or reliction. This type of rapid change ordinarily occurs in conjunction with a single, dynamic event such as a storm or flood.

Can you see why these categories of change are somewhat arbitrary? The following article explores this and other questions arising from the legal rules associated with each type of change.

Joseph L. Sax, The Accretion/Avulsion Puzzle: Its Past Revealed, Its Future Proposed

23 Tul. Envtl. L.J. 305 (2010)

The accretion/avulsion distinction embodies one of the baffling riddles of property law. Unfortunately, it cannot be dismissed as a mere artifact of antiquarian interest. The rule has serious contemporary relevance, for it determines ownership and use of our shorelines. The law provides that when the water's edge shifts "gradually and imperceptibly" (accretion), the property boundary moves with it. But where the shift is "sudden or violent" (avulsion), the boundary stays where it was. In general, the accretion rule accords with our contemporary view that water-adjacency is a primary value of private littoral/riparian titles, and that important public rights depend on the use of overlying water and the shore near the water's edge. Consequently, it has seemed to most modern observers that when a river shrinks or expands, or the sea rises or falls, title should move accordingly. That is the consequence of applying the accretion rule, and it traces back at least to Roman law set out in the Institutes of Justinian.

Why, then, do we have an avulsion rule, which has an equally long pedigree? Why should it matter whether the water's edge shifts as the result of a storm and the sudden deposit of alluvion, rather than from gradual accretion? Should avulsion be limited to situations where a river suddenly shifts to an entirely different channel, or to transient

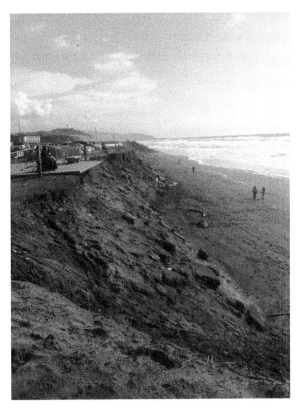

Photo: Amybekah/Wikimedia Commons

Figure 8-9. Erosion or Avulsion?
How could we tell whether the observed change to Ocean Beach in San Francisco was "gradual and imperceptibl[e]" or "sudden or violent"?

floodwaters? Notably, sudden changes are by no means always short-term, though that is the case with conventional flood overflows. Nor, as endless lawsuits have demonstrated, do notions like perceptibility or gradualness accord well with the actual behavior of water bodies. Often change is gradual, but quite perceptible; sometimes change isn't very gradual, but neither is it sudden or violent. Frequently, shorelines reconfigure themselves in myriad ways from a range of causes as variable as the wind and weather, and conform at different times to each of the different legal standards.

It remains something of a puzzle why the law did not slough off this doctrinal duality long ago and turn to developing a law of shorelands that addressed the various public and private interests that demand resolution in the dynamic areas where water and land meet. While it may be Utopian to hope for anything so fundamental, we do have many important questions to deal with, not least those that rising sea levels are beginning to generate. It is timely to look back to the historic evolution of these rules in England and America in an effort to understand something about how and why they developed as they did, with the hope that greater understanding might ultimately generate better outcomes. As we shall see, the history goes back a long way, and is more than a little obscure.

Nowadays one who wants to know about the English common law rules that shaped American law looks first to (and often not much beyond) Blackstone's Commentaries. So it may be useful to start by quoting the regularly cited passage in which he sets out the accretion/avulsion rules:

> And as to lands gained from the sea, either by alluvion, by the washing up of sand and earth, so as in time to make terra firma; or by dereliction, as when the sea shrinks back below the usual watermark; in these cases the law is held to be, that if this gain be by little and little, by small and imperceptible degrees, it shall go to the owner of the land adjoining. (o) For de minimis non curat lex: and, besides, these owners being often losers by the breaking in of the sea, or at charges to keep it out, this is possible gain is therefore a reciprocal consideration for such possible charge or loss. But if the alluvion or dereliction be sudden and considerable, in this case it belongs to the king: for, as the king is lord of the sea, and so owner of the soil while it is covered with water, it is but reasonable he should have the soil, when the water has left it dry. (p) So that the quantity of ground gained, and the time during which it is gaining, are what makes it either the king's, or the subject's property. In the same manner if a river, running between two lordships, by degrees gains upon the one, and thereby leaves the other dry; the owner who loses his ground thus imperceptibly has no remedy: but if the course of the river be changed by a sudden and violent flood, or other hasty means, and thereby a man loses his ground, he shall have what the river has left in any other place, as a recompense for this sudden loss. (q) And this law of alluvions and derelictions, with regard to rivers, is nearly the same in the imperial law; (r) from whence indeed those our determinations seem to have been drawn and adopted: but we ourselves, as islanders, have applied them to marine increases; and have given our sovereign the prerogative he enjoys, as well upon the particular reasons before-mentioned, as upon this other general ground of prerogative, which was formerly remarked, (s) that whatever hath no other owner is vested by the law in the king.

***

Blackstone's statement of the law raises a number of perplexing questions: Should the quantum of an accretive or avulsive change be determinative of the result? If not, what did he mean by speaking of "the quantity of ground gained" and of a sudden and "considerable" change? In what sense did he think accretive changes were necessarily "de minimis"? If "reciprocal considerations" justify a moving title for accretive changes, why aren't such considerations equally applicable to avulsive changes, which also go both ways, sometimes adding land and sometimes sweeping it away? Then there is the question of what is meant by the phrase "by little and little, by small and imperceptible degrees." Is that standard met if change, though not sudden as in a storm, is rapid enough that the change is obvious, measurable, and perceptible, such as the rising sea level on our coasts today? The more one thinks about these matters, and about Blackstone's famous passage, the more curious this little corner of the law becomes.

***

Essentially, the law regarding movement at the water's edge built on the general proposition that if land ownership were to change, the change must be pursuant to some lawful means for transferring property from one owner to another. Several such means existed, such as a grant from the sovereign, or a custom that legitimated long-standing uses of accreted or relicted land. At the time of the earliest known cases, in the fourteenth century, no avulsion or accretion rules had yet been developed in case law. The question then asked was simply how the claimant could have obtained title. In the earliest suits, the claim was that the littoral owner had appropriated land without the king's permission. Those cases most likely arose as attempts by Exchequer officials to raise money, rather than as specific concerns about rights at the seashore. But at least by the 1600s, it was clear that disputes concerning land at the edge of the sea (or in arms of the sea) where one of the owners at issue was the sovereign, were particularly sensitive: how had land previously owned by the king, land beneath the sea, somehow become vested in one of his subjects without his knowledge or consent?

... [A]ny such transfer would have been viewed as exceptional, and not — a priori — thought justifiable simply because it was fair to give accretions to owners who took the risk of submergence (reciprocity), or because it was deemed desirable to give such owners continued access to the water. A more convincing explanation, assuming its accuracy, would have been that the change was so insignificant that one could fairly say of it, "de minimis non curat Rex."

Some other ideas were put forward to justify a moving boundary that might have then satisfied jurists, or at least served as an acceptable legal fiction. One of them, as we shall see, is that where accretion or reliction occurred very slowly over a very long time, there was no longer evidence or knowledge of the location of the original boundary. That being the case, it could not be said with any confidence that land formerly owned by the king had been appropriated by the upland owner (I shall subsequently speak of this as the "lost boundary" rationale). This was a very important concern in the writings we shall examine, and it may help explain why early writers, including Blackstone, may have thought that both the speed of the change and its quantum could be significant. If the amount in contention was small, it might qualify as de minimis. And, even if the acreage in question was considerable, if no one could say how much — if any — had previously been the sovereign's property, and how much had been upland, there would be no proof that the sovereign had been dispossessed. Moreover, if the change occurred slowly enough, over a long enough time, it might have seemed that nothing was happening, so the king need not take notice of it. Of course, any such notions would indeed have been fictions. In fact, as we shall see, the sovereign actively litigated these cases, and the amounts of land in controversy were known, often substantial in size, and expressly described in the reports.

In any event, none of the above explanations speaks to the element that is central to modern thinking: that the original upland was granted to the water's edge, and that maintaining water-adjacency is central to the value and use of riparian/littoral property. As we shall see, that explanation is nowhere to be found in the early history of the accretion/avulsion doctrines; nor, notably, was it mentioned by Blackstone.

***

It is usual to mention first Bracton, a treatise called On the Laws and Customs of England, composed, for the most part, in the 1220s and 1230s. While the treatise, in many parts, was based on reports of actual cases in the king's court — the plea rolls — its references to accretion seem to have been derived entirely from Roman law. Bracton's statement of the rule would have been as familiar to ancient, as to present-day, writers:

> Alluvion is an imperceptible increment which is added so gradually that you cannot perceive [how much] the increase is from one moment of time to another. Indeed, though you fix your gaze on it for a whole day, the feebleness of human sight cannot distinguish such subtle increases, as may be seen in [the growth of] a gourd and other such things.

But Bracton appears not to have notably influenced the course of the English law governing shorelines, which through common law evolution developed its own rationales for the rules it adopted out of its own experience and its own perceived needs. That law was founded upon court decisions going back to the fourteenth century, beginning with three lawsuits. . . .

***

What is most revealing about [these cases], in retrospect, is that at a very early date, it had become established practice for seashore owners to treat accretions as their own, and that doing so did not apparently intrude on any other established uses or interests. The primary economic uses of such accreted lands in those days were for livestock grazing and, in marshy areas, for harvesting of reed and plover eggs. It must have seemed natural as solid land expanded simply to move one's uses down with the new land (and there was no doubt some diking and draining going on to help the alluvion along). As [Chief Justice Matthew] Hale said, the lesser (alluvion) simply became in fact — and then in law — a part of the greater (upland) tract.

In any event, the later-developed rationales for the accretion rule, such as the absence of a boundary dispute, and de minimis impact, seem to have been consistent with the experience of seashore communities in the fourteenth century. And even the notion of reciprocity seems to have been something the abbots' attorneys had in mind, inasmuch as their pleas spoke explicitly of the flux and ebb of the sea, implying that their clients were sometimes losers of land as well as gainers.

***

The first commentaries . . . on the issues raised by moving water boundaries are the lectures of Robert Callis delivered at Gray's Inn in August, 1622, and generally known as Callis on Sewers. Some forty-five years later, Hale is believed to have produced his much better-known treatise, De Jure Maris, though it was not then published. Callis is the more interesting writer. While Hale's work is presented as essentially descriptive of the law, Callis tries to work out inconsistencies among the precedents in an effort to come up with a coherent theory to use in a pending case where he was counsel.

Callis begins with an undisputed principle: that the sea, and the land beneath it, is the king's "in property, possession, and profit." That being the case, he says, it must be "that the ground which was the King's when it was covered with waters, is his also when the waters have left it." Thus, when the sea recedes or is pushed back by the accumulation of alluvion at the water's edge, it would seem that the area of the former sea bottom would continue to belong to the king. But, Callis says, things are not quite so simple.

First, in some places "frontagers [littoral owners] have claimed those grounds so left, by a pretended custom of frontagers." And, he says, there are good reasons for such customs, because such owners are subject to inundation when the water rises and are obliged to pay to hold back the water in some instances, "so if lands were left by the sea affront them [that is, if the sea recedes] that these land might accrue to them as a reciprocal consideration for their charge and loss." The problem, Callis says, is that there are also cases that go the other way.

***

Callis's conclusion appears to be that it is not the pace of change in itself that is critical (whether it is slow or sudden), but that when the pace of change is very gradual, the adjacent owner effectively takes over the newly exposed land unperceived and uses it as his own, so that it becomes . . . parcel of the manor; or, as is said in other writings, a perquisite to the littoral estate.

The gradualness of the process also diminishes the sense of loss by the loser. As Callis puts it, speaking of the Eyre of Nottingham case, "And so of petty and unperceivable increasements from the sea the King gains no property, for de minimis non curat Rex." While obviously not every gradual accretive or relictive change ultimately involves acreage or values that are de minimis, Callis seems to have concluded that when the process is slow enough, the diminution is so small as it happens, and occurs over so long a period, that it makes the loss of little consequence to the loser. . . .

***

It is virtually certain that when Blackstone picked up as standards pace and size, saying that "sudden and considerable" changes do not bring about changes of title, he was drawing on the just-described analysis of Callis; just as he picked up from Callis the reciprocity and de minimis notions as justifying the practice of giving gradual accretions to the upland owner.

Callis thus provided the rudiments of a theory for the law of moving shorelines. The first point is that change of location of the water's edge does not in and of itself change the ownership of the underlying soil (and emphatically so where title to the soil is in the sovereign). One must show a legally acceptable justification for a change of title. Under the precedents, that justification was the existence of a custom allowing the upland owner to acquire title to land at the water's edge that gradually added to his land and seamlessly came to function as part of his land.

The justification for such customs was that the littoral owner had long used and treated the added land as his own, a prescription-like notion. The gradualness of the change was simply evidentiary of such a claim of right by long use, not a reason in and of itself to divest the sovereign (or an adjacent riparian) of title. In the same way, the notions of reciprocity and de minimis were evidence of the justness of the customary practices, not legal defenses to the sovereign's claim in and of themselves.

By contrast, Callis points out, where the ocean recedes substantially, the title to the exposed soil remains in the sovereign; the legal reason is that there has been no opportunity to establish a pattern of private use. . . . As a policy matter, the use/prescription theory assured that large tracts of strategic land at the nation's frontier would not be lost to the sovereign. As Hale pointed out, the behavior of the shore, especially on the Channel side — where substantial declines in ocean elevations were observed and loss of strategically important shoreline was a real concern — made the distinction Callis drew of more than academic interest. By contrast, accretive-type changes, like those in the Abbot of Ramsey's case or where littoral owners acquire use rights in the land between high and low water, were necessarily less consequential in their potential impact on sovereign interests. Indeed, title shifts in cases of long-standing use seem more to confirm the status quo ante than to change it.

Callis then raises a more troublesome question: What about a rising sea that inundates what was formerly privately owned upland? It was apparently agreed by all that in such cases the king would have jurisdiction of the land newly submerged, and that public uses such as navigation would be available on such water. But what if the waters later receded? As to this he says:

> But put the case the sea overflow a field where divers men's grounds lie promiscuously, there continueth so long, that the same is accounted parcel of the sea, and then after many years the sea goes back and leaves the same, but the grounds are defaced, as the bounds thereof be clean extinct and grown out of knowledge. . . .

In such a case, he says, "it may be the King shall have those grounds." But the reason, it seems, is only because the original boundary has been lost, for he then says, rather wistfully, "I find that Nilus every year so overflows the grounds adjoining, that their bounds are defaced thereby; yet they are able to set them out by the art of Geometry." In a later edition of his book, in 1685, having found a precedent for his intuition, Callis says, "But if the bounds can be known in such a case, if the sea hath overflowed a man's land for forty years, and then goes back he shall have his land again, and not the King." The modern version of this doctrine is known as reemergence.

Callis's discussion is consistent with a general understanding that titles did not change simply because of natural events, as long as the original boundaries were identifiable. His lectures may be the first overt appearance of the lost boundary theory as the basis for justifying a permanent transfer of title. Apparently, at least in this situation, it was not thought that the sovereign obtained title by prescription. Once the area was no longer needed for public navigation, and as long as the original boundary was still known, the land could be returned to its former owner.

Notably, nothing in Callis suggests that adjacency to the water is the key to such cases and, as we shall see, none of the old cases or old writers justified results on that ground.

***

[In the nineteenth century], English jurisprudence came to the point where it maintained the legal distinction between accretion and avulsion, while the rationales that had historically justified different treatment of different situations faded away or were rejected. The result was that cases became disputes over what the term "imperceptible" means, and battlegrounds in which a variety of witnesses testified as to how they "perceived" the changing situation on the ground. Why, as a matter of fairness, public policy, economics, etc., one result rather than another should prevail, faded into the mists.

***

As one turns to the modern era and to the American cases, several features stand out. First, superficial appearances suggest that the old rules developed in England (and in the Roman law) are simply being taken up and applied to contemporary cases. The cases faithfully cite the standard rationales, such as reciprocity and de minimis; quote familiar passages from Lord Hale, Bracton, Blackstone, and Lord Yarborough's case; and duly cite the Institutes of Justinian and Gaius. But closer examination reveals two striking departures: the definition of what constitutes accretion, as contrasted with avulsion, has dramatically expanded; and a new justification for applying the accretion rule, maintaining water access for littoral/riparian owners, has become central.

***

As it happened, some of the leading nineteenth-century United States Supreme Court cases arose on the Mississippi and Missouri Rivers, both noted for their tumultuous behavior. In one case [*Nebraska v. Iowa*, 143 U.S. 359 (1892)], where the plaintiff claimed the benefit of the accretion rule to claim title to land added to his riparian tract, it was

> contended by the defendant that this well-settled rule is not applicable to land which borders on the Missouri river . . . the course of the river being tortuous, the current rapid, and the soil a soft, sandy loam, . . . the effect being that the river cuts away its banks, sometimes in a large body, and makes for itself a new course, while the earth thus removed is almost simultaneously deposited elsewhere, and new land is formed almost as rapidly as the former bank was carried away.

This sounds like the very definition of avulsion. Yet the Court says:

> But it has been held by this court that the general law of accretion is applicable to land on the Mississippi river; and, that being so, although the changes on the Missouri river are greater and more rapid than on the Mississippi, the difference does not constitute such a difference in principle as to render inapplicable to the Missouri river the general rule of law [applicable to accretions].

The Court here tightens the noose on avulsions beyond the strictures imposed in Lord Yarborough's case. Not only is imperceptibility shown by the inability to know at any given moment that change is happening (as that case ruled), but so long as it cannot be known at every moment what change is happening, the accretion test of imperceptibility will be met. In another Missouri River case, *Jefferis v. East Omaha Land Co.*, [134 U.S. 178 (1890)], the Court said:

> How much, if any of [the added soil], was formed between the date of the original survey, in 1851, and the time of the entry in . . . 1853, cannot be told; nor how much was formed between 1853 and 1856 . . . and so in regard to . . . each successive owner. There can be, in the nature of things, no determinate record, as to time, of the steps of the changes. . . . The very fact of the great changes in result, caused by imperceptible accretion, in the case of the Missouri river, makes even more imperative the application to that river of the law of accretion.

This is a most striking change. The test of imperceptibility in Lord Yarborough's case was the pace at which change was occurring (it must be very slow, even though, after some months or years, one could tell that change had taken place). Under the above standard, the pace of change — mostly rapid and sudden on the wild Missouri — was irrelevant. The question was whether one could identify (perceive) the exact amount of change that had occurred from each time period to the next, something that could presumably be done only if continuous monitoring of every site was occurring. This was a dramatic shift indeed from the older view of what constituted avulsive change. Apparently, only a single sudden event (like a hurricane, or a river breaking through an oxbow) would now qualify as an avulsion.

Though it used traditional terminology and citations in these cases, the Supreme Court set a standard significantly expanding the definition of accretion, and it made clear why it had done so, though not conceding that it had done so. While citing traditional justifications, such as reciprocity, it showed itself to be attentive to the problem of water accessibility for riparian and littoral owners, speaking of natural justice to those who own land "bounded" by the water, and "following title to the shore itself," notwithstanding the behavioral characteristics of the water body in question.

Because the accretion rule generally accords with contemporary intuitions about the right result for dealing with migrating shorelines, the approach of the Jefferis case has been followed quite consistently. . . .

***

However it came to pass, one benefit of the contemporary strong presumption in favor of accretion is that courts are often spared having to contend with the actual behavioral facts of river movements, which follow no simple duality like accretion vs. avulsion, but show instead every variety of movement along a continuum from extremely gradual and imperceptible to extremely sudden and violent. Nonetheless, one still finds cases where judges solemnly consider testimony and pore over factual evidence about river behavior in order to resolve the traditional doctrinal question: Was it accretion or was it avulsion?

***

Probably the reason our modern concern with riparian/littoral access to water was not a consideration in earlier times is that in those days, such land was used primarily as forage, rather than for boating or for access related to modern recreational use of the shore. Of course, there was a great deal of litigation and writing about littoral owners' use entitlements in the inter-tidal area (for example, a right to wreck washed up on the shore, or a right of fishing on the shore), but such entitlements did not generally rest on claims of title to the land.

By contrast, water access appears as a central concern even in early American cases. In one lawsuit, for example, counsel made an argument of the sort one never sees in the older English cases, though he invoked the old authorities as precedent:

> If the river is the boundary, the alluvion, as fast as it forms, becomes the property of the owner of the adjacent land to which it is attached. On a great public highway like the Mississippi, supporting an immense commerce and bearing it to every part of the globe, purchasers must have obtained lands for the beneficial use of the river as well as for the land. [*County of St. Clair v. Lovingston*, 90 U.S. 46, 56 (1874).]

While courts did not question the avulsion rule, by applying the accretion rule very generously, they effectively assured water access for littoral owners. The rationales given in the cases, however, range rather widely. One leading case gave a dual policy rationale for the accretion rules, reciprocity and water-adjacency, adding the civil law notion that land should not be left unowned. Another, after citing reciprocity as a principle of justice, also invoked the analogy of alluvion to the Roman idea of an owner's right to the fruit of his tree or the increase of his flock as a natural, not just a civil, right. One can also find cases invoking the lost-boundary rationale. But despite the various legal grounds cited, maintenance of water access has been the primary concern of American courts. A Minnesota case from 1893 [*Lamprey v. Metcalf*, 53 N.W. 1139 (Minn. 1893)] put it most plainly:

> Courts and text writers sometimes give very inadequate reasons, born of a fancy or conceit, for very wise and beneficent principles of the common law; and we cannot help thinking this is somewhat so as to the right of a riparian owner to accretions and relictions in front of his land. The reasons usually given for the rule are either that it falls within the maxim, de minimis lex non curat, or that, because the riparian owner is liable to lose soil by the action or encroachment of the water, he should also have the benefit of any land gained by the same action. But it seems to us that the rule rests upon a much broader principle, and has a much more important purpose in view, viz. to preserve the fundamental riparian right — on which all others depend, and which often constitutes the principal value of the land — of access to the water. The incalculable mischiefs that would follow if a riparian owner is liable to be cut off from access to the water, and another owner sandwiched in between him and it, whenever the water line had been changed by accretions or relictions, are self-evident, and have been frequently animadverted on by the courts.

***

points for discussion

1. *Presumptions and the burden of proof.* Given that there is likely to be significant uncertainty as to the cause of shoreline change, presumptions and the burden of proof likely will be outcome-determinative. In *Shulz v. Dania*, 156 So. 2d 520, 521 (Fla. 1963), the court quoted 93 C.J.S. Waters, § 83:

   "One claiming that the change in a bed or stream was by avulsion rather than accretion has the burden of showing the avulsion, by showing a sudden change, or by a preponderance of the evidence by showing that the changes were violent and subject to being perceived while they were going on." Therefore, the law seems clear as to these principles of law: in the event of erosion or submergence, the title to the land covered by water reverts to the State; erosion is presumed over avulsion; and the burden of proof is upon the party alleging avulsion.

2. *The opposite of reliction . . .* is not "dereliction," which is a synonym (as well as a variant on the name of a clothing line created in the classic movie, *Zoolander*). Perhaps "sea level rise," which has become widely used in recent years, is the most appropriate terminology. One would assume that the common law would treat gradual sea level rise (whether caused by increasing seas or subsiding land) as similar to erosion. Is there a reason one might treat it differently, particularly if scientists could document the exact amount of rise? The implications of climate change for coastal law are considered in Chapter 10.

3. *The upland owner's right to protect her property.* Should an upland owner have a legal right to combat erosion and avulsion by installing structures, for example, seawalls, or depositing sand in the adjacent submerged lands or on her own property? It would obviously be easier for a state to justify a ban on activities seaward of the legal coastline. Even if walls are built on the upland property, though, they can have significant effects on both neighbors and public trust areas: The only point of building them, after all, is in anticipation that erosion will eventually reach the structure. As we will see in Chapter 9, some states stringently regulate shoreline hard structures by statute.

   In the meantime, it is worth pointing out that an upland owner's right to protect his property from erosion is limited by the effect those efforts have on other upland owners. In early common law, the courts analogized threats from the storms and waves to the threat posed by other kinds of flooding, and held that, under the "common enemy doctrine," an upland owner could take any steps necessary to protect his property from damage. That is, he could act without regard for impacts on other upland owners. Modern cases, though, have modified the rule. Today, most courts will apply a nuisance-like rule: An upland owner can take steps to protect his property, for example, build a seawall, unless that action unreasonably interferes with another landowner's right to use and enjoy her property. *See, e.g., Lummis v. Lilly*, 429 N.E.2d 1146 (Mass. 1982); *Grundy v. Thurston Cty.*, 117 P.3d 1089 (Wash. 2005).

2. Natural versus Artificial Forces

The upland owner, Anne, is facing severe erosion problems. In order to combat these problems, she builds a rock jetty into the sea at the down-current end of her property. The project works as intended, trapping sand from the current and, more than halting erosion, results in accreted land. Should this land belong to the upland owner or to the state? What if the jetty is built — without Anne's complicity or knowledge — by her down-current neighbor, Bart? Should accretions to Anne's land resulting from Bart's jetty belong to Anne or to the state?

Brundage v. Knox

117 N.E. 123 (Ill. 1917)

Chief Justice CARTER delivered the opinion of the Supreme Court of Illinois.

The original information herein was filed in the circuit court of Cook County July 29, 1912, by the Attorney General, on behalf of the State, and the second amended information on February 2, 1916. Both the original and amended informations charged appellees with the erection of piers and other unlawful structures upon the submerged lands constituting a part of the bed of Lake Michigan and with the appropriation of a part of said submerged lands to private uses. All the defendants named in said informations filed answers which practically admitted the existence of piers and other artificial structures but all claiming title to said land by the process of natural accretions to the original shore line. Appellee Knox filed a cross-bill seeking affirmative relief. Thereafter a hearing was had before the judge in said circuit court and a decree was entered November 15, 1916, finding that the land in dispute had been formed by natural accretions caused by artificial structures, none of which were erected by appellees, and finding title to all of this artificially made land in Knox and the other appellees claiming under him; that the State of Illinois has no title to any part of said lands, and that Knox and the other persons claiming under him are, respectively, the riparian owners and entitled to all the riparian rights appertaining to their respective premises. From that decree an appeal was taken to this court.

* * *

The decree found the facts thus far stated, and, among other things, substantially as follows: That the State of Illinois upon its admission into the Union, in 1818, became vested with the title to that portion of the land underlying and forming the bed of Lake Michigan that is within the boundaries of said State, in trust for the people; that . . . at an early date the owners of lands along the shore of Lake Michigan, both north and south of the

Courtesy Northwestern University Library Archives

Figure 8-10. *Brundage v. Knox*
Mr. Knox was in the business of selling lake front lots.

premises in question, began the construction of pier structures, extending from a secure point back on their land out into the waters of the lake, for the purpose of protecting their said premises from the action of the waters of the lake; that Knox . . . purchased, in 1890, that part of the said northwest fractional quarter of section 20 that lies south of the north line of Lee street, in Evanston, extended to the waters of Lake Michigan. . . .

∗∗∗

The decree further finds that . . . the piers heretofore referred to, constructed north of the property in question, and the Main street pier on the southern limits of the property in question, formed a cove in front of said property and caused the sand of the lake to accumulate on the beach; that sand was carried into this cove by the currents of water before mentioned, these currents being doubtless caused, in part, by northeast winds; that the main cause of said accretions in front of the property in question has been the Main street pier; that a pier constructed on the west shore of the lake, extending into the water at substantially a right angle to the shore for a distance of approximately 75 feet or more from the shore, causes accretions to the shore on the north side of the pier; that the gentle slope of the lake bottom from the shore at this point, and the sand bars lying not far east of the shore, and the piers north and south of the property in question, have all contributed to the accretions which have formed on this property; that the pier constructed by Knox in 1890 was constructed for the purpose of protecting the property in question, and had no appreciable effect in causing accumulations to form on the shore because it did not extend far enough into the water.

. . . The decree further found that neither of the appellees is directly or indirectly responsible for the erection and maintenance of the piers north or south of the property in question, and the accretions which have taken place could not be attributed to anything that appellees have done; that the action of the water in making these accretions doubtless was caused to some extent, as shown by the evidence, by the artificial structures erected north and south of the property here in question. We think the weight of the evidence tends to support the findings of the decree as to the facts stated therein. . . .

∗∗∗

Counsel for the State argue that the evidence introduced by appellees tends to show that practically all of the accretions on this land, from the time of the original survey, in 1839, to the present time, were caused by artificial structures along the lake, and they contend, also, that the decree of the court is wrong in holding that these accretions were due to natural causes; that even though none of these accretions were the direct result of appellee Knox's own work or efforts, or those of his grantors or grantees, "yet the decree is wrong in holding that these accretions, which were caused by artificial structures by parties other than appellees on other property than that which is here in dispute, are not natural accretions but artificial, and in legal effect are no different, so far as affecting the title to its property, than if such accretions had been caused by artificial structures erected by appellee Knox or his grantors." This we deem the turning point in this case. . . .

It is undoubtedly the general rule that additions to land fronting on bodies of water, caused by artificial means by the owner of the adjoining shore land, do not come under the laws as to the ownership of accretions formed by purely natural causes. In *Bliss v. Ward*, 198 Ill. 104, 114 (1902), this court said "that a shore owner has no right to increase the boundary of his premises by building out into the lake for that purpose, and that the only rights which he has are the common law rights of access from the lake to his land and the right to natural accretions". . . . But the definitions for "accretion" do not always give as one of the essential elements that such deposit of land must be due to natural causes. . . .

***

The right to accretions or alluvion is a vested one. "Whether it is the effect of natural or artificial causes makes no difference. The result as to the ownership in either case is the same. . . . It is an inherent and essential attribute of the original property. The title to the increment rests in the law of nature. It is the same with that of the owner of a tree to its fruits and of the owner of flocks and herds to their natural increase." *Lovingston v. St. Clair County*, 90 U.S. 46, 69 (1874). This right is not mainly based, as argued by counsel for appellant, upon the right to the title to the submerged lands, but largely, if not chiefly, upon the right of access to the water, otherwise the owners of lands along Lake Michigan might, by losing their frontage by accretions, be debarred of valuable rights for which there would be no adequate redress. We think, therefore, by reason and by the great weight of authority, it must be held that the owner of land bordering on Lake Michigan has title to land formed adjacent to his property by accretions, even though the formation of such accretions is brought about, in part, by artificial conditions created by third parties. . . .

***

The decree of the circuit court will be affirmed.

State of California ex rel. State Lands Commission v. Superior Court of Sacramento County

900 P.2d 648 (Cal. 1995)

Justice ARABIAN delivered the opinion of the Supreme Court of California.

Beginning in 1848, and accelerating rapidly in 1849, gold lured fortune seekers to California. Hordes of prospectors panning or using other primitive methods quickly snatched up the wealth lying on the surface and in riverbeds. Soon, more advanced and environmentally intrusive techniques were utilized to reach the more inaccessible treasure hiding within the California hills. The era of hydraulic mining began. Miners washed the land away with water, extracting gold in the process.

Before being halted over 100 years ago, hydraulic mining caused enormous quantities of silt and other debris to be deposited into water systems, including the Sacramento River and its tributaries. This silt and debris then flowed downstream. Some came to rest along river banks far from the locale of the mining, changing forever the landscape of California. These events, and possibly human activities such as river dredging and the construction of wing dams and levees, contributed over many years to the imperceptible accumu-

Henry Sandham/Library of Congress

Figure 8-11. Hydraulic Mining
Hydraulic mining during the California gold rush.

lation, or "accretion," of 12 acres of dry land that used to be riverbed in a spot in Sacramento called Chicory Bend. The Sacramento River there is navigable and, even that far inland, is affected by the tides, making its shores tidelands. The river and tidelands belong to the state, as did the 12 acres when they were riverbed. The adjacent land, at least that not including the 12 acres, belongs to private parties. The question we address is who owns the 12 acres now.

. . . The general California rule is easy to state. If the accretion was *natural*, the private landowners own it; if it was *artificial*, the state owns it. But the specific application is far from easy. Is the accretion natural any time it is caused by the flow of the river, as the majority below found? Or is it artificial if caused by the hydraulic mining and by other human activities nearer the accreted land, as the state contends?

We conclude, as did the concurring justice of the Court of Appeal, that to adopt the test of the majority would effectively abandon California's longstanding "artificial accretion" rule. Instead, we reaffirm that rule. As between the state and private upland owners, land along tidelands and navigable rivers that accretes by artificial means, such as local dredging and construction of wing dams and levees, remains in state ownership, and does not go to the upland owner. We also conclude, however, that we should narrowly construe what is artificial under the California rule. Accretion is artificial if directly caused by human activities in the immediate vicinity of the accreted land. But accretion is not artificial merely because human activities far away and, in the case of hydraulic mining, long ago contributed to it.

We thus disagree with much of the analysis of the majority below. However, we agree with its result, which is to deny a petition for writ of mandate. Accordingly, we affirm the judgment of the Court of Appeal while rejecting the basis upon which it reached that judgment.

∗∗∗

The state filed the instant original writ proceeding in the Court of Appeal seeking to have the order granting summary adjudication vacated. . . . The state argued that the challenged order "is contrary to well-established controlling case authority which recognizes that deposition of materials washed into the water by human activities but deposited by the natural flow of the water constitute artificial accretion belonging to the state." The private landowners defended the trial court order, arguing that accretion is artificial only if "some man-made structure impedes the flow of water causing accumulation of sediment."

***

The majority of the Court of Appeal . . . found that in most jurisdictions, accreted land belongs to the upland owner whether or not the accretion is artificial, and concluded that California has deviated from this general rule "through a misapplication of judicial precedent." It argued that the decision commonly considered to be the genesis of the California rule, *Dana v. Jackson Street Wharf Co.*, 31 Cal. 118 (1866), has been misapplied ever since without critical analysis. "It is," the majority stated, "as if the post-*Dana* decisions have artificially accreted themselves on this point."

Based upon its historical review, and "principles of fairness and practical application . . . , recognizing that little in the California landscape or its significant waterways remains in a completely natural state," the majority concluded that "a fair, workable and legally supportable rule of accretion, for both [Civil Code] section 1014 and the tideland context, is that of a gradual and imperceptible accumulation of material that results from the action of the water, even if artificially influenced." Accordingly, it held that "to the extent that the land at Chicory Bend was once tideland but has now been covered by a gradual and imperceptible accumulation of material that has resulted from the action of the waters, even if artificially influenced, that land remains in private ownership — subject to new tideland at the water boundary of the accreted land (at the ordinary high-water mark) that is owned by the state in trust for the public." It therefore denied the state's petition for writ of mandate.

> **Quick Question**
>
> Is this one of the better judicial jokes you've ever heard, or one that doesn't bear repeating?

In a concurring and dissenting opinion, Justice Scotland agreed with the result — denying the mandate petition — but disagreed with the majority's analysis. He believed that "[w]hile the statutory construction adopted by the majority is logical, fair and arguably preferable, it does not wash because the majority's effort to avoid California Supreme Court precedent is unconvincing." He urged the rule "that alluvion belongs to the riparian owner except when accretion results from the placement in public waters of a structure or other artificial obstruction which alters the natural flow of the water and causes the gradual and imperceptible accumulation of land proximate to the obstruction. Under California's narrow artificial-accretion exception, it is the artificial nature of the ultimate cause of the accretion, not the artificial nature of the source of the resulting alluvion, which determines whether the alluvion inures to the benefit of the state or the riparian owner. Accordingly, although enormous quantities of debris were deposited artificially into the Sacramento River system after having been dislodged by hydraulic mining, any alluvion resulting from the gradual and imperceptible accumulation of mining debris transported to, and lodged at, Chicory Bend by the flow of the water was formed by 'natural causes' within the meaning of section 1014 assuming the accumulation was not caused by artificial structures placed in the water at Chicory Bend."

Justice Scotland thus agreed with the trial court's ruling, which "simply provides that, assuming any gradual and imperceptible accumulation of land at Chicory Bend consists of hydraulic mining debris carried by river water to that location, and not caused by any artificial obstruction in the water at or near Chicory Bend, it is accretion from 'natural causes' which inures to the benefit of the riparian owner."

We granted the state's petition for review.

***

B. The Merits

1. Background[1]

Under this doctrine, the "state holds [tidelands] in trust for the people for their use for commerce, navigation, fishing and other purposes. . . . " *State of California v. Superior Court (Lyon)*, 29 Cal. 3d 210, 214 (1981). Moreover, "the same incidents of the trust applicable to tidelands also apply to nontidal navigable waters and that the public's interest is not confined to the water, but extends also to the bed of the water." *Id.* at p. 231.

What this means here is that the state owns the land under the Sacramento River and adjacent tidelands to the ordinary line of high tide in trust for the public; the upland private landowners own the landward side of the ordinary line of high tide. The 12 acres in dispute used to be under the river, and thus originally

---

1. The following definitions apply. "Accretion" is the gradual and imperceptible accumulation of land due to the action of a boundary river, stream, lake, pond or tidal waters. "Alluvion" (also called "alluvium") is the material that is accreted and becomes the land. Although the two terms have sometimes been used interchangeably, "accretion" properly refers to the process, and "alluvion" to the substance. Accretion is distinguished from "reliction," the exposing of land by the gradual receding of the water, and "avulsion," a sudden and perceptible change in the location of a body of water. [Citations omitted.] "Tideland" is land between the lines of ordinary high and low tides, covered and uncovered by the ordinary ebb and flow of the tide. . . .

Because the legal principles of the case might involve either riparian property — that bordering a river — or littoral property — that bordering an ocean, sea or lake — we generally use the broader term "upland" to refer to both types of property or the owner of such property.

The river at Chicory Bend is both navigable and affected by the tides, making its shores tidelands. The following principles generally apply. The state owns all tidelands below the ordinary high-water mark. . . . The state also owns all land below the water of a navigable lake or stream. . . . Owners of upland bordering on tidewater take to the ordinary high-water mark. Owners of upland bordering on nontidal navigable water take to the low-water mark. Other upland owners take to the middle of the lake or stream. . . .

Both tidelands and the beds of navigable rivers are owned by the state in trust for the public. . . .

were owned by the state. They are now dry land. Did ownership shift to the upland owners?

The parties agree that the property was created by accretion rather than avulsion, that is, that it formed gradually and imperceptibly over time. . . .

The general rule that accretion belongs to the upland owner is venerable. . . .

***

In the common law, . . . it did not matter whether the accretion was natural or artificial (unless, possibly, the claimant caused the accretion). "It is insisted . . . that the accretion was caused wholly by obstructions placed in the river above, and that hence the rules upon the subject of alluvion do not apply. If the fact be so, the consequence does not follow. . . . The proximate cause was the deposits made by the water. The law looks no further. Whether the flow of the water was natural or affected by artificial means is immaterial." *County of St. Clair v. Lovingston*, 90 U.S. 46, 66 (1874). . . .

In California, the law regarding artificial accretion developed quite differently.

2. California's Artificial Accretion Rule

The state argues that in California, unlike most jurisdictions, it *does* matter whether accretion is natural or artificial, and that as to tidelands and navigable bodies of water, accretion that is not "from natural causes" but instead is artificial remains in the possession of the state. . . . The private landowners urge the position . . . adopted by the majority of [the Court of Appeal]. Resolving this question requires a historical review of the California rule.

In *Dana v. Jackson Street Wharf Co., supra,* . . . the landowner owned a waterfront lot in San Francisco. He built a wharf adjacent to the property that caused the disputed land to be "entirely reclaimed from the water," and to become "a permanent accretion by artificial and natural causes" to the lot. *Id.* at p. 120. We held that the common law rule that land gained by accretion belongs to the upland owner did not apply because the case was one of "purpresture, or encroachment, by the erection of a wharf in a public harbor, and not a case of marine increase by alluvion. . . ." *Ibid.* . . .

***

[The Court of Appeal found] that accretion caused by nonnatural structures belong[ed] to the upland owner, as long as the land was deposited gradually and imperceptibly through the action of the water. . . . It argued that *Dana*, properly analyzed, was not an artificial accretion case but a "purpresture (encroachment) case involving a waterfront landowner whose water boundary remained permanently fixed by statute," and that later cases misapplied it. . . . In effect, the majority held that the earlier decisions were incorrect, and that the artificial accretion rule should be abandoned in favor of a different but "fair, workable and legally supportable rule of accretion. . . ."

We disagree. California's artificial accretion rule was premised on, and is consistent with, the public trust doctrine and the inalienability of trust lands. Our cases

. . . have allowed *natural* accretion to go to private parties. The state has no control over nature; allowing private parties to gain by natural accretion does no harm to the public trust doctrine. But to allow accretion caused by artificial means to deprive the state of trust lands would effectively alienate what may not be alienated. . . . This, we believe, was the driving force behind the California doctrine, and the reason it remains vital today. We thus reaffirm the continuing validity of California's artificial accretion rule.

***

3. Whether California May Apply Its Rule

***

The landowners . . . argue that to allow the state to keep artificially accreted land would constitute a taking for which compensation must be provided. They rely on language [from U.S. Supreme Court decisions that] suggested, without deciding, that a judicial decision depriving a private party of property in favor of the state might constitute a taking without compensation in violation of due process. Whatever one may think of this question in the abstract (we express no view), it has no relevance here. As Justice Stewart himself stated, applying "established property rules with regard to the effects of avulsion, accretion, erosion, and reliction in resolving conflicting claims to the exposed riverbed" would "not involve a retroactive alteration of state law such as would constitute an unconstitutional taking of private property." *Bonelli Cattle Co. v. Arizona*, 414 U.S. 313, 337, fn. 2 (1973) (dis. opn. of Stewart, J.). . . . Applying California's long-standing artificial accretion rule would not constitute a taking of private property requiring compensation. . . .

We thus hold that California's artificial accretion rule may, and does, apply to this case.

4. The Scope of the Artificial Accretion Rule

It remains to define the scope of California's artificial accretion rule. In the trial court, the state cited four artificial influences it claims caused the 12 acres to accrete: hydraulic mining, wing dams, levees and dredging. The rule clearly applies to wing dams, levees and dredging in the immediate vicinity of the disputed property; the majority of the Court of Appeal erred in concluding otherwise. If these factors caused the accretion (which is yet to be determined in the superior court), it is artificial, and ownership would remain in the state. The cases discussed above admit of no other interpretation. Does the rule also apply to hydraulic mining, i.e., is accretion caused by those mining activities over a century ago artificial? This is itself an important question, for hydraulic mining had such widespread environmental effects that probably little along the Sacramento River and other rivers was unaffected by it.

Justice Scotland presented a brief historical overview. During a colorful time in California history, hydraulic gold mining altered both the wealth of miners and the character of California's waterways. Large quantities of water funneled with great pressure through monitors dislodged millions of cubic yards of earth in California's gold mining region. Along with the dislodged clay, sand, gravel and stone, mixed with particles of gold, the water was channeled through flumes, sluices and other conduits where the gold was extracted. The water and debris then were discharged into reservoirs and streams. Massive portions of the tailings were washed into Northern California rivers, including the Feather, American, and Sacramento rivers. By 1884, the bed of the American River had been raised 10 to 12 feet, and the bed of the Sacramento River had risen 6 to 12 feet. Due to the shallowing of these rivers, there was frequent flooding and thousands of acres of farmland were covered by mining debris. The flow of water also carried the debris through the Suisun Bay and into the San Pablo and San Francisco Bays. The adverse effect hydraulic mining had on state waterways was so great that the operations of certain mining companies were declared to be a public nuisance and were enjoined permanently. In 1893, Congress enacted legislation which prohibited hydraulic mining from harming state river systems and created the California Debris Commission. The commission was empowered to regulate hydraulic mining and prevent the discharge of mining debris into California waterways, and to commence the process of restoring the navigability of rivers and protecting their banks. . . .

The majority below, the concurring justice, and the superior court, all found that hydraulic mining does not make otherwise natural accretion artificial. We agree. California's artificial accretion exception to the general common law rule does not extend to human activities far from the site of the accretion.

Because the issue is before us on summary adjudication, the Attorney General argues first that we should not resolve it without a more developed factual record, but rather should remand the matter for a "trial on the merits." On this record, we cannot gauge the exact effect hydraulic mining had on the property at Chicory Bend. The parties agree it had some effect, but disagree how much. This is obviously a complex factual question. If it is legally relevant, evidence would have to be taken. But if it is not legally relevant, a needless trial should be avoided. We can decide that question now.

On the merits, we believe that, although theoretically alluvion placed in the river by hydraulic mining which eventually collects downstream might be viewed as artificial, the connection between the mining and the accretion at Chicory Bend is too attenuated to render the accretion artificial under California's rule. [The California rule is] that accretion goes to the upland owner. The exception must not swallow the rule. In one sense, much, if not everything, along the Sacramento River and other rivers is artificial. As the superior court stated, "very little remains natural in the strictest sense as to most California rivers. Dams regulate the flow and alter the extent to which banks are eroded, for example. But to consider the entire system an artificial one would be inappropriate." Over the years, numerous human activities have indirectly as well as directly caused a change in water flow and the accumulation of sediment in virtually every river and tideland in the state. To view all of this as artificial accretion would effectively eviscerate the general rule.

Moreover, as Justice Scotland noted, there would be difficult evidentiary problems if the upland owner had " 'to trace the accretions back to their source given the period of time which has elapsed since hydraulic mining took place. . . . [S]uch a burden would be monumental, if not impossible.' " Although potentially difficult problems of proof exist even as to local human activities, that has been the situation for a substantial part of the history of this state, and such problems undoubtedly are less onerous than trying to determine the effects of 19th century hydraulic mining or other human activities far from the site of the accretion. If the artificial activity or structure is in the immediate vicinity of the accreted area, the likelihood will be greater that it is the direct, proximate cause of the accretion, rather than an indirect cause, with natural elements constituting the direct cause. Problems of proof as to the direct cause of the accretion will be minimized if the artificial accretion rule is limited to human activities in the immediate vicinity of the accreted area.

Nothing in our cases requires the broad interpretation of the rule that the state urges. With one possible exception, all of the artificial accretion cases involved local conditions — generally structures built by humans in the immediate vicinity of the accretion, but also local dredging and dumping — not activities far away like mining operations (or, as hypothesized by the majority below, dams such as the Shasta Dam). There is no need to extend the rule beyond its historical bounds, and good reason not to. We thus will interpret the scope of the rule as narrowly as our cases permit.

***

Justice Scotland took the view that "it is the artificial nature of the ultimate cause of the accretion, not the artificial nature of the source of the resulting alluvion, which determines whether the alluvion inures to the benefit of the state or the riparian owner." The Attorney General challenges this, citing language in some of the cases suggesting that the *source* of the alluvion can also make it artificial. . . . We need not confront this, for we perceive the rule to be slightly different. The dichotomy is not between the source of the alluvion and the forces that caused it to accrete. For example, as indicated in the cases the Attorney General cites, local dumping as well as human structures or dredging might cause artificial accretion. (Dumping might also cause avulsion, but that need not be the determining point.) Rather, the cases have involved *local* human activity that directly caused the accretion. That is the critical distinction. Only if the artificial activity was near enough to the accretion to have directly caused it can the accretion be deemed artificial.

We thus hold, consistent with our prior cases, that accretion is artificial if directly caused by human activities, such as the dredging, wing dams or levees cited in this case, that occurred in the immediate vicinity of the accreted land. Accretion is not artificial merely because human activities far away contributed to it. The dividing line between what is and is not in the immediate vicinity will have to be decided on a case-by-case basis, keeping in mind that the artificial activity must have been the *direct* cause of the accretion before it can be deemed artificial. The larger the structure or the scope of human activity such as dredging or dumping, the farther away it can be and still be a direct cause of the accretion, although it must always be in the general location of the accreted property to come within the artificial accretion rule.

It is undisputed that Chicory Bend is many miles from the hydraulic mining areas. Therefore, the superior court properly granted summary adjudication on this issue. Because the summary adjudication applied only to hydraulic mining, and not to the other alleged causes of the accretion — which remain to be litigated — the Court of Appeal correctly denied the state's petition for writ of mandate.

***

points for discussion

1. *The four possible natural and artificial accretion rules.* Just like Calabresi and Melamed, we can come up with four different rules that courts might adopt to resolve disputes between neighboring landowners. *See* Guido Calabresi & A. Douglas Melamed, *Property Rules, Liability Rules and Inalienability: One View of the Cathedral*, 85 HARV. L. REV. 1089 (1972). First, the landowner is entitled to all accretion, regardless of whether it is artificial or natural and regardless of whether he did something to cause it. Second, the landowner is entitled to all accretion, unless he did something to cause it. Third, the landowner is entitled only to natural accretion. Fourth, the landowner is entitled to no accretion. Which of these rules seems the fairest? The most efficient?

2. *The California rule.* The above list can be expanded by playing with the definition of "artificial." A court could adopt the definition used by the lower court in *State of California ex rel. States Lands Commission*, that is, focus on the cause of the accretion rather than the source of the accreted material. Or, as the Supreme Court of California did, a court could focus on the proximity of the cause or source. Which definition makes more sense? Which seems more practical and predictable?

3. *Unwelcome accretion.* Ordinarily, upland owners welcome accretion. Who wouldn't? After all, it enlarges the amount of land that one owns, helps to serve as a buffer against storms and gradual erosion, creates more privacy by increasing the distance between the public wet sand and existing structures, and arrives free of charge. In *Los Angeles Athletic Club v. City of Santa Monica*, 63 Cal. App. 2d 795 (1944), the plaintiff was a littoral owner until the defendant's breakwaters caused sand to accrete along plaintiff's beach. Under California's artificial accretion rule, this accreted land belonged to the State of California. As its property no longer touched the water, plaintiff lost all of its littoral rights, including the right to future natural accretion. Which leads us to . . .

D. BRINGING IT ALL BACK HOME: *STOP THE BEACH RENOURISHMENT*

In late 2009, the U.S. Supreme Court heard oral arguments in a case that raised the issue of whether or not a court decision could result in a "judicial taking" of upland owners' rights. The Supreme Court's opinion, together with the preceding decision of the Florida Supreme Court, provides an excellent capstone to our discussion of upland owners' rights, tying together issues related to access, accretion, and the balance between private and public interests in public trust submerged lands. We begin with the decision of the Florida Supreme Court, which addressed an alleged regulatory taking.

1. A Regulatory Taking?

Walton County v. Stop the Beach Renourishment, Inc.

998 So. 2d 1102 (Fla. 2008)

Justice BELL delivered the opinion of the Florida Supreme Court.

We have for review the First District Court of Appeal's decision in *Save Our Beaches, Inc. v. Florida Department of Environmental Protection*, 27 So. 3d 48 (2006). . . . [The question before us is:]

> On its face, does the Beach and Shore Preservation Act unconstitutionally deprive upland owners of littoral rights without just compensation?

We answer [this question] in the negative and quash the decision of the First District. As explained below, we find that, on its face, the Beach and Shore Preservation Act does not unconstitutionally deprive upland owners of littoral rights without just compensation. At the outset, however, we emphasize that our decision in this case is strictly limited to the context of restoring critically eroded beaches under the Beach and Shore Preservation Act.

I. The Context

A. Factual and Procedural History

As the First District explained in its opinion,

> [t]he Gulf of Mexico beaches of the City of Destin and Walton County were [damaged] by Hurricane Opal in 1995. The . . . problem was identified by the Department [of Environmental Protection (Department)], which placed these beaches on its list of critically-eroded beaches. Destin and Walton County then initiated a lengthy process of beach restoration through renourishment. The process, which included extensive studies and construction design and pre-application conferences with Department staff, culminated in the filing of an Application for a Joint Coastal Permit and Authorization to Use Sovereign Submerged Lands on July 30, 2003.

The application proposed to dredge sand from an ebb shoal borrow area south of East Pass in eastern Okaloosa County, using either a cutter head dredge (which disturbs the sand on the bottom of the borrow area and vacuums it into a pipeline which delivers it to the project area) or a hopper dredge (which fills itself and is moved to the project

> **Quick Question**
>
> Why do you think beachfront owners would be opposed to state-funded beach renourishment that might protect their property from erosion or future storms? Do you think they value their littoral rights more highly than the net present value of the enhanced protection?

site). On the project site, heavy equipment moves the dredged sand as specified in the design plans. The project is executed in this manner and progresses along the beach, usually at a pace of about 300 to 500 feet a day. . . .

To determine the mean high water line (MHWL) for the restoration area, a coastline survey was completed in September 2003. The Board of Directors for the Internal Improvement Trust Fund (Board) subsequently established an erosion control line (ECL) at the surveyed MHWL. Pursuant to section 161.191(1) of the Beach and Shore Preservation Act, this ECL became the boundary between publicly owned land and privately owned upland after it was recorded. Then, on July 15, 2004, the Department issued a Notice of Intent to Issue the permit.

Stop the Beach Renourishment (STBR)[5] timely filed two petitions for formal administrative hearings, the first challenging the issuance of the permit and the second raising constitutional issues. A formal administrative hearing was held on STBR's permit challenge while its constitutional challenge was deferred for determination in court proceedings. . . .

On June 30, 2005, following the administrative hearing, the administrative law judge recommended that the Department enter a final order issuing the permit. The Department entered its final order on July 27, 2005, determining that the permit was properly issued pursuant to existing statutes and rules.

Photo: Andrea Booher/FEMA

Figure 8-12. Beach Renourishment
The process of beach renourishment.

---

5. STBR is a not-for-profit association that consists of six owners of beachfront property in the area of the proposed project. At the administrative and district level, Save Our Beaches, Inc. was a co-party. The administrative law judge and the First District determined that Save Our Beaches lacked standing to maintain its claims as its approximately 150 members were not necessarily owners of beachfront property in the affected area. . . . Save Our Beaches is no longer a party to the litigation.

Before the First District, STBR challenged the Department's final order, claiming in essence that the final order is unconstitutional because it was issued pursuant to an unconstitutional statute. Specifically, STBR asserted that section 161.191(1) of the Beach and Shore Preservation Act, which fixes the shoreline boundary after

> **Make the Connection**
>
> Section 161.201 purports to preserve the upland owners' rights so that they will still be entitled to enjoy them after they've lost their status as littoral owners. Can the state do this? Go back and have a look at point 5 after *Hayes v. Bowman*.

the ECL is recorded, unconstitutionally divests upland owners of all common law littoral rights by severing these rights from the uplands. According to STBR, after the recording of the ECL and by operation of section 161.191(1), the State becomes owner of the land to which common law littoral rights attach because it owns all lands seaward of the ECL. STBR further argued that the littoral rights, which are expressly preserved by section 161.201 of the Act, are an inadequate substitute for the upland owners' common law littoral rights that are eliminated by section 161.191.

The First District agreed the Act divests upland owners of their littoral right to receive accretions and relictions because section 161.191(2) provides that the common law rule of accretion and reliction no longer operates once the ECL is recorded. . . . The First District also agreed that the Act eliminates the right to maintain direct contact with the water since section 161.191(1) establishes the ECL as the shoreline boundary. . . . Furthermore, the First District found that:

> Although section 161.201 has language describing a preservation of common law riparian rights, it does not actually operate to preserve the rights at issue . . . [because] Florida's law is clear that riparian rights cannot be severed from riparian uplands absent an agreement with the riparian owner, not even by the power of eminent domain. . . .

Thus, the First District held that the final order issued pursuant to the Act results in an unconstitutional taking of the littoral rights to accretion and to contact with water without an eminent domain proceeding as required by section 161.141, Florida Statutes.

***

B. The Beach and Shore Preservation Act

Before addressing the rephrased certified question, it is helpful to provide the relevant portions of the Beach and Shore Preservation Act.

Recognizing the importance and volatility of Florida's beaches, the Legislature in 1961 enacted the Beach and Shore Preservation Act. . . . Determining that "beach erosion is a serious menace to the economy and general welfare of the people of [Florida] and has advanced to emergency proportions," the Legislature declared it "a necessary governmental responsibility to properly manage and protect Florida beaches . . . from erosion," and to provide funding for beach nourishment projects. . . . The Legislature then delegated to the Department the authority to determine "those beaches which are critically eroded and in need of restoration and nourishment"[7] and to "authorize appropriations to pay up to 75 percent of the actual costs for restoring and renourishing a critically eroded beach." [Citation omitted.]

Pursuant to section 161.141, when a local government applies for funding for beach restoration, a survey of the shoreline is conducted to determine the MHWL for the area. Once established, any additions to the upland property landward of the MHWL that result from the restoration project remain the property of the upland owner subject to all governmental regulations, including a public easement for traditional uses of the beach. . . .

After the MHWL is established, section 161.161(3) provides that the Board must determine the area to be protected by the project and locate an ECL. In locating the ECL, the Board is "guided by the existing line of mean high water, bearing in mind the requirements of proper engineering in the beach restoration project, the extent to which erosion or avulsion has occurred, and the need to protect existing ownership of as much upland as is reasonably possible." [Citation omitted.]

Pursuant to section 161.191(1), this ECL becomes the new fixed property boundary between public lands and upland property after the ECL is recorded. And, under section 161.191(2), once the ECL has been established, the common law no longer operates "to increase or decrease the proportions of any upland property lying landward of such line, either by accretion or erosion or by any other natural or artificial process."

However, section 161.201 expressly preserves the upland owners' littoral rights, including, but not limited to, rights of ingress, egress, view, boating, bathing, and fishing, and prevents the State from erecting structures on the beach seaward of the ECL except as required to prevent erosion. Section 161.141 further declares that the State has no intention "to extend its claims to lands not already held by it or to deprive any upland or submerged land owner of the legitimate and constitutional use and enjoyment of his or her property."

Moreover, section 161.141 explains that "[i]f an authorized beach restoration, beach nourishment, and erosion control project cannot reasonably be accomplished without the taking of private property, the taking must be made by the requesting authority by eminent domain proceedings." And, in the event the beach restoration is not commenced within a two-year period, is halted in excess of a

---

7. The Florida Administrative Code defines "critically eroded shoreline" as

> a segment of shoreline where natural processes or human activities have caused, or contributed to, erosion and recession of the beach and dune system to such a degree that upland development, recreational interests, wildlife habitat or important cultural resources are threatened or lost. Critically eroded shoreline may also include adjacent segments or gaps between identified critical erosion areas which, although they may be stable or slightly erosional now, their inclusion is necessary for continuity of management of the coastal system or for the design integrity of adjacent beach management projects. Fla. Admin. Code R. 62B-36.002(4).

six-month period, or the authorities do not maintain the restored beach, section 161.211 dictates that the ECL is cancelled.

II. Discussion

As stated earlier, the First District determined that section 161.191 of the Beach and Shore Preservation Act facially results in an unconstitutional taking of upland owners' littoral rights to receive accretions and to maintain direct contact with the water despite the express preservation of littoral rights in section 161.201. The determination of a statute's constitutionality and the interpretation of a constitutional provision are both questions of law reviewed *de novo* by this Court. . . . "While we review decisions striking state statutes *de novo*, we are obligated to accord legislative acts a presumption of constitutionality and to construe challenged legislation to effect a constitutional outcome whenever possible." *Fla. Dep't of Revenue v. Howard*, 916 So. 2d 640, 642 (Fla. 2005). Moreover, "a determination that a statute is facially unconstitutional means that no set of circumstances exists under which the statute would be valid." *Fla. Dep't of Revenue v. City of Gainesville*, 918 So. 2d 250, 256 (Fla. 2005).

After reviewing Florida's common law as well as the Beach and Shore Preservation Act's effect upon that common law, we find that the Act, on its face, does not unconstitutionally deprive upland owners of littoral rights without just compensation. In explaining our conclusion, we first describe the relationship at common law between the public and upland owners in regard to Florida's beaches. We then detail the Beach and Shore Preservation Act's impact upon this relationship. In particular, we explore how the Act effectuates the State's constitutional duty to protect Florida's beaches in a way that facially balances public and private interests. Finally, we address the First District's decision.

A. The Relationship at Common Law Between the Public and Upland Owners

Since the vast development of Florida's beaches, there has been a relative paucity of opinions from this Court that describe the nature of the relationship at common law between the public and upland owners in regard to Florida's beaches. It is important that we outline this relationship prior to resolving the specific issues in this case.

(1) The Public and Florida's Beaches

Under both the Florida Constitution and the common law, the State holds the lands seaward of the MHWL, including the beaches between the mean high and low water lines, in trust for the public for the purposes of bathing, fishing, and navigation. . . .

***

In addition to its duties under the public trust doctrine, the State has an obligation to conserve and protect Florida's beaches as important natural resources. As article II, section 7(a) of the Florida Constitution states,

[i]t shall be the policy of the state to conserve and protect its natural resources and scenic beauty. Adequate provision shall be made by law for the abatement of air and water pollution and of excessive and unnecessary noise and for the conservation and protection of natural resources.

Concisely put, the State has a constitutional duty to protect Florida's beaches, part of which it holds "in trust for all the people." Art. X, § 11, Fla. Const. [You can find this provision on pp. 562 of the casebook, in point 4.]

Having explained the State's interests and duties on behalf of the public in relation to Florida's beaches, we now describe the upland owners' interests and rights.

(2) The Upland Owners and Florida's Beaches

Private upland owners hold the bathing, fishing, and navigation rights described above in common with the public. . . . In fact, upland owners have no rights in navigable waters and sovereignty lands that are superior to other members of the public in regard to bathing, fishing, and navigation. . . . However, upland owners hold several special or exclusive common law littoral rights: (1) the right to have access to the water; (2) the right to reasonably use the water; (3) the right to accretion and reliction; and (4) the right to the unobstructed view of the water. . . . These special littoral rights "are such as are necessary for the use and enjoyment" of the upland property, but "these rights may not be so exercised as to injure others in their lawful rights." *Ferry Pass Inspectors' & Shippers' Ass'n v. White's River Inspectors' & Shippers' Ass'n*, 48 So. 643, 645 (Fla. 1909).

Though subject to regulation, these littoral rights are private property rights that cannot be taken from upland owners without just compensation. . . . Indeed, in *Thiesen v. Gulf, Florida & Alabama Railway Co.*, 78 So. 491, 506-07 (Fla. 1918), this Court considered and *rejected* the notion that littoral rights are subordinate to public rights and, as a result, could be eliminated without compensation. And, over the years, Florida courts have found unconstitutional takings when certain littoral rights were materially and substantially impaired. *See Lee County v. Kiesel*, 705 So. 2d 1013 (Fla. 1998) (holding that upland owners were entitled to compensation because bridge substantially and materially obstructed their littoral right to view); *Game & Fresh Water Fish Comm'n v. Lake Islands, Ltd.*, 407 So. 2d 189 (Fla. 1981) (holding that boating regulation was unconstitutional as to littoral owner because it substantially denied the right of access); *see also Webb v. Giddens*, 82 So. 2d 743 (Fla. 1955) (finding that culvert substantially impaired littoral owner's right of access); *cf. Duval Eng'g & Contracting Co. v. Sales*, 77 So. 2d 431 (Fla. 1954) (holding that upland owners had no right to compensation when there was only a slight impairment of littoral rights and owners did not show a material disturbance of the littoral rights to access and view).

While Florida case law has clearly defined littoral rights as constitutionally protected private property rights, the exact nature of these rights rarely has been described in detail. . . . Early on, this Court described the nature of littoral rights as follows:

These special rights are *easements* incident to the [littoral] holdings and are property rights that may be regulated by law, but may not be taken without just compensation and due process of law. The common-law [littoral] rights that arise by implication of law *give no title to the land under navigable waters except such as may be lawfully acquired by accretion, reliction*, and other similar rights. [Citations omitted.]

Based upon this early description, the littoral rights to access, use, and view are easements under Florida common law. Generally speaking, "[a]n easement creates a nonpossessory right to enter and use land in the possession of another and obligates the possessor not to interfere with the uses authorized by the easement." RESTATEMENT (THIRD) OF PROPERTY § 1.2(1) (2000). More specifically, the littoral rights to access and use are affirmative easements as they grant "rights to enter and use land in possession of another." *Id.* at § 1.2 cmt. a. In contrast, the littoral right to view is a negative easement as it "restrict[s] the uses that can be made of property." *Id.*

Furthermore, based upon this Court's early description of the nature of littoral rights, it is evident that the littoral right to accretion and reliction is distinct from the rights to access, use, and view. The rights to access, use, and view are rights relating to the present use of the foreshore and water. The same is not true of the right to accretion and reliction. The right to accretion and reliction is a contingent, future interest that only becomes a possessory interest if and when land is added to the upland by accretion or reliction.

At this point, we have described the upland owners' littoral rights and the State's duties in regard to Florida's beaches. We next explain how the common law attempts to bring order and certainty to the physical location where these often competing interests intersect.

(3) Dealing with a Dynamic Boundary

The boundary between public or sovereignty lands and private uplands is a dynamic boundary, which is located on a shoreline that, by its very nature, frequently changes. Florida's common law attempts to bring order and certainty to this dynamic boundary in a manner that reasonably balances the affected parties' interests.

> **Worth Noting**
>
> Notice how the court strengthens its argument by borrowing from another area of property law (future interests) to characterize the right to accretions. The use of such analogies can be an effective tool of persuasion.

***

The boundary between public lands and private uplands is the MHWL, which represents an average over a nineteen-year period. . . . This nineteen-year period for determining the MHWL is codified in [Florida law].

Under Florida common law, the legal effect of changes to the shoreline on the boundary between public lands and uplands varies depending upon whether the shoreline changes gradually and imperceptibly or whether it changes suddenly and perceptibly.

***

... [U]nder the doctrines of erosion, reliction, and accretion, the boundary between public and private land is altered to reflect gradual and imperceptible losses or additions to the shoreline.... In contrast, under the doctrine of avulsion, the boundary between public and private land remains the MHWL as it existed before the avulsive event led to sudden and perceptible losses or additions to the shoreline....

These common law doctrines reflect an attempt to balance the interests of the parties affected by inevitable changes in the shoreline.

***

While our common law has developed these specific rules that are intended to balance the interests in our ever-changing shoreline, Florida's common law has never fully addressed how public-sponsored beach restoration affects the interests of the public and the interests of the upland owners. We now turn to the legislative attempt to deal with this subject.

B. The Beach and Shore Preservation Act's Balancing of Public and Private Interests

As explained earlier, the State has a constitutional duty to protect Florida's beaches, part of which it holds in trust for public use. The Beach and Shore Preservation Act effectuates this constitutional duty when the State is faced with critically eroded, storm-damaged beaches.

Like the common law, the Act seeks a careful balance between the interests of the public and the interests of the private upland owners. By authorizing the addition of sand to sovereignty lands, the Act prevents further loss of public beaches, protects existing structures, and repairs prior damage. In doing so, the Act promotes the public's economic, ecological, recreational, and aesthetic interests in the shoreline. On the other hand, the Act benefits private upland owners by restoring beach already lost and by protecting their property from future storm damage and erosion. Moreover, the Act expressly preserves the upland owners' rights to access, use, and view, including the rights of ingress and egress.... The Act also protects the upland owners' rights to boating, bathing, and fishing.... Furthermore, the Act protects the upland owners' view by prohibiting the State from erecting structures on the new beach except those necessary to prevent erosion.... Thus, although the Act provides that the State may retain title to the newly created dry land directly adjacent to the water, upland owners may continue to access, use, and view the beach and water as they did prior to beach restoration. As a result, at least facially, there is no material or substantial impairment of these littoral rights under the Act....

Finally, the Act provides for the cancellation of the ECL if (1) the beach restoration is not commenced within two years; (2) restoration is halted in excess of a six-month period; or (3) the authorities do not maintain the restored beach.... Therefore, in the event the beach restoration is not completed and maintained, the rights of the respective parties revert to the status quo ante.

To summarize, the Act effectuates the State's constitutional duty to protect Florida's beaches in a way that reasonably balances public and private interests.

Without the beach renourishment provided for under the Act, the public would lose vital economic and natural resources. As for the upland owners, the beach renourishment protects their property from future storm damage and erosion while preserving their littoral rights to access, use, and view. Consequently, just as with the common law, the Act facially achieves a reasonable balance of interests and rights to uniquely valuable and volatile property interests.

Having explained how the Act effectuates the State's constitutional duty to protect Florida's beaches in a way that, at least facially, balances the interests and rights involved, we turn directly to the First District's decision.

C. The First District's Decision

As stated earlier, the First District determined that the Beach and Shore Preservation Act results in an unconstitutional taking of upland owners' rights to accretions and to contact with the water. . . . We disagree.

We find facially constitutional the provisions of the Act that fix the shoreline boundary and that suspend the operation of the common law rule of accretion but preserve the littoral rights of access, view, and use after an ECL is recorded. Therefore, we hold that the Act, on its face, does not unconstitutionally deprive upland owners of littoral rights without just compensation.

In explaining our disagreement with the First District, we first discuss how the First District failed to consider the doctrine of avulsion. The doctrine of avulsion is pivotal because, under that doctrine, the public has the right to reclaim its land lost by an avulsive event. We then address why, in the context of this Act, the littoral right to accretion is not an issue. Thereafter, we explain that there is no independent littoral right of contact with the water under Florida common law. . . .

(1) Doctrine of Avulsion

In its opinion, the First District stated that beach restoration under the Act "will cause the high-water mark to move seaward and ordinarily this would result in the upland landowners gaining property by accretion". . . . This statement fails to consider the doctrine of avulsion, most likely because the parties did not raise the issue before the First District. As a result, the First District never considered whether the Act is facially constitutional given the doctrine of avulsion.

Under Florida common law, hurricanes, such as Hurricane Opal in 1995, are generally considered avulsive events that cause avulsion. . . . As explained previously, avulsion is "the sudden or perceptible loss of or addition to the land by the action of the water or a sudden change in the bed of a lake or the course of a stream". . . .

Contrary to the First District's statement about accretion, under the doctrine of avulsion, the boundary between public lands and privately owned uplands remains the MHWL as it existed before the avulsive event. In *Bryant v. Peppe*, 238 So. 2d 836 (Fla. 1970), this Court expressly applied the doctrine of avulsion and held that title to a narrow strip of land that was submerged until a 1926 hurricane brought it to the surface remained in the State, not the adjoining landowners. 238 So. 2d at 838.

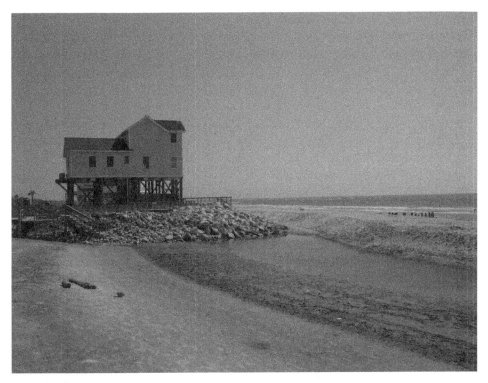

Photo: Emily Nellermoe

Figure 8-13. Explaining the Florida Supreme Court's Logic
Because this is a facial challenge, the court must identify one scenario in which
the statute does not effect a taking of property (littoral rights). The scenario the
court identifies is the post-avulsion scenario. The court finds that, pursuant to the
doctrine of avulsion, and specifically, the right of reclamation, the state is entitled to
"restore its shoreline" after an avulsion event. Once the state restores its wet-sand
beach (seaward of the MHWL), and once it fills in the now-submerged private land
(landward of the MHWL), everything will be just as it was before the avulsion —
the owner's rights have not been affected by the project. Why? Because the ECL
(property boundary) is, at least for a moment in time, located at the exact same spot
as the MHWL was before the avulsion. This means that the upland owner's land, for
that moment, touches the water, thus providing direct access. In order to wrap up
the case, the court still has to make the right of accretion a contingent right, that is,
not property. Do you see why? If you are wondering, the photo is of a renourishment
project on Folly Beach, South Carolina. Federally funded renourishment projects
require the beachfront owners to give the public a dry sand easement. The owner
of the property in the picture refused to grant the easement, so the renourishment
ended on the seaward side of the MHTL. You can see the pile of sand on the right.
This is not a good idea, if your goal is to have the renourishment project last for
a reasonable period of time — five to eight years is average on the Atlantic Coast.
Because of the numerous holdouts (and places for the ocean to breach), the Folly
Beach project pictured lasted less than a year.

This Court first determined that the hurricane was an avulsive event. *Id.* Then, we reasoned that the parcel in question "was originally sovereignty land; and it did not lose that character merely because, by avulsion, it became dry land." *Id.* Therefore, we found that "the plaintiff-respondents were charged with notice that the sudden avulsion of the parcel in controversy gave them no more title to it than they had to the water bottom before its emergence as dry land." *Id.* at 839.

Significantly, when an avulsive event leads to the loss of land, the doctrine of avulsion recognizes the affected property owner's right to reclaim the lost land within a reasonable time. . . . In *State v. Florida National Properties, Inc.*, 338 So. 2d 13 (Fla. 1976), this Court specifically explained that affected property owners can return their property to its pre-hurricane status. In *Florida National Properties*, littoral "owners had exercised self-help by dynamiting obstacles from a drainage canal to return [Lake Istokpoga] to an ordinary level . . . following the historic 1926 hurricane." *Id.* at 16. This Court stated that the "self-help by the [littoral] owners did not affect [sic] a lowering of the water level below the normal high-water mark; instead, as the survey notes show, the action merely returned the water to its normal level and did not expose any lake bottom." *Id.* at 18. In that circumstance, the Court determined that the littoral owners retained title to the present MHWL, which represented the pre-hurricane MHWL, and to the land they had reclaimed through lawful drainage of the lake. *Id.*

To summarize, when the shoreline is impacted by an avulsive event, the boundary between public lands and private uplands remains the pre-avulsive event MHWL. Consequently, if the shoreline is lost due to an avulsive event, the public has the right to restore its shoreline up to that MHWL.

In light of this common law doctrine of avulsion, the provisions of the Beach and Shore Preservation Act at issue are facially constitutional. In the context of restoring storm-ravaged public lands, the State would not be doing anything under the Act that it would not be entitled to accomplish under Florida's common law. Like the common law doctrine of avulsion, the Act authorizes the State to reclaim its storm-damaged shoreline by adding sand to submerged sovereignty lands. . . . And similar to the common law, the Act authorizes setting the ECL and the boundary between sovereignty lands and private uplands at "the existing line of mean high water, bearing in mind . . . the extent to which . . . avulsion has occurred." [Citation omitted.] In other words, when restoring storm-ravaged shoreline, the boundary under the Act should remain the pre-avulsive event boundary.[15] Thus, because the

---

15. It is not clear from the record whether or not the ECL recorded in this case represents the pre-hurricane MHWL. If it represents the pre-hurricane MHWL, there would be no difference between the boundary under the common law and the boundary under the Act. In contrast, if the ECL does not represent the pre-hurricane MHWL, the resulting boundary between sovereignty and private property might result in the State laying claim to a portion of land that, under the common law, would typically remain with the private owner. However, because STBR alleges what is essentially a facial challenge, it is unnecessary for this Court to address this as-applied issue. Indeed, it is possible that STBR is without standing to raise this as-applied issue since its resolution might depend upon the assessment of particular facts and defenses inuring to each parcel and each individual owner. . . .

Act authorizes actions to reclaim public beaches that are also authorized under the common law after an avulsive event, the Act is facially constitutional.

(2) Common Law Right to Accretion

Additionally, we disagree with the First District's determination that section 161.191(2) results in a facial and unconstitutional taking of the littoral right of accretion. We do not find the littoral right to accretion applicable in the context of this Act.

As we explained earlier, the right to accretion under Florida common law is a contingent right. It is a right that arises from a rule of convenience intended to balance public and private interests by automatically allocating small amounts of gradually accreted lands to the upland owner without resort to legal proceedings and without disturbing the upland owner's rights to access to and use of the water. . . .

[There are four reasons for the doctrine of accretion:]

> (1) *[D]e minimis non curat lex;* (2) he who sustains the burden of losses and of repairs imposed by the contiguity of waters ought to receive whatever benefits they may bring by accretion; (3) it is in the interest of the community that all land have an owner and, for convenience, the riparian is the chosen one; (4) the necessity for preserving the riparian right of access to the water. . . .

None of these doctrinal reasons apply here. First, the beach restoration provisions of the Act do not apply to situations involving *de minimis* additions or losses of land. . . . More specifically, critically eroded shorelines can hardly be characterized as trifles with which the law does not concern itself. . . . Similarly, the beach renourishment itself is a change to the shoreline that is more than *de minimis.* Second, by authorizing the creation of a buffer area of beach on sovereignty land, the Act removes the upland owner's concomitant risk of losses and repairs due to erosion. After renourishment, the risk of loss and repair lies more with the State than with the upland owner. Third, all land has an owner under the Act because the property line between private and public land is clearly and conveniently fixed at the ECL. . . . Fourth, the upland owner's littoral right of access is preserved under the Act. . . . Consequently, the common law rule of accretion, which is intended to balance private and public interests, is not implicated in the context of this Act.

Having explained our disagreement with the First District regarding the right to accretion, we now discuss the First District's analysis of the supposed independent right of contact with the water.

(3) Contact Is Ancillary to the Littoral Right of Access

The First District concluded that, under section 161.191(1), upland owners "lose the right to have the property's contact with the water remain intact". . . . However, under Florida common law, there is no independent right of contact with the water. Instead, contact is ancillary to the littoral right of access to the water.

The ancillary right to contact with the water exists to preserve the upland owner's core littoral right of access to the water. *See Board of Trustees of the Internal*

Improvement Trust Fund v. Sand Key Associates, Ltd., 512 So. 2d 934, 936 (Fla. 1987) (stating that littoral property rights include "the right of access to the water, including the right to have the property's contact with the water remain intact"); *see also* 1 Henry Philip Farnham, *The Law of Waters and Water Rights* § 62 (1904) ("The riparian owner is also entitled to have his contact with the water remain intact. This is what is known as the right of access."). We have never addressed whether littoral rights are unconstitutionally taken based solely upon the loss of an upland owner's direct contact with the water. But we have held that littoral rights are unconstitutionally taken when sovereignty lands are used in a way that deprives the upland owner of the right of access to the water. *See Thiesen, supra* 78 So. at 501 (finding that legislation allowing railway on sovereignty submerged lands unconstitutionally deprived upland owner of ingress and egress, *i.e.*, access to the water, without just compensation); *see also Webb, supra* 82 So. 2d 743 (finding that fill across small arm of lake constituted an infringement of upland owner's littoral right to access main part of lake); *Ferry Pass, supra* 48 So. at 646 (stating that the use of a river that deprived riparian owner of access to the water may be enjoined).

In this case, the Act expressly protects the right of access to the water, which is the sole justification for the subsidiary right of contact. The Act preserves the rights of ingress and egress and prevents the State from erecting structures upon the beach seaward of the ECL except as required to prevent erosion. . . . The Act also provides that the State has no intention "to extend its claims to lands not already held by it or to deprive any upland or submerged land owner of the legitimate and constitutional use and enjoyment of his or her property." [Citation omitted.] At least facially, these provisions ensure that the upland owner's access to the water remains intact. Therefore, the rationale for the ancillary right to contact is satisfied.

Furthermore, it is important to understand that contrary to what might be inferred from the First District's conclusion regarding contact, there is no littoral right to a seaward boundary at the water's edge in Florida. Rather, as explained previously, the boundary between sovereignty lands and private uplands is the MHWL, which represents an average over a nineteen-year period. Although the foreshore technically separates upland property from the water's edge at various times during the nineteen-year period, it has never been considered to infringe upon the upland owner's littoral right of access, which the ancillary right to contact is meant to preserve. Admittedly, the renourished beach may be wider than the typical foreshore, but the ultimate result is the same.[16] Direct access to the water is preserved under the Act. In other words, because the Act safeguards access to the water and because there is no right to maintain a constant boundary with the water's edge, the Act, on its face, does not unconstitutionally eliminate the ancillary right to contact.

***

16. Of course, the State is not free to unreasonably distance the upland property from the water by creating as much dry land between upland property and the water as it pleases. There is a point where such a separation would materially and substantially impair the upland owner's access, thereby resulting in an unconstitutional taking of littoral rights. . . .

In light of the above, we find that the Act, on its face, does not unconstitutionally deprive upland owners of littoral rights without just compensation. Consequently, we answer the rephrased certified question in the negative and quash the decision of the First District. And we again emphasize that our decision in this case is strictly limited to the context of restoring critically eroded beaches under the Beach and Shore Preservation Act.

It is so ordered.

Justice Lewis, dissenting.

I cannot join the majority because of the manner in which it has "butchered" Florida law in its attempted search for equitable answers to several issues arising in the context of beach restoration in Florida. In attempting to answer these questions, the majority has, in my view, unnecessarily created dangerous precedent constructed upon a manipulation of the question actually certified. Additionally, I fear that the majority's construction of the Beach and Shore Preservation Act is based upon infirm, tortured logic and a rescission from existing precedent under a hollow claim that existing law does not apply or is not relevant here. Today, the majority has simply erased well-established Florida law without proper analysis. . . .

First, the logic upon which the entire foundation of the majority opinion is based inherently assumes that contact with the particular body of water has absolutely no protection and is just some ancillary concept that tags along with access to the water and seemingly possesses little or no independent significance. I could not disagree more. By essential, inherent definition, riparian and littoral property is that which is contiguous to, abuts, borders, adjoins, or touches water. *See, e.g., Brickell v. Trammell*, 77 Fla. 544, 82 So. 221, 229-30 (Fla. 1919) (explaining that under Spanish civil law and English common law, private littoral ownership *extended to the high-water mark*); *Miller v. Bay-to-Gulf, Inc.*, 141 Fla. 452, 193 So. 425, 427 (Fla. 1940) ("[I]t is *essential* that [the property owners] show *the ordinary high-water mark* or ordinary high tide of the Gulf of Mexico *extended to their westerly boundary* in order *for them to be entitled to any sort of [littoral] rights. . . .*" (emphasis supplied)); *Thiesen v. Gulf, Fla. & Ala. Ry. Co.*, 75 Fla. 28, 78 So. 491, 500 (Fla. 1918) ("At common law lands which were *bounded by and extended to the high-water mark* of waters in which the tide ebbed and flowed *were riparian or littoral to such waters*." (emphasis supplied)). In this State, the legal essence of littoral or riparian land is contact with the water. Thus, the majority is entirely incorrect when it states that such contact has no protection under Florida law and is merely some "ancillary" concept that is subsumed by the right of access. In other words, the land *must touch* the water as a condition precedent to all other riparian or littoral rights and, in the case of littoral property, this touching must occur at the MHWL.

I agree with former Judge Hersey of the Fourth District Court of Appeal, who urged this Court to take action in *Belvedere Development Corp. v. Dep't of Transp. Administration*, 413 So. 2d 847 (Fla. 4th DCA 1982):

> To speak of riparian or littoral rights unconnected with ownership of the shore is to speak a *non sequitur*. Hopefully, the Supreme Court will take jurisdiction and extinguish this rather ingenious but *hopelessly illogical hypothesis*.

Id. at 851 (Hersey, J., specially concurring) (emphasis supplied). Later, this Court did act in *Belvedere* and agreed with Judge Hersey, quoting parts of his opinion at length. *See Belvedere Dev. Corp. v. Dep't of Transp.*, 476 So. 2d 649, 651-52 (Fla. 1985). Most assuredly, *Belvedere* established clear principles of law with regard to riparian and littoral property, which the majority views as an inconvenient detail of Florida legal precedent and simply unnecessarily discards with one sentence and no analysis as not "controlling or even particularly relevant." Majority op. at 35. Notwithstanding its apparent inconvenience to the majority, *Belvedere* continues to stand for the principle of law that riparian or littoral rights are generally inseparable from riparian or littoral uplands in this State. . . . Today, the majority has returned to a "hopelessly illogical hypothesis" without even an attempt to advance some rational analysis that conforms to the Florida Constitution, our common law, and [statutes].

Following *Belvedere* only a short two years later, this Court again directly addressed the fundamental principles of law applicable to riparian and littoral property, its owners, and their correlative rights in *Board of Trustees of the Internal Improvement Trust Fund v. Sand Key Associates, Ltd.*, 512 So. 2d 934 (Fla. 1987). In very clear and unmistakable language, we stated:

> This Court has expressly adopted the common law rule that a riparian or littoral owner *owns to the line of the ordinary high-water mark on navigable waters.* We have also held that riparian or littoral rights are *legal rights* and, for constitutional purposes, the common law rights of riparian and littoral owners *constitute property.* Riparian and littoral property rights consist not only of the right to use the water shared by the public, but include the following vested rights: (1) the right of access to the water, *including the right to have the property's contact with the water remain intact.* . . .

Id. at 936 (citations omitted) (emphasis supplied). The majority now avoids this inconvenient principle of law—and firmly recognized and protected property right—by improperly describing the littoral property and its owner as having "no *independent* right of contact with the water," and by mischaracterizing the significant right of *contact* as being only "ancillary" to the right of access. . . . Any claim that this existing precedent and law does not apply here is based upon empty, misguided logic that discounts the essential nature of littoral property. At least in theory, the MHWL is the location at which littoral property contacts the sea, and even the majority seems to accept this principle. As a definitional matter, without such contact with the water, littoral property does not exist in Florida. . . . Although the MHWL may be a "dynamic" boundary, until today, Florida has judicially and legislatively accommodated these variations without emasculating the underlying private-property rights and ownership principles. Our common law, statutes, and Constitution indicate that the right of contact with the water is neither "independent of," nor "ancillary to," riparian and littoral property, its ownership, and associated protected rights. That contact is inherent in, and essential to, the very heart of the property we discuss. Without bordering on, lying contiguous to, or abutting the water, the property ceases to be "riparian" or "littoral" by working definition:

The ordinary high-water mark is well established as the dividing line between private riparian and sovereign or public ownership of the land beneath the water. This dividing line was not chosen arbitrarily. . . . "Any other rule would leave riparian owners continually in danger of losing access to water which is often the most valuable feature of their property, and continually vulnerable to harassing litigation challenging the location of the original water lines."

Bd. of Trs. of the Internal Improvement Fund v. Medeira Beach Nominee, Inc., 272 So. 2d 209, 213 (Fla. 2d DCA 1973) (quoting *Hughes v. Washington*, 389 U.S. 290, 293-94 (1967)). . . .

The problem with the underlying logic and reasoning of the majority is not really a matter of just a few yards of sand but is, instead, its failure to acknowledge and account for the fundamental result that occurs in the absence of the inherent right of contact with the water. Under the legal principle adopted by the majority, the Sovereign could now create, widen, and extend "sovereign" land or a portion of beach between what should represent the status-quo-ante MHWL (also known as the ECL) and the water by hundreds or even thousands of yards without impacting the rights of riparian or littoral property owners. This new-found governmental power could be used to create extended state-owned or sovereign lands between the once-private riparian or littoral property and the water, thereby effectively severing private property from the sea, lakes, and rivers, which instantly converts ocean-front, gulf-front, lake-front, and river-front property into something far less.[24]

***

The same objective could be accomplished through the deposit of sand on the relevant beach with the understanding that the dividing line between sovereign and private lands would remain the dynamic MHWL. This would cost the State, our local governments, and Florida's taxpayers far less capital by avoiding the constant need to redistribute sand to maintain the restored MHWL at the recorded ECL or the need to exercise eminent-domain powers.

I recognize that beach restoration and renourishment are critical in Florida and present many difficult and complex issues. I have no doubt that the majority has attempted to balance the respective interests involved to reach a workable solution. However, this legislation has not been constitutionally applied in this case, and no matter the complexity or difficulty, I suggest that the private-property rights

---

24. In response, the majority states:

> Of course, the State is not free to unreasonably distance the upland property from the water by creating as much dry land between upland property and the water as it pleases. There is *a point* where such a separation would materially and substantially impair the upland owner's access, thereby resulting in an unconstitutional taking of littoral rights.

Majority op. at 34 n.16 (emphasis supplied). However, the majority never provides any guidance or a limiting principle concerning when governmental creation of new land seaward of the ECL would reach "a point" that materially impaired the upland owners' littoral rights. Further, the majority's interpretation of the Act is completely unsupported by Florida law, which provides that the right of contact is a condition precedent to all other littoral rights. . . .

destroyed today are also critical and of fundamental importance. As constitutionally protected rights slide, it becomes more difficult to protect others. The rights inherent in private-property ownership are at the foundation of this nation and this State. I simply cannot join a decision which, in my view, unnecessarily eliminates private-property rights without providing "full compensation" as required by article X, section 6 of the Florida Constitution. While the Act was applied in an unconstitutional manner here, it may be constitutionally applied under other circumstances in a manner that preserves both the intent of the Legislature and the quintessential nature of littoral and riparian property in Florida.

points for discussion

1. *Much ado about nothing?* At first blush, it is difficult to understand the practical concerns that might bring a plaintiff to file this lawsuit. One would guess that most beachfront landowners would welcome government-funded beach renourishment that would provide added security against future storms and erosion. The "costs" borne by the landowners also do not seem to be significant. Consider what they lost: the right to future accretion and physical contact with the water. In addition to the fact that future land gains through accretion are, by definition, speculative, it is unlikely that the amount of accretion would be such that, for example, the land could be subdivided for profit. What was really lost by losing contact with the water? For residential property, it cannot be argued that contact was necessary to load or unload cargo from ships. (Moreover, by reserving all littoral rights to the upland owners, the statute might permit this, if zoning allowed.) The upland owners could still walk to the water unabated, and see the waves as they had beforehand. The biggest impact of the renourishment — one that was never mentioned in the decision — was that it might create a strip of state-owned dry sand between the ECL and the MHWL upon which members of the public could walk or sit. Given that members of the public could walk or sit on the wet sand part of the beach before the renourishment, does the change wrought seem worth a lawsuit? What other factors might have motivated the upland owners?

2. *Another way to structure the renourishment law.* What if the Beach and Shore Preservation Act provided that, after the renourishment, the upland owners retained fee title to the new MHWL but the state retained a public easement over dry sand seaward of the ECL? Under this approach, the upland property would remain in contact with the water, and the upland owners would take title to land gained by future accretion. The net result would be the same: a strip of dry sand between the ECL and the water line upon which the public could walk or sit. Upland owners would be hard-pressed to claim that creation of the easement effected a taking, given that the state would be giving them title to the underlying land in the same transaction. Examples of this arrangement already exist in Florida: In the case of *Burkhart v. City of Fort Lauderdale*, 168 So. 2d 65 (Fla. 1964), the court held that while the

state held a road easement directly along the water's edge, the upland owners retained the right to any future accretion.

2. A Judicial Taking?

Act II of the drama began when the plaintiffs filed their petition for writ of certiorari with the United States Supreme Court. In its petition, the plaintiff asked the Supreme Court to reverse the Florida Supreme Court's decision that the Beach and Shore Preservation Act did not effect a regulatory taking of their littoral rights. In a surprising move, the plaintiffs also described one of the "questions presented" as follows:

> The Florida Supreme Court invoked "nonexistent rules of state substantive law" to reverse 100 years of uniform holdings that littoral rights are constitutionally protected. In doing so, did the Florida Court's decision cause a "judicial taking" proscribed by the Fifth and Fourteenth Amendments to the United States Constitution?

This was a surprising development for several reasons. First, the Supreme Court ordinarily reviews cases in order to determine whether the preceding court correctly resolved issues of law. Here, however, the plaintiffs were asking the court to review an issue that the preceding court did not consider. (In fact, it could not have considered the issue, because it did not arise until the Florida Supreme Court entered its final order.) Second, while the Supreme Court had recognized a cause of action for regulatory takings since the 1920s, it had never explicitly recognized a cause of action for judicial takings. Earlier opinions of the Court had hinted at the possibility. In a concurring opinion in *Hughes v. Washington*, 389 U.S. 290 (1967), Justice Stewart stated that:

> . . . it must be conceded as a general proposition that the law of real property is, under our Constitution, left to the individual States to develop and administer. And surely Washington or any other State is free to make changes, either legislative or judicial, in its general rules of real property law, including the rules governing the property rights of riparian owners. Nor are riparian owners who derive their title from the United States somehow immune from the changing impact of these general state rules. . . . For if they were, then the property law of a State like Washington, carved entirely out of federal territory, would be forever frozen into the mold it occupied on the date of the State's admission to the Union. . . . Like any other property owner, however, Mrs. Hughes may insist . . . that the State not take her land without just compensation.

***

> To the extent that the decision of the Supreme Court of Washington on that issue arguably conforms to reasonable expectations, we must of course accept it as conclusive. But to the extent that it constitutes a sudden change in state law, unpredictable in terms of the relevant precedents, no such deference would be appropriate. For a State cannot be permitted to defeat the constitutional prohibition against taking property without due process of law by the simple device of

asserting retroactively that the property it has taken never existed at all. Whether the decision here worked an unpredictable change in state law thus inevitably presents a federal question for the determination of this Court.

Id. at 295-98.

And, in dissenting from the Court's refusal to issue a writ of certiorari in the case of *Stevens v. City of Cannon Beach*, 854 P.2d 449 (Or. 1993), Justice Scalia had argued that the plaintiffs — whose dry sand beach Oregon courts had declared open to public access based on the common law doctrine of custom — should have an opportunity to challenge those courts' interpretation of Oregon property law in federal court.

> **Quick Question**
>
> *Hughes* and *Stevens* (and *Stop the Beach Renourishment*) involve beachfront property. Is this just a coincidence, or is there some reason why judicial takings claims seem to be linked to this kind of property?

In its Petition, Stop the Beach Renourishment argued that:

> [t]his Court should grant certiorari to halt the ever-increasing judicial nullification of private property rights by state courts (and especially the Florida Supreme Court) that "redefine" property rights to not exist under "background principles of state law" solely to accomplish public policy objectives that have no other purpose but to circumvent the Takings Clause of the United States Constitution. If a state court is free to "redefine" property interests so as to not exist, the Takings Clause no longer has a purpose or meaning. This case presents the perfect vehicle for the Court to address judicial takings.

Petition for Writ of Certiorari, *Stop the Beach Renourishment v. Florida Department of Environmental Protection*, 2008 U.S. Briefs 1151 at 45-6 (2008).

On June 15, 2009, the Supreme Court granted the petition. On June 17, 2010, it issued the following opinion.

Stop the Beach Renourishment, Inc. v. Florida Department of Environmental Protection

560 U.S. 702 (2010)

Justice SCALIA announced the judgment of the Court and delivered the opinion of the Court with respect to Parts I, IV, and V, and an opinion with respect to Parts II and III, in which THE CHIEF JUSTICE, Justice THOMAS, and Justice ALITO join.

> **FYI**
>
> You can listen to the oral argument in the case at www.oyez.org.

We consider a claim that the decision of a State's court of last resort took property without just compensation in violation of the Takings Clause of the Fifth Amendment, as applied against the States through the Fourteenth . . . .

I.

A.

Generally speaking, state law defines property interests, . . . including property rights in navigable waters and the lands underneath them. . . . In Florida, the State owns in trust for the public the land permanently submerged beneath navigable waters and the foreshore (the land between the low-tide line and the mean high-water line). . . . Thus, the mean high-water line (the average reach of high tide over the preceding 19 years) is the ordinary boundary between private beachfront, or littoral property, and state-owned land. . . .

Littoral owners have, in addition to the rights of the public, certain "special rights" with regard to the water and the foreshore, . . . rights which Florida considers to be property, generally akin to easements. . . . These include the right of access to the water, the right to use the water for certain purposes, the right to an unobstructed view of the water, and the right to receive accretions and relictions to the littoral property. . . . This is generally in accord with well-established common law, although the precise property rights vary among jurisdictions. . . .

At the center of this case is the right to accretions and relictions. Accretions are additions of alluvion (sand, sediment, or other deposits) to waterfront land; relictions are lands once covered by water that become dry when the water recedes. . . . (For simplicity's sake, we shall refer to accretions and relictions collectively as accretions, and the process whereby they occur as accretion.) In order for an addition to dry land to qualify as an accretion, it must have occurred gradually and imperceptibly — that is, so slowly that one could not see the change occurring, though over time the difference became apparent. . . . When, on the other hand, there is a "sudden or perceptible loss of or addition to land by the action of the water or a sudden change in the bed of a lake or the course of a stream," the change is called an avulsion. . . .

In Florida, as at common law, the littoral owner automatically takes title to dry land added to his property by accretion; but formerly submerged land that has become dry land by avulsion continues to belong to the owner of the seabed (usually the State). . . . Thus, regardless of whether an avulsive event exposes land previously submerged or submerges land previously exposed, the boundary between littoral property and sovereign land does not change; it remains (ordinarily) what was the mean high-water line before the event. . . . It follows from this that, when a new strip of land has been added to the shore by avulsion, the littoral owner has no right to subsequent accretions. Those accretions no longer add to *his* property, since the property abutting the water belongs not to him but to the State.

***

[The Court goes on to describe the terms and operation of the Beach and Shore Preservation Act and the procedural history of the case.]

The Florida Supreme Court answered the certified question in the negative, and quashed the First District's remand. . . . It faulted the Court of Appeal for not considering the doctrine of avulsion, which it concluded permitted the State to reclaim the restored beach on behalf of the public. . . . It described the right to accretions as a future contingent interest, not a vested property right, and held that there is no littoral right to contact with the water independent of the littoral right of access, which the Act does not infringe. . . . Petitioner sought rehearing on the ground that the Florida Supreme Court's decision itself effected a taking of the Members' littoral rights contrary to the Fifth and Fourteenth Amendments to the Federal Constitution.[4] The request for rehearing was denied. We granted certiorari. . . .

II.

A.

Before coming to the parties' arguments in the present case, we discuss some general principles of our takings jurisprudence. The *Takings Clause* — "nor shall private property be taken for public use, without just compensation," U.S. Const., Amendment 5 — applies as fully to the taking of a landowner's riparian rights as it does to the taking of an estate in land.[5] *See Yates v. Milwaukee*, 77 U.S. 497 (1871). Moreover, though the classic taking is a transfer of property to the State or to another private party by eminent domain, the Takings Clause applies to other state actions that achieve the same thing. Thus, when the government uses its own property in such a way that it destroys private property, it has taken that property. . . . Similarly, our doctrine of regulatory takings "aims to identify regulatory actions that are functionally equivalent to the classic taking." *Lingle v. Chevron U.S.A. Inc.*, 544 U.S. 528, 539 (2005). Thus, it is a taking when a state regulation forces a property owner to submit to a permanent physical occupation, *Loretto v. Teleprompter Manhattan CATV Corp.*, 458 U.S. 419, 425-426 (1982), or deprives him of all economically beneficial use of his property, *Lucas v. South Carolina Coastal Council*, 505 U.S. 1003, 1019 (1992). Finally (and here we approach the situation before us), States effect a taking if they recharacterize as public property what was previously private property. *See Webb's Fabulous Pharmacies, Inc. v. Beckwith*, 449 U.S. 155, 163-165 (1980).

The Takings Clause (unlike, for instance, the Ex Post Facto Clauses, see Art. I, § 9, cl. 3; § 10, cl. 1) is not addressed to the action of a specific branch or branches. It is concerned simply with the act, and not with the governmental actor ("nor shall private property *be taken*" (emphasis added)). There is no textual justification for saying that the existence or the scope of a State's power to expropriate private property without just compensation varies according to the branch of government

---

4. We ordinarily do not consider an issue first presented to a state court in a petition for rehearing if the state court did not address it. . . . But where the state-court decision itself is claimed to constitute a violation of federal law, the state court's refusal to address that claim put forward in a petition for rehearing will not bar our review. . . .

5. We thus need not resolve whether the right of accretion is an easement, as petitioner claims, or, as Florida claims, a contingent future interest.

effecting the expropriation. Nor does common sense recommend such a principle. It would be absurd to allow a State to do by judicial decree what the *Takings Clause* forbids it to do by legislative fiat. See *Stevens v. Cannon Beach*, 510 U.S. 1207 (1994) (Scalia, J., dissenting from denial of certiorari).

Our precedents provide no support for the proposition that takings effected by the judicial branch are entitled to special treatment, and in fact suggest the contrary. *PruneYard Shopping Center v. Robins*, 447 U.S. 74 (1980), involved a decision of the California Supreme Court overruling one of its prior decisions which had held that the California Constitution's guarantees of freedom of speech and of the press, and of the right to petition the government, did not require the owner of private property to accord those rights on his premises. The appellants, owners of a shopping center, contended that their private property rights could not "be denied by invocation of a state constitutional provision *or by judicial reconstruction of a State's laws of private property*," *id.*, at 79 (emphasis added). We held that there had been no taking, citing cases involving legislative and executive takings, and applying standard *Takings Clause* analysis. *See id.*, at 82-84. We treated the California Supreme Court's application of the constitutional provisions as a regulation of the use of private property, and evaluated whether that regulation violated the property owners' "right to exclude others," *id.*, at 80 (internal quotation marks omitted). Our opinion addressed only the claimed taking by the constitutional provision. Its failure to speak separately to the claimed taking by "judicial reconstruction of a State's laws of private property" certainly does not suggest that a taking by judicial action cannot occur, and arguably suggests that the same analysis applicable to taking by constitutional provision would apply.

Webb's Fabulous Pharmacies, supra, is even closer in point. There the purchaser of an insolvent corporation had interpleaded the corporation's creditors, placing the purchase price in an interest-bearing account in the registry of the Circuit Court of Seminole County, to be distributed in satisfaction of claims approved by a receiver. The Florida Supreme Court construed an applicable statute to mean that the interest on the account belonged to the county, because the account was "considered 'public money,' " *Beckwith v. Webb's Fabulous Pharmacies*, 374 So. 2d 951, 952-953 (1979) (*per curiam*). We held this to be a taking. We noted that "[t]he usual and general rule is that any interest on an interpleaded and deposited fund follows the principal and is to be allocated to those who are ultimately to be the owners of that principal," 449 U.S., at 162. "Neither the Florida Legislature by statute, nor the Florida courts by judicial decree," we said, "may accomplish the result the county seeks simply by recharacterizing the principal as 'public money.' " *Id.*, at 164.

In sum, the *Takings Clause* bars *the State* from taking private property without paying for it, no matter which branch is the instrument of the taking. To be sure, the manner of state action may matter: Condemnation by eminent domain, for example, is always a taking, while a legislative, executive, or judicial restriction of property use may or may not be, depending on its nature and extent. But the particular state *actor* is irrelevant. If a legislature *or a court* declares that what was once an established right of private property no longer exists, it has taken that property, no less than if the State had physically appropriated it or destroyed its value by regulation. "[A] State, by *ipse dixit*, may not transform private property into public property without compensation." *Ibid.*

***

III.

Respondents put forward a number of arguments which contradict, to a greater or lesser degree, the principle discussed above, that the existence of a taking does not depend upon the branch of government that effects it. First, in a case claiming a judicial taking they would add to our normal takings inquiry a requirement that the court's decision have no "fair and substantial basis." This is taken from our jurisprudence dealing with the question whether a state-court decision rests upon adequate and independent state grounds, placing it beyond our jurisdiction to review. . . . To assure that there is no "evasion" of our authority to review federal questions, we insist that the nonfederal ground of decision have "fair support." *Broad River Power Co. v. South Carolina ex rel. Daniel*, 281 U.S. 537, 540 (1930). . . . A test designed to determine whether there has been an evasion is not obviously appropriate for determining whether there has been a taking of property. But if it is to be extended there it must mean (in the present context) that there is a "fair and substantial basis" for believing that petitioner's Members did not have a property right to future accretions which the Act would take away. This is no different, we think, from our requirement that petitioners' Members must prove the elimination of an established property right.

Next, respondents argue that federal courts lack the knowledge of state law required to decide whether a judicial decision that purports merely to clarify property rights has instead taken them. But federal courts must often decide what state property rights exist in nontakings contexts. . . . And indeed they must decide it to resolve claims that legislative or executive action has effected a taking. For example, a regulation that deprives a property owner of all economically beneficial use of his property is not a taking if the restriction "inhere[s] in the title itself, in the restrictions that background principles of the State's law of property and nuisance already place upon land ownership." *Lucas*, 505 U.S., at 1029. A constitutional provision that forbids the uncompensated taking of property is quite simply insusceptible of enforcement by federal courts unless they have the power to decide what property rights exist under state law.

Respondents also warn us against depriving common-law judging of needed flexibility. That argument has little appeal when directed against the enforcement of a constitutional guarantee adopted in an era when . . . courts had no power to "change" the common law. But in any case, courts have no peculiar need of flexibility. It is no more essential that judges be free to overrule prior cases that establish property entitlements than that state legislators be free to revise pre-existing statutes that confer property entitlements, or agency-heads pre-existing regulations that do so. And insofar as courts merely clarify and elaborate property entitlements that were previously unclear, they cannot be said to have taken an established property right.

***

For its part, petitioner proposes an unpredictability test. Quoting Justice Stewart's concurrence in *Hughes v. Washington*, 389 U.S. 290, 296, 88 S. Ct. 438, 19 L. Ed. 2d 530 (1967), petitioner argues that a judicial taking consists of a decision that " 'constitutes a sudden change in state law, unpredictable in terms of relevant precedents.' " See Brief for Petitioner 17, 34-50. The focus of petitioner's test is misdirected. What counts is not whether there is precedent for the allegedly confiscatory decision, but whether the property right allegedly taken was established. A "predictability of change" test would cover both too much and too little. Too much, because a judicial property decision need not be predictable, so long as it does not declare that what had been private property under established law no longer is. A decision that clarifies property entitlements (or the lack thereof) that were previously unclear might be difficult to predict, but it does not eliminate established property rights. And the predictability test covers too little, because a judicial elimination of established private-property rights that is foreshadowed by dicta or even by holdings years in advance is nonetheless a taking. If, for example, a state court held in one case, to which the complaining property owner was not a party, that it had the power to limit the acreage of privately owned real estate to 100 acres, and then, in a second case, applied that principle to declare the complainant's 101st acre to be public property, the State would have taken an acre from the complainant even though the decision was predictable.

IV.

We come at last to petitioner's takings attack on the decision below. . . .

Petitioner argues that the Florida Supreme Court took two of the property rights of the Members by declaring that those rights did not exist: the right to accretions, and the right to have littoral property touch the water (which petitioner distinguishes from the mere right of access to the water). Under petitioner's theory, because no prior Florida decision had said that the State's filling of submerged tidal lands could have the effect of depriving a littoral owner of contact with the water and denying him future accretions, the Florida Supreme Court's judgment in the present case abolished those two easements to which littoral property owners had been entitled. This puts the burden on the wrong party. There is no taking unless petitioner can show that, before the Florida Supreme Court's decision, littoral-property owners had rights to future accretions and contact with the water superior to the State's right to fill in its submerged land. Though some may think the question close, in our view the showing cannot be made.

Two core principles of Florida property law intersect in this case. First, the State as owner of the submerged land adjacent to littoral property has the right to fill that land, so long as it does not interfere with the rights of the public and the rights of littoral landowners. *See Hayes v. Bowman*, 91 So. 2d 795, 799-800 (Fla. 1957) (right to fill conveyed by State to private party). . . . Second, . . . if an avulsion exposes land seaward of littoral property that had previously been submerged, that land belongs to the State even if it interrupts the littoral owner's contact with the water. . . . The issue here is whether there is an exception to this rule when the State is the cause of the avulsion. Prior law suggests there is not. In *Martin v. Busch*, 93 Fla. 535, 112 So. 274 (1927), the Florida Supreme Court held that when the State drained water from a lakebed belonging to the State, causing land that was formerly below the mean high-water line to become dry land, that land continued to belong to the State. . . . " 'The riparian rights doctrine of accretion and reliction,' " the Florida

> ### The Logic of the Opinion
>
> The Court's logic is as follows: First, the common law of Florida is that the state owns "positive avulsions," that is, sudden accretions, and that the state is not liable to upland owners simply because those positive avulsions cut off their riparian and littoral rights. Second, the common law of Florida does not distinguish between artificial and natural accretion or avulsion. (Unlike, say, Illinois or California, as we recently learned.) Third, the state's deposit of sand via renourishment is equivalent to an artificial avulsion. Thus, the state is not liable to upland owners for renourishment that eliminates riparian and littoral rights.

Supreme Court later explained, " 'does not apply to such lands.' " *Bryant v. Peppe*, 238 So. 2d 836, 839 (Fla. 1970). This is not surprising, as there can be no accretions to land that no longer abuts the water.

Thus, Florida law as it stood before the decision below allowed the State to fill in its own seabed, and the resulting sudden exposure of previously submerged land was treated like an avulsion for purposes of ownership. The right to accretions was therefore subordinate to the State's right to fill. *Thiesen v. Gulf, Florida & Alabama R. Co.*, 75 Fla. 28 (1918), suggests the same result. That case involved a claim by a riparian landowner that a railroad's state-authorized filling of submerged land and construction of tracks upon it interfered with the riparian landowners' rights to access and to wharf out to a shipping channel. The Florida Supreme Court determined that the claimed right to wharf out did not exist in Florida, and that therefore only the right of access was compensable. 75 Fla., at 58-65. Significantly, although the court recognized that the riparian-property owners had rights to accretion, . . . the only rights it even suggested would be infringed by the railroad were the right of access (which the plaintiff had claimed) and the rights of view and use of the water (which it seems the plaintiff had not claimed). . . .

The Florida Supreme Court decision before us is consistent with these background principles of state property law. . . . It did not abolish the Members' right to future accretions, but merely held that the right was not implicated by the beach-restoration project, because the doctrine of avulsion applied. . . . The Florida Supreme Court's opinion describes beach restoration as the reclamation by the State of the public's land, just as *Martin* had described the lake drainage in that case. Although the opinion does not cite *Martin* and is not always clear on this point, it suffices that its characterization of the littoral right to accretion is consistent with *Martin* and the other relevant principles of Florida law we have discussed.

What we have said shows that the rule of *Board of Trustees of Internal Improvement Trust Fund v. Sand Key Assoc., Ltd.*, 512 So. 2d 934 (Fla. 1987), which petitioner repeatedly invokes, is inapposite. There the Florida Supreme Court held that an artificial accretion does not change the right of a littoral-property owner to claim the accreted land as his own (as long as the owner did not cause the accretion himself). . . . The reason *Martin* did not apply, *Sand Key* explained, is that the drainage that had occurred in *Martin* did not lower the water level by " 'imperceptible degrees,' " and so did not qualify as an accretion. 512 So. 2d, at 940-941.

The result under Florida law may seem counter-intuitive. After all, the Members' property has been deprived of its character (and value) as oceanfront property by the State's artificial creation of an avulsion. Perhaps state-created avulsions ought to be treated differently from other avulsions insofar as the property right to accretion is concerned. But nothing in prior Florida law makes such a distinction, and *Martin* suggests, if it does not indeed hold, the contrary. Even if there might be different interpretations of *Martin* and other Florida property-law cases that would prevent this arguably odd result, we are not free to adopt them. The Takings Clause only protects property rights as they are established under state law, not as they might have been established or ought to have been established. We cannot say that the Florida Supreme Court's decision eliminated a right of accretion established under Florida law.

Petitioner also contends that the State took the Members' littoral right to have their property continually maintain contact with the water. To be clear, petitioner does not allege that the State relocated the property line, as would have happened if the erosion-control line were *landward* of the old mean high-water line (instead of identical to it). Petitioner argues instead that the Members have a separate right for the boundary of their property to be always the mean high-water line. Petitioner points to dicta in *Sand Key* that refers to "the right to have the property's contact with the water remain intact," 512 So. 2d, at 936. Even there, the right was included in the definition of the right to access . . . which is consistent with the Florida Supreme Court's later description that "there is no independent right of contact with the water" but it "exists to preserve the upland owner's core littoral right of access to the water," *Walton County v. Stop the Beach Renourishment, Inc.*, 998 So. 2d, 1102, 1119 (2008). Petitioner's expansive interpretation of the dictum in *Sand Key* would cause it to contradict the clear Florida law governing avulsion. One cannot say that the Florida Supreme Court contravened established property law by rejecting it.[1]

V.

Because the Florida Supreme Court's decision did not contravene the established property rights of petitioner's Members, Florida has not violated the Fifth and

---

1. Petitioner also argues that the Members' other littoral rights have been infringed because the Act replaces their common-law rights with inferior statutory versions. Petitioner has not established that the statutory versions are inferior; and whether the source of a property right is the common law or a statute makes no difference, so long as the property owner continues to have what he previously had.

Fourteenth Amendments. The judgment of the Florida Supreme Court is therefore affirmed.

[Justices Breyer, Ginsburg, Kennedy, and Sotomayor concurred with the result — that there was no taking. These justices did not agree with the plurality, however, that resolving the case required an inquiry into whether or not a "judicial taking" had occurred.]

points for discussion

1. *Judicial takings.* The Court addresses some of the practical difficulties of recognizing a cause of action for a judicial taking as well as the impacts that recognition of such a claim might have on future state court property decisions. What do you think of the arguments in favor and against recognition? For much more on these issues, see Barton H. Thompson, Jr., *Judicial Takings*, 76 Va. L. Rev. 1449, 1515 (1990).

2. *The new rule.* In addition to recognizing that property owners might be entitled to takings relief from state court decisions, a plurality of the Court creates a new rule for determining when such relief should be granted: when a state court decision "contravene[s] the established property rights" of a landowner. Given what we have learned about the qualified nature of upland owners' rights, will it ever be possible for a plaintiff to prove contravention? Consider the Oregon and New Jersey dry sand access cases we read in the previous chapter. Do these cases present stronger grounds for relief?

Problem Exercise: Balancing Upland Owners' Rights and the Public Trust

Mike owns a beachfront home in the town of Brown's Island, East Carolina. East Carolina is a state — one of the original 14 (!) colonies — located on the Atlantic Ocean between North and South Carolina. Mike's home is about 200 feet from the mean-high-tide line, just behind a row of large sand dunes. In 2007, Mike applied to the state for a permit to construct a rip-rap groin that would originate near the vegetation line on Mike's property and extend some 200 feet into the Atlantic. (The vegetation line is just seaward of the dunes.) The groin would be about eight feet wide and have a height of about four feet above sea level. According to Mike's application, the purpose of the groin would be to reduce erosion on his property and to give him fishing access to certain prized fish species that do not come within 100 feet from shore. Assume the state agreed to grant the permit if Mike granted the state an easement allowing the state to enlarge and maintain the dunes on Mike's property. The state wanted to make the dunes taller and wider in order to help protect private and public property from storm damage. Mike did not want the dunes enlarged because they will interfere with the views from his home.

- In requiring the grant of the easement, did the state violate the Fifth Amendment?
- On what grounds could Beachguardian, an environmental group, have challenged the issuance of the permit?
- How would the state have responded to these arguments?

Assume the state granted the permit and Beachguardian did not prevail on its challenge. Mike has the groin constructed in 2009. Between 2009 and 2014, a significant amount of sediment — up to 60 feet in some places — accumulated along both Mike's property and property belonging to Mike's next-door neighbor John. During that five-year period, the area experienced six to eight storm events. At the end of the summer in 2014, the state installed large (16-foot tall), permanent lifeguard chairs on the accumulated sediment. John and Mike both called to complain about the installation of the lifeguard chairs. State officials directed them to the state attorney general's office, where one of the deputy attorneys general told them that "the state now owns that property." Is that correct? Even if the state does own the property, can it build the chairs?

E. CHAPTER SUMMARY

1. **In general.** Upland owners' rights, also known as riparian and littoral rights, vary from state to state, although they generally include the right to access the adjacent public waterway, the right to wharf out, and the right to accretions (as well as the right to use the water, which we did not cover in this chapter).

2. **Rights in conflict.** Upland owners' rights only matter when there is a conflict with the public's rights or the rights of a neighboring upland owner. This means that rights can be defined only in the context of a conflict, and that it is best to think of them as qualified rights. Cases involving conflicts with the government generally manifest themselves as takings cases, while cases pitting upland owners against one another resemble private nuisance cases. The outcome of a given case will heavily depend on the particular facts in that case.

3. **Access.** Access is at the core of upland owners' rights. In this context, access means access from the upland property. In other words, it is a right distinct from the upland owner's right in common with the public. Access can mean visual access, and often includes derivative rights, such as the right to wharf out.

4. **Accretions.** The law distinguishes between gradual and sudden changes, although this is easier said than done. Depending on the state, the law also sometimes distinguishes between natural and artificial accretion (or avulsion). Neighbors may not subject their neighbors to unreasonable harm in the effort to protect their own property from erosion.

5. **Judicial takings.** To answer the question posed earlier, it is not a coincidence that the concept of a judicial taking is linked to beach cases. Because much coastal law is rooted in common law, courts make many of the important decisions regarding the public trust doctrine and upland owners' rights. Moreover, one can think of these court decisions as allocating property between the public and the upland owner. This is a "zero-sum game"; in other words, as the public's allocation is increased, the amount of private property necessarily is reduced. This somewhat unique circumstance sets the stage for the possibility of a judicial taking.

F. SUGGESTED READING

Donna R. Christie, *Of Beaches, Boundaries, and SOBs*, 25 J. LAND USE & ENVTL. L. 10 (2010).

A.E. McCordic, *The Right of Access and the Right to Wharf Out to Navigable Water*, 4 HARV. L. REV. 14 (1890).

George Sanford Parsons, *Public and Private Rights in the Foreshore*, 22 COLUM. L. REV. 706 (1922).

Volume 35 of the VERMONT LAW REVIEW (2010) contains a full range of papers assessing the U.S. Supreme Court's decision in *Stop the Beach Renourishment*.

chapter 9

The Coastal Zone Management Act and State Coastal Programs

As foreshadowed in Chapter 6, the federal Coastal Zone Management Act both provides the impetus for, and helps shape the parameters of, state statutes and programs. Thus, we begin this chapter with a brief description of the evolution and typology of federal environmental law, before turning our attention to state coastal statutes and programs.

A. A BRIEF HISTORY OF FEDERAL ENVIRONMENTAL LAW

Prior to the 1960s, the field of environmental law mostly consisted of state common law doctrines, such as private and public nuisance, and the occasional state water or air pollution statute. There were a few federal statutes, dating from the early 1900s, aimed at protecting wildlife, mainly migratory birds. Much of this law could be characterized as either reactive (common law) or fragmented (state statutes).

In the late 1960s, Congress began to develop a series of major environmental statutes that were both comprehensive and prescriptive. Two phenomena motivated Congress to act. First, improvements in scientists' ability to observe and quantify environmental impacts, such as the presence of toxic quantities of invisible chemicals in water and air, increased the amount of information available to lawmakers and the policy process. In some cases, such as when, in January and June of 1969 respectively, an oil rig off the Santa Barbara "blew out" and an oil slick on Ohio's Cuyahoga River caught fire, modern tools were not necessary to reveal disturbing impacts. Second, throughout the 1960s, public concern regarding the consequences of inadequate environmental regulation also increased, culminating in large, popular events such as Earth Day 1970. It is hard to say for certain whether new information led to heightened concern, or whether concerned citizens began to care more about damage to their environment. Both were probably true. The end result was a powerful congressional desire to create a sweeping set of major new environmental laws.

The Clean Air Act (1970), the Clean Water Act (1972), and the Endangered Species Act (1973), are what are sometimes referred to as "command and control" environmental laws. Although there are variations in the tools and approaches used, command and control laws share a common feature: They attempt to *preempt* excess environmental harm by all actors. Command and control laws work in two ways: First, "standard-based" laws prospectively limit the amount of harm an individual or firm (or a state government) can impose on the environment by, for example, releasing chemicals into water or air, or by killing endangered plants or animals. Second, "technology-based" laws require that firms or individuals engaged in harmful or polluting operations use specified devices aimed at reducing the amount of harm or pollution produced. Other federal environmental laws, such as the National Environmental Policy Act

> ### Optimal Pollution or Harm
>
> It is important to remember that, unless each marginal unit of pollution or harm produces extreme costs (e.g., release of enriched uranium), there is always what economists call an "optimal level of pollution or harm." The idea is that producing things that are valuable for society, such as chairs, might not be possible without some environmental harms — use of trees, release of chemicals from paints or stains, etc. When making the first few chairs, the benefit to society of producing a chair clearly outweighs the cost to society of enduring the pollution or harm. As production goes on, the marginal benefit of each additional chair declines — if there are four people in your home, the fifth chair in your house is not as valuable to you as the fourth. At the same time, each new chair imposes the same (or greater) amount of environmental cost. At a certain point, society begins to incur a loss every time a chair is made. From a societal perspective, the optimal production of chairs (and associated environmental harm) occurs just before this point.

> ### Quick Question
>
> What do you suppose "better" means in this context? What type of criteria would you use to determine whether one particular decision is better than another?

(1970), fit into a category that might be called "procedural" environmental law. Rather than addressing a particular environmental harm or attempting to limit incidents of harm, a procedural law establishes decision-making rules for government agencies. The idea behind such laws is that if agencies take the time to study the environmental aspects of a decision and to solicit and consider public input, then they will make better decisions than they would have had they not done so. What kinds of decisions are covered by procedural laws? NEPA, for example, applies whenever a federal government agency is deciding how to carry out a proposed, major activity. The word "activity" is broad in this context, and refers to activities carried out directly by an agency (construction of a new Army base), activities funded by an agency (the construction of an interstate highway), and activities that require the actor to apply for and receive a permit from the agency before proceeding (construction of a wharf that encroaches on a public waterway).

A third category of federal environmental laws incorporates a "planning" approach aimed at achieving efficient use of natural resources and avoiding wasteful and contentious user-group conflicts. The Federal Land Policy and Management Act (1976), for example, mandates that the Bureau of Land Management conduct studies of "tracts" and "areas" of public lands under its management authority, examining a variety of issues including natural resources present and competing uses of those resources. 43 U.S.C. § 1712(a). The Act further requires that, after the study phase, the Bureau prepare land management plans that explain how the Bureau intends to allocate resources and uses across the lands it manages. When, after a plan has been adopted, citizens request permission to engage in resource uses in the area covered by the plan, the Bureau must, prior to granting a permit, consider whether the proposed activity is "in accordance with" the terms of the plan. 43 U.S.C. § 1732(a).

The Coastal Zone Management Act (1972) (CZMA) combines features of all three of these kinds of environmental law, but with a twist. Although other federal statutes, such as the Clean Water Act and the Clean Air Act, allow states to partner with the federal government in implementation, the CZMA gives the states a leading role. The Act mandates that the command and control and planning activities be carried out not by any federal agency, but by the coastal states themselves; and the procedural component of the Act, known as "consistency review," is an interactive federal-state process.

It is perhaps a bit misleading to say that the CZMA "mandates" anything. Coastal states have a choice about whether or not to participate in the CZMA regime. Unlike other federal environmental statutes, such as the Clean Air Act or Clean Water Act, the CZMA neither imposes a penalty, nor requires a federal agency to step in, when a state refuses to participate. Instead, the CZMA offers coastal states two incentives to "get with the program." To date, these incentives have proven highly effective: Although some were slower to join than others, all 30 coastal states ultimately signed on. (Illinois was the last, becoming a CZMA state in 2005. The number of participating states dropped to 29 when Alaska withdrew in July 2011.)

Because of its unique governance structure, we approach the CZMA, state statutes and programs, and other coastal-relevant federal law as a complete and interwoven governance system. This chapter is laid out as follows:

First, we examine the overall structure of the Act. Like all environmental statutes, the Act contains goals and means for achieving those goals. Although Congress established a set of goals for coastal management, it gave the states significant discretion with respect to (1) how to prioritize among competing goals, and (2) how to regulate in furtherance of those priorities. The Act does require that coastal programs be developed and implemented in a consistent manner across all states.

Second, we will highlight some of the unique features in various states' coastal programs. This section illustrates the flexibility of the CZMA in allowing coastal states to tailor programs to reflect their own values and priorities. It also provides examples of "enforceable policies" in state programs. Those policies or provisions are the fulcrum of consistency review.

Third, we examine the consistency review process. While state statutes and coastal programs are the most important pieces of modern coastal law, consistency review also plays a very significant role, given the ubiquity of federal permitting.

Finally, we will take a closer look at one of the more stubborn problems in coastal law, that is, non-point source water pollution. Congress amended the statute in 1990 in an effort to address the issue.

We begin with a look at the basic framework of the Act.

1. The Coastal Zone Management Act

Congress walked a tightrope in designing the Coastal Zone Management Act (CZMA). In addition to working carefully around the fact that land use was traditionally an area of state and local primacy, Congress also had to respect the fact that some states had, in the early 1970s, begun to develop new coastal laws. Through the CZMA, Congress wanted to help shape the development of state coastal law, ensuring that national interests were protected, while at the same time avoiding the perception of federal heavy-handedness. As Senator Ernest "Fritz" Hollings, the driving force behind the Act, said at a conference in 1974:

Photo: Library of Congress

Figure 9-1. Senator Hollings

Coastal zone management and land use management are both, in a sense, land use management.

But the coastal zone is especially affected. The coastal zone is affected by the coastal waters and the Seven Seas. Like love, the coastal zone is a many splendored thing. Its ecosystem is a splendid relationship between ocean and beach, between marshlands — and uplands, and between man and his environment.

I wish I was an oceanographer or marine geologist or a poet so I could wax eloquently for a good 20 minutes about the beauty and delicate nature of the coastal zone. As a politician, I can give you only the people's side.

Everybody wants Coastal Zone Management. But substantial groups fear and are suspicious of Land Use Management. In fact, we in Coastal Zone Management cannot use the expression "land use."

When land use is mentioned, large groups in America voice concern on whether a particular area will be zoned residential or business, whether there will be a funeral home in a residential area, or a mammoth airport will be placed in a quiet nook. Land use means every local zoning headache over and over again; and there is but one thing that the average citizen is sure of — He doesn't want to have to deal with Washington on the property in his local area.

The words "Land Use" convey no national need; for if revenue sharing and the rhetoric from Washington about the New Federalism has any meaning, then certainly we do not need a national program to tell us how to zone in Cheyenne, Wyoming. But we may in the Durham, New Hampshire area.

For at Durham, an oil refinery has been planned. But if the citizens have their way, there will be no refinery at Durham. Adjacent communities have also considered ways to block the refinery.

The coast of New Hampshire is closing up. And, the same thing is happening elsewhere. I understand there are some compromises planned. Delaware moves to halt development of heavy industry in its coastal zone. Some cities pass ordinances running out, they think, 10 miles into the ocean. Maryland hangs out the unwelcome sign for oil refineries. So, right in the middle of environmental panic, here comes the energy crisis.

When I first started working on the Coastal Zone legislation, it was looked upon as a nice thing, not a necessary thing. We were trying to translate your feelings and concerns into legislation.

It was a little difficult to get attention, but we raised the specter of the 225 million Americans coming down to the sea and asked the obvious questions: What was to be done about urban sprawl? Energy facilities siting? Where would we locate water-consuming industries? What about fisheries? The recreational areas? The Ports Authorities? And how were we to locate these compatibly?

> ### Floating Nuclear?
>
> In 2007, 33 years after Senator Hollings's speech, Russia announced plans to build the first floating nuclear power plant. The size of a large ship, the plant would produce enough power to supply the electric power needs of a city of 200,000 people. Because they are mobile, floating nuclear plants could provide power as needed in remote locations on land and at sea (such as for offshore mining operations). Skeptics are concerned with safety issues related to both accidents and terrorist attacks. Tony Halpin, *Floating Nuclear Power Plants Raise Spectre of Chernobyl at Sea*, LONDON TIMES, Apr. 17, 2007.

At that time we were looking ahead. Now with the energy crisis, we are looking behind. Already in commission are 30 supertankers that have no United States ports of call. Offshore nuclear power plants already should have been constructed.

And with the oil shortage, we have yet to look at our whole card, the outer continental shelf along the Atlantic Coast. Thanks to the energy crisis, the pressure for increased offshore drilling, super power plants, and super ports now all create national needs and conflicts in the coastal zone.

Somewhere along the Northeast coast, we are eventually going to see floating nuclear power plants, offshore oil and gas drilling, and a superport.

There will be give and take between energy and environment. Neither need suffer. But neither can afford to wait. If coastal States do not act, the federal government will be compelled to act for them. Coastal Zone Management, therefore, is no longer merely desirable — it is necessary now.

So it is that we meet, charged with the acceleration of Coastal Zone Management, charged with keeping the States ahead of the federal government, charged with assisting the States in maintaining a flexibility in their approaches, charged with reordering the federal role so as to respond to the state guidelines, to completely change the customary practice of issuing "thou shalt" or "thou shalt not" directives from Washington, charged with proving that we in the coastal zone are the Land Use boys' best friend.

Sen. Ernest "Fritz" Hollings (D-SC), Keynote Address, "A National Ocean Policy — Our Last Chance?," at The Coastal Imperative: Developing a National Perspective for Coastal Decision Making, Charleston, SC, March 13, 1974.

2. Goals of the CZMA

If the CZMA does not mandate "thou shalt" or "thou shalt not," what does it do? Congress explained the Act's purposes and mechanisms as follows:

Coastal Zone Management Act

16 U.S.C. § 1452

The Congress finds and declares that it is the national policy —

(1) to preserve, protect, develop, and where possible, to restore or enhance, the resources of the Nation's coastal zone for this and succeeding generations;

(2) to encourage and assist the states to exercise effectively their responsibilities in the coastal zone through the development and implementation of management programs to achieve wise use of the land and water resources of the coastal zone, giving full consideration to ecological, cultural, historic, and esthetic values as well as the needs for compatible economic development, which programs should at least provide for —

(A) the protection of natural resources, including wetlands, floodplains, estuaries, beaches, dunes, barrier islands, coral reefs, and fish and wildlife and their habitat, within the coastal zone,

(B) the management of coastal development to minimize the loss of life and property caused by improper development in flood-prone, storm surge, geological hazard, and erosion-prone areas and in areas likely to be affected by or vulnerable to sea level rise, land subsidence, and saltwater intrusion, and by the destruction of natural protective features such as beaches, dunes, wetlands, and barrier islands,

(C) the management of coastal development to improve, safeguard, and restore the quality of coastal waters, and to protect natural resources and existing uses of those waters,

(D) priority consideration being given to coastal-dependent uses and orderly processes for siting major facilities related to national defense, energy, fisheries development, recreation, ports and transportation, and the location, to the maximum extent practicable, of new commercial and industrial developments in or adjacent to areas where such development already exists,

(E) public access to the coasts for recreation purposes,

(F) assistance in the redevelopment of deteriorating urban waterfronts and ports, and sensitive preservation and restoration of historic, cultural, and esthetic coastal features,

(G) the coordination and simplification of procedures in order to ensure expedited governmental decisionmaking for the management of coastal resources,

(H) continued consultation and coordination with, and the giving of adequate consideration to the views of, affected Federal agencies,

(I) the giving of timely and effective notification of, and opportunities for public and local government participation in, coastal management decisionmaking,

(J) assistance to support comprehensive planning, conservation, and management for living marine resources, including planning for the siting of pollution control and aquaculture facilities within the coastal zone, and improved coordination between State and Federal coastal zone management agencies and State and wildlife agencies, and

(K) the study and development, in any case in which the Secretary considers it to be appropriate, of plans for addressing the adverse effects upon the coastal zone of land subsidence and of sea level rise; and

(3) to encourage the preparation of special area management plans which provide for

---

Historical Note

Congress added language referencing global warming and its effects, such as sea level rise, in the Coastal Zone Management Act Reauthorization Amendments of 1990. As discussed later in this chapter, Congress also at that time added provisions addressing non-point source water pollution.

---

increased specificity in protecting significant natural resources, reasonable coastal-dependent economic growth, improved protection of life and property in hazardous areas, including those areas likely to be affected by land subsidence, sea level rise, or fluctuating water levels of the Great Lakes, and improved predictability in governmental decisionmaking;

(4) to encourage the participation and cooperation of the public, state and local governments, and interstate and other regional agencies, as well as of the Federal agencies having programs affecting the coastal zone, in carrying out the purposes of this title;

(5) to encourage coordination and cooperation with and among the appropriate Federal, State, and local agencies, and international organizations where appropriate, in collection, analysis, synthesis, and dissemination of coastal management information, research results, and technical assistance, to support State and Federal regulation of land use practices affecting the coastal and ocean resources of the United States; and

(6) to respond to changing circumstances affecting the coastal environment and coastal resource management by encouraging States to consider such issues as ocean uses potentially affecting the coastal zone.

3. Mandatory Elements of Qualifying State Programs

Congress does not ordinarily give money and power to the states without strings attached. So, the Act ensures that national interests are protected by specifying that the National Oceanic and Atmospheric Administration (NOAA) can only approve a state coastal program if it conforms to a set of requirements. As you read through the following list, mark

> **Was Congress Giving or Were Coastal States Taking?**
>
> Think back to the notes following *United States v. California* and the Submerged Lands Act of 1953, in Chapter 6. What is your intuition about the politics of coastal land use on Capitol Hill? What did populous and powerful coastal states, such as Texas, California, New York, and Florida, stand to gain and lose from passage of the CZMA?

requirements related to the process of developing the program with a "P," required substantive components with an "S," and mandates for implementation measures (such as dispute resolution procedures) with an "I." Think about the various ways in which states might meet each of these requirements.

Coastal Zone Management Act

16 U.S.C. § 1455(d)

Before approving a management program submitted by a coastal state, the Secretary [of Commerce — read NOAA — EDS.] shall find the following:

(1) The State has developed and adopted a management program for its coastal zone in accordance with rules and regulations promulgated by the Secretary, after notice, and with the opportunity of full participation by relevant Federal agencies, State agencies, local governments, regional organizations, port authorities, and other interested parties and individuals, public and private, which is adequate to carry out the purposes of this title and is consistent with the [policies of the Act].

(2) The management program includes each of the following required program elements:

(A) An identification of the boundaries of the coastal zone subject to the management program.

(B) A definition of what shall constitute permissible land uses and water uses within the coastal zone which have a direct and significant impact on the coastal waters.

(C) An inventory and designation of areas of particular concern within the coastal zone.

(D) An identification of the means by which the State proposes to exert control over the land uses and water uses referred to in subparagraph

(B), including a list of relevant State constitutional provisions, laws, regulations, and judicial decisions.

(E) Broad guidelines on priorities of uses in particular areas, including specifically those uses of lowest priority.

(F) A description of the organizational structure proposed to implement such management program, including the responsibilities and interrelationships of local, areawide, State, regional, and interstate agencies in the management process.

(G) A definition of the term "beach" and a planning process for the protection of, and access to, public beaches and other public coastal areas of environmental, recreational, historical, esthetic, ecological, or cultural value.

(H) A planning process for energy facilities likely to be located in, or which may significantly affect, the coastal zone, including a process for anticipating the management of the impacts resulting from such facilities.

(I) A planning process for assessing the effects of, and studying and evaluating ways to control, or lessen the impact of, shoreline erosion, and to restore areas adversely affected by such erosion.

(3) The State has —

(A) coordinated its program with local, areawide, and interstate plans applicable to areas within the coastal zone . . . [and]

(B) established an effective mechanism for continuing consultation and coordination between the management agency designated pursuant to paragraph (6) and with local governments, interstate agencies, regional agencies, and areawide agencies within the coastal zone to assure the full participation of those local governments and agencies in carrying out the purposes of this title. . . .

(4) The State has held public hearings in the development of the management program.

(5) The management program and any changes thereto have been reviewed and approved by the Governor of the State.

(6) The Governor of the State has designated a single State agency to receive and administer grants for implementing the management program.

(7) The State is organized to implement the management program.

(8) The management program provides for adequate consideration of the national interest involved in planning for, and managing the coastal zone, including the siting of facilities such as energy facilities which are of greater than local significance. In the case of energy facilities, the Secretary shall find that the State has given consideration to any applicable national or interstate energy plan or program.

(9) The management program includes procedures whereby specific areas may be designated for the purpose of preserving or restoring them for their conservation, recreational ecological, historical, or esthetic values.

(10) The State, acting through its chosen agency or agencies (including local governments, areawide agencies, regional agencies, or interstate agencies) has authority for the management of the coastal zone in accordance with the management program. Such authority shall include power —

    (A) to administer land use and water use regulations to control development[,] to ensure compliance with the management program, and to resolve conflicts among competing uses; and

    (B) to acquire fee simple and less than fee simple interests in land, waters, and other property through condemnation or other means when necessary to achieve conformance with the management program.

(11) The management program provides for any one or a combination of the following general techniques for control of land uses and water uses within the coastal zone:

    (A) State establishment of criteria and standards for local implementation, subject to administrative review and enforcement.

    (B) Direct State land and water use planning and regulation.

    (C) State administrative review for consistency with the management program of all development plans, projects, or land and water use regulations, including exceptions and variances thereto, proposed by any State or local authority or private developer, with power to approve or disapprove after public notice and an opportunity for hearings.

(12) The management program contains a method of assuring that local land use and water use regulations within the coastal zone do not unreasonably restrict or exclude land uses and water uses of regional benefit.

(13) The management program provides for —

    (A) the inventory and designation of areas that contain one or more coastal resources of national significance; and

    (B) specific and enforceable standards to protect such resources.

(14) The management program provides for public participation in permitting processes, consistency determinations, and other similar decisions.

(15) The management program provides a mechanism to ensure that all State agencies will adhere to the program.

(16) The management program contains enforceable policies and mechanisms to implement the applicable requirements of the Coastal Nonpoint Pollution Control Program of the State. . . .

a. Structure of State Programs

Following the 1974 speech excerpted above, and in response to a question from the audience regarding the costs involved in the development and implementation of state coastal programs, Senator Hollings noted that "the Act has sufficient flexibility to permit States to use existing State agencies for coastal management rather than requiring the organization of new State agencies." (One can easily find support for this claim in Section 1455(d).) In designing coastal programs, coastal states have employed a wide range of approaches.

Marc J. Hershman et al., The Effectiveness of Coastal Zone Management in the United States

27 Coastal Mgmt. 113 (1999)

A central feature of coastal management practice in the United States is the set of programs and activities at all levels of government that directly link to the federal CZMA. Under the CZMA all three levels of government, federal, state and local, are given important roles to play and considerable flexibility in defining those roles. This results in diverse coastal programs around the country which presents particular challenges for a systematic and national-scale program evaluation.

At the national level the OCRM is the administering office. [The Office of Ocean and Coastal Resource Management (OCRM) is part of NOAA. — EDS.] It interprets the statute through rules and regulations, interacts with oversight and reauthorizing committees in the Congress, and approves (or rejects) state coastal management programs and program amendments submitted to it for approval. Additionally, it awards grants to states for planning and administration of coastal programs, evaluates the progress of the states in implementation, and oversees implementation of the federal consistency provisions of the CZMA.

The states are the action arm of the coastal management system. The states follow the framework and guidelines laid out in the federal act. States, for example, determine the boundaries of the coastal zone, the key coastal problems, the policies and laws that address them, and the state and local organizations required to be involved in implementation.

Within each state, a designated lead agency is the author and lead implementor of the coastal management program and the recipient of federal grants and matching funds for planning or administration. Frequently, the states provide technical assistance to other entities, build constituencies, research coastal management issues and trends, and promote new policies.

Local governments, including cities, counties and substate regional entities, are often primary implementors of state coastal policies and programs. They use traditional land use powers and infrastructure improvements to achieve coastal policy objectives. Another important means of implementation is through state agencies with resource management mandates, such as state agencies with submerged lands, fish and wildlife, or environmental responsibilities. These implementing units work closely with the lead state agency, and as a result can receive federal CZMA funds and benefit from the federal consistency mandates under the CZMA.

***

The national structure for CZM anticipates considerable diversity at the state and local levels. Such diversity creates a host of different approaches to coastal problems, which complicates determination of whether national goals are being met. Each state must choose the level of importance to afford different CZMA objectives and the approach to take in addressing them. Similarly, the form of management states choose can vary widely. OCRM has identified five program types among the states ranging from direct regulatory control by a single state agency to a shared regulatory approach involving other state and local agencies.

***

The five are: Direct (a single state agency regulates); Direct/LCP (a single state agency regulates but may delegate power to a local government under a local coastal program [LCP]); Networked (a single state agency coordinates the activities of other state and local agencies who have regulatory power); Networked/

More Later

We will cover the different coastal program structures in more detail later in this chapter. The three important points to remember until then are that (1) the CZMA requires states to develop mechanisms for involving all relevant state agencies in coastal management; (2) the CZMA requires states to involve local governments, for example, cities and counties, in coastal management; and, (3) the CZMA gives states significant flexibility in structuring coastal programs to meet these two requirements.

LCP (same as Networked with the addition of enforceable LCP); Networked/Regulatory (a lead state agency shares regulatory authority with other state agencies).

***

b. Decision-Making

The primary goal of the Act might be described as "encouraging states to develop mechanisms for allocating coastal land and resources." The following excerpt argues that this is the case, explains the various decision-making mechanisms that states had, as of 1985, developed, and attempts to measure their impact.

Robert G. Healy & Jeffrey A. Zinn, Environment and Development Conflicts in Coastal Zone Management

51 J. Am. Planning Ass'n 299 (1985)

The 1972 federal Coastal Zone Management Act . . . was motivated by high rates of coastal development nationwide. But the extent of the development pressures varied greatly from place to place, as did the type of development anticipated and the nature of the coastal resources involved. In many places, prevailing growth patterns did not seem to pose an all-or-nothing choice between development and environmental protection; instead they posed the problem of how best to modify or locate developments so as to allow both economic and environmental objectives to be achieved. Although it would not have been impossible to set minimum national standards for some types of environmental protection (e.g., a national shoreline setback), the resolution of many development controversies depended critically on exact knowledge of the nature of the development and on prevailing conditions at the site. Intellectually, setting specific standards at the federal level would have been a truly formidable task; politically, it would have meant offending powerful developmental interests and endorsing a massive federal intrusion into an area — the regulation of private land use — that was traditionally the domain of state and local governments. The framers of the federal coastal act also faced the question of how to deal with the fact that while several states already had begun aggressively to address coastal problems, others had done nothing.

Congress responded to these issues by calling for a balance between environment and development and by carefully leaving the actual striking of the balance to the individual states and territories. That was in marked contrast to the contemporaneous federal pollution control laws, which set minimum federal standards (though most of the specific standard-setting was left to federal administrative agencies) and strove for uniformity in regulation among the states. Under the federal coastal act, the state coastal "managers" were not to be advocates for either environment or development, but were to provide a rational framework for organizing the use of coastal resources, emphasizing conflict avoidance through long-range, comprehensive planning and the advance designation of permitted uses in the coastal zone.

Examining the legislative history of the Coastal Zone Management Act of 1972, one cannot help but be struck by the explicitness of its mandate to simultaneously protect the environment of the coastal zone and permit continued economic development there. "S. 3507 has as its main purpose," said the Senate's committee report on its version of the act, "the encouragement and assistance of states in preparing and implementing management programs to preserve, protect, develop, *and* where possible restore the resources of the coastal zone of the United States." The House committee report said, "Your committee believes that it is of national importance that the Federal government encourage the states to arrange for the optimum utilization of coastal zone resources, coupled with an adequate protection of the zone's natural environment."

The notion of the federal coastal program not as another environmental protection program but as a means of balancing developmental and environmental interests also recurred in the testimony given while Congress was considering the coastal legislation. Walter Hickel, then Secretary of the Interior, pointed out the wildlife, recreational, and esthetic values of the coastal zone, but he also posed "the challenge to provide facilities to meet the requirements of a growing population — such as power plants, housing, and transportation systems." The legislation represented, one congressman declared, "a delicate but practical balance . . . a rational middle ground, where the forces of industry and ecology can live and work together."

Quick Questions

Think about this quote for a few minutes. Is there such a thing as a "rational middle ground"? Is there an objective definition of "rational"? How would you define that word? Also, think back to Chapter 5, in which we explored the competing interests in coastal land and resource use. If the goal is to maximize the value of coastal land and resources, how should we go about achieving that goal?

The federal act was quite explicit about the procedures states should follow in setting up their coastal management programs, but it gave them considerable leeway in program content. As the head of the federal agency administering the act put it in testimony before Congress, "... Our reading of the Federal act ... suggests that Congress wished States to carefully consider the future of their shorelines and the purposes *to which they wanted them to be put* and then to enact enforceable policies to achieve those goals."

This flexibility made it possible for states to incorporate their existing legislation and programs affecting coastal resources into a comprehensive program without necessarily changing any of the components. Indeed, the vast majority of state coastal management programs are made up of several discrete pieces of legislation, coordinated or "networked" to a greater or lesser degree. According to the federal coastal management office, more than one-third of the twenty-eight states with approved coastal programs did not have to pass any state legislation in order to meet requirements for participation in the federal program.

The lack of substantive federal standards does not necessarily mean state coastal programs are weak, but it does mean they are very diverse. That diversity greatly complicates the analysis of how coastal zone management has affected environment and development. First, because the individual states have a great deal of discretion in deciding whether environment or development should be favored, the striking of the "balance" naturally will vary from state to state. In most state coastal programs there are many decisionmakers — for example, one administrative agency may affect the intensity of building on dunes, while an entirely different agency may decide on the amount of oil drilling permitted on state-owned tidelands. Some states leave a great deal of discretionary authority to local officials, whose attitudes toward environment and development can differ greatly from one jurisdiction to another. Some variation also is likely in state and local decision-making over time in response to shifts in political alignments and public attitudes.

Second, as we will detail later in this article, states have implemented coastal management through a wide variety of planning and management tools. Even if two states were precisely alike in the intensity of their desire to protect coastal resources, they probably would differ in result because of the great variation in the tools employed by various states. This factor is even more important because where data on program implementation are available, they tend to describe the application of specific tools (*e.g.*, number of permits approved or denied) rather than actual effects on resources (*e.g.*, the status of coastal wildlife).

Third, considering the cumulative amount of money that has been spent on coastal zone management and the economic and environmental importance of the coastal resources that have been affected by decisions made under those programs, there is a surprising lack of evaluation literature. To be sure, there are numerous speeches, statements, and pieces of testimony by both developmental and environmental interests lauding or criticizing federal and state coastal programs. But rarely is systematic evidence of program effects presented. Perhaps the most that can be said of such material is that because neither environmentalists nor development interests are entirely happy with the federal program as a whole, we can assume that the "balance" has not tipped decisively in either direction.

Because of the diversity among states that we have described, it does not seem possible to identify, much less evaluate, the effects of coastal zone management in general. Yet there are many opportunities for analyzing the specific effects of components of state programs. There is much less such literature than one would expect, although it is notable that the most comprehensive (and arguably the most interesting) state program, California's, has been the subject of a number of evaluative studies.

What specific kinds of environment/development conflicts actually have become the subject matter of coastal zone management? The range of conflicts subject to the CZM process has varied tremendously among the states, depending partly on each state's physical characteristics and development pressures, partly on the geographic scope of its legally defined "coastal zone," and partly on how each state has defined "development" and identified "coastal resources." At one extreme of inclusiveness was California, which not only defined a very broad geographic limit for its coastal zone, but also defined the scope of coastal concerns to include such topics as farmland protection, historic preservation, and the provision of low-income housing. One California coastal commissioner has remarked that "the [California] coast is 1,100 miles long and there is every kind of pressure on us. The only thing we didn't have to deal with is glaciers."

Toward the other extreme are states such as Rhode Island, which initially extended the regulatory authority of its Coastal Resource Management Council only to the water area of the coastal zone and to a limited range of land-based activities potentially affecting tidal waters.

One source of substantial differences among the states in the concerns of their coastal programs was whether or not they faced the possibility of offshore oil and gas development. This type of development became an important subject of coastal management programs in such states as Alaska, California, Louisiana, New Jersey, New York, and Texas, while other states, such as Pennsylvania, Alabama, and Hawaii, paid it relatively little attention.

Although these variations among states are quite large, one might ask what developmental and environmental concerns have been of most importance in coastal zone management when the nation as a whole is considered. To answer that question, we examined the subjects covered by some 1,044 reports and studies produced by or for state coastal agencies (with federal coastal program funding) during the period from the beginning of the federal program through 1982. An annotated bibliography, published in 1983, presented a detailed list of subject headings for these documents. We theorized that the issues that the individual states considered worthy of study would be closely related to the issues most frequently encountered in coastal zone management.

Eliminating ambiguous or exclusively procedure-oriented index headings (*e.g.,* "federal consistency"), we divided the remainder into subjects primarily concerned with development or use of coastal resources (*e.g.*, "energy facility siting"), those primarily concerned with the coastal environment (*e.g.*, "barrier islands"), and those concerned with environment/development interactions (*e.g.*, "pollution"). The results, presented in the table below, give a broad picture of the subjects that have most concerned the state coastal programs thus far.

There is no particular significance in the fact that the number of reports concerned with environmental topics (844) is near the number concerned with development (778). What is significant is the distribution of topics within each category. It illustrates a breadth of state program issues that range from boating to agriculture and from estuaries to cultural and historical resources. Within the development category, the most common subject for study was recreation/tourism,

Table 1. Environment and development concerns in coastal management (number of citations out of possible 1,044)

Development concerns		Environmental concerns		Environment/development interactions	
Recreation/tourism	140	Coastal resources	118	Erosion/sedimentation	90
Petroleum industry	65	Wetlands	103	Environmental impact	38
Energy facility siting	65	Fish/fisheries	85	Conflicting uses	36
Facility siting	62	Public access	82	Floods/flooding	34
Ports/waterfronts	58	Critical areas	48	Oil Pollution/effects	29
Energy	45	Vegetation	47	Energy impacts	21
Transportation	43	Marine biology	46	Pollution	17
Industry/commerce	42	Wildlife	46	Water pollution	13
Population	29	Water quality	44		
Dredging	29	Beaches/dunes	36		
Marinas	28	Water resources	35		
Boating	25	Estuaries	34		
Growth	22	Aesthetics	28		
Shipping	18	Resource protection	22		
Agriculture	18	Living marine resources	21		
Water development projects	14	Cultural/historical resources	12		
Navigation	14	Groundwater	10		
Oil and gas	14	Barrier islands	8		
Marine mining	9	Open space	7		
Coal transportation/storage	9	Preservation	5		
Energy transportation/ storage	9	Coral reefs	4		
Forestry/logging	7	Air resources	3		
Waterfront development	7				
Aquaculture	6				
Total	778	Total	844	Total	278

followed by several aspects of energy and industrial development. Among environmental subjects, the ones most commonly dealt with in the 1,044 reports (aside from the broad subject "coastal resources") were wetlands, fish and fisheries, and public access. The prominence of the latter and of such subjects as aesthetics and cultural and historical resources illustrates how many of the state coastal programs went beyond protection of natural systems to encompass a wide range of "human environment" concerns.

The topics studied also illustrate the landward and seaward inclusiveness of the coastal zone. For example, eighteen studies dealt with agriculture, a land-based activity that can have significant effects on the quality of coastal waters. Another land-based activity, the subject of seven studies, is forestry/logging, which not only affects the visual quality of the coastal area but also may produce damaging soil erosion. Topics arising on the seaward side of the coastal zone included the fishing industry, marine mining, and development of the outer continental shelf. The number of possible ways in which the various forms of development can come into conflict with an equally wide range of environmental values offer yet another reason the impacts of coastal zone management have proven so difficult to measure.

The 1972 CZMA gave the states enormous leeway not only in the relative weight they could apply to environmental and development values but also in how the balance between them would be struck. The twenty-eight state coastal programs exhibit an extremely large number of permutations in (1) what tools are used to allocate the coast among alternative uses; (2) who actually makes which decisions; and (3) which parties, including developers, environmental organizations, local governments, and individual citizens, have standing to participate in the deliberations or otherwise to influence the decisions.

[Among the] principal tools that have come to be used in coastal management are regulatory permit systems, comprehensive planning, land use designations by zoning and subdivision ordinances, selective land acquisition and restoration, promotion of desirable coastal development, [and] negotiation. . . . States use these and other tools in various combinations to manage their coastal resources. . . .

Permit Systems

Requiring a permit for various types of coastal development has proved extremely popular as a coastal management tool, probably for two reasons. First, state and local governments traditionally have found permits useful in both land use and environmental regulation. Both the regulated and the regulators, as well as the state courts, are accustomed to permit systems and accept their legitimacy. Second, many of the state coastal programs are amalgams of existing special-purpose permit programs, particularly those requiring permits for dredging, using state-owned tidelands, depositing fill material, building bulkheads, installing water supply and sewage disposal, and modifying wetlands and dunes.

Some state programs are built from a patchwork of single-purpose permit requirements; others, such as in California, Rhode Island, and North Carolina, have created a general-purpose coastal permit (obtained from either a state or a local agency). The general purpose programs vary greatly in scope: California's applied (during the 1972-76 period) to all development in the entire coastal zone; Rhode Island's only to some forms of development; and North Carolina's only within state-designated "areas of environmental concern." Seven states have special programs for reviewing large-scale projects, usually resulting in a special permit.

Regulation inherently restricts development. Even if it results in no denial of permission, the cost of applying for a permit, the time consumed, and the increased uncertainty of approval present at least a modest disincentive to develop. Arguably, in some states, such as Massachusetts and Florida, coastal zone management under the federal law did not actually add to the preexisting regulatory burden, although it may have increased multiagency scrutiny of permit applications and raised the level of enforcement. But certainly there are several states, such as North Carolina, where participation in the federal program resulted in new substantive regulations and where it had an observable restricting effect on projects.

Examination of permit data offers one of the few opportunities for quantitative study of the degree to which coastal zone management has restricted development. That is extremely difficult in practice, however, not only because appropriate data are hard to find and difficult to interpret, but also because the state programs are so diverse. Probably the richest single data source is the record of the California Coastal Commission, which during 1973-76 operated a permit system covering virtually all coastal development. The coast was defined as a zone stretching from the three-mile limit of state territorial sovereignty to 1,000 yards inland of mean high tide. The California program is generally considered the most ambitious and among the most environmentally stringent of the state efforts.

> **Quick Questions**
>
> Does the imposition of conditions fully explain the high rate at which agencies grant permits? What other factors might help explain it?

Of the first 15,025 permits processed by the regional commissions in California, 488 (3.2 percent) were denied. The state commission denied 262 on appeal. Adjusting for double counting (permits denied on both levels), Healy and Rosenberg (1979) estimated that fewer than 4.5 percent of the total number of permits sought were ultimately denied.

Because a permit was required even for very small projects, such as a major addition to a single family house, it might be expected that larger, and hence more environmentally threatening, projects would have been more likely to be denied. There are no statewide figures on value of permits, but the busiest of the six regional commissions, in the Los Angeles-Orange County area, denied 13.5 percent of the dollar value of permits acted upon.

Development throughout the state's coastal zone was affected in two ways other than through outright denial of permits. First, planned projects, including some extremely large projects that can be identified specifically, were never submitted to the commissions, because denial was considered likely. Second, a large proportion of the projects, including virtually all the projects approved on appeal by the state commission, were subject to conditions ranging from various environmental protection features to deep cuts in project density.

Based on these permit data, it is clear that the California program did have a significant restrictive effect on development, but stopped well short of prohibiting all development in the coastal zone. The attachment of conditions to permits was crucial, both as a means of reducing densities and as a way of limiting specific environmental effects.

North Carolina's Division of Coastal Management operates two distinct permit systems, but unfortunately it does not separate its tally of dredge-and-fill permits from the more general permits required for major developments in areas of environmental concern. Between 1978 and 1983 the combined total of the two types of permits was 1,045 granted and 55 denied, an approval ratio of 95 percent. Part of the high approval ratio is a result of a state-operated preapplication counseling service, which identifies possible problems for applicants. Nearly all permits are subject to conditions.

Louisiana requires a permit for any activity that has a direct and significant effect on the state's coastal waters. The coastal zone section in the state's Department of Natural Resources processes an average of 2,000 permits yearly, about 80 percent of which are related to oil and gas development. In 1983, fewer than 1 percent of permits sought were denied, and 3.9 percent were withdrawn. But 45 percent were issued with conditions.

Journal articles, monographs, and papers presented at professional meetings describe or analyze specific permit cases. These, too, tend to show a mixed pattern of approvals and denials, considerable variation in environmental protection from state to state, and heavy reliance on conditional permits. A type of permit condition that has become increasingly popular is mitigation, that is, requiring some form of environmental enhancement to compensate for environmental damage caused by a development project. For example, projects causing unavoidable damage to wetlands may be allowed, provided that the project proponents restore degraded wetlands either offsite or nearby.

Comprehensive Planning

Comprehensive planning, in various forms, was a coastal management tool in almost all states and territories with approved programs. The level of government responsible for the initial planning, or for developing general guidelines, and the level of government responsible for detailed planning varies among states. As with permitting, California (in 1973-76) used a highly centralized form of planning: six regional coastal commissions prepared draft plans, which then were coordinated, and to a degree superseded, by a single state plan. After 1976, local governments were to draw up their own local comprehensive plans, but these, too, were subject to detailed review and possible amendment by the state coastal commission.

Oregon has relied on local comprehensive planning from the start, although it is subject to rather elaborate state guidelines and to state review. Washington's program is similar but has provided even more local leeway. Florida's coastal planning requirement leaves both the task and the authority to local government, simply specifying that all local comprehensive land use plans in coastal jurisdictions must contain "coastal zone protection elements." But there is no requirement that the state set minimum standards for the review and approval of coastal plan elements.

In recent years, a hybrid of comprehensive planning called "special area management planning" (SAMP) has appeared. SAMP refers to anticipatory planning for an area where many competing uses and values are concentrated, undertaken before decisions must be made that incrementally affect the area. The SAMP process is supposed to conclude with a plan that reflects trade-offs between development and environmental protection. All the important players (permitting agencies, development agencies, and environmental protection agencies) are involved in the planning process, so the result, if successful, is an informal agreement to allow the pattern of activities described in the plan. If development proposals are submitted that exceed the plan (*e.g.*, a larger fill area), several participants are likely to oppose the proposed action. The first attempt to implement the SAMP concept was at Grays Harbor, a small port along the ocean coast of Washington. Congress was sufficiently impressed with this concept, especially as it appeared to be working in Grays Harbor, to incorporate it into the Coastal Zone Management Improvement Act of 1980. More recently, SAMP processes have been initiated by coastal planners at a growing number of other coastal sites, but few have been completed.

Besides truly comprehensive planning, states also have used more detailed planning to anticipate and avoid possible environment/development conflicts. Michigan, for example, has used federal CZM funding to identify, designate, and manage more than 125 miles of high-risk erosion areas along the Lake Michigan shoreline. New Jersey has used planning as a means of balancing demand for housing in the fast-growing Atlantic City area with the protection of environmentally sensitive areas nearby. New Jersey also is developing a program to protect dune systems and limit development that would affect natural processes in those systems. And nearly all states practice specific planning for energy facilities.

In theory, planning, whether limited or comprehensive, is neutral with respect to environmental protection and to development. In practice, it probably favors environmental protection somewhat by identifying natural constraints that would not have been appreciated in the absence of planning. Planning's ability to identify possible conflicts very early in the siting process, however, means it may aid both environment and development simultaneously.

From the standpoint of environment, planning has been used frequently to identify critical areas where limitations or conditions should be imposed on development to protect natural systems. According to the federal coastal management office, eighteen of the states and territories with approved programs have specific provisions for identifying critical areas. Planning can aid developers as well, by helping them learn, before they spend too much money on a given site, where developments are likely to run afoul of environmental concerns. For example, comprehensive planning for the siting of oil refineries on the East Coast of the United States might well have avoided the dozens of unsuccessful attempts during the 1970s to site them individually. As one coastal planning researcher has commented, ". . . Planning and regulatory processes capable of anticipating and averting unwanted consequences of land use and development decisions should help the private sector meet its need to minimize future uncertainty."

Zoning and Subdivision Controls

Although coastal zone management is a newcomer among the concerns of planners, two very old tools — zoning and subdivision controls — have been used prominently in its implementation. These tools typically are used as ways of implementing the coastal policies newly introduced into local comprehensive plans. (They are important local plan implementation tools in California, Oregon, and Washington, for example.) Some states require their use in sensitive shoreline areas. For example, Maine requires local governments to have zoning and subdivision controls on all shorelands within 250 feet of the normal highwater mark. Delaware and Hawaii have what amounts to state-administered zoning on their shorelines. The former prohibits "heavy industry" in undeveloped portions of its coastal zone, while the latter has divided the entire state, including coastal areas, into broad land use categories (Hawaii's practice of state zoning antedates specific interest in coastal zone management.)

In theory, zoning and subdivision controls could promote development by reserving land for specified developed uses and preventing parcel divisions that would interfere with those uses. In practice, however, we must count those tools as primarily neutral or somewhat pro-environment, because they generally have been used to limit rather than promote the intensity of development in sensitive areas.

Acquisition and Restoration

The tool that is probably most unambiguously protective of the natural environment is acquisition of land by state and local government. Use of this tool has been promoted extensively, and sometimes funded, by coastal programs. The most obvious example is the estuarine sanctuaries program, created under section 315 of the 1972 CZMA. Under this program, states are given matching grants to acquire and operate estuarine areas as natural field laboratories. Often a portion of the sanctuary is already in protected status, and the designation is used to expand the area under protection or to develop user programs that show the public the value of these protected resources. By early 1985, fifteen sanctuaries had been designated. Outlays under this program totaled almost $19 million by the end of fiscal 1983. Although preservation of representative coastal ecosystems is the principal object, it is interesting to note that some of the sanctuaries have seen small amounts of development (trails, boardwalks, visitor centers) meant to enhance their usefulness in research and public education. Several states, notably California and Florida, have acquired lands for state parks or preserves as a result of coastal planning studies; the money usually has come from budgets outside the state coastal program.

In some cases, coastal programs have helped restore degraded lands and return them to uses that protect environmental values. The California Coastal Conservancy has been involved in acquisition to improve access to the coast, lot consolidation, agricultural land preservation, and stream and wetland restoration. And in Maine, the coastal program gave a grant to a local volunteer group to clean up and reseed clam flats on tidelands already owned by the state.

Promotion of Development

A modest, but by no means insignificant, amount of effort has been made by state coastal programs to actively promote certain uses of the coastal zone that they consider desirable, notably recreation, water transportation, and fisheries and other port uses. This effort often has involved assisting development that would aid those uses. In Maine, for example, localities have used coastal zone management funds for preliminary planning for fishing piers — and in two cases to leverage state and federal construction funding. Maine localities also have used coastal monies for waterfront development, recreation projects, and solid waste disposal projects.

The California Coastal Conservancy has initiated several urban waterfront projects, including a restoration of an important recreational pier in Santa Barbara. It also has accomplished more than 100 beach access improvements; for example, in Manhattan Beach, it constructed two access ramps for handicapped visitors. Coastal Energy Impact Program funds have been used to build boating slips and a marina in Massachusetts, and New Hampshire's coastal program has aided a port authority marketing and foreign trade zone program. A large portion of funds provided under the CEIP program has gone to community development projects that ameliorate impacts of past offshore energy activities, particularly Louisiana and Alaska. . . . Both California and New Jersey have tried to retain or increase low-income housing in the coastal zone, though in practice this generally has meant reserving units in proposed projects for low-income people rather than encouraging construction of more housing units. [In 1981, the California legislature removed language from the Coastal Act that allowed the Coastal Commission to protect or require below-market-rate housing.] Waterfront redevelopment has become the most prominent coastal activity in many urban areas in recent years.

Negotiation

Coastal zone management has had the unofficial effect of encouraging negotiation between proponents and opponents of development. Negotiation among staff members of various state agencies almost certainly was foreseen by the framers of the federal law. This negotiation frequently occurs between agencies that are likely to be pro-development, such as a public utilities commission, and others likely to be more pro-environmental protection, such as a department of fish and game.

Another, probably less well-anticipated, type of negotiation is a result of the large amount of public participation built into some coastal programs. This has brought developers and environmentalists into contact with each other as seldom has occurred before, in planning and regulatory hearings, not just in the courts after a decision has been made. It is likely that more frequent contact has led to at least a modicum of negotiation between those parties, either through face-to-face talks or through mutual attempts to anticipate the other's actions. On balance, increased negotiation should benefit the environmental interests, because previously their views had no place in the decision process. Measuring the benefits of negotiation is almost impossible, because unlike regulation or planning, this process does not leave a "paper trail" of official documents. Ball and Symons (1983) mention that

California Coastal Commission staff members trained in conflict management have acted as informal mediators between state air pollution regulators and an oil company in a dispute about air emissions associated with offshore oil drilling activities. The commission also has helped establish informal policy dialogues among various parties concerned with such drilling. The city of Long Beach, California, created a committee with representatives from twenty-nine environmental, development, and other groups to seek consensus on the "local coastal program" mandated under the state's coastal act.

Professional mediation also has been used in a number of coastal disputes. For example, mediation was an important tool in developing a management plan for the Columbia River estuary. Given the growing popularity of environmental negotiation as a means of reducing conflict about environmental issues, negotiation may prove to be an increasingly important function of the relatively open planning processes that are associated with coastal zone management.

✳✳✳

4. Incentives for State Participation

In order to entice states to, as Senator Hollings desired, stay ahead of the federal government, that is, to develop coastal programs before the exigencies of energy needs forced Congress to do it for them, the Act provides the states with two incentives. As noted, all eligible states and territories have now opted to participate in the CZMA program. Thus, the current role of these incentives is to keep states in the program. (A state could, if it so chose, leave the program.)

a. Funding

In the original version of the Act, Congress made three kinds of funding available to participating states. First, Section 305 provided that NOAA could make annual grants to coastal states "for the purpose of assisting in the development of" a state's coastal management program. Second, Section 306 authorized NOAA to make grants to states to be used in "administering the state's management program" once it had been developed and approved. Third, under Section 312, NOAA could make funds available to states for the "acquisition, development, and operation of estuarine sanctuaries for the purpose of creating natural field laboratories to gather data and make studies of the natural and human processes occurring within the estuaries of the coastal zone." (This provision marked the birth of what today is known as the National Estuarine Research Reserve Program. There are currently 28 reserves in 22 states and Puerto Rico.) Each of these programs required the applying state to commit to contributing some percentage of matching funds in order to receive federal funding. In later amendments to the Act, Congress repealed the provision relating to program development grants. Today, the Act authorizes NOAA to make six different kinds of grants to states (each of which requires state matching funds in various percentages). In addition to administration and estuarine reserve grants, Congress has given NOAA the power to make grants for the following:

- *Coastal resource improvement.* States may request funds to be used for one of four purposes: (1) preservation of special natural or historic resources; (2) redevelopment "of deteriorating and underutilized urban waterfronts and ports"; (3) the provision of access to public beaches and other public coastal areas and to coastal waters, e.g., by purchasing easements and land; and (4) to develop a coordinated process among state agencies to regulate and issue permits for aquaculture facilities in the coastal zone. 16 U.S.C. § 1455a(b).
- *Development of coastal non-point pollution control programs.* NOAA may make grants to help states develop programs aimed at reducing threats from non-point sources of pollution (run-off) to water quality in coastal areas, and to help states thus achieve water quality standards in those areas. (We will learn more about the non-point source water pollution provisions of the federal Clean Water Act, and about how states are addressing this problem, later in this chapter.) 16 U.S.C. § 1455b(f). States who do not develop such programs may lose their eligibility for administration grants and other federal funds.
- *Land acquisition.* Congress authorized funds for the acquisition of land for the purposes of acquiring natural areas of particular importance or whose acquisition furthers the goals of a state's coastal management or coastal land acquisition program. 16 U.S.C. § 1456-1(b).
- *Program modifications.* Given that all eligible states ultimately joined the CZMA system, the grant program created to help states develop coastal programs was no longer necessary. At the same time, new coastal uses are emerging and public values are changing. Thus, Congress replaced the original provision with one that allows NOAA to make grants to states in aid of revamping and improving existing coastal programs to meet evolving needs. 16 U.S.C. § 1456b(a).

To give a sense of the amount of money involved, NOAA reported that, in 2005, it made about $94 million in grants to the states under these programs. Because the states must provide matching funds, one can estimate that the total amount of federal and state money spent on these activities is somewhere in the range of (at least) $150 to $200 million, or an average of about $4 to $6 million per state.

b. Consistency Review

One might argue that the second incentive created by the Act, known as "consistency review," is an even greater enticement than the various federal grant programs. As you know from your other courses, including Constitutional Law, federal statutes may and often do preempt state law within the same substantive area. The consistency provisions of the CZMA turn the tables, allowing state coastal law to preempt federal law to a certain degree.

Specifically, Section 307 of the CZMA (16 U.S.C. § 1456) provides that federal agencies must ensure that all actions they conduct, fund, or permit, and that have a direct or indirect environmental, economic, or social impact on a state's coastal zone, are *consistent with the enforceable policies* contained in that state's management program. (The word "indirect" means that federal actions conducted in areas outside the coastal zone, either inland or in federal ocean waters, are covered by the consistency provisions.) Consistency review gives states the special power to avoid or shape the impact of federal actions. These federal actions include not only projects directed by a federal agency, but more important, permits for activities conducted by private firms and individuals. Activities that might require a federal permit include the dredging and filling of wetlands, the construction of ports and marinas, and the extraction of petroleum and other natural resources.

We will return later to the specific procedures of consistency review and to the question of how disputes about whether particular actions are consistent with an enforceable policy are resolved.

points for discussion

1. *National and local interests.* What are some examples of the national interests that Congress believed warranted federal involvement in coastal land use decision-making? How did Congress pay homage to the long-standing tradition of local control over land use? Congress, of course, is not a monolith of interests. What does your experience and intuition tell you about the diverse politics that shaped the final text? Which states, in other words, were likely to have had concerns about how other coastal states were regulating, or were going to regulate, use of their coastal resources?

2. *The CZMA model.* What do you think of the unique brand of federalism manifested in the CZMA? Do you think it might be applicable to other areas of environmental law, such as water or air pollution? What are the trade-offs to be considered in deciding how to allocate regulatory power between states and the federal government? Do you think the CZMA model would work as a model for regulating land use generally, that is, in non-coastal areas? Can you think of important national interests in the regulation and use of non-coastal lands? Why might Congress be more interested in shaping coastal land use law than non-coastal land use law?

3. *Checks on state action.* One potential downside of Congress's allocation of regulatory power to coastal states (through both consistency power and vague language in Section 1455(d)) is that states will implement coastal programs and policies that ultimately do not serve the national interest. What extra-statutory means does Congress have for ensuring that this does not happen?

4. *Structure of state programs.* Do you think a centralized state coastal program would work better or more efficiently than a networked program? Why or why not? What are the trade-offs involved?

5. *Permits and planning.* What are the limits on planning? Put differently, what are the up- and down-sides of very specific planning? Given these considerations, what is the ideal relationship between permits and planning?

6. A *"big picture" question.* Do you see the reflection of common law doctrines such as the public trust doctrine and upland owners' rights in the CZMA? Does state common law limit the design and implementation of state coastal programs? How should state common law inform design and implementation? Or, can and should states think of coastal programs as a substitute for coastal common law?

B. STATE COASTAL PROGRAMS AND STATUTES: A SAMPLER

Summarizing the specific contents of all state and territorial coastal programs would be an overwhelming, and thus not very useful, approach to learning. As an alternative, this section features a set of examples of interesting and controversial "enforceable policies" found within various state coastal programs. As you read through this section, refer back to Section 1452 of the CZMA and see if you can tie the state policies to one or more of the goals Congress enumerated in that section.

The court decisions in this section are meant to illustrate state coastal statutes and regulations. At the same time, these decisions are the result of litigation, usually between landowners and the state. Thus, in addition to providing some examples of state law, they will also give you some insight into the limits, constitutional and otherwise, on state regulatory power. As noted earlier, many of the most important Fifth Amendment takings cases have arisen out of coastal conflicts, specifically, conflicts between upland owners and their public neighbor on the other side of the legal coastline.

1. Erosion Policy

Erosion is obviously a central issue in coastal law. It not only shaped the development of the common law of the coast, but it continues to dominate the realm of statutes. You should be able to make the case that at least half of the goals Congress set out in Section 1452(2) of the CZMA are related to erosion policy.

What do we mean by erosion policy? By policy, we mean the objective that specific legal rules are meant to achieve. What are the policy options with respect to erosion? In order to begin the conversation about erosion policy, it is important to understand the status quo. In other words, what would the shoreline look like in the absence of an erosion policy? Fortunately (or unfortunately), answering this question is easy because, until the last 30 years, most states did not have a policy.

In the "no policy scenario," a landowner — faced with erosion caused by tides, currents, and storms — would be able to construct some form of hard "erosion control device," such as a seawall or bulkhead, along the seaward boundary of his property. These structures give some protection to the upland property and provide

Photo: Library of Congress

Figure 9-2. Seawall at St. Augustine, Florida

the owner with the incentive to build a more expensive home or building than he otherwise would. They also give landowners the sense (often inaccurate) that they can safely build structures close to the water's edge.

If erosion control devices protect and increase the value of private property, why is there a problem? As noted in Chapter 5, and as illustrated in Figures 9-2 and 9-3, these devices can have detrimental impacts on the public.

The effect of beachfront hard structures on the public is not limited to the decreased width of the public trust, wet sand beach. Loss of beach and aesthetic impacts can cause injury to the public in the form of lost tourism and tax revenues. Ecologically important intertidal and dune ecosystems vanish as well.

Most of these same concerns exist with respect to the use of hard structures on non-beachfront, estuarine, and marsh shorelines. Bulkheads can protect upland property, but also prevent the marsh from migrating toward the upland as sea levels rise. Marsh plants are eventually fully submerged, resulting in the elimination of highly productive ecosystems.

In addition to these kinds of costs, all of which result from gradual shoreline change, there are also social costs associated with sudden events such as hurricanes

> **Quick Question**
>
> Storms and tsunamis can obviously result in massive loss of life and private property. What other kinds of costs result?

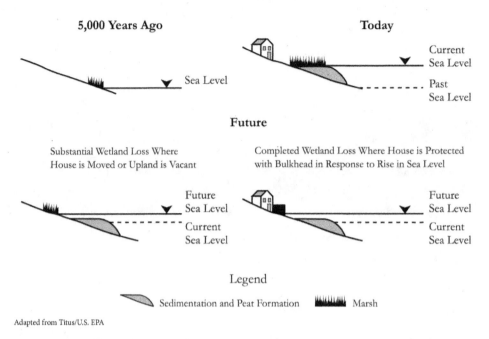

Evolution of a Marsh as Sea Level Rises

Adapted from Titus/U.S. EPA

Figure 9-3. Effect of Sea Level Rises on Marshes

and tsunamis. These costs are affected by erosion policy because the presence of structures close to the water and the absence of natural buffers such as dunes and marshes increase the amount of damage caused by such events.

The government has three erosion policy options. First, it can maintain the status quo by allowing upland owners to install erosion control devices and to build homes and other structures wherever they like. (The government could go further by subsidizing these activities or building public erosion control devices.) Second, the government can seek to maintain the beach, dunes, marshes, and estuaries by discouraging the use of some or all kinds of erosion control devices. This creates what some have dubbed a "rolling easement," allowing erosion (and accretion) to take its natural course. James G. Titus, *Rising Seas, Coastal Erosion, and the Takings Clause: How to Save Wetlands and Beaches Without Hurting Property Owners*, 57 MD. L. REV. 1279 (1998).[1] The state can discourage the use of erosion control devices by making their use illegal. It might also implement land-use measures, such as setbacks, which decrease upland owners' financial incentive to invest in erosion control. Subsidizing beach renourishment projects might have the same

---

1. The rolling easement described here is a negative easement; it would allow the holder (the state) to prevent activity (the use of erosion control devices) on the burdened parcel. You will see that the term "rolling easement" can also be used to describe an affirmative easement (a public right-of-way over dry sand). There is no reason the same term needs to be used for both types of easement, but this is unfortunately what has transpired.

effect. Finally, the state can encourage active retreat from the shoreline. Legal tools for accomplishing this include, again, setbacks that limit or prevent construction close to shorelines. The government might also embark on a program of purchasing vulnerable shoreline property through voluntary agreements or eminent domain.

Today, most coastal states employ a mixture of these policies and legal options. For example, a 1999 paper indicates that 27 of 29 coastal states studied have some form of law in place restricting upland owners' ability to construct hard structures. Tina Bernd-Cohen & Melissa Gordon, *State Coastal Program Effectiveness in Protecting Natural Beaches, Dunes, Bluffs, and Rocky Shores*, 27 COASTAL MGMT. 187, 196 (1999).

> **Quick Question**
>
> How do setbacks and limiting the size of buildings that can be constructed on upland parcels alter landowners' incentives?

The following materials illustrate state approaches to setbacks and erosion control devices and the legal issues these approaches raise.

a. Setbacks: South Carolina

In the coastal law context, a "setback rule" is a rule that limits or prevents construction within a specified distance from the legal coastline. Typically, these rules allow or require state coastal agencies to establish two different, imaginary lines running roughly parallel to the legal coastline. The line closest to the legal coastline, sometimes known as a "baseline," is drawn along the line of dunes or vegetation. Then, further landward, the agency draws a "setback line" parallel to the baseline. *See* Figure 9-4. The effect of the two lines is to create two zones for the spatial regulation of land use: the area seaward of the baseline and the area between the baseline and

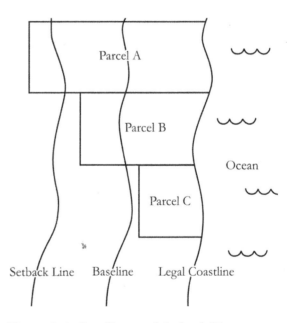

Figure 9-4. Baselines and Setback Lines
Oceanfront setbacks. Notice how the rules might differently affect Parcels A, B, and C.

the setback line. The law might require that the distance between the baseline and the setback line be uniform, for example, 100 feet, or that it be based on a variable, such as the annual erosion rate at each location. The rules might also tie the distance between the two lines to the size of a proposed structure. For example, under North Carolina law,

(A) A building or other structure less than 5,000 square feet requires a minimum setback of 60 feet or 30 times the shoreline erosion rate, whichever is greater;

(B) A building or other structure greater than or equal to 5,000 square feet but less than 10,000 square feet requires a minimum setback of 120 feet or 60 times the shoreline erosion rate, whichever is greater;

(C) A building or other structure greater than or equal to 10,000 square feet but less than 20,000 square feet requires a minimum setback of 130 feet or 65 times the shoreline erosion rate, whichever is greater . . .

. . . and so on. 15A N.C. Admin. Code 07H .0306: *General Use Standards for Ocean Hazard Areas.*

As noted above, there are several possible policy objectives behind these rules. First, limiting or banning construction is an alternative to limiting or banning the installation of hard erosion control structures. Titus explains:

> **Quick Question**
>
> How do the North Carolina ocean hazard setback rules affect landowners' incentives?

Setbacks and other development restrictions can protect natural shores for two reasons. First, they may reduce the value of the vulnerable land below the point where the land is worth protecting from the sea. For example, if an owner has a large lot and the setback requires her to build her house at the landward edge of the lot, the setback, from the owner's perspective, may reduce the value of the seaward land to zero.

Second, these restrictions may prevent the owner from increasing the value enough to make the land worth protecting. Consider a proposed $100,000 house on a $20,000 agricultural lot, for which a bulkhead costs $40,000. Once the house is built, the combined $120,000 property is worth protecting, but if a setback prevents construction, the land alone may not be worth protecting. Alternatively, if the house is built, but is designed so that it can be moved for $5,000, the land may still not be worth protecting.

James G. Titus, *supra*, at 1311-12.

In addition to altering landowners' incentives, setbacks have other benefits. Bernd-Cohen and Gordon argue that:

Setback laws have a dual purpose: (1) to protect the natural beach and dune or bluff systems as storm buffers; and (2) to reduce the loss of life and property from hurricanes and other storm events. Implementation of these laws has reduced the number and size of new structures that can be built on the shoreline and has located those structures that are built as far landward from the water's edge as possible to prevent erosion from reaching the structures during their expected useful life.

> **Quick Question**
>
> Although states can (and sometimes do) use setback rules for the development of property along non-oceanfront shorelines, they more commonly use them along the oceanfront. Why do you think this is?

Tina Bernd-Cohen & Melissa Gordon, *supra*, at 198. They can also enhance the ecological and aesthetic qualities of the beach environment.

As you would guess, the rules governing construction in the area seaward of the baseline are always more stringent than those applicable to the area between the baseline and the setback line. The 1988 amendments to South Carolina's coastal law put strict limits on construction seaward of the baseline. A landowner challenged those limits in the following case.

Lucas v. South Carolina Coastal Council

505 U.S. 1003 (1992)

Justice SCALIA delivered the opinion of the Court.

In 1986, petitioner David H. Lucas paid $975,000 for two residential lots on the Isle of Palms in Charleston County, South Carolina, on which he intended to build single-family homes. In 1988, however, the South Carolina Legislature enacted the Beachfront Management Act . . . , which had the direct effect of barring petitioner from erecting any permanent habitable structures on his two parcels. A state trial court found that this prohibition rendered Lucas's parcels "valueless." This case requires us to decide whether the Act's dramatic effect on the economic value of Lucas's lots accomplished a taking of private property under the Fifth and Fourteenth Amendments requiring the payment of "just compensation."

I.

A.

South Carolina's expressed interest in intensively managing development activities in the so-called "coastal zone" dates from 1977 when, in the aftermath of Congress's passage of the federal Coastal Zone Management Act of 1972 . . . , the legislature enacted a Coastal Zone Management Act of its own. . . . In its original form, the South Carolina Act required owners of coastal zone land that qualified as a "critical area" (defined in the legislation to include beaches and immediately adjacent sand dunes . . .) to obtain a permit from the newly created South Carolina Coastal Council (Council) (respondent here) prior to committing the land to a "use other than the use the critical area was devoted to on [September 28, 1977]". . . .

In the late 1970's, Lucas and others began extensive residential development of the Isle of Palms, a barrier island situated eastward of the city of Charleston. Toward the close of the development cycle for one residential subdivision known as "Beachwood East," Lucas in 1986 purchased the two lots at issue in this litigation for his own account. No portion of the lots, which were located approximately 300 feet from the beach, qualified as a "critical area" under the 1977 Act; accordingly, at the time Lucas acquired these parcels, he was not legally obliged to obtain a permit from the Council in advance of any development activity. His intention with respect to the lots was to do what the owners of the immediately adjacent parcels had already done: erect single-family residences. He commissioned architectural drawings for this purpose.

The Beachfront Management Act brought Lucas's plans to an abrupt end. Under that 1988 legislation, the Council was directed to establish a "baseline" connecting the landwardmost "points of erosion . . . during the past forty years" in the region of the Isle of Palms that includes Lucas's lots. . . .[1] In action not challenged here, the Council fixed this baseline landward of Lucas's parcels. That was significant, for under the Act construction of occupyable improvements[2] was flatly prohibited seaward of a line drawn 20 feet landward of, and parallel to, the baseline. . . . The Act provided no exceptions. [Baseline and setback rules are different in the current version of the BMA. — EDS.]

B.

Lucas promptly filed suit in the South Carolina Court of Common Pleas, contending that the Beachfront Management Act's construction bar effected a taking of his property without just compensation. Lucas did not take issue with the validity of the Act as a lawful exercise of South Carolina's police power, but contended that the Act's complete extinguishment of his property's value entitled him to compensation regardless of whether the legislature had acted in furtherance of legitimate police power objectives. Following a bench trial, the court agreed. Among its factual determinations was the finding that "at the time Lucas purchased the two lots, both were zoned for single-family residential construction and . . . there were no restrictions imposed upon such use of the property by either the State of South Carolina, the County of Charleston, or the Town of the Isle of Palms". . . . The trial court further found that the Beachfront Management Act decreed a permanent ban on construction insofar as Lucas's lots were concerned, and that this prohibition "deprived Lucas of any reasonable economic use of the lots, . . . eliminated the unrestricted right of use, and rendered them valueless". . . . The court thus concluded that Lucas's properties had been "taken" by operation of the Act, and it ordered respondent to pay "just compensation" in the amount of $1,232,387.50. . . .

The Supreme Court of South Carolina reversed. It found dispositive what it described as Lucas's concession "that the Beachfront Management Act [was] properly and validly designed to preserve . . . South Carolina's beaches". . . . Failing an attack on the validity of the statute as such, the court believed itself bound to accept the "uncontested . . . findings" of the South Carolina Legislature that new construction in the coastal zone — such as petitioner intended — threatened this public resource. The court ruled that when a regulation respecting the use of property is designed "to prevent serious public harm" . . . , no compensation is owing under the Takings Clause regardless of the regulation's effect on the property's value.

1. This specialized historical method of determining the baseline applied because the Beachwood East subdivision is located adjacent to a so-called "inlet erosion zone" (defined in the Act to mean "a segment of shoreline along or adjacent to tidal inlets which are directly influenced by the inlet and its associated shoals," S. C. Code Ann. § 48-39-270(7) (Supp. 1988)) that is "not stabilized by jetties, terminal groins, or other structures," § 48-39-280(A)(2). For areas other than these unstabilized inlet erosion zones, the statute directs that the baseline be established along "the crest of an ideal primary oceanfront sand dune." § 48-39-280(A)(1).

2. The Act did allow the construction of certain nonhabitable improvements, *e.g.*, "wooden walkways no larger in width than six feet," and "small wooden decks no larger than one hundred forty-four square feet." §§ 48-39-290(A)(1) and (2).

Two justices dissented. They acknowledged that our *Mugler v. Kansas*, 123 U.S. 623 (1887), line of cases recognizes governmental power to prohibit "noxious" uses of property — *i.e.*, uses of property akin to "public nuisances" — without having to pay compensation. But they would not have characterized the Beachfront Management Act's "*primary* purpose [as] the prevention of a nuisance". . . . To the dissenters, the chief purposes of the legislation, among them the promotion of tourism and the creation of a "habitat for indigenous flora and fauna," could not fairly be compared to nuisance abatement. . . . As a consequence, they would have affirmed the trial court's conclusion that the Act's obliteration of the value of petitioner's lots accomplished a taking.

We granted certiorari.

II.

As a threshold matter, we must briefly address the Council's suggestion that this case is inappropriate for plenary review. After briefing and argument before the South Carolina Supreme Court, but prior to issuance of that court's opinion, the Beachfront Management Act was amended to authorize the Council, in certain circumstances, to issue "special permits" for the construction or reconstruction of habitable structures seaward of the baseline. . . . According to the Council, this amendment renders Lucas's claim of a permanent deprivation unripe, as Lucas may yet be able to secure permission to build on his property. "[The Court's] cases," we are reminded, "uniformly reflect an insistence on knowing the nature and extent of permitted development before adjudicating the constitutionality of the regulations that purport to limit it." *MacDonald, Sommer & Frates v. Yolo County*, 477 U.S. 340 (1986). Because petitioner "has not yet obtained a final decision regarding how [he] will be allowed to develop [his] property," *Williamson County Regional Planning Comm'n v. Hamilton Bank of Johnson City*, 473 U.S. 172 (1985), the Council argues that he is not yet entitled to definitive adjudication of his takings claim in this Court.

We think these considerations would preclude review had the South Carolina Supreme Court rested its judgment on ripeness grounds, as it was (essentially) invited to do by the Council. The South Carolina Supreme Court shrugged off the possibility of further administrative and trial proceedings, however, preferring to dispose of Lucas's takings claim on the merits. . . . This unusual disposition does not preclude Lucas from applying for a permit under the 1990 amendment for *future* construction, and challenging, on takings grounds, any denial. But it does preclude, both practically and legally, any takings claim with respect to Lucas's *past* deprivation, *i.e.*, for his having been denied construction rights during the period before the 1990 amendment. *See generally First English Evangelical Lutheran Church of Glendale v. County of Los Angeles*, 482 U.S. 304 (1987) (holding that temporary deprivations of use are compensable under the *Takings* Clause). Without even so much as commenting upon the consequences of the South Carolina Supreme Court's judgment in this respect, the Council insists that permitting Lucas to press his claim of a past deprivation on this appeal would be improper, since "the issues of whether and to what extent [Lucas] has incurred a temporary taking . . . have simply never been addressed". . . . Yet Lucas had no reason to proceed on a "temporary taking" theory at trial, or even to seek remand for that purpose prior to submission of the case to the South Carolina Supreme Court, since as the Act then read, the taking was unconditional and permanent. Moreover, given the breadth of the South Carolina Supreme Court's holding and judgment, Lucas would plainly be unable (absent our intervention now) to obtain further state-court adjudication with respect to the 1988-1990 period.

***

A.

Prior to Justice Holmes's exposition in *Pennsylvania Coal Co. v. Mahon*, 260 U.S. 393 (1922), it was generally thought that the Takings Clause reached only a "direct appropriation" of property . . . or the functional equivalent of a "practical ouster of [the owner's] possession". . . . Justice Holmes recognized in *Mahon*, however, that if the protection against physical appropriations of private property was to be meaningfully enforced, the government's power to redefine the range of interests included in the ownership of property was necessarily constrained by constitutional limits. . . . If, instead, the uses of private property were subject to unbridled, uncompensated qualification under the police power, "the natural tendency of human nature [would be] to extend the qualification more and more until at last private property disappeared." *Id.*, at 415. These considerations gave birth in that case to the oft-cited maxim that, "while property may be regulated to a certain extent, if regulation goes too far it will be recognized as a taking." *Ibid.*

Nevertheless, our decision in *Mahon* offered little insight into when, and under what circumstances, a given regulation would be seen as going "too far" for purposes of the Fifth Amendment. In 70-odd years of succeeding "regulatory takings" jurisprudence, we have generally eschewed any " 'set formula' " for determining how far is too far, preferring to "engage in . . . essentially ad hoc, factual inquiries." *Penn Central Transportation Co. v. New York City*, 438 U.S. 104 (1978) (quoting *Goldblatt v. Hempstead*, 369 U.S. 590 (1962)). . . . We have, however, described at least two discrete categories of regulatory action as compensable without case-specific inquiry into the public interest advanced in support of the restraint. The first encompasses regulations that compel the property owner to suffer a physical "invasion" of his property. In general (at least with regard to permanent invasions), no matter how minute the intrusion, and no matter how weighty the public purpose behind it, we have required compensation. . . . *cf. Kaiser Aetna v. United States*, 444 U.S. 164 (1979) (imposition of navigational servitude upon private marina).

The second situation in which we have found categorical treatment appropriate is where regulation denies all economically beneficial or productive use of land. . . .[7]

___

7. Regrettably, the rhetorical force of our "deprivation of all economically feasible use" rule is greater than its precision, since the rule does not make clear the "property interest" against which the loss of value is to be measured. When, for example, a regulation requires a developer to leave 90% of a rural tract in its natural state, it is unclear whether we would analyze the situation as one in which

We have never set forth the justification for this rule. Perhaps it is simply, as Justice Brennan suggested, that total deprivation of beneficial use is, from the landowner's point of view, the equivalent of a physical appropriation. *See San Diego Gas & Electric Co. v. San Diego*, 450 U.S. at 652 (dissenting opinion). "For what is the land but the profits thereof[?]" 1 E. COKE, INSTITUTES, ch. 1, § 1 (1st Am. ed. 1812). Surely, at least, in the extraordinary circumstance when *no* productive or economically beneficial use of land is permitted, it is less realistic to indulge our usual assumption that the legislature is simply "adjusting the benefits and burdens of economic life," *Penn Central Transportation Co.*, 438 U.S. at 124, in a manner that secures an "average reciprocity of advantage" to everyone concerned, *Pennsylvania Coal Co. v. Mahon*, 260 U.S. at 415. And the *functional* basis for permitting the government, by regulation, to affect property values without compensation — that "Government hardly could go on if to some extent values incident to property could not be diminished without paying for every such change in the general law," *id.*, at 413 — does not apply to the relatively rare situations where the government has deprived a landowner of all economically beneficial uses.

On the other side of the balance, affirmatively supporting a compensation requirement, is the fact that regulations that leave the owner of land without economically beneficial or productive options for its use — typically, as here, by requiring land to be left substantially in its natural state — carry with them a heightened risk that private property is being pressed into some form of public service under the guise of mitigating serious public harm. *See, e.g., Annicelli v. South Kingstown*, 463 A.2d 133, 140-141 (R. I. 1983) (prohibition on construction adjacent to beach justified on twin grounds of safety and "conservation of open space"); *Morris County Land Improvement Co. v. Parsippany-Troy Hills Township*, 40 N.J. 539, 552-553 (1963) (prohibition on filling marshlands imposed in order to preserve region as water detention basin and create wildlife refuge). As Justice Brennan explained: "From the government's point of view, the benefits flowing to the public from preservation of open space through regulation may be equally great as from creating a wildlife refuge through formal condemnation or increasing electricity production through a dam project that floods private property." *San Diego Gas & Elec. Co., supra*, at 652 (dissenting opinion). The many statutes on the books, both state and federal, that provide for the use of eminent domain to impose servitudes on private scenic lands preventing developmental uses, or to acquire such lands altogether, suggest the practical equivalence in this setting of negative regulation and appropriation. . . .

---

the owner has been deprived of all economically beneficial use of the burdened portion of the tract, or as one in which the owner has suffered a mere diminution in value of the tract as a whole. . . . The answer to this difficult question may lie in how the owner's reasonable expectations have been shaped by the State's law of property — *i.e.*, whether and to what degree the State's law has accorded legal recognition and protection to the particular interest in land with respect to which the takings claimant alleges a diminution in (or elimination of) value. In any event, we avoid this difficulty in the present case, since the "interest in land" that Lucas has pleaded (a fee simple interest) is an estate with a rich tradition of protection at common law, and since the South Carolina Court of Common Pleas found that the Beachfront Management Act left each of Lucas's beachfront lots without economic value.

We think, in short, that there are good reasons for our frequently expressed belief that when the owner of real property has been called upon to sacrifice *all* economically beneficial uses in the name of the common good, that is, to leave his property economically idle, he has suffered a taking.[8]

The trial court found Lucas's two beachfront lots to have been rendered valueless by respondent's enforcement of the coastal-zone construction ban.[9] Under Lucas's theory of the case, which rested upon our "no economically viable use" statements, that finding entitled him to compensation. Lucas believed it unnecessary to take issue with either the purposes behind the Beachfront Management Act, or the means chosen by the South Carolina Legislature to effectuate those purposes. The South Carolina Supreme Court, however, thought otherwise. In its view, the Beachfront Management Act was no ordinary enactment, but involved an exercise of South Carolina's "police powers" to mitigate the harm to the public interest that petitioner's use of his land might occasion. . . . By neglecting to dispute the findings enumerated in the Act[10] or otherwise to challenge the legislature's purposes, petitioner "conceded that the beach/dune area of South Carolina's shores is

---

8. Justice Stevens criticizes the "deprivation of all economically beneficial use" rule as "wholly arbitrary," in that "[the] landowner whose property is diminished in value 95% recovers nothing," while the landowner who suffers a complete elimination of value "recovers the land's full value." *Post*, 505 U.S. at 1064. This analysis errs in its assumption that the landowner whose deprivation is one step short of complete is not entitled to compensation. Such an owner might not be able to claim the benefit of our categorical formulation, but, as we have acknowledged time and again, "the economic impact of the regulation on the claimant and . . . the extent to which the regulation has interfered with distinct investment-backed expectations" are keenly relevant to takings analysis generally. *Penn Central Transportation Co. v. New York City*, 438 U.S. 104, 124 (1978). It is true that in at least *some* cases the landowner with 95% loss will get nothing, while the landowner with total loss will recover in full. But that occasional result is no more strange than the gross disparity between the landowner whose premises are taken for a highway (who recovers in full) and the landowner whose property is reduced to 5% of its former value by the highway (who recovers nothing). Takings law is full of these "all-or-nothing" situations. Justice Stevens similarly misinterprets our focus on "developmental" uses of property (the uses proscribed by the Beachfront Management Act) as betraying an "assumption that the only uses of property cognizable under the Constitution are *developmental* uses." *Post*, 505 U.S. at 1065, n.3. We make no such assumption. Though our prior takings cases evince an abiding concern for the productive use of, and economic investment in, land, there are plainly a number of noneconomic interests in land whose impairment will invite exceedingly close scrutiny under the Takings Clause. *See, e.g., Loretto v. Teleprompter Manhattan CATV Corp.*, 458 U.S. 419, 436 (1982) (interest in excluding strangers from one's land).

9. This finding was the premise of the petition for certiorari, and since it was not challenged in the brief in opposition we decline to entertain the argument in respondent's brief on the merits . . . that the finding was erroneous. Instead, we decide the question presented under the same factual assumptions as did the Supreme Court of South Carolina. . . .

10. The legislature's express findings include the following:

"The General Assembly finds that:

"(1) The beach/dune system along the coast of South Carolina is extremely important to the people of this State and serves the following functions:

"(a) protects life and property by serving as a storm barrier which dissipates wave energy and contributes to shoreline stability in an economical and effective manner;

an extremely valuable public resource; that the erection of new construction, *inter alia*, contributes to the erosion and destruction of this public resource; and that discouraging new construction in close proximity to the beach/dune area is necessary to prevent a great public harm." *Lucas v. South Carolina Coastal Council*, 304 S.C. 376, 382-383 (1991). In the court's view, these concessions brought petitioner's challenge within a long line of this Court's cases sustaining against Due Process and Takings Clause challenges the State's use of its "police powers" to enjoin a property owner from activities akin to public nuisances. *See Mugler v. Kansas*, 123 U.S. 623 (1887) (law prohibiting manufacture of alcoholic beverages); *Hadacheck v. Sebastian*, 239 U.S. 394 (1915) (law barring operation of brick mill in residential area); *Miller v. Schoene*, 276 U.S. 272 (1928) (order to destroy diseased cedar trees to prevent infection of nearby orchards); *Goldblatt v. Hempstead*, 369 U.S. 590 (1962) (law effectively preventing continued operation of quarry in residential area).

"(b) provides the basis for a tourism industry that generates approximately two-thirds of South Carolina's annual tourism industry revenue which constitutes a significant portion of the state's economy. The tourists who come to the South Carolina coast to enjoy the ocean and dry sand beach contribute significantly to state and local tax revenues;

"(c) provides habitat for numerous species of plants and animals, several of which are threatened or endangered. Waters adjacent to the beach/dune system also provide habitat for many other marine species;

"(d) provides a natural health environment for the citizens of South Carolina to spend leisure time which serves their physical and mental well-being.

"(2) Beach/dune system vegetation is unique and extremely important to the vitality and preservation of the system.

"(3) Many miles of South Carolina's beaches have been identified as critically eroding.

"(4) . . . Development unwisely has been sited too close to the [beach/dune] system. This type of development has jeopardized the stability of the beach/dune system, accelerated erosion, and endangered adjacent property. It is in both the public and private interests to protect the system from this unwise development.

"(5) The use of armoring in the form of hard erosion control devices such as seawalls, bulkheads, and rip-rap to protect erosion-threatened structures adjacent to the beach has not proven effective. These armoring devices have given a false sense of security to beachfront property owners. In reality, these hard structures, in many instances, have increased the vulnerability of beachfront property to damage from wind and waves while contributing to the deterioration and loss of the dry sand beach which is so important to the tourism industry.

"(6) Erosion is a natural process which becomes a significant problem for man only when structures are erected in close proximity to the beach/dune system. It is in both the public and private interests to afford the beach/dune system space to accrete and erode in its natural cycle. This space can be provided only by discouraging new construction in close proximity to the beach/dune system and encouraging those who have erected structures too close to the system to retreat from it.

. . .

"(8) It is in the state's best interest to protect and to promote increased public access to South Carolina's beaches for out-of-state tourists and South Carolina residents alike."

S. C. Code Ann. § 48-39-250 (Supp. 1991).

It is correct that many of our prior opinions have suggested that "harmful or noxious uses" of property may be proscribed by government regulation without the requirement of compensation. For a number of reasons, however, we think the South Carolina Supreme Court was too quick to conclude that that principle decides the present case. The "harmful or noxious uses" principle was the Court's early attempt to describe in theoretical terms why government may, consistent with the Takings Clause, affect property values by regulation without incurring an obligation to compensate — a reality we nowadays acknowledge explicitly with respect to the full scope of the State's police power. *See, e.g., Penn Central Transportation Co.*, 438 U.S. at 125 (where State "reasonably concludes that 'the health, safety, morals, or general welfare' would be promoted by prohibiting particular contemplated uses of land," compensation need not accompany prohibition). . . .

"Harmful or noxious use" analysis was, in other words, simply the progenitor of our more contemporary statements that "land-use regulation does not effect a taking if it 'substantially advances legitimate state interests'. . . ." *Nollan v. California Coastal Commission*, 483 U.S. 825, 834, 834 (1987) (quoting *Agins v. Tiburon*, 447 U.S. 255, 260 (1980)). . . .

The transition from our early focus on control of "noxious" uses to our contemporary understanding of the broad realm within which government may regulate without compensation was an easy one, since the distinction between "harm-preventing" and "benefit-conferring" regulation is often in the eye of the beholder. It is quite possible, for example, to describe in *either* fashion the ecological, economic, and esthetic concerns that inspired the South Carolina Legislature in the present case. One could say that imposing a servitude on Lucas's land is necessary in order to prevent his use of it from "harming" South Carolina's ecological resources; or, instead, in order to achieve the "benefits" of an ecological preserve.[11] . . . Whether one or the other of the competing characterizations will come to one's lips in a particular case depends primarily upon one's evaluation of the worth of competing uses of real estate. *See* RESTATEMENT (SECOND) OF TORTS § 822, *Comment g*, p. 112 (1979) ("Practically all human activities unless carried on in a wilderness interfere to some extent with others or involve some risk of interference"). A given restraint will be seen as mitigating "harm" to the adjacent parcels or securing a "benefit" for them, depending upon the observer's evaluation of the relative importance of the use that the restraint favors. . . . Whether Lucas's construction of single-family residences on his parcels should be described as bringing

---

11. In the present case, in fact, some of the "[South Carolina] legislature's 'findings' " to which the South Carolina Supreme Court purported to defer in characterizing the purpose of the Act as "harm-preventing," 304 S.C. 376, 385 (1991), seem to us phrased in "benefit-conferring" language instead. For example, they describe the importance of a construction ban in enhancing "South Carolina's annual tourism industry revenue," S. C. Code Ann. § 48-39-250(1)(b) (Supp. 1991), in "providing habitat for numerous species of plants and animals, several of which are threatened or endangered," § 48-39-250(1)(c), and in "providing a natural healthy environment for the citizens of South Carolina to spend leisure time which serves their physical and mental well-being," § 48-39-250(1)(d). It would be pointless to make the outcome of this case hang upon this terminology, since the same interests could readily be described in "harm-preventing" fashion.

"harm" to South Carolina's adjacent ecological resources thus depends principally upon whether the describer believes that the State's use interest in nurturing those resources is so important that *any* competing adjacent use must yield.[12]

Justice Blackmun, however, apparently insists that we *must* make the outcome hinge (exclusively) upon the South Carolina Legislature's other, "harm-preventing" characterizations, focusing on the declaration that "prohibitions on building in front of the setback line are necessary to protect people and property from storms, high tides, and beach erosion." . . . He says "nothing in the record undermines [this] assessment," . . . apparently seeing no significance in the fact that the statute permits owners of *existing* structures to remain (and even to rebuild if their structures are not "destroyed beyond repair," S. C. Code Ann. § 48-39-290(B) (Supp. 1988)), and in the fact that the 1990 amendment authorizes the Council to issue permits for new construction in violation of the uniform prohibition, *see* S. C. Code Ann. § 48-39-290(D)(1) (Supp. 1991).

When it is understood that "prevention of harmful use" was merely our early formulation of the police power justification necessary to sustain (without compensation) *any* regulatory diminution in value; and that the distinction between regulation that "prevents harmful use" and that which "confers benefits" is difficult, if not impossible, to discern on an objective, value-free basis; it becomes self-evident that noxious-use logic cannot serve as a touchstone to distinguish regulatory "takings" — which require compensation — from regulatory deprivations that do not require compensation. *A fortiori* the legislature's recitation of a noxious-use justification cannot be the basis for departing from our categorical rule that total regulatory takings must be compensated. If it were, departure would virtually always be allowed. The South Carolina Supreme Court's approach would essentially nullify *Mahon*'s affirmation of limits to the noncompensable exercise of the police power. Our cases provide no support for this: None of them that employed the logic of "harmful use" prevention to sustain a regulation involved an allegation that the regulation wholly eliminated the value of the claimant's land. . . .

Where the State seeks to sustain regulation that deprives land of all economically beneficial use, we think it may resist compensation only if the logically antecedent inquiry into the nature of the owner's estate shows that the proscribed use interests were not part of his title to begin with. This accords, we think, with our "takings" jurisprudence, which has traditionally been guided by the understandings of our citizens regarding the content of, and the State's power over, the "bundle of rights" that they acquire when they obtain title to property. It seems to us that the property owner necessarily expects the uses of his property to be restricted,

---

12. In Justice Blackmun's view, even with respect to regulations that deprive an owner of all developmental or economically beneficial land uses, the test for required compensation is whether the legislature has recited a harm-preventing justification for its action. . . . Since such a justification can be formulated in practically every case, this amounts to a test of whether the legislature has a stupid staff. We think the Takings Clause requires courts to do more than insist upon artful harm-preventing characterizations.

from time to time, by various measures newly enacted by the State in legitimate exercise of its police powers; "as long recognized, some values are enjoyed under an implied limitation and must yield to the police power." *Pennsylvania Coal Co. v. Mahon*, 260 U.S. at 413. . . . In the case of land, . . . we think the notion pressed by the Council that title is somehow held subject to the "implied limitation" that the State may subsequently eliminate all economically valuable use is inconsistent with the historical compact recorded in the Takings Clause that has become part of our constitutional culture.

Where "permanent physical occupation" of land is concerned, we have refused to allow the government to decree it anew (without compensation), no matter how weighty the asserted "public interests" involved . . . though we assuredly *would* permit the government to assert a permanent easement that was a pre-existing limitation upon the landowner's title. *Compare Scranton v. Wheeler*, 179 U.S. 141, 163 (1900) (interests of "riparian owner in the submerged lands . . . bordering on a public navigable water" held subject to Government's navigational servitude), with *Kaiser Aetna v. United States*, 444 U.S. at 178-180 (imposition of navigational servitude on marina created and rendered navigable at private expense held to constitute a taking). We believe similar treatment must be accorded confiscatory regulations, *i.e.*, regulations that prohibit all economically beneficial use of land: Any limitation so severe cannot be newly legislated or decreed (without compensation), but must inhere in the title itself, in the restrictions that background principles of the State's law of property and nuisance already place upon land ownership. A law or decree with such an effect must, in other words, do no more than duplicate the result that could have been achieved in the courts — by adjacent landowners (or other uniquely affected persons) under the State's law of private nuisance, or by the State under its complementary power to abate nuisances that affect the public generally, or otherwise.[16]

On this analysis, the owner of a lakebed, for example, would not be entitled to compensation when he is denied the requisite permit to engage in a landfilling operation that would have the effect of flooding others' land. Nor the corporate owner of a nuclear generating plant, when it is directed to remove all improvements from its land upon discovery that the plant sits astride an earthquake fault. Such regulatory action may well have the effect of eliminating the land's only economically productive use, but it does not proscribe a productive use that was previously permissible under relevant property and nuisance principles. The use of these properties for what are now expressly prohibited purposes was *always* unlawful, and (subject to other constitutional limitations) it was open to the State at any point to make the implication of those background principles of nuisance and property law explicit. . . . When, however, a regulation that declares "off-limits" all economically

---

16. The principal "otherwise" that we have in mind is litigation absolving the State (or private parties) of liability for the destruction of "real and personal property, in cases of actual necessity, to prevent the spreading of a fire" or to forestall other grave threats to the lives and property of others. *Bowditch v. Boston*, 101 U.S. 16, 18-19 (1880). . . .

productive or beneficial uses of land goes beyond what the relevant background principles would dictate, compensation must be paid to sustain it.[17]

The "total taking" inquiry we require today will ordinarily entail (as the application of state nuisance law ordinarily entails) analysis of, among other things, the degree of harm to public lands and resources, or adjacent private property, posed by the claimant's proposed activities, *see, e.g.*, RESTATEMENT (SECOND) OF TORTS §§ 826, 827, the social value of the claimant's activities and their suitability to the locality in question, *see, e.g., id.*, §§ 828(a) and (b), 831, and the relative ease with which the alleged harm can be avoided through measures taken by the claimant and the government (or adjacent private landowners) alike, *see, e.g., id.*, §§ 827(e), 828(c), 830. The fact that a particular use has long been engaged in by similarly situated owners ordinarily imports a lack of any common-law prohibition (though changed circumstances or new knowledge may make what was previously permissible no longer so, *see id.*, § 827, Comment g. So also does the fact that other landowners, similarly situated, are permitted to continue the use denied to the claimant.

It seems unlikely that common-law principles would have prevented the erection of any habitable or productive improvements on petitioner's land; they rarely support prohibition of the "essential use" of land, *Curtin v. Benson*, 222 U.S. 78, 86 (1911). The question, however, is one of state law to be dealt with on remand. We emphasize that to win its case South Carolina must do more than proffer the legislature's declaration that the uses Lucas desires are inconsistent with the public interest, or the conclusory assertion that they violate a common-law maxim such as *sic utere tuo ut alienum non laedas*. As we have said, a "State, by *ipse dixit*, may not transform private property into public property without compensation. . . ." *Webb's Fabulous Pharmacies, Inc. v. Beckwith*, 449 U.S. 155, 164 (1980). Instead, as it would be required to do if it sought to restrain Lucas in a common-law action for public nuisance, South Carolina must identify background principles of nuisance and property law that prohibit the uses he now intends in the circumstances in which the property is presently found. Only on this showing can the State fairly claim that, in proscribing all such beneficial uses, the Beachfront Management Act is taking nothing.[18]

17. Of course, the State may elect to rescind its regulation and thereby avoid having to pay compensation for a permanent deprivation. *See First English Evangelical Lutheran Church*, 482 U.S. at 321. But "where the [regulation has] already worked a taking of all use of property, no subsequent action by the government can relieve it of the duty to provide compensation for the period during which the taking was effective." *Ibid.*

18. Justice Blackmun decries our reliance on background nuisance principles at least in part because he believes those principles to be as manipulable as we find the "harm prevention"/"benefit conferral" dichotomy. . . . There is no doubt some leeway in a court's interpretation of what existing state law permits — but not remotely as much, we think, as in a legislative crafting of the reasons for its confiscatory regulation. We stress that an affirmative decree eliminating all economically beneficial uses may be defended only if an *objectively reasonable application* of relevant precedents would exclude those beneficial uses in the circumstances in which the land is presently found.

The judgment is reversed, and the case is remanded for proceedings not inconsistent with this opinion. *So ordered.*

Justice KENNEDY concurs in the judgment.

***

The South Carolina Court of Common Pleas found that petitioner's real property has been rendered valueless by the State's regulation. . . . The finding appears to presume that the property has no significant market value or resale potential. This is a curious finding, and I share the reservations of some of my colleagues about a finding that a beachfront lot loses all value because of a development restriction. . . . Accepting the finding as entered, it follows that petitioner is entitled to invoke the line of cases discussing regulations that deprive real property of all economic value. . . .

The finding of no value must be considered under the Takings Clause by reference to the owner's reasonable, investment-backed expectations. . . . The Takings Clause, while conferring substantial protection on property owners, does not eliminate the police power of the State to enact limitations on the use of their property. . . . The rights conferred by the Takings Clause and the police power of the State may coexist without conflict. Property is bought and sold, investments are made, subject to the State's power to regulate. Where a taking is alleged from regulations which deprive the property of all value, the test must be whether the deprivation is contrary to reasonable, investment-backed expectations.

There is an inherent tendency towards circularity in this synthesis, of course; for if the owner's reasonable expectations are shaped by what courts allow as a proper exercise of governmental authority, property tends to become what courts say it is. Some circularity must be tolerated in these matters, however, as it is in other spheres. *E.g.,* *Katz v. United States,* 389 U.S. 347 (1967) (Fourth Amendment protections defined by reasonable expectations of privacy). The definition, moreover, is not circular in its entirety. The expectations protected by the Constitution are based on objective rules and customs that can be understood as reasonable by all parties involved.

In my view, reasonable expectations must be understood in light of the whole of our legal tradition. The common law of nuisance is too narrow a confine for the exercise of regulatory power in a complex and interdependent society. . . . The State should not be prevented from enacting new regulatory initiatives in response to changing conditions, and courts must consider all reasonable expectations whatever their source. The Takings Clause does not require a static body of state property law; it protects private expectations to ensure private investment. I agree with the Court that nuisance prevention accords with the most common expectations of property owners who face regulation, but I do not believe this can be the sole source of state authority to impose severe restrictions. Coastal property may present such unique concerns for a fragile land system that the State can go further in regulating its development and use than the common law of nuisance might otherwise permit.

The Supreme Court of South Carolina erred, in my view, by reciting the general purposes for which the state regulations were enacted without a determination that they were in accord with the owner's reasonable expectations and therefore sufficient to support a severe restriction on specific parcels of property. . . .

***

Justice BLACKMUN dissents.

Today the Court launches a missile to kill a mouse.

The State of South Carolina prohibited petitioner Lucas from building a permanent structure on his property from 1988 to 1990. Relying on an unreviewed (and implausible) state trial court finding that this restriction left Lucas' property valueless, this Court granted review to determine whether compensation must be paid in cases where the State prohibits all economic use of real estate. According to the Court, such an occasion never has arisen in any of our prior cases, and the Court imagines that it will arise "relatively rarely" or only in "extraordinary circumstances." Almost certainly it did not happen in this case.

***

I.

A.

In 1972 Congress passed the Coastal Zone Management Act. . . . The Act was designed to provide States with money and incentives to carry out Congress' goal of protecting the public from shoreline erosion and coastal hazards. In the 1980 amendments to the Act, Congress directed States to enhance their coastal programs by "preventing or significantly reducing threats to life and the destruction of property by eliminating development and redevelopment in high-hazard areas."[1] 16 U.S.C. § 1456b(a)(2) (1988 ed., Supp. II).

South Carolina began implementing the congressional directive by enacting the South Carolina Coastal Zone Management Act of 1977. Under the 1977 Act, any construction activity in what was designated the "critical area" required a permit from the South Carolina Coastal Council (Council), and the construction of any habitable structure was prohibited. The 1977 critical area was relatively narrow.

This effort did not stop the loss of shoreline. In October 1986, the Council appointed a "Blue Ribbon Committee on Beachfront Management" to investigate beach erosion and propose possible solutions. In March 1987, the Committee found that South Carolina's beaches were "critically eroding," and proposed land-use restrictions. . . . In response, South Carolina enacted the Beachfront Management

---

1. The country has come to recognize that uncontrolled beachfront development can cause serious damage to life and property. . . . Hurricane Hugo's September 1989 attack upon South Carolina's coastline, for example, caused 29 deaths and approximately $6 billion in property damage, much of it the result of uncontrolled beachfront development. . . . The beachfront buildings are not only themselves destroyed in such a storm, "but they are often driven, like battering rams, into adjacent inland homes." Natasha Zalkin, *Shifting Sands and Shifting Doctrines: The Supreme Court's Changing Takings Doctrine and South Carolina's Coastal Zone Statute*, 79 CALIF. L. REV. 205, 212-213 (1991). Moreover, the development often destroys the natural sand dune barriers that provide storm breaks. *Ibid.*

Act on July 1, 1988. . . . The 1988 Act did not change the uses permitted within the designated critical areas. Rather, it enlarged those areas to encompass the distance from the mean high watermark to a setback line established on the basis of "the best scientific and historical data" available.

B.

Petitioner Lucas is a contractor, manager, and part owner of the Wild Dune development on the Isle of Palms. He has lived there since 1978. In December 1986, he purchased two of the last four pieces of vacant property in the development. The area is notoriously unstable. In roughly half of the last 40 years, all or part of petitioner's property was part of the beach or flooded twice daily by the ebb and flow of the tide. Between 1957 and 1963, petitioner's property was under water. Between 1963 and 1973 the shoreline was 100 to 150 feet onto petitioner's property. In 1973 the first line of stable vegetation was about halfway through the property. Between 1981 and 1983, the Isle of Palms issued 12 emergency orders for sandbagging to protect property in the Wild Dune development. Determining that local habitable structures were in imminent danger of collapse, the Council issued permits for two rock revetments to protect condominium developments near petitioner's property from erosion; one of the revetments extends more than halfway onto one of his lots.

C.

The South Carolina Supreme Court found that the Beachfront Management Act did not take petitioner's property without compensation. The decision rested on two premises that until today were unassailable — that the State has the power to prevent any use of property it finds to be harmful to its citizens, and that a state statute is entitled to a presumption of constitutionality.

The Beachfront Management Act includes a finding by the South Carolina General Assembly that the beach/dune system serves the purpose of "protecting life and property by serving as a storm barrier which dissipates wave energy and contributes to shoreline stability in an economical and effective manner." S. C. Code Ann. § 48-39-250(1)(a) (Supp. 1990). The General Assembly also found that "development unwisely has been sited too close to the [beach/dune] system. This type of development has jeopardized the stability of the beach/dune system, accelerated erosion, and endangered adjacent property." § 48-39-250(4); *see also* § 48-39-250(6) (discussing the need to "afford the beach/dune system space to accrete and erode").

If the state legislature is correct that the prohibition on building in front of the setback line prevents serious harm, then, under this Court's prior cases, the Act is constitutional. "Long ago it was recognized that all property in this country is held under the implied obligation that the owner's use of it shall not be injurious to the community, and the Takings Clause did not transform that principle to one that requires compensation whenever the State asserts its power to enforce it." *Keystone Bituminous Coal Assn. v. DeBenedictis*, 480 U.S. 470, 491-492 (1987) (internal quotation marks omitted). . . . The Court consistently has upheld regulations imposed to arrest a significant threat to the common welfare, whatever their economic effect on the owner. . . .

Petitioner never challenged the legislature's findings that a building ban was necessary to protect property and life. Nor did he contend that the threatened harm was not sufficiently serious to make building a house in a particular location a "harmful" use, that the legislature had not made sufficient findings, or that the legislature was motivated by anything other than a desire to minimize damage to coastal areas. Indeed, petitioner objected at trial that evidence as to the purposes of the setback requirement was irrelevant. The South Carolina Supreme Court accordingly understood petitioner not to contest the State's position that "discouraging new construction in close proximity to the beach/dune area is necessary to prevent a great public harm," *Lucas v. South Carolina Coastal Council*, 304 S.C. 376, 383 (1991), and "to prevent serious injury to the community." *Id.*, at 387. The court considered itself "bound by these uncontested legislative findings . . . [in the absence of] any attack whatsoever on the statutory scheme." *Id.*, at 383.

Nothing in the record undermines the General Assembly's assessment that prohibitions on building in front of the setback line are necessary to protect people and property from storms, high tides, and beach erosion. Because that legislative determination cannot be disregarded in the absence of such evidence, . . . and because its determination of harm to life and property from building is sufficient to prohibit that use under this Court's cases, the South Carolina Supreme Court correctly found no taking.

[Justice Blackmun argues that the case should be dismissed, for want of jurisdiction (ripeness) because Lucas did not exhaust all of his administrative options, such as challenging the location of the baseline and applying for a special permit under the 1990 amendment to Section 48-39-290(A)(6).]

Even if I agreed with the Court that there were no jurisdictional barriers to deciding this case, I still would not try to decide it. The Court creates its new takings jurisprudence based on the trial court's finding that the property had lost all economic value. This finding is almost certainly erroneous. Petitioner still can enjoy other attributes of ownership, such as the right to exclude others, "one of the most essential sticks in the bundle of rights that are commonly characterized as property." *Kaiser Aetna v. United States*, 444 U.S. 164, 176 (1979). Petitioner can picnic, swim, camp in a tent, or live on the property in a movable trailer. State courts frequently have recognized that land has economic value where the only residual economic uses are recreation or camping. . . . Petitioner also retains the right to alienate the land, which would have value for neighbors and for those prepared to enjoy proximity to the ocean without a house.

Yet the trial court, apparently believing that "less value" and "valueless" could be used interchangeably, found the property "valueless." The court accepted no evidence from the State on the property's value without a home, and petitioner's appraiser testified that he never had considered what the value would be absent a residence. The appraiser's value was based on the fact that the "highest and best use of these lots . . . [is] luxury single family detached dwellings." . . . The trial court appeared to believe that the property could be considered "valueless" if it was not available for its most profitable use. Absent that erroneous assumption, . . . I find no evidence in the record supporting the trial court's conclusion that the damage to the lots by virtue of the restrictions was "total." . . . I agree with the Court that it has the power to decide a case that turns on an erroneous finding, but I question the wisdom of deciding an issue based on a factual premise that does not exist in this case, and in the judgment of the Court will exist in the future only in "extraordinary circumstances."

* * *

III.

The Court's willingness to dispense with precedent in its haste to reach a result is not limited to its initial jurisdictional decision. The Court also alters the long-settled rules of review.

The South Carolina Supreme Court's decision to defer to legislative judgments in the absence of a challenge from petitioner comports with one of this Court's oldest maxims: "The existence of facts supporting the legislative judgment is to be presumed." *United States v. Carolene Products Co.*, 304 U.S. 144, 152 (1938). Indeed, we have said the legislature's judgment is "well-nigh conclusive." *Berman v. Parker*, 348 U.S. 26, 32 (1954).

Accordingly, this Court always has required plaintiffs challenging the constitutionality of an ordinance to provide "some factual foundation of record" that contravenes the legislative findings. . . . In the absence of such proof, "the presumption of constitutionality must prevail." . . . We only recently have reaffirmed that claimants have the burden of showing a state law constitutes a taking. . . .

> **Quick Question**
>
> Is Justice Blackmun arguing that state legislators should be entitled to a presumption of correctness when they state (or include language in a statute to the effect) that:
>
> 1. This law does not constitute a taking; or,
> 2. The activity regulated by this law constitutes a public nuisance?

Rather than invoking these traditional rules, the Court decides the State has the burden to convince the courts that its legislative judgments are correct. Despite Lucas' complete failure to contest the legislature's findings of serious harm to life and property if a permanent structure is built, the Court decides that the legislative findings are not sufficient to justify the use prohibition. Instead, the Court "emphasizes" the State must do more than merely proffer its legislative judgments to avoid invalidating its law. . . . In this case, apparently, the State now has the burden of showing the regulation is not a taking. The Court offers no justification for its sudden hostility toward state legislators, and I doubt that it could.

IV.

The Court does not reject the South Carolina Supreme Court's decision simply on the basis of its disbelief and distrust of the legislature's findings. It also takes the opportunity to create a new scheme for regulations that eliminate all economic value. From now on, there is a categorical rule finding these regulations to be a taking unless the use they prohibit is a background common-law nuisance or property principle. . . .

A.

I first question the Court's rationale in creating a category that obviates a "case-specific inquiry into the public interest advanced," . . . if all economic value has been lost. If one fact about the Court's takings jurisprudence can be stated without contradiction, it is that "the particular circumstances of each case" determine whether a specific restriction will be rendered invalid by the government's failure to pay compensation. *United States v. Central Eureka Mining Co.*, 357 U.S. 155, 168 (1958). This is so because although we have articulated certain factors to be considered, including the economic impact on the property owner, the ultimate conclusion "necessarily requires a weighing of private and public interests." *Agins*, 447 U.S. at 261. When the government regulation prevents the owner from any economically valuable use of his property, the private interest is unquestionably substantial, but we have never before held that no public interest can outweigh it. Instead the Court's prior decisions "uniformly reject the proposition that diminution in property value, standing alone, can establish a 'taking.' " *Penn Central Transp. Co. v. New York City*, 438 U.S. 104, 131 (1978).

This Court repeatedly has recognized the ability of government, in certain circumstances, to regulate property without compensation no matter how adverse the financial effect on the owner may be. More than a century ago, the Court explicitly upheld the right of States to prohibit uses of property injurious to public health, safety, or welfare without paying compensation: "A prohibition simply upon the use of property for purposes that are declared, by valid legislation, to be injurious to the health, morals, or safety of the community, cannot, in any just sense, be deemed a taking or an appropriation of property." *Mugler v. Kansas*, 123 U.S. at 668-669. On this basis, the Court upheld an ordinance effectively prohibiting operation of a previously lawful brewery, although the "establishments will become of no value as property." *Id.*, at 664; see also *id.*, at 668.

Mugler was only the beginning in a long line of cases. . . .

***

The Court recognizes that "our prior opinions have suggested that 'harmful or noxious uses' of property may be proscribed by government regulation without the requirement of compensation," . . . but seeks to reconcile them with its categorical rule by claiming that the Court never has upheld a regulation when the owner alleged the loss of all economic value. Even if the Court's factual premise were correct, its understanding of the Court's cases is distorted. In none of the cases did the Court suggest that the right of a State to prohibit certain activities without paying compensation turned on the availability of some residual valuable use. Instead, the cases depended on whether the government interest was sufficient to prohibit the activity, given the significant private cost.

B.

Ultimately even the Court cannot embrace the full implications of its *per se* rule: It eventually agrees that there cannot be a categorical rule for a taking based on economic value that wholly disregards the public need asserted. Instead, the Court decides that it will permit a State to regulate all economic value only if the State prohibits uses that would not be permitted under "background principles of nuisance and property law."[15]

Until today, the Court explicitly had rejected the contention that the government's power to act without paying compensation turns on whether the prohibited activity is a common-law nuisance.[16] The brewery closed in *Mugler* itself was not a common-law nuisance, and the Court specifically stated that it was the role of the legislature to determine what measures would be appropriate for the protection of public health and safety. *See* 123 U.S. at 661. . . . In upholding the state action in *Miller*, the Court found it unnecessary to "weigh with nicety the question whether the infected cedars constitute a nuisance according to common law; or whether they may be so declared by statute." 276 U.S. at 280. . . . Instead the Court has relied in the past, as the South Carolina court has done here, on legislative judgments of what constitutes a harm.

The Court rejects the notion that the State always can prohibit uses it deems a harm to the public without granting compensation because "the distinction between 'harm-preventing' and 'benefit-conferring' regulation is often in the eye of the beholder." . . . Since the characterization will depend "primarily upon one's evaluation of the worth of competing uses of real estate," . . . the Court decides a legislative judgment of this kind no longer can provide the desired "objective, value-free basis" for upholding a regulation. . . . The Court, however, fails to explain how its proposed common-law alternative escapes the same trap.

***

. . . [T]he Court's reliance on common-law principles of nuisance in its quest for a valuefree takings jurisprudence [is perplexing]. In determining what is a nuisance

15. Although it refers to state nuisance and property law, the Court apparently does not mean just any state nuisance and property law. Public nuisance was first a common-law creation, *see* F. H. Newark, *The Boundaries of Nuisance*, 65 L. Q. Rev. 480, 482 (1949) (attributing development of nuisance to 1535), but by the 1800's in both the United States and England, legislatures had the power to define what is a public nuisance, and particular uses often have been selectively targeted. . . . The Court's references to "common-law" background principles, however, indicate that legislative determinations do not constitute "state nuisance and property law" for the Court.

16. Also, until today the fact that the regulation prohibited uses that were lawful at the time the owner purchased did not determine the constitutional question. The brewery, the brickyard, the cedar trees, and the gravel pit were all perfectly legitimate uses prior to the passage of the regulation. *See Mugler v. Kansas*, 123 U.S. at 654; *Hadacheck v. Sebastian*, 239 U.S. 394 (1915); *Miller*, 276 U.S. at 272; *Goldblatt v. Hempstead*, 369 U.S. 590 (1962). This Court explicitly acknowledged in *Hadacheck* that "[a] vested interest cannot be asserted against [the police power] because of conditions once obtaining. To so hold would preclude development and fix a city forever in its primitive conditions." 239 U.S. at 410 (citation omitted).

at common law, state courts make exactly the decision that the Court finds so troubling when made by the South Carolina General Assembly today: They determine whether the use is harmful. Common-law public and private nuisance law is simply a determination whether a particular use causes harm. *See* William L. Prosser, *Private Action for Public Nuisance*, 52 VA. L. REV. 997 (1966) ("*Nuisance* is a French word which means nothing more than harm"). There is nothing magical in the reasoning of judges long dead. They determined a harm in the same way as state judges and legislatures do today. If judges in the 18th and 19th centuries can distinguish a harm from a benefit, why not judges in the 20th century, and if judges can, why not legislators? There simply is no reason to believe that new interpretations of the hoary common-law nuisance doctrine will be particularly "objective" or "value free." Once one abandons the level of generality of *sic utere tuo ut alienum non laedas*, . . . one searches in vain, I think, for anything resembling a principle in the common law of nuisance.

***

V.

The Court makes sweeping and, in my view, misguided and unsupported changes in our takings doctrine. While it limits these changes to the most narrow subset of government regulation — those that eliminate all economic value from land — these changes go far beyond what is necessary to secure petitioner Lucas' private benefit. One hopes they do not go beyond the narrow confines the Court assigns them to today.

I dissent.

[Justice Stevens's dissent, and Justice Souter's statement, are omitted.]

points for discussion

1. *The case that launched 2,000 ships.* According to one study, law review authors cited the *Lucas* decision in their articles more than 2,000 times between 1992 and 2007. Josh Eagle, *A Window into the Regulated Commons: The Takings Clause, Investment Security, and Sustainability*, 34 ECOLOGY L.Q. 619, 620 (2007). Why do you think the decision generated so much controversy?

2. *A question of value(s).* Without question, the single most important fact in *Lucas* was that if Mr. Lucas couldn't build a habitable structure on the property, then it had no economic value. This fact was established at the state court trial. In order to establish that the property had value, the state's attorney put an expert witness (real estate appraiser) on the stand to testify as to the market value of the property with the Beachfront Management Act's restrictions in place. Mr. Lucas's counsel challenged this testimony, arguing that, while the witness was qualified to testify about real estate values, he was not qualified to testify about the value of real estate restricted by the

specific provisions in the Beachfront Management Act because he had never before appraised similarly restricted property. The trial court judge granted plaintiff's motion to strike the expert's testimony, rendering the absence of value a *legal* fact. Would you pay anything for it? Can you think of anyone else who might be interested in purchasing it? Think back to the New Jersey and Oregon beach access cases in Chapter 6! One noted scholar has argued that the no-value finding only makes sense if one assumes that land is valuable only because it can be developed. Joseph L. Sax, *Property Rights and the Economy of Nature: Understanding* Lucas v. South Carolina Coastal Council, 45 STAN. L. REV. 1433, 1446 (". . . *Lucas* represents the Court's rejection of pleas to engraft the values of the economy of nature onto traditional notions of the rights of land ownership."). Are the ecological values of undeveloped property valuable to the owner?

3. *Who says it's a nuisance?* The chances are small that, in the future, a court will make a factual finding that a particular regulation renders a piece of property completely valueless. Without that finding, courts will determine whether or not compensation is owed by applying the *Penn Central* balancing test. In other words, few cases are likely to fall into the *Lucas* category. The more important component of the *Lucas* decision is the Court's interpretation of the "nuisance defense"; more precisely, the Court's view that liability-insulating nuisance prevention must have a basis in something other than a statute or regulation:

> Any limitation so severe cannot be newly legislated or decreed (without compensation), but must inhere in the title itself, in the restrictions that background principles of the State's law of property and nuisance already place upon land ownership. A law or decree with such an effect must, in other words, do no more than duplicate the result that could have been achieved in the courts — by adjacent landowners (or other uniquely affected persons) under the State's law of private nuisance, or by the State under its complementary power to abate nuisances that affect the public generally, or otherwise.

This rule (or interpretation of a rule) raises many questions: Where should courts look to see whether the common law recognized the type of nuisance being legislated against? What if the nuisance in question is similar to other kinds of common law nuisances, but was simply never litigated (and thus never made it into reported common law)? How can private nuisance law inform landowners' expectations when private nuisances are almost always resolved on a case-by-case basis? What are we to make of the words "so severe" in the passage above? Do they mean that this particular interpretation of the nuisance defense only applies in *Lucas*-like, "100 percent wipe-out" cases?

4. *Information on "background."* What are "background principles of the State's law of property"? The idea here is that, like the law of nuisance, long-standing state property rules might similarly prevent a landowner from using his property

in certain ways. Some courts have found that the public trust doctrine is one such background principle; how might it limit the ways in which a landowner can use his property? *See* Michael C. Blumm & Lucus Ritchie, Lucas's *Unlikely Legacy: The Rise of Background Principles as Categorical Takings Defenses*, 29 HARV. ENVTL. L. REV. 321 (2005). Think back to the *Thornton* case in Chapter 6. Is "custom" a background principle?

5. *Retreat in action.* In the Beachfront Management Act, the South Carolina legislature explicitly adopted a policy of retreat from the oceanfront. As noted in the opinion, the mechanisms of the Act's zoning system are what it calls baselines and setback lines. In the case of most beachfront property, these two lines work as follows: OCRM's engineer draws a baseline (on a map) through the crest of the primary oceanfront dune. (Lines are re-drawn every eight to ten years.) Then, the engineer draws a setback line landward of the baseline, and parallel to it, at a distance that equals 40 times the average annual erosion rate in the area. (In no case can the distance between the baseline and the setback line be less than 20 feet.) New construction between the two lines is limited to 5,000 square feet of heated space, and the structure must be located as far landward on the lot as is practicable. Damaged buildings may be rebuilt, but are limited to the size of the original structure. As also noted in the opinion, construction seaward of the baseline is limited to the structures described in Section 48-39-290(A). How exactly will these measures lead to retreat?

6. *The aftermath of* Lucas. The Supreme Court remanded the case to the Supreme Court of South Carolina in order for that court to determine whether there were "background principles of the State's law of property and nuisance" that would have limited Mr. Lucas's right to construct a home on his land. The court held oral arguments on November 18, 1992. (These arguments are summarized in Blake Hudson, *The Public and Wildlife Trust Doctrines and the Untold Story of the* Lucas *Remand*, 34 COLUM. J. ENVTL. L. 99, 130-40 (2009).) The Supreme Court of South Carolina ruled that there were no such background principles, and that the state was liable. Before the subsequent hearing on damages could occur, the parties settled the case. South Carolina purchased the two lots from Mr. Lucas for $950,000 and paid him an additional $725,000 for litigation costs, attorneys' fees, and interest. "South Carolina later resold Mr. Lucas' property to another developer for $785,000." Douglas W. Kmiec, *At Last, the Supreme Court Solves the Takings Puzzle*, 19 HARV. J.L. PUB. POL'Y 147, 151 n.27 (1995).

b. Limits on the Construction of Erosion Control Devices: North Carolina

When the state prevents a landowner from protecting her property from the sea, establishing a "rolling easement," is it liable for the damage caused by the sea?

Photo: Bill Eiser

Figure 9-5. *Lucas*
The *Lucas* lots today (on either side of the modern home).

Shell Island Homeowners Association, Inc. v. Tomlinson

517 S.E.2d 406 (N.C. Ct. App. 1999)

Judge MARTIN delivered the opinion of the Court of Appeals of North Carolina.

Plaintiffs Casteen and Schnabel are owners of units at the Shell Island Resort Hotel Condominium ("Shell Island Resort"); plaintiff Shell Island Homeowners Association, Inc., is an association of all unit owners at Shell Island Resort, which is located at the north end of Wrightsville Beach, North Carolina, just south of Mason's Inlet. Plaintiffs filed this action on 7 January 1998 against Eugene B. Tomlinson, Chairman of the North Carolina Coastal Resources Commission, the North Carolina Coastal Resources Commission ("CRC"), the Department of Environment and Natural Resources for the State of North Carolina ("DENR"), Wayne McDevitt, Secretary of DENR, and the State of North Carolina (hereinafter "defendants"), challenging the "hardened structure rule" and variance provision adopted by the CRC and codified at 15A North Carolina Administrative Code ("NCAC") 7H.0308 and 7H.0301. The rule provides:

> Permanent erosion control structures may cause significant adverse impacts on the value and enjoyment of adjacent properties or public access to and use of the ocean beach, and, therefore, are prohibited. Such structures include, but are not limited to: bulkheads; seawalls; revetments; jetties; groins and breakwaters.

15A NCAC 7H.0308(a)(1)(B) (Specific Use Standards for Ocean Hazard Areas). . . .

. . . [P]laintiffs have sought permits to construct various hardened erosion control structures to protect Shell Island Resort from the southward migration of Mason's Inlet; defendants, enforcing the "hardened structure rule," have denied those applications and refused plaintiffs' requests for variances. Plaintiffs did not seek administrative review of any of defendants' decisions enforcing the hardened structure rules, and they have not applied for a permit for a permanent erosion control structure since their application for a variance was originally denied on 6 February 1996. Instead, on 7 January 1998, over two years after plaintiffs submitted their original permit request, plaintiffs filed the complaint in this action alleging twelve claims for declaratory and injunctive relief by which they (1) challenge the validity and enforcement of the hardened structure rules; (2) seek a declaration that plaintiffs have the right to build a permanent hardened erosion control structure of unspecified design; and (3) seek damages for a taking of their property without just compensation by reason of defendants' denial of their application for a CAMA permit for construction of a permanent erosion control structure.

The North Carolina Coastal Federation ("intervenor-defendant") was permitted to intervene as a party defendant on 4 March 1998. Defendants moved to dismiss plaintiff's complaint. . . . On 14 July 1998, the trial court entered an order dismissing plaintiffs' complaint. . . . Plaintiffs appeal.

***

[The Court discussed issues relating to standing and jurisdiction, including the question of whether plaintiffs had exhausted their administrative remedies.]

B.

The remaining issue for decision is whether plaintiffs' First, Second, and Fourth claims for relief in which they essentially allege that the hardened structure rules have effected a regulatory taking of plaintiffs' property without just compensation, for which taking they seek damages, state claims upon which relief can be granted. We hold these claims were also properly dismissed.

In their First claim for relief, plaintiffs allege that the rules both facially and as applied violate the Fifth and Fourteenth amendments of the Federal Constitution and similar state constitutional provisions in that the rules effect a taking of plaintiffs' property without just compensation. Plaintiffs' Second claim for relief seeks a declaratory judgment that defendants' actions constitute an inverse condemnation of their property, and damages. Their Fourth claim for relief alleges that defendants' permit and variance denials were contrary to G.S. § 113A-128, which provides that "nothing in this Article authorizes any governmental agency to adopt a rule or issue any order that constitutes a taking of property in violation of the Constitution of this State or of the United States."

However, plaintiffs have failed to identify, on the face of the complaint, any legally cognizable property interest which has been taken by defendants. The invasion of property and reduction in value which plaintiffs allege clearly stems from the natural migration of Mason's Inlet, and plaintiffs have based their takings claim on their need for "a permanent solution to the erosion that threatens its property," and the premise that "the protection of property from erosion is an essential right of property owners. . . ." The allegations in plaintiffs' complaint have no support in the law, and plaintiffs have failed to cite to this Court any persuasive authority for the proposition that a littoral or riparian landowner has a right to erect hardened structures in statutorily designated areas of environmental concern to protect their property from erosion and migration. The courts of this State have considered natural occurrences such as erosion and migration of waters to be, in fact, natural occurrences, a consequence of being a riparian or littoral landowner, which consequence at times operates to divest landowners of their property. Our Supreme Court has stated that when the location of a body of water constituting the boundary of a tract of land,

> is gradually and imperceptibly changed or shifted by accretion, reliction, or erosion, the margin or bed of the stream or body, as so changed, remains the boundary line of the tract, which is extended or restricted accordingly. The owner of the riparian land thus loses title to such portions as are so worn or washed away or encroached upon by the water. Thus the lots of the plaintiff were gradually worn away by the churning of the ocean on the shore and thereby lost. Its title was divested by "the sledge-hammering seas the inscrutable tides of God."

Carolina Beach Fishing Pier, Inc. v. Town of Carolina Beach, 277 N.C. 297, 304 (1970) (citations omitted).

In *Adams Outdoor Advertising of Charlotte v. North Carolina Dept. of Transp.*, 112 N.C. App. 120 (1993), this Court held that allegations of mere incidental or consequential interferences with property rights are insufficient to maintain an action for inverse condemnation. In *Adams*, a billboard owner sued the State for inverse condemnation, alleging that the State's planting of vegetation within its right-of-way adjacent to premises upon which plaintiff's billboards stood was a taking of the owner's property. This Court held that the plaintiff's action was properly dismissed pursuant to Rule 12(b)(6), stating,

> A plaintiff must show an actual interference with or disturbance of property rights resulting in injuries which are not merely consequential or incidental.
>
> While Black's Law Dictionary does not define the word consequential, it does define the term consequential damages, and from this definition, we may determine what the Supreme Court meant when it wrote of "injuries which are not merely consequential." Consequential damages means "such damage, loss or injury as does not flow directly and immediately from the act of the party, but only from some of the consequences or results of such act." Black's Law Dictionary 390 (6th ed. 1990). Black's Law Dictionary defines incidental as "depending upon or appertaining to something else as primary; something necessary, appertaining to, or depending upon another which is termed the principal; something incidental to the main purpose." Black's Law Dictionary 762. Using these definitions, we conclude that plaintiff's complaint fails to state a claim of inverse condemnation.
>
> . . .
>
> Defendant's planting of trees as part of its beautification project was defendant's primary act, of which the obscuring of plaintiff's billboards was only a

consequential or incidental result. Moreover, we note that defendant's use of its right-of-way to plant trees is consistent with its statutory powers.

112 N.C. App. at 122-23. . . .

Similarly, in the present case, plaintiffs' complaint does not allege that the migration of Mason's Inlet and the resulting erosion of plaintiffs' property have been caused by any regulatory action taken by defendants, and these naturally occurring phenomena are the primary causes of any loss sustained by plaintiffs. Defendants' consistent enforcement of the hardened structure rules, consistent with its statutory powers, is merely incidental to these naturally occurring events. Plaintiffs' complaint fails to allege any right supported by law to construct a hardened erosion control structure in an area designated by statute as one of environmental concern, nor does it allege that plaintiffs have lost all economically beneficial or productive use of their property; rather, plaintiffs have merely asserted that they have "experienced a significant reduction in use/value of the Hotel," which is insufficient to support a takings claim. . . .

In addition, plaintiffs' complaint specifically alleges that the hardened structure rules which they challenge were adopted in 1982, three years prior to issuance of the original CAMA permit for construction of the Shell Island Resort. The hardened structure rules were contained in the very regulatory scheme under which the original permit was issued, and the land upon which the hotel was constructed was subject to the restrictions at the time the permit was issued.

In *Bryant v. Hogarth*, 127 N.C. App. 79, *disc. review denied*, 347 N.C. 396 (1997), owners of an exclusive franchise to cultivate shellfish in a submerged tract of land sought a declaration that the Marine Fisheries Division's ("MFD") designation of the tract as a primary nursery area ("PNA"), and refusal to allow use of mechanical harvesting therein rendered their interest in the tract worthless, constituting a regulatory taking. This Court stated,

> plaintiffs' franchise was not acquired free of government regulation. See *State v. Sermons*, 169 N.C. 285, 287 (1915) (shellfish come well within police power of State and "are subject to rules and regulations reasonably designed to protect them and promote their increase and growth"). Indeed, the very statute granting the franchise to plaintiffs' predecessor in interest also gave the shellfish commissioners exclusive jurisdiction and control over shell-fisheries covered by the legislation.
>
> In addition, we note the tract was designated a PNA 1 November 1977 and that the administrative rules prohibiting mechanical harvesting of shellfish in such waters were adopted the same date. Plaintiffs' deed for purchase of the franchise was filed 25 August 1982, more than five years later. *Accordingly, plaintiffs' complaint failed to allege a claim of compensable taking under G.S. § 113-206(e) in consequence of the tract being subject to the challenged PNA restriction at the time of acquisition.* See *Lucas v. South Carolina Coastal Council*, 505 U.S. 1003, 1029 (1992) (existing regulation distinguished from future regulation for purposes of a "taking"; "newly legislated or decreed" regulation which prohibits all economically beneficial use of land without compensation constitutes a taking, but latter does not occur and no compensation required when one is barred by rules existing at time title to property acquired); *see also Hughes v. North Carolina State Hwy.*

Comm., 275 N.C. 121, 130 (1969) (purchaser with notice is chargeable with knowledge he would have acquired had he exercised ordinary care to ascertain truth concerning matters affecting his property interest).

***

Because plaintiffs have not exhausted nor properly pled justifiable avoidance of the legislatively established administrative remedies for denial of permit applications, they may not in the instant separate action mount a collateral attack by claiming such denial constituted a taking of the franchise. . . .

127 N.C. App. at 84-87 (emphasis added). Similarly, in this case, because plaintiff's tract was subject to the challenged restrictions at the time the original permit was issued and the hotel was constructed, there can be no claim of compensable taking by reason of the regulations. *Id.; see also, Lucas v. South Carolina Coastal Council,* at 1027 ("Where the State seeks to sustain regulation that deprives land of all economically beneficial use, we think it may resist compensation only if the logically antecedent inquiry into the nature of the owner's estate shows that the proscribed use interests were not part of his title to begin with."). . . .

Because plaintiffs have failed to state a viable claim for relief for a regulatory taking, their Second claim for relief alleging an inverse condemnation of their property also necessarily fails. . . .

Moreover, even assuming *arguendo* that plaintiffs had the ability to challenge the hardened structure rules on equal protection and due process grounds, the allegations in plaintiffs' complaint nevertheless fail to state a claim upon which relief can be granted. In *Town of Beech Mountain v. Watauga County,* 91 N.C. App. 87 (1988), *affirmed,* 324 N.C. 409, *cert. denied,* 493 U.S. 954 (1989), this Court upheld a Rule 12(b)(6) dismissal of an equal protection claim where, on the face of the complaint, the challenged statute bore a rational basis to a legitimate government interest. We stated:

> The Equal Protection Clause is not violated merely because a statute classifies similarly situated persons differently, so long as there is a reasonable basis for the distinction. When a statute is challenged on equal protection grounds, it is subjected to a two-tiered analysis. The first tier, or "strict scrutiny" provides the highest level of review and is employed only when the classification impermissibly interferes with the exercise of a fundamental right or operates to the peculiar disadvantage of a suspect class. To survive this level of review, the government must demonstrate that the classification created by statute is necessary to promote a compelling government interest. A class is suspect "when it is saddled with such disabilities, or subjected to such a history of purposeful unequal treatment, or relegated to such a position of political powerlessness as to command particular consideration from the judiciary." If a statute does not burden the exercise of a fundamental right or operate to the peculiar disadvantage of a suspect class, the statute is analyzed under the second tier and the government need only show that the classification in the challenged statute has some rational basis. A statute survives analysis under this level if it bears some rational relationship to a conceivable, legitimate interest of government. Statutes subject to this level of review come before the Court with a presumption of constitutionality.

91 N.C. App. at 90-91 (citations omitted).

Here, plaintiffs have not alleged their classification in any suspect class such as race, religion, or alienage, nor have they alleged that the hardened structure rules discriminate on such a basis. Furthermore, plaintiffs have not alleged that the rules burden any recognized fundamental personal right, and we discern none from the allegations of the complaint. Thus, in reviewing whether plaintiffs have stated an equal protection claim upon which relief may be granted, we must determine whether the hardened structure rules have a "rational relationship to a conceivable, legitimate interest of government," reviewed under a presumption of constitutionality. We hold that they do; the protection of lands of environmental concern is a conceivable and legitimate government interest, as is the preservation of value and enjoyment of adjacent properties and the need for the public to have access and use of the State's ocean beaches. The hardened structure rules, which prevent permanent structures from being erected in environmentally sensitive areas which may adversely impact the value of the land and adjacent properties, as well as the right to public enjoyment of such areas are clearly rationally related to the legitimate government end.

Plaintiffs' allegations that the hardened structure rules "deprive the Plaintiff of property without procedural and substantive due process of law" also fail to state a claim upon which relief can be granted. As earlier noted, plaintiffs have shown no established right to construct hardened structures in areas of environmental concern, thus, they have failed to plead a legally cognizable right to support a claim of due process. In addition, the allegations of the complaint detail the administrative process through which plaintiffs have been provided an ample opportunity to be heard and to seek review of defendants' permit and variance application decisions.

***

The order dismissing plaintiffs' complaint is affirmed.

points for discussion

1. *Right to move.* In *Tomlinson*, the court implies that the migratory legal coastline inheres in the title to upland property. If the state acted to prevent this boundary from moving, and the upland owner was thus ultimately physically disconnected from the sea, would the property owner have a claim against the state? (Recall *Stop the Beach Renourishment.*) In *United States v. Milner*, 583 F.3d 1174 (9th Cir. 2009), the government sought removal of seawall-like rip-rap structures that upland owners had at some point installed on their property. The government's argument was based on the theory that those structures were on public property because the legal coastline would have moved landward, but for those structures. The Ninth Circuit ruled in the government's favor on this issue on the ground that "the Homeowners cannot permanently fix the tideland boundary. . . ." *Id.* at 1191. Is the migratory boundary a private and public property right? What are the limits on these rights? *See* John D. Echeverria, *Managing Lands*

Behind Shore Protection Structures in the Era of Climate Change, 28 J. LAND USE & ENVTL. L. 71 (2012); Katrina M. Wyman & Nicholas R. Williams, *Migrating Boundaries*, 65 FLA. L. REV. 1957, 1969 (2013).

2. *Some hard (structure) questions.* While most coastal states have placed some limits on hard erosion control structures, no state has banned all types of structures along all kinds of shorelines. More states have placed limits on parallel structures, for example, seawalls and bulkheads, than on perpendicular structures, for example, groins and jetties. Why do you think this is the case? States are also far more likely to ban

Photo: Buddy and Dana Craig/Wikimedia Commons

Figure 9-6. Geotube on a Texas Beach

the construction of hard structures on beachfront properties than on other coastal waterfront properties, such as on land bordering estuaries. Why do you think this is so?

3. *Some harder questions.* While simple in theory, a legal ban on hard structures is very difficult to design. Here are four of many reasons: First, what is a hard structure? Statutes must define these carefully, as coastal engineers will always be developing new mechanisms. For example, would you call the geotube pictured in Figure 9-6 a "hard structure"? Second, how should laws deal with the fact that many hard structures already exist, that is, were constructed prior to the ban? Should (can?) the law require landowners to remove existing structures? Should owners of existing structures that are falling apart, or are destroyed, be permitted to maintain or rebuild them? Third, should state agencies be permitted to build or rebuild structures in order to protect infrastructure such as roads, water lines, or sewer systems? Fourth, *which* landowners should be prevented from building hard structures? It might be easy to rationalize a ban on new structures on waterfront property. But what if a future-conscious landowner who owned property one or two parcels back from the waterfront wanted to build a "seawall"?

4. *The right to protect one's property.* What property right did the plaintiffs in *Shell Island* allege had been taken? Is there a "right to protect one's property" in the bundle of sticks? One can find many analogous situations in other areas of law. What were the legal rules that you studied in Criminal Law relating to a person's right to protect her home from burglary? The common law version of the so-called common enemy doctrine allowed a landowner to take any steps necessary to protect her real property from flood waters, regardless of the impact on her neighbors. *See, e.g., White v. Pima*

Cty., 775 P.2d 1154 (Ariz. 1989). And, in the context of the Endangered Species Act, courts have held that a person may kill an endangered bear to protect his life, but not his sheep. *See Christy v. Hodel*, 857 F.2d 1324 (9th Cir. 1988); *see also* Justice White's dissent from the Supreme Court's decision to deny *certiorari* in that case, at 490 U.S. 1114 (1989). What are the best arguments for and against a state's authority to prevent the installation of hard structures? For and against compensation for the imposition of such a rule? *See Wooten v. S.C. Coastal Council*, 510 S.E.2d 716 (S.C. 1999). *See also* Frances H. Bohlen & John J. Burns, *The Privilege to Protect Property by Dangerous Barriers and Mechanical Devices*, 35 YALE L.J. 525 (1926).

5. *Setbacks versus rolling easements.* There is a good argument that rolling easements are more efficient than setbacks in terms of sending appropriate signals to upland property owners:

> In general, preventing development [through setbacks] will have a higher social cost than rolling easements, because the former prevents the property from being used between now and whenever the sea rises enough to erode it, which may be decades or centuries in the future. If a property owner wants to build in spite of the knowledge that the house will have to be abandoned a few decades hence, her reason may be that the rental value of a bayfront house — even for a short period of time — exceeds the cost of the structure.
>
> Consider a numerical example. A coastal lot would become tideland if sea level rises three feet. It is worth $20,000 as a site for a $180,000 house and $10,000 in an alternative use. Preventing development would thus impose a net cost of $10,000. A rolling easement, by contrast, would allow rent to be collected on the property for many decades. Assume further that the cost of moving the house (and cleaning up the site) would be $30,000, while the cost of a bulkhead would be $10,000. Given these assumptions, the bulkhead restriction would cost the property owner a total of $40,000 when the sea rises three feet. At a 5% interest rate, the impact of a rolling easement on the market value would thus be $300 if a three-foot rise was certain to occur in 100 years. But given EPA's estimate that such a rise has only a 5% probability, the expected cost would be $15. In this case, a rolling easement costs 1/666 as much as a setback, *i.e.*, 0.075% of the value of the land. If the property was four feet above mean high water, the rolling easement would cost only $3, or 0.015% of the land value.
>
> Setbacks are not always economically inefficient. If locating a house at the landward end of a given lot allows the house to last for sixty instead of thirty years, the long-term benefit is probably greater than the initial aesthetic cost a buyer attributes to being farther from the water. In those areas that are likely to be inundated soon, the cost of forgoing the use of the land would be small. But the setback implied by a four-foot rise in sea level would place an area the size of Massachusetts off limits to development, preventing any development on many parcels of land.

James G. Titus, *Rising Seas, Coastal Erosion, and the Takings Clause: How to Save Wetlands and Beaches Without Hurting Property Owners*, 57 MD. L. REV. 1279, 1322 (1998).

2. Maximizing Access

As we saw in Chapter 6, courts in some states, such as Oregon and New Jersey, have interpreted the common law in a way that enhances public access to the dry sand part of the beach. Among the goals of the CZMA is to encourage states to develop programs that "provide for . . . public access to the coasts for recreation purposes." 16 U.S.C. § 1452(2)(E). And NOAA may not approve a state program unless it includes: "A definition of the term 'beach' and a planning process for the protection of, and access to, public beaches and other public coastal areas of environmental, recreational, historical, esthetic, ecological, or cultural value." 16 U.S.C. § 1455(d)(2)(I). As the following materials illustrate, states have satisfied these requirements in various ways, incorporating existing laws and creating new ones.

a. Rolling Dry Sand Easements: Texas

In 1959, long before Congress passed the CZMA, the Texas legislature passed what is arguably Texas's most important coastal law, the Open Beaches Act. (Recall that the CZMA allows states to incorporate existing statutes and agencies into their CZMA coastal program.) The genesis of the Open Beaches Act was the Supreme Court of Texas's decision in *Luttes v. State*, 159 Tex. 500 (1958). In that case, the court interpreted Texas common law as setting the legal coastline at the mean-high-tide line rather than, as the state had argued, the highest high-tide (or vegetation) line. Movement of the legal coastline is a "zero-sum game." Thus, Luttes not only increased the amount of private property along the shore, but decreased (to an equal degree), the amount of public dry sand beach. In the Open Beaches Act, the Texas legislature sought to mitigate the impact of *Luttes* by making it unlawful for upland owners to obstruct public access to a dry sand area "if the public has acquired a right of use or easement to or over the area by prescription, dedication, or has retained a right by virtue of continuous right in the public." Tex. Nat. Res. Code § 61.013(a). (In 2009, Texas voters approved a ballot measure constitutionalizing the Open Beaches Act.)

Although it was driven by concerns over public access, the Open Beaches Act also serves as a form of erosion policy, effectively creating a construction setback. Given the reality of erosion, it was inevitable that some of the "public right" beaches in Texas would shrink or disappear over time. This led to the difficult question: If the beach disappeared, did the public's rights disappear as well?

In the 1980s, Texas courts issued several decisions establishing the rule that the public easement could move, or "roll," inland in order that the purpose of the public easement might still be satisfied. But, how far can the easement roll? There are (at least) three different scenarios. First, the easement (the gray-shaded strip in Figure 9-7) might have to move farther inland on owner *B*'s property, reducing the amount of purely private land owned by *B*. This is depicted in the figure as Scenario 1. Second, the easement might have to move so far inland that, while *B* still owned beachfront property, most or all of it would be sea-ward of the vegetation line (Scenario 2). Under this scenario, *B* could not build on the property because of the Act's prohibition on obstructing public access. Third, if the entire beachfront parcel were lost to erosion, then the public easement would have to shift onto *A*'s lot (Scenario 3).

In the first two cases, the common law of easements provides some support for the idea that an easement should be relocated on the servient parcel if necessary to accomplish its purposes. What happens in the third scenario? The Supreme Court of Texas answered this question (and revisited Scenarios 1 and 2, which had been addressed in prior decisions) in the following opinion.

Severance v. Patterson

345 S.W.3d 18 (Tex. 2010)

Justice WAINWRIGHT delivered the opinion of the Supreme Court of Texas.

This case comes before us in the form of certified questions from the United States Court of Appeals for the Fifth Circuit. Pursuant to Article V, Section 3-c of the Texas Constitution and Texas Rule of Appellate Procedure 58.1, we answer the following questions:

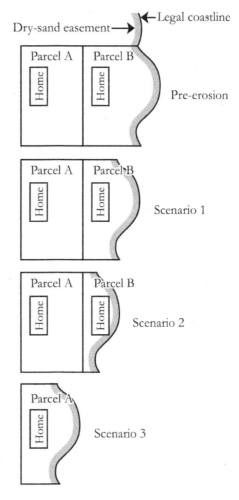

Figure 9-7. How Far Can a Texas Dry Sand Easement Roll?

1. Does Texas recognize a "rolling" public beachfront access easement, *i.e.*, an easement in favor of the public that allows access to and use of the beaches on the Gulf of Mexico, the boundary of which easement migrates solely according to naturally caused changes in the location of the vegetation line, without proof of prescription, dedication or customary rights in the property so occupied?

2. If Texas recognizes such an easement, is it derived from common law doctrines or from a construction of the [Open Beaches Act]?

3. To what extent, if any, would a landowner be entitled to receive compensation (other than the amount already offered for removal of the houses) under Texas's law or Constitution for the limitations on use of her property effected by the landward migration of a rolling easement onto property on which no public easement has been found by dedication, prescription, or custom?

Severance v. Patterson, 566 F.3d 490, 503-04 (5th Cir. 2009), *certified questions accepted*, 52 Tex. Sup. Ct. J. 741 (May 15, 2009). The central issue is whether private beachfront properties on Galveston Island's West Beach are impressed with a right of public use under Texas law without proof of an easement.

Oceanfront beaches change every day. Over time and sometimes rather suddenly, they shrink or grow, and the tide and vegetation lines make corresponding shifts. Beachfront property lines retract or extend as previously dry lands become submerged by the surf or become dry after being submerged. Accordingly, public easements that burden these properties along the sea are also dynamic. They may shrink or expand gradually with the properties they encumber. Once established, we do not require the State to re-establish easements each time boundaries move due to gradual and imperceptible changes to the coastal landscape. However, when a beachfront vegetation line is suddenly and dramatically pushed landward by acts of nature, an existing public easement on the public beach does not "roll" inland to other parts of the parcel or onto a new parcel of land. Instead, when land and the attached easement are swallowed by the Gulf of Mexico in an avulsive event, a new easement must be established by sufficient proof to encumber the newly created dry beach bordering the ocean. These public easements may gradually change size and shape as the respective Gulf-front properties they burden imperceptibly change, but they do not "roll" onto previously unencumbered private beachfront property when avulsive events cause dramatic changes in the coastline.

Legal encumbrances or reservations on private property titles on West Beach in Galveston Island dating from original land grants during the Republic of Texas or at the inception of the State of Texas could provide a basis for a public easement by custom or reveal inherent restrictions on the titles of the privately owned portions of these beaches. Under Mexican law, which governed Texas prior to 1836, colonization of beachfront lands was precluded for national defense and commercial purposes without approval of the "federal Supreme Executive Power" of Mexico, presumably the Mexican President. However, in 1840 the Republic of Texas, as later confirmed by the State of Texas, granted private title to West Galveston Island without reservation by the State of either title to beachfront property or any public right to use the now privately owned beaches. Public rights to use of privately owned property on West Beach in Galveston Island, if such rights existed at that time, were extinguished in the land patents by the Republic of Texas to private parties. In some states, background principles of property law governing oceanfront property provide a basis for public ownership or use of the beachfront property. Such expansive principles are not extant in the origins of Texas. Indeed, the original transfer by the Republic to private parties forecloses the argument that background principles in Texas common law provide a basis for impressing the West Beach area with a public easement, absent appropriate proof.

The Texas Open Beaches Act (OBA) provides the State with a means of enforcing public rights to use of State-owned beaches along the Gulf of Mexico and of privately owned beach property along the Gulf of Mexico where an easement is established in favor of the public by prescription or dedication, or where a right of public use exists "by virtue of continuous right in the public." Tex. Nat. Res. Code

§§ 61.012, .013(a). When promulgated in 1959, the OBA did not purport to create new substantive rights for public easements along Texas's ocean beaches and recognized that mere pronouncements of encumbrances on private property rights are improper. Because we find no right of public use in historic grants to private owners on West Beach, the State must comply with principles of law to encumber privately owned realty along the West Beach of Galveston Island.

I. Background

In April 2005, Carol Severance purchased three properties on Galveston Island's West Beach. "West Beach" extends from the western edge of Galveston's seawall along the beachfront to the western tip of the island. One of the properties, the Kennedy Drive property, is at issue in this case.[2] A rental home occupies the property. The parties do not dispute that no easement has ever been established on the Kennedy Drive property. A public easement for use of a privately owned parcel seaward of

Photo: Bob McMillan/FEMA.

Figure 9-8. Hurricane Rita's Effects on a Galveston Beach

Severance's Kennedy Drive property preexisted her purchase. That easement was established in a 1975 judgment in the case of *John L. Hill, Attorney General v. West Beach Encroachment, et al.*, Cause No. 108,156 in the 122nd District Court, Galveston County, Texas. Five months after Severance's purchase, Hurricane Rita devastated the property subject to the easement and moved the line of vegetation landward. The entirety of the house on Severance's property is now seaward of the vegetation line. The State claimed a portion of her property was located on a public beachfront easement and a portion of her house interfered with the public's use of the dry beach. When the State sought to enforce an easement on her private property pursuant to the OBA, Severance sued several State officials in federal district court. She argued that the State, in attempting to enforce a public easement, without proving its existence, on property not previously encumbered by an easement, infringed her federal constitutional rights and constituted (1) an unreasonable seizure under the Fourth

---

2. Severance owned three properties on West Beach — on Gulf Drive, Kennedy Drive and Bermuda Beach Drive. Her original lawsuit included all three properties, but she only appealed the trial court's judgment dismissing her claims as to two properties. After oral argument to this Court on the certified questions, Severance sold one of two remaining homes at issue in a FEMA-funded buyout program. Only the Kennedy Drive property remains subject to this litigation.

Amendment, (2) an unconstitutional taking under the Fifth and Fourteenth Amendments, and (3) a violation of her substantive due process rights under the Fourteenth Amendment.

The State officials filed motions to dismiss on the merits and for lack of jurisdiction. The district court dismissed Severance's case after determining her arguments regarding the constitutionality of a rolling easement were "arguably ripe," but deficient on the merits. Not presented with the information concerning the Republic's land grant, the court held that, according to Texas property law, an easement on a parcel landward [*sic*] of Severance's property pre-existed her ownership of the property and that after an easement to private beachfront property had been established between the mean high tide and vegetation lines, it "rolls" onto new parcels of realty according to natural changes to those boundaries. *Severance v. Patterson*, 485 F. Supp. 2d 793, 802-04 (S.D. Tex. 2007). Severance only appealed her Fourth and Fifth Amendment challenges to the rolling easement theory. On appeal, the United States Court of Appeals for the Fifth Circuit determined her Fifth Amendment takings claim was not ripe, but certified unsettled questions of state law to this Court to guide its determination on her Fourth Amendment unreasonable seizure claim. *Severance*, 566 F.3d at 500.

Public Use of Texas's Dry Sand Beaches

What kind of public use served as the basis for prescriptive easements on the dry sand of Galveston's West Beach? In one of the first cases arising under the Open Beaches Act, *Seaway Co. v. Attorney General of the State of Texas*, 375 S.W.2d 923, 933-34 (1964), the court described witnesses' accounts: "The effect of their testimony is that general use of the beach west of the 13 Mile Road was made by them and others as members of the public. People used the beach from the water line to the sand dunes to drive to the west end of the Island and return. While it is true that they generally drove near the water where the sand was packed the height of the water varied from time to time so the sand would be packed nearer the line of vegetation and thus people would drive along the waters near the sand dunes. Some witnesses testified there was a 'low road' and a 'high road.' When the tide produced high waters on part of the beach, travel was up near the sand dunes. Of course, there was at least one high tide a day and usually there were two high tides. Too, the evidence reflects some high tides were and are higher than others. In addition there are high waters which are the result of tide and winds. This situation would require and permit travel up above the line of mean high tide. The waters would pack the sand, from time to time, up to the sand dunes. Travel on the beach west of the 13 Mile Road, was, of course, heavier on weekends and holidays and particularly during the summer months and the springtime. . . . There is sufficient evidence also to show that each year, particularly in the summer months, in the springtime, and on holidays and weekends, the members of the public generally parked their automobiles, since the advent of automobiles, at various places on West Beach and personally went into the water to fish and swim. . . ." [*See also* Figure 9-9. — EDS.]

A. Texas Property Law in Coastal Areas

We have not been asked to determine whether a taking would occur if the State ordered removal of Severance's house, although constitutional protections of property rights fortify the conclusions we reach. The certified questions require us to address the competing interests between the State's asserted right to a migratory public easement to use privately owned beachfront property on Galveston Island's West Beach and the rights of the private property owner to exclude others from her property. The "law of real property is, under [the federal] Constitution, left to the individual states to develop and administer." *Phillips Petrol. Co. v. Mississippi*, 484 U.S. 469, 484 (1988) (quoting *Hughes v. Washington*, 389 U.S. 290, 295 (1967) (Stewart, J., concurring)); *Stop the Beach Renourishment, Inc. v. Fla. Dep't of Envtl. Prot.*, __ U.S. __, 130 S. Ct. 2592, 2612, 177 L. Ed. 2d 184 (2010) ("The Takings Clause only protects property rights as they are established under state law, not as they might have been established or ought to have been established."); *Oregon ex rel. State Land Bd. v. Corvallis Sand & Gravel Co.*, 429 U.S. 363, 377 (1977) (explaining that "subsequent changes in the contour of the land, as well as subsequent transfers of the land, are governed by the state law" (citation omitted)).

Texas has a history of public use of Texas beaches, including on Galveston Island's West Beach. *See, e.g., Matcha v. Mattox*, 711 S.W.2d 95, 99 (Tex. App. — Austin 1986, writ ref'd n.r.e.) (holding that "[n]o one doubts that proof exists from which the district court could conclude that the public acquired an easement over Galveston's West Beach by custom"), *cert. denied*, 481 U.S. 1024 (1987); *Feinman v. State*, 717 S.W.2d 106, 113 (Tex. App. — Houston [1st Dist.] 1986, writ ref'd n.r.e.) (discussing evidence presented at the trial court that showed "public use of West

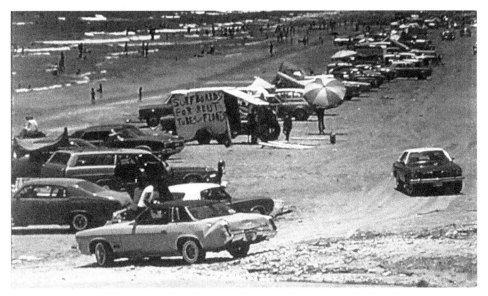

Photo: EPA/National Archives

Figure 9-9. Galveston's West Beach, 1973

Beach since before Texas gained its independence from Mexico"). These rights of use were proven in courtrooms with evidence of public enjoyment of the beaches dating to the nineteenth century Republic of Texas. But that history does not extend to use of West Beach properties, recently moved landward of the vegetation line by a dramatic event, that before and after the event have been owned by private property owners and were not impressed with pre-existing public easements. On one hand, the public has an important interest in the enjoyment of Texas's public beaches. But on the other hand, the right to exclude others from privately owned realty is among the most valuable and fundamental of rights possessed by private property owners.

1. Defining Public Beaches in Texas

The Open Beaches Act states the policy of the State of Texas for enjoyment of public beaches along the Gulf of Mexico. The OBA declares the State's public policy to be "free and unrestricted right of ingress and egress" to State-owned beaches and to private beach property to which the public "has acquired" an easement or other right of use to that property. . . . It defines public beaches as:

> any beach area, whether publicly or privately owned, extending inland from the line of mean low tide to the line of vegetation bordering on the Gulf of Mexico to which the public has acquired the right of use or easement to or over the area by prescription, dedication, presumption, or has retained a right by virtue of continuous right in the public since time immemorial, as recognized in law and custom. This definition does not include a beach that is not accessible by a public road or public ferry as provided in Section 61.021 of this code.

Id. § 61.001(8).[3] Privately owned beaches may be included in the definition of public beaches. *Id.* The Legislature defined public beach by two criteria: physical

---

3. In 2009, Texas voters approved an amendment to the Constitution to protect the public's right to "state-owned beach[es]" of the Gulf of Mexico. Tex. Const. Art. I, § 33. It protects public use of public beaches which, like the OBA, are defined as State-owned beaches and privately owned beachland "to which the public has acquired a right of use or easement. . . ." Although not at issue in this case, the amendment provides:

> Section 1. Article I, Texas Constitution, is amended by adding Section 33 to read as follows:
> Sec. 33. (a) In this section, "public beach" means a state-owned beach bordering on the seaward shore of the Gulf of Mexico, extending from mean low tide to the landward boundary of state-owned submerged land, and any larger area extending from the line of mean low tide to the line of vegetation bordering on the Gulf of Mexico to which the public has acquired a right of use or easement to or over the area by prescription or dedication or has established and retained a right by virtue of continuous right in the public under Texas common law.
> (b) The public, individually and collectively, has an unrestricted right to use and a right of ingress to and egress from a public beach. The right granted by this subsection is dedicated as a permanent easement in favor of the public.
> (c) The legislature may enact laws to protect the right of the public to access and use a public beach and to protect the public beach easement from interference and encroachments.
> (d) This section does not create a private right of enforcement.

location and right of use. A public beach under the OBA must border on the Gulf of Mexico. *Id.* The OBA does not specifically refer to inland bodies of water. Along the Gulf, public beaches are located on the ocean shore from the line of mean low tide to the line of vegetation, subject to the second statutory requirement explained below. *Id.* The area from mean low tide to mean high tide is called the "wet beach," because it is under the tidal waters some time during each day. The area from mean high tide to the vegetation line is known as the "dry beach."

The second requirement for a Gulf-shore beach to fall within the definition of "public beach" is the public must have a right to use the beach. This right may be "acquired" through a "right of use or easement" or it may be "retained" in the public by virtue of continuous "right in the public since time immemorial." *Id.*

The wet beaches are all owned by the State of Texas, which leaves no dispute over the public's right of use. . . . However, the dry beach often is privately owned and the right to use it is not presumed under the OBA.[5] The Legislature recognized that the existence of a public right to an easement in privately owned dry beach area of West Beach is dependent on the government's establishing an easement in the dry beach or the public's right to use of the beach "by virtue of continuous right in the public since time immemorial. . . ." Tex. Nat. Res. Code § 61.001(8). Accordingly, where the dry beach is privately owned, it is part of the "public beach" if a right to public use has been established on it. . . . Public beaches include Gulf-front wet beaches, State-owned dry beaches and private property in the dry beaches on which a public easement has been established.

In this case, before Hurricane Rita, Severance's Kennedy Drive property was landward of the vegetation line. After Hurricane Rita, because the storm moved the vegetation line landward, the property between Severance's land and the sea that was subject to a public easement was submerged in the surf or became part of the wet beach. Severance's Kennedy Drive parcel and her house are no longer behind the vegetation line but neither are they located in the wet beach owned by the State. At least a portion of Severance's Kennedy Drive property and all of her house are now located in the dry beach. The question is did the easement on the property seaward of Severance's property "roll" onto Severance's property? In other words, is Severance's house now located on part of the "public beach" and thereby subject to an enforcement action to remove it under the OBA? From the Fifth Circuit's statement of the case, we understand that no easement has been proven to exist on Severance's property under the OBA or the common law. We also presume that there are no express limitations or reservations in Severance's title giving rise to a public easement. The answer to the rolling easement question thus turns

---

5. The OBA includes two stated presumptions for purposes of ingress and egress to the sea. It provides that the title of private owners of dry beach area in Gulf beaches "does not include the right to prevent the public from using the area for ingress and egress to the sea." Tex. Nat. Res. Code § 61.020(a)(1). In 1991, the OBA was amended to add a second presumption that imposed "on the area a common law right or easement in favor of the public for ingress and egress to the sea." *Id.* § 61.020(a)(2). Although the constitutionality of these presumptions has been questioned, that issue is not before us. . . .

on whether Texas common law recognizes such an inherent limitation on private property rights along Galveston's West Beach, and if not, whether principles of Texas property law provide for a right of public use of beaches along the Gulf Coast.

2. History of Beach Ownership Along the Gulf of Mexico

Long-standing principles of Texas property law establish parameters for our analysis. It is well-established that the "soil covered by the bays, inlets, and arms of the Gulf of Mexico within tidewater limits belongs to the State, and constitutes public property that is held in trust for the use and benefit of all the people." *Lorino v. Crawford Packing Co.*, 142 Tex. 51 (Tex. 1943). . . . These lands are part of the public trust, and only the Legislature can grant to private parties title to submerged lands that are part of the public trust. . . .

Current title to realty and corresponding encumbrances on the property may be affected in important ways by the breadth of and limitations on prior grants and titles. . . . All the Gulf beachland in West Galveston Island that extended to the public trust was conveyed to private parties by the sovereign Republic of Texas as later affirmed by the State of Texas.

Having established that the State of Texas owned the land under Gulf tidal waters, the question remained how far inland from the low tide line did the public trust — the State's title — extend. We answered that question in *Luttes v. State*, 159 Tex. 500 (1958). This Court held that the delineation between State-owned submerged tidal lands (held in trust for the public) and coastal property that could be privately owned was the "mean higher high tide" line under Spanish or Mexican grants and the "mean high tide" line under Anglo-American law. . . . The wet beach is owned by the State as part of the public trust, and the dry beach is not part of the public trust and may be privately owned. . . .

These boundary demarcations are a direct response to the ever-changing nature of the coastal landscape because it is impractical to apply static real property boundary concepts to property lines that are delineated by the ocean's edge. The sand does not stay in one place, nor does the tide line. While the vegetation line may appear static because it does not move daily like the tide, it is constantly affected by the tide, wind, and other weather and natural occurrences.

A person purchasing beachfront property along the Texas coast does so with the risk that their property may eventually, or suddenly, recede into the ocean. When beachfront property recedes seaward and becomes part of the wet beach or submerged under the ocean, a private property owner loses that property to the public trust. . . . Likewise, if the ocean gradually recedes away from the land moving the high tide line seaward, a private property owner's land may increase at the expense of the public trust. . . . Regardless of these changes, the boundary remains fixed (relatively) at the mean high tide line. . . .

In 1959, the Legislature enacted the Open Beaches Act to address responses to the *Luttes* opinion establishing the common law landward boundary of State-owned beaches at the mean high tide line. The Legislature feared that this holding might "give encouragement to some overanxious developers to fence the seashore" as some private landowners had "erected barricades upon many beaches, some of these barricades extending into the water." Tex. Legis. Beach Study Comm., 57th Leg., R.S., The Beaches and Islands of Texas [hereinafter "Beach Study Comm., Beaches and Islands of Texas"] 1 (1961). . . . The OBA declared the State's public policy for the public to have "free and unrestricted access" to State-owned beaches, the wet beach, and the dry beach where the public "has acquired" an easement or other right to use that property. . . . To enforce this policy, the OBA prohibits anyone from creating, erecting, or constructing any "obstruction, barrier, or restraint that will interfere with the free and unrestricted right of the public" to access Texas beaches where the public has acquired a right of use or easement. . . . The Act authorizes the removal of barriers or other obstructions on

> state-owned beaches to which the public has the right of ingress and egress bordering on the seaward shore of the Gulf of Mexico or any larger area extending from the line of mean low tide to the line of vegetation bordering on the Gulf of Mexico *if the public has acquired* a right of use or easement to or over the area by prescription, dedication, or has *retained a right by virtue of continuous right in the public*.

Tex. Nat. Res. Code §§ 61.012, .013(a) (emphasis added).

The OBA does not alter *Luttes*. It enforces the public's right to use the dry beach on private property where an easement exists and enforces public rights to access and use State-owned beaches. Therefore, the OBA, by its terms, does not create or diminish substantive property rights. . . . In promulgating the OBA, the Legislature seemed careful to preserve private property rights by emphasizing that the enforcement of public use of private beachfront property can occur when a historic right of use is retained in the public or is proven by dedication or prescription. . . . The OBA also specifically disclaims any intent to take rights from private owners to Gulf-shore beach property. . . . Within these acknowledgments, the OBA proclaims that beaches should be open to the public. Certainly, the OBA guards the right of the public to use public beaches against infringement by private interests. But, as explained, the OBA is not contrary to private property rights at issue in this case under principles of Texas law. The public has a right to use the West Galveston beaches when the State owns the beaches or the government obtains or proves an easement for use of the dry beach under the common law or by other means set forth in the OBA.

***

B. Background on Severance's Property

Carol Severance purchased the Kennedy Drive property on Galveston Island's West Beach in 2005. The Fifth Circuit explained that "[n]o easement has ever been established on [her] parcel via prescription, implied dedication, or continuous right." 566 F.3d at 494. The State obtained the *Hill* judgment in 1975 that encumbered a strip of beach seaward of Severance's property. Severance's Kennedy Drive parcel was not included in the 1975 judgment. However, the parties dispute whether or not Severance's parcel was ever subject to a public easement.

In 1999, the Kennedy Drive house was on a Texas General Land Office (GLO) list of approximately 107 Texas homes located seaward of the vegetation line after Tropical Storm Frances hit the island in 1998. In 2004, the GLO again determined that the Kennedy Drive home was located "wholly or in part" on the dry beach in 2004, but did not threaten public health or safety and, at the time, was subject to a GLO two-year moratorium order. When Severance purchased the property, she received an OBA-mandated disclosure explaining that the property may become located on a public beach due to natural processes such as shoreline erosion, and if that happened, the State could sue seeking to forcibly remove any structures that come to be located on the public beach. . . . Winds attributed to Hurricane Rita shifted the vegetation line further inland in September 2005. In 2006, the GLO determined that Severance's house was entirely within the public beach.

The moratorium for enforcing the OBA on Severance's properties expired on June 7, 2006. Severance received a letter from the GLO requiring her to remove the Kennedy Drive home because it was located on a public beach. A second letter reiterated that the home was in violation of the OBA and must be removed from the beach, and offered her $40,000 to remove or relocate it if she acted before October 2006. She initiated suit in federal court. The Fifth Circuit certified questions of Texas law to this Court.

II. Dynamic Public Beachfront Easements

The first certified question asks if Texas recognizes "a 'rolling' public beachfront access easement, *i.e.*, an easement in favor of the public that allows access to and use of the beaches on the Gulf of Mexico, the boundary of which easement migrates solely according to naturally caused changes in the location of the vegetation line, without proof of prescription, dedication, or customary rights in the property so occupied?" 566 F.3d at 504. We have never held that the State has a right in privately owned beachfront property for public use that exists without proof of the normal means of creating an easement. And there is no support presented for the proposition that, during the time of the Republic of Texas or at the inception of our State, the State reserved the oceanfront for public use. . . . Therefore, considering the absence of any historic custom or inherent title limitations for public use on private West Beach property, principles of property law answer the first certified question.

Easements exist for the benefit of the easement holder for a specific purpose. An easement does not divest a property owner of title, but allows another to use the property for that purpose. . . . The existence of an easement "in general terms implies a grant of unlimited reasonable use such as is reasonably necessary and convenient and as little burdensome as possible to the servient owner." *Coleman v. Forister*, 514 S.W.2d 899, 903 (Tex. 1974). . . .

Easement boundaries are generally static and attached to a specific portion of private property. . . . "As a general rule, once the location of an easement has been established, neither the servient estate owner nor the easement holder may unilaterally relocate the servitude." Jon W. Bruce & James W. Ely, Jr., The Law of Easements and Licenses in Land § 7:13, at 7-30 (2009). Therefore, a new easement must be re-established for it to encumber a part of the parcel not previously encumbered. *See id.*

While the boundaries of easements on the beach are necessarily dynamic due to the composition of the beach and its constantly changing boundaries, easements for public use of privately owned dry beach do not necessarily burden the area between the mean high tide and vegetation lines when the land originally burdened by the easement becomes submerged by the ocean. They do not automatically move to the new properties; they must be proven.

Like easements, real property boundaries are generally static as well. But property boundaries established by bodies of water are necessarily dynamic. Because those boundaries are dynamic due to natural forces that affect the shoreline or banks, the legal rules developed for static boundaries are somewhat different. . . .

The nature of littoral property boundaries abutting the ocean not only incorporates the daily ebbs and flows of the tide, but also more permanent changes to the coastal landscape due to weather and other natural forces. Shoreline property ownership is typically delineated by boundaries such as the mean high tide and vegetation lines because they are easy to reference and locate. Sand and water are constantly moving and changing the landscape whether it is gradual and imperceptible or sudden and perceptible.

Courts generally adhere to the principle that littoral property owners gain or lose land that is gradually or imperceptibly added to or taken away from their banks or shores through erosion, the wearing away of land, and accretion, the enlargement of the land. . . . Avulsion, as derived from English common law, is the sudden and perceptible change in land and is said not to divest an owner of title. . . . We have never applied the avulsion doctrine to upset the mean high tide line boundary as established by *Luttes*.[16]

Property along the Gulf of Mexico is subjected to seasonal hurricanes and tropical storms, on top of the every-day natural forces of wind, rain, and tidal ebbs and flows that affect coastal properties and shift sand and the vegetation line. This is an ordinary hazard of owning littoral property. And, while losing property to the public trust as it becomes part of the wet beach or submerged under the ocean is an ordinary hazard of ownership for coastal property owners, it is far less reasonable to hold that a public easement can suddenly encumber an entirely new portion of a landowner's property that was not previously subject to that right of use. *See, e.g.*, *Phillips Petrol.*, 484 U.S. at 482 (discussing the importance of "honoring reasonable expectations in property interests[,]" but ultimately holding the property owner's expectations in that situation were unreasonable). Gradual movement of the vegetation line and mean high tide line due to erosion or accretion have very different practical implications.

---

16. Some states apply avulsion to determine that the mean high tide line as it existed before the avulsive event remains the boundary between public and private ownership of beach property after the avulsive event; therefore, allowing private property owners to retain ownership of property that becomes submerged under the ocean. . . . We have not accepted such an expansive view of the doctrine, but, we need not make that determination in this case.

Like littoral property boundaries along the Gulf Coast, the boundaries of corresponding public easements are also dynamic. The easements' boundaries may move according to gradual and imperceptible changes in the mean high tide and vegetation lines. However, if an avulsive event moves the mean high tide line and vegetation line suddenly and perceptibly causing the former dry beach to become part of State-owned wet beach or completely submerged, the private property owner is not automatically deprived of her right to exclude the public from the new dry beach. In those situations, when changes occur suddenly and perceptibly to materially alter littoral boundaries, the land encumbered by the easement is lost to the public trust, along with the easement attached to that land. Then, the State may seek to establish another easement as permitted by law on the newly created dry beach to enforce an asserted public right to use private land.

It would be an unnecessary waste of public resources to require the State to obtain a new judgment for each gradual and nearly imperceptible movement of coastal boundaries exposing a new portion of dry beach. These easements are established in terms of boundaries such as the mean high tide line and vegetation line; presumably public use moves according to and with those boundaries so the change in public use would likewise be imperceptible. Also, when movement is gradual, landowners and the State have ample time to reach a solution as the easement slowly migrates landward with the vegetation line. Conversely, when drastic changes expose new dry beach and the former dry beach that may have been encumbered by a public easement is now part of the wet beach or completely submerged under water, the State must prove a new easement on the area. Because sudden and perceptible changes by nature occur very quickly, it would be impossible to prove continued public use in the new dry beach, and it would be unfair to impose such drastic restrictions through the OBA upon an owner in those circumstances without compensation. . . .

If the public has an easement in newly created dry beach, as with any other property, the State must prove it. . . . [A] public beachfront easement in West Beach, although dynamic, does not roll. The public loses that interest in privately owned dry beach when the land to which it is attached becomes submerged underwater. While these boundaries are somewhat dynamic to accommodate the beach's everyday movement and imperceptible erosion and accretion, the State cannot declare a public right so expansive as to always adhere to the dry beach even when the land the easement originally attached to is eroded. . . .

On this issue of first impression, we hold that Texas does not recognize a "rolling" easement on Galveston's West Beach. Easements for public use of private dry beach property do change along with gradual and imperceptible changes to the coastal landscape. But, avulsive events such as storms and hurricanes that drastically alter pre-existing littoral boundaries do not have the effect of allowing a public use easement to migrate onto previously unencumbered property. This holding shall not be applied to use the avulsion doctrine to upset the long-standing boundary between public and private ownership at the mean high tide line. That result would be unworkable, leaving ownership boundaries to mere guesswork.

The division between public and private ownership remains at the mean high tide line in the wake of naturally occurring changes, even when boundaries seem to change suddenly. The State, as always, may act within a valid exercise of police power to impose reasonable regulations on coastal property or prove the existence of an easement for public use, consistent with the Texas Constitution and real property law.

***

A few Texas courts of appeals have reached results contrary to the holding in this opinion. In *Feinman*, the court held that public easements for use of dry beach can roll with movements of the vegetation line. . . .

The first Texas case to address the concept of a rolling easement in Galveston's West Beach is *Matcha v. Mattox*, 711 S.W.2d 95 (Tex. App. — Austin 1986, writ ref'd n.r.e.). In 1983, Hurricane Alicia shifted the vegetation line on the beach such that the Matchas' home had moved into the dry beach. The court held that legal custom — "a reflection in law of long-standing public practice" — supported the trial court's determination that a public easement had "migrated" onto private property. *Id.* at 101. The court reasoned that Texas law gives effect to the long history of recognized public use of Galveston's beaches, citing accounts of public use dating back to time immemorial, 1836 in this case. However, the legal custom germane to the matter is not the public use of beaches, it is whether the right in the public to a rolling easement has existed since time immemorial. The *Matcha* court's recognition of long-standing "custom" in public use of Galveston's beaches misses the point of whether a custom existed to give effect to a legal concept of a rolling beach, which would impose inherent limitations on private property rights. . . .

We disapprove of courts of appeals opinions to the extent they are inconsistent with our holding in this case. . . .

III. Conclusion

Land patents from the Republic of Texas in 1840, affirmed by legislation in the new State, conveyed the State's title in West Galveston Island to private parties and reserved no ownership interests or rights to public use in Galveston's West Beach. Accordingly, there are no inherent limitations on title or continuous rights in the public since time immemorial that serve as a basis for engrafting public easements for use of private West Beach property. Although existing public easements in the dry beach of Galveston's West Beach are dynamic, as natural forces cause the vegetation and the mean high tide lines to move gradually and imperceptibly, these easements do[] not migrate or roll landward to encumber other parts of the parcel or new parcels as a result of avulsive events. New public easements on the adjoining private properties may be established if proven pursuant to the Open Beach Act or the common law.[19]

---

19. We have not addressed in this opinion state police power, nuisance or other remedies that may authorize the government to act in the interests of the health, safety and welfare of the public.

Justice MEDINA, joined by Justice LEHRMANN, dissenting.

Texas beaches have always been open to the public. The public has used Texas beaches for transportation, commerce, and recreation continuously for nearly 200 years. The Texas shoreline is an expansive yet diminishing[2] public resource, and we have the most comprehensive public beach access laws in the nation. Since its enactment in 1959, the Texas Open Beaches Act ("OBA") has provided an enforcement mechanism for the public's common law right to access and to use Texas beaches.[3] The OBA enforces a reasoned balance between private property rights and the public's right to free and unrestricted use of the beach. Today, the Court's holding disturbs this balance and jeopardizes the public's right to free and open beaches.

After chronicling the history of Texas property law, the Court concludes that easements defined by natural boundaries are, by definition, dynamic. . . . Yet, in a game of semantics, the Court finds that such dynamic easements do not "roll." . . . The Court further distinguishes between movements by accretion and erosion and movements by avulsion, finding that gradual movements shift the easement's boundaries, but sudden movements do not. The Court's distinction protects public beach rights from so-called gradual events such as erosion but not from more dramatic events like storms, even though both events are natural risks known to the property owner. Because the Court's vague distinction between gradual and sudden or slight and dramatic changes to the coastline jeopardizes the public's right to free and open beaches, recognized over the past 200 years, and threatens to embroil the state in beach-front litigation for the next 200 years, I respectfully dissent.

I. Texas Coastal Property Ownership

. . . If this case were a matter of title, *Luttes* would provide the answer: the mean high tide separates public and private property ownership interests. But this case is about the enforcement of a common law easement that preserves the public's right to access the dry beach.

The mean low tide, mean high tide, and vegetation line are transitory.[7] Landowners may own property up to the mean high tide. But the exact metes and

---

2. Not only is Texas's coastline expansive, we also have the highest erosion rate in the nation, affecting "five to six feet of sand annually." Michael Hofrichter, *Texas's Open Beaches Act: Proposed Reforms Due to Coastal Erosion*, 4 ENVT'L & ENERGY L. & POL'Y J. 147, 148 (2009). This erosion rate causes coastal property lines to change annually.

3. It is important to note that the OBA only applies to public beaches that border the Gulf of Mexico and are accessible by public road or ferry. . . .

7. The mean low tide and high tide are averages assessed over a period of years. Their "actual determination at a given point on the coastline requires scientific measuring equipment and complex calculations extending over a lengthy period. Thus, as a practical matter, such physical determination of the landowner's actual boundary is not normally feasible." Richard Elliot, *The Texas Open Beaches Act: Public Rights to Beach Access*, 28 BAYLOR L. REV. 249, 383, 385 (1976). "The line of vegetation, on the other hand, is readily determinable with the naked eye at most points along the Gulf beaches." *Id.* However, all three lines are subject to the daily movements of ocean, which shift these lines both gradually and suddenly.

bounds of the beachfront property line cannot be ascertained with any specificity at any given time other than by reference to the mean high tide. Through shoreline erosion, hurricanes, and tropical storms, these lines are constantly moving both inland and seaward. In the West Bay system, whence this litigation arose, forty-eight percent of the shoreline is retreating, forty-seven percent is stable and six percent is advancing, at an average rate of –2.9 feet per year. The beaches on west Galveston Island, where Severance's property is located, have even higher retreat rates (a loss of over seven feet per year) because of their exposure to winds and waves. Natural erosion from waves and currents causes an overall shoreline retreat for the entire Texas coast.

These natural laws have compelled Texas common law to recognize rolling easements. Easements that allow the public access to the beach must roll with the changing coastline in order to protect the public's right of use. The dynamic principles that govern vegetation and tide lines must therefore apply to determine the boundaries of pre-existing public beachfront easements. *See Matcha v. Mattox*, 711 S.W.2d 95, 100 (Tex. App. — Austin 1986, writ ref'd n.r.e.) *cert. denied*, 481 U.S. 1024 (1987) ("An easement fixed in place while the beach moves would result in the easement being either under water or left high and dry inland, detached from the shore. Such an easement, meant to preserve the public right to use and enjoy the beach, would then cease functioning for that purpose"). "The law cannot freeze such an easement at one place anymore than the law can freeze the beach itself." *Id.*

II. Texas Recognizes Rolling Easements

The first certified question asks whether Texas recognizes rolling beachfront access easements that move with the natural boundaries by which they are defined. The answer is yes. The rolling easement "is not a novel idea." *Feinman*, 717 S.W.2d at 110. Courts consistently recognize the migrating boundaries of easements abutting waterways to uphold their purpose. *Id.* After all, "an easement is not so inflexible that it cannot accommodate changes in the terrain it covers." *Id.*

The law of easements, Texas law, and public policy support the enforcement of rolling easements. Such easements follow the movement of the dry beach in order to maintain their purpose and are defined by such purpose rather than geographic location. They are therefore affected by changes to the coast but never rendered ineffective by the change. The primary objective is not to ensure the easement's boundaries are fixed but rather that its purpose is never defeated.

A. Texas Easement Law

An easement is a non-possessory property interest that authorizes its holder to use the property of another for a particular purpose. . . . "A grant or reservation of an easement in general terms implies a grant of unlimited reasonable use such as is reasonably necessary and convenient and as little burdensome as possible to the servient owner." *Coleman v. Forister*, 514 S.W.2d 899, 903 (Tex. 1974). However, the burden on the servient estate is secondary to ensuring that the purpose of the easement is reasonably fulfilled. For example, oil and gas leases convey an implied easement to use the surface as reasonably necessary to fulfill the purpose of the lease. . . . The purpose of the easement cannot expand, but under certain circumstances, the geographic location of the easement may. . . .

Easements may be express or implied. Implied easements are defined by the circumstances that create the implication. . . . Express easements, however, must comply with the Statute of Frauds, which requires a description of the easement's location. . . . Under certain circumstances, even express easement boundaries may be altered to maintain the purpose of the easement. . . . [*See*] RESTATEMENT (THIRD) OF PROPERTY (SERVITUDES) § 4.1 (2000) (providing that an easement "should be interpreted to give effect to the intention of the parties ascertained from the language used in the instrument, or the circumstances surrounding the creation of the servitude, and to carry out the purpose for which it was created").

Rolling beachfront access easements are implied by prescription or continuous use of the dry beach and are defined by their purpose and their dynamic, non-static natural boundaries. To apply static real property concepts to beachfront easements is to presume their destruction. Hurricanes and tropical storms frequently batter Texas's coast. Avulsive events are not uncommon. The Court's failure to recognize the rolling easement places a costly and unnecessary burden on the state if it is to preserve our heritage of open beaches.

The Court's conclusion that beachfront easements are dynamic but do not roll defies not only existing law but logic as well. The definition of "roll" is "to impel forward by causing to turn over and over on a surface." Webster's Ninth New Collegiate Dictionary (Merriam-Webster Inc. 1983). "Dynamic" means "of or relating to physical force or energy" and "marked by continuous activity or change." *Id.* Both terms express movement, but neither term is limited by speed or degree of movement.

The Court also illogically distinguishes between shoreline movements by accretion and avulsion. On the one hand, the Court correctly declines to apply the avulsion doctrine to the mean high tide. . . . This means a property owner loses title to land if, after a hurricane or tropical storm, such land falls seaward of the mean high tide. On the other hand, this same hurricane, under the Court's analysis, requires the state to compensate a property owner for the land that now falls seaward of the vegetation line unless it was already a part of the public beachfront easement. Under the Court's analysis, the property line may be dynamic but beachfront easements must always remain temporary; the public's right to the beach can never be established and will never be secure.

The Court's distinctions nullify the purpose of rolling easements. I submit (in accord with several other Texas appellate courts that have addressed the issue of rolling easements) that natural movements of the mean high tide and vegetation line, sudden or gradual, re-establish the dynamic boundaries separating public and private ownership of the beach, as well as a pre-existing public beachfront access easement. So long as an easement was established over the dry beach before the avulsive event, it must remain over the new dry beach without the burden of having to re-establish a previously existing easement whose boundaries have naturally shifted.

Finally, I submit that once an easement is established, it attaches to the entire tract. . . . Regardless of how many times the original tract is subdivided, the easement remains. . . .

Private ownership of Galveston Island originated in two land grants issued by the Republic of Texas. First, it arose from the Menard Grant in 1838, which covers the east end of the Island. . . . Second, it issued from the Jones and Hall Grant in 1840, which encompasses 18,215 acres, and includes the West Beach, where Severance's property is located. . . .

The Court today reasons that because no *express* easement was made in these original land grants, no public easement can exist over the dry beach. . . . The Court, however, ignores the implied easement arising from the public's continuous use of the beach for nearly 200 years. The state may have relinquished title in these original grants, but it did not relinquish the public's right to access, use, and enjoy the beach. . . .

By implied prescription, implied dedication, or customary and continuous use, overwhelming evidence exists that Texans have been using the beach for nearly 200 years. *See Seaway Co. v. Att'y Gen.*, 375 S.W.2d 923, 936 (Tex. App.—Houston 1964, writ ref'd n.r.e.) (finding that "owners, beginning with the original ones, have thrown open the beach to public use and it has remained open"). . . . This evidence establishes that public beachfront access easements have been implied across this Texas coastline since statehood. As long as a dry beach exists, so too must beachfront access easements. Any other result deprives the public of its pre-existing, dominant right to unrestricted use and enjoyment of the public beach.

B. Texas Case Law

***

Before *Luttes*, the public assumed it had unrestricted access to use and enjoy the beach. After *Luttes*, in response to public concern over its right to access Texas beaches, the Texas Legislature passed the OBA to ensure that Texas beaches remained open for public use. Challenged five years later, the Houston Court of Civil Appeals found that a public easement existed on the West Beach of Galveston Island, forcing landowners to remove barriers and structures that prevented the public's access to and use of the public beach. . . .

In the years following the passage of the OBA, the shoreline naturally and predictably moved both gradually and suddenly. Texas courts have repeatedly held that once an easement is established, it expands or contracts ("rolls"), despite the sudden shift of the vegetation line. . . . *See Feinman*, 717 S.W.2d at 109-10 (after Hurricane Alicia); *Arrington v. Tex. Gen. Land Office*, 38 S.W.3d 764, 765 (Tex. App.—Houston [14th Dist.] 2001, no pet.) (after Tropical Storm Frances); *Brannan v. State*, No. 01-08-00179-CV, 2010 Tex. App. LEXIS 799, 2010 WL 375921, *2 (Tex. App. — Houston [1st Dist.] Feb. 4, 2010, pet. filed) (after unusually high tide or "bull tide"); *Matcha*, 711 S.W.2d at 100 (after hurricane of 1983); *Arrington v. Mattox*, 767 S.W.2d 957, 958 (1989) (after Hurricane Alicia). In short, Texas law has adopted "the rolling easement concept." *Feinman*, 717 S.W.2d at 110-11. The

Court's refusal to follow existing Texas law means that every hurricane season will bring new burdens not only on the public's ability to access Texas's beaches but on the public treasury as well.

✳✳✳

For almost twenty-five years, the state has taken the further step of informing beachfront property purchasers of the rolling nature of the easement burdening their property. Amendments to the OBA in 1985 make "pellucid that once an easement on the dry beach is established, its landward boundary may therefore 'roll,' *including over private property.*" *Severance v. Patterson*, 566 F.3d 490, 506 (5th Cir. 2009) (Wiener, J., dissenting) (emphasis in original). . . . Sellers of property on or near the coastline are required to include in the sales contract a "Disclosure Notice Concerning Legal and Economic Risks of Purchasing Coastal Real Property Near a Beach." Tex. Nat. Res. Code § 61.025(a). The notice specifically warns that

> If you own a structure located on coastal real property near a gulf coast beach, it may come to be located on the public beach *because of coastal erosion and storm events.* . . . Owners of structures erected seaward of the vegetation line (or other applicable easement boundary) or that *become seaward of the vegetation line as a result of natural processes* such as shoreline erosion are subject to a lawsuit by the State of Texas to remove the structures.

Tex. Nat. Res. Code § 61.025 (a) (emphasis added). The language of the Act itself clearly identifies the line of vegetation as an easement boundary and clearly recognizes the transient nature of these boundary lines. The vegetation line, "given the vagaries of nature, will always be in a state of intermittent flux[,]" and consequently, "[s]hifts in the vegetation line do not create new easements; rather they expand (or in the case of seaward shifts, reduce) the size and reach of one dynamic easement." *Severance v. Patterson*, 566 F.3d 490, 506 (5th Cir. 2009) (Wiener, J., dissenting). Severance purchased her properties with contracts that notified her of these risks and nature of the rolling easement.

✳✳✳

IV. No Compensation Owed to Beachfront Property Owners Whose Property Is Encumbered by a Rolling Easement

The third certified question asks whether compensation is owed to landowners whose property becomes subject to a public beachfront access easement after it rolls with natural shifts in the shoreline. When an act of nature destroys a piece of coastal property, no compensation is owed because there is no taking by the government. Likewise, when an act of nature changes the boundaries of the beach, no compensation is owed when the government seeks to protect the already existent public right of access to the beach. The government is merely enforcing an easement whose boundaries have shifted. The enforcement of rolling easements does not constitute a physical taking nor does it constitute a regulatory taking. Pre-existing rolling easements affect a property right that the landowner never owned, namely, excluding the public from the beach. Because no property is taken, no compensation is owed.

***

V. Conclusion

The Texas coastline is constantly changing and the risks of purchasing property abutting the ocean are well known. The OBA further mandates the disclosure of these risks in coastal purchase contracts. Insurance is available for some of these risks. It is unreasonable, however, to require the state and its taxpayers to shoulder the burden of these risks. In my view, coastal property is encumbered by a pre-existing rolling easement rooted in the common law. The state is not responsible for the ocean's movement and therefore owes no compensation when enforcing this existing easement. Because the Court requires the state to re-establish its easement after avulsive events and to pay landowners for risks they have voluntarily assumed, I must dissent. I would instead follow the constitution and the long-standing public policy of this state and hold that the beaches of Texas are, and forever will be, open to the public.

points for discussion

1. *The elements.* The public prescriptive easement, which you first heard about back in Chapter 6, is a tool that can be used in some states to create public rights-of-way over specific stretches of dry sand for which historical use can be proven. The public prescriptive easement is used to create public access in some states, like Texas, but many states do not recognize it as a legal tool for enhancing access, primarily because it seems unfair to the owner: Who should she sue to stop the trespassing when the trespassers are different people each day? Even in states, like Florida, that do recognize it as such, a public prescriptive easement can be difficult to prove in court. The elements needed to create a prescriptive public easement are the same as an ordinary prescriptive easement (held by one or a few parties): There must be open and notorious use, adverse to the interests of the landowner, that continues uninterrupted for some period of time. The most difficult element to establish is adversity. Given that most states prohibit building on the dry sand, active beach, why is public use adverse? For more on this question, see *City of Daytona Beach v. Tona-Rama, Inc.*, 294 So. 2d 73 (Fla. 1974).

2. *Reasonable investment-backed expectations.* As noted in the decision, the Supreme Court of Texas's decision in *Severance* represents, to some extent, a reversal of prior Texas case law. Is it fair to say that Ms. Severance was on notice that she might eventually be forced to allow the public onto part or all of her property? If so, should this fact be determinative? *See Palazzolo v. Rhode Island*, 533 U.S. 606 (2001) (The fact that a state statute is effective at the time a landowner acquired his property does not bar the

landowner from asserting that the statute effects a taking of his property. In other words, the fact that the landowner was "on notice" of a statutory restriction at the time of acquisition does not mean that an expectation of using the property in a way that would violate the restriction is necessarily unreasonable.).

3. *A national open beaches act?* In 1973, Congressman Robert Eckhardt of Texas introduced a bill that would have created a federal analogue to the Texas statute. Section 202 of the bill, H.R. 10394, 93d Cong., 1st Sess. (1973), provided that:

> By reason of their traditional use as a thoroughfare and haven for fishermen and sea ventures, the necessity for them to be free and open in connection with shipping, navigation, salvage, and rescue operations, as well as recreation, Congress declares and affirms that the beaches of the United States are impressed with a national interest and that the public shall have free and unrestricted right to use them as a common to the full extent that such public right may be extended consistent with such property rights of littoral landowners as may be protected absolutely by the Constitution. It is the declared intention of Congress to exercise the full reach of its constitutional power over the subject.

Representative Eckhardt explained the rationale for this legislation in a law review article he authored on the subject:

> For centuries men have used the beach . . . without making a precise distinction between the wet sand beach and the dry sand beach. Indeed, most of the traditional uses of the shore, if permissible only as to the tidelands or the wet shore, could not be enjoyed at all at high tide. Furthermore, the line between the foreshore and the dry sand beach is not clearly marked on the land, nor is it as constant, as is that between the beach and the uplands.

***

> . . . [O]nly certain uses are within the classification of uses traditionally relating to access to the sea. . . . Thus, one asserting a right to public use may bring with him a shovel and build a sand castle, but not a drilling rig and drill an oil well.

Robert C. Eckhardt, *A Rational National Policy on Public Use of the Beaches*, 24 Syracuse L. Rev. 967, 970-71 (1973). Do you think this is a good idea? Is it truly a matter of "national interest"? For more on the mechanics of the bill and an assessment of some of the legal issues it might raise, see both the Eckhardt article and Charles L. Black, Jr., *Constitutionality of the Eckhardt Open Beaches Bill*, 74 Colum. L. Rev. 439 (1974) (concluding the law would be constitutional).

4. *The latest on* Severance. In early 2012, after rehearing the case, the Supreme Court of Texas replaced the preceding opinion with a substantially similar one. *Severance v. Patterson*, 370 S.W.3d 705 (Tex. 2012). The most interesting difference in the second opinion is a dissent written by Justice Eva Guzman. Justice Guzman argued that, while the easement did move

onto Ms. Severance's property, the state could not require her to vacate or to remove her home: "The public can easily walk around the house in its ingress and egress to and from the water and enjoy beach recreation in the area around the house." *Id.* at 749. Justice Guzman's conclusion was based on the rationale that the beach is neither public nor private, and the interests of the public and landowners must be balanced.

After the Fifth Circuit received the second *Severance* opinion from the Texas Supreme Court, it then remanded the case back to the district court. At that point, the parties settled the case.

b. Public Access Rules: California and New Jersey

Another means by which states can enhance public access is by utilizing the leverage they have in coastal permitting processes. A permit is just that: permission to undertake an activity at the discretion of the state. Thus, when an upland owner applies for a permit, a state coastal agency may either grant or reject the permit application, so long as it has a rational basis for doing so and has treated the applicant fairly. The agency may also condition the permit on the upland owner carrying out the proposed project in a particular way or mitigating the impact that the project is likely to have on public assets, such as trust property or on public uses of that property. These conditions are sometimes known as "exactions," because the state is exacting something from the applicant in return for issuance of the permit.

The following materials show how two states have created similar rules for enhancing access, and how access rules can lead to conflict with upland owners.

California Coastal Act

Cal. Pub. Resources Code § 30212. Access from public roadway

(a) Public access from the nearest public roadway to the shoreline and along the coast shall be provided in new development projects except where (1) it is inconsistent with public safety, military security needs, or the protection of fragile coastal resources, (2) adequate access exists nearby, or (3) agriculture would be adversely affected. Dedicated accessway shall not be required to be opened to public use until a public agency or private association agrees to accept responsibility for maintenance and liability of the accessway.

(b) For purposes of this section, "new development" does not include:

***

(2) The demolition and reconstruction of a single-family residence; provided, that the reconstructed residence shall not exceed either the floor area, height or bulk of the former structure by more than 10 percent, and that the reconstructed residence shall be sited in the same location on the affected property as the former structure.

(3) Improvements to any structure which do not change the intensity of its use, which do not increase either the floor area, height, or bulk of the structure by more than 10 percent, which do not block or impede public access, and which do not result in a seaward encroachment by the structure.

(4) The reconstruction or repair of any seawall; provided, however, that the reconstructed or repaired seawall is not seaward of the location of the former structure.

(5) Any repair or maintenance activity for which the commission has determined, pursuant to Section 30610, that a coastal development permit will be required unless the commission determines that the activity will have an adverse impact on lateral public access along the beach.

As used in this subdivision, "bulk" means total interior cubic volume as measured from the exterior surface of the structure.

***

Nollan v. California Coastal Commission

483 U.S. 825 (1987)

Justice SCALIA delivered the opinion of the Court.

James and Marilyn Nollan appeal from a decision of the California Court of Appeal ruling that the California Coastal Commission could condition its grant of permission to rebuild their house on their transfer to the public of an easement across their beachfront property. 177 Cal. App. 3d 719 (1986). The California court rejected their claim that imposition of that condition violates the Takings Clause of the Fifth Amendment, as incorporated against the States by the Fourteenth Amendment. *Ibid.* . . .

I.

The Nollans own a beachfront lot in Ventura County, California. A quarter-mile north of their property is Faria County Park, an oceanside public park with a public beach and recreation area. Another public beach area, known locally as "the Cove," lies 1,800 feet south of their lot. A concrete seawall approximately eight feet high separates the beach portion of the Nollans' property from the rest of the lot. The historic mean high tide line determines the lot's oceanside boundary.

The Nollans originally leased their property with an option to buy. The building on the lot was a small bungalow, totaling 504 square feet, which for a time they rented to summer vacationers. After years of rental use, however, the building had fallen into disrepair, and could no longer be rented out.

The Nollans' option to purchase was conditioned on their promise to demolish the bungalow and replace it. In order to do so, under Cal. Pub. Res. Code Ann. §§ 30106, 30212, and 30600 (West 1986), they were required to obtain a coastal development permit from the California Coastal Commission. On February 25,

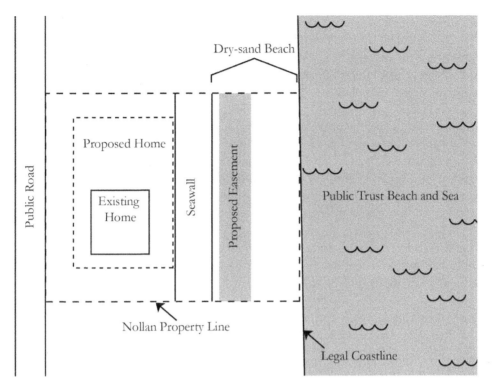

Figure 9-10. Diagram of the Facts in *Nollan*

1982, they submitted a permit application to the Commission in which they proposed to demolish the existing structure and replace it with a three-bedroom house in keeping with the rest of the neighborhood.

The Nollans were informed that their application had been placed on the administrative calendar, and that the Commission staff had recommended that the permit be granted subject to the condition that they allow the public an easement to pass across a portion of their property bounded by the mean high tide line on one side, and their seawall on the other side.

This would make it easier for the public to get to Faria County Park and the Cove. The Nollans protested imposition of the condition, but the Commission overruled their objections and granted the permit subject to their recordation of a deed restriction granting the easement. . . .

On June 3, 1982, the Nollans filed a petition for writ of administrative mandamus asking the Ventura County Superior Court to invalidate the access condition. They argued that the condition could not be imposed absent evidence that their proposed development would have a direct adverse impact on public access to the beach. The court agreed, and remanded the case to the Commission for a full evidentiary hearing on that issue. . . .

On remand, the Commission held a public hearing, after which it made further factual findings and reaffirmed its imposition of the condition. It found that the new house would increase blockage of the view of the ocean, thus contributing to the development of "a 'wall' of residential structures" that would prevent the public "psychologically . . . from realizing a stretch of coastline exists nearby that they have every right to visit." . . . The new house would also increase private use of the shorefront. These effects of construction of the house, along with other area development, would cumulatively "burden the public's ability to traverse to and along the shorefront." . . . Therefore the Commission could properly require the Nollans to offset that burden by providing additional lateral access to the public beaches in the form of an easement across their property. The Commission also noted that it had similarly conditioned 43 out of 60 coastal development permits along the same tract of land, and that of the 17 not so conditioned, 14 had been approved when the Commission did not have administrative regulations in place allowing imposition of the condition, and the remaining 3 had not involved shorefront property. . . .

The Nollans filed a supplemental petition for a writ of administrative mandamus with the Superior Court, in which they argued that imposition of the access condition violated the Takings Clause of the Fifth Amendment, as incorporated against the States by the Fourteenth Amendment. The Superior Court ruled in their favor on statutory grounds, finding, in part to avoid "issues of constitutionality," that the

> **Quick Question**
>
> Why is this a takings case? If the Nollans do not have the right to rebuild their house, what property is the State of California taking from them?

California Coastal Act of 1976 . . . authorized the Commission to impose public access conditions on coastal development permits for the replacement of an existing single-family home with a new one only where the proposed development would have an adverse impact on public access to the sea. . . . In the court's view, the administrative record did not provide an adequate factual basis for concluding that replacement of the bungalow with the house would create a direct or cumulative burden on public access to the sea. . . . Accordingly, the Superior Court granted the writ of mandamus and directed that the permit condition be struck.

The Commission appealed to the California Court of Appeal. While that appeal was pending, the Nollans satisfied the condition on their option to purchase by tearing down the bungalow and building the new house, and bought the property. They did not notify the Commission that they were taking that action.

The Court of Appeal reversed the Superior Court. 177 Cal. App. 3d 719 (1986). It disagreed with the Superior Court's interpretation of the Coastal Act, finding that it required that a coastal permit for the construction of a new house whose floor area, height or bulk was more than 10% larger than that of the house it was replacing be conditioned on a grant of access. *Id.*, at 723-724; *see* Cal. Pub. Res. Code Ann. § 30212. It also ruled that that requirement did not violate the Constitution under the reasoning of an earlier case of the Court of Appeal, *Grupe v. California Coastal Comm'n*, 166 Cal. App. 3d 148 (1985). In that case, the court had found that so long as a project contributed to the need for public access, even if the project standing alone had not created the need for access, and even if there was only an indirect relationship between the access exacted and the need to which the project contributed, imposition of an access condition on a development permit was sufficiently related to burdens created by the project to be constitutional. . . . The Court of Appeal ruled that the record established that that was the situation with respect to the Nollans' house. . . . It ruled that the Nollans' taking claim also failed because, although the condition diminished the value of the Nollans' lot, it did not deprive them of all reasonable use of their property. . . . Since, in the Court of Appeal's view, there was no statutory or constitutional obstacle to imposition of the access condition, the Superior Court erred in granting the writ of mandamus. The Nollans appealed to this Court, raising only the constitutional question.

II.

Had California simply required the Nollans to make an easement across their beachfront available to the public on a permanent basis in order to increase public access to the beach, rather than conditioning their permit to rebuild their house on their agreeing to do so, we have no doubt there would have been a taking. To say that the appropriation of a public easement across a landowner's premises does not constitute the taking of a property interest but rather (as Justice Brennan contends) "a mere restriction on its use," . . . is to use words in a manner that deprives them of all their ordinary meaning. Indeed, one of the principal uses of the eminent domain power is to assure that the government be able to require conveyance of just such interests, so long as it pays for them. . . . Perhaps because the point is so obvious, we have never been confronted with a controversy that required us to rule upon it, but our cases' analysis of the effect of other governmental action leads to the same conclusion. We have repeatedly held that, as to property reserved by its owner for private use, "the right to exclude [others is] 'one of the most essential sticks in the bundle of rights that are commonly characterized as property.' " *Loretto v. Teleprompter Manhattan CATV Corp.*, 458 U.S. 419, 433 (1982), quoting *Kaiser Aetna v. United States*, 444 U.S. 164, 176 (1979). In *Loretto* we observed that where governmental action results in "[a] permanent physical occupation" of the property, by the government itself or by others, see 458 U.S., at 432-433, n. 9, "our cases uniformly have found a taking to the extent of the occupation, without regard to whether the action achieves an important public benefit or has only minimal economic impact on the owner," *id.*, at 434-435. We think a "permanent physical occupation" has occurred, for purposes of that rule, where individuals are given a permanent and continuous right to pass to and fro, so that the real property may continuously be traversed, even though no particular individual is permitted to station himself permanently upon the premises.

***

Given, then, that requiring uncompensated conveyance of the easement outright would violate the Fourteenth Amendment, the question becomes whether requiring it to be conveyed as a condition for issuing a land-use permit alters the outcome. . . . The Commission argues that among [the legitimate governmental purposes for requiring the Nollans to dedicate the easement] are protecting the public's ability to see the beach, assisting the public in overcoming the "psychological barrier" to using the beach created by a developed shorefront, and preventing congestion on the public beaches. We assume, without deciding, that this is so — in which case the Commission unquestionably would be able to deny the Nollans their permit outright if their new house (alone, or by reason of the cumulative impact produced in conjunction with other construction) would substantially impede these purposes, unless the denial would interfere so drastically with the Nollans' use of their property as to constitute a taking. . . .

The Commission argues that a permit condition that serves the same legitimate police-power purpose as a refusal to issue the permit should not be found to be a taking if the refusal to issue the permit would not constitute a taking. We agree. Thus, if the Commission attached to the permit some condition that would have protected the public's ability to see the beach notwithstanding construction of the new house — for example, a height limitation, a width restriction, or a ban on fences — so

> **Quick Exercise**
>
> Draw Justice Scalia's "viewing spot" on Figure 9-10.

long as the Commission could have exercised its police power (as we have assumed it could) to forbid construction of the house altogether, imposition of the condition would also be constitutional. Moreover (and here we come closer to the facts of the present case), the condition would be constitutional even if it consisted of the requirement that the Nollans provide a viewing spot on their property for passersby with whose sighting of the ocean their new house would interfere. Although such a requirement, constituting a permanent grant of continuous access to the property, would have to be considered a taking if it were not attached to a development permit, the Commission's assumed power to forbid construction of the house in order to protect the public's view of the beach must surely include the power to condition construction upon some concession by the owner, even a concession of property rights, that serves the same end. If a prohibition designed to accomplish that purpose would be a legitimate exercise of the police power rather than a taking, it would be strange to conclude that providing the owner an alternative to that prohibition which accomplishes the same purpose is not.

The evident constitutional propriety disappears, however, if the condition substituted for the prohibition utterly fails to further the end advanced as the justification for the prohibition. When that essential nexus is eliminated, the situation becomes the same as if California law forbade shouting fire in a crowded theater, but granted dispensations to those willing to contribute $100 to the state treasury. While a ban on shouting fire can be a core exercise of the State's police power to protect the public safety, and can thus meet even our stringent standards for regulation of speech, adding the unrelated condition alters the purpose to one which, while it may be legitimate, is inadequate to sustain the ban. Therefore, even though, in a sense, requiring a $100 tax contribution in order to shout fire is a lesser restriction on speech than an outright ban, it would not pass constitutional muster. Similarly here, the lack of nexus between the condition and the original purpose of the building restriction converts that purpose to something other than what it was. The purpose then becomes, quite simply, the obtaining of an easement to serve some valid governmental purpose, but without payment of compensation. Whatever may be the outer limits of "legitimate state interests" in the takings and land-use context, this is not one of them. In short, unless the permit condition serves the same governmental purpose as the development ban, the building restriction is not a valid regulation of land use but "an out-and-out plan of extortion." *J. E. D. Associates, Inc. v. Atkinson,* 121 N. H. 581, 584 (1981). . . .[5]

The Commission claims that it concedes as much, and that we may sustain the condition at issue here by finding that it is reasonably related to the public need or burden that the Nollans' new house creates or to which it contributes. We can accept, for purposes of discussion, the Commission's proposed test as to how close a "fit" between the condition and the burden is required, because we find that this case does not meet even the most untailored standards. The Commission's principal contention to the contrary essentially turns on a play on the word "access." The Nollans' new house, the Commission found, will interfere with "visual access" to the beach. That in turn (along with other shorefront development) will interfere with the desire of people who drive past the Nollans' house to use the beach, thus creating a "psychological barrier" to "access." The Nollans' new house will also, by a process not altogether clear from the Commission's opinion but presumably potent enough to more than offset the effects of the psychological barrier, increase the use of the public beaches, thus creating the need for more "access." These burdens on "access" would be alleviated by a requirement that the Nollans provide "lateral access" to the beach.

Rewriting the argument to eliminate the play on words makes clear that there is nothing to it. It is quite impossible to understand how a requirement that people already on the public beaches be able to walk across the Nollans' property reduces any obstacles to viewing the beach created by the new house. It is also impossible to understand how it lowers any "psychological barrier" to using the public beaches, or how it helps to remedy any additional congestion on them caused by construction of the Nollans' new house. We therefore find that the Commission's imposition of the permit condition cannot be treated as an exercise of its land-use power for any of these purposes. Our conclusion on this point is consistent with the approach taken by every other court that has considered the question, with the exception of the California state courts. [Lengthy list of state court decisions omitted. — Eds.]

Justice Brennan argues that imposition of the access requirement is not irrational. In his version of the Commission's argument, the reason for the requirement is that in its absence, a person looking toward the beach from the road will see a street of residential structures including the Nollans' new home and conclude that

---

5. One would expect that a regime in which this kind of leveraging of the police power is allowed would produce stringent land-use regulation which the State then waives to accomplish other purposes, leading to lesser realization of the land-use goals purportedly sought to be served than would result from more lenient (but nontradeable) development restrictions. Thus, the importance of the purpose underlying the prohibition not only does not *justify* the imposition of unrelated conditions for eliminating the prohibition, but positively militates against the practice.

there is no public beach nearby. If, however, that person sees people passing and repassing along the dry sand behind the Nollans' home, he will realize that there is a public beach somewhere in the vicinity. . . . The Commission's action, however, was based on the opposite factual finding that the wall of houses completely blocked the view of the beach and that a person looking from the road would not be able to see it at all.

Even if the Commission had made the finding that Justice Brennan proposes, however, it is not certain that it would suffice. We do not share Justice Brennan's confidence that the Commission "should have little difficulty in the future in utilizing its expertise to demonstrate a specific connection between provisions for access and burdens on access," . . . that will avoid the effect of today's decision. We view the Fifth Amendment's Property Clause to be more than a pleading requirement, and compliance with it to be more than an exercise in cleverness and imagination. . . . We are inclined to be particularly careful [in identifying the government's purposes] where the actual conveyance of property is made a condition to the lifting of a land-use restriction, since in that context there is heightened risk that the purpose is avoidance of the compensation requirement, rather than the stated police-power objective.

We are left, then, with the Commission's justification for the access requirement unrelated to land-use regulation:

> Finally, the Commission notes that there are several existing provisions of pass and repass lateral access benefits already given by past Faria Beach Tract applicants as a result of prior coastal permit decisions. The access required as a condition of this permit is part of a comprehensive program to provide continuous public access along Faria Beach as the lots undergo development or redevelopment.

That is simply an expression of the Commission's belief that the public interest will be served by a continuous strip of publicly accessible beach along the coast. The Commission may well be right that it is a good idea, but that does not establish that the Nollans (and other coastal residents) alone can be compelled to contribute to its realization. Rather, California is free to advance its "comprehensive program," if it wishes, by using its power of eminent domain for this "public purpose," *see* U.S. Const., Amdt. 5; but if it wants an easement across the Nollans' property, it must pay for it.

Reversed.

Justice BRENNAN, joined by Justice MARSHALL, dissents.

Appellants in this case sought to construct a new dwelling on their beach lot that would both diminish visual access to the beach and move private development closer to the public tidelands. The Commission reasonably concluded that such "buildout," both individually and cumulatively, threatens public access to the shore. It sought to offset this encroachment by obtaining assurance that the public may walk along the shoreline in order to gain access to the ocean. The Court finds this an illegitimate exercise of the police power, because it maintains that there is no reasonable relationship between the effect of the development and the condition imposed.

The first problem with this conclusion is that the Court imposes a standard of precision for the exercise of a State's police power that has been discredited for the better part of this century. Furthermore, even under the Court's cramped standard, the permit condition imposed in this case directly responds to the specific type of burden on access created by appellants' development. Finally, a review of those factors deemed most significant in takings analysis makes clear that the Commission's action implicates none of the concerns underlying the Takings Clause. The Court has thus struck down the Commission's reasonable effort to respond to intensified development along the California coast, on behalf of landowners who can make no claim that their reasonable expectations have been disrupted. The Court has, in short, given appellants a windfall at the expense of the public.

I.

The Court's conclusion that the permit condition imposed on appellants is unreasonable cannot withstand analysis. First, the Court demands a degree of exactitude that is inconsistent with our standard for reviewing the rationality of a State's exercise of its police power for the welfare of its citizens. Second, even if the nature of the public-access condition imposed must be identical to the precise burden on access created by appellants, this requirement is plainly satisfied.

A.

There can be no dispute that the police power of the States encompasses the authority to impose conditions on private development. . . . It is also by now commonplace that this Court's review of the rationality of a State's exercise of its police power demands only that the State *"could rationally have decided"* that the measure adopted might achieve the State's objective. *Minnesota v. Clover Leaf Creamery Co.*, 449 U.S. 456, 466 (1981) (emphasis in original).[1] In this case, California has employed its police power in order to condition development upon preservation of public access to the ocean and tidelands. The Coastal Commission, if it had so chosen, could have denied the Nollans' request for a development permit, since the property would have remained economically viable without the requested new development.[2] Instead, the State sought to accommodate the Nollans' desire for new development, on the condition that the development not diminish the overall amount of public access to the coastline. Appellants' proposed development would

---

1. *See also Williamson v. Lee Optical of Oklahoma, Inc.*, 348 U.S. 483, 487-488 (1955) ("The law need not be in every respect logically consistent with its aims to be constitutional. It is enough that there is an evil at hand for correction, and that it might be thought that the particular legislative measure was a rational way to correct it"); *Day-Brite Lighting, Inc. v. Missouri*, 342 U.S. 421, 423 (1952) ("Our recent decisions make it plain that we do not sit as a super-legislature to weigh the wisdom of legislation nor to decide whether the policy which it expresses offends the public welfare. . . . State legislatures have constitutional authority to experiment with new techniques; they are entitled to their own standard of the public welfare"). . . .

2. As this Court declared in *United States v. Riverside Bayview Homes, Inc.*, 474 U.S. 121, 127 (1985):

"A requirement that a person obtain a permit before engaging in a certain use of his or her property does not itself 'take' the property in any sense: after all, the very existence of reduce public access by restricting visual access to the beach, by contributing to an increased need for community facilities, and by moving private development closer to public beach property. The Commission sought to offset this diminution in access, and thereby preserve the overall balance of access, by requesting a deed restriction that would ensure "lateral" access: the right of the public to pass and repass along the dry sand parallel to the shoreline in order to reach the tidelands and the ocean. In the expert opinion of the Coastal Commission, development conditioned on such a restriction would fairly attend to both public and private interests.

The Court finds fault with this measure because it regards the condition as insufficiently tailored to address the precise type of reduction in access produced by the new development. The Nollans' development blocks visual access, the Court tells us, while the Commission seeks to preserve lateral access along the coastline. Thus, it concludes, the State acted irrationally. Such a narrow conception of rationality, however, has long since been discredited as a judicial arrogation of legislative authority. "To make scientific precision a criterion of constitutional power would be to subject the State to an intolerable supervision hostile to the basic principles of our Government." *Sproles v. Binford*, 286 U.S. 374, 388 (1932). . . . As this Court long ago declared with regard to various forms of restriction on the use of property:

> "Each interferes in the same way, if not to the same extent, with the owner's general right of dominion over his property. All rest for their justification upon the same reasons which have arisen in recent times as a result of the great increase and concentration of population in urban communities and the vast changes in the extent and complexity of the problems of modern city life. State legislatures and city councils, who deal with the situation from a practical standpoint, are better qualified than the courts to determine the necessity, character, and degree of regulation which these new and perplexing conditions require; and their conclusions should not be disturbed by the courts unless clearly arbitrary and unreasonable." *Gorieb v. Fox*, 274 U.S. 603, 608 (1927) (citations omitted).

The Commission is charged by both the State Constitution and legislature to preserve overall public access to the California coastline. Furthermore, by virtue of its participation in the Coastal Zone Management Act (CZMA) program, the State must "exercise effectively [its] responsibilities in the coastal zone through the

---

a permit system implies that permission may be granted, leaving the landowner free to use the property as desired. Moreover, even if the permit is denied, there may be other viable uses available to the owner. Only when a permit is denied and the effect of the denial is to prevent 'economically viable' use of the land in question can it be said that a taking has occurred."

We also stated in *Kaiser Aetna v. United States*, 444 U.S. 164, 179 (1979), with respect to dredging to create a private marina:

> "We have not the slightest doubt that the Government could have refused to allow such dredging on the ground that it would have impaired navigation in the bay, or could have conditioned its approval of the dredging on petitioners' agreement to comply with various measures that it deemed appropriate for the promotion of navigation."

development and implementation of management programs to achieve wise use of the land and water resources of the coastal zone," 16 U.S.C. § 1452(2), so as to provide for, *inter alia*, "public access to the coas[t] for recreation purposes." § 1452(2)(D). The Commission has sought to discharge its responsibilities in a flexible manner. It has sought to balance private and public interests and to accept tradeoffs: to permit development that reduces access in some ways as long as other means of access are enhanced. In this case, it has determined that the Nollans' burden on access would be offset by a deed restriction that formalizes the public's right to pass along the shore. In its informed judgment, such a tradeoff would preserve the net amount of public access to the coastline. The Court's insistence on a precise fit between the forms of burden and condition on each individual parcel along the California coast would penalize the Commission for its flexibility, hampering the ability to fulfill its public trust mandate.

The Court's demand for this precise fit is based on the assumption that private landowners in this case possess a reasonable expectation regarding the use of their land that the public has attempted to disrupt. In fact, the situation is precisely the reverse: it is private landowners who are the interlopers. The public's expectation of access considerably antedates any private development on the coast. Article X, § 4, of the California Constitution, adopted in 1879, declares:

> No individual, partnership, or corporation, claiming or possessing the frontage or tidal lands of a harbor, bay, inlet, estuary, or other navigable water in this State, shall be permitted to exclude the right of way to such water whenever it is required for any public purpose, nor to destroy or obstruct the free navigation of such water; and the Legislature shall enact such laws as will give the most liberal construction to this provision, so that access to the navigable waters of this State shall always be attainable for the people thereof.

It is therefore private landowners who threaten the disruption of settled public expectations. Where a private landowner has had a reasonable expectation that his or her property will be used for exclusively private purposes, the disruption of this expectation dictates that the government pay if it wishes the property to be used for a public purpose. In this case, however, the State has sought to protect *public* expectations of access from disruption by private land use. The State's exercise of its police power for this purpose deserves no less deference than any other measure designed to further the welfare of state citizens.

Congress expressly stated in passing the CZMA that "in light of competing demands and the urgent need to protect and to give high priority to natural systems in the coastal zone, present state and local institutional arrangements for planning and regulating land and water uses in such areas are inadequate." 16 U.S.C. § 1451(h). It is thus puzzling that the Court characterizes as a "non-land-use justification" . . . the exercise of the police power to " 'provide continuous public access along Faria Beach as the lots undergo development or redevelopment.' " . . . The Commission's determination that certain types of development jeopardize public access to the ocean, and that such development should be conditioned on preservation of access, is the essence of responsible land-use planning. The Court's use of an unreasonably demanding standard for determining the rationality of state regulation in this area thus could hamper innovative efforts to preserve an increasingly fragile national resource.[3]

B.

Even if we accept the Court's unusual demand for a precise match between the condition imposed and the specific type of burden on access created by the appellants, the State's action easily satisfies this requirement. First, the lateral access condition serves to dissipate the impression that the beach that lies behind the wall of homes along the shore is for private use only. It requires no exceptional imaginative powers to find plausible the Commission's point that the average person passing along the road in front of a phalanx of imposing permanent residences, including the appellants' new home, is likely to conclude that this particular portion of the shore is not open to the public. If, however, that person can see that numerous people are passing and repassing along the dry sand, this conveys the message that the beach is in fact open for use by the public. Furthermore, those persons who go down to the public beach a quarter-mile away will be able to look down the coastline and see that persons have continuous access to the tidelands, and will observe signs that proclaim the public's right of access over the dry sand. The burden produced by the diminution in visual access—the impression that the beach is not open to the public—is thus directly alleviated by the provision for public access over the dry sand. The Court therefore has an unrealistically limited conception of what measures could reasonably be chosen to mitigate the burden produced by a diminution of visual access.

The second flaw in the Court's analysis of the fit between burden and exaction is more fundamental. The Court assumes that the only burden with which the Coastal Commission was concerned was blockage of visual access to the beach. This is incorrect. The Commission specifically stated in its report in support of the permit condition that "the Commission finds that the applicants' proposed development would present an increase in view blockage, *an increase in private use of the shorefront*, and that this impact would burden the public's ability to traverse to and along the shorefront." . . . (emphasis added). It declared that the possibility that "the public may get the impression that the beachfront is no longer available for public use" would be "due to *the encroaching nature of private use immediately adjacent to*

---

3. The list of cases cited by the Court as support for its approach . . . includes no instance in which the State sought to vindicate preexisting rights of access to navigable water, and consists principally of cases involving a requirement of the dedication of land as a condition of subdivision approval. Dedication, of course, requires the surrender of ownership of property rather than, as in this case, a mere restriction on its use. The only case pertaining to beach access among those cited by the Court is *MacKall v. White*, 445 N.Y.S.2d 486 (1981). In that case, the court found that a subdivision application could not be conditioned upon a declaration that the landowner would not hinder the public from using a trail that had been used to gain access to a bay. The trail had been used despite posted warnings prohibiting passage, and despite the owner's resistance to such use. In that case, unlike this one, neither the State Constitution, state statute, administrative practice, nor the conduct of the landowner operated to create any reasonable expectation of a right of public access.

the public use, as well as the visual 'block' of increased residential build-out impacting the visual quality of the beachfront." ... (emphasis added).

The record prepared by the Commission is replete with references to the threat to public access along the coastline resulting from the seaward encroachment of private development along a beach whose mean high-tide line is constantly shifting. As the Commission observed in its report: "The Faria Beach shoreline fluctuates during the year depending on the seasons and accompanying storms, and the public is not always able to traverse the shoreline below the mean high tide line." ... As a result, the boundary between publicly owned tidelands and privately owned beach is not a stable one, and "the existing seawall is located very near to the mean high water line." ... When the beach is at its largest, the seawall is about 10 feet from the mean high-tide mark; "during the period of the year when the beach suffers erosion, the mean high water line appears to be located either on or beyond the existing seawall." ... Expansion of private development on appellants' lot toward the seawall would thus "increase private use immediately adjacent to public tidelands, which has the potential of causing adverse impacts on the public's ability to traverse the shoreline." ... As the Commission explained:

> The placement of more private use adjacent to public tidelands has the potential of creating use conflicts between the applicants and the public. The results of new private use encroachment into boundary/buffer areas between private and public property can create situations in which landowners intimidate the public and seek to prevent them from using public tidelands because of disputes between the two parties over where the exact boundary between private and public ownership is located. If the applicants' project would result in further seaward encroachment of private use into an area of clouded title, new private use in the subject encroachment area could result in use conflict between private and public entities on the subject shorefront. . . .

The deed restriction on which permit approval was conditioned would directly address this threat to the public's access to the tidelands. It would provide a formal declaration of the public's right of access, thereby ensuring that the shifting character of the tidelands, and the presence of private development immediately adjacent to it, would not jeopardize enjoyment of that right. The imposition of the permit condition was therefore directly related to the fact that appellants' development would be "located along a unique stretch of coast where lateral public access is inadequate due to the construction of private residential structures and shoreline protective devices along a fluctuating shoreline." ... The deed restriction was crafted to deal with the particular character of the beach along which appellants sought to build, and with the specific problems created by expansion of development toward the public tidelands. In imposing the restriction, the State sought to ensure that such development would not disrupt the historical expectation of the public regarding access to the sea.

The Court is therefore simply wrong that there is no reasonable relationship between the permit condition and the specific type of burden on public access created by the appellants' proposed development. Even were the Court desirous of assuming the added responsibility of closely monitoring the regulation of development along the California coast, this record reveals rational public action by any conceivable standard.

II.

The fact that the Commission's action is a legitimate exercise of the police power does not, of course, insulate it from a takings challenge, for when "regulation goes too far it will be recognized as a taking." *Pennsylvania Coal Co. v. Mahon*, 260 U.S. 393, 415 (1922). Conventional takings analysis underscores the implausibility of the Court's holding, for it demonstrates that this exercise of California's police power implicates none of the concerns that underlie our takings jurisprudence.

In reviewing a Takings Clause claim, we have regarded as particularly significant the nature of the governmental action and the economic impact of regulation, especially the extent to which regulation interferes with investment-backed expectations. *Penn Central*, 438 U.S., at 124. The character of the government action in this case is the imposition of a condition on permit approval, which allows the public to continue to have access to the coast. The physical intrusion permitted by the deed restriction is minimal. The public is permitted the right to pass and repass along the coast in an area from the seawall to the mean high-tide mark. . . . This area is at its *widest* 10 feet . . . which means that *even without the permit condition*, the public's right of access permits it to pass on average within a few feet of the seawall. Passage closer to the 8-foot-high rocky seawall will make the appellants even less visible to the public than passage along the high-tide area farther out on the beach. The intrusiveness of such passage is even less than the intrusion resulting from the required dedication of a sidewalk in front of private residences, exactions which are commonplace conditions on approval of development. Furthermore, the high-tide line shifts throughout the year, moving up to and beyond the seawall, so that public passage for a portion of the year would either be impossible or would not occur on appellant's property. Finally, although the Commission had the authority to provide for either passive or active recreational use of the property, it chose the least intrusive alternative: a mere right to pass and repass. . . . As this Court made clear in *PruneYard Shopping Center v. Robins*, 447 U.S. 74, 83 (1980), physical access to private property in itself creates no takings problem if it does not "unreasonably impair the value or use of [the] property." Appellants can make no tenable claim that either their enjoyment of their property or its value is diminished by the public's ability merely to pass and repass a few feet closer to the seawall beyond which appellants' house is located.

PruneYard is also relevant in that we acknowledged in that case that public access rested upon a "state constitutional . . . provision that had been construed to create rights to the use of private property by strangers." *Id.*, at 81. In this case, of course, the State is also acting to protect a state constitutional right. . . . The constitutional provision guaranteeing public access to the ocean states that "the Legislature shall enact such laws as will give *the most liberal construction to this provision* so that access to the navigable waters of this State shall be always attainable for the people thereof." Cal. Const., Art. X, § 4 (emphasis added). This provision is the explicit basis for the statutory directive to provide for public access along the coast in new development projects, Cal. Pub. Res. Code Ann. § 30212 (West 1986), and has been construed by the state judiciary to permit passage over private land where necessary to gain access to the tidelands. *Grupe v. California Coastal Comm'n*, 166 Cal. App. 3d 148, 171-172 (1985). The physical access to the perimeter of appellants' property at issue in this case thus results directly from the State's enforcement of the State Constitution.

Finally, the character of the regulation in this case is not unilateral government action, but a condition on approval of a development request submitted by appellants. The State has not sought to interfere with any pre-existing property interest, but has responded to appellants' proposal to intensify development on the coast. Appellants themselves chose to submit a new development application, and could claim no property interest in its approval. They were aware that approval of such development would be conditioned on preservation of adequate public access to the ocean. The State has initiated no action against appellants' property; had the Nollans not proposed more intensive development in the coastal zone, they would never have been subject to the provision that they challenge.

Examination of the economic impact of the Commission's action reinforces the conclusion that no taking has occurred. Allowing appellants to intensify development along the coast in exchange for ensuring public access to the ocean is a classic instance of government action that produces a "reciprocity of advantage." *Pennsylvania Coal*, 260 U.S., at 415. Appellants have been allowed to replace a one-story, 521-square-foot beach home with a two-story, 1,674-square-foot residence and an attached two-car garage, resulting in development covering 2,464 square feet of the lot. Such development obviously significantly increases the value of appellants' property; appellants make no contention that this increase is offset by any diminution in value resulting from the deed restriction, much less that the restriction made the property less valuable than it would have been without the new construction. Furthermore, appellants gain an additional benefit from the Commission's permit condition program. They are able to walk along the beach beyond the confines of their own property only because the Commission has required deed restrictions as a condition of approving other new beach developments. Thus, appellants benefit both as private landowners and as members of the public from the fact that new development permit requests are conditioned on preservation of public access.

Ultimately, appellants' claim of economic injury is flawed because it rests on the assumption of entitlement to the full value of their new development. Appellants submitted a proposal for more intensive development of the coast, which the Commission was under no obligation to approve, and now argue that a regulation designed to ameliorate the impact of that development deprives them of the full value of their improvements. Even if this novel claim were somehow cognizable, it is not significant. "The interest in anticipated gains has traditionally been viewed as less compelling than other property-related interests." *Andrus v. Allard*, 444 U.S. 51, 66 (1979).

With respect to appellants' investment-backed expectations, appellants can make no reasonable claim to any expectation of being able to exclude members of the public from crossing the edge of their property to gain access to the ocean. It is axiomatic, of course, that state law is the source of those strands that constitute a property owner's bundle of property rights. "As a general proposition[,] the law of real property is, under our Constitution, left to the individual States to develop and administer." *Hughes v. Washington*, 389 U.S. 290, 295 (1967) (Stewart, J., concurring). *See also Borax Consolidated, Ltd. v. Los Angeles*, 296 U.S. 10, 22 (1935) ("Rights and interests in the tideland, which is subject to the sovereignty of the State, are matters of local law"). In this case, the State Constitution explicitly states that no one possessing the "frontage" of any "navigable water in this State, shall be permitted to exclude the right of way to such water whenever it is required for any public purpose." Cal. Const., Art. X, § 4. The state Code expressly provides that, save for exceptions not relevant here, "public access from the nearest public roadway to the shoreline and along the coast shall be provided in new development projects." Cal. Pub. Res. Code Ann. § 30212 (West 1986). The Coastal Commission Interpretative Guidelines make clear that fulfillment of the Commission's constitutional and statutory duty requires that approval of new coastline development be conditioned upon provisions ensuring lateral public access to the ocean. . . . At the time of appellants' permit request, the Commission had conditioned all 43 of the proposals for coastal new development in the Faria Family Beach Tract on the provision of deed restrictions ensuring lateral access along the shore. . . . Finally, the Faria family had leased the beach property since the early part of this century, and "the Faria family and their lessees [including the Nollans] had not interfered with public use of the beachfront within the Tract, so long as public use was limited to pass and repass lateral access along the shore." . . . California therefore has clearly established that the power of exclusion for which appellants seek compensation simply is not a strand in the bundle of appellants' property rights, and appellants have never acted as if it were. Given this state of affairs, appellants cannot claim that the deed restriction has deprived them of a reasonable expectation to exclude from their property persons desiring to gain access to the sea.

***

Standard Takings Clause analysis thus indicates that the Court employs its unduly restrictive standard of police power rationality to find a taking where neither the character of governmental action nor the nature of the private interest affected raise any takings concern. The result is that the Court invalidates regulation that represents a reasonable adjustment of the burdens and benefits of development along the California coast.

***

With respect to the permit condition program in general, the Commission should have little difficulty in the future in utilizing its expertise to demonstrate a specific connection between provisions for access and burdens on access produced by new development. Neither the Commission in its report nor the State in its briefs and at argument highlighted the particular threat to lateral access created by appellants' development project. In defending its action, the State emphasized the general point that *overall* access to the beach had been preserved, since the diminution of access created by the project had been offset by the gain in lateral access. This approach is understandable, given that the State relied on the reasonable assumption that its action was justified under the normal standard of review for determining legitimate exercises of a State's police power. In the future, alerted to the Court's apparently more demanding requirement, it need only make clear that a provision for public access directly responds to a particular type of burden on access created by a new development. Even if I did not believe that the record in this case satisfies this requirement, I would have to acknowledge that the record's documentation of the impact of coastal development indicates that the Commission should have little problem presenting its findings in a way that avoids a takings problem.

Nonetheless it is important to point out that the Court's insistence on a precise accounting system in this case is insensitive to the fact that increasing intensity of development in many areas calls for farsighted, comprehensive planning that takes into account both the interdependence of land uses and the cumulative impact of development. As one scholar has noted:

> Property does not exist in isolation. Particular parcels are tied to one another in complex ways, and property is more accurately described as being inextricably part of a network of relationships that is neither limited to, nor usefully defined by, the property boundaries with which the legal system is accustomed to dealing. Frequently, use of any given parcel of property is at the same time effectively a use of, or a demand upon, property beyond the border of the user. Joseph L. Sax, *Takings, Private Property, and Public Rights*, 81 YALE L.J. 149, 152 (1971) (footnote omitted).

As Congress has declared: "The key to more effective protection and use of the land and water resources of the coastal zone [is for the states to] develo[p] land and water use programs for the coastal zone, including unified policies, criteria, standards, methods, and processes for dealing with land and water use decisions of more than local significance." 16 U.S.C. § 1451(i). This is clearly a call for a focus on the overall impact of development on coastal areas. State agencies therefore require considerable flexibility in responding to private desires for development in a way that guarantees the preservation of public access to the coast. They should be encouraged to regulate development in the context of the overall balance of competing uses of the shoreline. The Court today does precisely the opposite, overruling an eminently reasonable exercise of an expert state agency's judgment, substituting its own narrow view of how this balance should be struck. Its reasoning is hardly suited to the complex reality of natural resource protection in the 20th century. I can only hope that today's decision is an aberration, and that a broader vision ultimately prevails.

* * *

Justice STEVENS, with whom Justice BLACKMUN joins, dissenting.

The debate between the Court and Justice Brennan illustrates an extremely important point concerning government regulation of the use of privately owned real estate. Intelligent, well-informed public officials may in good faith disagree about the validity of specific types of land-use regulation. Even the wisest lawyers would have to acknowledge great uncertainty about the scope of this Court's takings jurisprudence. Yet, because of the Court's remarkable ruling in *First English Evangelical Lutheran Church of Glendale v. Los Angeles County*, 482 U.S. 304 (1987), local governments and officials must pay the price for the necessarily vague standards in this area of the law.

> ### *First English*
>
> Prior to the Supreme Court's decision in *First English*, if a court found that a taking had occurred, the government had a choice: It could pay for the taken property (condemn it through eminent domain) or waive application of the challenged regulation to plaintiff's property. As the prior footnote indicates, the law after *First English* is that the government may be liable — regardless of whether it ultimately gives the plaintiff a waiver — for a "temporary taking." What is the measure of damages for a temporary taking? Under what circumstances should a court find that a temporary taking has occurred?

In his dissent in *San Diego Gas & Electric Co. v. San Diego*, 450 U.S. 621 (1981), Justice Brennan proposed a brand new constitutional rule.* He argued that a mistake such as the one that a majority of the Court believes that the California Coastal Commission made in this case should automatically give rise to pecuniary liability for a "temporary taking." . . . Notwithstanding the unprecedented chilling effect that such a rule will obviously have on public officials charged with the responsibility for drafting and implementing regulations designed to protect the environment and the public welfare, six Members of the Court recently endorsed Justice Brennan's novel proposal. *See First English Evangelical Lutheran Church, supra.*

I write today to identify the severe tension between that dramatic development in the law and the view expressed by Justice Brennan's dissent in this case that the public interest is served by encouraging state agencies to exercise considerable flexibility in responding to private desires for development in a way that threatens the preservation of public resources. . . . I like the hat that Justice Brennan has donned today better than the one he wore in *San Diego*, and I am persuaded that he has the

> ### Quick Question
>
> Good joke/bad joke?

---

* "The constitutional rule I propose requires that, once a court finds that a police power regulation has effected a 'taking,' the government entity must pay just compensation for the period commencing on the date the regulation first effected the 'taking,' and ending on the date the government entity chooses to rescind or otherwise amend the regulation." 450 U.S., at 658.

better of the legal arguments here. Even if his position prevailed in this case, however, it would be of little solace to land-use planners who would still be left guessing about how the Court will react to the next case, and the one after that. As this case demonstrates, the rule of liability created by the Court in *First English* is a shortsighted one. Like Justice Brennan, I hope that "a broader vision ultimately prevails." . . .

New Jersey Administrative Code

§ 7:7E-8.11 Public Trust Rights

(a) Public trust rights to tidal waterways and their shores (public trust rights) established by the Public Trust Doctrine include public access which is the ability of the public to pass physically and visually to, from and along lands and waters subject to public trust rights as defined at N.J.A.C. 7:7E-3.50, and to use these lands and waters for activities such as swimming, sunbathing, fishing, surfing, sport diving, bird watching, walking and boating. Public trust rights also include the right to perpendicular and linear access. Public accessways and public access areas provide a means for the public to pass along and use lands and waters subject to public trust rights.

***

(d) Except as otherwise provided at (f) below, development on or adjacent to all tidal waterways and their shores shall provide on-site, permanent, unobstructed public access to the tidal waterway and its shores at all times, including both visual and physical access. . . .

Public accessways and public access areas shall:

1. Include perpendicular access and a linear area along the tidal waterway and its entire shore; and

2. If located in a natural area of a tidal waterway, be designed to minimize the impacts to the natural area and tidal waterway including impacts to habitat value, vegetation and water quality.

***

Petrunis, Inc. v. New Jersey Department of Environmental Protection

OAL Dkt. No. ESA 6547-06, 2007 N.J. Agen. LEXIS 389 (Mar. 22, 2007)

Judge FIDLER delivered the opinion of the Administrative Law Court.

Petitioner A.J. Petrunis, Inc., seeks to remove Project Specific Condition No. 5 from a Coastal General Permit No. 15 issued by the Department of Environmental

Protection Land Use Regulation Program on November 23, 2005. The permit authorizes Petrunis to conduct remediation of oil and gasoline product soil contamination at a site it owns and operates in Cumberland County on the Cohansey River waterfront. Project Specific Condition No. 5 provides that Petrunis shall sign and record a Department approved conservation restriction for the entire waterfront portion of the site. This easement is intended to guarantee the public's ability to access the

Photo: Tim Kiser/Wikimedia Commons

Figure 9-11. The Cohansey River, Near Bridgeton, New Jersey

waterfront in the event of future development of the site. . . .

By its counsel, Petrunis expressed its disagreement with Condition No. 5 beginning in January 2006. The Department would not agree to eliminate the condition. On June 6, 2006, Petrunis submitted the materials required to formally request a hearing and the Department granted the hearing request on August 4, 2006. On September 8, 2006, the matter was transmitted to the Office of Administrative Law for determination as a contested case. . . .

The material facts are undisputed. Petrunis applied for a CAFRA [Coastal Area Facility Review Act] Coastal General Permit on August 29, 2005, proposing activities associated with the subsurface investigation, cleanup, and remediation of oil

> **CAFRA**
>
> CAFRA, N.J. STAT. ANN. §§ 13: 19-1 *et seq.*, is New Jersey's coastal permitting statute. The New Jersey Legislature passed the statute in 1973.

and gasoline product soil contamination associated with above-ground fuel storage tanks that used to be at its property. . . . The remediation project is within the filled water's edge of the Cohansey River. Petrunis acknowledges its obligation to remediate soil contamination in compliance with the New Jersey Spill Act and other New Jersey statutes and regulations, and fulfilling this obligation was its purpose for obtaining the permit.

The Coastal General Permit No. 15 issued to Petrunis specifies that the State of New Jersey does not relinquish tidelands ownership or claim to any portion of the subject property or adjacent properties. The Department's Bureau of Tidelands Management has documented three State tidelands conveyances, in 1883, 1894, and 1909, covering portions of the Petrunis property extending many feet inland of the current high water line of the Cohansey River. These Tidelands grants reveal that extensive portions of the subject lots were previously tidally flowed.

The challenged permit condition requires that

> In accordance with N.J.A.C. 7:7E-8.11 — Public Access to the Waterfront, the owner shall sign a Department approved conservation restriction for the entire waterfront portion of the site measured from the mean high water line to a width of 30 feet landward of the mean high water line. The said easement shall guarantee the public's ability to access the waterfront through the potential future development of the subject site. The restriction shall be included on the deed, and recorded in the office of the County Clerk (the Registrar of Deeds and Mortgages), in the county wherein the lands included in the waiver are located. Said restriction shall run with the land and be binding upon all successive owners. Any regulated activities undertaken on the site before a copy of this recorded restriction is submitted to the Department shall be considered in violation of the Waterfront Development Act. Please submit a copy of the draft restriction to the Land Use Regulation Program for review prior to recording. Send a copy of the recorded conservation restriction before beginning regulated activities.

The Petrunis site is in an industrial zone located in a heavily industrial area. The site is used for an energy business, involving the installation, storage, and repair of fuel oil, heating, air conditioning, and plumbing systems. Hazardous materials such as kerosene, propane, diesel and home heating oil are stored on site and pumped by employees into delivery trucks. Gasoline, oxygen, refrigerant, and acetylene are also used and handled on-site. Hazardous substance delivery trucks move on and off the property often and heavy equipment is operated on-site daily, including backhoes, large dump trucks, and flat-bed trucks. There are large stockpiles of sand and stone and there is a 40-yard dumpster where scrap metals, oil tanks, water heaters, air conditioning units, and other equipment are stored before disposal.

Petrunis has implemented a Safety and Security Plan pursuant to 49 C.F.R. 172, Final Rule HM-232 Haz-Mat Security Requirements. The site is a secured area, completely surrounded by barbed wire fence, including the waterfront. Hard-hats, safety goggles, and ear protection are provided to employees for their use at the site. Petrunis has no plans for development on the site.

N.J.A.C. 7:7E-8.11(b) states:

> Coastal development adjacent to all coastal waters, including both natural and developed waterfront areas, shall provide permanent perpendicular and linear access to the waterfront to the maximum extent practicable, including both visual and physical access. Development that limits public access and the diversity of the waterfront experiences is discouraged.

Petrunis has several arguments against the challenged permit condition. First, it contends that it would be dangerous to allow the public to enter onto its site, which is an active, industrial property in a heavily industrial area. Public access to the waterfront portion would potentially expose the public to hazardous materials and heavy equipment in use on-site, creating unsafe conditions that would dangerously interfere with business operations. In other words, no public waterfront access is practicable at this site within the plain meaning of N.J.A.C. 7:7E-8.11(b).

Petrunis further contends that application of the public access rule to its site under the existing circumstances is arbitrary and capricious. Because there will only be remediation of contamination under the permit sought, and no development from which it will gain a benefit, Petrunis asserts that it should not be burdened with a conservation restriction. The State and its waters will gain the benefit from the cleanup and Petrunis claims that it should not have to bear the burden of an easement on its property for some future property owner when the easement is unreasonable as to Petrunis.

Petrunis also contends that allowing general public access to the waterfront on its site will breach security requirements governed by federal regulation. As a hazardous materials transporter, Petrunis is required by the United States Department of Transportation to have a Safety and Security Plan that limits the access of "unauthorized persons" to the site, including the general public. The Petrunis site, including the waterfront, is completely surrounded by barbed-wire fence. Public access to the waterfront would breach the secured area and jeopardize the Safety and Security Plan. This could result in loss of DOT licenses and registrations and essentially put Petrunis out of business.

Petrunis concedes that New Jersey courts have recognized and expanded the public trust doctrine, holding that tidal waterways and their shores are held in trust by the State for the benefit of all people, allowing the public to enjoy these lands and waters for a variety of uses. *See Matthews v. Bay Head Improvement Ass'n*, 95 N.J. 306 (1984); *Raleigh Ave. Beach Ass'n v. Atlantis Beach Club, Inc.*, 185 N.J. 40 (2005). Petrunis argues, however, that the Department has recognized that properties such as the Petrunis site, where hazardous materials are routinely handled and stored, present an exception to the public trust doctrine. . . .

In its moving papers, the Department notes that the permit condition requiring an easement for future public access is fully supported by the public trust doctrine, but it emphasizes that public access to the waterfront within the subject site during its current land use is not the intent of the Department. Rather, the easement condition is intended only to guarantee future public access. The Department agrees that public access would be impracticable now under N.J.A.C. 7:7E-8.11(b), because of the existing business. Petrunis and its successors are entitled to continue such operations without any interference from public access to the waterfront. The essence of the permit condition is notice to potential future owners and users of the property that public access may be required if and when the land use changes.

The Appellate Division has upheld the Department's right to require deed restrictions under the Coastal Area Facility Review Act . . . and its implementing regulations, N.J.A.C. 7:7E-1.1 et seq. *In re Protest of Coastal Permit Program Rules*, 354 N.J. Super. 293, 367 (App. Div. 2002). CAFRA is primarily an environmental protection statute, but the powers delegated to the Department extend well beyond protection of the natural environment in the coastal area to cover land use regulations for the general welfare. . . . Public access to the waterfront is one of the Department's eight basic coastal policies, N.J.A.C. 7:7E-1.5(a)1v, and the permit condition in this matter is part of the Department's efforts to enhance water dependent uses along the shoreline. . . .

Having considered the parties' arguments, I agree with the Department that it has, consistent with the coastal zone management regulations, the public trust doctrine, and common sense, properly modified the standard public access requirement to accommodate the existing land use at the Petrunis property. This ensures that Petrunis and its successors can continue to operate the existing industrial business without any time limitation, while also securing possible future public access in the event that the property's land use changes. There is no present obligation to improve the property or construct any development to meet future public access requirements. Rather, the permit condition imposes only an easement recordation requirement giving notice to future owners or contract-purchasers of the potential future public access.

Based upon the foregoing, I conclude that Project Specific Condition No. 5 is a reasonable application of the Department's coastal zone management regulations and it should not be removed from the Coastal General Permit issued by the Department on November 23, 2005. Thus, the Department is entitled to summary decision, pursuant to N.J.A.C. 1:1-12.5, and petitioner's appeal should be dismissed.

points for discussion

1. *Understanding exactions.* As Justice Scalia writes, "the Commission unquestionably would be able to deny the Nollans their permit outright if their new house (alone, or by reason of the cumulative impact produced in conjunction with other construction) would substantially impede" a legitimate governmental objective, such as access. (This is why it is called a "permit," not a "right.") If the government can simply deny the request for a permit with no liability, why is it exposed to liability if it asks for something in return for the permit?

2. *Understanding* Nollan. Are the majority and dissent simply arguing about how close the relationship needs to be between the requested exaction and the public harm effected by the permitted activity? In other words, is this case simply about whether a permitted activity that blocks *visual* access can only give rise to an exaction that would enhance *visual* access?

3. *It rhymes with* Nollan. In a case decided seven years later, *Dolan v. City of Tigard*, 512 U.S. 374 (1994), the Supreme Court revisited the issue of exactions. In *Dolan*, the Court added a second requirement to *Nollan's* mandate that the permit condition be "reasonably related" to the harm effected: The condition must also be "roughly proportional" to that harm. For example, suppose a city predicts that a proposed project would increase traffic in the center of town. The city may request, as a condition of granting the permit, an exaction in the form of an easement for a bicycle path across the applicant's property (reasonably related), but only if it first shows that the traffic-reducing impact of the easement is about the same as (roughly proportional to) the predicted increase in traffic. How would the city show this?

4. *The Jersey approach.* Is New Jersey's approach to acquiring public access easements more or less likely to produce a winning takings claim than the California approach?

5. *Am I missing something?* Can you think of a better argument on behalf of Petrunis, Inc.? Exactly why do you think it wasn't made?

3. Protection of Special Areas

In Chapter 5, we read about the unique ecology of both submerged and upland coastal systems. Unlike erosion and access, the common law (other than several recent public trust decisions, such as *National Audubon*) had very little to say about the importance of protecting rare places and species. Moreover, the common law had no traction on upland areas, other than in the limited realm of public access.

On the other hand, the CZMA states as its first goal "the protection of natural resources, including wetlands, floodplains, estuaries, beaches, dunes, barrier islands, coral reefs, and fish and wildlife and their habitat, within the coastal zone. . . ." 16 U.S.C. § 1452(2)(A). Thus, where states define their coastal zones to include upland areas, state coastal programs should include measures aimed at the protection of upland wildlife and habitats. In addition, Section 1455(d)(2)(C) requires that state program documents include "[a]n inventory and designation of areas of particular concern within the coastal zone." The following cases illustrate — among other things — how New Hampshire and California provide additional protection for sensitive habitats.

a. Wetlands Protection: New Hampshire

Laws regulating activities that impact wetlands are an important part of state coastal programs for four reasons. First, wetlands are concentrated in coastal areas: Approximately 40 percent of wetlands in the United States are coastal wetlands. Second, wetlands are a dwindling resource: The total acreage of coastal wetlands in the United States today is less than half of what it was in the 1700s. Third, wetlands are extremely valuable in ecological and economic terms. They are both biodiverse and highly productive, and they provide a wealth of ecosystem services, supplying among other things recreational opportunities, support for commercial fisheries, beautiful scenery, and a buffer against storms and flooding. Finally, by limiting the scope of the Army Corps' wetlands jurisdiction (or at least increasing uncertainty regarding the scope of Corps' jurisdiction), the United States Supreme Court's decisions in *SWANCC* and *Rapanos* heightened the importance of *state* wetlands laws. *See* Jeanne Christie & Scott Hausmann, *Various State Reactions to the* SWANCC *Decision*, 23 WETLANDS 653 (2003).

In addition to providing an example of state wetlands regulation, the following opinion touches on some interesting issues regarding wetlands regulation and environmental regulation generally. Specifically, what are the appropriate geographic and temporal scales of a regulatory scheme?

Greenland Conservation Council v. New Hampshire Wetlands Council

913 A.2d 776 (N.H. 2006)

Chief Justice BRODERICK delivered the opinion of the Supreme Court of New Hampshire.

The plaintiffs, Greenland Conservation Commission (GCC) and Conservation Law Foundation (CLF), appeal an order of the Superior Court . . . affirming a decision and order (decision) of the New Hampshire Wetlands Council (wetlands council or council) that affirmed the issuance of a wetlands permit by the wetlands bureau (wetlands bureau or bureau) of the New Hampshire Department of Environmental Services (DES) to Endicott General Partnership (Endicott). That permit allows Endicott to fill 42,350 square feet of wetlands, at twelve locations, for the construction of roadways to serve a proposed housing development in Greenland. We affirm.

The following facts are drawn from the administrative record. Before DES issued the permit that gave rise to this suit, through its wetlands bureau, Endicott received subdivision approval from the Greenland Planning Board for a seventy-nine-lot housing development situated on a 212-acre parcel that includes approximately eighty-five acres of wetlands bordering Norton Brook, two unnamed tributaries to Norton Brook and several vernal pools. The remainder of the parcel consists of uplands. *See* N.H. Admin. Rules, Env-Wt 101.95 (defining "upland" as "an area of land that is not a jurisdictional area"); N.H. Admin. Rules, Env-Wt 101.50 (defining "jurisdictional area" as "an area that is subject to regulation under RSA chapter 482-A, as described therein"); RSA 482-A:4, II (2001) (describing the non-tidal waters and areas regulated by RSA chapter 482-A as encompassing "all surface waters of the state . . . which contain fresh water, including the portion of any bank or shore which borders such surface waters, and . . . any swamp or bog subject to periodical flooding by fresh water including the surrounding shore"). On June 12, 2002, Endicott filed a "standard dredge and fill application" with the DES wetlands bureau, pursuant to RSA 482-A:3, I (2001), for the construction of roadways across protected wetlands at thirteen locations.

On March 19, 2003, the bureau granted Endicott a permit that included the following project description:

> Fill a total of 61,150 sq. ft. of palustrine wetlands for roadway crossings at 13 locations for a 79-lot subdivision on 212 acres. [Palustrine wetlands are freshwater, non-tidal wetlands not directly connected to lakes or streams. — EDS.] Approve as mitigation preservation of a total of 98.6 acres, consisting of 20.7 acres of upland and 77.9 acres of wetland, to be placed in conservation easement and held by the Town of Greenland; and creation of 24,829 sq. ft. (one 10,890 sq. ft. area, and one 13,939 sq. ft. area) of flood plain scrub/shrub and emergent marsh wetlands constructed as compensation for wetland impacts within the 100 year flood plain.

The plaintiffs both requested reconsideration of the decision to issue the permit. After holding a public hearing on the petition for reconsideration, the bureau concurred on two of the four proposed grounds for reconsideration and revoked the permit by letter dated September 13, 2003.

Endicott, in turn, sought reconsideration of the permit revocation, and after holding a hearing on Endicott's petition for reconsideration, the bureau issued a new permit, dated February 4, 2004, that included the following project description:

> Fill a total of 42,350 sq. ft. of palustrine wetlands for roadway crossings at 12 locations, including 4,000 square feet for the construction of a 100 linear foot bridge, for a 79-lot subdivision on 212 acres. Approval includes, as mitigation, the preservation of a total of approximately 106 acres, consisting of approximately 27 acres of upland and approximately 79 acres of wetland, to be placed in conservation easement and held by the Town of Greenland; and, creation of 24,829 sq. ft. (one 10,890 sq. ft. area, and one 13,939 sq. ft. area) of flood plain scrub/shrub and emergent marsh wetlands constructed as compensation for wetland impacts within the 100 year flood plain; and, execution of the Atlantic White Cedar Management Plan as prepared by Carex Ecosystems dated 12/6/02, rec'd by DES 12/6/02.

The increased acreage under conservation easement in the new permit included three entire lots, and the new permit also called for establishment of a fifty-foot upland buffer that involved ten more lots.

The plaintiffs appealed the bureau's decision to the wetlands council . . . which affirmed. After the council denied their motions to reconsider, GCC and CLF filed separate appeals in the superior court . . . which were consolidated. The superior court affirmed the council's decision. This appeal followed.

On appeal, the plaintiffs contend that the trial court erred by: (1) ruling that DES' review authority (as exercised by the wetlands bureau) was limited to assessing the impact of construction activities in protected wetlands (*i.e.*, the twelve permitted wetland crossings) and did not include consideration of the impact that upland activities (*i.e.*, the entire subdivision) might have upon protected wetlands; (2) imposing on the plaintiffs the burden to develop and present alternative designs to the wetlands bureau; (3) affirming the wetlands council's decision when there was no evidence in the record of project alterations designed to address the issues raised by the wetlands bureau's September 13, 2003

Photo: Botteville/Wikimedia Commons

Figure 9-12. Newbury Marsh, Massachusetts Palustrine (upland) wetlands in New England.

permit revocation; (4) failing to address critical grounds for appeal concerning failures by Endicott and the bureau to properly address the impacts of the proposed project; and (5) affirming the council's decision, even though the council applied an overly deferential standard of review and failed to specify the factual and legal bases of its decision.

The trial court's review of wetlands council decisions is governed by RSA 482-A:10, XI (2001), which provides:

> On appeal to the superior court, the burden of proof shall be upon the party seeking to set aside the decision of the council to show that the decision is unlawful or unreasonable. The council's decision shall not be set aside or vacated, except for errors of law, unless the court is persuaded, by a preponderance of the evidence before it, that said decision is unjust or unreasonable.

Conservation Law Found. v. N.H. Wetlands Council, 150 N.H. 1, 3 (2003). We, in turn, will not disturb the trial court's decision unless it is unsupported by the evidence or legally erroneous. . . .

I.

The plaintiffs first argue that the wetlands bureau, the wetlands council, and the trial court all adopted an unlawfully narrow view of DES' statutory scope of review. On the plaintiffs' reading, RSA chapter 482-A . . . obligated the bureau to consider not just the effects of the filling necessary to construct the twelve approved wetland crossings, but also the effects of the housing development as a whole, including upland construction activities, on protected wetlands. Among other things, the plaintiffs point to the discharge of stormwater runoff and habitat fragmentation as neg-

---

Habitat Fragmentation

The term "habitat fragmentation" captures the idea that when we build, say, a road through a large habitat area, the impacts on habitat can be greater than the mere loss of area that has been paved. In other words, the road may also diminish the ecological value of the remaining habitat. There are many reasons why this might occur, among them the fact that the road could interfere with animals' ability to travel in search of food or shelter. *See* Lenore Fahrig, *Effects of Habitat Fragmentation on Biodiversity*, 34 ANN. REV. ECOLOGY, EVOLUTION & SYSTEMATICS 487 (2003).

---

ative effects that will result from the construction of seventy-six homes (seventy-nine lots minus the three lots placed under conservation easement) and related infrastructure. According to the plaintiffs, the trial court erred, as a matter of law, because its decision concerning the extent of DES' project review and permitting authority: (1) violated RSA 482-A:1; (2) violated DES' wetland rules; (3) is inconsistent with DES' prior implementation of RSA chapter 482-A and its wetland rules; and (4) is inconsistent with both the permit the wetlands bureau ultimately issued to Endicott and representations DES officials made during the permitting process. We address each argument in turn.

The plaintiffs' statutory argument rests upon the section of chapter 482-A titled "Finding of Public Purpose." According to that section:

> It is found to be for the public good and welfare of this state to protect and preserve its submerged lands under tidal and fresh waters and its wetlands, (both salt water and fresh-water), as herein defined, from despoliation and unregulated alteration, because such despoliation or unregulated alteration will adversely affect the value of such areas as sources of nutrients for finfish, crustacea, shellfish and wildlife of significant value, will damage or destroy habitats and reproduction areas for plants, fish and wildlife of importance, will eliminate, depreciate or obstruct the commerce, recreation and aesthetic enjoyment of the public, will be detrimental to adequate groundwater levels, will adversely affect stream channels and their ability to handle the runoff of waters, will disturb and reduce the natural ability of wetlands to absorb flood waters and silt, thus increasing general flood damage and the silting of open water channels, and will otherwise adversely affect the interests of the general public.

RSA 482-A:1. The plaintiffs argue that the language quoted above, "combined with basic principles of wetlands ecology," establishes the need for the review process outlined in chapter 482-A to consider not just the impacts of the twelve wetland crossings, but also the impacts of the subdivision as a whole, including both its upland and wetland components. We do not agree.

Chapter 482-A is titled "Fill and Dredge in Wetlands," and the permits granted under that chapter are referred to in the statute as "Excavating and Dredging Permit[s]." RSA 482-A:3, I. The title of a statute is not conclusive of its interpretation . . . , but it is a significant indication of the intent of the legislature in enacting a statute. . . . Here, the title of chapter 482-A strongly indicates that the legislature intended it to protect wetlands only from the effects caused by dredging and filling within their boundaries.

The part of the statute that describes the permitting process provides, in pertinent part:

> No person shall excavate, remove, fill, dredge or construct any structures in or on any bank, flat, marsh, or swamp in and adjacent to any waters of the state without a permit from the department. The permit application together with a detailed plan and a map showing the exact location of the proposed project . . . shall be submitted. . . . Fees for minor and major projects shall be assessed based on the area of dredge, fill, or construction proposed. . . .

RSA 482-A:3, I. This language plainly establishes the scope of the project review and permitting authority granted to DES and exercised by DES through its wetlands bureau. DES is authorized to grant permits for certain enumerated construction activities in or on banks, flats, marshes and swamps in and adjacent to state waters. *Id.* DES is not authorized to grant dredge and fill permits for construction activities not listed in the statute or conducted anywhere other than the places listed in the statute. . . . The permitting process described in RSA 482-A:3, I, is the way the legislature has determined that DES shall carry out the purposes described in RSA 482-A:1. We note, however, that while the scope of chapter 482-A limits

DES to the assessment of construction activities in wetlands when it issues dredge and fill permits, upland construction activities such as those proposed by Endicott in this case are subject to various other forms of DES review. *See, e.g.*, RSA 485-A:17 (DES permit required when "any person propos[es] to significantly alter the characteristics of the terrain, in such a manner as to impede the natural runoff or create an unnatural runoff"); RSA 485-A:29 (DES approval required for most sewage and waste disposal systems). Thus, our determination that chapter 482-A does not authorize DES to assess the impacts of upland construction does not mean that Endicott's upland construction activities are entirely free from DES review.

While it may be argued, based upon principles of wetlands ecology, that the purposes described in RSA 482-A:1 could be better served by the sort of review process the plaintiffs advocate — a matter upon which we offer no opinion — the proper place for making such arguments is before the legislature. . . .

The plaintiffs' regulatory argument is equally unavailing. According to the plaintiffs, the trial court erred by ruling that the wetlands bureau had no obligation to assess the effects of upland construction on protected wetlands because the administrative rules governing the wetlands bureau: (1) require the bureau to consider impacts on wetlands; (2) do not distinguish between direct and indirect impacts; and (3) do not define the term "project" to refer only to activities occurring within protected wetlands. While it is well settled that an administrative agency must follow its own rules and regulations, . . . the plaintiffs' argument fails for two reasons. First, when read as a whole, the regulations upon which the plaintiffs base their argument . . . do not authorize the bureau to assess the impacts of upland construction upon protected wetlands. . . . What those regulations do allow is for the bureau to assess the impact of construction in wetlands and to impose conditions, including mitigation, in order to protect wetlands. Moreover, any portion of those regulations that might purport to authorize the type of assessment advocated by the plaintiffs would be without effect, because agency regulations that contradict the terms of a governing statute exceed the agency's authority. . . . Accordingly, the trial court did not err by rejecting the plaintiffs' regulatory argument.

The plaintiffs next argue that the trial court's decision was erroneous because in the past, the wetlands bureau has considered the impacts of upland construction upon protected wetlands and, on at least one occasion, denied a permit on that ground. There are two problems with the plaintiffs' argument. First, the permitting decision upon which the plaintiffs rely, concerning a proposed highway bypass in Troy, did not address the impacts of upland development on protected wetlands; it addressed the impact of wetland destruction on the habitat value of upland areas connected by the 6.9 acres of wetlands that the department of transportation proposed to dredge and fill. In denying the Troy permit, DES explained:

> The project has severe impacts on significant wetland and surface water resources that play an integral role in the habitat value and viability of a large unfragmented forested ecosystem which includes forested wetlands of high functional value. Unnecessary destruction of vital wetland and surface water components of that larger ecosystem is contrary to the public purpose of RSA 482-A:1. . . .

Based upon the foregoing, the permit application for the Troy project is not analogous to the application in this case. If anything, it represents the converse. Second, even if the situation surrounding the Troy project were factually analogous, and DES had denied the application on the grounds advocated by the plaintiffs in this case, *i.e.*, the adverse impact upon wetlands resulting from upland construction, such a decision would have been unlawful, for reasons we have already explained, and there is no principle of law that would compel, or even allow, DES to overstep its statutory authority a second time, simply because it did so once before. . . .

The plaintiffs' final argument for requiring DES to consider the effects of upland construction on protected wetlands is that DES itself, both in the wetlands bureau's permit approval document and at the wetlands council hearing, took actions and made statements demonstrating that it believed it did have the authority to regulate upland activities to protect wetlands. In particular, the plaintiffs point to several conditions the wetlands bureau placed upon the permit approval, such as the requirement that three lots not be developed and the establishment of a fifty-foot buffer zone. Whatever various DES officials may have said, orally or in writing — and we do not interpret the actions and statements identified by the plaintiffs as conflicting with DES' statutory authority — those officials were without power to extend the scope of the agency's authority. . . .

Further, we disagree with the plaintiffs' argument that the trial court's decision was erroneous because its legal conclusions are inconsistent with the permit ultimately issued to Endicott. In support of that argument, the plaintiffs point to the fifty-foot buffer zone that was made a condition of approval and argue that if the bureau was without authority to consider or regulate activities conducted beyond the boundaries of protected wetlands, then it was also without authority to impose a condition that impinged upon uplands, a category of terrain that, by definition, falls outside DES' wetlands jurisdiction. . . .

The plaintiffs' argument is not persuasive. The plain meaning of the statute does not prohibit DES from imposing permit conditions that may have an effect on uplands. Rather, it limits DES to engaging in such consideration or regulation only when it arises directly from its assessment of proposed filling and dredging in wetlands — the activities that give DES jurisdiction in the first place, and for which an applicant seeks a permit. . . .

For all of the foregoing reasons, the trial court did not err by ruling that DES' review authority was limited to assessing the impacts of construction activities in protected wetlands, and did not extend to assessing the effects of upland construction activities upon such wetlands.

***

IV.

Next, the plaintiffs argue that the trial court erred by failing to address six "critical, potentially outcome-determinative grounds for appeal." Those grounds for appeal, discussed at length in the plaintiffs' post-hearing memorandum, include: (1) the wetlands bureau's failure to consider direct impacts upon an Atlantic white cedar wetland community; (2) the lack of baseline data on Norton Brook and projections concerning the discharge of pollutants into the brook; (3) DES' reliance upon its "site specific" division to analyze certain impacts upon water resources rather than having those impacts addressed by the wetlands bureau; (4) Endicott's failure to assess the impacts of wetland crossings upon the quality of water in adjacent vernal pools; (5) the bureau's failure to address significant project-specific wildlife concerns; and (6) the bureau's failure to assess either the cumulative impacts of the project . . . or the project's impacts upon the function and values of the total wetland complex. . . .

Review of the plaintiffs' post-hearing memorandum demonstrates that the first five arguments are without merit. Each relies, to a greater or lesser extent, upon a pair of legally untenable premises. One has already been addressed: the plaintiffs' incorrect belief that the RSA chapter 482-A permitting process authorizes DES to consider the impacts of upland construction upon protected wetlands. The second faulty premise is that DES is authorized to consider not just the impact of dredging and filling in wetlands, but also the impacts projected to result from the future use of a structure the construction of which required permitted dredging and filling. For example, the plaintiffs contend that DES was obligated to assess the impact of sand and salt runoff from roadways over wetland crossings constructed pursuant to the dredge and fill permit for which Endicott applied. As with their upland impact argument, the plaintiffs read the scope of RSA chapter 482-A too broadly. The impacts to wetlands that RSA chapter 482-A authorizes DES to consider are those created by excavating, removing, filling, dredging and constructing structures in or on banks, flats, marshes and swamps in and adjacent to state waters. RSA 482-A:3. The statute does not authorize DES to consider impacts created by the subsequent use of structures constructed under duly issued wetlands permits. Because the plaintiffs' first five arguments all depend upon one or both incorrect legal premises, they are all without merit.

According to the plaintiffs, the trial court also erred by failing to address their argument that Endicott failed to assess, and the wetlands bureau did not properly consider, the cumulative impacts of the project or its impacts upon the functions and values of the total wetland complex. The relevant DES regulations provide:

(a) For any major or minor project, the applicant shall demonstrate by plan and example that the following factors have been considered in the project's design in assessing the impact of the proposed project to areas and environments under the department's jurisdiction:

***

(16) The cumulative impact that would result if all parties owning or abutting a portion of the affected wetland or wetland complex were also permitted alterations to the wetland proportional to the extent of their property rights. For example, an applicant who owns only a portion of a wetland shall document the applicant's percentage of ownership of that wetland and the percentage of that ownership that would be impacted;

(17) The impact of the proposed project on the values and functions of the total wetland or wetland complex[.]

N.H. Admin. Rules, Env-Wt 302.04.

In its June 10, 2002 application to the wetlands bureau, Endicott described the wetlands on its property:

> For purposes of the functions and values assessment completed as part of this application, the wetland areas on-site were divided into areas A, B, and C. Area A corresponds to the Norton Brook drainage system, and areas B and C correspond to the drainage systems of two unnamed tributaries to Norton Brook. These wetlands areas are all part of one watershed.

According to the application, "[a]ll impacts to wetlands are associated with construction of access roadways to service the subdivision, and the construction of spans and/or box culverts over Norton Brook, unnamed tributaries to Norton Brook, and unnamed wetlands."

To address Rule 302.04(a)(16), the application provided: "This project has been designed to minimize the amount of wetland impact relative to the area of wetland on the property. Any cumulative impacts would be negligible providing the abutters impacted wetland proportional to their property rights[.]" Thus, notwithstanding the plaintiffs' argument to the contrary, Endicott did address the cumulative impact factor, and demonstrated in its application materials that it proposed to fill less than 1.7 percent of the wetlands on the site. That is sufficient to satisfy the requirements of Rule 302.04(a)(16). Because the factual basis for the plaintiffs' argument — that Endicott failed to address the cumulative impact factor — is plainly erroneous in light of the record, the trial court cannot be faulted for declining to address that argument.

So, too, with the plaintiffs' argument concerning the values and functions factor. To address Rule 302.04(a)(17), the application provided:

> Proposed impacts are minimal in relation to the overall size and character of the wetland areas. The project proposes to impact only 1.69% of the total wetlands on the site. Measures will be taken to minimize the effect on the functions or values of the wetland areas. A functions and values assessment is included in this application. The principal functions and values currently provided include groundwater recharge/discharge, floodflow alteration, fish and shellfish habitat, sediment/toxicant retention, nutrient removal, production export, sediment/shoreline stabilization, wildlife habitat, and uniqueness/heritage (the wetland system contains potential feeding and breeding habitat for two "special concern" turtle species and supports an Atlantic white cedar stand). The Conservation Easement areas associated with the project will ensure the large wetland areas on the property continue to provide these functions and are protected. The proposed roadways represent fragmentation of habitat from a wildlife perspective, but the wetlands will remain contiguous via appropriately sized spans and box culverts.

As suggested by the foregoing passage, the application materials did indeed include a "Wetland Function — Value Evaluation Form" for each of the three enumerated wetland areas on the property. Thus, the record does not support the plaintiffs' contention that Endicott failed to address the values and functions factor, which completely undermines any argument that the trial court erred in its treatment of that issue.

Moreover, because the plaintiffs' argument that the wetlands board did not properly consider the factors set out in Rules 302.04(a)(16) and (17) is premised exclusively upon the erroneous contention that Endicott did not address those factors in its application, there is no basis for arguing that the wetlands bureau failed to consider the project's cumulative impacts or its impacts upon the values and functions of the total wetland complex.

***

Because the order of the trial court is neither legally erroneous nor unsupported by the evidence, it is affirmed.

points for discussion

1. *Public trust and "private" wetlands.* Think back to Chapter 6: Are the wetlands at issue in *Greenland* subject to federal regulation under Section 404 of the Clean Water Act post-*Rapanos*? What would we need to know in order to answer this question? Are the wetlands at issue in *Greenland* public trust wetlands? (For a case involving state regulation of public trust wetlands, see *Palazzolo v. State of Rhode Island*, 2005 R.I. Super. LEXIS 108 (July 5, 2005).) Which other jurisdictional bases would the State of New Hampshire have for regulating the use or destruction of wetlands wholly located on private property? How would use or destruction of wetlands on private land impact public health, safety, welfare, or morals?

2. *Ulterior motives.* If the court in *Greenland* is correct that use and development of the uplands would be subject to regulation under other state environmental laws, why would the plaintiffs wish to see them also regulated under RSA 482-A?

3. *Dredge and fill.* The scope of activities covered by RSA 482-A is, despite the title of the code chapter ("Fill and Dredge in Wetlands"), broader than the scope of the federal wetlands statute, Section 404 of the Clean Water Act. That law, as you recall from Chapter 6, only covers "the discharge of dredged or fill material into the navigable waters." What activities result in the discharge of dredged or fill material? Would the construction of a dock, whose pilings are driven into the wetlands, require a federal wetlands permit? Are the pilings "filling" wetlands? (It would clearly require RSA 482-A permit, because that law covers construction activities.) *Cf. Nat'l Mining Ass'n v. U.S. Army Corps of Eng'rs*, 145 F.3d 1399 (D.C. Cir. 1998).

4. *The time/space continuum.* As noted above, this case highlights some issues that are central to wetlands regulation, and environmental regulation generally. Does it make sense to regulate use of uplands and use of wetlands separately? Does it make sense to consider the impacts of the proposed activity but not the future impacts of the development facilitated by the proposed activity? Professors Salzman and Thompson describe these "scale issues"

and the many forms in which they can arise. As you read this, consider how the examples Salzman and Thompson use are similar to, or different from, the regulatory issues raised in *Greenland*.

> Natural boundaries rarely track political boundaries. A map of the western United States shows states and counties with straight lines and right angles. Map the region's watersheds, ecosystems, or forests, however, and nary a straight line will appear. Ecological concerns were, not surprisingly, far from the politicians' and surveyors' minds when these political jurisdictions were created, but the mismatch of natural and political scales poses difficult challenges for environmental management. Air pollution, water pollution, and wildlife certainly pay no heed to state (or national) borders, with the result that often the generator of the pollution is politically distinct from those harmed.
>
> Acid rain was hard to control in the 1970s and 1980s because of political jurisdictions. The costs of reducing emissions downwind were borne by those who received no benefit and similarly, those benefiting from reduced pollution upwind did not have to pay for it. Midwestern power plants were far removed from the polluted lakes and forests of the Northeast and Canada. New York, Vermont, and certainly Canadian voters couldn't vote in Ohio or Pennsylvania. Thus those with the greatest cause for concern did not live in the areas where their concerns could be most effectively expressed. Similar problems of scale are evident in wildlife protection, where draining or filling prairie potholes in the Great Plains, for example, may benefit the local farmers but imperils migratory birds from Mexico to Canada. Pumping carbon dioxide in the air many not seem significant to someone driving an SUV in Montana, but to an islander on a low-lying Pacific atoll the prospects of sea-level rise are a good deal more unsettling.

***

> Problems of scale occur in time as well as space. Decisions must be made today that may prevent harm ten or twenty years from now or, indeed, in generations not yet born. Ozone depletion and climate change are two examples. CFCs (which are the major cause of stratospheric ozone depletion) and greenhouse gases we emit today will cause impacts over the next 50 years or longer. The same distributional asymmetry is at play here as with physical scale. The costs of refraining from an action fall on us today, while the benefits are enjoyed (most likely by others) far later. Yet these future beneficiaries can't express their preferences in today's voting booth or courtroom. Indeed, the temporal scale of many environmental problems makes it difficult even to hold current elected officials accountable, since many of their actions will not cause harms until they are no longer in office. . . . [M]any environmental advocates claim to be acting on behalf of the interests of future generations, but deciding what the proper sacrifice today should be for future benefits that may or may not be appreciated is easier said than done.

James Salzman & Barton H. Thompson, Jr., Environmental Law and Policy 25-28 (4th ed. 2014).

While wetlands might be the most common type of "special" habitat within coastal zone, each state's coastal zone is likely to feature other rare or unique habitats. The following case illustrates how the California Coastal Act, in addition to including special rules for protecting wetlands, also provides for the designation of what are known as "environmentally sensitive habitat areas," or "ESHAs."

b. Conservation of Other Rare, Vulnerable Habitats: California

Bolsa Chica Land Trust v. Superior Court of San Diego County

71 Cal. App. 4th 493 (1999)

Judge BENKE delivered the opinion of the Court of Appeal of California, Fourth Appellate District, Division One.

This case concerns development plans for a large tract of land in southern Orange County known as Bolsa Chica. Although the California Coastal Commission (Commission) approved a local coastal program (LCP) for Bolsa Chica, the trial court found defects in the program and remanded it to Commission for further proceedings. In this court both the opponents and proponents of the LCP contend that the trial court erred.

The opponents of the LCP contend the trial court erred in finding a planned relocation of a bird habitat was permissible under the Coastal Act. The proponents of the LCP contend the trial court erred in preventing residential development of a wetlands area and in requiring preservation of a pond that would have been eliminated under the LCP in order to make room for a street widening. . . .

We find the trial court erred with respect to relocation of the bird habitat. The Coastal Act does not permit destruction of an environmentally sensitive habitat area (ESHA) simply because the destruction is mitigated offsite. At the very least, there must be some showing the destruction is needed to serve some other environmental or economic interest recognized by the act.

We agree with the trial court's rulings as to the two substantive issues raised by the proponents of the LCP: on the record developed by Commission, neither residential development in the wetlands nor destruction of the pond is permissible. . . .

Factual Background

Bolsa Chica is a 1,588-acre area of undeveloped wetlands and coastal mesas. Urban development surrounds Bolsa Chica on three sides. On the fourth side is the Pacific Ocean, separated from Bolsa Chica by a narrow strip of beach, coastal dunes and coastal bluffs.

Approximately 1,300 acres of Bolsa Chica consist of lowlands ranging from fully submerged saltwater in Bolsa Bay to areas of freshwater and saltwater wetlands and islands of slightly raised dry lands used by local wildlife for nesting and foraging. However, a large part of the lowlands is devoted to an active oil field and at one time the area was farmed.

The lowlands are flanked by two mesas, the Bolsa Chica Mesa on the north and the Huntington Mesa on the south. The Bolsa Chica Mesa consists of 215 acres of uplands hosting a variety of habitat areas. Although much of Huntington Mesa is developed, a long narrow undeveloped strip of the mesa abutting the lowlands is the planned site of a public park.

Photo: NOAA

Figure 9-13. Bolsa Chica
Top box indicates location of Warner Pond; box just below indicates location of eucalyptus grove.

In 1973 the State of California acquired 310 contiguous acres of the Bolsa Chica lowlands in settlement of a dispute over its ownership of several separate lowland parcels and the existence of a public trust easement over other lowland areas.

In 1985 the County of Orange and Commission approved a land use plan for Bolsa Chica which contemplated fairly intense development. The 1985 plan allowed development of 5,700 residential units, a 75-acre marina and a 600-foot-wide navigable ocean channel and breakwater.

By 1988 substantial concerns had been raised with respect to the environmental impacts of the proposed marina and navigable ocean channel. Accordingly, a developer which owned a large portion of Bolsa Chica, a group of concerned citizens, the State Lands Commission, the County of Orange and the City of Huntington Beach formed the Bolsa Chica Planning Coalition (coalition). The coalition in turn developed an LCP for Bolsa Chica which substantially reduced the intensity of development. The coalition's LCP was eventually adopted by the Orange County Board of Supervisors. Commission approved the LCP with suggested modifications which were adopted by the board of supervisors.

As approved by Commission, the LCP eliminated the planned marina and navigable ocean channel, eliminated 3 major roads, reduced residential development from a total of 5,700 homes to 2,500 homes on Bolsa Chica Mesa and 900 homes in the lowlands and expanded planned open space and wetlands restoration to 1,300 acres.

The material features of the LCP which are in dispute here are: the replacement of a degraded eucalyptus grove on Bolsa Chica Mesa with a new raptor habitat consisting of nesting poles, native trees and other native vegetation on Huntington Mesa at the sight [*sic*] of the planned public park; the residential development in the lowland area which the LCP permits as a means of financing restoration of substantially degraded wetlands; and the elimination of Warner Pond on Bolsa Chica Mesa in order to accommodate the widening of Warner Avenue.

Throughout the approval process several interested parties and public interest groups, including the Bolsa Chica Land Trust, Huntington Beach Tomorrow, Shoshone-Gabrieleno Nation, Sierra Club and Surfrider Foundation (collectively the trust) objected to these and other portions of the LCP.

Procedural History

On March 6, 1996, the trust filed a timely petition for a writ of mandate challenging the LCP. In addition to Commission, the petition named two local agencies, the

---

The History of Eucalyptus in California

"From Australian miners Californians would learn of the huge tree that grew easily in temperate climates with little regard to soil or water. It seemed the perfect crop for construction timber and fuel in the rapidly growing state. The tree that one day would be called 'America's largest weed' was the 'wonder tree' of 19th century California.

"The first successful planting of eucalyptus in California probably occurred in San Francisco. W.C. Walker of the Golden Gate Nursery planted seeds from several species in 1853.

"By the 1870s, a eucalyptus boom was in full swing throughout the state. The Australian native was planted on thousands of acres....

"The eucalyptus seemed to offer several paths to fortune. Shipbuilders, who first saw the wood as it was used in Australian ships, were eager to try the timber. Regrettably, they discovered that California blue gum eucalyptus split and curled, unlike the old-growth trees used by Australian shipbuilders....

"The medicinal value of eucalyptus became a popular theme. As early as 1872, the California Pharmaceutical Society predicted products from the tree would 'ultimately supersede expensive drugs now in use.' Eucalyptus oil extracted from the leaves was touted as an antiseptic and anti-spasmodic and could be used as an expectorant, stimulant and deodorant. It could treat not only malaria but also insomnia, fevers, bladder infections, dysentery, diphtheria, tuberculosis, and venereal disease.

"But in San Diego, the greatest claim to fame for the eucalyptus was its large-scale production for railroad ties.

"In August 1906, the Santa Fe Land Improvement Co., a subsidiary of the Santa Fe Railway, bought the 9,000-acre San Dieguito Ranch in north San Diego County.

"'The question of lumber for ties is one that is being given a great deal of attention,' a company spokesman said. 'Experiments have shown that the eucalyptus tree makes first-class ties.... The work of planting these trees will be commenced without delay.'

> "The company took delivery of 6 million eucalyptus seeds shipped from Australia....
>
> "The eucalyptus railroad tie experiment ended in failure. The soft wood split from the rail spikes and tended to throw the tracks. Santa Fe recouped its investment by subdividing the ranch into hundreds of parcels for country estates...."
> Richard Crawford, *Eucalyptus Trees Have Deep Roots in California History*, SAN DIEGO UNION-TRIBUNE, August 31, 2008.

County of Orange and the Orange County Flood Control District, as real parties in interest. The petition also named a number of landowners as real parties in interest. Of those landowners, only real parties in interest Koll Real Estate Group (Koll) and Fieldstone Company (Fieldstone) actively participated in the litigation.

On April 16, 1997, before the matter could be heard on the merits, Commission made a motion to have the LCP remanded to it so that Commission could reconsider the plan in light of the state's recent acquisition of Koll's lowland property and the state's adoption of an independent plan to fund restoration of degraded portions of the lowlands.[1] All the other parties in the litigation opposed Commission's motion to remand. The trial court deferred ruling on the state's motion until it conducted a hearing on the merits.

Upon hearing the merits of the trust's challenge, the trial court determined that, consistent with the requirements of the Coastal Act, the eucalyptus grove on Bolsa Chica Mesa could be eliminated in order to permit residential development there and the habitat which existed at the grove regenerated on Huntington Mesa. However, the trial court found that residential development of wetlands was not permitted by the act, even if it would fund restoration of other portions of the wetlands. The court found that although wetlands could be eliminated if needed for a road or highway, Commission had not made a required finding that the need to widen Warner Road outweighed the value of preserving Warner Pond.

***

Eucalyptus Grove

History and Condition of the Grove

The LCP would permit residential development over five acres of a six-and-one-half-acre eucalyptus grove on Bolsa Chica Mesa. The five acres where development would be permitted is owned by Koll; the remainder of the grove is owned by the state.

The eucalyptus grove is not native to the area and was planted almost 100 years ago by a hunting club which owned large portions of Bolsa Chica. Since the time

---

1. Financing for the state's acquisition of Koll's lowland holdings as well as its restoration plan was provided by the Ports of Los Angeles and Long Beach as mitigation for the dredging and expansion that the ports planned.

of its planting, the original 20-acre grove has diminished considerably because of development in the area and the lack of any effort to preserve it. Indeed, although the eucalyptus grove was nine and two-tenths acres large as recently as 1989, it had shrunk to no more than six and one-half acres by 1994 and portions of it were under severe stress. According to expert testimony submitted to Commission, the grove is probably shrinking because of increased salinity in the soil.

Notwithstanding its current diminished and deteriorating condition, Commission identified the grove as an ESHA within the meaning of Public Resources Code section 30107.5. The ESHA identification was based on the fact the grove provided the only significant locally available roosting and nesting habitat for birds of prey (raptors) in the Bolsa Chica area. At least 11 species of raptors have been identified as utilizing the site, including the white-tailed kite, marsh hawk, sharp skinned hawk, Cooper's hawk and osprey. According to Commission, a number of the raptors are dependent upon the adjacent lowland wetlands for food and the eucalyptus grove provides an ideal nearby lookout location as well as a refuge and nesting site.

B. Section 30240

Under the Coastal Act, Commission is required to protect the coastal zone's delicately balanced ecosystem. . . . Thus in reviewing all programs and projects governed by the Coastal Act, Commission must consider the effect of proposed development on the environment of the coast. . . .

In terms of the general protection the Coastal Act provides for the coastal environment, we have analogized it to the California Environmental Quality Act (CEQA). . . . We have found that under both the Coastal Act and CEQA: " 'The courts are enjoined to construe the statute liberally in light of its beneficent purposes. . . . The highest priority must be given to environmental consideration in interpreting the statute.' "

In addition to the protection afforded by the requirement that Commission consider the environmental impact of all its decisions, the Coastal Act provides heightened protection to ESHA's. . . . Section 30107.5 identifies an ESHA as "any area in which plant or animal life or their habitats are either rare or especially valuable because of their special nature or role in an ecosystem and which could be easily disturbed or degraded by human activities and developments."

> The consequences of ESHA status are delineated in section 30240: "(a) Environmentally sensitive habitat areas shall be protected against any significant disruption of habitat values, and only uses dependent on those resources shall be allowed within those areas. (b) Development in areas adjacent to environmentally sensitive habitat areas and parks and recreation areas shall be sited and designed to prevent impacts which would significantly degrade those areas, and shall be compatible with continuance of those habitat and recreation areas." Thus development in ESHA areas themselves is limited to uses dependent on those resources, and development in adjacent areas must carefully safeguard their preservation. *Sierra Club v. California Coastal Com.*, 12 Cal. App. 4th 602, 611 (1993) ("Pygmy Forest").

Commission found that residential development in the eucalyptus grove was permissible under Section 30240 because the LCP required that an alternate raptor habitat be developed on Huntington Mesa. Commission reasoned that Section 30240 only requires that "habitat values" be protected and that given the deteriorating condition of the grove, creation of a new raptor habitat on Huntington Mesa was the best way to promote the "habitat values" of the eucalyptus grove.

The reasoning Commission employed is seductive but, in the end, unpersuasive. First, contrary to Koll's argument, we are not required to give great weight to the interpretation of Section 30240 set forth by Commission in its findings approving the LCP. The interpretation was not contemporaneous with enactment of Section 30240 or the result of any considered official interpretative effort and it did not carry any other of the indicia of reliability which normally requires deference to an administrative interpretation. . . .

Secondly, the language of section 30240 does not permit a process by which the habitat values of an ESHA can be isolated and then recreated in another location. Rather, a literal reading of the statute protects *the area* of an ESHA from uses which threaten the habitat values which exist in the ESHA. Importantly, while the obvious goal of section 30240 is to protect habitat values, the express terms of the statute do not provide that protection by treating those values as intangibles which can be moved from place to place to suit the needs of development. Rather, the terms of the statute protect habitat values by placing strict limits on the uses which may occur in an ESHA and by carefully controlling the manner uses in the area around the ESHA are developed. . . .

Thirdly, contrary to Commission's reasoning, Section 30240 does not permit its restrictions to be ignored based on the threatened or deteriorating condition of a particular ESHA. We do not doubt that in deciding whether a particular area is an ESHA within the meaning of Section 30107.5, Commission may consider, among other matters, its viability. . . . However, where, as is the case here, Commission has decided that an area is an ESHA, Section 30240 does not itself provide Commission power to alter its strict limitations. . . . There is simply no reference in Section 30240 which can be interpreted as diminishing the level of protection an ESHA receives based on its viability. Rather, under the statutory scheme, ESHA's, whether they are pristine and growing or fouled and threatened, receive uniform treatment and protection. . . .

In this regard we agree with the trust that Commission's interpretation of Section 30240 would pose a threat to ESHA's. As the trust points out, if, even though an ESHA meets the requirements of Section 30107.5, application of Section 30240's otherwise strict limitations also depends on the relative viability of an ESHA, developers will be encouraged to find threats and hazards to all ESHA's located in economically inconvenient locations. The pursuit of such hazards would in turn only promote the isolation and transfer of ESHA habitat values to more economically convenient locations. Such a system of isolation and transfer based on economic convenience would of course be completely contrary to the goal of the Coastal Act, which is to protect *all* coastal zone resources and provide heightened protection to ESHA's. . . .

In short, while compromise and balancing in light of existing conditions is appropriate and indeed encouraged under *other* applicable portions of the Coastal Act, the power to balance and compromise conflicting interests cannot be found in Section 30240.

C. Section 30007.5

Koll argues that even if transfer of habitat values was not permissible under Section 30240, such a transfer was permissible under the provisions of Section 30007.5 and our holding in *Sierra Club v. California Coastal Com.*, 19 Cal. App. 4th 547, 556-557 (1993) ("Batiquitos Lagoon"). Section 30007.5 states:

> The Legislature further finds and recognizes that conflicts may occur between one or more policies of the [Coastal Act]. The Legislature therefore declares that in carrying out the provisions of this division such conflicts be resolved in a manner which on balance is the most protective of significant coastal resources. In this context, the Legislature declares that broader policies which, for example, serve to concentrate development in close proximity to urban and employment centers may be more protective, overall, than specific wildlife habitat and other similar resource policies.

In *Batiquitos Lagoon* we were confronted with "the conflicting interests of fish and fowl." *Batiquitos Lagoon, supra*, 19 Cal. App. 4th at p. 550. Each interest was protected by a specific provision of the Coastal Act: The fish were protected by Section 30230 which directed that marine resources be preserved and, where feasible, restored; the fowl were protected by the requirement of Section 30233, subdivision (b), that the very substantial dredging needed to restore the fish habitat avoid significant disruption of the bird habitat. We found that under Section 30007.5, Commission could resolve these conflicting policy interests by favoring long-term restoration of the fish habitat over the short-term, but significant, disruption of the bird habitat. . . .

Here, in contrast to the situation in *Batiquitos Lagoon*, the record at this point will not support application of the balancing power provided by Section 30007.5. Unlike the record in that case, here our review of the proceedings before Commission does not disclose any policy or interest which directly conflicts with application of Section 30240 to the eucalyptus grove.

Although the Coastal Act itself recognizes the value and need for residential development . . . , nothing in the record or the briefs of the parties suggests there is such an acute need for development of residential housing in and around the eucalyptus grove that it cannot be accommodated elsewhere. Rather, the only articulated interests which the proposed transfer of the "habitat values" serves is Commission's expressed desire to preserve the raptor habitat values over the long term and Commission's subsidiary interest in replacing nonnative eucalyptus with native vegetation. However, as the trust points out, there is no evidence in the record that destruction of the grove is a prerequisite to creation of the proposed Huntington Mesa habitat. In the absence of evidence as to why preservation of the raptor habitat at its current location is unworkable, we cannot reasonably conclude that any genuine conflict between long-term and short-term goals exists.

In sum then the trial court erred in sustaining that portion of the LCP which permitted development of the eucalyptus grove.

V. Lowland Wetlands

The Coastal Act provides a separate protection regime for wetlands. Under Section 30121: " 'Wetland' means lands within the coastal zone which may be covered periodically or permanently with shallow water and include saltwater marshes, freshwater marshes, open or closed brackish water marshes, swamps, mudflats, and fens." Section 30233, subdivision (a), protects wetlands by providing:

> The diking, filling, or dredging of . . . wetlands . . . shall be permitted in accordance with other applicable provisions of this division, where there is no feasible less environmentally damaging alternative, and where feasible mitigation measures have been provided to minimize adverse environmental effects, and shall be limited to the following:
>
> (1) New or expanded port, energy, and coastal-dependent industrial facilities, including commercial fishing facilities.
>
> (2) Maintaining existing, or restoring previously dredged, depths in existing navigational channels, turning basins, vessel berthing and mooring areas, and boat launching ramps.
>
> (3) In wetland areas only, entrance channels for new or expanded boating facilities; and in a degraded wetland, identified by the Department of Fish and Game pursuant to subdivision (b) of Section 30411, for boating facilities if, in conjunction with such boating facilities, a substantial portion of the degraded wetland is restored and maintained as a biologically productive wetland. The size of the wetland area used for boating facilities, including berthing space, turning basins, necessary navigation channels, and any necessary support service facilities shall not exceed 25 percent of the degraded wetland.
>
> (4) In open coastal waters, other than wetlands, including streams, estuaries, and lakes, new or expanded boating facilities and the placement of structural pilings for public recreational piers that provide public access and recreational opportunities.
>
> (5) Incidental public service purposes, including, but not limited to, burying cables and pipes or inspection of pier and maintenance of existing and outfall lines.
>
> (6) Mineral extraction, including sand for restoring beaches, except in environmentally sensitive areas.
>
> (7) Restoration purposes.
>
> (8) Nature study, aquaculture, or similar resource-dependent activities.

Although Section 30233, subdivision (a), permits development of wetland areas when needed as a means of accommodating a whole host of varied uses, residential development is not a use permitted in wetlands. Nonetheless Commission found that residential development of portions of the Bolsa Chica lowlands was permissible, even though it would require destruction of otherwise protected wetlands, because the development would be used to finance needed restoration of other degraded portions of the wetlands.

Commission reasoned that, although Section 30233, subdivision (b), does not expressly permit residential development of wetlands, authority for such development can be found in the related provisions of Section 30411, subdivision (b). Section 30411, subdivision (b), states:

> The Department of Fish and Game, in consultation with the commission and the Department of Boating and Waterways, may study degraded wetlands and identify those which can most feasibly be restored in conjunction with development of a boating facility as provided in subdivision (a) of Section 30233. Any such study shall include consideration of all of the following:
>
> (1) Whether the wetland is so severely degraded and its natural processes so substantially impaired that it is not capable of recovering and maintaining a high level of biological productivity without major restoration activities.
>
> (2) Whether a substantial portion of the degraded wetland, but in no event less than 75 percent, can be restored and maintained as a highly productive wetland in conjunction with a boating facilities project.
>
> (3) Whether restoration of the wetland's natural values, including its biological productivity and wildlife habitat features, can most feasibly be achieved and maintained in conjunction with a boating facility or whether there are other feasible ways to achieve such values.

Commission found that Section 30411, subdivision (b)(3), permits wetland restoration to be achieved by way of any means which are more feasible than development of boating facilities. Because the county had previously found that development of a marina at Bolsa Chica was not feasible, Commission further reasoned that "residential development qualifies as a more feasible method of achieving restoration . . . since the construction and sale of the Lowland residential units would fund the restoration program and allow it to be implemented."

The trial court rejected Commission's reasoning. The trial court stated:

> Section 30411[, subdivision (b),] also does not authorize residential development. Rather, it authorizes the Department of Fish and Game to study and identify which degraded wetlands can feasibly be restored in conjunction with the development of a boating facility. In conducting its study, the Department of Fish and Game must consider whether the restoration of the wetlands' values can be achieved and maintained in conjunction with a boating facility "or whether there are other feasible ways to achieve such values." The most logical interpretation of the quoted language, construed in light of the Coastal Act as a whole, requires the Department of Fish and Game to consider whether alternatives less intrusive than developing a boating facility are feasible. The Commission's interpretation would open the door to any type of development in a wetland whenever a finding could be made that funds were otherwise unavailable to restore degraded wetlands.

We agree with the trial court. First, we note the trial court's interpretation comports with the plain meaning of Section 30411, subdivision (b), which expressly limits the power of the Department of Fish and Game to the *study* of boating projects authorized by Section 30233, subdivision (a). There is nothing on the face of Section 30411, subdivision (b), which *authorizes* the development of residential projects in wetland areas or for that matter authorizes any development which is not permitted by Section 30233.

Moreover, the alternative analysis required by Section 30411, subdivision (b)(3), cannot be read to inferentially permit the development of facilities which are not otherwise permitted by Section 30233, subdivision (a). By its terms Section 30233, subdivision (a), purports to set forth the purposes, in their entirety, for which coastal wetlands can be developed. If the Legislature intended that residential development of wetlands was to be permitted, logic would suggest that such a use be set forth unambiguously on the face of Section 30233, subdivision (a), rather than as an implied power under Section 30411, subdivision (b)(3).

Another difficulty with Commission's interpretation of Section 30411 is that the power to study the feasibility of boating facilities rests with the Department of Fish and Game, not Commission. We think it would be somewhat incongruous to provide the Department of Fish and Game with the power to determine, by way of a study, when residential development may occur in a coastal wetland. That power, it would seem, would be more appropriately directly exercised by Commission. Indeed Section 30411, subdivision (a), provides, in pertinent part: "The Department of Fish and Game and the Fish and Game Commission are the principal state agencies responsible for *the establishment and control of wildlife and fishery management programs.*" (Italics added.) There is nothing in the Coastal Act or any other provision of law, which suggests the Department of Fish and Game has any expertise with respect to the need for or impacts of residential development in the coastal zone.

We are also unpersuaded by the fact that Commission's interpretation has been set forth in interpretative guidelines it adopted pursuant to authority granted to Commission under section 30620, subdivision (b). . . . Although, because the guidelines were subject to a formal review and adoption process analogous to the Administrative Procedure Act . . . and for that reason are entitled to great weight . . . , here the guidelines themselves obliquely recognize that Commission's interpretation expands the uses and processes contemplated by Sections 30233 and 30411. The guidelines describe a process under which developers, agencies and Commission, rather than the Department of Fish and Game, consider alternatives to boating facilities. Importantly, however, the guidelines concede:

> The Coastal Act does not require the Department of Fish and Game to undertake studies which would set the process described in this section in motion. . . . This section is, however, included to describe, clarify, and encourage, public and private agencies to formulate innovative restoration projects to accomplish the legislative goals and objectives described earlier.

In light of the express limitation which appears on the face of Section 30233 and the express delegation of responsibility to the Department of Fish and Game under Section 30411, Commission's admittedly innovative interpretation cannot be sustained.

In short, the trial court's interpretation is supported by the plain language of the statute, the need to give significance to every word and phrase of the statute and the requirement that "statutes or statutory sections relating to the same subject must be harmonized, both internally and with each other, to the extent possible." *Dyna-Med, Inc. v. Fair Employment & Housing Com.*, 43 Cal. 3d 1379, 1387 (1987). Thus we find no error in the trial court's finding that residential development of the lowland wetlands was not permitted.

VI. Warner Avenue Pond

The parties agree Warner Avenue Pond, which is located on Bolsa Chica Mesa, is both an ESHA within the meaning of Section 30107.5 and a wetland within the meaning of Section 30121. As we have noted under Section 30240, the habitat values in an ESHA may not be significantly disrupted and no use of an ESHA may occur which is not dependent on resources which exist in the ESHA. As we have also noted under Section 30233, subdivision (a), wetlands are protected by specific limitations with respect to uses which may occur in a wetland and by the requirement that there be no feasible less environmentally damaging alternative to diking, filling or dredging of a wetland.

In approving the LCP, Commission found Warner Avenue Pond could be filled to permit the widening of Warner Avenue and that the filling could be mitigated by offsite restoration of other wetlands on a ratio of four to one. Commission found that widening of the road was an "[i]ncidental public service" within the meaning of Section 30233, subdivision (a)(5), and therefore a permissible use of the wetland. Commission's findings do not discuss the pond's status as an ESHA.

The trial court found Commission's findings were inadequate. The trial court reasoned that in this instance the protection provided by Section 30240 to ESHA's and the development permitted by Section 30233, subdivision (a)(5), were conflicting policies within the meaning of Section 30007.5 which empowered Commission to resolve such policy conflicts in a manner which is "most protective of coastal resources." § 30007.5, *Batiquitos Lagoon, supra*, 19 Cal. App. 4th at pp. 562-563. However the trial court further found that in order to exercise its power under Section 30007.5, Commission was required by Section 30200, subdivision (b), to make findings which identified and resolved the policy conflict. The trial court concluded Commission's findings did not meet these requirements.

We agree with the trial court that Commission's findings were inadequate with respect to Warner Avenue Pond. However, we reach that conclusion by way of a somewhat different analytical path. In particular, we do not believe the policies embodied in Sections 30240 and 30233 are in direct conflict necessitating resort to the power provided by Section 30007.5. Rather, in this instance we agree with Commission's guidelines that the ESHA protections provided by Section 30240 are more general provisions and the wetland protections provided by Section 30233 are more specific and controlling when a wetland area is also an ESHA. The guidelines state:

> The Commission generally considers wetlands, estuaries, streams, riparian habitats, lakes and portions of open coastal waters to be environmentally sensitive habitat areas because of the especially valuable role of these habitat areas in

maintaining the natural ecological functioning of many coastal habitat areas and because these areas are easily degraded by human developments. In acting on an application for development [of] one of these areas, the Commission considers all relevant information. The following specific policies apply to these areas: Sections 30230; 30231; 30233; and 30236. Section 30240, a more general policy, also applies, but the more specific language in the former sections is controlling where conflicts exist with general provisions of Section 30240 (*e.g.*, port facilities may be permitted in wetlands under Section 30233 even though they may not be resource dependent). This guideline addresses wet environmentally sensitive habitat areas only. The discussion in this section and in section VII is not intended to describe or include all environmentally sensitive habitat areas which may fall under Section 30240 of the Coastal Act.

The guidelines go on to provide:

Of all the environmentally sensitive habitat areas mentioned specifically in the Coastal Act, wetlands and estuaries are afforded the most stringent protection. In order to approve a project involving the diking, filling, or dredging of a wetland or estuary, the Commission must first find that the project is one of the specific, enumerated uses set forth in Section 30233 of the Act (these developments and activities are listed in section A. and B. below). The Commission must then find that the project meets all three requirements of Section 30233 of the Act. . . . In addition, permitted development in these areas must meet the requirements of other applicable provisions of the Coastal Act.

A. Developments and Activities Permitted in Wetlands and Estuaries

1. Port facilities.

***

5. Incidental public service purposes *which temporarily impact the resources of the area*, which include, but are not limited to, burying cables and pipes, inspection of piers, and maintenance of existing intake and outfall lines (*roads do not qualify*)." (Italics added, fns. omitted.)

Significantly, by way of a footnote Commission explains that "incidental services" may include, under certain circumstances, road expansion: "When no other alternative exists, and when consistent with the other provisions of this section, limited expansion of roadbeds and bridges necessary to maintain existing traffic capacity may be permitted."

We agree with these aspects of Commission's guidelines. We note Commission's determination that Section 30233, subdivision (a), was meant to supplant the provisions of Section 30240 is supported by Section 30233, subdivision (a)(6), which permits mineral development in wetlands "*except in environmentally sensitive areas.*" (Italics added.) Because none of the other permitted wetland uses set forth in Section 30233, subdivision (a), have such an express exception for ESHA's, the inference arises that had the drafters intended the uses permitted by Section 30233, subdivision (a), to be subject to ESHA protection, they would have made their intention explicit.

In addition to the inferential support found by reference to Section 30233, subdivision (a)(6), Commission's interpretation is also supported by a broader view of the statutory scheme. Wetland ESHA's are unique in that although like all ESHA's they need extraordinary protection, there are important activities such as fishing, boating, shipbuilding and other commercial and industrial activities which of necessity may occur on or near wetland areas. Importantly, the value of such activities is specifically recognized by the act and Commission is empowered to permit them to occur notwithstanding their adverse impact on coastal resources. . . .

The activities which may occur in wetland areas are, as Commission noted, set forth with great specificity and detailed limitation in Section 30233, subdivision (a). Such specificity and detail does not occur either in the general provisions accommodating industrial and commercial uses . . . or in the limitation on ESHA development set forth in Section 30240. Given that Section 30233, subdivision (a), provides specific and detailed limitation on the uses permitted in wetland areas, we believe it was reasonable for Commission to conclude that with respect to wetland ESHA's, Section 30233, subdivision (a), is a more specific guideline for what may occur in a wetland ESHA than either the accommodation of development expressed in Sections 30001.2 and 30708 or the more general limitation set forth in Section 30240.

Practicality, as well as the need to maintain a consistent level of wetland protection, suggests that development of wetland ESHA's is governed by the very specific and uniform limitations set forth in Section 30233, subdivision (a), rather than by way of the essentially ad hoc balancing process permitted by Section 30007.5. Given the myriad of wetland areas which exist in the coastal zone and the inherent conflict between the permissive policy expressed in Sections 30001.2 and 30708 and the restrictive policy of Section 30240, in the absence of the limitation set forth in section 30233, subdivision (a), case-by-case balancing of interests under Section 30007.5 would be repeatedly required.

Although we accept Commission's interpretation of Sections 30233 and 30240, we do not accept Commission's application of that interpretation to Warner Avenue Pond. In particular we note that under Commission's interpretation, incidental public services are limited to temporary disruptions and do not usually include permanent roadway expansions. Roadway expansions are permitted only when no other alternative exists and the expansion is necessary to maintain existing traffic capacity. As the trust points out, Commission found that the widening of Warner Avenue was needed to accommodate future traffic created by local and regional development in the area. Contrary to Koll's argument, this limited exception cannot be extended by finding that a roadway expansion is permissible when, although it increases the vehicle capacity of a roadway, it is designed to maintain an existing level of traffic service. Such an interpretation of the exception would entirely consume the limitation Commission has put on the incidental public services otherwise permitted by Section 30233, subdivision (a)(2).

In sum then, like the trial court we find that the LCP is defective insofar as it approves the filling of Warner Avenue Pond.

points for discussion

1. *The Coastal Commission's position.* Later in this chapter, we will learn more about the structure of California Coastal Commission membership. Without knowing anything about the makeup of the Commission at the time the LCP was approved, what else could explain its pro-development stance in this case?

2. *Rules of construction.* In *Bolsa Chica*, the court held — among other things — that the specific language of the ESHA provision trumped the more general balancing power that the legislature gave the Commission in Section 30007.5. This is consistent with the rule of statutory construction that "general policy does not trump specific legislative provisions." *R.T. Comm'ns v. FCC*, 201 F.3d 1264, 1269 (10th Cir. 2000). But isn't Section 30007.5 a "specific legislative provision[]"?

3. *What is "natural"?* As the court points out, "Section 30107.5 identifies an ESHA as 'any area in which plant or animal life or their habitats are either rare or especially valuable because of their special nature or role in an ecosystem and which could be easily disturbed or degraded by human activities and developments.'" Does the eucalyptus grove meet this test? Why do you suppose the ESHA designation for the grove was not challenged in the case? Is there a reason why the California legislature did not include the word "natural" in Section 30107.5? What is the purpose of "environmental zoning"? *See generally* Braxton C. Davis, *Regional Planning in the U.S. Coastal Zone: A Comparative Analysis of 15 Special Area Plans*, 47 OCEAN & COASTAL MGMT. 79 (2004).

4. Decision-Making Institutions

As described in the Healy and Zinn article we read at the beginning of this chapter, the implementation of state coastal programs requires making, on a near-daily basis, a large number and wide variety of small- and large-scale decisions. Depending on a variety of factors, permitting decisions might fit both of these descriptions. A permitting decision might be considered small-scale if, for example, it only affected one small area of public trust submerged lands: if an upland owner were applying for a permit to build a dock for personal use. Permitting decisions may also have large-scale impacts. Imagine that the proposed dock was to be quite large, or that it would impact a particularly sensitive or high-use area. Or, imagine that the state agency, in order to improve the efficiency of its administrative efforts, were considering issuing what is known as a "blanket permit," that is, a permit that would eliminate the need for individuals whose proposed projects met certain criteria to go through the normal permitting process. Such a blanket permit decision might result in significant impacts throughout the entire coastal zone.

It is critical to note that, regardless of the scale of the decision, the decision-making process will almost never be mechanical. In other words, making a decision will almost certainly require the application of values and judgment. Consider, for example, the decision to grant a "critical area permit" under applicable South Carolina law. The applicable regulations provide that, in assessing whether or not to grant the permit, the state coastal agency shall:

> . . . be guided by [among other things] the following ten considerations . . . :
>
> (1) The extent to which the activity requires a waterfront location or is economically enhanced by its proximity to the water;
>
> (2) The extent to which the activity would harmfully obstruct the natural flow of navigable water . . . ;
>
> (3) The extent to which the applicant's completed project would affect the production of fish, shrimp, oysters, crabs, or clams or any marine life or wildlife, or other natural resources in a particular area, including but not limited to water and oxygen supply;
>
> (4) The extent to which the activity could cause erosion, shoaling of channels or creation of stagnant water;
>
> (5) The extent to which the development could affect existing public access to tidal and submerged lands, navigable waters and beaches, or other recreational coastal resources;
>
> (6) The extent to which the development could affect the habitats for rare and endangered species of wildlife or irreplaceable historic and archeological sites of South Carolina's coastal zone;
>
> (7) The extent of the economic benefits as compared with the benefits from preservation of an area in its unaltered state;
>
> (8) The extent of any adverse environmental impact which cannot be avoided by reasonable safeguards;
>
> (9) The extent to which all feasible safeguards are taken to avoid adverse environmental impact resulting from a project;
>
> (10) The extent to which the proposed use could affect the value and enjoyment of adjacent owners.

S.C. Code Ann. Regs. 30.11(B).

By itself, the number of factors to be weighed ensures that each decision will be, almost purely, a matter of judgment. Each individual factor "asks" the agency to answer multiple difficult questions. Consider, for example, the last factor. Unless the project is proposed for an isolated area, it will almost certainly have an impact on neighbors, by reducing views, increasing vessel or car traffic, etc. At what point are these impacts so great that the agency should deny the permit application on this ground?

Section 1455(d) of the CZMA provides a few requirements for state decision-making procedures, for example, that there be a single body with final decision-making authority and that other state agencies, local governments, and the public have notice of, and the opportunity to comment on, decisions. Given these very limited guidelines, states—as noted at the outset of the chapter—have developed a wide range of decision-making structures. The two primary variables are

(1) whether the final decision-making authority is either an appointed coastal council (or commission) or a state agency, and (2) whether local governments are allowed to be final decision-makers within their respective jurisdictions or are simply offered the opportunity to comment on decisions made at the state level.

The materials immediately below provide two examples, from Rhode Island and California, of how a legislature might design a coastal council or commission. While you are reading through these statutory provisions, think about the kinds of values and judgment members of these bodies are likely to bring to permitting and other decisions.

a. Involvement of Elected Officials: Rhode Island

R.I. Water and Navigation Code

§ 46-23-2: Coastal Resources Management Council
Created – Appointment of Members diversity

(a) There is hereby created the coastal resources management council.

(1) The coastal resources management council shall consist of sixteen (16) members, two (2) of whom shall be members of the house of representatives, at least one of the members shall represent a coastal municipality, appointed by the speaker, two (2) of whom shall be members of the senate, each of whom shall represent a coastal municipality, appointed by the president of the senate, two (2) of whom shall be from the general public appointed by the speaker of the house for a term of two (2) years, two (2) of whom shall be from a coastal municipality appointed by the speaker of the house for a term of three (3) years.

(2) In addition, four (4) of the members shall be appointed or elected officials of local government appointed by the governor, one of whom shall be from a municipality of less than twenty-five thousand (25,000) population, appointed to serve until January 31, 1972, one of whom shall be from a coastal municipality of more than twenty-five thousand (25,000) population appointed to serve until January 31, 1973, and one of whom shall be from a coastal municipality of less than twenty-five thousand (25,000) population appointed to serve until January 31, 1974, and one of whom shall be from a coastal community of more than twenty-five thousand (25,000) population appointed to serve until January 31, 1975, the populations are to be determined by the latest federal census; all members shall serve until their successors are appointed and qualified; during the month of January, the governor shall appoint a member to succeed the member whose term will then next expire for a term of four (4) years commencing on the first day of February then next following and until his or her successor is named and qualified; each municipal appointment shall cease if the appointed or elected official shall no longer hold or change the office which he or she held upon appointment, and further, each appointee shall be eligible to succeed himself or herself.

(3) Three (3) members shall be appointed by the governor from the public, with the advice and consent of the senate, one of whom shall serve until January 1, 1972, one of whom shall serve until January 1, 1973 and one of whom shall serve until January 1, 1974; the members and their successors shall represent a coastal community.

(4) All members shall serve until their successors are appointed and qualified; during the month of January, the governor shall appoint, with the advice and consent of the senate, a member to succeed the members whose term will then next expire for a term of three (3) years commencing on the first day of February next following and until his or her successor is named and qualified. A member shall be eligible to succeed himself or herself. No more than two (2) persons on the council shall be from the same community.

(5) Appointments shall first be made by the governor, then by the president of the senate, and then by the speaker. The commissioner of the environmental protection branch or his or her designee within the department of environmental management shall serve ex officio. The ex-officio member shall not be counted as serving from any particular community.

b. Involvement of Elected Officials: California

California Coastal Act

Cal. Pub. Resources Code, § 30301: Membership [of California Coastal Commission]

The commission shall consist of the following 15 members:

(a) The Secretary of the Resources Agency.

(b) The Secretary of the Business and Transportation Agency.

(c) The Chairperson of the State Lands Commission.

(d) Six representatives of the public from the state at large. The Governor, the Senate Committee on Rules, and the Speaker of the Assembly shall each appoint two of these members.

(e) Six representatives selected from six coastal regions. The Governor shall select one member from the north coast region and one member from the south central coast region. The Speaker of the Assembly shall select one member from the central coast region and one member from the San Diego coast region. The Senate Committee on Rules shall select one member from the north central coast region and one member from the south coast region. For purposes of this division, these regions are defined as follows:

(1) The north coast region consists of the Counties of Del Norte, Humboldt, and Mendocino.

(2) The north central coast region consists of the Counties of Sonoma and Marin and the City and County of San Francisco.

(3) The central coast region consists of the Counties of San Mateo, Santa Cruz, and Monterey.

(4) The south central coast region consists of the Counties of San Luis Obispo, Santa Barbara, and Ventura.

(5) The south coast region consists of the Counties of Los Angeles and Orange.

(6) The San Diego coast region consists of the County of San Diego.

California Coastal Act

Cal. Pub. Resources Code, § 30310: Appointments; reflection of economic, social, and geographic diversity

In making their appointments pursuant to this division, the Governor, the Senate Rules Committee, and the Speaker of the Assembly shall make good faith efforts to assure that their appointments, as a whole, reflect, to the greatest extent feasible, the economic, social, and geographic diversity of the state.

c. Policy Issues in Design of Decision-Making Structures

The following excerpt weighs the strengths and weaknesses of various decision-making structures that states use in managing their natural resources. Although the author's focus is on wildlife, the article is useful in thinking about issues in coastal decision-making as well.

Martin Nie, State Wildlife Policy and Management: The Scope and Bias of Political Conflict

64 Pub. Admin. Rev. 221 (2004)

The controversy surrounding state wildlife policy making and management is likely to become more prevalent in the future. The move toward ecosystem management, conservation biology, and large-mammal restoration will place state wildlife agencies in a more visible public position. Many endangered species and fish and wildlife programs throughout the country are already illustrating the challenges facing wildlife managers. . . .

The goal of this article is to clarify issues and promote a more inclusive democratic debate among decision makers, stakeholders, and the public about the scope, structure, and process of state wildlife policy making and management. It uses the case of wildlife-centered political conflict to examine the important interactions among stakeholders, political institutions, decision-making processes, and approaches to conflict resolution. . . .

***

Theoretical Framework

State wildlife agencies have witnessed a number of controversial political conflicts in recent years. Debate over the hunting of black bears, predator-control measures, hunting and trapping practices, and other issues have placed state wildlife agencies in a difficult political and managerial position. There are a number of reasons for this increase in wildlife-related political conflict, including population growth, sprawl and development trends, urbanization, and changing American values and ethics toward wildlife. . . . This article argues there is another reason, and it is related to the scope of decision making.

Schattschneider describes the basic pattern of politics by emphasizing the scope, bias, and contagiousness of conflict:

> The first proposition is that the outcome of every conflict is determined by the extent to which the audience becomes involved in it. That is, the outcome of all conflict is determined by the scope of its contagion. The number of people involved in any conflict determines what happens; every change in the number of participants, every increase or reduction in the number of participants affects the result.

The nub of politics, according to Schattschneider, is the definition, spread, and control of conflict. "Therefore the contagiousness of conflict, the elasticity of its scope and the fluidity of the involvement of people are the X factors in politics." Furthermore, in political conflict, "every change in scope changes the equation."

Schattschneider provides a useful theoretical framework for this study and other cases in natural resource-wildlife political conflict. . . . While the causes of wildlife policy conflict are many, an important and often overlooked component is the scope of the wildlife policy-making process. Questions pertaining to the scope, structure, and process of wildlife policy must be asked: Who participates, who doesn't, and who cares? How do the institutions of wildlife policy making affect policy outcomes? Does the scope of decision making affect how wildlife policies are evaluated by key interest groups and stakeholders? And finally, what decision-making options and alternatives exist?

State Wildlife Management Paradigm

Ideas often become privileged when they are supported by key political state actors. These privileged ideas can become institutionalized, and, once in place, they are very difficult to dislodge. . . . Before federal and state regulation, fish and wildlife was exploited by commercial and other interests in a system that was characteristic of Hardin's "tragedy of the commons." State wildlife commissions were created in the 1930s by sport hunters and conservationists as a way to protect wildlife from widespread market hunting. To institutionalize such protection and to safeguard wildlife, sport hunters were placed on commissions that were to adopt and enforce wildlife laws. . . .

Forty-seven states have some sort of formal citizen board, commission, or advisory council which either makes, recommends, or advises fish, wildlife, park, and natural resource management decisions. There are several ways this is done, but most states have either some sort of fish and wildlife commission/board/council or a commission/board/council of natural resources. . . . Members are typically appointed by the governor and subject to state legislative approval. Most states also have requirements for commission membership, such as a general knowledge of wildlife issues, and political and geographic balance. . . . Some go even further. Prior to a ballot initiative in 1996, Massachusetts had a statutory requirement that five of seven fisheries and wildlife board members hold a sporting license. . . .

State wildlife agencies were also created as a way to protect wildlife and manage game species on a sustained-yield basis. A classic client-manager relationship has historically characterized state wildlife management. . . . Wildlife managers have seen their primary responsibility as providing resources (fish and game) to their clients — anglers, hunters, and trappers. Agency capture also characterizes this management paradigm. A large percentage of funding for state wildlife management comes directly from the sale of hunting and fishing licenses, or indirectly from federal assistance funds generated from excise taxes on fishing and hunting equipment. . . . Consequently, agencies often direct their resources toward the management of game species. Mangun (1986), for instance, shows that state expenditures for nongame species amount to roughly 3 percent of the amount spent on game species.

A Paradigm Challenged

The state wildlife management paradigm characterized by clientism and agency capture was challenged in the 1970s. Changes in the political landscape brought environmental values to the forefront, and these interests had new laws and procedural opportunities to have their voices heard. . . . An increasing number of Americans were expressing values toward wildlife that went beyond the utilitarian and consumptive. The more exclusive, traditional subgovernment that characterized state game management had been seriously challenged by nonconsumptive interests that did not hunt, fish, or trap. . . .

Of course, the state wildlife management paradigm is not the only paradigm to be challenged in recent years. The principles of ecosystem management, conservation biology, and the emergence of stakeholder-based collaborative conservation, among other things, have forced a number of public lands and natural resource agencies to reassess their mission and role. . . .

The most direct challenge to this paradigm has come from disgruntled interest groups that believe their values and perspectives do not receive serious consideration in the dominant wildlife commission decision-making framework. Many of these groups strike at what they see as the root of the problem: the wildlife policy-making process. The Humane Society of the United States, clearly prioritizing this issue, summarizes: "The 94 percent of Americans who do not hunt are effectively excluded from wildlife management decisions and policy development. Though non-hunters are increasingly knocking on the doors behind which these decisions are made, the states are fighting as never before to keep them closed" (Hagood 1997, 1). The Humane Society, among other critics, has a number of general complaints about the commission framework: (1) it runs counter to the idea of the public interest in wildlife because most Americans do not hunt, fish, or trap; (2) it favors consumptive values and interests; (3) commission members often have a conflict of interest because of their business interests in the consumptive use of wildlife, such as being guides, outfitters, and taxidermists; (4) nongame species and their habitat requirements are not prioritized; and (5) the public has the right to debate the values, ethics, and morality of hunting practices. . . .

***

Criticism has also come from those inside the wildlife professional subculture. . . . Like the professional history of American forestry, the wildlife profession has been characterized by a utilitarian, technorational philosophy, an emphasis on wise use, sustained yield, and scientific expert management. As such, it has been slow to respond to changing American values toward wildlife . . . .

***

Options, Alternatives, and Issues for Further Debate

This section explores some options and alternative approaches to state wildlife policy making and management. Four broad approaches are outlined in the hopes of promoting further discussion and debate: (1) the wildlife commission/no change alternative; (2) the authoritative expert alternative; (3) structural change alternatives; and (4) various stakeholder-based collaborative conservation alternatives. . . .

Wildlife Commission/No Change

This status quo/no change alternative continues to use the state wildlife commission process as a way to make wildlife policy and management decisions. . . . From a political standpoint, consumptive users of wildlife usually do quite well in this venue. Since wildlife commissions were first instituted, hunters, fishers and trappers have held a dominant position, and thus see no reason why they should be abandoned.

For many critics, it is not the commission as an institution, but the commissioners themselves that are the problem. In other words, critics of state wildlife commissions may simply be venue shopping, searching for a political venue that is more friendly to their interests. Critics may also be directing their criticism at the wrong source. After all, commission members are usually appointed by the governor and confirmed in some way by the state legislature. Therefore, these elected political representatives should receive their fair share of blame or credit for a commission's composition. Many . . . nonconsumptive stakeholders would have no problems with the board of game framework if their values were just better represented.

A dangerous precedent may be set if institutions are tinkered with simply because some groups and interests are currently not very well represented. Which institution is next? Because of issue intensity, salience, and superior organizing on the part of consumptive users, perhaps nonconsumptive users and critics of the process are simply being outmobilized. . . .

Authoritative Expert

This alternative emphasizes the importance of scientific knowledge and technical expertise in wildlife management. It would place biologists and wildlife managers in a preeminent decision-making position. In some states, wildlife commissions would be eliminated or play a more advisory role in making wildlife management decisions. Some biologists are uncomfortable with politicians, lay commission members, stakeholders, the public, or "barstool biologists" making wildlife management decisions, or they are uncomfortable with decisions that run counter to biological opinion. They would rather have a system in which wildlife biologists and professionals are given this responsibility.

This alternative will likely . . . be attacked as being undemocratic and elitist. Many critics will contend that the biologist-as-philosopher-king approach runs counter to the public interest in wildlife. Furthermore, many environmental and wildlife advocacy organizations believe biologists have their own consumptive values and agendas. These interests are suspicious of what they call "harvest biologists" — agency personnel who prioritize the manipulation and management of wildlife to favor consumptive users. . . . They also point out there is often no such thing as one definitive biological opinion.

***

Structural Change

Two possible changes are discussed here: changes in departmental organization, and changes in state wildlife commissions. The departmental (re)organization alternative would structurally reconfigure state wildlife departments, placing them within larger environmental or natural resource agencies while at the same time providing with them a broader base of funding. The restructuring alternative assumes that, if they were embedded in larger natural resource or environmental protection agencies, once-autonomous fish and wildlife departments would have a broader (nonconsumptive) constituency, more ecosystem-based management responsibilities, and a wider base of funding. It also assumes that nonconsumptive stakeholders would be less critical and have more trust in an agency serving more than their traditional (consumptive) clientele.

***

Securing a wider base of funding, one that is (more) independent of fish and game funds, is a critical part of this alternative. The bulk of fish and wildlife agency funding comes from consumptive users from the sale of licenses and excise taxes on sport hunting and fishing equipment. Providing alternative mechanisms for funding nongame wildlife conservation has long been a priority. . . . Many nonconsumptive stakeholders want the ability to pay for some of the costs associated with wildlife management and believe agency priorities will shift along with these new sources of funding.

Another possibility is to change the way that state wildlife commissions are appointed [so as to increase representation of non-consumptive users]. . . . Skeptics of [such proposals] . . . argue it is naive to believe wildlife policy making and management can somehow be depoliticized. Politics is inherent when managing a public resource, according to such a view . . . .

Stakeholder-Based Collaborative Conservation

An important change in environmental and natural resource policy making and management is the now-widespread use of stakeholder-based collaborative conservation. . . . A number of participatory models fall under this broad heading. Brick and Van de Wetering (quoted in Snow 2001, 2) summarize:

> Often called "collaborative conservation," this new movement represents the new face of American conservation as we enter the twenty-first century. Although no single strategy, process, or institutional arrangement characterizes this movement, collaborative conservation emphasizes the importance of local participation, sustainable natural and human communities, inclusion of disempowered voices, and voluntary consent and compliance rather than enforcement by legal and regulatory coercion. In short, collaborative conservation reaches across the great divide connecting preservation advocates and developers, commodity producers and conservation biologists, local residents, and natural interest groups to find working solutions to intractable problems that will surely languish unresolved for decades in the existing policy system.

***

There are a number of reasons and possible advantages to using stakeholder-based approaches in state wildlife management. . . . First, there is a public interest in wildlife. Stakeholding is one way the public's multiple values toward wildlife can be represented and expressed. Better information, open communication, increased understanding, and facilitated implementation is also possible. The process allows stakeholders to more effectively communicate their values, beliefs, and opinions to traditional adversaries and managing agencies. It also provides a venue in which nonscientific issues — often at the heart of wildlife-centered conflicts — can be communicated and worked through. It also provides a way to balance scientific understanding, technical expertise, and larger public democratic values. Citizen participation and local knowledge can be used constructively to identify and resolve complex problems. . . . It can also be used as a way to avoid adversarial analysis and the "dueling scientists" approach in which each stakeholder uses their science to forward their vision of the public interest. . . .

Decker and Chase (1997) and Chase, Schusler, and Decker (2000) provide a helpful typology to better understand wildlife management approaches to stakeholder input and involvement. At one end of the continuum is the authoritative expert approach discussed previously. Next is the passive-receptive approach, in which agencies are open to input when stakeholders take the initiative to be heard, such as by writing letters, making telephone calls, or testifying at commission meetings. The inquisitive approach occurs when agencies invite input from stakeholders through public meetings, listening sessions, and surveys. Here, human-dimensions inquiry can augment an agency's information base, informing them of stakeholder values, beliefs, and opinions. The transactional approach is a significant change in the way agencies interact with stakeholders. It allows stakeholders to become directly involved in making decisions, not just provide input. It also means that wildlife agencies must be willing to give up some managerial control. At the other end of the continuum is the next innovation in stakeholding, comanagement. This model differs from the transactional approach in that stakeholders are involved in multiple stages of the management process, not just in decision making.

points for discussion

1. *Agencies versus councils or commissions.* It is worth thinking about the strengths and weaknesses of each of these two models. Make a list of them, then decide which one you think will do a better job implementing state coastal law and policy. Next, think about what kinds of features you might build into your system in order to offset its weaknesses.

2. *The public trust doctrine.* Although it appears that no plaintiff has ever brought the case, it seems as though one might be able to make the argument that councils and commissions violate the public trust doctrine. Do you think a court might be convinced by this argument?

3. *The role of appointed citizens.* What role should citizens who are appointed to councils or commissions be given? For example, should the statute ask them to do their best to represent the general public or the public interest? Or, should the statute seek to fill a council with citizens who represent a wide range of interests, for example, developers or conservationists, then let them represent the views of their "constituents"? If the former, how would one ensure that members are "doing their best" to represent the public interest? Would an oath of office suffice? What is the "public interest"? Who decides? Does the latter model invite conflict-of-interest or bias problems? Is bias a problem?

4. *Constitutional issues with councils and commissions.* In *Marine Forests Society v. California Coastal Commission*, 113 P.3d 1062 (Cal. 2005), plaintiffs mounted a challenge to the appointment provisions of Section 30301. Specifically,

    > plaintiffs asserted that th[e] statutory structure—by authorizing members of the legislative branch to appoint a majority of the voting members of the Commission and enabling each appointing authority to remove its appointees at will—rendered the Coastal Commission a "legislative body" for purposes of the separation of powers clause of the California Constitution and that such a body was precluded from engaging in executive or judicial functions, such as granting, denying, or conditioning a development permit, or hearing and determining a cease and desist order.

    Id. at 1065-66. What do you suppose was the motivation behind this lawsuit? Take a look and see how the Supreme Court of California resolved it.

d. Decentralization and Local Permitting: Washington

In addition to the agency/council-commission variation, state programs also differ in the extent to which they delegate decision-making power to local governments. Some states, in accord with the CZMA, merely consult with local governments and offer them the opportunity to comment on decisions. Other states, like Washington and Connecticut, allow local governments, either counties or cities, to take the lead on coastal decision-making. This model—under which the state authorizes local governments to exercise state jurisdiction—is similar to the model used in zoning. One difference between delegation to local governments in the coastal zone management context and the zoning context is that, in the former, the state must—in order to ensure that the state program remains in compliance with *federal* CZMA rules—certify local government plans before they become effective.

Interestingly, the delegation of power from the state to the local level raises the same concerns that Senator Hollings and others sought to address in designing the federal/state relationship in the CZMA. On the one hand, land use is an area traditionally within the realm of local government; on the other hand, there are statewide interests in how coastal resources are allocated. The following case provides one example, in the context of a state program that delegates permitting authority to local governments, of the ways in which legislation and the courts attempt to resolve these tensions.

San Juan County v. Department of Natural Resources

626 P.2d 995 (Wash. Ct. App. 1981)

Judge Corbett delivered the opinion of the Court of Appeals of Washington, Division One.

This appeal is from a decision of the Superior Court, upholding an order of the Shorelines Hearings Board (SHB).

The Department of Natural Resources (DNR) applied to San Juan County for a substantial development permit, pursuant to the Shoreline Management Act of 1971. . . .* The proposed development consists of two mooring buoys, five campsites, a group fire ring, four picnic sites, two vault toilets, a well, signing, fencing, screening and improvement of the existing access road. The road is to be used for administrative purposes only and would be gated and locked to prevent public access from the uplands. The property fronts on Griffin Bay and is bounded on three sides by privately owned land. The purpose of the development is to provide a boating destination site.

DNR filed a declaration of nonsignificance pursuant to the State Environmental Policy Act of 1971 (SEPA). This negative threshold determination was based upon a checklist prescribed by the SEPA guidelines. The county planning department

---

* [The citizens of Washington adopted the Shoreline Management Act through a ballot initiative prior to enactment of the federal CZMA. — Eds.]

studied the application and recommended approval, subject to *10* conditions. The Board of County Commissioners then held a hearing at which no opposition was expressed by the county engineer or county sanitarian. However, neighbors and other citizens did voice objection. The county commissioners denied the application without stating any reasons. Thereafter DNR filed a request for review with SHB. The Department of Ecology, Firestone and Burden (owners of property near the site) appeared as intervenors.

SHB conducted a de novo proceeding, heard testimony, received exhibits, considered arguments, entered findings of fact and conclusions of law, and by order remanded the matter to San Juan County with instructions to issue a substantial development permit with *11* specific conditions (the added condition was to move the campsites from the forested area). The County and property owners appealed to the superior court. The decision of the Superior Court upholding the SHB order has been appealed to this court.

Appellants first argue

> **Washington's Shoreline Hearings Board**
>
> "The Shoreline Management Act . . . provides for the management of development along the state shorelines. Local government has the primary responsibility for initiating the planning required by the SMA and administering the regulatory program consistent with the policy and provisions of the Act. The Department of Ecology acts primarily in a supportive and review capacity with an emphasis on providing assistance to local government and on insuring compliance with the policy and provisions of the SMA.
>
> "Local government administers and issues shoreline substantial development, conditional use, and variance permits. Approvals by local government of shoreline conditional use and variance permits must be reviewed by Ecology, which then issues the final decision. Local government and Ecology can also issue fines under the SMA.
>
> "The Shorelines Hearings Board hears appeals from these permit decisions, and from those shoreline penalties jointly issued by local government and Ecology, or issued by Ecology alone. The Board is not affiliated with any other unit of government.
>
> "Three of the SHB members, who also serve as the Pollution Control Hearings Board, are full time employees, appointed by the governor and confirmed by the senate. At least one member is an attorney. The three other members, who serve part time are: the State Land Commissioner or designee, a representative from the Washington State Association of Counties, and one from the Association of Washington Cities." State of Washington, Environmental Hearings Office (2011).

that SHB review is limited to the record of proceedings before the county commissioners. We find that RCW 90.58.180(3) directs a broader scope of review by requiring a de novo adversary hearing pursuant to the administrative procedures act, RCW 34.04.

Appellants next argue that the standard of review to be applied by SHB is a determination of whether the county commissioners acted in an arbitrary and capricious or clearly erroneous manner. Therefore if there is a rational ground for the denial of the permit, the county commissioners must be upheld. They assert that this rational ground was impliedly found by SHB when it added the condition to the permit. Fire hazard was strenuously argued to SHB which made detailed findings that did not include fire hazard, thus negating the contended implication. Additionally, the standard of review is not that contended by appellants. The Board has adopted administrative rules as to the scope and standard of review.

WAC 461-08-174, Scope of review, provides:

> Hearings upon requests for review shall be quasijudicial in nature and shall be conducted *de novo* unless otherwise required by law.

WAC 461-08-175, Standard of review, provides in part:

> In deciding upon a request for review brought pursuant to RCW 90.58.180(1) and (2) the board shall make its decision considering the following standards:
>
> . . .
>
> (c) . . . whether the action of the local government unit is consistent with the applicable master program and the provisions of chapter 90.58 RCW.
>
> (2) Evidence that is material and relevant to determination of the matter consistent with the standards set out in subsection (1) above, subject to these rules, shall be admitted into the record whether or not such evidence had been submitted to the local government unit.

This statement by SHB of its interpretation of the statute is to be accorded great deference . . . . We find that WAC 461-08-174 and -175 correctly interpret the Shoreline Management Act of 1971.

Appellants object to SHB directing the commissioners to issue a permit, and complain that this is inconsistent with RCW 90.58.140(3), which provides:

> Local government shall establish a program, consistent with rules adopted by the department, for the administration and enforcement of the permit system provided in this section. *The administration of the system so established shall be performed exclusively by local government.* (Italics ours.)

The Shoreline Management Act of 1971 requires management of the shoreline by planning for and fostering all reasonable and appropriate uses. It calls for a planned, rational and concerted effort to be performed by federal, state and local governments to prevent the harm inherent in uncoordinated and piecemeal development . . . . It is apparent from the Act that SHB is the body charged with review of the local decisions to grant or deny a development permit and to determine whether such action is consistent with the master program adopted pursuant to the Shoreline Management Act of 1971. This responsibility necessarily requires that SHB have the power to approve or condition the approval of a permit. The administration of the permit system is not thereby removed from the local jurisdiction, but is made to be consistent with the Shoreline Management Act of 1971. Although there are several cases dealing with permits modified pursuant to the order of SHB, in none has the power of the Board been questioned. The power to review a permit decision does not remove from the local jurisdiction the general administration of a permit system.

* * *

Affirmed.

points for discussion

1. *The politics of coastal management.* As noted at the beginning of this chapter, land use control traditionally is a local government function. Although the authority to zone originates in the state legislature, states uniformly delegate this power to local governments. Thus, the Washington approach to coastal zone management — similar to approaches used in some other states — is consistent with, and parallels, the institutional structure of zoning, with one major difference. As illustrated in *San Juan County*, a state-level body, the Shoreline Hearings Board, has the power to override decisions made by local government. How is this power consistent with the idea of local control of land use? The California Coastal Act provides an interesting contrast. Like Washington's Shoreline Management Act, the California statute allows local governments with approved local coastal programs to issue permits. Unlike the Shoreline Hearings Board, however, the California Coastal Commission generally has no power to hear appeals from permit denials; rather, it can only hear objections to development permits issued by local governments. How does California's "double veto" structure affect the distribution of power between local and state government? *See* Robert Ellickson, *A Ticket to Thermidor: A Commentary on the Proposed California Coastal Plan*, 49 S. Cal. L. Rev. 715 (1976). For a discussion of how different structures affect the distribution of power, see Philip R. Berke & Steven P. French, *The Influence of State Planning Mandates on Local Plan Quality*, 13 J. Plan. Educ. & Res. 237 (1994).

2. *Externalities of local decisions.* Decisions made by local governments can impose costs on other nearby communities and on the entire state. In the zoning context, there are concerns that, when local governments zone in a way that prevents low-income housing, they are exporting the net costs of providing services to low-income families, that is, they are not carrying their fair share of state obligations. *See S. Burlington Cty. NAACP v. Twp. of Mount Laurel*, 336 A.2d 713 (N.J. 1975). How are the potential externalities of local, coastal land use decisions similar to, or different from, the potential externalities of run-of-the-mill zoning decisions?

3. *Initiative processes.* Both the Shoreline Management Act and the California Coastal Act were originally enacted through ballot measures. (Only some state constitutions permit laws to be created in this manner.) Interestingly, the Washington and California coastal statutes, compared to other states'

laws, incorporate more formal structures for delegating decision-making authority to local governments. Is there a connection between these structures and the origin of state laws in ballot measures?

4. *Coastal zoning.* So long as they operate within the authority given to them by state zoning enabling acts, cities and counties are free to include coastal management measures in their zoning ordinances. The use of this power is especially important in states without formal local delegation, such as South Carolina. The Town of Hilton Head, South Carolina has incorporated a variety of coastal protection measures into its zoning ordinance:

Erosion and Sedimentation Control

Erosion and sedimentation controls are required on all sites adjacent to waterbodies or drainage ways.

- Existing Uncovered Areas: Any site which has been substantially denuded of vegetation, and which is not in an active phase of development for more than 30 days, shall have functioning erosion and sediment control measures in place and shall be seeded or planted with an acceptable ground cover material. This provision applies to all ongoing development activities as of the effective date of this Title.
- Ground Cover Requirement: To help retain sediment generated by land-disturbing development activities within the boundaries of the development tract, all developers shall plant or otherwise provide a permanent dressed ground cover sufficient to restrain erosion after completion of construction or development within 30 calendar days following completion.
- Construction Buffer Zones: No land-disturbing activity except recreational uses which permit retention of grasses or other vegetation shall be permitted in proximity to a regulated wetland unless a vegetated strip is provided along the margin of the regulated wetlands of sufficient width as final minimum setbacks specified in Chapter 6, Article II, or unless other methods or structures of sediment control approved by the Town Engineer are used in place of a buffer zone to be created after construction which will prevent sediment from leaving the site and entering the watercourse.

Site Lighting Design Requirements

All lighting fixtures designed or placed so as to illuminate any portion of a site must meet the following requirements:

A. Fixture (luminaire). The light source shall be completely concealed within an opaque housing and shall not be visible from any street right of way.

B. Light Source (lamp). Only incandescent, florescent, metal halide, or color corrected high-pressure sodium may be used. The same type must be used for the same or similar types of lighting on any one site or Planned Unit Development.

C. Mounting. Fixtures must be mounted in such a manner that its cone of light does not cross any property line of the site.

D. Illumination Levels. All site lighting shall be designed so that the level of illumination as measured in foot candles (fc) at any one point meets the standards in the code.

Natural Resource Protection

Hilton Head has enacted zoning ordinances for the conservation or restoration of the natural resources found within the town. The ordinances are divided into sections specified for wetlands, beaches, and trees. (Sect. 16-6)

Wetlands (Sect. 16-6-201)

Buffers shall serve as an ecological transition zone from non-wetlands to freshwater or tidal wetlands which is an integral portion of the wetlands ecosystem, providing temporary refuge for wetlands fauna during high water episodes, critical habitat for animals dependent upon but not resident in wetlands, and slight variations of wetland boundaries over time due to hydrologic or climatologic effects. Buffers also serve as a sediment and storm water control zone to reduce the impacts of development upon wetlands and wetlands species.

To protect the wetlands, the ordinances provide for a system of wetland buffers which are required adjacent to all wetlands. Specifically, all structures, impervious and pervious paved surfaces, and lagoons and stormwater retention/detention areas shall be set back from wetlands in accordance with the following table.

Use	Tidal Wetland	Freshwater Wetland
Multifamily Residential/ Nonresidential Impervious Paved Surfaces	50-feet average 25-feet minimum	40-feet average 20-feet minimum
Multifamily Residential/ Nonresidential Pervious Paved Surfaces	35-feet average 15-feet minimum	35-feet average 10-feet minimum
Multifamily Residential/ Nonresidential Structures	40-feet average 20-feet minimum	35-feet average 20-feet minimum
Single Family Dwelling including accessory structures and impervious or pervious paved surfaces.	20 feet	—
Lagoons and Stormwater Retention/Detention Areas	—	20-feet minimum

Further, a number of activities are prohibited in the buffer area, such as grassed lawns and removal of dirt or trees.

C. CONSISTENCY

As noted, one of the primary inducements Congress gave states to join in the CZMA effort was what is known as "consistency review." This unique power gives participating states significant authority to control the activities of federal agencies within or affecting state coastal zones.

Coastal Zone Management Act

16 U.S.C. § 1456

(a) Federal agencies. In carrying out his functions and responsibilities under this chapter, the Secretary shall consult with, cooperate with, and, to the maximum extent practicable, coordinate his activities with other interested Federal agencies.

(b) Adequate consideration of views of Federal agencies. The Secretary shall not approve the management program submitted by a state pursuant to section 1455 of this title unless the views of Federal agencies principally affected by such program have been adequately considered.

(c) Consistency of Federal activities with State management programs; Presidential exemption; certification.

(1)(A) Each Federal agency activity within or outside the coastal zone that affects any land or water use or natural resource of the coastal zone shall be carried out in a manner which is consistent to the maximum extent practicable with the enforceable policies of approved State management programs. A Federal agency activity shall be subject to this paragraph unless it is subject to paragraph (2) or (3).

(B) After any final judgment, decree, or order of any Federal court that is appealable under section 1291 or 1292 of Title 28, or under any other applicable provision of Federal law, that a specific Federal agency activity is not in compliance with subparagraph (A), and certification by the Secretary that mediation under subsection (h) of this section is not likely to result in such compliance, the President may, upon written request from the Secretary, exempt from compliance those elements of the Federal agency activity that are found by the Federal court to be inconsistent with an approved State program, if the President determines that the activity is in the paramount interest of the United States . . . .

(C) Each Federal agency carrying out an activity subject to paragraph (1) shall provide a consistency determination to the relevant State agency designated under section 1455(d)(6) of this title at the earliest practicable time, but in no case later than 90 days before final approval of the Federal activity unless both the Federal agency and the State agency agree to a different schedule.

(2) Any Federal agency which shall undertake any development project in the coastal zone of a state shall insure that the project is, to the

maximum extent practicable, consistent with the enforceable policies of approved state management programs.

(3)(A) After final approval by the Secretary of a state's management program, any applicant for a required Federal license or permit to conduct an activity, in or outside of the coastal zone, affecting any land or water use or natural resource of the coastal zone of that state shall provide in the application to the licensing or permitting agency a certification that the proposed activity complies with the enforceable policies of the state's approved program and that such activity will be conducted in a manner consistent with the program. At the same time, the applicant shall furnish to the state or its designated agency a copy of the certification, with all necessary information and data. Each coastal state shall establish procedures for public notice in the case of all such certifications and, to the extent it deems appropriate, procedures for public hearings in connection therewith. At the earliest practicable time, the state or its designated agency shall notify the Federal agency concerned that the state concurs with or objects to the applicant's certification. If the state or its designated agency fails to furnish the required notification within six months after receipt of its copy of the applicant's certification, the state's concurrence with the certification shall be conclusively presumed. No license or permit shall be granted by the Federal agency until the state or its designated agency has concurred with the applicant's certification or until, by the state's failure to act, the concurrence is conclusively presumed, unless the Secretary, on his own initiative or upon appeal by the applicant, finds, after providing a reasonable opportunity for detailed comments from the Federal agency involved and from the state, that the activity is consistent with the objectives of this chapter or is otherwise necessary in the interest of national security.

(B) After the management program of any coastal state has been approved by the Secretary under section 1455 of this title, any person who submits to the Secretary of the Interior any plan for the exploration or development of, or production from, any area which has been leased under the Outer Continental Shelf Lands Act (43 U.S.C. 1331 et seq.) and regulations under such Act shall, with respect to any exploration, development, or production described in such plan and affecting any land or water use or natural resource of the coastal zone of such state, attach to such plan a certification that each activity which is described in detail in such plan complies with the enforceable policies of such state's approved management program and will be carried out in a manner consistent with such program. No Federal official or agency shall grant such person any license or permit for any activity described in detail in such plan until such state or its designated agency receives a copy of such certification and plan, together with any other necessary data and information, and until —

(i) such state or its designated agency, in accordance with the procedures required to be established by such state pursuant to subparagraph (A), concurs with such person's certification and notifies the Secretary and the Secretary of the Interior of such concurrence;

(ii) concurrence by such state with such certification is conclusively presumed as provided for in subparagraph (A), except if such state fails to concur with or object to such certification within three months after receipt of its copy of such certification and supporting information, such state shall provide the Secretary, the appropriate federal agency, and such person with a written statement describing the status of review and the basis for further delay in issuing a final decision, and if such statement is not so provided, concurrence by such state with such certification shall be conclusively presumed; or

(iii) the Secretary finds, pursuant to subparagraph (A), that each activity which is described in detail in such plan is consistent with the objectives of this chapter or is otherwise necessary in the interest of national security.

If a state concurs or is conclusively presumed to concur, or if the Secretary makes such a finding, the provisions of subparagraph (A) are not applicable with respect to such person, such state, and any Federal license or permit which is required to conduct any activity affecting land uses or water uses in the coastal zone of such state which is described in detail in the plan to which such concurrence or finding applies. If such state objects to such certification and if the Secretary fails to make a finding under clause (iii) with respect to such certification, or if such person fails substantially to comply with such plan as submitted, such person shall submit an amendment to such plan, or a new plan, to the Secretary of the Interior. With respect to any amendment or new plan submitted to the Secretary of the Interior pursuant to the preceding sentence, the applicable time period for purposes of concurrence by conclusive presumption under subparagraph (A) is 3 months.

***

See also 15 CFR Part 930.

The following excerpt provides an overview of the consistency provisions and process, highlights important changes to Section 1456 over time, and assesses the use and effect of consistency review. Although the paper is now more than 20 years old, the discussion and analysis is still useful in thinking about the function and efficacy of the CZMA.

Kem Lowry, Casey Jarman & Susan Machida, Federal-State Coordination in Coastal Management: An Assessment of the Federal Consistency Provision of the Coastal Zone Management Act

19 Ocean & Coastal Mgmt. 97 (1993)

The CZMA was based on several premises. First, state governments should play a major role in coastal resource management because they have the "resources, administrative machinery, enforcement powers, and constitutional authority on which to build a sound management program." This was an implicit critique of the prevailing pattern of coastal land use management by local governments. Second, each state should develop its own coastal management program around its own needs and objectives, subject to broad federal guidelines. Coastal zone management was not to be a federal regulatory program administered by the states as is the case with the Clean Air and Clean Water Acts.

Third, state participation in the program is voluntary. However, Congress constructed a set of incentives to encourage participation by the states. The primary incentive is financial: the offer of substantial matching grants for states to participate in a 3-year process of plan preparation, and additional implementation grants for state programs that receive formal approval from the Secretary of Commerce.

A fourth premise, and the focus of this article, is that state coastal management programs offer the opportunity to coordinate not only state and local planning, management and development activities in the coastal zone, but federal activities as well. Congress recognized that federal agencies exert an enormous influence over land and water uses in coastal areas, including the construction of facilities in coastal areas and the regulation of activities such as offshore mineral development, ocean incineration, and dredging and filling projects. In addition, they issue licenses for coastal energy facilities and own vast tracts of land. Hence the second important incentive to states — the federal consistency provision — was created. The consistency provision proved to be one of the most contentious of the CZMA. Prior to its recent amendment, federal activities undertaken in or directly affecting a state's coastal zone were to be consistent to the maximum extent practicable with the state's coastal program. In addition to those activities undertaken by the federal government itself, activities conducted by private or other governmental entities that require federal licenses or permits fall under the consistency rubric. As could be expected, coastal states sought to expand and federal agencies sought to restrict the activities requiring consistency determinations, often in the context of whether the activity in question was located within or outside the coastal zone boundary. In one instance, the controversy reached the U.S. Supreme Court, which affirmed the federal government's narrow interpretation. Disappointed states appealed to Congress, which, in 1990, overturned the Supreme Court decision by statutorily expanding the geographic scope of consistency coverage. [*See* 16 U.S.C. § 1456(c)(1)(A) — EDS.]

In 1988 we surveyed state coastal officials for data on consistency submissions reviewed during the 1987 calendar year. Surveys were sent to officials of the 30 federally approved coastal zone management programs in the US and affiliated territories. The surveys asked for basic descriptive information about consistency reviews conducted in each of their states. Officials were also asked to evaluate their relationships with federal agencies exercising jurisdiction and activities in the state's coastal zone . . . . Before turning to the results of this analysis, we first review the evolution of federal consistency followed by an assessment of the implementation of the process prior to the 1990 amendments.

Mechanics of Federal Consistency

An analysis of how this unique intergovernmental coordination technique works must necessarily begin with some discussion of the state plans against which determinations of federal consistency are made. Although state coastal resource management programs vary widely in how they address the general requirements of the CZMA, some common elements in state programs can be identified: each state has defined a coastal zone, the landward side of which may be as narrow as a few yards (e.g. Texas) or as broad as a coastal county (e.g. Oregon); each has defined the coastal resource issues it regards as important; each has developed a set of policies establishing how resources are to be used; and each has chosen a set of management techniques (e.g. zoning and permit systems) for achieving policy objectives. The pre-1990 CZMA Amendments empowered states to review the following five general activities for consistency:

(1) Federally conducted or supported activities directly affecting the coastal zone (e.g. fishery management plans and the designation of ocean dumping sites).
(2) Federal developments in the coastal zone (e.g. harbor construction).
(3) The issuance of federal licenses or permits for activities affecting land or water uses in the coastal zone (e.g. Army Corps of Engineers dredge and fill permits).
(4) Plans of exploration and development and production plans submitted for any area leased under the Outer Continental Shelf Lands Act affecting any land or water uses in the coastal zone.
(5) Applications for federal assistance by state and local governments to support activities affecting the coastal zone (e.g. Housing and Urban Development block grants).

The process and criteria for determining whether an activity is consistent with a state coastal resources management program vary somewhat for each type of federal activity listed above. For federal activities and developments, the federal agency proposing the activity makes the initial judgment about whether the proposed activity is consistent with the state coastal program. Until the passage of the 1990 Amendments, only activities "in" or "directly affecting" the state's designated coastal zone were subject to a consistency review. Once a consistency determination is made, it must be forwarded to the state agency responsible for review at least 90 days prior to federal agency action. The state has 45 days to respond. Disputes about whether a proposed activity is consistent with the state program that cannot be resolved by the relevant state and federal agencies may be forwarded to the Secretary of Commerce for mediation. If Secretarial mediation fails, recourse to the courts may be sought.

With regard to federal licenses or permits and outer continental shelf exploration and development plans, the applicant makes the initial consistency determination. The applicant must incorporate a statement in the application that the license or activity will be conducted "in a manner consistent with the program." 15 C.F.R. 930.57. The state review agency has 6 months to concur or object. The permit or license may not be issued if the state objects. If a dispute develops that cannot be resolved informally, applicants may appeal to the Secretary of Commerce. The Secretary has the authority to issue the permit on the basis of a finding that the activity is "consistent with the objectives of the CZMA" or "otherwise necessary in the interest of national security." 15 C.F.R. 930.64; 121; 122.

In the case of applications for federal assistance to support state or local planning efforts, the initial consistency determinations are made by the agency applicants. Federal agencies are prohibited from approving assistance for projects that are inconsistent with a state's coastal program. If objections are filed, the same appeal process and review criteria apply as in the case of applications for federal permits and licenses.

Evolution of Federal Consistency

To date, a body of legal scholarship has developed regarding federal consistency, with the primary emphasis on court-imposed limits on state demands for consistency. Yet the US Supreme Court has addressed the scope of consistency review only once, in its controversial 1984 opinion *Secretary of Interior v. California*, 464 U.S. 312 (1984). In addition, relatively few lower federal court decisions interpreting the consistency provision exist. Clearly then, most consistency determinations are being handled successfully at the administrative level.

The predominant issue in case law has centered on what types of federally conducted and federally permitted activities are subject to consistency. Prior to being amended in 1990, the CZMA required consistency determinations for federal activities directly affecting the coastal zone. 16 U.S.C. 1456(c). Prior to the *California* decision mentioned above, federal courts found the federal relocation of refugees, construction of docking facilities, federal highway projects, federal sewer grants and leasing of federal land to directly affect states' coastal zones. Other activities, such as transferring title of federal land to private interests, were found not to require consistency.

In its *California* decision, the Court was called upon to decide whether the sale of outer continental shelf (OCS) oil and gas leases located outside of California's legally defined coastal zone was an activity "directly affecting the coastal zone" under the CZMA. The lease sale was held pursuant to the DOI's authority under the Outer Continental Shelf Lands Act (OCSLA). The State of California and various conservation organizations attempted to stop the sale until a consistency determination was made. The DOI, asserting that lease sales were not covered by the consistency provision, refused to comply with their request. In the end, the DOI's position prevailed when a sharply divided Court (5-4 decision) held the consistency provision inapplicable to OCS lease sales.

Proponents of a narrow reading of the consistency doctrine heralded this opinion as standing for the proposition that activities occurring outside of the coastal zone are not subject to the consistency process. However, NOAA's own regulations and a 1989 NOAA General Counsel opinion belied such assertions. First, the Court refused to extend its holding beyond OCS lease sales. ". . . [T]he literal language of Section 307(c)(1), read without reference to its history, is sufficiently imprecise to leave open the possibility that some types of federal activities conducted on the OCS could fall within Section 307(c)(1)'s ambit." 464 U.S. at 324.

Second, NOAA's consistency rules, amended after the *California* decision, specifically excluded oil and gas leasing on the OCS from review. However, for other federal activities located outside the coastal zone, a case-by-case determination was mandated. "Federal activities outside the coastal zone . . . are subject to federal agency review to determine whether they directly affect the coastal zone." 15 C.F.R. 930.33. Similarly, federally issued licenses or permits for activities occurring outside the coastal zone potentially triggered the consistency process. "In the event the state agency chooses to review federal licenses and permits for activities outside of the coastal zone but likely to affect the coastal zone, it must generally describe the geographic location of such activities." 15 C.F.R. 930.53(b)).

***

A second, yet related, standard applied to federally permitted activities and OCS exploration and development affecting land and water uses in the coastal zone. Under this standard, courts have found that railroad abandonment permits issued by the Interstate Commerce Commission, right-of-way permits under the Mineral Lands Leasing Act and Clean Water Act Section 404 permits trigger consistency.

Another issue involved whether the CZMA's exclusion of federal lands from the definition of the coastal zone exempted federal activities occurring on those lands from the consistency provision. The one court that dealt with this issue held that "exclusion of the 'federal lands' (as indicated) from the term 'coastal zone' applies only to the land itself and not the effects on the surrounding non-federal lands." *Puerto Rico v. Muskee*, 507 F. Supp. 1035 (D.P.R. 1981). Thus, activities on federal lands directly affecting the coastal zone required a consistency statement.

In 1990, Congress severely weakened the effect of the *California* decision by requiring consistency determinations for all federal activities regardless of whether they fall within or outside the coastal zone. Congress also replaced the former "directly affecting the coastal zone" language with a broader standard: "affects land or water use or natural resource of the coastal zone." 16 U.S.C. Sec. 1456(c), as amended by Pub. L. No. 101-508. A third component of the amendment ensures consistency "to the maximum extent practicable with the enforceable policies of approved state management programs."

***

Data on Federal Consistency

The 1983 Draft Federal Consistency Study raised several questions about the implementation of the federal consistency process:

(1) What types of federal activities have been reviewed by the states?
(2) How many federal activities do the states review for consistency in a year?
(3) To what percentage of federal activities do states object?
(4) To what specific activities did the states object? Do certain types of activities receive more objections from the state than others?
(5) Which federal agencies are most actively involved in the federal consistency process? Which states are most active in reviewing federal projects for consistency?
(6) In cases in which a state objects to a project as being inconsistent, how often are differences resolved through further consultation and coordination?

For purposes of comparison, many of these same questions were addressed in the 1988 survey. In addition to these descriptive data, the 1988 survey raised several questions about the quality of the relationships between state coastal management agencies and specific federal agencies and the perceived effectiveness of the federal consistency review procedures. State officials were asked:

(1) How would you characterize the relationship between the state program and specific federal agencies? How has it changed in the last 5 years?
(2) How effective is consistency review for insuring that state program development and resource management objectives have been considered?
(3) What are the strengths and weaknesses of the federal consistency process?

Types of Federal Activities Reviewed by the States

***

Direct federal activities such as federal construction projects and harbor widening projects constitute only a small portion of all federal consistency reviews: 4% in 1983; 13% in 1987. Most of the direct federal activities (42% in 1983 and 33% in 1987) were harbor widening or deepening projects or maintenance and dredging of harbors.

Federal licenses and permits account for the bulk of federal consistency reviews, 68% in 1983 and 73% in the 1987 sample. Army Corps of Engineers dredge and fill permits accounted for 93% of the federal permits and licenses and 63% of all federal consistency reviews in 1983 (86% and 63%, respectively, in the 1987 data). The Army Corps of Engineers (COE) has broad regulatory authority in the nation's coastal waters. Until 1968 the COE's primary regulatory emphasis was the protection of navigation in coastal waters under the Rivers and Harbors Act of 1899.

More recent mandates under Section 404 of the Clean Water Act and Section 103 of the Marine Protection, Research and Sanctuaries Act give the COE important environmental management responsibilities. Section 404 gives the Corps responsibility for issuing permits for the discharge of dredged or fill material "into the waters of the United States at specified disposal sites." 33 C.F.R. 323.2. Under COE regulations "waters of the United States" includes wetlands. This gives the COE important regulatory authority in protecting wetlands. COE regulations require that agency officials consult with the US Fish and Wildlife Service, the National Marine Fisheries Service, state fish and wildlife agencies, and the Environmental Protection Agency. The COE also permits certain minor activities under "nationwide permits" or "regional permits." Such activities included placement of aids to navigation, fish and wildlife harvesting devices, such as crab traps and eel pots, certain structures for oil, gas and mineral exploration, production and transport, and some bank stabilization activities. The types of activities allowed under general or regional 404 permits has been the subject of much debate between individual states and the COE.

The third category of federal activities reviewed under the consistency provisions of the CZMA are offshore oil exploration, development, and production activities authorized by the Outer Continental Shelf Lands Act (OCSLA). As mentioned earlier, oil and gas offshore lease sales by the Interior Department were specifically exempted from state federal consistency review after a 1984 U.S. Supreme Court decision in *Secretary of the Interior v. California*. In 1983, 432 federal consistency reviews were conducted, accounting for 6% of the total volume of federal consistency reviews. In the states responding to the 1988 survey, 73 federal consistency reviews were conducted, again representing 6% of the total volume of consistency reviews.

The fourth category of federal activities reviewed for consistency was federal assistance in the form of loans, subsidies, grants, and insurance to state and county agencies. Federal assistance accounted for 22% of the consistency reviews in 1983 and 7% in 1987. Nearly 84% of the federal aid programs reviewed for consistency in the 1983 study were Housing and Urban Development programs, but only 33% of the programs reviewed in the 1987 study were HUD programs.

Five federal agencies — Army Corps of Engineers, Housing and Urban Development, Minerals Management Service, Federal Housing Administration and the Environmental Protection Agency — accounted for 97% of the federal activities subject to consistency reviews in the 1983 study and 85% in the 1988 survey. Five states — Alaska, Washington, South Carolina, Michigan and Louisiana — accounted for the largest volume of consistency reviews in 1983. In 1987, the five states accounting for the largest volume of reviews were Mississippi, Alabama, Massachusetts, Wisconsin and Washington (note: Louisiana did not respond to the 1988 survey).

State Objections to Federal Activities

States concurred with about 99% of all federal consistency applications in 1983 and 97% in 1987. Data from both the 1983 Draft Federal Consistency Study and the 1988 survey indicate that the greatest number of objections involved Army Corps of Engineers' dredge and fill permits (Section 10/404), with 49 state objections in

1983 and 26 in 1987. However, these objections represent only 1% of the dredge and fill permits reviewed in 1983 and 2% of those reported in the 1988 survey.

States also sought to exercise control over dredge and fill activities by imposing conditions on COE Section 10/404 permits in 17% of the consistency applications reviewed in 1983 and 30% of those reviewed in 1987. This suggests that some level of state concurrence with COE findings occurred in about 99% of the reviews. On the other hand, a rather high degree of disagreement by some states about the conditions under which dredge and fill activities should be allowed is evidenced by the fact that almost one-third of the 1987 consistency reviews had conditions attached. In 1983, state objections and conditional concurrences occurred most frequently in Louisiana (800 conditional concurrences), Alaska, Alabama, Washington, and Mississippi. In 1987, Washington, Oregon, Mississippi, Alabama, Massachusetts, and Wisconsin reported the largest number of objections or conditional concurrences — note again, Louisiana is not included in the 1988 survey results.

The frequency of objections is of course just one measure of the importance of federal-state conflicts over coastal management. The intensity of the conflict may be a more important indicator of the importance of these conflicts. In the 1988 survey, state officials were asked to identify the "types of federal projects or activities accounting for the most intense policy conflicts with state coastal management objections." Eleven of the 28 projects or activities (39%) identified as accounting for the most intense conflicts were dredge and fill activities. These activities were spread over nine states.

What is perhaps most noteworthy is that except for federal dredge and fill projects, no discernible pattern emerged in the data regarding intensity of conflict. However, the types of conflict that occur for activities under Category I Direct Federal Activities differs from those under Category II Federally Permitted/Licensed Activities. In general, it appears that "policy conflicts" arise between federal agencies and state coastal programs when activities fall under Category I. For example, activities conducted on federally excluded lands have led to conflicting interpretations of the phrase "directly affecting" and the applicability of federal consistency review procedures. By contrast, conflicts which involve federally permitted or licensed activities seem to be location-specific, having to do with particular circumstances or conditions, rather than general policy disputes. In addition, these disagreements are more often between the state program office and the applicants, rather than the federal agencies.

Several other activities accounted for the highest proportion of objections or concurrences with conditions:

(1) Of the 68 National Pollution Discharge Elimination system permits issued by the Environmental Protection Agency, five resulted in state objections and one received concurrence with conditions.

(2) Two of 51 harbor widening and deepening projects proposed by the COE were objected to by states and 18 were approved with conditions.

(3) Two of 19 Department of Transportation (Federal Highway Administration) assistance projects raised state objections and four were approved with conditions.

However, without knowing the details of these particular objections or conditional approvals, it is impossible to determine whether state concerns were location-specific or part of a larger structural problem with specific federal agencies.

Resolution of Consistency Disputes

The CZMA provides for two formal mechanisms for resolving federal-state disputes as to whether federal activities are consistent with a state coastal management program: mediation and administrative appeals. NOAA has developed regulations governing mediation, but participation in a mediation is voluntary. In five of the six cases in which a state agency has sought mediation, the federal agency has refused to participate. The sixth case eventually resulted in litigation (*Secretary of the Interior v. California*).

The CZMA also provides for appeals to the Secretary of Commerce to resolve state objections to federally permitted activities. The Secretary may override state objections based on a finding that the activity is necessary in the interest of national security or consistent with the objectives and purposes of the CZMA. To date, no appeals to the Secretary have been decided on national security grounds. To override on the basis of consistency with the objectives and purposes of the CZMA, the Secretary must find that the project meets several tests:

(1) It must further one or more of the national interest objectives listed in sections 302 and 303 of the CZMA (16 U.S.C. Secs. 1451 & 1452).

(2) Contributions of the activity to the national interest must outweigh its adverse individual and cumulative environmental impacts.

(3) The project or activity must not violate the Clean Air Act or Clean Water Act.

(4) There must be no reasonable alternatives available that would allow the activity to be conducted in a manner consistent with the state coastal plan.

. . . Of the 75 filed appeals, the Secretary has overridden six state objections and upheld eight. Five of the six overrides concerned OCS development, three in California and two in Alaska. Six of the denials were COE permit-related and two involved OCS exploration and development. Of the 61 remaining appeals, one has been stayed pending further negotiations, 26 were withdrawn by mutual consent, 16 are currently pending approval and 18 have been dismissed for good cause. . . . It appears that the Secretary is most likely to override state objections regarding OCS exploration and development and most likely to uphold state objections to Corps Section 10/404 permits. In addition, over one-half of the objections are resolved before the Secretary makes a decision. Appeals to the Secretary were taken most often from South Carolina (15) and California (14). Other states included North Carolina (9), New York (8), Alaska (8), Puerto Rico (4), Florida (4), Massachusetts (3), New Jersey (3), Connecticut (3), Washington (3) and Mississippi (1).

In addition to the Secretarial mediation of appeals, a variety of informal mechanisms are available to state and federal officials to resolve consistency issues . . . .

Both the 1983 study and the 1988 survey indicate that state and federal agency officials resolve many disputes through informal negotiation . . . .

In addition, a number of state programs have developed special procedures and/or mechanisms with specific federal agencies for coordinating activities affecting marine or coastal resources. These mechanisms include joint public notices (COE), special joint permit applications (COE) and memoranda of agreements.

***

Perceived Effectiveness of Consistency Review

State officials were asked to characterize the effectiveness of consistency reviews for insuring that state program development and resource management objectives have been considered in the planning and decision-making by federal agencies.

. . . [S]tate officials rate the federal consistency mechanisms as generally quite effective in insuring federal compliance with state coastal resource management and development objectives. The federal consistency review is perceived as particularly effective in insuring that COE Sections 10/404 permits are consistent with state resource management objectives. While federal consistency is regarded as generally effective, it is regarded as less effective for insuring that oil and gas exploration and drilling programs are consistent with state coastal management objectives.

Thirteen of 15 states also indicated that the federal consistency mechanism was "somewhat effective" or "very effective" for improving communication between federal and state agencies. Officials from the other two states reported that it helped improve communications for some agencies, but not for others.

When asked a follow-up question regarding what state programs felt OCRM should do to improve the consistency process and inter-agency coordination, the majority of states responding to the survey indicated that OCRM should work with the federal agencies to "re-inform" them of CZM and the federal consistency requirements.

***

Conclusions

Conclusions about the effectiveness of the federal consistency provisions for coordinating federal and state activities in the coastal areas depend on the evaluative criteria that are used. Analyzing federal-state coordination in terms of the gross percentage of state concurrence with federal activities, permits and licenses, plans and assistance suggests that the provisions are highly effective. States concurred with about 99% of all consistency applications reported in the 1983 Draft Federal Consistency Study and about 97% reported in the 1988 survey. This rate of concurrence suggests at best a high level of agreement between states and federal officials about the consistency of federal activities with state coastal policy or at least state acquiescence with federal activities because of perceived federal power (bearing in mind that some important federal activities such as military construction are exempt from the consistency provisions). Second, state coastal officials perceive the federal consistency provisions as effective. The effectiveness of the consistency provisions for intergovernmental coordination was rated higher for some agencies than for others, but generally those federal agencies with the most frequent interactions with state agencies were characterized by state officials as having the best relationships with the states. For example, the federal agency most actively involved in the federal consistency process is the Army Corps of Engineers. Their Section 10/404 permits accounted for about two-thirds of the federal consistency reviews in 1987. In absolute terms, most objections and administrative appeals involved Corps permits (although amounting to less than 1% of all COE permits reviewed). Nevertheless, officials in 13 of 15 states responding to the 1988 survey characterized their relationships with COE as "good" or "excellent."

A third, more compelling criterion has been the impact of the implementation of consistency provisions on communication between state and federal agencies. CZM officials in 13 of 15 states responding to the 1988 survey indicated that the provisions were "very effective" or "somewhat effective" for improving communication between federal and state agencies. In administrative practice, improved communication means that agency personnel learn the policy priorities of their colleagues in other agencies. They learn what matters to other agency officials and why.

Frequently they begin to search for ways to cooperate; to seek to assist each other in achieving policy objectives. The more frequent the interaction, the greater the incentives to collaborate. For example, officials in more states have collaborated with COE officials to devise other mechanisms for collaboration (i.e. joint public notices, special joint permit applications and memoranda of agreements) than any other agency (Draft Federal Consistency Study). The 1988 survey results indicated that other federal agencies including the Air Force, Environmental Protection Agency, Fish and Wildlife Service, Forestry Service, Minerals Management Service and Coast Guard have also developed collaborative mechanisms with various state programs.

While collaboration and informal negotiation have been the norm, they have not always been sufficient to bring activities subject to consistency review into compliance with state coastal management objectives. One popular device for expressing state concerns has been to attach conditions to state concurrences. The imposition of conditions is most likely to occur when state officials regard the information for making a consistency determination insufficient. There is no basis in the CZM law for attaching conditions and a number of states have found it difficult, if not impossible to enforce conditions once imposed. Appeals to the Secretary of Commerce for secretarial mediation are the most dramatic examples of state-federal consistency conflicts. Less than 1% of federal consistency decisions have been appealed to the Secretary for resolution. Again, the majority of those appeals involve COE 10/404 permits, usually cases in which a private applicant for the COE permit is appealing a state finding that a proposed pier, fill, dock or jetty would be inconsistent with state coastal management objectives. The most conflictful of these appeals have involved state findings that proposed OCS oil exploration would be inconsistent with the state objectives . . . .

points for discussion

1. *Two aspects of consistency.* The consistency mechanism can be viewed in two ways. First, it can be seen as a substantive device for ensuring that proposed projects are actually consistent with enforceable policies in state coastal programs. Second, it can be seen as a procedural mechanism for ensuring that state and federal agencies, as well as the public and permit applicants, have a real opportunity to consider and negotiate the impact of proposed projects. After reading the excerpt above, and considering the enforceable policies we have encountered throughout, which view do you think is more compelling?

2. *Problems with consistency.* Several commentators have raised concerns about the consistency mechanism. One author argues, in contrast to the authors of the excerpt, that the high rate of state concurrence with consistency determinations indicates that the consistency process is one of "routine, redundant reviews," and that nothing would "be lost, [n]or the environment harmed, if the CZMA consistency requirements were repealed." Bruce Kuhse, *The Federal Consistency Requirements of the Coastal Zone Management Act of 1972: It's Time to Repeal This Fundamentally Flawed Legislation*, 6 OCEAN & COASTAL L.J. 77, 106 (2001). Kuhse also argues that the consistency provisions undermine nationally uniform application of environmental laws. Another paper goes further, arguing that "state abuse of the consistency review process may violate the dormant commerce clause in cases where federal licenses and permits are related to proposed activities that affect interstate commerce." Scott C. Whitney et al., *State Implementation of the Coastal Zone Management Consistency Provisions — Ultra Vires or Unconstitutional?*, 12 HARV. ENVTL. L. REV. 67 (1988). How strong do you think these arguments are, given that the federal Secretary of Commerce — as will be seen in the next subsection — has the power to override state objections?

    The following subsection provides two examples of a Section 1456(a)(3)(A) controversy, that is, a disagreement between a permit applicant and a state on the issue of whether the applicant's proposed project is consistent with enforceable policies of the state's coastal program. Pursuant to the CZMA, an applicant who receives a "not consistent" determination from the state can appeal that determination to the Secretary of Commerce. 16 U.S.C. § 1456(a)(3)(A). As you will read, the Secretary does not review the decision of the state agency; rather, the question is whether the project is "consistent with the objectives of [the CZMA] or . . . necessary in the interest of national security." (The applicant would have to go to state court for a hearing on the merits of the state agency's decision.) As you read these opinions, think about why Congress might have created the option of an appeal to the Secretary of Commerce. Once you've figured that out, ask yourself whether it is possible for the Secretary to achieve what Congress had in mind and, if so, whether it actually happened in these appeals.

1. Private Projects

In the Consistency Appeal of Henry Crosby from an Objection by the State of South Carolina

U.S. Department of Commerce, Office of the Secretary
(December 29, 1992)

I. Background

In February, 1989, Henry Crosby (Appellant) applied to the U.S. Army Corps of Engineers for a permit under section 404 of the Clean Water Act to place fill material in a wetland for the purpose of constructing an impoundment and installing a water control structure. The objective of this project is to construct a "green tree reservoir" for private recreational use.[1] The excavation, filling, and impoundment will affect approximately 4.5 acres of freshwater wetlands. The proposed impoundment will be flooded to depths of 0.7 to 1.0 feet from October through February and will provide a static water level and aerial cover for migratory waterfowl. The site of the proposed project is approximately two miles from Willtown Bluff Landing, Colleton County, South Carolina. . . .

On September 8, 1989, the South Carolina Coastal Council (the State) objected to Appellant's consistency certification for the proposed project on the grounds that it violates certain policies of the State's coastal zone management program. Specifically, the policies against approval of projects deemed to have a significant negative impact on wildlife and fisheries resources, and against approval of projects which would require fill or other significant permanent alteration of a productive freshwater marsh. . . .

Under . . . 16 U.S.C. 1456(c)(3)(A) and 15 C.F.R. 930.131, the State's consistency objection precludes the Corps from issuing a permit for the activity unless the Secretary of Commerce (Secretary) finds that the activity may be federally approved, notwithstanding the State's objection, because the activity is either consistent with the objectives or purposes of the CZMA, or necessary in the interest of national security.

II. Appeal to the Secretary of Commerce

On October 17, 1989, Lafayette S. Lyle, III, of Agricadabra Land Counselors, filed an appeal with the Secretary on behalf of Henry Crosby. . . .

On December 26, 1989, Appellant informed the Department [of Commerce] that Appellant and the State were conducting discussions to informally resolve the dispute, in accordance with 15 C.F.R. 930.124, and asked that the appeal be held in abeyance while the discussions were being conducted.

---

1. Appellant explains that the term "green tree reservoir" refers to the manipulation of water in an area so that trees are able to stay alive, or "green."

Rice Field Impoundments in South Carolina

From the S.C. Department of Health and Environmental Control:

Before the tidal culture method was used, rice was grown as an upland crop, without irrigation. Then as the advantages of flooding became known, early in the 18th century, cultivation was moved into cleared swamp lands fed by freshwater streams so that water could be impounded and applied to the fields. Rain water was also impounded in "reserves" and used for flooding the crops. Flooding the rice greatly promoted its growth and killed the weeds and grass which formerly had to be cleared by hoeing.

". . . Consisting of a system of banks, ditches, floodgates and trunks, tidal culture provided a method whereby the rice fields could be kept as dry or as wet as the crop required. The following is a simple explanation of what was involved.

"Great acreages of land beyond the salt water reach of high tide were cleared along the coastal rivers, and with enormous labor, thousands of acres were diked by digging canals or ditches along the edges of the rivers and creeks and using the excavated mud to make an enclosing bank. Within this enclosed or impounded area, a network of smaller ditches was cut and cross banks were formed to divide the area into a number of fields and provide a means of drainage and irrigation.

"To control the systematic, precise flooding and subsequent draining of the fields for the maximum yield of rice, floodgates and trunks were installed perpendicular to the rivers and creeks and the adjacent canals. A trunk was essentially a rectangular wood box with a floodgate at either end. As the flood tide flowed in from the ocean and pushed the fresh water back up the distant reaches of the coastal rivers and creeks, the outside floodgate on the trunk was manually opened, allowing fresh water to flow in through the trunk and force the inside gate to swing open for the flooding of the fields. As the tide began to ebb, the lower water level in the creeks caused the water in the fields to begin flowing out and in so doing automatically forced the inner floodgate to swing shut, holding the water in the fields until such time as the rice was ready for a drying period. At this point, the inner gate was manually opened, on an ebb tide, to allow for drainage.

The rice industry in South Carolina died out in the 1890s. Since that time, some landowners (and wildlife agencies) have attempted to put the old impoundments to use (and to repair damaged impoundments) in furtherance of waterfowl conservation and recreational hunting.

In October, 1990, the parties agreed that the discussions had not been fruitful and that the appeals process should be reinitiated. . . .

After Appellant perfected the appeal by filing supporting data and information pursuant to 15 C.F.R. 930.125, the Department solicited comments on issues germane to the decision in the appeal by way of notices in the Federal Register, 56 Fed. Reg. 49173 (September 27, 1991) and the Charleston, South Carolina News and Courier (October 2, 3, and 4, 1991). The Department received no public comments.

On September 20, 1991, the Department solicited the views of other federal agencies on the four regulatory criteria the project must meet for the Secretary to find it consistent with the objectives or purposes of the CZMA. The criteria appear at 15 C.F.R. 930.121, and are discussed below. The Department requested comments from the National Marine Fisheries Service, the Environmental Protection Agency, the U.S. Army Corps of Engineers, and the Fish and Wildlife Service of the Department of Interior. All agencies responded.

***

III. Grounds for Reviewing an Appeal

Before I can determine whether the grounds for secretarial override have been satisfied, I must determine that the State's objection complies with the requirements of Section 307(c)(3)(A) of the CZMA and 15 C.F.R. 930.64(a) and (b). Those sections provide that the state's objection must describe how the proposed project is inconsistent with specific, enforceable elements of the State's coastal management program. The State cited its policies of opposing activities deemed to have a significant negative impact on wildlife and fisheries resources, and activities requiring fill or other permanent alteration of wetlands. Both of these policies are part of the State's coastal management program. . . . The State also explained how Appellant's project is inconsistent with those policies. Because the State's objection describes how Appellant's proposed activity is inconsistent with specific, enforceable elements of the management plan, I find that the State's objection was properly lodged.[2]

Section 307(c)(3)A) of the CZMA provides that federal licenses or permits required for a proposed activity may be granted despite a valid consistency objection if the Secretary finds that the activity is (1) consistent with the objectives of the CZMA or (2) otherwise necessary in the interest of national security. . . . Appellant has pleaded only the first ground.

To find that the proposed activity satisfies this ground, the Secretary must determine that the activity satisfies all four of the elements specified in 15 C.F.R. 930.121. These elements are:

1. The proposed activity furthers one or more of the competing national objectives or purposes contained in sections 302 or 303 of the CZMA [16 U.S.C. §§ 1451 and 1452]. . . .
2. When performed separately or when its cumulative effects are considered, [the proposed activity] will not cause adverse effects on the natural resources

---

2. . . . As in previous appeals, I do not consider whether the State properly applied its policies in determining that the proposed project is inconsistent with its coastal management program. I do not make my own determination as to whether the proposed project is actually inconsistent with the State's program. My review of the State's objection is limited to determining whether that objection was properly lodged, i.e., whether it complies with the requirements of the CZMA and its implementing regulations. For that, I need only determine that the State has cited policies that are part of its management program, and has explained how the proposed project will be inconsistent with those policies.

of the coastal zone substantial enough to outweigh its contribution to the national interest. . . .

3. The proposed activity will not violate any of the requirements of the Clean Water Act, as amended [*sic*] [should read "Clean Air Act" — EDS.], or the Federal Water Pollution Control Act, as amended. . . .

4. There is no reasonable alternative available (e.g., location[,] design, etc.) that would permit the activity to be conducted in a manner consistent with the [state's coastal zone] management program. . . .

Because Element Two is dispositive of this case, I turn immediately to that issue.

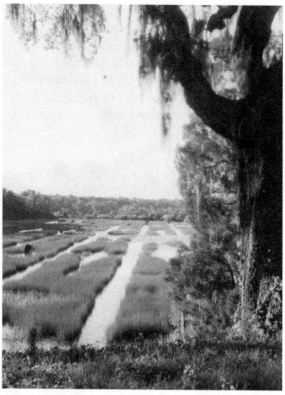

Photo: Frances Benjamin Johnston, Library of Congress

Figure 9-14. Rice Fields
Rice Fields in Berkeley County, South Carolina, 1938.

IV. Element Two

This element requires that the Secretary weigh the adverse effects of the objected-to activity on the natural resources of the coastal zone against its contribution to the national interest. To perform this balancing, the Secretary must first identify the proposed project's adverse effects and its contribution to the national interest.

A. Adverse Effects

Appellant's proposed project consists of constructing embankments, and improving existing embankments, for a total of 6,625 linear feet of embankments. The existing 1,000-foot embankment located along the south/west property line will not require any additional work. Fill will be required to improve the 4,425 feet of existing embankments on the north and south sides of the proposed impoundment. The remainder of the embankments will be new. Fill material for the proposed work will be obtained adjacent to the proposed embankments. . . .

Appellant argues that "no net loss of wetlands" will result from the proposed project. Appellant claims that 3.45 acres of wetlands on the site are already "disturbed," having been altered by the installation of existing embankments, and that the project will only add 1.1 more acres to those characterized as "disturbed." Appellant argues that therefore, the net result of the construction, which will cover 4.6 acres, is a net "disturbance, not loss, of 1.1 acres."

The State responds by challenging Appellant's argument that the wetlands on the site of the proposed construction are "disturbed." The State argues:

> The [South Carolina Coastal] Council looks at the current condition of the wetlands and they represent existing and undisturbed wetlands. Much of the coast of South Carolina prior to the passage of the 1977 Coastal Management Act has been altered by man. . . . This issue is the red herring because it would seek to characterize these wetlands as being disturbed when the more accurate description is that these are viable wetlands serving all of the purposes of wetlands having not been altered by man. State's Brief at 9.

It appears that Appellant is arguing that I should consider only the adverse effects of the proposed project on the 1.1 acres of wetlands he characterizes as "undisturbed," while the State is arguing that I should consider the adverse effects on the entire construction area. Appellant does not dispute that 4.5 acres of wetlands will be filled as part of the proposed project. I am not persuaded that I should disregard the proposed project's potential adverse effects on those portions of the site that Appellant calls "disturbed" wetlands. An analysis of a project's adverse effects on a particular resource will necessarily take into account the condition of the resource itself. I find nothing in the record to indicate that the proposed activity will affect some portions of these wetlands differently than other portions. I will therefore consider the proposed project's adverse effects on the 4.5 acres that will be filled.

Appellant claims that the proposed project will have no detrimental impact on the integrity of the impounded area. . . . Appellant argues that the purpose of the proposed green tree reservoir is "waterfowl and wading bird management," a use that would enhance the resource, while there is limited benefit in leaving the area in its current, "severely disturbed" state. . . .

In response, the State argues that permanent alteration of wetlands would result from Appellant's proposed excavation and filling activities. Additional permanent alteration would result from the proposed impoundment, which would change the area hydrologically. The State argues that these changes would affect "the basic functions of production and export as well as limiting passage of organisms in and out of the impounded area." Letter from H. Stephen Snyder, Director of Planning and Certification, South Carolina Coastal Council, to LTC James T. Scott, District Engineer, U.S. Army Corps of Engineers, September 8, 1989.

The South Carolina Wildlife and Marine Resources Department noted that the area in which the project is proposed consists of productive, freshwater wetlands:

> In their natural state, the wetlands in question perform a number of well documented ecological and water resource functions. Forested floodplain areas provide

an important link between upland watersheds and downstream aquatic environments. Detritus produced in these areas serves as an important energy source for aquatic food chains in adjoining creeks and receiving water bodies. Woody plant communities provide excellent food, cover, and nesting for a variety of wildlife species. Many wildlife species are attracted to the extensive edge and structurally heterogenous habitats found in forested areas. . . .

The Wildlife and Marine Resources Department concluded that "[i]n light of the direct, significant loss of productive wetlands and the loss of normal functions and values," the permit for Appellant's project should be denied. *Id.* at 3.

The State also submitted, in support of its position on this appeal, comments that were provided by the Fish and Wildlife Service of the U.S. Department of Interior (FWS) to the U.S. Army Corps of Engineers while the Corps was considering whether to approve Appellant's permit application. The FWS urged the Corps to deny the permit, stating:

> Long-term effects of greentree operation on the existing vegetation is uncertain. The potential exists for eventual conversion of forested wetland habitat to emergent wetlands, and the ultimate loss of this locally unique wetland habitat component to the wildlife dependent on it. . . .

In addition to the parties' submissions, the record contains the comments submitted by other federal agencies to the Department for purposes of this appeal. The FWS, in response to the Department's request for comments, submitted copies of its comments to the Corps, which are discussed above.

The Environmental Protection Agency (EPA) stated:

> The available evidence indicates that the proposed activity would cause adverse effects on the natural resources of this wetland area. In addition, it is general EPA policy to recommend that where any activity will adversely affect the natural functions of a wetland that activity should be avoided to the maximum extent practicable. As noted in the Clean Water Act Section 404(b)(1) Guidelines, "From a national perspective . . . filling operations in wetlands, is considered to be among the most severe environmental impacts covered by these Guidelines." 40 C.F.R. 230.1(d). . . .

The National Marine Fisheries Service recommended that Appellant's proposed project not be authorized, commenting:

> The wetlands at the project site support emergent, scrub/shrub, and forested plant assemblages that directly and indirectly support living marine resources that are of ecological, commercial, and recreational importance. The attached Field Investigation Report (FIR) . . . indicates that the area provides habitat for shad, herring, striped bass, and shrimp. The endangered shortnose sturgeon also migrates through the area. In addition, the wetlands provide food in the form of detritus and perform water quality maintenance functions that benefit downstream fisheries. . . .

A review of the record on this appeal indicates that permanent alteration of the wetlands will result from Appellant's proposed project. The submissions by the parties suggest that the change could result in the ultimate loss of this wetland habitat, which would adversely affect the natural resources of this area. The Appellant has not provided any evidence to contradict this. I therefore find that the proposed project will adversely affect the environment by permanently altering the wetlands, thus causing the loss of normal functions and values.

B. Contribution to the National Interest

With respect to the proposed project's contribution to the national interest, Appellant argues that the proposed project will further the desirable goal of water-fowl management and thus will create an enhanced resource. Appellant points out that the public benefits of waterfowl management, and the enhancement of the coastal zone, have been recognized in South Carolina's laws. . . .

Before I can weigh the proposed project's contribution to the national interest against the project's adverse effects, I must first define the national interests involved. As decided in a previous consistency appeal:

> The national interests to be balanced in Element Two are limited to those recognized in or defined by the objectives or purposes of the [Coastal Zone Management] Act. In other words, while a proposed activity may further (or impede) a national interest beyond the scope of the national interests recognized in or defined by the objectives or purposes of the Act, such a national interest may not be considered in the balancing. Decision and Findings in the Consistency Appeal of Korea Drilling Company, Ltd., January 19, 1989, at 16.

The CZMA includes, in section 303(1), enhancement of coastal zone resources as one of its objectives. Section 303(2)(A) mentions "protection of natural resources, including . . . fish and wildlife and their habitat" as another objective of the CZMA. Therefore, I find that waterfowl management, to the extent it involves "protection of . . . wildlife and their habitat," and enhancement of coastal zone resources are national interests that are properly considered for purposes of Element Two analysis. I now turn to an analysis of the extent to which Appellant's proposed project contributes to these interests.

The State argues that it "has consistently objected to the impounding of wetland areas except under rare circumstances," and that Appellant's claim that the proposed project would enhance the resource "meets with no agreement" on the part of the agencies that commented during the consistency determination process. . . .

The record does indicate that questions were raised regarding Appellant's argument that the proposed green tree reservoir would enhance the area. The South Carolina Wildlife and Marine Resources Department stated:

> We would question the suitability of this area for management as a greentree reservoir. The area contains very few mast producing plant species, a key part of a successful reservoir. With the proposed flooding regime, plant species requiring seasonal drawdown may be adversely impacted and eventually killed. . . .

The FWS also expressed reservations about the benefits of Appellant's proposed project:

> The area does not meet the criteria of a classic greentree reservoir. Although the existing tree species would provide some protective cover, the lack of mast-producing hardwoods severely limits its attraction to those waterfowl species most associated with this type of habitat, i.e., mallards, black ducks, wood ducks, and other dabblers. . . .

The EPA commented:

> The applicant has proposed the creation of a "greentree" reservoir. EPA finds this proposal has little merit since the project area does not contain any mast producing trees and has the potential to be converted to an emergent marsh due to long duration hydroperiods. . . . The applicant has stated that approximately 80% of the adjacent area is existing impoundments. EPA does not see the addition of another impoundment as an enhancement. . . .

Appellant presents no evidence to demonstrate how the "waterfowl management" aspects of his proposed project will contribute to the protection of any forms of wildlife and their habitat. Appellant does not present any other evidence demonstrating how his proposed project would contribute to the national interest in enhancing the resources of the coastal zone. In light of the agencies' above statements that the proposed green tree reservoir will not enhance the area, I find that Appellant's proposed project will contribute minimally, if at all, to the national interest.

C. Balancing

Above, I found that Appellant's proposed project would adversely affect the natural resources of the coastal zone by permanently altering wetlands, thus causing loss of normal functions and values. In addition, I found that the proposed activity's contribution to the national interest would be minimal. I now find that the evidence does not convince me that "[w]hen performed separately or when its cumulative effects are considered, [the activity] will not cause adverse effects on the coastal zone substantial enough to outweigh [the activity's] contribution to the national interest." 15 C.F.R. 930.121(b). Accordingly, the proposed project has failed to satisfy Element Two.

V. Conclusion

Because Appellant must satisfy all four elements of the regulations in order for me to sustain his appeal, failure to satisfy any one element precludes my finding that Appellant's project is "consistent with the objectives of the [CZMA]." Because I found that Appellant has failed to satisfy the second element of Ground I, it is unnecessary to examine the other three elements. Therefore, I will not override the State's objection to Mr. Crosby's consistency certification.

In the Consistency Appeal of Southern Pacific Transportation Company to an Objection from the California Coastal Commission

U.S. Department of Commerce, Office of the Secretary
(September 24, 1985)

Factual Background

Southern Pacific Transportation Company (Appellant), San Francisco, California, proposes to rehabilitate its railroad bridge located across the mouth of the Santa

Ynez River and on its right of way through Vandenberg Air Force Base (VAFB) near Surf, Santa Barbara County, California. . . . The bridge is part of the main coastal rail line that daily carries ten freight and two Amtrak passenger trains between Los Angeles and San Francisco, and serves to transport materials related to operations on VAFB. . . .

Originally constructed in 1896, the bridge has been modified and periodically repaired, primarily after sustaining storm or flood damage. The present structure is 549 feet long and consists of six 90-foot girder spans with a single track, supported by a combination of piers and temporary piles and by abutments built into the northern and southern embankments of the river. . . .

In March 1983, high river flows resulting from a series of winter storms destroyed a cement pier and a 90-foot steel girder span near the southern (Los Angeles) end of the bridge. . . . Emergency repairs included the replacement of the missing span and the installation of four steel pile piers as a temporary foundation for the new span. . . . The existing bridge foundation consists of a variety of supports including masonry, concrete and steel piles. . . .

Appellant proposes to rehabilitate the Santa Ynez River railroad bridge by modifying two existing concrete pile-supported piers, removing existing foundations, and installing four new concrete piers and two new abutments, anchored by piles extending below the scour line of the river and designed to withstand maximum flood events. . . . A new San Francisco abutment would be constructed 200 feet north of its present location, and the northern embankment excavated to eliminate the dogleg in the river so that the main flow of the river would be directed under the center of the bridge where a pilot channel would be dredged to provide a more direct flow to the ocean. . . . The new Los Angeles abutment would be constructed 160 feet north of its present location by extending the southern embankment into the river and filling in behind it. . . . As a result of the relocation of the two new abutments, the bridge would be lengthened by 40 feet and moved 200 feet to the north. . . . The increased length and relocation of the bridge would be accommodated by installing two new spans and repositioning the existing spans over the new foundation, including the two modified piers. . . .

The lengthening and relocation of the bridge and the excavation of the pilot channel are designed by Appellant to enhance the capacity of the river span beneath the bridge to carry flood flows, reduce the rate of flood waters rising at the bridge, and reduce existing erosion of the San Francisco abutment. . . . The project is also designed to eliminate the need for continual bridge repairs and to minimize the risk of bridge failure under extreme flow conditions. . . .

Construction would take six months to complete, during which Ocean Beach County Park, which provides access to the beach, would be closed to the public. . . .

At the mouth of the Santa Ynez River and southeast of the bridge is the largest salt marsh in Santa Barbara County. . . . Relatively undisturbed by human activity (with the exception of County Park roadway and several railroad embankments), it consists of over 200 acres of . . . marshlands traversed by a single main river channel. There is a sand bar at the mouth of the River, which is closed most of the year due to very low river flows. The closed sand bar forms a brackish lagoon that inundates the adjacent marshlands by sheet flow and subsurface seepage. This inundation is so widespread that the marsh areas south of the river channel, park roadway, and railroad embankment contain standing water for months. The water level of the lagoon and salt marsh during this period appears to be four to five feet above mean sea level. . . .

On July 25, 1984, Appellant, in connection with its application to the U.S. Army Corps of Engineers (COE), under Section 10 of the Rivers and Harbors Act and Section 404 of the Clean Water Act, for permits to conduct dredge and fill activities associated with the bridge rehabilitation project in the navigable waters of the Santa Ynez River, submitted a consistency certification to the California Coastal Commission (Commission) for review under Section 307(c)(3)(A) of the Coastal Zone Management Act . . . stating that "the proposed activity complies with the California approved coastal management program and will be conducted in a manner consistent with such program." . . . On September 24, 1984, following a public hearing, the Commission, as the federally approved coastal zone management agency for the State of California . . . , objected to Appellant's consistency certification. . . .

Existing and Projected River Mouth Configuration

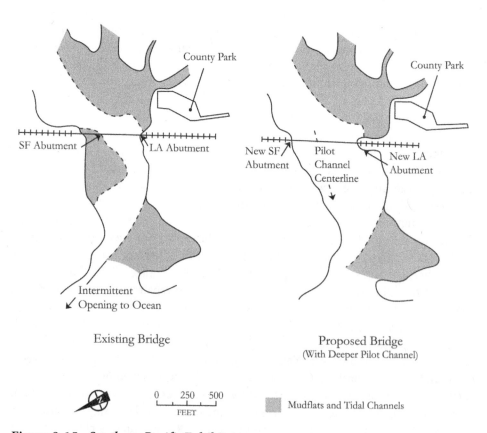

Existing Bridge

Proposed Bridge
(With Deeper Pilot Channel)

Mudflats and Tidal Channels

Figure 9-15. *Southern Pacific* **Exhibit**
An exhibit from the Secretary's opinion illustrating the railroad company's plans.

The Commission determined that Appellant's project as proposed did not comply with, and, therefore, was inconsistent with, the policies of the federally approved California Coastal Management Program (CCMP). . . . The Commission objected to Appellant's bridge rehabilitation project because it would alter the existing course of the Santa Ynez River. . . . In particular, the Commission objected to Appellant's filling in an area at the southern embankment, of 160 feet in length and 120 feet in width, and filling in the main channel of one of the few remaining unchannelized streams in southern California, making a "permanent commitment to armoring the channel," and substantially altering the sedimentary processes in the estuary. . . . The Commission also objected to the project's interference with public access to the beach during the construction period. . . . The Commission determined that the activities to which it objected failed to meet the enforceable policy requirements of the California Coastal Act (hereinafter CCA) relating to estuarine and wetland protection and coastal access. . . .

As provided at 15 CFR 930.64(b), the Commission identified alternative measures which, if adopted by Appellant, would permit the proposed activity to be conducted in a manner consistent with the CCMP. . . . Specifically, the Commission found that Appellant's project would be consistent with the CCMP if (1) the closure of the county park were mitigated by Appellant's providing the public use and notice of the availability of Appellant's nearby railroad switchyard for coastal access during the project's construction phase, and (2) the project were redesigned to relocate the Los Angeles abutment to its existing site, to eliminate all channelization, and to improve circulation along the north bank of the River. . . . The Commission also notified Appellant of its right to appeal the Commission's decision to the Secretary of Commerce (Secretary). . . .

Under [the CZMA], the Commission's consistency objection precludes Federal agencies from issuing any permit or license necessary for the Appellant's proposed activity to proceed, unless the Secretary determines that the activity may be federally approved notwithstanding the objection because the activity is consistent with the objectives or purposes of the CZMA, or is necessary in the interest of national security.

Appeal to the Secretary of Commerce

On October 24, 1984, Appellant . . . filed with the Secretary a Notice of Appeal and a supporting statement requesting that the Secretary find that Appellant's proposed Santa Ynez River railroad bridge rehabilitation activities are consistent with the objectives or purposes of the CZMA or are otherwise necessary in the interest of national security. . . .

Appellant also alleges that its project is consistent with the CCMP. . . . This last allegation, which this decision does not address for the reasons indicated, reflects a misunderstanding by Appellant of the appeals process. Under the CZMA, the authority and responsibility to determine whether a proposed activity is consistent with a federally approved State coastal management program is given to the State coastal management agency. The CZMA does not give the Secretary the authority to review the correctness of a State's consistency determination; rather, such determinations are subject to judicial review. All that Section 307(c)(3)(A) of the CZMA and the implementing regulations permit the Secretary to do is to determine whether Federal license or permit processes for a proposed project should be allowed to go forward despite a State consistency objection because the project is consistent with the objectives or purposes of the CZMA or is otherwise necessary in the interest of national security. If a consistency objection is properly filed by the State coastal management agency, the inconsistency of the proposed project is presumed valid for purposes of the appeal.

***

Ground I: Consistent with the Objectives of the CZMA

The first statutory ground (Ground I) for sustaining an appeal is to find that the activity "is consistent with the objectives of [the CZMA]." To make this finding, I must determine that the activity satisfies all four of the elements specified in 15 C.F.R. 930.121.

First Element

To satisfy the first of the four elements, I must find that: The activity furthers one or more of the competing national objectives or purposes contained in Sections 302 or 303 of the [CZMA]. . . .

Sections 302 and 303 of the CZMA identify a number of objectives and purposes which may be generally stated as follows:

1. To preserve, protect and where possible to restore or enhance the resources of the coastal zone . . . ;
2. To develop the resources of the coastal zone . . . ;
3. To encourage and assist the States to exercise their full authority over the lands and waters in the coastal zone, giving consideration to the need to protect as well as to develop coastal resources, in recognition by the Congress that State action is essential to more effective protection and use of the resources of the coastal zone. . . .

More specifically in the context of this appeal, the CZMA encourages coastal states to provide for orderly processes for siting major activities related to transportation that are coastal dependent. . . .

As I have stated in an earlier appeal, because Congress has broadly defined the national interest in coastal zone management to include both protection and development of coastal resources, this element will "normally" be found to be satisfied on appeal. . . .

Appellant's proposal involves the rehabilitation of a bridge carrying freight and passenger trains between northern and southern California. Materials for VAFB are also transported across this bridge. Both parties agree that the bridge needs to be rehabilitated. Since the goals of the CZMA include both development and protection of coastal resources, as well as siting of transportation facilities, I find that

Appellant's project to rehabilitate the bridge over the Santa Ynez River falls within and furthers one or more of the broad objectives of Sections 302 and 303 of the CZMA and therefore satisfies the first element of Ground I.

Second Element

To satisfy the second element of Ground I, I must find that:

> When performed separately or when its cumulative effects are considered, the activity will not cause adverse effects on the natural resources of the coastal zone substantial enough to outweigh its contribution to the national interest. . . .

This element requires that I weigh the adverse effects of the objected-to activity on the natural resources of the coastal zone against its contribution to the national interest.

In order to perform the weighing required by this element, I must identify the adverse effects, if any, of Appellant's project on the natural resources of the coastal zone as well as the project's contribution to the national interest.

Adverse Effects

The parties differ in their characterization of these effects. In response to the Written Questions, the Commission characterized these effects as follows:

1. Short-term adverse effects. Effects resulting directly from the construction activity itself and occurring during the construction phase. The smothering and disturbance of bottom-dwelling organisms and impairment of circulation in a sandy area of the River. Restabilization can be expected relatively soon after the construction phase. Closure, during the construction period, of Ocean Beach County Park, which provides public access to the beach, would interrupt the public's recreational use of the beach.

2. Mid-term adverse effects. Construction effects spanning at least several years, and possibly several decades, depending on the frequency of major River flow. Could be offset eventually by sediment due to the new configuration of the River mouth. Loss of a 2.5 acre mudflat habitat along the north bank caused by construction on that bank and from altered River processes which would deepen the estuary at the north end of the bridge. This loss could be offset by reestablishment of mudflat along the south bank; however, there would be a loss of habitat values while the River mouth adjusts to the changes in flow direction.

   During floods, the new southern abutment would constrict the flow of the River and exert tremendous force in altering water and sediment movement. Scour and erosion along the southern bank would be expected, damaging habitat values in the area. Sedimentation patterns would be changed with uncertain consequences for the adjacent wetlands.

   Because of the new southern abutment, changes could occur in the morphology of the lagoon, possibly changing the lagoon into mudflats, resulting in a loss of lagoon habitat or interference with the lagoon's function in the estuary.

3. Long-term adverse effects. The permanent loss of 0.8 acres of lagoon habitat, about 1.45 acres of bare sand adjacent to the River channel, up to 2.5 acres of shallow mudflat near the northern abutment, 0.8 acres of coastal strand and dune vegetation along the coast side of the railroad embankment, and disturbances to 0.2 acres of salt marsh near the northern embankment. Conversion of a portion of the lagoon into mudflats and possibly marsh lands. Conversion of a portion of wetlands into fastlands.

In its response to the Written Questions, Appellant has offset the adverse effects by netting them with alleged benefits of the proposed project and its proposed Marsh Enhancement and Mitigation Plan. Once the benefits are separated out, Appellant's characterization of the adverse effects of its project, as summarized in its response to the written questions and its Environmental Assessment, is as follows:

1. Short-term adverse effects. Effects which would cease or reverse upon completion of construction. Modification of surface topography and stream morphology near the railroad bridge. Minor adverse effects on air and water quality in the vicinity of the bridge. The temporary displacement of nearby fish and wildlife and degradation of aquatic habitat. The loss of small amounts of dune vegetation and shallow mudflat habitat. The possible reduction of local wildlife populations (mostly birds). The interruption of the recreational use of Santa Barbara County Ocean Beach Park. The degradation of the visual character of the River mouth because of the temporary presence of construction equipment, access berms, and an office trailer.
2. Long-term adverse effects. The loss of approximately 2.5 acres of shallow mudflats, 0.6-.08 acres of lagoon habitat, a few acres of salt marsh and a small amount of dune vegetation.

Besides information from the parties, the record contains an assessment of the project's adverse effects by Federal and State agencies. The California Department of Fish and Game (CDFG), in comments to the Corps of Engineers, the Federal permitting agency, indicated that it would have no objection to the issuance of the Federal permit if

> "[t]he proposed filling of 160 ft. of wetlands under the southern side of the trestle [were] deleted. This fill will cause a water slowdown and result in deposition of silt along the southeast side of the Santa Ynez estuary. That will eventually block circulation to the entire southern side of the salicornia marsh in this area and damage it." Letter from H. W. Carper, Director, California Department of Fish and Game, to U.S. Army Engineer District, Los Angeles, California, December 2, 1983. . . .

Similarly, the U.S. Fish and Wildlife Service (FWS), commenting on Appellant's application for a COE permit, identified the following unmitigated impacts associated with the project: 1) loss of some salt marsh (less than 0.1 acre) from the placement of riprap on the northern abutment; 2) increased sedimentation over about 100 acres of existing salt marsh and some conversion of wetlands to fastlands, resulting from the hydraulic diversion caused by the southern abutment; 3) suspended sediments and deterioration of water quality during the dredging and construction of the two temporary cofferdams; 4) conversion to tidal flat of coastal strand vegetation during the excavation of the pilot channel and removal of sand from a sandbar along the northern bank (about 4 acres); and 5) loss of 0.6 acres of habitat area resulting from the abutment addition on the southern bank (to be offset by a gain of 0.6 acres resulting from removal at the northern bank). . . . Of these impacts, the FWS considered the degradation or loss of salt marsh on the south bank resulting from increased sedimentation to be potentially significant. . . .

Based on the record, without implementation of marsh enhancement or mitigation measures, I find that the mid- or long-term adverse effects of Appellant's project, considered by itself, are the loss of a 2.5 acre mudflat habitat, the loss of approximately 0.8 acres of lagoon habitat, the loss of approximately 0.8 acres of coastal strand and dune vegetation, the substantial disturbance and possible destruction of approximately 0.2 acres of salt marsh, increased sedimentation over about 100 acres of salt marsh and some conversion of wetlands to fastlands (resulting from the fill at the southern abutment), and the potential of additional damaged habitat value due to increased scour and erosion. I find that the short-term effects, other than interference with the public's access to the beach during construction, are *de minimis.*

The adverse effects of Appellant's project are offset to some extent by the benefits of the project and by proposed marsh enhancement and other mitigation measures. The principal benefit of Appellant's proposed project is that the bridge would be designed to withstand maximum flood events, thus increasing public safety and decreasing the risk of rail traffic interruption due to bridge washout. . . .

Regarding the closure of Ocean Beach Park during the construction period, Appellant has agreed, in its submissions in the record of this appeal, to provide the public access to its switchyard, to construct a walkway under the bridge for beach access due to post signs at the County Park to direct beach-goers to the alternate access site. . . . Therefore, I find that the project's adverse effects on public access to the beach, a natural resource of the coastal zone, have been mitigated to the maximum extent feasible.

To compensate for the loss of habitat values, described above, Appellant has developed, in coordination with FWS, CDFG and the National Marine Fisheries Service, a Marsh Enhancement and Mitigation Plan. . . . Appellant's Mitigation Plan consists of enlarging the opening of two existing man-made channels that traverse the main salt marsh and connect to the main River channel, and monitoring these openings for 3 years; constructing a new 2,300-foot-long marsh channel adjacent to the road to the Ocean Beach County Park; installing several culverts under the County Park roadway and railroad at 4 locations in order to provide free water movement between the southern marshes and the main salt marsh; and excavating a 15-foot-wide channel to connect the River to a salt marsh along the new northern embankment. . . .

Appellant expects the Mitigation Plan to yield an expansion and improvement of the wetland habitat and, in turn, result in long-term increases in wetland species, especially resident and migrant bird species.

The Commission argues that the value of the Mitigation Plan is uncertain because little research exists on the ecology or morphology of estuarine systems like the Santa Ynez River system. According to the Commission, it is possible that implementation of the Plan would simply change high marsh habitat to open water, without enhancing habitat values or productivity at all. . . . Further, the Commission states that the Mitigation Plan would not create new habitat to offset habitat losses, but would only alter existing habitat. . . .

In summary, Appellant's Mitigation Plan is intended to offset the adverse impacts of the bridge rehabilitation project on the biological resources adjacent to the bridge, primarily the loss of wetlands and salt marsh habitat caused by increased fill at the southern embankment. . . . I cannot with certainty conclude whether these losses will be totally offset by the Plan, but they may be to some extent. At best, there will be no net gain in habitat value.

Also uncertain is the potential impact on the Estuary from the increased scour and erosion that the Commission believes may occur from the placement of the southern abutment 160 feet into the existing River channel. But this impact is likely to be offset by the widening of the channel under the Bridge and the removal of an existing obstruction (the northern embankment), thereby allowing more direct flow of the River to the sea.

Besides the adverse effects from the project by itself, I must consider any cumulative effects caused by the project and other nearby construction projects. According to Appellant's Environmental Assessment, which is not refuted in this respect by the Commission, there appears to be no future project of similar magnitude near the location of Appellant's proposed project, either by private industry, VAFB, or governmental agencies. Therefore, I find that there are no cumulative adverse impacts associated with Appellant's proposal.

Contribution to the National Interest

In order to help assess the contribution to the national interest of Appellant's project, I sought the views of certain Federal agencies. The views expressed by Federal agencies regarding the national interest in this project are summarized below.

The Department of Labor indicated that, in view of the small scale of the project, i.e., a total investment of less than $4 million, and the availability of other options, e.g., continual improvements of the existing bridge, the Department cannot find that the national interest would be adversely affected if the appeal is denied. . . .

The National Aeronautics and Space Administration (NASA) concluded that an investigation of the use of this bridge for transporting NASA Space Shuttle hardware and propellants reveals that none of these elements are required to cross the Santa Ynez River railroad bridge since, after arriving at VAFB, all Shuttle elements are routed off the main-line onto rail spurs prior to crossing the bridge. . . .

The Department of Transportation stated that since the issue is one of the physical and engineering approach chosen by Appellant and not whether the bridge will continue to fulfill its transportation function, no national interests are involved in this matter. . . .

The United States Air Force (USAF) advised that the bridge plays a significant role in support of national defense interests since items such as the solid rocket motor segments used for launch programs conducted at Space Launch Complex Four are routinely transported over the bridge. Transportation by other means would involve significant cost increases and could possibly impact vital missions of national significance. USAF expressed no opinion on the manner in which the project is carried out, by the Appellant's proposal or Commission's alternative, and acknowledged that environmental mitigation measures may be required for any potential environmental impacts. . . .

While no Federal agency stated that the national interest would be impaired if the bridge was not rehabilitated in the manner proposed by Appellant, the Federal agencies recognized that continuation of the bridge through some sort of rehabilitation or replacement would contribute to the national interest in having an efficient rail system.

Further, I note that the existing bridge is vulnerable to immediate failure should a storm/flood event occur, because most of the existing piers are not anchored below the potential scour line of the river. In March 1983, a pier and two spans were destroyed by high river flows, requiring emergency repairs and installation of temporary steel pipe piles. Failure of the bridge would result in loss of property, interrupted passenger and commercial rail traffic and, if the bridge failed while a train was crossing, could result in a further loss of property and possibly personal injury or death. . . . Because the bridge is used to transport equipment and materials used at Space Launch Complex Four at VAFB, failure of the bridge could raise transportation costs to the Air Force and could otherwise impede national defense interests.

Based on the record, I find that Appellant's proposed bridge rehabilitation project will contribute to the national interest in safe and efficient railway transportation and in maintenance of rail access to VAFB.

Weighing

Having described both the potential adverse effects on the natural resources of the coastal zone which may be caused by Appellant's bridge rehabilitation project and the national interest served by such a project, I am required to decide whether the project's adverse effects are substantial enough to outweigh its contribution to the national interest. 15 C.F.R. 930.121(b).

To recapitulate, the potential adverse effects of Appellant's proposal, absent the Mitigation Plan, consist of the direct loss of 2.5 acres of mudflat habitat, approximately 3 acres of sand and dune vegetation and less than one acre of lagoon habitat. The proposal, unmitigated, also could result in the deterioration or loss of salt marsh at the mouth of the River caused by increased sedimentation at the new southern abutment. These losses, while not negligible, may be offset to some extent by Appellant's Mitigation Plan, although no net gain in habitat values is anticipated. Appellant's Mitigation Plan does not directly address the potential adverse effect on adjacent wetlands of constructing the new southern abutment 160 feet into the existing River channel, but I find, based in part on Appellant's expert testimony in the record before the Commission, that the risk of significant erosion occurring is speculative and likely to be offset by the construction of the new northern abutment and excavation of a pilot channel under the bridge, which will tend to force the River to meander in a more northerly direction.

I have previously found that the national interest in safe and efficient rail transportation, including the transportation of materials to VAFB, will be served by reconstruction of the Santa Ynez River Bridge. When I weigh the loss of known but small quantities of mudflat and saltmarsh habitat, which may be offset by some extent by Appellant's Mitigation Plan, and the theoretical but low risk of additional loss of unknown quantities of saltmarsh habitat against its contribution to the national interest in safe rail transportation, I find that Appellant's proposal, as mitigated by Appellant's Mitigation Plan, will not cause adverse effects on the resources of the coastal zone substantial enough to outweigh its contribution to the national interest.

Third Element

To satisfy the third element of Ground I, I must find that: The activity will not violate any requirements of the Clean Air Act, as amended, or the Federal Water Pollution Control Act, as amended. . . .

* * *

The Clean Air Act

. . . The Commission has not objected to the air quality impacts of Appellant's project.

* * *

The Clean Water Act

Appellant's project will affect the water quality of the Santa Ynez River in two respects. During the construction period, as Appellant's Environmental Assessment acknowledges, water quality at the River mouth would be temporarily degraded by increased turbidity from fill and excavation activities within and adjacent to the lagoon, including the construction of the temporary access berms, excavation of the San Francisco embankment, and construction of the Los Angeles embankment. . . . The Commission has not objected to these temporary water quality impacts nor would they require a National Pollution Discharge Elimination System permit under the Clean Water Act. . . .

Appellant's project also entails the dredging and placement of filled materials in the Santa Ynez River. This activity requires a permit under both Section 10 of the Rivers and Harbors Act and Section 404 of the Clean Water Act (CWA). . . . The COE is the permitting agency for these permits and, pending my decision in this appeal, cannot issue them. If I decide this appeal in Appellant's favor, the COE can continue to process Appellant's application for these permits and decide whether to issue them. The COE cannot issue the Section 404 permit to Appellant if the activity were to violate the requirements of Section 404 of the CWA and the guidelines promulgated by the Administrator of EPA under Section 404(b)(1) of the CWA. Accordingly, I conclude that Appellant's proposed activity will not violate the CWA.

Fourth Element

To satisfy the fourth element of Ground I, I must find that: There is no reasonable alternative available (e.g., location[,] design, etc.) which would permit the activity to be conducted in a manner consistent with the [State coastal zone] management program. . . .

The Commission found that if Appellant's project were redesigned to retain the Los Angeles embankment at its existing location and to eliminate all channelization, the project would be consistent with the CCMP. . . . The Commission cites as advantages of its alternative: diminished interference with hydrological processes; lower flow velocities, resulting in lowering of risks to the bridge and affected habitat areas; less adverse effect of sedimentation on the wetlands; and less scouring and less erosion along the south embankment. . . .

The Commission also initially found that, for the project to be consistent with the CCMP, circulation improvements on the north bank would have to be included to mitigate channel changes . . . , but has not enumerated what improvements are required and, in its brief in this appeal, has stated that the Commission has no objection to the excavation on the north embankment. . . . Therefore, I find that there is no reasonable alternative for that part of Appellant's project which affects and circulation of the River at the northern embankment.

Appellant opposes the Commission's recommended alternative of extending the Los Angeles embankment (which would require adding an additional 160 feet to the bridge Span) because it would add approximately $750,000 to the project's construction costs and $20,000 per annum in additional maintenance costs, rendering the project economically infeasible and producing, according to Appellant, no demonstrated environmental benefit. . . . Appellant also states that a longer bridge would require a longer construction period, and could not be safely completed during the construction window allowed by other regulatory agencies (after Labor Day and before March 31) without the risk of a project washout due to high river flows during late winter. . . .

As I have stated in earlier appeals, regulations at 15 C.F.R. 930.121(d) indicate that an alternative to an objected-to activity may require major changes in the "location" or "design" of the project. Whether an alternative will be considered "reasonable" depends upon its feasibility and upon balancing the estimated increased costs of the alternative against its advantages. . . .

In addressing first whether the longer bridge alternative is feasible, some question exists whether the Commission's preferred alternative can be completed during the 7-month construction window allowed by wildlife agencies (September through March). Appellant has indicated that construction of the longer bridge will take an additional five to six weeks, thereby extending the construction period to the end of March, when floods are more likely to occur. . . . Appellant's Environmental Assessment indicates that the schedule for construction of a longer bridge would not differ substantially from the schedule for the Appellant's proposed project. . . . Therefore, I find that while the risk of winter flooding may increase as a result of constructing a longer bridge, it is feasible to complete construction during the seven-month window allowed by wildlife agencies. Further, I find based on the Administrative Record that Appellant has the financial resources or access to the financial resources to pay the $750,000 additional construction costs associated with the longer bridge and the annual increased maintenance cost of $20,000. Thus, I find that the longer bridge alternative is feasible and available to Appellant.

Next, I must balance the costs of the Commission's preferred alternative against its advantages. To perform this weighing I must consider, first, how much less adverse the alternative would be to the land and water resources of the coastal out and, second, the increased costs to Appellant of carrying out the rehabilitation project in a manner fully consistent with the CCMP.

The Commission's reasons for preferring the longer bridge were restated above. Appellant agrees that a wider span than it proposes to build would allow the River to meander more, but disputes that there is any value to this "benefit." . . . Although the record in this regard is not well documented to the parties, I find that implementing the Commission's preferred alternative, *i.e.*, leaving the southern abutment in situ, does have the advantage of decreasing sedimentation at the southern end and therefore reduces the risk of damage to the adjacent salt marsh. But, given my previous findings, that the risk of increased sedimentation may be offset to some extent by Appellant's Mitigation Plan and further that moving the northern embankment and excavating a pilot channel is likely to offset the risk of additional erosion and sedimentation at the southern embankment, I find that the Commission has not proven that its preferred alternative will have measurably less adverse effects on the land and water resources of the coastal zone.

***

Weighing the potential advantages of a longer bridge against the additional costs to be incurred in its construction, I find that the Commission's preferred alternative is not a reasonable alternative to Appellant's proposed rehabilitation of the Santa Ynez River bridge.

***

In summary, leaving aside the issue of beach access, I find that construction of a longer bridge or repairing the existing structure are feasible alternatives to Appellant's proposal, but that they are not reasonable alternatives in light of, in the case of the longer span, its additional costs when measured against its speculative advantages and, in the case of the repair work, its disadvantages over a permanent rehabilitation. Therefore, I find, based on the Administrative Record, that there is no reasonable alternative available to Appellant which would permit the reconstruction of the Santa Ynez River bridge to be conducted in a manner consistent with the CCMP.

The Commission also recommended that Appellant adopt certain mitigation measures necessary to offset the closure of Ocean Beach Park during the construction period, including adequate signing and access to the Southern Pacific Switchyard. . . . As noted above, Appellant has already agreed to these measures. Therefore, I find that there is no reasonable alternative to Appellant's proposed activity involving the temporary closure of beach access at Ocean Beach Park.

Conclusion for Ground I

On the basis of the findings I have made above, I find further that Appellant has satisfied the four elements of Ground I, and, therefore, that Appellant's proposed project, although presumptively inconsistent with the CCMP, is nevertheless consistent with the objective of the CZMA.

Conclusion

Because I have found that Appellant has satisfied the first of the two grounds set forth in the CZMA for allowing the objected-to activity to proceed notwithstanding an objection by the Commission, it is not necessary to address the second ground of "necessary in the interest of national security." The Appellant's project, including all of the elements of its proposed Mitigation Plan, may be permitted by federal agencies.

points for discussion

1. *The four "consistency objection override" elements.* Which of the four elements weighed in determining whether to overturn a consistency objection would seem to be most critical to the outcome? Why?
2. *The second element.* Applying the second element requires three steps. The first is an assessment of the extent to which the proposed activity will have an adverse effect on natural resources of the coastal zone. How should these be measured? Does the language of the regulations allow for a net assessment of impacts? For example, should the *Crosby* project's enhancement of wildlife habitat be subtracted from its negative impact on the undisturbed wetlands? Why did the Secretary take this approach in *Southern Pacific*, but not *Crosby*? Working through the second step seems similarly difficult: How should one measure "contribution to the national interest"? Given the imprecision in the first two steps, rationally applying the third, that is, deciding whether adverse impacts or national benefit is greater, seems impossible. Did the Secretary of Commerce make rational decisions?

2. Federal Activity

As noted, the CZMA provides for a different process when the proposed activity or project is to be carried out directly by a federal agency. What qualifies as a federal activity or project? How exactly is the consistency process different? How might the different process affect the outcome, that is, whether or not the project goes forward?

California Coastal Commission v. Department of the Navy

5 F. Supp. 2d 1106 (S.D. Cal. 1998)

Judge Jeffrey T. MILLER delivered the opinion of the United States District Court for the Southern District of California.

Order for a Conditional Preliminary Injunction

Plaintiff California Coastal Commission seeks a preliminary injunction against defendants United States of America, Department of the Navy, and Secretary of the Navy enjoining the disposal of dredged material from the San Diego Bay previously designated for coastal beach

Photo: U.S. Naval Historical Center

Figure 9-16. San Diego Bay, 1938

replenishment. This dredging of the bay is part of a Homeporting project by which the Navy will base a Nimitz class aircraft carrier. Defendants oppose the motion for a preliminary injunction. After careful consideration of all the pleadings, parties' arguments and applicable law, the court rules as follows:

Background

This case deals with the fundamental federal policy of conforming a federal coastal project to meet the dictates, to "the maximum extent possible," of state coastal management plans. This federal policy is codified in federal legislation known as the Coastal Zone Management Act (CZMA), 16 U.S.C. §§ 1451, 1456(c)(1).

Plaintiff California Coastal Commission (Commission) is the state agency responsible for review of federal agency projects for consistency with the federally approved California Coastal Management Program (CMP). The Commission reviewed and approved the Homeporting project of defendants United States of America, Department of the Navy, and Secretary of the Navy (collectively, the

Navy) which included the dredging of portions of the San Diego Bay and the use of dredged sandy material for beach replenishment along certain San Diego coastal communities.[1] In 1995, the Navy submitted Consistency Determination (CD) 95-95 which discussed the specifics of the dredging and disposal of the sandy material. Specifically, CD 95-95 called for the deposit of approximately 7.9 million cubic yards of material to Imperial Beach, Mission Beach, Del Mar and Oceanside to replenish areas affected by erosion. Additionally, 2 million cubic yards of other material not suitable for replenishment was to be disposed of in the ocean itself at site LA-5 approximately 4.5 miles off the coast of Point Loma. The remaining material, unsuitable for ocean disposal, would be confined to a new wharf structure at NASNI [Naval Air Station North Island].

On November 16, 1995 the Commission concurred with CD 95-95 and the Navy commenced its dredging project in September, 1997. Shortly thereafter, live ordnance and munitions were discovered in the dredged material deposited on the beach.

In October, 1997 the Navy requested that the Commission concur with modifications to the project which would permit the disposal of 2.5 million cubic yards

> **New Developments**
>
> Obviously, this changes things! Does the CZMA require project proponents to resubmit consistency determinations in light of changed circumstances? Why did the Navy do so here?

of dredged material earlier designated for beach replenishment at the LA-5 site. The Navy contends it requested the modifications in order to continue dredging while a long term solution was found. According to the Navy, an interruption of the dredging would result in excessive dredging expenses and a possible delay in the Homeporting project. On October 17, 1997 the Navy submitted a new CD (CD-140-97) which proposed that all remaining sediment be dumped into the ocean at LA-5 and that some inner channel materials be used for beach replenishment. The Navy asserts that CD 140-97 called for the use of a 3-inch ordnance grate to screen out larger ordnance in the outer channel. The Navy recognized however, that it did not know the exact size of the ordnance in the outer channel and the possibility existed that some of the ordnance was too small to be sifted through the grate. Thus, the Navy could not guarantee that all ordnance would be removed through its grating system proposed in CD 140-97. According to the Commission, CD 140-97 also discussed a second alternative whereby a 3/8 inch screen on the beach would be coupled with the 3 inch screen on the dredge to eliminate the public health risks from the ordnance. CD 140-97 indicated the second alternative would be more costly and time consuming than the first.

In late October, 1997 the Navy commissioned a consulting firm to examine available sand screening technologies and prepare a report of findings (Harris

1. The Navy's Homeporting project was undertaken to establish a home port for a Nimitz class aircraft carrier at Naval Air Station, North Island (NASNI) by August, 1998. In order to permit the unrestricted passage of the carrier in and out of the bay under any and all tide and load conditions approximately 9,000,000 cubic yards of sand must be removed from the bay through dredging.

Report). A preliminary report was submitted to the Navy in November, 1997. This report however, was not provided to the Commission until December 23, 1997. According to the Commission, this draft report outlines a number of alternatives to disposing of the dredged material at LA-5 which the Commission believes should be explored more fully by the parties for a possible solution to the problem posed by the ordnance.

In November, 1997 the Commission held a public hearing to discuss CD 140-97. During the hearing the Navy again modified the project to limit the disposal of materials at LA-5 to 500,000 cubic yards. The Commission objected to CD 140-97 stating that the amended project was not consistent with the requirement of the Coastal Zone Management Act (CZMA) that a project conform to a state coastal management plan to the maximum extent possible, that alternatives were available which would permit the Navy to complete the dredging as originally planned, and that the Navy had failed to document the cost of alternatives.

On November 13, 1997 the Navy submitted a further modified CD (CD 161-97) for Commission concurrence. CD 161-97 proposed disposal of up to 883,000 cubic yards of material at the LA-5 site for 30 days. The Navy also updated the potential costs involved in the delay of dredging activities. Finally, the Navy proposed further negotiations with the Commission to resolve the Commission's objections to CD 140-97 and explore reasonable alternatives to the disposal at LA-5. A public hearing was scheduled for December 11, 1997 regarding CD 161-97, but the proposal was withdrawn from Commission consideration by the Navy.

On November 19, 1997 the Navy sought and received a permit modification from the U.S. Army Corps of Engineers (Corps) which authorized the Navy to dispose of the remaining materials at LA-5. This modification was issued pursuant to § 404 of the Clean Water Act . . . which gives the Corps authority to regulate the Navy's dredging and disposal operations for the project. The Corps approved this modification without Commission concurrence which the Navy contends thereby became unnecessary.

On November 19, 1997 the Navy sent a letter to the Commission indicating that the Navy intended to continue dredging and disposal of previously designated beach replenishment at the LA-5 site without the Commission's concurrence. The Navy also indicated that it planned to "fully investigate beach nourishment options for placement of sand from the Homeporting project in coordination with the California Coastal Commission."

The Commission now moves for a preliminary injunction enjoining the Navy from further dredging and disposal of beach replenishment until the alternatives outlined in the Harris Report, CD 161-97 and other reports generated by the Commission are explored. The Commission submits the Navy is in violation of the CZMA as it has not demonstrated that the disposal of all material at the LA-5 site is consistent to the maximum extent practicable with the state's CMP under the CZMA. Further the Commission argues that the Navy has never demonstrated, as required by state and federal law, that alternatives to ocean dumping or other mitigation measures are unfeasible or impracticable. The Commission believes that injunctive relief is appropriate as the public will suffer irreparable injury from the continued dredging and disposal of beach replenishment which would otherwise be irretrievably lost. The Commission submits it is likely to ultimately succeed on the merits of its claim.

The Navy opposes the motion stating that the provisions of the CMP are not applicable as the ordnance-laden material is not suitable for beach replenishment, that consistency with the CMP does not require the Navy to violate other applicable federal or state laws (in this case § 404 of the CWA) and that the discovery of ordnance was an unforeseeable event which, under the CZMA, allows the Navy to deviate from the CMP. Additionally, the Navy argues that a preliminary injunction would impose a great hardship on the Navy and that the Commission has failed to establish the likelihood of success or that the balance of hardships tips in its favor.

Discussion

Requirements Under the CZMA and California Coastal Act

Federal agencies seeking to engage in project activity in a coastal zone must comply with the requirements of the CZMA. 16 U.S.C. § 1456(c)(1), (2). Section 307(c)(1)(A) of the CZMA states, in pertinent part:

> Each federal agency activity within or outside the coastal zone that affects any land or water use or natural resource of the coastal zone shall be carried out in a manner which is consistent to the maximum extent practicable with the enforceable policies of approved state management programs.

A federal agency is required to submit a "consistency determination" (as previously discussed "CD") to the state no later than 90 days before the proposed activity indicating that the federal activity would likely affect the coastal zone. 15 C.F.R. § 930.34.

The California Coastal Act (CCA) addresses the federal activity in this case. Under § 30233(a) of the CCA:

> the diking, filing, or dredging of open coastal waters . . . shall be permitted where there is no feasible less environmentally damaging alternative, and where feasible mitigation measures have been provided to minimize adverse environmental effects.

Section 30233(b) of the CCA further provides that:

> dredging and spoils disposal shall be planned and carried out to avoid significant disruption to marine and wildlife habitats and water circulation. Dredge spoils suitable for beach replenishment should be transported for such purposes to appropriate beaches or into suitable longshore current systems.

There is no private right of action under the CZMA itself. . . . Judicial review of a federal agency action under the CZMA is obtained through the Administrative Procedure Act (APA). 5 U.S.C. §§ 701-706. However, in a case such as this where Congress has provided in the CZMA more than one method in achieving the Act's purpose of protecting the nation's coastal zones, the principles of equitable discretion should be applied. . . .

Injunctive Relief

The threshold issue in the analysis of whether the Commission should be afforded equitable injunctive relief is what is the standard this court should employ for judicial review. The Navy urges this court to apply a deferential standard by which the Navy's determination to dump dredged material previous[ly] designated for beach replenishment must be upheld unless it was "arbitrary, capricious, an abuse of discretion, or otherwise not in accordance with the law." 5 U.S.C. § 706(2)(A). The Navy argues application of this narrow standard must result in affirmance of its action under the following rationale. The Navy, in effect, has the exclusive right to determine whether the sediments in question are "suitable for beach replenishment," the sediments as they exist in their pre-dredge state are not suitable for beach replenishment purposes, within the meaning of Cal. Pub. Res. Code § 30233, because of the presence of ordnance and munitions, and, therefore, disposal of these materials into deep ocean water complies with the CZMA and CCA. The Navy then concludes that because there is sufficient evidence (existence of ordnance and munitions) to support its conclusion, this court must defer.

Initially, as mentioned above, the deferential standard of review should not apply in this case. The Ninth Circuit has recognized that traditional equitable discretion should be applied in determining whether the Navy has complied with the requirement of the CZMA that a homeporting project conform to the relevant state coastal management plan. *See Friends of the Earth v. U.S. Navy*, 841 F.2d 927 (9th Cir. 1988). The CZMA was enacted by Congress to clearly encourage the wise use of coastal resources through adoption of state coastal plans. . . . Traditional judicial review subserves that stated legislative intent.

Moreover, even if the Navy was correct in its urging this court to apply a deferential standard, this court must still determine whether, on this record, the Navy's action has been in accordance with the law. Even by that standard, the focus becomes whether the CZMA and the CCA have been followed, not whether, as the Navy argues, it is obligated to follow the modified § 404 permit issued by the Corps. That permit, which is not existing federal law itself, was sought and obtained by the Navy upon the very same submission which must now be scrutinized by this court.

The next question which must be addressed in this analysis is, what *precisely* is the Commission seeking by way of a preliminary injunction. After careful consideration of the pleadings and oral arguments of the Commission, it appears the Commission seeks an order preventing the Navy from offshore dumping of dredged materials, previously designated for beach replenishment, until the Commission has a reasonable opportunity to consider the feasibility of alternatives which have been previously tendered by the Navy, including those in the Harris Report commissioned by the Navy. Further, the Commission, in oral argument, suggested the feasibility of alternatives can be explored in connection with a March, 1998 Commission hearing. For the reasons set forth below, this seems to be a reasonable request by the Commission.

Preliminary injunctive relief is available if the party meets one of two tests: (1) a combination of probable success and the possibility of irreparable harm, or (2) the party raises serious questions and the balance of hardship tips in its favor. *Arcamuzi v. Continental Air Lines, Inc.*, 819 F.2d 935, 937 (9th Cir. 1987). "These two formulations represent two points on a sliding scale in which the required degree of irreparable harm increases as the probability of success decreases." *Id.* Under both formulations, however, the party must demonstrate a "fair chance of success on the merits" and a "significant threat of irreparable injury." *Id.*

Likelihood of Success on the Merits

The Commission argues that the Navy cannot show, as required under the CCA, that no less environmentally damaging alternative exists or that feasible mitigation measures have been provided to minimize adverse environmental effects. Specifically, the Navy has submitted only CD 140-97 for consideration, has withdrawn CD 161-97, and has never submitted other analyses, including the Harris Report. Thus, the Navy's position that no feasible alternative exists other than to waste a valuable resource is predicated upon an incomplete factual record and unilateral determinations made by the Navy without the benefit of Commission input. On this record, the Navy has not shown that the dredging and disposal is consistent to the maximum extent practicable with the enforceable policies of approved state management programs in violation of the CZMA.

The Navy's position that it considered a reasonable range of alternatives as required under § 30233(a) of the CCA which it addressed in CD 140-97 and CD 161-97 simply does not answer the question. The Navy acknowledges in its pleadings and oral argument it "remains willing to negotiated reasonable solution" to offshore dumping. This position presupposes there may indeed be a feasible alternative to wasting this valuable beach replenishment resource. Until pending alternatives have at least been considered by both parties, it is illogical to conclude that offshore dumping is consistent with the CCA to the maximum extent possible. Finally, this portion of the analysis does not depend on whether the discovery of ordnance was an unforeseen event which warrants deviation from the CCA. As long as a reasonable alternative to dumping may be found with further expeditious study by the parties this factor is not material.

The Navy's contention that it has submitted feasible, less environmentally damaging alternatives, and has provided certain measures to mitigate the adverse environmental effects all in compliance with the CCA and CZMA, is not borne out by the record. Specifically, the Navy's alternatives are contained in CD 161-97 and other analyses which have either been withdrawn from consideration by the Navy or never submitted in final form to the Commission. The Navy cannot meritoriously argue that these alternatives contained in the CD 161-97 or the subsequent analyses are properly before the Commission at this time and therefore in compliance with the CCA or CZMA. Therefore, as the Navy has failed to demonstrate that it has complied with the requirements of the CZMA and CCA and has failed to allege an acceptable exemption from these requirements, the court finds that on the present record the Commission would likely succeed on the merits of its case against the Navy for disposing of beach replenishment materials off the coast of California in a manner inconsistent with the federal and state law.

Irreparable Harm and the Balancing of Hardships

Each side argues it will suffer irreparable harm if it does not prevail on the question of a preliminary injunction, and each argues the balancing of hardships tips in its favor. In this part of the analysis, the court should quickly dispose of the doomsday arguments made by both sides. The Commission argues if it does not obtain a preliminary injunction, beach replenishment materials will be forever lost resulting in beach users being swept into the sea while traversing narrow beaches. The Navy argues that a preliminary injunction may 1) imperil national security in the event the U.S.S. Stennis is delayed from its berth until high tide to maneuver, or 2) result in loss of or injury to seaman [sic] who must complete loading of the U.S.S. Stennis while underway in the open ocean during a military crisis. These considerations are far too speculative to consider. Moreover, prudent use of area beaches should not result in loss of life irrespective of beach depth, while Nimitz class carriers have negotiated safely the existing channels and berthings of San Diego Bay, and have been routinely refueled and resupplied at sea while underway.

Legitimate considerations of irreparable harm and hardship balance in favor of the Commission. One or more viable alternatives to ocean dumping of a valuable natural resource may presently exist and be quickly identified through further expeditious study and good faith negotiation by the parties. A reasonable additional period of time should be afforded for that contingency. Any offshore dumping of this resource during this period of study represents an irretrievable loss which such study and negotiation could prove to be an unnecessary and costly waste.

Any excess dredging fees to be paid by the Navy, as well as any short-term delay in the completion of dredging operations for this homeporting project are more than counterbalanced by the need to allow an additional period of expedited study and negotiation by the parties during which offshore dumping operations cease. Thus, a preliminary injunction is granted enjoining the Navy from disposing at LA-5 or any other offshore dumping site dredging material previously designated for beach replenishment purposes. This preliminary injunction is conditioned upon the Commission's expeditious study of proposed alternatives to offshore dumping, including those set forth in the Harris Report, and the good faith of the parties to negotiate a resolution which is the stated goal of both sides. The court reserves jurisdiction to modify or dissolve this preliminary injunction upon shortened notice.

points for discussion

1. *The* California Coastal Commission *case.* The Navy's proposed homeporting operation consisted of two phases: dredging the channel and disposing of the dredged material. The Commission objects only to the Navy's finding regarding the second phase of the operation. Can you imagine a reason why the first phase might also be inconsistent with a state policy? If so, why would the state be reluctant to object to it?

2. *Offshore energy and consistency.* As we saw in *Crosby* and *Southern Pacific*, the CZMA requires an "applicant for a required Federal license or permit" to submit a consistency certification to the state. 16 U.S.C. § 1456(a)(3)(A). Section 1456(3)(B) creates a special certification procedure for parties who submit plans to the Secretary of Interior for "the exploration or development of, or production from" areas leased under the Outer Continental Shelf Lands Act. This section is an odd hybrid: It gives states the opportunity to judge consistency, but it also allows the Secretary to make a finding that the proposed plan is consistent with the federal CZMA. When the Secretary of Interior is taking steps other than processing exploration, development, or production plans, her actions may require "agency self-certification" under Section 1456(a)(1). *See California v. Norton*, 311 F.3d 1162 (9th Cir. 2002) (state challenges Department of Interior decision to extend the lives of existing oil and gas leases in federal waters off California's coast).

D. NON-POINT SOURCE WATER POLLUTION CONTROL

In the 1990 amendments to the CZMA, known as the Coastal Zone Act Reauthorization Amendments (CZARA), Congress added Section 1455b, "Protecting Coastal Waters." (This provision is also frequently referred to as "Section 6217," in reference to its section number in the CZARA.) Pursuant to this provision, Congress required coastal states to develop plans for improving water quality within their coastal zones by reducing pollution from non-point sources. Non-point source water pollution most often takes the form of run-off from land, although it can also originate in air pollution that ultimately settles directly in the water. Pollutants in land-based run-off are generated by a variety of activities, such as agriculture, forestry, and urban and suburban land use. These pollutants include not only man-made chemicals, such as pesticides, but also sediments and other organic materials.

Subsections 1455b(a) and (b) mandate that states develop non-point plans within a certain time-frame and containing measures meant to address the full range of non-point sources:

Coastal Zone Management Act

16 U.S.C. § 1455b

(a) In general.

(1) Program development. Not later than 30 months after the date of the publication of [a final guidance document produced by the U.S. Environmental Protection Agency ("EPA Guidance Document")], each State for which a management program has been approved pursuant to section 306 of the Coastal Zone Management Act of 1972 . . . shall prepare

and submit to the Secretary and the Administrator a Coastal Nonpoint Pollution Control Program for approval pursuant to this section. The purpose of the program shall be to develop and implement management measures for nonpoint source pollution to restore and protect coastal waters, working in close conjunction with other State and local authorities.

(2) Program coordination. A State program under this section shall be coordinated closely with State and local water quality plans and programs developed pursuant to [the Clean Water Act] and with State plans developed pursuant to the Coastal Zone Management Act. . . . The program shall serve as an update and expansion of the State nonpoint source management program developed under [the Clean Water Act], as the program under that section relates to land and water uses affecting coastal waters.

(b) Program contents. Each State program under this section shall provide for the implementation, at a minimum, of management measures in conformity with the [EPA Guidance Document], to protect coastal waters generally, and shall also contain the following:

(1) Identifying land uses. The identification of, and a continuing process for identifying, land uses which, individually or cumulatively, may cause or contribute significantly to a degradation of—

(A) those coastal waters where there is a failure to attain or maintain applicable water quality standards or protect designated uses, as determined by the State pursuant to its water quality planning processes; or

(B) those coastal waters that are threatened by reasonably foreseeable increases in pollution loadings from new or expanding sources.

(2) Identifying critical coastal areas. The identification of, and a continuing process for identifying, critical coastal areas adjacent to coastal waters referred to in paragraph (1)(A) and (B), within which any new land uses or substantial expansion of existing land uses shall be subject to management measures in addition to those provided for in subsection (g).

(3) Management measures. The implementation and continuing revision from time to time of additional management measures applicable to the land uses and areas identified pursuant to paragraphs (1) and (2) that are necessary to achieve and maintain applicable water quality standards under [the Clean Water Act].

(4) Technical assistance. The provision of technical and other assistance to local governments and the public for implementing the measures referred to in paragraph (3), which may include assistance in developing ordinances and regulations, technical guidance, and modeling to predict and assess the effectiveness of such measures, training, financial incentives, demonstration projects, and other innovations to protect coastal water quality and designated uses.

(5) Public participation. Opportunities for public participation in all aspects of the program, including the use of public notices and opportunities for comment, nomination procedures, public hearings, technical and financial assistance, public education, and other means.

(6) Administrative coordination. The establishment of mechanisms to improve coordination among State agencies and between State and local officials responsible for land use programs and permitting, water quality permitting and enforcement, habitat protection, and public health and safety, through the use of joint project review, memoranda of agreement, or other mechanisms.

(7) State coastal zone boundary modification. A proposal to modify the boundaries of the State coastal zone as the coastal management agency of the State determines is necessary to implement the recommendations made pursuant to subsection (e). If the coastal management agency does not have the authority to modify such boundaries, the program shall include recommendations for such modifications to the appropriate State authority.

***

(g) Guidance for coastal nonpoint source pollution control.

(1) In general. The [EPA] Administrator, in consultation with the Secretary [of Commerce] and the Director of the United States Fish and Wildlife Service and other Federal agencies, shall publish (and periodically revise thereafter) guidance for specifying management measures for sources of nonpoint pollution in coastal waters.

(2) Content. Guidance under this subsection shall include, at a minimum —

(A) a description of a range of methods, measures, or practices, including structural and nonstructural controls and operation and maintenance procedures, that constitute each measure;

(B) a description of the categories and subcategories of activities and locations for which each measure may be suitable;

(C) an identification of the individual pollutants or categories or classes of pollutants that may be controlled by the measures and the water quality effects of the measures;

(D) quantitative estimates of the pollution reduction effects and costs of the measures;

(E) a description of the factors which should be taken into account in adapting the measures to specific sites or locations; and

(F) any necessary monitoring techniques to accompany the measures to assess over time the success of the measures in reducing pollution loads and improving water quality.

(3) Publication. The Administrator, in consultation with the Secretary, shall publish —

(A) proposed guidance pursuant to this subsection not later than 6 months after the date of the enactment of this Act [enacted Nov. 5, 1990]; and

(B) final guidance pursuant to this subsection not later than 18 months after such effective date.

(4) Notice and comment. The Administrator shall provide to coastal States and other interested persons an opportunity to provide written comments on proposed guidance under this subsection.

(5) Management measures. For purposes of this subsection, the term "management measures" means economically achievable measures for the control of the addition of pollutants from existing and new categories and classes of nonpoint sources of pollution, which reflect the greatest degree of pollutant reduction achievable through the application of the best available nonpoint pollution control practices, technologies, processes, siting criteria, operating methods, or other alternatives.

***

The following article assesses the success and future prospects of Section 1455b, also known as Section 6217.

Andrew Solomon, Comment: Section 6217 of the Coastal Zone Act Reauthorization Amendments of 1990: Is There Any Point?

31 Envtl. L. 152 (2001)

While the Clean Water Act (CWA) has achieved some measure of success at controlling point sources of pollution, it contains only weak provisions specifically designed to control nonpoint sources of pollution. This means that the CWA does not address significant sources of pollution, thereby allowing a large amount of pollution to be discharged unchecked into the nation's waterways. Nonpoint source pollution of coastal waters results in serious problems affecting both coastal ecosystems and local economies. In 1995, 3.5 billion acres of shellfish beds were closed to harvesting. According to the National Oceanic and Atmospheric Administration (NOAA), nonpoint source pollution caused eighty-five percent of these closures. Recent outbreaks of the dinoflagellate *Pfiesteria piscicida*, responsible for recent fish kills and detrimental effects to human health on the East Coast, are linked to increased nutrient loading from nonpoint source pollution. . . .

. . . [I]n recognition of serious coastal water quality problems, Congress enacted section 6217 as part of the Coastal Zone Reauthorization Amendments of 1990 (CZARA). The goal was to "strengthen the links between Federal and State coastal zone management and water quality programs and to enhance State and local efforts to manage land use activities which degrade coastal waters and coastal habitats." . . . Despite high expectations for the program, implementation of section 6217 has been very slow. At the time of this writing, the Environmental Protection Agency (EPA) and NOAA have given final approval to the coastal nonpoint programs of Maryland, Rhode Island, and California and are in the process of approving Puerto Rico's program. However, ten years after enactment of the statute, EPA and NOAA have yet to withhold a single dollar from any state.

The CZMA is currently due for reauthorization; in 1999 three bills were pending before Congress to reauthorize the statute. . . .

When Congress reauthorized and amended the CZMA as part of the Omnibus Budget Reconciliation Act of 1990, it perceived that the CZMA's goal of "control[ling] land use activities which have a direct and significant impact on the coastal waters" had not been achieved. To meet this goal more effectively, Congress created the section 6217 program.

Section 6217 has several purposes. Congress intended that the program enhance state and federal coordination, promote coordination between state coastal zone management programs and state water quality programs, and enhance state and local land use management efforts aimed at protecting coastal water quality. The coordination aspect of the program was critical to Congress. Congress did not intend to dictate the roles of the state coastal management program or the state water quality agency; however, it did intend that they would have a dual and coequal role in the implementation of section 6217. Congress wanted to encourage coordination between state coastal management programs and state water quality agencies because many states had established their coastal management programs under completely different agencies than their water quality agencies. For instance, Wisconsin's coastal management program is located in the State Department of Administration, the Governor's arm of state government, but the Department of Natural Resources contains the state's water quality program. Congress found a similar division in authority between NOAA and EPA. Congress was concerned about this separation not only because scientific expertise is more likely to reside in the water quality agencies, but also because it wanted to avoid redundant efforts. Congress designed section 6217 to complement the Clean Water Act's nonpoint source provisions, rather than to be duplicative or act as a surrogate to those provisions. Congress felt that by enlisting the land use capabilities of coastal management programs in conjunction with the powers of the water quality agencies, the creation of section 6217 would "advance the national goal of protecting our coastal resources."

To achieve the purposes of section 6217, Congress required that every state with an approved coastal management program develop and submit a Coastal Nonpoint Pollution Control Program (CNPCP) to NOAA and EPA for review. Congress further required that the program submittal provide for implementation of EPA-developed management measures. To that end, the states were to identify enforceable policies and mechanisms that would allow them to implement the management measures.

In 1993, NOAA and EPA jointly issued the Coastal Nonpoint Pollution Control Program Development and Approval Guidance (Program Guidance) to assist states in the development of program submittals. NOAA and EPA designed the Program Guidance to clarify the statutory requirements of the CZMA. The statute requires a state to make revisions to the coastal zone boundary that are "necessary to control the land and water uses that have a significant impact on coastal waters of the state." NOAA and EPA were to review the coastal zone boundary and then provide recommendations to the state regarding boundary modifications. The Program Guidance provided that NOAA and EPA would expect the state to incorporate the recommendation into its program submittal unless the state could demonstrate that a different boundary was warranted. Given NOAA and EPA's power to approve program submittals, these recommendations effectively resulted in a requirement for boundary modification, unless the state could demonstrate that the agencies were wrong.

As specified in the CZMA, EPA issued its Guidance Specifying Management Measures for Sources of Nonpoint Source Pollution in Coastal Waters (Management Measures Guidance) in 1993. The statute defined management measures as

> economically achievable measures for the control of the addition of pollutants from existing and new categories and classes of nonpoint sources of pollution, which reflect the greatest degree of pollutant reduction achievable through the application of the best available non-point pollution control practices. . . .

Congress selected this technology-based approach over a water-quality-based approach because it was concerned about the difficulty of establishing a causal relationship between land use practices and water quality. According to the statute, the Management Measures Guidance must contain the management measures, identify activities for which the measures were appropriate, determine which pollutants the measures would control, evaluate the pollution reduction of each measure, estimate the cost of each measure, describe considerations for adapting each measure to specific sites, and develop monitoring techniques necessary to determine the success of the measures. Congress wanted the Management Measures Guidance to be flexible so the states could adopt the measures that would best fit the local conditions and adapt them to their needs.

The Management Measures Guidance identifies six categories of land use activities that could contribute to nonpoint source pollution: agriculture, forestry, urbanization, marinas and recreational boating, hydromodification, and wetland and riparian area protection and restoration. Within these categories, the Management Measures Guidance identifies a number of subcategories of activities and associated management measures. The Program Guidance requires that each state program submittal identifies how it would implement management measures to address each subcategory identified in the Management Measures Guidance. The state could get an exemption from a subcategory if it could demonstrate that the subcategory or category was not present and was not anticipated to be present within the state's coastal zone. The state could also get an exemption if it could demonstrate that the category or subcategory "[did] not and [was] not reasonably expected to, individually or cumulatively, present significant adverse effects to living coastal resources or human health."

To have an approved program, a state must commit to implementing the management measures regardless of the quality of their coastal waters. Congress intentionally established the program this way because of the perceived failures of the nonpoint provisions of the Clean Water Act, which require that states identify waters where water quality standards could not be met because of nonpoint sources of pollution. Congress felt that a water-quality-based system like the one in the Clean Water Act would require the expenditure of too much money. Moreover, it felt that the money could be better spent on implementing management measures.

***

Under section 6217, failure to submit an approvable program by certain dates subjected states to a loss of federal funds. If a state did not submit an approvable program by 1996, NOAA was required to reduce the state's administrative grants under section 306 by ten percent. The amount withheld increased each subsequent year up to a maximum reduction of thirty percent. In addition to a reduction of section 306 funds, the statute also provided for an equivalent percentage reduction of funds awarded under section 319 of the Clean Water Act. EPA and NOAA were to make the withheld funds available to states with approved CNPCPs.

Although the Coastal Zone Act Reauthorization Amendments of 1990 set out a fairly clear process for implementation of section 6217, NOAA, EPA, and the states have not adhered to that process. Almost from the date Congress enacted the statute, states have pushed to alter its implementation. In response to pressure from the states, NOAA and EPA have changed the implementation of section 6217 from the requirements set out in the statute and in the Program Guidance.

The states resented section 6217 because they viewed it as an unfunded mandate. This is an absurd view because participation in coastal management is voluntary, not mandatory. However, the states did have a legitimate concern. In section 6217, Congress only provided funding for development of CNPCPs. It did not provide funding to the states for implementation of the CNPCPs nor did it provide funding to offset the costs of compliance with the management measures. In 1993, Congress only budgeted $1.8 million for development of CNPCPs, but the estimated yearly cost of compliance with the section 6217 management measures was between $390 and $590 million.

During the 1994 congressional hearings regarding the reauthorization of the Coastal Zone Management Act, representatives of coastal states lobbied for relief from the requirements of section 6217. They argued that the timetable established in the statute was impossible to meet, there was no federal funding to support implementation of the management measures, the program provided a disincentive to participate in the coastal management program for states not already participating, and the program in general was too inflexible. They recommended that the program be altered to 1) increase the length of time for development of programs, 2) allow for more state flexibility in development of management

> **Quick Questions**
>
> Why do states participate in the CZMA program to begin with? Do you think that the federal funding covers state implementation costs? How much is the consistency power worth? If it was worth enough to keep states in the CZMA fold, do threats in light of the prospective costs of implementing Section 6217 reveal anything about the value of the consistency power?

measures, 3) permit voluntary measures to be included, and 4) eliminate the funding reduction for failure to submit an approvable program or create a conditional approval process that would not result in the reduction of funding as long as a state was making reasonable progress. Even certain environmental organizations agreed with some of the states' concerns, supporting the states' requests for additional funding, changes in the timeframe for program submittal, and creation of incentives for state participation. However, the environmental organizations opposed the states' proposal to use voluntary measures; they were adamant that Congress maintain the federal funding reduction provisions. None of these suggestions were ultimately enacted in the Coastal Zone Protection Act of 1996, which reauthorized the Coastal Zone Management Act. The law made only a few minor changes to the CNPCP.

***

Amid complaints by the Coastal States Organization and threats by states like Wisconsin to withdraw from the coastal management program because of section 6217, NOAA and EPA decided to retreat from the program approval standards in the Program Guidance. In March 1995, NOAA and EPA published a document entitled Flexibility for State Coastal Nonpoint Programs (Flexibility Guidance), which contained significant revisions to the Program Guidance. First, it expanded the scope of conditional approvals. The Flexibility Guidance provided that if a state submitted a conditionally approvable program by July 1995, then EPA and NOAA would not reduce the state's funding as long as it fulfilled all of the conditions within five years of conditional approval. The Flexibility Guidance deleted the Program Guidance requirement that the state be able to demonstrate its ability to ensure adoption of the necessary regulations or ordinances in order to obtain conditional approval.

The Flexibility Guidance also greatly expanded the timeframe for implementation of the management measures. The Program Guidance originally provided states three years after program approval to implement the management measures. The Flexibility Guidance extended the deadline to the year 2004 for implementation of the management measures and 2009 for full program implementation. This schedule was adjusted again in 1998 to provide that states had to establish five-year implementation plans and fifteen-year program strategies. EPA and NOAA anticipated full implementation to occur within fifteen years of program approval.

In 1998, EPA and NOAA issued the Final Administrative Changes to the Coastal Nonpoint Pollution Program Guidance (Final Administrative Changes). This document essentially finalized the Flexibility Guidance. Importantly, the Final Administrative Changes clarified the voluntary measure approval standards initially established in the Flexibility Guidance. The Final Administrative Changes established that NOAA and EPA would approve voluntary or incentive-based measures when those measures are backed by existing state enforcement authorities. However, the state must provide a legal opinion that proves both that the state has back-up authority to enforce the management measures and that it commits to using those enforcement authorities where necessary. This appears to be a stricter requirement than the one in the Flexibility Guidance. The Flexibility Guidance only required states to provide an explanation of how they proposed to use existing state authorities as a backup to the voluntary program.

***

Although the Flexibility Guidance deadline for program submittal was July 1995, all twenty-nine states and territories with approved coastal management programs did not submit nonpoint source programs until July 1996. NOAA and EPA did not reduce the funding of any state that missed the deadline. Once states submitted programs, EPA and NOAA reviewed them for compliance with the requirements of section 6217. Between October 1997 and July 1998, all twenty-nine state and territorial coastal programs received conditional approval of their nonpoint programs. The majority of the submittals were deficient in almost every regard. Most of the state submittals did not provide for implementation of the management measures or identify enforceable authorities for their implementation. The conditions placed on the program submittals routinely required states to develop those mechanisms and authorities. In essence, these were not conditions but actually rejections of the state submittals because they merely required the states to submit an approvable program within three years, as defined in the statute. EPA and NOAA may have been willing to call these rejections "conditional approvals" because they were afraid the states would follow through on their threats to withdraw from the coastal management program.

Maryland and Rhode Island were the only states that came close to satisfying the Flexibility Guidance's weakened requirements. NOAA and EPA placed few conditions on those submittals, and by 1999 Maryland was able to satisfy all of the conditions to NOAA's and EPA's satisfaction. In October 1999, EPA and NOAA published a notice of intent to grant Maryland full approval of its Coastal Nonpoint Pollution Control Program. It had taken only nine years for a program to be approved — four years after the deadline set in section 6217.

***

States tried to avoid the program submittal requirements in several ways: 1) they attempted to alter the program boundary; 2) they tried to use purely voluntary measures; 3) they attempted to get exemptions from certain categories of management measures; 4) they failed to develop enforceable mechanisms of any kind; and 5) they proposed the use of management measures that did not conform to the Management Measures Guidance. Many of the state submittals contained some aspects of all of these factors.

Perhaps the most obvious and frustrating way that states attempted to avoid the program requirements was by submitting programs with boundaries that did not comply with NOAA and EPA's recommended boundary modifications. For instance, Alabama tried to establish a very limited program boundary that included only "the waters . . . and adjacent shorelands lying seaward of the continuous 10 foot contour." NOAA and EPA had determined that Alabama's boundary should include the entire area of Alabama's two coastal counties. Given that NOAA and EPA were required to recommend revisions to the state's coastal management boundary prior to program submittal, Alabama cannot claim that it simply did not understand what its boundary should be. Similarly, Maine's submittal attempted to exclude areas from the coastal zone requirements. It proposed to include in its boundaries only "those land areas that drain to waters downstream of lakes that flush less than 50 times per year or drain to the 'major' rivers at or below specific locations listed by the state." Likewise, Oregon attempted to exclude areas of the Umpqua, Rogue, and Columbia basins from its CNPCP boundary. The boundary determination provision has been controversial since the passage of section 6217, and states have lobbied for more flexibility to set program boundaries. However, it is clear that unless a state can demonstrate that NOAA and EPA's boundary recommendation is incorrect, it must incorporate that recommendation into the CNPCP to gain approval. In light of this explicit requirement, the submittal of programs with boundaries other than the recommended boundaries demonstrates the states' unwillingness to comply with the statute.

Some states continue to insist on the use of solely voluntary measures to implement aspects of their programs. Louisiana proposed using education, technical assistance, and voluntary initiatives to implement aspects of the agricultural management measures. While Louisiana has identified back-up authority that might apply if the voluntary program does not work, it is not clear that these back-up authorities would effectively implement the management measures. Mississippi also proposed implementing its agricultural management measures through solely voluntary mechanisms. It identified back-up mechanisms for implementing management measures if the voluntary measures fail; however, it has not demonstrated how these back-up mechanisms would be used to ensure implementation of the management measures. The problem with allowing voluntary mechanisms is the difficulty in measuring their success. It is clearly unreasonable to expect that all states will voluntarily comply immediately. There must be a period of development. Therefore, it is difficult to determine whether the program has failed or if it just needs more time to develop. If a state waits too long, it will fail to address the nonpoint pollution problem. If the state resorts to the back-up mechanism too quickly, it is not really a voluntary program. To ensure an effective nonpoint program, NOAA and EPA should require states to use enforceable mechanisms as a first step, supported by voluntary and educational programs that can aid in developing new approaches to the nonpoint pollution problem and ensure that citizens understand and support the CNPCP.

Even when states did not rely solely on voluntary measures, their program submittals frequently did not contain enforceable mechanisms. For example, Oregon's program submittal proposed to implement its New Urban Development Management Measures through local governments; the submittal, however, did not demonstrate how the state would get local governments to enact changes to their plans to implement those measures. There are numerous other examples of states failing to include enforceable mechanisms for the implementation of management measures.

***

States also attempted to avoid the section 6217 requirements by submitting programs that did not follow the Management Measures Guidance. For instance, Wisconsin proposed to implement an agricultural management measure that only limited the application of nitrogen, while the Management Measures Guidance specified that the management measure should address phosphorus as well. In freshwater aquatic ecosystems, phosphorus is frequently the limiting nutrient, which means that increases in algal blooms and the resultant decreases in oxygen content are the result of phosphorus pollution. Therefore, managing only for nitrogen in the Great Lakes Basin is not nearly as effective as managing for nitrogen and phosphorus. Most of the other states also have submitted programs that contain management measures not in conformance with the Management Measures Guidance. These deficiencies may be the result of genuine disagreements about the best way to manage nonpoint pollution; however, EPA and NOAA requirements generally call for stricter measures, such as designing urban water quality facilities to handle larger storm events than states presently require. As with states' failure to develop enforceable mechanisms, one possible reason for the lack of proper management measures may be that states ran out of time to change regulations and statutes to meet the Management Measures Guidance requirements.

While it is certainly easy to criticize a program like section 6217, it is much more difficult to design a successful program. Congress is constrained not only by constitutional limitations on its ability to act but also by political realities. The recommendations that follow are an attempt to improve the program while recognizing current political realities.

The federal funding reduction provision of section 6217 punishes states that do not submit approvable programs by reducing their coastal management and CWA section 319 funding. In addition to not providing a significant program participation incentive, this provision, if it were ever enforced, would do more harm to the environment than good because it takes away funding from programs that may be helping the environment . . . .

Instead of provisions that punish state environmental programs, Congress should include provisions that target budgets and programs promoting activities that contribute to nonpoint pollution. One of the categories of activity subject to management measures is forestry. Rather than punish the state by reducing coastal management funding, it would be more sensible to reduce the number of National Forest timber sales in the coastal zone. This would have the dual effect of reducing the amount of nonpoint pollution coming from timber lands and of encouraging timber interests to lobby for the development of a CNPCP so that they could return to previous harvest levels. Reducing harvest levels until the state develops a CNPCP would have the negative political effect of encouraging timber interests to lobby against section 6217 and for withdrawal from the coastal management program. However, without development and implementation of CNPCPs, there is little point to having section 6217.

To reduce agricultural nonpoint pollution, federal agencies could reduce federal agricultural subsidies and programs or could change the priorities for subsidy allocation in the coastal zone of states that do not develop CNPCPs. To reduce other types of pollution, such as those resulting from marina development and the filling of wetlands, EPA could limit the issuance of National Pollution Discharge Elimination System permits and section 404 permits that would affect pollution in the coastal zone. This would require not only amendment of the CZMA to permit EPA to impose these kinds of limitations for non-compliance with section 6217, but also amendment of the Clean Water Act to enable these limitations.

points for discussion

1. *High-hanging fruit.* As the excerpt implies, non-point source water pollution — while a very serious problem — is the most difficult to tackle, both politically and legally. What exactly are the political and legal obstacles to reducing non-point source pollution? Another way to think about it: Why is it easier to address point source pollution?
2. *Full circle.* Pondering non-point source pollution brings us back to some of the issues to which Senator Hollings referred. Some problems are within the traditional scope of state or local jurisdiction; at the same time, they have impacts that affect national interests. Is there a way — other than funding and consistency — for the federal government to encourage states and local governments to weigh the cost of these impacts into their coastal land use decisions? Would it be feasible or wise for Congress to consider more coercive measures? If so, where might Congress find the political will and constitutional authority to do this?

Problem Exercise: Permitting

Bob the Builder owns 1,200 acres in the coastal state of Pacifica, at the confluence of the Obokee and Goosen Rivers. Pursuant to the Pacifica Coastal Zone Management Act (PCZMA), Bob's land (known as "Goobo Corner") is located within Pacifica's "coastal zone," which is defined by the Act as including all of Pacifica's coastal counties. Also pursuant to the PCZMA, part of Bob's land is located within what the statute calls "critical area." The PCZMA defines "critical area" as "all marshes, wetlands, rivers, bays, estuaries, areas seaward of the high-water mark to three nautical miles from shore, and all other public trust areas; in addition, those upland lands, adjacent to any of the aforementioned submerged lands, and within 60 feet of the high-water mark."*

> * Section 16 of the PCZMA provides that:
>
> a permit is required for all substantial development activities within the critical area. For purposes of this section, "development" includes the construction of new structures with more than 400 square feet of heated space, the expansion of existing structures (heated or unheated) by more than 10 percent of the size at which said structures were originally constructed or the size of said structures as of the effective date of this Act (July 7, 1987), and the dredging, filling, or alteration of any public trust areas.

Despite heavy development along the Obokee and Goosen Rivers farther upstream, Goobo Corner remains undeveloped. For as long as the locals can remember, they have used the shores of Goobo Corner, along the Obokee side of the property, for fishing. The Obokee is a shallow, slow-moving, muddy river. The Goosen, on the other hand, is more accurately described (at least where it borders Goobo Corner) as a tidal marsh, filled with grassy islands and cut by dozens of narrow, braided streams. There is one, larger, 10-foot-wide stream that runs through the marsh, parallel to and about 400 feet from the bank along Goobo Corner. The upland portion of Goobo Corner is a mixture of coniferous forest and open meadows. There are approximately 16 small ponds on the property, ranging from .1 to .8 acres in size.

When he purchased Goobo Corner in 1986, Bob had ambitious plans for developing Goobo Corner; as it was the last, large undeveloped tract in the area, Bob saw a unique opportunity eventually to build 600 to 1,000 upscale residences; a small light-commercial center featuring restaurants, a gym, and a gourmet grocery; and, two world-class golf courses. Until a few years ago, when he sold his vast collection of rare stamps, Bob lacked the financial resources to bring his vision to fruition. Following the stamp sale, Bob hired a famous planner, Waldo, to help him design the layout of structures and golf courses across the entire property.

About six months ago, after an extensive process that included hiring a range of specialized consultants, Waldo brought his plan for Goobo Corner to Bob. The development would be known as Heritage Plantation at Goobo Corner. Waldo's plan entailed significant modification of the upland portions of the property. Nine of the sixteen ponds would be filled, and three others would be enlarged to serve as holding ponds for stormwater run-off. Although a significant number of trees would be left in place along roads, between homes, and on the golf courses, the development would reduce forested acreage on Goobo Corner by about 60 percent.

Waldo's plan also called for significant use of both the Goosen and Obokee riverfronts. Each of the forty 6,000+ square-foot homes built along the Obokee would have private docks extending into the river. Each of these docks would originate on the upland in separate, 350-square-foot "dock houses," which would be located near the river. Both golf courses would be routed along the Goosen River; Waldo's golf course design proposal called for filling approximately 90 acres of wetlands in order to provide a dramatic setting for the golf clubhouses and courses. Bob instantly recognized a problem: He did not own any of the tidal marsh in the Goosen River that was to be filled under Waldo's plan.

Section 17 of the PCZMA provides that the Pacifica Coastal Agency (PCA):

shall issue permits for substantial development in critical areas only to the extent that the proposed activity is consistent with continued use and enjoyment of Pacifica's public trust assets by the citizens of the state. To the extent that the proposed activity, or its cumulative impacts, will interfere with that use and enjoyment, the PCA may issue a permit; however, the agency shall ensure that all impacts are offset through mitigation or other measures that leave the public as well off as it was before commencement of the project.

Bob had one of his attorneys, Carolyn, conduct a title (not tidal!) search to determine whether any of that marsh area was privately owned. The search revealed that a man named Davis might hold some interest in that area. Searching further back, Carolyn found that Davis's interest in the marsh could be traced back to an 1876 grant from the State of Pacifica to a man named Ernest. The grant described the property transferred from the state to Ernest as "all those lands located along the western bank of the Goosen River, including wetlands, uplands, and islands, from the point where the Goosen and Obokee Rivers meet, then north eleven miles to the Johnsville Mill."

Carolyn suggested to Bob that he purchase Davis's interest in the marsh, but warned him that she couldn't be entirely sure, without further research, whether purchasing Davis's interest would give Bob the right to fill the area and then build his golf course. Bob purchased Davis's interest by quitclaim deed for a small sum of money.

Carolyn also had a back-up plan. During the course of her research, she had discovered that the Pacifica legislature had passed a "Riparian and Littoral Rights Act" in the early 1900s. That law provided, among other things, that "all owners of riparian and littoral property have the right to wharf out to the nearest navigable channel, by any available means including dock, pier, or the addition of earth, rocks or other materials to submerged lands." As far as Carolyn could tell, this law had never been repealed. Carolyn told Bob that he might be able to argue that the purpose of filling the tidal marsh in the Goosen River adjacent to his property was done in order to connect the upland portion of Goobo Corner to the ten-foot-wide "navigable" channel in the middle of the river.

Assignment

Please make a list of all of the permits Bob will likely need before beginning construction on the project. (You needn't list kinds of permits that were not touched upon in this class.) For each type of permit on your list, explain precisely why he will need that permit, and for which specific development activity.

E. CHAPTER SUMMARY

1. **The Coastal Zone Management Act.** Although some states, by the early 1970s, had begun to enact coastal legislation, the federal CZMA provided incentives and guidance for all coastal states (and territories) to develop coastal programs. While the CZMA includes some standards that state programs must meet in order to qualify for funding and consistency power, it gives states a great deal of flexibility in designing those programs.

2. **State coastal programs.** State coastal programs vary widely in both their structure and substantive priorities. These programs include statutes that codify common law doctrines and, oftentimes, expand on those doctrines in furtherance of CZMA objectives. Areas of focus include erosion policy,

public access, and the conservation of unique coastal habitats. State programs vary in terms of decision-making institutions, for example, agencies or appointed bodies, and the extent to which they delegate power to local governments.

3. **Consistency.** The consistency provisions of the CZMA give states some power over (1) federal activities, and (2) federally permitted or funded activities, in their coastal zones. The Act creates distinct processes for each of these two categories of activities. Although the consistency power is real, there are limits: The Act provides for a federal override under certain circumstances.

4. **Non-point source water pollution.** Congress did not attempt to tackle this issue in the original CZMA. In 1990, it amended the Act to address what might be considered one of the most serious threats to the coastal environment. To date, the effectiveness of these amendments has been limited by practical and political problems. Reducing the impacts of non-point source pollution on coastal waterways represents one of the biggest challenges to the next generation of coastal policymakers.

F. SUGGESTED READING

TIMOTHY BEATLEY ET AL., AN INTRODUCTION TO COASTAL ZONE MANAGEMENT (2002).

Edward M. Cheston, *An Overview of the Consistency Requirement Under the Coastal Zone Management Act*, 10 U. BALT. J. ENVTL. L. 135 (2003).

BILIANA CICIN-SAIN ET AL., INTEGRATED COASTAL AND OCEAN MANAGEMENT: CONCEPTS AND PRACTICES (1998).

SCOTT L. DOUGLASS, SAVING AMERICA'S BEACHES: THE CAUSES OF AND SOLUTIONS TO BEACH EROSION (2002).

JOHN RANDOLPH, ENVIRONMENTAL LAND USE PLANNING AND MANAGEMENT (2003).

chapter 10

Coastal Disasters, Climate Change, and the Future of Coastal Law

The first chapter of this book highlighted the fact that coastal areas are particularly vulnerable to natural disasters such as storms, flooding, and tsunamis. Factors contributing to this heightened vulnerability include proximity to the sea, low elevation, the concentration of rivers and other water bodies, and unstable geology. In addition to natural disasters, coastal areas are also vulnerable to damage — for many of these same reasons — resulting from manmade disasters such as oil and chemical spills. It is important to note that the impacts of both natural and manmade disasters are a product of natural and manmade factors. So, for example, the impacts of a storm will be shaped by prior human alteration of wetlands and shorelines, as well as the amount of investment in structures in the affected area. Along the same lines, the impacts of an oil spill will be shaped by natural forces such as wind, waves, and currents.

If the predictions made by climate change scientists are accurate, then coastal areas may experience more frequent and intense storm events in the future. While the exact nature of these events is uncertain, there appears to be cause for concern:

> [I]t is not yet possible to reliably predict how global climate change will affect hurricane and tropical-storm characteristics, nor is it apparent that we would be able to statistically detect any changes that might occur given the large natural variability and the relatively short historical record of meteorological observations. Nevertheless, some of the observed natural variability in tropical-storm and hurricane frequency and intensity has been related to long-term meteorological cycles including the multidecadal Sahel rainfall cycle, the quasi-biennial oscillation, and the El Niño-Southern Oscillation cycle. Thus, regardless of any effects of global climate change, we can expect changes in tropical-storm and hurricane activity as atmospheric and oceanic conditions respond to these long-term meteorological cycles. Furthermore, projected rising sea level alone will amplify the impacts of hurricane-attendant storm surges.

William K. Michener et al., *Climate Change, Hurricanes and Tropical Storms, and Rising Sea Level in Coastal Wetlands,* 7(3) ECOLOGICAL APPLICATIONS 770, 775 (1997) (citations omitted). Climate change may be thought of as a separate natural disaster, or as a factor increasing the threat posed by more "traditional" natural disasters. Either way, coastal lawyers and policymakers should be aware of the potential impacts, and should incorporate consideration of those impacts — even if they are uncertain — into their decision-making processes.

In this chapter, we look at some of the law and policy issues raised by coastal disasters. The first section addresses issues related to insuring coastal property against damage caused by natural disasters. Although the coverage is necessarily abbreviated — insurance law warrants its own course — this book will introduce you to the split nature of coastal property insurance: Wind coverage is generally offered by private insurers, while flood insurance is offered by the Federal Emergency Management Agency (FEMA). The second part of the chapter addresses global climate change and the future of coastal law. We will read some scientists' predictions about the possible impacts of global climate change on coastal areas as well as legal scholars' ideas as to how we might change policy and law in light of those potential threats.

A. INSURING COASTAL PROPERTY

Although storms and hurricanes often bring high winds and flood waters at the same time and in the same place, these two destructive forces are, in insurance terminology, separate "perils." Not only are wind and flood separate perils, they are covered by two different kinds of insurance policy. In the first part of this section, we will learn about these two kinds of policies, how courts interpret them, and what they do and do not cover. In the second part, we will take a broader view of insurance and consider the impacts that insurance markets, and federal participation in those markets, have on patterns of coastal development.

1. Wind Coverage

Ebert v. Pacific National Fire Insurance Company

40 So. 2d 40 (La. 1949)

Judge REGAN delivered the opinion of the Court of Appeal of Louisiana, Orleans.

This is a suit by Joseph F. Ebert, the plaintiff, and against Pacific National Fire Insurance Company, the defendant, to recover the sum of $1,000, the face value of a policy of windstorm insurance.

The defendant answered denying that the loss was caused by a peril covered by the policy.

There was judgment below dismissing plaintiff's suit and he has prosecuted this appeal.

The plaintiff alleged that his camp, located on the South side of Highway 90 between Chef Menteur and the Rigolets, was damaged by the hurricane of September 19, 1947, to the extent of $1,135, and that under his policy of extended coverage, he is entitled to recover the face value thereof or $1,000.

The defendant contends that the damage to the building was not a direct loss by wind-

Photo: Library of Congress

Figure 10-1. Trapper's Camp
Trapper's camp near Delacroix Island, Louisiana circa 1935.

storm within the meaning of the policy, but, on the contrary, was caused directly or indirectly by tidal wave, high water or overflow which accompanied the hurricane of September 19, 1947. In support of this contention it relies upon the following provisions of the policy:

> In consideration of the premium for this coverage shown in face of policy, and subject to provisions and stipulations (hereinafter referred to as provisions) herein and in the policy to which this extended coverage is attached, including riders and endorsements thereon, the coverage of this policy is extended to include direct loss by windstorm. . . .

***

> Provisions Applicable Only to Windstorm and Hail: This Company shall not be liable for loss caused directly or indirectly by (a) frost or cold weather or (b) snow storm, tidal wave, high water or overflow, whether driven by wind or not.

> This Company shall not be liable for loss to the interior of the building or the insured property therein caused, (a) by rain, snow, sand or dust, whether driven by wind or not, unless the building insured or containing the property insured shall first sustain an actual loss to roof or walls by the direct force of wind or hail and then shall be liable for loss to the interior of the building or the insured property therein as may be caused by rain, snow, or dust entering the building through openings in the roof or walls by direct action of wind or hail or (b) by water from sprinkling equipment or other piping, unless such equipment or piping be damaged as a direct result of wind or hail.

A careful analysis of the transcript indicates that the only question involved here is one of fact, and that is whether plaintiff's house was blown or floated off of its foundation.

The insured's building was located one hundred and sixty to one hundred and seventy feet from the South side of U.S. Highway 90, and twelve hundred feet from Lake Catherine, in the area between the Rigolets and Chef Menteur, in the Parish of Orleans. Lake Catherine is South of the Highway and beyond Lake Catherine is Lake Borgne and the Gulf of Mexico. North of the highway is Lake Pontchartrain. The Rigolets is the East pass from Lake Pontchartrain to Lake Borgne and Chef

Menteur is the West pass. The building was, therefore, practically surrounded by water and, for an additional orientation was approximately one mile from the Rigolets. It is an ordinary three room frame structure, colloquially designated as a "camp." It was built by the plaintiff himself about eighteen years before the hurricane, on a mound of earth about five feet higher than the surrounding marshland on pilings five feet above the ground, which were driven eighteen inches in the ground. The overall measurements of the camp were approximately fifty to fifty-five feet in length by twelve feet in width with nine and one half foot ceilings. It was constructed of one by twelve vertical boards covered with roofing felt and had a corrugated iron roof. When the camp was closed it was adequately protected from the wind and rain.

Photo: Infrogmation/Wikimedia Commons

Figure 10-2. U.S. Highway 90 Near Chef Menteur, Louisiana After Hurricane Katrina

We take judicial notice of the fact that the hurricane of September 19, 1947, was of unusual severity. According to the official record of the United States Weather Bureau, which we have examined in the record, the wind attained a velocity of approximately ninety-eight miles per hour in the New Orleans area. The camp, which we have described hereinabove, is situated in open marshland and we conclude that it is a reasonable assumption that the wind was of the same or greater intensity there than in the City of New Orleans.

Two witnesses testified at the trial who were in the area during the hurricane, namely, L. J. Rule, for the plaintiff, who resided at the Rigolets, and Dave Heilbron, for the defendant, who resided in a place known as Green's Ditch and situated approximately three miles from the insured camp in the general direction of Chef Menteur. Both these witnesses rode out the storm in their respective localities.

Heilbron, who is seventy-five years of age and five feet two inches tall, lived at Green's Ditch in a camp located about seventy-five feet from Lake Catherine and about one hundred and fifty feet from Highway 90. He testified that he abandoned his camp at about 1 o'clock on the morning of the hurricane and took refuge in a neighboring camp, occupied by Mr. and Mrs. Phynics which was located about twenty-five feet nearer the highway. Heilbron said that he remained at the Phynics' camp until 8 o'clock in the morning when, according to the record the storm had reached its greatest intensity, he and the Phynics, whom Heilbron described as "old folks" left and walked through the marsh, which was inundated with about four feet of water, to the highway, where he remained throughout the storm, taking refuge under some pilings measuring twelve by twelve. He testified that the wind tore the camps to pieces, hurling lumber, tin and miscellaneous articles across the highway and endangering his life. This is evidenced by the following testimony:

> Q. Then you went to the highway, and you said you sat behind a bunch of pilings, didn't you?
> A. Yes, big pilings, 12x12.
> Q. And you were sitting northward from these — on the lea side in other words, from the pilings?
> A. I was under them. The pilings was this way, slanted, and I was under them, dodging lumber and flying tin and all like that.
> Q. What did you say you were dodging?
> A. Timber and tin and everything was hitting on top of the highway; it was hitting on top of them pilings I was under and bouncing on the opposite side.
> Q. What was causing those things to fly in the air?
> A. That was the hurricane, that terrible wind. It knocked me down a couple of times before I made it under that piling. I had to crawl to get up under there.
> Q. You mean the wind knocked you down as you were going to the highway?
> A. Yes. I scrambled back to get to that piling there and it knocked me down and I had to crawl to get to them pilings.
> Q. And that was the force of the wind that was doing that?
> A. The force of the wind knocked me down.
> Q. Now, Mr. Heilbron, you testified about tin and debris flying through the air. Where was it coming from — from what structures?
> A. Oh, I couldn't tell you what structures it was coming from.
> Q. Well, I mean, it was coming from camps, wasn't it?
> A. Coming from camps. I don't know which camp it was. I couldn't say. But the things was coming that way and I says: "Well, a life is a life," and I started to save myself.

William L. Case, an engineer, who testified on behalf of the defendant, fixed the elevation of the Ebert camp, with respect to the elevation at Green's Ditch at about one foot, four inches above sea level. It will be recalled that Ebert's camp was built on a mound of earth which Mr. Case testified as being elevated four feet, ten inches above sea level and about five feet higher than the surrounding marshland, and the Ebert camp was further elevated by five foot pilings.

The testimony of defendant's witness Heilbron is in conformity, on vital facts, with the testimony of plaintiff's witness, Rule. Rule, a fisherman by occupation, resided at the Rigolets. He abandoned his camp about 2 o'clock on the morning of the hurricane and took refuge with other residents of that area in a building known as Maucele's Bar. He testified that he observed his camp blown down about ten minutes after eight that morning, which was before the water rose.

Q. Where were you during the hurricane?

A. Well, I was right at Maucele's barroom. That is right off from my place at Fort Pike.

Q. At the Rigolets?

A. At the Rigolets, yes sir. That is what they call it. They used to call it the Little Rigolets.

Q. Did you own a camp at the Rigolets? ˙

A. Yes, sir.

Q. What happened to that camp when the storm struck? . . .

A. The camp went down, and it went to wreck and when the water came up, it blowed it away. As the water came up, it washed the wreckage of it away.

Q. I want to know whether the wind blew your camp down or whether the water knocked it down . . . .

Q. Now, what camp were you in? Where were you, what building were you in when this hurricane struck?

A. When my camp went down?

The Court: Yes.

A. I was in Maucele's place, looking at my camp, watching all the time to see whether it would go down or not, and I saw it when it went down.

Q. How far is your camp from Maucele's place?

A. 350 feet, or 400 — not further than 400.

Q. You testified that you were looking at your camp when it went down. Did the wind blow it down or did the water knock it down? . . .

A. The wind blew it down, sir.

Q. Well, now, when your camp went down, had the water risen at the Rigolets in the area of your camp?

A. Well, they had a little water — not so much as we have in a regular high tide. *The water wasn't on the road from my camp up to the highway.*

Q. Well, was there any water in your camp at that time? . . .

A. No, sir.

Q. About what time of day was that?

A. My camp went down at exactly ten minutes after eight in the morning by the clock there . . . .

Q. Now, you testified that you were at Maucele's place. Why were you there?

A. Well, I was there because I figured mine was going down. I felt it was going and I wanted to get out before it did go down, and that seemed to be the most likely place to get out of the weather . . . .

Q. Now, why did you go to Maucele's camp?

A. To get out of the weather. I couldn't stay in mine. I was afraid it was going to fall on me. It was shaking there; it was a small camp.

Q. Well, was Maucele's building a stronger building than your camp?

A. Yes, sir; it is there yet.

Q. It didn't go down?

A. It didn't go down, no.

Q. Now, how far, measured by air line, is Mr. Ebert's camp from your camp, approximately?

A. Well, about nine-tenths of a mile.

Q. Well, now, was your camp on the same side of the highway as Mr. Ebert's?

A. Yes, sir.

Q. Now, was your camp built in the marsh like Mr. Ebert's?

A. Mine was in the marsh; Mr. Ebert's was up on a hill. It was in the marsh on a hill; mine wasn't.

Q. Well, now, is there any difference in the elevation of the marsh at your camp and the elevation of the marsh in the area of Mr. Ebert's camp? . . .

A. Well, the elevation of the marsh is no higher, but the hill pumped up there when the dredgeboat was there raised the elevation where his house was.

Q. Were there any other camps located near your camp at the Rigolets?

A. Yes, sir.

Q. Now, did any of these other camps — I am not speaking of Mr. Ebert's camp, but the other camps at the Rigolets — blow down? . . .

A. Yes, sir.

Q. Well, now Mr. Rule, about how many camps at the Rigolets were blown down by the wind before the high water came? . . .

A. Well, there were four camps right in the immediate neighborhood around mine that went down, besides mine.

Q. Well, now, did those camps go down before the water came — the high water?

A. Before the high water came to them. I saw Mrs. Pokorny's place go off the foundation; and I saw Dave Herring's place go off the foundation before the water ever got up to it. He has got a place of business right near the oyster factory there on the gulfcoast road . . . .

Q. Did you remain at Maucele's place during the entire storm?

A. No, sir. When the signs and stuff started blowing off the place, I hit the highway. I figured we was going to and I wanted to get where nothing was going to fall on me; so I walked down the side of the highway, which I couldn't walk on the highway, so I walked on up a piece of the way towards where Mr. Ebert's camp was.

Q. Now, you testified that you took to the highway.

A. Yes, sir.

Q. What did you mean by that?

A. Well, I figured it was safer on the highway than staying in that building.

Q. *About how high above the level of the marsh was that highway?*

A. *Well, right at that particular point, I will say it was 2 1/2 feet above the highest part of the water, the highest it came there, right there at Maucele's place.* (Italics ours.)

Rule testified further that at about 9:30 that morning he became frightened that Maucele's bar, in which he had taken refuge, would be destroyed by the storm, so he left this structure and walked out on the highway. The record reflects that Heilbron, defendant's witness, had taken refuge on the same highway and was still there at 8:45 A.M., so, at this time, the highway could not have been under water. Rule further stated that on the highway he had a clear view of Ebert's camp across the open marsh and that it was then off its foundation and this was before the water rose. When asked by the Court "whether the water had risen in the area of Mr. Ebert's camp," Rule replied, "I will say up as far as the top of the hill where his foundation was, yes."

The evidence reflects that the front of the Ebert camp received the greatest damage. The camp faced north and the hurricane wind struck from the Northeast. The flood waters came from the opposite direction, that is, from the general direction of the South or Lake Catherine. The defendant insurance company took photographs of all parts of the camp with the exception of the front. The insurance adjuster testified that the reason he did not take pictures of the front of the camp was that he ran out of film.

Heilbron, a man seventy-five years of age and five feet, two inches tall, accompanied by "old folks" (Mr. and Mrs. Phynics) walked through the marsh to the highway at Green's Ditch at about 8 o'clock on the morning of the hurricane. He testified that the water in the marsh was up to his shoulders, therefore, the water could not have been very rough nor more than four to four and one half feet deep. He took refuge on the highway behind some piling and there was no water on the highway at that time. Rule testified that he walked to the highway at about 9:30 that morning and the insured's camp was off of its foundation at that time and the water had risen to about the level of the mound of earth in which the pilings supporting the camp were driven. It will be remembered that Heilbron and Rule were the only witnesses produced at the trial who testified that they were in this area during the hurricane.

We have examined the entire record and after a careful analysis of the testimony, we are of the opinion that the evidence preponderates in favor of the plaintiff and is to the effect that the direct cause of the damage to plaintiff's camp was the intensity of the wind on the morning of September 19, 1947.

Counsel for defendant maintain that the damage to the insured's property would not have occurred except for the action of the flood water reaching the property before it had been removed from its foundation by the wind and, in support of this contention cite what they term the [two] leading cases on this subject, which are, of course, Texas cases growing out of the Galveston Hurricane of 1915 . . . .

In the two cited cases the conditions of the wind and the height of the water during the course of the hurricane are vividly and picturesquely described in the opinions. In each instance the appellate court rendered judgment in favor of the defendant insurer on the ground that the exception in the policy clearly indicated that the insurer undertook to insure against loss by wind alone and not loss as a result of the action of wind and water. In each opinion the court stated that the plaintiff bore the burden of proving that his loss was the result of the wind and not caused directly or indirectly by the water.

However, in *Pennsylvania Fire Insurance Company v. Sikes*, 197 Okl. 137 (1946), a case decided by the Supreme Court of Oklahoma in 1946, which, in our opinion is analogous to the case which we are presently considering, it was held:

The policy covering the household effects contains the following: "This company shall not be liable for any loss or damage caused by snowstorm, blizzard, frost or cold weather; . . . nor for loss or damage occasioned directly or indirectly by or through any explosion, tidal wave, high water, overflow, cloudburst, theft; nor for any loss or damage, caused by water or rain, whether driven by wind or not, unless the building insured, or containing the property insured, shall first sustain an actual damage to the roof or walls by the direct force of the wind, and shall then be liable only for such damage to the interior of the building or the insured property therein, as may be caused by water or rain entering the building through openings in the roof or walls made by the direct action of the wind, or by water from sprinkler or other piping broken by such damage to roof or walls." . . .

Defendant says that by virtue of the above quoted provisions of the policies it is not liable for water damage under the facts here. [Citations to a variety of cases cited by defendant omitted.] Those are cases wherein the trier of facts found that the damage was caused by flood, or there was no sufficient evidence upon which to base a conclusion that the wind alone was the proximate cause of the damage. The cases would be applicable had the jury here found that the house was removed from its foundations and carried away by the rising flood waters. The jury herein found to the contrary. [Some of the] cases concern losses occasioned by tidal waves — where great bodies of gulf waters were blown into and against the houses and they were in fact inundated and flooded thereby where they stood upon their foundations. In [another of the cited cases] it is pointed out that the policy excepted from its coverage damage caused by action of water driven by the wind. Here that damage which may have occurred to plaintiff's property after it had been deposited in the flood waters by the wind was not caused by water driven by the wind. Much the same may be said of the other cited cases. They contain some showing that the damage would not have occurred but for the action of the flood waters reaching the property itself before it had been displaced by action of the wind. They merely hold that the proximate and efficient cause of the damage was by flood as commonly known and accepted, and as agreed upon in the contracts of the parties. Here the wind directly damaged the property and was alone the proximate and efficient cause of the same being deposited in the flood waters where it likely was damaged further. We think it would be far-fetched to reason that the parties to these contracts would have contemplated such damage to be a flood damage. We have the view that the exceptions above noted in the policies relate to flood damage as commonly known.

In the cited cases the facts were that flood waters were the proximate cause rather than the contributing or incidental cause of the disturbance of the houses, or was a major factor with the wind in making up the initial cause, or agency, which caused the houses to be disturbed and removed from their anchorage. Therein there was flood damage as the proximate cause of the damage as contemplated by the contracting parties. The houses were in fact flooded by bodies of water which flood water caused or was an efficient element in the cause of the entire disturbance of the houses.

In the present case neither the house nor the truck was affected by the flood water until the wind had blown them from their sites and anchorage. Whatever flood damage may have resulted thereafter was incidental, and a somewhat logical sequence to the wind disturbance. No unusual or unexpected thing occurred thereafter to cause the water damage. Common experience and

> understanding suggest that when personal property of this nature is blown into a body of water that some water damage will likely result before the property can be recovered. It is fair to assume that under these facts this incidental water damage was within the terms of the policies and contracts of the parties at the time they were made.

Id. at 137-41.

In our opinion the instant case is distinguished from the case cited by the defendant by the *Sikes* case, and we feel that the distinction is clear, unequivocal and appropriate and that, in this case, our conclusion of fact is supported by sound reason and equity.

The description of the situs of the insured's camp readily conveys the associated idea that the camp is surrounded by water, and it is inconceivable to us, who have lived all of our lives in this general area, to believe that a storm or hurricane could occur of any sort whatsoever, without a corresponding rise in the tide. There is not one scintilla of evidence in the record of a tidal wave — where great bodies of gulf waters were blown into and against the camps causing them to be inundated and swept away by the mad fury of gargantuan waves of water. The damage to the insured's camp, in our opinion, was not occasioned by the action of flood waters, in the common and accepted sense of that phrase, reaching the property itself before it had been displaced by the intense action of the wind. Here the wind directly damaged the property and was alone the proximate and efficient cause of the camp being deposited in the water. If a tornado or windstorm policy does not afford protection from a storm accompanied by winds of ninety-eight miles per hour or more, it occurs to us that authors of the contracts of windstorm insurance may just as well insert a clause in the policy to the effect that it should not be operative when a hurricane is accompanied by high tides.

As stated the vital issue of fact in this case was whether the plaintiff's camp was blown or floated off of its foundation and we have concluded and found as a fact that the camp was blown into the flood waters by the intense force of the winds prevailing in that area at the time of the hurricane.

We said in *Owens v. Felder*, 35 So. 2d 671, 672 (La. 1948), that:

> We are reluctant to reverse the finding of a trial court based primarily on questions of fact, but in a case, such as we are presently analyzing, it is a self evident principle that it is occasionally easier to perceive fallacies and inconsistencies contained in the record by a comparison of the various portions of the transcribed record with other pertinent portions than it is to accurately observe and catalogue them while listening to the oral evidence of the various witnesses who testified during the course of the trial.

For the reasons assigned the judgment appealed from is annulled, avoided and reversed and it is now ordered that there be judgment herein in favor of Joseph F. Ebert, the plaintiff, and against Pacific National Fire Insurance Company, defendant, in the full sum of $1,000, together with legal interest from judicial demand until paid, and for all costs.

Reversed.

Tuepker v. State Farm Fire & Casualty Company

507 F.3d 346 (5th Cir. 2007)

Judge GARWOOD delivered the opinion of the United States Court of Appeals for the Fifth Circuit.

This case arises from the unprecedented destruction brought to the Mississippi Gulf Coast by Hurricane Katrina in August 2005. The hurricane completely destroyed the home of plaintiffs-appellees-cross-appellants, John and Claire Tuepker ("the Tuepkers"). Their residence and the property contained therein were insured by defendant-appellant-cross-appellee, State Farm Fire and Casualty Company ("State Farm"). When State Farm refused to compensate the Tuepkers for their losses, the Tuepkers on November 21, 2005 sued State Farm in the district court below, federal jurisdiction being based on diversity of citizenship. State Farm filed a motion to dismiss the complaint. . . . The district court denied the motion. This interlocutory appeal is before us under 28 U.S.C. § 1292(b).

Context Facts and Proceedings Below

(a) Proceedings

The Tuepkers' complaint identified their State Farm issued "Homeowner's Policy," with policy period August 9, 2005 to August 9, 2006, and attached a "representative copy of the subject policy." The complaint alleged, *inter alia*, that "[o]n August 29, 2005 . . . the insured residence and the personal contents therein were completely destroyed by hurricane wind, rain, and/or storm surge from Hurricane Katrina . . . . This loss was covered under the subject policy. There is nothing left of the insured residence or contents but a slab." The complaint further included the allegations that

> . . . regardless of whether the total damage to Plaintiffs' insured property was caused by hurricane wind, storm surge proximately caused by hurricane wind, or both, the so-called "flood" exclusion, which State Farm defines in the subject policy and in its denial letter as "flood, surface water, waves, tidal water, tsunami, seiche, or overflow of a body of water, or spray from any of these, all whether or not driven by wind," is not applicable here and in any event, is modified by the "Hurricane Deductible"

and that "[t]his 'flood' exclusion is ambiguous and deceiving when read in conjunction with . . . the 'Hurricane Deductible.' " The relief sought in the complaint includes, *inter alia*, declaratory relief, and the declarations sought include a declaration "that any damage to Plaintiffs' insured residence and property caused by 'storm surge' is not excluded under the subject policy" and "that the subject policy's 'flood' exclusion is not applicable and is ambiguous."

State Farm, in late December 2005, filed a motion to dismiss the complaint . . . asserting, *inter alia*, that in respect to the declaratory relief sought, the complaint "fail[s] as a matter of law, because the claims for insurance coverage are

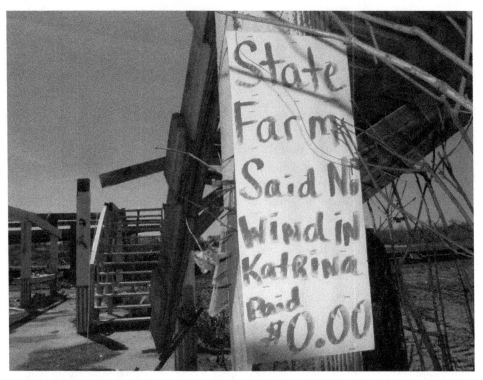

Photo: Tim Isbell/Biloxi Sun Herald

Figure 10-3. Sign Posted by Homeowner, Biloxi, Mississippi
Is this an accurate summary of State Farm's legal argument?

barred by the plain language of the Plaintiffs' policy," that the policy's "water damage exclusion is valid and enforceable, and unambiguously excludes losses that would not have occurred 'in the absence' of water damage" and "applies to water damage from 'hurricane' and 'storm surge,'" and that "[t]he hurricane deductible endorsement does not provide coverage for hurricane damage not covered under the policy, including 'storm surge' damage, nor does it render the policy ambiguous."

The district court, in its May 23, 2006 order, denied State Farm's motion to dismiss "in accordance with" its Memorandum Opinion of the same date, in which the court, *inter alia*, construed, as a matter of law, a number of the relevant provisions of the State Farm policy, primarily including the policy's "Water Damage" exclusion clause and the clause, which introduces that and other related exclusions, commonly known as the "anti-concurrent-causation clause" or "ACC Clause." The court also addressed the policy's hurricane deductible endorsement and its personal property coverage "windstorm or hail" peril, as well as the burden of proof. The opinion holds that "interpretation of the terms of an insurance policy present questions of law, not fact" and that "where the terms of an insurance policy are clear and unambiguous, they are to be enforced as written." It further holds that

Losses directly attributable to water in the form of a "storm surge" are excluded from coverage because this damage was caused by the inundation of plaintiffs' home by tidal water from the Mississippi Sound driven ashore during Hurricane Katrina. This is water damage within the meaning of that [the "Water Damage"] policy exclusion. The exclusion found in the policy for water damage is a valid and enforceable policy prevision (*sic*). . . .

Under applicable Mississippi law, where there is damage caused by both wind and rain (covered losses) and water (losses excluded from coverage) the amount payable under the insurance policy becomes a question of which is the proximate cause of the loss. To the extent that the State Farm policy is inconsistent with this settled rule of Mississippi law, the exclusionary language is invalid.

The court also held the "anti-concurrent-causation clause" ambiguous and ineffective to exclude damage proximately caused by wind or rain, stating:

I also find that the language in the State Farm policy that introduces subsection 2 of SECTION I — LOSSES NOT COVERED is ambiguous. The provisions in question purport to exclude from coverage losses that would otherwise be covered, such as wind damage, when that covered loss happens to accompany water damage (an excluded loss). . . .

I find that this language in the State Farm policy creates ambiguities in the context of damages sustained by the insured during a hurricane. These provisions purport to exclude coverage for wind and rain damage, both of which are covered losses under this policy, where an excluded cause of loss, *e.g.* water damage, also occurs. I find that these two exclusions are ambiguous in light of the other policy provisions granting coverage for wind and rain damage and in light of the inclusion of a "hurricane deductible" as part of the policy.

To the extent that plaintiffs can prove their allegations that the hurricane winds (or objects driven by those winds) and rains entering the insured premises through openings caused by the hurricane winds proximately caused damage to their insured property, those losses will be covered under the policy, and this will be the case even if flood damage, which is not covered, subsequently or simultaneously occurred.

The court further held that State Farm had "the burden of proving that the [Water Damage] exclusion applies to the plaintiffs' claims."

State Farm, after the court denied its motion to alter or amend, then moved the court to certify to this court . . . its May 23, 2006 order and opinion as involving the controlling legal question of whether "the anti-concurrent cause language in State Farm's homeowner's policies is ambiguous and unenforceable." The Tuepkers opposed the motion as limited to that one particular issue but acknowledged that the criteria for . . . certification were met "provided . . . that *all* of the rulings made by the Court on the substantive *legal* issues surrounding interpretation of the State Farm contract are also certified for appeal." Thereafter, the district court, on September 27, 2006 issued its order certifying . . . its May 23, 2006 order and opinion interpreting the State Farm policy in the noted respects as involving controlling questions of law as to which there is substantial ground for difference of opinion and that an appeal will materially advance the ultimate termination of the litigation.[1] The order states that "This certification is limited to the interpretation of the various provisions of the subject insurance policy under the factual circumstances presented."

In October 2006, both State Farm and the Tuepkers timely filed with this court their respective petitions for permissions to appeal . . . , and on November 21, 2006 a motions panel of this court granted those petitions.

(b) Policy Provisions

The State Farm homeowner's policy had two relevant property coverage provisions. These are contained in its "SECTION I — YOUR PROPERTY COVERAGES" and are as follows:

SECTION I — LOSSES INSURED

COVERAGE A — DWELLING

We insure for accidental direct physical loss to the property described in Coverage A, except as provided in SECTION I — LOSSES NOT INSURED.

COVERAGE B — PERSONAL PROPERTY

We insure for accidental direct physical loss to property described in Coverage B caused by the following perils, except as provided in SECTION I — LOSSES NOT INSURED.

There next appear subparagraphs "1." through "16." in each of which a Coverage B covered peril is listed and described, subparagraph "2" of which is as follows:

2. Windstorm or hail. This peril does not include loss to property contained in a building caused by rain, snow, sleet, sand or dust. This limitation does not apply when the direct force of wind or hail damages the building causing an opening in a roof or wall and the rain, snow, sleet, sand or dust enters through this opening.

This peril includes loss to watercraft of all types and their trailers, furnishings, equipment, and outboard motors, only while inside a fully enclosed building.

The next portion of the property coverages section of the policy is entitled "SECTION I — LOSSES NOT INSURED." It consists of three parts (numbers "1.", "2." and "3."), the second of which ("2.") commences as follows:

2. We do not insure under any coverage for any loss which would not have occurred in the absence of one or more of the following excluded events. We do not insure for such loss regardless of: (a) the cause of the excluded event; or (b) other causes of the loss; or (c) whether other causes acted concurrently or in

---

1. The order notes, *inter alia*, that in the May 23 opinion: "The Court determined that the water damage exclusion is valid and that storm surge is nothing more than a flood, but that the anti-concurrent cause clause (especially when combined with a hurricane deductible endorsement) does not negate coverage for damage which is caused by the covered risk of wind. In addition, this Court held that Plaintiffs bear the burden of proving allegations that hurricane wind (and resulting damages when the direct force of wind causes an opening in a roof or wall and the rain enters through this opening), while the exclusion is an affirmative defense on which the Defendant carries the burden."

any sequence with the excluded event to produce the loss; or (d) whether the event occurs suddenly or gradually, involves isolated or widespread damage, arises from natural or external forces, or occurs as a result of any combination of these.

This is the noted "anti-concurrent-causation clause" or "ACC Clause." Immediately after it there next appear subparagraphs "a" through "f" in each of which an excluded event under "2." is listed and described, subparagraph "c." of which is as follows:

c. Water Damage, meaning:

(1) flood, surface water, waves, tidal water, tsunami, seiche, overflow of a body of water, or spray from any of these, all whether driven by wind or not;

(2) water or sewage from outside the residence premises plumbing system that enters through sewers or drains, or water which enters into and overflows from within a sump pump, sump pump well or any other system designed to remove subsurface water which is drained from the foundation area; or

(3) water below the surface of the ground, including water which exerts pressure on, or seeps or leaks through a building, sidewalk, driveway, foundation, swimming pool or other structure.

However, we do insure for any direct loss by fire, explosion or theft resulting from water damage, provided the resulting loss is itself a Loss Insured.

The policy also includes a "Hurricane Deductible Endorsement" which provides:

The following Deductible language is added to the policy:

Deductible
The Hurricane deductible percentage (%) shown in the Declarations applies only for direct physical loss or damage to coverage property caused by wind, wind gusts, hail, rain, tornadoes, or cyclones caused by or resulting from a hurricane as defined above. The deductible for loss caused by each hurricane occurrence is the amount determined by applying the deductible percentage (%) shown in the Declarations to the COVERAGE A — DWELLING limit shown in the Declarations.

In the event of a hurricane loss, this deductible will apply in place of any other deductible stated in the policy. In no event will this deductible be less than the Section I deductible amount shown in the Declarations.

All other policy provisions apply.[4]

4. This endorsement begins with the following definitions:

Definitions
As used in this endorsement hurricane means a storm system that has been declared to be a hurricane by the National Hurricane Center of the National Weather Service. The duration of the hurricane includes the time period, in this state:

1. beginning at the time a hurricane watch or hurricane warning is issued for any part of this state by the National Hurricane Center of the National Weather Service;
2. continuing for the time period during which the hurricane conditions exist anywhere in this state; and
3. ending 24 hours following the termination of the last hurricane watch or hurricane warning for any part of this state by the National Hurricane Center of the National Weather Service.

Discussion

As the court below correctly ruled, and as all parties recognize, the governing substantive law is that of Mississippi. We address the proper interpretation and legal effect of the State Farm policy under Mississippi law, and hence our review is *de novo.* . . .

We limit our discussion to the issues raised by the parties on appeal: Whether damage resulting to the Tuepkers' home from the storm surges is an excluded peril that is not covered by the policy, whether the ACC Clause in the State Farm policy is ambiguous; and whether the efficient proximate cause doctrine applies in this case. For the reasons stated below, we affirm in part, reverse in part, and remand.

A. Water Damage Exclusion

State Farm urges this court to affirm the district court's conclusion that the Water Damage Exclusion is valid under Mississippi law and that it includes losses attributable to storm surge. The Tuepkers argue that damages caused by storm surge are not excluded from coverage by the Water Damage Exclusion.

The Water Damage Exclusion states that water damage includes damages caused by, among other things, flood, waves, tidal water, and overflow of a body of water, "all whether driven by wind or not." These words accurately describe the influx of water into the Tuepkers' home that was caused by the Katrina storm surge. Furthermore, courts have held that similarly worded water damage exclusions apply to flooding that occurs during a hurricane. *See In re Katrina Canal Breaches Litig.*, 495 F.3d 191, 214 (5th Cir. 2007) (concluding that under Louisiana law, similar water damage exclusions in insurance policies are unambiguous and that flooding resulting from the damage to the levees during Hurricane Katrina "fits squarely within the generally prevailing meaning of the term 'flood,' " and is, thus, excluded from coverage by the policies). . . . In interpreting an almost identical water damage exclusion and applying Mississippi law,[6] this court has found that "storm surge" is "little more than a synonym for a 'tidal wave' or wind-driven flood," both of which are perils excluded by the State Farm policy. *Leonard*, 499 F.3d 419, 437 (5th Cir. 2007). In *Leonard*, we concluded that the lack of a specific reference to a "storm surge" in the water damage exclusion did not render the policy ambiguous or allow the insured party to recover for losses caused by the storm surge associated with Hurricane Katrina. *Id.* at 435. Our opinion in *Leonard* specifically relied on the *Katrina Canal Breaches Litigation* opinion *and* on the district court's opinion here for the holding that the Katrina "storm surge" was unambiguously excluded water damage.

We conclude that under Mississippi law, the Water Damage Exclusion is valid and that the storm surge that damaged the Tuepkers' home is a peril that is

---

6. The water damage exclusion at issue in *Leonard* "explicitly exempt[ed] from coverage damage caused by 'flood . . . waves, tidal waves, [and] overflow of a body of water . . . *whether or not driven by wind.*' " *Leonard v. Nationwide Mutual Ins. Co.*, 499 F.3d 419, 437 (5th Cir. 2007).

unambiguously excluded from coverage under State Farm's policy. Therefore, we affirm the district court's ruling on this issue.

B. Anti-Concurrent-Causation Clause

The Tuepkers urge this court to uphold the district court's conclusion that the ACC Clause was ambiguous. They argue that the ACC clause is unenforceable because it conflicts with other provisions in the policy, namely the express coverage for losses attributable to wind and the Hurricane Deductible Endorsement. State Farm argues that the ACC Clause is not ambiguous because it cannot be construed to have two or more reasonable meanings and it does not conflict with any other provisions in the policy. We agree with State Farm.

Under Mississippi law, if the words of an insurance policy are plain and unambiguous, courts will afford them their ordinary meaning. . . .

This court has recently ruled that a Nationwide Mutual Insurance Company ACC Clause, which is similar to that in the State Farm insurance policy in this case, is not ambiguous under Mississippi law. *Leonard*, 499 F.3d at 430. The ACC Clause and subsequent water damages exclusion at issue in *Leonard* read:

> 1. We do not cover loss to any property resulting directly or indirectly from any of the following. Such a loss is excluded even if another peril or event contributed concurrently or in any sequence to cause the loss. . . .
> 2. Water or damage caused by water-borne material . . .
>
> (1) flood, surface water, waves, tidal waves, overflow of a body of water, spray from these, whether or not driven by wind. *Id.* at 430 (emphasis deleted).

The State Farm ACC Clause does differ from the Nationwide ACC Clause in that it states that the policy does not cover "any loss which would not have occurred in the absence of one or more of the following excluded events." However, this difference does not introduce any ambiguity or significantly differentiate the clause from the ACC Clause at issue in *Leonard*. Both clearly state that excluded losses —

here, any loss which would not have occurred in the absence of one or more of the excluded events — will not be covered even if a nonexcluded event or peril acts "concurrently or in any sequence" with the excluded event to cause the loss in question. Thus, *Leonard* governs this case, and compels the conclusion that the ACC Clause in State Farm's policy is not ambiguous, and should be enforced under Mississippi law. As the *Leonard*

Quick Question

Is the debate between the trial court and Fifth Circuit really about the perspective from which ambiguity should be judged? In other words, did the trial court's decision view the language in the policy from the perspective of the Tuepkers (at the time they purchased it)?

---

opinion directs, any damage caused *exclusively* by a nonexcluded peril or event such as wind, not concurrently or sequentially with water damage, is covered by the policy, while all damage caused by water or by wind acting concurrently or sequentially with water, is excluded. *Id.* Thus, the ACC Clause in combination with the

Water Damage Exclusion clearly provides that indivisible damage caused by both excluded perils and covered perils or other causes is not covered. However, as State Farm has conceded in its briefs here and below, the ACC Clause by its terms applies only to "any loss which would not have occurred in the absence of one or more of the below listed excluded events," and thus, for example, if wind blows off the roof of the house, the loss of the roof is not excluded merely because a *subsequent* storm surge later completely destroys the entire remainder of the structure; such roof loss *did* occur in the absence of any listed excluded peril.

Furthermore, contrary to the ruling of the district court, the Hurricane Deductible Endorsement in the State Farm policy does not in any way render the ACC Clause ambiguous. The Hurricane Deductible Endorsement clearly states that a higher deductible percentage will apply for losses attributable to hurricane occurrences. There is nothing in the language of the endorsement, even when read in conjunction with the loss exclusion provisions, that expands or changes any other aspect of the policy.

We addressed this issue in *In re Katrina*, 495 F.3d 191. There, the plaintiffs argued that similar hurricane deductible endorsements would lead a reasonable policyholder to expect their policy to cover damage resulting from a storm surge caused by a hurricane despite the fact that the policies excluded coverage for water damage. *Id.* at 220. Applying Louisiana law, this court held that "the plain language of the hurricane-deductible endorsements indicates that they do nothing more than alter the deductible for damage caused by a hurricane." *Id.* We also found that the endorsements do not extend the scope of the policies to cover floods. *Id.* . . .

In pertinent part, the instant Hurricane Deductible Endorsement states:

> The Hurricane deductible percentage . . . applies only for direct physical loss or damage to covered property caused by wind, wind gusts, hail, rain, tornadoes, or cyclones caused by or resulting from a hurricane . . . . In the event of a hurricane loss, this deductible will apply in place of any other deductible stated in the policy. . . . All other policy provisions apply.

Like the hurricane deductible endorsements at issue in *In re Katrina*, this clause clearly only applies to the deductible, and does not affect the scope of coverage under the policy. The list of enumerated perils covered by the Hurricane Deductible Endorsement only includes perils that are covered under the policy like wind, rain, and hail damage. It does not include any perils related to flooding or any peril covered under the Water Damage Exclusion. The fact that water damage is explicitly excluded from coverage and that the endorsement concludes by stating that "[a]ll other policy provisions apply," unambiguously reflects that the endorsement does not enlarge or change the scope of coverage under the policy.

In light of all of the relevant policy provisions, the ACC Clause is unambiguous and enforceable. We accordingly reverse the holding of the district court that State Farm's ACC Clause is ambiguous under Mississippi law.

C. Efficient Proximate Cause Doctrine

The Tuepkers argue that the ACC Clause is not enforceable because it conflicts with the "efficient proximate cause doctrine." The district court agreed to the extent of refusing to apply that clause when it might deny coverage that would have been allowed under the "efficient proximate cause doctrine." Under that doctrine, when a loss is caused by the combination of both covered and excluded perils, the loss is fully covered by the insurance policy if the covered risk proximately caused the loss. *See Leonard*, 499 F.3d at 432. Under this doctrine, if a policy covers wind damage but excludes water damage, the insured may recover for damages if it can show that the wind (the covered peril) proximately or efficiently caused the loss, notwithstanding that there were other excluded causes contributing to that loss like flooding. *Id.* . . .

Mississippi courts have yet to indicate whether a homeowner's insurance policy may preclude recovery for damages resulting from the concurrent action of wind and water in a hurricane. *Id.* at 431. However, in *Leonard*, we made an "*Erie* guess" as to how the Mississippi Supreme Court would rule on the issue. *Id.* The efficient proximate cause doctrine is the "default causation rule in Mississippi regarding damages caused concurrently by a covered and an excluded peril under an insurance policy." *Id.* However, *Leonard* concludes that ACC Clauses are enforceable under Mississippi law, and that they circumvent the efficient proximate cause doctrine. *See id.* at 436 ("[W]e conclude that use of an ACC clause to supplant the default causation regime is not forbidden by Mississippi caselaw . . . , statutory law, or public policy.").

> **Quick Question**
>
> Should parties to an insurance contract be prohibited by law from contracting around the efficient proximate cause rule?

Therefore, under *Leonard*, which binds us, and with which we in any event agree, the ACC Clause in State Farm's policy overrides the efficient proximate cause doctrine. Accordingly, we reverse the district court's holding that the ACC Clause in the State Farm policy is invalid to the extent that it conflicts with the efficient proximate cause doctrine.

D. Proper Assignment of Burdens of Proof

State Farm contends that the district court erred in assigning the parties' respective burdens of proof under the "open peril" coverage for the residence and the "named peril" coverage for the personal property. Under Mississippi law, the plaintiff bears the burden of proving his right to recover under an insurance policy. . . . For "named peril" coverage — here Coverage B — Personal Property — the plaintiff has the burden of proving that any losses were caused by a peril covered by the policy. . . . Under "open peril" coverage — here Coverage A — Dwelling — the plaintiff still has the basic burden of proving his right to recover. . . . However, under "open peril" coverage "the insurer bears the burden of proving that a particular peril falls within a policy exclusion," and "must plead and prove the applicability of an exclusion as an affirmative defense." *Leonard*, 499 F.3d at 429. . . . State Farm argues that once an insurer has provided evidence that an item of claimed damage resulted at least in part from an excluded peril, the burden shifts to the insured to produce evidence as to what portion of the damages were caused by perils covered by the policy. However, the parties here entered into a "High-Low Agreement" under which the Tuepkers will, for specified consideration varying in amount depending on the outcome of this appeal, release State Farm from all claims related to this case at the conclusion of all appeals, so this case will never return to the district court for an actual trial.[11] Thus, the questions that the parties raise regarding the burden of proof are not relevant to the case and controversy at issue in this court, and we will not expand upon previous precedents regarding those issues.

Conclusion

For the foregoing reasons, we affirm the judgment of the district court in part, reverse it in part, and remand the case for further proceedings not inconsistent with this opinion.

AFFIRMED in part; REVERSED in part; and REMANDED.

points for discussion

1. *"Just say no."* One of the issues in *Tuepker* was whether the existence of a "hurricane deductible" provision in the insurance contract "affect[ed] the scope of coverage under the policy." Within days after Sandy hit the shores of Connecticut, Maryland, New Jersey, and New York, the governors of those states issued statements that officially classified Sandy as something other than a hurricane. These declarations were meant to relieve state residents from paying the higher deductibles. Homeowners in other states, where rule policies are written to have "named-storm" deductibles, were not as lucky. According to NOAA, the storm, or the relevant part of the 900-mile-wide storm, was a post-tropical cyclone with hurricane force winds at the time it landed on the Atlantic Coast.
2. *"Proximate and efficient cause."* As two insurance lawyers, Mark Wuerfel and Mark Koop, explain:

   > . . . [T]he efficient proximate cause rule is the all but universal method used in the United States for resolving coverage issues involving the concurrence of covered and excluded perils. . . .

***

11. On February 6, 2007, State Farm and the Tuepkers agreed to the amount of liquidated damages that State Farm will pay the Tuepkers upon "the outcome of all appeals" ("the High-Low Agreement"), one specified amount if "the final appellate decision on coverage issues is favorable to State Farm," and a significantly greater amount if that decision favors the Tuepkers. The Tuepkers agreed to release State Farm from all claims at the conclusion of all appeals of the case, so the case will not continue in lower courts. This type of agreement, which liquidates damages to be paid upon the outcome of a case while maintaining a live case and controversy between the parties with respect to the issues on appeal is permissible under *Havens Realty Corp. v. Coleman*, 455 U.S. 363 (1982), and *Nixon v. Fitzgerald*, 457 U.S. 731 (1982).

[I]n *Bird v. St. Paul Fire & Marine Insurance*, 120 N.E. 86 (N.Y. 1918), . . . a freight yard fire, after about 30 minutes, caused some rail cars loaded with explosives to explode. That explosion caused another fire, which then caused a much greater explosion of dynamite stores in the freight yard. The second explosion damaged an insured canal boat about 1,000 feet away from the freight yard. The canal boat was insured against the perils of "the sounds, harbors, bays, rivers, canals and fires." There was no specific exclusion for damage from an explosion.

New York's intermediate appellate court gave judgment for the insured, but the Court of Appeals reversed. "The problem before us is not one of philosophy," [Judge] Cardozo wrote. "Our guide is the reasonable expectation and purpose of the ordinary business man when making an ordinary business contract."

. . . Even though the specified peril of fire caused the explosion that caused the concussion that damaged the insured canal boat, the fire was not a "proximate" cause. Reasonable insureds would not have contracted for "fire" insurance with the expectation that the policy would cover a web of causation that included a fire at a significant distance from the insured property.

Cardozo [explained] the essentially fact-specific nature of the inquiry into the "efficient proximate cause" of property insurance loss . . . :

> From this complex web, the law picks out now this cause and now that one. The same cause producing the same effect may be proximate or remote as the contract of the parties seems to place it in light or shadow. That cause is to be held predominant which they would think of as predominant. A common-sense appraisement of everyday forms of speech and modes of thought must tell us when to stop. . . .
>
> This view of the problem of causation shows how impossible it is to set aside as immaterial the element of proximity in space. The law solves these problems pragmatically. There is no use in arguing that distance ought not to count, if life and experience tell us that it does. The question is not what men ought to think of as a cause. The question is what they do think of as a cause. We must put ourselves in the place of the average owner whose boat or building is damaged by the concussion of a distant explosion, let us say a mile away. Some glassware in his pantry is thrown down and broken. It would probably never occur to him that within the meaning of his policy of insurance, he had suffered loss by fire. A philosopher or a lawyer might persuade him that he had, but he would not believe it until they told him. He would expect indemnity, of course, if fire reached the thing insured.
>
> The case comes, therefore, to this: Fire must reach the thing insured, or come within such proximity to it that damage, direct or indirect, is within the compass of reasonable probability. Then only is it the proximate cause because then only may we suppose that it was within the contemplation of the contract. In last analysis, therefore, it is something in the minds of men, in the will of the contracting parties, and not merely in the physical bond of union between events, which solves, at least for the jurist, this problem of causation. In all this, there is nothing anomalous. Everything in nature is cause and effect by turns.

Id. at 87-88.

3. *The anti-concurrent causation clause.* Professor Adam Scales explains:

> Read literally, the clause eliminates coverage wherever water acts alongside a covered peril such as wind. Unsurprisingly, the leading authorities emerging from Hurricane Katrina decline to do so.
>
> In gracious correspondence with the author, one of the drafters of the ACC (a senior officer with State Farm) pointed out that it has been widely upheld. State Farm and other insurers have made the same claim in briefs filed throughout the Katrina litigation. While true, this overlooks the particular evil the ACC was designed to eliminate: The judicially-created uncertainty regarding the border between earth movement and other perils such as explosion or negligent construction. An insurer undertakes to cover explosions due to earthquake (such as a ruptured gas main) because it would be patently ridiculous to describe a house consumed by fire as not having been lost due to fire simply because the fire was antecedently caused by an excluded peril. The problem arose when courts construed "explosion" to refer to the underlying earth movement itself, an act of judicial sophistry that has few parallels. No one but a homeowner lacking earthquake insurance would think to describe such a loss as a covered "explosion" as that term is conventionally understood. It is unsurprising that many of the cases upholding the ACC — upholding the right of the insurer to specify coverage defined outside of the general rule of proximate causation — have in fact arisen in the context of earth movement.
>
> In the Katrina cases, the issue is more complicated. Hurricane Katrina resulted in several distinct types of losses, not all of which, it appears, can be reliably distinguished after the fact. A rough taxonomy of catastrophe would include: Homes apparently washed away by the surge of the Gulf Coast or nearby bodies of water; homes damaged by such surges, then destroyed by hurricane winds; homes damaged by hurricane winds, then destroyed by flooding; and homes destroyed entirely by flood. This taxonomy does not lend itself to the market-segmenting function of the ACC because two of its categories are highly indeterminate. Moreover, if the insurance industry's interpretation is correct, there is no insurance product available for losses caused partially by flood and partly by wind.

Adam F. Scales, *A Nation of Policyholders: Governmental and Market Failure in Flood Insurance*, 26 Miss. C. L. Rev. 3, 23 (2006).

4. *Other approaches?* Professor Scales's article, written before the Fifth Circuit's opinion in *Tuepker*, suggests that at least some courts will, in order to protect what they consider to be the homeowner's reasonable expectations, find a way to invalidate anti-concurrent causation clauses. Would invalidating the ACC result in an all-or-nothing factual battle over "efficient proximate cause"? Is there another approach? Why do you think insurance companies would not support a seemingly fair-sounding rule that losses be apportioned in relation to damage caused by the various covered and non-covered perils at play?

5. *Follow the money.* Given that many homes are subject to mortgages, why don't banks exercise their political power to negotiate more generous standard homeowners' coverage?

2. Federal Flood Insurance

The private insurance market is unwilling to offer affordable coverage for the flood peril associated with storms such as hurricanes, The following materials explain the reasons for this, the history and administration of the federal flood insurance program, the kind of flood coverage offered by the standard policy issued under the auspices of this program, and some of the policy issues associated with the dual system of wind/flood insurance.

a. History and Administration

Rawle O. King, Federal Flood Insurance: The Repetitive Loss Problem

Cong. Research Serv., CRS Rep. RL32972 (June 30, 2005)

Floods and Insurance Coverage

Of the two types of floods — riverine or inland stream flooding and coastal flooding — riverine floods typically cause the highest economic losses. On the other hand, coastal floods often cause greater loss of life. The Great Flood of 1993 that occurred along the Missouri and Upper Mississippi River basins is considered the most costly and devastating flood to ravage the United States. Its size and

Photo: Steve Nicklas/NOAA

Figure 10-4. Cape Girardeau, Missouri During the Great Flood of 1927 impact surpassed the 1927 flood disaster, noted earlier, in most categories: number of record river levels; the number of persons displaced, amount of crop and property damage; and, duration. A tragic combination of unique extreme weather and hydrologic conditions led to the flood of 1993.

Flooding is not confined to just a few geographic areas; almost every region of the country is subject to flooding. Some of the principal economic consequences of flooding are: (1) the cost of emergency services borne by state and local governments; (2) reductions in government revenue due to business interruption or business destruction (sales taxes) foregone and lower property tax revenues; (3) dollar value of flood-related deaths, bodily injury and mental anguish suffered by victims; and (4) post-disaster outlays by the federal government, such as loans and direct financial assistance to individuals for emergency housing, food, and clothing. Property damage caused by a general condition of flooding is explicitly excluded under most homeowner insurance policies sold in the private sector.

Property insurance companies insist that flood insurance is not commercially feasible. As a general rule, property insurance markets will provide coverage (capacity) when insurers are confident that they can identify the risk and set insurance rates that cover expected losses. Insurers generally lack the ability to spread flood hazard risk sufficiently to safeguard their assets against catastrophic flood losses. Moreover, only people living in flood hazard areas would be expected to purchase flood insurance (so-called adverse selection) and these people would have frequent claims, making the coverage prohibitively expensive and, hence, not marketable.

Private insurance companies have been unable or unwilling to pre-fund and diversify flood risks through insurance, reinsurance agreements or securitization.

National Flood Insurance Program

In 1968, Congress created the NFIP in response to the trend of development and redevelopment in flood-prone areas, the increasing damages caused by floods, and rising cost of taxpayer funded disaster relief for flood victims. Today, the NFIP is among the nation's largest domestic liabilities, along with the Social Security System and federal health programs such as Medicare and Medicaid. The NFIP involves a partnership among FEMA specialists and contractors, thousands of insurance agents and claims adjusters, private insurance companies, floodplain managers, and other public officials, lenders, and real estate agents. Federal flood insurance is currently offered to homeowner, renters, and business owners in over 20,000 participating communities that adopt and enforce floodplain management regulations which conform to NFIP standards.

. . . [B]y the end of the FY2004, almost five million (4,498,324) flood insurance policies were in effect for homeowners, renters, and business owners, representing $723 billion of insurance in force. Federal flood insurance coverage is available on almost all types of buildings up to $350,000 for residential types ($250,000 for residential building coverage and $100,000 for residential contents coverage), and $1,000,000 for non-residential structures ($500,000 building and $500,000 contents.)

The NFIP serves two major functions: underwriting flood insurance and leading floodplain management. Various entities have specific roles to play under the NFIP.

The federal government assumes all liability for the insurance coverage, sets the rates, coverage limitations, and eligibility requirements, designates special flood hazard areas (SFHA) with the issuance of flood insurance rate maps (FIRMs) and provides grant funding for mitigation planning activities. The private insurance sector sells insurance, adjusts and pays claims, and performs engineering and planning studies. The states coordinate the program and provide technical assistance to local participating communities. Finally local communities with jurisdiction over land use adopt, administer, and enforce floodplain development regulations. The NFIP does not operate on the traditional insurance definition of fiscal solvency; rather, it operates under a statutory mandate that premiums on pre-FIRM structures — i.e., structures built before the issuance of a FIRM or before 1975, whichever is later — must be reasonable and, if necessary, be subsidized. The subsidy is provided by charging premium rates discounted from full actuarial rates.

In order to make up the subsidized premium shortfall, NFIP has established a rating methodology consisting of a target level of premium income for the program as a whole that is at least sufficient to cover expenses and losses relative to what FEMA calls the "average historical loss year." The premium level generated to cover the average historical loss year must accommodate the combined effect of the portion of NFIP business paying less than full risk premiums and the portion of the business paying full risk premiums. In the event that premium and investment income are inadequate in a given year, the NFIP can exercise its statutory authority to borrow up to $1.5 billion from the U.S. Treasury to cover losses. Borrowed funds must be repaid with interest.

Identification and Mapping of Special Hazard Areas

The first step in assessing a community's flood hazards is identifying and mapping the special flood hazard areas. Flood maps provide the basis for establishing floodplain management ordinances (i.e., building standards), setting insurance rates, and identifying properties whose owners are required to purchase flood insurance.

FEMA issues FIRMs that delineate areas within the "100-year flood" boundary, called Special Flood Hazard Areas (SFHA), and flood insurance risk rate zones. The SFHA is based on NFIP's "1%-annual chance flood" standard commonly called the "100 year flood." A "100-year flood" is a calculation of the maximum stream discharge or coastal storm surge and resultant level of flood water that has a "one chance in 100" of occurring in any given year. The occurrence of a flood of this magnitude is independent of all other floods; indeed, a

> **Make Your Own**
>
> FEMA's website allows you to create a flood map for the place you live (or anywhere else). Go to www.msc.fema.gov.

"100-year flood" may occur more than once in a given year, and even a number of times in a 10 or 20 year period. FEMA uses statistical methods or hydrologic calculations to determine the 100-year stream flow or coastal storm height based upon stream gauge records of river flows, storm tides, and rainfall. That information is related to topographic maps and field surveys using hydraulic analysis to then determine the predicted elevation of floodwaters.

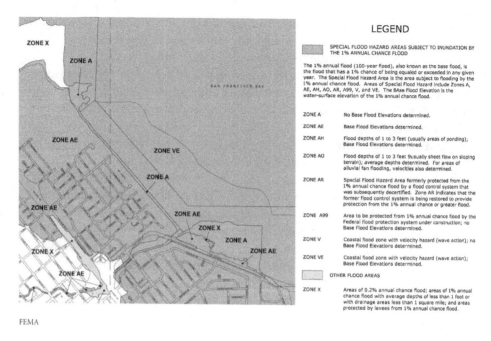

FEMA

Figure 10-5. Detail of FEMA Flood Map of San Mateo, California

Based on the expected flood elevation for a 100-year flood, the NFIP then delineates the area of inundation (i.e., SFHA) relative to elevation above sea level. These SFHAs receive a particular insurance risk zone designation. FIRMs also serve as guiding documents for communities as they regulate development in floodplains and for lenders that enforce mandatory flood insurance purchase requirements. Insurance companies and agents use the FIRMs as the source of risk information for underwriting and rating applications for flood insurance under the NFIP.

Accuracy of Flood Maps. An important policy issue for state and local officials, insurers, mortgage lenders, and property owners is that many flood maps have not been updated with detailed topography or more accurate methodologies or reflect real estate growth. Growth tends to increase runoff and alter drainage patterns on floodplains and, thus, increase flood hazard risk. An inaccurate flood map could result in flood damages to uninsured properties and larger than expected expenditures of federal disaster assistance.

Not all structures that lie within the same flood zone on a FIRM are subject to the same risk. The flood risk depends on factors such as how the home is built, elevation, and drainage. There are also instances where individual properties are inadvertently shown on an SFHA. The NFIP has made it possible through a flood zone correction process for homeowners to remove their homes from the SFHA, removing the mandatory flood insurance purchase requirement.

***

Policy Issuance and Claims Adjusting

Unlike the practice in private insurance markets, the NFIP accepts all insurance applicants and is not selective in evaluating individual applicants for flood insurance coverage. There is no individual risk analysis to determine the likelihood of a future loss, and individual property loss experience is not used as a rating criterion. The sole criterion for accepting an applicant is that the insured property is located in a community that participates in the NFIP. The Standard Flood Insurance Policy (SFIP) is issued for all insured properties. Federal flood insurance coverage is sold to eligible homeowners, renters, and business owners, either directly from the NFIP or through the "Write Your Own" (WYO) program. Under the WYO program, private insurers enter into a "Financial Assistant/Subsidy Arrangement" whereby they agree to issue flood policies in their own name and take responsibility for policy administration, claims processing, marketing and sales. Private insurers handle all claims issued in their name, and adjust and settle flood loss claims consistent with their general claims practices. In adjusting flood insurance claims, which are binding upon the federal government, a WYO insurer is authorized to use staff adjusters or independent contractors selected and supervised by the company. The WYO insurer also determines when and how adjusters will be compensated for their work on flood claims.

WYO insurers are compensated by the federal government for providing services, but assume no financial risk in settling claims. First, the WYO insurers collect the flood premiums and retain approximately 30% as an administrative fee to pay general administrative expenses associated with issuing the policy (e.g., agent commissions, marketing, operations). Second, they are reimbursed for loss adjustment expenses (i.e., direct and indirect expenses associated with settling claims). Third, WYO insurers are reimbursed by the NFIP for the services provided by claims adjusters according to a fee schedule. The balance of the premium that remains, if any, is sent to the NFIP. In the event retained premiums are not sufficient to pay claims and cover expenses, the WYO insurers may draw against Letters of Credit made available by FEMA with a bank.

b. Coverage

The following cases explore what is covered, and not covered, by the standard WYO flood insurance policy.

Quesada v. Director, Federal Emergency Management Agency

753 F.2d 1011 (11th Cir. 1985)

PER CURIAM opinion.

This is an appeal by the Federal Emergency Management Agency (FEMA) from an adverse judgment in favor of the plaintiffs G. Frank and Rosa A. Quesada (the Quesadas). The trial court found that FEMA's flood insurance policy covered the damage sustained to the Quesadas' home as a result of tropical storm "Dennis". . . . We affirm.

I. Background

There is no real dispute over the facts. On August 18, 1981, tropical storm Dennis passed through Florida, causing exceptionally heavy rainfall. It is undisputed that

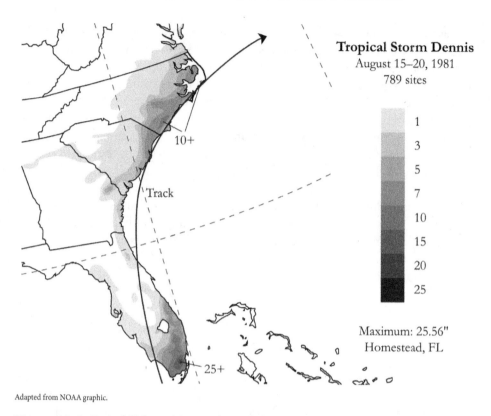

Adapted from NOAA graphic.

Figure 10-6. Rainfall from Tropical Storm Dennis

there was flooding in the area surrounding the Quesadas' home. It is also undisputed that no water actually entered the interior of the Quesadas' home. Rather, their home sustained damage due to the settling or compacting of the fill underneath the foundation of their home, which occurred as a result of the saturation of the fill by the water from the storm. When the saturated fill compacted, the floor slab underneath the Quesadas' home shifted, causing extensive cracking of the floors and walls.

The Quesadas had a flood insurance policy with FEMA. The pertinent provisions of that policy provide as follows:

DEFINITION OF "FLOOD"

Wherever in this policy the term "flood" occurs, it shall be held to mean:

A. A general and temporary condition of partial or complete inundation of normally dry land areas from:

1. The overflow of inland or tidal waters.

2. The unusual and rapid accumulation or runoff of surface waters from any source.

3. Mudslide (i.e. mudflow), a river of flow of liquid mud proximately caused by flooding as defined in subparagraph A-2 above or by the accumulation of water under the ground.

B. The collapse or subsidence of land along the shore of a lake or other body of water as a result of erosion or undermining caused by waves or currents of water exceeding the anticipated cyclical levels.

Perils Excluded:

The insurer shall not be liable for loss;

. . .

> d. By theft or by fire, windstorm, explosion, earthquake, landslide or any other earth movement [except] such mudslides or erosion as is covered under the peril of flood.

The policy issued to plaintiffs was the result of a federally subsidized program, which was designed to provide flood insurance at an affordable price. The program was established by the National Flood Insurance Act of 1968, 42 U.S.C. §§ 4001-4127, which is now administered by FEMA.[2]

The claims adjuster for FEMA testified that he saw fresh looking cracks inside the house during an inspection of appellees' home two days after the storm. Appellees' expert testified that appellees' house was built on sand fill above limerock; such sand fill being the material commonly used for the construction of houses in this area. He also explained that if the house had been built improperly, then this type of structural damage would have occurred prior to the storm. The house was approximately four years old. In assessing appellees' evidence, the district court stated that "there is no question that this [the damage to appellees' home] was an extremely rapid event directly associated with and caused by the flood."

On cross-examination, appellees' expert acknowledged that it was the compaction of the soil, not the water itself, which was the immediate cause of the damage to appellees' home. That is, the sudden and total saturation of the sand fill beneath appellees' home by the flood waters from the tropical storm caused the compaction of that fill which caused the damage incurred by appellees.

II. The Law

Appellant makes two arguments in support of denial of coverage: first, that the definition of "flood" in this policy does not cover the instant situation, and second, that the "earth movement" exclusion applies. The district court concluded that the policy's definition of flood did cover the facts presented here and that the exclusion was not applicable. We agree.

As to the first argument, FEMA basically contends that the flood water must actually inundate the home in order for there to be coverage. That is, a predicate for coverage is that the water must physically enter the house. In our view, this position is untenable and flies in the face of the clear language of the policy. There is no question that the water produced by the tropical storm thoroughly "inundated," to use appellant's terminology, the foundation of appellees' home. We discern no sound reason why coverage should be denied solely because the water did not rise so high as to actually enter the living area of appellees' home. . . .

---

2. At oral argument, the government asserted that the policy's coverage was intended to be limited in scope. We conclude that denial of coverage in this factual context would unduly limit coverage to an extremely narrow class of situations, in contravention with the congressional intent. . . .

In support of its second argument, that the "earth movement" exclusion applies,[4] appellant urges us to follow *West v. Harris*, 573 F.2d 873 (5th Cir. 1978), *cert. denied*, 440 U.S. 946 (1979). Though we agree that the *West* case is facially similar to the instant case, we also agree with the district court that it is factually distinguishable in several significant respects. First and most importantly, in both cases encompassed in the *West* decision, the houses were built on reclaimed swampland, which was supported by a soil which expanded and contracted with normal changes in the soil moisture. The evidence in *West* showed that those "soil movements cause[d] houses built on slabs to heave and settle slightly with soil moisture changes." 573 F.2d at 876. There was clear evidence that damage to these houses would probably have occurred regardless of any flood. In contrast, there is no evidence in the instant case that the soil underneath appellees' home was susceptible to any such compaction due to normal moisture fluctuations. The Quesadas' expert testified that had the house been built on an improper foundation, the cracking of the walls and floors would have occurred sooner. Second, as the trial court noted, in one of the *West* claims, the water had never actually reached the insured's home. . . . In this matter, all agree that the water from tropical storm Dennis actually rose to within inches of the concrete slab and completely saturated the fill constituting the foundation of appellees' home. In sum, we agree with the district court that "the flood and the draining of the canals [in *West*] accelerated a process that was *already* taking place, e.g., the shifting or 'heaving' of the reclaimed swampland and clay-humus fill under the plaintiffs' houses." . . . No such condition was present in the Quesada home.

We note additionally, as did the district court, that since *West* was decided, the flood insurance policy issued by FEMA has undergone some broadening of coverage. As an example, these policies now cover loss due to erosion as caused by flooding, whereas erosion was specifically excluded from coverage in earlier versions. Because of the unique circumstances present in *West*, it does not control the disposition of the instant case.

The government's contention that the "earth movement" exclusion precludes recovery is really grounded on a very strained proximate cause theory, to wit, the nearest and most immediate "cause" of the damage was the compaction of the soil beneath appellees' home. Though in the most literal sense this may be true, we cannot ignore the uncontradicted fact that the compaction would not have occurred but for the flooding[6] and did in fact occur simultaneously therewith. If we deny

4. Of course, all exclusions will be "strictly construed against the insurer and in favor of coverage." *Smith v. Horace Mann Ins. Co.*, 713 F.2d 674, 676 (11th Cir. 1983).

6. A similar proximate cause argument was raised in *Atlas Pallet, Inc. v. Gallagher*, 725 F.2d 131 (1st Cir. 1984), where the court denied coverage, based on the following scenario. The Clear River had flooded, which caused the milldam to collapse, which then rendered insured's sprinkler system inoperative. The court held that the damage to the sprinkler system was not a "direct loss by flood." *Id.* at 137-38. In contrast, we conclude that the damage to appellees' home was directly attributable to the flooding which occurred as a result of tropical storm Dennis. We do not view the compaction of soil in the instant case as a form of "superseding cause," which is how the First Circuit apparently viewed the collapse of the milldam.

coverage in this factual situation, we are hard pressed to imagine a scenario, other than the actual washing away of a house, where coverage would exist.

Because we conclude that the definition of "flood" in the Quesadas' flood insurance policy covers the factual situation presented here and that the "earth movement" exclusion is not applicable, the district court's judgment is AFFIRMED.

Judge TJOFLAT dissents.

In 1968, the Congress passed the National Flood Insurance Act, establishing a federally subsidized program to provide flood insurance to American citizens at an affordable price. Congress took this action because private insurance companies were unable to write flood insurance policies on an economically feasible basis and something had to be done to alleviate some of the extreme hardships suffered by flood victims. The insurance policy the Federal Emergency Management Agency (FEMA) issued Frank and Rosa Quesada was the standard flood insurance policy provided by this program.

I am compelled to dissent. . . . [T]he majority's interpretation of FEMA's standard policy affords much wider coverage than is contemplated by the National Flood Insurance Program FEMA administers and could result in premiums beyond the pocketbooks of many of our citizens the program was designed to reach. The majority has expanded the policy's coverage by eliminating the policy exclusion which precludes coverage when the insured's loss is caused, as it was here, by earth movement. . . .

Wagner v. Director, Federal Emergency Management Agency

847 F.2d 515 (9th Cir. 1988)

Judge KOZINSKI delivered the opinion of the United States Court of Appeals for the Ninth Circuit.

Plaintiffs sue to recover benefits under a Standard Flood Insurance Policy (SFIP) issued pursuant to the National Flood Insurance Act. . . . We consider whether they have satisfied the procedural requirements for maintaining the action and whether the SFIP covers losses caused by a flood-induced landslide.

Facts

Plaintiffs own homes in the Big Rock Mesa area of Malibu, California. Their properties are situated on an ancient landslide that had been dormant. Unusually heavy rainfall during the winter of 1982-1983 and the discharge of effluent from defective septic systems raised the ground water level in the Big Rock Mesa area, saturating and destabilizing the subsurface soil. The rise in ground water thus contributed to the reactivation of the landslide, damaging plaintiffs' property and threatening further damage should the landslide continue.

Each of the plaintiffs had insured his property against "all direct physical loss by flood" with an SFIP issued by the National Flood Insurance Program (NFIP), which provides federally subsidized flood insurance at or below actuarial rates. . . . In order to qualify for flood insurance benefits, a claimant must submit a signed and sworn proof of loss to FEMA within 60 days after the loss has occurred. . . .

Plaintiffs advised FEMA informally of the loss and eventually most of them filed the required formal proofs of loss. None did so, however, until April 1984, seven months after Los Angeles County officials had notified them that their homes were located in an unstable area. In

Photo: John Shea/FEMA

Figure 10-7. Landslide
Rain-induced landslide, La Conchita, California.

February 1984, FEMA sent adjusters and an engineering firm to conduct a limited investigation of plaintiffs' claims. The investigators determined that the properties had not been inundated by flowing surface waters and that all of the damage resulted from the landslide. FEMA thereupon sent letters to plaintiffs denying coverage on the ground that the policy excluded the type of loss they had suffered.

Plaintiffs filed four separate actions against FEMA for breach of the insurance contract. After the actions were consolidated, both sides filed motions for summary judgment. The district court granted plaintiffs' motion and then granted final judgment in the amount of each plaintiff's policy limit.

Contentions of the Parties

. . . FEMA argues that [plaintiffs'] losses were caused not by a flood but by a landslide, a hazard specifically excluded by the SFIP.

[P]laintiffs contend that the subsurface saturation constituted a flood within the meaning of the policy and that their losses were the direct, proximate result of that flood.

Discussion

We now turn to the merits. . . . The SFIP is a single-risk insurance policy: It "only provide[s] coverage for direct, physical loss by flood," SFIP, art. III, which, the policy further explains, must be "directly and proximately caused by a 'flood.'" *Id.*, art. II. At the same time, the SFIP expressly excludes coverage for "loss caused by . . . earthquake, land sinkage, land subsidence, landslide, gradual erosion or any other earth movement except such mudslides (i.e., mudflows) or erosion as is covered under the peril of flood." *Id.*, art. III, para. A(1).

The parties vigorously dispute whether the saturation of the subsurface soil by rainwater and effluent constituted a flood, and, if it did, whether that flood "directly and proximately" caused plaintiffs' losses by contributing to the reactivation of the landslide. While we have doubts about the district court's decision granting judgment for plaintiffs on these two issues, we need not address them here. Plaintiffs admit that flood waters did not damage their properties directly and that all of their losses were caused by the shifting of the earth beneath their homes. The issue of coverage in this case is therefore determined, in our view, by the SFIP's earth movement exclusion, which expressly precludes coverage for losses caused by landslides. *See Quesada v. Director, FEMA,* 753 F.2d 1011, 1015 (11th Cir. 1985) (Tjoflat, J., dissenting) ("the 'earth movement' policy exclusion is dispositive").

Plaintiffs argue that even if the landslide was the immediate cause of the damage, the flood was a direct and proximate cause. The district court adopted this reasoning, holding that the SFIP covered the loss because the " 'flood' set in motion the events leading to the damage to plaintiffs' homes. . . . Although the landslide, an excluded risk, was in a 'strained' sense, the immediate cause of the damage, the water saturation was and is the proximate cause." . . . The district court erred. While the regulations and federal common law govern construction of the SFIP, *see* SFIP, art. X, "Congress did not intend to abrogate standard insurance law principles." *Brazil v. Giuffrida,* 763 F.2d 1072, 1075 (9th Cir. 1985). Where the insurer exercises its right to limit coverage of risks, the plain language of that limitation must be observed. . . . As the courts have all but universally held, federal flood insurance policies do not cover losses stemming from water-caused earth movements. . . .

Plaintiffs point to the one exception in the case law, *Quesada v. Director, FEMA,* 753 F.2d 1011 (11th Cir. 1985). In *Quesada,* the Eleventh Circuit held that the SFIP covered property damage caused by the settlement and compaction of sand fill under plaintiff's home where the settlement resulted from saturation of the fill by water from a tropical storm. The court concluded that although an earth movement may have been the immediate cause "in the most literal sense," the flood was still a proximate cause. *Id.* at 1014. We do not find *Quesada* persuasive. . . .

In the most recent appellate decision in this area, the Seventh Circuit also rejected *Quesada. Sodowski v. NFIP,* 834 F.2d 653, 657-59 (7th Cir. 1987). In *Sodowski,* FEMA paid a claim for the damaged contents of a home inundated by a flood but refused to pay for structural damage "caused by 'settlement of the ground beneath the house.' " *Id.* at 654-55. Rejecting *Quesada*'s expansion of the SFIP's coverage as "an act of judicial activism," *id.* at 659, the Seventh Circuit concluded that the earth movement exclusion applies even where the earth movement was itself caused by a flood. We agree.

Conclusion

The judgment of the district court is reversed and the case is remanded with instructions that judgment be entered for defendant against all plaintiffs.

c. "Policy" and Policy Issues

Kenneth J. Bagstad, Kevin Stapleton & John R. D'Agostino, Taxes, Subsidies, and Insurance as Drivers of United States Coastal Development

63 Ecology Econ. 285 (2007)

Subsidized insurance allows landholders to develop areas that the market alone might otherwise deem too risky for construction — floodplains, coastal zones, and areas prone to earthquakes, mudslides, or wildfire. By matching pooled risk to premiums, private insurers maintain the viability of their industry. Government-subsidized insurance, through the National Flood Insurance Program, was originally intended to reduce flood zone development and risk. It has instead encouraged risky development while providing a subsidy to coastal and floodplain developers, repetitive loss property owners, and the private insurance industry. The decision to provide insurance and other reconstruction aid by federal, state, and local governments can lead to development of places that would otherwise be economically unsuitable for construction.

Tax, subsidy, and government-sponsored insurance programs distort market outcomes; in this way, they can lead to economic inefficiency. A key question with these policies, then, is whether they provide accompanying economic, social, and environmental benefits to justify their existence. On the U.S. Gulf Coast, particularly in Louisiana and Mississippi, the development patterns that arose prior to Hurricane Katrina took place under the influence of a variety of tax, subsidy, and insurance programs, many with ambiguous or conflicting goals.

***

The National Flood Insurance Program (NFIP) was established in 1968 as an economic means to address the insufficient floodplain management practices of levee, dike, and dam construction that characterized the preceding decades. Its creation was also at least partly in response to damage to New Orleans by Hurricane Betsy in 1965. By the 1960s, there was growing recognition that despite decades of spending on levee construction and other structural flood control measures, the nation's flood damage risk had not been reduced. This led to support for the NFIP. The NFIP was expanded in 1973 to include coastal hazard zones (as part of the 1973 Flood Disaster Act) and was amended again in 1994 and 2004. The NFIP has the ability to pay about $700 million per year (which it defines as a historical average loss year). Since 1969, the NFIP has paid $11.9 billion that would have otherwise come from disaster relief payments . . . .

Theoretically, for the NFIP to function properly, three important assumptions must be met. . . . First, the buyer and builder of floodplain or coastal property must know the costs of flood insurance. Second, enrollment in the insurance program must be compulsory for properties located in flood zones. Third, the flood insurance premium must be tied to the risk of paying the claim, so the system is actuarially sound and aligned with social costs of floodplain development. An ecological economics perspective also requires a fourth assumption—that development occurs on a sustainable scale and does not negatively impact distribution and allocation.

There is substantial evidence, both anecdotal and quantitative, that the first two assumptions are rarely met. Chivers and Flores (2002) found that 70% of purchasers learned of the flood insurance rates at closing, and 21% learned after that time. Evidence also suggests that undeveloped flood-prone land sells at a discount (due to perceived flood risk) but developed flood-prone land sells at a premium, creating an incentive for developers to build in flood-prone areas in order to maximize profit. . . . Although developed floodplain property does sometimes sell at a discount (reducing development incentives) and elevation requirements do reduce damage, ongoing floodplain development continues to increase overall risk due to floods and storms. . . . Most studies agree that a combination of improved local land use planning, actuarially sound rates, mandatory participation in the flood insurance program, and improved information to prospective buyers would strengthen the NFIP. Weak building code enforcement has also plagued flood risk areas, particularly in Florida, exacerbating the challenges of reducing premiums paid by the NFIP. . . . Regulations mandating insurance are also routinely avoided because local governments are responsible for enforcement and policies are often allowed to lapse because of a lack of oversight.

The third assumption, that the system is self supporting and actuarially sound, is also not met. George Bernstein, the first Flood Insurance Administrator, testified to Congress in 1973 that "the combination of effective land use controls and full actuarial based rates for new construction . . . makes the NFIP an insurance program rather than a reckless and unjustifiable giveaway program that could impose an enormous burden on the vast majority of taxpayers." FEMA asserts that the NFIP is designed to be self-sufficient—a claim that today is hard to justify upon examining the program's performance. Before 2005, various estimates put program losses at $450 million annually. . . . Congress also forbids the program to charge enough to cover catastrophic losses (hence the unsound rates for the riskiest participants). In doing so, they leave the program vulnerable to massive losses, as the Katrina cleanup is proving. Estimated NFIP payments from damage induced by Hurricane Katrina were approximately $23 billion. Prior to Katrina, the NFIP had authority to borrow up to $1.5 billion from the Treasury Department, which must be repaid with interest. Katrina was the first time the NFIP's financial obligations surpassed this ceiling; the borrowing limit was subsequently raised to $20.7 billion

> ## Quick Questions
>
> Why must the program be compulsory? Does it have to do with pooling risk, or to prevent a moral hazard, with some property owners depending on what they might perceive as inevitable government disaster relief? Would a compulsory program raise the same kind of policy issues as the Affordable Care Act or mandatory auto insurance requirements?

with passage of the NFIP Enhanced Borrowing Act of 2006. The $23 billion in estimated claims from the 2005 hurricane season is more than the total amount paid in claims by the NFIP through its entire history. In order to internally absorb catastrophic risk such as the 2005 hurricane season, revenues from policyholders would have to double. FEMA's own study of the economic effects of removing subsidies predicts that the average premiums for residential properties exposed to considerable flood risk would likely increase from $585 to about $2000 . . . .

Left to the market, flood insurance would not be offered or at best would be offered at far higher rates. For example, the Office of Technology Assessment (1993) estimates that premiums run approximately $800/year in high-risk coastal areas, while private insurers would need a $12,000/year premium to maintain a viable private program. . . . Insurance companies cannot underwrite such predictable and catastrophic loss to large areas at rates that would make development feasible. The concept of pooling risk is not efficient when the only purchasers of a policy are those at great and predictable risk.

Unlike private insurance, the NFIP also pays claims multiple times for the same property, and does not raise rates with additional claims, which encourages rebuilding in the most flood-prone areas. When disaster strikes, developers are able to buy up large amounts of land at steeply discounted rates, knowing they can rebuild and sell that property at rates that do not reflect the site's propensity for flooding. This rebuilding process costs the NFIP hundreds of millions of dollars each year. Repetitive loss properties account for about 2% of policyholders (approximately 82,000 of 4.1 million participating households) but almost 30% of all claims, totaling over $200 million per year. Absent from the NFIP's authority is the ability to condemn houses or require they be moved. Those decisions remain in the hands of local officials. If the NFIP can demonstrate that damage has reduced the market value of the property by at least 50%, it can require that owners elevate the structure when they rebuild. It cannot, however, require the building to be moved or reject reinsuring the property upon rebuilding.

The 2004 Flood Insurance Reform Act sought to address the problem of repetitive loss properties. A "three strikes and you're out of the government's pocket" program was established to deal with properties that incur three claims of $3000 or more with cumulative claim damages of $15,000 or more, making them no longer eligible for NFIP insurance reimbursement for losses. Because so many participating NFIP homeowners were grandfathered into the program at subsidized rates, they have minimal incentive to conform to stronger recent floodplain building codes, leading to the repetitive loss cycle. Grand Isle, Louisiana's only inhabited barrier island, is a prime example of the problems of repetitive loss and perverse economic incentives provided by the NFIP. Grand Isle has been hit by 50 major storms in the past 130 years. According to Tulane University's Oliver Houck . . . the total federal spending in Grand Isle amounted to $439,000 per home. Subtracting the many vacation homes increases the subsidy to $1.28 million for each of its 622 year round residents. Houck concluded that the government is funding high-risk coastal development, and suggested ending this subsidy, buying up flood-prone areas, and moving people back to low-risk zones.

Generally, private insurers have a strong interest in risk prevention and minimization, and devote considerable resources to disaster planning and mitigation. Well before Katrina, there was substantial concern among the insurance industry that exposures are increasing due to a relocation of large numbers of wealthy people to coastal areas. With short-term memory for disasters and short economic horizons, particularly for real estate speculators or transient residents who stay in their home for only several years, there is a strong disincentive to buy insurance or make structural improvements to mitigate for potential disaster loss. . . . Given the statement by reinsurers that $45-50 billion in claims would lead to major insolvencies in the insurance industry . . . perhaps it is fortuitous for these industries that most damage from Katrina came from flooding, and not wind damage.

> **Quick Question**
>
> But if courts uphold the validity of ACCs, why would insurers worry?

Finally, perhaps the largest fault of the NFIP is that it encourages development in environmentally sensitive areas, decreasing the likelihood of development at a sustainable scale. The program externalizes the risk associated with building while imposing the added social cost of foregone ecosystem services. In providing flood protection, even the best structural measures usually fail as sufficient substitutes for intact natural capital.

The NFIP currently fails all four of the aforementioned requirements to properly function. Buyers and sellers have asymmetric information about the actual cost of flood insurance. Though nominally mandatory, many people avoid maintaining coverage, leading to moral hazard. The program is not actuarially sound, as a substantial number of policy holders do not pay premiums commensurate with risk. Finally, the program acts as a subsidy to encourage unsustainable development in high-risk areas, depleting natural capital and externalizing the inherent risks of building in flood zones.

Adam F. Scales, A Nation of Policyholders: Governmental and Market Failure in Flood Insurance

26 Miss. C. L. Rev. 3 (2006)

In the United States, it is time for insurers to recognize that, despite their efforts, they are . . . already in the business of providing flood insurance. One of the effects of the NFIP is to "reclaim" what might otherwise be financially uninhabitable flood-prone areas. Not only are existing communities sustained, but they are enhanced and new ones developed because the risk of disaster has been intermediated. From the perspective of private insurance companies, this appears to be a positive development, as it enhances the demand for their products. Homes that otherwise would not be built or maintained require appropriate homeowners coverage. Prudence may also require appropriate flood insurance, yet the public-private asymmetry continues here. As described earlier, many homes that ought to have flood insurance do not, and many of those homes are privately insured. The result is that insurers' growth in high-risk areas comes at a substantial implied cost — the risk that when catastrophe strikes, the private insurer will be the only available target. This risk is obviously greatest with respect to coastal (rather than riverine) flooding.

But because insurers' exposure to flood risk is somewhat opaque, they may perceive little immediate self-interest in pushing for flood-mitigation efforts. It is clear that communities and the federal government have failed to police flood risk adequately, Katrina merely being a rather spectacular example of a longstanding problem. I suggest that part of the solution to this problem is to bring other interests into play. NFIP incentives are compromised and moderated by its inability to discipline wayward communities and policyholders. Absent a more robust federal land use planning role that seems plausible, some other mechanism must be found to govern flood risk. That mechanism is the insurance market.

Consider the ways in which the structure of the NFIP inhibits optimal flood-risk mitigation. Currently, the NFIP relies on nearly 100,000 floodplain maps to determine risk and premium cost. Upon this superstructure rest the development efforts of approximately 20,000 participating communities. These maps first developed over thirty years ago, and they were largely outdated or inaccurate even then because the baseline data was already ten to twenty years old. The NFIP is slowly addressing this problem, but it should be no surprise that it has not acted more decisively. After all, there simply is no penalty to the NFIP for making a mistake. Because it has no real competitors, the NFIP has no incentive to prioritize remapping (an extraordinarily costly and time-consuming process) over other, seemingly more urgent agency needs. As remapping is likely to expand the number of households nominally required to obtain what will be unsubsidized flood insurance, an agency sensitive to political pressures may be disinclined to press vigorously.

Relatedly, NFIP actuarial projections and subsidies do not provide a transparent picture of risk. NFIP's retrospective risk assessment tends to mask the increasingly risky portfolio of policies in force (as has housing price appreciation). Moreover, while the "grandfathering" subsidy is understandable, it does a poor job of communicating to high-risk insureds the cost of ownership and fails to capture the criterion that would ordinarily be most relevant for the provision of a subsidy — namely income.

Most importantly, private insurers (as well as banks and the secondary mortgage market) do not perceive themselves as being directly threatened by flood risk. Whereas windstorm insurers are at least active (if not always effective) in the inevitable post-hurricane tightening of building codes, only the NFIP is heard to urge that repetitively-flooded properties be elevated or floodplain development be redirected in the wake of a catastrophe. That signal is designed to be weak, and the results are predictable.

At the same time, the NFIP discourages what is admittedly not a particularly encouraging market for private flood insurance. It is unlikely that private insurers could compete meaningfully with the NFIP, inasmuch as the NFIP pays no taxes, generates no reserves, and is indifferent to losing money. Yet the program fails in its basic mission to pre-fund flood losses. Surely, the private market can do better.

I propose that flood risk be incorporated as a mandatory term into all home-owners policies. Several steps are needed to complete this expansion of coverage. First, the federal government should underwrite the remapping of all known or suspected floodplains. Once this is complete, the task of mapping can be turned over to the insurance industry, which can maintain and update this data dynamically (reflecting changing meteorological and development patterns). The NFIP would retain oversight responsibility to ensure that this function is performed accurately and timely. This regulatory jurisdiction could profitably be shared with local insurance commissioners, though they would be required to develop the actuarial expertise and resources necessary to play a meaningful role (i.e., something beyond lobbying NFIP for local exemptions). Private insurers will have an incentive to maintain accurate information because they will lose money to the extent that they do not.

At the same time, the market must be given a freer hand in setting rates. Perhaps the biggest impediment to the creation of a private insurance market is insurers' legitimate fear that, once in, they will be expected to subsidize flood losses much as the NFIP does now. Already allergic to regulatory rate setting, insurers' confidence in the process is not enhanced when state governments allow their own residual pool premium increases but deny them to private market participants.

Something approaching the market rate is absolutely essential to signal to consumers that lakeshore views are expensive. It is debatable whether federal policy should be to facilitate high-risk development at all, but that is a discussion left for another day. The assumption of this Article is that governmental policy will continue to subsidize, even if implicitly, the construction and maintenance of communities in places of high risk. The question is how to enlighten that policy without fundamentally undermining it.

There are two categories of subsidies that my proposal requires, one of which will likely be permanent. Eliminating the grandfathering provisions overnight would cause a collapse in home values, as a home's price reflects the implicit subsidy. The effect would be similar if, overnight, an additional million homes currently considered outside SFHA were redesignated to reflect their true risk. The creators of the NFIP envisioned a twenty-five year subsidy phaseout but provided no mechanism for ensuring this. Recent amendments to the NFIP have purported to speed up this process, but it is unclear if they will be effective.

My solution is to phase out all location-specific subsidies over a fifteen-year period. The declining subsidy must remain transferable to new purchasers to moderate the impact on housing prices. By that point, homeowners will be accustomed to paying near-market rates for flood insurance.

It is unlikely, however, that relatively poor homeowners will ever be able to afford market rates for catastrophic coverage. It is appropriate to redirect the impulse to subsidize toward consumers based on their income. These subsidies may be effectuated in the form of tax credits (hateful as it is to this author to countenance governance via the tax code).

Although imperfect from the standpoint of the free market ideal, the redirected subsidy should unfold against a background of competitive, risk-based ratemaking. One of the great ironies of the NFIP is that it obscures the fact that nearly everyone is at risk for flood-related losses. Flooding is not limited to coastal or midwestern states. Not only are there rivers that occasionally overflow nearly everywhere, but homeowners in western states are at risk for fire-induced mudslides and subsidence. By substantially expanding the policy base, insurers can underwrite flood risk with more manageable loss exceedance probabilities, making the business more attractive. Although risk-based premiums imply substantial variation in rates, a broad portfolio of relatively uncorrelated policies in force reduces the risk of catastrophic loss to insurers.

* * *

One of the virtues of a modest proposal such as this is inevitability. Certainly, it is not inevitable that the federal-state compact on insurance regulation should be breached; nor is it inevitable that private insurers should be required to offer particular coverage. It is not inevitable that the scope of the federal government should be expanded in this way, nor must all homeowners tend unswervingly to the prudent course of full insurance against the spectrum of risks they face.

What is inevitable is that our society will continue to assess premiums opaquely through ad hoc post-disaster relief; that insurers will opaquely remain in the flood insurance business to an extent they cannot transparently acknowledge; that communities will elect the benefits of development now when the risks are to be borne elsewhere; and that the NFIP will be reluctant to upset the constituencies of key members of Congress — for who else would choose the focus on NFIP oversight, save for representatives from coastal and alluvial plains? All these processes are inevitable unless a considered decision to act is taken. At the end of the day, "when all else fails," we are already a nation of policyholders. The only question is whether we are to act as one.

points for discussion

1. *Policy policy.* The dissent in *Quesada* argues courts should interpret SFIP coverage narrowly as a matter of policy. Somewhat ironically, perhaps, the majority in *Wagner* cites approvingly to the dissent in *Quesada*, but then accuses the majority of judicial activism — a term ordinarily used to describe the triumph of policy over law. At the same time, as Professor Scales infers, the ordinary rule in interpreting ambiguous provisions in insurance cases is that such provisions are to be construed in favor of the insured. (Of course, as *Tuepker* illustrates, a court must first decide that a provision is ambiguous before applying that rule of construction. Which raises the question: Should there be a rule of construction to the effect that if a provision might be ambiguous, it is?) Are there good reasons for interpreting obviously dense insurance contracts in favor of one party or the other? Or, is this simply an

ideological battlefield, pitting more "free market"-oriented courts against more "consumer protection"-oriented courts?

2. *The preexisting condition problem.* Is the real problem in the flood insurance arena the fact that there are already (and were already, at the time the NFIP was inaugurated) a very large number of structures constructed in flood-prone areas? The government is faced with a choice: continue to pay out disaster relief moneys post-flood or attempt to offset some of these inevitable costs with premiums from a "flood insurance program." The NFIP cannot charge actuarially accurate rates because that would reduce property owners' incentive to buy a policy in the first place. Why doesn't Congress simply refuse to fund disaster relief after the next big storm or flood? Would that completely solve the problem? The remainder of Professor Scales's article provides excellent discussions of these (and many other) issues.

3. *NFIP reform.* In 2012, Congress passed the Biggert-Waters Insurance Reform Act, which made significant changes to the NFIP. (President Obama signed it into law in July of that year.) The primary goal of Biggert-Waters was to move the federal flood program toward actuarial soundness; in other words, to ensure that homeowners' insurance premiums matched the financial risks being underwritten by the federal government. The Act attempted to do this by eliminating subsidies from pre-1968 structures, appropriating funds for updated risk-mapping, and requiring that rates be adjusted as new flood maps were generated. In early 2013, the combination of Sandy and updated flood maps, many of which showed increased risk levels, drew attention to Biggert-Waters. Newspapers reported that, in some cases, individual annual rates would rise from under $1,000 to over $15,000. In March 2014, President Obama signed the Homeowners Flood Insurance Affordability Act, which delayed or eliminated many of the changes made by Biggert-Waters. For detailed analysis of the two laws and suggestions for how Congress should move forward, see Robert R.M. Verchick & Lynsey R. Johnson, *When Retreat Is the Best Option: Flood Insurance After* Biggert-Waters *and Other Climate Change Puzzles*, 47 JOHN MARSHALL L. REV. 695 (2014).

B. CLIMATE CHANGE IMPACTS AND THE FUTURE OF COASTAL LAW

Without delving into the science of climate change, that is, our understanding of whether or not human-generated gases are contributing to a large-scale, potentially catastrophic shift in the earth's climate, we can still think about what governments (and the private sector) ought to be doing right now in order to prepare for change. Paraphrasing the late, famous climate scientist (and champion birdwatcher) Steven Schneider, just because we don't know it is going to happen with 100 percent certainty doesn't mean we shouldn't do anything to prepare for it. It is rational to spend some resources now in order to avoid or to prepare for a catastrophe; this is the nature of insurance.

Along the same lines, many have written about the fact that actions aimed at reducing greenhouse gases produce many other benefits for society, such as reducing our dependence on foreign oil, encouraging the growth of new businesses, and decreasing other forms of harmful air pollution. In the coastal context, this is probably true as well. As described below, many predicted coastal impacts of climate change are simply more intense, exaggerated versions of the kinds of hazards and threats we've been reading about throughout this course. So, for example, we might have more and more serious storms, faster and more substantial erosion, and deeper and more dangerous flooding. One question that you might think about as you read through the following materials is whether potential coastal climate change impacts represent a qualitative or quantitative change from the kinds of issues coastal law is already meant to address. For example, do we simply need more aggressive versions of our current erosion policies, or do we need altogether new forms of regulation?

This section is organized as follows: First, we will learn about the specific impacts that climate change might bring to coastal areas. Second, we will read a brief excerpt from a very lengthy court opinion in a case in which several states sued large power companies, claiming that the companies' activities constituted a nuisance. The excerpt focuses on states' factual claims about coastal impacts. The remainder of the section explores the idea of adaptation and, specifically, ideas about coastal adaptation. These readings are meant to stimulate thinking and discussion about how we might start changing our coastal policies and laws in order to minimize the potential future harms of climate change.

1. Potential Impacts

Maryland Commission on Climate Change Adaptation and Response Working Group, Comprehensive Strategy for Reducing Maryland's Vulnerability to Climate Change

(2008)

The [Intergovernmental Panel on Climate Change, or IPCC] defines *vulnerability* as the degree to which a system is susceptible to or unable to cope with adverse effects of climate change, including climate variability or extremes. Vulnerability is a function of the character, magnitude, and rate of climate change and variation to which a system is exposed, its sensitivity, and its adaptive capacity. With over 3,000 miles of coastline, Maryland is poised in a very precarious position when it comes to the impacts of climate change. Maryland's coast is particularly vulnerable to both episodic storm events, such as hurricanes and nor'easters and chronic hazards associated with shore erosion, coastal flooding, storm surge, and inundation. These coastal hazards are both driven and exacerbated by climate change and sea-level rise.

Rising sea levels over the last 20,000 years formed the Chesapeake Bay that we know today. While the rapid rate of sea-level rise that occurred over the past

5,000 years has slowed, historic tide-gauge records show that levels are still rising and have increased by one foot within Maryland's coastal waters in the last 100 years. Such a rate of rise is nearly twice that of the global average over the same time period. Maryland is experiencing more of a rise in sea level than other parts of the world, due to naturally occurring regional land subsidence.

Measurement of sea level at any particular location is *relative*. Relative sea-level rise is the sum of global (eustatic) sea level change plus changes in vertical land movement at a particular location. In support of this report, the MCCC Scientific and Technical Working Group (STWG) assessed the 2007 IPCC global sea-level rise projections, along with regional land subsidence variables, and provided a conservative estimate that by the end of this century, Maryland may experience a relative sea-level rise of 2.7 feet under a lower-emission scenario, and as much as 3.4 feet under the higher-emission scenario.

Due to its geography and geology, the Chesapeake Bay region is considered the third most vulnerable to sea-level rise, behind Louisiana and southern Florida. . . . In fact, sea-level rise impacts are already being detected all along Maryland's coast.

Shore erosion. Erosion is a significant problem currently facing Maryland's diverse coastal environment. Approximately 31% of Maryland's coastline is currently experiencing some degree of erosion, with some areas losing as much as 8 ft of upland per year. State-wide, approximately 580 acres of land is lost per year due to shore erosion processes. Sea-level rise is a causal force which influences the ongoing coastal processes that drive erosion, in turn making coastal areas ever more vulnerable to both chronic erosion and episodic storm events.

Coastal flooding. As demonstrated by Tropical Storm Isabel in 2003, Maryland's coast is extremely vulnerable to coastal flood events. Sea-level rise increases the height of storm waves, enabling them to extend further inland. In low-lying coastal areas, a one-foot rise in sea level translates into a one-foot rise in flood level, intensifying the impact of coastal flood waters and storm surge. The risk of damage to properties and infrastructure all along Chesapeake Bay and the Atlantic coast will be heightened as sea level continues to rise.

Inundation. For many coastal areas, slope is the primary variable controlling the magnitude and range of sea-level rise impact over time. In areas such as Maryland's Eastern Shore where elevation change may only be as much as one foot per mile, gradual submergence of a large geographic area, including large expanses of tidal wetlands, is quite likely over time. Land inundation due to sea-level rise is already occurring along low-lying coastal areas in Dorchester and Somerset Counties.

Impacts to barrier and bay islands. Barrier islands are highly dynamic coastal landforms, under constant pressure from the driving forces of waves, wind, ocean currents, and storm surge. These forces, coupled with rising sea levels, act to continually reshape barrier islands, as well as to advance landward migration of the island itself. Fenwick and Assateague Islands form the barrier between Maryland's mainland and the Atlantic Ocean. Extensive development in Ocean City, located on Fenwick Island, restricts the natural process of barrier island migration and in turn puts billions of dollars of public and private infrastructure at risk. Islands, such as James Island in Chesapeake Bay, are also extremely vulnerable to sea-level rise.

Thirteen charted Chesapeake Bay islands have completely disappeared beneath the water's surface.

Higher water tables and salt water intrusion. As sea level rises, the groundwater table, in general, will also rise and salt water will begin to intrude into fresh water aquifers. Evidence of these gradual processes has already started to appear along Maryland's Eastern Shore. Analysis of aerial photography taken over the last 50 years confirms that large expanses of upland areas in Dorchester County are being converted to nontidal wetlands and, as the mean high tide has begun to encroach further inland, these freshwater wetlands are becoming infiltrated with saline water. Over time, these impacts will grow to be ever more problematic as fresh water drinking water supplies are diminished, septic tanks and associated drainfields begin to fail, and non-salt-tolerant plants and crops start to die off in surrounding agricultural fields and forests.

Two to three feet of additional sea-level rise will result in a dramatic intensification of coastal flood events, increase shore erosion, cause the intrusion of salt water into freshwater aquifers, and submerge thousands of acres of tidal wetlands, low-lying lands and Chesapeake Bay's last inhabited island community in Maryland — Smith Island. Sea-level rise poses a significant threat to resources and infrastructure in Maryland's coastal zone. As growth and development continues, especially within low-lying Eastern Shore communities, these impacts are likely to escalate. In the short-term, coastal areas already under natural and human-induced stress are most vulnerable. Of these, barrier and bay islands and the lower Eastern Shore of Chesapeake Bay are in critical need of protection. However, much larger portions of Maryland's coast will become threatened over time.

2. Addressing the Threat

In our discussion of the *Exxon Valdez* litigation, we explored the elements of a common law public nuisance action. In the following decision, the court assesses — among other things — whether the plaintiff states have stated a claim for a public nuisance caused by emission of greenhouse gases.

a. A Lawsuit?

Connecticut v. American Electric Power Co.

582 F.3d 309 (2d Cir. 2009)

Judge HALL delivered the opinion of the United States Court of Appeals for the Second Circuit.

In 2004, two groups of Plaintiffs, one consisting of eight States and New York City, and the other consisting of three land trusts (collectively "Plaintiffs"), separately sued the same six electric power corporations that own and operate fossil-fuel-fired power plants in twenty states (collectively "Defendants"), seeking abatement of Defendants' ongoing contributions to the public nuisance of global warming. Plaintiffs claim that global warming, to which Defendants contribute as the "five largest emitters of carbon dioxide in the United States and . . . among the largest in the world," *Connecticut v. American Electric Power Co.*, 406 F. Supp. 2d 265, 268 (S.D.N.Y. 2005), by emitting 650 million tons per year of carbon dioxide, is causing and will continue to cause serious harms affecting human health and natural resources. They explain that carbon dioxide acts as a greenhouse gas that traps heat in the earth's atmosphere, and that as a result of this trapped heat, the earth's temperature has risen over the years and will continue to rise in the future. Pointing to a "clear scientific consensus" that global warming has already begun to alter the natural world, Plaintiffs predict that it "will accelerate over the coming decades unless action is taken to reduce emissions of carbon dioxide."

Plaintiffs brought these actions under the federal common law of nuisance or, in the alternative, state nuisance law, to force Defendants to cap and then reduce their carbon dioxide emissions. Defendants moved to dismiss on a number of grounds. The district court held that Plaintiffs' claims presented a non-justiciable political question and dismissed the complaints. *See id.*

On appeal, Plaintiffs argue that the political question doctrine does not bar adjudication of their claims; that they have standing to assert their claims; that they have properly stated claims under the federal common law of nuisance; and that their claims are not displaced by federal statutes. Defendants respond that the district court's judgment should be upheld, either because the complaints present non-justiciable political questions or on a number of alternate grounds: lack of standing; failure to state a claim; and displacement of federal common law. . . .

We hold that the district court erred in dismissing the complaints on political question grounds; that all of Plaintiffs have standing; that the federal common law of nuisance governs their claims; that Plaintiffs have stated claims under the federal common law of nuisance; [and] that their claims are not displaced. . . . We therefore vacate the judgment of the district court and remand for further proceedings.

***

I. Background

The States' Complaint

In July 2004, eight States — California, Connecticut, Iowa, New Jersey, New York, Rhode Island, Vermont, and Wisconsin — and the City of New York (generally, hereinafter, "the States") filed a complaint against Defendants American Electric Power Company Inc., American Electric Power Service Corporation, Southern Company, TVA, Xcel Energy, and Cinergy Corporation. The complaint sought "abatement of defendants' ongoing contributions to a public nuisance" under federal common law, or in the alternative, under state law. Specifically, the States assert that Defendants are "substantial contributors to elevated levels of carbon dioxide and global warming," as their annual emissions comprise "approximately one quarter of the U.S. electric power sector's carbon dioxide emissions and approximately ten percent of all carbon dioxide emissions from human activities in the United States." Moreover, the rate of increase of emissions from the U.S. electric power sector is expected to rise "significantly faster than the projected growth rate of emissions from the economy as a whole" from now until the year 2025. At the same time, the States contend that Defendants have "practical, feasible and economically viable options for reducing emissions without significantly increasing the cost of electricity for their customers."

The complaint cites reports from the Intergovernmental Panel on Climate Change and the U.S. National Academy of Sciences to support the States' claims of a causal link between heightened greenhouse gas concentrations and global warming, explaining that carbon dioxide emissions have persisted in the atmosphere for "several centuries and thus have a lasting effect on climate." The States posit a proportional relationship between carbon dioxide emissions and injury: "The greater the emissions, the greater and faster the temperature change will be, with greater resulting injuries. The lower the level of emissions, the smaller and slower the total temperature change will be, with lesser injuries." The States caution that the earth's climate "can undergo an abrupt and dramatic change when a 'radiative forcing agent' causes the Earth's climate to reach a tipping point". . . .

As a result, the States predict that these changes will have substantial adverse impacts on their environments, residents, and property, and that it will cost billions of dollars to respond to these problems.

The complaint details the harms that will befall the States, plaintiff by plaintiff. Not only does the complaint spell out expected future injuries resulting from the increased carbon dioxide emissions and concomitant global warming, but it also highlights current injuries suffered by the States. As an example of global warming having already begun to alter a State's climate, the complaint refers to the reduction of California's mountain snowpack, "the single largest freshwater source, critical to sustaining water to the State's 34 million residents during the half of each year when there is minimal precipitation." The complaint goes on to explain that

> [d]iminished summer runoff from mountain snow will cause water shortages and disruptions to the interrelated water systems and hydroelectric plants on which the State's residents rely. Flooding will increase in California as a result of the earlier melting. This process of reduced mountain snowpack, earlier melting and associated flooding, and reduced summer streamflows already has begun.

Other current injuries resulting from climate changes that the States allege they have already begun to experience include warmer average temperatures, later fall freezes and earlier spring thaws, and the decrease in average snowfall and duration of snow cover on the ground in New England and California. While the complaint does not articulate the impact of these changes on the States currently, it does discuss the effect of these changes in the context of future injuries.

With regard to future injuries, the complaint categorizes in detail a range of injuries the States expect will befall them within a span of 10 to 100 years if global warming is not abated. Among the injuries they predict are: increased illnesses and deaths caused by intensified and prolonged heat waves; increased smog, with a concomitant increase in residents' respiratory problems; significant beach erosion; accelerated sea level rise and the subsequent inundation of coastal land and damage to coastal infrastructure; salinization of marshes and water supplies; lowered Great Lakes water levels, and impaired shipping, recreational use, and hydropower generation; more droughts and floods, resulting in property damage; increased wildfires, particularly in California; and the widespread disruption of ecosystems, which would seriously harm hardwood forests and reduce biodiversity. The States claim that the impact on property, ecology, and public health from these injuries will cause extensive economic harm.

Seeking equitable relief, the States seek to hold Defendants jointly and severally liable for creating, contributing to, or maintaining a public nuisance. They also seek permanently to enjoin each Defendant to abate that nuisance first by capping carbon dioxide emissions and then by reducing emissions by a specified percentage each year for at least ten years.

***

III. The District Court's Amended Opinion and Order

In district court, Defendants moved to dismiss both complaints on several grounds. They asserted that Plaintiffs failed to state a claim because: "(1) there is no recognized federal common law cause of action to abate greenhouse gas emissions that allegedly contribute to global warming; (2) separation of powers principles preclude this Court from adjudicating these actions; and (3) Congress had displaced any federal common law cause of action to address the issue of global warming." *Am. Elec. Power Co.*, 406 F. Supp. 2d at 270. They also contended that the court lacked jurisdiction over Plaintiffs' claims because: "(1) Plaintiffs do not have standing to sue on account of global warming and (2) Plaintiffs' failure to state a claim under federal law divests the court of § 1331 jurisdiction." *Id.* In addition, four of the defendants moved to dismiss for lack of personal jurisdiction. . . . *Id.*

In an Amended Opinion and Order, the district court dismissed the complaints, interpreting Defendants' argument that "separation-of-powers principles foreclosed recognition of the unprecedented 'nuisance' action plaintiffs assert" as an argument that the case raised a non-justiciable political question. *Id.* at 271. Drawing on *Baker v. Carr*, 369 U.S. 186, 198 (1962), in which the Supreme Court enumerated six factors that may indicate the existence of a non-justiciable political question, the district court stated that "[a]lthough several of these [*Baker v. Carr*] indicia have formed the basis for finding that Plaintiffs raise a non-justiciable political question, the third indicator is particularly pertinent to this case." *Am. Elec. Power Co.*, 406 F. Supp. 2d at 271-72. The court based its conclusion that the case was non-justiciable solely on that third *Baker* factor, finding that Plaintiffs' causes of action were " 'impossib[le] [to] decid[e] without an initial policy determination of a kind clearly for nonjudicial discretion.' " *Id.* . . . In the court's view, this factor counseled in favor of dismissal because it would not be able to balance those "interests seeking strict schemes to reduce pollution rapidly to eliminate its social costs" against "interests advancing the economic concern that strict schemes [will] retard industrial development with attendant social costs." *Id.* . . . The district court concluded that balancing those interests required an " 'initial policy determination' first having been made by the elected branches to which our system commits such policy decisions, *viz.*, Congress and the President." *Id.*

In addition, the district court rejected Plaintiffs' arguments that they were presenting "simple nuisance claim[s] of the kind courts have adjudicated in the past," observing that none of the other public nuisance cases involving pollution "touched on so many areas of national and international policy." *Id.* According to the district court, the broad reach of the issues presented revealed the "transcendently legislative nature of this litigation." *Id.* If it were to grant the relief sought by Plaintiffs — capping carbon dioxide emissions — the court believed that it would be required, at a minimum, to: determine the appropriate level at which to cap the emissions and the appropriate percentage reduction; create a schedule to implement the reductions; balance the implications of such relief with the United States' ongoing climate change negotiations with other nations; and assess and measure available alternative energy resources, "all without an 'initial policy determination' having been made by the elected branches." *Id.* at 272-73. The district court pointed to the "deliberate

> **Quick Question**
>
> Is it accurate to call the inaction "deliberate"?

inactions of Congress and the Executive," both in the domestic and international arena "in response to the issue of climate change," and remonstrated Plaintiffs for seeking to impose by "judicial fiat" the kind of relief that Congress and the Executive had specifically refused to impose. *Id.* at 273-74. That fact underscored for the court that the "initial policy determination addressing global climate change" was an undertaking for the political branches, which were charged with the "identification and balancing of economic, environmental, foreign policy, and national security interests." *Id.* at 274.

***

Discussion

***

V. Stating a Claim Under the Federal Common Law of Nuisance

A. Standard of Review

Defendants have also argued — here and before the district court — that Plaintiffs have failed to state a claim under the federal common law of nuisance. *Connecticut v. Am. Elec. Power Co.*, 406 F. Supp. 2d 265, 267 (S.D.N.Y. 2005). The district court did not reach this issue, dismissing the cases on the ground that they presented political questions. In the interest of judicial economy, we exercise our discretion to address the question now, which has been fully briefed to this Court. . . .

***

B. The Federal Common Law of Nuisance and the Restatement's Definition of Public Nuisance

The American colonies imported public nuisance law from England. One of the earliest definitions of public nuisance (then known as "common nuisance") included any "act not warranted by law, or omission to discharge a legal duty, which obstructs or causes inconvenience or damage to the public in the exercise of rights common to all Her Majesty's subjects." *Restatement (Second) of Torts* § 821B cmt. a (1977) (quoting J. Stephen, A General View of the Criminal Law of England 105 (1890)). Originally, public nuisance was a crime, and

> it was used against those who interfered with a public right of way, or ran "noisome trades," but its flexibility became apparent in the varied activities prosecuted under its name over the years: digging up a wall of a church, helping a "homicidal maniac" to escape, being a common scold, keeping a tiger in a pen next to a highway . . . .

Robert Abrams & Val Washington, *The Misunderstood Law of Public Nuisance: A Comparison with Private Nuisance Twenty Years after Boomer*, 54 ALB. L. REV. 359, 362 (1990). In *Mugler v. Kansas*, 123 U.S. 623 (1887), Justice Harlan took the opportunity to wax eloquent on nuisance law and its equitable roots:

> The ground of this jurisdiction, in cases of purpresture, as well as of public nuisances, is the ability of courts of equity to give a more speedy, effectual, and permanent remedy than can be had at law. They cannot only prevent nuisances that are threatened, and before irreparable mischief ensues, but arrest or abate those in progress, and, by perpetual injunction, protect the public against them in the future. . . . This is a salutary jurisdiction, especially where a nuisance affects the health, morals, or safety of the community. Though not frequently exercised, the power undoubtedly exists in courts of equity thus to protect the public against injury.

Id. at 673. Public nuisance eventually became a source of common law civil liability.

The earliest Supreme Court public nuisance cases, brought by States pursuant to the Court's original jurisdiction, did not define what constituted a "public nuisance," as the damage or threatened damage caused by air or water pollution was readily apparent from the pleadings and testimony. For example, the noxious, "sulphurous acid gas" released from the Tennessee Copper Company foundry was alleged to cause "wholesale destruction of forests, orchards and crops." *Georgia v. Tenn. Copper Co.*, 206 U.S. 230, 236, 238 (1907). Similarly, "large quantities of undefecated sewage" were seen as "poison[ing] the water supply of the inhabitants of Missouri and injuriously affect[ing] that portion of the bed or soil of the Mississippi river which lies within its territory." *Missouri v. Illinois* ("*Missouri I*"), 180 U.S. 208, 243 (1901). In each instance, the effect of the nuisance was widespread — injuring the public-at-large — and States as *parens patriae* acted to protect their citizens from the harms caused by the pollution.

United States v. Bushey & Sons, Inc., 363 F. Supp. 110 (D. Vt. 1973), *aff'd* 487 F.2d 1393 (2d Cir. 1973), *cert. denied*, 417 U.S. 976 (1974), was one of the first cases to apply the standards of public nuisance, as defined in Restatement § 821B, to the federal common law of nuisance. Judge Oakes, then a member of this Court sitting by designation in Vermont's district court, examined the federal common law of nuisance and recognized the reshaping of "the old law of public nuisance . . . to fit the 'realities of modern technology.'" *Id.* at 120. He updated federal nuisance law by adopting the Restatement (Second) of Torts's definition of public nuisance: "an unreasonable interference with a right common to the general public." Judge Oakes opined that the oil spills at issue in the *Bushey* case interfered "with the right of the public in the waters of Lake Champlain to have those waters preserved from oil-spill pollution." *Id.* at 116-17, 120. He determined that the defendants' inter- ference with that public right was "unreasonable" because the oil-spill pollution was proscribed by both the Refuse Act, 33 U.S.C. § 407, and by the fact that it "has been of a recurring nature, although not continuous, producing long-lasting effects and substantial detriment upon the public right, with the actor — in this case, the defendants — knowing or having reason to know of that effect." *Bushey*, 363 F. Supp. at 120-21. . . . Judge Oakes's approach proved both practical and feasi- ble in forging an equitable remedy, and was upheld on appeal. . . .

***

In keeping with the precedents discussed above, we will apply the Restatement's principles of public nuisance as the framework within which to examine the fed- eral common law of nuisance question presented by the instant cases. We believe the Restatement definition provides a workable standard for assessing whether the parties have stated a claim under the federal common law of nuisance. . . . The Restatement definition of public nuisance set out in § 821B(1) has two elements: an "unreasonable interference" and "a right common to the general public." Section 821B(2) further explains:

> Circumstances that may sustain a holding that an interference with a public right is unreasonable include the following:
> (a) Whether the conduct involves a significant interference with the pub- lic health, the public safety, the public peace, the public comfort or the public convenience, or
> (b) whether the conduct is proscribed by a statute, ordinance or administrative regulation, or
> (c) whether the conduct is of a continuing nature or has produced a permanent and long-lasting effect, and, as the actor knows or has reason to know, has a signif- icant effect upon the public right.

Restatement § 821B(2).

***

C. Have the States Stated a Claim Under the Federal Common Law of Nuisance?

1. Applying the Public Nuisance Definition to the States

The States have sued in both their *parens patriae* and proprietary capacities. As quasi-sovereigns and as property owners, they allege that Defendants' emissions, by contributing to global warming,

> constitute a substantial and unreasonable interference with public rights in the plaintiffs' jurisdictions, including, *inter alia*, the right to public comfort and safety, the right to protection of vital natural resources and public property, and the right to use, enjoy, and preserve the aesthetic and ecological values of the natural world.

These grievances suffice to allege an "unreasonable interference" with "public rights" within the meaning of § 821B(2)(a).... The States have additionally asserted that the emissions constitute continuing conduct that may produce a permanent or long lasting effect, and that Defendants know or have reason to know that their emissions have a significant effect upon a public right, satisfying § 821B(2)(c). We hold that the States, in their *parens patriae* and proprietary capacities, have properly alleged public nuisance under Restatement § 821B, and therefore have stated a claim under the federal common law of nuisance as it incorporates the Restatement's definition of public nuisance.

2. Defendants' Arguments

***

The Character of the Alleged Nuisance

Defendants' next argument is based on a reference to *North Dakota v. Minnesota*, in which the Supreme Court wrote: "It is the creation of a public nuisance of simple type for which a State may properly ask an injunction." 263 U.S. 365 (1923). North Dakota had sought to enjoin Minnesota's continued use of "cut-off ditches," which had the net effect of causing a river to overflow and harm valuable North Dakota farmland. In discussing whether it had jurisdiction over the dispute, the Supreme Court reviewed the public nuisance cases it had previously decided and, in that context, referred to public nuisances "of simple type." Defendants seize upon the phrase and contend that *only* a public nuisance of a simple type may constitute a valid claim for public nuisance. They then create their own definition for the phrase in an attempt to show that the States have not stated a claim. According to Defendants, nuisances of a "simple type" involve "immediately noxious or harmful substances [that] cause severe localized harms that can be directly traced to an out-of-state source." They assert that carbon dioxide is not "poisonous or noxious" and does not "immediately harm anyone (as contagious and pathogenic bacteria do), or destroy forests, crops and farms (as sulphuric gases and floodwaters do)." Defendants also point out that their carbon dioxide emissions mix "with other greenhouse gases from innumerable sources across the planet." Because the States do not claim that any alleged future harm can be directly traced to their emissions, Defendants submit that the States have not alleged a "simple type" nuisance entitling them to relief.

The *North Dakota* Court did not otherwise explain or define the phrase "simple type." *Id.* An earlier Supreme Court case, however, provides some clue as to what the *North Dakota* Court meant. In *Missouri v. Illinois*, 200 U.S. 496 (1906) ("*Missouri II*"), the Supreme Court analyzed whether the alleged nuisance—typhoid bacillus from Illinois's discharge of sewage into the Mississippi River—could survive the 357-mile journey to the St. Louis drinking water intake area. In assessing whether Missouri had proved a nuisance claim, the Court examined scientific data specifically directed to the issues, listened to dueling experts, and ultimately held that Missouri did not prove its case. *Id.* at 522-26. The Court wrote:

> [I]f this suit had been brought fifty years ago it almost necessarily would have failed. There is no pretense that there is a *nuisance of the simple kind* that was known to the older common law. There is nothing that can be *detected by the unassisted senses*—no visible increase of filth, no new smell.... The plaintiff's case depends upon *an inference of the unseen.*

Id. at 522 (emphases added).

The phrase "simple type" thus appears to describe a kind of rudimentary nuisance that could easily be detected by "the unassisted senses"—apparently the only kind of pollution-related nuisance claim that had been actionable in the mid-1850s—which a complaining State would have little difficulty in proving. But rather than limiting what nuisances were actionable, the Court in *Missouri II* was, in fact, asserting the opposite. The Court never held that the complexity of Missouri's claim precluded Illinois's legal responsibility or, conversely, that a nuisance of a "simple type" was a *sine qua non* for a nuisance claim. It was merely making the point that the law of public nuisance had already evolved from the era when only easily perceived nuisances had been actionable. The *Missouri II* Court's use of the phrase did not operate to divide nuisances into those that were simple or complex so as to cull out the latter, nor did it otherwise imply that only the "simple" type of nuisances were actionable.

As a corollary to their "simple type" of nuisance argument, Defendants additionally contend that the challenged pollution must be directly traced to an out-of-state source in order to be actionable. Because Defendants' emissions "mix with other greenhouse gases from innumerable sources across the planet and contribute to a global process that will allegedly cause a variety of future harms" and pose "the same alleged threat to every sovereign," Defendants assert that Plaintiffs cannot properly complain of a "simple type" nuisance. Defendants contest the States' argument that "[n]atural resources injuries due to pollution—the 'paradigmatic' federal common law case—rarely occur because of just one polluter," and that many sources often contribute to the alleged harm....

Defendants have cited no case law that supports their reasoning.... The Court has not imposed a requirement upon all federal common law of nuisance cases that the challenged pollution must be "directly traced" or that Plaintiffs must sue all sources of the pollution complained of in order to state an actionable claim. On the contrary, "the fact that other persons contribute to a nuisance is not a bar to the defendant's liability for his own contribution." Restatement (Second) of Torts § 840E (note that Comment a. states that this provision applies to both public and private nuisance); *see also, e.g., Illinois ex rel. Scott v. Milwaukee*, No. 72 C 1253, 1973 U.S. Dist. LEXIS 15607, at *20-22 (N.D. Ill. Nov. 1, 1973) ("[I]t is sufficient for plaintiffs to show that defendants' nutrient discharges [leading to eutrophication of Lake Michigan] constitute a significant portion of the total nutrient input to the lake. The correct rule would seem to be that any discharger who contributes an aliquot of a total combined discharge which causes a nuisance may be enjoined from continuing his discharge. Either that is true or it is impossible to enjoin point dischargers."), *aff'd in relevant part* and *rev'd in part*, 599 F.2d 151 (7th Cir. 1979), *vacated on other grounds, Milwaukee II*, 451 U.S. 304. . . .

Yet another limitation that Defendants seek to impose on the federal common law of nuisance is that the nuisance must be "poisonous" or "noxious" in order to be actionable. They insist that because carbon dioxide is neither, Plaintiffs' claim must fail. But none of the federal common law of nuisance cases impose this requirement. Defendants' position, moreover, runs counter to the holding in *North Dakota*, for example, where the Court held that a life-giving substance such as water could be a nuisance under certain circumstances, such as when it flooded farmland. 263 U.S. at 374.

Nor does public nuisance theory require that the harm caused must be immediate, as even threatened harm is actionable under the federal common law of nuisance. *See Mugler v. Kansas*, 123 U.S. 623 (1887) (observing that courts of equity, in adjudicating public nuisance cases, can both prevent threatened nuisances, "before irreparable mischief ensues," as well as abate those in progress). Judge Oakes, in *Bushey*, recognized this attribute of nuisance law, writing that " '[o]ne distinguishing feature of equitable relief is that it may be granted upon the threat of harm which has not yet occurred.' " *Bushey*, 346 F. Supp. at 150 (quoting William Prosser, Handbook of the Law of Torts 624 (3d ed. 1964)). . . .

Defendants' assertion that the federal common law of nuisance mandates that the harm be localized is similarly misplaced. The touchstone of a common law public nuisance action is that the harm is widespread, unreasonably interfering with a right common to the general public. *See Tenn. Copper Co.*, 206 U.S. at 238-39 ("[W]e are satisfied, by a preponderance of evidence, that the sulphurous fumes cause and threaten damage on so considerable a scale to the forests and vegetable life, if not health, with the plaintiff State as to make out a case . . . ."); *Missouri I*, 180 U.S. at 241 ("The health and comfort of the large communities inhabiting those parts of the state situated on the Mississippi river are not alone concerned, but contagious and typhoidal diseases introduced in the river communities may spread themselves throughout the territory of the state.").

The only qualification that the Supreme Court has placed upon a state bringing a nuisance action against another state was that "the case should be of serious magnitude, clearly and fully proved." *Missouri II*, 200 U.S. at 521. As discussed above, this statement was not intended to limit the scope of the nuisance cause of action, but to recognize the sensitivity with which the Court must undertake, pursuant to its original jurisdiction, adjudication of disputes involving a state's quasi-sovereign interests. But even assuming, *arguendo*, that the Court intended such a limitation to apply more broadly, the Court in *Missouri II* immediately went on to characterize as "a question of the first magnitude whether the destiny of the great rivers is to be the sewers of the cities along their banks or to be protected against everything which threatens their purity." *Id.* In this case, the States have properly asserted *parens patriae* standing with respect to a public nuisance, and the "serious magnitude" of the nuisance caused by climate change, as it has been alleged, is apparent.

In sum, the States have stated a claim under the federal common law of nuisance.

***

The judgment of the district court is VACATED, and the cases are REMANDED for further proceedings.

points for discussion

1. *Displaced.* In 2011, the Supreme Court reversed the Second Circuit's decision in *American Electric Power*. In a unanimous decision, the Court found that the Clean Air Act displaced federal common law of nuisance claims. In a 2007 decision, *Massachusetts v. Environmental Protection Agency*, 549 U.S. 497 (2007), the Court held that the Clean Air Act allowed the EPA to regulate carbon dioxide emissions. Given that holding, there was no remaining room or purpose for nuisance claims relating to those emissions.

2. *The powers of the common law.* One of the virtues of the public trust doctrine, at least as it is often described, is that it empowers courts as watchdogs of, or backstops to, legislative or agency decision-making. Are the arguments the same in the context of public nuisance regulation? In other words, should courts have a role in policing environmentally harmful activities, or should such matters be left to the realm of environmental laws and agency administration? Interestingly, a separate set of lawsuits is underway, arguing that the states have a responsibility to limit carbon emissions based on the theory that they are trustees of a "sky trust." In an interview with the High Country News, Professor Mary Wood of the University of Oregon School of Law explains how that litigation might work:

    > **HCN:** Let's turn now to the specifics of the atmospheric trust litigation.
    > **Wood:** The other piece the public needs to understand is the concept of orphan shares. That is, every single level of government has to reduce carbon (emissions from all sources within its jurisdiction). Otherwise, it leaves its share on the table without anybody taking responsibility for it. I call that an orphan share. If we have any significant orphan shares left out there, we can't reduce the carbon in time to prevent catastrophic climate heating . . . because no other government is going to take a deadbeat sovereign's orphan share.

So virtually every city, county, every state, every nation must accept its own responsibility for carbon reduction, and that's not happening right now. . . . There's a patchwork quilt of carbon reduction and people are treating this as a political choice. It's not. . . . The scientists have defined the fiduciary obligation, and now it's up to every level of government as trustee to carry out that fiduciary obligation in a uniform manner so that all of the carbon reduction will add up to the amount we need. So this is a matter of carbon math. It all must add up, and if there is a piece missing it won't add up.

***

HCN: And you believe the way to do this is atmospheric trust litigation?
Wood: Well, that's only one piece of it. The trust approach . . . is part of an overall paradigm shift which demands that our government, every level of it, start protecting the resources that we, the public, own. . . . (This awareness) must happen in the communities, the agencies, the churches, the schools, all of that, and in other countries as well.

The atmospheric trust litigation part is a road map for citizens to bring suit against their government, (whether) city, state, or federal, to enforce the fiduciary obligation. We still have three branches of government in this country, last time I checked. But the courts have been passive observers to this monumental destruction that now threatens, literally, the future of human civilization and our children. The courts . . . must provide a check against runaway politicization by the other two branches. They have been on the sidelines in climate crisis. So this atmospheric trust litigation puts the courts as the appropriate enforcers of governments' basic duty.
HCN: So how would it work?
Wood: The court would declare this trust obligation, which is well-rooted in law. And then it could craft a declaratory judgment, setting forth these principles. That alone would go a long ways, because suddenly the public would have clarity on its own government's responsibility.

But second, a judge can order an accounting against any level of government. An accounting is a very standard tool . . . and it basically means the government would have to measure its carbon footprint, which is very feasible these days, and it would have to show the court that it's reducing carbon in accordance with the scientifically defined fiduciary obligation. So a court would not tell the jurisdiction how to accomplish carbon reduction. That would be up to the political branches, and the citizens. But the court would enforce that carbon reduction, and have a method by which the citizens can know whether their government is squandering their future . . . or protecting their resources, through this accounting.

And finally there could be injunctive backstops. If the officials do not perform as trustees, they would be subject to contempt of court, or injunctions such as prohibitions on logging, road building, and other activities that contribute carbon.

***

> **HCN:** Given the science that says we have to be acting right now, is there really time for this legal strategy to bear fruit in two years or less? Don't lawsuits sometimes take decades?
>
> **Wood:** Lawsuits often take decades, but judges have the power to structure their lawsuits to provide expeditious or even emergency relief. Every judge has the power to organize his or her docket to address climate crisis with the urgency that it demands. And my own feeling is that there will be judges out there who recognize that they are part of the third branch of government and that our government is sending the entire world into disaster by not dealing with climate. So there will be judges there that will accept this responsibility.
>
> **HCN:** So you actually believe this is a realistic approach and that this could help to prevent climate meltdown as you call it?
>
> **Wood:** Oh, I do. But I would never say that this is the silver bullet. Because, as Bill McKibben has said . . . if climate is to be solved, it's going to be solved with silver buckshot, not with a silver bullet, and this is my buckshot. This is just one little buckshot, but it's my buckshot, and it's something people hadn't thought of.

High Country News (May 12, 2008). What do you think of this approach? For an update on the atmospheric trust litigation, see *Juliana v. United States*, OUR CHILDREN'S TRUST, https://www.ourchildrenstrust.org/us/federal-lawsuit/ (last visited Feb. 27, 2019).

3. Adaptation

In the climate change context, "adaptation" refers to the actions taken to respond to climate change impacts. ("Mitigation" refers to actions taken to prevent or slow climate change itself.) The following materials discuss adaptation generally, then provide some examples of more and less conventional thinking about coastal adaptation.

a. Generally

William E. Easterling, III, Brian H. Hurd & Joel B. Smith, Coping with Climate Change: The Role of Adaptation in the United States

(2004)

What History Tells Us About Adaptation to Climate Variability

Historic responses to changes in socioeconomic or environmental conditions can serve as analogues for social adaptation to future climate change. Although historical environmental changes were not — until recently — caused by anthropogenic climate change, many are similar to climate change because they were gradual and irreversible or resulted in large changes in the location of activities. For example, the nation's natural resource managers, including farmers, foresters, civil engineers, and their supporting institutions, have been forced to adapt to numerous historical challenges either to overcome adversity or to remove important impediments to sustained productivity. Many analysts argue that the ways in which those managers and institutions responded to past challenges may provide insights into how they might respond in the future to climate variability and change. . . . The following case studies illustrate the potential for technology, human ingenuity, and institutional innovation to deal with changes analogous to climate change: translocation of crops to new environments; resource substitution in response to scarcity; and response to geophysical events similar to climate change.

***

Sea-Level Rise Analogue: The Rising Great Salt Lake

Societies respond to climate change, but often not in the most efficient manner possible. Thus the process of adaptation can often be a case of "muddling through." Incremental decisions may be adopted to address immediate threats, but changes that could address long-term threats, but may be politically difficult to adopt, are avoided.

Between 1982 and 1986, the Great Salt Lake rose 12 feet due to heavy precipitation in northern Utah. . . . This rise resulted in flooding and damage to lakeshore mineral industries, highways and railroads, ecosystems, wildlife and recreation areas, and residential developments bordering the lake. The Great Salt Lake's level had not risen substantially before 1982, and models based on the previous 30 to 40 years of data predicted variability in lake levels only as high as 4,202 feet. Problems arose when actual lake-level variability exceeded historical and modeled variability — by 1986, the actual level reached almost 4,212 feet.

When the lake began rising in 1982, decision-makers assumed it was a one-season anomaly, and chose to take no action. As the lake continued to rise over the next several years, the state government faced uncertainty regarding the nature of the lake change (whether it was an anomaly or a trend). The government decided to adopt a "wait and see" approach to dealing with the problem, choosing short-term structural mitigation over long-term adaptations. The state pursued immediate fixes such as diking and raising highways. These fixes addressed the immediate lake-level

Photo: Utah Division of Water Resources

Figure 10-8. Pumping Station in the Great Salt Lake

rise, but did not necessarily protect the infrastructure from future rises. These solutions also failed to address threats to shoreline development.

As the Great Salt Lake continued to rise in 1986, however, the state government decided to construct a system to pump excess water to a large adjacent evaporative pond that would increase the effective evapotranspiration rate and lower the lake, at a cost of $60 million. Shortly after the pumping project was constructed, precipitation subsided, the lake level began dropping, and the project was then criticized as unnecessary. Interestingly, this pumping project was engineered to be effective in reducing lake levels up to 4,215 feet. If the lake continued to rise above this level — only 3 feet above the high mark in 1986 — the pumping project would have no longer been able to reduce the level further. Thus, the project that many viewed as a long-term solution was only effective within a relatively small range of conditions, illustrating the limitations of even long-term structural fixes if actual variability exceeds anticipated limits.

An alternative adaptation option that was proposed, The Beneficial Development Area (BDA), would have established floodplain and hazard zones in the region. The BDA, which potentially would have removed land from development, was proposed by the Federal Emergency Management Agency (FEMA) and had some support at the local level. Localities were reluctant to adopt it, however, because they were wary of surrendering autonomy or restricting development in valuable lands.

Case Study Lessons

Unlike the elegance and simplicity of models, case studies demonstrate that actual adaptation can be complex, varied, and imperfect. [They] illustrate that society has a high capacity for adaptation and *eventually* can make adaptations to accommodate changing conditions. . . . The Great Salt Lake example shows that society can, to some degree, address immediate and pressing problems brought about by a changing climate.

Yet these examples . . . demonstrate that adaptation is not necessarily seamless or efficient and can be filled with many mistakes and costs. . . . The Great Salt Lake example is an interesting study of what Glantz (1988) would refer to as "muddling through." At first, decision-makers considered the lake's rise to be an extreme event and anticipated that conditions would soon return to "normal." Perhaps this view reflected the "wishful thinking" of the decision-makers and possibly the sentiments of the wider community — completely understandable positions in the face of significant scientific uncertainty about the fate of the lake. However, though "muddling through" is not unusual, it can impede recognition of long-term change. This can result in delayed actions and, consequently, higher adjustment costs (or incurred damages). In the Great Salt Lake, adaptations were made incrementally to address problems as they arose, but decision-makers had difficulty with anticipatory adaptations to address risks from a continued rise in lake levels. They avoided the BDA, perhaps because it would have resulted in short-term economic harm. The investment in the pumping station turned out to be costly and, ultimately, unnecessary for the immediate problem. However, given the potential for a continued rise in lake levels, the investment still may have been appropriate. Such large investments, which could be necessary for adaptation to climate change, can be risky for decision-makers. Governments may have more incentive to engage in incremental responses that provide only short-term solutions rather than more comprehensive changes that can better position society to cope with larger events in the future.

On the whole, the case studies suggest that society has a substantial capacity to adapt to climate change but may in many instances fall short of using the capacity to its full extent. The necessity of coping with adverse impacts from climate change will force adaptations, but decision-makers may miss many opportunities to adapt more effectively and efficiently.

Reactive Adaptation: How Successful Will It Be?

A central question in the assessment of the potential impacts of climate change to the United States is the extent to which adaptation can reduce the vulnerability of societal systems. A review of quantitative studies of reactive adaptation to climate change can help assess whether reactive adaptation may be successful in offsetting adverse impacts of climate change. The literature as a whole offers an opportunity to garner broader lessons concerning the general effectiveness of reactive adaptation.

Reactive Adaptation as Assessed in Quantitative Studies

The published literature offers limited analysis on what damages would occur to U.S. societal systems if there were no adaptation to future climate change, and it does not address the extent to which damages could be avoided and the cost of such avoidance measures. The analysis necessary to compare scenarios with and without adaptation has only been conducted for coastal resources and agriculture. Given that these are societal sectors that demonstrate high potential for adaptation, analysis of the relative effectiveness of adaptation in these sectors alone should not be extrapolated to other sectors — such as natural ecosystems — where adaptation may be less successful.

Coastal Development

A small number of studies analyze the implications of sea-level rise for coastal communities and the potential for adaptation to ameliorate damages. Yohe (1989) estimates that a half-meter rise in sea level would place $185 billion of property and infrastructure in jeopardy by 2100, and a one-meter rise in sea level would place $429 billion in jeopardy by 2100. Titus and Greene (1989) estimate that the financial cost of protecting all developed areas from a half-meter sea-level rise would be $50 to $66 billion, and protecting against a one-meter sea-level rise would cost $115 to $174 billion. This analysis suggests that appropriate adaptation could reduce the severity of damages to development by about three-fifths to three-quarters, compared with no adaptation. Neumann et al. (2000) point out that some areas may have relatively low property value relative to the cost of protection and thus further savings are possible by limiting the scope of protection to exclude low value areas. Therefore, the relative reduction in damages from adaptation could be larger. However, even areas with relatively low property values may be valued for cultural, ecological, or aesthetic reasons. The Cajun parishes of the low-lying Louisiana bayous are a prime example.

***

Effectiveness of Reactive Adaptation — General Findings

Can the United States adapt to climate change without incurring excessive social and environmental costs? As mentioned above, limited quantitative information is available to address this question. However, on a qualitative basis, some general conclusions can be drawn regarding the capacity of the United States to adapt to future climate change. Adequate adaptive capacity is required across a range of scales from the micro (place-based) to the macro (national). . . .

The Path of Climate Change

The more rapid and varied the change in climate, the more challenging it will be for society to adapt. The path of climate change incorporates the rate of change, the variability of change, and the magnitude of change (*e.g.*, whether climate becomes monotonically wetter or drier, or whether it fluctuates). Experience with historical analogs of climate change suggests that agricultural and other societal land-use systems are fully capable of responding to long-term change that occurs gradually and consistently. Given the time to depreciate and replace aging capital stock with new stock and production systems, there is little reason to doubt the ability of American farmers to switch to crops that are better adapted to the changing climate, assuming, of course, that such changes are supported by prevailing economic conditions. The key will be the successful identification of the signal of climate change such that farmers make the right decisions in a timely way. If farmers fail in this regard, then they may face substantial costs of adapting. The same conclusions apply to the replacement of coastal infrastructure and buildings in response to climate variability and sea-level rise.

A more rapid rate of climate change is likely to make adaptation more difficult and result in net damages. One of the underlying problems with a more rapid change is that the pace of adaptation needs to speed up. With a more rapid change in climate, infrastructure and other investments will need to be replaced or modified more rapidly and, in many cases, before the end of design lifetimes are reached. Replacing investments early will also increase the cost of adaptation.

Changes in variability, especially increases in extreme events, likely would pose an even greater challenge for adaptation. Extreme events such as floods and droughts cause extensive damage to many parts of society, and thus a critical issue for adaptation is the degree to which frequency, intensity, and persistence of extreme events change. Such changes portend a more difficult and costly transition compared with that based solely on marginal changes in average conditions.

***

The Portfolio of Tools for Adaptation

The United States currently is endowed with a large portfolio of tools for adapting to climate change. Results of model simulations of simple reactive agronomic strategies, such as switching crops and cultivars, planting earlier, and changing land-use allocations, suggest that the nation's farmers have a high potential to adjust to the early stages of warming. Moreover, the nation's water managers and other natural resource professionals have developed strategies for coping with climate risk. Such strategies, which include increasing storage, improving conservation, and increasing water transfers may provide a measure of protection against climate variability and a first line of defense against climate change. Much is still unknown, however, such as the long-term success of these tools for mitigating climate change, and the ease with which the tools will be employed. In particular, it is not clear if these tools alone will be sufficient to adapt to a rapid change in climate or a change that involves a significant increase in intensity or frequency of extreme events.

***

Uptake of Adaptive Strategies

Resource managers and policy-makers will be challenged to identify, observe, and react to climate change appropriately. This challenge stems partly from the difficulty in properly identifying and distinguishing climate change from natural climate variability. . . . There is some indication that the process of adapting to climate change has already begun, among both societal and natural systems. However, the earlier case study of the Great Salt Lake exemplifies the trouble that managers may encounter with detecting a climate-change trend from background climatic fluctuations. Compounding this identification challenge, inappropriate management strategies and institutional constraints on decision-makers — such as the need to give due consideration to the rights of property owners — may result in delayed adaptation and outright maladaptation — that is, long-term adaptation to short-term climate variability that is inconsistent with long-term climate change. Over the long term, some inefficiency in adaptation is bound to happen, at least initially. In the case of agriculture, Schneider et al. (2000) demonstrate that crop yields could be reduced by several percentage points if farmers delay their response to climate change or misread the direction that climate change takes. Another critical issue is how quickly new technologies will be diffused into common use.

Yet another important facet is the role of public policy in promoting or inhibiting adaptation. Policies that encourage experimentation and change could promote adaptation, while those that discourage change can discourage adaptation. For example, agricultural policies that reward farmers for planting specific crops in specific locations can discourage farmers from changing their planting regime in response to climate change. Water policies that encourage users to consume or waste water can inhibit the adoption of water-saving technologies and practices and even the transfer of water to more efficient uses in response to climate change. In contrast, water allocation policies that enable prices to fluctuate with water availability and allow water to be traded among users tend to encourage more efficient use of water. Market-oriented water transfers can provide valuable flexibility in adapting to changes in water scarcity. The value of this flexibility and the adaptive capacity it provides must, however, be weighed against the possible adverse and unintended consequences such transfers often entail because of water's interconnectedness to water users whose values are difficult to reflect in economic markets (*e.g.*, the value of instream flows for fish and wildlife habitat, the aesthetic and spiritual values held by some groups, and the value of quantity and quality changes to downstream water users).

It is important to note that complete adaptation by all regions, populations, or individuals is not a necessary condition for society on the whole to adapt successfully. Indeed, successful adaptation can entail a loss of livelihood and migration for many people. For example, the agricultural sector is expected to adapt to climate change in part by expanding production in northern parts of the United States and reducing production of many crops in many southern areas. . . . This geographic shift could result in reduction of acreage or loss of employment for many farmers in areas that experience shrinking production. . . .

The Case for Proactive Adaptation

The nature and extent of expected climate change may reveal inadequacies in existing institutions and reactive responses. Waiting to act until changes have occurred can be more costly than making forward-looking responses that anticipate climate change, especially with respect to long-lived assets and infrastructure such as bridges and dams, coastal development, and floodplain development. A "wait-and-see" approach would be particularly unsuccessful in coping with:

- Irreversible impacts, such as species extinction or unrecoverable ecosystem changes;
- Unacceptably high costs and damages, such as inappropriate coastal zone development that exposes lives and property to intense storm damages; and
- Long-lived investments and infrastructure that may be costly or prohibitive to change in response to climate change. . . .

Proactive adaptation, unlike reactive adaptation, is forward-looking and takes into account the inherent uncertainties associated with anticipating change. Successful proactive adaptation strategies are therefore flexible; that is, they are designed to be effective under a wide variety of potential climate conditions, to be economically justifiable (*i.e.*, benefits exceed costs), and to increase adaptive capacity.

When and where climate change risks loom large, long-run societal goals may benefit from a thorough and comprehensive consideration of the adequacy of institutions and infrastructure in providing necessary services in light of climate change. Perhaps the clearest and strongest cases for incorporating proactive adaptation into long-term planning are those of long-lived investments and the design and organization of institutions.

Proactive adaptation could be best facilitated through a range of possible mechanisms including knowledge and learning, risk and disaster management and response, infrastructure planning and development, institutional design and reform, increased flexibility of sensitive managed and unmanaged systems, avoidance of maladaptation, and technological innovation. In addition, all of these mechanisms are routinely influenced or governed by public institutions and public policy, allowing governments to play an active role in enhancing the uptake of proactive adaptation strategies. These mechanisms and their intersection with public policy are briefly discussed below. . . .

Knowledge and Learning

Knowledge is key to adaptive capacity. . . . Knowledge is dynamic; it accumulates through observation, monitoring, and analysis. It can also degrade, however, if the learning process is neglected. For example, knowledge degrades if monitoring and data collection systems collapse, if research and development are not continually supported, if literacy and education levels diminish, or if basic societal infrastructure decays.

Adapting knowledge proactively involves choosing the type and level of learning from a spectrum of pathways, ranging from passive to active learning. Passive learning is akin to reactive adaptation. Passive knowledge is desirable when short-run and long-run priorities are in agreement and when reaction times for adjusting to external disturbances are relatively swift. In the context of climate change, passive learning presupposes that climate change will behave in a predictable and smooth manner and that any surprises can be "muddled through" with minimal disruption. However, climate change could involve sudden and unpredictable changes in extreme events, which could limit the capacity of nonstructural changes to cope with impacts.

At the other end of the spectrum, active learning is more experimental. Active processes may involve periodic testing such as providing a shock to the system and observing the resulting behavior. Such testing supports the possibility for feedback to update and revise the system, thus enlivening the process of adaptive capacity building.

Risk and Disaster Management and Response

Proactive adaptation to climate change may necessitate periodic reassessment of the adequacy and preparedness of relief systems and programs, particularly in light of changing frequency and intensity of extreme events. Governments and insurance companies provide relief for such extreme climate events as hurricanes, floods, and droughts. Even though these programs appear to be the very essence of reactive response, they can involve risk-reduction measures. For example, insurance companies may require the adoption of certain practices to reduce exposure of people and property to climate extremes or they drop insurance.

Insurance rates are driven by actuarial tables and probability estimates, which heavily depend on knowledge and information gathered from government agencies. Updating risk tables may require anticipation of future changes in risk. Disaster assistance agencies such as FEMA must be able to assess their financial exposure to risk in order to identify budgetary needs.

An example of proactive preparedness is the ability to fight and control fires during the explosive summer fire season. With hotter summers, the extent, magnitude, and length of the fire season can reasonably be expected to rise. . . . Proactive adaptation, therefore, may include fire mitigation programs such as prescribed burns and land use controls.

Infrastructure Planning and Development

Among the most visible components of adaptive capacity are the infrastructure systems that support economic activities and social functioning. In many cases, flexibility, durability, and resiliency to climatic variability and change can be enhanced via changes in infrastructure design characteristics and building codes . . . , similar to the approach taken in earthquake-prone areas. Weighing the economic tradeoffs, however, is the principal difficulty. Designing infrastructure to enhance flexibility, durability, and resiliency is often relatively inexpensive. . . . Getting the balance correct is challenging in the face of an uncertain climate future and a planning process that often focuses on short-term and least-cost solutions. Questions of the "sufficiency" of building design and the possibility of ex post adaptation (*i.e.*, reactive adaptations) are pertinent and contribute to the complexity.

Institutional Design and Reform

Institutional effectiveness is another key element to promoting adaptive capacity. Institutions can provide information to affected actors on how climate is changing and how they can alter their behavior to adapt to the change. . . . For example, weather services can provide information on changes in climate means and variability, while agriculture extension services can inform farmers about changes in crop varieties and practices that may be better suited to changing climate conditions.

Institutions can also inhibit adaptation. One way they do so is to distort information that could encourage adaptation. Water allocation institutions that fix the prices consumers pay effectively mask changes in water availability that could be communicated to consumers through changes in prices. Institutions can also encourage behavior that is destructive or risky. For example, flood insurance programs can encourage development in flood-prone areas by insuring homes against flood risk, rather than having consumers bear the full risks and therefore presumably adopt more risk-averse behavior (see the discussion of maladaptation below).

Changing institutions so they can better address climate change can be a difficult and costly matter. Institutions are long-lived and often lack the internal mechanisms for self-assessment and revision. Vested interests are often effective at lobbying to protect and preserve their economic stakes and the real or perceived "value" of their property, the value of which in turn is determined in part by the economic benefits of the institution or program. . . . Thus, maintaining or restoring institutional effectiveness raises its own challenges, not the least of which are claims by property owners for "takings" compensation.

Better design, reform, and coordination of government policies and programs can be appropriate vehicles for proactive adaptation. The most suitable reforms can also generate additional benefits that improve resource planning and economic efficiency. Hurd et al. (1999a, 2004) and Frederick and Gleick (1999) suggest that improving the viability and functioning of active water markets, for example, contributes to increased water use efficiency under current climate conditions, and also helps mitigate the adverse impacts of climate change. Such "no regrets" or win-win approaches lead the list of improvements and changes worthy of consideration. . . .

***

Avoidance of "Maladaptations"

The avoidance of "maladaptations" is an important consideration for climate change adaptation. Maladaptations are situations where management of natural resources is already leading to undue harm to ecosystems or society. . . . For example, the current practices of development of low-lying coastal areas and areas prone to flooding and the continued cropping of marginal agricultural areas are examples of trends that increase exposure to current climate and climate change risks. Limiting development of low-lying coastal areas, applying innovative approaches such as "rolling easements" (Titus, 1998), or using such programs as the Conservation Reserve Program to discourage cropping of marginal agriculture areas are examples of approaches that can address maladaptation.

Technological Innovation

Technological change is a principal route of many recent human adaptations. Innovations in transportation, agriculture, and information systems have advanced adaptive capacity in significant ways. Technology has propelled U.S. agriculture to ever-greater production levels over the past century. . . . Adams et al. (2001) and Reilly (1999) conclude that technological innovation coupled with appropriate advances and changes in management will enable the U.S. agricultural system to rise to the challenges posed by climate change. However, that is predicated on maintaining and possibly enhancing both private and public research capacity, which may require that both government and industry take proactive positions.

The Role of Public Policy

Public institutions and policies wield considerable power in shaping technology development, resource and land use, information collection and dissemination, risk management, and disaster relief. As a result, governments can substantially influence the magnitude and distribution of climate change impacts and social preparedness. For example, the U.S. experience during the Dust Bowl era of the 1930s shaped the design and direction of government efforts to assist in managing the nation's soil and agricultural resources. Research was pursued to understand the causes and contributing factors of the Dust Bowl, and to develop technologies, management systems, and support programs to minimize the reoccurrence of such a calamity. Had the reaction been limited to simply providing immediate disaster relief and restoration of existing practices, the country might have faced an even worse set of outcomes during the severe drought that later hit the region in the 1950s. However, that potentially more extreme disaster was avoided because of the proactive steps that had been taken by the federal government. . . .

Barton H. Thompson, Jr., Tragically Difficult: The Obstacles to Governing the Commons

30 Envtl. L. 241 (2000)

Why has it proven so difficult to adopt solutions to . . . commons tragedies? Why have people who would seemingly benefit from mandated solutions often actively opposed them? It is often tempting to blame the people themselves when they are locked in a political battle over fishing, groundwater use, or global climate change. It is also tempting to believe that those who are opposing a solution are selfish, shortsighted, anti-environmental, or overly focused on immediate material gain. But most people trapped in commons dilemmas are good people who want to do what is right for their community, for society at large, and for the environment.

In [his book] SONG FOR A BLUE OCEAN, Carl Safina goes out of his way to give readers a sense for the morality of the fishermen who are the root of the overfishing problem. Fisherman after fisherman in his book describe how they love the very fish that they are catching. These fishermen often label themselves conservationists and decry obviously destructive activities. Many of the fishermen throughout the book claim they would be among the first to stop fishing, if they thought the fish were really in trouble. Farmers say the same thing about their water resources. People worldwide say the same thing about the climatic balance that nurtures and protects them.

If you believe these resource users, the problem is not the people locked in the commons dilemmas, but the situations in which they find themselves. When put in a commons dilemma, most of us behave in a similar fashion. To help understand and overcome the difficulties involved in gaining support for commons solutions, we must turn away from attribution of blame and look to recent research conducted by psychologists, economists, sociologists, and anthropologists both in the field and in experimental simulations on why people sometimes do not behave in their best interest.

Although each of my three examples has its own unique characteristics that make a solution difficult, they share three important features that make it difficult for people locked in tragic overuse to act "rationally" in trying to come up with an acceptable solution. First, solving each dilemma requires people to reduce the level of resource use that they historically have enjoyed. Second, each dilemma is characterized by significant scientific and social uncertainty. Finally, each dilemma involves an intertemporal trade-off: to what degree are people willing to sacrifice today in order to preserve resources for the future?

Framing: Losses Versus Gains

The first point may seem obvious. The tragedy would be easy to resolve if the user of a common resource did not have to sacrifice anything to avoid the tragedy of the commons. However, my premise is not simply that the tragedy is difficult to resolve because solutions involve giving up higher consumption today in order to preserve the resource for the future. In the cases that I've discussed, many "rational" resource users should find the necessary trade-off worthwhile. The problem is that most resource users view the trade-off as requiring them to give up a current right. And most people will accept a high degree of risk to avoid giving up a current right.

Psychologists have long recognized that the framing of an action as either a gain or a loss can make a great difference. In particular, people are more risk-averse when dealing with gains (they prefer sure payoffs to gambles) and are more willing to take risks when dealing with potential losses (they will risk much to avoid an otherwise sure loss). In evaluating proposed solutions to commons dilemmas, most resource users appear to start with their historic level of resource use and ask how the solution affects that level of use. Thus they see most proposed solutions, such as caps on use, as constituting losses rather than restricted gains. These solutions, in the eyes of the resource users, require the users to give up something that they currently have. And as researchers have predicted, resource users are therefore willing to risk sizable future losses to avoid the sure immediate loss. Repeatedly, experimental simulations of commons dilemmas have found that participants have a harder time resolving the commons in a loss framework than in a gains framework. In real life, moreover, resource users believe that they have achieved their historic level of resource use through their own industry and skills, strengthening the framing effect and making the resource users more willing to risk potentially catastrophic future losses to avoid a sure cutback in their current use of the resource.

Governments make the problem worse where they recognize property rights in common access to a resource, as many states have done with groundwater. Property rights can help solve the tragedy of the commons when the rights result in the effective internalization of the cost of excessive harvesting, but property rights turn harmful when they reinforce a sense of entitlement to an unlimited harvest. Not only do such property rights reinforce the framing effect, but they also can cause resource users, as a matter of fairness, to reject out of hand even the suggestion that they should reduce their current usage. Property rights are sensible and important societal tools, but in thinking about potential solutions to the tragedy of the commons, resource users often convert property rights from practical tools into absolute moral rights that prevent them from thinking carefully about the potential benefits of averting the tragedy. Moreover, property rights may focus resource users on their individual interests rather than on total societal well-being, undermining social norms of cooperation and reinforcing the very dichotomy between individual and social welfare that underlies the tragedy of the commons.

The Problem of Uncertainty

The second problem that prevents people from thinking "rationally" about solutions to the tragedy of the commons is uncertainty. Two types of uncertainty often plague commons dilemmas. The first is scientific uncertainty regarding the current health of the resource, the impact of human actions on the resource, and the potential future of the resource. The second is social uncertainty regarding what is a fair or proper means of allocating the burden of trying to save the commons.

. . . [T]hree . . . examples of commons dilemmas involve significant scientific uncertainty. All involve hidden resources. Fisheries are cloaked beneath the ocean. Groundwater is concealed beneath the surface of the Earth. Although we can see the results of climate change, we cannot see the actual climatic process and thus cannot see how our actions actually affect the climate. To varying degrees, moreover, science is uncertain about how grave a danger each resource actually faces. We probably know the most about groundwater, but often there is still considerable uncertainty regarding the safe yield of any particular aquifer. Extreme scientific uncertainty characterizes our knowledge of most fisheries; indeed, we do not know the status of 544 fish species in the United States — sixty percent of the fish that U.S. fisheries target commercially. Although virtually all scientists agree that we are affecting the climate, there is sharp disagreement as to the nature and extent of the likely impact and its implications for the world's peoples. In all of these settings, scientists often give the impression that there is even more uncertainty than there really is by qualifying their opinions. Scientists are trained to be cautious in their conclusions, and to many resource users, that cautiousness sounds a lot like uncertainty.

Unfortunately, when there is scientific uncertainty, people faced with a tough solution to a commons dilemma engage in tremendous wishful thinking. If scientists estimate that there are between one thousand and thirty thousand fish in any given population, most fishermen assume that there are thirty thousand fish in that population. The fishermen find confirmation for their views in their own personal experience, no matter how unsupportable. One good day of fishing will convince them that the more cautious estimates are wrong. The fact that fish are hard to catch the rest of the year serves as evidence merely that fish are getting smarter and learning to stay away from the boats.

Scientific simulations of fishery problems duplicate this phenomenon. As uncertainty increases regarding the exact size of a pool of fish, participants in fishery simulations increasingly overestimate the likely number of fish and boost their harvesting accordingly. Uncertainty over the regeneration rate of the fish population leads to a similar jump in harvesting. According to some psychologists, mathematic misperceptions might be at work. Because people often have found in the past that mean and variance are positively correlated, they mistakenly believe that increased variance justifies an upward shift in their estimate of the size of both current and future fish populations. But a more likely explanation is that people use uncertainty to willingly fool themselves that the resource is in better shape and under less threat than it is in fact. Once one resource user engages in wishful thinking, the wishful thinking might have a spiraling effect. When faced by ambiguity, people often look to the statements and behavior of others to see how to resolve that ambiguity. To the degree that some resource users either claim that the common pool is large or act as if it is large by using a large quantity of the resource, their behavior may signal to other resource users that they should resolve the ambiguity in pool size by assuming a high level of the resource.

Assuming that resource users believe there is a problem, they must determine the fair means of allocating the burden of solving the tragedy. In each of my examples, this is difficult because the tragedy is asymmetric. People contribute in different degrees to the problem, and people benefit to different degrees from a solution. In these settings, there are multiple ways to allocate the burden of reducing resource use and no generally accepted societal norms for how to choose between the various allocations. What, for example, is the fairest means of limiting emission of greenhouse gases? All nations could reduce their 1990 emissions by an equal percentage on the principle that everyone should share the burden equally. All nations could be limited to a uniform per capita emission level on the principle that each nation should share in the resource equally. Those nations that would be hurt the most by global warming could undertake the bulk of the necessary reductions on the principle that those who benefit the most should make the largest contribution to a solution. A myriad of potential rules could be suggested, each with its own reasonable justification.

Unfortunately, where there are multiple fairness rules, people suffer from what some psychologists have labeled "egocentric interpretations of fairness." People assume that the rule that benefits them is the fairest. As a result, agreeing on a common solution becomes difficult if not impossible. In one group of fishing simulations, for example, researchers found that most participants were able to agree on equal reductions in catches where the dilemma was symmetric so that the participants benefited equally from cooperation. If some participants balked at equal reduction, the other participants were able to argue effectively that any approach other than an equal reduction was unfair; the dissenters quickly dropped their opposition when their position was criticized. Where the dilemma was asymmetric, however, both egocentrism and harvesting levels increased. Explaining the phenomenon to people, moreover, does not cure the problem. When told of the phenomenon, people assume that others' fairness perceptions, but not their own, suffer from an egocentric bias. The problem, moreover, is not merely theoretical. . . . [B]iased interpretations of fairness have plagued efforts to address global climate change. Developing countries argue that the developed countries should resolve the problem because they are overwhelmingly "at fault" for current greenhouse gas levels and have more resources with which to address the problem. Developed countries argue that it is only fair that all nations share in the burden because all will benefit.

The scientific and social uncertainties, when combined, also permit resource users to indulge in what some psychologists have called "self-enhancing attribu-tional biases," or what I call a "halo effect." Because bad behavior is hard to define and determine, everyone assumes that they are more cooperative than they are in reality. In one experimental simulation of a fishery, for example, eighty-four per-cent of the participants thought that they had acted in a socially "cooperative" fash-ion, even though a review of the experiment's results showed that a majority of the participants had engaged in varying degrees of gluttonous behavior. Seventy-seven percent of the participants thought they had been "cooperative," even though they had not left sufficient fish for an optimal fishery; thirty-two percent reported they had been "cooperative" even though they took more than their proportionate share of all the fish in the fishery.

Not surprisingly, the halo effect frequently does not extend to people's eval-uations of other resource users' behavior — particularly where the other resource users are outside the person's own community. When the user of a resource believes that there is a human-based problem at all, the user blames the source of the prob-lem on someone else. New England fishermen of blue fin tuna blame the decline in tuna stocks on long line fishermen in the Gulf of Mexico, who blame the problem on Mediterranean fishermen catching the blue fin tuna when the fish cross the Atlantic, who blame the problem back on the fishermen in New England.

This one-sided halo effect makes it even more difficult to solve the tragedy of the commons in two ways. First, the halo effect magnifies the egocentric inter-pretation of a fair solution. When participants in a resources simulation are told that a shortage of the resource is attributable to a purely natural phenomenon, it is much easier to persuade them to limit their usage of the resource than when they are told that the shortage is attributable to a man-made cause. Participants who believe that a shortage is the result of a purely natural cause generally think it is fair to assume part of the burden of the shortage. But when the participants believe that the shortage is man-made, they assume that somebody else is the true culprit and that the culprit should cure the problem. Second, when dealing with this type of a one-sided halo effect, it becomes much harder to appeal to people's altruism or conscience, because resource users already think that they are acting for the social good. . . . [T]his problem is central to determining whether we can increase support for solutions to commons dilemmas by trying to change resource users' environmental views.

Intertemporal Tradeoffs

Getting resource users to come to grips with the tragedy of the commons is also dif-ficult because the resource users must engage in an intertemporal tradeoff: should they accept a loss today in order to avoid a bigger loss at some point distant in the future? Homo sapiens are better than most mammals at considering the future consequences of their current actions — but not much better. We do care about the future, including the well-being of future generations. But we suffer from a variety of temporal anomalies. In particular, individuals trapped in a commons dilemma appear to extravagantly discount the future consequences of their current actions.

I want to avoid the standard debate about whether or not private discount rates are appropriate for making intertemporal trade-offs involving environmental consequences. As others have discussed, there is tremendous disagreement as to whether market discount rates are socially proper, particularly when discounting across generations. Professor Cass Sunstein, for example, has argued that market discount rates do not fully account for effects on future generations, because future generations are not involved in the discounting decision.

My concern is that people have difficulty making any sacrifice to avoid uncertain future losses. Several factors may be at work here. First, people tend to focus myopically on current costs in evaluating the wisdom of conservation measures. In the energy crunch years of the late 1970s and early 1980s a number of economists studied people's willingness to purchase energy efficient appliances. It should have been relatively easy, one might think, for people to make rational trade-offs between the increase in the current purchase price of an appliance and the future energy savings they would enjoy by buying that appliance. Governmentally mandated labels supplied consumers with all the basic information necessary to make those trade-offs. But the studies found that people nonetheless were highly biased towards buying the cheaper, energy consumptive appliances. Depending on the particular study, the "applied discount rates" — the discount rates reflected in the actual purchases people were making — ranged from a low of 17% (a high discount rate, even for the inflation-prone 1970s) to an astronomical 243%. Because people had trouble making complex discounting decisions, they focused on the most obvious statistic confronting them: how much they could save immediately by buying the cheaper appliance. In a similar fashion, resource users confronted by a commons dilemma may decide that it is easiest to treat current harvesting decisions as if they were the last.

Second, several experiments have shown that people often tend to minimize the risk of future losses, willingly gambling on the future, where the risk is characterized by significant uncertainty and avoiding the risk would require giving up something today. Interestingly, this result is in marked contrast to the way that people generally respond to the tradeoff between current and future losses that are certain to occur. Psychologists have found that most people tend to employ lower discount rates when choosing between losses than when choosing between gains; indeed, some subjects demonstrate negative discounting when choosing between losses, preferring an immediate loss over a delayed loss of the same amount. Distant losses, in short, appear to weigh far more heavily in peoples' decision-making than distant gains. But where the loss is risky and uncertain, people often act as if there's virtually no future risk to them at all. Why the reversal?

A major explanation is that, when confronted by an uncertain future, most people assume that they will be able to avoid, reduce, or ameliorate future risks. We tend to be optimists about the future, at least when taking precautionary steps today is costly. Part of the optimism is an unrealistic belief that tragedy will befall others but not ourselves. A number of experiments, for example, have shown that people faced with various health risks, such as cancer from radon exposure in their homes, optimistically discount the personal risk to them. A greater factor is the optimistic belief that the risk is controllable. An everyday example is the interest rate on credit cards. When you last applied for a credit card, did you consider the interest rate that the credit card company will charge you if you fail to pay your bills on time — or did you focus on whether you would receive frequent flyer mileage or get a discount at your local grocery store? Studies suggest that most consumers do not pay much attention to the interest rate charged on outstanding balances. One of the reasons appears to be that most people underestimate their future credit card debts. Or if they recognize that they will have future debts, they think they will be able to pay them off fairly quickly.

Psychological studies have found that this innate optimism about the future is even more pronounced in business settings. Business managers, who have typically advanced to their current positions because they have been successful in overcoming problems in the past, believe that they can also effectively control the odds and magnitudes of future risks. One suspects that fishermen and farmers, who have repeatedly confronted and overcome severe risks in their businesses, might be particularly prone to believe that they can avoid future risks.

We as a society have frequently reinforced resource users' natural sense of optimism by bailing out the people who take on risks and turn out to have bet wrong. Most groundwater users, if you talk to them about overdepleting their aquifer, will probably tell you "yes, it's a problem, but we don't worry too much about running out of groundwater because if we end up depleting our aquifer, the government will bail us out." Based on past experience, groundwater users believe that the government will build a project to import needed water if the farmers ultimately run out of economically withdrawable groundwater. In a similar fashion, fishermen expect that the government will provide "transition relief" if a fishery is ultimately depleted.

A final reason for expecting high discounting of the future risk of resource tragedy is people's uncanny ability either to totally ignore problems that are not immediate and visible — what Sandra Postel has called the "out-of-sight, out-of-mind syndrome" — or to see them in their rosiest light. The phenomenon here is similar, but slightly different from, people's over-optimism. When I agreed a year ahead of time to deliver the speech from which this Essay grew, I knew that I would have to spend considerable time researching, writing, and polishing the talk. But it seemed like a lot less work a year ahead of time than when I finally sat down to prepare the talk, and I quickly put the issue out of my mind because it was so far off in the future. If I had seriously thought about how much work would really be involved, I might have hesitated a bit more before agreeing to give the speech. I was not tricked by an overoptimistic belief that I could avoid the work or be more efficient than I had been in the past (although I probably hoped that I would be more efficient, despite all evidence to the contrary from my past efforts at writing speeches). I simply conveniently forgot how much work is really involved, the same way that women discount the pains of childbirth when they decide whether to have another baby. In a similar fashion, resource users may well find it easy to put future problems out of their mind. As Sandra Postel has noted, "[w]hen looking at say, a field of golden wheat, it can be difficult to imagine why crops like that can't just go on forever." Even where resource users think about the problem, they are likely to "underimagine" the consequences of overusing the resource, placing the best face on the potential tragedy. Indeed, most resource users do not even have a past experience upon which to draw in trying to imagine the import to them of exhausting the fishery or aquifer. Resource users may find it even more difficult to imagine the full scope of the negative impact where future generations will suffer the consequences.

points for discussion

1. *Now what?* Given Professor Thompson's analysis, what private and public strategies might be useful for encouraging proactive adaptation?
2. *After Sandy.* In the (literal) wake of Hurricane Sandy, the U.S. Army Corps of Engineers offered funds and technical assistance to local communities interested in proactive adaptation: using the storm as an opportunity to reinforce natural storm-mitigation features. Specifically, the projects entailed building systems of large sand dunes along the shoreline. The Corps required local communities to obtain the necessary easements over the privately owned dry sand beaches where the dunes would be built. In cases where the upland owners did not consent to easements, the local government would use its eminent domain powers. Several homeowners in New Jersey ultimately challenged easement condemnations on just compensation grounds, arguing that the dunes would significantly lower property values by blocking views of the ocean. In *Borough of Harvey Cedars v. Karan*, 70 A.3d 524 (N.J. 2013), the Supreme Court of New Jersey effectively quashed such claims by requiring trial courts and juries to take into account, in valuing the easements, the benefits provided by increased storm-mitigation.

b. Coastal Adaptation Strategies

i. Conventional

Florida Atlantic University Center for Urban and Environmental Studies, Florida's Resilient Coasts: A State Policy Framework for Adaptation to Climate Change

(2010)

Beaches and Beach Management

Of the 1250 miles of Florida coastline, 825 miles are beaches. The beaches throughout the state are loved by residents and visitors alike. They are a critical component of the statewide, regional, and local economies. This is why 192 miles of

Florida's beaches are managed for restoration by federal, state, and local entities, governed by a Strategic Beach Management Plan. And, since 1964, the Legislature has appropriated nearly $600 million for beach erosion control activities and hurricane recovery. However, according to the state Department of Environmental Protection, 485 miles of beaches (59%) already are experiencing erosion, with 387 miles experiencing "critical erosion." Heretofore, some of this erosion is the result of natural forces, but mostly it's the result of human activity: the construction and management of navigation inlets (some 60 across the state) and imprudent coastal development. This erosion could be considered just a warm-up for the potential impact on beaches induced by climate change.

Sea level rise and the climate-change-induced increase in the frequency and severity of hurricanes put all of Florida's beaches and beach management programs at risk. There are only three known responses to beach erosion: structural ("armoring" or hardening, with controversial environmental and "bad neighbor" consequences); nourishment, essentially replacing sand lost to hurricanes, which is an increasingly expensive choice because of the diminution of sand supply; and retreat, which is controversial among coastal residents and visitors alike.

Critical Issues

1. Should Florida reassess, in light of the permanence and irreversibility of impacts projected by climate change science, the purposes and priorities of its strategic beach management plans and investments?

2. Is there a "rebalancing" of human and environmental concerns, particularly for sea turtles whose effective reproduction is beach-dependent, to ensure that humans and nature are well protected against the impacts of climate change?

3. What process involving the wide array of stakeholders might effectively establish a new consensus on beach protection and restoration strategies?

4. Because substantial private property interests are involved here, what state strategies and incentives could be established to fairly compensate land and property owners if there is a major shift in beach protection and restoration strategies?

5. How should new beach management priorities be factored into the comprehensive land-use planning of Florida's coastal regions and communities?

6. How can Florida and its Caribbean neighbors collaborate on this issue, given that it affects both Florida and its island nation neighbors?

7. What economic value might Florida capture through its new climate-sensitive beach management strategies for export to other countries facing similar climate change impacts? Is this an "industry cluster" worthy of encouragement and support?

State Policy Options to Be Considered

1. Florida should undertake, perhaps in partnership with the Florida Shore and Beach Preservation Association, a major reassessment of its beach management strategies.

2. Florida should explore alternative, but cost-effective, engineering for navigation inlets to minimize beach impacts. A long-time issue for coastal Florida, it becomes even more significant in the context of predicted climate impacts.

3. Beach "hardening" may be required for the beachfront developments of greatest value to owners or the public, and the trade-offs to surrounding communities may require compensatory action and financing.

4. Relocation of some beach developments, where retreat is the optimal choice, will be necessary for some at-risk beachfront developments. With enough lead time for implementation, and a "no fault" compensation program for innocent victims, Florida could ensure sensible responses to climate change without causing a rupture in its beach-dependent economy or a property owner's backlash.

5. Where beach nourishment is still the optimal response to erosion, Florida state government should explore the creation of a public entity to negotiate least-cost contracts for sand.

James G. Titus, Rising Seas, Coastal Erosion, and the Takings Clause: How to Save Wetlands and Beaches Without Hurting Property Owners

57 Md. L. Rev. 1279 (1998)

Development and rising sea levels are eliminating tidelands, but the loss is slow, almost imperceptible. There is no crisis. Addressing the issue is urgent only because there are inexpensive opportunities to solve the problem now — opportunities that will be prohibitively costly if we wait until housing developments replace our shorefront farms and forests.

The common law has long assumed that, except for extraordinary circumstances, states will keep their tidal shores in the hands of the public. This policy has been reaffirmed in the last few decades by state and federal laws prohibiting the filling of wetlands both above and

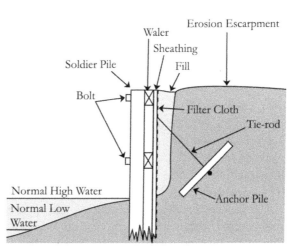

Bulkhead
(view from side)

Adapted from N.C. Dept. of Envt. and Nat. Res. drawing.

Figure 10-9. Bulkhead Illustration

below the mean high-water mark. The failure to consider rising sea level and coastal erosion would frustrate these policies.

[Earlier, this Article] presented three general approaches for protecting tidelands as shores retreat: preventing development, rolling easements, and deferring action. Because history provides little or no evidence that the tidelands will be protected by a policy of deferring action, the real choice is among rolling easements, preventing development, and losing the tidelands. But even where shores are bulkheaded and our bay beaches and wetlands are lost, states need not automatically terminate the public's right to access along the shore.

The rising sea has put two legal interests on a collision course. Advancing inland is the public interest in access for navigation, fishing, and hunting, as well as the environmental, recreational, and aesthetic benefits of tidal marshes, swamps, and sandy beaches. In the past, as these interests migrated inland, they met little resistance as long as most of the land was undeveloped. But as land is developed, homeowners increasingly assert a commonly assumed (if legally unproven) right to defend their property. In doing so, they cannot help but assert that their interest is superior to that of the public.

This conflict could be settled piecemeal under various common law doctrines, but unless policy makers confront the issue directly, current trends suggest that some ocean shores and the overwhelming majority of estuarine shores will be eliminated. The type of comprehensive shoreline plan necessary to protect natural shores in perpetuity would probably involve a combination of setbacks, density restrictions, building codes, and rolling easements. In many cases, states may prefer to compensate coastal landowners for the impact of these policies. Nevertheless, any legislative or regulatory response is likely to raise the question: Is the policy a taking?

A. Rolling Easements Will Rarely Be Takings, But Setbacks and Deferred Action Will Often Require Compensation

1. Setbacks and Other Immediate Limitations. — Setbacks will not require compensation in areas where the setback line is fairly close to today's high-water mark, compared with the size of coastal lots, *i.e.*, where erosion is slow and the land is steep. Moreover, if farming, forestry, and other uses are profitable, the existence of an alternative use may defeat a takings claim.

A taking is more likely in areas where land is held for speculation or lots have been subdivided, because setbacks are more likely to render the property economically unusable. Still, the likelihood of a taking can be minimized if setbacks are incorporated into the subdivision process, because large parcels are more likely to have enough land to develop inland of the setback line.

2. Deferred Action. — In general, the government may not evict people from their homes if they are willing and able to cure any threats to health and safety that their dwellings may pose. The law on the coast is different: Land has always changed hands as the shore eroded, and in at least a few states governments have required the removal of private seawalls that impair public access along the ocean

coast. Along bay shores, however, the demand for public access is less, and states have not prohibited shore protection.

The public trust doctrine holds that the state has not given away its tidelands unless it explicitly decided to do so. Would this doctrine allow people to be evicted if the alternative were an unintended privatization of the public shoreline? Because courts have stretched and squeezed the doctrine, this question will probably remain unclear in most states until the problems of the rising sea level are upon us. Regardless of what old cases and statutes say, would a court really resurrect an ancient common law doctrine in order to allow the government to evict people from their homes?

3. Rolling Easements. — The uncertainties regarding the public trust doctrine cut the other way for rolling easements. Because the law of erosion has long held that the public tidelands migrate inland as sea level rises, legislation saying that this law will apply in the future takes nothing. Even without the public trust doctrine and the law of erosion, rolling easements would rarely be takings. They are inexpensive conditions that counteract an inevitable problem caused by coastal development. Rolling easements do not render property economically useless — they merely warn the owner that some day, environmental conditions may render the property useless, and that if this occurs, the state will not allow the owner to protect her investment at the expense of the public. By the time the sea threatens the property, owners will have had decades and perhaps centuries to factor this expectation into their plans — and into the price they paid for their property.

Rolling easements do not interfere with private economic activities. Instead, they merely allocate the risk of shoreline retreat to the riparian owner. They would be constitutional in most cases even without the public trust doctrine. With that doctrine, a rolling easement policy with a reasonable advance warning is unlikely to be a taking anywhere.

B. Good Policy Is Also Consistent with the Constitution

Setbacks have been the most popular technique to address erosion along the ocean coast. But along bay shores, they seem advisable only in some circumstances. If the land is steep enough for the ten- or twenty-foot contour to be within a hundred feet or so of the high-water mark, and if the typical riparian parcel has substantial land above this elevation, setbacks may suffice for two reasons. First, landowners could still develop their property. Second, there would be no need to quibble about how fast the sea will rise or how far into the future the tidelands should be protected.

In many areas, however, the land is too flat for even a one-thousand-foot setback to protect the tidelands into the distant future. The government would have to weigh risks and benefits in locating the setback line. But where should that line be? Landowners would have a strong incentive to dispute the government's scientific projections. Even if everyone agreed to assume, for example, a three-foot rise, purchasing all of that land — or forcing property owners to bear the cost — would be very expensive. Furthermore, eventually the shore would erode up to that line and the tidelands would be eliminated anyway.

Rolling easements, by contrast, face none of these limitations. Landowners are not prevented from using their property; they simply are prevented from protecting it when doing so eliminates tidelands. Thus, there is no need to draw a particular line on the map. Property owners do not suffer large economic deprivations, and the many decades that will pass before the property is lost imply a small present discounted value for whatever future loss one expects. Rolling easements also foster consensus, because only landowners who expect a significant rise in sea level would have a reason to be concerned about their cost. Perhaps most importantly, however, the government could acquire rolling easements through eminent domain for less than one percent of current land values. This makes it possible for governments to avoid hurting property owners and, thus, avoid the takings issue.

Setbacks and rolling easements are not mutually exclusive. In some cases, setbacks may be useful for protecting tidelands threatened over the next forty to seventy-five years, while rolling easements could be employed to ensure that bulkheads are not subsequently built at the setback line. It would be premature to conclude that any single approach will be appropriate everywhere. The analysis supporting rolling easements demonstrates, however, that the long-term and uncertain nature of sea level rise need not prevent policy makers from laying out the rules of the game so that social and political institutions will be prepared for a rising sea.

C. Recommendations

The fact that society decided not to eliminate its tidelands during the last part of the twentieth century does not automatically imply that they should be retained during the twenty-first century. But it does imply that their resources are valuable enough to (1) decide where tidelands should be eliminated and where they should be retained, and (2) retain them wherever the cost of doing so is a tiny fraction of what it would cost to prevent their immediate elimination. Toward those ends, the author presents the following ten recommendations for states, local governments, and the private sector.

States

1. State legislatures should direct the appropriate cabinet officers to undertake long-term public trust tideland planning studies that develop legislative recommendations on which shorelines should be privatized and which should remain in their natural condition as shores erode. These studies should produce maps showing the likely loss of natural shorelines over the next hundred years given current development trends, alternative scenarios of future sea level rise, and alternative policies of coastal management, such as setbacks, rolling easements, various engineering strategies, and existing policies. They also should examine implementation issues and estimate the costs associated with each policy. Special attention should be given to unique cultural resources, including inhabited islands, lighthouses, forts, and archaeological sites, as well as environmental resources.

In Maryland, a planning study would be particularly useful along Chesapeake Bay. The legislatively recognized right to bulkhead, along with the Critical Area

Act's limitation of development along rural bay shores, already provides a skeletal structure for deciding which shores to privatize. But the state's Tidal Wetlands Act contains a statutory right to hold back the sea, a right that could be read as approving an eventual elimination of all wetlands and beaches other than those adjacent to conservation areas.

2. State coastal zone agencies should develop access policies for new development along bay shores and otherwise expand the portion of the bay beaches to which the public has access. The constituency for protecting shores will grow if people can reach the water, but it will wither if they cannot. Both the layout of roads and the existence of public paths to the shore could have important long-term implications for coastal access.

Along the ocean coast, roads leading to the sea provide access to the shore, and they ensure that as the beach erodes, all houses will still have road access. Along estuarine shores, by contrast, roads parallel to the shore limit access and may make retreat impossible if they provide the sole access to some properties.

In theory, Maryland has a policy to promote access to the waters of Chesapeake Bay. It does not, however, have a policy to increase substantially the portion of the shore to which the public has access. Nor does it have a policy of retaining public access along the shore when issuing permits for erosion control structures.

3. State legislatures should ask their attorneys general to analyze which tidelands policies can be implemented under state law and whether current development and bulkhead policies are likely to foreclose any options. The success and takings implications of tidelands policies will depend ultimately on the quality of legal advice provided before the policy development. Even in areas that are developed, retaining public access along the shore may be worthwhile.

Local Governments

4. Local governments should modify their master plans to indicate explicitly which shorelines will eventually be armored and which will remain natural. A good initial plan would be to assume that previously developed or subdivided areas will eventually be protected, and areas zoned for agriculture, resource conservation, or otherwise not yet subdivided will retain natural shorelines forever even if rezoned. A possible compromise for undeveloped residential areas would be to maintain access along the shore in perpetuity, even if the shore is eventually armored.

5. Zoning regulations should also specify which shorelines will remain armored and which will remain natural. Because the designated natural shorelines are often agricultural and are not likely to be developed for several decades, local development interests may find these changes to be reasonable. While the natural shoreline designation might be revoked if and when the agricultural lands are rezoned, the inevitable compromises involved in rezoning might lead to their retention. Moreover, the designation would eventually become one of the background principles of land ownership in the county and would alert out-of-town developers about the need to consider tideland preservation.

6. Local governments should factor sea level rise and erosion trends into their guidelines for subdividing coastal property. Setbacks are less costly and less likely to be takings when the coastal lot is relatively deep. Even in areas where shorelines will eventually be armored, a deeper lot will lengthen the life of the natural shoreline environment. In areas where the public wants shorelines to remain natural, subdivision presents a realistic opportunity to warn the property owner of the requirements to protect natural shorelines. Where state law permits, it may be the last opportunity to add covenants or easements to the deed without compensation.

7. In areas likely to be protected, local governments should decide how the shore would be protected, even if erosion will not threaten developed areas for several decades. If the area would be protected by a levee, then setbacks along the shore should be increased to make room for that eventuality. If the area would be raised with fill, the proper height for roads, utilities, and building lots may be different. Environmental officials desiring to protect the tidelands must take an active interest in these related issues. Otherwise, they risk losing credibility among the moderate elements of the community.

Private Sector

8. Builders should reserve or purchase rolling easements when seeking permits for development in coastal counties and donate those easements to conservancies. This temporal extension of wetland mitigation is a cost-effective way to guarantee that a project will have a positive net impact on the environment. It need not be limited to those who seek to fill a wetland. Privately created rolling easements could also include non-development buffers above the high-water mark to limit pollution runoff.

9. Conservancies should reserve rolling easements from lands they sell and consider purchasing rolling easements from farmers who own land along the shore. In addition to the direct benefits, private activities can help to flush out the legal issues and thereby reduce institutional inertia elsewhere.

10. Activists should take regular walks along estuarine shores. The public's failure to visit these often-inaccessible tidelands leads many private property owners to assume incorrectly that they own the shore. This failure also leads many officials to conclude that, as with an abandoned roadway, there is no harm to privatizing the shore.

This Article has focused on state, local, and private arrangements for protecting tidelands. The federal Clean Water Act was the primary motivator for protecting wetlands, and amending the Act to protect these wetlands as sea level rises would be a logical extension. But the federal government's role in wetlands protection was justified by its traditional power to regulate the waters of the United States. Although wetlands are part of those waters, setbacks and rolling easements involve land use, which has always been a matter for state and local government. Certainly the Army Corps of Engineers and the Environmental Protection Agency should reexamine existing programs so that they are less vulnerable to rising sea level. Environmental Impact Statements associated with expanding access to sewage treatment plants in low areas should acknowledge that these projects will cause a large long-term net loss of wetlands, both because the projects encourage development in low areas and because flooded septic systems will no longer force people to abandon homes as the sea rises. A federal regulatory solution to this problem, on the other hand, is probably impractical and definitely premature.

Although a federal regulatory role seems premature, the national government could help the process in its role as a property owner. The National Park Service, the Fish and Wildlife Service, and other agencies that purchase lands for conservation purposes in coastal areas could keep shorelines natural through the purchase of rolling easements. Undeveloped farmland is still found along the mainland shores of many bays that lie behind federally owned barrier islands, such as Assateague Island National Seashore along the Atlantic Coast of Maryland. For less than one percent of the cost of buying the land, the federal government could ensure that even if these areas become developed some day, the shore will still be composed of wetlands and beaches.

ii. Less Conventional

R.K. Turner et al., A Cost–Benefit Appraisal of Coastal Managed Realignment Policy

17 Global Envtl. Change 397 (2007)

Traditional sea defence and coastal erosion strategies in England and Wales have sought to provide long-run engineered "hold-the-line" fixed protection for people, property and other assets against the vagaries of dynamic coastal environments. Since at least Roman times the British coast has been heavily modified by flood and coastal defences to protect existing human activities on coastal land and to claim land for agricultural, industrial, port and residential development. Currently, the English coastline is protected by over 2000 km of flood defences; 860 km protect the coast from erosion while 2347 km^2 of former coastal floodplains are protected from flooding by 1259 km of sea defences. Many of these structures are now reaching the end of their design lives. The expenditure of public funds on the implementation of this approach has been justified by reference to a rank ordering system underpinned by standard economic cost–benefit analysis (CBA) applied on a project by project basis. However, set against a contemporary and likely future context of increasing sea levels and increasing severity and frequency of storm conditions, both the cost and the effectiveness of traditional coastal management must be seriously questioned. This line of argument is further strengthened by growing evidence of the current unsustainability of coastal management practice such as beach denudation and coastal steepening.

As our knowledge of coastal dynamics and climate change improves it has become increasingly apparent that sole reliance on engineered "hard" defences is unlikely to be sustainable. Instead emphasis is switching to a "coping strategy" based on a mixed approach, with protection focused on strategic and high-value areas and the rest of the coastline left to adapt to change more naturally. Measures such as "managed realignment" which involves the deliberate breaching of engineered defences to allow coastal migration with the creation of extended intertidal marshes and mudbanks is typical of this new approach.

This re-orientation towards a more flexible management process will not be a straightforward transition. In principle, future management should be better able to cope with changing circumstances, changing social tastes, improvements in knowledge about coastal processes, human behaviour and ecosystem "values," as well as changing technology, factor prices and political ideology. In practice, because of the range of stakeholders and competing resource usages typical of coastal areas, a number of challenges need to be urgently addressed. The politics of coastal management has become increasingly polarised and contested. Consultation processes seeking to take forward new shoreline management plans in England, for example, have stalled and controversy surrounding compensation, planning and development and equity and natural justice has intensified. . . .

***

Managed Realignment Policy Appraisal

The analysis presented below must be viewed as preliminary and partial but as also providing one significant component of a more comprehensive coastal policy appraisal. The managed realignment example that is focused on has a number of particular characteristics which may not always be typical of a more extensive managed realignment strategy. People and property assets, as well as nature conservation designation sites, are not part of the trade-off in this set of realignments. The sites have been deliberately chosen, following a GIS-based study, to avoid such conflicts and only involve the loss of agricultural land for a compensating gain of saltmarsh and mudflat habitats. In the longer term future, a mixed approach to coastal management may well have to face up to more "politically sensitive" and highly "contested" trade-offs, especially if the more severe climate change modelling predictions are accurate. But this only serves to emphasise the argument in favour of economic CBA as a complementary component within a policy analysis-based decision support system which will have to grapple with compensation, planning law and regulations, public trust and social norms of fairness and accountability dimensions of decision making. With these caveats in mind we turn to the application of the CBA model to managed realignment policy.

The construction of coastal defences effectively immobilises a naturally dynamic and adaptive ecosystem at the land–sea interface. In response to rising sea levels, a modified coast is unable to adapt by migrating landwards with the result that valuable intertidal habitats are eventually lost through inundation and erosion ("coastal squeeze"). There are two main consequences of this "squeeze" effect. It can be argued that the ability of the intertidal zone to absorb energy and water and thereby contribute to sea defence will be diminished. The loss of a "first line" of defence against waves and tides, especially during storm conditions, can result in increased capital and maintenance costs for engineered defences. Secondly, "squeeze" results in degraded or destroyed mudflats, sandflat and saltmarsh habitats. These habitats provide a number of ecosystem services, they are significant reservoirs of biodiversity, and have attracted a range of conservation designations. Under the EU Water Framework Directive, loss of conservation area must be compensated for on a "like-for-like" basis. Managed retreat seems to offer a way of mitigating this problem by deliberately breaking defences, allowing the coastline to recede and the intertidal zone to expand. However, the situation is further complicated because many freshwater coastal sites protected by coastal defences are also designated as protected areas on nature conservation grounds. Pethick (2002) has claimed that a stalemate might develop between the requirements of freshwater and intertidal habitats conservation. If sea defences are removed the freshwater habitat is compromised; if the defences are maintained then the intertidal habitat is reduced.

While managed realignment seems to provide a number of benefits, the realignment process also incurs engineering costs and other opportunity costs (e.g. the unsubsidised value of any land lost which was previously protected). . . .

Managed Realignment in the Humber Estuary, England

Cave et al. (2003) have undertaken a scoping study . . . to examine the complex interplay of factors in the Humber estuary and catchment. The macro-tidal Humber estuary is one of the largest in the UK, fed by two principal river systems, the Ouse and the Trent. With a maximum tidal length of 147 km from Cromwell Weir on the Trent to the Humber's mouth, and maximum width of 15 km, it is comparable with the Thames and Severn estuaries. Draining over a fifth of the land area of England (24,000 km²), the Humber estuary is the largest source of freshwater (approximately 250 m³ s⁻¹) into the North Sea from all the British rivers. Much of the land surrounding the estuary is the result of historical land reclamation, created from the enclosure of saltmarshes and mudflats. Consequently, approximately 90,000 ha of land surrounding the Humber estuary is below high spring tide level and is currently protected by 235 km of flood and coastal defences (405 km including those defences along the tidal reaches of the rivers Trent and Ouse). This area is comprised of agricultural land (85%), housing (8%) and commercial or industrial activities (3%).

The Humber estuary is of international importance for wildlife, particularly birds, with a large area of intertidal habitat of between 10,000 and 11,000 ha of which around 90% consists of mudflats and sandflats with the remainder being mainly saltmarsh. This intertidal habitat plays an important role within the estuary, through the recycling of nutrients within the estuary, and their role as soft sea defences, dissipating wave energy. They are highly productive biologically in terms of bird species — the Humber is recognised internationally for its breeding, passage and wintering birds. The entire estuary has been proposed as a marine "Special Area of Conservation" (SAC) while the Humber flats are designated a "Special Protection Area" (SPA), "Site of Special Scientific Interest" (SSSI) and Ramsar site.

However, through land-claim, the Humber estuary has an uncharacteristically low extent of saltmarsh for an English estuary. Jickells et al. (2000) have estimated that more than 90% of the intertidal area and sediment accumulation capacity of the

Humber estuary has been lost over the last 300 years with protected areas becoming threatened. In areas with extensive seawalls and commercial development, such as around Grimsby and Hull, tidal flats are narrow (<100 m wide) or absent. The natural succession of marine to terrestrial environments has been truncated by the construction of seawalls. Before extensive human involvement the vegetation succession probably incorporated much wider tracts of saltmarsh, progressing to less saline fen and carr environments. It now ends at mature saltmarsh. These types of marginal marine–terrestrial environments are no longer present in the Humber system.

In addition to the loss of intertidal habitats through reclamation and coastal squeeze, there is also concern regarding the state of traditional sea defences within the Humber estuary. As many of the defences in the estuary were built following the 1953 flooding disaster on the East Coast, they are now reaching the end of their design life and are currently unsatisfactory and in need of repair or replacing. Both of these problems are likely to be exacerbated by climate-change-related sea level rise and increased storm conditions. With the reduction of intertidal habitats and increasing costs of maintaining defences, the flood defence strategies for the Humber estuary are being reassessed and a limited amount of realignment work has begun. In 2003, the EA undertook the first realignment of the flood and coastal defences in the Humber, by breeching the defences at Thorngumbald, on the north bank of the Humber, east of Hull creating 80 ha of intertidal habitat, having identified a further 11 potential sites.

Ledoux et al. (2005) have applied futures scenario analysis to help scope possible management strategies for the Humber estuary. The case study presented here builds on this existing body of work and adopts the five scenarios (a "hold-the-line" approach versus four other possible states of the world with increasing reliance on managed realignment measures) of possible futures set out by Ledoux et al. (2005). It then combines a GIS-based analysis with a cost–benefit economic valuation model to assess the management options.

Managed Realignment Scenarios

The five scenarios are based on the following assumptions:

1. *Hold-the-line (HTL):* The existing defences are maintained to a satisfactory standard, but intertidal habitat will be lost due to continued development and coastal squeeze.

2. *Business-as-usual (BAU):* This option takes into account existing realignment schemes; however compliance with the Habitats Directive is lax, with continued economic development possibly leading to a loss of habitat due to coastal squeeze.

3. *Policy targets (PT):* Economic growth is combined with environmental protection, with realignment undertaken to reduce flood defence expenditure and compensate for past and future intertidal habitat loss in compliance with the Habitats Directive.

4. *Deep green (DG):* Environmental protection takes priority over economic growth, while development continues; the maximum feasible area of intertidal habitat is created.

Table 1. Details of areas suitable for realignment

	Scenarios				
	HTL	BAU	PT	DG	EDG
Length of defences before realignment (km)	405.3	405.3	405.3	405.3	405.3
Length of defences after realignment (km)	405.3	396.8	361.6	318.2	284.5
Length of realigned defences (km)	0.0	7.0	30.8	69.0	102.7
Length of unsatisfactory defences after realignment (km)	64.6	61.9	42.2	38.2	34.0
Amount of intertidal habitat created by realignment (ha)	0.0	80.0	1320.9	2332.4	7493.6
Estimated tonnes of Carbon stored each year	0	38.4	634.1	1119.4	3597.1

5. *Extended deep green (EDG):* A greater emphasis is placed on habitat creation, with less restrictive criteria being used to identify suitable areas for realignment.

To identify areas suitable for future possible realignment in the Humber for each of the scenarios outlined in the above sections, five key criteria were considered in the GIS mapping . . . .

Details of the areas that were identified as suitable for realignment, for each of the scenarios, are illustrated in Table 1. The table shows the implications of realignment on defence length, the amount of habitat that could be created and the subsequent impacts on carbon sequestration. . . .

Marc R. Poirier, A Very Clear Blue Line: Behavioral Economics, Public Choice, Public Art and Sea Level Rise

16 Southeastern Envtl. L.J. 83 (2007)

Now let us consider sea level rise and blue line projects. In the wake of recent publicity about global climate change, artists in Santa Barbara and New York City decided to inscribe the reality of sea level rise right there on the ground. Bruce Caron of Santa Barbara proposed to paint a line seven meters above current sea level, which was to represent sea level if the Greenland ice sheet were to melt and flow into the ocean. He calls his project "lightblueline." Eve S. Mosher, in Brooklyn and lower Manhattan, demarcated a more modest ten foot rise in chalk powder, to represent the reach of a storm surge under current conditions. She used the governmentally

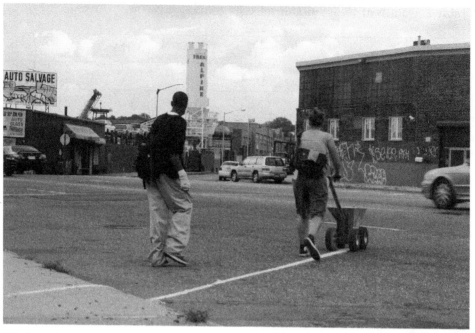

Photo: Hose Cedeno/Eve Mosher/HighWaterLine

Figure 10-10. Artist Eve Mosher Applies a "High Water Line" in Brooklyn, New York

established elevation of 9.7 feet for a 100-year storm surge in her area, without any projected sea level rise at all. Mosher's project also involved placing beacons in parks, linked by the chalk line. Her project also provides information on the website about possible direct individual actions around global warming, and links to other information about global warming and climate change. Mosher calls her project the High Water Line. Other similar projects are emerging, even as this essay is being finalized. I will collectively call projects of this type blue line projects.

The lightblueline project website describes Caron's project as "a public information project to paint on the streets the message that human-induced climate change will impact coastal cities." It is significant that it is a visual message, not a verbal one, and that it is a message in a particular place. The line is to be affixed to the ground, in public, in Santa Barbara. It cannot be tossed out, tucked away in a drawer, or, in our internet age, turned off. As a semi-permanent visual cue (the paint in Caron's project is to dissipate in two to three years), blue line projects seem an effective refinement of the idea of "persistent publicity" about coastal hazard.

The fate of Caron's lightblueline project is also instructive. The Santa Barbara City Council approved it by a 6-1 vote in July 2007. It was also approved by the Santa Barbara Historic Landmarks Committee on a 5-2 vote in August 2007, and the city even appropriated some money for it as a public art project. Then the real estate lobby moved in. The lobby announced the formation of a committee dedicated to keeping the lightblueline project off Santa Barbara's streets. Two days later, the artist announced he was withdrawing his application from City Hall. As communicated by the artist to me, this move was actually part of a plan to regroup in light of media opposition, not a concession of defeat; he is waiting for the right moment to move forward. The principal concern of real estate interests was, of course, the diminution of property values. Buyers might see more clearly that some property in Santa Barbara could be inundated, lowering property values and prices. To be sure, part of the articulated opposition to the project was that the seven-meter level was based on a speculative event, the melting of Greenland's ice cap. But I am quite sure that a similar project at the well-accepted ten-foot current storm surge elevation that Mosher selected would have generated similar opposition. This circumstance illustrates what I am calling public choice mobilization to counter a proposed attempt to address a risk perception defect through a particularly effective form of risk communication.

Let us consider now why blue line projects might be especially effective as part of a strategy to address sea level rise; then catalog a couple of legal concerns; then consider the lessons of such projects for giving environmental debates over to specific places and communities.

The Signal Visibility of Landscape

While maps, animations, and movies about sea level rise are all available, none of these has the immediacy and unavoidability of a message inscribed directly on and in the landscape. Carol Rose has noted that property law has "peculiar links with vision." A landscape can "dramatically affect the way one thinks about what can be done on, with, and to [the] landscape, and about what is changeable and what is not." "Vision mediates between what is given by the surroundings and what the viewers think that they and other can do, either to accommodate to their surrounding or to shape them anew." Quoting Justice Oliver Wendell Holmes, she suggests, "[t]he fact that tangible property is also visible tends to give rigidity to our conception of our rights in it that we do not attach to others less concretely clothed."

As Rose points out in her recent reflections on coastal development, there are other important natural resources that are less fixed and that are, by the same token, less permanently visible. Rose contrasts the visibility and tangibility of land with the mobility and elusiveness of air and water. "[L]and is the most visible and tangible of things you can own, and that quality captures your attention, and enhances your sense of entitlement." Air, water and wildlife are "elusive, spread-out, hard to capture, easily subject to invasion. . . ." She suggests that this difference explains the recurrent regulatory takings litigation over environmental land use regulations at the water's edge. As a result of our perception of land as stable and of other natural resources as fugitive and transitory, land is subject to "imbalanced propertization."

The visibility of landscape is also associated with changelessness and indefinite duration, and ignores time. In contrast, I suggest, the coastal hazards present by sea level rise, storms, and erosion are quintessentially time-bounded and episodic in nature. Their threat is not always visible. Without permanent visual cues, this episodic risk inherent in the coastal landscape is forgettable, concealable or deniable. What is visually present most of the time is the land. And it is land that looks like developed or developable land, not the high water or the raging storm.

Rose's focus on the importance of permanent visibility to landscape and of landscape to one's sense of property helps us to understand why the blue line concept is potentially effective and, by the same token, why it is potentially so threatening to those who wish to deny or conceal the risk of unwise coastal development. A blue line is more effective at communicating risk than a flood map or a mandated disclosure buried in a sheaf of closing documents. It is also more effective at communicating to the unwilling than any of the computer-drawn sea level rise projects, which one must actively seek out, and which do not confront a person at the moment she or he is in the landscape itself. The blue line is public, encountered daily, viscerally understandable, and in your face. If we were to have a blue line clearly indicating the threat of storm surge (at ten feet) or of the melting of one of the land based polar ice sheets (at twenty-two feet) inscribed on the landscape around the country, I believe much of the resistance to other precautions about sea level rise and global climate change would weaken. It would certainly change the dynamics of coastal hazard management, both in their behavioral economic and public choice aspects.

Blue Line Projects: Law and Politics

Is this kind of blue line public art/public information project possible on a large scale? It is contentious from a political perspective, precisely because it is likely to be effective and to threaten property values. If it were an approach that made everyone happy, it would already be here, given its comparatively low cost. Yet Eve Mosher completed her project in Brooklyn and Lower Manhattan without incident. Bruce Caron won approval from all the relevant governing bodies in Santa Barbara; and despite the resistance being mounted by real estate interests, he is not ready to abandon the fray. Evidently, in some places the local politics are workable.

The next question, then, is whether widespread blue line projects could be done legally. The answer to that question is mostly yes. Public property could be blue lined easily enough, at the say-so of whatever governmental owner controlled each property. To be sure, there could be some harmful effect on a coastal town's economy if it went forward and its neighbors did not. This observation suggest that, to address the holdout problem, blue line projects probably need to be implemented eventually at a state level. The federal government might give the project a super boost by requiring a blue line on all its coastal property. The effect of a blue line on property values is not as likely to concern Uncle Sam. Moreover, Congress itself would not even have to act, since a blue line project on federal land would likely be the proper subject matter of an Executive Order of a future, green president.

Inscribing a blue line on private property is trickier. After *Loretto v. Teleprompter Manhattan CATV Corp.*, [458 U.S. 419 (1982),] a regulation imposing a permanent physical invasion on unwilling property owners is going to be understood to effect a taking and therefore to require compensation. One possible response to this doctrinal consequence of requiring blue lines on private property would be to impose a blue line easement or servitude as an exaction, in exchange for some required coastal land use or building permit. Wherever a permit is required for either fill or development along the coast, the blue line could probably be imposed as a permit condition, as it is reasonably related (roughly proportional) to problems created by the activity being permitted.

Another, complementary means of permanently inscribing the blue line is available wherever coastal private property owners who are sympathetic to the project voluntarily agree to blue line their properties. A standard form easement for a blue line across private property could be developed, so as to make such agreements stick from one owner to the next. This method would create a dominant tenement in favor of the public or a suitable conservation-oriented non-profit — basically a mini-conservation easement. The blue line agreement should not be a mere license, revocable subsequently simply at the will of the holder of the land; the point is permanence. In this way, environmentally-minded property owners could impose the blue line project on their successors so long as the dominant tenement holder did not agree to release the property from the servitude. Bit by bit, the coast would acquire a blue line.

In the most significant areas — low-lying and urban, for example — a governmental entity could also simply bite the Loretto bullet. The property being blue lined is still as useful as it ever was. Nothing has changed except that the information about its susceptibility to flooding and erosion is out in the open. If this information is true and already public, how does making the information more available cause harm? How much compensable loss can there be in that? It is perhaps important to keep in mind that the damages that Mrs. Loretto received for New York City's imposition of a cable box and wiring on her apartment building, after she won in the Supreme Court, amounted to one dollar. If there is comparably little just compensation cost per property, even the physical invasion/takings/compensation issue might well not be an insurmountable one.

For the truly recalcitrant property owner, perhaps we still need a substitute for the physical blue line. A jurisdiction could require a very clear statement in the deed of where the blue line would fall. Just as a few states require deed records to disclose toxic contamination and California requires notification of natural hazards in property transactions, a sympathetic jurisdiction could impose a virtual blue line requirement via a truly salient deed notice — something more than the flood maps that a potential purchaser might now have to confront. A deed notice would not be as effective as the physical, tangible blue line, for the reasons of landscape visibility and tangibility discussed above. Still, suppose that in a given community (or eventually a state or country, one might hope) the blue line appeared physically on more and more coastal property. The question of where a non-lined property was located vis-à-vis sea level rise and storm surge might become more salient. In turn, this salience would make more effective a virtual blue line consisting of a deed or document notice.

Blue Line Projects, Particular Local Places and the Evolution of Environmental Norms

I now would like to draw in themes of place and localism in political dialogue over global warming, in order to situate public and place-based art such as blue line projects at an important intersection of global processes and specific local places and communities. Blue line projects attempt to redirect cultural attitudes and political priorities around natural resource use and coastal development, in view of the apparent inevitability of climate change and concomitant sea level rise. In addition to their artistic character, they are also a public information campaign about natural resources management and land use, contributing to a discussion of issues simultaneously local and global in scale.

Changing culture and related social practice is inevitably a piecemeal thing. It typically occurs in a piecemeal fashion locally before it occurs on a larger scale. We have already seen that blue line projects could be politically and legally embraced and implemented at many levels. At the small end are the actions of artists like Bruce Caron and Eve Mosher, along with the potential consent of individual private property owners who might allow a permanent blue line on their property. Then, one level of scale up, we might have localities like Santa Barbara, which granted all the necessary permits and even found funding for the lightblueline project. State and national arenas could also come into play, though we might expect them to do so piecemeal and perhaps later, as public opinion trends are established.

Cities and states sometimes indeed do serve as laboratories of policy experimentation. We currently see, for example, coastal states driving United States policy on greenhouse gases in a particular direction, in an attempt to force national norms and policies. Many of the nation's mayors are also considering what steps they can take to reduce global warming by acting locally. The United States Conference of Mayors recently convened a Climate Protection Summit, attended by more than 100 mayors. In addition, more than 700 U.S. mayors have signed a pledge to reduce their cities' emissions of carbon dioxide and other greenhouse gases to the levels of the Kyoto Protocol. Such small or smallish groups can set out to seed cultural and economic shifts.

Where environmental and natural resource policies are concerned, this localism arises in part from the nature of the feedback from the natural resources and environmental processes themselves. A number of property theorists have pointed out that we shift our notions of property rights and environmental obligations (as well as other community-regarding obligations that limit private property rights) on an ongoing basis, even though that renegotiation process is not always clearly acknowledged. Some of these theorists usefully distinguish between types of evolutionary dialectic around property. Thus, Eric Freyfogle contrasts a narrative of "property and the evolving community" and a "narrative of natural use." In the narrative of natural use, "the land itself is the lawgiver"; a proper understanding of the natural world dictates that certain basic principles of natural resource management are not debatable. Similarly, in an article analyzing the crosscurrents in *Lucas v. South Carolina Coastal Council*, [505 U.S. 1003 (1992),] Joseph Sax distinguishes between a transformative economy and an economy of nature, with property rights in tension as between these two visions. The economy of nature requires one to take account of ecological services and interconnectedness in discerning how to parcel out land and regulate land uses, and makes property rights less absolute and more subject to community needs as they are discerned. One can find a number of other articulations of similar ideas, all identifying the need to temper classic absolute property rights to account for communal dependence on shared environmental services or other shared resources such as public health and safety.

How do Freyfogle's "narrative of natural use" or Sax's "economy of nature" work themselves out as we become more and more aware of the issues posed by global warming and climate change? The problems of global warming, including those due to sea level rise, occur at a number of different levels of scale simultaneously, as do also attempts to slow global warming and to adapt to its effects. The problem and the possible responses are local and global at the same time. Sea level rise will affect many parts of the world in many different ways; but each individual locality will be affected individually, community by community — even, one could say, property by property, house by house. And each community will be called to respond just as locally. The problem can be described abstractly and generally, but it also is inevitably local and concrete. Beaches erode. Buildings fall down. Then communities try to figure out what to do about it.

At the local, place-based community level, land-based political art such as a blue line project takes on an edge and holds an advantage that some other kinds of climate change advocacy do not. Consider, in contrast to blue line projects, the Canary Project, another attempt to use public art to bring home to a public the effects of global warming. The Canary Project publishes on the internet compelling pictures of a number of the effects of climate change; images of some possible solutions or mitigation measures; and contacts for further information. Yet consider its audience: individuals who voluntarily sign in to its website. While it thus can help to inform and motivate those who already are more or less persuaded, or at least open minded, it will not reach those who do not access it. One could say the same thing about the web-based blue line projects. They too reach only the converted and the curious. They do not reach the entirety of the local, place-based community that actually encounters the resource and has to deal with the laws of nature.

In contrast, Caron's lightblueline project occurs in and communicates physically in Santa Barbara, California, USA. Mosher's High Water Line project occurs in and communicates physically in New York City, New York, USA. Santa Barbara and New York City are shared places, in contrast to a shared information space like a website. One cannot escape communication planted in such a place by websurfing over to a different channel.

The community that inhabits a particular place is not necessarily like-minded in the way that the community of an internet space can be. Its members are not bound by interest, but by necessity, the necessity of their shared physical space and resources. Generally speaking, human communities encounter, conceptualize and approach issues of natural resource management through time- and space-specific encounters and problems. Blue line projects, then, provoke encounters and dialogues about one specific place and its resources, in that place, with others who share the same spatial and political community, although not necessarily the same views. Blue line projects force the inhabitants of a local, place-based community to engage in a dialogue over the management of shared natural resources and socioeconomic processes such as coastal development. They foster locally focused awareness in a way that something like the Canary Project, for all its potential persuasive value, cannot. In Santa Barbara, Caron engaged the city leaders in dialog over the project and hence over sea level rise and global warming, with the public watching through the local media. In New York City, Mosher discussed her projects with passers-by as well as in her blog. Here is what Mosher writes generally about her project:

> High Water Line seeks to engage people on the street, in the neighborhoods where they live, work and play. People will encounter the chalk line and the beacons while going about their daily lives. The work is an intervention in routine — the public's as well as my own. This aspect of the piece ensures catching the public's attention, and it assures easy and direct access. The simplicity of the project, aesthetically and visually, will appeal to people of all ages, ethnicities and economic backgrounds. Climate change is a silent, invisible threat — High Water Line gives voice and makes visible the affects [sic] of this threat. High Water Line is designed to engage the community and promote thoughtful, informed dialogue and action.

point for discussion

The shotgun approach. Recall Professor Wood's argument that mitigating climate change would require a multi-pellet, rather than a single-bullet, approach. Given what you've just read, what strategies for coastal adaptation would you advocate for in front of your state legislature?

C. CHAPTER SUMMARY

1. **Insuring coastal property.** Coastal property is insured, as a general matter, against wind damage by private insurers and against flood damage by the National Flood Insurance Program. The former provides limited protection from storm effects, and the latter is fraught with significant funding and incentive problems.
2. **Climate change impacts.** Global climate change presents a slew of potential impacts unique to coastal areas, including more and more frequent storms, higher erosion rates, and the salinization of important ground water supplies.
3. **Coastal adaptation.** Preparing for the potential coastal impacts of global climate change will not be easy. It will require overcoming many obstacles, including human nature. However, the costs of not preparing adequately will likely be substantial.

D. SUGGESTED READING

Timothy Beatley, Planning for Coastal Resilience (2009).

Michael B. Gerard, ed., Climate Change and U.S. Law (2007).

The Intergovernmental Panel on Climate Change, Climate Change 2007: Working Group II: Impacts, Adaptation and Vulnerability, https://www.ipcc.ch/site/assets/uploads/2018/03/ar4_wg2_full_report.pdf.

Howard C. Kunreuther, At War with the Weather: Managing Large-Scale Risks in a New Era of Catastrophes (2009).

Joseph Lavitt, *The Doctrine of Efficient Proximate Cause, the Katrina Disaster, Prosser's Folly, and the Third Restatement of Torts: Cracking the Conundrum*, 54 Loy. L. Rev. 1 (2008).

Margaret E. Peloso & Margaret R. Caldwell, *Dynamic Property Rights: The Public Trust Doctrine and Takings in a Changing Climate*, 30 Stanford Envtl. L.J. 51 (2011).

Orrin H. Pilkey & Rob Young, The Rising Sea (2009).

U.S. Environmental Protection Agency, Synthesis of Adaptation Options for Coastal Areas (2009), https://www.epa.gov/sites/production/files/2014-04/documents/cre_synthesis_1-09.pdf.

Table of Cases

Table of Authors

Index

Bold numbers indicate references to cases, statutes, and state-specific materials.